PRO FO
GUIDE

1988 EDITION

Editor/Pro Football Guide
DAVE SLOAN

Contributing Editors/Pro Football Guide
HOWARD BALZER
BARRY SIEGEL

President-Chief Executive Officer
RICHARD WATERS

Editor
TOM BARNIDGE

Director of Books and Periodicals
RON SMITH

Published by

The Sporting News

1212 North Lindbergh Boulevard
P.O. Box 56 — St. Louis, MO 63166

Copyright © 1988
The Sporting News Publishing Company

A Times Mirror
Company

IMPORTANT NOTICE

The Pro Football Guide is protected by copyright. All information was compiled by the publishers and proof is available.

Information from the Pro Football Guide must not be used elsewhere without special written permission, and then only with full credit to the Pro Football Guide, published by THE SPORTING NEWS, St. Louis, Missouri.

ISBN 0-89204-285-0   ISSN 0732-1902

MW01506281

TABLE OF CONTENTS

Club Directories, 1988 Schedules, 1987 Results, Veteran Rosters, Rookie & First-Year Rosters, 1988 Draft Choices

ON THE COVER: Denver quarterback John Elway led the Broncos to their second consecutive Super Bowl last season and was voted to the AFC Pro Bowl squad for the second time in his career.

Photograph by Rich Pilling

THE NATIONAL FOOTBALL LEAGUE

WELLINGTON MARA President National Football Conference	**PETE ROZELLE** Commissioner National Football League	**LAMAR HUNT** President American Football Conference

COMMISSIONER'S OFFICE

PETE ROZELLE, Commissioner
JAY MOYER, Executive V.P./Counsel to Commissioner
DON WEISS, Executive Director
JOE RHEIN, Director of Administration
JOHN SCHOEMER, Treasurer
JAN VAN DUSER, Director of Operations
JOE BROWNE, Director of Communications
JIM HEFFERNAN, Director of Public Relations
VAL PINCHBECK, Jr., Director of Broadcasting
NANCY DEHAR, Asst. Dir. of Broadcasting
WARREN WELSH, Director of Security
CHARLES R. JACKSON, Assistant Director of Security
JOEL BUSSERT, Director of Player Personnel
ART McNALLY, Supervisor of Officials
JACK READER, Assistant Supervisor of Officials
JIM STEEG, Director of Special Events
SUSAN McCANN-MINOGUE, Asst. Dir. of Special Events
BILL GRANHOLM, Director of Special Projects
TOM SULLIVAN, Controller
DAVE CORNWELL, Asst. Counsel/Dir. of Equal Employment
MEL BLOUNT, Director of Player Relations

AMERICAN FOOTBALL CONFERENCE

LAMAR HUNT, President
ROGER GOODELL, Assistant to the President
PETE ABITANTE, Director of Information

NATIONAL FOOTBALL CONFERENCE

WELLINGTON MARA, President
JAMES NOEL, Assistant to the President
DICK MAXWELL, Director of Information

LEAGUE OFFICES
410 Park Avenue
New York, New York 10022

TELEPHONE (Area Code 212)
Commissioner's Office: 758-1500

NATIONAL FOOTBALL LEAGUE

FINAL STANDINGS OF THE TEAMS—1987

AMERICAN CONFERENCE

EASTERN DIVISION

	W.	L.	T.	Pct.	Pts.	Opp.
*Indianapolis	9	6	0	.600	300	238
New England	8	7	0	.533	320	293
Miami	8	7	0	.533	362	335
Buffalo	7	8	0	.467	270	305
N.Y. Jets	6	9	0	.400	334	360

CENTRAL DIVISION

	W.	L.	T.	Pct.	Pts.	Opp.
*Cleveland	10	5	0	.667	390	239
†Houston	9	6	0	.600	345	349
Pittsburgh	8	7	0	.533	285	299
Cincinnati	4	11	0	.267	285	370

WESTERN DIVISION

	W.	L.	T.	Pct.	Pts.	Opp.
*Denver	10	4	1	.700	379	288
†Seattle	9	6	0	.600	371	314
San Diego	8	7	0	.533	253	317
L.A. Raiders	5	10	0	.333	301	289
Kansas City	4	11	0	.267	273	388

*Division champion.
†Wild-card team.

NATIONAL CONFERENCE

EASTERN DIVISION

	W.	L.	T.	Pct.	Pts.	Opp.
*Washington	11	4	0	.733	379	285
Dallas	7	8	0	.467	340	348
St. Louis	7	8	0	.467	362	368
Philadelphia	7	8	0	.467	337	380
N.Y. Giants	6	9	0	.400	280	312

CENTRAL DIVISION

	W.	L.	T.	Pct.	Pts.	Opp.
*Chicago	11	4	0	.733	356	282
†Minnesota	8	7	0	.533	336	335
Green Bay	5	9	1	.367	255	300
Tampa Bay	4	11	0	.267	286	360
Detroit	4	11	0	.267	269	384

WESTERN DIVISION

	W.	L.	T.	Pct.	Pts.	Opp.
*San Francisco	13	2	0	.867	459	253
†New Orleans	12	3	0	.800	422	283
L.A. Rams	6	9	0	.400	317	361
Atlanta	3	12	0	.200	205	436

*Division champion.
†Wild-card team.

AFC PLAYOFFS

WILD CARD
Houston 23, Seattle 20 (OT)

SEMIFINALS
Cleveland 38, Indianapolis 21
Denver 34, Houston 10

NFC PLAYOFFS

WILD CARD
Minnesota 44, New Orleans 10

SEMIFINALS
Minnesota 36, San Francisco 24
Washington 21, Chicago 17

AFC CHAMPIONSHIP
Denver 38, Cleveland 33

NFC CHAMPIONSHIP
Washington 17, Minnesota 10

NFL CHAMPIONSHIP
Washington 42, Denver 10

NATIONAL FOOTBALL LEAGUE CHAMPIONS

Year—Team	Coach
1921—Chicago Staleys†	George Halas
1922—Canton Bulldogs	Guy Chamberlin
1923—Canton Bulldogs	Guy Chamberlin
1924—Cleveland Bulldogs‡	Guy Chamberlin
1925—Chicago Cardinals	Norman Barry
1926—Frankford Yellowjackets	Guy Chamberlin
1927—New York Giants	Earl Potteiger
1928—Providence Steamrollers	Jim Conzelman
1929—Green Bay Packers	Curly Lambeau
1930—Green Bay Packers	Curly Lambeau
1931—Green Bay Packers	Curly Lambeau
1932—Chicago Bears	Ralph Jones
1933—Chicago Bears	George Halas
1934—New York Giants	Steve Owen
1935—Detroit Lions	Potsy Clark
1936—Green Bay Packers	Curly Lambeau
1937—Washington Redskins	Ray Flaherty
1938—New York Giants	Steve Owen
1939—Green Bay Packers	Curly Lambeau
1940—Chicago Bears	George Halas
1941—Chicago Bears	George Halas
1942—Washington Redskins	Ray Flaherty
1943—Chicago Bears	Luke Johnsos & Hunk Anderson
1944—Green Bay Packers	Curly Lambeau
1945—Cleveland Rams	Adam Walsh
1946—Chicago Bears	George Halas
1947—Chicago Cardinals	Jim Conzelman
1948—Philadelphia Eagles	Greasy Neale
1949—Philadelphia Eagles	Greasy Neale
1950—Cleveland Browns	Paul Brown
1951—Los Angeles Rams	Joe Stydahar
1952—Detroit Lions	Buddy Parker
1953—Detroit Lions	Buddy Parker
1954—Cleveland Browns	Paul Brown
1955—Cleveland Browns	Paul Brown
1956—New York Giants	Jim Lee Howell
1957—Detroit Lions	George Wilson
1958—Baltimore Colts	Weeb Ewbank
1959—Baltimore Colts	Weeb Ewbank
1960—Philadelphia Eagles	Buck Shaw
1961—Green Bay Packers	Vince Lombardi
1962—Green Bay Packers	Vince Lombardi
1963—Chicago Bears	George Halas
1964—Cleveland Browns	Blanton Collier
1965—Green Bay Packers	Vince Lombardi
1966—Green Bay Packers*	Vince Lombardi
1967—Green Bay Packers*	Vince Lombardi
1968—Baltimore Colts	Don Shula
1969—Minnesota Vikings	Bud Grant
1970—Baltimore Colts	Don McCafferty
1971—Dallas Cowboys	Tom Landry
1972—Miami Dolphins	Don Shula
1973—Miami Dolphins	Don Shula
1974—Pittsburgh Steelers	Chuck Noll
1975—Pittsburgh Steelers	Chuck Noll
1976—Oakland Raiders	John Madden
1977—Dallas Cowboys	Tom Landry
1978—Pittsburgh Steelers	Chuck Noll
1979—Pittsburgh Steelers	Chuck Noll
1980—Oakland Raiders	Tom Flores
1981—San Francisco 49ers	Bill Walsh
1982—Washington Redskins	Joe Gibbs
1983—Los Angeles Raiders	Tom Flores
1984—San Francisco 49ers	Bill Walsh
1985—Chicago Bears	Mike Ditka
1986—New York Giants	Bill Parcells
1987—Washington Redskins	Joe Gibbs

†Later called the Chicago Bears.

‡Franchise moved from Canton.

*Won AFL-NFL Championship Game.

ATLANTA FALCONS
(Western Division, National Conference)

Marion Campbell

Chairman of the Board—Rankin M. Smith, Sr.
President—Rankin M. Smith, Jr.
Executive Vice-President—Taylor Smith
Director of College Player Personnel—Ken Herock
Director of Pro Personnel—Bill Jobko
Head Coach—Marion Campbell (7 years: 26-60-1)
Assistant Coaches:
  Defensive Line—Tom Brasher
  Assistant Head Coach—Fred Bruney
  Administrative Assistant—Scott Campbell
  Linebackers—Chuck Clausen
  Running Backs—Steve Crosby
  Offensive Coordinator—Rod Dowhower
  Tight Ends/Special Teams—Foge Fazio
  Asst. Head Coach/Offense—Jim Hanifan
  Defensive Assistant—Claude Humphrey
  Strength & Conditioning—Tim Jorgensen
  Receivers—Jimmy Raye
Public Relations Director—Charlie Taylor
  (Office Phone: 945-1111—Area Code 404)
Offices—I-85 & Suwanee Rd., Suwanee, Ga. 30174
Stadium—Atlanta-Fulton County Stadium (Capacity: 59,643)
Team Colors—Red, Black, Silver and White
Training Site—Atlanta Falcon Complex, Suwanee, Ga.

1988 SCHEDULE
(All times local.
All games Sunday unless noted otherwise.)

Sept. 4	at Detroit	1:00
Sept. 11	NEW ORLEANS	1:00
Sept. 18	at San Francisco	1:00
Sept. 25	at Dallas	12:00
Oct. 2	SEATTLE	1:00
Oct. 9	LOS ANGELES RAMS	1:00
Oct. 16	at Denver	2:00
Oct. 23	NEW YORK GIANTS	1:00
Oct. 30	at Philadelphia	1:00
Nov. 6	GREEN BAY	1:00
Nov. 13	S..N DIEGO	1:00
Nov. 20	at Los Angeles Raiders	1:00
Nov. 27	TAMPA BAY	1:00
Dec. 4	SAN FRANCISCO	1:00
Dec. 11	at Los Angeles Rams	1:00
Dec. 18	at New Orleans	12:00

1987 RESULTS—(Won 3, Lost 12)

Falcons	Opp.		Att.
10 Tampa Bay	48	(A)	51,250
21 Washington	20	(H)	50,882
New Orleans*		(A)	
12 Pittsburgh	*28*	*(H)*	*16,667*
17 San Francisco	*25*	*(H)*	*8,684*
24 L.A. Rams	*20*	*(H)*	*15,813*
33 Houston	37	(A)	29,062
0 New Orleans	38	(H)	42,196
3 Cleveland	38	(A)	71,135
10 Cincinnati	16	(H)	25,758
13 Minnesota	24	(A)	53,866
21 St. Louis	34	(H)	15,909
21 Dallas	10	(A)	40,103
0 L.A. Rams	33	(A)	43,310
7 San Francisco	35	(A)	54,698
13 Detroit	30	(H)	13,906

*Game cancelled due to strike.
Italics denote strike replacement games.

1987 GAMES STARTED
(NOTE: Players with an asterisk (*) following their names made starts only in strike-replacement games.)

  12 games: Bobby Butler, Floyd Dixon, Bill Fralic, Mike Gann, Mike Kenn, Leonard Mitchell, Robert Moore, Wayne Radloff, Gerald Riggs, John Scully.

  11 games: John Rade.

  10 games: Scott Case, Arthur Cox.

  9 games: Rick Bryan, Scott Campbell, Tony Casillas.

  8 games: Tim Gordon, Rich Kraynak, Joel Williams.

  7 games: Ken Whisenhunt.

  6 games: Stacey Bailey, Aubrey Matthews.

  5 games: Greg Brown, Tim Green, Dennis Harrison, Reggie Wilkes.

  4 games: Joe Costello, Buddy Curry, Ron Middleton, Jessie Tuggle.

  3 games: Milton Barney*, Randy Clark*, Jim Hendley*, Lawrence Jackson*, Jim Laughlin*, Mike Lush*, Doug Mackie*, Gary Moss*, Pat Saindon*.

  2 games: Rick Badanjek*, Sylvester Byrd*, Wendell Cason, David Croudip, Charles Huff*, Lyndell Jones*, Erik Kramer*, Chris Miller*, Buddy Moor*, Dwaine Morris*, Herb Spencer*, Mark Studaway*, Lenny Taylor*, Leon Thomasson*, Emanuel Weaver*.

  1 game: David Archer, Aaron Brown*, Bret Clark, John Evans*, Kenny Flowers, Norm Granger*, Billy Johnson, John Kamana*, Andrew Provence, John Settle, James Shibest*, Jeff Van Raaphorst*, Michael Williams*, Brenard Wilson, Leonard Wingate*, Geno Zimmerlink*.

ATLANTA FALCONS 1988 VETERAN ROSTER

No.	Name	Pos.	Ht.	Wt.	NFL Exp.	Birth-date	College	Games in '87	How Acquired
	Anderson, Anthony	DB	6-2	208	2	10-24-64	Grambling	*3	FA, '88
	Armstrong, John	DB	5-10	195	2	7- 7-63	Richmond	*3	FA, '88
47	Badanjek, Rick	RB	5-8	217	2	4-25-62	Maryland	2	FA, '88
82	Bailey, Stacey	WR	6-0	157	7	2-10-60	San Jose State	7	D3, '82
93	Bohm, Ron	DE	6-3	253	2	9- 3-64	Illinois	*3	FA, '88
98	Brown, Greg	DE	6-5	265	8	1- 5-57	Kansas State	12	T-Phi, '87
	Brown, Ken	WR	5-8	175	2	3-10-65	Southern Arkansas	*3	FA, '88
77	†Bryan, Rick	DE	6-4	265	5	3-20-62	Oklahoma	9	D1, '84
23	†Butler, Bobby	CB	5-11	182	8	5-28-59	Florida State	12	D1, '81
	Byrd, Sylvester	TE	6-2	240	2	5- 1-63	Kansas	3	FA, '88
10	Campbell, Scott	QB	6-0	195	5	4-15-62	Purdue	12	FA, '86
25	†Case, Scott	CB	6-0	178	5	5-17-62	Oklahoma	11	D2, '84
75	Casillas, Tony	NT	6-3	280	3	10-26-63	Oklahoma	9	D1, '86
28	Clark, Bret	S	6-3	198	2	2-24-61	Nebraska	1	T-Rai, '88
	Colton, George	G	6-3	279	2	7-28-63	Maryland	*3	W-NE, '88
56	Costello, Joe	LB	6-3	244	3	6- 1-60	Central Connecticut St.	9	FA, '86
30	†Croudip, David	CB	5-8	183	5	1-25-59	San Diego State	12	FA, '85
	Davis, Greg	P	5-11	190	2	10-29-65	The Citadel	*3	FA, '88
86	Dixon, Floyd	WR	5-9	170	3	4- 9-64	Stephen F. Austin	12	D6, '86
	Dixon, Willie	DT	6-2	275	1	1- 8-64	Tulsa	*2	FA, '88
3	†Donnelly, Rick	P	6-0	190	4	5-17-62	Wyoming	12	FA, '85
64	†Dukes, Jamie	G	6-1	278	3	6-14-64	Florida State	4	OFA, '86
24	Emery, Larry	RB	5-9	195	2	7-13-64	Wisconsin	5	D12, '87
39	Everett, Major	RB	5-10	218	5	1- 4-60	Mississippi College	*11	FA, '87
48	Flowers, Kenny	RB	6-0	210	2	3-14-64	Clemson	8	D2, '87
79	Fralic, Bill	T/G	6-5	280	4	10-31-62	Pittsburgh	12	D1, '85
76	Gann, Mike	DE	6-5	275	4	10-19-63	Notre Dame	12	D2, '85
41	Gordon, Tim	S	6-0	188	2	5- 7-65	Tulsa	11	OFA, '87
99	Green, Tim	LB	6-2	245	3	12-16-63	Syracuse	9	D1a, '86
	Griffin, Steve	RB	5-10	185	1	12-24-64	Clemson	2	FA, '88
96	Hall, James	LB	6-1	252	2	1-27-63	Northwestern State, La.	3	FA, '88
	Hinson, Billy	G	6-1	278	1	1- 8-63	Florida	*0	FA, '88
21	Huff, Charles	CB	5-11	195	2	2-24-63	Presbyterian	3	FA, '88
68	Jackson, Lawrence	G	6-1	275	2	8-10-64	Presbyterian	3	FA, '88
	Johnson, Walter	DL	6-1	250	1	9-13-65	Pittsburgh	*1	FA, '88
84	†Jones, Joey	WR	5-8	165	2	10-29-62	Alabama	*0	SupD, '84
78	Kenn, Mike	T	6-7	277	11	2- 9-56	Michigan	12	D1, '78
	Knight, Leander	DB	6-1	193	1	2-16-63	Montclair State	1	FA, '88
14	Kramer, Erik	QB	6-0	192	2	11- 6-64	North Carolina State	3	FA, '87
52	†Kraynak, Rich	LB	6-1	230	6	1-20-61	Pittsburgh	9	FA, '87
	Land, Dan	RB	6-0	190	2	7- 3-65	Albany State	*3	FA, '88
	Lavette, Robert	RB	5-11	190	3	9- 8-63	Georgia Tech	*5	FA, '88
	Liter, Greg	DE	6-6	275	1	12-31-63	Iowa State	*1	FA, '88
83	†Matthews, Aubrey	WR	5-7	165	3	9-15-62	Delta State	12	OFA, '86
87	†Middleton, Ron	TE	6-2	252	3	7-17-65	Auburn	12	OFA, '86
62	Miller, Brett	T	6-7	300	6	10- 2-58	Iowa	2	D5, '83
12	Miller, Chris	QB	6-2	195	2	8- 9-65	Oregon	3	D1, '87
73	†Mitchell, Leonard	T	6-7	295	8	10-12-58	Houston	12	T-Phi, '87
	Mobley, Stacey	WR	5-8	170	2	9-15-65	Jackson State	*3	FA, '88
34	†Moore, Robert	S	5-11	190	3	8-15-64	Northwestern State, La.	12	OFA, '86
67	Mraz, Mark	DE	6-4	255	2	2- 9-65	Utah State	11	D5, '87
	Padjen, Gary	LB	6-2	241	4	7- 2-58	Arizona State	*1	FA, '88
59	†Rade, John	LB	6-1	240	6	8-31-60	Boise State	11	D8, '83
55	Radloff, Wayne	C	6-5	277	4	5-17-61	Georgia	12	FA, '85
95	Reid, Michael	LB	6-2	226	2	6-25-64	Wisconsin	11	D7, '87
42	Riggs, Gerald	RB	6-1	232	7	11- 6-60	Arizona State	12	D1, '82
	Schamel, Duke	LB	6-2	220	2	11- 3-63	South Dakota	*3	FA, '88
61	Scully, John	G	6-6	270	8	8- 2-58	Notre Dame	12	D4, '81
44	Settle, John	RB	5-9	207	2	6- 2-65	Appalachian	9	OFA, '87
37	Shelley, Elbert	S	5-11	180	2	12-24-64	Arkansas State	4	D11, '87
	Small, Fred	LB	5-11	227	2	7-15-63	Washington	*0	FA, '88
	Smith, Matt	LB	6-2	226	2	9- 1-65	West Virginia	*3	FA, '88
29	†Stamps, Sylvester	RB	5-7	171	4	2-24-61	Jackson State	7	FA, '85
	Strauthers, Tom	DL	6-4	265	5	4- 6-61	Jackson State	*0	FA, '88
45	†Whisenhunt, Ken	TE	6-3	240	4	2-28-62	Georgia Tech	7	D12, '85
	Wilkins, Gary	TE	6-1	235	2	11-23-63	Georgia Tech	*1	FA, '88
54	Williams, Joel	LB	6-1	227	10	12-13-56	Wisconsin-LaCrosse	8	T-Phil, '86
	Williams, Joel	TE	6-3	242	2	3-16-65	Notre Dame	*3	FA, '88

No.	Name	Pos.	Ht.	Wt.	NFL Exp.	Birth-date	College	Games in '87	How Acquired
	Witt, Billy	DE	6-5	265	1	4-15-64	North Alabama	*2	FA, '88
	Young, Mitchell	DL	6-4	260	1	7-18-64	Arkansas State	1	FA, '88

*Anderson played 3 games with Chargers in '87; Armstrong played 3 games with Bills in '87; Bohm played 3 games with Cardinals in '87; K. Brown played 3 games with Bengals in '87; Colton played 3 games with Patriots in '87; Davis played 3 games with Falcons, inactive for 2 games with Dolphins in '87; W. Dixon played 2 games with Oilers in '87; Everett played 4 games with Browns, 7 with Falcons in '87; Hinson missed '87 season due to injury, active for 2 games with Falcons in '86, but did not play; Johnson played 1 game with Cowboys in '87; Jones missed '87 season due to injury; Land played 3 games with Buccaneers in '87; Lavette played 4 games with Cowboys, 1 with Eagles in '87; Liter played 1 game with 49ers in '87; Mobley played 3 games with Rams in '87; Padjen played 1 game with Colts in '87; Schamel played 3 games with Dolphins in '87; Small last active with Steelers in '85; Smith played 3 games with Broncos in '87; Strauthers last active with Eagles in '86; Wilkins played 1 game with Bills in '87; Williams played 3 games with Dolphins in '87; Witt played 2 games with Bills in '87.

†Option playout; subject to developments.

Retired—Buddy Curry, 9-year linebacker, 4 games in '87; Mick Luckhurst, 8-year kicker, 12 games in '87.

D—Draft; T—Trade; FA—Free Agent; OFA—Original Free Agent; SupD—Supplemental Draft. Also played with Falcons in '87, see page 386.

ATLANTA FALCONS
1988 DRAFT CHOICES

(Number following name designates order of selection among 333 players drafted.)

Round and Player		Position	College
1. BRUCE, Aundray	1	LB	Auburn
2. COTTON, Marcus	28	LB	Southern Cal
3. HIGDON, Alex	56	TE	Ohio State
4. Choice to Tampa Bay through Philadelphia (a)			
5. DIMRY, Charles	110	DB	Nev.-Las Vegas
6. THOMAS, George	138	WR	Nev.-Las Vegas
6. HOOVER, Houston from Tampa Bay (b)	140	G	Jackson State
7. HAYNES, Michael	166	WR	Northern Arizona
8. BROWN, Phillip	194	LB	Alabama
9. PRIMUS, James	222	RB	UCLA
10. CLAYTON, Stan	250	T	Penn State
11. MILLING, James	278	WR	Maryland
12. WILEY, Carter	306	DB	Virginia Tech

(a) Falcons traded pick to Eagles for tackle Leonard Mitchell, August 7, 1987; Eagles traded pick and 2nd-round pick in 1988 to Buccaneers for 2nd-round pick in 1988, April 24, 1988.

(b) Acquired pick for running back Cliff Austin, September 7, 1987.

ATLANTA FALCONS
1988 ROOKIE AND FIRST-YEAR ROSTER

Name	Pos.	Hgt.	Wgt.	Birth-date	College	How Acquired
Bates, Ted	DE	6-3	255	9- 4-65	Norfolk State	FA
Bayless, Gerald	TE	6-3	235	7- 5-64	Bowling Green	*FA
Broussard, Pat	K	5-7	173	9-27-66	Southwestern Louisiana	FA
Brown, Phillip	LB	6-2	230	5-30-64	Alabama	D8
Bruce, Aundray	LB	6-5	245	4-30-66	Auburn	D1
Carter, James	G	6-3	260	10-21-63	Georgia Southern	*FA
Clayton, Stan	T	6-3	265	1-31-65	Penn State	D10
Comalander, Mark	QB	6-4	205	1-24-66	Rice	FA
Cotton, Marcus	LB	6-3	214	8-11-66	Southern California	D2
Dimry, Charles	CB	6-0	175	1-31-66	Nevada-Las Vegas	D5
Fiala, Doug	T	6-6	280	3-24-65	Colorado State	FA
Fleming, Flint	DE	6-4	270	3-17-65	North Dakota State	FA
Foley, Tim	K	5-10	210	2-22-65	Georgia Southern	*T-SF, '88
Haynes, Michael	WR	6-0	180	12-24-65	Northern Arizona	D7
Higdon, Alex	TE	6-5	247	9- 9-66	Ohio State	D3
Hoover, Houston	G	6-2	262	6- 2-65	Jackson State	D6a
Houghtlin, Robert	K	5-11	170	1- 4-65	Iowa	FA
James, Danny	WR	5-10	175	11-22-65	Morehouse	FA
McGuire, Gary	LB	6-3	240	5-25-65	Houston	*Wv.-Den.
Meyers, Eddie	RB	5-9	210	1- 7-59	Navy	*FA, '82
Miller, Ken	K	6-1	195	5- 2-64	North Carolina	FA
Milling, James	WR	5-9	156	2-14-65	Maryland	D11
Parham, Daryl	T	6-6	253	7- 1-65	North Carolina	FA
Primus, James	RB	5-11	196	5-18-64	UCLA	D9
Reese, Jerry	TE	6-2	230	8-17-63	Illinois	*FA
Simon, Kevin	WR	6-0	190	11-11-66	Lamar	FA
Smith, Vinson	LB	6-0	219	7- 3-65	East Carolina	FA
Thomas, George	WR	5-9	169	6-11-64	Nevada-Las Vegas	D6
Thompson, Scott	DT	6-5	270	11-14-65	The Citadel	FA
Ward, Jeffrey	P	5-10	171	12- 4-64	Texas	*FA
Wiley, Carter	S	6-2	213	4-26-64	Virginia Tech	D12

*Bayless: FA Cleveland '87, released 9/7; Carter: FA Chicago '87, injured reserve 9/2 through 12/6, released 12/7; Foley: D10 San Francisco '88, rights traded to Falcons for conditional 10th-round pick in '89 6/8; McGuire: FA Denver '88, released 5/13, awarded on waivers to Atlanta 5/23; Meyers on military reserve '82 through '86 seasons and missed '87 season due to injury; Reese: D10 Atlanta '87, injured reserve 8/31 through 11/9, released 11/10; Ward: D11 Dallas '87, released 8/25.

BUFFALO BILLS
(Eastern Division, American Conference)

Marv Levy

President—Ralph C. Wilson, Jr.
General Manager/V.P., Administration—Bill Polian
Vice-President/Head Coach—Marv Levy (7 years: 40-54)
Director of Pro Personnel—Bob Ferguson
Director of College Scouting—John Butler
Director of Public & Community Relations—Denny Lynch
Director of Media Relations—Dave Senko
　(Office Phone: 648-1800—Area Code 716)
Assistant Coaches:
　Def. Coord./Linebackers—Walt Corey
　Defensive Line—Ted Cottrell
　Special Teams—Bruce DeHaven
　Special Asst. to Head Coach/Tight Ends—Chuck Dickerson
　Strength & Conditioning—Rusty Jones
　Defensive Assistant—Chuck Lester
　Quarterbacks/Passing Game—Ted Marchibroda
　Running Backs—Elijah Pitts
　Off. Coord./Offensive Line—Jim Ringo
　Defensive Backs—Dick Roach
　Receivers—Ted Tollner
Offices: One Bills Drive, Orchard Park, N. Y. 14127
Stadium—Rich Stadium (Capacity: 80,290)
Team Colors—Royal Blue, White and Scarlet
Training Site—Fredonia State University, Fredonia, N. Y.

1988 SCHEDULE
(All times local.
All games Sunday unless noted otherwise.)

Sept. 4	MINNESOTA	1:00
Sept. 11	MIAMI	1:00
Sept. 18	at New England	1:00
Sept. 25	PITTSBURGH	1:00
Oct. 2	at Chicago	12:00
Oct. 9	INDIANAPOLIS	1:00
Oct. 17	at New York Jets (Mon.)	9:00
Oct. 23	NEW ENGLAND	1:00
Oct. 30	GREEN BAY	1:00
Nov. 6	at Seattle	1:00
Nov. 14	at Miami (Mon.)	9:00
Nov. 20	NEW YORK JETS	1:00
Nov. 27	at Cincinnati	1:00
Dec. 4	at Tampa Bay	1:00
Dec. 11	LOS ANGELES RAIDERS	1:00
Dec. 18	at Indianapolis	1:00

1987 RESULTS—(Won 7, Lost 8)

Bills		Opp.		Att.
28	New York Jets	31	(H)	76,718
34	Houston	30	(H)	56,534
	Dallas*		(A)	
6	*Indianapolis*	47	(H)	*9,860*
7	*New England*	14	(A)	*11,878*
6	*New York Giants (OT)*	3	(H)	*15,737*
34	Miami (OT)	31	(A)	61,295
7	Washington	27	(H)	71,640
21	Denver	14	(H)	63,698
21	Cleveland	27	(A)	78,409
17	New York Jets	14	(A)	58,407
27	Miami	0	(H)	68,055
21	L.A. Raiders	34	(A)	43,143
27	Indianapolis	3	(A)	60,253
7	New England	13	(H)	74,945
7	Philadelphia	17	(A)	57,547

*Game cancelled due to strike.
Italics denote strike replacement games.

1987 GAMES STARTED

(NOTE: Players with an asterisk (*) following their names made starts only in strike-replacement games.)

12 games: Chris Burkett, Derrick Burroughs, Shane Conlan, Joe Devlin, Kent Hull, Jim Kelly, Mark Kelso, Sean McNanie, Pete Metzelaars, Nate Odomes, Andre Reed, Jim Ritcher, Fred Smerlas, Bruce Smith, Darryl Talley, Tim Vogler.

10 games: Ronnie Harmon.

9 games: Scott Radecic, Will Wolford.

8 games: Carl Byrum.

7 games: Cornelius Bennett.

6 games: Dwight Drane, Jamie Mueller.

4 games: Ray Bentley, Eugene Marve.

3 games: Leonard Burton, Will Cokeley*, Sean Dowling*, Sheldon Gaines*, Lawrence Johnson, Bob LeBlanc*, Ron Pitts, Scott Schankweiler*, Rick Schulte*, Don Sommer*, Richard Tharpe*, Scott Watters*.

2 games: John Armstrong*, Veno Belk*, Greg Bell, Tony Brown*, Scott Garnett*, Scott Hernandez*, Bruce King*, Dave Martin*, Thad McFadden*, Kerry Parker*, Durwood Roquemore*, Billy Witt*.

1 game: Gerald Bess*, Reggie Bynum*, Bill Callahan*, Steve Clark*, Will Grant*, Kevin Lamar*, Dan Manucci*, Brian McClure*, Keith McKeller*, Robb Riddick*, Leon Seals*, Johnny Shepherd*, Mark Shupe*, Joe Silipo*, Willie Totten*.

BUFFALO BILLS 1988 VETERAN ROSTER

No.	Name	Pos.	Ht.	Wt.	NFL Exp.	Birth-date	College	Games in '87	How Acquired
	Beecher, Willie	K	5-10	170	2	4-14-63	Utah State	*3	FA, '87
55	Bennett, Cornelius	LB	6-2	235	2	8-25-66	Alabama	8	T-Ind, '87
50	Bentley, Ray	LB	6-2	245	3	11-25-60	Central Michigan	9	FA, '86
	Brady, Kerry	K	6-1	205	1	8-27-63	Hawaii	*1	FA, '88
81	Broughton, Walter	WR	5-10	180	3	10-20-62	Jacksonville State	9	FA, '86
	Brown, Tony	OT	6-5	285	1	7-11-64	Pittsburgh	2	FA, '87
85	Burkett, Chris	WR	6-4	210	4	8-21-62	Jackson State	12	D2a, '85
29	Burroughs, Derrick	CB	6-1	180	4	5-18-62	Memphis State	12	D1a, '85
61	Burton, Leonard	T	6-3	275	3	6-18-64	South Carolina	12	D3, '86
80	Butler, Jerry	WR	6-0	178	8	10-12-57	Clemson	*0	D1a, '79
	Bynum, Reggie	WR	6-1	185	1	2-10-64	Oregon State	1	FA, '87
35	Byrum, Carl	RB	6-0	235	3	6-29-63	Mississippi Valley State	13	D5, '86
69	Christy, Greg	G	6-4	285	2	4-29-62	Pittsburgh	*0	OFA, '85
58	Conlan, Shane	LB	6-3	230	2	4- 3-64	Penn State	12	D1, '87
21	Davis, Wayne	CB	5-11	175	4	7-17-63	Indiana State	10	T-SD, '87
70	†Devlin, Joe	T	6-5	280	12	2-23-54	Iowa	12	D2a, '76
45	Drane, Dwight	S	6-2	205	3	5- 6-62	Oklahoma	11	SupD, '84
	Duliban, Chris	LB	6-2	216	2	1- 9-63	Texas	*3	FA, '88
	†Fox, Chas	WR/KR	5-11	190	2	10- 3-63	Furman	*0	FA, '87
59	Frerotte, Mitch	G	6-3	280	2	3-30-65	Penn State	12	OFA, '87
53	Furjanic, Tony	LB	6-1	228	3	2-26-64	Notre Dame	8	D8, '86
99	Garner, Hal	LB	6-4	235	3	1-18-62	Utah State	*0	D3a, '85
8	Gelbaugh, Stan	QB	6-3	207	2	12- 4-62	Maryland	*0	FA, '86
75	Hamby, Mike	DE	6-4	270	2	11- 2-62	Utah State	*0	D6, '85
	Hammond, Steve	LB	6-4	225	1	2-25-60	Wake Forest	*0	FA, '87
33	Harmon, Ronnie	RB	5-11	192	3	5- 7-64	Iowa	12	D1, '86
71	Hellestrae, Dale	T	6-5	275	3	7-11-62	Southern Methodist	*0	D4a, '85
	Hendel, Andy	LB	6-1	230	2	3- 4-61	North Carolina State	*0	FA, '88
67	Hull, Kent	C	6-4	275	3	1-13-61	Mississippi State	12	FA, '86
	Jackson, Kirby	CB	5-10	180	2	2- 2-65	Mississippi State	*5	FA, '87
86	Johnson, Trumaine	WR	6-1	196	4	1-16-60	Grambling State	12	T-SD, '87
52	†Kaiser, John	LB	6-3	227	5	6- 6-62	Arizona	12	W-Sea, '87
12	Kelly, Jim	QB	6-3	218	3	2-14-60	Miami (Fla.)	12	D1a, '83
38	Kelso, Mark	S	5-11	177	3	7-23-63	William & Mary	12	FA, '86
4	Kidd, John	P	6-3	208	5	8-22-61	Northwestern	12	D5, '84
	Leach, Scott	LB	6-2	221	2	9-18-63	Ohio State	*3	FA, '88
63	Lingner, Adam	C	6-4	260	6	11- 2-60	Illinois	12	W-Den, '87
	Loving, Warren	FB	6-1	230	1	11-12-61	William Penn	2	FA, '88
54	Marve, Eugene	LB	6-2	240	7	8-14-60	Saginaw Valley State	5	D3, '82
	McClure, Brian	QB	6-6	222	1	12-28-63	Bowling Green	1	D12, '86
95	McNanie, Sean	DE	6-5	270	5	9- 9-61	San Diego State	12	D3a, '84
74	Mesner, Bruce	NT	6-5	280	2	3-21-64	Maryland	11	D8, '87
88	Metzelaars, Pete	TE	6-7	243	7	5-24-60	Wabash	12	T-Sea, '85
25	Mitchell, Roland	CB/KR	5-11	180	2	3-15-64	Texas Tech	11	D2a, '87
39	Mueller, Jamie	RB	6-1	225	2	10- 4-64	Benedictine College	12	D3a, '87
11	Norwood, Scott	K	6-0	207	4	7-17-60	James Madison	12	FA, '85
37	Odomes, Nate	CB/KR	5-9	188	2	8-25-65	Wisconsin	12	D2, '87
	Partridge, Rick	P	6-1	175	4	8-26-57	Utah	3	FA, '87
57	Pike, Mark	LB	6-4	257	2	12-27-63	Georgia Tech	3	D7a, '87
27	Pitts, Ron	CB/S	5-10	175	3	10-14-62	UCLA	12	D7, '85
30	Porter, Kerry	RB	6-1	210	2	9-23-64	Washington State	6	D7, '87
26	†Porter, Ricky	RB	5-10	210	4	1-14-60	Slippery Rock State	9	FA, '87
79	†Prater, Dean	DE	6-4	260	7	9-28-58	Oklahoma State	10	FA, '84
97	Radecic, Scott	LB	6-3	242	5	6-14-62	Penn State	12	W-KC, '87
83	Reed, Andre	WR	6-0	190	4	1-29-64	Kutztown State	12	D4, '85
14	Reich, Frank	QB	6-3	208	4	12- 4-61	Maryland	*0	D3, '85
40	Riddick, Robb	RB	6-0	195	7	4-26-57	Millersville State	6	D9, '81
	Ridgle, Elston	DL	6-6	260	2	8-24-63	Nevada-Reno	*3	FA, '88
51	†Ritcher, Jim	G	6-3	265	9	5-21-58	North Carolina State	12	D1, '80
87	†Rolle, Butch	TE	6-3	242	3	8-19-64	Michigan State	12	D7b, '86
	†Sampson, Clint	WR	5-11	183	5	1- 4-61	San Diego State	*0	T-Den, '87
96	Seals, Leon	DE	6-4	265	2	1-30-64	Jackson State	13	D4, '87
	Simmons, Tony	DE	6-4	270	3	12-18-62	Tennessee	*3	FA, '88
76	†Smerlas, Fred	NT	6-3	280	10	4- 8-57	Boston College	12	D2, '79
78	Smith, Bruce	DE	6-4	285	4	6-18-63	Virginia Tech	12	D1, '85
	Starks, Kevin	TE	6-4	226	1	9-14-63	Minnesota	*1	FA, '88
	Strenger, Rich	OT	6-7	285	6	3-10-60	Michigan	*3	FA, '88
56	Talley, Darryl	LB	6-4	227	6	7-10-60	West Virginia	12	D2, '83

No.	Name	Pos.	Ht.	Wt.	NFL Exp.	Birth-date	College	Games in '87	How Acquired
89	†Tasker, Steve	WR/KR	5-9	185	4	4-10-62	Northwestern	12	W-Hou, '86
62	Traynowicz, Mark	G	6-5	280	4	11-20-62	Nebraska	11	D2, '85
	Vital, Lionel	RB	5-9	195	2	7-15-63	Nicholls State	*3	FA, '87
65	Vogler, Tim	G	6-3	285	10	10- 2-56	Ohio State	12	OFA, '79
	Winslow, George	P	6-4	205	2	7-28-63	Villanova	*5	W-Cle, '88
73	Wolford, Will	T	6-5	276	3	5-18-64	Vanderbilt	12	D1a, '86

*Beecher played 3 games with Dolphins in '87; Brady played 1 game with Cowboys in '87; Butler, Christy, Fox, Garner, Gelbaugh, Hamby, Hellestrae and Sampson missed '87 season due to injury; Duliban played 3 games with Cowboys in '87; Fox last active with Chiefs in '86; Hammond missed '87 season due to injury, last active with Memphis-USFL in '85; Hendel last active with Dolphins in '86; Jackson played 5 games with Rams, inactive for 5 games with Bills in '87; Leach played 3 games with Saints in '87; Reich active for 12 games with Bills in '87, but did not play; Ridgle played 3 games with 49ers in '87; Simmons played 3 games with Chargers in '87; Starks played 1 game with Vikings in '87, active for 1 game with Bills in '87, but did not play; Strenger played 3 games with Lions in '87; Vital played 3 games with Redskins, inactive for 3 games with Bills in '87; Winslow played 5 games with Browns in '87.

†Option playout; subject to developments.

D—Draft; T—Trade; W—Waivers; FA—Free Agent; OFA—Original Free Agent; SupD—Supplemental Draft.

Also played with Bills in '87, see page 386.

BUFFALO BILLS
1988 DRAFT CHOICES

(Number following name designates order of selection among 333 players drafted.)

Round and Player		Position	College
1. Choice to L.A. Rams (a)			
2. THOMAS, Thurman	40	RB	Oklahoma State
3. FORD, Bernard	65	WR	Central Florida
4. Choice to San Diego			
5. GADSON, Ezekial	123	DB	Pittsburgh
5. ROACH, Kirk from San Francisco (b)	135	K	Western Carolina
6. MURRAY, Dan	150	LB	E. Stroudsburg, Pa.
7. BORCKY, Tim	177	T	Memphis State
7. WRIGHT, Bo from San Diego (c)	184	RB	Alabama
8. HAGY, John	204	DB	Texas
8. WRIGHT, Jeff from Indianapolis (d)	213	NT	Central Missouri
9. BAILEY, Carlton	235	NT	North Carolina
10. MAYHEW, Martin	262	DB	Florida State
11. CURKENDALL, Pete	289	NT	Penn State
12. DRISCOLL, John from Kansas City (e)	309	T	New Hampshire
12. ERLANDSON, Tom	316	LB	Washington

(a) Traded pick, 1st- and 2nd-round picks in 1989 and running back Greg Bell to Rams in deal in which Bills acquired rights to linebacker Cornelius Bennett from Colts and Colts acquired running back Eric Dickerson from Rams, October 31, 1987. Colts traded 1st- and 2nd-round picks in 1988, 2nd-round pick in 1989 and running back Owen Gill to Rams.

(b) Acquired pick and 3rd-round pick in 1987 for running back Joe Cribbs, August 19, 1986.

(c) Acquired pick and wide receiver Trumaine Johnson for linebacker David Brandon and 4th-round pick in 1988, August 31, 1987.

(d) Acquired pick for tackle Roger Caron, who Colts traded to Bills for 8th-round pick in 1987, April 13, 1987, but did not report to training camp.

(e) Acquired pick for cornerback Charles Romes, July 14, 1987.

BUFFALO BILLS
1988 ROOKIE AND FIRST-YEAR ROSTER

Name	Pos.	Hgt.	Wgt.	Birth-date	College	How Acquired
Amoia, Vince	RB	5-11	218	3-30-63	Arizona State	*FA
Bailey, Carlton	LB	6-2	240	12-15-64	North Carolina	D9
Ballard, Howard	T	6-6	300	11- 3-63	Alabama A&M	*D11, '87
Borcky, Tim	T	6-7	295	12-10-65	Memphis State	D7
Cain, Dean	S	6-0	185	7-31-66	Princeton	FA
Curkendall, Pete	NT	6-2	280	3- 8-66	Penn State	D11
Dial, Alan	S	6-1	188	2- 2-65	UCLA	FA
Driscoll, John	T	6-5	285	9- 4-64	New Hampshire	D12
Erlandson, Tom	LB	6-1	220	6-19-66	Washington	D12a
Ford, Bernard	WR	5-9	168	2-27-66	Central Florida	D3
Gadson, Ezekial	S	6-0	205	5-13-66	Pittsburgh	D5
Hagy, John	S	5-11	190	12- 9-65	Texas	D8
Howard, Joe	WR	5-9	165	12-21-62	Notre Dame	*FA, '87
Johnson, Flip	WR-KR	5-10	185	7-13-63	McNeese State	*FA, '87
Mayhew, Martin	CB	5-8	172	10- 8-65	Florida State	D10
McKeller, Keith	TE	6-6	230	7- 9-64	Jacksonville State	*D9, '87
Miller, Alvin	WR	6-4	212	10- 5-64	Notre Dame	FA
Murray, Dan	LB	6-1	240	10-20-66	East Stroudsburg	D6
Roach, Kirk	K	6-1	217	11- 8-66	Western Carolina	D5a
Smith, Troy	S/LB	6-2	220	10-12-65	Jacksonville State	FA
Taggart, Ed	TE	6-3	222	12-19-64	Ohio State	*W-Mia, '88
Thomas, Thurman	RB	5-10	198	5-16-66	Oklahoma State	D2
Tucker, Erroll	DB	5-8	170	7- 6-64	Utah	*FA
Wright, Bo	RB	5-10	210	9-16-65	Alabama	D7a
Wright, Jeff	NT	6-2	270	6-13-63	Central Missouri St.	D8a

*Amoia: D11 New York Jets '86; injured reserve entire '86 season, physically unable to perform 8/31/87 through 11/2, released 11/3; Ballard: Played college football (NAIA) in '87; Howard: FA Tampa Bay '85, released 8/20, FA Buffalo '86, released 8/18, FA Buffalo '87, released 8/31, FA replacement Buffalo 9/24, injured reserve 10/1 through remainder of season; Johnson and McKeller missed '87 season due to injury; Taggart: FA Chicago '87, released 9/7, FA Miami '88, released 5/26, awarded on waivers to Bills 6/7; Tucker: D5 Pittsburgh '86, injured reserve entire '86 season, released (failed physical) 7/31/87.

CHICAGO BEARS
(Central Division, National Conference)

Mike Ditka

Chairman of the Board—Edward McCaskey
President and Chief Executive Officer—Michael McCaskey
Vice-President/Player Personnel—Bill Tobin
Director of Administration—Bill McGrane
Director of Finance—Ted Phillips
Head Coach—Mike Ditka (6 years: 61-27)
Assistant Coaches:
  Research and Quality Control—Jim Dooley
  Offensive Coordinator—Ed Hughes
  Special Teams/Tight Ends—Steve Kazor
  Quarterbacks/Receivers—Greg Landry
  Defensive Backs—Jim LaRue
  Defensive Line—John Levra
  Linebackers—Dave McGinnis
  Running Backs—Johnny Roland
  Offensive Line—Dick Stanfel
  Defensive Coordinator—Vince Tobin
Director of Public Relations—Ken Valdiserri
  (Office Phone 295-6600 Area Code 312)
Offices—250 N. Washington Rd., Lake Forest, Ill. 60045
Stadium—Soldier Field (Capacity: 65,793)
Team Colors—Orange, Navy Blue and White
Training Site—Halas Hall, Lake Forest, Ill.

1988 SCHEDULE
(All times local.
All games Sunday unless noted otherwise.)

Sept. 4	MIAMI	12:00
Sept. 11	at Indianapolis	12:00
Sept. 18	MINNESOTA	12:00
Sept. 25	at Green Bay	12:00
Oct. 2	BUFFALO	12:00
Oct. 9	at Detroit	1:00
Oct. 16	DALLAS	12:00
Oct. 24	SAN FRANCISCO (Mon.)	8:00
Oct. 30	at New England	1:00
Nov. 6	TAMPA BAY	12:00
Nov. 13	at Washington	1:00
Nov. 20	at Tampa Bay	1:00
Nov. 27	GREEN BAY	12:00
Dec. 5	at Los Angeles Rams (Mon.)	6:00
Dec. 11	DETROIT	12:00
Dec. 19	at Minnesota (Mon.)	8:00

1987 RESULTS—(Won 11, Lost 5)

Bears		Opp.		Att.
34	New York Giants	19	(H)	65,704
20	Tampa Bay	3	(H)	63,551
	Detroit*		(A)	
35	*Philadelphia*	*3*	*(A)*	*4,073*
27	*Minnesota*	*7*	*(H)*	*32,111*
17	*New Orleans*	*19*	*(H)*	*46,813*
27	Tampa Bay	26	(A)	70,747
31	Kansas City	28	(H)	63,498
26	Green Bay	24	(A)	53,320
29	Denver	31	(A)	75,783
30	Detroit	10	(H)	63,357
23	Green Bay	10	(H)	61,638
30	Minnesota	24	(A)	62,331
0	San Francisco	41	(A)	63,509
21	Seattle	34	(H)	62,518
6	L.A. Raiders	3	(A)	78,019
	NFC SEMIFINAL GAME			
17	Washington	21	(H)	66,030

*Game cancelled due to strike.
Italics denote strike replacement games.

1987 GAMES STARTED

(NOTE: Players with an asterisk (*) following their names made starts only in strike-replacement games.)

12 games: Mark Bortz, Richard Dent, Dave Duerson, Willie Gault, Jay Hilgenberg, Vestee Jackson, Wilber Marshall, Steve McMichael, Emery Moorehead, Ron Morris, Walter Payton, Mike Singletary, Keith Van Horne.

11 games: Todd Bell, William Perry, Tom Thayer.

10 games: Neal Anderson.

9 games: Jim Covert.

8 games: Dan Hampton.

7 games: Otis Wilson.

6 games: Jim McMahon, Mike Richardson, Mike Tomczak.

5 games: Al Harris, Reggie Phillips, Ron Rivera.

4 games: John Wojciechowski.

3 games: Egypt Allen*, Jim Althoff,*, Bobby Bell*, Lakei Heimuli*, Mike January*, Ken Knapczyk*, Glen Kozlowski*, Bruce McCray*, Sean McInerney*, Jon Norris*, Jay Norvell*, Jack Oliver*, Mark Rodenhauser*, Jon Roehlk*, Steve Trimble*.

2 games: Paul Blair, Chuck Harris*, Mike Hohensee*, Don Kindt*, Lorenzo Lynch*, Anthony Mosley*, Matt Suhey, Guy Teafatiller*.

1 game: John Arp*, Kurt Becker, Steve Bradley*, Chris Brewer*, Maurice Douglass, Gary Fencik, Brian Glasgow*, Gene Rowell*, Mike Stoops*.

CHICAGO BEARS 1988 VETERAN ROSTER

No.	Name	Pos.	Ht.	Wt.	NFL Exp.	Birth-date	College	Games in '87	How Acquired
54	Adickes, John	C	6-3	264	2	6-29-64	Baylor	6	D6, '87
47	†Allen, Egypt	CB/S	6-0	203	2	7-28-64	Texas Christian	6	OFA, '87
70	Althoff, Jim	DT	6-3	278	2	9-27-61	Winona State	4	FA, '87
35	Anderson, Neal	RB	5-11	210	3	8-14-64	Florida	11	D1, '86
81	Barnes, Lew	WR	5-8	163	2	12-27-62	Oregon	*0	D5, '86
17	Barnhardt, Tommy	P	6-3	205	2	6-11-63	North Carolina	*5	FA, '87
79	Becker, Kurt	G	6-5	270	7	12-22-58	Michigan	12	D6, '82
	Berry, Louis	P	5-11	180	1	7-21-65	Florida State	*2	FA, '88
68	Blair, Paul	T	6-4	295	3	3- 8-63	Oklahoma State	10	D4, '86
62	Bortz, Mark	G	6-6	269	6	2-12-61	Iowa	12	D8a, '83
86	Boso, Cap	TE	6-3	224	2	9-10-62	Illinois	12	W-StL, '87
6	†Butler, Kevin	K	6-1	204	4	7-24-62	Georgia	12	D4, '85
94	Chapura, Dick	DT	6-3	280	2	6-15-64	Missouri	2	D10, '87
74	Covert, Jim	T	6-4	271	6	3-22-60	Pittsburgh	9	D1, '83
95	Dent, Richard	DE	6-5	263	6	12-13-60	Tennessee State	12	D8, '83
36	†Douglass, Maurice	CB/S	5-11	200	3	2-12-64	Kentucky	12	D8, '86
22	Duerson, Dave	S	6-1	203	6	11-28-60	Notre Dame	12	D3, '83
83	†Gault, Willie	WR	6-1	183	6	9- 5-60	Tennessee	12	D1a, '83
23	Gayle, Shaun	CB	5-11	193	5	3- 8-62	Ohio State	8	D10, '84
29	†Gentry, Dennis	WR	5-8	181	7	2-10-59	Baylor	12	D4, '82
	Goode, Conrad	T	6-6	285	4	1-19-62	Missouri	*11	FA, '88
99	Hampton, Dan	DE	6-5	267	10	9-19-57	Arkansas	8	D1, '79
4	Harbaugh, Jim	QB	6-3	202	2	12-23-63	Michigan	6	D1, '87
90	Harris, Al	LB	6-5	253	9	12-31-56	Arizona State	12	D1a, '79
63	†Hilgenberg, Jay	C	6-2	260	8	3-21-60	Iowa	12	OFA, '81
24	Jackson, Vestee	CB	6-0	186	3	8-14-63	Washington	12	D2, '86
31	Jeffries, Eric	CB/S	5-10	161	1	7-25-64	Texas	1	D12, '87
93	Johnson, Will	LB	6-4	245	2	12- 4-64	Northeast Louisiana	11	D5a, '87
88	†Kozlowski, Glen	WR	6-1	193	2	12-31-62	Brigham Young	3	D11, '86
	Lashar, Tim	K	5-9	160	2	9- 5-64	Oklahoma	3	FA, '88
43	Lynch, Lorenzo	CB/S	5-9	197	2	4- 6-63	Cal State-Sacramento	2	FA, '87
85	McKinnon, Dennis	WR	6-1	185	5	8-22-61	Florida State	12	OFA, '83
9	McMahon, Jim	QB	6-1	190	7	8-21-59	Brigham Young	7	D1, '82
76	†McMichael, Steve	DT	6-2	260	9	10-17-57	Texas	12	FA, '81
87	†Moorehead, Emery	TE	6-2	220	12	3-22-54	Colorado	12	W-Den, '81
84	Morris, Ron	WR	6-1	187	2	11-14-64	Southern Methodist	12	D2, '87
51	Morrissey, Jim	LB	6-3	215	4	12-24-62	Michigan State	10	D11, '85
46	†Mosley, Anthony	RB	5-9	204	1	12-25-65	Fresno State	2	FA, '87
	Norris, Jon	DT	6-3	260	2	11- 1-62	American International	3	FA, '88
91	Norvell, Jay	LB	6-2	232	2	3-28-63	Iowa	6	FA, '87
89	Ortego, Keith	WR	6-0	180	4	8-30-63	McNeese State	8	OFA, '85
72	Perry, William	DT	6-2	345	4	12-16-62	Clemson	12	D1, '85
48	Phillips, Reggie	CB	5-10	170	4	12-12-60	Southern Methodist	12	D2, '85
27	†Richardson, Mike	CB	6-0	188	6	5-23-61	Arizona State	11	D2, '83
59	†Rivera, Ron	LB	6-3	239	5	1- 7-62	California	12	D2, '84
53	Rodenhauser, Mark	C	6-5	260	2	6- 1-61	Illinois State	9	FA, '87
52	†Rubens, Larry	C	6-2	262	4	1-25-59	Montana State	*0	FA, '86
20	†Sanders, Thomas	RB	5-11	203	4	1- 4-62	Texas A&M	12	D9, '85
50	Singletary, Mike	LB	6-0	228	8	10- 9-58	Baylor	12	D2, '81
97	Smith, Sean	DE	6-4	275	2	3-27-65	Grambling	10	D4, '87
26	Suhey, Matt	RB	5-11	216	9	7- 7-58	Penn State	12	D2, '80
57	Thayer, Tom	G	6-4	261	4	8-16-61	Notre Dame	11	D4, '83
33	†Thomas, Calvin	RB	5-11	245	7	1- 7-60	Illinois	12	OFA, '82
18	†Tomczak, Mike	QB	6-1	195	4	10-23-62	Ohio State	12	OFA, '85
78	†Van Horne, Keith	T	6-6	280	8	11- 6-57	Southern California	12	D1, '81
15	Wagner, Bryan	P	6-2	195	2	3-28-62	Cal. State-Northridge	10	T-Den, '87
55	Wilson, Otis	LB	6-2	232	9	9-15-57	Louisville	7	D1, '80
73	Wojciechowski, John	G	6-4	262	2	7-30-63	Michigan State	4	FA, '87

*Barnes and Rubens missed '87 season due to injury; Barnhardt played 3 games with Saints, 2 with Bears in '87; Berry played 2 games with 49ers in '87; Goode played 11 games with Buccaneers in '87.

†Option playout; subject to developments.

Retired—Gary Fencik, 12-year safety, 12 games in '87; Walter Payton, 13-year running back, 12 games in '87.

D—Draft; T—Trade; W—Waivers; FA—Free Agent; OFA—Original Free Agent.

Also played with Bears in '87, see page 386.

CHICAGO BEARS
1988 DRAFT CHOICES

(Number following name designates order of selection among 333 players drafted.)

Round and Player		Position	College
1. MUSTER, Brad	23	RB	Stanford
1. DAVIS, Wendell from Washington (a)	27	WR	Louisiana State
2. JONES, Dante	51	LB	Oklahoma
3. JARVIS, Ralph	78	DE	Temple
4. THORNTON, Jim	105	TE	Fullerton State
5. JOHNSON, Troy	133	LB	Oklahoma
6. STINSON, Lemuel	161	DB	Texas Tech
7. RENTIE, Caesar	189	T	Oklahoma
8. TATE, David from New England (b)	208	DB	Colorado
8. REED, Harvey	217	RB	Howard
9. MAGEE, Rogie	245	WR	Louisiana State
10. PORTER, Joel	273	G	Baylor
11. FORCH, Steve	301	LB	Nebraska
12. CLARK, Greg	329	LB	Arizona State

(a) Acquired pick and 1st-round pick in 1989 as compensation for Redskins' signing of free agent linebacker Wilber Marshall, March 18, 1988.

(b) Acquired pick for quarterback Doug Flutie, October 13, 1987.

CHICAGO BEARS
1988 ROOKIE AND FIRST-YEAR ROSTER

Name	Pos.	Hgt.	Wgt.	Birth-date	College	How Acquired
Barnard, Mike	T	6-5	259	12-26-64	San Jose State	FA
Bell, William	S	6-0	194	2-20-65	Hawaii	FA
Blue, Keith	G	6-2	253	12-16-64	Western Illinois	FA
Burger, Jeff	QB	6-0	208	5-22-65	Auburn	FA
Clark, Greg	LB	6-0	221	3- 5-65	Arizona State	D12
Davis, Wendell	WR	5-11	188	1- 3-66	Louisiana State	D1a
Deckard, Jerry	S	6-1	210	10- 5-65	Oklahoma State	FA
Ehmke, Richard	K	5-10	170	11-30-65	Eastern Illinois	FA
Forch, Steve	LB	6-1	238	12-29-64	Nebraska	D11
Jarvis, Ralph	DE	6-3	240	6- 1-65	Temple	D3
Johnson, Troy	LB	6-0	228	11-10-64	Oklahoma	D5
Jones, Dante	LB	6-1	228	3-23-65	Oklahoma	D2
Lilja, David	TE	6-4	240	8-14-64	Indiana	*FA
Magee, Rogie	WR	6-2	203	8-28-64	Louisiana State	D9
McBride, Mike	G	6-2	261	9- 5-64	Texas Tech	FA
Muster, Brad	RB	6-3	231	4-11-65	Stanford	D1
Novoselsky, Brent	TE	6-3	235	1- 8-66	Penn	FA
Patterson, Votie	WR	5-11	185	3-11-64	West Texas State	*FA '87
Porter, Joel	T	6-3	268	9-11-65	Baylor	D10
Pruitt, Mickey	S	6-1	210	1-10-65	Colorado	FA
Reed, Harvey	RB	5-11	181	9- 2-65	Howard	D8a
Rentie, Caesar	T	6-3	293	11-10-64	Oklahoma	D7
Shannon, John	DE	6-3	250	1-18-65	Kentucky	FA
Siebler, Bryan	S	5-11	194	4-10-64	Nebraska	*FA
Smith, Keith	DE-TE	6-5	240	2-18-58	Texas-El Paso	*FA '87
Solatka, Phil	DL	6-2	246	6- 1-64	Eastern Michigan	FA
Starr, Eric	RB	5-9	199	2- 2-66	North Carolina	FA
Stewart, Curtis	RB	5-11	204	6- 4-63	Auburn	FA
Stinson, Lemuel	DB	5-9	165	5-10-66	Texas Tech	D6
Tate, David	DB	6-0	178	11-22-64	Colorado	D8
Thornton, James	TE	6-2	245	2- 8-65	Cal State-Fullerton	D4
Webb, Phil	RB	5-11	200	3-15-65	Michigan	FA
Woody, Darrin	S	5-11	169	10- 9-65	Virginia Union	FA
Young, Dan	LB	6-1	253	4- 4-66	Virginia Military	FA

*Lilja: FA Miami '87, injured reserve 8/31 through 10/19, released 10/20; Patterson missed '87 season due to injury; Siebler: FA Chicago '87, left squad and released, 5/27; Smith: FA Washington '85, released 8/17, FA Denver (Arena Football) '87; granted free agency 8/15, FA replacement Chicago 9/24, injured reserve 10/1 through remainder of season.

CINCINNATI BENGALS
(Central Division, American Conference)

Sam Wyche

Chairman of the Board—Austin E. Knowlton
President—John Sawyer
Vice-President, General Manager—Paul E. Brown
Assistant General Manager—Michael Brown
Director of Player Personnel—Pete Brown
Assistant Director of Player Personnel—Frank Smouse
Head Coach—Sam Wyche (4 years: 29-34)
Assistant Coaches:
 Offensive Backfield—Jim Anderson
 Offensive Coordinator—Bruce Coslet
 Tight Ends—Bill Johnson
 Defensive Coordinator—Dick LeBeau
 Offensive Line—Jim McNally
 Linebackers—Dick Selcer
 Special Teams—Mike Stock
 Defensive Line—Bill Urbanik
 Strength—Kim Wood
Director of Public Relations—Allan Heim
 (Office Phone: 621-3550 Area Code 513)
Offices—200 Riverfront Stadium, Cincinnati, O. 45202
Stadium—Riverfront Stadium (Capacity: 59,755)
Team Colors—Orange, Black and White
Training Site—Wilmington College, Wilmington, O.

1988 SCHEDULE
(All times local.
All games Sunday unless noted otherwise.)

Sept. 4	PHOENIX	1:00
Sept. 11	at Philadelphia	4:00
Sept. 18	at Pittsburgh	1:00
Sept. 25	CLEVELAND	1:00
Oct. 2	at Los Angeles Raiders	1:00
Oct. 9	NEW YORK JETS	1:00
Oct. 16	at New England	1:00
Oct. 23	HOUSTON	1:00
Oct. 30	at Cleveland	1:00
Nov. 6	PITTSBURGH	1:00
Nov. 13	at Kansas City	12:00
Nov. 20	at Dallas	12:00
Nov. 27	BUFFALO	1:00
Dec. 4	SAN DIEGO	1:00
Dec. 11	at Houston	12:00
Dec. 17	WASHINGTON (Sat.)	12:30

1987 RESULTS—(Won 4, Lost 11)

Bengals		Opp.		Att.
23	Indianapolis	21	(A)	59,387
26	San Francisco	27	(H)	53,490
	L.A. Rams*		(A)	
9	*San Diego*	*10*	*(H)*	*18,074*
17	*Seattle*	*10*	*(A)*	*31,739*
0	*Cleveland*	*34*	*(H)*	*40,170*
20	Pittsburgh	23	(A)	53,692
29	Houston	31	(H)	52,700
14	Miami	20	(H)	53,847
16	Atlanta	10	(A)	25,758
16	Pittsburgh	30	(H)	52,795
20	New York Jets	27	(A)	41,135
30	Kansas City (OT)	27	(A)	46,489
24	Cleveland	38	(A)	77,331
24	New Orleans	41	(H)	43,424
17	Houston	21	(A)	49,275

*Game cancelled due to strike.
Italics denote strike replacement games.

1987 GAMES STARTED

(NOTE: Players with an asterisk (*) following their names made starts only in strike-replacement games.)

15 games: Reggie Williams.

14 games: Eddie Edwards.

12 games: Eddie Brown, Boomer Esiason, Rodney Holman, Robert Jackson, Emanuel King, Tim Krumrie, Jim Skow, Joe Walter, Carl Zander.

11 games: Lewis Billups, David Fulcher, Anthony Munoz.

10 games: Joe Kelly.

9 games: Max Montoya.

8 games: Ray Horton, Larry Kinnebrew, Bruce Reimers, Dave Rimington.

7 games: James Brooks.

6 games: Cris Collinsworth.

5 games: Stanford Jennings, Tim McGee.

4 games: Brian Blados, David Douglas, Bill Johnson, Bruce Kozerski.

3 games: Chris Barber*, Bill Berthusen*, Kenneth Brown*, Keith Cupp*, Tom Flaherty*, Gary Hunt*, Tim Inglis*, Mark Johnson*, Marc Logan*, Sam Manos*, David McCluskey*, Greg Meehan*, Billy Poe*, Bob Riley*, Dave Romasko*, Lance Sellers*, Daryl Smith*, Eric Thomas, Mark Tigges*.

2 games: Louis Breeden, Kiki DeAyala, Jeffrey Smith*, Dave Walter*.

1 game: Adrian Breen*, Barney Bussey, Willie Fears*, Jeff Reinke*.

CINCINNATI BENGALS 1988 VETERAN ROSTER

No.	Name	Pos.	Ht.	Wt.	NFL Exp.	Birth-date	College	Games in '87	How Acquired
61	Aronson, Doug	G	6-3	290	2	8-14-64	San Diego State	2	OFA, '87
35	Barber, Chris	S	6-0	187	2	1-15-64	North Carolina A&T	3	FA, '88
53	Barker, Leo	LB	6-2	227	5	11- 7-59	New Mexico State	12	D7, '84
24	Billups, Lewis	CB	5-11	190	3	10-10-63	North Alabama	11	D2, '86
74	Blados, Brian	G	6-5	295	5	1-11-62	North Carolina	11	D1b, '84
55	†Brady, Ed	LB	6-2	235	5	6-17-60	Illinois	12	W-Ram, '86
3	Breech, Jim	K	5-6	161	10	4-11-56	California	12	FA, '80
21	Brooks, James	RB	5-10	182	8	12-28-58	Auburn	9	T-SD, '84
81	Brown, Eddie	WR	6-0	185	4	12-17-62	Miami (Fla.)	12	D1, '85
	Brown, Gordon	RB	5-11	211	2	3-19-63	Tulsa	*3	FA, '88
99	Buck, Jason	DE	6-5	264	2	7-27-63	Brigham Young	12	D1, '87
27	†Bussey, Barney	S	6-0	195	3	5-20-62	South Carolina	12	D5, '84
80	Collinsworth, Cris	WR	6-6	192	8	1-27-59	Florida	8	D2, '81
93	†DeAyala, Kiki	LB	6-1	225	3	10-23-61	Texas	12	D6, '83
67	Douglas, David	T	6-4	280	3	3-20-63	Tennessee	12	D8, '86
73	Edwards, Eddie	DE	6-5	256	12	4-25-54	Miami (Fla.)	14	D1, '77
7	Esiason, Boomer	QB	6-4	220	5	4-17-61	Maryland	12	D2, '84
33	†Fulcher, David	S	6-3	228	3	9-28-64	Arizona State	11	D3b, '86
17	Fulhage, Scott	P	5-11	191	2	11-17-61	Kansas State	11	FA, '87
	Gaffney, Jeff	K	6-2	200	2	10-22-64	Virginia	*3	FA, '88
	Goode, John	TE	6-2	243	3	11- 5-62	Youngstown State	*0	FA, '88
71	Hammerstein, Mike	DE	6-4	270	3	3-29-63	Michigan	11	D3a, '86
89	†Hillary, Ira	WR	5-11	190	2	11-13-62	South Carolina	11	FA, '86
82	Holman, Rodney	TE	6-3	238	7	4-20-60	Tulane	12	D3, '82
20	Horton, Ray	CB	5-11	190	6	4-12-60	Washington	12	D2, '83
92	Inglis, Tim	LB	6-3	232	2	3-10-64	Toledo	8	OFA, '87
37	†Jackson, Robert	S	5-10	186	7	10-10-58	Central Michigan	12	D11, '81
36	†Jennings, Stanford	RB	6-1	205	5	3-12-62	Furman	12	D3, '84
30	Johnson, Bill	RB	6-2	230	4	10-31-60	Arkansas State	11	SupD, '84
84	Kattus, Eric	TE	6-5	235	3	3- 4-63	Michigan	11	D4, '86
58	Kelly, Joe	LB	6-2	227	3	12-11-64	Washington	10	D1, '86
90	King, Emanuel	LB	6-4	251	4	8-15-63	Alabama	12	D1a, '85
28	†Kinnebrew, Larry	RB	6-1	258	6	6-11-59	Tennessee State	11	D6a, '83
64	Kozerski, Bruce	G	6-4	275	5	4- 2-62	Holy Cross	8	D9, '84
69	Krumrie, Tim	NT	6-2	262	6	5-20-60	Wisconsin	12	D10, '83
52	Manos, Sam	C	6-3	265	2	10- 2-63	Marshall	3	FA, '88
88	†Martin, Mike	WR	5-10	186	6	11-18-60	Illinois	12	D8, '83
72	McClendon, Skip	DE	6-6	270	2	4- 9-64	Arizona State	12	D3a, '87
85	McGee, Tim	WR	5-10	175	3	8- 7-64	Tennessee	11	D1a, '86
47	Meehan, Greg	WR	6-0	191	2	4-27-63	Bowling Green	3	FA, '87
65	Montoya, Max	G	6-5	275	10	5-12-56	UCLA	10	D7, '79
78	Munoz, Anthony	T	6-6	278	9	8-19-58	Southern California	11	D1, '80
12	†Norseth, Mike	QB	6-2	200	2	8-22-64	Kansas	*0	FA, '87
75	Reimers, Bruce	T	6-7	280	5	9-18-60	Iowa State	10	D8, '84
	Reinke, Jeff	DE	6-5	275	1	9-12-62	Mankato State	1	FA, '87
46	Rice, Dan	RB	6-1	241	2	11- 9-63	Michigan	3	FA, '88
87	Riggs, Jim	TE	6-5	245	2	9-29-63	Clemson	9	D4, '87
50	†Rimington, Dave	C	6-3	288	6	5-22-60	Nebraska	8	D1, '83
	Rothschild, Doug	LB	6-5	250	2	4-27-65	Wheaton	*3	FA, '88
15	Schonert, Turk	QB	6-1	196	9	1-15-57	Stanford	11	FA, '87
70	Skow, Jim	DE	6-3	250	3	6-29-63	Nebraska	12	D3, '86
25	Smith, Daryl	CB	5-9	185	2	5- 8-63	North Alabama	3	FA, '87
22	Thomas, Eric	CB	5-11	175	2	9-11-60	Tulane	12	D2, '87
	Thompson, Robert	WR	5-9	175	1	9- 9-62	Youngstown State	*2	FA, '88
63	Walter, Joe	T	6-6	290	4	6-18-63	Texas Tech	12	D7a, '85
51	White, Leon	LB	6-2	236	3	10- 4-63	Brigham Young	12	D5, '86
41	Wilcots, Solomon	CB	5-11	180	2	10- 9-64	Colorado	12	D8, '87
57	Williams, Reggie	LB	6-0	228	13	9-19-54	Dartmouth	15	D3a, '76
	Wilson, Stanley	RB	5-10	210	4	8-23-61	Oklahoma	*0	FA, '87
49	Wright, Dana	RB	6-1	219	2	6- 2-63	Findlay College	5	FA, '87
91	Zander, Carl	LB	6-2	235	4	3-23-63	Tennessee	12	D2, '85

*G. Brown played 3 games with Colts in '87; Gaffney played 3 games with Chargers in '87; Goode last active with Eagles in '85; Norseth active for 3 games with Bengals in '87, but did not play; Rothschild played 3 games with Bears in '87; Thompson played 2 games with Broncos in '87; Wilson missed '87 season due to suspension.

†Option playout; subject to developments.

D—Draft; T—Trade; W—Waivers; FA—Free Agent; OFA—Original Free Agent; SupD—Supplemental Draft.

Also played with Bengals in '87, see page 386.

CINCINNATI BENGALS
1988 DRAFT CHOICES

(Number following name designates order of selection among 333 players drafted.)

Round and Player		Position	College
1. DIXON, Rickey	5	DB	Oklahoma
2. WOODS, Ickey	31	RB	Nev.-Las Vegas
3. WALKER, Kevin	57	LB	Maryland
4. GRANT, David	84	NT	West Virginia
5. WESTER, Herb	114	T	Iowa
6. JETTON, Paul	141	G	Texas
7. ROMER, Rich	168	LB	Union, N.Y.
8. MAXEY, Curtis	195	NT	Grambling
9. WELLS, Brandy	226	DB	Notre Dame
10. DILLAHUNT, Ellis	253	DB	East Carolina
11. HICKERT, Paul	280	K	Murray State
12. PARKER, Carl	307	WR	Vanderbilt

CINCINNATI BENGALS
1988 ROOKIE AND FIRST-YEAR ROSTER

Name	Pos.	Hgt.	Wgt.	Birth-date	College	How Acquired
Cepicky, Scott	P	6-4	217	7-29-66	Wisconsin	FA
Dickinson, Steve	S	6-0	180	11-28-65	Hillsdale	FA
Dillahunt, Ellis	S	5-11	200	11-25-64	East Carolina	D10
Dixon, Rickey	CB	5-11	177	12-26-66	Oklahoma	D1
Grant, David	NT	6-4	277	9-17-65	West Virginia	D4
Hickert, Paul	K	6-3	186	3-30-66	Murray State	D11
Holifield, John	RB	6-0	202	7-14-64	West Virginia	*FA
Jetton, Paul	G	6-4	288	10- 6-64	Texas	D6
Lee, Darryl	NT	6-3	270	10-12-63	Ohio State	*FA
Maxey, Curtis	NT	6-3	285	6-28-65	Grambling	D8
McConnell, Andrew	NT	6-3	300	12-17-64	St. Francis Xavier	*FA
Parker, Carl	WR	6-2	201	2- 5-65	Vanderbilt	D12
Romer, Rich	LB	6-3	214	2-27-66	Union College	D7
Smith, Dave	T	6-6	290	12-12-64	Southern Illinois	FA
Stewart, Vernon	WR	6-2	192	3- 1-64	Akron	*FA
Thatcher, Chris	G	6-4	275	10-10-64	Lafayette	*D7 '87
Tiefenthaler, Jeff	WR	6-1	185	6- 6-63	South Dakota State	*FA
Walker, Kevin	LB	6-2	238	12-24-65	Maryland	D3
Wells, Brandy	CB	5-10	184	6-12-65	Notre Dame	D9
Wester, Herb	T	6-7	300	5- 7-65	Iowa	D5
Willis, Steve	PK	6-3	200	4-28-62	Kansas State	*FA
Woods, Ickey	RB	6-0	231	2-28-66	Nevada-Las Vegas	D2

*Holifield: D12 Cincinnati '87, released 8/18; Lee: FA Dallas '87, released 8/25, FA replacement Dallas 9/23, released 10/7; McConnell: FA Cincinnati '87, released 8/18; Stewart: FA Pittsburgh '87, released 8/1, FA replacement Pittsburgh '87, released 10/5; Thatcher missed '87 season due to injury; Tiefenthaler: FA Atlanta '87, released 8/5, FA replacement San Francisco 9/24, released 10/3, awarded on waivers Buffalo 10/5, on inactive list for 1 game, released 10/19; Willis: FA Los Angeles Raiders '85, released 8/20, FA Washington '86, released 8/6, FA San Francisco 8/12, released 8/19, FA Atlanta '87, released 8/11, FA replacement Philadelphia 10/14, on inactive list for 1 game, released 10/19.

CLEVELAND BROWNS
(Central Division, American Conference)

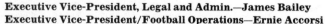

President—Arthur B. Modell
Executive Vice-President, Legal and Admin.—James Bailey
Executive Vice-President/Football Operations—Ernie Accorsi
Vice President/Director of Finance—Mike Poplar
Vice President/Director of Public Relations—Kevin Byrne
   (Office Phone: 696-5555 Area Code 216)
Director of Player Relations—Ricky Feacher
Head Coach—Marty Schottenheimer (4 years: 34-21)
Assistant Coaches:
   Def. Coord./Linebackers—Dave Adolph
   Special Asst./Offense—Ray Brown
   Secondary—Bill Cowher
   Receivers—Richard Mann
   Offensive Line—Howard Mudd
   Running Backs—Joe Pendry
   Defensive Line—Tom Pratt
   Strength & Conditioning—Dave Redding
   Special Teams—Kurt Schottenheimer
   Quarterbacks—Marc Trestman
   Special Asst./Defense—Darvin Wallis

Marty Schottenheimer

Offices—Cleveland Stadium, Cleveland, O. 44114
Stadium—Cleveland Stadium (Capacity: 80,098)
Team Colors—Brown, Orange and White
Training Site—Lakeland Community College, Mentor, O.

1988 SCHEDULE
(All times local.
All games Sunday unless noted otherwise.)

Sept. 4	at Kansas City	3:00
Sept. 11	NEW YORK JETS	4:00
Sept. 19	INDIANAPOLIS (Mon.)	8:00
Sept. 25	at Cincinnati	1:00
Oct. 2	at Pittsburgh	1:00
Oct. 9	SEATTLE	1:00
Oct. 16	PHILADELPHIA	1:00
Oct. 23	at Phoenix	1:00
Oct. 30	CINCINNATI	1:00
Nov. 7	at Houston (Mon.)	8:00
Nov. 13	at Denver	2:00
Nov. 20	PITTSBURGH	1:00
Nov. 27	at Washington	1:00
Dec. 4	DALLAS	1:00
Dec. 12	at Miami (Mon.)	9:00
Dec. 18	HOUSTON	1:00

1987 RESULTS—(Won 11, Lost 6)

Browns		Opp.		Att.
21	New Orleans	28	(A)	59,900
34	Pittsburgh	10	(H)	79,543
	Denver*		(H)	
20	New England	10	(A)	14,830
10	Houston	15	(H)	38,927
34	Cincinnati	0	(A)	40,170
30	L.A. Rams	17	(H)	76,933
24	San Diego (OT)	27	(A)	55,381
38	Atlanta	3	(H)	71,135
27	Buffalo	21	(H)	78,409
40	Houston	7	(A)	51,161
24	San Francisco	38	(A)	60,248
7	Indianapolis	9	(H)	70,661
38	Cincinnati	24	(H)	77,331
24	L.A. Raiders	17	(A)	40,275
19	Pittsburgh	13	(A)	56,394
AFC SEMIFINAL GAME				
38	Indianapolis	21	(H)	78,586
AFC CHAMPIONSHIP GAME				
33	Denver	38	(A)	75,993

*Game cancelled due to strike.
Italics denote strike replacement games.

1987 GAMES STARTED

(NOTE: Players with an asterisk (*) following their names made starts only in strike-replacement games.)

14 games: Carl Hairston.

13 games: Ozzie Newsome, Cody Risien.

12 games: Mike Baab, Earnest Byner, Hanford Dixon, Paul Farren, Dan Fike, Bob Golic, Bernie Kosar, Reggie Langhorne, Kevin Mack, Clay Matthews, Frank Minnifield, Webster Slaughter.

11 games: Eddie Johnson.

10 games: Ray Ellis, Mike Johnson.

8 games: Sam Clancy, Lucius Sanford, Larry Williams.

7 games: Felix Wright.

5 games: Rickey Bolden, Reggie Camp, David Grayson, Al Gross.

4 games: Darryl Sims.

3 games: Tim Crawford*, Brian Dudley*, Major Everett*, Cliff Hannemann*, Alvin Horn*, Mike Katolin*, Perry Kemp*, Mark Krerowicz*, Larry Mason*, DeJuan Robinson*, Mike Rusinek*, Troy Wilson*.

2 games: Keith Bosley*, Jeff Christensen*, Anthony Griggs, Tom Polley*, Derek Tennell*, Ralph Van Dyke*, Blake Wingle*.

1 game: Al Baker, Brian Brennan*, Alex Carter*, Gary Danielson*, Darryl Haley*, Nick Miller*, Dave Puzzuoli, Chris Rockins, Keith Tinsley*, David Verser*.

CLEVELAND BROWNS 1988 VETERAN ROSTER

No.	Name	Pos.	Ht.	Wt.	NFL Exp.	Birth-date	College	Games in '87	How Acquired
61	Baab, Mike	C	6-4	270	7	12- 6-59	Texas	12	D5, '82
9	Bahr, Matt	K	5-10	175	10	7- 6-56	Penn State	3	T-SF, '81
60	†Baker, Al	DE	6-6	270	11	12- 9-56	Colorado State	12	T-StL, '87
43	Baker, Tony	RB	5-10	175	2	6-11-64	East Carolina	*0	W-Atl, '86
77	Bolden, Rickey	T	6-6	280	5	9- 8-61	Southern Methodist	5	D4, '84
75	Bosley, Keith	T	6-5	320	2	6-19-63	Eastern Kentucky	3	FA, '88
36	Braggs, Stephen	CB/S	5-9	173	2	8-29-65	Texas	12	D6, '87
86	Brennan, Brian	WR	5-9	178	5	2-15-62	Boston College	13	D4a, '84
44	Byner, Earnest	RB	5-10	215	5	9-15-62	East Carolina	12	D10, '84
96	†Camp, Reggie	DE	6-4	280	6	2-28-61	California	6	D3, '83
91	†Clancy, Sam	DE	6-7	260	5	5-29-58	Pittsburgh	13	T-Sea, '85
47	Crawford, Mike	RB	5-10	215	2	1- 3-64	Arizona State	3	FA, '88
18	Danielson, Gary	QB	6-2	196	11	9-10-51	Purdue	6	T-Det, '85
29	Dixon, Hanford	CB	5-11	186	8	12-25-58	Southern Mississippi	12	D1, '81
	Dressel, Chris	TE	6-4	238	5	2- 7-61	Stanford	*1	FA, '88
26	Dudley, Brian	S	6-1	180	2	8-30-60	Bethune-Cookman	3	FA, '88
74	†Farren, Paul	T/G	6-5	280	6	12-24-60	Boston University	12	D12, '83
69	Fike, Dan	G	6-7	280	4	6-16-61	Florida	12	FA, '85
28	Fontenot, Herman	RB	6-0	206	4	9-12-63	Louisiana State	12	OFA, '85
79	Golic, Bob	NT	6-2	270	9	10-26-57	Notre Dame	12	FA, '82
56	Grayson, David	LB	6-2	229	2	2-27-64	Fresno State	11	FA, '87
53	Griggs, Anthony	LB	6-3	230	7	2-12-60	Ohio State	12	T-Phi, '86
27	†Gross, Al	S	6-3	195	6	1- 4-61	Arizona	6	W-Dal, '83
78	Hairston, Carl	DE	6-4	260	13	12-15-52	Maryland-Eastern Shore	14	T-Phi, '84
65	†Haley, Darryl	T/G	6-4	265	6	2-16-61	Utah	9	FA, '87
23	†Harper, Mark	CB	5-9	174	3	11- 5-61	Alcorn State	12	FA, '86
	Holmes, Bruce	LB	6-3	235	2	10-24-64	Minnesota	*3	FA, '88
38	Horn, Alvin	S	5-11	185	2	3- 7-65	Nevada-Las Vegas	3	FA, '88
	Jackson, David	WR	5-9	174	1	1- 2-65	Southeast Missouri State	*1	FA, '88
8	Jaeger, Jeff	K	5-11	189	2	11-26-64	Washington	10	D3a, '87
51	†Johnson, Eddie	LB	6-1	225	8	2- 3-59	Louisville	12	D7, '81
11	†Johnson, Lee	P	6-2	198	4	11-27-61	Brigham Young	*12	W-Buf, '87
59	†Johnson, Mike	LB	6-1	228	3	11-26-62	Virginia Tech	11	SupD, '84
95	Jones, Marlon	DE	6-4	260	2	7- 1-64	Central State, Ohio	1	FA, '87
54	Junkin, Mike	LB	6-3	238	2	11-21-64	Duke	4	D1, '87
	Knox, Darryl	LB	6-3	230	2	9- 3-62	Nevada-Las Vegas	*3	FA, '88
19	Kosar, Bernie	QB	6-5	210	4	11-25-63	Miami (Fla.)	12	SupD, '85
88	Langhorne, Reggie	WR	6-2	195	4	4- 7-63	Elizabeth City State	12	D7, '85
	Logan, Marc	RB	5-11	204	2	5- 9-65	Kentucky	*3	FA, '88
34	Mack, Kevin	RB	6-0	225	4	8- 9-62	Clemson	12	SupD, '84
42	Manoa, Tim	RB	6-1	227	2	9- 9-64	Penn State	12	D3, '87
57	†Matthews, Clay	LB	6-2	235	11	3-15-56	Southern California	12	D1, '78
89	McNeil, Gerald	WR/KR	5-7	147	3	3-27-62	Baylor	12	SupD, '84
52	†Miller, Nick	LB	6-2	238	2	10-26-63	Arkansas	9	D5, '86
31	Minnifield, Frank	CB	5-9	180	5	1- 1-60	Louisville	12	FA, '84
82	Newsome, Ozzie	TE	6-2	232	11	3-16-56	Alabama	13	D1a, '78
10	Pagel, Mike	QB	6-2	206	7	9-13-60	Arizona State	4	T-Ind, '86
	Patterson, Reno	NT	6-2	255	1	4-22-61	Bethune-Cookman	*1	FA, '88
	Price, Mitchell	DE	6-3	260	R	7-29-61	Livingston	*10	FA, '88
72	†Puzzuoli, Dave	NT	6-3	260	6	1-12-61	Pittsburgh	12	D6a, '83
73	Rakoczy, Gregg	T	6-6	290	2	5-18-65	Miami (Fla.)	12	D2, '87
	Redick, Corn	WR	5-11	187	1	1- 7-64	Fullerton State	*1	FA, '88
63	Risien, Cody	T	6-7	280	9	3-22-57	Texas A&M	13	D7, '79
37	†Rockins, Chris	S	6-0	195	5	5-18-62	Oklahoma State	12	D2, '84
98	Rusinek, Mike	NT	6-3	250	2	5- 1-63	California	3	FA, '88
	Shelley, JoNathan	DB	5-11	180	1	8- 6-64	Mississippi	*1	FA, '88
99	Sims, Darryl	DE	6-3	282	4	7-23-61	Wisconsin	10	FA, '87
84	Slaughter, Webster	WR	6-0	170	3	10-19-64	San Diego State	12	D2, '86
38	Swarn, George	RB	5-10	205	2	2-15-64	Miami, Ohio	1	FA, '87
50	Teifke, Mike	C	6-4	255	2	12-29-63	Akron	3	FA, '88
81	Tennell, Derek	TE	6-5	245	2	2-12-64	UCLA	11	FA, '87
87	Tucker, Travis	TE	6-3	240	4	9-19-63	So. Connecticut State	4	D11, '85
5	Watson, Louis	WR	5-11	173	1	1-11-63	Mississippi Valley State	2	FA, '88
6	Watson, Remi	WR	6-0	174	1	8-11-64	Bethune-Cookman	1	OFA, '87
85	Weathers, Clarence	WR	5-9	170	6	1-10-62	Delaware State	12	W-NE, '85
70	Williams, Larry	G	6-5	290	3	7- 3-63	Notre Dame	12	D10, '85
64	Winters, Frank	C	6-3	290	2	1-23-64	Western Illinois	12	D10, '87
22	†Wright, Felix	S	6-2	190	4	6-22-59	Drake	12	FA, '85
83	Young, Glen	WR/KR	6-2	205	5	10-11-60	Mississippi State	10	FA, '87

*T. Baker missed '87 season due to injury; Dressel played 1 game with 49ers and inactive for 3 games with Browns in '87; Holmes played 3 games with Chiefs in '87; Jackson played 1 game with Buccaneers in '87; L. Johnson played 9 games with Oilers, inactive for 1 game with Bills and played 3 games with Browns in '87; Knox played 3 games with Steelers in '87; Logan played 3 games with Bengals and on inactive list for 2 games with Browns in '87; Patterson played 1 game with 49ers in '87; Price played 10 games with Ottawa-CFL in '87; Redick played 1 game with Packers in '87; Shelley played 1 game with 49ers in '87.

†Option playout; subject to developments.

D—Draft; T—Trade; W—Waivers; FA—Free Agent; OFA—Original Free Agent; SupD—Supplemental Draft.

Also played with Browns in '87, see page 386.

CLEVELAND BROWNS
1988 DRAFT CHOICES

(Number following name designates order of selection among 333 players drafted.)

Round and Player		Position	College
1. CHARLTON, Clifford	21	LB	Florida
2. PERRY, Michael Dean	50	DT	Clemson
3. WAITERS, Van	77	LB	Indiana
4. BLAYLOCK, Anthony	103	DB	Winston-Salem
5. Choice to Phoenix (a)			
6. Choice to Philadelphia (b)			
7. GASH, Thane	188	DB	E. Tenn. St.
8. BIRDEN, J.J.	216	WR	Oregon
9. COPELAND, Danny	244	DB	East Kentucky
10. WASHINGTON, Brian	272	DB	Nebraska
11. HAWKINS, Hendley	300	WR	Nebraska
12. SLAYDEN, Steve	328	QB	Duke

(a) Traded pick for defensive end Al Baker, September 3, 1987.

(b) Traded pick, conditional pick in 1989 and cornerback D.D. Hoggard for rights to defensive tackle Chris Pike, March 25, 1988.

CLEVELAND BROWNS
1988 ROOKIE AND FIRST-YEAR ROSTER

Name	Pos.	Hgt.	Wgt.	Birth-date	College	How Acquired
Bauer, Trey	LB	6-1	215	11-28-64	Penn State	FA
Bell, Albert	WR	6-0	170	4-23-64	Alabama	*FA, '87
Birden, J.J.	WR	5-9	160	5-16-65	Oregon	D8
Blaylock, Anthony	CB	5-11	190	2-21-65	Winston-Salem	D4
Buchanan, Charles	DE	6-3	245	9-20-64	Tennessee State	*FA
Bullitt, Steve	LB	6-2	228	4-21-65	Texas A&M	*D8, '87
Burdick, Shaun	P	6-4	185	5-28-63	Cincinnati	*FA
Caston, Willie	RB	5-10	191	6- 3-66	Idaho State	FA
Charlton, Clifford	LB	6-2	238	2-16-65	Florida	D1
Conyers, Lorne	RB	5-10	185	3- 1-66	Baldwin-Wallace	FA
Copeland, Danny	S	6-2	210	1-24-66	Eastern Kentucky	D9
Cullity, Dave	OL	6-7	275	6-15-64	Utah	*FA, '87
Gash, Thane	S	6-0	200	9- 9-65	East Tennessee State	D7
Grooms, Greg	RB	6-2	198	10-16-64	Richmond	*FA
Hawkins, Hendley	WR	5-9	190	1- 3-65	Nebraska	D11
Hill, Will	DB	6-0	197	3- 5-63	Bishop College	*FA, '87
Incollingo, John	C	6-2	280	5- 2-65	Temple	FA
Jones, Tony	T	6-5	280	5-24-66	Western Carolina	FA
McKee, Eric	TE	6-4	243	4- 2-65	Southern California	*FA
Meech, Pat	T	6-3	270	12-10-64	Northern Arizona	FA
Negrin, Rich	G	6-3	275	5-29-66	Wagner College	FA
Perry, Michael Dean	DL	6-1	280	8-27-65	Clemson	D2
Pike, Chris	DL	6-7	291	1-13-64	Tulsa	*T-Phi.
Sam, Aaron	RB	5-9	196	1-17-66	Florida Central	*FA, '87
Slayden, Steve	QB	6-1	185	1-22-66	Duke	D12
Sorrells, Tyrone	G	6-3	280	5-10-63	Georgia Tech	*FA
Stephens, Tony	LB	6-1	226	9- 7-65	Kent State	FA
Taylor, Greg	WR	5-10	180	1-23-66	Bethune-Cookman	FA
Waiters, Van	LB	6-4	240	2-27-65	Indiana	D3
Wall, Jerry	LB	6-3	220	8- 5-66	Pittsburgh	FA
Washington, Brian	S	6-0	225	9-10-65	Nebraska	D10
Watson, Troy	WR	6-0	172	7-27-63	East Tennessee State	FA
White, Bobby	LB	6-2	242	1- 7-64	Penn State	*FA
Wisnosky, John	T	6-4	280	5-16-65	Western Illinois	FA

*Bell, Bullitt, Cullity, Hill and Sam missed '87 season due to injury; Buchanan: D8 Pittsburgh '87, released 9/7; Burdick: FA Cincinnati '87, released 7/31; Grooms: FA Washington '87, injured reserve 9/1 through 10/26, released 10/27; McKee: FA San Francisco '87, released 8/1, FA Miami 8/10, released 8/31; Pike: D6 Philadelphia '87, reserve/unsigned entire '87 season, rights traded for CB D.D. Hoggard, 6th-round pick in '88 draft and conditional pick in '89 draft 3/25/88; Sorrels: D12 New Orleans '87, released 8/24, FA Indianapolis 8/27, released 9/1, FA replacement Denver 9/23, released 9/29, awarded on waivers Cleveland 9/30, left squad 10/5 (exempt), reserve/left squad 10/28 through remainder of season; White: D6 San Francisco '87, released 8/28.

DALLAS COWBOYS
(Eastern Division, National Conference)

Tom Landry

General Partner—H.R. (Bum) Bright
President and General Manager—Texas E. Schramm
Vice-President, Personnel Development—Gil Brandt
Vice President, Pro Personnel—Bob Ackles
Vice-President, Administration—Joe Bailey
Vice-President, Treasurer—Don Wilson
Head Coach—Tom Landry (28 years: 247-149-6)
Assistant Coaches:
  Kickers—Ben Agajanian
  Research & Development—Neill Armstrong
  Offensive Line—Jim Erkenbeck
  Pass Offense Coord.—Paul Hackett
  Running Backs—Al Lavan
  Receivers—Alan Lowry
  Defensive Backs—Dick Nolan
  Special Teams/Off. Line—Mike Solari
  Defensive Coordinator/Def. Line—Ernie Stautner
  Linebackers—Jerry Tubbs
  Conditioning—Bob Ward
Public Relations Director—Doug Todd
  (Office Phone: 556-9900—Area Code 214)
Offices—One Cowboys Parkway, Irving, Tex. 75063
Stadium—Texas Stadium (Capacity: 63,855)
Team Colors—Royal Blue, Metallic Blue and White
Training Site—California Lutheran University, Thousand Oaks, Calif.

1988 SCHEDULE
(All times local.
All games Sunday unless noted otherwise.)

Sept. 4	at Pittsburgh	1:00
Sept. 12	at Phoenix (Mon.)	6:00
Sept. 18	NEW YORK GIANTS	3:00
Sept. 25	ATLANTA	12:00
Oct. 3	at New Orleans (Mon.)	8:00
Oct. 9	WASHINGTON	12:00
Oct. 16	at Chicago	12:00
Oct. 23	at Philadelphia	1:00
Oct. 30	PHOENIX	12:00
Nov. 6	at New York Giants	1:00
Nov. 13	MINNESOTA	7:00
Nov. 20	CINCINNATI	12:00
Nov. 24	HOUSTON (Thanksgiving)	3:00
Dec. 4	at Cleveland	1:00
Dec. 11	at Washington	1:00
Dec. 18	PHILADELPHIA	12:00

1987 RESULTS—(Won 7, Lost 8)

Cowboys		Opp.		Att.
13 St. Louis	24	(A)		47,241
16 New York Giants	14	(A)		73,426
Buffalo*		(H)		
38 *New York Jets*	24	(A)		*12,370*
41 *Philadelphia*	22	(H)		*40,622*
7 *Washington*	13	(H)		*60,415*
20 Philadelphia	37	(A)		61,630
33 New York Giants	24	(H)		55,730
17 Detroit	27	(A)		45,325
23 New England (OT)	17	(A)		60,567
14 Miami	20	(H)		56,519
38 Minnesota (OT)	44	(H)		54,229
10 Atlanta	21	(H)		40,103
20 Washington	24	(A)		54,882
29 Los Angeles Rams	21	(A)		60,700
21 St. Louis	16	(H)		36,788

*Game cancelled due to strike.
Italics denote strike replacement games.

1987 GAMES STARTED

(NOTE: Players with an asterisk (*) following their names made starts only in strike-replacement games.)

14 games: Ed Jones, Randy White.

12 games: Kevin Brooks, Doug Cosbie, Michael Downs, Jim Jeffcoat, Crawford Ker, Tom Rafferty, Jeff Rohrer, Everson Walls.

11 games: Bill Bates, Ron Francis, Nate Newton, Mike Renfro, Herschel Walker.

10 games: Kevin Gogan, Mike Hegman.

9 games: Kelvin Edwards, Eugene Lockhart, Danny White.

8 games: Timmy Newsome, Mark Tuinei.

7 games: Daryle Smith.

6 games: Tony Dorsett.

4 games: Gordon Banks, Steve Pelluer.

3 games: Rich Borresen*, Sal Cesario*, Steve Cisowski*, Chris Duliban*, Mike Dwyer*, Alex Green*, Tommy Haynes*, Dale Jones*, Don Smerek*, Russ Swan*, Bob White*, Gerald White*, Robert Williams*, Mike Zentic*.

2 games: Jimmy Armstrong*, Alvin Blount*, Cornell Burbage*, Ron Burton, Steve DeOssie, Phil Pozderac, Kevin Sweeney*.

1 game: Vince Albritton, Rod Barksdale, Thornton Chandler, John Dutton, Todd Fowler, Manny Hendrix, Bill Hill*, Jesse Penn, Rayotis Perkins*, Sebron Spivey*, Jeff Zimmerman.

DALLAS COWBOYS 1988 VETERAN ROSTER

No.	Name	Pos.	Ht.	Wt.	NFL Exp.	Birth-date	College	Games in '87	How Acquired
36	Albritton, Vince	S	6-2	217	5	7-23-62	Washington	11	OFA, '87
2	Alexander, Ray	WR	6-4	196	2	1- 8-62	Florida A&M	*0	FA, '87
87	Banks, Gordon	WR	5-10	170	6	3-12-58	Stanford	5	FA, '85
80	Barksdale, Rod	WR	6-1	193	3	9- 8-62	Arizona	12	T-Rai, '87
40	Bates, Bill	S	6-1	199	6	6- 6-61	Tennessee	12	OFA, '83
99	Brooks, Kevin	DE	6-6	278	4	2- 9-63	Michigan	13	D1, '85
15	Burbage, Cornell	WR	5-10	181	2	2-22-65	Kentucky	3	FA, 88
57	Burton, Ron	LB	6-1	245	2	5- 2-64	North Carolina	12	OFA, '87
85	Chandler, Thornton	TE	6-5	242	3	11-27-63	Alabama	12	D6, '86
70	Cisowski, Steve	T	6-5	275	2	1-23-63	Santa Clara	3	FA, '87
42	Clack, Darryl	RB	5-10	220	3	10-29-63	Arizona State	12	D2, '86
	Clark, Steve	S	6-3	186	2	12-14-62	Liberty	*3	FA, '88
84	Cosbie, Doug	TE	6-6	241	10	3-27-56	Santa Clara	12	D3, '79
55	†DeOssie, Steve	LB	6-2	249	5	11-22-62	Boston College	11	D4, '84
26	†Downs, Michael	S	6-3	212	8	6- 9-59	Rice	12	OFA, '81
81	Edwards, Kelvin	WR	6-2	205	3	7-19-64	Liberty	13	FA, '87
85	Folsom, Steve	TE	6-5	236	3	3-21-58	Utah	9	FA, '87
46	Fowler, Todd	RB	6-3	222	4	6- 9-62	Stephen F. Austin	12	SupD, '84
38	Francis, Ron	CB	5-9	199	2	4- 7-64	Baylor	11	D2, '87
66	Gogan, Kevin	T	6-7	310	2	11- 2-64	Washington	11	D8, '87
	Harris, Archie	T	6-6	270	2	11-17-64	William & Mary	*3	FA, '88
27	Haynes, Tommy	S	6-0	190	2	2- 6-63	Southern California	3	FA, '88
58	Hegman, Mike	LB	6-1	226	13	1-17-53	Tennessee State	10	D7, '75
45	Hendrix, Manny	CB/S	5-10	181	3	10-20-64	Utah	12	OFA, '86
52	Hurd, Jeff	LB	6-2	245	2	5-25-64	Kansas State	5	OFA, '87
53	Jax, Garth	LB	6-2	222	3	9-16-63	Florida State	3	D11, '86
77	Jeffcoat, Jim	DE	6-5	263	6	4- 1-61	Arizona State	12	D1, '83
72	Jones, Ed	DE	6-9	275	14	2-23-51	Tennessee State	15	D1, '74
68	Ker, Crawford	G	6-3	283	4	5- 5-62	Florida	12	D3, '85
67	Lilja, George	C	6-4	282	7	3- 3-58	Michigan	5	FA, '87
56	Lockhart, Eugene	LB	6-2	230	5	3- 8-61	Houston	9	D6, '84
83	Martin, Kelvin	WR	5-9	163	2	5-14-65	Boston College	7	D4, '87
14	†McDonald, Paul	QB	6-2	182	9	2-23-58	Southern California	*0	FA, '86
30	Newsome, Timmy	RB	6-1	235	9	5-17-58	Winston-Salem State	11	D6, '80
67	Newton, Nate	G	6-3	315	3	12-20-61	Florida A&M	11	FA, '86
73	Noonan, Danny	DT	6-4	270	2	7-14-65	Nebraska	11	D1, '87
	Oswald, Paul	C	6-3	273	1	4- 9-64	Kansas	*2	FA, '88
16	Pelluer, Steve	QB	6-4	208	5	7-29-62	Washington	12	D5, '84
59	Penn, Jesse	LB	6-3	224	4	9- 6-62	Virginia Tech	11	D2, '85
64	Rafferty, Tom	C	6-3	263	13	8- 2-54	Penn State	12	D4, '76
82	Renfro, Mike	WR	6-0	184	11	6-19-55	Texas Christian	14	T-Hou, '84
50	Rohrer, Jeff	LB	6-2	222	7	12-25-58	Yale	12	D2, '82
9	Ruzek, Roger	K	6-1	190	2	12-17-60	Weber State	12	FA, '87
4	Saxon, Mike	P	6-3	193	4	7-10-62	San Diego State	12	FA, '85
22	Scott, Victor	CB/S	6-0	203	5	6- 1-62	Colorado	6	D2, '84
	Sherrard, Mike	WR	6-2	187	2	6-21-63	UCLA	*0	D1, '86
60	Smerek, Don	DT	6-7	266	7	12-10-57	Nevada-Reno	8	OFA, '80
79	Smith, Daryle	T	6-5	278	2	1-18-64	Tennessee	9	FA, '87
	Smith, Robert	DE	6-7	270	2	12-3-62	Grambling	*0	FA, '87
19	Sweeney, Kevin	QB	6-0	193	2	11-16-63	Fresno State	3	D7, '87
63	Titensor, Glen	G	6-4	275	7	2-21-58	Brigham Young	*0	D3, '81
71	Tuinei, Mark	C	6-5	282	6	3-31-60	Hawaii	8	OFA, '83
95	Walen, Mark	DT	6-5	262	2	3-10-63	UCLA	9	D3, '86
34	Walker, Herschel	RB	6-1	225	3	3- 3-62	Georgia	12	D5, '85
24	Walls, Everson	CB	6-1	192	8	12-28-59	Grambling	12	OFA, '81
94	Watts, Randy	DE	6-6	305	2	6-22-63	Catawba	5	FA, '88
	Westberry, Gary	C	6-2	268	1	11- 1-64	Hampton Institute	*0	FA, '88
65	White, Bob	T	6-5	267	2	4- 9-63	Rhode Island	4	FA, '87
11	White, Danny	QB	6-3	198	13	2- 9-52	Arizona State	11	D3, '74
37	White, Gerald	RB	5-11	223	2	12- 9-64	Michigan	3	OFA, '87
54	White, Randy	DT	6-4	263	14	1-15-53	Maryland	15	D1, '75
23	Williams, Robert	CB/S	5-10	195	2	10- 2-62	Baylor	11	FA, '87
	Wright, Charles	DB	5-9	178	2	4- 5-64	Tulsa	*3	FA, '88
76	Zimmerman, Jeff	T	6-3	316	2	1-10-65	Florida	11	D3, '87

*Alexander, Sherrard and Titensor missed '87 season due to injury; Clark played 3 games with Bills in '87; Harris played 3 games with Broncos in '87; McDonald active for 12 games with Cowboys in '87, but did not play; Oswald played 2 games with Steelers in '87; R. Smith missed '87 season due to injury, last active with Vikings in '85; Westberry active for 1 game with Cowboys in '87, but did not play; Wright played 3 games with Cardinals in '87.

†Option playout; subject to developments.

Retired—Kurt Petersen, 7-year guard, missed '87 season due to injury; Phil Pozderac, 6-year tackle, 2 games in '87.

D—Draft; T—Trade; FA—Free Agent; OFA—Original Free Agent; SupD—Supplemental Draft.

Also played with Cowboys in '87, see page 386.

DALLAS COWBOYS
1988 DRAFT CHOICES

(Number following name designates order of selection among 333 players drafted.)

Round and Player		Position	College
1. IRVIN, Michael	11	WR	Miami (Fla.)
2. NORTON, Ken	41	LB	UCLA
3. HUTSON, Mark	67	G	Oklahoma
4. WIDELL, Dave	94	T	Boston College
5. Choice to Phoenix through Seattle (a)			
6. SECULES, Scott	151	QB	Virginia
7. HOOVEN, Owen	178	T	Oregon State
8. HIGGS, Mark	205	RB	Kentucky
9. BEDFORD, Brian	232	WR	California
10. OWENS, Billy	263	DB	Pittsburgh
11. HENNINGS, Chad	290	DE	Air Force
12. HUMMEL, Ben	317	LB	UCLA

(a) Cowboys traded pick to Seahawks for tackle Ron Essink, August 25, 1987; Seahawks traded pick and 1st- and 5th-round picks in 1989 to Cardinals for rights to quarterback Kelly Stouffer, April 22, 1988.

DALLAS COWBOYS
1988 ROOKIE AND FIRST-YEAR ROSTER

Name	Pos.	Hgt.	Wgt.	Birth-date	College	How Acquired
Adams, Mike	S	6-0	189	11- 4-64	N.E. Oklahoma State	FA
Austin, Jean	CB	5-9	186	1-26-65	Rutgers	FA
Beach, Sanjay	WR	6-0	184	2-21-66	Colorado State	FA
Bedford, Brian	WR	6-3	209	6-29-65	California	D9
Blacknell, Kenny	LB	6-2	236	4-21-66	Appalachian State	FA
Branch, Rodney	CB	5-9	184	11-24-65	Grambling	FA
Briggs, Alvin	S	5-10	184	10- 7-64	Auburn	FA
Brown, Chase	WR	6-2	218	4-15-65	Idaho State	FA
Burnett, Craig	QB	6-1	188	12-30-65	Wyoming	FA
Chappell, Curtis	WR	5-11	151	1-16-66	Howard	FA
Clark, Matt	WR	5-10	183	11- 1-64	Baylor	FA
Clark, Steven	S	6-3	190	12-14-62	Liberty	FA
Coleman, Ray	DL	6-2	240	8-13-64	Florida A&M	FA
Crawford, James	RB	5-11	194	11-30-64	Eastern Kentucky	FA
Dean, Kent	TE	6-4	234	9- 4-64	Kansas State	FA
Demore, David	LB	6-2	227	4-26-65	Duke	FA
DenBraber, Dave	QB	6-1	188	8-20-66	Ferris State	FA
Driscoll, Bob	TE	6-2	235	6- 3-66	Northwestern	FA
Duhart, Tommy	DT	6-4	281	11-29-64	S.E. Oklahoma	FA
Dunlap, Jerry	DB	5-8	175	2- 4-65	Youngstown State	FA
Friewald, Todd	DE	6-5	233	7-19-66	Virginia Military	FA
Garrett, John	WR	5-11	172	3- 2-65	Princeton	FA
Gay, Everett	WR	6-2	204	10-23-64	Texas	*D5, '87
Gibson, Boomer	LB	6-3	220	2-26-65	Arizona	FA
Gillies, Ed	G	6-4	258	6-16-64	Fullerton State	FA

Name	Pos.	Hgt.	Wgt.	Birth-date	College	How Acquired
Griffin, Tony	CB	5-8	174	11-21-64	Texas	FA
Hardman, James	G	6-3	276	11-28-64	Appalachian State	FA
Harmon, Victor	LB	6-2	220	1-19-65	Louisiana Tech	FA
Hennings, Chad	DL	6-5	251	10-20-65	Air Force	D11
Higgs, Mark	RB	5-7	188	4-11-66	Kentucky	D8
Hooker, Alan	WR	6-1	191	10-15-65	North Carolina A&T	FA
Hooven, Owen	T	6-8	302	8-11-66	Oregon State	D7
Huge, Al	DT	6-3	261	6- 1-66	Hillsdale	FA
Hummel, Ben	LB	6-4	234	8-22-66	UCLA	D12
Hutson, Mark	G	6-3	292	8-29-66	Oklahoma	D3
Irvin, Michael	WR	6-2	198	3- 5-66	Miami (Fla.)	D1
Johnson, Carl	CB	5-7	163	6-14-65	Jackson State	FA
Johnson, Eric	DT	6-7	267	12-12-65	Rice	FA
Johnson, Scott	DE	6-5	240	9-27-66	Nebraska-Omaha	FA
Jones, Karl	RB	6-1	226	11-22-65	Louisiana State	FA
Jones, Mack	WR	5-8	183	9-17-64	North Carolina State	FA
Jones, Reggie	RB	6-1	238	9- 7-63	Florida A&M	FA
Jones, Robert	DB	6-1	203	6-22-65	Houston	FA
Kremer, Jeff	LB	6-2	241	4-18-65	Kentucky	FA
Kropke, John	DT	6-4	261	1- 3-66	Illinois State	FA
LeBel, Harper	TE	6-4	245	7-14-63	Colorado State	*FA
Leet, Scott	P	6-1	184	12-26-62	San Francisco State	*FA
Malosky, Jim	QB	6-3	204	11-20-65	Minnesota-Duluth	FA
Manzullo, Mike	WR	6-0	183	4-26-66	N.E. Louisiana	FA
Marlatt, Andrew	DE	6-4	262	5- 1-65	Miami (O.)	FA
McClendon, Tyrone	DE	6-4	258	10-10-65	Georgia	FA
Miller, Jim	S	6-1	194	3- 7-66	New Mexico State	FA
Minear, Chris	G	6-2	273	5-22-65	Virginia	FA
Monk, Stanley	RB	6-0	196	12-22-66	Duke	FA
Morris, Terry	QB	6-1	195	9-29-64	Miami (O.)	FA
Moss, Zefross	T	6-6	315	8-17-66	Alabama State	FA
Norton, Ken	LB	6-2	224	9-29-66	UCLA	D2
Owens, Billy	DB	6-1	198	12- 2-65	Pittsburgh	D10
Patterson, Melvin	WR	6-2	190	9- 7-65	Stephen F. Austin	FA
Phillips, James	TE	6-4	218	3-21-65	Wake Forest	FA
Pulley, Lonnie	RB	5-10	220	10-12-65	Winston-Salem	FA
Richmond, Jim	G	6-5	289	10-21-64	Purdue	FA
Rinehart, Jeff	OL	6-1	316	6- 6-65	Arizona	FA
Robinson, Toren	S	6-1	184	7-29-65	Southern	FA
Rose, Terry	WR	5-9	165	11-26-64	Grambling	FA
Ryan, Kelly	QB	6-1	198	2- 5-66	Yale	FA
Sampson, Steve	P	6-3	211	9-12-65	Arkansas State	FA
Schell, David	DT	6-4	258	10-24-66	Arkansas	FA
Scheller, Sean	DT	6-5	250	9-27-65	Stanford	FA
Schmidt, Derek	K	5-8	183	7-20-65	Florida State	FA
Scott, Sean	LB	6-1	226	4-10-66	Maryland	FA
Secules, Scott	QB	6-3	220	11- 8-64	Virginia	D6
Simmons, Jimmie	LB	6-1	218	12- 7-65	Wake Forest	FA
Smith, Jeffrey	CB	5-10	178	11-10-66	Grambling	FA
Smith, Mark	LB	6-2	220	10-16-64	North Carolina State	FA
Smith, Vernice	G	6-2	275	10-24-65	Florida A&M	*FA
Terry, Dewayne	S	6-1	185	7-16-66	Duke	FA
Thieneman, Chris	DE	6-4	248	6- 6-65	Louisville	FA
Thomas, Chris	RB	5-8	199	2- 4-65	Miami (O.)	FA
Thomas, Franky	S	6-2	208	12- 9-65	Houston	FA
Tillman, James	LB	6-1	213	7-19-64	Alabama State	FA
Wallace, Mark	LB	6-1	210	12-12-64	Winston-Salem	FA
Warnick, Russ	OL	6-5	272	6- 1-66	UCLA	FA
Warren, Terry	LB	6-2	227	2-11-64	Florida State	FA
Washington, Sean	CB	5-11	190	3-31-66	Rutgers	FA
Webb, Charles	RB	6-0	226	10-21-64	Arizona	FA
Widell, Dave	T	6-6	297	5-14-65	Boston College	D4
Worley, Joe	K	5-10	169	9-15-66	Kentucky	FA

*Gay missed '87 season due to injury; LeBel: D12 Kansas City '85, released 8/12, FA San Francisco '86, released failed physical 4/7, FA replacement San Diego 9/29/87, (on inactive list for 1 game), released 10/20; Leet: FA Los Angeles Rams '86, released 7/25; V. Smith: FA Miami '87, released 9/7.

DENVER BRONCOS

(Western Division, American Conference)

Dan Reeves

President and Chief Executive Officer—Patrick D. Bowlen
General Manager—John Beake
Vice-President/Head Coach—Dan Reeves (7 years: 66-37-1)
Assistant Coaches:
Special Assistant—Marvin Bass
Asst. Defensive Line—Rubin Carter
Asst. Head Coach/Defensive Coord.—Joe Collier
Running Backs—Mo Forte
Quarterbacks—Chan Gailey
Offensive Line—George Henshaw
Defensive Line—Stan Jones
Wide Receivers—Larry Kennan
Tight Ends/Asst. Off. Line—Pete Mangurian
Strength & Conditioning—Al Miller
Linebackers—Myrel Moore
Special Teams/Asst. Linebackers—Mike Nolan
Special Teams/Asst. Defensive Backs—Charlie Waters
Defensive Backs—Charlie West
Director of Media Relations—Jim Saccomano
(Office Phone: 296-1982—Area Code 303)
Offices—5700 Logan St., Denver, Colo. 80216
Stadium—Mile High Stadium (Capacity: 76,273)
Team Colors—Orange, Blue and White
Training Site—University of Northern Colorado, Greeley, Colo.

1988 SCHEDULE

(All times local.
All games Sunday unless noted otherwise.)

Sept. 4	SEATTLE	2:00
Sept. 11	SAN DIEGO	2:00
Sept. 18	at Kansas City	12:00
Sept. 26	L.A. RAIDERS (Mon.)	6:00
Oct. 2	at San Diego	1:00
Oct. 9	at San Francisco	1:00
Oct. 16	ATLANTA	2:00
Oct. 23	at Pittsburgh	1:00
Oct. 31	at Indianapolis (Mon.)	9:00
Nov. 6	KANSAS CITY	2:00
Nov. 13	CLEVELAND	2:00
Nov. 20	at New Orleans	12:00
Nov. 27	LOS ANGELES RAMS	2:00
Dec. 4	at Los Angeles Raiders	1:00
Dec. 11	at Seattle	5:00
Dec. 17	NEW ENGLAND (Sat.)	2:00

1987 RESULTS—(Won 12, Lost 5, Tied 1)

Broncos		Opp.		Att.
40	Seattle	17	(H)	75,999
17	Green Bay (OT)	17	(A)	50,624
	Cleveland*		(A)	
10	Houston	40	(H)	38,494
30	L.A. Raiders	14	(H)	61,230
26	Kansas City	17	(A)	20,296
27	Minnesota	34	(A)	51,011
34	Detroit	0	(H)	75,172
14	Buffalo	21	(A)	63,698
31	Chicago	29	(H)	75,783
23	L.A. Raiders	17	(A)	61,318
31	San Diego	17	(A)	61,880
31	New England	20	(H)	75,794
21	Seattle	28	(A)	61,759
20	Kansas City	17	(H)	75,053
24	San Diego	0	(A)	21,189
	AFC SEMIFINAL GAME			
34	Houston	10	(H)	75,968
	AFC CHAMPIONSHIP GAME			
38	Cleveland	33	(H)	75,993
	NFL CHAMPIONSHIP GAME			
10	Washington	42	(†)	73,302

*Game cancelled due to strike.
(†) Jack Murphy Stadium, San Diego, Calif.
Italics denote strike replacement games.

1987 GAMES STARTED

(NOTE: Players with an asterisk (*) following their names made starts only in strike-replacement games.)

14 games: Jim Ryan, Dave Studdard.

12 games: Keith Bishop, John Elway, Simon Fletcher, Mike Harden, Mark Haynes, Ricky Hunley, Rulon Jones, Clarence Kay, Ken Lanier, Karl Mecklenburg.

11 games: Andre Townsend.

10 games: Sammy Winder.

9 games: Mike Freeman, Mark Jackson, Vance Johnson, Greg Kragen, Tony Lilly.

7 games: Stefan Humphries.

6 games: Gene Lang, Orson Mobley, Dennis Smith.

5 games: John Ayers, Larry Lee, Steve Wilson.

4 games: Bill Bryan, Rick Massie, Randy Robbins.

3 games: Mitch Andrews*, Walt Bowyer, Steve Bryan*, Kevin Clark*, Freddie Gilbert, Earl Johnson*, Tim Joiner*, Ken Karcher*, Keith Kartz*, Tim Lucas*, Bobby Micho, Ricky Nattiel, Jeff Tupper*, Bryant Winn*.

2 games: Joe Dudek*, Winford Hood*, Roger Jackson*, Shane Swanson*.

1 game: Kevin Belcher*, Ken Bell, Laron Brown*, Scott Caldwell*, Kirk Dodge*, Steve Fitzhugh*, Daryll Jones*, David Jones*, Leonard Jones*, Jack Peavey*, Martin Rudolph*, Steve Watson*, Gerald Willhite, Ray Woodard*.

DENVER BRONCOS 1988 VETERAN ROSTER

No.	Name	Pos.	Ht.	Wt.	NFL Exp.	Birth-date	College	Games in '87	How Acquired
	Ackerman, Rick	DE	6-4	250	5	6-16-59	Memphis State	*3	FA, '88
86	Andrews, Mitch	TE	6-2	239	2	3- 4-64	Louisiana State	8	FA, '87
	Araposthasis, Evan	P	5-10	165	2	10-30-63	Eastern Illinois	*0	FA, '88
35	†Bell, Ken	RB	5-10	190	3	11-16-64	Boston College	12	OFA, '86
54	Bishop, Keith	C/G	6-3	265	8	3-10-57	Baylor	12	D6, '80
24	Boddie, Tony	RB	5-11	198	2	11-11-60	Montana State	5	FA, '87
65	Bowyer, Walt	DE	6-4	260	4	9- 8-60	Arizona State	15	FA, '87
34	Braxton, Tyrone	S	5-11	174	2	12-17-64	North Dakota State	2	D12, '87
56	Brooks, Michael	LB	6-1	235	2	10- 2-64	Louisiana State	12	D3, '87
	Brown, Arnold	DB	5-11	185	2	8-27-62	North Carolina Central	*2	FA, '88
64	†Bryan, Bill	C	6-2	255	12	9-21-55	Duke	4	D4, '77
95	Bryan, Steve	NT	6-2	256	2	5- 6-64	Oklahoma	4	FA, '87
	Buford, Maury	P	6-1	191	6	2-18-60	Texas Tech	*0	FA, '88
28	†Castille, Jeremiah	CB/S	5-10	175	6	1-15-61	Alabama	11	W-TB, '87
27	Clark, Kevin	S	5-10	185	2	6- 8-64	San Jose State	11	OFA, '87
69	†Colorito, Tony	NT	6-5	260	2	9- 8-64	Southern California	*0	D5, '86
	Davis, Tyrone	DB	6-1	190	2	11-17-61	Clemson	*0	FA, '88
55	Dennison, Rick	LB	6-3	220	7	6-22-58	Colorado State	12	FA, '82
	Dorsett, Tony	RB	5-11	188	12	4- 7-54	Pittsburgh	*12	T-Dal, '88
7	Elway, John	QB	6-3	210	6	6-28-60	Stanford	12	T-Bal, '83
73	Fletcher, Simon	DE/LB	6-5	240	4	2-18-62	Houston	12	D2b, '85
62	Freeman, Mike	G	6-3	256	4	10-13-61	Arizona	13	OFA, '84
90	†Gilbert, Freddie	DE	6-4	275	3	4-8-62	Georgia	7	SupD, '84
83	Graddy, Sam	WR	5-10	165	2	2-10-64	Tennessee	1	OFA, '87
31	Harden, Mike	CB/S	6-1	192	9	2-16-59	Michigan	12	D5, '80
36	Haynes, Mark	CB	5-11	195	9	11- 6-58	Colorado	12	T-NYG, '86
	Hendley, Jim	C	6-3	275	2	10-25-64	Florida State	*3	FA, '88
78	Hood, Winford	G	6-3	265	5	3-29-62	Georgia	3	FA, '87
2	†Horan, Mike	P	5-11	190	5	2- 1-59	Long Beach State	12	FA, '86
	Hudson, Gordon	TE	6-4	241	2	6-22-62	Brigham Young	*0	FA, '88
79	†Humphries, Stefan	G	6-3	268	5	1-20-62	Michigan	7	T-Chi, '87
98	†Hunley, Ricky	LB	6-2	238	5	11-11-61	Arizona	12	T-Cin, '84
80	Jackson, Mark	WR	5-9	174	3	7-23-63	Purdue	12	D6a, '86
82	Johnson, Vance	WR	5-11	174	4	3-13-63	Arizona	11	D2, '85
20	Jones, Daryll	S	6-0	193	3	3-23-62	Georgia	1	FA, '87
75	Jones, Rulon	DE	6-6	260	9	3-25-58	Utah State	12	D2, '80
	Jordan, David	G	6-6	276	4	7-14-62	Auburn	*3	FA, '88
12	Karcher, Ken	QB	6-3	205	2	7- 1-63	Tulane	3	FA, '87
3	†Karlis, Rich	K	6-0	180	7	5-23-59	Cincinnati	12	FA, '82
72	Kartz, Keith	T	6-4	270	2	5- 5-63	California	12	FA, '87
88	Kay, Clarence	TE	6-2	237	5	7-30-61	Georgia	12	D7, '84
	Kiser, Paul	G	6-3	275	1	11-19-63	Wake Forest	*1	FA, '88
97	†Klostermann, Bruce	LB	6-4	225	2	4-17-63	South Dakota State	9	D8, '86
71	Kragen, Greg	NT	6-3	245	4	3- 4-62	Utah State	12	FA, '85
8	Kubiak, Gary	QB	6-0	192	6	8-15-61	Texas A&M	12	D8, '83
33	Lang, Gene	RB	5-10	196	5	3-15-62	Louisiana State	12	D11, '84
76	Lanier, Ken	T	6-3	269	8	7- 8-59	Florida State	12	D5, '81
	Leach, William	OL	6-5	280	1	7- 2-64	North Carolina State	*1	FA, '88
68	†Lee, Larry	G/C	6-2	263	8	9-10-59	UCLA	9	T-Mia, '87
22	†Lilly, Tony	S	6-0	199	5	2-16-62	Florida	13	D3, '84
59	Lucas, Tim	LB	6-3	230	2	4- 3-61	California	11	FA, '87
29	Marshall, Warren	RB	6-0	216	2	7-24-64	James Madison	1	D6, '87
85	Massie, Rick	WR	6-1	190	2	1-16-60	Kentucky	9	FA, '87
	McMillen, Dan	LB	6-4	235	1	2-23-64	Colorado	*2	FA, '88
77	Mecklenburg, Karl	DE/LB	6-3	230	6	9- 1-60	Minnesota	12	D12, '83
46	Micho, Bobby	RB	6-3	235	4	3- 7-62	Texas	15	W-SD, '86
89	Mobley, Orson	TE	6-5	256	3	3- 4-63	Salem College	10	D6, '86
51	Munford, Marc	LB	6-2	231	2	2-14-65	Nebraska	12	D4, '87
84	Nattiel, Ricky	WR	5-9	180	2	1-25-66	Florida	12	D1, '87
	Nugent, Terry	QB	6-4	218	2	12- 5-61	Colorado State	*1	FA, '88
	Phillips, Raymond	LB	6-3	240	2	7-24-64	North Carolina State	*3	FA, '88
	Plummer, Bruce	CB	6-1	197	2	9- 1-64	Mississippi State	11	D9, '87
	Provence, Andrew	DL	6-3	267	6	3- 8-61	South Carolina	*5	T-Atl, '88
74	Remsberg, Dan	T	6-8	275	3	4- 7-62	Abilene Christian	5	FA, '86
48	†Robbins, Randy	S	6-2	189	5	9-14-62	Arizona	10	D4, '84
50	Ryan, Jim	LB	6-1	225	10	5-18-57	William & Mary	14	OFA, '79
30	Sewell, Steve	RB	6-3	210	4	4- 2-63	Oklahoma	7	D1, '85
49	†Smith, Dennis	S	6-3	200	8	2- 3-59	Southern California	6	D1, '81
70	Studdard, Dave	T	6-4	260	10	11-22-55	Texas	14	FA, '79

No.	Name	Pos.	Ht.	Wt.	NFL Exp.	Birth- date	College	Games in '87	How Acquired
61	Townsend, Andre	DE/NT	6-3	265	5	10- 8-62	Mississippi	12	D2, '84
81	Watson, Steve	WR	6-4	195	10	5-28-57	Temple	5	OFA, '79
47	Willhite, Gerald	RB	5-10	200	7	5-30-59	San Jose State	3	D1, '82
45	†Wilson, Steve	CB	5-10	195	10	8-25-57	Howard	11	FA, '82
23	Winder, Sammy	RB	5-11	203	7	7-15-59	Southern Mississippi	12	D5, '82
	Winn, Bryant	LB	6-4	230	2	11- 7-62	Houston	3	FA, '88

*Ackerman played 3 games with Raiders in '87; Araposthasis last active with Cardinals in '86, inactive for 1 game with Broncos in '87; Brown played 2 games with Seahawks in '87; Buford last active with Bears in '86; Colorito missed '87 season due to injury; Davis last active with Giants in '85; Dorsett played 12 games with Cowboys in '87; Hendley played 3 games with Falcons in '87; Hudson last active with Seahawks in '86; Jordan played 3 games with Buccaneers in '87; Kiser played 1 game with Lions in '87; Leach played 1 game with Saints in '87; McMillen played 1 game with Raiders and 1 game with Eagles in '87; Nugent played 1 game with Colts in '87; Phillips played 3 games with Eagles in '87; Provence played 5 games with Falcons in '87.

†Option playout; subject to developments.

D—Draft; T—Trade; W—Waivers; FA—Free Agent; OFA—Original Free Agent; SupD—Supplemental Draft.

Also played with Broncos in '87, see page 386.

DENVER BRONCOS
1988 DRAFT CHOICES

(Number following name designates order of selection among 333 players drafted.)

Round and Player		Position	College
1. GREGORY, Ted	26	NT	Syracuse
2. PERRY, Gerald from Minnesota (a)	45	T	Southern U.
2. Choice to Minnesota (b)			
3. GUIDRY, Kevin from New Orleans (c)	79	DB	Louisiana State
3. Choice to New Orleans (d)			
4. Choice to Minnesota (b)			
5. ERVIN, Corris	136	DB	Central Florida
6. Choice to Minnesota (b)			
7. KELLY, Pat from L.A. Rams (e)	174	TE	Syracuse
7. FRANK, Garry	192	G	Mississippi State
8. Choice to Miami (f)			
9. FARR, Mel	248	RB	UCLA
10. WILLIAMS, Channing from Pittsburgh (g)	268	RB	Arizona State
10. Choice to New Orleans (d)			
11. CALVIN, Richard	304	RB	Washington State
12. CARTER, Johnny	332	NT	Grambling

(a) Acquired pick for 2nd-, 4th- and 6th-round picks in 1988, April 24, 1988.

(b) See (a).

(c) Acquired pick for 3rd- and 10th-round picks in 1988, April 24, 1988.

(d) See (c).

(e) Acquired pick and 11th-round pick in 1987 for linebacker Steve Busick, September 2, 1986.

(f) Traded pick for offensive lineman Larry Lee, August 19, 1987.

(g) Acquired pick for linebacker Ken Woodard, August 27, 1987.

DENVER BRONCOS
1988 ROOKIE AND FIRST-YEAR ROSTER

Name	Pos.	Hgt.	Wgt.	Birth-date	College	How Acquired
Abraham, Gerald	RB	5-10	207	7- 4-65	Wyoming	FA
Aldridge, Thomas	LB	6-2	219	11-24-64	Texas	FA
Alexander, Jeff	RB	6-0	232	1-15-65	Southern University	FA
Amend, David	OL	6-4	274	5-18-65	Maryland	FA
Baran, Dave	OL	6-5	280	6-28-63	UCLA	*FA, '87
Barker, Bryan	K	6-1	175	6-28-64	Santa Clara	FA
Borgia, John	OL	6-2	278	1-13-65	Brigham Young	FA
Calvin, Richard	RB	6-0	198	9- 1-65	Washington State	D11
Carter, Johnny	NT	6-3	295	4-23-65	Grambling	D12
Cooke, Troy	TE	6-4	227	5- 9-62	Arizona	FA
Cooper, Cary	P	5-10	160	8-18-66	Oklahoma State	FA
Corrington, Kip	S	6-0	175	4-12-65	Texas A&M	*T-Det, '88
Croteau, David	K	6-5	200	10- 9-63	Cal. St. Poly-SLO	*FA
Davis, Fred	TE	6-4	226	8-24-65	Colorado State	FA
DeFrank, Matt	P	6-2	191	8- 8-66	Louisiana State	FA
Demerritt, James	RB	6-0	225	5-31-63	Jackson State	*FA, '87
Ervin, Corris	CB	5-11	173	8-30-66	Central Florida	D5
Farr, Mel, Jr.	RB	6-0	223	8-12-66	UCLA	D9
Frank, Garry	G	6-2	289	12-20-64	Mississippi State	D7a
Gregory, Ted	NT	6-1	265	2-11-65	Syracuse	D1
Guidry, Kevin	CB	6-0	176	5-16-64	Louisiana State	D3
Harris, Clinton	DB	5-11	210	8-19-62	East Carolina	*FA
Harris, Reggie	DL	6-2	267	7-18-65	Northern Illinois	FA
Howard, Bryan	OL	6-5	266	1-11-64	Kansas	FA
Humphreys, Brad	DB	6-2	195	1-19-66	Stanford	FA
Johnson, Jason	WR	5-10	178	11- 8-65	Illinois State	FA
Juriga, Jim	G/T	6-6	269	9-12-64	Illinois	*D4, '86
Kelly, Jon	RB	6-0	195	8- 5-65	Nebraska	FA
Kelly, Pat	TE	6-6	239	10-29-65	Syracuse	D7
Kilpatrick, Darren	DL	6-4	237	2-28-65	Oklahoma	FA
Kmet, Jim	DE	6-2	250	1-16-64	Wisconsin	*FA
Marks, Richard	OL	6-4	237	12-29-64	Oklahoma	FA
Marquez, Michael	RB	5-11	185	11- 8-64	Colorado	FA
Merritt, Charles	LB	6-2	235	1-13-63	Carson-Newman	*FA
Miles, David	WR	6-2	182	3- 7-65	Brigham Young	FA
Moore, Victor	WR	5-9	180	5-19-64	Missouri	FA
Myers, Woody	OL	6-4	254	12-23-64	South Carolina	FA
Perry, Gerald	T	6-6	311	11-12-64	Southern University	D2
Reed, Richard	DL	6-4	260	11-18-63	Oklahoma	*FA, '87
Riggs, Bryan	LB	6-0	232	11- 5-64	Cal. St.-Fullerton	FA
Roberts, Steve	TE	6-4	240	12- 8-63	Washington	*FA
Rolle, Gary	WR	5-11	180	2-16-62	Florida	*FA
Sanders, Sean	RB	5-11	204	7- 7-66	Weber State	FA
Sargent, Mike	TE	6-1	262	12-30-65	Michigan State	FA
Scales, Chuck	WR	6-0	185	11-19-64	Pittsburgh	FA
Schmidt, Mark	OL	6-5	255	12-10-65	UCLA	FA
Thornton, Randy	LB	6-3	220	12-23-64	Houston	FA
Torretta, Geoff	QB	6-2	203	7- 1-64	Miami (Fla.)	*FA
Treadwell, David	K	6-1	165	2-27-65	Clemson	FA
Waltman, Chris	TE	6-7	255	11-25-61	Oregon State	*FA
Wilkinson, Rafe	LB	6-3	235	12-28-65	Richmond	*D10, '87
Williams, Channing	RB	5-10	227	2-22-64	Arizona State	D10
Wilson, Scott	DL	6-7	257	1-18-64	North Carolina State	FA

*Baran: FA Denver '85, released (failed physical) 7/16, FA Denver '86, released 8/11, FA Denver '87, injured reserve 8/20 through entire season; Corrington: D9 Detroit '88, failed mini-camp physical, rights traded Denver for conditional 9th-round pick in '89 draft 5/13; Croteau: FA Philadelphia '87, released 7/31; Demerritt: FA Denver '87, released 7/30, resigned 7/30, injured reserve 8/26 through entire season; C. Harris: D5 New York Giants '84, injured reserve 8/27 through entire season, released 8/19/85, FA replacement Minnesota 9/24/87, released 10/3; Juriga missed '86 and '87 seasons due to injury; Kmet: FA Washington '87, released (failed physical) 5/14; Merritt: FA Kansas City '85, released 8/26, FA Atlanta '86, released (failed physical) 5/13, FA Kansas City '87, injured reserve 9/7 through 10/26, released 10/27; Reed: FA Denver '87, injured reserve 9/1 through entire season; Roberts: D11 Denver '87, released 8/26; Rolle: D11 Denver '85, released 8/20, FA Denver '86, injured reserve 8/25 through 9/6, released 9/7; Torretta: FA Tampa Bay '87, released 8/17, FA replacement Miami 9/23 (on inactive list for 1 game), released 10/19; Waltman: FA Dallas '85, injured reserve 8/20 through entire season, released 8/18/86; Wilkinson: D10 Denver '87, injured reserve 9/1 through entire season.

DETROIT LIONS
(Central Division, National Conference)

Darryl Rogers

Owner and President—William Clay Ford
Executive Vice-President and G.M.—Russ Thomas
Head Coach/Dir. of Football Oper.—Darryl Rogers
(3 years: 16-31)
Assistant Coaches:
Offensive Coordinator—Bob Baker
Special Teams—Carl Battershell
Receivers—Lew Carpenter
Strength & Conditioning—Don Clemons
Administrative Assistant/Tight Ends—Don Doll
Defensive Coordinator/Secondary—Wayne Fontes
Defensive Line—Dick Modzelewski
Offensive Line—Bill Muir
Inside Linebackers—Mike Murphy
Offensive Backfield—Vic Rapp
Outside Linebackers—Willie Shaw
Public Relations Director—Bill Keenist
(Office Phone: 335-4131—Area Code 313)
Offices—1200 Featherstone Road, Box 4200, Pontiac, Mich. 48057
Stadium—Pontiac Silverdome (Capacity: 80,638)
Team Colors—Honolulu Blue and Silver
Training Site—Oakland University, Rochester, Mich.

1988 SCHEDULE
(All times local.
All games Sunday unless noted otherwise.)

Date	Opponent	Time
Sept. 4	ATLANTA	1:00
Sept. 11	at Los Angeles Rams	1:00
Sept. 18	NEW ORLEANS	1:00
Sept. 25	NEW YORK JETS	1:00
Oct. 2	at San Francisco	1:00
Oct. 9	CHICAGO	1:00
Oct. 16	at New York Giants	1:00
Oct. 23	at Kansas City	12:00
Oct. 30	NEW YORK GIANTS	1:00
Nov. 6	at Minnesota	12:00
Nov. 13	TAMPA BAY	1:00
Nov. 20	vs. Green Bay at Milwaukee	12:00
Nov. 24	MINNESOTA (Thanksgiving)	12:30
Dec. 4	GREEN BAY	1:00
Dec. 11	at Chicago	12:00
Dec. 18	at Tampa Bay	1:00

1987 RESULTS—(Won 4, Lost 11)

Lions		Opp.		Att.
19	Minnesota	34	(A)	57,061
7	L.A. Raiders	27	(A)	50,300
	Chicago*		(H)	
27	*Tampa Bay*	*31*	*(H)*	*4,919*
19	*Green Bay (OT)*	*16*	*(A)*	*35,779*
14	*Seattle*	*37*	*(H)*	*8,310*
33	Green Bay	34	(H)	27,278
0	Denver	34	(A)	75,172
27	Dallas	17	(H)	45,325
13	Washington	20	(A)	53,593
10	Chicago	30	(A)	63,357
20	Kansas City	27	(H)	43,820
16	L.A. Rams	37	(H)	33,143
20	Tampa Bay	10	(A)	41,699
14	Minnesota	17	(H)	27,693
30	Atlanta	13	(A)	13,906

*Game cancelled due to strike.
Italics denote strike replacement games.

1987 GAMES STARTED

(NOTE: Players with an asterisk (*) following their names made starts only in strike-replacement games.)

12 games: Jerry Ball, Dennis Gibson, James Griffin, Chuck Long, Pete Mandley, Bruce McNorton, Shelton Robinson, Jimmy Williams.

11 games: Lomas Brown, Mike Cofer, James Jones, Steve Mott, Harvey Salem, Eric M. Williams.

10 games: Scott Barrows, Rafael Cherry.

9 games: Keith Ferguson, Kevin Glover.

8 games: Jeff Chadwick, Rob Rubick.

7 games: Duane Galloway, George James.

5 games: Keith Dorney, William Gay, Bobby Watkins.

3 games: Charles Benson*, Karl Bernard, Thomas Boyd*, Carl Carr*, Jerome Davis*, Stan Edwards*, Anthony Fields*, Alvin Hall*, Todd Hons*, Gary Lee, Greg Orton*, Jerry Quaerna*, Rich Strenger, Eric Truvillion*, Jim Warne*, Mark Witte*.

2 games: Pat Cain*, Gary Ellerson*, Creig Federico*, Joe Felton*, Darrell Grymes*, Maurice Harvey*, Vyto Kab, George McDuffie*, Anthony Office*, Robert Thompson*, Scott Williams.

1 game: John Bostic*, Danny Bradley*, Tony Dollinger*, Chris Geile*, Jimmie Giles, William Graham, Steve Hirsch*, Angelo King*, Mark Lewis, Danny Lockett*, Vernon Maxwell, Mark Nichols, Chuck Steele*, Ivory Sully, Cleve Wester*.

DETROIT LIONS 1988 VETERAN ROSTER

No.	Name	Pos.	Ht.	Wt.	NFL Exp.	Birth-date	College	Games in '87	How Acquired
6	†Arnold, Jim	P	6-3	211	6	1-31-61	Vanderbilt	11	FA, '86
68	†Baack, Steve	G	6-4	265	5	11-16-60	Oregon	7	D3b, '84
93	Ball, Jerry	NT	6-1	283	2	12-15-64	Southern Methodist	12	D3, '87
61	Barrows, Scott	G/C	6-2	278	3	3-31-63	West Virginia	12	FA, '86
	Beemer, Bob	DT	6-5	231	1	5-14-63	Toledo	2	FA, '88
	Benson, Charles	DE	6-1	267	4	11-21-60	Baylor	3	FA, '88
25	Bernard, Karl	RB	5-11	205	2	10-12-64	Southwestern Louisiana	8	OFA, '87
80	Bland, Carl	WR	5-11	182	5	8-17-61	Virginia Union	10	OFA, '84
75	Brown, Lomas	T	6-4	282	4	3-30-63	Florida	11	D1, '85
	Brown, Raynard	WR	5-9	185	1	7-25-65	South Carolina	*1	FA, '88
96	Butcher, Paul	LB	6-0	219	3	11- 8-63	Wayne State	12	FA, '86
	Carr, Carl	LB	6-3	230	2	3-26-64	North Carolina	3	FA, '88
	Carthens, Milt	OT	6-4	305	1	12-22-60	Michigan	*1	FA, '88
89	Chadwick, Jeff	WR	6-3	190	6	12-16-60	Grand Valley State	8	OFA, '83
45	Cherry, Raphel	S	6-0	194	3	12-19-61	Hawaii	10	FA, '87
55	Cofer, Michael	LB	6-5	245	6	4- 7-60	Tennessee	11	D3, '83
	Davis, Jerome	NT	6-1	260	2	2-27-62	Ball State	3	FA, '88
70	Dorney, Keith	G/T	6-5	285	10	12- 3-57	Penn State	5	D1, '79
42	†Ellerson, Gary	RB/KR	5-11	220	4	7-17-63	Wisconsin	8	FA, '87
77	†Ferguson, Keith	DE	6-5	260	8	4- 3-59	Ohio State	12	W-SD, '85
40	†Galloway, Duane	CB/S	5-8	181	3	11- 7-61	Arizona State	10	FA, '85
98	Gibson, Dennis	LB	6-2	240	2	2- 8-64	Iowa State	12	D8, '87
53	Glover, Kevin	C/G	6-2	267	4	6-17-63	Maryland	12	D2, '85
62	†Green, Curtis	DE/NT	6-3	265	8	6- 3-57	Alabama State	12	D2, '81
34	Griffin, James	S	6-2	197	6	9- 7-61	Middle Tennessee State	12	FA, '86
	Grymes, Darrell	WR	6-2	186	1	12- 4-62	Central State (O.)	2	FA, '87
	Hill, David	TE	6-2	240	12	1- 1-54	Texas A&I	*12	FA, '88
17	Hipple, Eric	QB	6-2	198	8	9-16-57	Utah State	*0	D4, '80
32	James, Garry	RB	5-10	214	3	9- 4-63	Louisiana State	8	D2, '86
95	Jamison, George	LB	6-1	226	2	9-30-62	Cincinnati	12	SupD, '87
	Johnson, Earl	CB	6-0	190	2	10-20-63	South Carolina	*3	FA, '88
	Johnson, Rick	OT	6-6	255	1	12-12-63	Grand Valley State	1	FA, '88
30	Jones, James	RB	6-2	229	6	3-21-61	Florida	11	D1, '83
87	†Kab, Vyto	TE	6-5	240	6	12-23-59	Penn State	7	W-Cle, '87
83	Lee, Gary	WR/KR	6-1	202	2	2-12-65	Georgia Tech	12	D12, '87
81	Lewis, Mark	TE	6-2	250	3	5- 5-61	Texas A&M	*10	FA, '87
50	Lockett, Danny	LB	6-2	228	2	7-11-64	Arizona	13	D6, '87
16	Long, Chuck	QB	6-4	211	3	2-18-63	Iowa	12	D1, '86
82	Mandley, Pete	WR/KR	5-10	191	5	7-29-61	Northern Arizona	12	D2, '84
57	Maxwell, Vernon	LB	6-2	235	6	10-25-61	Arizona State	12	FA, '85
	McDuffie, George	DE	6-6	270	2	1-20-63	Findlay	3	FA, '88
29	McNorton, Bruce	CB	5-11	175	7	2-28-59	Georgetown (Ky.)	12	D4, '82
74	Milinichik, Joe	G/T	6-5	275	2	3-30-63	North Carolina State	11	D3, '86
31	Mitchell, Devon	S	6-1	194	2	12-30-62	Iowa	*0	D4, '86
52	Mott, Steve	C	6-3	270	6	3-24-61	Alabama	11	D5a, '83
3	Murray, Ed	K	5-10	175	9	8-29-56	Tulane	12	D7, '80
86	Nichols, Mark	WR	6-2	208	7	10-29-59	San Jose State	12	D1, '81
49	†Paige, Tony	RB	5-10	230	5	10-14-62	Virginia Tech	5	FA, '87
51	†Robinson, Shelton	LB	6-2	236	7	9-14-60	North Carolina	12	T-Sea, '86
60	Rogers, Reggie	DE	6-6	272	2	1-21-64	Washington	6	D1, '87
84	Rubick, Rob	TE	6-3	234	7	9-27-60	Grand Valley State	9	D12a, '82
97	Saleaumua, Dan	NT	6-0	285	2	11-11-65	Arizona State	9	D7, '87
73	Salem, Harvey	G	6-6	285	6	1-15-61	California	11	T-Hou, '86
64	Sanders, Eric	T/G	6-7	280	8	10-22-58	Nevada-Reno	12	W-Atl, '87
28	Sheffield, Chris	CB	6-1	200	3	1- 9-63	Albany State	*11	FA, '87
41	Smith, Ricky	WR/CB	6-0	188	5	7-20-60	Alabama State	12	FA, '87
	Walker, Kevin	DB	5-11	180	3	10-20-63	East Carolina	*3	FA, '88
	Warren, John	DB	5-9	174	1	4-25-63	Virginia Union	*0	FA, '88
27	Watkins, Bobby	CB	5-10	184	7	5-31-60	Southwest Texas State	5	D2, '82
	Wester, Cleve	RB	5-8	188	2	6-14-64	Concordia (Neb.)	3	FA, '88
	Wheeler, Mark	TE	6-2	232	2	6-15-66	Kentucky	3	FA, '88
76	Williams, Eric	NT	6-4	280	5	2-24-62	Washington State	11	D3, '84
59	Williams, Jimmy	LB	6-3	230	7	11-15-60	Nebraska	12	D1, '82
38	†Williams, Scott	RB	6-2	234	3	7-21-62	Georgia	5	FA, '86
21	†Woolfolk, Butch	RB	6-1	212	7	3- 1-60	Michigan	12	W-Cle, '87

*R. Brown played 1 game with 49ers in '87 and on inactive list for 5 games with Lions in '87; Carthens played 1 game with Colts in '87; Hill played 12 games with Rams in '87; Hipple and Mitchell missed '87 season due to injury; Johnson played 3 games with Broncos, active for 2 games with Lions in

'87; Lewis played 1 game with Packers, 9 with Lions in '87; Sheffield played 5 games with Steelers, 6 with Lions in '87; Walker played 3 games with Buccaneers in '87; Warren last active with Los Angeles-USFL in '85.

†Option playout; subject to developments.

D—Draft; T—Trade; W—Waivers; FA—Free Agent; OFA—Original Free Agent; SupD—Supplemental Draft.

Also played with Lions in '87, see page 386.

DETROIT LIONS
1988 DRAFT CHOICES

(Number following name designates order of selection among 333 players drafted.)

Round and Player		Position	College
1. Choice to Kansas City (a)			
1. BLADES, Bennie from Kansas City (b)	3	DB	Miami (Fla.)
2. SPIELMAN, Chris from Kansas City (b)	29	LB	Ohio State
2. CARTER, Pat	32	TE	Florida State
3. ROUNDTREE, Ray	58	WR	Penn State
4. WHITE, William	85	DB	Ohio State
5. ANDOLSEK, Eric	111	G	Louisiana State
6. PAINTER, Carl	142	RB	Hampton (Va.)
7. JAMES, Jeff	169	WR	Stanford
8. HADD, Gary	196	DE	Minnesota
9. CORRINGTON, Kip (c)	223	DB	Texas A&M
9. IRVIN, Todd from Philadelphia (d)	234	T	Mississippi
10. CRAIG, Paco	254	WR	UCLA
11. McCOIN, Danny	281	QB	Cincinnati
12. Choice to Indianapolis (e)			

(a) Traded pick for 1st- and 2nd-round picks in 1988, April 20, 1988.
(b) See (a).
(c) Rights traded to Denver for conditional 9th-round pick in 1989 draft, May 13, 1988.
(d) Acquired pick for tight end Jimmie Giles, November 3, 1987.
(e) Traded pick for tight end Derrick Ramsey, September 1, 1987.

DETROIT LIONS
1988 ROOKIE AND FIRST-YEAR ROSTER

Name	Pos.	Hgt.	Wgt.	Birth-date	College	How Acquired
Andolsek, Eric	G	6-2	281	8-22-66	Louisiana State	D5
Beaty, Douglas	RB	6-1	221	9-17-65	Appalachian State	FA
Blades, Bennie	S	6-1	216	9- 3-66	Miami (Fla.)	D1
Bostic, Carl	LB	6-2	231	5-12-65	Michigan	FA
Brasco, Mark	K	5-10	175	3-30-66	Pittsburgh	FA
Bryant, Willie	DB	6-0	195	3-10-66	Louisiana State	FA
Bulger, L.C.	FB	5-11	205	7-20-64	Wayne State	FA
Carter, Pat	TE	6-4	263	8- 1-66	Florida State	D2a
Craig, Paco	WR	5-10	170	2- 2-65	UCLA	D10
Garner, Dene	K	5-9	165	9-21-64	Utah State	FA
Giuliano, Joe	G	6-4	282	1- 1-65	Maryland	FA
Hadd, Gary	NT	6-4	270	10-19-65	Minnesota	D8
Holinka, Jeff	G	6-3	270	9-19-63	Maryland	*FA
Hughes, William	C	6-5	285	6- 6-65	Maryland	FA
Irvin, Todd	T	6-5	288	2- 1-65	Mississippi	D9a
James, Jeff	WR	5-11	179	3-25-65	Stanford	D7
Johnson, Greg	P	6-2	190	2- 9-63	Bowling Green	FA
Johnson, Michael	LB	6-2	222	3- 2-66	Texas Tech	FA
Kosor, Ron	C	6-2	270	12- 2-62	North Carolina State	*FA-'87
McCoin, Danny	QB	6-3	206	8-31-64	Cincinnati	D11
Painter, Carl	RB	5-9	184	5-10-64	Hampton Institute	D6
Peppers, Victor	DB	5-8	155	5-29-66	Tennessee	FA
Reveiz, Louis	K	5-10	175	11-14-65	Carson-Newman	FA
Roundtree, Ray	WR	6-0	180	4-19-66	Penn State	D3
Saltz, Lee	QB	6-1	195	9-25-63	Temple	*FA-'87
Schmidt, Mark	WR	6-1	190	4-27-64	Buffalo	FA
Shafer, Donald	K	5-10	175	6-15-64	Southern California	*FA
Spence, Marvin	DB	5-10	179	12-25-63	Notre Dame	FA
Spielman, Chris	LB	6-0	234	10-11-65	Ohio State	D2
Spielman, Rick	LB	6-0	230	12- 2-62	Southern Illinois	*FA
Stafford, Angelo	WR	6-6	213	1-12-65	Alabama	FA
White, William	CB	5-10	189	2-19-66	Ohio State	D4

*Holinka: FA New York Giants '86, released 8/11; Kosor: FA New England '86, injured reserve 8/18 through 9/15, released 9/16, FA Detroit '87, injured reserve 9/1 through entire season; Saltz on injured reserve 9/1 through entire season; Shafer: FA Atlanta '87, released 9/1, FA replacement Los Angeles Rams 9/23, released 10/3; R. Spielman: FA San Diego '87, released 7/30.

GREEN BAY PACKERS
(Central Division, National Conference)

Lindy Infante

President—Hon. Robert J. Parins
Executive V.P./Administration—Bob Harlan
Head Coach—Lindy Infante (First Year)
Vice President/Football Operations—Tom Braatz
Director of College Scouting—Dick Corrick
Assistant Coaches:
  Defensive Coordinator—Hank Bullough
  Defensive Line—Greg Blache
  Offensive Line—Charlie Davis
  Receivers—Wayne (Buddy) Geis
  Defensive Backfield—Dick Jauron
  Stren./Cond./Off. Line—Virgil Knight
  Outside Linebackers—Richard Moseley
  Offensive Backfield—Willie Peete
  Special Teams—Howard Tippett
Public Relations Director—Lee Remmel
  (Office Phone: 494-2351—Area Code 414)
Offices—1265 Lombardi Ave., Green Bay, Wis. 54303
Mailing Address—P.O. Box 10628, Green Bay, Wis. 54307-0628
Stadium—Lambeau Field, Green Bay (Capacity: 57,063); County Stadium, Milwaukee (Capacity: 56,051)
Team Colors—Green, Gold and White
Training Site—St. Norbert College, De Pere, Wis. (food and lodging only; workouts at Lambeau Field, Green Bay)

1988 SCHEDULE
(All times local.
All games Sunday unless noted otherwise.)

Sept. 4	LOS ANGELES RAMS	12:00
Sept. 11	TAMPA BAY	12:00
Sept. 18	at Miami	1:00
Sept. 25	CHICAGO	12:00
Oct. 2	at Tampa Bay	1:00
Oct. 9	NEW ENGLAND at Milwaukee	12:00
Oct. 16	at Minnesota	12:00
Oct. 23	WASHINGTON at Milwaukee	12:00
Oct. 30	at Buffalo	1:00
Nov. 6	at Atlanta	1:00
Nov. 13	INDIANAPOLIS	12:00
Nov. 20	DETROIT at Milwaukee	12:00
Nov. 27	at Chicago	12:00
Dec. 4	at Detroit	1:00
Dec. 11	MINNESOTA	12:00
Dec. 18	at Phoenix	2:00

1987 RESULTS—(Won 5, Lost 9, Tied 1)

Packers		Opp.		Att.
0	L.A. Raiders	20	(H)	54,983
17	Denver (OT)	17	(H)	50,624
	Tampa Bay*		(A)	
23	*Minnesota*	*16*	*(A)*	*13,911*
16	*Detroit (OT)*	*19*	*(H)*	*35,779*
16	*Philadelphia (OT)*	*10*	*(H)*	*35,842*
34	Detroit	33	(A)	27,278
17	Tampa Bay	23	(H)	50,308
24	Chicago	26	(H)	53,320
13	Seattle	24	(A)	60,963
23	Kansas City	3	(A)	34,611
10	Chicago	23	(A)	61,638
12	San Francisco	23	(H)	51,118
16	Minnesota	10	(H)	47,059
10	New York Giants	20	(A)	51,013
24	New Orleans	33	(A)	68,364

*Game cancelled due to strike.
Italics denote strike replacement games.

1987 GAMES STARTED

(NOTE: Players with an asterisk (*) following their names made starts only in strike-replacement games.)

12 games: John Anderson, Dave Brown, Robert Brown, Mark Cannon, Alphonso Carreker, Ron Hallstrom, Tim Harris, Johnny Holland, Mark Lee, Rich Moran, Mark Murphy, Brian Noble, Ken Ruettgers, Walter Stanley.

11 games: Ken Stills, Ed West.

10 games: Jessie Clark.

9 games: Phillip Epps.

8 games: Jerry Boyarsky, Kenneth Davis, Keith Uecker.

7 games: Randy Wright.

6 games: Steve Collier.

5 games: Paul Ott Carruth, Don Majkowski.

3 games: David Caldwell*, Anthony Harrison*, Jim Hobbins*, Ed Konopasek*, Rydell Malancon*, Lee Morris*, Frankie Neal, John Pointer*, Vince Rafferty*, Louis Rash*, Alan Risher*, Patrick Scott*, Carl Sullivan*, Charles Washington*, Kevin Willhite*.

2 games: Todd Auer*, Ross Browner, Putt Choate*, Jimmy Hargrove*, Craig Jay*, Charles Martin, Sylvester McGrew*, Jim Bob Morris*, Alan Veingrad.

1 game: Tony Elliott*, Brent Fullwood, Tiger Greene, Perry Hartnett*, Kenneth Jordan*, Tony Leiker*, Mark Lewis, John McGarry*, Ron Monaco*, Don Summers*, Lavale Thomas*.

GREEN BAY PACKERS 1988 VETERAN ROSTER

No.	Name	Pos.	Ht.	Wt.	NFL Exp.	Birth-date	College	Games in '87	How Acquired
59	Anderson, John	LB	6-3	228	11	2-14-56	Michigan	12	D1a, '78
61	†Boyarsky, Jerry	NT	6-3	290	8	5-15-59	Pittsburgh	12	FA, '87
17	Bracken, Don	P	6-0	211	4	2-16-62	Michigan	12	FA, '85
32	Brown, Dave	CB	6-1	197	14	1-16-53	Michigan	12	T-Sea, '87
93	†Brown, Robert	DE	6-2	267	7	5-21-60	Virginia Tech	12	D4, '82
79	†Browner, Ross	DE	6-3	265	11	3-22-54	Notre Dame	11	FA, '87
58	†Cannon, Mark	C	6-3	258	5	6-14-62	Texas-Arlington	12	D11, '84
76	†Carreker, Alphonso	DE	6-6	271	5	5-25-62	Florida State	12	D1, '84
30	Carruth, Paul Ott	RB	6-1	220	3	7-22-61	Alabama	12	FA, '86
69	†Cherry, Bill	C/G	6-4	277	3	1- 5-61	Middle Tennessee St.	12	FA, '86
33	†Clark, Jessie	RB	6-0	228	6	1- 3-60	Arkansas	12	D7, '83
64	Collier, Steve	T	6-7	342	2	4-19-63	Bethune-Cookman	10	FA, '87
20	Cook, Kelly	RB	5-10	225	2	8-20-62	Oklahoma State	11	FA, '87
36	Davis, Kenneth	RB	5-10	209	3	4-16-62	Texas Christian	10	D2, '86
56	Dent, Burnett	LB	6-1	236	3	3-16-63	Tulane	9	D6, '86
99	Dorsey, John	LB	6-2	243	5	8-31-60	Connecticut	12	D4, '84
	Drost, Jeff	NT	6-5	286	1	1-27-64	Iowa	2	FA, '87
	Dwyer, Mike	DT	6-3	280	2	6-13-63	Massachusetts	*3	FA, '88
	Elliott, Tony	DB	5-10	195	1	1-10-64	Central Michigan	1	FA, '87
85	†Epps, Phillip	WR	5-10	165	7	11-11-59	Texas Christian	10	D12, '82
21	Fullwood, Brent	RB	5-11	209	2	10-10-63	Auburn	11	D1, '87
23	†Greene, Tiger	CB/S	6-0	194	4	2-15-62	Western Carolina	11	FA, '86
89	Hackett, Joey	TE	6-5	267	3	9-29-58	Elon College	11	FA, '87
65	†Hallstrom, Ron	G	6-6	290	7	6-11-59	Iowa	12	D1, '82
97	Harris, Tim	LB	6-5	235	3	9-10-64	Memphis State	12	D4, '86
50	Holland, Johnny	LB	6-2	221	2	3-11-65	Texas A&M	12	D2, '87
38	Jefferson, Norman	CB/S	5-10	183	2	8- 7-64	Louisiana State	12	D12, '87
39	Johnson, Kenneth	CB	6-0	185	2	12-28-63	Mississippi State	12	FA, '87
	Kemp, Perry	WR	5-11	170	2	12-31-61	California State (Pa.)	*3	FA, '88
	Kiel, Blair	QB	6-0	200	4	11-29-61	Notre Dame	*4	FA, '88
	King, Don	DB	5-11	200	1	2-10-64	Southern Methodist	1	FA, '87
22	†Lee, Mark	CB/S	5-11	189	9	3-20-58	Washington	12	D2, '80
7	Majkowski, Don	QB	6-2	197	2	2-25-64	Virginia	7	D10, '87
44	Mandeville, Chris	S	6-1	213	2	2- 1-65	California-Davis	4	OFA, '87
	Mataele, Stan	NT	6-2	290	1	6-24-63	Arizona	2	FA, '88
	Mayes, Tony	S	6-0	195	2	5-19-64	Kentucky	*3	FA, '88
98	Moore, Brent	LB	6-5	242	2	1- 9-63	Southern California	4	D9, '86
57	†Moran, Rich	C/G	6-2	275	4	3-19-62	San Diego State	12	D3, '85
47	Morris, Jim Bob	CB/S	6-3	211	2	5-17-61	Kansas State	11	FA, '87
81	Morris, Lee	WR	5-10	180	2	7-14-64	Oklahoma	5	FA, '87
37	Murphy, Mark	S	6-2	201	7	4-22-58	West Liberty	12	OFA, '80
80	Neal, Frankie	WR	6-1	202	2	10- 1-65	Fort Hays State	12	D3b, '87
	Nelson, Bob	NT	6-4	275	2	3- 3-59	Miami (Fla.)	*0	FA, '88
72	†Neville, Tom	T/G	6-5	306	3	9- 4-61	Fresno State	12	FA, '86
91	†Noble, Brian	LB	6-3	252	4	9- 6-62	Arizona State	12	D5, '85
82	Paskett, Keith	WR	5-11	180	2	12- 7-64	Western Kentucky	12	OFA, '87
	Porell, Tom	NT	6-3	275	1	9-23-64	Boston College	*1	FA, '88
	Powe, Karl	WR	6-2	175	3	1-17-62	Alabama State	*0	FA, '88
	Preston, John	S	6-0	207	2	8-28-62	Central State (O.)	*5	FA, '88
77	Robison, Tommy	G	6-4	290	2	11-17-61	Texas A&M	3	T-Cle, '85
75	Ruettgers, Ken	T	6-5	280	4	8-20-62	Southern California	12	D1, '85
83	Scott, Patrick	WR	5-10	170	2	9-13-64	Grambling	8	OFA, '81
	Simpkins, Ron	LB	6-1	235	7	4- 2-58	Michigan	*0	FA, '88
87	†Stanley, Walter	WR/KR	5-9	179	4	11- 5-62	Mesa College (Colo.)	12	D4, '85
54	Stephen, Scott	LB	6-2	232	2	6-18-64	Arizona State	8	D3a, '87
29	Stills, Ken	CB/S	5-10	186	4	9- 6-63	Wisconsin	11	D8, '85
48	Summers, Don	TE	6-4	235	3	2-22-61	Boise State	3	FA, '87
92	Thomas, Ben	DE/NT	6-4	275	3	7- 2-61	Auburn	*0	W-NE, '86
	Thomas, Lavale	RB	6-0	205	1	12-12-63	Fresno State	1	FA, '88
	Twombly, Darren	C-G	6-4	270	1	5-14-65	Boston College	*1	FA, '88
70	Uecker, Keith	G/T	6-5	284	6	6-29-60	Auburn	8	W-Den, '84
73	†Veingrad, Alan	T-G	6-5	277	3	7-24-63	East Texas State	11	FA, '86
	Walter, Dave	QB	6-3	220	2	12- 9-64	Michigan Tech	*3	FA, '88
28	Watts, Elbert	CB	6-1	205	2	3-20-63	Southern California	*0	W-Ram, '87
52	†Weddington, Mike	LB	6-4	245	3	10- 9-60	Oklahoma	12	FA, '86
51	Weishuhn, Clayton	LB	6-1	218	5	10- 7-59	Angelo State	9	W-NE, '87
86	West, Ed	TE	6-1	243	5	8- 2-61	Auburn	12	OFA, '84
35	Willhite, Kevin	RB	5-11	208	2	5- 4-63	Oregon	3	OFA, '87

No.	Name	Pos.	Ht.	Wt.	NFL Exp.	Birth-date	College	Games in '87	How Acquired
16	Wright, Randy	QB	6-2	203	5	1-12-61	Wisconsin	9	D6, '84
8	Zendejas, Max	K	5-11	184	3	9- 2-63	Arizona	10	FA, '87

*Dwyer played 3 games with Cowboys in '87; Kemp played 3 games with Browns in '87; Kiel played 4 games with Colts in '87; Mayes played 3 games with Cardinals in '87; Nelson last active with Buccaneers in '86; Porell played 1 game with Patriots in '87; Powe last active with Cowboys in '86; Preston played 5 games with Cardinals in '87; Simpkins last active with Bengals in '86; Thomas and Watts missed '87 season due to injury; Twombly played 1 game with Patriots in '87; Walter played 3 games with Bengals in '87.

†Option playout; subject to developments.

D—Draft; T—Trade; W—Waivers; FA—Free Agent; OFA—Original Free Agent.

Also played with Packers in '87, see page 386.

GREEN BAY PACKERS
1988 DRAFT CHOICES

(Number following name designates order of selection among 333 players drafted.)

Round and Player		Position	College
1. SHARPE, Sterling	7	WR	South Carolina
2. PATTERSON, Shawn	34	DT	Arizona State
3. WOODSIDE, Keith	61	RB	Texas A & M
4. PUTZIER, Rollin from L.A. Raiders (a)	88	DT	Oregon
4. CECIL, Chuck	89	DB	Arizona
5. REED, Darrell	116	LB	Oklahoma
6. HILL, Nate	144	DE	Auburn
7. RICHARD, Gary	173	DB	Pittsburgh
8. COLLINS, Patrick	200	RB	Oklahoma
9. WILKINSON, Neal	228	TE	James Madison
10. KEYES, Bud	256	QB	Wisconsin
11. Choice to Seattle (b)			
12. BOLTON, Scott	312	WR	Auburn

(a) Acquired pick and 3rd-round pick in 1987 for wide receiver James Lofton, April 13, 1987.

(b) Traded pick for cornerback Dave Brown, August 26, 1987.

GREEN BAY PACKERS
1988 ROOKIE AND FIRST-YEAR ROSTER

Name	Pos.	Hgt.	Wgt.	Birth-date	College	How Acquired
Albergamo, Nacho	C/G	6-2	265	11-19-66	Louisiana State	FA
Armentrout, Joe	RB	6-0	225	11- 4-64	Wisconsin	*FA
Avery, Stephone	DB	6-0	188	8- 1-65	Northeast Louisiana	FA
Bolton, Scott	WR	6-0	188	1- 4-65	Auburn	D12
Bosco, Robbie	QB	6-2	198	1-11-63	Brigham Young	*D3-'86
Campbell, Erik	DB	5-10	173	1-21-66	Michigan	FA
Castellanos, Hugo	K	5-10	190	10-20-64	Texas-El Paso	FA
Cecil, Chuck	S	6-0	184	11- 8-64	Arizona	D4a
Collins, Patrick	RB	5-9	197	8- 4-66	Oklahoma	D8
Croston, Dave	T	6-5	280	11-10-63	Iowa	*D3-'87
Dorough, Dewey	WR	5-11	170	3- 4-65	Colorado State	FA
Fitzgerald, Pat	WR	6-3	197	10-13-63	Boise State	*FA-'87
Flesher, Thomas	DL	6-5	250	9-28-66	Weber State	FA
Gregoire, Todd	K	6-0	190	9- 3-65	Wisconsin	FA
Gross, Wes	OL	6-7	290	4- 2-63	Utah State	*FA
Hardy, Eugene	CB	5-10	185	4-14-66	Arizona	FA
Harper, Robert	LB	6-2	243	10- 6-65	Houston	FA
Harris, Frankie	TE	6-2	227	8-27-65	Northern Michigan	FA
Harris, Gregg	G	6-4	279	4- 8-66	Wake Forest	*D9-'87
Hill, Nate	DE	6-4	273	2-22-66	Auburn	D6
Keyes, Bud	QB	6-2	211	3- 3-66	Wisconsin	D10
Kidder, John	G	6-5	305	1-25-65	UCLA	FA
Mancini, Michael	P	5-10	173	4- 3-63	Fresno State	*FA
Marshall, Willie	WR	6-1	190	5-23-64	Temple	*D6-'87
McComb, Jeff	P	5-10	185	5-18-65	Southern Utah State	FA
Murino, Louis	T	6-6	301	1-14-66	Cal State-Northridge	FA
Nairn, John	S	6-1	187	12- 7-64	Colorado	FA
Parker, Eddie	DB	5-11	185	10-14-65	Temple	FA
Patterson, Shawn	DL	6-5	261	4- 6-65	Arizona State	D2
Phillips, John	G	6-4	275	9-29-65	Clemson	FA
Pomfret, Paul	TE	6-5	242	3-27-64	Penn State	FA
Putzier, Rollin	NT	6-4	279	12-10-65	Oregon	D4
Reed, Darrell	LB	6-1	225	7-28-65	Oklahoma	D5
Richard, Gary	CB	5-9	171	10- 9-65	Pittsburgh	D7
Russell, Sean	WR	6-3	210	10-25-65	California	FA
Sharpe, Sterling	WR	5-11	202	4- 6-65	South Carolina	D1
Shurmur, Patrick	C	6-2	252	4-14-65	Michigan State	FA
Soraghan, Matt	LB	6-2	233	11-18-65	Southwest Missouri St.	FA
Taylor, Pat	LB	6-2	223	3-19-64	Arizona State	FA
Weishuhn, Doyle	C	6-2	280	9-10-65	Angelo State	FA
Whelihan, Tom	K	5-10	198	8-15-66	Missouri	FA
Wilkinson, Neal	TE	6-5	226	10- 2-64	James Madison	D9
Woodside, Keith	RB	5-11	203	7-29-64	Texas A&M	D3
Zielinski, Phil	LB	6-3	233	5-15-65	Central Michigan	FA

*Armentrout: D9 Tampa Bay '87, released 8/5, FA Los Angeles Rams 8/11, injured reserve 8/27 through 9/13, released 9/14, FA replacement Green Bay 10/14 (on active list for 1 game), released 10/20; Bosco missed '86 and '87 seasons due to injury; Croston, G. Harris and Marshall missed '87 season due to injury; Fitzgerald: FA Green Bay '86, released 8/25, FA Green Bay '87, injured reserve 8/10 through entire season; Gross: FA Houston '86, released 7/27; Hopkins: FA replacement Green Bay (on inactive list for 1 game), released 10/20; Mancini: FA San Francisco '86, released 8/19, FA Pittsburgh '87, released 8/7, FA replacement Detroit 9/24, released 9/29; Veldman; FA Miami '87, injured reserve 8/31 through 10/19, released 10/20.

HOUSTON OILERS
(Central Division, American Conference)

Jerry Glanville

Owner-President—K. S. (Bud) Adams, Jr.
Executive Vice-President and G.M.—Ladd Herzeg
Vice-President, Player Personnel—Mike Holovak
Director of Administration—Rick Nichols
Director of Media Relations—Chip Namias
Public Relations Director—Gregg Stengel
 (Office Phone: 797-9111—Area Code 713)
Head Coach—Jerry Glanville (3 years: 14-19)
Assistant Coaches:
 Offensive Line—Kim Helton
 Receivers—Milt Jackson
 Quarterbacks—June Jones
 Linebackers—Floyd Reese
 Defensive Backs—Nick Saban
 Running Backs—Ray Sherman
 Defensive Line—Doug Shively
 Special Teams/Tight Ends—Richard Smith
 Strength/Rehabilitation—Steve Watterson
Offices—6910 Fannin, Houston, Tex. 77030
Mailing Address—P. O. Box 1516, Houston, Tex. 77251
Stadium—Astrodome (Capacity: 50,599)
Team Colors—Scarlet, Columbia Blue and White
Training Site—Angelo State University, San Angelo, Tex.

1988 SCHEDULE
(All times local.
All games Sunday unless noted otherwise.)

Sept.	4	at Indianapolis	3:00
Sept.	11	LOS ANGELES RAIDERS	3:00
Sept.	18	at New York Jets	1:00
Sept.	25	NEW ENGLAND	12:00
Oct.	2	at Philadelphia	1:00
Oct.	9	KANSAS CITY	12:00
Oct.	16	at Pittsburgh	1:00
Oct.	23	at Cincinnati	1:00
Oct.	30	WASHINGTON	7:00
Nov.	7	CLEVELAND (Mon.)	8:00
Nov.	13	at Seattle	1:00
Nov.	20	PHOENIX	12:00
Nov.	24	at Dallas (Thanksgiving)	3:00
Dec.	4	PITTSBURGH	7:00
Dec.	11	CINCINNATI	12:00
Dec.	18	at Cleveland	1:00

1987 RESULTS—(Won 10, Lost 7)

Oilers		Opp.		Att.
20	L.A. Rams	16	(H)	33,186
30	Buffalo	34	(A)	56,534
	L.A. Raiders*		(H)	
40	*Denver*	*10*	*(A)*	*38,494*
15	*Cleveland*	*10*	*(A)*	*38,927*
7	*New England*	*21*	*(H)*	*26,294*
37	Atlanta	33	(H)	29,062
31	Cincinnati	29	(A)	52,700
20	San Francisco	27	(A)	59,740
23	Pittsburgh	3	(A)	56,177
7	Cleveland	40	(H)	51,161
27	Indianapolis	51	(A)	54,999
33	San Diego	18	(H)	31,714
10	New Orleans	24	(A)	68,257
24	Pittsburgh	16	(H)	38,683
21	Cincinnati	17	(H)	49,275

AFC WILD-CARD GAME

23	Seattle (OT)	20	(H)	49,622

AFC SEMIFINAL GAME

10	Denver	34	(A)	75,968

*Game cancelled due to strike.
Italics denote strike replacement games.

1987 GAMES STARTED

(NOTE: Players with an asterisk (*) following their names made starts only in strike-replacement games.)

13 games: Ray Childress, Doug Smith.

12 games: Keith Bostic, Jeff Donaldson, Ernest Givins, John Grimsley, Drew Hill, Robert Lyles, Johnny Meads, Warren Moon, Mike Munchak, Jay Pennison, Jamie Williams.

11 games: Patrick Allen, Richard Byrd, Mike Rozier, Al Smith, Dean Steinkuhler.

10 games: Steve Brown.

9 games: Ray Wallace.

7 games: Bruce Davis, Doug Williams.

6 games: Kent Hill, Bruce Matthews.

4 games: Eugene Seale.

3 games: Tom Briehl*, Domingo Bryant*, Jerrell Franklin*, Mark Gehring*, Leonard Harris*, Alonzo Highsmith, Andrew Jackson*, Thad Jefferson*, Byron Johnson*, Kenny Johnson*, Billy Kidd*, Charles Martin, Ricky Moore*, Tony Newsom*, Brent Pease*, Vince Stroth*, Bucky White*, Almon Young*.

2 games: Jesse Baker*, Audrey McMillian, Clay Miller*, Oliver Williams*.

1 game: Rayford Cooks*, William Fuller, Haywood Jeffires*, Richard Johnson, Eric Larkin*, Spencer Tillman.

HOUSTON OILERS 1988 VETERAN ROSTER

No.	Name	Pos.	Ht.	Wt.	NFL Exp.	Birth-date	College	Games in '87	How Acquired
29	†Allen, Patrick	CB	5-10	180	5	8-26-61	Utah State	11	D4a, '84
36	Birdsong, Craig	S	6-2	217	2	8-16-64	North Texas State	3	FA, '87
25	Bostic, Keith	S	6-1	223	6	1-17-61	Michigan	12	D2a, '83
	Brown, Sonny	S	6-2	200	1	11-12-63	Oklahoma	2	OFA, '87
24	†Brown, Steve	CB	5-11	187	6	3-20-60	Oregon	10	D3b, '83
38	Bryant, Domingo	S	6-3	175	2	12- 8-63	Texas A&M	13	FA, '87
71	Byrd, Richard	DE	6-4	265	4	3-20-62	Southern Mississippi	12	D2, '85
	Carlson, Cody	QB	6-3	203	2	11- 5-63	Baylor	*0	D3, '87
90	Caston, Toby	LB	6-1	235	2	7-17-65	Louisiana State	6	D6a, '87
79	Childress, Ray	DE	6-6	276	4	10-20-62	Texas A&M	13	D1, '85
	Clinton, Charles	CB	5-8	170	1	1-26-62	San Jose State	2	FA, '88
98	†Cooks, Rayford	DE	6-3	245	2	8-25-62	North Texas State	10	FA, '87
	Darrington, Chris	WR	5-10	180	2	7-13-64	Weber State	3	FA, '88
77	Davis, Bruce	T	6-6	280	10	6-21-56	UCLA	*11	T-Rai, '87
73	Davis, John	T/G	6-4	304	2	8-22-65	Georgia Tech	6	D11, '87
31	Donaldson, Jeff	S	6-0	194	5	4-19-62	Colorado	12	D9, '84
82	Drewrey, Willie	WR/KR	5-7	164	4	4-28-63	West Virginia	12	D11, '85
80	Duncan, Curtis	WR/KR	5-11	184	2	1-26-65	Northwestern	10	D10, '87
1	†Fairs, Eric	LB	6-3	238	3	2-17-64	Memphis State	12	OFA, '86
95	†Fuller, William	DE	6-3	260	3	3- 8-62	North Carolina	12	T-Ram, '86
81	Givins, Ernest	WR	5-9	172	3	9- 3-64	Louisville	12	D2, '86
8	Gossett, Jeff	P	6-2	200	7	1-25-57	Eastern Illinois	*9	FA, '87
59	Grimsley, John	LB	6-2	236	5	2-25-62	Kentucky	12	D6, '84
83	Harris, Leonard	WR	5-8	165	3	11-27-60	Texas Tech	3	FA, '87
32	Highsmith, Alonzo	RB	6-1	235	2	2-26-65	Miami (Fla.)	8	D1, '87
85	Hill, Drew	WR	5-9	170	9	2- 5-56	Georgia Tech	12	T-Ram, '85
49	James, Arrike	TE	6-4	238	2	12-31-64	Delta State	3	FA, '87
84	Jeffires, Haywood	WR	6-2	198	2	12-12-64	North Carolina State	9	D1a, '87
	Jefferson, Thad	LB	5-11	225	2	3-11-64	Hawaii	3	FA, '88
22	†Johnson, Kenny	S	5-10	175	9	1- 7-58	Mississippi State	12	W-Atl, '86
23	Johnson, Richard	CB	6-1	190	4	9-16-63	Wisconsin	5	D1a, '85
57	Johnson, Walter	LB	6-0	241	2	11-13-63	Louisiana Tech	10	D2, '87
	Jones, Sean	DE	6-7	265	5	12-19-62	Northeastern	*12	T-Rai, '88
	Kafentzis, Kurt	S	6-1	189	1	12-31-62	Hawaii	2	FA, '88
	Kidd, Billy	T	6-4	260	2	11-28-59	Houston	7	FA, '88
	Loveall, Calvin	CB	5-9	182	R	7-23-62	Idaho	*17	FA, '88
93	Lyles, Robert	LB	6-1	223	5	3-21-61	Texas Christian	12	D5, '84
78	Maggs, Don	T/G	6-5	277	2	11- 1-61	Tulane	*0	SupD, '84
94	Martin, Charles	NT	6-4	280	5	8-31-59	Livingston	*14	W-GB, '87
74	Matthews, Bruce	T/G	6-5	280	6	8- 8-61	Southern California	8	D1, '83
	McDonald, Keith	WR	5-8	165	2	11- 7-63	San Jose State	3	FA, '88
26	†McMillian, Audrey	CB	6-0	190	4	8-13-62	Houston	12	W-NE, '85
91	†Meads, Johnny	LB	6-2	230	5	6-25-61	Nicholls State	12	D3, '84
	Miller, Clay	G	6-4	280	2	8-27-63	Michigan	3	W-NYJ, '88
1	Moon, Warren	QB	6-3	210	5	11-18-56	Washington	12	FA, '84
63	Munchak, Mike	G	6-3	280	7	3- 5-60	Penn State	12	D1, '82
	Nordgren, Fred	NT	5-11	245	2	12-11-59	Portland State	*3	FA, '88
89	Parks, Jeff	TE	6-4	240	3	9-14-64	Auburn	7	D5, '86
10	Pease, Brent	QB	6-2	200	2	10- 8-64	Montana	6	FA, '87
52	†Pennison, Jay	C	6-1	275	3	9- 9-61	Nicholls State	12	FA, '86
	Petersmark, Brett	G	6-3	280	2	3- 5-64	Eastern Michigan	3	FA, '88
20	Pinkett, Allen	RB	5-9	185	3	1-25-64	Notre Dame	8	D3, '86
30	Rozier, Mike	RB	5-10	211	4	3- 1-61	Nebraska	11	SupD, '84
53	Seale, Eugene	LB	5-10	250	2	6- 3-64	Lamar	9	FA, '87
54	Smith, Al	LB	6-1	230	2	11-26-64	Utah State	12	D6, '87
99	†Smith, Doug	NT	6-5	282	4	6-13-60	Auburn	14	D2, '84
70	†Steinkuhler, Dean	T/G	6-3	278	5	1-27-61	Nebraska	11	D1, '84
33	Tillman, Spencer	RB	5-11	206	2	4-21-64	Oklahoma	5	D5, '87
45	Valentine, Ira	RB	6-0	212	2	6- 4-63	Texas A&M	7	D12, '87
35	Wallace, Ray	RB	6-0	220	3	12- 3-63	Purdue	12	D6, '86
69	Williams, Doug	T/G	6-5	288	3	10- 1-62	Texas A&M	8	W-NYJ, '86
87	†Williams, Jamie	TE	6-4	245	6	2-25-60	Nebraska	12	W-TB, '84
	Young, Almon	G	6-3	290	2	7- 3-62	Bethune-Cookman	3	FA, '88
7	†Zendejas, Tony	K	5-8	165	4	5-15-60	Nevada-Reno	13	T-Was, '85

*Carlson active for 4 games with Oilers in '87, but did not play; B. Davis played 4 games with Raiders, 7 with Oilers in '87; Gossett played 5 games with Browns, 4 with Oilers in '87; Jones played 12 games with Raiders in '87; Loveall played 17 games with Ottawa-CFL in '87; Maggs active for 1 game with Oilers in '87, but did not play; Martin played 2 games with Packers, 12 with Oilers in '87; Nordgren played 3 games with Buccaneers in '87.

†Option playout; subject to developments.

D—Draft; T—Trade; W—Waivers; FA—Free Agent; OFA—Original Free Agent; SupD—Supplemental Draft.

Also played with Oilers in '87, see page 386.

HOUSTON OILERS
1988 DRAFT CHOICES

(Number following name designates order of selection among 333 players drafted.)

Round and Player		Position	College
1. WHITE, Lorenzo	22	RB	Michigan State
2. JONES, Quintin	48	DB	Pittsburgh
3. MONTGOMERY, Greg from San Diego (a)	72	P	Michigan State
3. Choice to N.Y. Jets through L.A. Raiders (b)			
4. Choice to San Francisco through L.A. Raiders (c)			
5. DISHMAN, Cris from San Diego (a)	125	DB	Purdue
5. VERHULST, Chris	130	TE	Chico State
6. CRAIN, Kurt	157	LB	Auburn
7. EATON, Tracey	187	DB	Portland State
8. VIAENE, Dave	214	C	Minn.-Duluth
9. SPRADLIN, David	241	LB	Texas Christian
10. JOHNSON, Marco	271	WR	Hawaii
11. FRANKLIN, Jethro	298	DE	Fresno State
12. BRANTLEY, John	325	LB	Georgia

(a) Acquired picks for 3rd-round pick in 1988, April 24, 1988.

(b) Oilers traded pick and 1st- and 4th-round picks in 1988 to Raiders for defensive end Sean Jones and 2nd- and 3rd-round picks in 1988, April 21, 1988; Raiders traded pick to Jets for 4th- and 5th-round picks in 1988, April 24, 1988.

(c) Oilers traded pick to Raiders: see first part of (b); Raiders traded pick, 2nd-round pick in 1988 and wide receiver Dokie Williams to 49ers for 1st-round pick in 1988, April 24, 1988.

HOUSTON OILERS
1988 ROOKIE AND FIRST-YEAR ROSTER

Name	Pos.	Hgt.	Wgt.	Birth-date	College	How Acquired
Banks, Robert	DE	6-5	254	12-10-63	Notre Dame	*D7, '87
Booker, Andre	WR	6-3	195	2-13-64	Texas Southern	FA
Brantley, John	LB	6-2	229	10-23-65	Georgia	D12
Brazil, David	T	6-4	275	7-15-64	Texas Christian	FA
Burt, Kerry	S	6-1	207	12-17-64	Iowa	FA
Crain, Kurt	LB	6-2	228	12-31-64	Auburn	D6
Dabrow, Chris	RB	5-9	210	11-25-65	Claremont	FA
Dishman, Cris	CB	6-0	173	8-13-65	Purdue	D5
Dusbabek, Mark	LB	6-3	232	6-23-64	Minnesota	*D4, '87
Eaton, Tracey	S	6-1	190	7-19-65	Portland State	D7
Endre, Pete	T	6-5	265	9- 7-66	Indiana State	FA
Franklin, Jethro	DE	6-1	260	10-25-65	Fresno State	D11
Hoover, Alex	LB	6-1	225	6-29-64	Colorado State	*FA
Johnson, Marco	WR/KR	5-9	170	9- 4-65	Hawaii	D10
Jones, Quintin	CB	5-11	193	7-28-66	Pittsburgh	D2
Lee, Ivery	NT	6-1	271	3- 5-64	Georgia Tech	FA
Lockley, Andre	T	6-6	282	9-15-65	Tulane	FA
Malbrough, Darren	LB	6-1	228	11- 8-64	Louisiana State	FA
McCarty, Eric	LB	6-1	230	11-16-64	Colorado	FA
Montgomery, Greg	P	6-3	210	10-29-64	Michigan State	D3
O'Brient, Sammy	NT	6-4	270	10-14-65	Texas A&M	FA
Owens, Edwin	CB	6-2	193	9-21-65	North Texas State	FA
Pickett, David	G	6-0	284	2-14-65	Texas Tech	FA
Rhone, Mike	CB	6-0	200	9-24-65	North Texas State	FA
Spradlin, David	LB	6-3	239	9-23-64	Texas Christian	D9
Terrell, Floyd	LB	6-1	235	8-22-64	Texas Christian	FA
Thomas, Steve	NT	6-1	280	9- 2-64	Iowa	FA
Verhuist, Chris	TE	6-2	239	5-16-66	Chico State	D5a
Viaene, David	C	6-5	291	7-14-65	Minnesota-Duluth	D8
White, Lorenzo	RB	5-11	207	4-12-66	Michigan State	D1
Willis, Keith	WR	5-8	170	6-14-65	Sam Houston State	FA

*Banks and Dusbabek missed '87 season due to injuries; Hoover: FA Tampa Bay '87, injured reserve 8/5 through 11/23, released 11/24.

INDIANAPOLIS COLTS
(Eastern Division, American Conference)

Ron Meyer

President and Treasurer—Robert Irsay
General Manager—Jim Irsay
Assistant General Manager—Bob Terpening
Player Personnel Director—Jack Bushofsky
Head Coach—Ron Meyer (5 years: 30-22)

Assistant Coaches:
Offensive Coordinator—John Becker
Running Backs—Leon Burtnett
Secondary—George Catavolos
Defensive Coordinator—George Hill
Assistant Head Coach/Off. Line—Tom Lovat
Defensive Line—John Marshall
Receivers—Chip Myers
Special Teams/Asst. Off Line—Keith Rowen
Linebackers—Rick Venturi
Strength & Conditioning—Tom Zupancic

Public Relations Director—Craig Kelley
  (Office Phone: 297-2658—Area Code 317)
Mailing Address—P. O. Box 535000 Indianapolis, Ind. 46253
Stadium—Hoosier Dome (Capacity: 60,127)
Team Colors—Royal Blue and White
Training Site—Anderson University, Anderson, Ind.

1988 SCHEDULE
(All times local.
All games Sunday unless noted otherwise.)

Sept. 4	HOUSTON	3:00
Sept. 11	CHICAGO	12:00
Sept. 19	at Cleveland (Mon.)	8:00
Sept. 25	MIAMI	12:00
Oct. 2	at New England	1:00
Oct. 9	at Buffalo	1:00
Oct. 16	TAMPA BAY	12:00
Oct. 23	at San Diego	1:00
Oct. 31	DENVER (Mon.)	9:00
Nov. 6	NEW YORK JETS	4:00
Nov. 13	at Green Bay	12:00
Nov. 20	at Minnesota	12:00
Nov. 27	NEW ENGLAND	4:00
Dec. 4	at Miami	1:00
Dec. 10	at New York Jets (Sat.)	12:30
Dec. 18	BUFFALO	1:00

1987 RESULTS—(Won 9, Lost 7)

Colts		Opp.		Att.
21	Cincinnati	23	(H)	59,387
10	Miami	23	(H)	57,524
	St. Louis*		(A)	
47	*Buffalo*	*6*	*(A)*	*9,860*
6	*New York Jets*	*0*	*(H)*	*34,927*
7	*Pittsburgh*	*21*	*(A)*	*34,627*
30	New England	16	(A)	48,850
19	New York Jets	14	(A)	60,863
13	San Diego	16	(H)	60,459
40	Miami	21	(A)	65,433
0	New England	24	(A)	56,906
51	Houston	27	(H)	54,999
9	Cleveland	7	(A)	70,661
3	Buffalo	27	(H)	60,253
20	San Diego	7	(A)	46,211
24	Tampa Bay	6	(H)	60,468
AFC SEMIFINAL GAME				
21	Cleveland	38	(A)	78,586

*Game cancelled due to strike.
Italics denote strike replacement games.

1987 GAMES STARTED

(NOTE: Players with an asterisk (*) following their names made starts only in strike-replacement games.)

12 games: Pat Beach, Duane Bickett, Matt Bouza, Bill Brooks, Kevin Call, Ray Donaldson, Chris Hinton, Cliff Odom, Ron Solt, Donnell Thompson, Willie Tullis, Ben Utt.

11 games: Eugene Daniel, Nesby Glasgow, Jon Hand, Barry Krauss.

10 games: Johnie Cooks.

9 games: Freddie Robinson.

8 games: Eric Dickerson, Jerome Sally, Jack Trudeau.

7 games: Mike Prior.

6 games: Mark Boyer, Gary Hogeboom.

5 games: Tim Sherwin.

4 games: Albert Bentley, Byron Darby.

3 games: Sid Abramowitz*, Jeff Criswell*, Marsharne Graves*, Ed Grimsley*, Greg Hawthorne*, Bryant Jones*, Steve Knight*, Jeff Leiding*, Walter Murray*, Bob Ontko*, Jim Perryman*, Ron Plantz*, Chris Scott*, Don Thorp*.

2 games: Dave Ahrens, Bill Benjamin*, John Brandes, Joe Jones*, Scott Kellar*, Chris McLemore*, James Noble*, Terry Wright*.

1 game: Harvey Armstrong, Pat Ballage*, Chuck Banks,* Mark Bellini*, Brian Bulluck*, Bill Elko*, Blair Kiel*, Orlando Lowry.

INDIANAPOLIS COLTS 1988 VETERAN ROSTER

No.	Name	Pos.	Ht.	Wt.	NFL Exp.	Birth-date	College	Games in '87	How Acquired
57	Ahrens, Dave	LB	6-4	249	8	12- 5-58	Wisconsin	12	T-StL, '85
78	†Armstrong, Harvey	NT	6-3	268	6	12-29-59	Southern Methodist	11	FA, '86
35	Banks, Chuck	RB	6-1	227	3	1- 4-64	West Virginia Tech	3	FA, '87
81	Beach, Pat	TE	6-4	252	6	12-28-59	Washington State	12	D6, '82
87	Bellini, Mark	WR	5-11	185	2	1-19-64	Brigham Young	10	D7, '87
20	Bentley, Albert	RB	5-11	214	4	8-15-60	Miami (Fla.)	12	SupD, '84
4	†Biasucci, Dean	K	6-0	191	4	7-25-62	Western Carolina	12	FA, '86
50	Bickett, Duane	LB	6-5	243	4	12- 1-62	Southern California	12	D1, '85
85	†Bouza, Matt	WR	6-3	212	7	4- 8-59	California	12	FA, '82
84	†Boyer, Mark	TE	6-4	242	4	9-16-62	Southern California	7	D9, '85
88	Brandes, John	TE	6-2	237	2	4- 2-64	Cameron University	12	OFA, '87
80	Brooks, Bill	WR	6-0	191	3	4- 6-64	Boston University	12	D4, '86
74	†Brotzki, Bob	T	6-5	293	3	12-24-62	Syracuse	11	D9, '86
68	†Broughton, Willie	DE	6-5	281	3	9- 9-64	Miami (Fla.)	*0	D4, '85
	Brown, Charlie	WR	5-10	184	7	10-29-58	South Carolina State	*6	T-Atl, '88
72	†Call, Kevin	T	6-7	302	5	11-13-61	Colorado State	12	D5a, '84
31	Coleman, Leonard	S	6-2	202	4	1-30-62	Vanderbilt	4	D1, '84
98	Cooks, Johnie	LB	6-4	252	7	11-23-58	Mississippi State	10	D1, '82
38	Daniel, Eugene	CB	5-11	178	5	6- 4-61	Louisiana State	12	D8, '84
72	†Darby, Byron	DE	6-4	260	6	6- 4-60	Southern California	12	FA, '87
29	Dickerson, Eric	RB	6-3	217	6	9- 2-60	Southern Methodist	*12	T-Ram, '87
69	Dixon, Randy	T	6-3	293	2	3-12-65	Pittsburgh	3	D4, '87
53	Donaldson, Ray	C	6-3	288	9	5-17-58	Georgia	12	D2, '80
	Ellis, Ray	S	6-1	196	8	4-27-59	Ohio State	*12	FA, '88
25	Glasgow, Nesby	S	5-10	187	10	4-15-57	Washington	11	D8a, '79
37	Goode, Chris	CB/S	6-0	193	2	9-17-63	Alabama	8	D10, '87
51	Hancock, Kevin	LB	6-2	225	1	1- 8-62	Baylor	1	FA, '87
78	Hand, Jon	DE	6-7	298	3	11-13-63	Alabama	12	D1, '86
	Herrmann, Mark	QB	6-4	207	8	1- 8-59	Purdue	*3	T-SD, '88
75	Hinton, Chris	G	6-4	295	6	7-31-61	Northwestern	12	T-Den, '83
7	Hogeboom, Gary	QB	6-4	208	9	8-21-58	Central Michigan	6	T-Dal, '86
21	†Holt, John	CB	5-10	179	8	6-14-59	West Texas State	12	T-TB, '86
58	James, June	LB	6-1	236	3	12- 2-62	Texas	11	FA, '87
94	Kellar, Scott	NT	6-3	279	3	12-31-63	Northern Illinois	3	D5, '86
	Klecko, Joe	NT	6-3	263	12	10-15-53	Temple	*7	FA, '88
55	Krauss, Barry	LB	6-3	269	10	3-17-57	Alabama	12	D1, '79
59	Lowry, Orlando	LB	6-4	236	4	8-14-61	Ohio State	8	FA, '85
49	McCloskey, Mike	TE	6-5	246	4	2- 2-61	Penn State	*1	W-Phi, '87
32	McMillan, Randy	RB	6-0	220	7	12-17-58	Pittsburgh	*0	D1, '81
86	Murray, Walter	WR	6-4	202	3	12-13-62	Hawaii	14	T-Was, '86
93	Odom, Cliff	LB	6-2	245	8	9-15-58	Texas-Arlington	12	FA, '82
65	Patten, Joel	T	6-7	307	3	2- 7-58	Duke	12	FA, '87
43	Perryman, Jim	CB/S	6-0	187	3	12-23-60	Millikin	14	FA, '87
39	†Prior, Mike	CB/S	6-0	200	3	11-14-63	Illinois State	13	FA, '87
47	Robinson, Freddie	CB/S	6-1	191	2	2- 1-64	Alabama	9	D6, '87
13	†Salisbury, Sean	QB	6-5	215	3	3- 9-63	Southern California	2	FA, '87
76	†Sally, Jerome	NT	6-3	270	3	2-24-59	Missouri	12	T-NYG, '87
83	Sherwin, Tim	TE	6-5	252	8	5- 4-58	Boston College	8	D4, '81
66	†Solt, Ron	G	6-3	285	5	5-19-62	Maryland	12	D1a, '84
3	Stark, Rohn	P	6-3	204	7	5- 4-59	Florida State	12	D2a, '82
26	Swoope, Craig	CB/S	6-1	200	3	2- 3-64	Illinois	*4	W-TB, '87
99	Thompson, Donnell	DE	6-4	275	8	10-27-58	North Carolina	12	D1a, '81
62	Thorp, Don	DT/DE	6-4	260	3	7-10-62	Illinois	5	FA, '87
10	Trudeau, Jack	QB	6-3	213	3	9- 9-62	Illinois	10	D2, '86
42	†Tullis, Willie	CB	5-11	195	8	4- 5-58	Troy State	12	FA, '87
64	Utt, Ben	G	6-6	286	7	6-13-59	Georgia Tech	12	FA, '82
	Verdin, Clarence	WR	5-8	160	3	6-14-63	Southwestern Louisiana	*3	T-Was, '88
34	Wonsley, George	RB	5-10	219	5	11-23-60	Mississippi State	11	D4a, '84
27	Wright, Terry	CB/S	6-0	195	2	7-17-65	Temple	13	OFA, '87

*Broughton and McMillan missed '87 season due to injury; Brown played 6 games with Falcons in '87; Dickerson played 3 games with Rams, 9 with Colts in '87; Ellis played 12 games with Browns in '87; Herrmann played 3 games with Chargers in '87; Klecko played 7 games with Jets in '87; McCloskey played 1 game with Eagles, inactive for 1 game with Colts in '87; Swoope played 1 game with Buccaneers, 3 with Colts in '87; Verdin played 3 games with Redskins in '87.

†Option playout; subject to developments.

D—Draft; T—Trade; W—Waivers; FA—Free Agent; OFA—Original Free Agent; SupD—Supplemental Draft.

Also played with Colts in '87, see page 386.

INDIANAPOLIS COLTS
1988 DRAFT CHOICES

(Number following name designates order of selection among 333 players drafted.)

Round and Player		Position	College
1. Choice to L.A. Rams (a)			
2. Choice to L.A. Rams (a)			
3. CHANDLER, Chris	76	QB	Washington
4. BALL, Michael	104	DB	Southern U.
5. BAYLOR, John	129	DB	So. Mississippi
6. Choice to Washington (b)			
7. Choice to N.Y. Giants (c)			
8. Choice to Buffalo (d)			
9. HERROD, Jeff	243	LB	Mississippi
10. ALSTON, O'Brien	270	LB	Maryland
11. DEE, Donnie	297	TE	Tulsa
12. KENNEY, Aatron from Detroit (e)	308	WR	Stevens Point, Wis.
12. VESLING, Tim	327	K	Syracuse

(a) Traded picks, 2nd-round pick in 1989 and running back Owen Gill for running back Eric Dickerson, October 31, 1987 (as part of deal, Colts traded rights to linebacker Cornelius Bennett to Bills with Buffalo sending 1st-round pick in 1988, 1st- and 2nd-round picks in 1989 and running back Greg Bell to Rams).

(b) Traded pick for wide receiver Clarence Verdin, March 29, 1988.

(c) Traded pick for nose tackle Jerome Sally, September 2, 1987.

(d) Returned pick acquired for tackle Roger Caron, April 13, 1987 when Caron did not report to training camp.

(e) Acquired pick for tight end Derrick Ramsey, September 1, 1987.

INDIANAPOLIS COLTS
1988 ROOKIE AND FIRST-YEAR ROSTER

Name	Pos.	Hgt.	Wgt.	Birth-date	College	How Acquired
Alston, O'Brien	LB	6-6	241	12-21-65	Maryland	D10
Ball, Michael	CB/S	6-0	211	8- 5-64	Southern University	D4
Baylor, John	CB/S	6-0	192	3- 5-65	Southern Mississippi	D5
Chandler, Chris	QB	6-4	215	10-12-65	Washington	D3
Coyne, Christopher	C	6-2	280	1-10-66	Delaware	FA
Cunningham, Tim	LB	6-4	235	7-21-64	Indiana State	*FA
Dee, Donnie	TE	6-4	235	3-17-65	Tulsa	D11
Gambol, Chris	T	6-6	303	9-14-64	Iowa	*D3, '87
Garza, Louis	T	6-5	290	11-17-62	New Mexico State	*FA
Herrod, Jeff	LB	6-0	237	7-29-66	Mississippi	D9
Kenney, Aatron	WR	5-11	171	9- 6-63	Wisconsin-Stevens Point	D12a
Miller, Chuckie	DB	5-8	173	5- 9-65	UCLA	*D8, '87
Moon, Micah	LB	6-0	232	11-15-62	North Carolina	*FA, '87
Pizzo, Joe	QB	6-3	215	6-25-64	Mars Hill College	*FA
Polite, Stoney	RB	5-10	210	1-24-66	North Carolina A&T	FA
Sims, Richie	DB	5-11	187	12-19-65	Louisiana Tech	FA
Summers, Michael	RB	6-2	218	9-29-65	South Carolina State	FA
Vesling, Tim	K	5-11	178	11-20-64	Syracuse	D12b

*Cunningham: FA New Orleans '87, released 8/27; Gambol and Miller missed '87 season due to injuries; Garza: D12 Cincinnati '85, released 8/12, FA Houston '87, released 8/17, FA replacement Houston '87 (on inactive list for 1 game), released 10/19; Moon: D9 Atlanta '85, released 8/19, FA Baltimore Stars '86, FA 8/7, FA Indianapolis '87, injured reserve 8/11 through entire season; Pizzo: FA Pittsburgh '87, released 8/3, FA replacement Cleveland 9/23 (on inactive list for 2 games), released 10/15.

KANSAS CITY CHIEFS
(Western Division, American Conference)

Frank Gansz

Owner—Lamar Hunt
President—Jack Steadman
General Manager and Vice-President—Jim Schaaf
Director of Player Personnel—Whitey Dovell
Head Coach—Frank Gansz (1 year: 4-11)
Assistant Coaches:
 Special Teams—Ed Beckman
 Defensive Backs—Tom Bettis
 Linebackers—Dave Brazil
 Tight Ends—J.D. Helm
 Strength & Conditioning/Linemen—C.T. Hewgley
 Defensive Line—Don Lawrence
 Running Backs—Billie Matthews
 Offensive Line—Carl Mauck
 Defensive Coordinator—Rod Rust
 Offensive Coordinator—George Sefcik
 Receivers—Dick Wood
Public Relations Director—Gary Heise
 (Office Phone: 924-9300—Area Code 816)
Offices—One Arrowhead Drive, Kansas City, Mo. 64129
Stadium—Arrowhead Stadium (Capacity: 78,067)
Team Colors—Red, Gold and White
Training Site—William Jewell College, Liberty, Mo.

1988 SCHEDULE
(All times local.
All games Sunday unless noted otherwise.)

Sept. 4	CLEVELAND	3:00
Sept. 11	at Seattle	1:00
Sept. 18	DENVER	12:00
Sept. 25	SAN DIEGO	3:00
Oct. 2	at New York Jets	4:00
Oct. 9	at Houston	12:00
Oct. 16	LOS ANGELES RAIDERS	12:00
Oct. 23	DETROIT	12:00
Oct. 30	at Los Angeles Raiders	1:00
Nov. 6	at Denver	2:00
Nov. 13	CINCINNATI	12:00
Nov. 20	SEATTLE	12:00
Nov. 27	at Pittsburgh	1:00
Dec. 4	NEW YORK JETS	3:00
Dec. 11	at New York Giants	1:00
Dec. 18	at San Diego	1:00

1987 RESULTS—(Won 4, Lost 11)

Chiefs		Opp.		Att.
20	San Diego	13	(H)	56,940
14	Seattle	43	(A)	61,667
	Minnesota*		(H)	
17	L.A. Raiders	35	(A)	10,708
0	Miami	42	(A)	25,867
17	Denver	26	(H)	20,296
21	San Diego	42	(A)	47,972
28	Chicago	31	(A)	63,498
16	Pittsburgh	17	(H)	45,249
9	New York Jets	16	(H)	40,718
3	Green Bay	23	(H)	34,611
27	Detroit	20	(A)	43,820
27	Cincinnati (OT)	30	(A)	46,489
16	L.A. Raiders	10	(H)	63,834
17	Denver	20	(A)	75,053
41	Seattle	20	(H)	20,370

*Game cancelled due to strike.
Italics denote strike replacement games.

1987 GAMES STARTED

(NOTE: Players with an asterisk (*) following their names made starts only in strike-replacement games.)

12 games: Mark Adickes, Mike Bell, Carlos Carson, Albert Lewis, Christian Okoye, Art Still.

11 games: Rich Baldinger, Lloyd Burruss, Dino Hackett, Bill Maas, Stephone Paige, Kevin Ross.

9 games: John Alt, Aaron Pearson.

8 games: Deron Cherry, Irv Eatman, Bill Kenney.

7 games: Jack Del Rio, Jonathan Hayes, Dave Lutz.

6 games: Tom Baugh, Louis Cooper, Rick Donnalley, Herman Heard, Pete Koch.

5 games: Tim Cofield.

4 games: Walt Arnold, James Harrell, Larry Moriarty, Mark Robinson.

3 games: Bob Harris*, James Harvey*, Bruce Holmes*, Doug Hoppock*, Chris Lindstrom*, Ted Nelson*, Steve Rogers*, Chris Smith*, Arland Thompson*, John Trahan*.

2 games: Bill Acker*, Todd Blackledge, Trent Bryant*, Jack Epps*, Leonard Griffin, Mark Keel, Stein Koss*, Dave Montague*, Lloyd Mumphrey*, Robert Parker*, J.C. Pearson, Jim Pietrzak*, Frank Seurer, Matt Stevens*, Carlton Thomas*, John Walker*.

1 game: Eric Brown*, Sherman Cocroft, Paul Coffman, Jeff Faulkner*, Eric Holle, Tony Holloway*, Doug Hudson*, Glenn Hyde*, Ken Johnson*, Rod Jones*, Brian Jozwiak, Ken Lacy*, Garcia Lane*, Paul Palmer, Blane Smith*, Gary Spann.

KANSAS CITY CHIEFS 1988 VETERAN ROSTER

No.	Name	Pos.	Ht.	Wt.	NFL Exp.	Birth-date	College	Games in '87	How Acquired
61	Adickes, Mark	G	6-4	270	3	4-22-61	Baylor	12	SupD, '84
76	†Alt, John	T	6-7	290	5	5-30-62	Iowa	9	D1a, '84
91	Baldinger, Gary	NT/DE	6-3	265	3	10- 4-63	Wake Forest	7	D9, '86
77	Baldinger, Rich	G/T	6-4	285	7	12-31-59	Wake Forest	12	FA, '83
58	Baugh, Tom	C	6-3	274	3	12- 1-63	Southern Illinois	12	D4, '86
99	Bell, Mike	DE	6-4	260	8	8-30-57	Colorado State	12	D1, '79
34	Burruss, Lloyd	S	6-0	209	8	10-31-57	Maryland	11	D3b, '81
88	†Carson, Carlos	WR	5-11	180	9	12-28-58	Louisiana State	12	D5, '80
20	Cherry, Deron	S	5-11	193	8	9-12-59	Rutgers	8	OFA, '81
46	Clemons, Michael	RB/KR	5-5	166	2	1-15-65	William & Mary	8	D8, '87
22	Cocroft, Sherman	S/CB	6-1	192	4	8-29-61	San Jose State	12	FA, '85
54	Cofield, Tim	LB	6-2	245	3	5-18-63	Elizabeth City State	12	OFA, '86
81	Colbert, Darrell	WR	5-10	174	2	11-16-64	Texas Southern	12	OFA, '87
5	Colbert, Lewis	P	5-11	179	2	8-23-63	Auburn	2	D8, '86
55	†Cooper, Louis	LB	6-2	240	4	8- 5-63	Western Carolina	12	FA, '85
	Cupp, Keith	T	6-6	305	2	6-20-64	Findlay	*3	FA, '88
	DeBerg, Steve	QB	6-3	210	12	1-19-54	San Jose State	*12	T-TB, '88
50	†Del Rio, Jack	LB	6-4	238	4	4- 4-63	Southern California	10	T-NO, '87
	DiGiacomo, Curt	C	6-4	275	2	10-24-63	Arizona	*0	FA, '88
75	Eatman, Irv	T	6-7	293	3	1- 1-61	UCLA	12	D8, '83
	Espinoza, Alex	QB	6-1	193	1	5-31-64	Iowa State	1	FA, '88
40	†Fields, Jitter	CB/S/KR	5-9	180	3	8-16-62	Texas	*6	FA, '87
2	Goodburn, Kelly	P	6-2	195	2	4-14-62	Emporia State	13	FA, '87
98	Griffin, Leonard	DE	6-4	258	3	9-22-62	Grambling	12	D3, '86
	Guthrie, Keith	NT	6-4	275	2	8-17-62	Texas A&M	*0	FA, '87
56	Hackett, Dino	LB	6-3	228	3	6-28-64	Appalachian State	11	D2, '86
57	†Harrell, James	LB	6-2	240	9	7-19-57	Florida	11	FA, '87
86	†Harry, Emile	WR	5-11	175	2	4- 5-63	Stanford	*0	FA, '86
64	Harvey, James	G	6-3	265	2	11-27-65	Jackson State	3	OFA, '87
	Hawkins, Andy	LB	6-2	230	7	3-31-58	Texas A&I	*2	FA, '88
85	Hayes, Jonathan	TE	6-5	240	4	8-11-62	Iowa	12	D2, '85
44	†Heard, Herman	RB	5-10	182	5	11-24-61	Southern Colorado	12	D3, '84
23	†Hill, Greg	CB	6-1	197	6	2-12-61	Oklahoma State	*6	W-Hou, '84
93	†Holle, Eric	NT	6-5	265	5	9- 5-60	Texas	8	D5, '85
	Hooper, Trell	DB	5-11	182	2	12-22-61	Memphis State	*3	FA, '88
53	Howard, Todd	LB	6-2	235	2	2-18-65	Texas A&M	12	D3, '87
	Hudson, Doug	QB	6-2	201	1	9-11-64	Nicholls State	1	D7, '87
	Ingram, Byron	G	6-2	295	1	11-17-64	Eastern Kentucky	1	FA, '87
	Jenkins, Keyvan	RB	5-10	192	2	1-6-61	Nevada-Las Vegas	*3	FA, '88
81	Jones, Rod	TE	6-4	242	2	3- 3-64	Washington	3	FA, '88
73	Jozwiak, Brian	G	6-5	310	3	6-20-63	West Virginia	10	D1, '86
80	Keel, Mark	TE	6-4	228	2	10- 1-62	Arizona	*10	FA, '87
9	Kenney, Bill	QB	6-4	207	10	1-20-55	Northern Colorado	11	FA, '79
74	Koch, Pete	DE	6-6	265	5	1-23-62	Maryland	6	W-Cin, '85
29	Lewis, Albert	CB	6-2	192	6	10- 6-60	Grambling	12	D3, '83
8	Lowery, Nick	K	6-4	189	9	5-27-56	Dartmouth	12	FA, '80
72	Lutz, David	T	6-6	290	6	12-30-59	Georgia Tech	12	D2, '83
63	†Maas, Bill	NT	6-5	268	5	3- 2-62	Pittsburgh	11	D1, '84
	MacDonald, Dan	LB	6-3	240	2	9-2-63	Idaho State	*3	FA, '88
89	†Marshall, Henry	WR	6-2	216	13	8- 9-54	Missouri	12	D3b, '76
	Monaco, Ron	LB	6-1	225	2	5- 3-63	South Carolina	*2	FA, '88
32	†Moriarty, Larry	RB	6-1	237	6	4-24-58	Notre Dame	12	T-Hou, '86
	Nelson, Ted	S	5-10	190	2	1-1-63	Nevada-Las Vegas	3	FA, '88
35	Okoye, Christian	RB	6-1	253	2	8-16-61	Azusa Pacific	12	D2, '87
83	Paige, Stephone	WR	6-2	185	6	10-15-61	Fresno State	12	OFA, '83
26	Palmer, Paul	RB/KR	5-9	184	2	10-14-64	Temple	12	D1, '87
43	Parker, Robert	RB	6-1	190	2	1- 7-63	Brigham Young	3	OFA, '87
96	Pearson, Aaron	LB	6-0	240	3	8-22-64	Mississippi State	12	D11, '86
24	Pearson, J. C.	CB	5-11	183	3	8-17-63	Washington	12	FA, '86
	Readon, Ike	NT	6-0	273	2	5-16-63	Hampton Institute	*3	FA, '88
31	Ross, Kevin	CB	5-9	182	5	1-16-62	Temple	12	D7, '84
10	Seurer, Frank	QB	6-1	195	3	8-16-62	Kansas	8	FA, '86
97	Snipes, Angelo	LB	6-0	215	3	1-11-63	West Georgia	*6	FA, '87
	Spann, Gary	LB	6-2	217	1	2-3-63	Texas Christian	2	FA, '87
	Standifer, Bob	DT	6-5	265	1	6-3-63	Tennessee-Chattanooga	*0	FA, '88
67	Still, Art	DE	6-7	255	11	12- 5-55	Kentucky	12	D1, '78
38	Thomas, Carlton	CB	6-0	195	2	11-25-63	Elizabeth City State	4	OFA, '87
62	Tupper, Jeff	NT	6-5	269	3	12-26-62	Oklahoma	*4	FA, '87
70	Woodard, Ray	DE	6-6	290	2	1-22-60	Texas	*8	FA, '87

*Cupp played 3 games with Bengals in '87; DeBerg played 12 games with Buccaneers in '87; DiGiacomo last active with Chargers in '86; Fields played 1 game with Colts, 5 with Chiefs in '87; Guthrie missed '87 season due to injury, last active with Chargers in '84; Harry missed '87 season due to injury; Hawkins played 2 games with Chargers in '87; Hill played 2 games with Raiders, 4 with Chiefs in '87; Hooper played 3 games with Dolphins in '87; Jenkins played 3 games with Chargers in '87; Keel played 3 games with Seahawks, 7 with Chiefs in '87; MacDonald played 3 games with Broncos in '87; Monaco played 2 games with Packers in '87; Readon played 3 games with Dolphins in '87; Snipes played 2 games with Chargers, 4 with Chiefs in '87; Standifer last active with Oakland-USFL in '85; Tupper played 4 games with Broncos, active for 1 game with Chiefs in '87, but did not play; Woodard played 3 games with Broncos, 5 with Chiefs in '87.

†Option playout; subject to developments.

D—Draft; T—Trade; W—Waivers; FA—Free Agent; OFA—Original Free Agent; SupD—Supplemental Draft.

Also played with Chiefs in '87, see page 386.

KANSAS CITY CHIEFS
1988 DRAFT CHOICES

(Number following name designates order of selection among 333 players drafted.)

Round and Player	Position		College
1. SMITH, Neil from Detroit (a)	2	DE	Nebraska
1. Choice to Detroit (b)			
2. Choice to Detroit (b)			
3. PORTER, Kevin	59	DB	Auburn
4. Choice to Tampa Bay (c)			
4. AMBROSE, J.R. from Pittsburgh (d)	96	WR	Mississippi
5. Choice to New Orleans (e)			
6. SAXON, James	139	RB	San Jose State
7. STEDMAN, Troy	170	LB	Washburn (Kan.)
8. ROBERTS, Alfredo	197	TE	Miami (Fla.)
9. ABDUR-RA'OOF, Azizuddin	224	WR	Maryland
10. GAMBLE, Kenny	251	RB	Colgate
11. McMANUS, Danny	282	QB	Florida State
12. Choice to Buffalo (f)			

(a) Acquired pick for 1st- and 2nd-round picks in 1988, April 20, 1988.
(b) See (a).
(c) Traded pick, 8th-round pick in 1988 and safety Mark Robinson for quarterback Steve DeBerg, March 31, 1988.
(d) Acquired pick for quarterback Todd Blackledge, March 29, 1988.
(e) Traded pick for linebacker Jack Del Rio, August 17, 1987.
(f) Traded pick for cornerback Charles Romes, July 14, 1987.

KANSAS CITY CHIEFS
1988 ROOKIE AND FIRST-YEAR ROSTER

Name	Pos.	Hgt.	Wgt.	Birth-date	College	How Acquired
Abdur-Ra'oof, Azizuddin ...	WR	6-0	200	4- 8-65	Maryland	D9
Ambrose, J.R.	WR	6-0	188	4-19-64	Mississippi	D4
Brock, Ray	C	6-3	270	8-30-63	Louisiana State	*FA
Chambers, James	RB	5-11	193	4-19-65	Northern Arizona	FA
Collier, Willie	CB	5-10	190	8-31-64	Fort Valley State	FA
DeLine, Dave	K	5-10	167	1-12-65	Colorado	FA
Freeman, Tom	G	6-4	275	3- 9-65	Notre Dame	FA
Gaines, Darryl	CB/S	5-11	197	11- 9-64	Mississippi Valley State	FA
Gamble, Kenny	RB	5-10	197	3- 8-65	Colgate	D10
Hobbs, Stephen	WR	5-11	190	11-14-65	North Alabama	FA
Holt, Daryl	C	6-2	257	8-30-64	Vanderbilt	FA
Johnson, Sidney	CB	5-9	170	3- 7-65	California	*FA, '87
Kantner, Craig	C	6-3	272	4-23-65	Ball State	FA
Leonard, Thomas	RB	6-0	219	3-17-65	Mississippi Valley State	FA
Lowery, Thomas	G	6-4	276	2- 5-62	Jackson State	FA
McDowell, Willard	DE	6-4	250	9-16-65	Norwich	FA
McManus, Danny	QB	6-0	205	6-17-65	Florida State	D11
Montoya, Mark	P	5-9	175	4-17-64	Eastern New Mexico	FA
Norman, Kurt	LB	6-2	230	8-12-63	Hillsdale	*FA
Porter, Kevin	CB/S	5-10	210	4-11-66	Auburn	D3
Randolph, Paul	LB	6-0	234	6-22-66	Tennessee-Martin	FA
Ray, Mickey	LB	6-2	230	11- 2-65	Appalachian State	FA
Roberts, Alfredo	TE	6-3	246	3- 1-65	Miami (Fla.)	D8
Saxon, James	RB	5-11	195	3-23-66	San Jose State	D6
Schnitzius, Brett	T	6-6	282	10- 6-63	Utah State	FA
Smith, Neil	DE	6-4	260	4-10-66	Nebraska	D1
Stedman, Troy	LB	6-3	235	5-19-65	Washburn	D7
Stevens, Tim	K	6-2	219	5-30-62	Southern Oregon State	*FA
Stewart, Michael	CB/S	6-0	191	7-30-64	Yale	FA
Taylor, Kitrick	WR	5-10	183	7-22-64	Washington State	*D5, '87
Thetford, Pat	TE	6-3	245	9- 2-63	Missouri	*FA
Van Drutten, Richard	T	6-5	270	9-23-62	Abilene Christian	FA
White, Terry	CB	5-8	170	12-20-64	West Virginia	FA

*Brock: FA Kansas City '87, released 8/31; Johnson and Taylor missed '87 season due to injury; Norman: FA Cleveland '86, released (failed physical) 7/22; Stevens: FA Green Bay '86, released 8/4; Thetford: FA Kansas City '87, released 8/31.

LOS ANGELES RAIDERS
(Western Division, American Conference)

Mike Shanahan

Managing General Partner—Al Davis
Executive Assistant—Al LoCasale
Personnel Operations—Ron Wolf
Senior Executive—John Herrera
Senior Administrators—Irv Kaze, Mike Ornstein
Head Coach—Mike Shanahan (First Year)
Assistant Coaches:
  Defensive Backfield—Willie Brown
  Strength & Conditioning—John Dunn
  Special Asst. to Head Coach—Alex Gibbs
  Linebackers—Sam Gruneisen
  Defensive Line—Earl Leggett
  Receivers—Nick Nicolau
  Coaches Assistant—Terry Robiskie
  Special Teams—Pete Rodriguez
  Offensive Backfield—Joe Scannella
  Offensive Line—Art Shell
  Linebackers—Charlie Sumner
  Quarterbacks—Tom Walsh
  Defensive Backfield—Jimmy Warren
  (Office Phone: 322-3451—Area Code 213)
Offices—332 Center St., El Segundo, Calif. 90245
Stadium—Los Angeles Memorial Coliseum (Capacity: 92,488)
Team Colors—Silver and Black
Training Site—Oxnard, Calif.

1988 SCHEDULE
(All times local. All games Sunday unless noted otherwise.)

Sept. 4	SAN DIEGO	1:00
Sept. 11	at Houston	3:00
Sept. 18	LOS ANGELES RAMS	1:00
Sept. 26	at Denver (Mon.)	6:00
Oct. 2	CINCINNATI	1:00
Oct. 9	MIAMI	1:00
Oct. 16	at Kansas City	12:00
Oct. 23	at New Orleans	12:00
Oct. 30	KANSAS CITY	1:00
Nov. 6	at San Diego	5:00
Nov. 13	at San Francisco	1:00
Nov. 20	ATLANTA	1:00
Nov. 28	at Seattle (Mon.)	6:00
Dec. 4	DENVER	1:00
Dec. 11	at Buffalo	1:00
Dec. 18	SEATTLE	1:00

1987 RESULTS—(Won 5, Lost 10)

Raiders		Opp.		Att.
20	Green Bay	0	(A)	54,983
27	Detroit	7	(H)	50,300
	Houston*		(A)	
35	*Kansas City*	*17*	*(H)*	*10,708*
14	*Denver*	*30*	*(A)*	*61,230*
17	*San Diego*	*23*	*(H)*	*23,541*
13	Seattle	35	(H)	52,735
23	New England	26	(A)	60,664
20	Minnesota	31	(A)	57,150
14	San Diego	16	(A)	60,639
17	Denver	23	(H)	61,318
37	Seattle	14	(A)	62,802
34	Buffalo	21	(H)	43,143
10	Kansas City	16	(A)	63,834
17	Cleveland	24	(H)	40,275
3	Chicago	6	(H)	78,019

*Game cancelled due to strike.
Italics denote strike replacement games.

1987 GAMES STARTED

(NOTE: Players with an asterisk (*) following their names made starts only in strike-replacement games.)

14 games: Howie Long.

12 games: Marcus Allen, Todd Christensen, Sean Jones, James Lofton, Rod Martin, Vann McElroy, Matt Millen, Don Mosebar, Jerry Robinson, Stacey Toran.

11 games: Bill Pickel.

10 games: Dean Miraldi, Lionel Washington.

9 games: John Clay.

8 games: Brian Holloway, Linden King.

7 games: Mervyn Fernandez, Mike Haynes, Marc Wilson.

6 games: Bill Lewis, Steve Wright.

5 games: Charley Hannah, Rusty Hilger, Bo Jackson, Reggie McKenzie, Sam Seale, Bruce Wilkerson, Dokie Williams.

4 games: Bruce Davis.

3 games: Carl Aikens*, Eddie Anderson*, Darryl Byrd*, Vince Evans*, Rod Hill*, Shawn Regent*, Steve Smith, Steve Strachan, John Tautolo*, Malcolm Taylor.

2 games: Rick Ackerman*, Barry Black*, Jim Ellis*, Ron Fellows, Ron Foster*, Darryl Goodlow*, Greg Hill*, Ethan Horton*, Mario Perry*, David Williams*.

1 game: Jim Browne*, Ted Chapman*, Joe Cormier*, James Davis*, Craig Ellis*, John Gesek*, Rick Goltz*, Rob Harrison*, Frank Hawkins, Leonard Jackson*, Trey Junkin, Mike Noble*, Tony Tillmon*, Greg Townsend*, Ronnie Washington*, Dwight Wheeler, Ron Wheeler*, Chris Woods.

LOS ANGELES RAIDERS 1988 VETERAN ROSTER

No.	Name	Pos.	Ht.	Wt.	NFL Exp.	Birth-date	College	Games in '87	How Acquired
	Adams, David	RB	5-6	168	2	6-24-64	Arizona	*3	W-Ram, '88
44	Adams, Stefon	S	5-10	185	3	8-11-63	East Carolina	9	D3a, '85
32	Allen, Marcus	RB	6-2	205	7	3-26-60	Southern California	12	D1, '82
33	Anderson, Eddie	S	6-1	200	3	7-22-63	Fort Valley State	13	FA, '87
10	Bahr, Chris	K	5-10	170	13	2- 3-53	Penn State	13	FA, '80
56	Barnes, Jeff	LB	6-2	230	12	3- 1-55	California	7	D5a, '77
	Bennett, Barry	DE	6-4	260	11	12-10-55	Concordia	*13	T-NYJ, '88
	Black, Mel	LB	6-2	225	3	2- 7-62	Eastern Illinois	*3	FA, '88
82	†Branton, Gene	TE	6-5	245	2	11-23-60	Texas Southern	*0	FA, '86
95	Buczkowski, Bob	DE	6-5	270	2	5- 5-64	Pittsburgh	2	D1, '86
	Budde, Brad	G	6-4	271	8	5-9-58	Southern California	*0	FA, '88
	Caldwell, David	DL	6-1	261	2	2-28-65	Texas Christian	*3	FA, '88
	Carter, Russell	CB	6-2	195	5	2-10-62	Southern Methodist	*8	T-NYJ
46	Christensen, Todd	TE	6-3	230	10	8- 3-56	Brigham Young	12	FA, '79
78	Clay, John	T	6-5	295	2	5- 1-64	Missouri	10	D1, '87
	Cooper, Scott	DE	6-5	275	1	6-20-64	Kearney State	*0	FA, '88
45	†Davis, James	S	6-0	195	7	6-12-57	Southern	12	D5, '81
	Doig, Steve	LB	6-2	240	5	3-28-60	New Hampshire	*1	FA, '88
11	Evans, Vince	QB	6-2	200	9	6-14-55	Southern California	3	FA, '87
21	Fellows, Ron	CB	6-0	175	8	11- 7-58	Missouri	12	T-Dal, '87
86	Fernandez, Mervyn	WR	6-3	200	2	12-29-59	San Jose State	7	D10, '83
63	Gesek, John	C/G	6-5	275	2	2-18-63	Cal State-Sacramento	3	D10a, '87
	Giacomarro, Ralph	P	6-1	190	4	1-17-61	Penn State	*3	FA, '88
	Goebel, Hank	T	6-7	270	2	11-1-64	Fullerton State	*3	FA, '88
73	Hannah, Charley	G	6-5	265	12	7-26-55	Alabama	5	T-NE, '83
22	†Haynes, Mike	CB	6-2	190	13	7- 1-53	Arizona State	8	T-NE, '83
	Heimuli, Lakei	RB	5-11	219	2	6-24-65	Brigham Young	*3	W-Ram, '88
84	Hester, Jessie	WR	5-11	170	4	1-21-63	Florida State	10	D1, '85
12	Hilger, Rusty	QB	6-4	205	4	5- 9-62	Oklahoma State	5	D6, '85
76	†Holloway, Brian	T	6-7	285	8	7-25-59	Stanford	12	T-NE, '87
34	Jackson, Bo	RB	6-1	230	2	11-30-62	Auburn	7	D7, '87
	Johnson, James	LB	6-2	235	2	6-21-62	San Diego State	*1	FA, '88
74	Jordan, Shelby	T	6-7	285	12	1-23-52	Washington (Mo.)	*0	T-NE, '83
87	Junkin, Trey	TE	6-2	230	6	1-23-61	Louisiana Tech	12	FA, '85
59	Kimmel, Jamie	LB	6-3	235	3	3-28-62	Syracuse	15	D4, '85
52	King, Linden	LB	6-4	250	11	6-28-55	Colorado State	12	FA, '86
	Lee, Byron	LB	6-2	230	3	9-8-64	Ohio State	*3	FA, '88
	Lee, John	K	5-11	182	2	5-19-64	UCLA	*0	FA, '88
40	†Lee, Zeph	RB	6-3	210	2	6-17-63	Southern California	*3	D9, '86
51	Lewis, Bill	G/C	6-7	275	3	7-12-63	Nebraska	8	D7, '86
80	Lofton, James	WR	6-3	190	11	7- 5-56	Stanford	12	T-GB, '87
75	Long, Howie	DE	6-5	265	8	1- 6-60	Villanova	14	D2, '81
	Malone, Ralph	LB	6-5	225	2	1-12-64	Georgia Tech	*0	FA, '88
53	Martin, Rod	LB	6-2	225	12	4- 7-54	Southern California	12	D12, '77
65	†Marvin, Mickey	G	6-4	270	11	10- 5-55	Tennessee	1	D4, '77
26	McElroy, Vann	S	6-2	195	7	1-13-60	Baylor	12	D3, '82
54	McKenzie, Reggie	LB	6-1	235	4	2- 8-63	Tennessee	10	D10, '85
20	McLemore, Chris	RB	6-1	230	2	12-31-63	Arizona	*5	D11, '87
55	†Millen, Matt	LB	6-2	245	9	3-12-58	Penn State	12	D2, '80
64	†Miraldi, Dean	G	6-6	280	5	4- 8-58	Utah	10	FA, '87
72	Mosebar, Don	C	6-6	275	6	9-11-61	Southern California	12	D1, '83
42	Mueller, Vance	RB	6-0	210	3	5- 5-64	Occidental	12	D4a, '86
81	Parker, Andy	TE	6-5	245	5	9- 8-61	Utah	12	D5, '84
71	Pickel, Bill	DT	6-5	260	6	11- 5-59	Rutgers	12	D2, '83
16	Plunkett, Jim	QB	6-2	225	17	12- 5-47	Stanford	*0	FA, '78
77	†Riehm, Chris	G	6-6	275	2	4- 4-61	Ohio State	1	FA, '86
57	Robinson, Jerry	LB	6-2	225	10	12-18-56	UCLA	12	T-Phi, '85
43	Seale, Sam	CB	5-9	185	5	10- 6-62	Western State (Colo.)	12	D8, '84
35	Smith, Steve	RB	6-1	235	2	8-30-64	Penn State	7	D3, '87
39	†Strachan, Steve	RB	6-1	220	4	3-22-63	Boston College	11	D11, '85
5	Talley, Stan	P	6-5	220	2	9- 5-58	Texas Christian	12	FA, '87
61	Tautolo, John	T	6-4	280	4	5-29-59	UCLA	3	FA, '88
96	†Taylor, Malcolm	DT	6-0	280	5	6-20-60	Tennessee State	12	FA, '87
30	†Toran, Stacey	S	6-3	200	5	10-11-61	Notre Dame	12	D6, '84
93	Townsend, Greg	DE	6-3	250	6	11- 3-61	Texas Christian	13	D4, '83
48	Washington, Lionel	CB	6-0	185	6	10-21-60	Tulane	11	T-StL, '87
67	†Wheeler, Dwight	G/C	6-3	280	8	1- 3-55	Tennessee State	*7	FA, '84
68	Wilkerson, Bruce	G	6-5	280	2	7-28-64	Tennessee	11	D2, '87

No.	Name	Pos.	Ht.	Wt.	NFL Exp.	Birth-date	College	Games in '87	How Acquired
98	†Willis, Mitch	DT	6-8	275	4	3-16-62	Southern Methodist	10	D7, '84
90	Wise, Mike	DE	6-7	265	2	6- 5-64	California-Davis	*0	D4, '86
88	Woods, Chris	WR	5-11	190	2	7-19-62	Auburn	9	SupD, '84
66	†Wright, Steve	T	6-6	270	6	4- 8-59	Northern Iowa	9	FA, '87

*Adams played 3 games with Cowboys and on inactive list for 2 games with Rams in '87; Bennett played 13 games with Jets in '87; Black played 3 games with Patriots in '87; Branton active for 1 game with Raiders in '87, but did not play; Budde missed '87 season with Chiefs due to injury; Caldwell played 3 games with Packers in '87; Carter played 8 games with Jets in '87; Cooper active for 1 game with Browns in '87, but did not play; Doig played 1 game with Patriots in '87; Giacomarro played 3 games with Broncos in '87; Goebel played 3 games with Rams in '87; Heimuli played 3 games with Bears and on inactive list for 2 games with Rams in '87; Johnson played 1 game with 49ers in '87; Jordan and Plunkett missed '87 season due to injury; B. Lee played 3 games with Eagles in '87; J. Lee last active with Cardinals in '86; Zeph Lee played 1 game with Broncos, 2 with Raiders in '87; Malone last active with Browns in '86; McLemore played 2 games with Colts, 3 with Raiders in '87; Wheeler played 3 games with Chargers, 4 with Raiders in '87; Wise active for 1 game with Raiders in '87, but did not play.

†Option playout; subject to developments.

D—Draft; T—Trade; FA—Free Agent; SupD—Supplemental Draft.

Also played with Raiders in '87, see page 386.

LOS ANGELES RAIDERS
1988 DRAFT CHOICES

(Number following name designates order of selection among 333 players drafted.)

Round and Player		Position	College
1. BROWN, Tim	6	WR	Notre Dame
1. McDANIEL, Terry from L.A. Rams through Houston (a)	9	DB	Tennessee
1. DAVIS, Scott from San Francisco (b)	25	DE	Illinois
2. Choice to San Francisco (c)			
3. Choice to San Diego through Houston (d)			
4. Choice to Green Bay (e)			
4. ROTHER, Tim from N.Y. Jets (f)	90	DT	Nebraska
5. Choice to New England (g)			
5. PRICE, Dennis from Sea. through S.F. & N.Y. Jets (h)	131	DB	UCLA
6. GRABISNA, Erwin	143	LB	Case Western (O.)
7. CRUDUP, Derrick	171	DB	Oklahoma
8. ALEXANDER, Mike	199	WR	Penn State
9. WARE, Reggie	227	RB	Auburn
9. TABOR, Scott from N.Y. Giants (i)	229	P	California
10. HARRELL, Newt	255	T	West Texas St.
11. WEBER, David	283	QB	Carroll (Wis.)
12. KUNKEL, Greg	311	G	Kentucky

(a) Oilers acquired pick, guard Kent Hill, defensive end William Fuller and 1st- and 5th-round picks in 1987 from Rams for rights to quarterback Jim Everett, September 18, 1986; Raiders acquired pick and 3rd- and 4th-round picks in 1988 from Oilers for defensive end Sean Jones and 2nd- and 3rd-round picks in 1988, April 21, 1988.

(b) Acquired pick for wide receiver Dokie Williams and 2nd- and 4th-round picks in 1988, April 24, 1988.

(c) See (b).

(d) Raiders traded pick to Oilers: see second part of (a); Oilers traded pick to Chargers for 3rd- and 5th-round picks in 1988, April 24, 1988.

(e) Traded pick and 3rd-round pick in 1987 for wide receiver James Lofton, April 13, 1987.

(f) Acquired pick and 5th-round pick in 1988 for 3rd-round pick in 1988, April 24, 1988.

(g) Traded pick and conditional 1989 pick for tackle Brian Holloway, September 1, 1987.

(h) 49ers acquired pick from Seahawks for quarterback Jeff Kemp, May 19, 1987; Jets acquired pick from 49ers for wide receiver Johnny (Lam) Jones, July 23, 1987; Raiders acquired pick from Jets: see (f).

(i) Acquired pick for two 12th-round picks in 1987, April 30, 1987.

LOS ANGELES RAIDERS
1988 ROOKIE AND FIRST-YEAR ROSTER

Name	Pos.	Hgt.	Wgt.	Birth-date	College	How Acquired
Alexander, Mike	WR/TE	6-3	215	3-19-65	Penn State	D8
Beuerlein, Steve	QB	6-2	205	3- 7-65	Notre Dame	*D4, '87
Brown, Tim	WR	6-0	190	7-22-66	Notre Dame	D1
Carroll, Sam	DE	6-4	260	8- 2-65	Hawaii	FA
Clark, Craig	TE	6-3	230	10-25-64	Iowa	FA
Crudup, Derrick	CB	6-2	210	2-15-65	Oklahoma	D7
Davis, Scott	DE	6-7	270	8- 7-65	Illinois	D1b
Dyal, Mike	TE	6-2	235	5-20-66	Texas A&I	FA
Grabisna, Erwin	LB	6-3	250	8-28-66	Case Western Reserve	D6
Graves, Rory	T	6-6	290	7-21-63	Ohio State	*FA
Greenwood, Marcus	RB	6-0	210	3- 7-63	UCLA	*FA
Harrell, Newt	G	6-5	295	9- 7-64	West Texas State	D10
Harvey, Stacy	LB	6-4	230	3- 8-65	Arizona State	FA
Hatcher, Mark	QB	6-0	185	1-27-66	Colorado	FA
Henry, Ken	WR	6-3	200	10- 7-65	Southern California	*W-Det, '88
Hutson, Brian	S	6-1	195	2-20-65	Mississippi State	*FA, '87
Jackson, Milt	WR	5-10	178	12-10-63	Notre Dame	*FA
Johnson, Matt	S	6-2	205	9-10-62	Southern California	*FA
Johnson, Rory	RB	5-10	220	3-23-65	St. Joseph's (Ind.)	FA
Knapp, Greg	QB	6-4	200	3-15-63	Cal State-Sacramento	*FA
Kunkel, Greg	G	6-5	285	2- 9-64	Kentucky	D12
McDaniel, Terence	CB	5-10	170	2- 8-65	Tennessee	D1a
Odom, Walter	TE	6-4	233	3-30-65	Florida	FA
Price, Dennis	CB	6-1	170	6-14-65	UCLA	D5
Reynosa, Jim	LB	6-5	255	5-19-64	Arizona State	*FA
Rother, Tim	DT	6-7	265	9-28-65	Nebraska	D4
Shapiro, John	WR	6-4	200	2-11-65	Brown	FA
Short, Stanley	G	6-4	270	9-20-63	Penn State	*FA
Smith, Brock	WR	6-1	175	10- 2-63	Fresno State	FA
Smith, Rod	WR	6-2	195	5-23-65	Nebraska	FA
Snelson, Eric	TE	6-3	235	7-20-65	Stanford	FA
Stone, Tim	T	6-5	290	11-24-60	Kansas State	*FA
Stoney, John	CB	5-9	175	10-24-64	Occidental	FA
Tabor, Scott	P	6-3	195	6-15-65	California	D9a
Toy, David	S	6-1	200	10- 2-65	Washington	FA
Ware, Reggie	RB	6-1	240	2- 8-65	Auburn	D9
Weber, David	QB	6-3	215	6-23-65	Carroll, Wisconsin	D11
Zayas, Rich	WR	6-0	172	2-23-64	Brigham Young	FA
Zumwalt, Rich	LB	6-3	224	5-19-65	Arizona State	FA

*Beuerlein and Hutson missed '87 season due to injury; Graves: FA Seattle '86, injured reserve 8/19 through entire season, released 9/1/87; Greenwood: D12 San Diego '87, released 8/27; Henry: FA Detroit '88, released 5/13, awarded on waivers to Raiders 5/24; Jackson: FA Cleveland '87, released 6/1, FA Kansas City 6/27, released 8/3; Johnson: D5 San Diego '86, rights released (failed physical) 7/10, FA Tampa Bay 7/17, released 8/17, FA Seattle '87, released 9/7; Knapp: FA Kansas City '86, released 8/18, FA Los Angeles Raiders '87, released 8/20; Reynosa: D11 Indianapolis '87, released 8/31; Short: D6 Detroit '85, released 8/27, FA Denver '86, injured reserve 8/18 through entire season, released 8/26/87; Stone: D11 Cincinnati '86, released 8/18, FA Kansas City '87, injured reserve 8/21 through 10/26, released 10/27.

LOS ANGELES RAMS
(Western Division, National Conference)

John Robinson

President—Georgia Frontiere
Vice-President, Finance—John Shaw
General Counsel—Jay Zygmunt
Administrator of Football Operations—Jack Faulkner
Director of Operations—Dick Beam
Director of Player Personnel—John Math
Head Coach—John Robinson (5 years: 46-33)
Assistant Coaches:
  Asst. Defensive Line—Larry Brooks
  Quarterbacks—Dick Coury
  Special Teams—Artie Gigantino
  Defensive Line—Marv Goux
  Running Backs—Gil Haskell
  Offensive Line—Hudson Houck
  Defensive Backfield—Steve Shafer
  Defensive Coordinator—Fritz Shurmur
  Wide Receivers/Tight Ends—Norval Turner
  Outside Linebackers—Fred Whittingham
  Offensive Coordinator—Ernie Zampese
Director of Public Relations—John Oswald
(Office Phones: 535-7267—Area Code 714; 585-5400—Area Code 213)
Offices—2327 W. Lincoln Ave., Anaheim, Calif. 92801
Stadium—Anaheim Stadium (Capacity: 69,008)
Team Colors—Royal Blue, Gold and White
Training Site—California State University, Fullerton, Calif.

1988 SCHEDULE
(All times local.
All games Sunday unless noted otherwise.)

Sept. 4	at Green Bay	12:00
Sept. 11	DETROIT	1:00
Sept. 18	at Los Angeles Raiders	1:00
Sept. 25	at New York Giants	4:00
Oct. 2	PHOENIX	1:00
Oct. 9	at Atlanta	1:00
Oct. 16	SAN FRANCISCO	1:00
Oct. 23	SEATTLE	1:00
Oct. 30	at New Orleans	12:00
Nov. 6	at Philadelphia	1:00
Nov. 13	NEW ORLEANS	1:00
Nov. 20	SAN DIEGO	1:00
Nov. 27	at Denver	2:00
Dec. 5	CHICAGO (Mon.)	6:00
Dec. 11	ATLANTA	1:00
Dec. 18	at San Francisco	5:00

1987 RESULTS—(Won 6, Lost 9)

Rams		Opp.		Att.
16 Houston	20	(A)		33,186
16 Minnesota	21	(H)		63,567
Cincinnati*		(H)		
10 New Orleans	37	(A)		29,745
31 Pittsburgh	21	(H)		20,218
20 Atlanta	24	(A)		15,813
17 Cleveland	30	(A)		76,933
10 San Francisco	31	(H)		55,328
14 New Orleans	31	(H)		43,379
27 St. Louis	24	(A)		27,730
30 Washington	26	(A)		53,614
35 Tampa Bay	3	(H)		45,188
37 Detroit	16	(A)		33,143
33 Atlanta	0	(H)		43,310
21 Dallas	29	(H)		60,700
0 San Francisco	48	(A)		57,950

*Game cancelled due to strike.
Italics denote strike replacement games.

1987 GAMES STARTED

(NOTE: Players with an asterisk (*) following their names made starts only in strike-replacement games.)

15 games: Jim Collins, Greg Meisner.

12 games: Henry Ellard, Jerry Gray, David Hill, Tom Newberry, Mel Owens, Irv Pankey, Doug Reed, Jackie Slater, Doug Smith, Charles White, Mike Wilcher.

11 games: Ron Brown, Carl Ekern, Jim Everett.

9 games: Reggie Doss, LeRoy Irvin.

8 games: Nolan Cromwell, Mike Guman, Dennis Harrah, Vince Newsome.

7 games: Johnnie Johnson.

6 games: Shawn Miller.

5 games: Damone Johnson.

4 games: Steve Dils, Duval Love, Michael Stewart.

3 games: Rick DiBernardo*, Hank Goebel*, Kirby Jackson*, James McDonald*, Joe Murray*, Reggie Richardson*, Mickey Sutton*, Tom Taylor*, Kelly Thomas*, Navy Tuiasosopo*, Kyle Whittingham*, Greg Williamson*, Alvin Wright*.

2 games: Kyle Borland*, Eric Dickerson, Bernard Henry*, Phil Smith*.

1 game: Greg Bell, Neil Hope*, Kevin House, Sam Johnson*, Larry Kelm, Buford McGee, Stacey Mobley*, Malcolm Moore*.

LOS ANGELES RAMS 1988 VETERAN ROSTER

No.	Name	Pos.	Ht.	Wt.	NFL Exp.	Birth-date	College	Games in '87	How Acquired
84	†Baty, Greg	TE	6-5	241	3	8-28-64	Stanford	*9	W-NE, '87
42	Bell, Greg	RB	5-10	210	5	8- 1-62	Notre Dame	*4	T-Buf, '87
92	Brown, Richard	LB	6-3	240	2	9-21-65	San Diego State	8	OFA, '87
50	Collins, Jim	LB	6-2	230	7	6-11-58	Syracuse	15	D2, '81
72	Cox, Robert	T	6-5	258	2	12-30-63	UCLA	10	D6, '86
21	†Cromwell, Nolan	S	6-1	200	12	1-30-55	Kansas	15	D2, '77
	Diaz-Infante, David	OL	6-2	272	2	3-31-64	San Jose State	*3	FA, '88
8	Dils, Steve	QB	6-1	191	10	12- 8-55	Stanford	15	T-Min, '84
55	Ekern, Carl	LB	6-3	222	12	5-27-54	San Josc State	11	D5, '76
80	Ellard, Henry	WR	5-11	175	6	7-21-61	Fresno State	12	D2, '83
	Embree, Jon	TE	6-2	230	1	10-15-65	Colorado	1	D6, '87
11	Everett, Jim	QB	6-5	212	3	1- 3-63	Purdue	11	T-Hou, '86
35	Francis, Jon	RB	5-11	207	2	6-21-64	Boise State	9	FA, '87
19	Gaynor, Doug	QB	6-2	205	2	7- 5-63	Long Beach State	*0	FA, '88
25	Gray, Jerry	CB	6-0	185	4	12- 2-62	Texas	12	D1, '85
91	†Greene, Kevin	LB	6-3	238	4	7-31-62	Auburn	9	D5, '85
44	Guman, Mike	RB	6-2	218	9	4-21-58	Penn State	12	D6, '80
5	†Hatcher, Dale	P	6-2	200	4	4- 5-63	Clemson	15	D3, '85
	Henley, Thomas	WR	5-10	173	1	7-28-65	Stanford	*1	FA, '88
28	Hicks, Cliff	CB	5-10	188	2	8-18-64	Oregon	11	D3, '87
	Holohan, Pete	TE	6-4	232	8	7-25-59	Notre Dame	*2	T-SD, '88
83	†House, Kevin	WR	6-1	185	9	12-20-57	Southern Illinois	12	W-TB, '86
47	Irvin, LeRoy	CB	5-11	184	9	9-15-57	Kansas	10	D3a, '80
59	†Jerue, Mark	LB	6-3	232	6	1-15-60	Washington	4	T-Bal, '83
77	Jeter, Gary	DE	6-4	260	12	3-24-55	Southern California	12	T-NYG, '83
86	†Johnson, Damone	TE	6-4	230	3	3- 2-62	Cal Poly-SLO	12	FA, '86
20	Johnson, Johnnie	S	6-1	183	9	10- 8-56	Texas	7	D1, '80
52	Kelm, Larry	LB	6-4	226	2	11-29-64	Texas A&M	12	D4a, '87
1	Lansford, Mike	K	6-0	183	7	7-20-58	Washington	15	FA, '82
67	Love, Duval	G	6-3	263	4	6-24-63	UCLA	10	D10, '85
90	McDonald, Mike	LB	6-1	235	4	6-22-58	Southern California	10	FA, '87
24	McGee, Buford	RB	6-0	206	5	8-16-60	Mississippi	3	T-SD, '87
69	†Meisner, Greg	NT	6-3	253	8	4-23-59	Pittsburgh	15	D3, '81
12	Millen, Hugh	QB	6-5	216	2	11-22-63	Washington	1	D8, '86
98	†Miller, Shawn	NT	6-4	255	5	3-14-61	Utah State	6	FA, '84
45	Moore, Malcolm	TE	6-3	236	2	6-24-61	Southern California	3	FA, '88
66	Newberry, Tom	G	6-2	279	3	12-20-62	Wisconsin-LaCrosse	12	D2, '86
22	Newsome, Vince	S	6-1	179	6	1-22-61	Washington	8	D4a, '83
58	Owens, Mel	LB	6-2	224	8	12- 7-58	Michigan	12	D1, '81
75	Pankey, Irv	T	6-4	267	9	12-15-58	Penn State	12	D2, '80
93	†Reed, Doug	DE	6-3	262	5	7-16-60	San Diego State	12	D4, '83
63	Shields, Jon	G	6-5	285	2	4-30-64	Portland State	*1	OFA, '87
78	Slater, Jackie	T	6-4	271	13	5-27-54	Jackson State	12	D3, '76
61	Slaton, Tony	C	6-3	265	4	4-12-61	Southern California	11	FA, '84
56	Smith, Doug	C	6-3	260	11	11-25-56	Bowling Green	12	OFA, '78
23	Stewart, Michael	S	5-11	195	2	7-21-65	Fresno State	12	D8, '87
65	Stokes, Fred	DE	6-3	262	2	3-14-64	Georgia Southern	8	D12a, '87
49	†Sutton, Mickey	CB	5-8	165	3	8-28-60	Montana	12	FA, '86
70	Teafatiller, Guy	NT	6-2	185	2	5-10-64	Illinois	*3	FA, '88
68	Tuiasosopo, Navy	C	6-2	285	2	5-24-64	Utah State	3	FA, '88
32	†Tyrrell, Tim	RB	6-1	201	5	2-19-61	Northern Illinois	11	FA, '86
51	†Vann, Norwood	LB	6-1	237	5	2-18-62	East Carolina	11	D10, '84
73	Walker, Jeff	T	6-4	295	2	1-22-63	Memphis State	*0	T-SD, '87
41	Wattelet, Frank	S	6-0	190	8	10-25-58	Kansas	*7	FA, '87
33	White, Charles	RB	5-10	190	8	1-22-58	Southern California	15	FA, '85
54	†Wilcher, Mike	LB	6-3	235	6	3-20-60	North Carolina	12	D2a, '83
99	†Wright, Alvin	NT	6-2	265	3	2- 5-61	Jacksonville State	15	FA, '86
88	Young, Michael	WR	6-1	185	4	2- 2-62	UCLA	12	D6, '85

*Baty played 5 games with Patriots, 4 with Rams in '87; Bell played 2 games with Bills, 2 with Rams in '87; Diaz-Infante played 3 games with Chargers in '87; Gaynor last active with Bengals in '86; Henley played 1 game with Saints in '87; Holohan played 12 games with Chargers in '87; Shields played 1 game with Cowboys in '87; Teafatiller played 3 games with Bears in '87; Walker missed '87 season due to injury; Wattelet played 2 games with Saints, 5 with Rams in '87.

†Option playout; subject to developments.

Retired—Wide receiver Ron Brown, 4-year veteran, 12 games in '87; guard Dennis Harrah, 13-year veteran, 8 games in '87.

D—Draft; T—Trade; W—Waivers; FA—Free Agent; OFA—Original Free Agent.

Also played with Rams in '87, see page 386.

LOS ANGELES RAMS
1988 DRAFT CHOICES

(Number following name designates order of selection among 333 players drafted.)

Round and Player		Position	College
1. Choice to L.A. Raiders through Houston (a)			
1. GREEN, Gaston from Buffalo (b)	14	RB	UCLA
1. COX, Aaron from Indianapolis (b)	20	WR	Arizona State
2. NEWMAN, Anthony	35	DB	Oregon
2. ANDERSON, Willie from San Diego (c)	46	WR	UCLA
2. STRICKLAND, Fred from Indianapolis (b)	47	LB	Purdue
3. Choice to Washington (d)			
3. PIEL, Mike from Washington (e)	82	DT	Illinois
4. Choice to San Diego (f)			
5. DELPINO, Robert	117	RB	Missouri
5. WASHINGTON, James from Washington (e)	137	DB	UCLA
6. JONES, Keith	147	RB	Nebraska
6. KNAPTON, Jeff from Washington (e)	165	DT	Wyoming
7. Choice to Denver (g)			
8. FRANKLIN, Darryl	201	WR	Washington
9. FOSTER, Pat	231	DT	Montana
10. MULLIN, R.C.	258	T	S.W. Louisiana
11. Choice to San Diego (h)			
12. Choice to Washington (i)			
12. BEATHARD, Jeff from Washington (j)	333	WR	Southern Oregon

(a) Rams traded pick, guard Kent Hill, defensive end William Fuller and 1st- and 5th-round picks in 1987 to Oilers for rights to quarterback Jim Everett, September 18, 1986; Oilers traded pick and 3rd- and 4th-round picks in 1988 to Raiders for defensive end Sean Jones and 2nd- and 3rd-round picks in 1988, April 21, 1988.

(b) Acquired picks, October 31, 1987 in deal which sent running back Eric Dickerson to Colts and rights to linebacker Cornelius Bennett from Colts to Bills; Rams also acquired 1st- and 2nd-round picks in 1989 and running back Greg Bell from Bills and 2nd-round pick in 1989 and running back Owen Gill from Colts.

(c) Acquired pick, conditional 1989 pick and running back Buford McGee for running back Barry Redden, June 9, 1987.

(d) Traded pick for 3rd-, 5th- and 6th-round picks in 1988, April 24, 1988.

(e) Acquired picks: See (d).

(f) Traded pick for tight end Pete Holohan, April 24, 1988.

(g) Traded pick and 11th-round pick in 1987 for linebacker Steve Busick, September 2, 1986.

(h) Traded pick for guard Jeff Walker, September 8, 1987.

(i) Traded pick for 12th-round pick in 1988 and 11th-round pick in 1989, April 25, 1988.

(j) See (i).

LOS ANGELES RAMS
1988 ROOKIE AND FIRST-YEAR ROSTER

Name	Pos.	Hgt.	Wgt.	Birth-date	College	How Acquired
Anderson, Gary	C/G	6-4	265	2-19-64	Utah	FA
Anderson, Willie	WR	6-0	169	3- 7-65	UCLA	D2a
Bartlett, Doug	NT	6-2	257	2-22-57	Northern Illinois	*D4, '87
Beathard, Jeff	RB	5-9	190	6- 9-64	Southern Oregon State	D12
Brookhart, Joe	WR	5-11	195	10-17-64	Colorado State	FA
Cox, Aaron	WR	5-9	174	3-13-65	Arizona State	D1a
Delpino, Robert	RB	6-0	198	11- 2-65	Missouri	D5
Esene, Levi	NT	5-11	270	7-31-63	San Diego State	*FA
Foster, Pat	DE	6-5	255	12- 2-64	Montana	D9
Franklin, Darryl	WR	5-10	187	2- 4-65	Washington	D8
Frasch, Phillip	S/CB	6-3	200	7-19-66	Bakersfield (J.C.)	FA
Glenn, Ledell	CB	5-11	185	7-28-63	Oklahoma	FA
Green, Gaston	RB	5-10	189	8- 1-66	UCLA	D1
Jones, Keith	RB	5-9	179	2- 5-66	Nebraska	D6
Knapton, Jeff	NT	6-5	236	8-28-66	Wyoming	D6a
Lambert, Darren	LB	5-9	170	8-31-65	Brigham Young	FA
Moore, William	G	6-0	285	7- 4-65	Elizabeth City State	FA
Mullin, R.C.	T	6-6	316	6-28-65	S.W. Louisiana	D10
Myers, Bryan	P	6-2	200	9-29-59	Ball State	*FA
Newman, Anthony	S/CB	6-0	199	11-21-65	Oregon	D2
Nicholas, Rey	WR	6-1	185	2- 6-65	California	FA
Piel, Mike	NT	6-4	263	9-21-65	Illinois	D3
Richardson, Craig	WR	5-11	189	11-11-63	Eastern Washington	*FA, '87
Rill, David	LB	6-0	220	6-30-66	Washington	FA
Seawright, James	LB	6-3	236	3-30-62	South Carolina	*FA
Smith, David	LB	6-6	235	3-14-65	Northern Arizona	*D10, '87
Strickland, Fred	LB	6-2	244	8-15-66	Purdue	D2b
Tanner, Randy	WR	5-11	190	1-29-66	Southern California	FA
Terry, Joe	LB	6-2	229	11-10-65	Texas-El Paso	FA
Washington, James	S	6-1	191	1-10-65	UCLA	D5a

*Bartlett and Smith missed '87 season due to injury; Esene: FA replacement San Diego 9/24/87 (on inactive list for 1 game), released 10/20; Myers: FA Washington '84, released 7/31, FA Indianapolis '85, released 7/27; Richardson: D11 Kansas City '87, released 8/24, FA Los Angeles Rams 8/29, injured reserve 9/5 through entire season; Seawright: D11 Buffalo '85, injured reserve 9/2 through entire season, injured reserve 8/18 through entire '86 season, released 9/7/87.

MIAMI DOLPHINS
(Eastern Division, American Conference)

Don Shula

President—Joseph Robbie
Executive Vice-President and G.M.—J. Michael Robbie
Head Coach—Don Shula (25 years: 255-101-6)
Director, Pro Scouting—Charley Winner
Director, College Personnel—Chuck Connor
Assistant Coaches:
　Defense—Tom Olivadotti
　Defensive Backfield—Mel Phillips
　Offense/Offensive Line—John Sandusky
　Receivers—Larry Seiple
　Defensive Line—Dan Sekanovich
　Assistant Head Coach—David Shula
　Linebackers—Chuck Studley
　Offensive Backfield—Carl Taseff
　Strength & Conditioning—Junior Wade
　Special Teams—Mike Westhoff
Director of Publicity—Eddie White
　(Office Phone: 576-1000—Area Code 305)
Offices—4770 Biscayne Blvd., (Suite 1440) Miami, Fla. 33137
Stadium—Joe Robbie Stadium (Capacity: 75,000)
Team Colors—Aqua and Orange
Training Site—St. Thomas University, Miami, Fla.

1988 SCHEDULE
(All times local.
All games Sunday unless noted otherwise.)

Sept. 4	at Chicago	12:00
Sept. 11	at Buffalo	1:00
Sept. 18	GREEN BAY	1:00
Sept. 25	at Indianapolis	12:00
Oct. 2	MINNESOTA	4:00
Oct. 9	at Los Angeles Raiders	1:00
Oct. 16	SAN DIEGO	1:00
Oct. 23	NEW YORK JETS	4:00
Oct. 30	at Tampa Bay	1:00
Nov. 6	at New England	1:00
Nov. 14	BUFFALO (Mon.)	9:00
Nov. 20	NEW ENGLAND	8:00
Nov. 27	at New York Jets	1:00
Dec. 4	INDIANAPOLIS	1:00
Dec. 12	CLEVELAND (Mon.)	9:00
Dec. 18	at Pittsburgh	1:00

1987 RESULTS—(Won 8, Lost 7)

Dolphins		Opp.		Att.
21	New England	28	(A)	54,642
23	Indianapolis	10	(A)	57,524
	New York Giants*		(H)	
20	*Seattle*	*24*	*(A)*	*19,448*
42	*Kansas City*	*0*	*(H)*	*25,867*
31	*New York Jets (OT)*	*37*	*(A)*	*18,249*
31	Buffalo (OT)	34	(H)	61,295
35	Pittsburgh	24	(H)	52,578
20	Cincinnati	14	(A)	53,847
21	Indianapolis	40	(H)	65,433
20	Dallas	14	(A)	56,519
0	Buffalo	27	(A)	68,055
37	New York Jets	28	(H)	58,879
28	Philadelphia	10	(A)	63,841
23	Washington	21	(H)	65,715
10	New England	24	(H)	61,192

*Game cancelled due to strike.
Italics denote strike replacement games.

1987 GAMES STARTED

(NOTE: Players with an asterisk (*) following their names made starts only in strike-replacement games.)

12 games: John Bosa, Mark Brown, Mark Clayton, Roy Foster, Bruce Hardy, William Judson, Paul Lankford, Dan Marino, Jackie Shipp, Brian Sochia, Tom Toth, T.J. Turner.

11 games: Woody Bennett, Mark Duper.

10 games: Glenn Blackwood.

9 games: Jon Giesler, Ronnie Lee, John Offerdahl, Dwight Stephenson.

8 games: Bob Brudzinski.

7 games: Bud Brown.

6 games: Jeff Dellenbach, Lorenzo Hampton, Liffort Hobley.

5 games: Rick Graf, Troy Stradford.

3 games: Bill Bealles*, Charles Bennett*, Dennis Fowlkes*, Trell Hooper*, Scott Kehoe*, Mike Lambrecht*, David Lewis*, Kyle Mackey*, Vic Morris*, Greg Ours*, Tim Pidgeon*, Lawrence Sampleton*, Duke Schamel*, Robert Sowell*, Derek Wimberly*, Jeff Wiska*.

2 games: Mark Dennis, Leland Douglas*, Jim Gilmore*, Demetrious Johnson*, Ronald Scott*.

1 game: Clarence Bailey*, Mike Caterbone*, Eddie Chavis*, Ron Davenport, David Frye*, Hugh Green, Rickey Isom*, Greg Koch, Louis Oubre*, James Pruitt, Tate Randle*, Dameon Reilly*, Donovan Rose, John Swain*, John Tagliaferri*, Reyna Thompson.

MIAMI DOLPHINS 1988 VETERAN ROSTER

No.	Name	Pos.	Ht.	Wt.	NFL Exp.	Birth-date	College	Games in '87	How Acquired
	Anderson, Aric	LB	6-2	225	2	4-9-65	Millikin	*3	FA, '88
	Archer, David	QB	6-2	208	5	2-15-62	Iowa State	*9	FA, '88
86	Banks, Fred	WR	5-10	180	3	5-26-62	Liberty	3	FA, '87
	Bennett, Charles	DE	6-5	255	2	2- 9-63	Southwestern Louisiana	3	FA, '87
34	Bennett, Woody	RB	6-2	244	10	3-24-56	Miami (Fla.)	12	W-NYJ, '80
75	†Betters, Doug	DE	6-7	265	11	6-11-56	Nevada-Reno	12	D6, '78
47	†Blackwood, Glenn	S	6-0	190	10	2-23-57	Texas	10	D8a, '79
97	Bosa, John	DE	6-4	263	2	1-10-64	Boston College	12	D1, '87
43	Brown, Bud	S	6-0	194	5	4-19-61	Southern Mississippi	9	D11, '84
51	Brown, Mark	LB	6-2	235	6	7-18-61	Purdue	12	D9, '83
	Brown, Tom	RB	6-1	225	1	11-20-64	Pittsburgh	1	D7, '87
59	†Brudzinski, Bob	LB	6-4	223	12	1- 1-55	Ohio State	12	T-Ram, '81
	Burgess, Marvell	S	6-3	195	1	10-7-65	Henderson State	1	FA, '88
	Caterbone, Mike	WR/KR	5-11	180	2	2-17-62	Franklin and Marshall	3	FA, '88
	Cesario, Sal	T/G	6-4	255	2	7- 4-63	Cal Poly-SLO	*3	FA, '88
83	Clayton, Mark	WR	5-9	175	6	4- 8-61	Louisville	12	D8, '83
98	Cline, Jackie	NT	6-5	276	2	3-13-60	Alabama	*8	W-Pit, '87
67	Conlin, Chris	G/C	6-4	290	2	6- 7-65	Penn State	3	D5, '87
30	†Davenport, Ron	RB	6-2	230	4	12-22-62	Louisville	10	D6a, '85
65	†Dellenbach, Jeff	T/C	6-6	280	4	2-14-63	Wisconsin	11	D4a, '85
74	Dennis, Mark	T	6-6	291	2	4-15-65	Illinois	5	D8a, '87
85	†Duper, Mark	WR	5-9	187	7	1-25-59	Northwestern (La.) St.	11	D2, '82
	Flaherty, Tom	LB	6-3	227	2	9-24-64	Northwestern	*3	FA, '88
61	Foster, Roy	G	6-4	275	7	5-24-60	Southern California	12	D1, '82
53	†Frye, David	LB	6-2	227	6	6-21-61	Purdue	12	FA, '86
79	†Giesler, Jon	T	6-5	265	10	12-23-56	Michigan	10	D1, '79
66	Gilmore, Jim	G	6-5	275	3	12-19-62	Ohio State	3	FA, '87
58	Graf, Rick	LB	6-5	239	2	8-29-63	Wisconsin	12	D2, '87
55	Green, Hugh	LB	6-2	225	8	7-27-59	Pittsburgh	9	T-TB, '85
71	Gruber, Bob	T	6-5	280	2	6- 7-58	Pittsburgh	*1	FA, '87
27	Hampton, Lorenzo	RB	6-0	203	4	3-12-62	Florida	12	D1, '85
84	Hardy, Bruce	TE	6-5	234	11	6- 1-56	Arizona State	12	D9, '78
	Harris, Gerald	RB	5-9	200	1	4-11-64	Georgia Southern	*1	FA, '88
29	Hobley, Liffort	S	6-0	199	3	5-12-62	Louisiana State	14	FA, '87
	Holloway, Steve	TE	6-3	235	2	8-23-64	Tennessee State	*6	FA, '88
	Hunley, LaMonte	LB	6-1	240	3	1-31-63	Arizona	*0	FA, '88
17	Jaworski, Ron	QB	6-1	195	14	3-23-51	Youngstown State	*0	FA, '87
11	Jensen, Jim	WR/RB	6-4	215	8	11-14-58	Boston University	12	D11, '81
87	†Johnson, Dan	TE	6-3	245	6	5-17-60	Iowa State	7	D7, '82
	Jordan, Kenneth	LB	6-2	235	2	4-29-64	Tuskegee	*3	FA, '88
49	Judson, William	CB	6-2	190	7	3-26-59	South Carolina State	12	D8, '81
	Kehoe, Scott	T	6-4	282	2	9-20-64	Illinois	3	FA, '87
54	Kolic, Larry	LB	6-1	238	2	8-31-63	Ohio State	7	D7, '86
69	Lambrecht, Mike	NT	6-1	271	2	5- 2-63	St. Cloud State	5	OFA, '87
44	†Lankford, Paul	CB	6-2	184	7	6-15-58	Penn State	12	D3, '82
72	Lee, Ronnie	T	6-4	265	10	12-24-56	Baylor	9	T-Atl, '84
99	†Little, George	DE/NT	6-4	270	4	6-27-63	Iowa	9	D3, '85
13	Marino, Dan	QB	6-4	214	6	9-15-61	Pittsburgh	12	D1, '83
78	Marrone, Doug	G/C	6-5	269	2	7-25-64	Syracuse	4	FA, '87
	Mathis, Mark	CB	5-8	183	1	8-23-65	Liberty	*2	FA, '88
28	McNeal, Don	CB	5-11	192	8	5- 6-58	Alabama	12	D1, '80
	McNeil, Mark	DB	6-0	195	1	8-25-61	Houston	*0	FA, '88
	Middleton, Frank	RB	5-11	205	4	10-28-60	Florida A&M	*3	FA, '88
52	†Nicolas, Scott	LB	6-3	226	7	8- 7-60	Miami (Fla.)	12	FA, '87
56	Offerdahl, John	LB	6-2	232	3	8-17-64	Western Michigan	9	D2, '86
82	Pruitt, James	WR	6-2	199	3	1-29-64	Fullerton State	12	D4, '86
7	Reveiz, Fuad	K	5-11	217	4	2-24-63	Tennessee	11	D7, '85
4	Roby, Reggie	P	6-2	242	6	7-30-61	Iowa	10	D6, '83
	Russell, Darryl	CB	6-0	195	2	12-14-64	Appalachian State	*3	FA, '88
81	Schwedes, Scott	WR/KR	6-0	174	2	6-30-65	Syracuse	12	D2a, '87
	Scott, Chris	DE	6-4	250	4	12-11-61	Purdue	*3	FA, '88
50	†Shipp, Jackie	LB	6-2	236	5	3-19-62	Oklahoma	12	D1, '84
	Simpson, Travis	C/G	6-2	265	2	11-19-63	Oklahoma	*3	FA, '88
25	Smith, Mike	CB	6-0	175	4	10-24-62	Texas-El Paso	8	D4, '85
70	†Sochia, Brian	NT	6-3	274	6	7-21-61	N.W. Oklahoma State	12	FA, '86
	Stark, Chad	RB	6-1	225	1	4-4-65	North Dakota State	*2	FA, '88
57	Stephenson, Dwight	C	6-2	258	9	11-20-57	Alabama	9	D2, '80
23	Stradford, Troy	RB	5-9	191	2	9-11-64	Boston College	12	D4, '87

No.	Name	Pos.	Ht.	Wt.	NFL Exp.	Birth-date	College	Games in '87	How Acquired
10	†Strock, Don	QB	6-5	225	15	11-27-50	Virginia Tech	12	D5, 73
	Thomas, Derrick	RB	6-0	224	1	3-8-65	Arkansas	*1	FA, '88
24	Thompson, Reyna	CB	5-11	194	3	8-28-63	Baylor	9	D9, '86
76	Toth, Tom	G	6-5	275	3	5-23-62	Western Michigan	12	FA, '86
95	Turner, T.J.	DE	6-4	275	3	5-16-63	Houston	12	D3, '86
	Warren, Vince	WR	6-0	180	2	2-18-63	San Diego State	*0	FA, '88
	Watters, Scott	LB	6-2	230	2	1- 1-65	Wittenberg	*3	FA, '88
	Wimberly, Derek	DE	6-4	265	2	1- 4-64	Purdue	3	FA, '88

*Anderson played 3 games with Packers in '87; Archer played 9 games with Falcons in '87; Cesario played 3 games with Cowboys in '87; Cline played 1 game with Steelers, 7 games with Dolphins in '87; Flaherty played 3 games with Bengals in '87; Gruber played 1 game with Packers, active for 2 games with Dolphins in '87, but did not play; Harris played 1 game with Hamilton-CFL in '87; Holloway played 6 games with Buccaneers in '87; Hunley last active with Colts in '86; Jaworski active for 2 games with Dolphins in '87, but did not play; Jordan played 3 games with Packers in '87; Mathis played 2 games with Cardinals in '87; McNeil last active with San Antonio-USFL in '85; Middleton played 3 games with Chargers in '87; Russell played 3 games with Broncos in '87; Scott played 3 games with Colts in '87; Simpson played 3 games with Packers in '87; Stark played 2 games with Seahawks in '87; Thomas played 1 game with Buccaneers in '87; Warren last active with Giants in '86; Watters played 3 games with Bills in '87.

†Option playout; subject to developments.

D—Draft; T—Trade; W—Waivers; FA—Free Agent.

Also played with Dolphins in '87, see page 386.

MIAMI DOLPHINS
1988 DRAFT CHOICES

(Number following name designates order of selection among 333 players drafted.)

Round and Player		Position	College
1. KUMEROW, Eric	16	DE	Ohio State
2. WILLIAMS, Jarvis	42	DB	Florida
3. EDMUNDS, Ferrell	73	TE	Maryland
4. JOHNSON, Greg	99	T	Oklahoma
5. THOMAS, Rodney	126	DB	Brigham Young
6. BRATTON, Melvin	153	RB	Miami (Fla.)
6. COOPER, George from Minnesota (a)	156	RB	Ohio State
7. BELL, Kerwin	180	QB	Florida
8. GALBREATH, Harry	212	G	Tennessee
8. CHEEK, Louis from Denver (b)	220	T	Texas A & M
9. CROSS, Jeff	239	DE	Missouri
10. JACKSON, Artis	266	NT	Texas Tech
11. KELLEHER, Tom	292	RB	Holy Cross
12. KINCHEN, Brian	320	TE	Louisiana State

(a) Acquired pick and conditional 1989 pick for tackle Greg Koch, October 20, 1987.

(b) Acquired pick for guard Larry Lee, August 19, 1987.

MIAMI DOLPHINS
1988 ROOKIE AND FIRST-YEAR ROSTER

Name	Pos.	Hgt.	Wgt.	Birth-date	College	How Acquired
Andrade, Eric	WR	6-1	194	9-28-65	Boise State	FA
Beals, Shawn	WR	5-10	178	8-16-66	Idaho State	FA
Beasley, Jerry	LB	6-1	220	2-13-65	Arizona	FA
Bell, Kerwin	QB	6-2	200	6-15-65	Florida	D7
Bratton, Melvin	RB	6-1	225	2- 2-65	Miami (Fla.)	D6
Brown, Jeff	QB	6-3	205	3- 5-66	Southeast Missouri	FA
Brown, Selwyn	S	5-11	200	9-28-65	Miami (Fla.)	FA
Cannon, Willie	RB	6-1	206	9-28-64	Murray State	FA
Cheek, Louis	T	6-6	288	10- 6-64	Texas A&M	D8a
Clayton, McCarthon	CB	5-11	190	5-24-64	Nebraska	FA
Cooper, George	RB	6-1	245	12- 8-65	Ohio State	D6a
Cox, Greg	K	6-5	200	1-10-66	Miami (Fla.)	FA
Cross, Jeff	DE	6-4	261	3-25-66	Missouri	D9
Edmunds, Ferrell	TE	6-6	241	4-16-65	Maryland	D3
Galbreath, Harry	G	6-1	271	1- 1-65	Tennessee	D8
Hansen, James	T	6-5	265	9-17-64	Utah	*FA
Hulsey, Gary	DE	6-5	286	4- 3-66	Utah State	FA
Jackson, Artis	NT	6-5	309	8- 9-65	Texas Tech	D10
Jackson, Chris	RB	5-9	179	9-25-64	Boise State	FA
James, Michel	WR	6-0	180	11-19-63	Washington State	*FA
Jenkins, DeShon	S	6-1	198	12-19-64	Northwestern St. La.	*FA, '87
Johnson, Greg	T	6-4	311	12-19-64	Oklahoma	D4
Karsatos, Jim	QB	6-4	225	5-26-63	Ohio State	*D12, '87
Kelleher, Tom	RB	6-1	230	8-24-65	Holy Cross	D11
Keller, Ron	P	6-0	182	9-10-64	New Mexico State	*FA
Kinchen, Brian	TE	6-2	227	8- 6-65	Louisiana State	D12
Kumerow, Eric	DE	6-7	264	4-17-65	Ohio State	D1
Manu, Tika	DE	6-3	250	12- 5-64	Utah	FA
McCormick, John	G	6-1	274	1-28-65	Nebraska	FA
Reherman, Leo	C	6-3	274	7- 4-66	Cornell	FA
Scriber, Stephen	FB	6-3	230	11-13-64	Maryland	*FA
Smith, Harvey	WR	5-10	165	11- 5-64	West Virginia	FA
Thomas, Rodney	CB	5-10	196	12-21-65	Brigham Young	D5
Vlatas, Tony	TE	6-7	235	5-24-65	Princeton	FA
Williams, Jarvis	S	6-0	195	5-16-65	Florida	D2

*Hansen: FA Pittsburgh '87, injured reserve 9/7 through 10/19, released 10/20; James: D8 Houston '87, released 9/6, FA replacement Denver 9/25, released 10/6; Jenkins and Karsatos missed '87 season due to injury; Keller: FA Dallas '87, released 7/30; Scriber: FA San Diego '87, released 7/30.

MINNESOTA VIKINGS
(Central Division, National Conference)

Jerry Burns

President—Wheelock Whitney
Executive Vice-President and General Manager—Mike Lynn
Director of Football Operations—Jerry Reichow
Player Personnel Director—Frank Gilliam
Director of Pro Personnel—Bob Hollway
Head Coach—Jerry Burns (2 years: 17-14)
Assistant Coaches:
  Tight Ends/Special Teams—Tom Batta
  Running Backs—John Brunner
  Secondary—Pete Carroll
  Linebackers—Monte Kiffin
  Offensive Line—John Michels
  Defensive Coordinator—Floyd Peters
  Receivers—Dick Rehbein
  Offensive Coordinator—Bob Schnelker
  Defensive Line—Paul Wiggin
Public Relations Director—Merrill Swanson
  (Office Phone: 828-6500—Area Code 612)
Offices—9520 Viking Drive, Eden Prairie, Minn. 55344
Stadium—Metrodome, Minneapolis, Minn. (Capacity: 63,000)
Team Colors—Purple, Gold and White
Training Site—Mankato State University, Mankato, Minn.

1988 SCHEDULE
(All times local.
All games Sunday unless noted otherwise.)

Sept. 4	at Buffalo	1:00
Sept. 11	NEW ENGLAND	3:00
Sept. 18	at Chicago	12:00
Sept. 25	PHILADELPHIA	12:00
Oct. 2	at Miami	4:00
Oct. 9	TAMPA BAY	12:00
Oct. 16	GREEN BAY	12:00
Oct. 23	at Tampa Bay	1:00
Oct. 30	at San Francisco	1:00
Nov. 6	DETROIT	12:00
Nov. 13	at Dallas	7:00
Nov. 20	INDIANAPOLIS	12:00
Nov. 24	at Detroit (Thanksgiving)	12:30
Dec. 4	NEW ORLEANS	12:00
Dec. 11	at Green Bay	12:00
Dec. 19	CHICAGO (Mon.)	8:00

1987 RESULTS—(Won 10, Lost 8)

Vikings		Opp.		Att.
34	Detroit	19	(H)	57,061
21	L.A. Rams	16	(A)	63,567
	Kansas City*		(A)	
16	*Green Bay*	*23*	*(H)*	*13,911*
7	*Chicago*	*27*	*(A)*	*32,111*
10	*Tampa Bay*	*20*	*(A)*	*20,850*
34	Denver	27	(H)	51,011
17	Seattle	28	(A)	61,134
31	L.A. Raiders	20	(H)	57,150
23	Tampa Bay	17	(H)	48,605
24	Atlanta	13	(H)	53,866
44	Dallas (OT)	38	(A)	54,229
24	Chicago	30	(H)	62,331
10	Green Bay	16	(A)	47,059
17	Detroit	14	(A)	27,693
24	Washington (OT)	27	(H)	59,166
NFC WILD-CARD GAME				
44	New Orleans	10	(A)	68,127
NFC SEMIFINAL GAME				
36	San Francisco	24	(A)	62,547
NFC CHAMPIONSHIP GAME				
10	Washington	17	(A)	55,212

*Game cancelled due to strike.
Italics denote strike replacement games.

1987 GAMES STARTED

(NOTE: Players with an asterisk (*) following their names made starts only in strike-replacement games.)

12 games: Joey Browner, Chris Doleman, John Harris, David Huffman, Tim Irwin, Steve Jordan, Carl Lee, Leo Lewis, Kirk Lowdermilk, Doug Martin, Jesse Solomon, Gary Zimmerman.

11 games: Anthony Carter, Scott Studwell, Henry Thomas.

10 games: Alfred Anderson.

9 games: Darrin Nelson.

8 games: Wymon Henderson, Keith Millard.

7 games: David Howard, Stafford Mays, Wade Wilson.

6 games: Issiac Holt, Greg Koch.

5 games: Tommy Kramer, Terry Tausch.

4 games: Chris Martin.

3 games: Tony Adams*, James Brim*, Derek Burton*, D.J. Dozier, David Evans*, Fletcher Loual-len*, Marc May*, Mike McCurry*, Phil Micech*, Peter Najarian*, Frank Ori*, Ted Rosnagle*, John Scardina*, Kevin Webster*.

2 games: Rufus Bess*, Jim Dick*, Kelly Quinn*, Allen Rice, Jimmy Walker*.

1 game: Don Bramlett*, Dan Coleman*, Fabrey Collins*, Steve Finch*, Phil Frye*, Willie Gille-spie*, Neal Guggemos, Sam Harrell*, Carl Hilton, Mark MacDonald, Leonard Moore*, Ricky Parks*, Kurt Ploeger*, Randy Scott*, Jimmy Smith*, Wayne Smith*, Joe Stepanek*, Brad White*, Brett Wilson*, Jeff Womack*.

MINNESOTA VIKINGS 1988 VETERAN ROSTER

No.	Name	Pos.	Ht.	Wt.	NFL Exp.	Birth-date	College	Games in '87	How Acquired
46	Anderson, Alfred	RB	6-1	219	5	8- 4-61	Baylor	10	D3, '84
53	Anno, Sam	LB	6-2	230	2	1-26-65	Southern California	*9	FA, '87
58	Ashley, Walker Lee	LB	6-0	240	5	7-28-60	Penn State	12	D3, '83
50	Berry, Ray	LB	6-2	230	2	10-28-63	Baylor	11	D2, '87
19	Brim, James	WR	6-3	187	2	2-28-63	Wake Forest	3	FA, '87
47	Browner, Joey	S/CB	6-2	212	6	5-15-60	Southern California	12	D1, '83
60	Burton, Derek	T	6-2	280	2	8-10-63	Oklahoma State	3	FA, '88
81	Carter, Anthony	WR	5-11	166	4	9-17-60	Michigan	12	T-Mia, '85
8	Coleman, Greg	P	6-0	181	12	9- 9-54	Florida A&M	9	FA, '78
56	Doleman, Chris	DE	6-5	250	4	10-16-61	Pittsburgh	12	D1, '85
42	Dozier, D.J.	RB	6-0	198	2	9-21-65	Penn State	9	D1, '87
	Durrette, Michael	OL	6-4	280	3	8-11-57	West Virginia	*3	FA, '88
31	Fenney, Rick	RB	6-1	240	2	12- 7-64	Washington	11	D8, '87
43	Fitzgerald, Jamie	CB	6-1	187	1	4-30-65	Idaho State	2	FA, '88
62	†Foote, Chris	C	6-4	265	6	12- 2-56	Southern California	6	T-NYG, '87
22	Freeman, Steve	S	5-11	185	14	5- 8-53	Mississippi State	12	T-Buf, '87
16	Gannon, Rich	QB	6-3	197	2	12-20-65	Delaware	4	T-NE, '87
	Gay, William	DE	6-5	260	11	5-28-55	Southern California	*11	FA, '88
41	†Guggemos, Neal	S	6-0	187	3	6-14-64	St. Thomas	12	OFA, '86
80	†Gustafson, Jim	WR	6-1	181	3	3-16-61	St. Thomas	12	FA, '85
44	Harris, John	S	6-2	198	11	6-13-56	Arizona State	12	T-Sea, '86
24	Henderson, Wymon	CB/S	5-10	186	2	12-15-61	Nevada-Las Vegas	12	FA, '87
82	Hilton, Carl	TE	6-3	232	3	2-28-64	Houston	11	D7, '86
30	Holt, Issiac	CB	6-1	197	4	10- 4-62	Alcorn State	9	D2, '85
51	Howard, David	LB	6-2	228	4	12- 8-61	Long Beach State	10	SupD, '84
72	†Huffman, David	G	6-6	283	9	4- 4-57	Notre Dame	12	D2, '79
76	Irwin, Tim	T	6-6	289	8	12-13-58	Tennessee	12	D3, '81
84	Jones, Hassan	WR	6-0	195	3	7- 2-64	Florida State	12	D5, '86
83	Jordan, Steve	TE	6-3	236	7	1-10-61	Brown	12	D7, '82
68	†Koch, Greg	T	6-4	276	12	6-14-55	Arkansas	*10	T-Mia, '87
9	Kramer, Tommy	QB	6-2	207	12	3- 7-55	Rice	6	D1, '77
39	Lee, Carl	CB	5-11	184	6	4- 6-61	Marshall	12	D7, '83
93	Leiker, Tony	DT	6-5	250	1	9-26-64	Stanford	*1	FA, '88
87	Lewis, Leo	WR	5-8	171	8	9-17-56	Missouri	12	FA, '81
38	Louallen, Fletcher	DB	6-0	190	2	9-12-62	Livingston State	3	FA, '88
63	†Lowdermilk, Kirk	C	6-3	263	4	4-10-63	Ohio State	12	D3, '85
71	MacDonald, Mark	G	6-4	267	4	4-30-61	Boston College	12	D5, '85
56	†Martin, Chris	LB	6-2	233	6	12-19-60	Auburn	12	W-NO, '84
79	†Martin, Doug	DE	6-3	270	9	5-22-57	Washington	12	D1, '80
73	†Mays, Stafford	DE	6-2	264	9	3-13-58	Washington	12	FA, '87
	McQuaid, Dan	T	6-7	278	3	10- 4-60	Nevada-Las Vegas	*1	W-Wsh, '88
75	Millard, Keith	DT	6-6	260	4	3-18-62	Washington State	9	D1, '84
90	Molden, Fred	DE	6-2	272	1	8-12-63	Jackson State	2	FA, '88
86	Mularkey, Mike	TE	6-4	238	6	11-19-61	Florida	9	W-SF, '83
77	Mullaney, Mark	DE	6-6	246	13	4-30-53	Colorado State	*0	D1, '75
1	Nelson, Chuck	K	5-11	172	5	2-23-60	Washington	12	FA, '86
20	Nelson, Darrin	RB	5-9	183	7	1- 2-59	Stanford	10	D1, '82
96	Newton, Tim	DT	6-0	283	4	3-23-63	Florida	9	D6a, '85
52	Rasmussen, Randy	C/G	6-1	254	5	9-27-60	Minnesota	5	FA, '87
36	Rice, Allen	RB	5-10	203	5	4- 5-62	Baylor	12	D5a, '84
89	Richardson, Greg	WR	5-7	172	1	10- 6-64	Alabama	2	FA, '87
95	†Robinson, Gerald	DE	6-3	256	3	5- 4-63	Auburn	4	D1, '86
48	Rutland, Reggie	S	6-1	195	2	6-20-64	Georgia Tech	7	D4, '87
13	Scribner, Bucky	P	6-0	205	4	7-11-60	Kansas	4	FA, '87
98	Sellers, Lance	LB	6-2	236	2	2-24-63	Boise State	*3	FA, '88
40	†Smith, Wayne	CB	6-0	170	9	5- 9-57	Purdue	6	FA, '87
54	Solomon, Jesse	LB	6-0	235	3	11- 4-63	Florida State	12	D12, '86
55	Studwell, Scott	LB	6-2	228	12	8-27-54	Illinois	12	D9, '77
67	†Swilley, Dennis	C	6-3	257	11	6-28-55	Texas A&M	6	D2, '77
66	Tausch, Terry	T	6-5	275	7	2- 5-59	Texas	5	D2, '82
97	Thomas, Henry	NT	6-2	268	2	1-12-65	Louisiana State	12	D3, '87
37	Williams, Perry	CB	6-2	200	2	4- 2-62	Clemson	*3	FA, '88
11	Wilson, Wade	QB	6-3	208	8	2- 1-59	East Texas State	12	D8, '81
65	†Zimmerman, Gary	T	6-6	277	3	12-13-61	Oregon	12	T-NYG, '86

*Anno played 3 games with Rams, 6 with Vikings in '87; Durrette played 3 games with 49ers, inactive for 2 games with Vikings in '87; Gay played 11 games with Lions in '87; Koch played 1 game with Dolphins, 9 with Vikings in '87; Leiker played 1 game with Packers in '87; McQuaid played 1 game with Redskins in '87; Mullaney missed '87 season due to injury; Sellers played 3 games with Bengals in

'87; Williams played 3 games with Patriots in '87.
    †Option playout; subject to developments.
    D—Draft; T—Trade; W—Waivers; FA—Free Agent; OFA—Original Free Agent; SupD—Supplemental Draft.
    Also played with Vikings in '87, see page 386.

MINNESOTA VIKINGS
1988 DRAFT CHOICES

(Number following name designates order of selection among 333 players drafted.)

Round and Player		Position	College
1. McDANIEL, Randall	19	G	Arizona State
2. Choice to Denver (a)			
2. EDWARDS, Brad from Denver (b)	54	DB	South Carolina
3. NOGA, Al	71	DT	Hawaii
4. Choice to New England (c)			
4. KALIS, Todd from Denver (b)	108	G	Arizona State
5. FULLINGTON, Darrell	124	DB	Miami (Fla.)
6. Choice to Miami (d)			
6. WHITE, Derrick from Denver (b)	164	DB	Oklahoma
7. BECKMAN, Brad	183	TE	Nebraska-Omaha
8. CAIN, Joe	210	LB	Oregon Tech
9. McGOWAN, Paul	237	LB	Florida State
10. HABIB, Brian	264	DT	Washington
11. FLOYD, Norman from Minnesota through New England (e)	296	DB	South Carolina
12. Choice to N.Y. Giants (f)			

(a) Traded pick for 2nd-, 4th- and 6th-round picks in 1988, April 24, 1988.

(b) Acquired picks: See (a).

(c) Traded pick and 11th-round pick in 1988 for rights to quarterback Rich Gannon, May 6, 1987.

(d) Traded pick and conditional 1989 pick for tackle Greg Koch, October 20, 1987.

(e) Vikings traded pick to Patriots: see (c); Patriots traded pick to Vikings for 9th-round pick in 1989, April 25, 1988.

(f) Traded pick for center Chris Foote, May 7, 1987.

MINNESOTA VIKINGS
1988 ROOKIE AND FIRST-YEAR ROSTER

Name	Pos.	Hgt.	Wgt.	Birth-date	College	How Acquired
Beckman, Brad	TE	6-2	236	12-31-64	Nebraska-Omaha	D7
Belli, Barry	K	5-10	168	8- 7-65	Fresno State	FA
Cain, Joe	LB	6-1	228	6-11-65	Oregon Tech	D8
Edwards, Brad	S	6-1	198	2-22-66	South Carolina	D2
Esqu, Roketi	RB	6-0	180	1-12-66	Northeast Missouri State	FA
Eyl, Steve	TE	6-6	215	2- 1-66	Indiana	FA
Floyd, Norman	S	5-11	198	2-10-66	South Carolina	D11
Fullington, Darrell	S	6-1	183	4-17-64	Miami (Fla.)	D5
Furlong, Bob	G	6-1	273	5- 1-62	Wisconsin-Stevens Point	FA
Greenfield, Mike	QB	6-0	180	4-30-66	Northwestern	FA
Habib, Brian	NT	6-6	271	12- 2-64	Washington	D10
Harris, Darryl	RB	5-10	173	2-20-66	Arizona State	FA
Jenkins, Jeff	WR	6-0	169	5-31-66	Utah	FA
Kalis, Todd	G	6-5	269	5-10-65	Arizona State	D4
McDaniel, Randall	G	6-3	268	12-19-64	Arizona State	D1
McGowan, Paul	LB	5-11	221	1-13-66	Florida State	D9
Noga, Al	NT	6-1	245	9-16-66	Hawaii	D3
Rice, Mike	P	5-11	196	8-12-65	Montana	*FA
Salmon, Craig	P	6-2	205	5-16-65	North Carolina State	FA
Sheppard, Von	WR	5-10	185	2-28-65	Nebraska	FA
Truelove, Tony	RB	5-11	205	3-24-64	Livingston	*FA
White, Derrick	CB	5-8	185	11-11-65	Oklahoma	D6
Wilson, Charles	RB	5-11	215	12-28-64	Tennessee	FA
Yancey, Lloyd	T	6-4	275	12- 8-62	Temple	*FA

*Rice: D8 New York Jets '87, released 8/27, FA replacement Washington 9/23 (on inactive list for 1 game), released 10/20; Truelove: D6 Birmingham-USFL '86, signed 6/9, granted free agency when operations suspended 8/7, FA Minnesota '87, injured reserve 9/7 through 10/19, activated 10/20 (on inactive list for 2 games), released 11/15; Yancey: D6 Dallas '86, injured reserve 8/18 through entire season, released 8/25/87.

NEW ENGLAND PATRIOTS
(Eastern Division, American Conference)

Raymond Berry

President—William H. Sullivan, Jr.
Executive Vice-President—Charles W. Sullivan
Vice-President—Francis (Bucko) Kilroy
General Manager—Patrick Sullivan
Director of Player Development—Dick Steinberg
Vice-President/Finance—Richard M. Regan
Head Coach—Raymond Berry (4 years: 34-21)
Assistant Coaches:
    Assistant Linebackers—Don Blackmon
    Defensive Backfield—Jim Carr
    Off. Backfield/Running Game—Bobby Grier
    Asst. Defensive Line—Ray Hamilton
    Asst. Head Coach/Off. Coord.—Rod Humenuik
    Receivers—Harold Jackson
    Defensive Line—Eddie Khayat
    Special Asst. to Head Coach—John Polonchek
    Special Teams/Tight Ends—Dante Scarnecchia
    Linebackers—Don Shinnick
    Quarterbacks/Passing Game—Les Steckel
Director of Publicity—Jim Greenidge
    (Office Phone: 543-7911 or 543-8200—Area Code 508)
Offices—Sullivan Stadium, Route 1, Foxboro, Mass. 02035
Stadium—Sullivan Stadium, Foxboro, Mass. (Capacity: 60,794)
Team Colors—Red, White and Blue
Training Site—Bryant College, Smithfield, R. I.

1988 SCHEDULE
(All times local.
All games Sunday unless noted otherwise.)

Sept. 4	NEW YORK JETS	4:00
Sept. 11	at Minnesota	3:00
Sept. 18	BUFFALO	1:00
Sept. 25	at Houston	12:00
Oct. 2	INDIANAPOLIS	1:00
Oct. 9	vs. Green Bay at Milwaukee	12:00
Oct. 16	CINCINNATI	1:00
Oct. 23	at Buffalo	1:00
Oct. 30	CHICAGO	1:00
Nov. 6	MIAMI	1:00
Nov. 13	at New York Jets	1:00
Nov. 20	at Miami	8:00
Nov. 27	at Indianapolis	4:00
Dec. 4	SEATTLE	1:00
Dec. 11	TAMPA BAY	1:00
Dec. 17	at Denver (Sat.)	2:00

1987 RESULTS—(Won 8, Lost 7)

Patriots		Opp.		Att.
28	Miami	21	(H)	54,642
24	New York Jets	43	(A)	70,847
	Washington*		(A)	
10	*Cleveland*	*20*	*(H)*	*14,830*
14	*Buffalo*	*7*	*(H)*	*11,878*
21	*Houston*	*7*	*(A)*	*26,294*
16	Indianapolis	30	(A)	48,850
26	L.A. Raiders	23	(H)	60,664
10	New York Giants	17	(A)	73,817
17	Dallas (OT)	23	(H)	60,567
24	Indianapolis	0	(H)	56,906
31	Philadelphia (OT)	34	(H)	54,198
20	Denver	31	(A)	75,794
42	New York Jets	20	(H)	60,617
13	Buffalo	7	(A)	74,945
24	Miami	10	(A)	61,192

*Game cancelled due to strike.
Italics denote strike replacement games.

1987 GAMES STARTED

(NOTE: Players with an asterisk (*) following their names made starts only in strike-replacement games.)

14 games: Sean Farrell.

13 games: Andre Tippett, Ron Wooten.

12 games: Bruce Armstrong, Irving Fryar, Ronnie Lippett, Fred Marion, Lawrence McGrew, Garin Veris, Toby Williams.

11 games: Tony Collins, Lin Dawson, Steve Nelson.

10 games: Raymond Clayborn.

9 games: Stanley Morgan, Mosi Tatupu.

8 games: Jim Bowman, Kenneth Sims.

7 games: Guy Morriss, Danny Villa, Ed Williams.

6 games: Steve Grogan.

5 games: Ernest Gibson.

4 games: Don Blackmon, Roland James, Cedric Jones, Trevor Matich, Steve Moore, Brent Williams.

3 games: Pete Brock, George Colton*, Reggie Dupard, Tony Eason, Darryl Holmes*, Larry Linne*, Jerry McCabe*, Greg Moore*, Joe Peterson*, Tom Ramsey, Benton Reed*, Greg Robinson*, Ron Shegog*, Steve Wilburn*.

2 games: Rogers Alexander*, Mel Black*, Bob Bleier*, Wayne Coffey*, Paul Fairchild, Todd Frain*, John Guzik*, Bruce Hansen*, Michael LeBlanc*.

1 game: Doug Flutie*, Dennis Gadbois*, Chuck McSwain*, Bob Perryman, Art Plunkett, Tom Porell*, Johnny Rembert, Ed Reynolds, Willie Scott*, Randall Sealby*, Stephen Starring, Eric Stokes*, Darren Twombly*.

NEW ENGLAND PATRIOTS 1988 VETERAN ROSTER

No.	Name	Pos.	Ht.	Wt.	NFL Exp.	Birth-date	College	Games in '87	How Acquired
78	Armstrong, Bruce	T	6-4	284	2	9- 7-65	Louisville	12	D1, '87
28	Bowman, Jim	S	6-2	210	4	10-26-63	Central Michigan	12	D2a, '85
58	Brock, Pete	C	6-5	275	13	7-14-54	Colorado	4	FA, '87
	Calhoun, Rick	RB	5-7	185	2	5-30-63	Fullerton State	*3	FA, '88
3	Camarillo, Rich	P	5-11	185	8	11-29-59	Washington	12	OFA, '81
26	Clayborn, Raymond	CB	6-0	186	12	1- 2-55	Texas	10	D1, '77
	Davis, Chris	LB	6-1	225	2	7-26-63	San Diego State	*3	FA, '88
40	Davis, Elgin	RB	5-10	192	2	10-23-65	Central Florida	4	D12, '87
87	Dawson, Lin	TE	6-3	240	7	6-24-59	North Carolina State	12	D8a, '81
21	Dupard, Reggie	RB	5-11	205	3	10-30-63	Southern Methodist	8	D1, '86
11	†Eason, Tony	QB	6-4	212	6	10- 8-59	Illinois	4	D1, '83
66	Fairchild, Paul	G/C	6-4	270	5	9-14-61	Kansas	11	D5, '84
62	Farrell, Sean	G	6-3	260	7	5-25-60	Penn State	14	T-TB, '87
2	Flutie, Doug	QB	5-10	175	3	10-23-62	Boston College	*2	T-Chi, '87
49	Francis, Russ	TE	6-6	242	13	4- 3-53	Oregon	*9	FA, '87
1	Franklin, Tony	K	5-8	182	10	11-18-56	Texas A&M	14	T-Phi, '84
80	†Fryar, Irving	WR	6-0	200	5	9-28-62	Nebraska	12	D1, '84
48	Gadbois, Dennis	WR	6-1	183	2	9-18-63	Boston University	3	OFA, '87
43	Gibson, Ernest	CB	5-10	185	5	10- 3-61	Furman	12	D6, '84
14	Grogan, Steve	QB	6-4	210	14	7-24-53	Kansas State	7	D5, '75
35	Hansen, Bruce	RB	6-1	225	2	9-18-61	Brigham Young	6	FA, '87
	Hodge, Milford	DE	6-3	278	3	3-11-61	Washington State	12	FA, '88
41	Holmes, Darryl	S	6-2	190	2	9- 6-64	Fort Valley State	15	OFA, '87
32	James, Craig	RB	6-0	215	4	1- 2-61	Southern Methodist	2	D7, '83
38	James, Roland	S	6-2	191	9	2-18-58	Tennessee	9	D1, '80
83	†Jones, Cedric	WR	6-1	184	7	6- 1-60	Duke	12	D3, '82
93	Jordan, Tim	LB	6-3	226	2	4-26-64	Wisconsin	5	D4b, '87
	Kelley, Chris	TE	6-3	236	1	11-13-64	Akron	*2	FA, '88
	Lewis, Walter	QB	6-0	198	1	4-26-62	Alabama	*0	SupD, '84
42	†Lippett, Ronnie	CB	5-11	180	6	12-10-60	Miami (Fla.)	12	D8, '83
31	Marion, Fred	S	6-2	191	7	8- 2-59	Miami (Fla.)	12	D5, '82
64	Matich, Trevor	C	6-4	270	4	10- 9-61	Brigham Young	6	D1, '85
48	McCabe, Jerry	LB	6-1	225	2	1-25-65	Holy Cross	3	OFA, '87
50	†McGrew, Lawrence	LB	6-5	233	8	7-23-57	Southern California	12	D2, '80
23	†McSwain, Rod	CB	6-1	198	5	1-28-62	Clemson	12	T-Atl, '84
67	Moore, Steve	T	6-5	305	6	10- 1-60	Tennessee State	5	D3a, '83
86	Morgan, Stanley	WR	5-11	181	12	2-17-55	Tennessee	10	D1a, '77
75	Morriss, Guy	C/G	6-4	260	16	5-13-51	Texas Christian	11	FA, '84
	Ours, Greg	OL	6-5	279	2	10-29-63	Muskingum	*3	FA, '88
34	Perryman, Bob	RB	6-1	233	2	10-16-64	Michigan	9	D3, '87
	Peterson, Joe	CB	5-10	180	2	8-15-64	Nevada-Reno	3	OFA, '87
	Pickering, Clay	WR	6-5	215	4	6- 2-61	Maine	1	FA, '88
70	Plunkett, Art	T	6-8	282	7	3- 8-59	Nevada-Las Vegas	7	FA, '85
22	Profit, Eugene	CB	5-10	175	3	11-11-64	Yale	7	OFA, '86
12	†Ramsey, Tom	QB	6-1	189	4	7- 9-61	UCLA	9	D10b, '83
52	†Rembert, Johnny	LB	6-3	234	6	1-19-61	Clemson	11	D4, '83
95	Reynolds, Ed	LB	6-5	242	6	9-23-61	Virginia	12	OFA, '83
	Riley, Eric	TE	6-3	230	1	10-10-64	Eastern Washington	*2	FA, '88
65	Ruth, Mike	NT	6-1	266	2	2-25-64	Boston College	2	D2, '86
	Sealby, Randall	LB	6-2	225	1	5-16-60	Missouri	2	FA, '87
77	†Sims, Kenneth	DE	6-5	271	7	10-31-59	Texas	12	D1, '82
81	†Starring, Stephen	WR	5-10	172	6	7-30-61	McNeese State	11	D3, '83
	Staurovsky, Jason	K	5-9	162	1	3-23-63	Tulsa	*2	FA, '88
30	Tatupu, Mosi	RB	6-0	227	11	4-26-55	Southern Methodist	12	D8a, '78
56	Tippett, Andre	LB	6-3	241	7	12-27-59	Iowa	13	D2a, '82
60	Veris, Garin	DE	6-4	255	4	2-27-63	Stanford	12	D2, '85
73	Villa, Danny	T	6-5	305	2	9-21-64	Arizona State	11	D5, '87
	Ward, David	LB	6-2	232	2	3-10-64	Southern Arkansas	*3	FA, '88
24	Weathers, Robert	RB	6-2	225	6	9-13-60	Arizona State	*0	D2, '82
	Wichard, Murray	DL	6-2	260	2	11-16-63	Frostburg State	3	FA, '88
	Wilburn, Steve	DE	6-4	266	2	2-25-61	Lincoln College	3	FA, '88
96	Williams, Brent	DE	6-3	278	3	10-23-64	Toledo	12	D7a, '86
54	†Williams, Ed	LB	6-4	244	5	9- 8-61	Texas	12	D2, '84
90	†Williams, Toby	NT	6-4	270	6	11-19-59	Nebraska	12	D10a, '83
61	†Wooten, Ron	G	6-4	273	7	6-28-59	North Carolina	13	D6, '81

*Calhoun played 3 games with Raiders in '87; C. Davis played 3 games with Giants in '87; Flutie played 1 game with Bears, 1 with Patriots in '87; Francis played 8 games with 49ers, 1 with Patriots in '87; Kelley played 2 games with Browns in '87; Lewis missed '87 season due to injury, last active with

Montreal-CFL in '86; Ours played 3 games with Dolphins in '87; Riley played 2 games with Jets in '87; Staurovsky played 2 games with Cardinals in '87; Ward played 3 games with Bengals in '87; Weathers missed '87 season due to injury.

†Option playout; subject to developments.

Retired—Don Blackmon, 7-year linebacker, 4 games in '87; Steve Nelson, 14-year linebacker, 11 games in '87.

D—Draft; T—Trade; FA—Free Agent; OFA—Original Free Agent.

Also played with Patriots in '87, see page 386.

NEW ENGLAND PATRIOTS
1988 DRAFT CHOICES

(Number following name designates order of selection among 333 players drafted.)

Round and Player		Position	College
1. STEPHENS, John	17	RB	N.W. Louisiana
2. BROWN, Vincent	43	LB	Mississippi Valley St.
3. REHDER, Tom	69	T	Notre Dame
4. GOAD, Tim from Tampa Bay (a)	87	NT	North Carolina
4. MARTIN, Sammy from Minnesota (b)	97	WR	Louisiana State
4. GARCIA, Teddy	100	K	N.E. Louisiana
5. WOLKOW, Troy from L.A. Raiders (c)	115	G	Minnesota
5. Choice to Washington (d)			
6. JOHNSON, Steve	154	TE	Virginia Tech
7. USHER, Darryl	181	WR	Illinois
8. Choice to Chicago (e)			
9. GALBRAITH, Neil	240	DB	Central (Okla.) St.
10. LOSSOW, Rodney	267	C	Wisconsin
11. ALLEN, Marvin	294	RB	Tulane
12. NUGENT, Dave	321	NT	Boston College

(a) Acquired pick for 5th-round pick in 1987, April 29, 1987.

(b) Acquired pick and 11th-round pick in 1988 for rights to quarterback Rich Gannon, May 6, 1987.

(c) Acquired pick and conditional 1989 pick for tackle Brian Holloway, September 1, 1987.

(d) Traded pick for 4th-round pick in 1989, April 24, 1988.

(e) Traded pick for quarterback Doug Flutie, October 13, 1987.

NEW ENGLAND PATRIOTS
1988 ROOKIE AND FIRST-YEAR ROSTER

Name	Pos.	Hgt.	Wgt.	Birth-date	College	How Acquired
Allen, Marvin	RB	5-10	215	11-26-65	Tulane	D11
Beasley, Derrick	S	6-1	205	7-13-65	Winston-Salem State	*D4, '87
Brantley, LaRoy	LB	6-5	237	5-17-66	Amherst	FA
Brown, Vincent	LB	6-2	245	1- 9-65	Mississippi Valley State	D2
Crumpler, Bobby	RB	5-11	200	4-22-65	North Carolina State	FA
Dickens, Gerold	LB	6-2	230	11-19-64	Florida	FA
Feagles, Jeff	P	6-0	198	3- 7-66	Miami (Fla.)	FA
Feggins, Howard	CB	5-9	198	5- 6-65	North Carolina	FA
Flynn, Chris	RB	5-9	185	10-15-65	Pennsylvania	FA
Galbraith, Neil	CB	6-0	170	10-25-65	Central State, Okla.	D9
Garcia, Teddy	K	5-10	190	6- 4-64	Northeast Louisiana	D4b
Gibson, Tom	DE	6-7	250	12-20-63	Northern Arizona	*D5, '87
Goad, Tim	NT	6-3	280	2- 6-66	North Carolina	D4
Goldammer, Duane	G	6-4	268	2-19-65	Mankato State	FA
Henning, Dan	QB	6-0	188	6-22-65	Maryland	FA
Heren, Dieter	LB	6-3	230	8- 9-64	Michigan	*FA
Hull, Lee	WR	6-0	185	12-31-65	Holy Cross	FA
Johnson, Steve	TE	6-6	245	6-22-65	Virginia Tech	D6
Kirker, Bill	G	6-4	280	10-12-65	U.S. Merchant Marines	FA
Knighten, Billy	P	6-1	188	3- 5-64	Southern Mississippi	FA
Knizner, Matt	QB	6-3	203	1-17-65	Penn State	FA
Lloyd, Andre	LB	6-2	240	6-29-65	Jackson State	FA
Lossow, Rodney	C	6-3	275	8-28-65	Wisconsin	D10
Martin, Sammy	WR/KR	5-11	175	8-21-65	Louisiana State	D4a
McPhearson, Gerrick	CB	5-9	173	5-31-66	Boston College	FA
Naposki, Eric	LB	6-2	230	12-20-66	Connecticut	FA
Nugent, David	NT	6-3	275	7-19-65	Boston College	D12
Parker, Barry	WR	5-9	160	6-25-65	Texas-El Paso	FA
Rehder, Tom	T	6-7	280	1-27-65	Notre Dame	D3
Richardson, Bruce	S	6-1	195	5-24-66	Stanford	FA
Rundle, Todd	LB	6-3	240	3-21-66	Massachusetts	FA
Smith, David	CB	5-11	186	2-12-65	North Alabama	FA
Stephens, John	RB	6-1	220	2-23-66	Northwestern St., La.	D1
Stokes, Dan	C	6-4	255	7- 9-65	Northeastern	FA
Texeira, David	K	5-9	212	3- 2-61	American International	*FA
Thompson, Bill	LB	6-3	230	3- 7-66	Boston College	FA
Tumey, Terry	LB	6-2	230	10-29-65	UCLA	FA
Usher, Darryl	WR	5-8	170	1- 3-65	Illinois	D7
Vercheval, Pierre	C	6-1	275	11-22-64	Western Ontario	FA
Walker, Mike	DE	6-3	260	1- 7-62	Fresno State	FA
White, Kevin	WR	5-11	203	6-30-65	South Carolina	FA
Wilkins, Peter	LB	6-4	225	9-27-65	Idaho	FA
Wolkow, Troy	G	6-4	280	6-25-66	Minnesota	D5
Yahn, Tom	RB	5-10	205	9- 9-64	Penn State	FA

*Beasley and Gibson missed '87 season due to injury; Heren: FA New England '87, injured reserve 9/1 through 11/2, released 11/3; Texeira: FA Green Bay '85, released 8/19, FA Denver '86, released 7/31.

NEW ORLEANS SAINTS
(Western Division, National Conference)

Jim Mora

Managing General Partner—Tom Benson
President/General Manager—Jim Finks
Director of Player Personnel—Bill Kuharich
Vice-President/Administration—Jim Miller
Head Coach—Jim Mora (2 years: 19-12)
Assistant Coaches:
  Offensive Line—Paul Boudreau
  Secondary—Dom Capers
  Linebackers—Vic Fangio
  Tight Ends/Special Teams—Joe Marciano
  Strength & Conditioning—Russell Paternostro
  Defensive Line—John Pease
  Defensive Coordinator—Steve Sidwell
  Running Backs—Jim Skipper
  Offensive Coordinator—Carl Smith
  Receivers—Steve Walters
Director of Media Services—Rusty Kasmiersky
  (Office Phone: 733-6147—Area Code 504)
Offices—6928 Saints Dr., Metairie, La. 70003
Stadium—Louisiana Superdome (Capacity: 69,551)
Team Colors—Old Gold, Black and White
Training Site—University of Wisconsin, LaCrosse, Wis.

1988 SCHEDULE
**(All times local.
All games Sunday unless noted otherwise.)**

Sept. 4	SAN FRANCISCO	12:00
Sept. 11	at Atlanta	1:00
Sept. 18	at Detroit	1:00
Sept. 25	TAMPA BAY	12:00
Oct. 3	DALLAS (Mon.)	8:00
Oct. 9	at San Diego	1:00
Oct. 16	at Seattle	1:00
Oct. 23	LOS ANGELES RAIDERS	12:00
Oct. 30	LOS ANGELES RAMS	12:00
Nov. 6	at Washington	4:00
Nov. 13	at Los Angeles Rams	1:00
Nov. 20	DENVER	12:00
Nov. 27	NEW YORK GIANTS	7:00
Dec. 4	at Minnesota	12:00
Dec. 11	at San Francisco	1:00
Dec. 18	ATLANTA	12:00

1987 RESULTS—(Won 12, Lost 4)

Saints		Opp.		Att.
28	Cleveland	21	(H)	59,900
17	Philadelphia	27	(A)	57,485
	Atlanta*		(H)	
37	*L.A. Rams*	*10*	*(H)*	*29,745*
19	*St. Louis*	*24*	*(A)*	*11,795*
19	*Chicago*	*17*	*(A)*	*46,813*
22	San Francisco	24	(H)	60,497
38	Atlanta	0	(A)	42,196
31	L.A. Rams	14	(A)	43,379
26	San Francisco	24	(A)	60,436
23	New York Giants	14	(H)	67,639
20	Pittsburgh	16	(A)	47,896
44	Tampa Bay	34	(H)	66,471
24	Houston	10	(H)	68,257
41	Cincinnati	24	(A)	43,424
33	Green Bay	24	(H)	68,364
NFC WILD-CARD GAME				
10	Minnesota	44	(H)	68,127

*Game cancelled due to strike.
Italics denote strike replacement games.

1987 GAMES STARTED

(NOTE: Players with an asterisk (*) following their names made starts only in strike-replacement games.)

15 games: Bruce Clark.

14 games: Tony Elliott.

12 games: Stan Brock, Bobby Hebert, Joel Hilgenberg, Rickey Jackson, Vaughan Johnson, Rueben Mayes, Sam Mills, Pat Swilling, Dave Waymer, Jim Wilks.

11 games: Eric Martin, Steve Trapilo.

10 games: Hoby Brenner, Jim Dombrowski, Antonio Gibson, Van Jakes, Brett Maxie.

9 games: Brad Edelman.

8 games: John Tice.

7 games: Mike Jones.

5 games: Gene Atkins, Daren Gilbert.

4 games: Chuck Commiskey, Buford Jordan, Mark Pattison.

3 games: Michael Adams*, Cliff Benson, Dwight Beverly*, James Campen*, Stacey Dawsey*, Joe Deforest*, John Fourcade*, Phillip James*, Ken Kaplan*, Larry McCoy*, Jeff Rodenberger*, Bill Roe*, Malcolm Scott*, Reggie Sutton*, Pat Swoopes*, Derrick Taylor*.

2 games: Scott Leach*, Johnnie Poe, Henry Thomas*, Frank Wattelet.

1 game: Sheldon Andrus*, Mel Gray, Lonzell Hill, Dalton Hilliard, Greg Loberg*, Ken Marchiol*, Barry Word.

NEW ORLEANS SAINTS 1988 VETERAN ROSTER

No.	Name	Pos.	Ht.	Wt.	NFL Exp.	Birth-date	College	Games in '87	How Acquired
40	Adams, Michael	CB	5-10	195	2	4- 5-64	Arkansas State	7	D3, '87
7	Andersen, Morten	K	6-2	221	7	8-19-60	Michigan State	12	D4, '82
28	Atkins, Gene	CB/S	6-1	200	2	8-31-64	Florida A&M	13	D7, '87
83	Benson, Cliff	TE	6-4	240	4	8-28-61	Purdue	*10	W-Was, '87
	Brannon, Robert	DE	6-7	245	1	3-26-61	Arkansas	*2	FA, '88
85	†Brenner, Hoby	TE	6-4	240	8	6- 2-59	Southern California	12	D3a, '81
67	Brock, Stan	T	6-6	292	9	6- 8-58	Colorado	12	D1, '80
	Burks, Shawn	LB	6-1	230	2	2-10-63	Louisiana State	*0	FA, '88
59	Campen, James	C	6-3	260	2	6-11-64	Tulane	3	FA, '87
	Caron, Roger	G	6-5	275	3	6- 3-62	Harvard	*0	FA, '88
75	Clark, Bruce	DE	6-3	275	7	3-31-58	Penn State	15	T-GB, '82
89	Clark, Robert	WR	5-11	175	1	8- 6-65	North Carolina Central	2	D10, '87
	Coffman, Paul	TE	6-3	225	11	3-29-56	Kansas State	*12	FA, '88
66	Commiskey, Chuck	G	6-4	290	3	3- 2-58	Mississippi	12	FA, '86
70	Contz, Bill	T	6-5	270	3	5-12-61	Penn State	3	FA, '86
41	Cook, Toi	S	5-11	188	2	12- 3-64	Stanford	7	D8, '87
26	Dawsey, Stacey	WR	5-9	154	2	10-24-65	Indiana	3	OFA, '87
	DeForest, Joe	LB	6-1	240	2	4-17-65	Southwestern Louisiana	3	FA, '88
72	Dombrowski, Jim	T	6-5	298	3	10-19-63	Virginia	10	D1, '86
63	†Edelman, Brad	G	6-6	270	7	9- 3-60	Missouri	11	D2, '82
99	Elliott, Tony	NT	6-2	295	7	4-28-59	North Texas State	14	D5, '82
11	Fourcade, John	QB	6-1	208	2	10-11-60	Mississippi	3	FA, '87
	Fourcade, Keith	LB	5-11	225	1	10-20-61	Mississippi	2	FA, '88
97	†Geathers, James	DE	6-7	290	4	4-26-60	Wichita State	1	D2, '84
27	†Gibson, Antonio	S	6-3	204	3	7- 5-62	Cincinnati	10	FA, '86
77	Gilbert, Daren	T	6-6	295	4	10- 3-63	Fullerton State	6	D2, '85
37	†Gray, Mel	RB	5-9	166	3	3-16-61	Purdue	12	SupD, '84
10	Hansen, Brian	P	6-3	209	5	10-18-60	Sioux Falls	12	D9, '84
	Harris, Herbert	WR	6-1	206	2	5- 4-61	Lamar	2	FA, '86
92	Haynes, James	LB	6-2	233	5	8- 9-60	Mississippi Valley	12	FA, '84
3	Hebert, Bobby	QB	6-4	215	4	8-19-60	Northwestern St. (La.)	12	FA, '85
61	Hilgenberg, Joel	C/G	6-2	252	5	7-10-62	Iowa	12	D4, '84
87	Hill, Lonzell	WR	5-11	189	2	9-25-65	Washington	10	D2, '87
21	Hilliard, Dalton	RB	5-8	204	3	1-21-64	Louisiana State	12	D2, '86
57	Jackson, Rickey	LB	6-2	243	8	3-20-58	Pittsburgh	12	D2a, '81
22	†Jakes, Van	CB	6-0	190	5	5-10-61	Kent State	12	FA, '86
	Jean-Batiste, Garland	FB	6-0	208	2	4- 2-65	Louisiana State	3	FA, '88
53	†Johnson, Vaughan	LB	6-3	235	3	3-24-62	North Carolina State	12	SupD, '84
	Jones, Kirk	RB	5-9	204	1	1- 5-65	Nevada-Las Vegas	*1	FA, '88
86	Jones, Mike	WR	5-11	183	6	4-14-60	Tennessee State	12	T-Min, '86
23	†Jordan, Buford	RB	6-0	223	3	6-26-62	McNeese State	12	FA, '86
71	Kaplan, Ken	T	6-5	270	4	1-12-60	New Hampshire	3	FA, '88
78	Knight, Shawn	DE	6-6	288	2	6- 4-64	Brigham Young	10	D1, '87
55	†Kohlbrand, Joe	LB	6-4	242	4	3-18-63	Miami (Fla.)	12	D8, '85
60	†Korte, Steve	C	6-2	260	6	1-15-60	Arkansas	3	D2, '83
24	Mack, Milton	CB	5-11	182	2	9-20-63	Alcorn State	13	OFA, '87
	Mandarich, John	NT	6-4	265	R	8-1-61	Kent State	*12	FA, '88
84	Martin, Eric	WR	6-1	207	4	11- 8-61	Louisiana State	15	D7, '85
39	†Maxie, Brett	S	6-2	194	4	1-13-62	Texas Southern	12	OFA, '85
36	Mayes, Rueben	RB	5-11	200	3	6-16-63	Washington State	12	D3, '86
51	Mills, Sam	LB	5-9	225	3	6- 3-59	Montclair State	12	FA, '86
	Nelson, Edmund	DL	6-3	266	7	4-30-60	Auburn	*10	W-Pit, '88
88	†Pattison, Mark	WR	6-2	190	3	12-12-61	Washington	9	W-Rai, '87
56	Swilling, Pat	LB	6-3	242	3	10-25-64	Georgia Tech	12	D3a, '86
69	Swoopes, Patrick	NT	6-4	280	2	3- 4-64	Mississippi State	9	FA, '87
82	Tice, John	TE	6-5	249	6	6-22-60	Maryland	12	D3, '83
54	Toles, Alvin	LB	6-1	227	4	3-23-63	Tennessee	12	D1, '85
65	Trapilo, Steve	G	6-5	281	2	9-20-64	Boston College	11	D4, '87
73	†Warren, Frank	DE	6-4	290	8	9-14-59	Auburn	12	D3, '81
33	Waters, Mike	TE	6-2	230	3	3-15-62	San Diego State	5	FA, '87
44	Waymer, Dave	CB	6-1	188	8	7- 1-58	Notre Dame	12	D2, '80
94	Wilks, Jim	DE	6-5	266	8	3-12-58	San Diego State	12	D12, '81
18	Wilson, Dave	QB	6-3	206	7	4-27-59	Illinois	4	SupD, '81
34	Word, Barry	RB	6-2	220	2	7-17-64	Virginia	12	D3, '86

*Benson played 2 games with Redskins, 8 with Saints in '87; Brannon played 1 game with Browns and 1 game with Saints in '87; Burks last active with Redskins in '86; Caron last active with Colts in '86; Coffman played 12 games with Chiefs in '87; K. Jones played 1 game with Browns and on inactive list for 1 game with Saints in '87; Mandarich played 12 games with Edmonton-CFL in '87; Nelson played 10

games with Steelers in '87.
†Option playout; subject to developments.
D—Draft; T—Trade; W—Waivers; FA—Free Agent; OFA—Original Free Agent; SupD—Supplemental Draft.
Also played with Saints in '87, see page 386.

NEW ORLEANS SAINTS
1988 DRAFT CHOICES

(Number following name designates order of selection among 333 players drafted.)

Round and Player		Position	College
1. HEYWARD, Craig	24	RB	Pittsburgh
2. PERRIMAN, Brett	52	WR	Miami (Fla.)
3. Choice to Denver (a)			
3. STEPHENS, Tony from Denver (b)	81	NT	Clemson
4. CARR, Lydell	106	RB	Oklahoma
5. SCALES, Greg from Kansas City (c)	112	TE	Wake Forest
5. TAYLOR, Keith	134	DB	Illinois
6. SIMS, Bob	162	G	Florida
7. FORDE, Brian	190	LB	Washington State
8. DERBY, Glenn	218	T	Wisconsin
9. NUNN, Clarence	246	DB	San Diego State
10. SANTOS, Todd	274	QB	San Diego State
10. FIZER, Vincent from Denver (b)	276	LB	Southern U.
11. COUCH, Gary	302	WR	Minnesota
12. JURGENSEN, Paul	330	DE	Georgia Tech

(a) Traded pick for 3rd- and 10th-round picks in 1988, April 24, 1988.
(b) See (a).
(c) Acquired pick for linebacker Jack Del Rio, August 17, 1987.

NEW ORLEANS SAINTS
1988 ROOKIE AND FIRST-YEAR ROSTER

Name	Pos.	Hgt.	Wgt.	Birth-date	College	How Acquired
Booker, Darrell	LB	5-11	221	12-19-64	Delaware	FA
Carr, Lydell	RB	6-0	226	5-27-65	Oklahoma	D4
Cephus, Marvin	WR	5-10	170	3-10-65	Tulane	FA
Couch, Gary	WR	5-11	171	1- 2-66	Minnesota	D11
Crow, Mike	P	6-2	200	6-16-64	Northwestern St., La.	*FA
Derby, Glenn	T	6-6	290	6- 7-64	Wisconsin	D8
Evans, Vince	RB	5-10	216	9- 8-63	North Carolina State	*FA, '87
Fizer, Vincent	LB	6-4	250	10-10-65	Southern	D10a
Forde, Brian	LB	6-2	225	11- 1-63	Washington State	D7
Genilla, Sal	QB	6-2	207	1- 8-65	Pittsburgh	FA
Hammond, Darryl	CB/S	6-1	207	9-24-66	Virginia	FA
Henderson, Keith	CB	5-9	183	9-11-65	Texas Tech	FA
Heyward, Craig	RB	5-11	251	9-26-66	Pittsburgh	D1
Hopkins, Joe	WR	5-9	181	4-28-65	East Texas State	FA
Jurgensen, Paul	DE	6-5	243	11-16-65	Georgia Tech	D12
Keith, Jeff	G	6-2	274	10-26-65	Texas Tech	FA
McCabe, Jim	LB	6-2	223	1-16-65	Morningside	FA
McKinley, James	CB	5-8	175	7-18-66	Tulane	FA
Nunn, Clarence	CB	5-10	176	12-29-64	San Diego State	D9
Orndorff, Dave	C	6-0	285	4- 4-64	Oregon State	FA
Perriman, Brett	WR	5-9	175	10-10-65	Miami (Fla.)	D2
Robinson, Anthony	WR	6-3	178	4-15-66	Elizabeth City State	FA
Santos, Todd	QB	6-2	207	2-12-64	San Diego State	D10
Scales, Greg	TE	6-4	253	5- 9-66	Wake Forest	D5
Sims, Bob	G	6-3	269	9- 2-66	Florida	D6
Solon, Dave	T	6-5	268	2-15-66	St. Cloud State	FA
Squires, Chris	LB	6-1	223	9-21-64	Tennessee Tech	FA
Steele, Todd	RB	6-3	245	12- 3-63	Southern California	*FA, '87
Stephens, Tony	NT	6-3	306	12-13-64	Clemson	D3
Taylor, Keith	CB/S	5-11	193	12-21-64	Illinois	D5a
Young, Nay	CB/S	5-9	187	2-10-65	Georgia Southern	FA

*Crow: FA Pittsburgh '87, released 8/24, FA replacement St. Louis '87, released 10/6; Evans and Steele missed '87 season due to injury.

NEW YORK GIANTS
(Eastern Division, National Conference)

Bill Parcells

President—Wellington T. Mara
Vice-President and Treasurer—Timothy J. Mara
Vice-President and Secretary—Raymond J. Walsh
Vice-President and General Manager—George Young
Assistant General Manager—Harry Hulmes
Director of Player Personnel—Tom Boisture
Director of Pro Personnel—Tim Rooney
Head Coach—Bill Parcells (5 years: 42-36-1)
Assistant Coaches:
 Defensive Coordinator/Linebackers—Bill Belichick
 Receivers—Tom Coughlin
 Special Teams—Romeo Crennel
 Offensive Coordinator—Ron Erhardt
 Defensive Backs—Len Fontes
 Running Backs—Ray Handley
 Offensive Line—Fred Hoaglin
 Defensive Line—Lamar Leachman
 Strength & Conditioning—Johnny Parker
 Tight Ends—Mike Pope
 Defensive Assistant—Mike Sweatman
Director of Media Services—Ed Croke
 (Office Phone: 935-8111—Area Code 201)
Offices—Giants Stadium, East Rutherford, N. J. 07073
Stadium—Giants Stadium (Capacity: 76,891)
Team Colors—Royal Blue, Red and White
Training Site—Fairleigh-Dickinson University (Madison),
 Florham Park, N.J.

1988 SCHEDULE
(All times local.
All games Sunday unless noted otherwise.)

Sept. 5	WASHINGTON (Mon.)	9:00
Sept. 11	SAN FRANCISCO	1:00
Sept. 18	at Dallas	3:00
Sept. 25	LOS ANGELES RAMS	4:00
Oct. 2	at Washington	1:00
Oct. 10	at Philadelphia (Mon.)	9:00
Oct. 16	DETROIT	1:00
Oct. 23	at Atlanta	1:00
Oct. 30	at Detroit	1:00
Nov. 6	DALLAS	1:00
Nov. 13	at Phoenix	2:00
Nov. 20	PHILADELPHIA	4:00
Nov. 27	at New Orleans	7:00
Dec. 4	PHOENIX	1:00
Dec. 11	KANSAS CITY	1:00
Dec. 18	at New York Jets	1:00

1987 RESULTS—(Won 6, Lost 9)

Giants		Opp.		Att.
19	Chicago	34	(A)	65,704
14	Dallas	16	(H)	73,426
	Miami*		(A)	
21	San Francisco	41	(H)	16,471
12	Washington	38	(H)	9,123
3	Buffalo (OT)	6	(A)	15,737
30	St. Louis	7	(H)	74,391
24	Dallas	33	(A)	55,730
17	New England	10	(H)	73,817
20	Philadelphia	17	(A)	66,172
14	New Orleans	23	(A)	67,639
19	Washington	23	(A)	45,815
23	Philadelphia (OT)	20	(H)	65,874
24	St. Louis	27	(A)	29,623
20	Green Bay	10	(H)	51,013
20	New York Jets	7	(H)	68,318

*Game cancelled due to strike.
Italics denote strike replacement games.

1987 GAMES STARTED

(NOTE: Players with an asterisk (*) following their names made starts only in strike-replacement games.)

12 games: Bill Ard, Carl Banks, Mark Bavaro, Brad Benson, Harry Carson, Kenny Hill, Pepper Johnson, Terry Kinard, Lionel Manuel, Bart Oates, William Roberts.

11 games: Mark Collins, Lawrence Taylor.

10 games: Leonard Marshall, Joe Morris, Perry Williams.

9 games: George Martin, Phil Simms.

8 games: Jim Burt.

7 games: George Adams, Damian Johnson.

5 games: Stephen Baker, Maurice Carthon, Chris Godfrey.

4 games: Erik Howard, Stacy Robinson, Jeff Rutledge.

3 games: Lewis Bennett*, Donald Brown*, Reginald Carr*, Eric Dorsey, Bill Dugan*, Curtis Garrett*, Chris Jones*, Edwin Lovelady*, Steve Rehage*, Douglas Smith*, Jeffrey Smith*, Warren Thompson*, Van Williams*.

2 games: Mike Black*, Dennis Borcky*, Chris Davis*, Dan DeRose*, Andy Headen, Jerry Kimmel*, Dan Morgan*, Kaulana Park*, Lee Rouson, Frank Sutton*, Odessa Turner, John Washington, Herb Welch.

1 game: Mike Busch*, Jim Crocicchia*, Kelvin Davis*, Robert DiRico*, Anthony Howard*, Kevin Meuth*, Pat Morrison*, Zeke Mowatt, Frank Nicholson*, Elvis Patterson, Rob Porter*, Jeff Tootle*, Scott Urch*, Adrian White*.

NEW YORK GIANTS 1988 VETERAN ROSTER

No.	Name	Pos.	Ht.	Wt.	NFL Exp.	Birth-date	College	Games in '87	How Acquired
	Abraham, Robert	LB	6-1	236	6	7-13-60	North Carolina State	*2	W-Hou, '88
33	Adams, George	RB	6-1	255	3	12-22-62	Kentucky	12	D1, '85
2	Allegre, Raul	K	5-10	167	6	6-15-59	Texas	12	FA, '86
24	Anderson, Ottis	RB	6-2	225	10	11-19-57	Miami (Fla.)	4	T-StL, '86
67	Ard, Bill	G	6-3	270	8	3-12-59	Wake Forest	12	D8b, '81
85	Baker, Stephen	WR	5-8	160	2	8-30-64	Fresno State	12	D3, '87
58	†Banks, Carl	LB	6-4	235	5	8-29-62	Michigan State	12	D1, '84
89	†Bavaro, Mark	TE	6-4	245	4	4-28-63	Notre Dame	12	D4, '85
	Belk, Veno	TE	6-3	229	1	3- 7-63	Michigan State	*2	FA, '88
79	Berthusen, Bill	NT	6-5	285	2	6-26-64	Iowa State	*4	D12, '87
69	Black, Mike	T	6-4	280	1	8-24-64	Cal State-Sacramento	2	FA, '88
	Borcky, Dennis	NT	6-3	284	1	9-14-64	Memphis State	2	FA, '88
47	Brown, Don	CB	5-11	189	3	11-28-63	Maryland	3	FA, '87
64	Burt, Jim	NT	6-1	260	8	6- 7-59	Miami (Fla.)	8	OFA, '81
	Byrd, Boris	CB/S	6-0	210	2	4-15-62	Austin Peay	3	FA, '88
53	Carson, Harry	LB	6-2	240	13	11-26-53	South Carolina State	12	D4a, '76
44	†Carthon, Maurice	RB	6-1	225	4	4-24-61	Arkansas State	11	FA, '85
21	†Clayton, Harvey	CB	5-9	186	5	4- 4-61	Florida State	2	FA, '87
25	Collins, Mark	CB	5-10	190	3	1-16-64	Fullerton State	11	D2, '86
	Cummings, Mack	WR	6-0	195	1	3- 3-60	East Tennessee State	1	FA, '87
77	Dorsey, Eric	DE	6-5	280	3	8- 5-64	Notre Dame	12	D1, '86
28	Flynn, Tom	S	6-0	195	5	3-24-62	Pittsburgh	12	FA, '86
61	†Godfrey, Chris	G	6-3	265	6	5-17-58	Michigan	8	FA, '84
37	Haddix, Wayne	CB	6-1	203	2	7-23-65	Liberty	5	OFA, '87
54	†Headen, Andy	LB	6-5	242	6	7- 8-60	Clemson	12	D8, '83
48	Hill, Kenny	S	6-0	195	8	7-25-58	Yale	12	T-Rai, '84
15	Hostetler, Jeff	QB	6-3	212	4	4-22-61	West Virginia	*0	D3, '84
74	Howard, Erik	NT	6-4	268	3	11-12-64	Washington State	12	D2a, '86
57	Hunt, Byron	LB	6-5	242	8	12-17-58	Southern Methodist	12	D9, '81
82	Ingram, Mark	WR	5-10	188	2	8-23-65	Michigan State	9	D1, '87
68	†Johnson, Damian	T	6-5	290	3	12-18-62	Kansas State	12	OFA, '85
52	Johnson, Pepper	LB	6-3	248	3	7-29-64	Ohio State	12	D2b, '86
43	Kinard, Terry	S	6-1	200	6	11-24-59	Clemson	12	D1, '83
5	†Landeta, Sean	P	6-0	200	4	1- 6-62	Towson State	12	FA, '85
46	Lasker, Greg	S	6-0	200	3	9-28-64	Arkansas	11	D2c, '86
86	Manuel, Lionel	WR	5-11	180	5	4-13-62	Pacific	12	D7, '84
70	Marshall, Leonard	DE	6-3	285	6	10-22-61	Louisiana State	10	D2, '83
75	Martin, George	DE	6-4	255	14	2-16-53	Oregon	12	D11, '75
80	McConkey, Phil	WR	5-10	170	5	2-24-57	Navy	12	FA, '83
	McLean, Ron	DE	6-3	274	2	3-16-63	Fullerton State	*3	FA, '88
	Morgan, Dan	G	6-6	285	1	2- 2-64	Penn State	2	FA, '88
20	Morris, Joe	RB	5-7	195	7	9-15-60	Syracuse	11	D2, '82
84	Mowatt, Zeke	TE	6-3	240	5	3- 5-61	Florida State	12	OFA, '83
	Nave, Steve	G	6-2	265	1	8-29-63	Kansas	*2	FA, '88
63	†Nelson, Karl	T	6-6	285	4	6-14-60	Iowa State	*0	D3, '83
65	Oates, Bart	C	6-3	265	4	12-16-58	Brigham Young	12	FA, '85
55	Reasons, Gary	LB	6-4	234	5	2-18-62	Northwestern (La.) St.	10	D4a, '84
72	Riesenberg, Doug	T	6-5	275	2	7-22-65	California	8	D6a, '87
66	†Roberts, William	T	6-5	280	4	8- 5-62	Ohio State	12	D1a, '84
81	Robinson, Stacy	WR	5-11	186	4	2-19-62	North Dakota State	5	D2, '85
22	Rouson, Lee	RB	6-1	222	4	10-18-62	Colorado	12	D8, '85
17	Rutledge, Jeff	QB	6-1	195	10	1-22-57	Alabama	13	T-Ram, '82
	Sanders, Charles	RB	6-1	230	3	4-24-64	Slippery Rock	*5	FA, '88
	Schippang, Gary	T	6-4	254	1	4-16-63	West Chester State	*0	FA, '88
11	Simms, Phil	QB	6-3	214	9	11- 3-56	Morehead State	9	D1, '79
	Sisley, Brian	DE	6-4	250	2	1-18-64	South Dakota State	3	FA, '88
56	Taylor, Lawrence	LB	6-3	243	8	2- 4-59	North Carolina	12	D1, '81
83	Turner, Odessa	WR	6-3	205	2	10-12-64	Northwestern (La.) St.	7	D4, '87
34	†Varajon, Michael	RB	6-1	232	2	7-12-64	Toledo	*3	W-SF, '87
73	Washington, John	DE	6-4	275	3	2-20-63	Oklahoma State	12	D3, '86
27	Welch, Herb	DB	5-11	180	4	1-12-61	UCLA	12	D12, '85
36	White, Adrian	S	6-0	200	2	4- 6-64	Florida	6	D2, '87
23	Williams, Perry	CB	6-2	203	5	5-12-61	North Carolina State	10	D7, '83

*Abraham played 2 games with Oilers in '87; Belk played 2 games with Bills in '87; Berthusen played 3 games with Bengals, 1 with Giants in '87; Hostetler active for 2 games with Giants in '87, but did not play; McLean played 3 games with Broncos in '87; Nave played 2 games with Broncos in '87; Nelson missed '87 season due to illness; Sanders played 5 games with Steelers in '87; Schippang active for 1 game with Chargers in '87, but did not play; Varajon played 3 games with 49ers in '87.

†Option playout; subject to developments.
Retired—Brad Benson, 10-year tackle, 12 games in '87.
D—Draft; T—Trade; W—Waivers; FA—Free Agent; OFA—Original Free Agent.
Also played with Giants in '87, see page 386.

NEW YORK GIANTS
1988 DRAFT CHOICES

(Number following name designates order of selection among 333 players drafted.)

Round and Player		Position	College
1. MOORE, Eric	10	T	Indiana
2. ELLIOTT, John	36	T	Michigan
3. WHITE, Sheldon	62	DB	Miami (O.)
4. SHAW, Ricky	92	LB	Oklahoma State
5. CARTER, Jon	118	DE	Pittsburgh
6. HOULE, David	145	G	Michigan State
7. PEREZ, Mike	175	QB	San Jose State
7. WHITAKER, Danta from Indianapolis (a)	186	TE	Mississippi Valley St.
8. LILLY, Sammy	202	DB	Georgia Tech
9. Choice to L.A. Raiders (b)			
10. HICKERSON, Eric	259	DB	Indiana
10. WILKES, Steve from San Diego (c)	265	TE	Appalachian State
11. HARRIS, Greg	286	WR	Troy State
12. FUTRELL, David	313	NT	Brigham Young
12. McCORMACK, Brendan from Minnesota (d)	323	DT	South Carolina

(a) Acquired pick for nose tackle Jerome Sally, September 2, 1987.
(b) Traded pick for two 12th-round picks in 1987, April 30, 1987.
(c) Acquired pick for wide receiver Bobby Johnson, August 20, 1987.
(d) Acquired pick for center Chris Foote, May 7, 1987.

NEW YORK GIANTS
1988 ROOKIE AND FIRST-YEAR ROSTER

Name	Pos.	Hgt.	Wgt.	Birth-date	College	How Acquired
Ariey, Mike	T	6-6	285	3-12-64	San Diego State	FA
Brown, Henry	NT	6-3	265	10- 1-65	Florida	FA
Brownlee, Brandy	K	6-1	225	12- 9-65	Washington	FA
Carter, Jon	DE	6-4	260	3-12-65	Pittsburgh	D5
Compton, J.R.	RB	6-0	214	11- 4-65	West Texas State	FA
Dominic, Steve	DE	6-5	262	6-10-66	Cal State-Northridge	FA
Donovan, Mark	QB	6-4	205	2-15-66	Brown	FA
Elliott, John	T	6-7	305	4- 1-65	Michigan	D2
Futrell, David	DE	6-1	265	3-20-66	Brigham Young	D12
Harris, Greg	WR	5-9	160	12-30-65	Troy State	D11
Hickerson, Eric	CB/S	6-2	215	10- 4-65	Indiana	D10
Howard, Stanley	WR	5-10	171	5-22-65	Murray State	FA
Houle, David	G	6-4	278	1-20-65	Michigan State	D6
Johnson, Thomas	TE	6-6	257	7- 9-64	New Hampshire	FA
Lilly, Sammy	CB/S	5-9	172	2-12-65	Georgia Tech	D8
Martin, Andrew	LB	6-3	245	6-24-66	Holy Cross	FA
McCormack, Brendan	DE	6-6	270	3-17-66	South Carolina	D12a
Medlock, James	RB	6-2	225	11-17-66	Purdue	FA
Morrow, Terry	RB	5-8	198	3-17-66	Central State	FA
Moore, Eric	T	6-5	290	1-21-65	Indiana	D1
Mulcahy, Phil	DT	6-4	285	11- 6-64	Rhode Island	*FA
Neal, Michael	DE	6-3	273	9-26-64	Weber State	FA
Oglesby, Eric	WR	5-9	168	7-30-65	Northern Colorado	FA
Oliver, Tommy	DE	6-4	257	8- 4-64	Alabama State	FA
Perez, Mike	QB	6-1	210	3- 7-65	San Jose State	D7
Richardson, Tim	RB	6-0	215	2-23-64	Pacific	*D6, '87
Salonoa, Thor	LB	6-1	249	7- 9-65	Brigham Young	FA
Shaw, Ricky	LB	6-4	240	7-28-65	Oklahoma State	D4
Stewart, Michael	WR	6-3	198	11- 1-64	Pittsburgh	FA
Thaxton, Galand	LB	6-1	240	10-23-64	Wyoming	FA
Williams, John	WR	6-0	180	4- 5-64	Kansas State	FA
Whitaker, Danta	TE	6-3	240	3-14-65	Mississippi Valley State	D7a
White, Sheldon	CB/S	5-11	188	3- 1-65	Miami (O.)	D3
Wilkes, Steve	TE	6-5	250	5-18-66	Appalachian State	D10a
Wimbley, Keenan	LB	6-1	234	7- 9-66	Central Florida	FA

*Mulcahy: FA New England '87, injured reserve 9/1 through 10/19, released 10/20; Richardson missed '87 season due to injury.

NEW YORK JETS

(Eastern Division, American Conference)

Joe Walton

Chairman of the Board—Leon Hess
President—Jim Kensil
Secretary & Admin. Manager—Steve Gutman
Director of Player Personnel—Mike Hickey
Director of Pro Personnel—Jim Royer
Head Coach—Joe Walton (5 years: 41-38)
Assistant Coaches:
    Quarterbacks—Zeke Bratkowski
    Quality Control—Ray Callahan
    Defensive Coordinator—Bud Carson
    Defensive Line—Wally Chambers
    Secondary—Mike Faulkiner
    Running Backs—Bobby Hammond
    Offensive Coordinator/Receivers—Rich Kotite
    Special Teams—Larry Pasquale
    Offensive Line—Dan Radakovich
    Linebackers—Jim Vechiarella
Director of Public Relations—Frank Ramos
    (Office Phone: 421-6600—Area Code 212)
Offices—598 Madison Ave., New York, N.Y. 10022
Stadium—Giants Stadium (Capacity: 76,891)
Team Colors—Kelly Green and White
Training Site—Hofstra University, Hempstead, N.Y.

1988 SCHEDULE

(All times local.
All games Sunday unless noted otherwise.)

Sept.	4	at New England	4:00
Sept.	11	at Cleveland	4:00
Sept.	18	HOUSTON	1:00
Sept.	25	at Detroit	1:00
Oct.	2	KANSAS CITY	4:00
Oct.	9	at Cincinnati	1:00
Oct.	17	BUFFALO (Mon.)	9:00
Oct.	23	at Miami	4:00
Oct.	30	PITTSBURGH	1:00
Nov.	6	at Indianapolis	4:00
Nov.	13	NEW ENGLAND	1:00
Nov.	20	at Buffalo	1:00
Nov.	27	MIAMI	1:00
Dec.	4	at Kansas City	3:00
Dec.	10	INDIANAPOLIS (Sat.)	12:30
Dec.	18	NEW YORK GIANTS	1:00

1987 RESULTS—(Won 6, Lost 9)

Jets		Opp.		Att.
31	Buffalo	28	(A)	76,718
43	New England	24	(H)	70,847
	Pittsburgh*		(A)	
24	*Dallas*	*38*	*(H)*	*12,370*
0	*Indianapolis*	*6*	*(A)*	*34,927*
37	*Miami (OT)*	*31*	*(H)*	*18,249*
16	Washington	17	(A)	53,497
14	Indianapolis	19	(H)	60,863
30	Seattle	14	(H)	60,452
16	Kansas City	9	(A)	40,718
14	Buffalo	17	(H)	58,407
27	Cincinnati	20	(H)	41,135
28	Miami	37	(A)	58,879
20	New England	42	(A)	60,617
27	Philadelphia	38	(H)	30,752
7	New York Giants	20	(A)	68,318

*Game cancelled due to strike.
Italics denote strike replacement games.

1987 GAMES STARTED

(NOTE: Players with an asterisk (*) following their names made starts only in strike-replacement games.)

13 games: Marty Lyons.

12 games: Dan Alexander, Alex Gordon, Harry Hamilton, Ken O'Brien, Jim Sweeney.

11 games: Barry Bennett, Troy Benson, Guy Bingham, Bob Crable, Rich Miano, Al Toon.

10 games: Joe Fields, Mickey Shuler, Roger Vick.

9 games: Ted Banker.

8 games: Kyle Clifton, Freeman McNeil.

7 games: Mark Gastineau, Jerry Holmes, Carl Howard, Joe Klecko.

6 games: Russell Carter, Johnny Hector, Rocky Klever.

5 games: Reggie McElroy, Gerald Nichols.

4 games: Ken Jones, Scott Mersereau, Kurt Sohn, Wesley Walker.

3 games: Jay Brophy*, Trent Collins*, Eric Coss*, Marc Hogan*, Tom Humphrey*, Eddie Hunter*, Kevin McArthur, George Radachowsky*, Ken Rose*, John Thomas*.

2 games: Dennis Bligen*, Sean Dykes*, Kerry Glenn, Michael Harper*, Jim Haslett*, Scott Holman*, Bobby Humphery, Jamie Kurisko*, Lance Mehl, David Norrie*, Larry Robinson*, Tony Sweet*.

1 game: Tony Chickillo*, John Chirico*, Billy Griggs, Mike Haight, Vince Jasper*, Lester Lyles, Pete McCartney*, Eric Riley*, Pat Ryan*, Ladell Wills*.

NEW YORK JETS 1988 VETERAN ROSTER

No.	Name	Pos.	Ht.	Wt.	NFL Exp.	Birth-date	College	Games in '87	How Acquired
60	Alexander, Dan	G/T	6-4	274	12	6-17-55	Louisiana State	12	D8, '77
97	Baldwin, Don	DE	6-3	263	2	7- 9-64	Purdue	8	FA, '87
95	Baldwin, Tom	DT	6-4	270	4	5-13-61	Tulsa	*0	D9, '84
63	Banker, Ted	G/C	6-2	275	5	2-17-61	Southeast Missouri	13	OFA, '83
31	Barber, Marion	RB	6-3	228	7	12- 6-59	Minnesota	12	D2, '81
54	†Benson, Troy	LB	6-2	235	3	7-30-63	Pittsburgh	11	D5a, '85
64	Bingham, Guy	C/G	6-3	260	9	2-25-58	Montana	12	D10, '80
23	Bligen, Dennis	RB	5-11	215	5	3- 3-62	St. John's	6	FA, '87
	Caldwell, Darryl	T	6-5	245	2	2- 2-60	Tennessee State	*0	FA, '87
	Chickillo, Tony	DT	6-3	257	2	7- 8-60	Miami (Fla.)	2	FA, '88
59	†Clifton, Kyle	LB	6-4	236	5	8-23-62	Texas Christian	12	D3, '84
50	Crable, Bob	LB	6-3	230	7	9-22-59	Notre Dame	12	D1, '82
	Davis, Kelvin	G	6-3	265	1	2- 7-63	Johnson C. Smith	*1	FA, '88
	Davis, Lee	DB	5-11	198	3	12-18-62	Mississippi	3	FA, '88
	Dennison, Glenn	TE	6-3	225	2	11-17-61	Miami (Fla.)	*2	FA, '88
	Dunn, K.D.	TE	6-3	235	4	4-28-63	Clemson	*3	FA, '88
22	Dykes, Sean	CB	5-10	170	2	8- 8-64	Bowling Green	6	FA, '87
52	Elam, Onzy	LB	6-2	225	2	12- 1-64	Tennessee State	5	D3, '87
30	†Faaola, Nuu	RB	5-11	210	3	1-15-64	Hawaii	12	D9, '86
8	Flick, Tom	QB	6-2	190	5	9-30-58	Washington	*0	FA, '87
98	Foster, Jerome	DE/DT	6-2	275	4	7-25-60	Ohio State	4	FA, '86
99	Gastineau, Mark	DE	6-5	255	10	11-20-56	East Central Oklahoma	15	D2, '79
35	Glenn, Kerry	CB	5-9	175	3	3-31-62	Minnesota	8	D10, '85
55	Gordon, Alex	LB	6-5	246	2	9-14-64	Cincinnati	12	D2, '87
81	Griggs, Billy	TE	6-3	230	4	8- 4-62	Virginia	12	D8, '84
79	Haight, Mike	G/T	6-4	270	3	10- 6-62	Iowa	6	D1, '86
39	†Hamilton, Harry	S	6-0	195	5	11-29-62	Penn State	12	D7, '84
84	Harper, Michael	WR	5-10	180	3	5-11-61	Southern California	3	FA, '86
51	Haslett, Jim	LB	6-3	236	9	12- 9-56	Indiana (Pa.)	3	FA, '87
34	Hector, Johnny	RB	5-11	200	6	11-26-60	Texas A&M	11	D2, '83
47	†Holmes, Jerry	CB	6-2	175	7	12-22-57	West Virginia	8	OFA, '80
28	†Howard, Carl	CB/S	6-2	190	5	9-20-61	Rutgers	12	FA, '85
	Howe, Glenn	T	6-7	298	3	10-18-61	Southern Mississippi	*0	FA, '88
48	Humphery, Bobby	CB/KR	5-10	180	5	8-23-61	New Mexico State	12	D9, '83
	Jones, Ken	T	6-5	285	13	12- 1-52	Arkansas	5	FA, '88
89	†Klever, Rocky	TE	6-3	230	6	7-10-59	Montana	12	D9, '82
	Krerowicz, Mark	T	6-4	282	3	3- 1-63	Ohio State	*3	FA, '88
5	Leahy, Pat	K	6-0	193	15	3-19-51	St. Louis	12	FA, '74
21	Lewis, Sid	CB	5-11	180	2	5-30-64	Penn State	2	D10, '87
	Lindstrom, Chris	DE	6-7	260	4	8- 3-60	Boston University	*3	FA, '88
26	Lyles, Lester	S	6-3	218	4	12-27-62	Virginia	4	D2, '85
93	Lyons, Marty	DE/DT	6-5	269	10	1-15-57	Alabama	13	D1, '79
	Mackey, Kyle	QB	6-3	220	3	3- 2-62	East Texas State	*3	FA, '88
86	Martin, Tracy	WR/KR	6-3	205	2	12- 4-64	North Dakota	12	D6, '87
57	McArthur, Kevin	LB	6-2	245	3	5-11-63	Lamar	12	FA, '86
68	McElroy, Reggie	T	6-6	275	6	3- 4-60	West Texas State	8	D2, '82
24	McNeil, Freeman	RB	5-11	214	8	4-22-59	UCLA	9	D1, '81
56	Mehl, Lance	LB	6-3	233	9	2-14-58	Penn State	3	D3, '80
94	Mersereau, Scott	DE	6-3	278	2	4- 8-65	Southern Connecticut	13	FA, '87
36	†Miano, Rich	S	6-0	200	4	9- 3-62	Hawaii	12	D6a, '85
58	Monger, Matt	LB	6-1	238	4	11-15-61	Oklahoma State	12	D8, '85
77	Nichols, Gerald	DT	6-2	261	2	2-10-64	Florida State	13	D7, '87
7	O'Brien, Ken	QB	6-4	208	6	11-27-60	California-Davis	12	D1, '83
	Prokop, Joe	P	6-3	225	3	7- 7-60	Cal Poly-Pomona	*3	FA, '88
25	†Radachowsky, George	S	5-11	190	4	9- 7-62	Boston College	8	FA, '87
	Renner, Bill	P	6-0	198	3	5-23-59	Virginia Tech	*3	FA, '88
92	Rose, Ken	LB	6-1	215	2	6- 9-61	Nevada-Las Vegas	10	FA, '87
10	Ryan, Pat	QB	6-3	210	11	9-16-55	Tennessee	13	D11, '78
82	Shuler, Mickey	TE	6-3	231	11	8-21-56	Penn State	11	D3, '78
87	†Sohn, Kurt	WR/KR	5-11	180	7	6-26-57	Fordham	12	FA, '81
53	†Sweeney, Jim	T/G	6-4	275	5	8- 8-62	Pittsburgh	12	D2, '84
88	Toon, Al	WR	6-4	205	4	4-30-63	Wisconsin	12	D1, '85
83	†Townsell, JoJo	WR/KR	5-9	180	4	11- 4-60	UCLA	12	D3, '83
43	Vick, Roger	RB	6-3	232	2	8-11-64	Texas A&M	12	D1, '87
85	Walker, Wesley	WR	6-0	182	12	5-26-55	California	5	D2, '77
	Witkowski, John	QB	6-1	205	3	6-18-62	Columbia	*0	FA, '88
38	Zordich, Mike	S	5-11	207	2	10-12-63	Penn State	10	FA, '87

*T. Baldwin and Caldwell missed '87 season due to injury; Davis played 1 game with Giants in '87;

Dennison played 2 games with Redskins, inactive for 4 games with Jets in '87; Dunn played 3 games with Redskins in '87; Flick active for 1 game with Jets in '87, but did not play; Howe active for 1 game with Cowboys in '87, but did not play; Krerowicz played 3 games with Browns in '87; Lindstrom played 3 games with Chiefs in '87; Mackey played 3 games with Dolphins in '87; Prokop played 3 games with Chargers in '87; Renner played 3 games with Packers in '87; Witkowski active for 3 games with Oilers in '87, but did not play.

†Option playout; subject to developments.

D—Draft; FA—Free Agent; OFA—Original Free Agent.

Also played with Jets in '87, see page 386.

NEW YORK JETS
1988 DRAFT CHOICES

(Number following name designates order of selection among 333 players drafted.)

Round and Player		Position	College
1. CADIGAN, Dave	8	T	Southern Cal
2. WILLIAMS, Terry	37	DB	Bethune-Cookman
3. McMILLAN, Erik	63	DB	Missouri
3. HASTY, James from Houston through L.A. Raiders (a)	74	DB	Washington State
4. Choice to L.A. Raiders (b)			
5. WITHYCOMBE, Mike	119	T	Fresno State
6. FRASE, Paul	146	DE	Syracuse
7. PATTON, Gary	172	RB	Eastern Michigan
8. NEUBERT, Keith	203	TE	Nebraska
9. TAMM, Ralph	230	G	West Chester (Pa.)
10. BOOTY, John	257	DB	Texas Christian
11. GALVIN, John	287	LB	Boston College
12. GOSS, Albert	314	NT	Jackson State

(a) Raiders acquired pick and 1st- and 4th-round picks in 1988 from Oilers for defensive end Sean Jones and 2nd- and 3rd-round picks in 1988, April 21, 1988; Jets acquired pick from Raiders for 4th- and 5th-round picks in 1988, April 24, 1988.

(b) See second part of (a).

NEW YORK JETS
1988 ROOKIE AND FIRST-YEAR ROSTER

Name	Pos.	Hgt.	Wgt.	Birth-date	College	How Acquired
Alfieri, Phil	DE	6-3	265	1-13-65	Oregon State	FA
Averitt, Kelly	T/G	6-4	260	10-24-64	Tennessee Tech	FA
Booty, John	CB	6-1	180	10- 9-65	Texas Christian	D10
Cadigan, Dave	T	6-4	280	4- 6-65	Southern California	D1
Calcagno, Greg	QB	6-2	187	9- 5-64	Santa Clara	FA
Collins, Harold	WR	6-2	205	2-16-65	Texas-El Paso	FA
Dixon, Byron	DB	6-0	191	3-13-66	Holy Cross	FA
Douglas, Donnie	CB	5-9	180	3-29-65	East Central Oklahoma	FA
Farris, Ray	CB	5-8	161	1-14-65	Utah State	FA
Flowers, Ricky	WR	6-0	200	9- 5-64	Jackson State	FA
Frase, Paul	DE	6-5	270	5- 5-65	Syracuse	D6
Gallimore, Jeff	TE	6-2	232	6-14-64	Arizona State	*FA
Galvin, John	LB	6-2	226	7- 9-65	Boston College	D11
Garrett, John	C	6-1	263	7-13-65	Syracuse	FA
Goss, Albert	NT	6-7	355	11-15-64	Jackson State	D12
Green, Doug	WR	5-11	182	10- 9-65	Duke	FA
Hall, Leon	DL	6-3	263	7- 5-65	East Carolina	FA
Hasty, James	CB	6-0	200	5-23-65	Washington State	D3a
Hatfield, Bruce	LB	6-3	238	10-12-65	Tennessee Tech	FA
Ingalls, Dave	C	6-3	267	12- 7-64	Maine	FA
Johns, Gregg	LB	6-2	233	4- 3-65	Penn State	FA
Kemper, Matt	G/T	6-5	295	10-31-65	Miami (O.)	FA
Kingston, Mike	DL	6-3	274	4- 5-64	Eastern Washington	*FA, '87
Lambert, Brad	DB	5-10	180	1-14-65	Kansas State	FA
Lewis, Eric	WR	5-9	186	12- 2-64	North Carolina	FA
Makins, Mike	DE	6-4	260	10-19-65	Tennessee-Chattanooga	*FA
McCarthy, Tom	P	6-2	200	6-25-62	Hawaii	*FA
McMillan, Erik	S	6-2	200	5- 3-65	Missouri	D3
Metcalf, Major	WR	6-4	215	11-20-63	Central Michigan	FA
Neubert, Keith	TE	6-5	250	9-13-64	Nebraska	D8
O'Brien, Chris	P-K	5-10	187	8- 5-64	San Diego State	*FA
O'Malley, Tom	LB	6-3	225	9-14-64	Hofstra	FA
Patton, Gary	RB	5-9	195	1-20-66	Eastern Michigan	D7
Pearson, Darryl	WR	6-2	197	3- 9-66	Alabama State	FA
Petitbon, Richie	LB	6-4	236	8- 3-64	Maryland	FA
Ross, Edwin	S	6-2	201	12-30-66	Alabama State	FA
Sanders, Bill	TE	6-3	229	9-25-64	Cal State-Sacramento	*FA
Schulting, Tom	S	5-10	172	5- 4-66	Iowa State	FA
Sheffield, Russell	DL	6-3	279	12-16-64	Baylor	FA
Tamm, Ralph	G-DE	6-3	275	3-11-66	West Chester State	D9
Williams, Keith	LB	6-3	249	4-30-64	Clemson	*FA
Williams, Terry	CB	5-11	205	10-14-65	Bethune-Cookman	D2
Withycombe, Mike	T	6-5	310	11-18-64	Fresno State	D5

*Gallimore: FA St. Louis '87, released 8/10; Kingston missed '87 season due to injury; Makins: FA Dallas '87, injured reserve 9/1 through 9/6, released 9/7; McCarthy: FA Dallas '85, released 8/12, FA Kansas City '86, released 8/18, FA Seattle '87, released 8/7; Nowinski: FA San Diego '86, released 8/18, FA New York Jets '87, injured reserve 8/27 through 9/20, released 9/21, returned injured reserve 10/20 through remainder of season; O'Brien: FA Philadelphia '86, released 8/26, FA Denver '87, released 7/30; Price: FA Chicago '85, released 5/21, FA San Diego 6/12, released 7/28, FA New York Jets '87, injured reserve 8/27 through entire season; Sanders: FA New York Jets '87, injured reserve 8/21 through 11/2, released 11/3; K. Williams: FA Dallas '86, released 7/21, FA Los Angeles Raiders '87, released 8/20, FA replacement Los Angeles Raiders 9/24, released 10/6.

PHILADELPHIA EAGLES
(Eastern Division, National Conference)

Buddy Ryan

Owner—Norman Braman
President—Harry T. Gamble
Head Coach—Buddy Ryan (2 years: 12-18-1)
V.P.-Player Personnel—Bill Davis
Director of Player Personnel—Joe Woolley
Assistant Coaches:
  Offensive Backfield—Dave Atkins
  Secondary—Jeff Fisher
  Defensive Line—Dale Haupt
  Strength & Conditioning—Ronnie Jones
  Asst. Offensive Line—Dan Neal
  Defensive Coord./Linebackers—Wade Phillips
  Asst. Head Coach/Offense—Ted Plumb
  Special Teams—Al Roberts
  Quarterbacks—Doug Scovil
  Offensive Line—Bill Walsh
Director of Public Relations—Ron Howard
  (Office Phone: 463-2500—Area Code 215)
Offices—Veterans Stadium, Philadelphia, Pa. 19148
Stadium—Veterans Stadium (Capacity: 66,356)
Team Colors—Kelly Green, White and Silver
Training Site—West Chester University, West Chester, Pa.

1988 SCHEDULE
(All times local.
All games Sunday unless noted otherwise.)

Sept. 4	at Tampa Bay	1:00
Sept. 11	CINCINNATI	4:00
Sept. 18	at Washington	1:00
Sept. 25	at Minnesota	12:00
Oct. 2	HOUSTON	1:00
Oct. 10	NEW YORK GIANTS (Mon.)	9:00
Oct. 16	at Cleveland	1:00
Oct. 23	DALLAS	1:00
Oct. 30	ATLANTA	1:00
Nov. 6	LOS ANGELES RAMS	1:00
Nov. 13	at Pittsburgh	1:00
Nov. 20	at New York Giants	4:00
Nov. 27	PHOENIX	1:00
Dec. 4	WASHINGTON	1:00
Dec. 10	at Phoenix (Sat.)	2:00
Dec. 18	at Dallas	12:00

1987 RESULTS—(Won 7, Lost 8)

Eagles		Opp.		Att.
24	Washington	34	(A)	52,128
27	New Orleans	17	(H)	57,485
	San Francisco*		(A)	
3	*Chicago*	*35*	*(H)*	*4,073*
22	*Dallas*	*41*	*(A)*	*40,622*
10	*Green Bay (OT)*	*16*	*(A)*	*35,842*
37	Dallas	20	(H)	61,630
28	St. Louis	23	(A)	24,586
31	Washington	27	(H)	63,609
17	New York Giants	20	(H)	66,172
19	St. Louis	31	(H)	55,592
34	New England (OT)	31	(A)	54,198
20	New York Giants (OT)	23	(A)	65,874
10	Miami	28	(H)	63,841
38	New York Jets	27	(A)	30,752
17	Buffalo	7	(H)	57,547

*Game cancelled due to strike.
Italics denote strike replacement games.

1987 GAMES STARTED

(NOTE: Players with an asterisk (*) following their names made starts only in strike-replacement games.)

12 games: Joe Conwell, Randall Cunningham, Matt Darwin, Gerry Feehery, Kenny Jackson, Seth Joyner, Mike Quick, Adam Schreiber, Clyde Simmons, John Spagnola, Andre Waters, Reggie White.

11 games: Terry Hoage, Anthony Toney, Roynell Young.

10 games: Ron Baker, Ken Clarke.

9 games: Mike Reichenbach.

8 games: Jerome Brown, Keith Byars, Elbert Foules.

7 games: Garry Cobb.

6 games: Mike Pitts.

5 games: William Frizzell, Dwayne Jiles.

4 games: Michael Haddix.

3 games: Eric Bailey*, Vic Bellamy*, Kevin Bowman*, Reggie Brown*, Byron Evans, Otis Grant*, Elois Grooms*, Angelo James*, Byron Lee*, Matt Long*, Randall Mitchell*, Mike Perrino*, Jacque Robinson*, Fred Smalls*, Scott Tinsley*, Pete Walters*, Jeff Wenzel*, Troy West*.

2 games: Matt Battaglia*, Jeff Griffin*, Scott Leggett*, Ray Phillips*.

1 game: Marvin Ayers*, Carlos Bradley*, Ray Conlin*, Evan Cooper, Chuck Gorecki*, Michael Kullman*, Bob Landsee, Dan McMillen*, Mike Nease*, Ben Tamburello, Junior Tautalatasi.

PHILADELPHIA EAGLES 1988 VETERAN ROSTER

No.	Name	Pos.	Ht.	Wt.	NFL Exp.	Birth-date	College	Games in '87	How Acquired
72	Alexander, David	T	6-3	275	2	7-28-64	Tulsa	12	OFA, '87
58	Allert, Ty	LB	6-2	233	3	7-23-63	Texas	*10	W-SD, '87
87	Bailey, Eric	TE	6-5	240	2	5-12-63	Kansas State	3	FA, '88
63	†Baker, Ron	G	6-4	274	11	11-19-54	Oklahoma State	10	T-Bal, '80
23	†Brown, Cedrick	CB	5-10	182	2	9- 6-64	Washington State	12	FA, '86
99	Brown, Jerome	DT	6-2	288	2	2- 4-65	Miami (Fla.)	12	D1, '87
41	Byars, Keith	RB	6-1	238	3	10-14-63	Ohio State	10	D1, '86
80	Carter, Cris	WR	6-3	194	2	11-25-65	Ohio State	9	SupD, '87
6	Cavanaugh, Matt	QB	6-2	210	11	10-27-56	Pittsburgh	3	T-SF, '86
27	Clemmons, Topper	RB	5-11	205	2	9-16-63	Wake Forest	3	FA, '88
50	†Cobb, Garry	LB	6-2	230	10	3-16-57	Southern California	12	T-Det, '85
79	†Conwell, Joe	T	6-5	286	3	2-24-61	North Carolina	12	T-SF, '86
21	Cooper, Evan	S	5-11	194	5	6-28-62	Michigan	12	D4, '84
45	Crawford, Charles	RB	6-2	243	2	3- 8-64	Oklahoma State	2	SupD, '86
12	†Cunningham, Randall	QB	6-4	201	4	3-27-63	Nevada-Las Vegas	12	D2, '85
78	Darwin, Matt	T	6-4	275	3	3-11-63	Texas A&M	12	D4, '86
	Dorsey, Dean	K	5-11	190	1	3-13-57	Univ. of Toronto	*16	FA, '88
93	Dumbauld, Jonathan	DE	6-4	259	3	2-14-63	Kentucky	6	W-NO, '87
56	Evans, Byron	LB	6-2	225	2	2-23-64	Arizona	12	D4, '87
67	Feehery, Gerry	C	6-2	270	6	3- 9-60	Syracuse	12	OFA, '83
29	Foules, Elbert	CB	5-11	193	6	7- 4-61	Alcorn State	9	OFA, '83
33	Frizzell, William	S	6-3	205	5	9- 8-62	North Carolina Central	12	FA, '86
86	Garrity, Gregg	WR	5-10	169	6	11-24-61	Penn State	12	FA, '84
38	Gary, Russell	S	5-11	200	8	7-31-59	Nebraska	12	FA, '87
83	†Giles, Jimmie	TE	6-3	240	12	11- 8-54	Alcorn State	*12	T-Det, '87
90	Golic, Mike	DE/DT	6-5	275	3	12-12-62	Notre Dame	*8	FA, '87
26	Haddix, Michael	RB	6-2	227	6	12-27-61	Mississippi State	12	D1, '83
34	†Hoage, Terry	S	6-3	201	5	4-11-62	Georgia	11	FA, '86
	Hoggard, D.D.	CB	6-0	188	3	5-20-61	North Carolina State	*1	T-Cle, '88
48	Hopkins, Wes	S	6-1	212	6	9-26-61	Southern Methodist	*0	D2, '83
53	†Jiles, Dwayne	LB	6-4	250	4	11-23-61	Texas Tech	9	D5, '85
54	Johnson, Alonzo	LB	6-3	222	3	4- 4-63	Florida	3	D2a, '86
85	Johnson, Ron	WR	6-3	186	4	9-21-58	Long Beach State	3	FA, '85
59	†Joyner, Seth	LB	6-2	248	3	11-18-64	Texas-El Paso	12	D8, '86
64	Kelley, Mike	G/C	6-5	280	2	2-27-62	Notre Dame	*1	FA, '87
97	Klingel, John	DE	6-3	267	2	12-21-63	Kentucky	5	OFA, '87
65	†Landsee, Bob	G/C	6-4	273	2	3-21-64	Wisconsin	2	D6, '86
89	†Little, Dave	TE	6-2	226	5	4-18-61	Middle Tennessee State	12	FA, '85
8	†McFadden, Paul	K	5-11	166	5	9-24-61	Youngstown State	12	D12, '84
36	Morse, Bobby	RB/KR	5-10	213	2	10- 3-65	Michigan State	11	D12, '87
74	Pitts, Mike	DT	6-5	277	6	9-25-60	Alabama	12	T-Atl, '87
82	Quick, Mike	WR	6-2	190	7	5-14-59	North Carolina State	12	D1, '82
66	†Reeves, Ken	T/G	6-5	270	4	10- 4-61	Texas A&M	10	D6, '85
55	Reichenbach, Mike	LB	6-2	230	5	9-14-61	East Stroudsburg	11	OFA, '84
	Reid, Alan	RB	5-8	197	1	9- 6-60	Minnesota	1	FA, '87
76	Schreiber, Adam	G	6-4	277	5	2-20-62	Texas	12	FA, '86
96	Simmons, Clyde	DE	6-6	276	3	8- 4-64	Western Carolina	12	D9, '86
68	Singletary, Reggie	G	6-3	280	3	1-17-64	North Carolina State	12	D12, '86
88	Spagnola, John	TE	6-4	242	9	8- 1-57	Yale	12	FA, '79
	Tamburello, Ben	G/C	6-3	278	1	9- 9-64	Auburn	2	D3, '87
37	Tautalatasi, Junior	RB	5-10	210	3	3-24-62	Washington State	12	D10, '86
10	Teltschik, John	P	6-2	209	3	3- 8-64	Texas	12	FA, '86
	Tinsley, Scott	QB	6-2	195	2	11-14-59	Southern California	3	FA, '88
25	Toney, Anthony	RB	6-0	227	3	9-23-62	Texas A&M	11	D2, '86
20	Waters, Andre	S	5-11	199	5	3-10-62	Cheyney	12	OFA, '84
	Wenzel, Jeff	T	6-7	270	2	10-21-63	Tulane	3	FA, '88
92	White, Reggie	DE	6-5	285	4	12-19-61	Tennessee	12	SupD, '84
43	Young, Roynell	CB	6-1	185	9	12- 1-57	Alcorn State	11	D1, '80

*Allert played 3 games with Chargers, 7 with Eagles in '87; Dorsey played 16 games with Ottawa-CFL in '87; Giles played 4 games with Lions, 8 with Eagles in '87; Golic played 2 games with Oilers, 6 with Eagles in '87; Hopkins missed '87 season due to injury; Hoggard played 1 game with Browns in '87; Kelley played 1 game with Oilers and inactive for 3 games with Eagles in '87.

†Option playout; subject to developments.

D—Draft; T—Trade; W—Waivers; FA—Free Agent; OFA—Original Free Agent; SupD—Supplemental Draft.

Also played with Eagles in '87, see page 386.

PHILADELPHIA EAGLES
1988 DRAFT CHOICES

(Number following name designates order of selection among 333 players drafted.)

Round and Player		Position	College
1. JACKSON, Keith	13	TE	Oklahoma
2. ALLEN, Eric from Tampa Bay (a)	30	DB	Arizona State
2. Choice to San Francisco through Tampa Bay (b)			
3. PATCHAN, Matt	64	T	Miami (Fla.)
4. Choice exercised in 1987 Supplemental Draft for Cris Carter, WR, Ohio State			
5. EVERETT, Eric	122	DB	Texas Tech
6. McPHERSON, Don	149	QB	Syracuse
6. STERLING, Rob from Cleveland (c)	160	DB	Maine
7. WHITE, Todd	176	WR	Fullerton State
8. SMITH, David	207	RB	Western Kentucky
9. Choice to Detroit (d)			
10. SCHUSTER, Joe	261	DT	Iowa
11. JENKINS, Izel	288	DB	North Carolina St.
12. KAUFUSI, Steve	319	DE	Brigham Young

(a) Acquired pick for 2nd- and 4th-round picks in 1988, April 24, 1988.

(b) Eagles traded pick to Buccaneers: See (a); Buccaneers traded pick to 49ers for 2nd- and 4th-round picks in 1988, April 24, 1988.

(c) Acquired pick, conditional pick in 1989 and cornerback D.D. Hoggard for rights to defensive tackle Chris Pike, March 25, 1988.

(d) Traded pick for tight end Jimmie Giles, November 3, 1987.

PHILADELPHIA EAGLES
1988 ROOKIE AND FIRST-YEAR ROSTER

Name	Pos.	Hgt.	Wgt.	Birth-date	College	How Acquired
Allen, Eric	CB	5-10	181	11-11-65	Arizona State	D2
Anglim, Patrick	G	6-4	255	4- 6-65	Connecticut	FA
Antoine, Tamlin	WR	5-11	185	9-25-64	Morehouse	FA
Booker, Martin	WR	6-1	191	3- 8-63	Villanova	*FA, '86
Curtis, Scott	LB	6-1	230	12-26-64	New Hampshire	FA
Everett, Eric	CB	5-10	161	7-13-66	Texas Tech	D5
Folkertsma, David	DT	6-5	255	8-31-65	Michigan	FA
Gilmore, Corey	RB	6-1	220	12- 9-64	San Diego State	*FA
Giongo, Michael	LB	6-2	245	12-27-64	Syracuse	FA
Hedgeman, Karl	LB	6-4	242	10-18-63	Iowa	FA
Jackson, Keith	TE	6-2	250	4-19-65	Oklahoma	D1
Jackson, Troy	LB	6-2	225	4-12-64	Indiana, Pennsylvania	FA
Jenkins, Izel	CB	5-10	191	5-27-64	North Carolina State	D11
Kaufusi, Steve	DE	6-4	260	10-17-63	Brigham Young	D12
Lambiotte, Ken	QB	6-3	191	10-17-63	William & Mary	*D9, '87
Loving, James	WR	5-9	180	6-22-66	Wyoming	FA
McPherson, Don	QB	6-1	183	4- 2-65	Syracuse	D6
Moten, Ron	LB	6-1	230	9-15-64	Florida	*D6, '87
Patchan, Matt	T	6-4	275	8-11-65	Miami (Fla.)	D3
Powers, Scott	P	6-2	185	10- 5-65	Williams	FA
Schuster, Joe	DT	6-4	260	12-30-64	Iowa	D10
Smith, David	RB	6-1	225	11- 3-65	Western Kentucky	D8
Sterling, Rob	CB/S	5-11	195	2-11-66	Maine	D6a
Tiller, Bruce	WR	6-2	188	5-10-63	Kutztown State	*FA
Walsh, Steven	T/G/C	6-4	315	3-22-65	Western Kentucky	FA
White, Todd	WR/KR	6-0	196	9-15-65	Fullerton State	D7
Widmeyer, Kelly	T	6-7	315	7- 3-60	Weber State	FA
Yates, Bo	LB	6-1	222	1- 2-65	Washington	FA

*Booker missed '86 and '87 seasons due to injury; Gilmore: FA Pittsburgh '87, released 8/24, FA replacement Cleveland 9/23, released 10/15; Lambiotte and Moten missed '87 season due to injury; Tiller: FA Cleveland '87, released 8/9, FA San Francisco '88, released 5/10, FA Philadelphia 5/21.

PHOENIX CARDINALS
(Eastern Division, National Conference)

Gene Stallings

Chairman/President—William V. Bidwill
Vice-President—Curt Mosher
Director of Pro Personnel—Larry Wilson
Director of Player Personnel—George Boone
Head Coach—Gene Stallings (2 years: 11-19-1)
Assistant Coaches:
  Special Teams—Marv Braden
  Offensive Line—Tom Bresnahan
  Strength & Conditioning—LeBaron Caruthers
  Defensive Line—Jim Johnson
  Running Backs—Hank Kuhlmann
  Special Assistant/Quality Control—Leon McLaughlin
  Receivers—Mal Moore
  Linebackers—Joe Pascale
  Offensive Coordinator—Jim Shofner
  Defensive Backs—Dennis Thurman
Director of Public Relations—Bob Rose
  (Office Phone: 967-1010—Area Code 602)
Offices—51 W. Third, Tempe, Ariz. 85281
Stadium—Sun Devil Stadium (Capacity: 72,000)
Team Colors—Cardinal Red, Black and White
Training Site—Northern Arizona University, Flagstaff, Ariz.

1988 SCHEDULE
(All times local.
All games Sunday unless noted otherwise.)

Sept.	4	at Cincinnati	1:00
Sept.	12	DALLAS (Mon.)	6:00
Sept.	18	at Tampa Bay	1:00
Sept.	25	WASHINGTON	1:00
Oct.	2	at Los Angeles Rams	1:00
Oct.	9	PITTSBURGH	1:00
Oct.	16	at Washington	1:00
Oct.	23	CLEVELAND	1:00
Oct.	30	at Dallas	12:00
Nov.	6	SAN FRANCISCO	2:00
Nov.	13	NEW YORK GIANTS	2:00
Nov.	20	at Houston	12:00
Nov.	27	at Philadelphia	1:00
Dec.	4	at New York Giants	1:00
Dec.	10	PHILADELPHIA (Sat.)	2:00
Dec.	18	GREEN BAY	2:00

1987 RESULTS—(Won 7, Lost 8)

Cardinals		Opp.		Att.
24	Dallas	13	(H)	47,241
24	San Diego	28	(A)	47,988
	Indianapolis*		(H)	
21	*Washington*	*28*	*(A)*	*27,728*
24	*New Orleans*	*19*	*(H)*	*11,795*
28	*San Francisco*	*34*	*(A)*	*38,094*
7	New York Giants	30	(A)	74,391
23	Philadelphia	28	(H)	24,586
31	Tampa Bay	28	(H)	22,449
24	L.A. Rams	27	(H)	27,730
31	Philadelphia	19	(A)	55,592
34	Atlanta	21	(A)	15,909
17	Washington	34	(H)	31,324
27	New York Giants	24	(H)	29,623
31	Tampa Bay	14	(A)	32,046
16	Dallas	21	(A)	36,788

*Game cancelled due to strike.
Italics denote strike replacement games.

1987 GAMES STARTED

(NOTE: Players with an asterisk (*) following their names made starts only in strike-replacement games.)

15 games: Lance Smith, Leonard Smith.

14 games: Tootie Robbins, J.T. Smith.

13 games: E.J. Junior.

12 games: Anthony Bell, Carl Carter, Bob Clasby, Roy Green, Neil Lomax, Stump Mitchell, Niko Noga, Freddie Joe Nunn, Luis Sharpe, Lonnie Young.

11 games: Earl Ferrell, Derek Kinnard.

10 games: Cedric Mack.

9 games: Robert Awalt, Curtis Greer.

8 games: Todd Peat.

6 games: Steve Alvord.

4 games: Joe Bostic, Mark Jackson, Jay Novacek, Ron Wolfley.

3 games: Charlie Baker, Ron Bohm*, Ray Brown*, Mark Duda, Gary Dulin*, David Galloway, Mark Garalczyk*, William Harris*, Peter Noga*, Keith Radecic*, Rod Saddler, Colin Scotts, Tom Welter*.

2 games: Shawn Halloran*, Troy Johnson*, Tony Mayes*, Derrick McAdoo*, Ken Sims*.

1 game: Tony Buford*, Travis Curtis*, Wayne Davis, Sammy Garza*, Johnny Holloway, Don Holmes, Mark Mathis*, Mike Ruether, Broderick Sargent*, Charles Vatterott*.

PHOENIX CARDINALS 1988 VETERAN ROSTER

No.	Name	Pos.	Ht.	Wt.	NFL Exp.	Birth-date	College	Games in '87	How Acquired
60	Alvord, Steve	DT	6-4	272	2	10- 2-64	Washington	12	D8, '87
80	Awalt, Robert	TE	6-5	248	2	4- 9-64	San Diego State	12	D3, '87
52	Baker, Charlie	LB	6-2	234	9	9-26-57	New Mexico	14	D3a, '80
55	Bell, Anthony	LB	6-3	231	3	7- 2-64	Michigan State	12	D1, '86
71	Bostic, Joe	G	6-3	268	10	4-20-57	Clemson	9	D3, '79
62	Brown, Ray	G/T	6-5	280	3	12-12-62	Arkansas State	7	D8, '86
82	Brown, Ron	WR	5-10	186	2	1-11-63	Colorado	3	FA, '87
41	Carter, Carl	CB	5-11	180	3	3- 7-64	Texas Tech	12	D4, '86
74	Chilton, Gene	T	6-3	271	3	3-27-64	Texas	11	D3, '86
79	†Clasby, Bob	DT	6-5	260	3	9-28-60	Notre Dame	12	FA, '86
20	Curtis, Travis	S	5-10	180	2	9-27-65	West Virginia	13	OFA, '87
53	Davis, Wayne	LB	6-1	213	2	3-10-64	Alabama	12	D9, '87
17	Del Greco, Al	K	5-10	191	5	3- 2-62	Auburn	*8	FA, '87
73	Duda, Mark	DT	6-3	279	6	2- 4-61	Maryland	3	D4, '83
31	†Ferrell, Earl	RB	6-0	240	7	3-27-58	East Tennessee State	11	D5a, '82
13	Gallery, Jim	K	6-1	190	2	9-15-61	Minnesota	13	FA, '87
65	Galloway, David	DE	6-3	279	7	2-16-59	Florida	4	D2, '82
76	Garalczyk, Mark	DT	6-5	272	2	8-12-65	Western Michigan	11	D6, '87
10	Garza, Sammy	QB	6-1	184	2	9-30-65	Texas-El Paso	2	FA, '87
81	Green, Roy	WR	6-0	195	10	6-30-57	Henderson State	12	D4, '79
75	Greer, Curtis	DE	6-4	258	8	11-10-57	Michigan	10	D1, '80
89	Harris, William	TE	6-4	243	2	2-10-65	Texas	10	D7a, '87
82	†Holmes, Don	WR	5-10	180	3	4- 1-61	Mesa College (Colo.)	11	FA, '86
11	Horne, Greg	P	6-0	188	2	11-22-64	Arkansas	*9	FA, '87
21	Jackson, Mark	CB	5-9	180	2	3-16-62	Abilene Christian	11	OFA, '87
50	Jarostchuk, Ilia	LB	6-3	231	2	8- 1-64	New Hampshire	12	D5b, '87
27	†Johnson, Greggory	CB/S	6-1	195	6	10-20-58	Oklahoma State	8	FA, '87
87	†Johnson, Troy	WR	6-1	175	3	10-20-62	Southern	14	FA, '86
	Jones, Tyrone	LB	6-0	220	R	8- 3-61	Southern	*18	FA, '88
54	Junior, E. J.	LB	6-3	235	8	12- 8-59	Alabama	13	D1, '81
70	Kennard, Derek	C	6-3	285	3	9- 9-62	Nevada-Reno	12	SupD, '84
15	Lomax, Neil	QB	6-3	215	8	2-17-59	Portland State	12	D2, '81
47	†Mack, Cedric	CB	6-0	194	6	9-14-60	Baylor	10	D2, '83
	Mack, Terence	LB	6-3	240	2	9- 9-64	Clemson	5	FA, '88
33	McAdoo, Derrick	RB	5-10	198	2	4- 2-65	Baylor	15	OFA, '87
46	McDonald, Tim	S	6-2	207	2	1- 6-65	Southern California	3	D2, '87
30	Mitchell, Stump	RB	5-9	188	8	3-15-59	The Citadel	12	D9, '81
	Moore, Ricky	FB	5-11	253	3	4-7-63	Alabama	*3	FA, '88
68	Morris, Michael	G	6-5	275	2	2-22-61	Northeast Missouri St.	14	OFA, '87
	Neighbors, Wes	C	6-2	250	1	2-28-64	Alabama	*0	FA, '88
57	Noga, Niko	LB	6-1	235	5	3- 2-62	Hawaii	12	D8, '84
85	†Novacek, Jay	TE	6-4	235	4	10-24-62	Wyoming	7	D6, '85
78	Nunn, Freddie Joe	DE	6-4	255	4	4- 9-62	Mississippi	12	D1, '85
64	Peat, Todd	G	6-2	294	2	5-20-64	Northern Illinois	12	D11, '87
63	Robbins, Tootie	T	6-5	302	7	6- 2-58	East Carolina	14	D4, '82
	Royals, Mark	P	6-5	216	1	6-22-63	Appalachian State	*2	FA, '88
51	†Ruether, Mike	C	6-4	275	3	9-20-62	Texas	12	SupD, '84
72	Saddler, Rod	DE	6-5	276	2	9-26-65	Texas A&M	12	D4, '87
39	†Sargent, Broderick	RB	5-10	215	3	9-16-62	Baylor	15	OFA, '86
69	Scotts, Colin	DT	6-5	263	2	4-26-63	Hawaii	7	D3a, '87
67	Sharpe, Luis	T	6-4	260	7	6-16-60	UCLA	12	D1, '82
36	Sikahema, Vai	RB/KR	5-9	191	3	8-29-62	Brigham Young	15	D10, '86
84	Smith, J.T.	WR	6-2	185	11	10-29-55	North Texas State	15	FA, '85
61	Smith, Lance	G	6-2	262	4	11- 1-63	Louisiana State	15	D3, '85
45	Smith, Leonard	S	5-11	202	6	9- 2-60	McNeese State	15	D1, '83
18	†Stoudt, Cliff	QB	6-4	215	10	3-27-55	Youngstown State	12	T-Pit, '86
	Thurman, Junior	DB	6-1	180	2	9- 8-64	Southern California	*3	FA, '88
	Van Dyke, Ralph	T	6-6	270	1	1-19-64	Southern Illinois	*2	FA, '88
	Vatterott, Charles	OL	6-4	263	2	1-31-64	Southwest Texas State	2	FA, '87
66	Welter, Tom	T	6-5	280	2	2-24-64	Nebraska	3	OFA, '87
24	†Wolfley, Ron	RB	6-0	222	4	10-14-62	West Virginia	12	D4, '85
43	Young, Lonnie	S	6-1	182	4	7-18-63	Michigan State	12	D12, '85

*Del Greco played 5 games with Packers, 3 with Cardinals in '87; Horne played 4 games with Bengals, 5 with Cardinals in '87; Jones played 18 games with Winnipeg-CFL in '87; Moore played 3 games with Oilers in '87; Neighbors active for 1 game with Colts in '87, but did not play; Royals played 1 game with Cardinals and 1 game with Eagles in '87; Thurman played 3 games with Saints in '87; Van Dyke played 2 games with Browns in '87.
†Option playout; subject to developments.

D—Draft; T—Trade; FA—Free Agent; OFA—Original Free Agent; SupD—Supplemental Draft.
Also played with Cardinals in '87, see page 386.

PHOENIX CARDINALS
1988 DRAFT CHOICES

(Number following name designates order of selection among 333 players drafted.)

Round and Player		Position	College
1. HARVEY, Ken	12	LB	California
2. JEFFERY, Tony	38	RB	Texas Christian
3. TUPA, Tom	68	P	Ohio State
4. BRIM, Michael	95	DB	Virginia Union
5. GAINES, Chris from Dallas through Seattle (a)	120	LB	Vanderbilt
5. Choice to Pittsburgh (b)			
5. JORDAN, Tony from Cleveland (c)	132	RB	Kansas State
6. PHILLIPS, Jon	148	G	Oklahoma
7. JONES, Ernie	179	WR	Indiana
8. MOORE, Tim	206	LB	Michigan State
9. DILL, Scott	233	G	Memphis State
10. SCHILLINGER, Andy	260	WR	Miami (O.)
11. McCOY, Keith	291	DB	Fresno State
12. CARRIER, Chris	318	DB	Louisiana State

(a) Seahawks acquired pick from Cowboys for tackle Ron Essink, August 25, 1987;
Cardinals acquired pick and 1st- and 5th-round picks in 1989 from Seahawks for
rights to quarterback Kelly Stouffer, April 22, 1988.

(b) Traded pick for quarterback Cliff Stoudt, September 2, 1986.

(c) Acquired pick for defensive end Al Baker, September 3, 1987.

PHOENIX CARDINALS
1988 ROOKIE AND FIRST-YEAR ROSTER

Name	Pos.	Hgt.	Wgt.	Birth-date	College	How Acquired
Andrews, Derek	LB	6-2	228	6-20-64	Delaware State	FA
Bates, Mike	QB	6-3	200	7- 2-65	Miami (O.)	FA
Belton, Steve	S	6-0	190	4-10-65	Nebraska-Omaha	FA
Brim, Michael	CB	6-0	186	1-23-66	Virginia Union	D4
Brown, Willie	DB	5-9	180	1- 3-65	Grambling	FA
Camper, Scott	DT	6-3	260	10-27-65	Montana	FA
Carrier, Chris	S	6-5	215	4- 4-64	Louisiana State	D12
Clement, John	G	6-4	280	2- 5-66	Northeast Louisiana	FA
Connors, Michael	T	6-4	275	7-11-65	Purdue	FA
Davis, Lorenzo	RB	5-10	190	1-25-66	DuPage	FA
Dill, Scott	G	6-5	272	4- 5-66	Memphis State	D9
Dorsey, Alfred	WR	5-7	169	7-19-65	Nicholls State	FA
Gaines, Chris	LB	6-0	238	2- 3-65	Vanderbilt	D5
Haggerty, Richard	DT	6-2	270	4-18-65	Oregon State	FA
Hardy, Anthony	WR	5-9	162	4-13-66	Purdue	FA
Harvey, Ken	LB	6-2	225	5- 6-65	California	D1
Henry, Calvin	CB	5-10	190	1-23-65	New Mexico State	FA
Jeffery, Tony	RB	5-11	208	7- 8-64	Texas Christian	D2
Jenkins, Alfred	TE	6-4	227	4- 1-64	Arizona	*FA
Johnson, Michael	DT	6-2	270	9-19-63	Temple	FA
Johnson, Scott	LB	6-2	230	10-13-64	Northern Arizona	FA
Jones, Ernie	WR	5-11	186	12-15-64	Indiana	D7
Jones, Lee	DE	6-1	255	10-12-64	Nebraska	FA
Jordan, Tony	RB	6-2	220	5- 5-65	Kansas State	D5a
Lane, Fred	WR	5-8	157	2-27-65	Georgia	*FA, '87
Maynard, Scot	WR	6-0	185	2-10-64	Texas-El Paso	*FA
McCoy, Keith	CB	5-11	172	11-27-64	Fresno State	D11
Mimbs, Robert	RB	5-10	197	8- 6-64	Kansas	*FA
Moore, Tim	LB	6-2	218	1- 1-65	Michigan State	D8
Peoples, Tim	DB	6-0	200	7-26-64	Washington	*D7, '87
Phillips, Jon	G	6-3	280	12-30-64	Oklahoma	D6
Rogers, Rodney	S	6-1	195	1-11-65	Colorado	FA
Schillinger, Andy	WR	5-11	179	11-22-64	Miami (O.)	D10
Simmons, Michael	DT	6-4	280	11-14-65	Mississippi State	FA
Spachman, Chris	DT	6-5	275	12-25-63	Nebraska	*FA
Tupa, Tom	QB-P	6-4	220	9- 6-66	Ohio State	D3
Wahlheim, Pete	S	6-1	205	9-27-64	Southern Utah State	FA
Webster, Kennedy	DB	6-1	200	11-28-63	Texas-El Paso	*FA
Wilburn, Fred	DB	5-10	185	6-30-63	Fresno State	FA

*Jenkins: D9 Washington '87, injured reserve 9/1 through 10/26, released 10/27, FA San Francisco '88, released 5/10: Lane: FA Atlanta '87, released 8/5, FA replacement St. Louis 9/25, left squad 10/5, reserve/left squad 10/29 through remainder of season; Maynard: FA San Francisco '87, released 7/29; Mimbs: FA Dallas '86, released 8/18, FA New York Jets '87, released 8/10, FA replacement St. Louis 9/25 (on inactive list for 1 game), released 10/20; Peoples missed '87 season due to injury; Spachman: FA Washington '87, injured reserve 9/1 through 11/16, released 11/17; Webster: FA replacement Denver 9/25/87, released 10/2.

PITTSBURGH STEELERS
(Central Division, American Conference)

Chuck Noll

Chairman of the Board—Arthur J. Rooney
President—Daniel M. Rooney
Vice-President—John R. McGinley
Vice-President—Arthur J. Rooney, Jr.
Director of Player Personnel—Dick Haley
Head Coach—Chuck Noll (19 years: 163-114-1)
Assistant Coaches:
   Offensive Line (Tackles/Tight Ends)—Ron Blackledge
   Defensive Coordinator—Tony Dungy
   Special Teams/Def. Asst.—Dennis Fitzgerald
   Defensive Line—Joe Greene
   Offensive Backfield—Dick Hoak
   Linebackers—Jed Hughes
   Offensive Line (Centers/Guards)—Hal Hunter
   Special Teams/Off. Asst.—Jon Kolb
   Offensive Coordinator—Tom Moore
   Receivers—Dwain Painter
Publicity Director—Dan Edwards
   (Office Phone: 323-1200—Area Code 412)
Offices—Three Rivers Stadium, 300 Stadium Circle, Pittsburgh, Pa. 15212
Stadium—Three Rivers Stadium (Capacity: 59,000)
Colors—Black and Gold
Training Site—St. Vincent's College, Latrobe, Pa.

1988 SCHEDULE
(All times local.
All games Sunday unless noted otherwise.)

Sept. 4	DALLAS	1:00
Sept. 11	at Washington	1:00
Sept. 18	CINCINNATI	1:00
Sept. 25	at Buffalo	1:00
Oct. 2	CLEVELAND	1:00
Oct. 9	at Phoenix	1:00
Oct. 16	HOUSTON	1:00
Oct. 23	DENVER	1:00
Oct. 30	at New York Jets	1:00
Nov. 6	at Cincinnati	1:00
Nov. 13	PHILADELPHIA	1:00
Nov. 20	at Cleveland	1:00
Nov. 27	KANSAS CITY	1:00
Dec. 4	at Houston	7:00
Dec. 11	at San Diego	1:00
Dec. 18	MIAMI	1:00

1987 RESULTS—(Won 8, Lost 7)

Steelers		Opp.		Att.
30	San Francisco	17	(H)	55,735
10	Cleveland	34	(A)	79,543
	New York Jets*		(H)	
28	*Atlanta*	*12*	*(A)*	*16,667*
21	*L.A. Rams*	*31*	*(A)*	*20,218*
21	*Indianapolis*	*7*	*(H)*	*34,627*
23	Cincinnati	20	(H)	53,692
24	Miami	35	(A)	52,578
17	Kansas City	16	(A)	45,249
3	Houston	23	(H)	56,177
30	Cincinnati	16	(A)	52,795
16	New Orleans	20	(H)	47,896
13	Seattle	9	(H)	48,881
20	San Diego	16	(A)	51,605
16	Houston	24	(A)	38,683
13	Cleveland	19	(H)	56,394

*Game cancelled due to strike.
Italics denote strike replacement games.

1987 GAMES STARTED
(NOTE: Players with an asterisk (*) following their names made starts only in strike-replacement games.)

15 games: Mike Webster.

13 games: Gary Dunn, Danzell Lee, Terry Long, Donnie Shell.

12 games: Walter Abercrombie, Robin Cole, Delton Hall, Bryan Hinkle, David Little, Mark Malone, Mike Merriweather, Craig Wolfley, Dwayne Woodruff.

11 games: Tunch Ilkin, John Stallworth.

10 games: Keith Willis.

9 games: Thomas Everett, Earnest Jackson.

8 games: Edmund Nelson.

7 games: Frank Pollard.

6 games: Keith Gary, Ray Pinney, Calvin Sweeney.

5 games: Buddy Aydelette.

3 games: Steve Apke*, Craig Bingham*, Brian Blankenship*, Steve Bono*, Jim Boyle*, Joey Clinkscales*, Dave Edwards*, Cornell Gowdy*, Larry Griffin*, Jeff Lucas*, Lupe Sanchez, Tyronne Stowe*, Weegie Thompson, Bert Williams*.

2 games: Rodney Carter*, Tommy Dawkins*, Preston Gothard, Russell Hairston*, Louis Lipps, Michael Minter*, Ted Petersen*, John Rienstra, Cameron Riley*.

1 game: Lyneal Alston*, Alan Huff*, Charles Lockett, Dave Opfar*, Bret Shugarts*, Gerald Williams*, Theo Young.

PITTSBURGH STEELERS 1988 VETERAN ROSTER

No.	Name	Pos.	Ht.	Wt.	NFL Exp.	Birth-date	College	Games in '87	How Acquired
34	Abercrombie, Walter	RB	6-0	210	7	9-26-59	Baylor	12	D1, '82
81	Alston, Lyneal	WR	6-1	205	2	7-23-64	Southern Mississippi	3	OFA, '87
1	Anderson, Gary	K	5-11	170	7	7-16-59	Syracuse	12	W-Buf, '82
72	Aydelette, Buddy	T/C	6-4	262	3	8-19-56	Alabama	12	W-Min, '87
66	Behning, Mark	T	6-6	277	2	9-26-61	Nebraska	*0	D2, '85
	Blackledge, Todd	QB	6-3	223	6	2-25-61	Penn State	*3	T-KC,'88
60	Blankenship, Brian	G/C	6-1	281	2	4- 7-63	Nebraska	13	FA, '87
15	Bono, Steve	QB	6-4	215	4	5-11-62	UCLA	3	FA, '87
65	Boyle, Jim	T	6-5	270	2	7-27-62	Tulane	3	FA, '88
6	Brister, Bubby	QB	6-3	195	3	8-15-62	Northeast Louisiana	2	D3, '86
10	Bruno, John	P	6-2	190	2	9-10-64	Penn State	3	FA, '88
91	†Carr, Gregg	LB	6-2	224	4	3-31-62	Auburn	12	D6, '85
44	Carter, Rodney	RB	6-0	212	2	10-30-64	Purdue	11	D7, '86
88	Clinkscales, Joey	WR	6-0	204	2	5-21-64	Tennessee	7	D9, '87
56	Cole, Robin	LB	6-2	225	12	9-11-55	New Mexico	12	D1, '77
67	Dunn, Gary	NT	6-3	278	12	8-24-53	Miami (Fla.)	13	D6, '76
27	Everett, Thomas	S	5-9	179	2	11-21-64	Baylor	12	D4, '87
68	Freeman, Lorenzo	NT/DT	6-5	270	2	5-23-64	Pittsburgh	6	FA, '87
92	†Gary, Keith	DE	6-3	260	6	9-14-59	Oklahoma	11	D1, '81
86	Gothard, Preston	TE	6-4	242	4	2-23-62	Alabama	2	OFA, '85
29	Gowdy, Cornell	S/CB	6-1	197	3	10- 2-63	Morgan State	13	FA, '87
22	Griffin, Larry	S/CB	6-0	199	3	1-11-63	North Carolina	7	FA, '87
35	Hall, Delton	CB	6-1	205	2	1-16-65	Clemson	12	D2, '87
96	Henton, Anthony	LB	6-1	234	2	7-27-63	Troy State	*0	D9, '86
53	Hinkle, Bryan	LB	6-2	215	7	6- 4-59	Oregon	12	D6, '81
33	Hoge, Merril	RB	6-2	212	2	1-26-65	Idaho State	13	D10, '87
62	Ilkin, Tunch	T	6-3	265	9	9-23-57	Indiana State	11	D6, '80
43	Jackson, Earnest	RB	5-9	219	6	12-18-59	Texas A&M	12	FA, '86
78	Johnson, Tim	DE/DT	6-3	260	2	1-29-65	Penn State	12	D6, '87
84	Lee, Danzell	TE	6-2	229	2	3-16-63	Lamar	13	FA, '87
83	Lipps, Louis	WR	5-10	190	5	8- 9-62	Southern Mississippi	4	D1, '84
50	Little, David	LB	6-1	230	8	1- 3-59	Florida	12	D7, '81
89	Lockett, Charles	WR	6-0	179	2	10- 1-65	Long Beach State	11	D3, '87
74	Long, Terry	G	5-11	275	5	7-21-59	East Carolina	13	D4a, '84
	Lucas, Jeff	T	6-7	288	2	5-30-64	West Virginia	3	OFA, '87
57	Merriweather, Mike	LB	6-2	221	7	11-26-60	Pacific	12	D3, '82
	Minter, Michael	DT	6-3	275	2	8-13-65	North Texas State	3	FA, '88
18	Newsome, Harry	P	6-0	189	4	1-25-63	Wake Forest	12	D8, '85
54	Nickerson, Hardy	LB	6-2	224	2	9- 1-65	California	12	D5, '87
30	Pollard, Frank	RB	5-10	230	9	6-15-57	Baylor	12	D11, '80
76	Quick, Jerry	T/G	6-5	273	2	12-30-63	Wichita State	1	FA, '86
79	Rienstra, John	G	6-5	269	3	3-22-63	Temple	12	D1, '86
47	Riley, Cameron	S	6-1	195	1	5-13-64	Missouri	2	FA, '88
28	Sanchez, Lupe	S/KR	5-10	195	3	10-28-61	UCLA	12	FA, '86
20	Stone, Dwight	RB/KR	6-0	188	2	1-28-64	Middle Tennessee State	14	OFA, '87
90	Stowe, Tyronne	LB	6-1	232	2	5-30-65	Rutgers	13	FA, '87
87	†Thompson, Weegie	WR	6-6	210	5	3-21-61	Florida State	12	D4, '84
52	Webster, Mike	C	6-2	254	15	3-18-52	Wisconsin	15	D5, '74
98	Williams, Gerald	DE/DT	6-3	270	3	9- 3-63	Auburn	9	D2, '86
93	Willis, Keith	DE	6-1	260	7	7-29-59	Northeastern	11	OFA, '82
73	Wolfley, Craig	G	6-1	272	9	5-19-58	Syracuse	12	D5, '80
49	†Woodruff, Dwayne	CB	6-0	198	9	2-18-57	Louisville	12	D6a, '79
26	Woodson, Rod	CB/S/KR	6-0	202	2	3-10-65	Purdue	8	D1, '87
80	Young, Theo	TE	6-2	237	2	4-25-65	Arkansas	12	D12, '87

*Behning and Henton missed '87 season due to injury; Blackledge played 3 games with Chiefs in '87.
†Option playout; subject to developments.
Retired—Donnie Shell, 14-year safety, 13 games in '87; John Stallworth, 14-year wide receiver, 12 games in '87.
D—Draft; T—Trade; W—Waivers; FA—Free Agent; OFA—Original Free Agent.
Also played with Steelers in '87, see page 386.

PITTSBURGH STEELERS
1988 DRAFT CHOICES

(Number following name designates order of selection among 333 players drafted.)

Round and Player		Position	College
1. JONES, Aaron	18	DE	Eastern Kentucky
2. DAWSON, Dermontti	44	G	Kentucky
3. LANZA, Chuck	70	C	Notre Dame
4. Choice to Kansas City (a)			
5. JORDAN, Darin	121	LB	Northeastern
from Phoenix (b)			
5. REESE, Jerry	128	NT	Kentucky
6. WILLIAMS, Warren	155	RB	Miami (Fla.)
7. ZENO, Marc	182	WR	Tulane
8. NICHOLS, Mark	209	NT	Michigan State
8. HINNANT, Mike	211	TE	Temple
from San Diego (c)			
9. LOCKBAUM, Gordie	236	RB	Holy Cross
10. JACKSON, John	252	T	Eastern Kentucky
from Tampa Bay (d)			
10. Choice to Denver			
11. DAWSON, Bobby	295	DB	Illinois
12. EARLE, James	322	LB	Clemson

(a) Traded pick for quarterback Todd Blackledge, March 29, 1988.

(b) Acquired pick for quarterback Cliff Stoudt, September 2, 1986.

(c) Acquired pick and conditional 1989 pick for quarterback Mark Malone, April 12, 1988.

(d) Acquired pick for safety Rick Woods, September 1, 1987.

PITTSBURGH STEELERS
1988 ROOKIE AND FIRST-YEAR ROSTER

Name	Pos.	Hgt.	Wgt.	Birth-date	College	How Acquired
Bain, Tolbert	S	6-2	207	7-29-64	Miami (Fla.)	FA
Calcagno, Jim	T	6-4	270	10 -1-65	Southwestern Louisiana	FA
Clark, David	RB	6-0	205	10- 7-62	Penn State	*FA
Cobb, Brian	WR	6-0	183	2-12-66	Rutgers	FA
Dawson, Bobby	S	5-11	211	2-18-86	Illinois	D11
Dawson, Dermontti	C/G	6-2	272	6-17-65	Kentucky	D2
Dominic, Jim	DL	6-2	260	7-20-65	Syracuse	FA
Earle, James	LB	6-4	224	3-26-66	Clemson	D12
Gainer, Herb	WR	6-2	195	8-25-65	Florida State	FA
Garczynski, Andy	WR	6-0	205	6- 2-66	Temple	FA
Giftopoulos, Pete	LB	6-3	240	6-14-65	Penn State	FA
Green, Jonathan	RB	5-11	201	7-25-63	Waynesburg	FA
Hinnant, Mike	TE	6-3	254	9- 8-66	Temple	D8a
Jackson, John	T	6-6	287	1- 4-65	Eastern Kentucky	D10
Jones, Aaron	DE	6-5	258	12-18-66	Eastern Kentucky	D1
Jones, Earnest	RB	5-9	210	10-15-64	Virginia Tech	FA
Jordan, Darin	LB	6-1	245	12- 4-64	Northeastern	D5
Lanza, Chuck	C	6-2	270	9-20-64	Notre Dame	D3
Lee, Greg	CB/S	6-1	204	1-15-65	Arkansas State	FA
Lloyd, Greg	LB	6-2	224	5-26-65	Fort Valley State	*D6-'87
Lockbaum, Gordie	RB	5-11	195	11-16-65	Holy Cross	D9
Markland, Jeff	TE	6-3	245	11-16-65	Illinois	FA
Mattioli, Keith	WR	5-11	175	6 -6-65	Virginia	FA
Nichols, Mark	DT	6-2	262	8-29-64	Michigan State	D8
Osborn, Cassius	WR	6-0	192	8-26-66	Georgia	FA
Reese, Jerry	DT/DE	6-2	270	7-11-64	Kentucky	D5a
Sindlinger, Mark	C	6-1	250	2-15-65	Iowa	FA
Sistrunk, Dwight	S	6-1	185	12-12-64	Iowa	FA
Strom, Rick	QB	6-3	206	3-11-65	Georgia Tech	FA
Walker, Chad	LB	6-2	223	8-11-66	Arkansas Tech	FA
Williams, Al	LB	6-5	237	6-17-65	James Madison	FA
Williams, Warren	RB	6-0	203	7-29-65	Miami (Fla.)	D6
Zeno, Marc	WR	6-3	202	5-21-65	Tulane	D7

*Clark: FA Buffalo '87, released 7/30; Lloyd missed '87 season due to injury.

SAN DIEGO CHARGERS
(Western Division, American Conference)

Al Saunders

Chairman of the Board/President—Alex G. Spanos
Vice-Chairman—Dean A. Spanos
Director of Football Operations—Steve Ortmayer
Director of Administration—Jack Teele
Director of Player Personnel—Chet Franklin
Assistant to Chairman—Warren Jones
Head Coach—Al Saunders (2 years: 11-12)
Assistant Coaches:
  Assistant Coach—Gunther Cunningham
  Assistant Coach—Mike Haluchak
  Assistant Coach—Bobby Jackson
  Assistant Coach—Charlie Joiner
  Assistant Coach—Dave Levy
  Defensive Coordinator—Ron Lynn
  Defensive Assistant—Jim Mora, Jr.
  Offensive Coordinator—Jerry Rhome
  Special Teams—Wayne Sevier
  Strength Coach—Phil Tyne
  Assistant Coach—Jerry Wampfler
Public Relations Director—Rick Smith
  (Office Phone: 280-2111—Area Code 619)
Offices—San Diego Jack Murphy Stadium, P. O. Box 20666, San Diego, Calif. 92120
Stadium—San Diego Jack Murphy Stadium (Capacity: 60,750)
Team Colors—Navy Blue, White and Gold
Training Site—University of California, San Diego

1988 SCHEDULE
(All times local.
All games Sunday unless noted otherwise.)

Sept. 4	at Los Angeles Raiders	1:00
Sept. 11	at Denver	2:00
Sept. 18	SEATTLE	1:00
Sept. 25	at Kansas City	3:00
Oct. 2	DENVER	1:00
Oct. 9	NEW ORLEANS	1:00
Oct. 16	at Miami	1:00
Oct. 23	INDIANAPOLIS	1:00
Oct. 30	at Seattle	1:00
Nov. 6	LOS ANGELES RAIDERS	5:00
Nov. 13	at Atlanta	1:00
Nov. 20	at Los Angeles Rams	1:00
Nov. 27	SAN FRANCISCO	1:00
Dec. 4	at Cincinnati	1:00
Dec. 11	PITTSBURGH	1:00
Dec. 18	KANSAS CITY	1:00

1987 RESULTS—(Won 8, Lost 7)

Chargers	Opp.		Att.
13 Kansas City	20	(A)	56,940
28 St. Louis	24	(H)	47,988
Seattle*		(H)	
10 Cincinnati	*9*	*(A)*	*18,074*
17 Tampa Bay	*13*	*(A)*	*23,873*
23 L.A. Raiders	*17*	*(A)*	*23,541*
42 Kansas City	21	(H)	47,972
27 Cleveland (OT)	24	(H)	55,381
16 Indianapolis	13	(A)	60,459
16 L.A. Raiders	14	(H)	60,639
3 Seattle	34	(A)	62,444
17 Denver	31	(H)	61,880
18 Houston	33	(A)	31,714
16 Pittsburgh	20	(H)	51,605
7 Indianapolis	20	(H)	46,211
0 Denver	24	(A)	21,189

*Game cancelled due to strike.
Italics denote strike replacement games.

1987 GAMES STARTED

(NOTE: Players with an asterisk (*) following their names made starts only in strike-replacement games.)

12 games: Chip Banks, Gill Byrd, Vencie Glenn, Jim Lachey, Dennis McKnight, Billy Ray Smith, Lee Williams, Kellen Winslow.

11 games: Martin Bayless, Wes Chandler, Lionel James, Don Macek, Elvis Patterson.

10 games: Mike Charles, Dan Fouts.

9 games: James FitzPatrick, Gary Kowalski.

8 games: Thomas Benson.

7 games: Gary Anderson, Joe Phillips, Gary Plummer, Tim Spencer.

6 games: Jeffery Jackson.

5 games: Mike Humiston, Danny Walters.

4 games: Curtis Adams, Sam Claphan, Chuck Ehin, Pete Holohan, Les Miller.

3 games: Greg Feasel*, Walter Harris*, Harry Holt*, Dan Rosado*, Curtis Rouse*, Tony Simmons*, John Stadnik*, John Taylor*, Broderick Thompson, Dwight Wheeler*, Al Williams*, Blaise Winter*.

2 games: Rod Bernstine, Carl Brazley*, Mark Herrmann, Darrel Hopper*, Keyvan Jenkins*, Frank Middleton*, Rick Neuheisel*, Todd Spencer*, Terry Unrein.

1 game: Keith Baldwin, Ed Berry*, David Brandon, Chuck Faucette*, Andy Hawkins, Brian Ingram*, Mike Kelley*, Randy Kirk*, Tim Moffett*, Tag Rome*, Martin Sartin*, Eric Sievers, King Simmons*, Timmie Ware, Karl Wilson.

SAN DIEGO CHARGERS 1988 VETERAN ROSTER

No.	Name	Pos.	Ht.	Wt.	NFL Exp.	Birth-date	College	Games in '87	How Acquired
10	Abbott, Vince	K	5-11	206	2	5-31-59	Fullerton State	12	FA, '87
42	†Adams, Curtis	RB	5-11	194	3	4-30-62	Central Michigan	12	D8, '85
40	Anderson, Gary	RB	6-0	181	4	4-18-61	Arkansas	12	D1a, '83
96	Baldwin, Keith	DE	6-4	270	6	10-13-60	Texas A&M	6	FA, '87
56	†Banks, Chip	LB	6-4	236	7	9-18-59	Southern California	12	T-Cle, '87
44	Bayless, Martin	S	6-2	200	5	11-11-62	Bowling Green	12	T-Buf, '87
	Bennett, Roy	CB	6-2	200	1	7- 5-61	Jackson State	*18	FA, '88
57	†Benson, Thomas	LB	6-2	235	5	9- 6-61	Oklahoma	11	T-Atl, '86
82	Bernstine, Rod	TE	6-3	235	2	2- 8-65	Texas A&M	10	D1, '87
	Borland, Kyle	LB	6-3	228	1	7- 5-61	Wisconsin	*2	FA, '88
58	Brandon, David	LB	6-4	225	2	2- 9-65	Memphis State	8	T-Buf, '87
	Briehl, Tom	LB	6-3	247	3	9- 8-62	Stanford	*3	FA, '88
	Brookins, Mitchell	WR	5-11	192	3	12-10-60	Illinois	*0	FA, '88
	Browner, Keith	LB	6-6	245	4	1-24-62	Southern California	*2	FA, '88
55	Busick, Steve	LB	6-4	227	8	12-10-58	Southern California	1	FA, '87
22	Byrd, Gill	CB/S	5-11	196	6	2-20-61	San Jose State	12	D1b, '83
71	†Charles, Mike	NT	6-4	287	6	9-23-62	Syracuse	11	W-TB, '87
77	Claphan, Sam	G/T	6-6	288	8	10-10-56	Oklahoma	9	FA, '81
	Cox, Arthur	TE	6-2	262	6	2- 5-61	Texas Southern	*12	FA, '88
37	Dale, Jeff	S	6-3	213	3	10- 6-62	Louisiana State	*0	D2a, '85
61	Dallafior, Ken	G	6-4	278	4	8-26-59	Minnesota	8	FA, '85
78	†Ehin, Chuck	NT	6-4	266	6	7- 1-61	Brigham Young	12	D12a, '83
70	FitzPatrick, James	G/T	6-7	286	3	2- 1-64	Southern California	10	D1a, '86
	Fletcher, John	DE	6-3	280	2	8-22-65	Texas A&I	*3	FA, '88
	Foster, Ron	S	6-1	200	2	11-25-63	Cal State-Northridge	*3	FA, '88
	Franklin, Pat	RB	6-1	230	3	8-16-63	Southwest Texas State	*2	FA, '88
	Fuller, Steve	QB	6-4	198	9	1- 5-57	Clemson	*0	FA, '88
	Glaze, Charles	DB	5-11	198	2	9-12-65	South Carolina State	*3	FA, '88
25	Glenn, Vencie	S	6-0	187	3	10-26-64	Indiana State	12	T-NE, '86
	Goodlow, Eugene	WR	6-2	186	5	12-19-58	Kansas State	*0	FA, '88
	Greene, Danny	WR	5-11	190	2	12-26-61	Washington	*0	FA, '88
92	Hardison, Dee	DE	6-4	291	11	5- 2-56	North Carolina	3	W-NYG, '86
86	Holland, Jamie	WR	6-1	186	2	2- 1-64	Ohio State	12	D7, '87
	Hudson, Mike	DB	6-1	205	2	12-25-63	Oklahoma State	3	FA, '88
27	Hunter, Daniel	CB	5-11	178	4	9- 1-62	Henderson State	12	FA, '86
	Jackson, Enis	CB	5-9	175	1	5-16-63	Memphis State	*1	FA, '88
52	Jackson, Jeffery	LB	6-1	230	4	10- 9-61	Auburn	11	FA, '87
26	James, Lionel	WR	5-6	170	5	5-25-62	Auburn	12	D5, '84
	Johnson, Demetrious	S	6-0	196	6	7-21-61	Missouri	*3	FA, '88
10	Kelley, Mike	QB	6-3	195	2	12-31-59	Georgia Tech	3	FA, '88
	Keys, Tyrone	DE	6-7	267	7	10-24-59	Mississippi State	*5	FA, '88
94	Kirk, Randy	LB	6-2	235	2	12-27-64	San Diego State	13	FA, '87
68	Kowalski, Gary	G/T	6-6	273	5	7- 2-60	Boston College	12	T-Ram, '85
74	Lachey, Jim	T	6-6	289	4	6- 4-63	Ohio State	12	D1, '85
	Laufenberg, Babe	QB	6-2	195	4	12- 5-59	Indiana	*0	FA, '88
	Linne, Larry	WR	6-1	185	2	7-20-62	Texas-El Paso	*3	W-NE, '88
62	Macek, Don	C	6-2	270	13	7- 2-54	Boston College	11	D2, '76
	Malone, Mark	QB	6-4	224	9	11-22-58	Arizona State	12	T-Pit, '88
60	McKnight, Dennis	C/G	6-3	270	7	9-12-59	Drake	12	FA, '82
69	Miller, Les	DE	6-7	285	2	3- 1-65	Fort Hays State	9	FA, '87
	Moffett, Tim	WR	6-2	190	4	2- 8-62	Mississippi	2	FA, '88
2	Mojsiejenko, Ralf	P	6-3	212	4	1-28-63	Michigan State	12	D4, '85
91	O'Neal, Leslie	DE	6-4	255	2	5- 7-64	Oklahoma State	*0	D1, '86
34	Patterson, Elvis	CB	5-11	198	5	10-21-60	Kansas	*14	FA, '87
93	Pettitt, Duane	DE	6-4	265	2	11- 2-64	San Diego State	3	FA, '88
75	†Phillips, Joe	DE	6-5	275	3	7-15-63	Southern Methodist	13	FA, '87
50	Plummer, Gary	LB	6-2	240	3	1-26-60	California	8	FA, '86
53	Price, Stacey	LB	6-2	194	2	3- 3-62	Arkansas State	3	FA, '88
	Quillan, Fred	C	6-5	266	11	1-27-56	Oregon	*11	T-SF, '88
20	Redden, Barry	RB	5-10	219	7	7-21-60	Richmond	12	T-Ram, '87
66	Rosado, Dan	G/T	6-3	280	2	7- 6-59	Northern Illinois	4	FA, '87
79	Rouse, Curtis	G/T	6-3	340	7	7-13-60	Tennessee-Chattanooga	10	FA, '87
	Rubbert, Ed	QB	6-5	225	2	5-28-65	Louisville	*3	FA, '88
	Sataele, Alvis	LB	6-1	230	1	4-30-63	Hawaii	*9	FA, '88
85	Sievers, Eric	TE	6-4	230	8	11- 9-58	Maryland	12	D4a, '81
54	Smith, Billy Ray	LB	6-3	236	6	8-10-61	Arkansas	12	D1, '83
43	†Spencer, Tim	RB	6-1	227	4	12-10-60	Ohio State	12	D11a, '83
	Stadnik, John	C/G	6-4	265	2	2-18-60	Western Illinois	3	FA, '87

No.	Name	Pos.	Ht.	Wt.	NFL Exp.	Birth-date	College	Games in '87	How Acquired
59	Taylor, John	LB	6-4	235	4	6-21-61	Hawaii	7	FA, '87
76	Thompson, Broderick	G/T	6-4	290	3	8-14-60	Kansas	8	FA, '87
98	Unrein, Terry	NT/DE	6-5	280	3	10-24-62	Colorado State	9	D3, '86
13	Vlasic, Mark	QB	6-3	206	2	10-25-63	Iowa	1	D4, '87
	Walczak, Mark	TE	6-6	246	2	4-26-62	Arizona	*10	FA, '88
81	Ware, Timmie	WR	5-10	170	2	4- 2-63	Southern California	12	FA, '86
84	Williams, Al	WR	5-10	180	2	2- 4-62	Nevada-Reno	3	FA, '87
	Williams, Kevin	CB	5-9	169	2	11-28-61	Iowa State	*0	FA, '88
99	†Williams, Lee	DE	6-5	263	5	10-15-62	Bethune-Cookman	12	SupD, '84
72	Wilson, Karl	DE	6-4	268	2	9-10-64	Louisiana State	7	D3, '87
80	Winslow, Kellen	TE	6-5	251	10	11- 5-57	Missouri	12	D1, '79
97	†Winter, Blaise	NT	6-3	274	4	1-31-62	Syracuse	3	FA, '86
33	Zachary, Ken	RB	6-0	222	2	11-19-63	Oklahoma State	3	FA, '88

*Bennett played 18 games with Winnipeg-CFL in '87; Borland played 2 games with Rams in '87; Briehl played 3 games with Oilers in '87; Brookins last active with Bills in '85; Browner played 1 game with 49ers and 1 game with Raiders in '87; Cox played 12 games with Falcons in '87; Dale and O'Neal missed '87 season due to injury; Fletcher played 3 games with Bengals in '87; Foster played 3 games with Raiders in '87; Franklin played 2 games with Bengals in '87; Fuller missed '87 season with Bears due to injury; Glaze played 3 games with Seahawks in '87; Goodlow last active with Saints in '86; Greene last active with Seahawks in '85 and inactive for 3 games with Chargers in '87; Jackson played 1 game with Browns in '87; Johnson played 3 games with Dolphins in '87; Keys played 5 games with Buccaneers in '87; Laufenberg active for 1 game with Redskins in '87, but did not play; Linne played 3 games with Patriots in '87; Patterson played 1 game with Giants, 13 with Chargers in '87; Quillan played 11 games with 49ers in '87; Rubbert played 3 games with Redskins in '87; Sataele played 9 games with British Columbia-CFL in '87; Walczak played 2 games with Bills and 8 games with Colts in '87; K. Williams last active with Bills in '86.

†Option playout; subject to developments.

Retired—Dan Fouts, 16-year quarterback, 11 games in '87.

D—Draft; T—Trade; W—Waivers; FA—Free Agent; SupD—Supplemental Draft.

Also played with Chargers in '87, see page 386.

SAN DIEGO CHARGERS
1988 DRAFT CHOICES

(Number following name designates order of selection among 333 players drafted.)

Round and Player		Position	College
1. MILLER, Anthony	15	WR	Tennessee
2. Choice to L.A. Rams (a)			
3. EARLY, Quinn from L.A. Raiders through Houston (b)	60	WR	Iowa
3. Choice to Houston (c)			
4. CAMPBELL, Joe from L.A. Rams (d)	91	DE	New Mexico St.
4. SEARELS, Stacy from Buffalo (e)	93	T	Auburn
4. RICHARDS, David	98	T	UCLA
5. Choice to Houston (c)			
6. FIGARO, Cedric	152	LB	Notre Dame
7. Choice to Buffalo (f)			
8. Choice to Pittsburgh (g)			
9. HOWARD, Joey	238	T	Tennessee
10. Choice to N.Y. Giants (h)			
11. MILLER, Ed from L.A. Rams (i)	285	C	Pittsburgh
11. HINKLE, George	293	NT	Arizona
12. PHILLIPS, Wendell	324	DB	North Alabama

(a) Traded pick, conditional pick in 1989 and running back Buford McGee for running back Barry Redden, June 9, 1987.

(b) Oilers acquired pick, 2nd-round pick in 1988 and defensive end Sean Jones from Raiders for 1st-, 3rd- and 4th-round picks in 1988, April 21, 1988; Chargers acquired pick from Oilers for 3rd- and 5th-round picks in 1988, April 24, 1988.

(c) Traded picks: See second part of (b).

(d) Acquired pick for tight end Pete Holohan, April 24, 1988.

(e) Acquired pick and linebacker David Brandon for wide receiver Trumaine Johnson and 7th-round pick in 1988, August 31, 1987.

(f) See (e).

(g) Traded pick and conditional pick in 1989 for quarterback Mark Malone, April 12, 1988.

(h) Traded pick for wide receiver Bobby Johnson, August 20, 1987.

(i) Acquired pick for guard Jeff Walker, September 8, 1987.

SAN DIEGO CHARGERS
1988 ROOKIE AND FIRST-YEAR ROSTER

Name	Pos.	Hgt.	Wgt.	Birth-date	College	How Acquired
Campbell, Joe	DE/NT	6-3	242	12-28-66	New Mexico State	D4
DeLine, Steve	K	5-11	185	8-19-61	Colorado State	*FA
Early, Quinn	WR	6-0	190	4-13-65	Iowa	D2
Figaro, Cedric	LB	6-2	250	8-17-66	Notre Dame	D6
Flagg, Mike	TE	6-6	250	4-15-65	Iowa	FA
Floyd, Eric	OL	6-5	290	10-28-65	Auburn	FA
Flutie, Darren	WR	5-10	185	11-18-66	Boston College	FA
Franklin, Eric	RB	5-11	193	2-21-65	Fullerton State	FA
Hinkle, George	DE/NT	6-5	269	3-17-65	Arizona	D11a
Howard, Joey	T	6-5	285	9-14-65	Tennessee	D9
Hudson, Robert	TE	6-4	256	1- 6-64	Nevada-Reno	FA
Jackson, Kenny	RB	5-11	198	5-20-65	San Jose State	FA
Jones, Nelson	DB	6-1	190	2-13-64	North Carolina State	*D5 '87
MacEsker, Joe	T	6-7	305	9-21-65	Texas-El Paso	*D8 '87
Mattox, Marvin	S	6-4	205	8 -7-65	Kansas	FA
Miller, Anthony	WR	5-11	180	4-15-65	Tennessee	D1
Miller, Ed	OL	6-3	275	8- 4-65	Pittsburgh	D11
Phillips, Wendell	CB/S	5-11	195	4- 3-66	Northern Arizona	D12
Scott, Kevin	RB	5-9	181	10-24-63	Stanford	*FA '87
Searels, Stacy	T/G/C	6-5	281	5-19-65	Auburn	D4a

*DeLine: D7 San Francisco '87, released 8/31, awarded on waivers to Philadelphia 9/1, injured reserve 9/6 through 10/21, released 10/22; Jones, MacEsker and Scott missed '87 season due to injury.

SAN FRANCISCO 49ers
(Western Division, National Conference)

Bill Walsh

Owner-President—Edward J. DeBartolo, Jr.
Head Coach—Bill Walsh (9 years: 82-53-1)
Vice President and General Manager—John McVay
Director of College Scouting—Tony Razzano
Director of Pro Personnel—Allan Webb
Assistant Coaches:
    Strength & Conditioning—Jerry Attaway
    Receivers—Dennis Green
    Quarterbacks—Mike Holmgren
    Running Backs—Sherm Lewis
    Offensive Line—Bobb McKittrick
    Linebackers—Bill McPherson
    Secondary—Ray Rhodes
    Defensive Coordinator—George Seifert
    Special Teams—Lynn Stiles
    Defensive Line—Fred vonAppen
Public Relations Director—Jerry Walker
    (Office Phone: 365-3420—Area Code 415)
Offices—4949 Centennial Blvd., Santa Clara, Calif. 95054
Stadium—Candlestick Park (Capacity: 64,252)
Team Colors—49er Gold and Scarlet
Training Site—Sierra Community College, Rocklin, Calif.

1988 SCHEDULE
(All times local.
All games Sunday unless noted otherwise.)

Sept. 4	at New Orleans	12:00
Sept. 11	at New York Giants	1:00
Sept. 18	ATLANTA	1:00
Sept. 25	at Seattle	1:00
Oct. 2	DETROIT	1:00
Oct. 9	DENVER	1:00
Oct. 16	at Los Angeles Rams	1:00
Oct. 24	at Chicago (Mon.)	8:00
Oct. 30	MINNESOTA	1:00
Nov. 6	at Phoenix	2:00
Nov. 13	LOS ANGELES RAIDERS	1:00
Nov. 21	WASHINGTON (Mon.)	6:00
Nov. 27	at San Diego	1:00
Dec. 4	at Atlanta	1:00
Dec. 11	NEW ORLEANS	1:00
Dec. 18	LOS ANGELES RAMS	5:00

1987 RESULTS—(Won 13, Lost 3)

49ers		Opp.		Att.
17	Pittsburgh	30	(A)	55,735
27	Cincinnati	26	(A)	53,490
	Philadelphia*		(H)	
41	*New York Giants*	*21*	*(A)*	*16,471*
25	*Atlanta*	*17*	*(A)*	*8,684*
34	*St. Louis*	*28*	*(H)*	*38,094*
24	New Orleans	22	(A)	60,497
31	L.A. Rams	10	(A)	55,328
27	Houston	20	(H)	59,740
24	New Orleans	26	(H)	60,436
24	Tampa Bay	10	(A)	63,211
38	Cleveland	24	(H)	60,248
23	Green Bay	12	(A)	51,118
41	Chicago	0	(H)	63,509
35	Atlanta	7	(H)	54,698
48	L.A. Rams	0	(H)	57,950

NFC SEMIFINAL GAME

24	Minnesota	36	(H)	62,547

*Game cancelled due to strike.
Italics denote strike replacement games.

1987 GAMES STARTED

(NOTE: Players with an asterisk (*) following their names made starts only in strike-replacement games.)

14 games: Roger Craig.

13 games: Jeff Fuller.

12 games: Dwaine Board, Michael Carter, Randy Cross, Ronnie Lott, Tim McKyer, Jerry Rice, Michael Walter.

11 games: Joe Montana.

10 games: Jim Fahnhorst, Don Griffin, Milt McColl, Keena Turner.

9 games: Harris Barton, Jesse Sapolu.

8 games: Bruce Collie, Pete Kugler, Bubba Paris, Mike Wilson.

7 games: Russ Francis, Tom Rathman.

6 games: John Frank, Ron Heller.

5 games: Jeff Stover.

4 games: Fred Quillan, Steve Wallace.

3 games: Dwight Clark, Mark Cochran*, Matt Courtney*, Tom Cousineau*, Michael Durrette*, Keith Fahnhorst, Tracy Franz*, Guy McIntyre, Kevin Reach*, Chuck Thomas*, Steve Young.

2 games: George Cooper*, Joe Cribbs, Kevin Fagen, Ron Hadley*, Charles Haley, Dana McLemore*, Doug Mikolas*, Carl Monroe*, Darryl Pollard*, Elston Ridgle*, Larry Roberts, Todd Shell, John Taylor, Eric Wright.

1 game: Keith Browner*, Tony Cherry*, Glen Collins*, Kevin Dean*, Joe Drake*, Riki Ellison, Terrence Flagler, Bob Gagliano*, Clyde Glover*, Terry Greer*, Thomas Henley*, Jerry Keeble*, Derrick Martin*, Jonathan Shelley*, John Sullivan*, Mike Varajon*, Mike Wells*, Carlton Williamson.

SAN FRANCISCO 49ers 1988 VETERAN ROSTER

No.	Name	Pos.	Ht.	Wt.	NFL Exp.	Birth-date	College	Games in '87	How Acquired
	Apke, Steve	LB	6-1	222	2	8- 3-65	Pittsburgh	*3	FA, '88
	Bartalo, Steve	RB	5-9	200	2	7-15-64	Colorado State	*9	W-TB, '88
79	Barton, Harris	T	6-4	280	2	4-19-64	North Carolina	12	D1, '87
	Berry, Ed	DB	5-10	183	2	9-28-63	Utah State	*2	FA, '88
76	Board, Dwaine	DE	6-5	248	9	11-29-56	North Carolina A&T	14	W-Pit, '79
65	Bregel, Jeff	G	6-4	280	2	5- 1-64	Southern California	5	D2, '87
	Burnett, Victor	DE	6-5	258	2	10- 5-62	Fresno State	*3	FA, '88
95	Carter, Michael	NT	6-2	285	5	10-29-60	Southern Methodist	12	D5, '84
	Chandler, Wes	WR	6-0	188	11	8-22-56	Florida	*12	T-SD, '88
	Cochran, Mark	T	6-5	285	2	5- 6-63	Baylor	3	FA, '88
	Cofer, Mike	K	6-1	190	1	2-19-64	North Carolina State	*2	FA, '88
69	†Collie, Bruce	T/G	6-6	275	4	6-27-62	Texas-Arlington	11	D5, '85
59	Comeaux, Darren	LB	6-1	227	7	4-15-60	Arizona State	8	FA, '87
52	Cooper, George	LB	6-2	225	2	12-24-58	Michigan State	10	FA, '87
33	Craig, Roger	RB	6-0	224	6	7-10-60	Nebraska	14	D2, '83
83	†Crawford, Derrick	WR/KR	5-10	185	2	9- 3-60	Memphis State	*0	SupD, '86
28	Cribbs, Joe	RB	5-11	193	8	1- 5-58	Auburn	11	T-Buf, '86
51	Cross, Randy	G	6-3	265	13	4-25-54	UCLA	12	D2, '76
57	Dean, Kevin	LB	6-1	235	2	2- 5-65	Texas Christian	4	OFA, '87
25	DuBose, Doug	RB	5-11	190	1	3-14-64	Nebraska	2	OFA, '87
	Eason, Bo	S	6-2	205	5	3-10-61	California-Davis	*3	T-Hou., '88
	Eccles, Scott	TE	6-4	240	1	6-28-63	Eastern New Mexico	*1	FA, '88
50	Ellison, Riki	LB	6-2	225	6	8-15-60	Southern California	3	D5, '83
75	Fagan, Kevin	DE	6-3	260	2	4-25-63	Miami (Fla.)	7	D4c, '86
32	Flagler, Terrence	RB	6-0	200	2	9-24-64	Clemson	3	D1a, '87
86	Frank, John	TE	6-3	225	5	4-17-62	Ohio State	12	D2, '84
49	Fuller, Jeff	S/LB	6-2	216	5	8- 8-62	Texas A&M	14	D5a, '84
11	Gagliano, Bob	QB	6-3	205	5	9- 5-58	Utah State	3	FA, '88
	Gamache, Vince	P	5-11	176	3	11-18-61	Fullerton State	*3	FA, '88
93	Glover, Clyde	DE	6-6	280	2	7-16-60	Fresno State	13	FA, '87
	Greer, Terry	WR	6-1	192	3	9-27-57	Alabama State	3	FA, '88
29	Griffin, Don	CB	6-0	176	3	3-17-64	Middle Tennessee State	12	D6, '86
54	Hadley, Ron	LB	6-2	240	2	11- 9-63	Washington	3	FA, '87
94	Haley, Charles	DE/LB	6-5	230	3	1- 6-64	James Madison	12	D4, '86
89	Heller, Ron	TE	6-3	235	2	9-18-62	Oregon State	13	FA, '86
46	Holmoe, Tom	S	6-2	195	5	3- 7-60	Brigham Young	11	D4, '83
88	Jones, Brent	TE	6-4	230	2	2-12-63	Santa Clara	4	FA, '87
67	Kugler, Pete	NT/DE	6-4	255	6	8- 9-59	Penn State	11	D6, '81
	Lewis, David	TE	6-3	235	5	6- 8-61	California	*5	FA, '88
42	†Lott, Ronnie	S	6-0	200	8	5- 8-59	Southern California	12	D1, '81
	Manca, Massimo	K	5-10	192	2	3-18-64	Penn State	*3	FA, '88
	Marchiol, Ken	LB	6-2	251	2	8-27-65	Mesa (Ariz.)	*3	FA, '88
84	Margerum, Ken	WR	6-0	180	6	10- 5-58	Stanford	2	FA, '86
53	†McColl, Milt	LB	6-6	230	8	8-28-59	Stanford	12	OFA, '81
62	McIntyre, Guy	G	6-3	264	5	2-17-61	Georgia	3	D3, '84
22	McKyer, Tim	CB	6-0	174	3	9- 5-63	Texas-Arlington	12	D3a, '86
97	Mikolas, Doug	NT	6-1	270	2	6- 7-62	Portland State	8	FA, '87
16	Montana, Joe	QB	6-2	195	10	6-11-56	Notre Dame	13	D3, '79
20	Nixon, Tory	CB	5-11	186	4	2-24-62	San Diego State	12	T-Was, '85
	O'Connor, Paul	G	6-3	258	1	11- 7-62	Miami (Fla.)	*2	FA, '88
77	Paris, Bubba	T	6-6	299	6	10- 6-60	Michigan	11	D2, '82
	Perry, Mario	TE	6-5	235	2	12-20-63	Mississippi	*3	FA, '88
	Poe, Johnnie	S	6-0	194	8	8-29-59	Missouri	*12	FA, '88
44	Rathman, Tom	RB	6-1	232	3	10- 7-62	Nebraska	12	D3, '86
80	Rice, Jerry	WR	6-2	200	4	10-13-62	Mississippi Valley State	12	D1, '85
	Riley, Bob	T	6-6	270	2	6-23-64	Indiana	*3	FA, '88
	Rivers, Garland	DB	6-1	181	1	11- 3-64	Michigan	*2	FA, '88
91	Roberts, Larry	DE	6-3	264	3	6- 2-63	Alabama	11	D2, '86
	Robinson, Greg	T	6-5	285	3	12-25-62	Cal St.-Sacramento	*3	FA, '88
	Rodgers, Del	RB	5-10	202	4	6-22-60	Utah	7	FA, '88
4	†Runager, Max	P	6-1	189	10	3-24-58	South Carolina	12	FA, '84
61	†Sapolu, Jesse	G/C	6-4	260	3	3-10-61	Hawaii	12	D11, '83
	Scott, Chuck	WR	6-2	202	2	5-24-63	Vanderbilt	*2	FA, '88
90	†Shell, Todd	LB	6-4	225	4	6-24-62	Brigham Young	6	D1, '84
72	Stover, Jeff	DE	6-5	275	7	5-22-58	Oregon	12	OFA, '82
24	Sydney, Harry	RB	6-0	217	2	6-26-59	Kansas	14	FA, '87
82	Taylor, John	WR	6-1	185	2	3-31-62	Delaware State	12	D3c, '86
60	Thomas, Chuck	C	6-3	280	3	12-24-60	Oklahoma	7	FA, '87

No.	Name	Pos.	Ht.	Wt.	NFL Birth- Exp. date	College	Games in '87	How Acquired
58	†Turner, Keena	LB	6-2	222	9 10-22-58	Purdue	10	D2, '80
74	Wallace, Steve	T	6-5	276	3 12-27-64	Auburn	11	D4a, '86
99	Walter, Michael	LB	6-3	238	6 11-30-60	Oregon	12	W-Dal, '84
14	Wersching, Ray	K	5-11	215	16 8-21-50	California	12	FA, '77
	Williams, Dokie	WR	5-11	180	6 8-25-60	UCLA	*11	T-Rai, '88
27	†Williamson, Carlton	S	6-0	204	8 6-12-58	Pittsburgh	8	D3, '81
85	Wilson, Mike	WR	6-3	215	8 12-19-58	Washington State	11	FA, '81
21	Wright, Eric	CB	6-1	185	7 4-18-59	Missouri	2	D2a, '81
8	Young, Steve	QB	6-2	200	4 10-11-61	Brigham Young	8	T-TB, '87

*Apke played 3 games with Steelers in '87; Bartalo played 9 games with Buccaneers in '87; Berry played 2 games with Chargers in '87; Burnett played 3 games with Cardinals in '87; Chandler played 12 games with Chargers in '87; Cofer played 2 games with Saints in '87; Crawford missed '87 season due to injury; Eason played 3 games with Oilers in '87; Eccles played 1 game with Oilers in '87; Gamache played 3 games with Raiders in '87; Lewis played 5 games with Dolphins in '87; Manca played 3 games with Bengals in '87; Marchiol played 3 games with Saints in '87; O'Connor played 2 games with Buccaneers in '87; Perry played 3 games with Raiders in '87; Poe played 12 games with Saints in '87; Riley played 3 games with Bengals in '87; Rivers played 2 games with Bears and on inactive list for 1 game with Bills in '87; Robinson played 3 games with Patriots in '87; Scott played 2 games with Cowboys in '87; Williams played 11 games with Raiders in '87.

†Option playout; subject to developments.

Retired—Dwight Clark, 9-year wide receiver, 13 games in '87; Keith Fahnhorst, 14-year tackle, 3 games in '87.

D—Draft; T—Trade; W—Waivers; FA—Free Agent; OFA—Original Free Agent; SupD—Supplemental Draft.

Also played with 49ers in '87, see page 386.

SAN FRANCISCO 49ers
1988 DRAFT CHOICES

(Number following name designates order of selection among 333 players drafted.)

Round and Player		Position	College
1. Choice to L.A. Raiders (a)			
2. STUBBS, Danny from L.A. Raiders (b)	33	DE	Miami (Fla.)
2. HOLT, Pierce from Philadelphia through Tampa Bay (c)	39	DT	Angelo State
2. Choice to Tampa Bay (d)			
3. ROMANOWSKI, Bill	80	LB	Boston College
4. HELTON, Barry from Houston through L.A. Raiders (e)	102	P	Colorado
4. Choice to Tampa Bay (d)			
5. Choice to Buffalo (f)			
6. Choice to Tampa Bay (g)			
7. BRYANT, Kevin	191	LB	Delaware State
8. CLARKSON, Larry	219	T	Montana
9. BONNER, Brian (h)	247	LB	Minnesota
10. FOLEY, Tim (i)	275	K	Georgia Southern
11. BROOKS, Chet	303	DB	Texas A & M
12. MIRA, George	331	LB	Miami (Fla.)

(a) Traded pick for wide receiver Dokie Williams and 2nd- and 4th-round picks in 1988, April 24, 1988.

(b) See (a).

(c) Buccaneers acquired pick and 4th-round pick in 1988 from Eagles for 2nd-round pick in 1988, April 24, 1988; 49ers acquired pick from Buccaneers for 2nd- and 4th-round picks in 1988, April 24, 1988.

(d) See second part of (c).

(e) Raiders acquired pick and 1st- and 3rd-round picks in 1988 from Oilers for defensive end Sean Jones and 2nd- and 3rd-round picks in 1988, April 21, 1988; 49ers acquired pick from Raiders: See (a).

(f) Traded pick and 3rd-round pick in 1987 for running back Joe Cribbs, August 19, 1986.

(g) Traded pick for linebacker Keith Browner, February 27, 1987.

(h) Placed on waivers after failing physical, June 8, 1988.

(i) Rights traded to Falcons for conditional 10th-round pick in 1989 draft, June 8, 1988.

SAN FRANCISCO 49ers
1988 ROOKIE AND FIRST-YEAR ROSTER

Name	Pos.	Hgt.	Wgt.	Birth-date	College	How Acquired
Allen, Dennis	WR	6-1	182	7- 7-63	Kansas State	*FA
Bankston, Bobby	WR	5-7	170	1-20-63	East Texas State	*FA
Belluomini, Paul	C	6-0	210	3-31-57	California-Davis	*FA
Biggers, Kevin	CB	5-11	185	5- 6-62	Nebraska	*FA
Brooks, Chet	CB	5-11	191	1- 1-66	Texas A&M	D11
Bryant, Kevin	LB	6-2	223	4-19-65	Delaware State	D7
Clarkson, Larry	T	6-7	303	3-11-65	Montana	D8
Cox, Greg	DB	6-0	223	1- 6-65	San Jose State	FA
Davis, Jeff	LB	6-5	235	1-19-66	Nevada-Reno	FA
Gilcrest, Stacey	CB/S	5-10	185	9- 5-63	San Jose State	FA
Hammond, Curtis	CB	6-1	195	8-31-66	Southeast Missouri	FA
Helton, Barry	P	6-3	205	1- 2-65	Colorado	D4
Holt, Pierce	DE/NT	6-4	280	1- 1-62	Angelo State	D2a
Hooper, Mike	DE	6-3	275	10- 7-65	San Diego State	FA
Kennedy, Sam	LB	6-3	235	7-10-64	San Jose State	*FA
Liggins, Guy	WR	6-2	200	6- 4-66	San Jose State	FA
Lilly, Kevin	DE	6-4	265	5-14-63	Tulsa	*FA '87
Miller, Mike	DE	6-4	275	9- 8-64	California Lutheran	*FA
Mira, George, Jr.	LB	6-0	230	6-13-65	Miami (Fla.)	D12
Nicholas, Calvin	WR	6-4	208	6-11-64	Grambling	*D11, '87
Paye, John	QB	6-3	205	3-30-65	Stanford	*D10, '87
Romanowski, Bill	LB	6-4	231	4- 2-66	Boston College	D3
Spangler, Rich	K	6-1	195	10-29-63	Ohio State	*FA
Stubbs, Danny	DE	6-4	260	1- 3-65	Miami (Fla.)	D2

*Allen: FA replacement San Francisco 9/24/87, released 10/2; Bankston: FA Tampa Bay '87, injured reserve 9/3 through 11/2, released 11/3; Belluomini: FA San Francisco '81, released 7/28, FA San Francisco '82, released 8/23, FA San Francisco '83, released 8/16, FA San Francisco '84, released 8/20, FA San Francisco '85, released 8/20, FA San Francisco '86, released 8/19, FA San Francisco '88, released 8/14; Biggers: FA Edmonton '87, released 6/17, FA replacement San Francisco 9/24/87, released 10/14; Kennedy: FA San Francisco '87, injured reserve 8/28 through 10/25, released 10/26; Lilly: FA San Diego '86, released (failed physical) 7/20, FA San Diego 8/11, released 8/25, FA San Francisco '87, injured reserve 8/28 through entire '87 season; Miller: FA Los Angeles Raiders '87, released 8/12, FA replacement Los Angeles Raiders 9/24, released 10/5; Nicholas and Paye missed '87 season due to injury; Spangler: FA Dallas '86, released 7/21, FA St. Louis '87, released 8/25.

SEATTLE SEAHAWKS
(Western Division, American Conference)

Chuck Knox

President/General Manager—Mike McCormack
V.P./Asst. General Manager—Chuck Allen
Director of Player Personnel—Mike Allman
V.P./Public Relations—Gary Wright
  (Office Phone: 827-9777—Area Code 206)
Head Coach—Chuck Knox (15 years: 139-82-1)
Assistant Coaches:
  Asst. Head Coach/Def. Coord./Linebackers—Tom Catlin
  Defensive Line—George Dyer
  Offensive Backs—Chick Harris
  Defensive Backs—Ralph Hawkins
  Quarterbacks—Ken Meyer
  Offensive Coordinator/Receivers—Steve Moore
  Tight Ends/Asst. Special Teams—Russ Purnell
  Offensive Line—Kent Stephenson
  Linebackers/Special Teams—Rusty Tillman
  Special Assignments—Joe Vitt
Offices—11220 N.E. 53rd St., Kirkland, Wash. 98033
Stadium—The Kingdome (Capacity: 64,984)
Team Colors—Blue, Green and Silver
Training Site—Eastern Washington University, Cheney, Wash.

1988 SCHEDULE
(All times local.
All games Sunday unless noted otherwise.)

Sept. 4	at Denver	2:00
Sept. 11	KANSAS CITY	1:00
Sept. 18	at San Diego	1:00
Sept. 25	SAN FRANCISCO	1:00
Oct. 2	at Atlanta	1:00
Oct. 9	at Cleveland	1:00
Oct. 16	NEW ORLEANS	1:00
Oct. 23	at Los Angeles Rams	1:00
Oct. 30	SAN DIEGO	1:00
Nov. 6	BUFFALO	1:00
Nov. 13	HOUSTON	1:00
Nov. 20	at Kansas City	12:00
Nov. 28	L.A. RAIDERS (Mon.)	6:00
Dec. 4	at New England	1:00
Dec. 11	DENVER	5:00
Dec. 18	at Los Angeles Raiders	1:00

1987 RESULTS—(Won 9, Lost 7)

Seahawks		Opp.		Att.
17	Denver	40	(A)	75,999
43	Kansas City	14	(H)	61,667
	San Diego*		(A)	
24	Miami	20	(H)	19,448
10	Cincinnati	17	(H)	31,739
37	Detroit	14	(A)	8,310
35	L.A. Raiders	13	(A)	52,735
28	Minnesota	17	(H)	61,134
14	New York Jets	30	(A)	60,452
24	Green Bay	13	(A)	60,963
34	San Diego	3	(H)	62,444
14	L.A. Raiders	37	(H)	62,802
9	Pittsburgh	13	(A)	48,881
28	Denver	21	(H)	61,759
34	Chicago	21	(A)	62,518
20	Kansas City	41	(A)	20,370
	AFC WILD-CARD GAME			
20	Houston (OT)	23	(A)	49,622

*Game cancelled due to strike.
Italics denote strike replacement games.

1987 GAMES STARTED

(NOTE: Players with an asterisk (*) following their names made starts only in strike-replacement games.)

13 games: Steve Largent, Fredd Young.

12 games: Edwin Bailey, Brian Bosworth, Jeff Bryant, Jacob Green, Dave Krieg, Ron Mattes, Bryan Millard, Joe Nash, Eugene Robinson, Terry Taylor, Mike Tice, Curt Warner, Mike Wilson.

11 games: Blair Bush, Kenny Easley, Patrick Hunter.

10 games: Greg Gaines, John L. Williams.

8 games: Daryl Turner.

7 games: Bruce Scholtz, Tony Woods.

3 games: Tim Burnham*, Ray Butler, Julio Cortes*, Dale Dorning*, Don Fairbanks*, Matt Hanousek*, Mark Keel*, John McVeigh*, Dallis Smith*, Wilbur Strozier, Renard Young*.

2 games: Harvey Allen*, Tom Andrews*, Grant Feasel, Charles Glaze*, David Graham*, Boyce Green*, Kevin Juma*, Eric Lane*, Bruce Mathison*, Howard Richards*, Jack Sims*, Jimmy Teal*, Rico Tipton*.

1 game: Tony Caldwell*, Fred Davis*, Mike Hagen*, Doug Hire*, Van Hughes*, Melvin Jenkins*, Jeff Kemp*, Paul Lavine*, Paul Moyer, Rick Parros*, Ken Sager*, Garth Thomas*, Ricky Thomas*, Charles Wiley*.

SEATTLE SEAHAWKS 1988 VETERAN ROSTER

No.	Name	Pos.	Ht.	Wt.	NFL Exp.	Birth-date	College	Games in '87	How Acquired
65	Bailey, Edwin	G	6-4	276	8	5-15-59	South Carolina State	12	D5, '81
62	Barbay, Roland	NT	6-4	260	2	10- 1-64	Louisiana State	5	D7, '87
76	†Borchardt, Jon	T	6-5	272	10	8-13-57	Montana State	12	T-Buf, '85
55	Bosworth, Brian	LB	6-2	248	2	3- 9-65	Oklahoma	12	SupD, '87
77	†Bryant, Jeff	DE	6-5	272	7	5-22-60	Clemson	12	D1, '82
97	Burnham, Tim	T	6-5	280	2	5- 6-63	Washington	*6	FA, '88
34	Burse, Tony	RB	6-0	220	2	4- 4-65	Middle Tennessee State	12	D12a, '87
59	†Bush, Blair	C	6-3	272	11	11-25-56	Washington	11	T-Cin, '83
53	†Butler, Keith	LB	6-4	239	11	5-16-56	Memphis State	12	D2, '78
83	Butler, Ray	WR	6-3	206	9	6-28-56	Southern California	12	FA, '85
84	Clark, Louis	WR	6-0	206	2	7- 3-64	Mississippi State	2	D10, '87
	Daum, Mitch	TE	6-4	230	1	11-13-63	Wyoming	*2	FA, '88
	Dove, Wes	DE	6-7	270	1	2-9-64	Syracuse	2	D12, '87
45	Easley, Kenny	S	6-3	198	8	1-15-59	UCLA	12	D1, '81
30	Edmonds, Bobby Joe	RB	5-11	186	3	9-26-64	Arkansas	11	D5, '86
	Eisenhooth, Stan	C	6-6	300	1	7-8-63	Towson State	1	OFA, '86
54	Feasel, Grant	C	6-7	280	4	6-28-60	Abilene Christian	12	FA, '87
88	†Franklin, Byron	WR	6-1	183	7	9- 3-58	Auburn	6	T-Buf, '85
56	†Gaines, Greg	LB	6-3	222	7	10-16-58	Tennessee	11	OFA, '81
79	Green, Jacob	DE	6-3	252	9	1-21-57	Texas A&M	12	D1, '80
47	Hardy, Andre	RB	6-1	233	3	11-28-61	St. Mary's (Calif.)	*1	T-SF, '87
78	Heller, Ron	T	6-6	280	5	8-25-62	Penn State	*12	T-TB, '88
	Hollie, Doug	DE	6-4	265	1	12-15-60	Southern Methodist	2	FA, '88
25	Hollis, David	CB	5-11	175	2	7- 4-65	Nevada-Las Vegas	11	OFA, '87
29	Holloway, Johnny	CB	5-11	182	3	11- 8-63	Kansas	*3	FA, '88
	Hood, James	WR	6-1	175	1	9-9-61	Arizona State	*9	FA, '87
23	Hunter, Patrick	CB	5-11	185	3	10-24-64	Nevada-Reno	11	D3, '86
24	Jenkins, Melvin	CB	5-10	170	2	3-16-62	Cincinnati	12	FA, '87
52	Johnson, M.L.	LB	6-3	225	2	1-24-64	Hawaii	8	D9, '87
9	†Johnson, Norm	K	6-2	198	7	5-31-60	UCLA	13	OFA, '82
26	Justin, Kerry	CB	5-11	185	9	5- 3-55	Oregon State	7	OFA, '78
15	Kemp, Jeff	QB	6-0	201	8	7-11-59	Dartmouth	13	T-SF, '87
17	Krieg, Dave	QB	6-1	196	9	10-20-58	Milton	12	OFA, '80
37	†Lane, Eric	RB	6-0	201	8	1- 6-59	Brigham Young	12	D8, '81
80	Largent, Steve	WR	5-11	184	13	9-28-54	Tulsa	13	T-Hou, '76
13	Mathison, Bruce	QB	6-3	205	5	4-25-59	Nebraska	3	FA, '87
70	†Mattes, Ron	T	6-6	306	3	8- 8-63	Virginia	12	D7, '85
	McGarry, John	G	6-5	288	1	11-24-63	St. Joseph's (Ind.)	*2	FA, '88
51	†Merriman, Sam	LB	6-3	232	6	5- 5-61	Idaho	9	D7, '83
71	Millard, Bryan	G	6-5	284	5	12- 2-60	Texas	12	FA, '84
61	Mitz, Alonzo	DE	6-3	273	3	6- 5-63	Florida	6	D8, '86
35	Moore, Mark	S	6-0	194	2	9- 3-64	Oklahoma State	5	D4, '87
43	Morris, Randall	RB	6-0	200	5	4-22-62	Tennessee	10	D10, '84
	Morrison, Tim	CB	6-1	195	3	4- 3-63	North Carolina	*7	T-Was, '88
21	†Moyer, Paul	S	6-1	201	6	7-26-61	Arizona State	12	OFA, '83
72	†Nash, Joe	NT	6-2	257	7	10-11-60	Boston College	12	OFA, '82
73	†Powell, Alvin	G	6-5	296	2	11-19-59	Winston-Salem State	12	SupD, '84
41	Robinson, Eugene	S	6-0	186	4	5-28-63	Colgate	12	OFA, '85
5	Rodriguez, Ruben	P	6-2	220	2	3- 3-65	Arizona	12	D5a, '87
27	†Romes, Charles	CB	6-1	190	12	12-16-53	North Carolina Central	*5	FA, '87
58	Scholtz, Bruce	LB	6-6	242	7	9-26-58	Texas	8	D2, '82
74	Singer, Curt	T	6-5	279	2	11- 4-61	Tennessee	*0	FA, '86
82	†Skansi, Paul	WR	5-11	183	6	1-11-61	Washington	12	FA, '84
87	Strozier, Wilbur	TE	6-4	255	2	11-12-64	Georgia	12	FA, '87
20	†Taylor, Terry	CB	5-10	191	5	7-18-61	Southern Illinois	12	D1, '84
85	Teal, Jimmy	WR	5-11	175	4	8-18-62	Texas A&M	4	FA, '87
86	†Tice, Mike	TE	6-7	247	8	2- 2-59	Maryland	12	OFA, '81
90	Tipton, Rico	LB	6-2	240	2	7-31-61	Washington State	3	FA, '88
81	†Turner, Daryl	WR	6-3	194	5	12-15-61	Michigan State	12	D2, '84
28	Warner, Curt	RB	5-11	205	5	3-18-61	Penn State	12	D1, '83
32	Williams, John L.	RB	5-11	226	3	11-23-64	Florida	12	D1, '86
91	Williams, Lester	NT	6-3	290	6	1-19-59	Miami (Fla.)	2	FA, '88
75	Wilson, Mike	T	6-5	280	11	5-28-55	Georgia	12	T-Cin, '86
57	Woods, Tony	LB	6-4	244	2	9-11-65	Pittsburgh	12	D1, '87
92	Wyman, David	LB	6-2	229	2	3-31-64	Stanford	4	D2, '87
50	Young, Fredd	LB	6-1	233	5	11-14-61	New Mexico State	13	D3, '84

*Burnham played 3 games with Seahawks and 3 games with British Columbia CFL in '87; Daum played 2 games with Oilers in '87; Hardy played 1 game with 49ers in '87; Heller played 12 games with

Buccaneers in '87; Holloway played 3 games with Cardinals in '87; Hood played 9 games with Ottawa-CFL in '87; McGarry played 2 games with Packers in '87; Morrison played 7 games with Redskins in '87; Romes played 5 games with Chargers in '87; Singer missed '87 season due to injury.

†Option playout; subject to developments.

D—Draft; T—Trade; FA—Free Agent; OFA—Original Free Agent; SupD—Supplemental Draft.

Also played with Seahawks in '87, see page 386.

SEATTLE SEAHAWKS
1988 DRAFT CHOICES

(Number following name designates order of selection among 333 players drafted.)

Round and Player		Position	College
1. Choice exercised in 1987 supplemental draft for Brian Bosworth, LB, Oklahoma			
2. BLADES, Brian	49	WR	Miami (Fla.)
3. KANE, Tommy	75	WR	Syracuse
4. HARMON, Kevin	101	RB	Iowa
5. Choice to L.A. Raiders through San Francisco and N.Y. Jets (a)			
6. HART, Roy	158	NT	South Carolina
7. JACKSON, Ray	185	DB	Ohio State
8. TYLER, Robert	215	TE	South Carolina St.
9. WISE, Deatrich	242	NT	Jackson State
10. JONES, Derwin	269	DE	Miami (Fla.)
11. McLEOD, Rick from Green Bay (b)	284	T	Washington
11. HARPER, Dwayne	299	DB	South Carolina St.
12. DesROCHERS, Dave	326	T	San Diego State

(a) Seahawks traded pick to 49ers for quarterback Jeff Kemp, May 19, 1987; 49ers traded pick to Jets for wide receiver Johnny (Lam) Jones, July 23, 1987; Jets traded pick and 4th-round pick in 1988 to Raiders for 3rd-round pick in 1988, April 24, 1988.

(b) Acquired pick for cornerback Dave Brown, August 26, 1987.

SEATTLE SEAHAWKS
1988 ROOKIE AND FIRST-YEAR ROSTER

Name	Pos.	Hgt.	Wgt.	Birth-date	College	How Acquired
Agee, Tommie	RB	6-0	220	2-22-64	Auburn	*D5, '87
Bess, Terry	NT	6-5	250	3-30-65	Tennessee-Chattanooga	FA
Blades, Brian	WR	5-11	182	7-24-65	Miami (Fla.)	D2
Breeland, Garrett	LB	6-1	230	5-31-63	Southern California	*FA
Burdett, David	T	6-5	283	7- 9-64	Linfield	FA
Condon, Bill	G	6-3	265	4-18-66	Alabama	FA
Cooper, Richard	DE	6-5	285	11- 1-64	Tennessee	FA
DesRochers, Dave	T	6-7	290	12- 1-64	San Diego State	D12
Floyd, Lucius	RB	6-0	195	4- 7-66	Nevada-Reno	FA
Hairston, Ray	LB	6-2	235	7- 6-63	Illinois	*FA, '87
Harmon, Kevin	RB	6-0	190	10-26-65	Iowa	D4
Harper, Dwayne	CB	5-11	165	3-29-66	South Carolina State	D11a
Hart, Roy	NT	6-1	280	7-10-65	South Carolina	D6
Hines, John	DE	6-4	250	5- 1-66	Alabama State	FA
Hosea, Cedric	RB	5-11	195	9- 2-64	Eastern Washington	FA
Jackson, Ray	CB	5-11	190	1-11-65	Ohio State	D7
Jones, Derwin	DE	6-3	270	9- 4-64	Miami (Fla.)	D10
Kane, Tommy	WR	5-11	180	1-14-64	Syracuse	D3
Knight, Ryan	RB	6-0	210	3-16-66	Southern California	FA
MacInnes, Angus	C	6-3	260	1- 6-65	Weber State	FA
McLean, Kevin	QB	6-3	200	12-12-64	Southern California	FA
McLeod, Rick	T	6-6	280	8-29-64	Washington	D11
Mokofisi, Filipo	LB	6-1	230	10-22-62	Utah	*FA, '87
Parharm, Larry	CB	5-11	175	10-29-64	Tuskegee	FA
Patterson, Ian	DB	5-10	190	1-31-65	Central Florida	FA
Pearson, Pat	G	6-4	270	3- 2-65	Southern Mississippi	FA
Poinsett, David	G	6-5	277	5- 5-66	South Carolina	FA
Porter, Rufus	LB	6-1	207	5-18-65	Southern	FA
Stein, Eric	K	6-1	176	8-12-66	Eastern Washington	FA
Stouffer, Kelly	QB	6-3	210	7- 6-64	Colorado State	*T (Phx)
Tyler, Robert	TE	6-5	259	10-12-65	South Carolina State	D8
Vickers, David	S	6-4	204	8-10-64	Oklahoma	FA
Waiters, Garey	P	5-10	220	2- 2-65	Jacksonville State	FA
Weathers, Monte	KR	5-8	165	1-20-66	Pittsburgh State	FA
White, Arthur	LB	6-1	220	11-18-65	Florida	FA
Williams, Bob	TE	6-3	235	9-22-63	Penn State	*FA, '87
Wilson, Don	DB	6-0	190	11-25-65	Penn	FA
Wise, Deatrich	NT	6-4	280	5- 6-65	Jackson State	D9

*Agee and Hairston missed '87 season due to injury; Breeland: D10 Los Angeles Rams '86, injured reserve 8/25 through 10/6, released 10/7; Mokofisi: D8 New Orleans '86, released 8/26, FA Seattle '87, injured reserve 8/5 through entire season; Stouffer: D1 St. Louis '87, reserve/unsigned entire season, rights traded 4/22/88; Williams: D7 Buffalo '86; injured reserve 8/26 through entire season, released 9/8/87, FA Seattle 10/21 (on inactive list for 10 games).

TAMPA BAY BUCCANEERS
(Central Division, National Conference)

Ray Perkins

Owner/President—Hugh F. Culverhouse
Vice President/Head Coach—Ray Perkins (5 years: 27-45)
Vice-President—Joy Culverhouse
Assistant to the President—Phil Krueger
Director of Player Personnel—Jerry Angelo
Director of Pro Personnel—Erik Widmark
Assistant Coaches:
    Offensive Line—Larry Beightol
    Offensive Assistant—John Bobo
    Running Backs—Sylvester Croom
    Defensive Line—Mike DuBose
    Def. Coord./Secondary—Doug Graber
    Strength & Conditioning—Kent Johnston
    Inside Linebackers—Joe Kines
    Outside Linebackers—Herb Paterra
    Special Teams—Rodney Stokes
    Receivers—Richard Williamson
Director of Public Relations—Rick Odioso
    (Office Phone: 870-2700—Area Code 813)
Offices—One Buccaneer Place, Tampa, Fla. 33607
Stadium—Tampa Stadium (Capacity: 74,317)
Team Colors—Florida Orange, White and Red
Training Site—University of Tampa, Tampa, Fla.

1988 SCHEDULE
(All times local.
All games Sunday unless noted otherwise.)

Sept. 4	PHILADELPHIA	1:00
Sept. 11	at Green Bay	12:00
Sept. 18	PHOENIX	1:00
Sept. 25	at New Orleans	12:00
Oct. 2	GREEN BAY	1:00
Oct. 9	at Minnesota	12:00
Oct. 16	at Indianapolis	12:00
Oct. 23	MINNESOTA	1:00
Oct. 30	MIAMI	1:00
Nov. 6	at Chicago	12:00
Nov. 13	at Detroit	1:00
Nov. 20	CHICAGO	1:00
Nov. 27	at Atlanta	1:00
Dec. 4	BUFFALO	1:00
Dec. 11	at New England	1:00
Dec. 18	DETROIT	1:00

1987 RESULTS—(Won 4, Lost 11)

Buccaneers		Opp.		Att.
48	Atlanta	10	(H)	51,250
3	Chicago	20	(A)	63,551
	Green Bay*		(H)	
31	*Detroit*	*27*	*(A)*	*4,919*
13	*San Diego*	*17*	*(H)*	*23,873*
20	*Minnesota*	*10*	*(H)*	*20,850*
26	Chicago	27	(H)	70,747
23	Green Bay	17	(A)	50,308
28	St. Louis	31	(A)	22,449
17	Minnesota	23	(A)	48,605
10	San Francisco	24	(H)	63,211
3	L.A. Rams	35	(A)	45,188
34	New Orleans	44	(A)	66,471
10	Detroit	20	(H)	41,699
14	St. Louis	31	(H)	32,046
6	Indianapolis	24	(A)	60,468

*Game cancelled due to strike.
Italics denote strike replacement games.

1987 GAMES STARTED

(NOTE: Players with an asterisk (*) following their names made starts only in strike-replacement games.)

12 games: Gerald Carter, Randy Grimes, Bobby Kemp, Rick Mallory, Ervin Randle, Ricky Reynolds, Mike Stensrud, Chris Washington, James Wilder.

11 games: John Cannon, Rod Jones, Calvin Magee.

10 games: Jeff Davis, Ron Heller.

9 games: Jeff Smith.

8 games: Steve DeBerg, Ron Holmes, George Yarno.

6 games: Ray Isom, Winston Moss, Jackie Walker.

5 games: Mark Carrier, Phil Freeman, Rob Taylor, Rick Woods.

4 games: Marvin Powell, Vinny Testaverde, Paul Tripoli.

3 games: Mike Clark*, Brian Gant*, Ron Hall, Steve Holloway*, David Jordan*, J.D. Maarleveld, Fred McCallister*, Sankar Montoute*, Fred Nordgren*, Donald Pumphrey*, Marcus Quinn*, Reggie Smith*, Eric Streater*, Dan Turk, Kevin Walker*, Adrian Wright*.

2 games: Cliff Austin, Scot Brantley, Mark Cooper, Ivory Curry*, Conrad Goode, Roy Harris*, Curt Jarvis, Dan Land*, Paul O'Connor*, Chuck Pitcock*, John Reaves*, Harry Swayne, Miles Turpin*, Herkie Walls*.

1 game: Steve Carter*, Walter Carter*, Bobby Futrell, Jeff George*, Bruce Hill, James Huddleston*, Kevin Kellin, Harold Ricks*, Pat Teague*, Jim Zorn*.

TAMPA BAY BUCCANEERS 1988 VETERAN ROSTER

No.	Name	Pos.	Ht.	Wt.	NFL Exp.	Birth-date	College	Games in '87	How Acquired
20	†Austin, Cliff	RB	6-0	190	6	3- 2-60	Clemson	3	T-Atl, '87
	Bellinger, Rodney	CB	5-8	189	4	6- 4-62	Miami (Fla.)	*0	FA, '88
6	Brown, Kevin	P	6-1	185	2	1-11-63	West Texas State	*3	FA, '88
78	†Cannon, John	DE	6-5	260	7	7-30-60	William & Mary	11	D3a, '82
89	Carrier, Mark	WR	6-0	182	2	10-28-65	Nicholls State	10	D3, '87
87	Carter, Gerald	WR	6-1	190	9	6-19-57	Texas A&M	12	FA, '80
	Coleman, Dan	DT	6-4	249	2	8-14-62	Murray State	*3	FA, '88
71	†Cooper, Mark	T	6-5	270	6	2-14-60	Miami (Fla.)	*9	FA, '87
13	Criswell, Ray	P	6-0	189	2	8-16-63	Florida	3	FA, '88
58	†Davis, Jeff	LB	6-0	230	7	1-26-60	Clemson	11	D5, '82
	Edwards, Randy	NT	6-4	267	4	3- 9-61	Alabama	*7	T-Sea, '88
29	Elder, Donnie	CB	5-9	175	3	12-13-63	Memphis State	*0	FA, '88
38	Evans, James	RB	6-0	220	2	8-14-63	Southern	*2	W-KC, '87
	Ferguson, Joe	QB	6-1	195	16	4-23-50	Arkansas	*0	T-Ind, '88
81	†Freeman, Phil	WR	5-11	185	4	12- 9-62	Arizona	8	D8, '85
36	Futrell, Bobby	CB/S	5-11	190	3	8- 4-62	Elizabeth City State	12	FA, '86
91	Gant, Brian	LB	6-0	235	2	9- 6-65	Illinois State	11	FA, '87
31	Gordon, Sonny	S	5-11	192	2	7-30-65	Ohio State	7	FA, '87
53	Graham, Don	LB	6-2	244	2	1-31-64	Penn State	2	D4, '87
60	†Grimes, Randy	C	6-4	270	6	7-20-60	Baylor	12	D2, '83
82	Hall, Ron	TE	6-4	238	2	3-15-64	Hawaii	11	D4a, '87
	Heffernan, Dave	OL	6-4	255	1	10-28-62	Miami (Fla.)	2	FA, '88
5	Herline, Alan	P	6-0	170	2	9-16-64	Vanderbilt	*3	FA, '88
84	Hill, Bruce	WR	6-0	175	2	2-29-64	Arizona State	8	D4b, '87
7	Hold, Mike	QB	5-11	190	2	3-16-63	South Carolina	2	FA, '88
90	Holmes, Ron	DE	6-4	255	4	8-26-63	Washington	10	D1, '85
25	Howard, Bobby	RB	6-0	210	3	6- 1-64	Indiana	12	FA, '86
37	Hunter, Eddie	RB	5-10	195	2	1-20-65	Virginia Tech	*6	FA, '87
1	Igwebuike, Donald	K	5-9	185	4	12-27-60	Clemson	12	D10, '85
28	Isom, Ray	S	5-9	190	2	12-27-65	Penn State	6	OFA, '87
24	Jackson, Andrew	RB	5-10	190	2	5- 6-64	Iowa State	*7	FA, '88
95	Jarvis, Curt	DT/DE	6-2	266	2	1-28-65	Alabama	2	D7, '87
	Jones, Bruce	DB	6-1	195	1	12-26-62	North Alabama	*2	FA, '88
46	Jones, Dale	LB	6-1	240	2	3- 8-63	Tennessee	*3	FA, '88
22	Jones, Rod	CB	6-0	175	3	3-31-64	Southern Methodist	11	D1a, '86
75	Kellin, Kevin	DE	6-5	250	3	11-16-59	Minnesota	7	FA, '86
77	†Maarleveld, J.D.	T	6-6	300	3	10-24-61	Maryland	11	D5, '86
86	Magee, Calvin	TE	6-3	240	4	4-23-63	Southern	11	OFA, '85
68	†Mallory, Rick	G	6-2	265	4	10-21-60	Washington	12	D9, '84
99	McHale, Tom	DE	6-4	275	2	2-25-63	Cornell	3	OFA, '87
98	McInerney, Sean	DE	6-3	260	2	12-27-60	Frostburg State	*3	FA, '88
83	Miller, Solomon	WR	6-1	185	3	12- 6-64	Utah State	8	FA, '87
57	Moss, Winston	LB	6-3	235	2	12-24-65	Miami (Fla.)	12	D2a, '87
76	Mumphrey, Lloyd	DE	6-3	270	2	2-14-61	Mississippi Valley State	*3	FA, '88
59	Murphy, Kevin	LB	6-2	230	3	9- 8-63	Oklahoma	9	D2a, '86
50	Najarian, Pete	LB	6-2	232	2	12-22-63	Minnesota	*5	FA, '88
74	Pettey, Phil	G	6-4	270	2	4-17-61	Missouri	*3	FA, '88
	Pidgeon, Tim	LB	5-11	237	2	9-20-64	Syracuse	*3	FA, '88
2	Prindle, Mike	K	5-11	160	2	11-12-63	Western Michigan	*3	FA, '88
	Pumphrey, Donald	OL	6-4	275	2	11-22-63	Valdosta State	3	FA, '88
54	Randle, Ervin	LB	6-1	250	4	10-12-62	Baylor	12	D3, '85
29	Reynolds, Ricky	CB	5-11	182	2	1-19-65	Washington State	12	D2, '87
	Robinson, Mark	S	5-11	206	4	9-13-62	Penn State	*12	T-KC, '88
26	Shegog, Ronald	CB/S	6-0	195	2	3- 2-64	Austin Peay	10	FA, '88
93	Sileo, Dan	NT	6-2	282	2	1- 3-64	Miami (Fla.)	*3	FA, '88
42	Smalls, Fred	LB	6-2	235	2	1- 7-63	West Virginia	12	T-KC, '88
35	Smith, Jeff	RB	5-9	204	4	3-22-62	Nebraska	8	D7a, '87
70	Swayne, Harry	DE	6-5	268	2	2- 2-65	Rutgers	7	W-NE, '87
85	Taylor, Gene	WR	6-2	189	2	11-12-62	Fresno State	5	FA, '86
72	Taylor, Rob	T	6-6	285	3	11-14-60	Northwestern	1	FA, '88
	Teague, Pat	LB	6-1	230	2	10-22-63	North Carolina State	6	D1, '87
14	Testaverde, Vinny	QB	6-5	220	2	11-13-63	Miami (Fla.)	*1	FA, '88
	Tiffin, Van	K	5-9	155	1	9-6-55	Alabama	13	FA, '87
24	†Tripoli, Paul	S	6-0	197	2	12-14-61	Alabama	13	T-Pit, '87
50	Turk, Dan	C	6-4	260	4	6-25-62	Wisconsin	3	FA, '88
45	Turpin, Miles	LB	6-4	230	2	5-15-64	California	12	D2, '86
56	Walker, Jackie	LB	6-5	245	3	11- 3-62	Jackson State	*3	FA, '88
69	Warne, Jim	T	6-7	300	2	11-27-64	Arizona State	12	D6, '84
51	Washington, Chris	LB	6-4	230	2	3- 6-62	Iowa State		

No.	Name	Pos.	Ht.	Wt.	NFL Exp.	Birth-date	College	Games in '87	How Acquired
32	Wilder, James	RB	6-3	225	8	5-12-58	Missouri	12	D2, '81
	Williams, Derwin	WR	6-1	185	4	5- 6-61	New Mexico	*10	FA, '88
3	Williams, Keith	RB	5-10	173	2	9- 8-63	Southwest Missouri	*0	T-Atl, '87
19	Wilson, Teddy	WR	5-9	170	2	7-14-64	Central Florida	*3	FA, '88
34	†Wright, Adrian	RB	6-1	230	2	10-13-61	Virginia Union	3	FA, '87

*Bellinger last active with Bills in '86; Brown played 3 games with Bears in '87; Coleman played 3 games with Vikings in '87; Cooper played 5 games with Denver, 4 with Tampa Bay in '87; R. Edwards played 7 games with Seahawks in '87; Elder last active with Lions and Steelers in '86; J. Evans played 2 games with Chiefs in '87, active for 1 game with Buccaneers in '87, but did not play; Ferguson active for 12 games with Lions in '87, but did not play; Herline played 3 games with Patriots in '87; Hunter played 3 games with Jets, 3 games with Buccaneers in '87; Jackson played 7 games with Oilers in '87; B. Jones played 3 games with Steelers in '87; D. Jones played 3 games with Cowboys in '87; McInerney played 3 games with Bears in '87; Mumphrey played 3 games with Chiefs in '87; Najarian played 5 games with Vikings in '87; Pettey played 3 games with Redskins in '87; Pidgeon played 3 games with Dolphins in '87; Prindle played 3 games with Lions in '87; Robinson played 12 games with Chiefs in '87; Shegog played 3 games with Patriots in '87; Smalls played 3 games with Eagles in '87; Tiffin played 1 game with Dolphins in '87; Warne played 3 games with Lions in '87; D. Williams played 10 games with Patriots in '87; K. Williams missed '87 season due to injury; Wilson played 3 games with Redskins in '87.

†Option playout; subject to developments.

D—Draft; T—Trade; W—Waivers; FA—Free Agent; OFA—Original Free Agent; SupD—Supplemental Draft.

Also played with Buccaneers in '87, see page 386.

TAMPA BAY BUCCANEERS
1988 DRAFT CHOICES

(Number following name designates order of selection among 333 players drafted.)

Round and Player	Position		College
1. GRUBER, Paul	4	T	Wisconsin
2. Choice to Philadelphia (a)			
2. TATE, Lars from San Francisco (b)	53	RB	Georgia
3. Choice exercised in 1987 Supplemental Draft for Dan Sileo, DT, Miami (Fla.)			
4. GOFF, Robert from Atlanta through Philadelphia (c)	83	DT	Auburn
4. BRUHIN, John from Kansas City (d)	86	G	Tennessee
4. Choice to New England (e)			
4. ROBBINS, Monte from San Francisco (b)	107	P	Michigan
5. HOWARD, William	113	RB	Tennessee
6. Choice to Atlanta (f)			
6. LEE, Shawn from San Francisco (g)	163	DT	North Alabama
7. GOODE, Kerry	167	RB	Alabama
8. SIMPSON, Anthony from Tampa Bay through Kansas City (h)	198	RB	East Carolina
9. DAVIS, Reuben	225	DT	North Carolina
10. Choice to Pittsburgh (i)			
11. PILLOW, Frank	279	WR	Tennessee State
12. JONES, Victor	310	LB	Virginia Tech

(a) Traded pick for 2nd- and 4th-round picks in 1988, April 24, 1988.

(b) Acquired picks for 2nd-round pick in 1988, April 24, 1988.

(c) Eagles acquired pick from Falcons for tackle Leonard Mitchell, August 7, 1987; Buccaneers acquired pick from Eagles: See (a).

(d) Acquired pick, 8th-round pick in 1988 and safety Mark Robinson for quarterback Steve DeBerg, March 31, 1988.

(e) Traded pick for 5th-round pick in 1987, April 29, 1987.

(f) Traded pick for running back Cliff Austin, September 7, 1987.

(g) Acquired pick for linebacker Keith Browner, February 27, 1987.

(h) Buccaneers traded pick to Chiefs for running back Jeff Smith, September 3, 1987; Chiefs traded pick to Buccaneers: See (d).

(i) Traded pick for safety Rick Woods, September 1, 1987.

TAMPA BAY BUCCANEERS
1988 ROOKIE AND FIRST-YEAR ROSTER

Name	Pos.	Hgt.	Wgt.	Birth-date	College	How Acquired
Allen, Doug	RB	5-9	195	5- 2-65	Alabama	FA
Bruhin, John	G	6-4	285	12- 9-64	Tennessee	D4a
Carney, John	K	5-11	170	4-20-64	Notre Dame	*FA
Casparriello, Peter	TE	6-3	235	7- 9-65	Boston College	FA
Clapp, Tommy	DL	6-4	280	7- 2-65	Louisiana State	FA
Coleman, Sidney	LB	6-2	250	1-14-64	Southern Mississippi	FA
Crawford, Everett	RB	5-10	190	12- 3-65	Vanderbilt	FA
Creamer, Andre	DB	6-0	185	10- 9-66	Tennessee	FA
Davis, Reuben	DE	6-3	295	5- 7-65	North Carolina	D9
Drew, Peter	K	5-10	172	4-15-64	Troy State	*FA
Ford, Gary	TE	6-5	240	3-30-65	Texas Christian	FA
Francis, Cazzy	WR	5-10	175	12-17-63	Arkansas State	*FA
Frazier, Ed	WR	5-11	185	3-31-64	Florida	FA
Goff, Robert	DE	6-3	265	10- 2-65	Auburn	D4
Goode, Kerry	RB	6-1	200	7-28-64	Alabama	D7
Graham, Dan	C	6-2	270	5-10-65	Northern Illinois	D1
Gruber, Paul	T	6-5	290	2-24-65	Wisconsin	D1
Harris, Odie	DB	6-0	190	4- 1-66	Sam Houston State	FA
Howard, William	RB	6-0	245	6- 2-64	Tennessee	D5
Jones, Victor	LB	6-2	245	10-19-66	Virginia Tech	D12
Lee, Shawn	NT	6-3	265	10-24-66	North Alabama	D6
Lightner, Kevin	T	6-2	285	7- 4-65	Nebraska	FA
Marsh, Marvin	RB	5-10	195	10-20-63	North Alabama	FA
Maye, Mark	QB	6-3	200	1-30-65	North Carolina	FA
Morgan, Sylvester	TE	6-3	235	7-22-65	Texas A&M	FA
Morton, James	RB	6-0	220	2- 6-65	West Texas State	FA
Moses, Cedric	DB	5-11	185	2-10-64	Jacksonville State	FA
Pillow, Frank	WR	5-10	170	4-11-65	Tennessee State	D11
Ransdell, Bill	QB	6-2	210	4-15-63	Kentucky	*FA
Robbins, Monte	P	6-4	200	9-19-64	Michigan	D4b
Rolling, Henry	LB	6-2	210	9- 8-65	Nevada-Reno	*D5, '87
Seals, Ray	TE	6-3	245	6-17-65	None	FA
Simmonds, Mike	G	6-4	281	8-12-64	Indiana State	*D10, '87
Simpson, Anthony	RB	5-10	245	12-21-64	East Carolina	D8
Smith, Bill	P	6-3	225	6- 9-65	Mississippi	*FA
Smith, Danny	WR	6-3	205	5-27-66	South Carolina	FA
Smith, Don	RB	5-11	200	10-30-63	Mississippi State	*D2, '87
Sowell, Brent	T/G	6-5	285	3-27-63	Alabama	*FA
Symington, Chris	G	6-2	290	3-14-64	Colorado	FA
Tate, Lars	RB	6-2	215	2- 2-66	Georgia	D2
Thomas, Kevin	C	6-2	268	7-27-64	Arizona State	*FA, '87
White, Randy	WR	6-0	180	1- 1-66	Florida State	FA
Whitehurst, Clay	WR	6-0	185	12-20-65	Alabama	FA

*Carney: FA Cincinnati '87, released 8/10, FA replacement Tampa Bay 9/24, released 10/14; Drew: FA New England '87, released 8/19; Francis: FA Tampa Bay '87, did not report and released 7/18; Ransdell: D12 New York Jets '87, injured reserve 8/25 through 11/2, released 11/3; Rolling, Simmonds, Don Smith and Thomas missed '87 season due to injury; B. Smith: D7 Green Bay '87, released 9/7; Sowell: D6 Miami '86, released 8/25, FA Chicago '87, injured reserve 9/2 through 11/8, released 11/9.

WASHINGTON REDSKINS
(Eastern Division, National Conference)

Joe Gibbs

Chairman, Chief Operating Officer—Jack Kent Cooke
Executive Vice President—John Kent Cooke
General Manager—Bobby Beathard
Director of Player Personnel—Dick Daniels
Head Coach—Joe Gibbs (7 years: 74-30)
Assistant Coaches:
  Special Teams—Chuck Banker
  Offensive Backfield—Don Breaux
  Assistant Head Coach-Offense—Joe Bugel
  Offensive Assistant—Dan Henning
  Defensive Coordinator—Larry Peccatiello
  Assistant Head Coach-Defense—Richie Petitbon
  Strength & Conditioning—Dan Riley
  Tight Ends—Warren Simmons
  Receivers—Charley Taylor
  Defensive Assistant—Emmitt Thomas
  Defensive Line—LaVern Torgeson
Director of Media Relations—John Konoza
  (Office Phone: 471-9100—Area Code 703)
Offices—Redskin Park, 13832 Redskin Drive, Herndon, Va., 22071; Mailing Address: P. O. Box 17247, Dulles International Airport, Washington, D. C. 20041
Stadium—RFK Memorial Stadium (Capacity: 55,642)
Team Colors—Burgundy and Gold
Training Site—Dickinson College, Carlisle, Pa.

1988 SCHEDULE
(All times local.
All games Sunday unless noted otherwise.)

Sept.	5	at New York Giants (Mon.)	9:00
Sept.	11	PITTSBURGH	1:00
Sept.	18	PHILADELPHIA	1:00
Sept.	25	at Phoenix	1:00
Oct.	2	NEW YORK GIANTS	1:00
Oct.	9	at Dallas	12:00
Oct.	16	PHOENIX	1:00
Oct.	23	vs. Green Bay at Milwaukee	12:00
Oct.	30	at Houston	7:00
Nov.	6	NEW ORLEANS	4:00
Nov.	13	CHICAGO	1:00
Nov.	21	at San Francisco (Mon.)	6:00
Nov.	27	CLEVELAND	1:00
Dec.	4	at Philadelphia	1:00
Dec.	11	DALLAS	1:00
Dec.	17	at Cincinnati (Sat.)	12:30

1987 RESULTS—(Won 14, Lost 4)

Redskins		Opp.		Att.
34	Philadelphia	24	(H)	52,128
20	Atlanta	21	(A)	50,882
	New England*		(H)	
28	*St. Louis*	*21*	*(H)*	*27,728*
38	*New York Giants*	*12*	*(A)*	*9,123*
13	*Dallas*	*7*	*(A)*	*60,415*
17	New York Jets	16	(H)	53,497
27	Buffalo	7	(A)	71,640
27	Philadelphia	31	(A)	63,609
20	Detroit	13	(H)	53,593
26	L.A. Rams	30	(H)	53,614
23	New York Giants	19	(H)	45,815
34	St. Louis	17	(A)	31,324
24	Dallas	20	(H)	54,882
21	Miami	23	(A)	65,715
27	Minnesota (OT)	24	(A)	59,166
	NFC SEMIFINAL GAME			
21	Chicago	17	(A)	66,030
	NFC CHAMPIONSHIP GAME			
17	Minnesota	10	(H)	55,212
	NFL CHAMPIONSHIP GAME			
42	Denver	10	(†)	73,302

*Game cancelled due to strike.
(†)Jack Murphy Stadium, San Diego, Calif.
Italics denote strike replacement games.

1987 GAMES STARTED

(NOTE: Players with an asterisk (*) following their names made starts only in strike-replacement games.)

12 games: Todd Bowles, Dave Butz, Monte Coleman, Darrell Green, Joe Jacoby, Mel Kaufman, Charles Mann, Raleigh McKenzie, R.C. Thielemann, Alvin Walton, Don Warren, Barry Wilburn.

11 games: Gary Clark, Darryl Grant.

10 games: Dexter Manley, Mark May, Jay Schroeder.

9 games: Art Monk, George Rogers.

6 games: Clint Didier, Neal Olkewicz.

5 games: Jeff Bostic, Joe Caravello, Russ Grimm, Rich Milot, Ricky Sanders.

4 games: Darrick Brilz.

3 games: Anthony Allen*, Dan Benish*, Mark Carlson*, Eric Coyle*, Bob Curtis*, Alec Gibson*, Skip Lane*, Steven Martin*, Craig McEwen*, Mike Mitchell*, Phil Pettey*, Ed Rubbert*, Willard Scissum*, Ed Simmons, Lionel Vital*, Eric Wilson*, Dennis Woodberry*.

2 games: Keith Griffin, Markus Koch, Carlton Rose*, Tony Sagnella*, Doug Williams, Ted Wilson*.

1 game: Kelvin Bryant, Joe Cofer*, Glenn Dennison, Steve Gage*, Kurt Gouveia, Dean Hamel, Charles Jackson*, Ted Karras*, Jamie Kimmel*, Terry Orr, Derrick Shepard*, Clarence Verdin.

WASHINGTON REDSKINS 1988 VETERAN ROSTER

No.	Name	Pos.	Ht.	Wt.	NFL Exp.	Birth-date	College	Games in '87	How Acquired
89	Allen, Anthony	RB	5-11	182	4	6-29-59	Washington	3	FA, '87
4	Atkinson, Jess	K	5-9	168	4	12-11-61	Maryland	1	FA, '86
95	†Benish, Dan	DT	6-5	275	6	11-21-60	Clemson	3	FA, '87
53	Bostic, Jeff	C	6-2	260	9	9-18-58	Clemson	12	FA, '80
23	Bowles, Todd	S	6-2	203	3	11-18-63	Temple	12	OFA, '86
29	†Branch, Reggie	RB	5-11	235	3	10-22-62	East Carolina	12	OFA, '85
	Brilz, Darrick	G	6-3	264	2	2-14-64	Oregon State	7	OFA, '87
24	Bryant, Kelvin	RB	6-2	195	3	9-26-60	North Carolina	11	D7, '83
65	Butz, Dave	DT	6-7	295	15	6-23-50	Purdue	12	VFA, '75
50	Caldwell, Ravin	LB	6-3	229	2	8- 4-63	Arkansas	12	D5, '86
88	Caravello, Joe	TE	6-3	270	2	6- 6-63	Tulane	11	FA, '87
	Carlson, Mark	T	6-6	284	2	6- 6-63	Southern Conn. State	3	OFA, '87
84	Clark, Gary	WR	5-9	173	4	5- 1-62	James Madison	12	SupD, '84
51	†Coleman, Monte	LB	6-2	230	10	11- 4-57	Central Arkansas	12	D11, '79
12	Cox, Steve	P/K	6-4	195	8	5-11-58	Arkansas	12	FA, '85
	Coyle, Eric	C	6-3	260	2	10-26-63	Colorado	3	OFA, '87
	Curtis, Bobby	LB	6-2	235	2	10-23-64	Savannah State	3	FA, '88
34	Davis, Brian	CB	6-2	190	2	8-31-63	Nebraska	7	D2, '87
86	†Didier, Clint	TE	6-5	240	7	4- 4-59	Portland State	9	D12, '81
48	Gage, Steve	S	6-3	210	2	5-10-64	Tulsa	4	D6, '87
	Gehring, Mark	TE	6-4	235	2	4-16-64	Eastern Washington	*6	FA, '88
54	Gouveia, Kurt	LB	6-1	227	2	9-14-64	Brigham Young	11	D8, '86
77	†Grant, Darryl	DT	6-1	275	8	11-22-59	Rice	12	D9, '81
28	Green, Darrell	CB	5-8	170	6	2-15-60	Texas A&I	12	D1, '83
35	†Griffin, Keith	RB	5-8	185	5	10-26-61	Miami (Fla.)	9	D10, '84
68	†Grimm, Russ	C/G	6-3	275	8	5- 2-59	Pittsburgh	6	D3, '81
6	†Haji-Sheikh, Ali	K	6-0	172	5	1-11-61	Michigan	11	FA, '87
78	Hamel, Dean	DT	6-3	290	4	7- 7-61	Tulsa	12	D12, '85
64	†Hamilton, Steve	DE/DT	6-4	270	4	9-28-61	East Carolina	12	D2a, '84
	Hitchcock, Ray	C/G	6-2	289	2	6-20-65	Minnesota	5	D12, '87
66	Jacoby, Joe	T	6-7	305	8	7- 6-59	Louisville	12	OFA, '81
21	Jessie, Tim	RB	5-11	190	2	3- 1-63	Auburn	3	OFA, '87
82	Jones, Anthony	TE	6-3	248	4	5-16-60	Wichita State	2	D11, '84
55	Kaufman, Mel	LB	6-2	230	7	2-24-58	Cal Poly-SLO	12	OFA, '81
61	Kehr, Rick	G	6-3	285	2	6-18-59	Carthage	5	FA, '87
74	Koch, Markus	DE	6-5	275	3	2-13-63	Boise State	12	D2, '86
72	Manley, Dexter	DE	6-3	257	8	2- 2-59	Oklahoma State	11	D5, '81
71	Mann, Charles	DE	6-6	270	6	4-12-61	Nevada-Reno	12	D3, '83
58	Marshall, Wilber	LB	6-1	225	5	4-18-62	Florida	*12	VFA, '88
73	May, Mark	T	6-6	295	8	11- 2-59	Pittsburgh	10	D1, '81
	McEwen, Craig	TE	6-1	220	2	12-16-65	Utah	4	OFA, '87
63	McKenzie, Raleigh	G	6-2	275	4	2- 8-63	Tennessee	12	D11, '85
81	Monk, Art	WR	6-3	209	9	12- 5-57	Syracuse	9	D1, '80
52	†Olkewicz, Neal	LB	6-0	233	10	1-30-57	Maryland	10	OFA, '79
	Ontko, Bob	LB	6-3	236	2	3-21-64	Penn State	*3	FA, '88
87	†Orr, Terry	TE	6-3	227	3	9-27-61	Texas	10	D10, '85
	Rose, Carlton	LB	6-2	220	1	2- 8-62	Michigan	2	FA, '88
11	†Rypien, Mark	QB	6-4	234	2	10- 2-62	Washington State	*0	D6a, '86
83	Sanders, Ricky	WR	5-11	180	5	8-30-62	Southwest Texas State	12	T-NE, '86
10	Schroeder, Jay	QB	6-4	215	5	6-28-61	UCLA	11	D3, '84
	Scott, Ronald	RB	6-0	205	2	3- 3-63	Southern	*3	FA, '88
	Shepard, Derrick	WR	5-11	183	1	1-22-64	Oklahoma	2	FA, '88
76	Simmons, Ed	T	6-5	280	2	12-31-63	Eastern Washington	5	D6a, '87
36	Smith, Timmy	RB	5-11	216	2	1-21-64	Texas Tech	7	D5, '87
	Stanley, Jack	QB	6-4	212	2	4-26-64	Nevada-Reno	*0	FA, '88
69	†Thielemann, R.C.	G	6-4	272	12	8-12-55	Arkansas	12	T-Atl, '85
	Thompson, Gary	DB	6-0	180	3	2-23-59	San Jose State	1	FA, '88
31	Vaughn, Clarence	S	6-0	202	2	7-17-64	Northern Illinois	5	D8, '87
40	Walton, Alvin	S	6-0	180	3	3-14-64	Kansas	12	D3, '86
85	Warren, Don	TE	6-4	242	10	5- 5-56	San Diego State	12	D4, '77
45	†Wilburn, Barry	CB	6-3	186	4	12- 9-63	Mississippi	12	D8, '85
17	Williams, Doug	QB	6-4	220	8	8- 9-55	Grambling State	5	T-TB, '86
46	Woodberry, Dennis	CB	5-10	183	3	4-22-61	Southern Arkansas	12	FA, '87
80	Yarber, Eric	WR/KR	5-8	156	2	9-22-63	Idaho	12	D12, '86

*Gehring played 6 games with Oilers in '87; Marshall played 12 games with Bears in '87; Ontko played 3 games with Colts in '87; Rypien active for 1 game with Redskins in '87, but did not play; Scott played 3 games with Dolphins in '87; Stanley active for 3 games with Redskins in '87, but did not play.

†Option playout; subject to developments.

WASHINGTON REDSKINS
1988 DRAFT CHOICES

(Number following name designates order of selection among 333 players drafted.)

Round and Player		Position	College
1. Choice to Chicago (a)			
2. LOHMILLER, Chip	55	K	Minnesota
3. OLIPHANT, Mike from L.A. Rams (b)	66	KR	Puget Sound
3. Choice to L.A. Rams (c)			
4. MORRIS, Jamie	109	RB	Michigan
5. MIMS, Carl from New England (d)	127	DB	Sam Houston St.
5. Choice to L.A. Rams (c)			
6. HUMPHRIES, Stan from Indianapolis (e)	159	QB	N.E. Louisiana
6. Choice to L.A. Rams (c)			
7. HICKS, Harold	193	DB	San Diego State
8. McGILL, Darryl	221	RB	Wake Forest
9. PETERSON, Blake	249	LB	Mesa (Colo.)
10. BROWN, Henry	277	T	Ohio State
11. KOCH, Curt	305	DE	Colorado
12. ROSS, Wayne from L.A. Rams (f)	315	P	San Diego State
12. Choice to L.A. Rams (g)			

(a) Pick and 1st-round pick in 1989 sent as compensation for free agent signing of linebacker Wilber Marshall, March 18, 1988.

(b) Acquired pick for 3rd-, 5th- and 6th-round picks in 1988, April 24, 1988.

(c) See (b).

(d) Acquired pick for 4th-round pick in 1989, April 24, 1988.

(e) Acquired pick for wide receiver Clarence Verdin, March 29, 1988.

(f) Acquired pick for 12th-round pick in 1988 and 11th-round pick in 1989, April 25, 1988.

(g) See (f).

WASHINGTON REDSKINS
1988 ROOKIE AND FIRST-YEAR ROSTER

Name	Pos.	Hgt.	Wgt.	Birth-date	College	How Acquired
Adams, Marvin	DE	6-5	270	12-30-64	Washington State	FA
Alexander, Dave	G	6-2	264	7-19-64	Iowa	FA
Annexstad, Scott	G	6-4	272	7- 8-64	Mankato State	FA
Austin, Teryl	S	6-0	195	3- 3-65	Pittsburgh	FA
Banderas, Tom	TE	6-2	247	6- 6-65	Nebraska	FA
Berkemeier, Roy	T	6-3	285	3-21-65	Austin Peay	FA
Blondell, Jim	DT	6-2	270	2-17-65	Illinois	FA
Brown, Henry	T	6-4	262	1-27-65	Ohio State	D10
Carl, Lance	WR	6-1	190	9-13-65	Colorado	FA
Corse, Cedric	LB	6-2	227	12-24-64	Mississippi State	FA
Davis, Donald	CB	5-9	177	1-23-65	Idaho State	FA
Demerest, Chris	S	6-2	200	2- 9-65	Northeastern	FA
Donaldson, Duke	WR	5-10	170	5-16-66	Auburn	FA
Duckens, Mark	DT	6-4	260	3- 4-65	Arizona State	FA
Dumpson, Jeffrey	S	5-11	190	10-21-64	Towson State	FA
Grant, African	CB	6-0	198	8- 2-65	Illinois	FA
Green, Rod	WR	5-8	168	3-23-65	Oregon	FA
Harbour, Dave	G/C	6-4	265	10-23-65	Illinois	FA
Hawkins, Gilbert	WR	5-10	180	10-24-64	Oregon State	FA
Hicks, Harold	S/CB	6-0	200	12- 7-65	San Diego State	D7
Holmes, Carl	T	6-6	280	5-29-65	Temple	FA
Humphries, Stan	QB	6-2	223	4-14-65	N.E. Louisiana	D6
Jackson, Cecil	LB	6-3	212	11-13-63	Eastern New Mexico	FA
Karamanos, Ted	G	6-2	282	6-12-65	Northern Illinois	FA
Kleine, Wally	DT	6-9	320	10-22-64	Notre Dame	*D2, '87
Knighton, Rodney	RB	5-11	205	5-17-65	Louisville	FA
Koch, Curt	DE	6-8	270	8- 3-65	Colorado	D11
Krumm, Todd	S	6-0	189	12-18-65	Michigan State	FA
Lohmiller, Chip	K	6-3	213	7-16-66	Minnesota	D2
Maiden, Petey	TE	6-2	220	9- 7-65	Utah State	FA
Manusky, Greg	LB	6-1	242	8-12-66	Colgate	FA
McDonald, Tim	DE	6-3	260	2-16-65	Kansas State	FA
McGill, Darryl	RB	5-10	210	3-28-66	Wake Forest	D8
Mims, Carl	CB	5-10	180	10-28-65	Sam Houston State	D5
Morris, Jamie	RB	5-7	188	6- 6-65	Michigan	D4
Newton, Grady	LB	6-1	225	12-20-64	Kansas State	FA
Oliphant, Mike	RB/KR	5-10	183	5-19-63	Puget Sound	D3
Peterson, Blake	LB	6-4	245	5-14-66	Mesa (Colo.)	D9
Reese, Albert	TE	6-4	245	2-15-65	Southern Methodist	*FA, '87
Robinson, Kenneth	LB	6-1	234	12- 4-63	South Carolina	*FA, '87
Robison, Doug	P	6-4	217	5-29-66	Stanford	FA
Ross, Wayne	P	6-3	210	2- 8-65	San Diego State	D12
Scully, Mike	C	6-5	280	11- 1-65	Illinois	FA
Shepard, Derrick	WR	5-10	187	1-22-64	Oklahoma	FA
Smith, Warren	CB	5-11	175	6-12-65	Wake Forest	FA
Stewart, Chris	S/CB	5-10	183	2-20-66	Bethune-Cookman	FA
Thomas, Johnny	CB	5-9	190	7- 3-64	Baylor	*D7, '87
Thompson, Steve	DT	6-2	285	6-24-65	Minnesota	*FA
Tramel, Kent	DT	6-2	260	2-22-65	Texas Christian	FA
White, Kelvin	RB	5-11	205	6- 1-62	Oklahoma	FA
White, Robb	DE	6-4	270	5-26-65	South Dakota	FA

*Kleine, Reese, Robinson and Thomas missed '87 season due to injury; Thompson: FA Washington '87, released 8/31, FA replacement Washington 9/23, released 10/8.

Anything But Normal in 1987

By VITO STELLINO

The National Football League's 1987 season was an upside-down year, a season of inexplicable twists and turns that had to be seen to be believed.

While such perennial doormats as New Orleans, Indianapolis and Houston made the playoffs, such traditional contenders as the Los Angeles Raiders, Dallas Cowboys, Miami Dolphins and Pittsburgh Steelers watched the playoffs on television for the second straight year.

Whether all this was an aberration or the new wave of football parity won't be known until 1988, when the NFL gets back to the normalcy of a 16-game season.

The 1987 season was a lot of things, but normal wasn't one of them.

It was a two-tier season, a three-game season of strike games played by—depending on your viewpoint—replacement players or scabs and a 12-game season played by the regular players.

It added up to 15 games, one short of a normal NFL schedule. Lost forever was the third weekend of the season that was cancelled when the players went on strike September 22.

After the players struck for 57 days in 1982 and wiped out seven games of that season, both sides expressed the belief that it would never happen again.

Both sides were wrong. They hadn't learned their lessons.

The owners, though, had learned one thing: They weren't about to be shut down again. After taking one week off to put together hastily assembled teams consisting of former NFL and United States Football League players, castoffs and amateur dreamers willing to cross the picket lines, the league picked up the schedule with the fourth weekend.

The games were something less than artistic successes and featured strange-looking plays by NFL standards. San Francisco even ran the Wishbone offense.

But the owners gave the games, which counted in the standings, credit for shortening the strike. As Commissioner Pete Rozelle said, "The replacement games troubled me, but they played a major part in shortening the strike. There's no easy answer during a strike."

After watching two weeks of strike games, the players were ready to come back for the sixth weekend of the season. They ended the strike without a contract October 15 when they filed an antitrust lawsuit against the owners in Minneapolis.

But the owners didn't allow the regular players to return to the field for that weekend be-

Striking NFL players (in foreground) didn't appreciate the replacement players who took over their jobs.

cause they hadn't reported for work by the 1 p.m. Wednesday, October 14 deadline.

Cris Collinsworth, the Cincinnati receiver, summed up the owners' hard-line attitude when he said, "It's the end of the Civil War here and they're taking Atlanta. Let's get the furniture before it burns, too."

The National Labor Relations Board subsequently filed an unfair labor practice charge against the owners for not letting the players put on their uniforms that weekend. If the union prevails on the issue, the players may still get paid. That could cost the owners about $20 million.

As it stands now, each player who stayed out for the entire strike lost 25 percent of his base salary for the season. The player suffering the biggest loss was Cincinnati quarterback Boomer Esiason. The strike cost him $300,000 of his $1.2 million base salary.

For a rookie making the $50,000 minimum, the strike cost $12,500. A player making the average NFL salary of $230,000 lost $57,500.

The owners also lost millions in ticket revenue and had to rebate money to the television networks because the ratings dropped during the replacement games.

Those fans who attended games during the three weekends of strike replacement football didn't have much trouble finding available seats.

Rozelle said that more than half the teams lost money for the season.

The fans, though, showed remarkable tolerance for the wrangling of the owners and players. Although overall attendance dropped in all games from the 1986 record level of 17,223,212 to 15,180,013 because of the replacement games and the lost weekend that was wiped out, the average per game attendance for the 12 non-strike weekends was 59,717. Only twice has the NFL averaged more than 60,000.

The network television ratings also bounced back quickly and the league's first cable package—Sunday night games on ESPN the final eight weekends of the season—was a success and set cable records.

The key issue in the strike was the players' attempt to gain unrestricted free agency at some point in their careers so they could switch teams without compensation.

When the strike started, only one player, defensive back Norm Thompson, who went from the Cardinals to the Colts for a third-round pick in 1977, had switched teams with compensation since the current system was put in place in 1977.

It was an ironic touch that after the strike in March, Washington signed Chicago linebacker Wilber Marshall to a five-year, $6 million contract. When Chicago declined to match the offer, Marshall went to Washington and the Bears got the Redskins' first-round picks for the next two years.

The owners said the Marshall signing was an indication the system can work and more players would move under the revised compensation limits the owners were offering the players. The players insisted one signing doesn't start a trend.

The free agency question will now be decided by the courts, but there's no question the replacement games had a major impact on the season. For the defending-champion New York Giants, they played a critical role in their downfall.

The Giants started the season 0-2, lost all three replacement games to drop to 0-5 and never recovered. They wound up with a 6-9 record.

It has now been almost a decade since a defending champion has repeated in the NFL. The Pittsburgh Steelers of 1978-79 were the last to do it.

In fact, the last four champions (the 1983 Raiders, the '84 49ers, the '85 Bears and the '86 Giants) have failed to win a playoff game in any season since winning the Vince Lombardi Trophy. The only team to show much consistency in this decade has been the Washington Redskins, a team that profited handsomely from the replacement games.

Even though not a single Redskin veteran crossed the picket line, General Manager Bobby Beathard and his staff managed to round up a competitive replacement team featuring quarterbacks Ed Rubbert and Tony

All-Pro linebacker Wilber Marshall became the first free agent to switch teams in 11 years when he left the Bears to join the Redskins.

Robinson and running back Lionel Vital that won all three replacement games.

Vital rushed for 346 yards in the three games and wound up 21st in the NFC in rushing for the season, even though he didn't get a carry after the strike.

The three strike wins helped the Redskins win their division with an 11-4 record and they went on to win the Super Bowl for the second time in the last six seasons.

Even though they've gone from Joe Theismann to Jay Schroeder to Doug Williams at quarterback and from John Riggins to George Rogers to Timmy Smith at running back in Joe Gibbs' seven years as a head coach, the Redskins have managed to make the playoffs five times in the last six years.

After winning the Super Bowl in the 1982 strike season, they came back to make the Super Bowl again in 1983 and the NFC title game in 1986.

They join the 49ers and the Raiders as the only three teams to win two Super Bowls in this decade.

The Redskins kept alive a tradition in the Super Bowl when they blew out the Denver Broncos, 42-10. It was the fifth straight year that the Super Bowl has been a blowout. The scores of the previous four games won by the Raiders, 49ers, Bears and Giants were 38-9, 38-16, 46-10 and 39-20.

Nobody can explain why the sport's showcase game tends to be so disappointing. It was particularly frustrating for the Broncos, who were routed for the second straight year. Two years ago, they lost to the Giants, 39-20.

In both games, their wunderkind quarterback, John Elway, gave his team an early lead and then was trumped by the opposing quarterback. First, it was the Giants' Phil Simms. Last year it was the Redskins' Doug Williams.

Williams, the first black quarterback to play in a Super Bowl, directed a 35-point second-period explosion, a playoff record. Williams threw four touchdown passes in that quarter to tie the Super Bowl record for four quarters of play.

Records fell like leaves on a windy autumn day as the Redskins ran up 602 yards and scored five touchdowns on just 18 offensive plays in the second period.

Williams passed for more yards (340), rookie Timmy Smith ran for more yards (204) and Ricky Sanders caught passes for more yards (193) than any players in Super Bowl history.

Two other teams, San Francisco and Cleveland, were as disappointed by their season-ending games as the Broncos.

San Francisco won its three strike games, posted the best record in football (13-2) during the regular season and was favored to win its third Super Bowl of the decade.

Instead, the 49ers were stunned at home in their first playoff game by the Minnesota Vikings, 36-24. It may or may not be a coincidence, but after the season, when Owner Edward DeBartolo Jr. extended Coach Bill Walsh's contract for two years, he removed the additional title of president.

Cleveland suffered the frustration of losing the AFC title game to the Broncos for the second straight year. Two years ago, Elway engineered a clutch 98-yard drive in the final quarter to send the game into overtime and the Broncos won, 23-20. Last year, Cleveland's Earnest Byner fumbled as he was attempting to score the tying touchdown with 1:05 left. The Broncos then took a safety and won, 38-33.

For New Orleans, Indianapolis and Houston, it was an accomplishment just to make the playoffs.

The Saints, who had never recorded a winning season and had never gone to the playoffs, enjoyed a remarkable 12-3 season under Coach Jim Mora, who was just in his second

The October 31 trade that landed disgruntled running back Eric Dickerson (left) in Indianapolis and rookie linebacker Cornelius Bennett in Buffalo was one of the biggest in recent NFL history.

season with the team after winning a pair of championships in the United States Football League with the Philadelphia-Baltimore Stars.

The fact that the Saints were beaten, 44-10, in their first playoff game by Minnesota didn't diminish the fact that the Saints finally turned their program around.

Minnesota had a topsy-turvy season that was a microcosm of what the league went through as a whole. The Vikings won their first two games before the strike, lost all three strike games and won five of their next six after the strike to get back into contention. At that point, the Vikings' regular players were 7-1.

The Vikings then slumped, losing three of their last four playoff games and control of their playoff destiny. They needed help from Dallas, which upset St. Louis in the regular-season finale, to get into the playoffs.

Once the Vikings got in, they upset New Orleans and San Francisco on the road and came within a Darrin Nelson fourth-down dropped pass of pushing the Redskins into overtime in the NFC title game. They lost, 17-10.

The Indianapolis Colts hadn't made the playoffs or posted a winning season since 1977 when the team was in Baltimore. It seemed like more of the same when the team lost its first two games last year.

But with the help of quarterback Gary Hogeboom, one of the first starting players to cross the picket line, the Colts won their first two strike games.

After the strike, on Halloween, the Colts then pulled off one of the most talked-about trades in recent years. After sending unsigned rookie linebacker Cornelius Bennett to the Buffalo Bills for two first-round picks, a second-round pick and running back Greg Bell, they shipped three first-round picks, three seconds, Bell and running back Owen Gill to the Los Angeles Rams for running back Eric Dickerson.

Dickerson, who was unhappy with his Ram contract, quickly agreed to a four-year $5.55 million deal with the Colts. He had played under Indianapolis Coach Ron Meyer in his college days at SMU, and quickly rejuvenated the Colt attack. The team won the AFC East with a 9-6 record before losing to Cleveland, 38-21, in the playoffs.

Buffalo, however, prefers to view the deal as the Cornelius Bennett trade instead of the Eric Dickerson trade. Combining with rookie Shane Conlan and Bruce Smith to form the heart of the Buffalo defense, Bennett recorded 8½ sacks in half a season to tie for fifth in the AFC in that department.

Buffalo is now more than the Jim Kelly Show. The team finished 7-8 and may be a contender in 1988.

The Los Angeles Rams, meanwhile, think they'll have a bright future with all the draft picks they collected in the Dickerson deal. They also showed they can run the ball without Dickerson.

Bo Jackson's 221 yards rushing against Seattle on November 30 was the season's high.

While Dickerson led the AFC in rushing with 1,288 yards, Charles White, who overcame a drug problem, stepped into Dickerson's shoes and led the NFL with 1,376.

Houston hadn't made the playoffs since the Bum Phillips era ended in 1981, but the 1987 Oilers went 9-6 and beat Seattle, 23-20, in the wild-card game before losing to Denver, 34-10.

Four teams accustomed to victory—the Raiders, Cowboys, Dolphins and Steelers—continued to experience hard times. The Raiders started out 3-0 and then lost seven straight and finished 5-10. Dallas went 7-8 while Miami and Pittsburgh were 8-7. These four teams had combined to win 10 straight Super Bowls in the 1970s and early '80s.

The most colorful team continued to be the Chicago Bears, aided by their controversial coach, Mike Ditka. Although the Bears lost their playoff opener at home to Washington for the second straight year, they were never dull. Among other things, Ditka threw gum in the stands in San Francisco and said Washington's Dexter Manley had the "IQ of a grapefruit." He also knocked the Metrodome in Minneapolis as a "Rollerdome."

The season featured many individual exploits. The San Francisco passing combination of Joe Montana to Jerry Rice was spectacular all year long. Montana passed for 31 touchdowns and Rice made 22 touchdown catches.

Steve Largent of Seattle, who seems destined to break every pass receiving record in the book, caught six passes in his final game to boost his lifetime total to 752 and surpass Charlie Joiner's old mark of 750.

Philadelphia's Reggie White also solidified his standing as the game's finest defensive player, collecting 21 sacks in just 12 games. No other player had more than 12½.

The Raiders' Bo Jackson, also a major league baseball player with the Kansas City Royals, rushed for 221 yards against Seattle, but later injured his ankle in Kansas City and sat out the final two games.

Off the field, the major development was the St. Louis Cardinals' move to Phoenix at the end of the year. It was the third franchise move of this decade—the Raiders went from Oakland to Los Angeles in 1982 and the Colts from Baltimore to Indianapolis in 1984. But this was the first move to be approved by the league since the Cardinals went from Chicago to St. Louis in 1960. The Cardinals were in St. Louis 28 years and never won or hosted a playoff game.

The United States Football League also lost its appeal of the loss of its antitrust lawsuit to the NFL. The USFL went out of business in the fall of 1986 after being awarded only $3 in damages.

Instant replay was used for a second straight year and continued to be popular with the fans, though there still were several glitches in the operation. After some debate, the owners approved it for a third season by a 23-5 margin. In one change, the replay official will be a member of the officiating crew. League personnel will no longer be used in that capacity.

Only two coaching changes were made at the end of the season. Forrest Gregg resigned in Green Bay to go to his college alma mater, SMU, and Tom Flores resigned the Los Angeles Raider job, saying he was "tired." There was much speculation that he was given a push by Raider boss Al Davis.

Lindy Infante, a Cleveland assistant who had been a head coach in the USFL, got the Green Bay job, and Mike Shanahan, a Denver assistant, was named the Raiders coach.

One of the game's greatest players, Chicago running back Walter Payton, retired as the league's all-time leading rusher and immediately stepped into the team's front office to begin a second career.

Billy Sullivan, who founded the New England Patriots in 1960, was forced to sell the team because of financial problems. After prolonged negotiations with several interested parties, Sullivan sold the team to Reebok shoe executive Paul Fireman. Sullivan's son, Patrick, remains the team's general manager. The Patriots were the only team to change ownership.

'87 REGULAR SEASON GAMES

FIRST WEEK

RESULTS OF WEEK 1
Sunday, September 13

Cincinnati 23, Indianapolis 21 at Ind.
Denver 40, Seattle 17 at Den.
Houston 20, L.A. Rams 16 at Hous.
Kansas City 20, San Diego 13 at K.C.
L.A. Raiders 20, Green Bay 0 at G.B.
Minnesota 34, Detroit 19 at Minn.
New England 28, Miami 21 at N.E.
New Orleans 28, Cleveland 21 at N.O.
N.Y. Jets 31, Buffalo 28 at Buff.
Pittsburgh 30, San Francisco 17 at Pitt.
St. Louis 24, Dallas 13 at St. L.
Tampa Bay 48, Atlanta 10 at T.B.
Washington 34, Philadelphia 24 at Wash.

Monday, September 14

Chicago 34, N.Y. Giants 19 at Chi.

The 68th National Football League season opened September 13 in much the same manner it would end some 4½ months later in the Super Bowl: The Washington Redskins would be winners and quarterback Doug Williams would be their star.

Williams, who was acquired by the Redskins as a backup signal-caller to Jay Schroeder in August 1986, climaxed the '87 season by being named Most Valuable Player in Washington's 42-10 destruction of the Denver Broncos in Super Bowl XXII. But Williams gave a preview of his later heroics in the Redskins' 34-24 victory over Philadelphia in Week 1.

Schroeder, who was named to the Pro Bowl in 1986 after his first full season as an NFL starting quarterback, suffered a sprained right shoulder on Washington's second possession after a hit by the Eagles' Reggie White. In came Williams, the former Tampa Bay quarterback who had not completed a pass in the NFL since 1982.

The 32-year-old veteran responded by completing 17 of 27 passes for 272 yards and two touchdowns, including a 39-yard strike to Art Monk on the first play of the fourth quarter to break a 24-24 tie.

"It's tough to sit, having been a starter, and having to play the backup role," Williams said. "I just hope some of the people who never called to give Doug Williams a chance, I hope they hurt."

Williams, who was a starter during his five years with the Buccaneers (1978-82) and two seasons in the United States Football League (1984-85), had been shopped around the league by the Redskins the previous off-season in hopes of getting him a starting job. But when only the Los Angeles Raiders showed interest

(reportedly offering a second-round draft choice), Washington decided to keep the veteran as a backup to Schroeder.

"Doug and I have had several hard-fought discussions because you talk about his future, what's best for him and all that," said Redskins Coach Joe Gibbs, who was an assistant coach with the Bucs in 1978 during Williams' rookie season. "It's kind of tough, but this is why you have him."

Four and a half months later, Redskin fans were glad they did.

Veteran Steve DeBerg beat out celebrated rookie Vinny Testaverde for Williams' old Tampa Bay position and celebrated by setting a club record with five touchdown passes in the Buccaneers' 48-10 rout of Atlanta. DeBerg, named the starter by Coach Ray Perkins just one week before the opening game, completed 24 of 34 passes for 333 yards to lead the Bucs to their most lopsided victory in club history. It was the Buccaneers' first opening-day win since 1981 and Perkins' first as an NFL head coach since 1982, when he left the New York Giants to take the University of Alabama coaching job.

DeBerg, who threw seven interceptions in Tampa Bay's 31-7 season-opening loss to San Francisco in 1986, had a big day against the Falcons despite ailing from both a pulled back muscle and the flu.

Ironically, Testaverde, the 1986 Heisman Trophy winner from the University of Miami, was the only player from either team who didn't play in the game.

The player who finished second to Testaverde in the '86 Heisman balloting, Temple running back Paul Palmer, returned a kickoff 95 yards for a touchdown with 3:19 remaining to lead the Kansas City Chiefs to a 20-13 victory over AFC West Division rival San Diego. The win was the Chiefs' fifth straight on opening day and the first as an NFL head coach for Frank Gansz, the team's former special teams coach who succeeded John Mackovic after the 1986 season.

Palmer, Kansas City's No. 1 choice in the '87 draft, was outplayed for most of the afternoon by the team's No. 2 selection, Christian Okoye of Azusa Pacific. Okoye, a 6-foot-1, 253-pound fullback, rushed for 105 yards on 21 carries and scored on a 43-yard run. It was just the second 100-yard rushing performance by a Chiefs running back since 1981.

Palmer, the NCAA's rushing leader in 1986, rushed for just six yards on two carries.

The most celebrated rookie to make his NFL debut in Week 1 was Seattle linebacker

Tampa Bay quarterback Steve DeBerg threw a club-record five touchdown passes in leading the Buccaneers to their most lopsided victory ever, 48-10 over Atlanta in Week 1.

Brian Bosworth, who was drafted by the Seahawks in the league's supplemental draft in June. Bosworth, a consensus All-America at the University of Oklahoma, avoided the NFL's regular draft in April by graduating from college with a year of eligibility remaining.

Bosworth, whose punk hairdo, outrageous talk and flamboyant style made him one of the most recognized athletes in all of sports, at first balked at the idea of playing in Seattle. But a 10-year, $11 million contract changed his mind. Bosworth announced before his first NFL game that he'd like nothing better than to get in a few clean licks against Denver quarterback John Elway, whose own pro debut with the Broncos in 1983 generated perhaps as many headlines as Bosworth's.

Bosworth did get two clean hits on Elway early in the game—sparking a momentary war of words between the two—but the Broncos ended up rolling to a relatively easy 40-17 victory. Denver led by three points at the half (20-17) but took command by converting two third-period Seattle turnovers into touchdowns. At one point, the Broncos scored points on five straight possessions.

Elway finished the game with 338 yards passing and four touchdowns and placekicker Rich Karlis booted four field goals before a record opening-day crowd of 75,999 at Mile High Stadium. Bosworth forced one fumble and had nine tackles for Seattle.

Another rookie defender, cornerback Delton Hall of the Pittsburgh Steelers, had a memorable NFL debut in his club's 30-17 upset of the San Francisco 49ers.

Hall, Pittsburgh's second-round draft choice from Clemson, returned a fumble 50 yards for the Steelers' first touchdown and intercepted a Joe Montana pass to set up a field goal. The interception was one of three thrown by Montana. Steelers quarterback Mark Malone didn't throw an interception but completed just nine of 33 passes for 99 yards.

The victory was Chuck Noll's 171st as an NFL head coach, moving him past the legendary Paul Brown into fifth place on the all-time list. George Halas (326), Don Shula (265), Tom Landry (261) and Curly Lambeau (234) are the four winningest coaches in NFL history.

The player selected right after Hall in the second round of the 1987 draft, Baylor defensive back Ron Francis, had a fourth quarter he'd like to forget in the Dallas Cowboys' 24-13 opening-day loss at St. Louis. Francis was burned for one touchdown and called for pass interference on another scoring drive as the Cardinals rallied for three touchdowns in the final two minutes to pull out the victory.

The Cowboys led, 13-3, before St. Louis quarterback Neil Lomax hit wide receiver Roy Green with a 16-yard touchdown pass with 1:58 left to cut the deficit to 13-10. Francis was covering Green on the play.

After the Cowboys failed to get a first down on their next possession, Lomax drove the Cardinals from their own 39-yard line to the Dallas 31 with a minute to play. Francis was called for pass interference against Cardinal tight end Jay Novacek on the next play and the 9-yard penalty put the ball on the Dallas 22. Lomax and Green then hooked up for what proved to be the game-winning touchdown against cornerback Everson Walls.

Quarterback Danny White fumbled after being sacked for the eighth time on Dallas' next possession, setting up the final Cardinal touchdown—a 15-yard run by fullback Earl Ferrell with 19 seconds left.

The loss was only the Cowboys' second in their last 23 season-opening games.

Texas' other NFL team, the Houston Oilers, rallied from a 16-3 fourth-quarter deficit by scoring 17 unanswered points to edge the visiting Los Angeles Rams, 20-16.

Quarterback Warren Moon and safety Keith Bostic led Houston's fourth-quarter comeback. Moon threw a three-yard touchdown pass to tight end Jamie Williams midway through the quarter and connected with wide receiver Ernest Givins for a 59-yard touchdown with three minutes left. They were the only touchdowns scored by either offense in the game.

Bostic, a fifth-year player from Michigan, intercepted two Jim Everett passes in the final quarter to kill Ram drives, the second coming with 28 seconds remaining. Everett, who was drafted by Houston in 1986 and then traded to L.A. in a contract dispute, completed just nine of 26 passes for 125 yards.

Another homecoming of sorts took place in Green Bay, where former Packers receiver James Lofton returned as a member of the Los Angeles Raiders and helped his new team to a 20-0 interconference victory. Lofton, a Pro Bowl player in seven of his nine years with the Packers, was traded to the Raiders in April after his alleged involvement in a sexual assault case. He later was acquitted.

Lofton caught two passes for 32 yards but the Raiders' top gun was running back Marcus Allen, who rushed a career-high 33 times for 136 yards and scored one touchdown. Allen's performance was necessitated by a poor showing by Raiders' quarterback Rusty Hilger, who was making his first NFL start. Hilger, who entered the season as L.A.'s best hope at its most troubling position, completed just two of seven passes for 12 yards before being replaced by veteran Marc Wilson.

Packers quarterback Randy Wright wasn't any better. Wright completed eight of 21 attempts for 99 yards, threw three interceptions and was sacked four times. The Green Bay offense mustered its fewest total yards in nearly six years (147) and was shut out for the first time in 122 games.

There was little wrong with the Cincinnati

offense in the Bengals' 23-21 victory at Indianapolis. The offense, which finished the 1986 season ranked No. 1 in the league, rolled up 403 yards against the Colts. Running back James Brooks ran and caught passes for 115 yards and scored two touchdowns.

Cincinnati, which began its last four seasons with records of 0-3, 0-5, 0-3 and 0-1, won its first season opener since 1982. The Colts lost their opener for the fourth straight year.

The Bengals' defense held Indianapolis to 15 first downs and intercepted three Jack Trudeau passes. Safety Robert Jackson intercepted two Trudeau passes, including one at the Cincinnati 37-yard line with 1:12 remaining.

Minnesota quarterback Wade Wilson also threw three interceptions—all in the first half —but rebounded to throw three touchdown passes while leading the Vikings to a 34-19 NFC Central Division victory over Detroit. Two of Wilson's interceptions skipped through the hands of wide receiver Anthony Carter, who made amends by catching a 73-yard touchdown pass in the third quarter.

Wilson, whose mistakes helped the Lions grab a 16-3 lead in the first 20 minutes, opened the season as the Vikings' starting quarterback after 11-year veteran Tommy Kramer went through alcohol rehabilitation and suffered a pinched nerve in his neck during the preseason.

The New Orleans Saints got their season off to a rousing start by twice sacking Cleveland quarterback Bernie Kosar in the end zone for safeties in a 28-21 interconference victory at the Superdome. Both of the Saints' team-record two safeties came in the final 10 minutes of the game to break a 21-21 tie.

Defensive end Bruce Clark registered the first when he grabbed Kosar around the ankles, a call that incensed Kosar and the Browns' coaching staff. Brett Maxie got the second safety when he blindsided Kosar with 3:09 left, causing the ball to squirt through the back of the end zone. The safeties culminated a frustrating day for the Cleveland offense, which despite 376 total yards never started a drive beyond its 20-yard line.

New Orleans' opening-day win was only its fourth in 21 seasons.

The New York Jets won for the seventh straight time against AFC East Division rival Buffalo, 31-28. Quarterback Ken O'Brien and running back Johnny Hector led the Jets assault, O'Brien passing for two touchdowns and Hector running for two others. O'Brien's two touchdowns matched his total for the Jets' final five regular-season games in 1986—all New York defeats.

The Jets' final touchdown—and what proved to be the game-winning points—came after linebacker Bob Crable intercepted a Jim Kelly pass late in the game and returned it eight yards to the Buffalo 4-yard line. Hector scored

from a yard out four plays later.

In a game played in a near-constant downpour, the New England Patriots rallied from a 21-7 second-quarter deficit to upend AFC East rival Miami, 28-21. It was the Patriots' fourth win in succession against the Dolphins.

New England scored the tying and go-ahead touchdowns in less than a minute of the third quarter. Tony Collins ran seven yards for a touchdown at 6:18 of the period and cornerback Ronnie Lippett returned a Dan Marino pass 20 yards for a score 50 seconds later. Miami tight end Bruce Hardy tipped Marino's pass before it landed in the arms of Lippett, who returned it for his first NFL touchdown.

In a game that was as hyped as most Super Bowls, the Chicago Bears and the New York Giants—the previous two Super Bowl winners —were pitted against each other in the season's first Monday night game. And as is the case with most Super Bowls, the game turned into a blowout.

The Bears won at home in convincing fashion, 34-19, behind a superb performance by quarterback Mike Tomczak and a fierce defense. Tomczak, subbing for an injured Jim McMahon, completed 20 of 34 passes for 292 yards and two touchdowns. He also scored the Bears' go-ahead touchdown on a one-yard plunge with eight seconds left in the first half.

Prior to the game, Tomczak's NFL resume consisted of two touchdown passes and 10 interceptions in 19 games over a two-year period.

Although both teams had defenses recognized among the best in the league, Chicago's clearly had the better of it in this game. The Bears sacked Giants quarterbacks Phil Simms and Jeff Rutledge eight times while the Giants' defense was held without a sack.

The loss snapped a 12-game winning streak for New York, which also lost its 1986 season-opener on a Monday night before rebounding to win 17 of its next 18 games and the league title.

Lions-Vikings
SUNDAY, SEPTEMBER 13
SCORE BY PERIODS

Detroit	6	10	3	0—19
Minnesota	0	10	21	3—34

SCORING

Detroit—Field goal Murray 26, 9:56 1st.

Detroit—Field goal Murray 27, 5:47 1st.

Minnesota—Field goal C. Nelson 27, 14:58 2nd.

Detroit—Field goal Murray 24, 12:21 2nd.

Detroit—Mandley 5 pass from Long (Murray kick), 9:59 2nd.

Minnesota—Dozier 2 pass from Wilson (C. Nelson kick), 2:59 2nd.

Detroit—Field goal Murray 34, 9:12 3rd.

Minnesota—Carter 73 pass from Wilson (C. Nelson kick), 8:30 3rd.

Minnesota—Dozier 1 run (C. Nelson kick), 6:30 3rd.

Minnesota—Lewis 24 pass from Wilson (C. Nelson kick), 1:23 3rd.

Minnesota—Field goal C. Nelson 22, 3:35 4th.

TEAM STATISTICS

	Detroit	Minnesota
First downs	17	21
Rushes-Yards	26-83	32-113
Passing yards	189	240
Sacked-Yards lost	1-6	1-8
3rd down eff	4-14	7-10
Passes	24-38-2	12-22-3
Punts	3-47.7	1—31.0
Fumbles-Lost	1-0	1-0
Penalties-Yards	8-56	6-36
Time of possession	31:45	28:15

Attendance—57,061.

INDIVIDUAL STATISTICS

Rushing—Detroit, Jones 15-58, Long 3-3, S. Williams 5-21, Bernard 2-7, Chadwick 1-minus 6; Minnesota, Anderson 11-53, Dozier 12-57, Wilson 4-0, Rice 5-3.

Passing—Detroit, Long 24-38-2—195; Minnesota, Wilson 12-22-3—248.

Receiving—Detroit, S. Williams 3-14, Jones 6-26, Mandley 7-79, Bernard 4-20, Rubick 1-9, Chadwick 1-26, Giles 1-7, Lee 1-14; Minnesota, Rice 2-30, Jordan 3-43, Lewis 3-72, Dozier 1-2, Anderson 1-7, Carter 2-94.

Kickoff Returns—Detroit, Bernard 2-54, Lee 3-69; Minnesota, Richardson 2-36, Guggemos 2-39.

Punt Returns—Detroit, Mandley 1-13; Minnesota, Richardson 1-3.

Interceptions—Detroit, Galloway 2-25; Griffin 1-11; Minnesota, Guggemos 1-26, Henderson 1-0.

Punting—Detroit, Erxleben 1-52.0; Minnesota, Coleman 1-31.0.

Field Goals—Detroit, Murray 4-5 (missed: 54); Minnesota, C. Nelson 2-2.

Sacks—Detroit, Gibson; Minnesota, Millard ½, D. Martin ½.

49ers-Steelers
SUNDAY, SEPTEMBER 13
SCORE BY PERIODS

San Francisco	0	3	7	7—17
Pittsburgh	7	10	3	10—30

SCORING

Pittsburgh—Hall 50 fumble return (Anderson kick), 5:57 1st.

San Francisco—Field goal Wersching 43, 4:52 2nd.

Pittsburgh—Gothard 2 pass from Malone (Anderson kick), 9:50 2nd.

Pittsburgh—Field goal Anderson 50, 14:54 2nd.

Pittsburgh—Field goal Anderson 41, 7:30 3rd.

San Francisco—Frank 1 pass from Montana (Wersching kick), 12:18 3rd.

Pittsburgh—Field goal Anderson 44, 5:52 4th.

Pittsburgh—Abercrombie 28 run (Anderson kick), 9:35 4th.

San Francisco—Rice 3 pass from Montana (Wersching kick), 14:02 4th.

TEAM STATISTICS

	San Francisco	Pittsburgh
First downs	24	21
Rushes-Yards	20-47	41-183
Passing yards	309	83
Sacked-Yards lost	1-7	2-16
3rd down eff	2-10	5-17
Passes	34-49-3	9-33-0
Punts	7-42.1	7-43.4
Fumbles-Lost	3-1	4-0
Penalties-Yards	6-67	3-25
Time of possession	29:17	30:43

Attendance—55,735.

INDIVIDUAL STATISTICS

Rushing—San Francisco, Cribbs 9-33, Craig 10-16, Montana 1-minus 2; Pittsburgh, Jackson 25-103, Abercrombie 7-44, Malone 6-minus 1, Pollard 2-21, Newsome 1-16.

Passing—San Francisco, Montana 34-49-3—316; Pittsburgh, Malone 9-33-0—99.

Receiving—San Francisco, Rice 8-106, Wilson 4-40, Taylor 1-17, Craig 10-61, Heller 2-40, Cribbs 4-30, Frank 4-15, Clark 1-7; Pittsburgh, Stallworth 2-26, Hoge 1-27, Gothard 1-2, Lipps 3-44, Abercrombie 1-5, Pollard 1-minus 5.

Kickoff Returns—San Francisco, Sydney 1-18, Flagler 1-4, Cribbs 4-86; Pittsburgh, Sanchez 2-51, Jones 1-16.

Punt Returns—San Francisco, Griffin 3-50; Pittsburgh, Lipps 6-42.

Interceptions—Pittsburgh, Woodruff 1-25, Hall 1-4, Merriweather 1-15.

Punting—San Francisco, Runager 7-42.1; Pittsburgh, Newsome 1-43.4.

Field Goals—San Francisco, Wersching 1-1; Pittsburgh, Anderson 3-4 (missed: 42).

Sacks—San Francisco, Kugler, Haley; Pittsburgh, Gary.

Cowboys-Cardinals
SUNDAY, SEPTEMBER 13
SCORE BY PERIODS

Dallas	0	6	0	7—13
St. Louis	3	0	0	21—24

SCORING

St. Louis—Field goal Gallery 23, 3:08 1st.

Dallas—Field goal Ruzek 22, 2:37 2nd.

Dallas—Field goal Ruzek 29, 14:35 2nd.

Dallas—Banks 20 pass from D. White (Ruzek kick), 1:42 4th.

St. Louis—Green 16 pass from Lomax (Gallery kick), 13:02 4th.

St. Louis—Green 22 pass from Lomax (Gallery kick), 14:07 4th.

St. Louis—Ferrell 15 run (Gallery kick), 14:41 4th.

TEAM STATISTICS

	Dallas	St. Louis
First downs	19	20
Rushes-Yards	32-125	27-108
Passing yards	197	252
Sacked-Yards lost	8-59	3-18
3rd down eff	5-15	4-14
Passes	21-32-0	17-33-0
Punts	8-46.0	8-45.6
Fumbles-Lost	1-1	1-0
Penalties-Yards	5-34	6-38
Time of possession	34:38	25:22

Attendance—47,241.

INDIVIDUAL STATISTICS

Rushing—Dallas, Walker 13-62, Dorsett 18-60, D. White 1-3; St. Louis, Ferrell 10-71, Mitchell 14-41, Lomax 3-minus 4.

Passing—Dallas, D. White 20-32-0—256; St. Louis, Lomax 17-33-0—270.

Receiving—Dallas, Walker 7-90, Cosbie 4-44, Renfro 4-42, Dorsett 2-49, Banks 1-20, Fowler 1-6, Barksdale 1-5; St. Louis, J.T. Smith 5-78, Green 4-90, Novacek 4-43, Mitchell 2-35, Holmes 2-24.

Kickoff Returns—Dallas, Clack 1-24; St. Louis, Sikahema 1-14.

Punt Returns—Dallas, Banks 1-2; St. Louis, Sikahema 7-44.

Interceptions—None.

Punting—Dallas, Saxon 8-46.0; St. Louis, Cater 8-45.6.

Field Goals—Dallas, Ruzek 2-2; St. Louis, Gallery 1-1.

Sacks—Dallas, Bates, Jeffcoat, Walen; St. Louis, Greer 3, Clasby, Scotts 2, Saddler, Leonard Smith.

Eagles-Redskins
SUNDAY, SEPTEMBER 13
SCORE BY PERIODS

Philadelphia	0	10	14	0—24
Washington	10	7	7	10—34

Washington—Field goal Atkinson 27, 3:30 1st.
Washington—Monk 6 pass from Williams (Atkinson kick), 10:42 1st.
Philadelphia—Quick 30 pass from Cunningham (McFadden kick), 4:02 2nd.
Philadelphia—Field goal McFadden 43, 9:28 2nd.
Washington—Rogers 1 run (Cox kick), 14:22 2nd.
Washington—Branch 1 run (Cox kick), 3:48 3rd.
Philadelphia—Cunningham 2 run (McFadden kick), 10:41 3rd.
Philadelphia—White 70 fumble return (McFadden kick), 14:52 3rd.
Washington—Monk 39 pass from Williams (Cox kick), 0:07 4th.
Washington—Field goal Cox 40, 9:40 4th.

TEAM STATISTICS

	Philadelphia	Washington
First downs	24	19
Rushes-Yards	30-112	27-110
Passing yards	239	264
Sacked-Yards lost	4-30	1-8
3rd down eff	5-13	6-14
Passes	21-36-2	17-30-0
Punts	4-42.0	5-49.2
Fumbles-Lost	3-2	2-2
Penalties-Yards	8-61	6-55
Time of possession	32:36	27:24

Attendance—52,128.

INDIVIDUAL STATISTICS

Rushing—Philadelphia, Toney 2-0, Haddix 14-60, Tautalatasi 6-3, Teltschik 1-10, Cunningham 7-39; Washington, Rogers 7-15, Bryant 7-32, Monk 1-5, Schroeder 1-31, Griffin 8-21, Branch 3-6.

Passing—Philadelphia, Cunningham 21-36-2—269; Washington, Schroeder 0-3-0—0, Williams 17-27-0—272.

Receiving—Philadelphia, Quick 4-69, Spagnola 6-61, Jackson 2-45, Little 1-8, Haddix 3-24, Tautalatasi 4-44, Garrity 1-18; Washington, Monk 3-53, Clark 8-102, Bryant 1-34, Sanders 4-81, Warren 1-2.

Kickoff Returns—Philadelphia, Tautalatasi 1-32, Cooper 2-37, Alexander 1-6; Washington, Griffin 4-109.

Punt Returns—Philadelphia, Garrity 1-10; Washington, Yarber 4-18.

Interceptions—Washington, Bowles 1-0, Wilburn 1-0.

Punting—Philadelphia, Teltschik 4-42.0; Washington, Cox 5-49.2.

Field Goals—Philadelphia, McFadden 1-2 (missed: 56); Washington, Cox 1-1, Atkinson 1-1.

Sacks—Philadelphia, White; Washington, Koch, Mann 2, Walton.

Seahawks-Broncos
SUNDAY, SEPTEMBER 13
SCORE BY PERIODS

Seattle	14	3	0	0—17
Denver	7	13	14	6—40

SCORING

Seattle—Turner 20 pass from Krieg (N. Johnson kick), 4:36 1st.
Denver—Sewell 72 pass from Elway (Karlis kick), 5:47 1st.
Seattle—Warner 10 pass from Krieg (N. Johnson kick), 10:25 1st.
Seattle—Field goal N. Johnson 25, 4:42 2nd.
Denver—Field goal Karlis 37, 9:29 2nd.
Denver—Field goal Karlis 42, 13:43 2nd.
Denver—Watson 4 pass from Elway (Karlis kick), 14:25 2nd.
Denver—Mobley 5 pass from Elway (Karlis kick), 4:36 3rd.
Denver—Johnson 59 pass from Elway (Karlis kick), 13:28 3rd.
Denver—Field goal Karlis 25, 6:33 4th.
Denver—Field goal Karlis 29, 11:38 4th.

TEAM STATISTICS

	Seattle	Denver
First downs	15	25
Rushes-Yards	20-108	41-166
Passing yards	169	338
Sacked-Yards lost	1-16	0-0
3rd down eff	3-7	7-14
Passes	14-28-3	22-31-1
Punts	3-43.7	1-37.0
Fumbles-Lost	2-2	1-1
Penalties-Yards	7-45	4-35
Time of possession	23:07	36:53

Attendance—75,999.

INDIVIDUAL STATISTICS

Rushing—Seattle, Warner 11-83, Williams 5-18, Morris 2-6, Krieg 2-1; Denver, Winder 17-79, Willhite 6-19, Elway 4-16, Lang 12-46, Bell 2-6.

Passing—Seattle, Krieg 14-28-3—185; Denver, Elway 22-32-1—338.

Receiving—Seattle, Largent 4-73, Turner 1-20, Warner 2-29, Millard 1-minus 5, Butler 2-27, Tice 2-25, Skansi 1-11, R. Williams 1-5; Denver, Johnson 4-96, Sewell 2-83, Nattiel 2-15, Kay 3-32, Watson 4-47, Willhite 1-minus 1, Mobley 4-49, Lang 2-17.

Kickoff Returns—Seattle, Edmonds 3-91, Morris 1-15; Burse 1-1; Denver, Nattiel 1-25.

Punt Returns—Denver, Nattiel 3-11.

Interceptions—Seattle, Easley 1-0; Denver, Smith 1-15, Mecklenburg 1-minus 2, Harden 1-32.

Punting—Seattle, Rodriguez 3-43.7; Denver, Horan 1-37.0.

Field Goals—Seattle, N. Johnson 1-1; Denver, Karlis 4-4.

Sacks—Denver, Brooks.

Jets-Bills
SUNDAY, SEPTEMBER 13
SCORE BY PERIODS

New York Jets	0	14	3	14—31
Buffalo	0	7	7	14—28

SCORING

Buffalo—T. Johnson 26 pass from Kelly (Norwood kick), 3:13 2nd.
New York—Walker 55 pass from O'Brien (Leahy kick), 11:47 2nd.
New York—Shuler 4 pass from O'Brien (Leahy kick), 14:34 2nd.
New York—Field goal Leahy 29, 8:46 3rd.
Buffalo—Burkett 6 pass from Kelly (Norwood kick), 12:33 3rd.
New York—Hector 2 run (Leahy kick), 3:01 4th.
Buffalo—Riddick 2 run (Norwood kick), 5:18 4th.
New York—Hector 1 run (Leahy kick), 12:02 4th.
Buffalo—Riddick 1 pass from Kelly (Norwood kick), 13:44 4th.

TEAM STATISTICS

	New York	Buffalo
First downs	26	23
Rushes-Yards	44-133	16-67
Passing yards	261	292
Sacked-Yards lost	4-15	2-13
3rd down eff	8-18	6-12
Passes	24-35-1	25-42-1
Punts	5-41.2	5-46.8
Fumbles-Lost	0-0	0-0
Penalties-Yards	15-103	5-42
Time of possession	38:03	21:57

Attendance—76,718.

INDIVIDUAL STATISTICS

Rushing—New York, McNeil 21-68, Vick 12-34, Jennings 1-4, O'Brien 4-7, Faaola 2-11, Hector 4-9; Buffalo, Bell 10-39, Byrum 3-9, Reed 1-1, Riddick 2-18.

Passing—New York, O'Brien 24-35-1—276; Buffalo, Kelly 25-42-1—305.

Receiving—New York, Walker 4-91, Hector 4-51, Shuler 7-63, McNeil 2-13, Toon 6-59, Sohn 1-minus 1; Buffalo, Reed 3-47, Riddick 2-3, Metzelaars 4-37, T. Johnson 3-63, Bell 4-37, Burkett 3-47, Harmon 5-51, Byrum 1-20.

Kickoff Returns—New York, Barber 1-0, Humphery 1-11, Townsell 1-12; Buffalo, Harmon 1-30, Riddick 1-21.

Punt Returns—New York, Townsell 4-28.

Interceptions—New York, Crable 1-8; Buffalo, Kelso 1-0.

Punting—New York, Jennings 5-41.2; Buffalo, Kidd 5-46.8.

Field Goals—New York, Leahy 1-1; Buffalo, none attempted.

Sacks—New York, Gastineau, Nichols ½, Bennett ½; Buffalo, Smith, McNanie 2, Seals.

Dolphins-Patriots

SUNDAY, SEPTEMBER 13
SCORE BY PERIODS

Miami	7	14	0	0—21
New England	7	7	14	0—28

SCORING

Miami—Duper 9 pass from Marino (Reveiz kick), 4:01 1st.
New England—Collins 4 run (Franklin kick), 9:57 1st.
Miami—Duper 25 pass from Marino (Reveiz kick), 2:44 2nd.
Miami—Davenport 1 pass from Marino (Reveiz kick), 10:18 2nd.
New England—Fryar 17 pass from Grogan (Franklin kick), 13:12 2nd.
New England—Collins 7 run (Franklin kick), 6:18 3rd.
New England—Lippett 20 interception return (Franklin kick), 7:08 3rd.

TEAM STATISTICS

	Miami	New England
First downs	20	18
Rushes-Yards	25-64	39-159
Passing yards	221	150
Sacked-Yards lost	0-0	0-0
3rd down eff.	1-12	5-12
Passes	24-43-2	14-21-2
Punts	7-33.6	4-47.3
Fumbles-Lost	3-0	5-3
Penalties-Yards	3-19	5-26
Time of possession	29:21	30:39
Attendance—54,642.		

INDIVIDUAL STATISTICS

Rushing—Miami, Hampton 19-55, Davenport 3-6, Bennett 1-3, Marino 1-0, Hardy 1-0; New England, Collins 22-95, Tatupu 10-45, Grogan 4-8, Perryman 2-6, James 1-5.

Passing—Miami, Marino 19-37-2—165, Strock 5-6-0—56; New England, Grogan 14-21-2—150.

Receiving—Miami, Duper 9-123, Jensen 4-24, Hardy 4-23, Davenport 3-5, Clayton 2-36, Hampton 2-10; New England, Morgan 6-76, Collins 3-22, Fryar 2-33, Tatupu 2-8, Dawson 1-11.

Kickoff Returns—Miami, Stradford 1-2, Schwedes 2-26; New England, Starring 3-54, Perryman 1-14.

Punt Returns—Miami, Schwedes 2-40; New England, Fryar 1-0.

Interceptions—Miami, Lankford 1-0, Blackwood 1-0; New England, Lippett 1-20, Marion 1-9.

Punting—Miami, Strock 7-33.6; New England, Camarillo 4-47.3.

Field Goals—Miami, none attempted; New England, Franklin 0-2 (missed: 39, 47).

Sacks—None.

Browns-Saints

SUNDAY, SEPTEMBER 13
SCORE BY PERIODS

Cleveland	0	7	7	7—21
New Orleans	7	0	14	7—28

SCORING

New Orleans—Brenner 5 pass from Hebert (Andersen kick), 11:38 1st.
Cleveland—Weathers 7 pass from Kosar (Jaeger kick), 9:05 2nd.
New Orleans—Brenner 16 pass from Hebert (Andersen kick), 1:37 3rd.
Cleveland—Brennan 30 pass from Kosar (Jaeger kick), 5:44 3rd.
New Orleans—Hilliard 5 run (Andersen kick), 12:38 3rd.
Cleveland—Kosar 3 run (Jaeger kick), 2:23 4th.
New Orleans—Safety, Kosar tackled in end zone, 5:15 4th.
New Orleans—Safety, Kosar tackled in end zone, 11:51 4th.
New Orleans—Field goal Andersen 39, 13:17 4th.

TEAM STATISTICS

	Cleveland	New Orleans
First downs	25	21
Rushes-Yards	23-93	34-191
Passing yards	283	147
Sacked-Yards lost	4-31	1-2
3rd down eff.	4-8	5-11
Passes	28-39-1	13-22-2
Punts	0-0.0	5-41.6
Fumbles-Lost	1-1	0-0
Penalties-Yards	2-20	7-74
Time of possession	29:24	30:36
Attendance—59,900.		

INDIVIDUAL STATISTICS

Rushing—Cleveland, Mack 11-37, Byner 10-45, Manoa 1-8, Kosar 1-3; New Orleans, Mayes 24-147, Jordan 5-12, Word 1-3, Gray 1-11, Hebert 1-13, Hilliard 2-5.

Passing—Cleveland, Kosar 28-39-1—314; New Orleans, Hebert 13-22-2—149.

Receiving—Cleveland, Newsome 5-43, Mack 2-17, Slaughter 2-28, Langhorne 5-85, Byner 8-61, Manoa 1-8, Weathers 1-7; New Orleans, Martin 2-29, Brenner 5-68, Gray 2-18, Jordan 1-2, R. Clark 1-11, Tice 1-10, Jones 1-11.

Kickoff Returns—Cleveland, Young 2-39; New Orleans, Gray 5-108, Martin 1-15.

Punt Returns—Cleveland, McNeil 1-4.

Interceptions—New Orleans, Johnson 1-0.

Punting—New Orleans, Hansen 5-41.6.

Field Goals—Cleveland, Jaeger 0-1 (missed: 49); New Orleans, Andersen 1-1.

Sacks—Cleveland, Matthews; New Orleans, B. Clark, Warren, Maxie, Swilling.

Raiders-Packers

SUNDAY, SEPTEMBER 13
SCORE BY PERIODS

Los Angeles Raiders	0	7	7	6—20
Green Bay	0	0	0	0— 0

SCORING

Los Angeles—Allen 1 run (Bahr kick), 12:48 2nd.
Los Angeles—McElroy 35 interception return (Bahr kick), 7:31 3rd.
Los Angeles—Field goal Bahr 40, 0:50 4th.
Los Angeles—Field goal Bahr 27, 11:53 4th.

TEAM STATISTICS

	Los Angeles	Green Bay
First downs	21	9
Rushes-Yards	48-193	17-66
Passing yards	100	81
Sacked-Yards lost	4-9	4-33
3rd down eff.	7-20	1-12
Passes	11-23-0	10-28-3
Punts	7-46.7	10-48.9
Fumbles-Lost	1-0	0-0
Penalties-Yards	6-45	12-72
Time of possession	38:32	21:28
Attendance—54,983.		

INDIVIDUAL STATISTICS

Rushing—Los Angeles, Allen 33-136, Hilger 1-6, Hawkins 4-24, Wilson 2-4, Mueller 3-4, Smith 1-0, Strachan 4-19; Green Bay, J. Clark 3-15, Davis 8-40, Fullwood 3-8, Carruth 3-3.

Passing—Los Angeles, Hilger 2-7-0—12, Wilson 9-16-0—97; Green Bay, Wright 8-21-3—99, Majkowski 2-7-0—15.

Receiving—Los Angeles, Christensen 3-29, Hawkins 1-6, Fernandez 2-33, Lofton 2-32, Allen 2-0, D. Williams 1-9; Green Bay, J. Clark 2-31, Stanley 3-30, Neal 2-33, Davis 1-1, Epps 1-20, Carruth 1-minus 1.

Kickoff Returns—Los Angeles, Mueller 1-24; Green Bay, Cook 2-58, Fullwood 2-38.

Punt Returns—Los Angeles, Adams 5-39; Green Bay, Stanley 5-32.

Interceptions—Los Angeles, Haynes 1-2, McElroy 1-35, Millen 1-6.

Punting—Los Angeles, Talley 7-46.7; Green Bay, Bracken 10-48.9.

Field Goals—Los Angeles, Bahr 2-3 (missed: 47); Green Bay, none attempted.

Sacks—Los Angeles, Martin 1½, King ½, Taylor, Townsend; Green Bay, Martin, Anderson, R. Brown, Carreker.

Falcons-Buccaneers
SUNDAY, SEPTEMBER 13
SCORE BY PERIODS

Atlanta	0	3	0	7—10
Tampa Bay	14	13	7	14—48

SCORING

Tampa Bay—Freeman 11 pass from DeBerg (Igwebuike kick), 6:04 1st.

Tampa Bay—Carter 6 pass from DeBerg (Igwebuike kick), 14:17 1st.

Atlanta—Field goal Luckhurst 50, 3:25 2nd.

Tampa Bay—Magee 11 pass from DeBerg (Igwebuike kick), 9:42 2nd.

Tampa Bay—Carter 3 pass from DeBerg (kick failed), 12:23 2nd.

Tampa Bay—Austin 1 run (Igwebuike kick), 9:17 3rd.

Tampa Bay—Carrier 2 pass from DeBerg (Igwebuike kick), 1:22 4th.

Atlanta—Bailey 34 pass from Campbell (Luckhurst kick), 5:26 4th.

Tampa Bay—Bartalo 3 run (Igwebuike kick), 11:28 4th.

TEAM STATISTICS

	Atlanta	Tampa Bay
First downs	13	30
Rushes-Yards	16-63	41-127
Passing yards	134	333
Sacked-Yards lost	4-37	0-00
3rd down eff.	3-10	14-16
Passes	14-33-2	24-34-1
Punts	6-45.5	1-40.0
Fumbles-Lost	2-1	2-1
Penalties-Yards	8-50	6-35
Time of possession	21:48	38:12
Attendance—51,250.		

INDIVIDUAL STATISTICS

Rushing—Atlanta, Riggs 12-52, Archer 2-8, Flowers 2-3; Tampa Bay, Wilder 7-13, Austin 9-20, Freeman 1-1, J. Smith 5-23, Howard 12-47, Bartalo 7-23.

Passing—Atlanta, Archer 8-22-2—94, Campbell 6-11-0—77; Tampa Bay, DeBerg 24-34-1—333.

Receiving—Atlanta, Bailey 3-56, Matthews 1-4, Dixon 1-33, Riggs 4-27, Whisenhunt 1-14, Flowers 1-4, Johnson 3-33; Tampa Bay, Carrier 6-50, Magee 3-46, Wilder 4-62, Freeman 1-11, Carter 6-60, Austin 1-15, Howard 1-45, Hall 2-44.

Kickoff Returns—Atlanta, Stamps 6-117; Tampa Bay, Futrell 1-8.

Punt Returns—Tampa Bay, Futrell 4-39.

Interceptions—Atlanta, Case 1-12; Tampa Bay, Futrell 1-23, Woods 1-42.

Punting—Atlanta, Donnelly 6-45.5; Tampa Bay, Garcia 1-40.0.

Field Goals—Atlanta, Luckhurst 1-1; Tampa Bay, none attempted.

Sacks—Tampa Bay, Kellin 2½, Holmes 1½.

Rams-Oilers
SUNDAY, SEPTEMBER 13
SCORE BY PERIODS

Los Angeles Rams	6	7	3	0—16
Houston	0	3	0	17—20

SCORING

Los Angeles—Field goal Lansford 28, 5:28 1st.

Los Angeles—Field goal Lansford 44, 12:42 1st.

Los Angeles—Greene 25 interception return (Lansford kick), 10:39 2nd.

Houston—Field goal Zendejas 44, 13:58 2nd.

Los Angeles—Field goal Lansford 47, 6:28 3rd.

Houston—J. Williams 3 pass from Moon (Zendejas kick), 7:28 4th.

Houston—Givins 59 pass from Moon (Zendejas kick), 12:01 4th.

Houston—Field goal Zendejas 19, 13:59 4th.

TEAM STATISTICS

	Los Angeles	Houston
First downs	13	22
Rushes-Yards	30-147	27-113
Passing yards	97	287
Sacked-Yards lost	3-28	2-23
3rd down eff.	2-13	5-15
Passes	9-26-2	21-43-2
Punts	7-46.4	7-37.1
Fumbles-Lost	2-1	3-1
Penalties-Yards	8-72	9-70
Time of possession	27:56	32:04
Attendance—33,186.		

INDIVIDUAL STATISTICS

Rushing—Los Angeles, Dickerson 27-149, White 2-minus 9, Guman 1-7; Houston, Rozier 20-93, Pinkett 4-17, Moon 2-0, Wallace 1-3.

Passing—Los Angeles, Everett 9-26-2—125; Houston, Moon 21-43-2—310.

Receiving—Los Angeles, Brown 2-48, Dickerson 1-3, Ellard 6-74; Houston, Rozier 4-29, Givins 6-117, J. Williams 2-11, Hill 5-98, Duncan 1-6, Jeffires 3-49.

Kickoff Returns—Los Angeles, White 2-47; Houston, Pinkett 3-48, Duncan 1-18.

Punt Returns—Los Angeles, Ellard 3-24; Houston, Duncan 3-11, Drewrey 1-2.

Interceptions—Los Angeles, J. Johnson 1-0, Greene 1-25; Houston, Bostic 2-0.

Punting—Los Angeles, Hatcher 7-46.4; Houston, L. Johnson 7-37.1.

Field Goals—Los Angeles, Lansford 3-3; Houston, Zendejas 2-2.

Sacks—Los Angeles, Miller, Greene; Houston, D. Smith, Byrd, Childress.

Bengals-Colts
SUNDAY, SEPTEMBER 13
SCORE BY PERIODS

Cincinnati	13	0	0	10—23
Indianapolis	7	0	7	7—21

SCORING

Cincinnati—Brooks 18 pass from Esiason (Breech kick), 8:39 1st.

Cincinnati—Holman 61 pass from Esiason (kick failed), 11:01 1st.

Indianapolis—Brooks 52 pass from Trudeau (Biasucci kick), 13:35 1st.

Indianapolis—Bentley 2 run (Biasucci kick), 12:31 3rd.
Cincinnati—Field goal Breech 20, 4:24 4th.
Cincinnati—Brooks 1 run (Breech kick), 7:10 4th.
Indianapolis—Sherwin 1 pass from Trudeau (Biasucci kick), 12:27 4th.

TEAM STATISTICS

	Cincinnati	Indianapolis
First downs	25	15
Rushes-Yards	42-187	27-85
Passing yards	216	206
Sacked-Yards lost	2-20	0-0
3rd down eff.	9-14	5-10
Passes	17-26-0	13-23-3
Punts	3-52.0	4-52.3
Fumbles-Lost	4-1	2-0
Penalties-Yards	5-50	2-26
Time of possession	27:16	32:44

Attendance—59,387.

INDIVIDUAL STATISTICS

Rushing—Cincinnati, Brooks 19-86, Kinnebrew 12-57, Esiason 5-20, Jennings 3-18, Brown 1-0, Johnson 2-6; Indianapolis, Bentley 25-77, Kiel 1-8, Trudeau 1-0.

Passing—Cincinnati, Esiason 17-26-0—236; Indianapolis, Trudeau 13-23-3—206.

Receiving—Cincinnati, Holman 3-79, Collinsworth 3-38, Brown 3-22, Kinnebrew 2-31, Brooks 2-29, Kattus 2-2, Martin 1-20, Hillary 1-15; Indianapolis, Brooks 6-146, Bouza 3-32, Beach 2-27, Sherwin 2-1.

Kickoff Returns—Cincinnati, Fulcher 1-0, Bussey 1-34; Indianapolis, K. Daniel 5-121.

Punt Returns—Cincinnati, Martin 2-23; Indianapolis, Tullis 1-8.

Interceptions—Cincinnati, Jackson 2-49, Fulcher 1-28.

Punting—Cincinnati, Horne 3-52.0; Indianapolis, Stark 4-52.3.

Field Goals—Cincinnati, Breech 1-2 (missed: 42); Indianapolis, none attempted.

Sacks—Indianapolis, Hand, Darby.

Chargers-Chiefs
SUNDAY, SEPTEMBER 13
SCORE BY PERIODS

San Diego	0	0	3	10	13
Kansas City	3	7	0	10	20

SCORING

Kansas City—Field goal Lowery 25, 13:37 1st.
Kansas City—Okoye 43 run (Lowery kick), 12:04 2nd.
San Diego—Field goal Abbott 32, 7:13 3rd.
Kansas City—Field goal Lowery 29, 2:15 4th.
San Diego—Anderson 34 pass from Fouts (Abbott kick), 7:23 4th.
San Diego—Field goal Abbott 33, 11:23 4th.
Kansas City—Palmer 95 kickoff return (Lowery kick), 11:41 4th.

TEAM STATISTICS

	San Diego	Kansas City
First downs	19	15
Rushes-Yards	23-84	40-174
Passing yards	258	58
Sacked-Yards lost	2-12	4-21
3rd down eff.	4-12	3-12
Passes	21-40-3	6-15-1
Punts	4-43.8	6-39.2
Fumbles-Lost	2-1	0-0
Penalties-Yards	9-55	9-70
Time of possession	27:29	32:31

Attendance—56,940.

INDIVIDUAL STATISTICS

Rushing—San Diego, Anderson 12-43, Spencer 7-24, James 3-17, Redden 1-0; Kansas City, Okoye 21-105, Heard 10-42, Moriarty 4-15, Blackledge 2-6, Palmer 2-6, Clemons 1-0.

Passing—San Diego, Fouts 21-39-2—270, Smith 0-1-1—0; Kansas City, Blackledge 6-15-1—79.

Receiving—San Diego, James 6-100, Anderson 6-68, Winslow 4-42, Holohan 3-43, Spencer 2-17; Kansas City, Paige 2-29, Arnold 2-20, Marshall 1-19, Carson 1-11.

Kickoff Returns—San Diego, Anderson 3-77; Kansas City, Palmer 3-115.

Punt Returns—San Diego, James 2-11; Kansas City, Clemons 2-7.

Interceptions—San Diego, Plummer 1-2; Kansas City, Cherry 2-28, Lewis 1-0.

Punting—San Diego, Mojsiejenko 4-43.8; Kansas City, L. Colbert 6-39.2.

Field Goals—San Diego, Abbott 2-3 (missed: 44); Kansas City, Lowery 2-2.

Sacks—San Diego, Smith 2, Bayless, Banks; Kansas City, Ross, Hackett.

Giants-Bears
MONDAY, SEPTEMBER 14
SCORE BY PERIODS

New York Giants	7	0	6	6	19
Chicago	3	7	14	10	34

SCORING

New York—Flynn recovered blocked punt in end zone (Allegre kick), 4:41 1st.
Chicago—Field goal Butler 24, 13:21 1st.
Chicago—Tomczak 1 run (Butler kick), 14:52 2nd.
Chicago—Morris 42 pass from Tomczak (Butler kick), 6:40 3rd.
Chicago—Gault 56 pass from Tomczak (Butler kick), 8:43 3rd.
New York—Kinard 70 interception return (kick failed), 14:19 3rd.
Chicago—McKinnon 94 punt return (Butler kick), 2:20 4th.
New York—Robinson 5 pass from Simms (pass failed), 5:30 4th.
Chicago—Field goal Butler 25, 13:55 4th.

TEAM STATISTICS

	New York	Chicago
First downs	14	17
Rushes-Yards	21-75	39-124
Passing yards	128	292
Sacked-Yards lost	8-53	0-0
3rd down eff.	3-14	8-19
Passes	15-30-0	20-34-2
Punts	9-42.1	5-34.0
Fumbles-Lost	2-1	1-0
Penalties-yards	4-19	4-31
Time of possession	24:49	35:11

Attendance—65,704.

INDIVIDUAL STATISTICS

Rushing—New York, Morris 14-54, Carthon 2-4, Galbreath 1-11, Rutledge 1-minus 2, Adams 2-14, Simms 1-minus 6; Chicago, Payton 18-42, Anderson 13-62, Thomas 4-10, Tomczak 3-5, Gentry 1-5.

Passing—New York, Simms 15-28-0—181, Rutledge 0-2-0—0; Chicago, Tomczak 20-34-2—292.

Receiving—New York, Manuel 3-41, Bavaro 5-86, Carthon 1-7, Morris 1-4, Robinson 2-18, Anderson 1-9, Galbreath 1-7, Baker 1-9; Chicago, Moorehead 3-43, McKinnon 1-9, Anderson 6-81, Payton 3-12, Suhey 2-11, Morris 2-61, Gault 3-75.

Kickoff Returns—New York, Adams 4-71, Rouson 1-25; Chicago, Sanders 1-42, Gentry 3-84.

Punt Returns—New York, McConkey 2-25; Chicago, McKinnon 5-134.

Interceptions—New York, Kinard 1-70, Welch 1-7.

Punting—New York, Landeta 9-42.1; Chicago, Wagner 4-42.5.

Field Goals—New York, none attempted; Chicago, Butler 2-2.

Sacks—Chicago, Singletary 2, Marshall 2, Dent, Wilson, Hampton, Bell.

SECOND WEEK

Sunday, September 20

Atlanta 21, Washington 20 at Atl.
Buffalo 34, Houston 30 at Buff.
Chicago 20, Tampa Bay 3 at Chi.
Cleveland 34, Pittsburgh 10 at Cleve.
Dallas 16, N.Y. Giants 14 at N.Y.
Denver 17, Green Bay 17 (OT) at Milw.
L.A. Raiders 27, Detroit 7 at L.A.
Miami 23, Indianapolis 10 at Ind.
Minnesota 21, L.A. Rams 16 at L.A.
Philadelphia 27, New Orleans 17 at Phila.
San Diego 28, St. Louis 24 at S.D.
San Francisco 27, Cincinnati 26 at Cin.
Seattle 43, Kansas City 14 at Sea.

Monday, September 21

N.Y. Jets 43, New England 24 at N.Y.

Just like the men who officiate the games, NFL head coaches seldom receive credit for the things they do right and often endure criticism for the things they do wrong.

Such was the predicament Cincinnati Coach Sam Wyche found himself in following the Bengals' 27-26 loss to the San Francisco 49ers in Week 2. That the 49ers—one of the league's better teams—defeated the Bengals was not the problem. San Francisco, after all, had won two of the previous six Super Bowls and entered the 1987 season favored by many to win a third. But the way the 49ers beat the Bengals was enough to make the stomach of even the most hardened NFL coach churn.

The Bengals led, 26-20, and had a first down at their own 45-yard line with 54 seconds remaining. Cincinnati quarterback Boomer Esiason took a two-yard loss on first down and the 49ers stopped the clock with 49 seconds left. Esiason took a three-yard loss on second down and San Francisco used its final timeout with 45 seconds remaining. Esiason lost five yards on third down, giving the Bengals a fourth-and-20 at the 35-yard line.

The Bengals took a five-yard delay of game penalty as the clock ticked down to the final six seconds. On fourth down, Wyche decided against a punt or a safety and ordered a sweep to run out the final seconds. But San Francisco's Kevin Fagen hauled down the ballcarrier, James Brooks, before the Cincinnati running back could run out the clock. Two seconds remained and the 49ers—who trailed 20-7 at halftime—had one final chance.

San Francisco lined up three receivers on the left side and All-Pro Jerry Rice on the right. The only player covering Rice was rookie cornerback Eric Thomas, who already had been beaten by Rice and Mike Wilson for touchdowns earlier in the game.

Rice took Thomas deep into the end zone and came back for quarterback Joe Montana's pass, catching it with no time left to tie the game at 26-26. Ray Wersching's extra point gave the 49ers an improbable win.

"I miscalculated two seconds," Wyche said later in defense of his strategy. "I made a miscalculation that cost us the win. I don't blame anyone but me. This is a game of inches and seconds and that's what it was today.

"We decided to pitch to Brooks on our last play, figuring it would eat up the last few seconds. We had thought about a punt and thought about taking a safety. But we were afraid of something going wrong with either one."

The 49ers were confused by Wyche's strategy, but thankful.

"I can't believe they ran the ball on their last play," Rice said. "I thought for sure they would punt."

Rice was likewise confused by the coverage he received on the final play.

"He (Thomas) was covering me all by himself. At least you might expect them to give him some help," Rice said.

"I expected help," Thomas said. "Rice ran, stopped and the ball was in the air. It didn't matter at that point."

"I knew the pass was there," Montana said. "The problem is, it's tough to make the catch in that situation. The receiver has to outjump anybody around him. But what's really amazing is that we got a chance to get a play like that off."

That wasn't the only Week 2 fantastic finish, however. The visiting Minnesota Vikings stunned the Los Angeles Rams, 21-16, on quarterback Wade Wilson's 41-yard touchdown pass to Hassan Jones with 30 seconds remaining. The touchdown came four plays after the pair had combined on a desperation fourth-and-16 pass that netted 20 yards and kept Minnesota's drive alive.

The Vikings, who had managed but one second-half first down prior to their game-winning 12-play, 80-yard drive with 4:19 left, got three first downs on the march, including two on fourth down. Wilson's touchdown pass was his third of the day, marking the second straight week the seven-year veteran from East Texas State had thrown for three touchdowns in relief of regular quarterback Tommy Kramer.

Another close game took place down the California coast in San Diego, where the Chargers jumped out to a 28-0 halftime lead before withstanding a St. Louis comeback and holding on for a 28-24 victory. The Cardinals, who had rallied for three touchdowns in the final two minutes of their opening game to defeat Dallas, nearly won it in the closing seconds. Quarterback Neil Lomax threw three incompletions from the Chargers' 5-yard line in the final seconds, fullback Earl Ferrell dropping a sure touchdown pass at the goal line on the game's final play.

San Diego scored two touchdowns in the first 5:24 to take control early. Lionel James returned a punt 81 yards for a score 2:35 into the contest, and linebacker Billy Ray Smith recovered a Lomax fumble on the next Cardinal possession. Gary Anderson's five-yard touchdown run gave the Chargers a 14-0 lead.

Chicago's Walter Payton set the 10th NFL record of his illustrious career in helping the Bears to a 20-3 victory over Tampa Bay. The win was the Bears' ninth straight over the Buccaneers and Chicago's 25th in its last 27 NFC Central Division games.

Payton, who didn't practice during the week before the game because of an ankle injury, rushed 15 times for only 24 yards but scored the Bears' first touchdown on a one-yard run in the opening period. The rushing touchdown was the 107th of Payton's career, surpassing Jim Brown's record of 106 that had stood for more than two decades.

Ironically, in the same game that Payton set the rushing touchdown record, Neal Anderson, Chicago's No. 1 draft choice in 1986 and Payton's heir apparent in the Bears' backfield, scored the first rushing touchdown of his young career. Anderson's 27-yard, second-quarter touchdown helped Chicago to a 14-3 half-time lead. Anderson finished with 115 yards rushing on 16 carries for the first 100-yard rushing game of his career.

Chicago's Walter Payton (above) scored his NFL-record 107th rushing touchdown in Week 2 while team-mate Neal Anderson scored his first in a 20-3 triumph over Tampa Bay.

The Bucs, who scored 48 points against Atlanta in their opening game, failed to score a touchdown against Chicago despite moving inside the Bears' 30-yard line on four occasions. Starting quarterback Steve DeBerg, who had five touchdown passes against the Falcons, was replaced by rookie Vinny Testaverde in the final three minutes. Testaverde, the first player chosen in the 1987 draft, completed one of four passes for 14 yards in his professional debut.

Another rookie quarterback who made his NFL debut in Week 2 was Don Majkowski, a 10th-round draft pick from Virginia and the 13th quarterback taken in the '87 draft. The youngster got the nod from Green Bay Coach Forrest Gregg after Randy Wright had been ineffective in the Packers' 20-0 loss to the Los Angeles Raiders in Week 1.

Majkowski completed 10 of 20 passes for 121 yards and one touchdown in guiding the Packers to a 17-17 tie with the Denver Broncos. Majkowski's seven-yard touchdown pass to Paul Ott Carruth put Green Bay ahead 14-0 in the second quarter. But the Broncos, despite committing six turnovers on a wet, soggy field, came back to tie the game for the final time on Steve Sewell's two-yard run with 5:53 left.

Placekickers on both teams missed potential game-winning field goals in overtime. The Packers' Al Del Greco missed a 47-yard attempt on Green Bay's first possession and the

Fullback John L. Williams rushed for a career-high 112 yards in Seattle's 43-14 win over Kansas City.

Broncos' Rich Karlis missed a 40-yard try with nine seconds left in overtime.

The week's biggest upset took place in Atlanta, where the Falcons—coming off a 38-point loss to Tampa Bay the week before—stunned the Washington Redskins, 21-20. Journeyman quarterback Scott Campbell made his first start for Atlanta and threw for 271 yards and two touchdowns. Campbell, subbing for David Archer, was making just the third start of his five-year career and his first since 1985 with Pittsburgh.

Campbell led the Falcons on 80-yard drives for their final two touchdowns. Atlanta took its first lead at 9:47 of the third quarter when Campbell capped a scoring march with a 23-yard touchdown pass to Stacey Bailey for a 14-13 lead. Campbell later connected with Floyd Dixon for a 33-yard gain on a touchdown drive that was capped by Gerald Riggs' four-yard run with 6:47 remaining.

Riggs finished with 120 yards on 23 carries.

One game that went according to script took place in Indianapolis, where the Miami Dolphins defeated the Colts for the 14th straight time, 23-10. It is the longest current domination in the NFL and the Colts have not beaten the Dolphins at home since a 45-28 victory on October 9, 1977, when the Colts franchise was located in Baltimore.

Quarterback Dan Marino led the Dolphins on an 11-play, 81-yard scoring drive on their first possession, throwing 18 yards to rookie Troy Stradford for the touchdown. Marino later added touchdown passes of six yards to Jim Jensen and 10 yards to Mark Clayton.

The Cleveland Browns posted their largest victory margin over the Pittsburgh Steelers in 21 years with a 34-10 triumph in Week 2. The Browns' victory was their sixth straight over the Steelers at Cleveland Stadium and marked the first time Cleveland had won its home-opening game since 1979.

The Browns exploded for 17 points in a 2:25 span of the fourth quarter to transform a close game into a rout. The big play in the sequence was linebacker Clay Matthews' 26-yard interception return for a touchdown to give the

Browns a 27-10 lead. For good measure, Matthews intercepted another Mark Malone pass on Pittsburgh's next play from scrimmage.

Malone was intercepted five times and Pittsburgh's offense was held to just 29 total yards in the second half and 58 yards rushing in the game. Earnest Jackson, who rushed for 103 yards against San Francisco in Week 1, managed just 19 yards against the Browns.

Jackson could find a sympathizer in New Orleans' Rueben Mayes, who was held to only 20 yards rushing in the Saints' 27-17 loss to Philadelphia. Mayes ran for 147 yards the previous week against Cleveland, the same team that shut Jackson down.

The Eagles' defense was a terror for most of the game with three interceptions, three sacks and two fumble recoveries. Linebacker Seth Joyner accounted for Philadelphia's final touchdown with an 18-yard fumble return in the fourth quarter.

The Seattle Seahawks also used a strong defense to post a 43-14 AFC West Division victory over Kansas City. The Seahawks forced five Chiefs turnovers, all coming in Kansas City territory and leading to Seattle points.

The Seahawks took advantage of two Kansas City turnovers early in the second half to score 10 points and take a commanding 27-7 lead. Chiefs running back Michael Clemons fumbled after a hit by Paul Moyer and Eugene Robinson recovered for Seattle at the Kansas City 25-yard line. Seven plays later, Dave Krieg and Mike Tice hooked up for a two-yard touchdown pass. On the Chiefs' next possession, quarterback Bill Kenney fumbled after a hit by Jacob Green and Moyer recovered on the K.C. 5-yard line. That set up a 25-yard Norm Johnson field goal.

Johnson booted a team-record five field goals while Krieg threw for three touchdowns to pace a Seattle offense that didn't commit a turnover. Running back John L. Williams added a career-high 112 yards rushing on 15 attempts.

Although he didn't score, Seattle wide receiver Steve Largent caught two passes to become only the second player in NFL history to reach the 700 mark in career receptions. Charlie Joiner retired after the 1986 season with 750.

The Dallas Cowboys snapped a six-game losing streak—the club's longest in 23 years—with a 16-14 upset victory over the New York Giants. The Cowboy defense intercepted four passes by Giants quarterback Phil Simms and held the Giants' running attack to just 60 yards on 20 attempts. It marked the Giants' first loss at home in 13 games.

Two of the interceptions were made by strong safety Bill Bates, with his 22-yard interception return in the first period setting up the Cowboys' first touchdown and his second thwarting a New York drive in the fourth quarter.

Dallas quarterback Danny White also threw four interceptions and was sacked five times. But he still completed 23 of 38 passes for 276 yards. Tony Dorsett rushed 18 times for 75 yards and finished the game with 15,064 career rushing yards, only the third player (after Payton and Brown) to reach the 15,000-yard plateau.

Dallas' Roger Ruzek kicked three field goals, including a 28-yard game-winner with 5:26 remaining. His counterpart, Raul Allegre, was wide left on a 46-yard attempt with six seconds left.

Buffalo quarterback Jim Kelly threw three touchdown passes, including a 10-yarder to Ronnie Harmon with 57 seconds left, to lead the Bills to a 34-30 triumph over the Houston Oilers.

After the Oilers had taken a 30-20 lead with 4:58 left on Tony Zendejas' 30-yard field goal, the Bills cut the deficit to three points by driving 80 yards, with Robb Riddick scoring from two yards out with 3:31 left.

After Houston failed to score on its next possession, Kelly drove Buffalo 54 yards on eight plays before connecting with Harmon for the game-winning score. Kelly completed four of five passes on the drive.

The Los Angeles Raiders had little trouble defeating the Detroit Lions, 27-7, in an interconference game. Quarterback Rusty Hilger had his best game as a pro, completing 20 of 39 passes for 234 yards, including a 14-yard touchdown pass to Dokie Williams that gave the Raiders the lead for good.

In what turned out to be the final game played prior to the strike, the New York Jets coasted to a 43-24 victory over AFC East Division rival New England in the Monday night game. Jets quarterback Ken O'Brien completed 19 of 26 passes for 313 yards, including a 58-yard touchdown pass to wide receiver Al Toon.

O'Brien completed 13 consecutive passes at one point, including all seven in the third quarter as the Jets exploded for 21 points.

The Jets' win gave them a 2-0 record prior to the strike, one of four teams (the Bears, Raiders and Vikings were the others) to be undefeated going in to the work stoppage. On the other hand, the Colts, Giants, Lions and Rams were winless prior to the strike.

Vikings-Rams
SUNDAY, SEPTEMBER 20
SCORE BY PERIODS

Minnesota	7	7	0	7—21
Los Angeles Rams	0	0	7	9—16

SCORING
Minnesota—Hilton 8 pass from Wilson (C. Nelson kick), 4:39. 1st.

Minnesota—Carter 46 pass from Wilson (C. Nelson kick), 1:47 2nd.

Los Angeles—McGee 2 run (Lansford kick), 8:52 3rd.

Los Angeles—J. Johnson 20 run with blocked punt (kick failed), 2:45 4th.
Los Angeles—Field goal Lansford 27, 5:05 4th.
Minnesota—H. Jones 41 pass from Wilson (C. Nelson kick), 14:30 4th.

TEAM STATISTICS

	Minnesota	Los Angeles
First downs	17	15
Rushes-Yards	25-96	35-122
Passing yards	257	88
Sacked-Yards lost	4-28	2-17
3rd down eff.	2-15	5-15
Passes	17-38-0	15-25-1
Punts	8-36.3	7-43.3
Fumbles-Lost	4-2	3-1
Penalties-Yards	7-81	9-51
Time of possession	28:02	31:58

Attendance—63,567.

INDIVIDUAL STATISTICS

Rushing—Minnesota, D. Nelson 8-58, Anderson 7-31, Dozier 5-13, Wilson 2-2, Fenney 1-1, Lewis 2-minus 9; Los Angeles, Dickerson 26-90, Everett 4-16, Guman 3-10, Ellard 1-4, McGee 1-2.

Passing—Minnesota, Wilson 17-38-0—285; Los Angeles, Everett 15-25-1—105.

Receiving—Minnesota, Carter 4-117, H. Jones 3-76, Jordan 1-38, Dozier 3-21, D. Nelson 3-13, Anderson 2-12, Hilton 1-8; Los Angeles, Dickerson 4-35, McGee 3-22, Hill 3-18, Guman 1-11, Ellard 3-10, Young 1-9.

Kickoff Returns—Minnesota, Guggemos 1-16, Richardson 2-40, D. Nelson 1-20; Los Angeles, White 1-26, Sutton 2-37.

Punt Returns—Minnesota, Richardson 3-16; Los Angeles, Ellard 4-49.

Interceptions—Minnesota, Solomon 1-30.

Punting—Minnesota, Coleman 7-41.4; Los Angeles, Hatcher 7-43.3.

Field Goals—Minnesota, none attempted; Los Angeles, Lansford 1-1.

Sacks—Minnesota, Studwell, D. Martin; Los Angeles, Wright, Jeter, Miller, Owens.

Cowboys-Giants
SUNDAY, SEPTEMBER 20
SCORE BY PERIODS

Dallas	3	7	3	3—16
New York Giants	7	0	7	0—14

SCORING

New York—Robinson 5 pass from Simms (Allegre kick), 8:01 1st.
Dallas—Field goal Ruzek 46, 9:34 1st.
Dallas—Chandler 1 pass from D. White (Ruzek kick), 3:20 2nd.
New York—Bavaro 1 pass from Simms (Allegre kick), 6:54 3rd.
Dallas—Field goal Ruzek 43, 11:40 3rd.
Dallas—Field goal Ruzek 28, 9:44 4th.

TEAM STATISTICS

	Dallas	New York
First downs	21	14
Rushes-Yards	38-114	20-60
Passing yards	242	205
Sacked-Yards lost	5-34	2-14
3rd down eff.	9-21	4-12
Passes	23-38-4	17-37-4
Punts	4-41.8	4-40.3
Fumbles-Lost	1-0	1-1
Penalties-Yards	9-70	5-51
Time of possession	41:42	18:18

Attendance—73,426.

INDIVIDUAL STATISTICS

Rushing—Dallas, Walker 17-27, Dorsett 18-75, New-

some 2-14, D. White 1-minus 2; New York, Morris 8-26, Carthon 2-3, Adams 2-1, Anderson 2-6, Rouson 5-22, Simms 1-2.

Passing—Dallas, D. White 23-38-4—276; New York, Simms 17-36-4—219, Rutledge 0-1-0—0.

Receiving—Dallas, Banks 6-96, Dorsett 4-12, Walker 3-50, Cosbie 4-67, Barksdale 1-20, Chandler 1-1, Newsome 3-19, Renfro 1-11; New York, Manuel 2-24, Robinson 3-31, Bavaro 3-64, Anderson 1-7, McConkey 1-12, Galbreath 5-59, Rouson 1-8, Ingram 1-14.

Kickoff Returns—Dallas, Clack 1-26, Lavette 2-40; New York, Ingram 1-12, Adams 1-14, Rouson 3-53.

Punt Returns—Dallas, Banks 4-31; New York, McConkey 2-7.

Interceptions—Dallas, Scott 1-1, Bates 2-28, Walls 1-6; New York, Taylor 1-minus 2, Kinard 3-93.

Punting—Dallas, Saxon 4-41.8; New York, Landeta 4-40.3.

Field Goals—Dallas, Ruzek 3-3; New York, Allegre 0-1 (missed: 46).

Sacks—Dallas, Rohrer, Hegman; New York, Hill, Taylor, Martin, Burt, Marshall.

Redskins-Falcons
SUNDAY, SEPTEMBER 20
SCORE BY PERIODS

Washington	7	0	6	7—20
Atlanta	7	0	7	7—21

SCORING

Washington—Bryant 17 pass from Williams (Haji-Sheikh kick), 7:49 1st.
Atlanta—Dixon 19 pass from Campbell (Luckhurst kick), 13:31 1st.
Washington—Clark 19 pass from Williams (kick failed), 5:06 3rd.
Atlanta—Bailey 23 pass from Campbell (Luckhurst kick), 9:47 3rd.
Washington—Monk 6 pass from Williams (Haji-Sheikh kick), 3:12 4th.
Atlanta—Riggs 4 run (Luckhurst kick), 8:13 4th.

TEAM STATISTICS

	Washington	Atlanta
First downs	21	18
Rushes-Yards	32-145	29-125
Passing yards	190	269
Sacked-Yards lost	1-8	1-2
3rd down eff.	8-13	6-15
Passes	18-30-2	17-34-1
Punts	5-51.6	6-40.3
Fumbles-Lost	2-1	2-0
Penalties-Yards	5-54	9-65
Time of possession	33:02	26:58

Attendance—50,882.

INDIVIDUAL STATISTICS

Rushing—Washington, Griffin 14-73, Bryant 15-70, Williams 1-3, Branch 1-3, Monk 1-minus 4; Atlanta, Riggs 23-120, Campbell 4-8, Dixon 1-minus 1, Griffin 1-minus 2.

Passing—Washington, Williams 18-30-2—198; Atlanta, Campbell 17-34-1—271.

Receiving—Washington, Bryant 6-76, Sanders 4-45, Clark 3-52, Monk 2-12, Dennison 2-8, Yarber 1-5; Atlanta, Whisenhunt 6-68, Dixon 5-105, Bailey 3-45, Matthews 1-37, Stamps 1-10, Riggs 1-6.

Kickoff Returns—Washington, Griffin 3-28; Atlanta, Stamps 1-24, Croudip 1-18.

Punt Returns—Washington, Yarber 4-61; Atlanta, Johnson 5-27.

Interceptions—Washington, Wilburn 1-22; Atlanta, Butler 1-7, Gordon 1-1.

Punting—Washington, Cox 5-51.6; Atlanta, Donnelly 5-48.4, Luckhurst 1-37.0.

Field Goals—Washington, Haji-Sheikh 0-1 (missed: 33); Atlanta, none attempted.

Sacks—Washington, Hamilton; Atlanta, Bryan.

49ers-Bengals

SUNDAY, SEPTEMBER 20
SCORE BY PERIODS

San Francisco	0	7	13	7—27
Cincinnati	10	10	0	6—26

SCORING

Cincinnati—Kinnebrew 2 run (Breech kick), 8:25 1st.
Cincinnati—Field goal Breech 23, 14:09 1st.
San Francisco—Wilson 38 pass from Montana (Wersching kick), 11:42 2nd.
Cincinnati—Holman 46 pass from Esiason (Breech kick), 13:14 2nd.
Cincinnati—Field goal Breech 42, 14:58 2nd.
San Francisco—Rice 34 pass from Montana (Wersching kick), 2:30 3rd.
San Francisco—Field goal Wersching 24, 5:47 3rd.
San Francisco—Field goal Wersching 31, 11:43 3rd.
Cincinnati—Field goal Breech 41, 6:55 4th.
Cincinnati—Field goal Breech 46, 13:06 4th.
San Francisco—Rice 25 pass from Montana (Wersching kick), 15:00 4th.

TEAM STATISTICS

	San Francisco	Cincinnati
First downs	16	19
Rushes-Yards	20-56	50-128
Passing yards	205	164
Sacked-Yards lost	5-45	3-16
3rd down eff	3-13	8-22
Passes	21-37-0	14-29-1
Punts	8-39.5	6-40.3
Fumbles-Lost	1-1	1-0
Penalties-Yards	3-25	4-30
Time of possession	25:46	34:14

Attendance—53,490.

INDIVIDUAL STATISTICS

Rushing—San Francisco, Craig 12-35, Cribbs 5-14, Flagler 2-3, Rice 1-4; Cincinnati, Kinnebrew 22-84, Brooks 16-31, Esiason 10-5, Johnson 1-1, Jennings 1-7.

Passing—San Francisco, Montana 21-37-0—250; Cincinnati, Esiason 14-29-1—180.

Receiving—San Francisco, Cribbs 2-11, Heller 3-22, Craig 4-23, Rice 4-86, Wilson 7-104, Flagler 1-4; Cincinnati, Brooks 3-28, Collinsworth 3-32, Jennings 1-7, Munoz 1-12, Brown 2-32, Holman 2-55, Martin 1-9, Kinnebrew 1-5.

Kickoff Returns—San Francisco, Flagler 2-27, Cribbs 2-50, Sydney 3-75; Cincinnati, Martin 3-51.

Punt Returns—San Francisco, Griffin 3-17; Cincinnati, Martin 3-36.

Interceptions—San Francisco, Turner 1-15.

Punting—San Francisco, Runager 8-39.5; Cincinnati, Horne 6-40.3.

Field Goals—San Francisco, Wersching 2-2; Cincinnati, Breech 4-4.

Sacks—San Francisco, Kugler, Stover, Haley; Cincinnati, Fulcher, Krumrie, Skow 2, Zander.

Chiefs-Seahawks

SUNDAY, SEPTEMBER 20
SCORE BY PERIODS

Kansas City	0	7	0	7—14
Seattle	3	14	20	6—43

SCORING

Seattle—Field goal Johnson 34, 7:44 1st.
Seattle—Turner 9 pass from Krieg (N. Johnson kick), 5:13 2nd.
Kansas City—Carson 10 pass from Blackledge (Lowery kick), 11:04 2nd.
Seattle—Turner 17 pass from Krieg (N. Johnson kick), 14:09 2nd.
Seattle—Tice 2 pass from Krieg (N. Johnson kick), 4:54 3rd.
Seattle—Field goal N. Johnson 25, 6:55 3rd.
Seattle—Williams 1 run (N. Johnson kick), 10:18 3rd.
Seattle—Field goal N. Johnson 46, 14:17 3rd.
Seattle—Field goal N. Johnson 27, 6:32 4th.
Seattle—Field goal N. Johnson 49, 10:54 4th.
Kansas City—Carson 10 pass from Kenney (Lowery kick), 13:53 4th.

TEAM STATISTICS

	Kansas City	Seattle
First downs	12	23
Rushes-Yards	20-75	44-225
Passing yards	107	135
Sacked-Yards lost	4-27	3-17
3rd down eff	4-11	7-15
Passes	14-26-1	16-22-0
Punts	4-35.5	1-33.0
Fumbles-Lost	5-4	0-0
Penalties-Yards	4-37	3-15
Time of possession	22:50	37:10

Attendance—61,667.

INDIVIDUAL STATISTICS

Rushing—Kansas City, Okoye 11-30, Moriarty 2-16, Blackledge 3-15, Clemons 1-7, Heard 3-7; Seattle, Williams 15-112, Warner 18-53, Morris 6-34, Krieg 2-22, Burse 2-5, Kemp 1-minus 1.

Passing—Kansas City, Blackledge 8-15-0—59, Kenney 6-11-1—75; Seattle, Krieg 16-22-0—152.

Receiving—Kansas City, Carson 5-83, Okoye 3-15, Hayes 2-10, Heard 1-7, Arnold 1-6, Marshall 1-4, Paige 1-9; Seattle, R. Butler 4-50, Williams 3-38, Turner 3-27, Largent 2-17, Tice 2-4, Skansi 1-12, Warner 1-4.

Kickoff Returns—Kansas City, Palmer 9-221, Moriarty 1-9; Seattle, Edmonds 2-36.

Punt Returns—Kansas City, Clemons 1-1; Seattle, Edmonds 2-28.

Interceptions—Seattle, Hunter 1-3.

Punting—Kansas City, L. Colbert 4-35.5; Seattle, Rodriguez 1-33.0.

Field Goals—Kansas City, none attempted; Seattle, N. Johnson 5-6 (missed: 39).

Sacks—Kansas City, Bell 1½, Still, G. Baldinger ½; Seattle, Young 1½, Bosworth, Green 1½.

Broncos-Packers

SUNDAY, SEPTEMBER 20
SCORE BY PERIODS

Denver	0	3	7	7	0—17
Green Bay	7	7	0	3	0—17

SCORING

Green Bay—Fullwood 3 run (Del Greco kick), 4:22 1st.
Green Bay—Carruth 7 pass from Majkowski (Del Greco kick), 12:37 2nd.
Denver—Field goal Karlis 38, 15:00 2nd.
Denver—Lang 3 run (Karlis kick), 2:47 3rd.
Green Bay—Field goal Del Greco 32, 0:48 4th.
Denver—Sewell 2 run (Karlis kick), 9:07 4th.

TEAM STATISTICS

	Denver	Green Bay
First downs	29	14
Rushes-Yards	45-197	41-134
Passing yards	281	100
Sacked-Yards lost	1-4	3-21
3rd down eff	12-19	4-15
Passes	30-49-3	10-20-0
Punts	4-34.3	9-35.7
Fumbles-Lost	5-3	1-1
Penalties-Yards	10-63	8-68
Time of possession	40:49	34:11

Attendance—50,624.

INDIVIDUAL STATISTICS

Rushing—Denver, Winder 21-89, Willhite 12-65, Elway 4-36, Lang 5-9, Sewell 2-6, Johnson 1-minus 8; Green Bay, Fullwood 13-57, Davis 16-38, Majkowski 3-16, Carruth 5-12, Clark 4-11.

Passing—Denver, Elway 30-48-3—285, Willhite 0-1-0 —0; Green Bay, Majkowski 10-20-0—121.

Receiving—Denver, Willhite 8-26, Mobley 4-64, Kay 4-50, Watson 4-44, Jackson 3-39, Johnson 3-34, Sewell 2-7, Lang 1-15, Nattiel 1-6; Green Bay, Carruth 3-27, Stanley 2-59, Davis 2-7, Epps 1-17, Neal 1-7, West 1-4.

Kickoff Returns—Denver, Nattiel 1-20, Lang 1-15, Ryan 2-9; Green Bay, Fullwood 1-28, Cook 1-20, Weishuhn 1-1.

Punt Returns—Denver, Willhite 4-22, Nattiel 2-5; Green Bay, Stanley 1-1.

Interceptions—Green Bay, Johnson 1-2, Noble 1-10, Anderson 1-9.

Punting—Denver, Horan 4-34.4; Green Bay, Bracken 9-35.7.

Field Goals—Denver, Karlis 1-2 (missed: 40); Green Bay, Del Greco 1-2 (missed: 47).

Sacks—Denver, Robbins, Fletcher, Ryan; Green Bay, Holland.

Saints-Eagles
SUNDAY, SEPTEMBER 20
SCORE BY PERIODS

New Orleans	10	0	0	7—17
Philadelphia	0	17	3	7—27

SCORING

New Orleans—Field goal Andersen 45, 7:19 1st.

New Orleans—Tice 6 pass from Hebert (Andersen kick), 11:37 1st.

Philadelphia—Field goal McFadden 30, 6:35 2nd.

Philadelphia—Quick 19 pass from Cunningham (McFadden kick), 11:10 2nd.

Philadelphia—Jackson 25 pass from Cunningham (McFadden kick), 14:38 2nd.

Philadelphia—Field goal McFadden 30, 12:40 3rd.

Philadelphia—Joyner 18 fumble return (McFadden kick), 0:23 4th.

New Orleans—Tice 27 pass from Wilson (Andersen kick), 11:09 4th.

TEAM STATISTICS

	New Orleans	Philadelphia
First downs	14	19
Rushes-Yards	18-32	43-161
Passing yards	188	175
Sacked-Yards lost	3-22	3-20
3rd down eff.	2-13	6-17
Passes	18-39-3	19-34-1
Punts	6-33.0	7-34.1
Fumbles-Lost	2-2	5-2
Penalties-Yards	8-47	4-45
Time of possession	24:40	35:20
Attendance—57,485.		

INDIVIDUAL STATISTICS

Rushing—New Orleans, Mayes 13-20, Hilliard 2-3, Hebert 1-9, Jordan 1-2, Word 1-minus 2; Philadelphia, Tautalatasi 13-54, Cunningham 8-32, Haddix 12-28, Teltschik 1-23, Morse 6-14, Jackson 1-6, Byars 1-7.

Passing—New Orleans, Hebert 14-32-3—127, Wilson 4-7-0—83; Philadelphia, Cunningham 19-34-1—195.

Receiving—New Orleans, Tice 5-64, Jones 3-38, R. Clark 2-27, Brenner 2-27, Mayes 2-3, Martin 2-41, Jordan 1-11, Gray 1-minus 1; Philadelphia, Quick 7-83, Spagnola 4-37, Tautalatasi 3-16, Jackson 2-46, Haddix 2-3, Byars 1-10.

Kickoff Returns—New Orleans, Word 1-17, Gray 1-12, Hilliard 1-16; Philadelphia, Cooper 2-38, Tautalatasi 2-21.

Punt Returns—New Orleans, Gray 1-0, Martin 2-13.

Interceptions—New Orleans, Waymer 1-17; Philadelphia, Foules 2-0, Waters 1-0.

Punting—New Orleans, Hansen 6-33.0; Philadelphia, Teltschik 7-34.1.

Field Goals—New Orleans, Andersen 1-1; Philadelphia, McFadden 2-2.

Sacks—New Orleans, Warren, Jackson, Swilling; Philadelphia, Simmons 1½, White 1½.

Oilers-Bills
SUNDAY, SEPTEMBER 20
SCORE BY PERIODS

Houston	3	14	3	10—30
Buffalo	3	10	0	21—34

SCORING

Buffalo—Field goal Norwood 45, 4:23 1st.

Houston—Field goal Zendejas 52, 11:59 1st.

Houston—D. Hill 2 pass from Moon (Zendejas kick), 1:54 2nd.

Buffalo—Field goal Norwood 38, 5:28 2nd.

Houston—Rozier 8 run (Zendejas kick), 11:07 2nd.

Buffalo—Riddick 11 pass from Kelly (Norwood kick), 14:54 2nd.

Houston—Field goal Zendejas 27, 11:06 3rd.

Buffalo—Reed 9 pass from Kelly (Norwood kick), 6:23 4th.

Buffalo—Givins 12 pass from Moon (Zendejas kick), 8:33 4th.

Houston—Field goal Zendejas 30, 10:02 4th.

Buffalo—Riddick 2 run (Norwood kick), 11:29 4th.

Buffalo—Harmon 10 pass from Kelly (Norwood kick), 14:03 4th.

TEAM STATISTICS

	Houston	Buffalo
First downs	19	30
Rushes-Yards	37-197	31-133
Passing yards	130	248
Sacked-Yards lost	1-12	5-45
3rd down eff.	4-14	6-13
Passes	13-27-1	26-43-2
Punts	6-39.0	5-32.6
Fumbles-Lost	2-0	1-0
Penalties-Yards	10-113	7-55
Time of possession	30:02	29:58
Attendance—56,534.		

INDIVIDUAL STATISTICS

Rushing—Houston, Rozier 29-150, Moon 1-0, Wallace 4-31, Pinkett 3-16; Buffalo, Bell 4-21, Mueller 9-45, Harmon 12-46, Kelly 3-10, Riddick 3-11.

Passing—Houston, Moon 13-27-1—142; Buffalo, Kelly 26-43-2—293.

Receiving—Houston, D. Hill 4-48, Rozier 3-3, Givins 5-66, J. Williams 1-25; Buffalo, Harmon 8-82, Burkett 7-115, Riddick 4-30, Reed 6-62, Metzelaars 1-4.

Kickoff Returns—Houston, Drewrey 2-19, Pinkett 5-105; Buffalo, Riddick 1-31.

Punt Returns—Houston, Duncan 3-4; Buffalo, Pitts 3-21.

Interceptions—Houston, Bostic 1-4, Donaldson 1-9; Buffalo, Pitts 1-12.

Punting—Houston, L. Johnson 6-39.0; Buffalo, Kidd 5-32.6.

Field Goals—Houston, Zendejas 3-3; Buffalo, Norwood 2-2.

Sacks—Houston, Donaldson, Childress, Lyles, Fuller; Buffalo, Smith.

Dolphins-Colts
SUNDAY, SEPTEMBER 20
SCORE BY PERIODS

Miami	7	9	7	0—23
Indianapolis	0	7	3	0—10

SCORING

Miami—Stradford 18 pass from Marino (Reveiz kick), 9:23 1st.

Miami—Field goal Reveiz 27, 2:23 2nd.

Indianapolis—Bouza 17 pass from Hogeboom (Biasucci kick), 8:48 2nd.

Miami—Jensen 6 pass from Marino (kick failed), 13:48 2nd.

Miami—Clayton 10 pass from Marino (Reveiz kick), 7:41 3rd.

Indianapolis—Field goal Biasucci 50, 13:28 3rd.

TEAM STATISTICS

	Miami	Indianapolis
First downs	20	20
Rushes-Yards	34-130	23-84
Passing yards	245	258
Sacked-Yards lost	1-9	2-24
3rd down eff.	8-15	4-12
Passes	23-32-0	27-43-1
Punts	5-34.2	4-37.5
Fumbles-Lost	2-2	4-3
Penalties-Yards	1-5	4-30
Time of possession	33:16	26:44

Attendance—57,524.

INDIVIDUAL STATISTICS

Rushing—Miami, Hampton 13-44, Bennett 8-42, Stradford 8-34, Davenport 5-10; Indianapolis, Bentley 22-84, Wonsley 1-0.

Passing—Miami, Marino 23-32-0—254; Indianapolis, Hogeboom 27-43-1—282.

Receiving—Miami, Clayton 4-69, Hardy 4-48, Duper 2-36, Stradford 2-22, Jensen 3-21, Pruitt 1-9, Hampton 7-49; Indianapolis, Bentley 9-69, Brooks 7-80, Bouza 6-85, Beach 3-27, Sherwin 2-21.

Kickoff Returns—Miami, Schwedes 1-33; Indianapolis, K. Daniel 5-104.

Punt Returns—Miami, Schwedes 1-26; Indianapolis, Tullis 2-9.

Interceptions—Miami, Blackwood 1-17.

Punting—Miami, Hayes 4-42.8; Indianapolis, Stark 4-37.5.

Field Goals—Miami, Reveiz 1-1; Indianapolis, Biasucci 1-1.

Sacks—Miami, Sochia 2; Indianapolis, Bickett.

Buccaneers-Bears
SUNDAY, SEPTEMBER 20
SCORE BY PERIODS

Tampa Bay	0	3	0	0— 3
Chicago	7	7	0	6—20

SCORING

Chicago—Payton 1 run (Butler kick), 9:41 1st.
Tampa Bay—Field goal Igwebuike 43, 2:37 2nd.
Chicago—Anderson 27 run (Butler kick), 6:29 2nd.
Chicago—Payton 9 pass from Tomczak (run failed), 11:40 4th.

TEAM STATISTICS

	Tampa Bay	Chicago
First downs	18	18
Rushes-Yards	25-89	36-166
Passing yards	173	133
Sacked-Yards lost	4-36	1-17
3rd down eff.	4-15	6-14
Passes	19-40-2	15-27-2
Punts	7-47.8	5-42.8
Fumbles-Lost	2-2	2-2
Penalties-Yards	9-100	8-65
Time of possession	28:21	31:39

Attendance—63,551.

INDIVIDUAL STATISTICS

Rushing—Tampa Bay, Wilder 17-80, Austin 7-9, DeBerg 1-0; Chicago, Anderson 16-115, Payton 15-24, Sanders 2-11, Thomas 2-6, Tomczak 1-10.

Passing—Tampa Bay, DeBerg 18-36-2—195, Testaverde 1-4-0—14; Chicago, Tomczak 15-27-2—150.

Receiving—Tampa Bay, Carter 4-55, Austin 4-36, Wilder 4-29, Magee 3-34, Carrier 2-27, Hall 1-14, Freeman 1-14; Chicago, Moorehead 6-53, Anderson 4-28, Payton 2-2, Gault 1-46, McKinnon 1-6, Morris 1-15.

Kickoff Returns—Tampa Bay, Futrell 3-61; Chicago, Gentry 2-38.

Punt Returns—Chicago, McKinnon 5-81.

Interceptions—Tampa Bay, Kemp 1-11, Jones 1-0; Chicago, Jackson 1-0, Phillips 1-1.

Punting—Tampa Bay, Garcia 7-47.8; Chicago, Wagner 5-42.8.

Field Goals—Tampa Bay, Igwebuike 1-2 (missed: 46); Chicago, Butler 0-2 (missed: 50, 55).

Sacks—Tampa Bay, Team; Chicago, Wilson 2, Dent, Perry.

Cardinals-Chargers
SUNDAY, SEPTEMBER 20
SCORE BY PERIODS

St. Louis	0	0	10	14—24
San Diego	14	14	0	0—28

SCORING

San Diego—James 81 punt return (Abbott kick), 2:35 1st.
San Diego—Anderson 5 run (Abbott kick), 5:24 1st.
San Diego—Chandler 26 pass from Fouts (Abbott kick), 4:16 2nd.
San Diego—James 7 run (Abbott kick), 13:32 2nd.
St. Louis—Green 8 pass from Lomax (Gallery kick), 8:13 3rd.
St. Louis—Field goal Gallery 38, 14:58 3rd.
St. Louis—Novacek 21 pass from Lomax (Gallery kick), 7:35 4th.
St. Louis—Mitchell 17 pass from Lomax (Gallery kick), 13:12 4th.

TEAM STATISTICS

	St. Louis	San Diego
First downs	24	17
Rushes-Yards	20-59	37-130
Passing yards	412	152
Sacked-Yards lost	5-45	0-0
3rd down eff.	8-20	6-13
Passes	32-61-1	13-19-1
Punts	3-39.0	6-45.0
Fumbles-Lost	2-1	3-1
Penalties-Yards	5-13	3-27
Time of possession	32:40	27:20

Attendance—47,988.

INDIVIDUAL STATISTICS

Rushing—St. Louis, Mitchell 13-42, Lomax 2-2, Ferrell 5-15; San Diego, Spencer 12-34, James 2-14, Anderson 19-79, Fouts 3-minus 1, Adams 1-4.

Passing—St. Louis, Lomax 32-61-1—457; San Diego, Fouts 13-19-1—152.

Receiving—St. Louis, Novacek 7-101, Mitchell 5-54, Green 7-139, Ferrell 4-32, J.T. Smith 6-92, Holmes 3-39; San Diego, Winslow 1-8, Chandler 5-77, Anderson 2-28, James 3-27, Holohan 1-12, Spencer 1-0.

Kickoff Returns—St. Louis, Ferrell 1-10, Sikahema 3-63; San Diego, James 1-21, Adams 1-11, Anderson 2-28.

Punt Returns—St. Louis, Sikahema 2-29; San Diego, James 1-81.

Interceptions—St. Louis, Mack 1-0; San Diego, Smith 1-5.

Punting—St. Louis, Cater 3-39.0; San Diego, Mojsiejenko 6-45.0.

Field Goals—St. Louis, Gallery 1-3 (missed: 29, 41); San Diego, none attempted.

Sacks—San Diego, Banks 1½, Snipes, Williams ½, Unrein, K. Wilson.

Steelers-Browns
SUNDAY, SEPTEMBER 20
SCORE BY PERIODS

Pittsburgh	0	3	7	0—10
Cleveland	0	10	7	17—34

SCORING

Cleveland—Field goal Jaeger 29, 3:05 2nd.
Cleveland—Mack 1 run (Jaeger kick), 11:24 2nd.
Pittsburgh—Field goal Anderson 27, 14:56 2nd.
Pittsburgh—Shell 19 fumble return (Anderson kick), 0:34 3rd.
Cleveland—McNeil 11 pass from Kosar (Jaeger kick), 10:17 3rd.
Cleveland—Field goal Jaeger 22, 4:43 4th.

Cleveland—Matthews 26 interception return (Jaeger kick), 5:49 4th.

Cleveland—Weathers 37 pass from Kosar (Jaeger kick), 7:08 4th.

TEAM STATISTICS

	Pittsburgh	Cleveland
First downs	17	18
Rushes-Yards	23-58	35-124
Passing yards	127	180
Sacked-Yards lost	4-34	1-8
3rd down eff.	7-17	6-17
Passes	13-41-6	18-30-1
Punts	6-41.0	6-40.8
Fumbles-Lost	1-0	1-1
Penalties-Yards	13-102	10-83
Time of possession	26:25	33:35

Attendance—79,543.

INDIVIDUAL STATISTICS

Rushing—Pittsburgh, Jackson 10-19, Stone 1-21, Abercrombie 6-25, Pollard 4-minus 4, Malone 2-minus 3; Cleveland, Byner 12-53, Mack 14-53, Kosar 1-3, Manoa 5-14, Fontenot 3-1.

Passing—Pittsburgh, Malone 12-36-5—151, Brister 1-5-1—10; Cleveland, Kosar 17-29-1—174, Fontenot 1-1-0—14.

Receiving—Pittsburgh, Lipps 5-68, Stallworth 1-22, Abercrombie 3-24, Lockett 1-17, Hoge 2-23, Gothard 1-7; Cleveland, Slaughter 3-37, Mack 8-45, Langhorne 1-12, Byner 2-35, Fontenot 1-5, McNeil 1-11, Newsome 1-6, Weathers 1-37.

Kickoff Returns—Pittsburgh, Sanchez 4-65, Hoge 1-13, Jones 1-22; Cleveland, Fontenot 1-3, Young 2-33.

Punt Returns—Pittsburgh, Lipps 1-4; Cleveland, McNeil 3-43.

Interceptions—Pittsburgh, Hinkle 1-4; Cleveland, Rockins 2-25, M. Johnson 1-3, Matthews 2-26, Minnifield 1-27.

Punting—Pittsburgh, Newsome 6-41.0; Cleveland, Gossett 6-40.8.

Field Goals—Pittsburgh, Anderson 1-2 (missed: 29); Cleveland, Jaeger 2-2.

Sacks—Pittsburgh, Hinkle; Cleveland, Baker, Puzzuoli, Hairston, Camp.

Lions-Raiders
SUNDAY, SEPTEMBER 20
SCORE BY PERIODS

Detroit	0	7	0	0— 7
Los Angeles Raiders	6	0	7	14—27

SCORING

Los Angeles—Field goal Bahr 38, 3:45 1st.

Los Angeles—Field goal Bahr 34, 14:38 1st.

Detroit—S. Williams 2 pass from Long (Murray kick), 5:21 2nd.

Los Angeles—Williams 14 pass from Hilger (Bahr kick), 2:14 3rd.

Los Angeles—Allen 1 run (Bahr kick), 3:27 4th.

Los Angeles—Mueller 1 run (Bahr kick), 13:07 4th.

TEAM STATISTICS

	Detroit	Los Angeles
First downs	16	25
Rushes-Yards	15-47	41-171
Passing yards	244	234
Sacked-Yards lost	2-11	1-0
3rd down eff.	2-10	7-15
Passes	21-35-2	20-40-1
Punts	4-36.0	4-20.0
Fumbles-Lost	2-1	1-0
Penalties-Yards	8-70	9-62
Time of possession	22:56	37:04

Attendance—50,300.

INDIVIDUAL STATISTICS

Rushing—Detroit, Jones 9-23, James 4-21, S. Williams 2-3; Los Angeles, Allen 22-79, Mueller 7-58, Strachan 7-33, Horton 2-3, Hilger 3-minus 2.

Passing—Detroit, Long 21-35-2—255; Los Angeles,

Hilger 20-39-1—234, Allen 0-1-0—0.

Receiving—Detroit, Mandley 7-110, Giles 2-37, Woolfolk 3-28, Chadwick 2-27, Rubick 2-26, Jones 3-20, Nichols 1-5, S. Williams 1-2; Los Angeles, Christensen 6-88, Lofton 3-44, Williams 3-33, Hester 1-30, Fernandez 2-24, Allen 3-6, Horton 1-6, Mueller 1-3.

Kickoff Returns—Detroit, Bernard 2-0, Lee 3-69; Los Angeles, Mueller 1-33, Williams 1-25.

Punt Returns—Detroit, Mandley 2-23.

Interceptions—Detroit, Griffin 1-29; Los Angeles, Haynes 1-7, Toran 1-0.

Punting—Detroit, Arnold 3-35.7, Murray 1-37.0; Los Angeles, Talley 3-26.3.

Field Goals—Detroit, Murray 0-3 (missed: 45, 37, 30); Los Angeles, Bahr 2-3 (missed: 33).

Sacks—Detroit, J. Williams; Los Angeles, Jones, Taylor.

Patriots-Jets
MONDAY, SEPTEMBER 21
SCORE BY PERIODS

New England	0	3	7	14—24
New York Jets	6	0	21	16—43

SCORING

New York—Field goal Leahy 22, 5:59 1st.

New York—Field goal Leahy 34, 13:54 1st.

New England—Field goal Franklin 32, 7:43 2nd.

New York—Toon 58 pass from O'Brien (Leahy kick), 3:30 3rd.

New York—Hector 5 run (Leahy kick), 7:25 3rd.

New England—Tippett 29 fumble return (Franklin kick), 8:40 3rd.

New York—Hector 9 run (Leahy kick), 12:53 3rd.

New York—Safety, Lyons tackled Tatupu in end zone, 1:09 4th.

New England—Baty 1 pass from Eason (Franklin kick), 7:12 4th.

New York—Faaola 1 run (Leahy kick), 11:01 4th.

New England—Starring 12 pass from Eason (Franklin kick), 11:57 4th.

New York—Faaola 1 run (Leahy kick), 14:45 4th.

TEAM STATISTICS

	New England	New York
First downs	17	21
Rushes-Yards	20-48	42-127
Passing yards	145	281
Sacked-Yards lost	5-41	5-38
3rd down eff.	4-13	9-18
Passes	18-34-1	20-27-0
Punts	6-40.2	4-37.3
Fumbles-Lost	2-1	3-2
Penalties-Yards	7-83	7-63
Time of possession	22:52	37:08

Attendance—70,847.

INDIVIDUAL STATISTICS

Rushing—New England, Collins 10-32, Tatupu 7-11, James 3-5; New York, Hector 17-75, McNeil 8-30, Vick 10-18, Faaola 5-4, O'Brien 1-0, Ryan 1-0.

Passing—New England, Eason 18-34-1—186; New York, O'Brien 19-26-0—313, Ryan 1-1-0—6.

Receiving—New England, Baty 5-37, Morgan 3-72, Starring 3-38, Collins 3-10, Tatupu 2-18, Jones 1-7, Fryar 1-4; New York, Shuler 6-57, Walker 4-88, McNeil 4-56, Hector 3-29, Toon 3-89.

Kickoff Returns—New England, Perryman 1-13, Starring 4-83, Collins 1-18; New York, Townsell 4-106, Sohn 1-16.

Punt Returns—New England, Fryar 1-4; New York, Townsell 5-41.

Interceptions—New York, Miano 1-3.

Punting—New England, Camarillo 6-40.2; New York, Jennings 4-37.3.

Field Goals—New England, Franklin 1-2 (missed: 48); New York, Leahy 2-2.

Sacks—New England, Blackmon, B. Williams, Sims, T. Williams 2; New York, Crable 2, Gordon 2, Nichols.

FOURTH WEEK

RESULTS OF WEEK 4

Sunday, October 4

Chicago 35, Philadelphia 3 at Phila.
Cleveland 20, New England 10 at N.E.
Dallas 38, N.Y. Jets 24 at N.Y.
Green Bay 23, Minnesota 16 at Minn.
Houston 40, Denver 10 at Den.
Indianapolis 47, Buffalo 6 at Buff.
L.A. Raiders 35, Kansas City 17 at L.A.
New Orleans 37, L.A. Rams 10 at N.O.
Pittsburgh 28, Atlanta 12 at Atl.
San Diego 10, Cincinnati 9 at Cin.
Seattle 24, Miami 20 at Sea.
Tampa Bay 31, Detroit 27 at Det.
Washington 28, St. Louis 21 at Wash.

Monday, October 5

San Francisco 41, N.Y. Giants 21 at N.Y.

The second National Football League players' strike in six years disrupted play after the second weekend of games. The sticking point this time was free agency, with NFL Players Association Executive Director Gene Upshaw demanding freedom of movement from team to team for his members. The collective bargaining agreement between the players and the owners had expired August 31, and the union wanted a new agreement—including unlimited free agency—before going back to work.

But the owners, represented in the negotiations by its Management Council, would have none of it. They wanted to keep the status quo, with a limited form of free agency that had seen just one player (defensive back Norm Thompson, who left St. Louis for Baltimore in 1977) switch teams in 10 years.

About the only thing the NFLPA and the Management Council agreed on were their many disagreements, and so, following the September 21 New England Patriots-New York Jets game, the players walked out.

But unlike 1982, when the first in-season strike in NFL history forced the cancellation of eight regular-season weekends of football, the owners this time would attempt to play the games as scheduled. The rosters would be comprised largely of free agents, former United States Football League players, untested rookies and aged veterans.

The owners believed that some union members would cross the picket lines set up around the league, and they were right. By the deadline for those players wishing to play in the first "strike replacement" games, 101 striking players representing 17 teams had reported for work. However, 43 of those players were on injured reserve lists when the strike was called, unable to play in the games even if they wanted to.

In a development that had to please Upshaw and his supporters, the only players reporting on four teams—the Bears, 49ers, Packers and Seahawks—were on injured reserve. Thirteen teams had no players on active rosters cross picket lines.

The players did succeed in forcing the cancellation of one weekend of games. The NFL announced that those games scheduled for September 27 and 28 would not be played—nor made up at a later date—and that the regular season would consist of 15 games.

Beginning with the games of October 4 and 5, replacement players wearing NFL uniforms began playing in NFL stadiums with the results to count in the league standings. For the most part, the media, striking players and sympathetic union members nationwide harshly criticized the owners for staging the games. But the owners held firm.

Said Jets President Jim Kensil, speaking for many NFL owners: "The NFL can afford as many of these weeks as necessary."

★   ★   ★

The first week of replacement football and the official third week of the 1987 season began October 4 with striking players manning picket lines outside sparsely filled stadiums. The total attendance for the 13 games was 220,827, for an average of 16,987. The largest single-game attendance was in Denver, where 38,494 people turned out for the Broncos game with the Houston Oilers. It was the first non-sellout at 76,142-seat Mile High Stadium in 18 years.

The smallest fan turnout came in Philadelphia, where just 4,073 people braved a nasty pre-game atmosphere outside Veterans Stadium to watch the Eagles play the Chicago Bears. A large convoy of 18-wheelers sympathetic to the players' cause circled the stadium for an hour prior to the game. Philadelphia police estimated that some 1,500 pickets were set up around Veterans Stadium in the more than four-hour demonstration, with hundreds at each gate.

People trying to enter the stadium were pelted with eggs and numerous car windshields were broken in the skirmish. The replacement players themselves were spared much of the same indignity because managements of the two teams had hustled them to the stadium between 6 and 6:30 that morning to avoid such problems.

"The hooliganism which took place outside our stadium is a tragedy for the city of Philadelphia, especially after this city took such pride in the 200th anniversary of the Constitution," said an incensed Eagles Owner Norman Braman. "Everything our founding fathers tried to accomplish, we saw the exact opposite."

The Players Association was quick to point

Former Bears quarterback Vince Evans returned to the NFL as a result of the strike and threw for two touchdowns and ran for another to lead the Raiders' replacement team to a 35-17 victory over the Chiefs.

out the fans' indifference and, in some cases, outright hostility, to what often was called "scab" football.

"It's a clear indication the fans reject this brand of football and aren't going to pay NFL prices for poor-quality games with players they've never heard of," said NFLPA Assistant Executive Director Doug Allen.

The games themselves resembled regular NFL football only in the final scores. At first glance, it appeared the Bears, Colts, 49ers, Oilers, Raiders, Redskins and Saints had the best replacement squads while the Bills, Broncos, Eagles, Giants and Rams had the worst. It was obvious from the beginning which general managers had prepared best for a strike.

The week's biggest blowout occurred in Buffalo, where the visiting Indianapolis Colts destroyed the Bills, 47-6. Regular Colts quarterback Gary Hogeboom crossed the picket line and bombarded the replacement Bills, exiting the game after throwing his team record-tying

fifth touchdown pass in the first minute of the second half.

Two other Colt regulars played and both were pivotal to the game's outcome. Joining Hogeboom were wide receiver Walter Murray, who caught seven passes for 161 yards and two touchdowns, and defensive back Jim Perryman, who intercepted one pass to set up a touchdown and blocked a punt that led to a safety.

Buffalo had no veteran players in uniform and played like it. Willie Totten was one of three quarterbacks for the Bills and accounted for the team's only touchdown with an eight-yard pass to Marc Brown. But the former Mississippi Valley State star also fumbled five times and lost three of them.

Despite the tension outside Veterans Stadium, the game went on and the Bears pounded the Eagles, 35-3. Former USFL and Canadian Football League player Mike Hohensee started at quarterback for the Bears and completed 12 of 22 passes for 157 yards and three touchdowns. Chicago outgained Philadelphia in total yards, 318-170.

Though no regulars from either team played, the Eagles lost to the Bears for the 22nd time in 26 regular-season meetings. The Eagles gave up 11 quarterback sacks for 70 yards in losses and were penalized 11 times for 65 more yards.

Philadelphia quarterback Guido Merkens had a particularly rough day. He was sacked 10 times, rushed three times for minus eight yards, had a punt blocked for a touchdown, passed for a nine-yard loss from punt formation, was injured on the next-to-last play of the game and had his name mispelled (Merkins) on his uniform.

"If it wasn't so embarrassing, it would have been fun," he said.

The week's closest game was played in Cincinnati, where the San Diego Chargers scored 10 fourth-quarter points to upend the Bengals, 10-9. Replacement kicker Jeff Gaffney's 24-yard field goal with 2:44 left won it for the Chargers.

Gaffney also was involved in the game's most memorable play and one of the most unusual during the strike. Gaffney was in to kick the extra point after San Diego's only touchdown when he was forced to field the ball after a bad snap from center. Gaffney ran to his left with Rick Neuheisel, the Chargers' quarterback and the holder on the play, trailing him. After hearing Neuheisel yell for the ball, Gaffney pitched it back to the quarterback, who then ran back across the field before diving into the right corner of the end zone to complete the point after.

The only regular player on either team to defy the strike and play was Cincinnati linebacker Reggie Williams, a 12-year veteran.

Having a large number of regular players in the strike games was not an automatic formula for success, however, as the St. Louis Cardinals found out. The Cardinals had 11 veteran players suit up and play in their game at Washington and still lost to a Redskins team without a single union member. The final score was 28-21 and marked the 10th consecutive victory at RFK Stadium for the Redskins in the divisional rivalry, strike or no strike.

The Redskins were led by quarterback Ed Rubbert, a rookie from Louisville who was released in the preseason, and wide receiver Anthony Allen, a 28-year-old veteran who had played the previous two NFL seasons in Atlanta before getting cut in training camp. Allen, who had signed as a free agent with Washington just two days before the game, caught three touchdown passes from Rubbert and set a club record with 255 yards in receptions.

The game's final touchdown came on a 60-yard interception return by Cardinal linebacker Peter Noga, whose brother, Niko, was walking the Cardinals' picket line back in St. Louis. Peter not only played his brother's position, but also wore Niko's uniform No. 57.

The Redskins' NFL record of 159 straight sellouts ended with a crowd of 27,728 at 55,642-seat RFK Stadium.

The smallest home crowd in the 54-year history of the Detroit Lions watched as the Lions dropped an NFC Central Division game to Tampa Bay, 31-27. The Pontiac Silverdome, where the Lions have played their home games since 1975, has a capacity of 80,638 for football.

The Bucs were led by defensive back Paul Tripoli, a player who had been cut by both the Toronto Argonauts of the CFL and the Buccaneers in training camp. Tripoli intercepted two passes, returning one for a touchdown and setting up a field goal with another.

Others also made the most of their pro football opportunity.

John Fourcade, a former star quarterback at the University of Mississippi who had played in the USFL, the CFL and even the Arena Football League, got the nod from the New Orleans Saints as their signal-caller in a game against the Los Angeles Rams.

Fourcade didn't disappoint. He threw three touchdown passes, including an 82-yarder to Mike Waters in the third period for the longest scoring play in Saints history. Fourcade completed 16 of 21 passes for 222 yards and the Saints played so well in a 37-10 victory that the Superdome crowd of 29,745 began chanting, "Stay on strike," in reference to the striking Saints players outside the stadium.

Alan Risher had been working as a stockbroker in the New Orleans area before becoming an NFL starting quarterback as a result of the strike. Risher, a former standout at Louisiana State University who had played in the USFL, threw for one touchdown and ran for another to lead the Green Bay Packers to a 23-16 triumph over Minnesota. Risher drove the Pack 61 yards for a touchdown on its second possession, throwing 31 yards to Lavale Thomas for the score.

Risher's counterpart with the Vikings, 37-year-old Tony Adams, was a real veteran of pro football wars. Adams had played previously in the NFL, the CFL, the USFL and was the World Football League's Most Valuable Player in 1974 with the Southern California Sun. For the previous six autumns, Adams was playing touch football in Kansas City and selling industrial supplies.

Another former NFL quarterback to make a return in strike football was 32-year-old Vince Evans, who played with the Chicago Bears for seven seasons before bolting to the newly formed USFL in 1983. Evans threw for two touchdowns and ran for a third to lead the Los Angeles Raiders to a 35-17 victory over Kansas City.

Evans started for the Raiders despite the presence of Marc Wilson, a $1 million-a-year player who crossed the picket line and was used only to hold for kicks against the Chiefs. Evans' first pass of the game went for a 27-yard touchdown to wide receiver Carl Aikens.

A crowd of 10,708 watched the game in 106-degree heat at the 92,516-seat Los Angeles Coliseum.

For the second straight game, the Miami Dolphins took their first possession of the game and drove downfield for a touchdown. Only this time it was Kyle Mackey at the controls, not Dan Marino.

Mackey, who had been with the Cardinals and the Eagles in recent seasons but never played, completed 17 of 26 passes for 179 yards against the Seattle Seahawks but it wasn't enough. The Seahawks prevailed, 24-20, behind their own replacement quarterback, Bruce Mathison.

Mathison, a 10th-round draft pick of the Chargers in 1983 who had signed with the Seahawks just four days earlier, threw for 326 yards and two touchdowns. His 47-yard bomb to Jimmy Teal to the Miami 2-yard line set up Rick Parros' game-winning, one-yard touchdown run with 1:30 left.

Kevin Sweeney, the NCAA's career passing yardage leader and a seventh-round draft choice, threw three touchdown passes to lead the Dallas Cowboys to a 38-24 victory over the New York Jets. Sweeney, who was waived by the Cowboys in their final training camp cut, completed just six passes in the game.

The contest was one of the sloppiest played in the first week of strike games. The Jets and Cowboys combined were penalized 26 times for 281 yards. Five Jets turnovers led to 17 Dallas points and four Cowboys giveaways produced 14 New York points.

Regular players Ed Jones and Randy White started for a Dallas defense that had 11 quarterback sacks.

Another sloppy game was played in Foxboro, Mass., where the visiting Cleveland Browns rallied from a 10-0 halftime deficit to defeat the New England Patriots, 20-10. Patriots regular running back Tony Collins fumbled on the game's first, third and sixth plays from scrimmage but the Browns failed to recover any of the three. The Cleveland defense also blew a possible interception on the game's fourth play.

The Browns, who didn't have any regular players in the game, were led on the comeback trail by running back Larry Mason, who played two seasons with the Jacksonville Bulls of the USFL. Mason, who rushed for just 27 yards in the first half, exploded for 106 yards and two touchdowns in the second.

New England was held to three first downs and 35 total yards in the second half and finished with just 31 yards rushing in the game.

The Pats had just 10 first downs and failed on all 13 of their third-down conversion opportunities.

The Pittsburgh Steelers beat the Atlanta Falcons, 28-12, behind replacement quarterback Steve Bono. Bono, a UCLA product who played briefly with Minnesota in 1985-86, passed for one touchdown and ran for another. Steelers wide receiver Joey Clinkscales caught six passes for 150 yards.

Houston Coach Jerry Glanville said he was so worried about his team's first strike replacement game at Denver that he was sick from 4 a.m. until the opening kickoff.

He needn't have worried. The Oilers pounded the Broncos, 40-10, behind quarterback Brent Pease and kicker John Diettrich. Pease, an 11th-round draft choice and a late cut by the Minnesota Vikings, threw for 260 yards and one touchdown and ran for another. Diettrich, who had been acquired by the Oilers in a trade with Green Bay only the day before, connected on all four of his field-goal attempts.

Denver quarterbacks Ken Karcher and Dean May didn't fare so well. Karcher threw two interceptions and fumbled three snaps and May threw one interception.

The first strike game played before a national television audience was definitely not a ready-for-prime-time affair. The San Francisco 49ers, with 17 players having at least some NFL game experience, pounded the New York Giants, 41-21. It was the first non-sellout for a Giants game at Giants Stadium in 87 games.

New York, which damaged its chances of repeating as league champs when its regular team lost its first two games, got little help from its strike team. The Giants employed what was generally considered to be the league's worst replacement team, with just two players—fullback Van Williams and tackle Bill Dugan—ever having played in the NFL.

But the Giants' strikers amassed 77 rushing yards against the 49ers—17 more yards than the regulars had against Dallas two weeks earlier.

Rams-Saints
SUNDAY, OCTOBER 4
SCORE BY PERIODS

Los Angeles Rams	0	0	3	7—10
New Orleans	7	20	3	7—37

SCORING

New Orleans—O'Neal 1 pass from J. Fourcade (Cofer kick), 13:28 1st.

New Orleans—R. Sutton 13 blocked punt return (kick failed), 1:51 2nd.

New Orleans—Martin 11 pass from J. Fourcade (Cofer kick), 6:24 2nd.

New Orleans—Alexander 1 run (Cofer kick), 13:50 2nd.

Los Angeles—Field goal Lansford 37, 5:12 3rd.

New Orleans—Field goal Cofer 27, 12:37 3rd.

New Orleans—Waters 82 pass from J. Fourcade (Cofer kick), 1:35 4th.

Los Angeles—Mobley 40 pass from Quarles (Lansford kick), 5:44 4th.

TEAM STATISTICS

	Los Angeles	New Orleans
First downs	12	19
Rushes-Yards	22-72	43-154
Passing yards	135	195
Sacked-Yards lost	2-14	1-27
3rd down eff.	5-15	14-18
Passes	11-30-1	16-21-1
Punts	4-32.5	3-47.0
Fumbles-Lost	1-1	2-0
Penalties-Yards	4-38	9-87
Time of possession	22:25	37:35

Attendance—29,745.

INDIVIDUAL STATISTICS

Rushing—Los Angeles, White 9-18, Guman 1-0, Dils 1-0, Francis 8-37, Quarles 1-8, Williams, 2-9; New Orleans, Beverly 8-32, Rodenberger 8-12, J. Fourcade 6-39, Alexander 21-71.

Passing—Los Angeles, Dils 10-27-0—109, Quarles 1-3-1—40; New Orleans, J. Fourcade 16-21-1—222.

Receiving—Los Angeles, Guman 3-29, McDonald 1-5, White 2-5, Moore 2-44, Henry 1-13, Mobley 2-53; New Orleans, Walker 2-15, Dawsey 6-79, Alexander 2-15, O'Neal 1-1, Martin 2-21, Scott 2-9, Waters 1-82.

Kickoff Returns—Los Angeles, Williams 4-103, Tiumalu 3-71.

Punt Returns—Los Angeles, Mobley 1-12; New Orleans, Martin 3-19.

Interceptions—Los Angeles, Williamson 1-28; New Orleans, Atkins 1-8.

Punting—Los Angeles, Hatcher 3-32.5; New Orleans, Barnhardt 3-47.0.

Field Goals—Los Angeles, Lansford 1-1; New Orleans, Cofer 1-1.

Sacks—Los Angeles, Cromwell; New Orleans, Clark 2.

Oilers-Broncos
SUNDAY, OCTOBER 4
SCORE BY PERIODS

Houston	7	10	10	13—40
Denver	0	10	0	0—10

SCORING

Houston—Pease 1 run (Diettrich kick), 9:52 1st.
Denver—Field goal Clendenen 28, 0:13 2nd.
Houston—Field goal Diettrich 43, 5:17 2nd.
Houston—Jackson 16 run (Diettrich kick), 12:33 2nd.
Denver—Massie 21 pass from Karcher (Clendenen kick), 14:51 2nd.
Houston—Field goal Diettrich 39, 6:35 3rd.
Houston—Seale 73 interception return (Diettrich kick), 8:03 3rd.
Houston—Gehring 31 pass from Pease (Diettrich kick), 0:06 4th.
Houston—Field goal Diettrich 44, 4:28 4th.
Houston—Field goal Diettrich 27, 11:43 4th.

TEAM STATISTICS

	Houston	Denver
First downs	20	14
Rushes-Yards	42-154	16-38
Passing yards	260	182
Sacked-Yards lost	0-0	5-44
3rd down eff.	5-12	4-17
Passes	15-25-0	22-45-3
Punts	2-31.0	8-40.8
Fumbles-Lost	3-2	3-0
Penalties-Yards	9-89	7-60
Time of possession	31:52	28:8

Attendance—38,494.

INDIVIDUAL STATISTICS

Rushing—Houston, Jackson 21-99, R. Moore 5-19, Hunter 2-4, Pease 6-12, Cobble 8-20; Denver, Caldwell 10-30, Micho 4-8, Karcher 2-0.

Passing—Houston, Pease 15-25-0—260; Denver, Karcher 22-40-2—226, McGuire 0-1-0—0, May 0-4-1—0.

Receiving—Houston, Jackson 1-3, Walters 2-37, Harris 3-51, O. Williams 2-41, McDonald 2-31, James 1-14, R. Moore 2-14, Darrington 1-38, Gehring 1-31; Denver, Brown 3-39, Andrews 3-33, Massie 3-55, Micho 9-69, Payne 1-8, Caldwell 3-22.

Kickoff Returns—Houston, Harris 2-71; Denver, Swanson 4-91, Brown 1-28.

Punt Returns—Houston, K. Johnson 6-56; Denver, Swanson 1-0.

Interceptions—Houston, Seale 1-73, Bryant 1-28, Small 1-3.

Punting—Houston, Superick 2-31.0; Denver, Giacomarro 8-40.8.

Field Goals—Houston, Diettrich 4-4; Denver, none attempted.

Sacks—Houston, B. Johnson 2, Fox, Cooks, D. Smith.

Packers-Vikings
SUNDAY, OCTOBER 4
SCORE BY PERIODS

Green Bay	7	13	0	3—23
Minnesota	0	7	7	2—16

SCORING

Green Bay—Thomas 31 pass from Risher (Zendejas kick), 5:18 1st.
Green Bay—Field goal Zendejas 35, 2:29 2nd.
Green Bay—Field goal Zendejas 43, 4:35 2nd.
Minnesota—Brim 63 pass from Adams (Dawson kick), 6:33 2nd.
Green Bay—Risher 13 run (Zendejas kick), 10:53 2nd.
Minnesota—Brim 38 run (Dawson kick), 12:22 3rd.
Minnesota—Safety, Risher tackled in end zone, 1:21 4th.
Green Bay—Field goal Zendejas 34, 7:32 4th.

TEAM STATISTICS

	Green Bay	Minnesota
First downs	16	17
Rushes-Yards	40-147	25-96
Passing yards	153	219
Sacked-Yards lost	2-11	3-17
3rd down eff.	2-12	2-12
Passes	12-21-0	15-26-1
Punts	6-32.2	8-34.3
Fumbles-Lost	3-0	2-1
Penalties-Yards	8-97	6-60
Time of possession	33:15	26:45

Attendance—13,911.

INDIVIDUAL STATISTICS

Rushing—Green Bay, Willhite 19-72, Risher 6-25, Parker 8-33, Thomas 5-19, Hunter 1-0, Lee Morris 1-minus 2; Minnesota, Moore 4-11, Miller 1-minus 1, Smith 7-13, A. Walker 3-13, Adams 5-19, S. Harris 4-3, Brim 1-38.

Passing—Green Bay, Risher 12-21-0—164; Minnesota, Adams 14-23-1—234, Miller 1-3-0—2.

Receiving—Green Bay, Scott 2-13, Thomas 2-52, Parker 3-22, Lee Morris 3-46, Summers 2-31; Minnesota, Brim 6-144, Moore 1-8, A. Walker 2-3, S. Harris 2-17, Schenk 1-10, Finch 3-54.

Kickoff Returns—Green Bay, Lee Morris 2-46, Harden 1-15; Minnesota, Smith 2-42, Bess 5-77.

Punt Returns—Green Bay, Lee Morris 1-1, Scott 1-0; Minnesota, Bess 3-47.

Interceptions—Green Bay, J.B. Morris 1-73.

Punting—Green Bay, Renner 6-32.2; Minnesota, Bruno 8-34.3.

Field Goals—Green Bay, Zendejas 3-3; Minnesota, Dawson 0-1 (missed: 41).

Sacks—Green Bay, Drost 2, Caldwell ½, Sullivan ½; Minnesota, Coleman, Molden.

Cardinals-Redskins
SUNDAY, OCTOBER 4
SCORE BY PERIODS

St. Louis	0	7	7	7—21
Washington	7	7	14	0—28

SCORING

Washington—Allen 34 pass from Rubbert (Toibin kick), 13:40 1st.
St. Louis—Ferrell 1 run (Staurovsky kick), 5:32 2nd.
Washington—Allen 88 pass from Rubbert (Toibin kick), 5:55 2nd.
St. Louis—Ferrell 1 run (Staurovsky kick), 6:59 3rd.
Washington—Vital 8 run (Toibin kick), 9:36 3rd.
Washington—Allen 48 pass from Rubbert (Toibin kick), 12:58 3rd.
St. Louis—P. Noga 60 interception return (Staurovsky kick), 2:43 4th.

TEAM STATISTICS

	St. Louis	Washington
First downs	27	18
Rushes-Yards	44-167	33-118
Passing yards	231	334
Sacked-Yards lost	4-27	0-0
3rd down eff	7-16	5-12
Passes	16-35-0	14-24-1
Punts	6-37.0	5-30.8
Fumbles-Lost	1-0	0-0
Penalties-Yards	5-35	6-54
Time of possession	36:55	23:05
Attendance—27,728.		

INDIVIDUAL STATISTICS

Rushing—St. Louis, Ferrell 27-87, Sargent 14-78, Ron Brown 1-9, Halloran 2-minus 7; Washington, Vital 27-82, Rubbert 4-29, Holman 2-7.
Passing—St. Louis, Halloran 16-35-0—258; Washington, Rubbert 14-24-1—334.
Receiving—St. Louis, J.T. Smith 6-116, Ferrell 3-13, Green 1-16, Ron Brown 2-16, Johnson 4-97; Washington, T. Wilson 1-23, McEwen 4-43, Allen 7-255, R. Johnson 1-5, Jessie 1-8.
Kickoff Returns—St. Louis, McAdoo 2-35, Sikahema 2-61; Washington, Vital 2-31, Wilson 1-20, Shepard 1-20.
Punt Returns—St. Louis, Sikahema 2-11; Washington, Wilson 1-1, Shepard 3-118.
Interceptions—St. Louis, P. Noga 1-60.
Punting—St. Louis, Royals 6-37.0; Washington, Weil 5-30.8.
Field Goals—St. Louis, Staurovsky 0-2 (missed: 25, 41); Washington, Toibin 0-2 (missed: 37, 42).
Sacks—Washington, Karras, Cofer, Benish, Martin.

Bears-Eagles
SUNDAY, OCTOBER 4
SCORE BY PERIODS

Chicago	7	28	0	0—35
Philadelphia	0	3	0	0— 3

SCORING

Chicago—Mosley 9 pass from Hohensee (Lasher kick), 7:37 1st.
Philadelphia—Field goal Jacobs 27, 3:33 2nd.
Chicago—Kozlowski 20 pass from Hohensee (Lashar kick), 7:04 2nd.
Chicago—Brewer 1 run (Lashar kick), 10:41 2nd.
Chicago—Mosley 9 blocked punt return (Lashar kick), 11:41 2nd.
Chicago—Kindt 3 pass from Hohensee (Lashar kick), 14:45 2nd.

TEAM STATISTICS

	Chicago	Philadelphia
First downs	22	14
Rushes-Yards	35-134	29-105
Passing yards	184	65
Sacked-Yards lost	4-24	11-70
3rd down eff	4-14	6-19
Passes	17-33-1	14-36-0
Punts	5-40.8	8-30.0
Fumbles-Lost	2-1	5-2
Penalties-Yards	7-50	11-65
Time of possession	30:34	29:26
Attendance—4,073.		

INDIVIDUAL STATISTICS

Rushing—Chicago, Mosley 8-28, Payton 1-28, Heimuli 6-24, F. Harris 2-21, Clark 4-12, Hohensee 5-11, Brewer 8-9, Wolden 1-1; Philadelphia, Robinson 11-58, R. Brown 11-34, Grant 1-20, Tinsley 1-1, Clemons 2-0, Merkens 3-minus 8.
Passing—Chicago, Hohensee 12-22-1—157, Payton 5-11-0—51; Philadelphia, Tinsley 7-22-0—65, Merkens 7-14-0—70.
Receiving—Chicago, Kozlowski 5-65, Heimuli 3-31, Knapczyk 2-31, Kindt 2-10, Wolden 1-26, Mullen 1-20, Brewer 1-14, Bowers 1-6, Glasgow 1-5; Philadelphia, Grant 4-48, Renko 3-26, Siano 2-20, Bailey 2-20, R. Brown 2-17, Bowman 1-4.
Kickoff Returns—Chicago, Lynch 2-54, Mosley 1-17; Philadelphia, Bowman 3-45, Turral 1-21.
Punt Returns—Chicago, Duarte 3-25; Philadelphia, Caterbone 1-13, Bowman 3-43.
Interceptions—Philadelphia, Coleman 1-13.
Punting—Chicago, Brown 5-40.8; Philadelphia, Jacobs 5-37.6, Merkens 2-30.5.
Field Goals—Chicago, none attempted; Philadelphia, Jacobs 1-2 (missed: 42).
Sacks—Chicago, Morris, Teafatiller 1½, McInerney 2, Althoff 2½, Norvell 2, Norris, Bell; Philadelphia, Grooms, Mitchell, Phillips ½, Auer ½, Battaglia.

Colts-Bills
SUNDAY, OCTOBER 4
SCORE BY PERIODS

Indianapolis	7	21	19	0—47
Buffalo	0	0	0	6— 6

SCORING

Indianapolis—Murray 37 pass from Hogeboom (Jordan kick), 12:12 1st.
Indianapolis—Murray 11 pass from Hogeboom (Jordan kick), 7:56 2nd.
Indianapolis—Jones 4 pass from Hogeboom (Jordan kick), 13:22 2nd.
Indianapolis—Noble 18 pass from Hogeboom (Jordan kick), 14:42 2nd.
Indianapolis—Noble 18 pass from Hogeboom (Jordan kick), 0:50 3rd.
Indianapolis—Safety, Perryman tackled in end zone, 2:30 3rd.
Indianapolis—Field goal Jordan 36, 7:49 3rd.
Indianapolis—Brown 18 run (Jordan kick), 10:10 3rd.
Buffalo—Brown 8 pass from Totten (kick failed), 6:08 4th.

TEAM STATISTICS

	Indianapolis	Buffalo
First downs	28	14
Rushes-Yards	41-166	28-81
Passing yards	297	82
Sacked-Yards lost	1-9	6-66
3rd down eff	5-13	5-16
Passes	20-30-0	12-35-3
Punts	3-20.3	7-27.6
Fumbles-Lost	3-2	7-4
Penalties-Yards	5-30	10-70
Time of possession	31:44	28:16
Attendance—9,860.		

INDIVIDUAL STATISTICS

Rushing—Indianapolis, Banks 16-69, McLemore 17-58, Nugent 2-1, Brown 6-38; Buffalo, King 5-9, Williams 8-22, Manucci 3-10, Shepherd 7-38, Totten 5-2.
Passing—Indianapolis, Hogeboom 17-25-0—259, Nugent 3-5-0—47; Buffalo, Manucci 7-20-2—68, Totten 4-12-0—71, Miller 1-3-1—9.
Receiving—Indianapolis, Banks 3-27, McLemore 1-4, Noble 4-50, Murray 7-161, Jones 2-17, Hawthorne 1-14, Kearse 1-21, Bryant 1-12; Buffalo, McFadden 3-28, Williams 1-5, Gaines 6-98, M. Brown 1-8, Chetti 1-9.
Kickoff Returns—Indianapolis, Johnson 3-66; Buffalo, Brown 2-35, Armstrong 1-7, McFadden 2-28.

Punt Returns—Indianapolis, Johnson 4-12; Buffalo, McFadden 1-7.

Interceptions—Indianapolis, Perryman 1-0, Prior 1-15, Curry 1-0.

Punting—Indianapolis, Jordan 1-33.0, Colquitt 1-28.0; Buffalo, Partridge 6-32.2.

Field Goals—Indianapolis, Jordan 1-1; Buffalo, none attempted.

Sacks—Indianapolis, Prior, Wright, Benjamin, Mattiace, Elko, Thorp; Buffalo, Armstrong.

Buccaneers-Lions
SUNDAY, OCTOBER 4
SCORE BY PERIODS

Tampa Bay	0	21	10	0—31
Detroit	17	7	0	3—27

SCORING

Detroit—Grymes 36 pass from Hons (Prindle kick), 6:49 1st.

Detroit—Field goal Prindle 23, 9:44 1st.

Detroit—King 9 fumble return (Prindle kick), 10:44 1st.

Tampa Bay—Wright 15 pass from Hold (Tiffin kick), 0:11 2nd.

Tampa Bay—Tripoli 15 interception return (Tiffin kick), 3:27 2nd.

Detroit—Truvillion 53 pass from Hons (Prindle kick), 13:09 2nd.

Tampa Bay—Streater 61 pass from Hold (Tiffin kick), 13:28 2nd.

Tampa Bay—Field goal Tiffin 21, 6:57 3rd.

Tampa Bay—Ricks 1 run (Tiffin kick), 12:43 3rd.

Detroit—Field goal Prindle 35, 3:19 4th.

TEAM STATISTICS

	Tampa Bay	Detroit
First downs	12	12
Rushes-Yards	39-113	32-101
Passing yards	106	161
Sacked-Yards lost	1-12	5-40
3rd down eff.	4-16	1-12
Passes	8-23-0	10-26-3
Punts	10-38.4	6-38.8
Fumbles-Lost	4-1	5-1
Penalties-Yards	9-55	5-45
Time of possession	31:31	28:29
Attendance—4,919.		

INDIVIDUAL STATISTICS

Rushing—Tampa Bay, Wright 21-67, Hold 3-18, Land 7-16, Ricks 6-10, Thomas 1-2, Criswell 1-0; Detroit, Wester 12-46, Edwards 13-28, Dollinger 5-16, Hons 1-11, Black 1-0.

Passing—Tampa Bay, Reaves 2-8-0—16, Hold 6-15-0—102; Detroit, Hons 10-26-3—201.

Receiving—Tampa Bay, Wright 4-29, Streater 1-61, Walls 1-13, Holloway 1-3, Ricks 1-12; Detroit, Truvillion 4-99, Grymes 3-81, Wheeler 2-17, Dollinger 1-4.

Kickoff Returns—Tampa Bay, Gladman 1-16, Wright 1-17, Walls 4-104; Detroit, Hall 4-73, Bradley 2-42.

Punt Returns—Tampa Bay, Walls 4-12; Detroit, Bradley 5-30.

Interceptions—Tampa Bay, Tripoli 2-17, Gant 1-5.

Punting—Tampa Bay, Criswell 10-38.4; Detroit, Black 6-38.8.

Field Goals—Tampa Bay, Tiffin 1-1; Detroit, Prindle 2-2.

Sacks—Tampa Bay, McCallister, Harris, Montoute, Riggins, M. Clark; Detroit, Carr.

Chiefs-Raiders
SUNDAY, OCTOBER 4
SCORE BY PERIODS

Kansas City	0	0	14	3—17
Los Angeles Raiders	14	7	7	7—35

SCORING

Los Angeles—Aikens 27 pass from Evans (Hardy kick), 0:55 1st.

Los Angeles—C. Ellis 2 run (Hardy kick), 5:28 1st.

Los Angeles—Evans 4 run (Hardy kick), 4:56 2nd.

Kansas City—Harris 23 blocked punt return (Hamrick kick), 5:33 1st.

Los Angeles—Horton 32 pass from Evans (Hardy kick), 9:54 3rd.

Kansas City—Jones 4 pass from Stevens (Hamrick kick), 14:01 3rd.

Los Angeles—C. Ellis 8 run (Hardy kick), 0:16 4th.

Kansas City—Field goal Hamrick 40, 6:49 4th.

TEAM STATISTICS

	Kansas City	Los Angeles
First downs	22	21
Rushes-Yards	35-131	39-252
Passing yards	137	248
Sacked-Yards lost	3-25	0-0
3rd down eff.	4-11	5-10
Passes	14-25-0	10-18-0
Punts	4-43.8	2-20.0
Fumbles-Lost	3-3	3-2
Penalties-Yards	4-30	9-79
Time of possession	31:10	28:50
Attendance—10,708.		

INDIVIDUAL STATISTICS

Rushing—Kansas City, Lacy 13-45, Parker 12-39, C. Smith 8-39, Stevens 1-6, Stockemer 1-2; Los Angeles, C. Ellis 12-70, Evans 4-63, Harrison 9-49, Calhoun 7-36, Horton 7-34.

Passing—Kansas City, Stevens 14-25-0—162; Los Angeles, Evans 10-18-0—248.

Receiving—Kansas City, Brown 5-69, Jones 3-25, Koss 2-25, Nash 2-22, Montagne 1-16, Parker 1-5; Los Angeles, Lathan 2-66, David Williams 2-64, Aikens 2-48, Horton 1-32, Harrison 1-15, C. Ellis 1-15, Wheeler 1-8.

Kickoff Returns—Kansas City, Wyatt 4-100, Lacy 2-35; Los Angeles, Calhoun 3-58.

Punt Returns—Kansas City, Wyatt 1-0; Los Angeles, Harkey 2-17.

Interceptions—None.

Punting—Kansas City, Goodburn 4-43.8; Los Angeles, Gamache 1-40.0.

Field Goals—Kansas City, Hamrick 1-1; Los Angeles, Hardy 0-1 (missed: 34).

Sacks—Los Angeles, McMillen, Brown 2.

Chargers-Bengals
SUNDAY, OCTOBER 4
SCORE BY PERIODS

San Diego	0	0	0	10—10
Cincinnati	7	2	0	0— 9

SCORING

Cincinnati—Russell 4 pass from Breen (Manca kick), 14:06 1st.

Cincinnati—Safety, Schutt tackled Neuheisel in end zone, 7:51 2nd.

San Diego—Middleton 1 run (Neuheisel run), 3:42 4th.

San Diego—Field goal Gaffney 24, 12:16 4th.

TEAM STATISTICS

	San Diego	Cincinnati
First downs	15	11
Rushes-Yards	34-92	50-219
Passing yards	169	—13
Sacked-Yards lost	3-25	3-23
3rd down eff.	6-16	6-19
Passes	17-28-1	5-13-0
Punts	6-37.6	10-46.5
Fumbles-Lost	3-1	1-0
Penalties-Yards	2-10	4-14
Time of possession	28:44	31:16
Attendance—18,074.		

INDIVIDUAL STATISTICS

Rushing—San Diego, Jenkins 3-6, Middleton 16-61, Zachary 1-3, Steels 1-3, Spencer 11-20, Kelley 2-minus 1; Cincinnati, McCluskey 10-19, Logan 14-95, Rice 7-23, Meehan 3-25, Wright 10-32, Walter 2-17, Breen 4-8.

Passing—San Diego, Neuheisel 10-19-1—84, Kelley 7-9-0—110; Cincinnati, Breen 3-5-0—9, Walter 2-8-0—1.

Receiving—San Diego, Spencer 2-47, Jenkins 1-7, Holt 1-8, Williams 5-73, Steels 1-4, Rome 3-29, Middleton 3-1, Moffett 1-25; Cincinnati, Meehan 1-6, Russell 1-4, Logan 2-minus 4, Wright 1-4.

Kickoff Returns—San Diego, Sartin 2-46; Cincinnati, Meehan 1-9, Logan 3-31.

Punt Returns—San Diego, Williams 3-47, Rome 3-8; Cincinnati, Brown 2-4.

Interceptions—Cincinnati, D. Smith 1-0.

Punting—San Diego, Prokop 6-37.6; Cincinnati, Fulhage 10-46.5.

Field Goals—San Diego, Gaffney 1-2 (missed: 30); Cincinnati, Manca 0-1 (missed: 45).

Sacks—San Diego, Phillips, Winter, T. Simmons; Cincinnati, Berthusen, Catchings, Schutt.

Cowboys-Jets
SUNDAY, OCTOBER 4
SCORE BY PERIODS

Dallas	7	17	14	0—38
New York Jets	3	7	7	7—24

SCORING

New York—Field goal Ragusa 20, 2:24 1st.
Dallas—Burbage 13 pass from Sweeney (Zendejas kick), 10:06 1st.
Dallas—Field goal Zendejas 33, 2:43 2nd.
Dallas—Adams 27 run (Zendejas kick), 4:32 2nd.
Dallas—Edwards 33 pass from Sweeney (Zendejas kick), 13:06 2nd.
New York—Kurisko 41 pass from Norrie (Ragusa kick), 14:50 2nd.
New York—Chirico 3 run (Ragusa kick), 3:31 3rd.
Dallas—Blount 1 run (Zendejas kick), 8:01 3rd.
Dallas—Edwards 35 pass from Sweeney (Zendejas kick), 13:32 3rd.
New York—Harper 78 punt return (Ragusa kick), 13:21 4th.

TEAM STATISTICS

	Dallas	New York
First downs	14	22
Rushes-Yards	37-114	30-82
Passing yards	132	159
Sacked-Yards lost	2-7	11-54
3rd down eff.	4-12	6-15
Passes	6-15-1	18-35-2
Punts	6-42.5	4-25.8
Fumbles-Lost	4-3	4-3
Penalties-Yards	16-131	10-150
Time of possession	29:36	30:24

Attendance—12,370.

INDIVIDUAL STATISTICS

Rushing—Dallas, Blount 28-72, Sweeney 3-3, Adams 5-43, G. White 1-minus 4; New York, E. Hunter 15-48, Chirico 9-16, Norrie 4-5, Briggs 1-4, Foster 1-9.

Passing—Dallas, Sweeney 6-14-1—139, Snyder 0-1-0 —0; New York, Norrie 18-33-1—213, Briggs 0-2-1—0.

Receiving—Dallas, Burbage 3-46, Edwards 2-68, Spivey 1-25; New York, Harper 6-89, Holman 4-40, Chirico 4-18, Kurisko 1-41, Gaffney 1-10, Foster 1-9, E. Hunter 1-6.

Kickoff Returns—Dallas, Spivey 2-49, Adams 2-23, Borreson 1-5; New York, Harper 4-75, E. Hunter 2-47.

Punt Returns—Dallas, Livingston 1-0, Burbage 1-13; New York, Collins 1-0, Harper 3-88.

Interceptions—Dallas, Green 1-0, Haynes 1-0; New York, Radachowsky 1-0.

Punting—Dallas, Sawyer 6-42.5; New York, O'Connor 4-25.8.

Field Goals—Dallas Zendejas 1-1; New York, Ragusa 1-1.

Sacks—Dallas, Haynes 2, Duliban 2, E. Jones 2, Perkins 2, Dwyer, Watts, Johnson; New York, Brophy, Rose.

Dolphins-Seahawks
SUNDAY, OCTOBER 4
SCORE BY PERIODS

Miami	7	0	6	7—20
Seattle	7	3	0	14—24

SCORING

Miami—Douglas 14 pass from Mackey (Beecher kick), 5:15 1st.
Seattle—Pardridge 25 pass from Mathison (Hagler kick), 8:16 1st.
Seattle—Field goal Hagler 20, 15:00 2nd.
Miami—Field goal Beecher 34, 3:48 3rd.
Miami—Field goal Beecher 40, 11:05 3rd.
Seattle—Keel 24 pass from Mathison (Hagler kick), 4:45 4th.
Miami—Tagliaferri 2 run (Beecher kick), 11:49 4th.
Seattle—Parros 1 run (Hagler kick), 13:30 4th.

TEAM STATISTICS

	Miami	Seattle
First downs	19	20
Rushes-Yards	35-164	25-76
Passing yards	160	326
Sacked-Yards lost	3-12	0-0
3rd down eff.	8-16	7-15
Passes	18-30-1	20-42-3
Punts	5-37.8	5-38.2
Fumbles-Lost	3-1	1-0
Penalties-Yards	9-91	9-74
Time of possession	33:28	26:32

Attendance—19,448.

INDIVIDUAL STATISTICS

Rushing—Miami, Scott 9-55, Bailey 10-55, Tagliaferri 9-28, Konecny 2-13, Mackey 5-13; Seattle, Parros 13-32, Morton 7-24, Mathison 2-17, Hagen 2-3, Griffin 1-0.

Passing—Miami, Mackey 17-26-0—179, Stankavage 1-4-1—minus 7; Seattle, Mathison 20-42-3—326.

Receiving—Miami, Chavis 4-58, Tagliaferri 4-51, Douglas 4-37, Sampleton 2-15, Reilly 1-8, Farmer 1-5, Scott 1-5, Konecny 1-minus 7; Seattle, Teal 9-137, Pardridge 5-83, Keel 3-56, Bengen 1-24, Juma 1-19, Parros 1-7.

Kickoff Returns—Miami, Farmer 3-56, Roth 1-26; Seattle, Teal 4-55, Bengen 1-11.

Punt Returns—Miami, Caterbone 4-45.

Interceptions—Miami, Randle 2-16, Hooper 1-0; Seattle, Glaze 1-0.

Punting—Miami, Gore 5-37.8; Seattle, Griffith 5-38.2.

Field Goals—Miami, Beecher 2-2; Seattle, Hagler 1-1.

Sacks—Seattle, Glaze 2, Wiley.

Steelers-Falcons
SUNDAY, OCTOBER 4
SCORE BY PERIODS

Pittsburgh	0	14	0	14—28
Atlanta	3	0	2	7—12

SCORING

Atlanta—Field goal Davis 27, 5:43 1st.
Pittsburgh—Jackson 1 run (Trout kick), 5:23 2nd.
Pittsburgh—Hairston 5 pass from Bono (Trout kick), 13:38 2nd.
Atlanta—Safety, Moor sacked Bono in end zone, 11:19 3rd.
Pittsburgh—Bono 1 run (Trout kick), 4:35 4th.
Pittsburgh—Clinkscales 11 pass from Collier (Trout kick), 10:51 4th.
Atlanta—Barney 19 pass from Van Raaphorst (Davis kick), 13:03 4th.

TEAM STATISTICS

	Pittsburgh	Atlanta
First downs	19	13
Rushes-Yards	41-142	21-67
Passing yards	214	148
Sacked-Yards lost	2-10	2-13
3rd down eff.	9-15	5-13
Passes	14-25-1	18-34-3
Punts	4-36	7-31
Fumbles-Lost	3-2	2-1
Penalties-Yards	3-20	7-54
Time of possession	33:24	26:36

Attendance—16,667.

INDIVIDUAL STATISTICS

Rushing—Pittsburgh, Jackson 29-104, Bono 3-13, Sanders 3-12, Reeder 2-8, Carter 3-7, Collier 1-minus 2; Atlanta, Williams 13-49, Granger 5-11, Van Raaphorst 1-6, Butler 1-1, Oliver 1-0.

Passing—Pittsburgh, Bono 12-22-1—164, Collier 2-3-0—60; Atlanta, Kramer 5-13-2—48, Van Raaphorst 13-21-1—113.

Receiving—Pittsburgh, Clinkscales 6-150, Lee 2-29, Carter 2-18, Hairston 2-16, Sanders 1-11, Boyle 1-0; Atlanta, Williams 9-70, Barney 4-66, Butler 2-7, Granger 1-8, Evans 1-8, Oliver 1-2.

Kickoff Returns—Pittsburgh, Clark 1-18, Gowdy 1-0; Atlanta, Butler 1-13, Moss 1-23, Oliver 4-72.

Punt Returns—Pittsburgh, Anderson 3-19; Atlanta, Morris 1-11, Butler 2-10.

Interceptions—Pittsburgh, Griffin 2-2, Williams 1-0; Atlanta, Huff 1-14.

Punting—Pittsburgh, Bruno 4-36.5; Atlanta, Starnes 6-33.8, Davis 1-19.0.

Field Goals—Pittsburgh, none attempted; Atlanta, Davis 1-1.

Sacks—Pittsburgh, Warren, Dawkins; Atlanta, Moor 2.

Browns-Patriots
SUNDAY, OCTOBER 4
SCORE BY PERIODS

Cleveland	0	0	6	14—20
New England	0	10	0	0—10

SCORING

New England—Field goal Schubert 23, 1:26 2nd.
New England—Linne 6 pass from Bleier (Schubert kick), 9:29 2nd.
Cleveland—Field goal Franco 28, 4:33 3rd.
Cleveland—Field goal Franco 21, 12:22 3rd.
Cleveland—Mason 1 run (Kelley pass from Walters), 4:37 4th.
Cleveland—Mason 1 run (Franco kick), 13:19 4th.

TEAM STATISTICS

	Cleveland	New England
First downs	22	10
Rushes-Yards	54-217	27-31
Passing yards	131	110
Sacked-Yards lost	1-4	3-28
3rd down eff.	8-19	0-13
Passes	10-30-0	10-26-0
Punts	5-33.8	9-30.9
Fumbles-Lost	3-3	5-1
Penalties-Yards	8-60	1-15
Time of possession	37:01	22:59

Attendance—14,830.

INDIVIDUAL STATISTICS

Rushing—Cleveland, Mason 32-133, Everett 14-52, Christensen 7-32, Katolin 1-0; New England, Collins 15-24, McSwain 7-20, Woods 1-0, Bleier 3-minus 6, LeBlanc 1-minus 7.

Passing—Cleveland, Christensen 10-30-0—135; New England, Bleier 10-26-0—138.

Receiving—Cleveland, Tennell 3-39, Everett 3-23, Kemp 2-58, Tinsley 1-17, Mason 1-minus 2; New England,

Linne 4-45, Coffey 3-66, Collins 2-16, Frain 1-11.

Kickoff Returns—Cleveland, Beauford 1-22, Mason 1-0; New England, McSwain 2-32, LeBlanc 1-24, Alexander 1-4.

Punt Returns—Cleveland, Wilson 3-32; New England, Linne 1-16.

Interceptions—None.

Punting—Cleveland, Walters 5-33.8; New England, Herline 9-30.9.

Field Goals—Cleveland, Franco 2-3 (missed: 37); New England, Schubert 1-2 (missed: 40).

Sacks—Cleveland, T. Crawford 2, Carter; New England, Wichard.

49ers-Giants
MONDAY, OCTOBER 5
SCORE BY PERIODS

San Francisco	3	14	10	14—41
New York Giants	0	7	0	14—21

SCORING

San Francisco—Field goal Brockhaus 39, 13:06 1st.
New York—Bennett 46 pass from Crocicchia (Benyola kick), 6:33 2nd.
San Francisco—Rodgers 2 run (Brockhaus kick), 14:10 2nd.
San Francisco—Wells 1 blocked punt return (Brockhaus kick), 14:38 2nd.
San Francisco—Monroe 39 pass from Stevens (Brockhaus kick), 7:42 3rd.
San Francisco—Field goal Brockhaus 22, 12:02 3rd.
San Francisco—Stevens 9 run (Brockhaus kick), 0:05 4th.
New York—McGowan 63 pass from Busch (Benyola kick), 6:00 4th.
San Francisco—Cherry 13 run (Brockhaus kick), 11:34 4th.
New York—Lovelady 7 pass from Busch (Benyola kick), 12:40 4th.

TEAM STATISTICS

	San Francisco	New York
First downs	28	14
Rushes-Yards	49-242	22-77
Passing yards	191	154
Sacked-Yards lost	2-11	3-30
3rd down eff.	6-14	1-7
Passes	14-23-0	9-21-1
Punts	4-30.3	5-23.6
Fumbles-Lost	3-1	6-3
Penalties-Yards	8-84	3-14
Time of possession	40:17	19:43

Attendance—16,471.

INDIVIDUAL STATISTICS

Rushing—San Francisco, Monroe 1-9, Cherry 13-65, Varajon 16-75, A. Hardy 7-48, Rodgers 4-9, Stevens 7-36, Blount 1-0; New York, Beecham 5-22, Williams 6-31, DiRico 5-11, Lovelady 1-3, Direnzo 1-5, Crocicchia 4-5.

Passing—San Francisco, Gagliano 12-21-0—150, Stevens 2-2-0—52; New York, Crocicchia 6-15-0—89, Busch 3-6-1—95.

Receiving—San Francisco, Monroe 3-66; Varajon 3-25, A. Hardy 1-7, Rodgers 1-24, Greer 1-12, Gladney 4-60, Dressel 1-8; New York, Williams 1-5, Lovelady 2-15, Bennett 4-87, J. Smith 1-14, McGowan 1-63.

Kickoff Returns—San Francisco, Monroe 2-32, Rodgers 1-12, Henley 1-21; New York, Cummings 1-11, Coleman 1-20, Beecham 3-70, Dirico 2-31.

Punt Returns—San Francisco, Martin 2-12; New York, Lovelady 2-2.

Interceptions—San Francisco, Martin 1-12.

Punting—San Francisco, Asmus 4-30.3; New York, Moore 4-29.5.

Field Goals—San Francisco, Brockhaus 2-3 (missed: 45); New York, none attempted.

Sacks—San Francisco, Collins, Browner ½, Korff ½; New York, Thompson 2.

FIFTH WEEK

RESULTS OF WEEK 5
Sunday, October 11

Chicago 27, Minnesota 7 at Chi.
Cincinnati 17, Seattle 10 at Sea.
Dallas 41, Philadelphia 22 at Dall.
Detroit 19, Green Bay 16 (OT) at G.B.
Houston 15, Cleveland 10 at Cleve.
Indianapolis 6, N.Y. Jets 0 at Ind.
L.A. Rams 31, Pittsburgh 21 at L.A.
Miami 42, Kansas City 0 at Mia.
New England 14, Buffalo 7 at N.E.
St. Louis 24, New Orleans 19 at St.L.
San Diego 17, Tampa Bay 13 at T.B.
San Francisco 25, Atlanta 17 at Atl.
Washington 38, N.Y. Giants 12 at N.Y.

Monday, October 12
Denver 30, L.A. Raiders 14 at Den.

National Football League replacement games moved into their second week October 11 with larger crowds, usually depending on whether the home team had won its first strike game. The total attendance for the 13 Sunday afternoon games was 825,564, an increase of 104,737 from the 13 Sunday games played the previous week. Not counting Monday night games, stadiums were filled to 37.8 percent capacity in the second week of strike games, compared with 24.4 percent the first week.

The highest single-game figures were reported in Dallas, Cleveland and Green Bay, where in each instance the home team was coming off a win on the road.

The day's largest crowd, 40,622, filled Texas Stadium for the Dallas Cowboys' game with the Philadelphia Eagles and gave the Cowboys replacement team a standing ovation in pregame introductions.

The only Dallas player to be booed was veteran running back Tony Dorsett, who had crossed his teammates' picket line during the week. Dorsett, the NFL's fourth all-time leading rusher, was booed every time he touched the ball, even after he scored a third-quarter touchdown.

The game was a mismatch, mainly because the Cowboys played eight veteran regulars to the Eagles' none. Dallas scored touchdowns on three of its first five offensive plays and had scoring drives that lasted 13, nine, one and two seconds. A 62-yard flanker reverse by Kelvin Edwards on the first play of the game gave the Cowboys a 7-0 lead en route to a 41-22 victory.

A crowd of 38,927 showed up at Cleveland Stadium to watch the replacement Browns take on the Houston Oilers in an AFC Central game. But the crowd didn't like what it saw as the Oilers defeated the Browns, 15-10, to snap a six-game losing streak in the divisional series.

The Houston defense held Cleveland to just 50 yards rushing, including a paltry five yards on four carries for running back Larry Mason, who had scorched New England for 133 yards the previous week. The Oilers' Herman Hunter, a former Philadelphia and Detroit player, rushed 28 times for 121 yards.

It marked the first time an Oilers team had won two consecutive road games since 1981.

The day's third-largest crowd, 35,779, turned out at Lambeau Field in Green Bay to watch the Packers duel the Detroit Lions. The Lions won, 19-16, on placekicker Mike Prindle's fourth field goal of the game, a 31-yarder with 2:34 left in overtime. Prindle had missed a 42-yard attempt earlier in the overtime.

The game was a dream come true for the Grand Rapids, Mich., native who attended Western Michigan University. But it was a nightmare for Green Bay cornerback Chuck Washington. Washington was penalized 38 yards for pass interference on a drive that set up Prindle's 27-yard field goal with 1:20 left in regulation time and was penalized 15 yards for the same infraction to set up Prindle's overtime game-winner.

The Indianapolis Colts registered their first shutout in nearly 11 years with a 6-0 triumph over the New York Jets. It was the Colts' first shutout since a 20-0 victory over the Jets on October 24, 1976.

In two strike games, the Indianapolis defense had allowed just six points while registering 10 quarterback sacks, six interceptions and six fumble recoveries.

Colts replacement kicker Steve Jordan kicked two field goals to account for the game's only points. Running back Chuck Banks rushed 25 times for 159 yards, including 35 yards to set up Jordan's first field goal.

Another successful replacement defense belonged to the Chicago Bears, who registered nine sacks in a 27-7 victory over the Minnesota Vikings to increase their two-week total to 20. Defensive end Sean McInerney had 3½ sacks against Minnesota and 5½ in two games. The Bears held the Vikings to just 43 yards rushing.

The victory was Chicago's second straight in strike play and fourth of the season. Minnesota lost its second strike game after its regular team had won its first two games.

Another defensive domination took place in Miami, where the Dolphins christened $100 million Joe Robbie Stadium by pounding the Kansas City Chiefs, 42-0. The stadium's grand-opening festivities were cancelled because of the strike and the crowd of 25,867 was Miami's smallest in 18 seasons. Even Dolphins Owner Joe Robbie, the man responsible for building the facility, had to cross his own players' picket line to watch the game.

What he saw was a blowout, with Kansas

Replacement running back Ronald Scott scored three Miami touchdowns in the Dolphins' 42-0 romp over the Kansas City Chiefs in Week 5.

City never advancing inside the Miami 40-yard line. Safety Liffort Hobley, the only regular player from either team, intercepted two passes, knocked down two others and returned a fumble 55 yards for a touchdown. Less than three minutes later, teammate Trell Hooper returned another Kansas City fumble 59 yards for the fifth of Miami's six touchdowns.

Running back Ronald Scott scored three Dolphin touchdowns and rushed for 99 yards on 18 carries. The Dolphins tied a team record with four rushing touchdowns.

The St. Louis Cardinals also returned two fumbles for touchdowns in a 24-19 victory over the New Orleans Saints. Defensive backs Mark Jackson (77 yards) and Leonard Smith (29) accounted for two of St. Louis' three touchdowns to help overcome an anemic effort by the Cardinal offense.

The Cardinals were outgained in total yards (368-143) and first downs (29-10) while running 87 offensive plays to 42 for New Orleans. St. Louis quarterbacks Shawn Halloran and Sammy Garza combined for a net passing total

of four yards and the Cardinals' only two offensive scores came on drives that began at the New Orleans 17- and 26-yard lines.

The crowd of 11,795 was the smallest ever to watch a pro football game at Busch Stadium.

The San Diego Chargers' replacement squad recorded a comeback victory for the second straight week, defeating Tampa Bay, 17-13. The Chargers scored 17 second-half points to overcome a 10-0 halftime deficit. A week earlier, the Chargers scored 10 points in the fourth quarter for a 10-9 victory at Cincinnati.

Rick Neuheisel completed 18 of 22 passes to break veteran quarterback Dan Fouts' team record for single-game completion percentage. Neuheisel's .818 percentage bettered Fouts' mark of .800 (28 for 35) set against Seattle in 1979.

New England quarterback Bob Bleier had a completion percentage of just 31 percent against Buffalo (4 for 13), but it didn't prove to be a factor in the Patriots' 14-7 victory over the Bills. That's because the Pats stayed on the ground, running the ball 55 times, with Mike

Bengal regulars Reggie Williams (above) and Eddie Edwards combined for three sacks in Cincinnati's 17-10 strike victory over Seattle.

LeBlanc carrying 35 times for 146 yards.

Not surprisingly, the Patriots' two touchdowns also came on the ground, with Bleier scoring what proved to be the game-winner from a yard out midway through the third period.

Another team to shun the pass and run their way to victory was the Cincinnati Bengals, who ran the ball on 61 of 72 offensive plays en route to a 17-10 victory over Seattle. Marc Logan led the Bengals' ground attack with 103 yards on 16 carries.

The Bengals' use of a ball-control running attack came one week after replacement quarterbacks Dave Walter and Adrian Breen combined for a net passing total of minus-13 yards in a loss to San Diego.

The Cincinnati defense sacked Seattle quarterback Bruce Mathison five times, with regular Reggie Williams getting two sacks and Eddie Edwards one.

Veteran regulars Joe Montana, Roger Craig and Joe Cribbs were instrumental in helping the San Francisco 49ers grab a 20-0 halftime lead in their NFC West Division game against the Falcons at Atlanta. The 49ers dominated the Falcons in the first half, outdistancing them in total yardage, 261-56, and rushing yardage, 139-6.

But San Francisco Coach Bill Walsh's plan to rest his regular players in the second half was abandoned when the Falcons scored 10 points in the third quarter to cut the deficit in half.

Montana and Co. reentered the game at that point and, although the trio didn't score, the 49ers held on for a 25-17 victory.

The Los Angeles Rams played 11 veteran regulars in their interconference game against Pittsburgh and two of them—quarterback Steve Dils and running back Charles White—led the Rams to a 31-21 triumph. Dils completed 13 of 19 passes for 148 yards and two touchdowns while White rushed for a career-high 166 yards on 33 carries.

The Washington Redskins had lost their previous four games at Giants Stadium in East Rutherford, N.J.—including a 17-0 defeat in the 1986 NFC championship game—but snapped the string with a 38-12 victory over the Giants in Week 5. The Redskins entered the game with one of the best strike teams in the NFL, while the Giants fielded one of the worst.

Redskins running back Lionel Vital rolled up 128 yards rushing and scored one touchdown as Washington finished with a 376-171 edge in total yards. And the Redskin defense was just as impressive, sacking New York quarterback Mike Busch six times and limiting him to just 14 completions in 41 attempts.

The Giants, on the other hand, had allowed 809 total yards and 79 points in two strike games. The Giants were the only NFL team without a victory after four weeks.

The largest crowd by far—61,230—turned

out at Denver's Mile High Stadium for the Broncos' AFC Western Division game with the Los Angeles Raiders on Monday night. The Broncos had the largest crowds on each of the first two strike football weekends.

Running back Joe Dudek, a former star at Division III Plymouth State, scored two first-quarter touchdowns to lead the Broncos to a 30-14 victory. Dudek, who was released by Denver in training camp after spending the entire 1986 season on injured reserve, rushed for 128 yards on 23 carries.

Lions-Packers
SUNDAY, OCTOBER 11
SCORE BY PERIODS

Detroit	3	0	3	10	3—19
Green Bay	0	6	0	10	0—16

SCORING
Detroit—Field goal Prindle 23, 14:03 1st.
Green Bay—Field goal Zendejas 39, 5:03 2nd.
Green Bay—Field goal Zendejas 28, 14:46 2nd.
Detroit—Field goal Prindle 32, 8:57 3rd.
Green Bay—Summers 10 pass from Risher (Zendejas kick), 1:42 4th.
Detroit—Grymes 7 pass from Hons (Prindle kick), 9:29 4th.
Detroit—Field goal Prindle 27, 13:40 4th.
Green Bay—Field goal Zendejas 45, 15:00 4th.
Detroit—Field goal Prindle 31, 12:26 OT.

TEAM STATISTICS

	Detroit	Green Bay
First downs	21	16
Rushes-Yards	42-122	36-151
Passing yards	220	122
Sacked-Yards lost	1-4	7-42
3rd down eff	6-19	8-20
Passes	19-39-0	17-29-1
Punts	7-34.0	8-38.9
Fumbles-Lost	4-2	4-2
Penalties-Yards	6-39	11-114
Time of possession	36:03	36:23
Attendance—35,779.		

INDIVIDUAL STATISTICS
Rushing—Detroit, Wester 19-50, Edwards 17-28, Hons 3-38, Dollinger 3-6; Green Bay, Willhite 18-79, Risher 3-30, Hargrove 4-10, Weigel 9-26, Scott 1-2, Lee Morris 1-4.

Passing—Detroit, Hons 19-39-0—224; Green Bay, Risher 17-29-1—164.

Receiving—Detroit, Grymes 6-59, Edwards 4-40, Witte 1-19, Truvillion 6-85, Dollinger 2-21; Green Bay, Lee Morris 7-81, Scott 3-27, Willhite 4-24, Summers 3-32.

Kickoff Returns—Detroit, Hall 2-32, Bradley 3-70; Green Bay, Sterling 1-0, Harden 1-20, Lee Morris 3-41, Willhite 0-37.

Punt Returns—Detroit, Bradley 4-11; Green Bay, Scott 3-35.

Interceptions—Detroit, Benson 1-2.

Punting—Detroit, Kinzer 7-34.0; Green Bay, Renner 8-38.9.

Field Goals—Detroit, Prindle 4-5 (missed: 42); Green Bay, Zendejas 3-3.

Sacks—Detroit, Boyd, Carr, Benson, Federico, McDuffie, Ross, Thompson; Green Bay, Jordan.

Jets-Colts
SUNDAY, OCTOBER 11
SCORE BY PERIODS

New York Jets	0	0	0	0—0
Indianapolis	0	3	3	0—6

SCORING
Indianapolis—Field goal Jordan 35, 13:03 2nd.
Indianapolis—Field goal Jordan 25, 7:32 3rd.

TEAM STATISTICS

	New York	Indianapolis
First downs	16	14
Rushes-Yards	28-66	32-174
Passing yards	145	96
Sacked-Yards lost	4-18	3-19
3rd down eff	4-15	2-15
Passes	17-35-3	15-31-1
Punts	8-39.4	7-34.6
Fumbles-Lost	5-2	2-1
Penalties-Yards	8-65	7-70
Time of possession	30:00	30:00
Attendance—34,927.		

INDIVIDUAL STATISTICS
Rushing—New York, Bligen 12-35, E. Hunter 13-27, Chirico 2-4, Norrie 1-0; Indianapolis, Banks 25-159, Brown 4-15, Hogeboom 2-1, Kiel 1-minus 1.

Passing—New York, Norrie 17-35-3—163; Indianapolis, Hogeboom 15-28-1—115, Kiel 0-3-0—0.

Receiving—New York, Harper 5-56, Bligen 2-29, Holman 3-23, S. Hunter 4-19, Riley 2-19, Sweet 1-17; Indianapolis, Murray 4-52, Banks 5-22, Kearse 1-20, Noble 3-11, McLemore 1-5, Brandes 1-5.

Kickoff Returns—New York, E. Hunter 3-46; Indianapolis, Nobles 1-17.

Punt Returns—New York, Harper 1-5, Foster 2-8, Rose 1-1; Indianapolis, Johnson 3-30, Simmons 1-0.

Interceptions—New York, Rose 1-1; Indianapolis, B. Jones 2-26, Prior 1-3.

Punting—New York, O'Connor 8-39.4; Indianapolis, Kiel 7-34.6.

Field Goals—New York, Ragusa 0-2 (missed: 46, 33); Indianapolis, Jordan 2-4 (missed: 42, 42).

Sacks—New York, Lyons, Mersereau 2; Indianapolis, Grimsley, Bulluck, Thorp, Leiding.

Eagles-Cowboys
SUNDAY, OCTOBER 11
SCORE BY PERIODS

Philadelphia	3	7	6	6—22
Dallas	21	6	14	0—41

SCORING
Dallas—Edwards 62 run (Zendejas kick), 2:44 1st.
Dallas—Blount 8 run (Zendejas kick), 5:09 1st.
Dallas—Burbage 77 pass from Sweeney (Zendejas kick), 8:40 1st.
Philadelphia—Field goal Jacobs 40, 12:07 1st.
Philadelphia—Bowman 62 pass from Tinsley (Jacobs kick), 5:33 2nd.
Dallas—Field goal Zendejas 45, 14:18 2nd.
Dallas—Field goal Zendejas 50, 15:00 2nd.
Dallas—Dorsett 10 run (Zendejas kick), 4:18 3rd.
Dallas—Blount 1 run (Zendejas kick), 4:44 3rd.
Philadelphia—Siano 13 pass from Tinsley (kick failed), 14:12 3rd.
Philadelphia—Clemons 13 pass from Tinsley (kick failed), 4:30 4th.

TEAM STATISTICS

	Philadelphia	Dallas
First downs	24	19
Rushes-Yards	30-72	31-160
Passing yards	362	240
Sacked-Yards lost	5-44	2-15
3rd down eff	6-18	4-12
Passes	29-45-0	15-25-0
Punts	6-30.1	5-42.2
Fumbles-Lost	4-3	3-2
Penalties-Yards	9-68	10-71
Time of possession	33:37	26:23
Attendance—40,622.		

INDIVIDUAL STATISTICS

Rushing—Philadelphia, Brown 17-43, Ross 7 24, Robinson 2-6, Clemons 1-0, Horn 1-0, Tinsley 2-minus 1; Dallas, Edwards 1-62, Blount 18-53, Dorsett 4-27, E.J. Jones 2-7, Adams 2-6, Sweeney 2-5, Snyder 2-0.

Passing—Philadelphia, Tinsley 24-34-0—338, Horn 5-11-0—68; Dallas, Sweeney 8-14-0—152, D. White 3-3-0 —59, Snyder 4-8-0—44.

Receiving—Philadelphia, Siano 6-83, Bowman 5-123, Grant 5-97, Ross 5-41, Brown 4-20, Bailey 2-17, Clemons 1-13, Repko 1-12; Dallas, Edwards 6-100, Burbage 3-110, G. White 1-11, Spivey 1-9, Scott 1-11, Lavette 1-6, Blount 1-5, E.J. Jones 1-3.

Kickoff Returns—Philadelphia, Bowman 4-108, Clemons 1-0; Dallas, Adams 3-70.

Punt Returns—Philadelphia, Bowman 1-0, Caterbone 1-0; Dallas, Burbage 2-9.

Interceptions—None.

Punting—Philadelphia, Jacobs 5-36.2; Dallas, Sawyer 5-42.2.

Field Goals—Philadelphia, Jacobs 1-2 (missed: 38); Dallas, Zendejas 2-3 (missed: 49).

Sacks—Philadelphia, West, Grooms; Dallas, R. White 2, E. Jones, Watts 2.

Steelers-Rams

SUNDAY, OCTOBER 11

SCORE BY PERIODS

Pittsburgh	7	7	0	7—21
Los Angeles Rams	7	14	7	3—31

SCORING

Los Angeles—Jackson recovered blocked punt in end zone (Lansford kick), 2:35 1st.

Pittsburgh—Alston 22 pass from Bono (Trout kick), 8:22 1st.

Pittsburgh—Carter 10 pass from Bono (Trout kick), 0:44 2nd.

Los Angeles—White 2 run (Lansford kick), 3:42 2nd.

Los Angeles—McDonald 1 pass from Dils (Lansford kick), 14:44 2nd.

Los Angeles—Moore 11 pass from Dils (Lansford kick), 0:40 3rd.

Los Angeles—Field goal Lansford 39, 12:51 4th.

Pittsburgh—Alston 42 pass from Collier (Trout kick), 14:04 4th.

TEAM STATISTICS

	Pittsburgh	Los Angeles
First downs	16	15
Rushes-Yards	28-149	38-172
Passing yards	170	141
Sacked-Yards lost	4-16	1-7
3rd down eff.	4-13	4-12
Passes	13-32-1	13-19-1
Punts	7-31.7	5-38.0
Fumbles-Lost	3-0	3-1
Penalties-Yards	6-40	6-3
Time of possession	27:06	32:54
Attendance—20,218.		

INDIVIDUAL STATISTICS

Rushing—Pittsburgh, Pollard 15-77, E. Jackson 8-24, Bono 1-23, Collier 3-22, Carter 1-9; Los Angeles, White 33-166, Francis 1-4, Guman 1-2, Dils 3-0.

Passing—Pittsburgh, Bono 11-28-0—136, Collier 2-4-1—50; Los Angeles, Dils 13-19-1—148.

Receiving—Pittsburgh, Alston 3-84, Carter 4-39, Lee 3-37, Clinkscales 1-19, Pollard 1-5, Bono 1-2; Los Angeles, P. Smith 1-51, Mobley 4-35, Guman 2-31, McDonald 2-14, Moore 1-11, Francis 1-6, White 2-0.

Kickoff Returns—Pittsburgh, Britt 2-9, A. Riley 1-0, Stone 2-38, M. Anderson 1-8; Los Angeles, Williams 1-11, Tiumalu 2-29.

Punt Returns—Pittsburgh, M. Anderson 4-19; Los Angeles, S. Johnson 4-minus 4.

Interceptions—Pittsburgh, Gowdy 1-5; Los Angeles, H.

Johnson 1-49.

Punting—Pittsburgh, Bruno 6-37.0; Los Angeles, Hatcher 5-38.0.

Field Goals—Pittsburgh, Trout 0-1 (missed: 32); Los Angeles, Lansford 1-2 (missed: 50).

Sacks—Pittsburgh, J. Williams; Los Angeles, Meisner, Borland, Edwards, Wright.

Saints-Cardinals

SUNDAY, OCTOBER 11

SCORE BY PERIODS

New Orleans	0	6	6	7—19
St. Louis	10	7	0	7—24

SCORING

St. Louis—Jackson 77 fumble return (Staurovsky kick), 8:38 1st.

St. Louis—Field goal Staurovsky 24, 14:15 1st.

St. Louis—Leonard Smith 29 fumble return (Staurovsky kick), 9:18 2nd.

New Orleans—Martin 5 pass from Ingram (kick blocked), 14:42 2nd.

New Orleans—Beverly 3 run (kick failed), 10:31 3rd.

St. Louis—Garza 2 run (Staurovsky kick), 4:01 4th.

New Orleans—Beverly 5 run (Cofer kick), 8:04 4th.

TEAM STATISTICS

	New Orleans	St. Louis
First downs	29	10
Rushes-Yards	48-213	31-139
Passing yards	155	4
Sacked-Yards lost	3-27	1-7
3rd down eff.	12-18	1-8
Passes	17-36-1	3-10-1
Punts	2-43.0	5-35.4
Fumbles-Lost	4-3	0-0
Penalties-Yards	8-70	11-72
Time of possession	39:35	20:25
Attendance—11,795.		

INDIVIDUAL STATISTICS

Rushing—New Orleans, Beverly 35-139, Fourcade 5-57, Rodenberger 5-16, Barnhardt 1-minus 13, Ingram 2-14; St. Louis, McAdoo 20-94, Ferrell 7-34, Garza 3-13, Halloran 1-minus 2.

Passing—New Orleans, Fourcade 16-34-1—177, Ingram 1-2-0—5; St. Louis, Halloran 2-7-1—5, Garza 1-3-0—6.

Receiving—New Orleans, Dawsey 3-19, Waters 2-33, Scott 2-14, Rodenberger 1-6, O'Neal 2-9, Martin 7-101; St. Louis, J.T. Smith 2-5, McAdoo 1-6.

Kickoff Returns—New Orleans, Beverly 3-46, Adams 2-29; St. Louis, Sikahema 3-59, Sargent 1-10.

Punt Returns—New Orleans, Martin 3-25; St. Louis, Sikahema 1-29.

Interceptions—New Orleans, Leach 1-10; St. Louis, Mathis 1-4.

Punting—New Orleans, Barnhardt 2-43.0; St. Louis, Cater 5-35.4.

Field Goals—New Orleans, none attempted; St. Louis, Staurovsky 1-1.

Sacks—New Orleans, Swoopes; St. Louis, Garalczyk 2, Leonard Smith.

Bills-Patriots

SUNDAY, OCTOBER 11

SCORE BY PERIODS

Buffalo	0	0	0	7— 7
New England	7	0	7	0—14

SCORING

New England—Woods 4 run (Franklin kick), 8:34 1st.

New England—Bleier 1 run (Franklin kick), 6:36 3rd.

Buffalo—McFadden 13 pass from Totten (Schlopy kick), 3:03 4th.

TEAM STATISTICS

	Buffalo	New England
First downs	14	15
Rushes-Yards	37-107	55-213
Passing yards	61	43
Sacked-Yards lost	2-23	0-0
3rd down eff.	2-12	7-19
Passes	9-21-2	4-13-1
Punts	6-40.0.	9-34.6
Fumbles-Lost	7-3	2-0
Penalties-Yards	5-40	3-26
Time of possession	25:40	34:20
Attendance—11,878.		

INDIVIDUAL STATISTICS

Rushing—Buffalo, Byrum 19-59, King 4-19, Partridge 1-13, Totten 7-9, Sheppard 5-4, Williams 1-3; New England, LeBlanc 35-146, Hansen 13-43, Woods 3-20, McSwain 2-3, Bleier 2-1.

Passing—Buffalo, Totten 9-21-2—84; New England, Bleier 4-13-1—43.

Receiving—Buffalo, M. Brown 2-44, Gaines 2-19, McFadden 1-13, Belk 1-7, King 1-3, Sheppard 1-2, Byrum 1-minus 4; New England, Linne 3-32, Frain 1-11.

Kickoff Returns—Buffalo, McFadden 3-60; New England, LeBlanc 1-7.

Punt Returns—Buffalo, McFadden 3-25; New England, Linne 1-3.

Interceptions—Buffalo, Schankweiler 1-17; New England, P. Williams 1-0, Petersen 1-0.

Punting—Buffalo, Partridge 6-40.0; New England, Herline 9-34.6.

Field Goals—None attempted.

Sacks—New England, Mangiero, Wilburn ½, Wichard ½.

Chiefs-Dolphins
SUNDAY, OCTOBER 11
SCORE BY PERIODS

Kansas City	0	0	0	0—	0
Miami	7	7	21	7—	42

SCORING

Miami—Isom 6 run (Beecher kick), 8:59 1st.
Miami—R. Scott 2 run (Beecher kick), 12:07 2nd.
Miami—R. Scott 4 run (Beecher kick), 3:06 3rd.
Miami—Hobley 55 fumble return (Beecher kick), 3:42 3rd.
Miami—Hooper 59 fumble return (Beecher kick), 6:33 3rd.
Miami—R. Scott 3 run (Beecher kick), 4:49 4th.

TEAM STATISTICS

	Kansas City	Miami
First downs	8	25
Rushes-Yards	30-90	35-202
Passing yards	42	142
Sacked-Yards lost	4-32	0-0
3rd down eff.	4-14	8-14
Passes	10-18-2	17-31-0
Punts	8-35.8	4-37.3
Fumbles-Lost	3-2	2-1
Penalties-Yards	6-85	7-60
Time of possession	27:57	32:03
Attendance—25,867.		

INDIVIDUAL STATISTICS

Rushing—Kansas City, Parker 20-46, C. Smith 5-19, Lacy 1-4, Espinoza 1-5, Pippens 3-16; Miami, Tagliaferri 3-11, R. Scott 18-99, Isom 6-25, Konecny 1-19, Mackey 4-38, Roth 3-10.

Passing—Kansas City, Stevens 1-4-0—5, Espinoza 9-14-2—69; Miami, Mackey 14-28-0—127, Stankavage 3-3-0—15.

Receiving—Kansas City, Trahan 2-15, Montagne 2-13, C. Smith 2-21, Parker 1-9, Stockemer 1-4, Pippens 2-12; Miami, Konecny 4-24, Reilly 1-16, Tagliaferri 4-29, Sampleton 5-45, Douglas 1-17, W. Smith 1-8, Lewis 1-3.

Kickoff Returns—Kansas City, Wyatt 1-21, Parker 3-49, B. Smith 1-10, S. Griffin 1-16; Miami, Roth 1-23.

Punt Returns—Kansas City, Wyatt 1-4, Montagne 1-8; Miami, Caterbone 3-14.

Interceptions—Miami, Hobley 2-7.

Punting—Kansas City, Goodburn 8-35.8; Miami, Gore 4-37.3.

Field Goals—Kansas City, none attempted; Miami, Beecher 0-1 (missed: 49).

Sacks—Miami, Lambrecht, Readon, S. Scott.

Redskins-Giants
SUNDAY, OCTOBER 11
SCORE BY PERIODS

Washington	3	21	7	7—	38
New York Giants	3	0	9	0—	12

SCORING

New York—Field goal Benyola 45, 3:12 1st.
Washington—Field goal Ariri 22, 8:03 1st.
Washington—W. Wilson 1 run (Ariri kick), 5:10 2nd.
Washington—Vital 22 run (Ariri kick), 9:55 2nd.
Washington—W. Wilson 3 run (Ariri kick), 13:45 2nd.
New York—Lovelady 23 pass from Busch (kick failed), 4:06 3rd.
Washington—T. Wilson 64 pass from Rubbert (Ariri kick), 5:24 3rd.
New York—Field goal Benyola 20, 8:58 3rd.
Washington—Jessie 14 run (Ariri kick), 13:05 4th.

TEAM STATISTICS

	Washington	New York
First downs	24	13
Rushes-Yards	48-200	19-47
Passing yards	176	124
Sacked-Yards lost	0-0	6-59
3rd down eff.	6-14	5-17
Passes	11-23-0	14-41-1
Punts	6-34.7	10-36.8
Fumbles-Lost	4-2	3-2
Penalties-Yards	5-59	9-79
Time of possession	33:33	26:27
Attendance—9,123.		

INDIVIDUAL STATISTICS

Rushing—Washington, Vital 27-128, W. Wilson 15-56, Jessie 1-14, Rubbert 5-2; New York, Williams 12-36, Lovelady 1-8, Park 4-5, Covington 2-minus 2.

Passing—Washington, Rubbert 11-23-0—176; New York, Busch 14-41-1—183.

Receiving—Washington, Allen 4-51, C. Wilson 2-76, W. Wilson 2-16, McEwen 1-13, Vital 1-13, Caravello 1-7; New York, Bennett 2-21, Coleman 1-5.

Kickoff Returns—Washington, W. Wilson 2-32, Jessie 2-32; New York, Byrd 3-99, Norris 3-59, Urch 1-13.

Punt Returns—Washington, T. Wilson 7-142; New York, Lovelady 4-20.

Interceptions—Washington, Gage 1-7.

Punting—Washington, Weil 6-34.7; New York, Moore 10-36.8.

Field Goals—Washington, Ariri 1-2 (missed: 42); New York, Benyola 2-2.

Sacks—Washington, Martin 2, Benish 2, Sagnella, Curtis.

Bengals-Seahawks
SUNDAY, OCTOBER 11
SCORE BY PERIODS

Cincinnati	0	17	0	0—	17
Seattle	0	0	3	7—	10

SCORING

Cincinnati—Logan 5 run (Manca kick), 1:59 2nd.
Cincinnati—McCluskey 1 run (Manca kick), 11:11 2nd.
Cincinnati—Field goal Manca 28, 14:51 2nd.
Seattle—Field goal Hagler 24, 6:06 3rd.
Seattle—Teal 8 pass from Mathison (Hagler kick), 11:31 4th.

TEAM STATISTICS

	Cincinnati	Seattle
First downs	22	17
Rushes-Yards	61-270	21-90
Passing yards	97	126
Sacked-Yards lost	0-0	5-41
3rd down eff.	7-15	3-12
Passes	6-11-0	15-32-2
Punts	5-45.2	6-32.5
Fumbles-Lost	7-3	0-0
Penalties-Yards	8-75	6-43
Time of possession	35:27	24:33

Attendance—31,739.

INDIVIDUAL STATISTICS

Rushing—Cincinnati, Logan 16-103, McCluskey 15-70, Rice 8-35, Wright 10-35, Walter 11-33, Meehan 1-minus 6; Seattle, B. Green 15-68, Lane 5-19, Mathison 1-3.

Passing—Cincinnati, Walter 6-11-0—97; Seattle, Mathison 15-32-2—167.

Receiving—Cincinnati, Pleasant 2-45, Wright 2-17, Russell 1-23, Meehan 1-12; Seattle, Teal 4-49, Juma 3-53, Keel 3-32, Lane 3-18, Pardridge 2-15.

Kickoff Returns—Cincinnati, Wright 2-43, K. Brown 1-13; Seattle, Teal 2-40, Lane 1-12, B. Green 1-20.

Punt Returns—Cincinnati, K. Brown 3-12; Seattle, Teal 2-15.

Interceptions—Cincinnati, Niehoff 1-19, D. Smith 1-0.

Punting—Cincinnati, Fulhage 5-45.2; Seattle, Griffith 6-32.5.

Field Goals—Cincinnati, Manca 1-1; Seattle, Hagler 1-1.

Sacks—Cincinnati, Williams 2, Catchings, Edwards, Berthusen.

Oilers-Browns
SUNDAY, OCTOBER 11
SCORE BY PERIODS

Houston	0	7	6	2—15
Cleveland	3	0	0	7—10

SCORING

Cleveland—Field goal Franco 26, 6:09 1st.

Houston—McDonald 15 pass from Pease (Diettrich kick), 3:45 2nd.

Houston—Field goal Diettich 45, 7:01 3rd.

Houston—Field goal Diettich 23, 13:40 3rd.

Cleveland—Mason 5 pass from Christensen (Franco kick), 3:48 4th.

Houston—Safety, Baker tackled Christensen in end zone, 7:43 4th.

TEAM STATISTICS

	Houston	Cleveland
First downs	17	9
Rushes-Yards	46-174	18-50
Passing yards	148	119
Sacked-Yards lost	1-7	4-33
3rd down eff.	10-19	3-12
Passes	13-25-2	13-27-3
Punts	6-34.5	6-38.5
Fumbles-Lost	2-0	3-1
Penalties-Yards	9-75	7-60
Time of possession	40:36	19:24

Attendance—38,927.

INDIVIDUAL STATISTICS

Rushing—Houston, Jackson 11-40, Pease 5-10, Hunter 28-121, Moore 2-3; Cleveland, Mason 4-5, Everett 10-27, Christensen 3-9, Verser 1-9.

Passing—Houston, Pease 13-25-2—155; Cleveland, Christensen 13-27-3—152.

Receiving—Houston, Harris 6-104, Gehring 3-21, Jackson 1-9, McDonald 1-15, Hunter 2-6; Cleveland, Watson 1-9, Everett 3-10, Mason 2-16, Pierce 2-21, Kemp 5-96.

Kickoff Returns—Houston, Harris 1-16, Walters 1-18; Cleveland, Grayson 1-6, Driver 1-16, Tinsley 1-13.

Punt Returns—Houston, Walters 1-12; Cleveland, Wilson 3-25.

Interceptions—Houston, Newsom 1-minus 3, Bryant 2-18; Cleveland, Horn 1-28, D. Robinson 1-0.

Punting—Houston, Superick 6-34.5; Cleveland, Walters 6-38.5.

Field Goals—Houston, Diettrich 2-2; Cleveland, Franco 1-1.

Sacks—Houston, Baker 1½, Martin 2, D. Smith ½; Cleveland, T. Crawford.

Chargers-Buccaneers
SUNDAY, OCTOBER 11
SCORE BY PERIODS

San Diego	0	0	10	7—17
Tampa Bay	7	3	0	3—13

SCORING

Tampa Bay—Streater 26 pass from Reaves (Tiffin kick), 4:03 1st.

Tampa Bay—Field goal Tiffin 41, 14:23 2nd.

San Diego—Field goal Gaffney 27, 4:58 3rd.

San Diego—Sartin 2 run (Gaffney kick), 11:47 3rd.

San Diego—Moffett 19 pass from Neuheisel (Gaffney kick), 2:00 4th.

Tampa Bay—Field goal Tiffin 45, 7:07 4th.

TEAM STATISTICS

	San Diego	Tampa Bay
First downs	22	7
Rushes-Yards	33-125	30-129
Passing yards	260	72
Sacked-Yards lost	1-10	2-16
3rd down eff.	7-13	3-13
Passes	23-33-0	6-17-1
Punts	4-37.3	8-43.6
Fumbles-Lost	5-3	1-0
Penalties-Yards	6-35	9-60
Time of possession	32:50	27:10

Attendance—23,873.

INDIVIDUAL STATISTICS

Rushing—San Diego, Jenkins 8-32, Middleton 6-10, Spencer 3-4, Sartin 12-50, Kelley 1-10, Moffett 1-1, Neuheisel 2-18; Tampa Bay, Wright 11-26, Land 2-4, Boone 1-2, Ricks 10-43, Hold 5-49, Streater 1-5.

Passing—San Diego, Kelley 5-11-0—53, Neuheisel 18-22-0—217; Tampa Bay, Reaves 4-8-0—67, Hold 2-9-1—21.

Receiving—San Diego, Muhammad 1-20, Middleton 4-34, Sartin 4-13, Jenkins 2-13, Williams 5-110, Holt 2-17, Moffett 3-46, Rome 2-17; Tampa Bay, Streater 2-41, Wright 2-18, Holloway 1-17, S. Carter 1-12.

Kickoff Returns—San Diego, Rome 2-28, Jenkins 2-46; Tampa Bay, Walls 2-32, Ricks 1-26, Curry 1-15.

Punt Returns—San Diego, Williams 4-20.

Interceptions—San Diego, Brazley 1-0.

Punting—San Diego, Prokop 4-37.7; Tampa Bay, Criswell 8-43.6.

Field Goals—San Diego, Gaffney 1-2 (missed: 38); Tampa Bay, Tiffin 2-2.

Sacks—San Diego, Phillips, Winter; Tampa Bay, Riggins.

Vikings-Bears
SUNDAY, OCTOBER 11
SCORE BY PERIODS

Minnesota	0	0	0	7— 7
Chicago	0	7	10	10—27

SCORING

Chicago—Kozlowski 9 pass from Hohensee (Lashar kick), 10:04 2nd.

Chicago—Brewer 1 run (Lashar kick), 10:05 3rd.

Chicago—Field goal Lashar 26, 12:53 3rd.

Minnesota—Brim 11 pass from Adams (Dawson kick), 1:30 4th.

Chicago—Field goal Lashar 27, 5:24 4th.

Chicago—McCray 23 interception return (Lashar kick), 14:34 4th.

TEAM STATISTICS

	Minnesota	Chicago
First downs	15	26
Rushes-Yards	22-43	41-185
Passing yards	108	159
Sacked-Yards lost	9-70	4-27
3rd down eff.	6-16	5-16
Passes	15-32-1	16-31-0
Punts	5-38.0	5-41.0
Fumbles-Lost	3-1	3-1
Penalties-Yards	9-80	9-82
Time of possession	24:33	35:27

Attendance—32,111.

INDIVIDUAL STATISTICS

Rushing—Minnesota, Wilson 4-13, Thomas 6-4, Womack 5-7, Adams 4-10, Brim 1-minus 2, A. Walker 2-11; Chicago, Mosley 10-52, Heimuli 13-67, Hohensee 4-45, Brewer 8-12, F. Harris 4-2, Wolden 1-7, Brown 1-0.

Passing—Minnesota, Adams 15-29-0—178, L. Miller 0-3-1—0; Chicago, Hohensee 16-30-0—186, S. Payton 0-1-0—0.

Receiving—Minnesota, Brim 8-89, Parks 3-46, A. Thomas 2-13, May 1-22, Daugherty 1-8; Chicago, Kozlowski 7-87, Kindt 3-24, Mosley 2-16, Knapczyk 1-22, Heimuli 1-17, Brewer 1-9, Glasgow 1-11.

Kickoff Returns—Minnesota, Bess 3-50, Womack 3-53; Chicago, Lynch 1-12, Knapczyk 1-14.

Punt Returns—Minnesota, Bess 1-21; Chicago, Duarte 1-16, Jeffries 1-5.

Interceptions—Chicago, McCray 1-23.

Punting—Minnesota, Bruno 5-38.0; Chicago, Brown 5-41.0.

Field Goals—Minnesota, Dawson 0-1 (missed: 31); Chicago, Lashar 2-3 (missed: 42).

Sacks—Minnesota, Mays 2, D. Coleman, J. Walker; Chicago, McInerney 3½, Althoff, B. Bell 1½, Norvell 2, January.

49ers-Falcons
SUNDAY, OCTOBER 11
SCORE BY PERIODS

San Francisco	6	14	0	5	25
Atlanta	0	0	10	7	17

SCORING

San Francisco—Craig 1 run (kick failed), 8:38 1st.

San Francisco—Clark 6 pass from Montana (Brockhaus kick), 6:13 2nd.

San Francisco—Greer 5 pass from Gagliano (Brockhaus kick), 14:42 2nd.

Atlanta—Badanjek 2 run (Davis kick), 6:24 3rd.

Atlanta—Field goal Davis 42, 14:13 3rd.

San Francisco—Field goal Brockhaus 20, 3:06 4th.

San Francisco—Safety, Kramer sacked in end zone, 3:34 4th.

Atlanta—Kamana 4 pass from Kramer (Davis kick), 13:29 4th.

TEAM STATISTICS

	San Francisco	Atlanta
First downs	20	20
Rushes-Yards	43-239	20-50
Passing yards	122	188
Sacked-Yards lost	3-20	6-49
3rd down eff.	5-14	3-16
Passes	9-18-1	18-46-2
Punts	5-32.4	5-34.4
Fumbles-Lost	0-0	0-0
Penalties-Yards	10-79	7-50
Time of possession	32:17	27:43

Attendance—8,684.

INDIVIDUAL STATISTICS

Rushing—San Francisco, Craig 17-91, Cribbs 9-67, Rodgers 7-37, Monroe 1-17, Sydney 4-11, Stevens 3-9, Varajon 2-7; Atlanta, Badanjek 15-45, Kramer 1-11, McIntosh 2-7, Williams 1-0, Taylor 1-13.

Passing—San Francisco, Montana 5-8-0—63, Gagliano 4-8-1—79, Stevens 0-2-0—0; Atlanta, Van Raaphorst 5-13-1—61, Kramer 13-33-1—176.

Receiving—San Francisco, Greer 2-55, Clark 2-27, Rodgers 1-21, Francis 1-17, Craig 1-12, Heller 1-7, Sydney 1-3; Atlanta, Taylor 6-94, Byrd 4-68, Kamana 3-19, Gonzalez 2-28, Granger 1-26, McIntosh 1-5, Badanjek 1-3.

Kickoff Returns—San Francisco, McLemore 1-23, Rodgers 1-18, Heller 1-0, Sydney 2-38; Atlanta, M. Williams 2-18, McIntosh 2-37.

Punt Returns—San Francisco, McLemore 1-6, Pollard 1-0; Atlanta, Moss 2-4.

Interceptions—San Francisco, Courtney 1-30, McLemore 1-10; Atlanta, Moss 1-18.

Punting—San Francisco, Asmus 5-32.4; Atlanta, Davis 5-34.4.

Field Goals—San Francisco, Brockhaus 1-3 (missed: 23, 39); Atlanta, Davis 1-2 (missed: 45).

Sacks—San Francisco, Glover 2, Collins, Fuller, Kugler, Courtney; Atlanta, Moor, Green, Morris ½, Studaway ½.

Raiders-Broncos
MONDAY, OCTOBER 12
SCORE BY PERIODS

Los Angeles Raiders	0	14	0	0	14
Denver	14	3	6	7	30

SCORING

Denver—Dudek 8 run (Clendenen kick), 2:25 1st.

Denver—Dudek 3 run (Clendenen kick), 9:01 1st.

Los Angeles—Perry 3 pass from Evans (Hardy kick), 0:54 2nd.

Los Angeles—Calhoun 55 punt return (Hardy kick), 2:47 2nd.

Denver—Field goal Clendenen 31, 14:55 2nd.

Denver—Massie 10 pass from Karcher (kick failed), 12:59 3rd.

Denver—Poole 1 run (Clendenen kick), 12:17 4th.

TEAM STATISTICS

	Los Angeles	Denver
First downs	16	24
Rushes-Yards	29-102	43-204
Passing yards	168	142
Sacked-Yards lost	2-7	1-8
3rd down eff.	6-13	3-12
Passes	18-34-3	11-26-0
Punts	6-37.0	6-41.3
Fumbles-Lost	2-2	3-2
Penalties-Yards	8-97	8-61
Time of possession	31:04	28:56

Attendance—61,230.

INDIVIDUAL STATISTICS

Rushing—Los Angeles, Horton 15-35, C. Ellis 9-32, Evans 3-34, Browne 2-1; Denver, Karcher 3-minus 2, Dudek 23-128, Poole 10-63, Caldwell 5-19, May 2-minus 4.

Passing—Los Angeles, Evans 18-34-3—175; Denver, Karcher 9-23-0—127, May 0-1-0—0, McGuire 2-2-0—23.

Receiving—Los Angeles, Harrison 1-3, Aikens 3-38, Perry 1-3, Lathan 3-32, Browne 2-8, Wheeler 1-24, Williams 1-20, C. Ellis 4-24, Horton 1-6, Calhoun 1-17; Denver, Watson 1-49, Dudek 2-19, Micho 6-62, Massie 2-20.

Kickoff Returns—Los Angeles, Calhoun 3-85, Harkey 1-20, Foster 1-12, R. Washington 1-0; Denver, Swanson 2-52, Brown 1-7.

Punt Returns—Los Angeles, Calhoun 4-59; Denver, Swanson 2-20.

Interceptions—Denver, Clark 1-50, Ryan 1-1, Lucas 1-11.

Punting—Los Angeles, Gamache 6-37.0; Denver, Giacomarro 6-41.3.

Field Goals—Los Angeles, none attempted; Denver, Clendenen 1-2 (missed: 40).

Sacks—Los Angeles, Ackerman; Denver, Lucas, Tupper.

SIXTH WEEK

RESULTS OF WEEK 6
Sunday, October 18

Atlanta 24, L.A. Rams 20 at Atl.
Buffalo 6, N.Y. Giants 3 (OT) at Buff.
Cleveland 34, Cincinnati 0 at Cin.
Denver 26, Kansas City 17 at K.C.
Green Bay 16, Philadelphia 10 (OT) at G.B.
New England 21, Houston 7 at Hous.
New Orleans 19, Chicago 17 at Chi.
N.Y Jets 37, Miami 31 (OT) at N.Y.
Pittsburgh 21, Indianapolis 7 at Pitts.
San Diego 23, L.A. Raiders 17 at L.A.
San Francisco 34, St. Louis 28 at S.F.
Seattle 37, Detroit 14 at Det.
Tampa Bay 20, Minnesota 10 at T.B.

Monday, October 19

Washington 13, Dallas 7 at Dall.

The National Football League players' strike ended October 15 when Players Association chief Gene Upshaw, unable to get a new collective bargaining agreement and faced with the prospect of many of his members crossing the picket lines, ordered an end to the 24-day work stoppage.

Upshaw's announcement was not a surprise. And neither was his decision to file an antitrust lawsuit against the NFL owners in a Minneapolis federal court. When the players walked out of training camps for 41 days in a similar dispute over free agency in 1974, then-union head Ed Garvey—also faced with many players crossing picket lines—ordered the players back to work and filed an antitrust lawsuit against the owners.

Upshaw's decision was forced. With 247 of nearly 1,600 NFLPA members already having returned, his union was not solid. The average player had lost four paychecks at $15,000 each and had nothing to show for it.

Once again in an NFL player-management dispute, the owners held firm while the players gave in.

The dam broke when the Washington Redskins, the only team that hadn't had a single defector, voted as a team to go back. When they reported en masse on Thursday, October 15, the strike effectively was over. Other teams followed suit and by the end of the day, Upshaw had declared the strike over.

The owners were not magnanimous in victory. Although three days remained before the next scheduled games, they remained steadfast in refusing to allow the regulars to play. The owners had established a 1 p.m. Wednesday reporting deadline for games during the strike and weren't willing to change that scenario once the strike ended.

The third and final week of replacement football drew 344,645 fans for the 13 Sunday games, with stadiums filled to 38.5 percent capacity. The largest single-game crowd turned out in Chicago, where 46,813 watched the Bears battle the New Orleans Saints. The day's smallest crowd of 8,310 watched the Lions and visiting Seattle Seahawks do battle in Detroit.

The large crowd at Chicago's Soldier Field left disappointed when the Bears lost their first game of the season, 19-17, to the Saints. The Bears had been the NFL's last unbeaten team.

The Chicago offense was almost non-existent in the absence of quarterback Mike Hohensee, who had directed the replacement team to victories in the first two weeks of strike football. Hohensee sat out because of a knee injury and his replacements, Steve Bradley and Sean Payton, were able to muster just 133 yards of offense. Chicago's three scores came after a fumbled kickoff, a fumbled punt and an interception deep in New Orleans territory.

The Saints, who suited up 11 regular players (the Bears had none), got 12 points on four field goals by placekicker Florian Kempf, including a 21-yard game-winner with 4:30 remaining.

Field goals accounted for the game's only points as the Buffalo Bills beat the New York Giants, 6-3, in an interconference game. Bills kicker Todd Schlopy hit a 27-yard field goal with 19 seconds left in overtime after the Giants' George Benyola had missed a 40-yard attempt with five seconds left in regulation time. Schlopy's kick was set up by a 23-yard interception return by Steve Clark and a 30-yard run by Carl Byrum.

The Giants lost their third strike game to remain the league's only winless team after five weeks. Their 0-5 start was the worst ever for a Super Bowl champion.

The Bills and Giants combined for five missed field goals, nine turnovers and 26 penalties for 258 yards in a sloppily played game.

Another sloppy game was played in Tampa, where the Bucs and Minnesota Vikings combined for eight turnovers and 21 penalties in a game won by the Bucs, 20-10. Tampa Bay's only two touchdowns came on a fumble recovery in the end zone and an interception return.

The victory was the Bucs' second in three strike games and gave Tampa Bay a 3-2 record overall, the club's best start since 1981. The Vikings lost their third strike game in succession following two season-opening wins by their regular players.

Besides the Giants and Vikings, the NFL's other two winless strike teams were the Kansas City Chiefs and Philadelphia Eagles.

The Chiefs lost to AFC West Division rival Denver, 26-17, as Broncos quarterback Ken Karcher completed 25 of 39 passes for 275 yards and three touchdowns. Two of Karcher's touchdown passes went to wide receiver

Gene Upshaw (right), head of the NFL players union, announces the end of the players' strike at a press conference in Washington, D.C., on October 15.

Bobby Micho, who caught nine passes for 105 yards.

The Eagles lost to the Green Bay Packers in overtime, 16-10, as Packers running back James Hargrove capped a 10-play drive with a five-yard touchdown run 5:04 into the extra period. The Eagles had forced the extra period when placekicker Dave Jacobs connected on a 44-yard field goal with 4:58 remaining.

The overtime was Green Bay's third in five games and improved their overtime record to 1-1-1.

Another overtime game took place in East Rutherford, N.J., where the New York Jets defeated Miami, 37-31, in an AFC East Division game. Jets quarterback Pat Ryan's fourth touchdown pass of the game—an eight-yard toss to Eddie Hunter—won it for New York with 34 seconds left in overtime. The touchdown came after defensive back George Radachowsky intercepted a pass by Miami quarterback Kyle Mackey and returned it 45 yards to the Dolphin 31.

Mackey, who ran for two touchdowns and threw for two more, tied a Miami record by throwing five interceptions.

The Jets, who played eight regular players to the Dolphins' one, set a team record with 17 penalties.

The Los Angeles Raiders had a 17-2 edge in veteran regulars when they met AFC West Division rival San Diego in the final strike game for both teams. But the Chargers prevailed, 23-17, when cornerback Elvis Patterson intercepted a pass by L.A. quarterback Vince Evans and returned it 75 yards for a touchdown with 18 seconds remaining.

Patterson, a starter for the Super Bowl-champion Giants in 1986 who was released after a poor season-opening game against Chicago, stepped in front of an Evans pass intended for wide receiver Mervyn Fernandez and sprinted down the left sideline.

Raider placekicker Chris Bahr, who crossed his team's picket line earlier in the week, had missed a 37-yard field-goal attempt with 1:56 left in regulation.

The Chargers' third straight strike victory equaled that of the San Francisco 49ers, who edged St. Louis, 34-28, behind quarterback Joe Montana. Montana completed 31 of 39 passes for 334 yards and four touchdowns, including two to wide receiver Dwight Clark, who caught nine passes for 99 yards.

The Cardinals, who opened the game with an eight-play, 80-yard scoring drive, were led by rookie running back Derrick McAdoo, who rushed 23 times for 111 yards and three touchdowns.

Another player to score three touchdowns in Week 6 was veteran Seattle receiver Steve Largent, who scored on the Seahawks' first three possessions in a 37-14 victory at Detroit. Largent, who did not play after the midway point of the third period, set team records with 15 receptions for 261 yards and had six catches for 116 yards in the first period alone.

Largent's three touchdowns gave him 90 in his 12-year career and moved him past Don Maynard (88) into second place behind Don Hutson (99) on the NFL's all-time list.

Another veteran receiver, Pittsburgh's John Stallworth, caught the 500th pass of his 14-year career as the Steelers defeated the Indianapolis Colts, 21-7. Stallworth's milestone catch came on a four-yard touchdown toss from quarterback Steve Bono and gave Pittsburgh a 7-0 first-quarter lead.

The key to the Steelers' victory, however, was their defense, which forced five turnovers. All three Pittsburgh touchdowns were scored after Colt turnovers.

The game attracted 34,627 fans and was the first non-sellout at Three Rivers Stadium in 119 games.

Cleveland quarterback Gary Danielson had not thrown a pass in an NFL regular-season game in 22 months, but against a woeful Cincinnati Bengals strike replacement team, it really didn't matter. Danielson, a 10-year veteran who had crossed the picket line the previous week, completed 25 of 31 passes for 281 yards and four touchdowns as the Browns crushed the Bengals, 34-0. It was the first shutout in the 34-game regular-season series between the teams and Cleveland's first shutout victory since 1980.

In contrast to Danielson's performance, three Cincinnati quarterbacks—Dave Walter, Ben Bennett and Adrain Breen—combined to complete just four of 11 passes for 40 yards.

The Browns dominated from the start, with huge edges in first downs (29-6), total yards (410-95) and time of possession (42:12 to 17:48). Perhaps most telling was that Cleveland did not have to punt until 1:32 remained in the game.

New England quarterback Doug Flutie celebrated his trade from the Chicago Bears earlier in the week by driving the Patriots to touchdowns on each of their first two possessions in a 21-7 victory over Houston. Flutie, who grew up in Natick, Mass., and won the 1984 Heisman Trophy at Boston College, hit wide receiver Larry Linne for a 27-yard touchdown on the first possession and then completed a 30-yard pass to Linne to set up a three-yard scoring run by running back Michael LeBlanc.

Linebacker Andre Tippett also was a big contributor to the New England victory. Tippett sacked Oilers quarterback Brent Pease three times and blocked a 48-yard field-goal attempt by Tony Zendejas late in the first half. Raymond Clayborn scooped up the loose ball after the block and returned it 71 yards for the game's final score.

Erik Kramer is as unknown around pro football circles as Doug Flutie is well-known. But the 6-foot-1, 196-pound Kramer, a free agent released by New Orleans in the preseason, was given a second chance by the players' strike. He completed 27 of 46 passes for 335 yards to lead the Atlanta Falcons to a 24-20 comeback victory over the Los Angeles Rams.

The Falcons trailed, 17-0, at halftime before Kramer—a former standout at North Carolina State—brought them back. Kramer threw a five-yard scoring pass to Milton Barney in the third quarter; a one-yard TD pass to Joe McIntosh in the fourth period and a 19-yard touchdown pass to Lenny Taylor with 5:40 left to play.

The Rams drove from their own 20 to the Atlanta 4 in the closing moments before Steve Dils was intercepted in the end zone by the Falcons' Lyndell Jones.

The 42nd and last strike replacement game was played at Texas Stadium on Monday night. The matchup pitted a team with many veteran regulars in the lineup (Dallas) against the league's only team that hadn't had a single player cross the picket line (Washington).

The Redskins won, 13-7, despite everything seemingly working against them, including an injury to replacement quarterback Ed Rubbert, who was hurt after attempting just two passes. The replacement quarterback was replaced by former Tennessee star Tony Robinson, who completed 11 of his 18 attempts against the Cowboys.

Dallas regulars Tony Dorsett and Danny White were booed loudly by a crowd of 60,415 during pregame introductions. Dorsett compounded his problems by fumbling twice in the opening period, with his first fumble leading to a field goal and 3-0 Washington lead. The Redskins built their lead to 10-0 with a seven-play, 80-yard drive at the beginning of the second half, with Ted Wilson scoring from 16 yards out.

Washington's victory improved its record to 4-1 and the record of its strike replacement squad to 3-0. Only the Redskins, Chargers and 49ers fielded teams that went undefeated during the strike games of 1987.

Vikings-Buccaneers
SUNDAY, OCTOBER 18
SCORE BY PERIODS

Minnesota	3	0	7	0—10
Tampa Bay	3	0	14	3—20

SCORING

Minnesota—Field goal Dawson 34, 4:25 1st.
Tampa Bay—Field goal Tiffin 50, 10:49 1st.
Tampa Bay—Wells recovered fumble in end zone (Tiffin kick), 1:50 3rd.
Minnesota—Womack 23 pass from Adams (Dawson kick), 4:34 3rd.
Tampa Bay—Walker 30 interception return (Tiffin kick), 9:00 3rd.
Tampa Bay—Field goal Tiffin 37, 6:26 4th.

TEAM STATISTICS

	Minnesota	Tampa Bay
First downs	16	15
Rushes-Yards	17-23	29-75
Passing yards	152	193
Sacked-Yards lost	7-43	1-6
3rd down eff.	4-15	5-16
Passes	20-37-4	20-36-2
Punts	5-46.0	8-39.1
Fumbles-Lost	5-2	4-0
Penalties-Yards	10-89	11-109
Time of possession	28:42	31:18

Attendance—20,850.

INDIVIDUAL STATISTICS

Rushing—Minnesota, Frye 4-4, Harrell 5-8, Wilson 1-3, Womack 4-13, Adams 2-2, Scribner 1-minus 7; Tampa Bay, Ricks 8-23, Gladman 12-29, Wright 5-19, Zorn 4-4.

Passing—Minnesota, Adams 20-37-4—195; Tampa Bay, Zorn 20-36-2—199.

Receiving—Minnesota, Frye 3-25, Harrell 3-20, Gillespie 2-28, Brim 4-49, Wilson 2-14, Womack 5-46, Daugherty 1-13; Tampa Bay, Wright 7-51, Holloway 8-107, Dixon 1-18, Streater 2-15, Gladman 2-8.

Kickoff Returns—Minnesota, Harrell 1-4, Womack 2-24, Bess 2-42; Tampa Bay, Curry 2-38, K. Walker 1-0.

Punt Returns—Minnesota, Bess 3-18; Tampa Bay, Curry 3-32.

Interceptions—Minnesota, W. Smith 1-24, Louallen 1-16; Tampa Bay, K. Walker 2-30, Tripoli 1-0, Montoute 1-0.

Punting—Minnesota, Scribner 5-46.0; Tampa Bay, Criswell 8-39.1.

Field Goals—Minnesota, Dawson 1-3 (missed: 44, 47); Tampa Bay, Tiffin 1-2 (missed: 32).

Sacks—Minnesota, Mays; Tampa Bay, Turner 3, Turpin 2, Nordgren, Montoute.

Colts-Steelers
SUNDAY, OCTOBER 18
SCORE BY PERIODS

Indianapolis	0	7	0	0— 7
Pittsburgh	7	0	0	14—21

SCORING

Pittsburgh—Stallworth 4 pass from Bono (Trout kick), 7:54 1st.
Indianapolis—Murray 20 pass from Kiel (Jordan kick), 13:06 2nd.
Pittsburgh—Hoge 20 pass from Bono (Trout kick), 4:59 4th.
Pittsburgh—Sanders 10 run (Trout kick), 12:00 4th.

TEAM STATISTICS

	Indianapolis	Pittsburgh
First downs	15	23
Rushes-Yards	22-75	47-252
Passing yards	195	126
Sacked-Yards lost	0-0	2-12
3rd down eff.	2-9	6-14
Passes	17-30-3	11-23-1
Punts	5-39.6	6-41.8
Fumbles-Lost	2-2	4-0
Penalties-Yards	8-69	6-57
Time of possession	23:21	36:39

Attendance—34,627.

INDIVIDUAL STATISTICS

Rushing—Indianapolis, Banks 9-17, Kiel 2-23, Brown 9-32, Carver 2-3; Pittsburgh, Bono 4-minus 9, Jackson 24-134, Stone 9-67, Sanders 8-53, Hoge 2-7.

Passing—Indianapolis, Kiel 17-30-3—195; Pittsburgh, Bono 11-23-1—138.

Receiving—Indianapolis, Bellini 5-69, Hawthorne 2-27, Noble 3-17, Kearse 1-15, Banks 1-1, Murray 3-43, Johnson 1-15, J. Jones 1-8; Pittsburgh, Hoge 2-29, Stone 1-22, Stallworth 5-54, Jackson 2-12, Lee 1-21.

Kickoff Returns—Indianapolis, Johnson 3-38, Noble 1-18; Pittsburgh, Stone 2-53.

Punt Returns—Indianapolis, Simmons 1-5, Johnson 2-0; Pittsburgh, Lockett 2-3.

Interceptions—Indianapolis, Davis 1-7; Pittsburgh, A. Riley 1-4, Edwards 1-0, Sheffield 1-2.

Punting—Indianapolis, Kiel 5-39.6; Pittsburgh, Bruno 6-41.8.

Field Goals—Indianapolis, none attempted; Pittsburgh, Trout 0-1 (missed: 29).

Sacks—Indianapolis, Thorp, Chatman.

Seahawks-Lions
SUNDAY, OCTOBER 18
SCORE BY PERIODS

Seattle	21	9	7	0—37
Detroit	0	7	0	7—14

SCORING

Seattle—Largent 19 pass from Kemp (N. Johnson kick), 2:12 1st.
Seattle—Largent 21 pass from Kemp (N. Johnson kick), 4:11 1st.
Seattle—Largent 2 pass from Kemp (N. Johnson kick), 11:25 1st.
Detroit—Bradley 5 pass from Hons (Prindle kick), 1:21 2nd.
Seattle—Teal 12 pass from Kemp (kick failed), 3:58 2nd.
Seattle—Field goal N. Johnson 43, 15:00 2nd.
Seattle—Morton 1 run (N. Johnson kick), 5:34 3rd.
Detroit—Bradley 3 pass from Hons (Prindle kick), 5:07 4th.

TEAM STATISTICS

	Seattle	Detroit
First downs	24	15
Rushes-Yards	34-80	22-93
Passing yards	324	104
Sacked-Yards lost	4-28	3-23
3rd down eff.	9-13	3-10
Passes	21-30-1	14-27-2
Punts	3-34.7	6-40.3
Fumbles-Lost	5-1	2-0
Penalties-Yards	6-51	3-41
Time of possession	36:28	23:32

Attendance—8,310.

INDIVIDUAL STATISTICS

Rushing—Seattle, Morton 12-28, Lane 8-21, Moore 3-15, Kemp 3-12, Green 6-9, Mathison 2-minus 5; Detroit, Ellerson 16-61, Wester 2-17, Edwards 2-13, Kowgios 1-2, Hons 1-0.

Passing—Seattle, Kemp 20-27-1—344, Mathison 1-2-0—8, Largent 0-1-0—0; Detroit, Hons 14-27-2—127.

Receiving—Seattle, Largent 15-261, Juma 3-23, Pardridge 1-47, Teal 1-12, Bengen 1-9; Detroit, Bradley 7-50, Edwards 3-42, Truvillion 2-23, Ellerson 1-9, Kowgios 1-3.

Kickoff Returns—Seattle, Pardridge 2-29, Bengen 1-36; Detroit, Bradley 4-76.

Punt Returns—Seattle, Teal 4-23; Detroit, Bradley 3-12.

Interceptions—Seattle, Glaze 1-53, Caldwell 1-4; Detroit, Hall 1-0.

Punting—Seattle, Bowman 3-34.7; Detroit, Misko 6-40.3.

Field Goals—Seattle, N. Johnson 1-1; Detroit, none attempted.

Sacks—Seattle, F. Young ½, L. Williams, Dorning 1½; Detroit, Lockett, Gay, Thompson, McDuffie.

Chargers-Raiders
SUNDAY, OCTOBER 18
SCORE BY PERIODS

San Diego	7	0	0	16	23
Los Angeles Raiders	0	14	0	3	17

SCORING
San Diego—Neuheisel 8 run (Gaffney kick), 3:30 1st.
Los Angeles—Aikens 7 pass from Evans (Bahr kick), 8:13 2nd.
Los Angeles—Aikens 32 pass from Evans (Bahr kick), 14:59 2nd.
San Diego—Field goal Gaffney 21, 0:50 4th.
Los Angeles—Field goal Bahr 33, 4:19 4th.
San Diego—Williams 7 pass from Kelley (Gaffney kick), 6:53 4th.
San Diego—Patterson 75 interception return (kick failed), 14:42 4th.

TEAM STATISTICS

	San Diego	Los Angeles
First downs	14	19
Rushes-Yards	30-97	30-138
Passing yards	147	176
Sacked-Yards lost	7-61	5-31
3rd down eff.	6-17	4-13
Passes	17-27-0	11-31-1
Punts	7-39.9	6-42.8
Fumbles-Lost	0-0	2-2
Penalties-Yards	6-31	4-25
Time of possession	31:12	28:48
Attendance—23,541.		

INDIVIDUAL STATISTICS
Rushing—San Diego, Jenkins 11-50, Neuheisel 4-23, Williams 1-11, Kelley 1-8, Middleton 6-3, Sartin 7-2; Los Angeles, Evans 4-47, Ellis 12-36, Strachan 6-31, Horton 4-23, Aikens 1-1.

Passing—San Diego, Neuheisel 12-18-0—66, Kelley 5-9-0—142; Los Angeles, Evans 11-31-1—207.

Receiving—San Diego, Jenkins 5-20, Holt 4-31, Williams 2-64, Sartin 2-6, Muhammad 1-67, Moffett 1-9, Middleton 1-8, Rome 1-3; Los Angeles, Fernandez 4-94, Aikens 3-48, Strachan 2-16, Wheeler 1-29, David Williams 1-20.

Kickoff Returns—San Diego, Sartin 3-71, Zachary 1-2; Los Angeles, Calhoun 3-74.

Punt Returns—San Diego, Williams 3-29; Los Angeles, Calhoun 4-33.

Interceptions—San Diego, Patterson 1-75.

Punting—San Diego, Prokop 7-39.9; Los Angeles, Gamache 6-42.8.

Field Goals—San Diego, Gaffney 1-2 (missed: 36); Los Angeles, Bahr 1-2 (missed: 37).

Sacks—San Diego, T. Simmons, Jackson, Kirk, Winter, K. Simmons 1½, Anderson 1½; Los Angeles, Robinson 2, Cormier, Pickel, Washington, Townsend, Buczkowski.

Rams-Falcons
SUNDAY, OCTOBER 18
SCORE BY PERIODS

Los Angeles Rams	7	10	3	0	20
Atlanta	0	0	7	17	24

SCORING
Los Angeles—Francis 2 pass from Dils (Lansford kick), 8:35 1st.
Los Angeles—McDonald 13 pass from Dils (Lansford kick), 6:27 2nd.
Los Angeles—Field goal Lansford 40, 14:35 2nd.
Atlanta—Barney 5 pass from Kramer (Davis kick), 9:37 3rd.
Los Angeles—Field goal Lansford 40, 12:45 3rd.

Atlanta—McIntosh 1 pass from Kramer (Davis kick), 2:10 4th.
Atlanta—Field goal Davis 35, 6:04 4th.
Atlanta—Taylor 19 pass from Kramer (Davis kick), 9:20 4th.

TEAM STATISTICS

	Los Angeles	Atlanta
First downs	21	22
Rushes-Yards	36-186	19-46
Passing yards	164	296
Sacked-Yards lost	2-10	5-39
3rd down eff.	5-13	3-13
Passes	14-29-2	27-46-2
Punts	7-38.7	7-36.9
Fumbles-Lost	3-3	3-3
Penalties-Yards	7-63	10-99
Time of possession	28:25	31:35
Attendance—15,813.		

INDIVIDUAL STATISTICS
Rushing—Los Angeles, White 31-155, Francis 3-28, Bryant 1-2, Dils 1-1; Atlanta, Badanjek 14-42, McIntosh 3-4, Granger 1-1, Kramer 1-minus 1.

Passing—Los Angeles, Dils 14-29-2—174; Atlanta, Kramer 27-46-2—335.

Receiving—Los Angeles, Moore 3-52, White 3-35, Francis 3-12, Smith 2-44, Mobley 2-19, McDonald 1-12; Atlanta, Barney 6-109, Taylor 6-77, Badanjek 5-38, Kamana 4-32, Byrd 3-57, McIntosh 2-10, Gonzalez 1-12.

Kickoff Returns—Los Angeles, Tiumalu 3-38; Atlanta, Badanjek 2-27, Oliver 1-18, McIntosh 1-71.

Punt Returns—Los Angeles, P. Smith 2-5, Rutledge 3-10; Atlanta, Barney 5-28.

Interceptions—Los Angeles, Jackson 1-36, Cromwell 1-0; Atlanta, Huff 1-0, Jones 1-0.

Punting—Los Angeles, Hatcher 7-38.7; Atlanta, Berry 7-36.9.

Field Goals—Los Angeles, Lansford 2-2; Atlanta, Davis 1-1.

Sacks—Los Angeles, Miller 3, Meisner, Borland; Atlanta, Moor 2.

Browns-Bengals
SUNDAY, OCTOBER 18
SCORE BY PERIODS

Cleveland	7	17	3	7	34
Cincinnati	0	0	0	0	0

SCORING
Cleveland—Brennan 6 pass from Danielson (Jaeger kick), 10:01 1st.
Cleveland—Tennell 3 pass from Danielson (Jaeger kick), 3:47 2nd.
Cleveland—Field goal Jaeger 45, 6:04 2nd.
Cleveland—Kemp 22 pass from Danielson (Jaeger kick), 12:04 2nd.
Cleveland—Field goal Jaeger 33, 12:10 3rd.
Cleveland—Kemp 19 pass from Danielson (Jaeger kick), 8:09 4th.

TEAM STATISTICS

	Cleveland	Cincinnati
First downs	29	6
Rushes-Yards	42-123	25-65
Passing yards	287	30
Sacked-Yards lost	2-4	2-10
3rd down eff.	10-15	2-10
Passes	26-32-0	4-11-1
Punts	1-44.0	6-40.1
Fumbles-Lost	7-4	3-2
Penalties-Yards	5-53	7-55
Time of possession	42:12	17:48
Attendance—40,170.		

INDIVIDUAL STATISTICS
Rushing—Cleveland, Mason 20-69, Everett 10-16, Danielson 1-0, Driver 9-31, Davis 1-7, Christensen 1-0; Cincin-

nati, Walter 3-20, Logan 7-5, McCluskey 4-5, Rice 3-1, Wright 4-7, Bennett 2-17, Breen 2-10.

Passing—Cleveland, Danielson 25-31-0—281, Christensen 1-1-0—10; Cincinnati, Walter 2-2-0—15, Bennett 2-6-1—25, Breen 0-3-0—0.

Receiving—Cleveland, Mason 2-12, Brennan 10-139, Kemp 5-70, Newsome 4-29, Tennell 2-20, Everett 2-8, Watson 1-13; Cincinnati, McCluskey 1-8, Meehan 1-7, Wright 1-7, Logan 1-18.

Kickoff Returns—Cleveland, Tinsley 1-13; Cincinnati, K. Brown 2-32, Wright 3-60.

Punt Returns—Cleveland, Wilson 4-44.

Interceptions—Cleveland, Wilson 1-0.

Punting—Cleveland, Gossett 1-44.0; Cincinnati, Fulhage 6-40.1.

Field Goals—Cleveland, Jaeger 2-2; Cincinnati, none attempted.

Sacks—Cleveland, Hairston, Rusinek; Cincinnati, Berthusen ½, Catchings ½, Ward.

Saints-Bears

SUNDAY, OCTOBER 18

SCORE BY PERIODS

New Orleans	0	10	3	6—19
Chicago	10	7	0	0—17

SCORING

Chicago—Field goal Lashar 22, 8:11 1st.

Chicago—Brewer 8 pass from Bradley (Lashar kick), 8:28 1st.

New Orleans—Field goal Kempf 48, 2:41 2nd.

Chicago—Kozlowski 18 pass from Bradley (Lashar kick), 6:48 2nd.

New Orleans—Martin 14 pass from Fourcade (Kempf kick), 14:18 2nd.

New Orleans—Field goal Kempf 31, 9:32 3rd.

New Orleans—Field goal Kempf 42, 0:50 4th.

New Orleans—Field goal Kempf 21, 10:30 4th.

TEAM STATISTICS

	New Orleans	Chicago
First downs	18	11
Rushes-Yards	40-112	25-67
Passing yards	179	66
Sacked-Yards lost	3-19	5-39
3rd down eff.	5-19	1-14
Passes	16-35-1	9-29-4
Punts	6-42.7	9-36.7
Fumbles-Lost	5-2	1-0
Penalties-Yards	6-68	3-18
Time of possession	34:13	25:47

Attendance—46,813.

INDIVIDUAL STATISTICS

Rushing—New Orleans, Beverly 19-46, Fourcade 8-38, Batiste 8-18, Rodenberger 4-7, Riordan 1-3; Chicago, Heimuli 15-37, Brewer 8-34, Bradley 1-minus 3, Clark 1-minus 1.

Passing—New Orleans, Fourcade 16-34-1—198, Riordan 0-1-0—0; Chicago, Bradley 6-18-3—77, Payton 3-11-1—28.

Receiving—New Orleans, Martin 5-84, Dawsey 4-44, Waters 2-25, Beverly 1-8, Scott 2-12, Rodenberger 1-11, C. Thomas 1-14; Chicago, Brewer 3-33, Kozlowski 3-47, Heimuli 1-3, Mullen 1-13, Knapczyk 1-9.

Kickoff Returns—New Orleans, Adams 2-23, C. Thomas 1-11; Chicago, Milton 1-10, White 1-17, Kozlowski 3-72.

Punt Returns—New Orleans, C. Thomas 1-11, Martin 5-20; Chicago, Duarte 4-23.

Interceptions—New Orleans, R. Sutton 3-42, Mack 1-3; Chicago, Norris 1-6.

Punting—New Orleans, Barnhardt 5-43.0, Kempf 1-41.0; Chicago, Brown 8-41.3.

Field Goals—New Orleans, Kempf 4-5 (missed: 33); Chicago, Lashar 1-1.

Sacks—New Orleans, McCoy 2, S. Leach 1½, DeForest, Taylor ½; Chicago, B. Bell, Norris, McInerney.

Patriots-Oilers

SUNDAY, OCTOBER 18

SCORE BY PERIODS

New England	14	7	0	0—21
Houston	7	0	0	0— 7

SCORING

New England—Linne 27 pass from Flutie (Franklin kick), 2:55 1st.

Houston—Williams 36 pass from Pease (Zendejas kick), 7:40 1st.

New England—LeBlanc 3 run (Franklin kick), 12:19 1st.

New England—Clayborn 71 blocked field goal return (Franklin kick), 14:05 2nd.

TEAM STATISTICS

	New England	Houston
First downs	17	17
Rushes-Yards	30-114	26-113
Passing yards	196	221
Sacked-Yards lost	1-3	4-29
3rd down eff.	4-12	8-17
Passes	15-25-0	21-49-2
Punts	7-38.9	6-42.7
Fumbles-Lost	2-0	1-1
Penalties-Yards	4-35	5-30
Time of possession	29:07	30:53

Attendance—26,294.

INDIVIDUAL STATISTICS

Rushing—New England, Flutie 6-43, LeBlanc 13-31, Davis 7-47, Hansen 2-minus 1, Whitten 2-minus 6; Houston, Jackson 18-69, Harris 1-17, Pease 2-5, Cobbie 1-3, Hunter 4-19.

Passing—New England, Flutie 15-25-0—199; Houston, Pease 21-49-2—250.

Receiving—New England, Scott 4-32, Gadbois 3-51, Linne 4-81, Pickering 1-10, Hansen 1-22, LeBlanc 2-3; Houston, Jeffires 1-8, Jackson 3-7, Williams 9-124, Walters 3-62, Harris 1-9, Moore 1-7, McDonald 1-10, Gehring 1-12, Hunter 1-11.

Kickoff Returns—New England, Hansen 1-14; Houston, Hunter 4-79.

Punt Returns—New England, Linne 3-3; Houston, Walters 1-7.

Interceptions—New England, Shegog 1-7, Holmes 1-4.

Punting—New England, Herline 7-38.9; Houston, L. Johnson 6-42.7.

Field Goals—New England, Franklin 0-1 (missed: 52); Houston, Zendejas 0-2 (missed: 48, 34).

Sacks—New England, Tippett 3, McCabe; Houston, Seale.

Dolphins-Jets

SUNDAY, OCTOBER 18

SCORE BY PERIODS

Miami	10	0	7	14	0—31
New York Jets	0	17	0	14	6—37

SCORING

Miami—Field goal Beecher 19, 8:57 1st.

Miami—Smith 5 pass from Mackey (Beecher kick), 10:40 1st.

New York—Harper 35 pass from Ryan (Ragusa kick), 2:59 2nd.

New York—Hunter 7 pass from Ryan (Ragusa kick), 12:34 2nd.

New York—Field goal Ragusa 34, 13:56 2nd.

Miami—Mackey 1 run (Beecher kick), 6:52 3rd.

New York—Bligen 7 run (Ragusa kick), 1:48 4th.

New York—Hunter 5 pass from Ryan (Ragusa kick), 8:42 4th.

Miami—Mackey 5 run (Beecher kick), 11:22 4th.

Miami—Lewis 1 pass from Mackey (Beecher kick), 13:59 4th.

New York—Hunter 8 pass from Ryan (no kick), 14:26 OT.

TEAM STATISTICS

	Miami	New York
First downs	30	24
Rushes-Yards	35-128	40-183
Passing yards	286	294
Sacked-Yards lost	1-12	1-7
3rd down eff.	11-17	10-21
Passes	26-55-5	30-49-2
Punts	5-32.8	6-30.7
Fumbles-Lost	2-1	4-3
Penalties-Yards	5-50	17-100
Time of possession	33:15	41:11
Attendance—18,249.		

INDIVIDUAL STATISTICS

Rushing—Miami, R. Scott 20-45, Mackey 8-47, Isom 3-16, Konecny 3-14, Tagliaferri 1-6; New York, E. Hunter 20-94, Bligen 17-90, Chirico 1-2, Ryan 2-minus 3.

Passing—Miami, Mackey 26-55-5—298; New York, Ryan 30-49-2—301.

Receiving—Miami, Chavis 3-50, Lewis 5-50, Tagliaferri 4-37, Douglas 4-38, Reilly 3-46, Caterbone 2-46, Isom 1-11, Konecny 1-9, R. Scott 1-2, Smith 1-5, Sampleton 1-4; New York, E. Hunter 2-15, Holman 8-92, Harper 7-80, Bligen 5-29, Sweet 2-28, S. Hunter 4-34, Riley 2-23.

Kickoff Returns—Miami, Isom 1-11, R. Scott 1-22; New York, R. Smith 4-60, E. Hunter 3-30.

Punt Returns—Miami, Caterbone 2-19, Hooper 1-0; New York, R. Smith 2-9.

Interceptions—Miami, Sowell 1-29, Hooper 1-11; New York, Heath 1-29, Robinson 1-38, Hogan 1-5, Haslett 1-9, Radachowsky 1-45.

Punting—Miami, Gore 5-32.8; New York, O'Connor 6-30.7.

Field Goals—Miami, Beecher 1-1; New York, Ragusa 1-1.

Sacks—Miami, Lambrecht ½, Wimberly ½; New York, Gastineau.

Broncos-Chiefs
SUNDAY, OCTOBER 18
SCORE BY PERIODS

Denver	9	10	0	7—26
Kansas City	7	7	3	0—17

SCORING

Denver—Safety, Hudson falls on own fumble in end zone, 4:12 1st.

Denver—Micho 26 pass from Karcher (Clendenen kick), 7:52 1st.

Kansas City—Fields 85 punt return (Hamrick kick), 11:52 1st.

Denver—Field goal Clendenen 35, 1:35 2nd.

Kansas City—Parker 4 run (Hamrick kick), 5:37 2nd.

Denver—Swanson 35 pass from Karcher (Clendenen kick), 14:23 2nd.

Kansas City—Field goal Hamrick 25, 5:26 3rd.

Denver—Micho 5 pass from Karcher (Clendenen kick), 4:25 4th.

TEAM STATISTICS

	Denver	Kansas City
First downs	23	16
Rushes-Yards	35-98	31-122
Passing yards	275	125
Sacked-Yards lost	0-0	2-23
3rd down eff.	6-13	4-13
Passes	25-39-2	17-29-1
Punts	4-45.8	6-45.5
Fumbles-Lost	3-2	4-2
Penalties-Yards	6-50	7-60
Time of possession	32:45	27:15
Attendance—20,296.		

INDIVIDUAL STATISTICS

Rushing—Denver, Poole 18-63, Dudek 12-26, Karcher 4-5, Caldwell 1-4; Kansas City, Parker 15-65, C. Smith 13-56, Stevens 2-1, Hudson 1-0.

Passing—Denver, Karcher 25-39-2—275; Kansas City, Hudson 0-1-0—0, Stevens 17-28-1—148.

Receiving—Denver, Micho 9-105, Swanson 6-87, Dudek 5-22, Andrews 1-20, Massie 1-19, Caldwell 1-12, Poole 1-9, Brown 1-1; Kansas City, Jones 5-51, Parker 5-30, Estell 3-24, Trahan 2-25, Montagne 2-18.

Kickoff Returns—Denver, Swanson 3-91, Clark 1-25, Brown 1-22; Kansas City, Lane 2-37, Fields 1-13, Lacy 2-9.

Punt Returns—Denver, Swanson 6-112; Kansas City, Fields 2-123.

Interceptions—Denver, Clark 1-35; Kansas City, Bryant 1-0, Ross 1-0.

Punting—Denver, Giacomarro 4-45.8; Kansas City, Goodburn 6-45.5.

Field Goals—Denver, Clendenen 1-1; Kansas City, Hamrick 1-1.

Sacks—Denver, Lucas, Tupper ½, Woodard ½.

Cardinals-49ers
SUNDAY, OCTOBER 18
SCORE BY PERIODS

St. Louis	7	14	7	0—28
San Francisco	0	14	7	13—34

SCORING

St. Louis—McAdoo 1 run (Gallery kick), 9:48 1st.

St. Louis—Johnson 38 pass from Garza (Gallery kick), 2:51 2nd.

San Francisco—Clark 22 pass from Montana (Brockhaus kick), 7:16 2nd.

St. Louis—McAdoo 6 run (Gallery kick), 12:04 2nd.

San Francisco—Clark 8 pass from Montana (Brockhaus kick), 14:07 2nd.

San Francisco—Craig 1 run (Brockhaus kick), 7:47 3rd.

St. Louis—McAdoo 1 run (Gallery kick), 15:00 3rd.

San Francisco—Craig 36 pass from Montana (Brockhaus kick), 2:31 4th.

San Francisco—Heller 3 pass from Montana (kick failed), 10:21 4th.

TEAM STATISTICS

	St. Louis	San Francisco
First downs	18	28
Rushes-Yards	36-160	32-121
Passing yards	164	327
Sacked-Yards lost	1-13	1-7
3rd down eff.	2-8	8-13
Passes	10-17-2	31-39-2
Punts	2-54.0	3-33.7
Fumbles-Lost	3-1	1-1
Penalties-Yards	5-30	7-60
Time of possession	28:29	31:31
Attendance—38,094.		

INDIVIDUAL STATISTICS

Rushing—St. Louis, McAdoo 23-111, Ferrell 7-22, Garza 5-18, Johnson 1-9; San Francisco, Craig 17-71, Du-Bose 7-24, Montana 5-19, Sydney 3-7.

Passing—St. Louis, Garza 10-17-2—177; San Francisco, Montana 31-39-2—334.

Receiving—St. Louis, J.T. Smith 7-96, Johnson 2-73, Harris 1-8; San Francisco, Clark 9-99, Craig 7-99, Francis 6-46, DuBose 4-37, Greer 3-44, Heller 2-9.

Kickoff Returns—St. Louis, Sargent 1-0, Sikahema 3-61, McAdoo 0-5, Ron Brown 1-40; San Francisco, Varajon 1-13, Rodgers 1-38, Monroe 3-59.

Punt Returns—St. Louis, Sikahema 2-22; San Francisco, McLemore 2-13.

Interceptions—St. Louis, T. Curtis 2-50; San Francisco, Cousineau 1-11, McLemore 1-25.

Punting—St. Louis, Cater 2-54.0; San Francisco, Asmus 3-33.7.

Field Goals—St. Louis, Gallery 0-2 (missed: 32, 48); San Francisco, none attempted.

Sacks—St. Louis, Garalczyk ½, Dulin ½; San Francisco, Board.

Giants-Bills
SUNDAY, OCTOBER 18
SCORE BY PERIODS

New York Giants	0	0	0	3	0—3
Buffalo	0	0	0	3	3—6

SCORING
New York—Field goal Benyola 22, 5:12 4th.
Buffalo—Field goal Schlopy 31, 11:57 4th.
Buffalo—Field goal Schlopy 27, 14:41 OT.

TEAM STATISTICS

	New York	Buffalo
First downs	19	22
Rushes-Yards	36-128	40-167
Passing yards	180	164
Sacked-Yards lost	3-23	2-17
3rd down eff	6-21	5-15
Passes	17-46-2	20-39-3
Punts	10-34.5	6-40.8
Fumbles-Lost	4-0	5-4
Penalties-Yards	15-145	11-113
Time of possession	33:15	41:26
Attendance—15,737.		

INDIVIDUAL STATISTICS
Rushing—New York, Williams 11-41, Rutledge 1-0, Covington 2-2, DiRico 20-79, Park 2-6; Buffalo, Riddick 11-29, Byrum 25-139, McClure 2-4, Porter 1-minus 1, Manucci 1-minus 4.

Passing—New York, Rutledge 17-46-2—203; Buffalo, McClure 20-38-3-181, Manucci 0-1-0—0.

Receiving—New York, Lovelady 5-59, Williams 2-10, McGowan 3-48, Bennett 2-31, Covington 1-9, DiRico 2-22, Park 1-6, Smith 1-18; Buffalo, Park 1-6, M. Brown 6-68, McKeller 9-80, Gaines 1-minus 2, Byrum 2-24.

Kickoff Returns—New York, Norris 1-11, Byrd 1-0; Buffalo, McFadden 2-33, Armstrong 1-18.

Punt Returns—New York, Lovelady 4-16; Buffalo, McFadden 4-51.

Interceptions—New York, DeRose 1-10, Rehage 1-14, Brown 1-4; Buffalo, Cokeley 1-4, Clark 1-23.

Punting—New York, Miller 10-34.5; Buffalo, Partridge 6-40.8.

Field Goals—New York, Benyola 1-3 (missed: 37, 40); Buffalo, Schlopy 2-5 (missed: 30, 44, 35).

Sacks—New York, Taylor 2; Buffalo, Armstrong, Martin, Seals.

Eagles-Packers
SUNDAY, OCTOBER 18
SCORE BY PERIODS

Philadelphia	7	0	0	3	0—10
Green Bay	0	3	7	0	6—16

SCORING
Philadelphia—Ross 5 run (Jacobs kick), 9:31 1st.
Green Bay—Field goal Zendejas 42, 8:26 2nd.
Green Bay—Lee Morris 46 pass from Risher (Zendejas kick), 9:24 3rd.
Philadelphia—Field goal Jacobs 44, 11:02 4th.
Green Bay—Hargrove 5 run (no kick), 5:04 OT.

TEAM STATISTICS

	Philadelphia	Green Bay
First downs	17	20
Rushes-Yards	30-141	39-175
Passing yards	224	226
Sacked-Yards lost	1-10	6-38
3rd down eff	4-13	7-17
Passes	17-31-4	17-28-2
Punts	5-41.8	6-34.7
Fumbles-Lost	2-1	4-2
Penalties-Yards	10-89	8-70
Time of possession	27:04	38:00
Attendance—35,842.		

INDIVIDUAL STATISTICS
Rushing—Philadelphia, Robinson 11-50, Brown 11-59, Ross 7-30, Tinsley 1-2; Green Bay, Willhite 16-100, Sterling 5-20, Larry Morris 8-18, Hargrove 7-28, Risher 2-9, Weigel 1-0.

Passing—Philadelphia, Tinsley 17-30-4—234, Grant 0-1-0—0; Green Bay, Risher 15-23-2—236, Gillus 2-5-0—28.

Receiving—Philadelphia, Repko 1-8, Robinson 2-9, Bailey 4-32, Grant 7-135, Brown 2-16, Siano 1-34; Green Bay, Redick 1-18, Weigel 1-17, Scott 2-29, Harden 2-29, Lee Morris 6-132, Willhite 2-13, Summers 2-20, Hargrove 1-6.

Kickoff Returns—Philadelphia, R. Brown 1-20, Ulmer 1-8, Siano 1-13; Green Bay, Lee Morris 1-17, Scott 1-9.

Punt Returns—Philadelphia, Ulmer 2-10, Green Bay, Harden 2-39, Scott 2-36.

Interceptions—Philadelphia, West 1-0, Kullman 1-12; Green Bay, Harrison 1-0, Melka 1-0, Mansfield 1-14, J.B. Morris 1-12.

Punting—Philadelphia, Royals 5-41.8; Green Bay, Renner 6-34.7.

Field Goals—Philadelphia, Jacobs 1-1; Green Bay, Zendejas 1-1.

Sacks—Philadelphia, Griffin, Smalls 2½, Lee, Phillips 1½; Green Bay, J.B. Morris.

Redskins-Cowboys
MONDAY, OCTOBER 19
SCORE BY PERIODS

Washington	3	0	7	3—13
Dallas	0	0	7	0— 7

SCORING
Washington—Field goal Ariri 19, 6:11 1st.
Washington—Wilson 16 run (Ariri kick), 4:25 3rd.
Dallas—Edwards 38 pass from D. White (Brady kick), 6:50 3rd.
Washington—Field goal Ariri 39, 8:47 4th.

TEAM STATISTICS

	Washington	Dallas
First downs	19	18
Rushes-Yards	42-186	21-93
Passing yards	153	222
Sacked-Yards lost	3-21	6-40
3rd down eff	8-16	7-13
Passes	12-20-2	21-36-1
Punts	3-40.0	6-34.6
Fumbles-Lost	1-1	2-2
Penalties-Yards	8-55	5-31
Time of possession	36:05	23:55
Attendance—60,415.		

INDIVIDUAL STATISTICS
Rushing—Washington, Vital 26-136, T. Wilson 2-28, Jessie 9-23, Robinson 2-0, W. Wilson 3-minus 1; Dallas, Dorsett 19-81, D. White 2-12.

Passing—Washington, Robinson 11-18-2—152, Rubbert 1-2-0—22; Dallas, D. White 21-36-1—262.

Receiving—Washington, McEwen 7-108, Allen 2-31, T. Wilson 2-13; Dallas, Edwards 6-104, Renfro 5-79, G. White 4-35, Dorsett 2-11, E.J. Jones 2-13, Burbage 1-12, Adams 1-8.

Kickoff Returns—Washington, Jessie 2-41; Dallas, Lavette 2-32, Adams 1-20.

Punt Returns—Washington, Shepard 3-28; Dallas, Burbage 2-7.

Interceptions—Washington, Mitchell 1-17; Dallas, Haynes 2-7.

Punting—Washington, Weil 3-40.0; Dallas, Sawyer 5-34.6.

Field Goals—Washington, Ariri 2-3 (missed: 43); Dallas, none attempted.

Sacks—Washington, Rose, Cofer; Dallas, R. White, Haynes, Brooks.

SEVENTH WEEK

RESULTS OF WEEK 7

Sunday, October 25

Buffalo 34, Miami 31 (OT) at Mia.
Chicago 27, Tampa Bay 26 at T.B.
Green Bay 34, Detroit 33 at Det.
Houston 37, Atlanta 33 at Hous.
Indianapolis 30, New England 16 at Ind.
N.Y. Giants 30, St. Louis 7 at N.Y.
Philadelphia 37, Dallas 20 at Phila.
Pittsburgh 23, Cincinnati 20 at Pitts.
San Diego 42, Kansas City 21 at S.D.
San Francisco 24, New Orleans 22 at N.O.
Seattle 35, L.A. Raiders 13 at L.A.
Washington 17, N.Y. Jets 16 at Wash.

Monday, October 26

Cleveland 30, L.A. Rams 17 at Cleve.
Minnesota 34, Denver 27 at Minn.

After three weeks of replacement games, the National Football League resumed play in Week 7 with regular, unionized personnel.

As expected, there were hurt feelings between those players who honored the strike for the full three weeks and those veteran performers who returned to work in defiance of their union. Some teams retained a few of their strike replacement players on their regular rosters, and the inclusion of those players made for some tense situations.

But the fear of ugly incidents was unfounded. Petty jealousies and resentment were evident on most teams, but actual physical violence never occurred.

"The war is over and we have to get down to the business of playing football," said San Diego Chargers running back Lionel James, who did not play in any strike games. "Those guys (replacement players) are part of our team now. We play as a team and we stay together as a team."

But while all sides tried to put the past behind them, that didn't mean that everything that occurred the previous three weeks was forgotten—or forgiven.

The best example of that came in Philadelphia, where Eagles Coach Buddy Ryan got a measure of revenge against the Dallas Cowboys, a team that had beaten his Eagles, 41-22, in a strike game in Dallas two weeks earlier.

In the teams' first game October 11, Philadelphia, which had no regular players in the contest, was trailing by 19 points late in the game and was driving. However, the drive was snuffed out when Dallas Coach Tom Landry reinserted veteran defensive linemen Ed Jones and Randy White into the game. Eight regular Cowboys played in that first game.

Ryan vowed revenge and he got it. With a 30-20 lead late in the teams' second meeting, the Eagles took over on downs at the Dallas 28-yard line. On first and second downs, quarterback Randall Cunningham dropped to one knee, losing a total of five yards. Then, with 11 seconds left in the game, Cunningham faked going down, stood up and attempted a pass to Mike Quick in the end zone. Cowboys rookie Ron Francis was called for interference and the ball was moved to the Dallas 1-yard line. Running back Keith Byars then scored a touchdown with one second left for a 37-20 Philadelphia victory.

"I've been dreaming of that one for two weeks," Ryan said. "It's like the old cliche. What goes around comes around."

The Dallas players were livid.

"It was the pathetic ravings of a semi-senile old man," said linebacker Steve DeOssie. "If it makes him feel good. . . .they only did it to satisfy Buddy Ryan's overinflated ego."

Cunningham admitted as much. "It wasn't my idea," said the quarterback. "But Buddy called it, so I had to do it."

"I don't want to comment," said Landry, who in 28 years as an NFL head coach has probably seen just about everything. "It's not worthy of comment. Everybody has to live with themselves. I don't have to live with it. I was afraid it might be like this."

The Eagles weren't the only team to rebound with a Week 7 victory after its strike team lost three straight games.

The defending Super Bowl champion New York Giants, who entered the week as the NFL's only winless club, relieved their frustrations with a 30-7 thumping of St. Louis. The Giants dominated from start to finish, with the Cardinals' only touchdown coming in the final two minutes.

The play of New York's defense was reminiscent of their championship season, with four turnovers and five sacks of St. Louis quarterback Neil Lomax. Lomax, who had been sacked 55 times in his last 12 games against New York, threw two interceptions, fumbled a snap from center and fumbled on a sack.

Phil Simms, meanwhile, completed 17 of 21 passes to set a Giants team record for single-game pass completion percentage (80.9). Simms threw two touchdown passes to wide receiver Lionel Manuel and one to tight end Mark Bavaro.

Jim McMahon replaced Mike Tomczak as the Chicago quarterback with the Bears trailing NFC Central Division rival Tampa Bay, 23-14, at halftime. McMahon, who had won his last 23 games as a starter before an injury, went on to complete 17 of 24 passes for 195 yards to lead the Bears to a 27-26 victory.

The Buccaneers scored a team-record 20 first-quarter points on two touchdown passes by Steve DeBerg and a fumble recovery in the end zone by rookie Winston Moss. But the Bears, who won for the 10th straight time in the series, scored two touchdowns in the final six minutes to overcome a 26-14 deficit.

McMahon, who had not played in an NFL game since suffering a separated right shoulder on a late hit by Green Bay's Charles Martin 11 months earlier, cut the Tampa Bay lead to six points with a one-yard touchdown run with 5:31 left. He then completed six consecutive passes on the game-winning drive, throwing six yards to Neal Anderson for the touchdown with 1:28 left.

McMahon completed 12 of 14 passes for 145 yards on the two scoring drives.

In contrast to McMahon, Indianapolis' Jack Trudeau had never won a game as a starting quarterback. Trudeau broke that string in the 13th start of his NFL career, a 30-16 AFC East Division triumph over New England.

Trudeau, who helped the Colts snap a six-game losing streak to the Patriots, completed 17 of 28 passes for 239 yards and one touchdown.

The Indianapolis defense broke the game open with a touchdown midway through the third period to give the Colts a 23-6 lead. Linebacker Duane Bickett hit Pats quarterback Tony Eason, forcing a fumble, and end Donnell Thompson returned the loose ball 28 yards for a touchdown.

The victory was sweet for Colts Coach Ron Meyer, who exactly three years earlier had been fired as the New England head coach despite a 5-3 record.

The San Diego Chargers, one of three teams to go undefeated during the strike, continued their winning ways with a 42-21 victory over Kansas City. It was the Chargers' fifth straight win overall and the Chiefs' fifth straight loss. The Chargers' last loss and the Chiefs' last win came in Kansas City's 20-13 triumph over San Diego in Week 1.

San Diego kept eight players on its roster from the strike and one of them, defensive lineman Les Miller, recovered a fumble by Chiefs quarterback Bill Kenney in the end zone for a touchdown.

The Charger offense showed no ill effects from its month-long layoff. The unit rolled up 391 total yards, with quarterback Dan Fouts throwing for two scores and running for another while halfback Gary Anderson chipped in with two touchdown runs.

Another offense that didn't seem to have suffered from the strike belonged to Seattle, which converted nine of 10 third-down plays in the first two periods en route to a 28-0 halftime lead over the Los Angeles Raiders. The last of those four touchdowns, however, was scored by the Seahawk defense, with linebacker Fredd Young returning an interception 50 yards for a touchdown.

Seattle finished 14 of 19 in third-down conversions and running back Curt Warner rushed for 112 yards on 29 attempts to hand the

Jim McMahon (above) came off the bench to lead the Bears to victory while Curt Warner ran over the Raiders for 112 yards in Seattle's Week 7 victory.

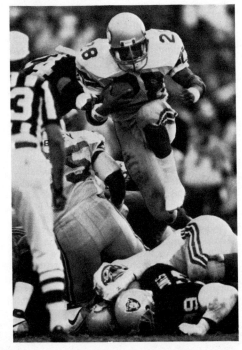

Raiders their third straight defeat, 35-13. It marked the first time in the last nine games between the AFC West Division rivals that the home team did not win.

For the second straight week, the Buffalo Bills won in overtime with a 27-yard field goal. Scott Norwood's field goal 4:12 into the extra period gave the Bills a 34-31 AFC East Division victory over Miami. A week earlier, replacement kicker Todd Schlopy had hit a 27-yarder with 19 seconds left in overtime for a 6-3 win over the New York Giants.

Buffalo's victory was its first over Miami since October 1983 and only the second in the last 12 meetings between the teams. Miami's overtime defeat was its second in as many weeks and 10th in 15 such games in club history.

The Dolphins never got the ball on offense in the overtime as Buffalo won the coin toss and drove 65 yards in eight plays to set up Norwood's winning kick.

Dolphins rookie Scott Schwedes, a second-round draft pick from Syracuse, fumbled a punt and a kickoff in the fourth quarter to help the Bills, trailing 24-17 at the time, score two touchdowns to take a 31-24 lead with 4:04 left. Miami then drove 80 yards in 11 plays and quarterback Dan Marino's fourth touchdown pass of the game, a 12-yarder to Mark Clayton with 1:03 left, sent the game into overtime.

Morten Andersen kicked field goals of 39, 49, 19, 19 and 37 yards before missing on a 52-yard attempt with seven seconds left that cemented New Orleans' 24-22 loss to San Francisco in an NFC West Division game.

New Orleans had to settle for field goals after driving inside the 49ers' 10-yard line two times in the third period. The Saints' only touchdown came on linebacker Alvin Toles' 11-yard return of a blocked punt.

The 49ers, who won for the fifth straight week, were led by quarterback Joe Montana's three touchdown passes, the last a 14-yarder to Mike Wilson for the game-winning points. That score came just five plays after Toles' touchdown had given the Saints a 19-17 lead with 13:24 left.

Pittsburgh's Gary Anderson, who was supplanted as the NFL's most accurate placekicker of all-time (minimum 100 field goals) by Morten Andersen in Week 7, kicked a 20-yard field goal with 1:47 left to lead the Steelers to a 23-20 victory over Cincinnati.

Anderson's winning kick was set up by the second of two interceptions by linebacker Bryan Hinkle, who fumbled trying to lateral the football. Teammate Thomas Everett recovered and, after Mark Malone and John Stallworth combined for a 45-yard completion to the Bengal 8-yard line, Anderson kicked the winning field goal.

Steelers rookie Delton Hall scored from 25 yards out after a Hinkle lateral following the linebacker's first interception in the third quarter.

The Steelers, who trailed the entire game, tied the game at 20-20 on Malone's 12-yard touchdown pass to Stallworth with 5:27 left.

Another interdivisional game that went down to the wire was played in Detroit, where the Green Bay Packers nipped the Lions, 34-33, on Al Del Greco's 45-yard field goal with a minute left. The Packers, who once led 31-7 before falling behind 33-31, drove 42 yards on nine plays to set up Del Greco's winning kick.

Detroit's Eddie Murray missed a 45-yard field goal as time expired.

Green Bay quarterback Don Majkowski was steady if not spectacular in his second NFL start, completing 19 of 29 attempts for 323 yards and a 70-yard touchdown pass to Walter Stanley. His counterpart, the Lions' Chuck Long, set career highs with 33 completions in 47 attempts for 362 yards and three touchdowns in a losing effort.

The Lions rushed for just 17 yards on 12 attempts.

A crowd of 53,497 at Washington's RFK Stadium booed the Redskins when they took the field for their Week 7 interconference game with the New York Jets. And the boos got louder when the Redskins—whose strike replacement team spoiled the fans by going undefeated—fell behind and trailed the Jets for most of the game.

But the boos turned to cheers when the Redskins, behind quarterback Jay Schroeder, scored 10 points in the final 5:15 to pull out a 17-16 victory. Schroeder, who completed just nine of his first 28 passes, connected on six of his final 10 in the two late scoring drives. Schroeder's two-yard touchdown pass to Kelvin Bryant cut the Jets' lead to 16-14 before Ali Haji-Sheikh's 28-yard field goal with 54 seconds remaining won it for Washington.

The Jets, who have never beaten the Redskins in four meetings, converted just one of 14 third-down attempts.

Warren Moon of the Houston Oilers could empathize with the Redskins. Moon, the Oilers' quarterback and player rep, was booed loudly by a crowd of 29,062 at the Astrodome before the Oilers-Atlanta Falcons game. But Moon, a $1 million-a-year player who lost a lot of money because of the strike, won over at least some of his detractors by driving the Oilers 80 yards on seven plays for the game-winning touchdown in a 37-33 victory.

After Mick Luckhurst, the Falcons' player rep, kicked his fourth field goal to give Atlanta a 33-30 lead with 2:24 left, the Oilers took over at their own 20-yard line with no timeouts. Moon completed 29-yard passes to Drew Hill and Ernest Givins before climaxing the drive with a 14-yard touchdown pass to Curtis Duncan with 27 seconds remaining.

The touchdown catch was the second of the

Washington quarterback Jay Schroeder turned boos to cheers by rallying the Redskins to 10 points in the final 5:15 for a 17-16 victory over the New York Jets.

game for Duncan, who had just one NFL reception prior to the game.

Because of the Minnesota Twins' appearance in the World Series, there were two Monday night games instead of the customary one.

The Minnesota Vikings, who had their Sunday afternoon game at the Metrodome moved to Monday because of the seventh game of the Series, edged the Denver Broncos, 34-27, in an interconference game. Rookie running back D.J. Dozier scored three touchdowns for the Vikings despite rushing for just 15 yards.

Teammate Darrin Nelson, however, rushed for 98 yards and set up two of Dozier's touchdowns with runs of 76 and 16 yards.

The regularly scheduled and nationally televised Monday night game saw the Cleveland Browns defeat the Los Angeles Rams, 30-17. The Browns blew open the game by scoring 20 points in the second period, with safety Felix Wright's 40-yard interception return giving the Browns a commanding 17-0 lead.

It was the second interception of the game for Wright, who earlier returned an interception of a Jim Everett pass at the Cleveland goal line 68 yards to set up the first of rookie Jeff Jaeger's three field goals.

The game marked the final appearance in a Rams uniform for running back Eric Dickerson, who was dealt to the Indianapolis Colts five days later in one of the biggest trades in recent NFL history. Dickerson, who won the league rushing title in three of his four seasons with the Rams, asked to be traded after the team would not meet his salary demands.

In his final game with Los Angeles, Dickerson played only in the second quarter because of an aggravated charley horse and rushed seven times for 38 yards. He scored the Rams' first points on a 27-yard touchdown run late in the first half. His replacement in the L.A. backfield, Charles White, rushed for 54 yards on 13 carries and scored the team's only other touchdown.

Patriots-Colts
SUNDAY, OCTOBER 25
SCORE BY PERIODS

New England	3	3	7	3—16
Indianapolis	0	10	13	7—30

SCORING

New England—Field goal Franklin 38, 9:01 1st.
New England—Field goal Franklin 31, 7:18 2nd.
Indianapolis—Bouza 25 pass from Trudeau (Biasucci kick), 13:06 2nd.
Indianapolis—Field goal Biasucci 48, 14:32 2nd.
Indianapolis—Field goal Biasucci 38, 3:49 3rd.
Indianapolis—Field goal Biasucci 24, 8:04 3rd.
Indianapolis—Thompson 28 fumble return (Biasucci kick), 9:46 3rd.
New England—Morgan 27 pass from Eason (Franklin kick), 13:18 3rd.
New England—Field goal Franklin 49, 6:08 4th.
Indianapolis—Bentley 12 run (Biasucci kick), 11:35 4th.

TEAM STATISTICS

	New England	Indianapolis
First downs	18	17
Rushes-Yards	27-79	25-87
Passing yards	225	213
Sacked-Yards lost	2-21	3-26
3rd down eff	6-17	3-12
Passes	22-43-1	17-28-0
Punts	5-36.0	5-44.6
Fumbles-Lost	2-2	3-1
Penalties-Yards	5-40	9-65
Time of possession	32:54	27:06
Attendance—48,850.		

INDIVIDUAL STATISTICS

Rushing—New England, Tatupu 12-39, Collins 11-23, Eason 2-21, Davis 2-minus 4; Indianapolis, Bentley 16-65,

Wonsley 7-27, Trudeau 1-minus 2, Brooks 1-minus 3.

Passing—New England, Eason 22-42-1—246, Jones 0-1-0-0; Indianapolis, Trudeau 17-28-0—239.

Receiving—New England, Morgan 7-102, Baty 4-49, Starring 3-42, Collins 4-32, Fryar 2-13, Dawson 2-8; Indianapolis, Bentley 4-53, Bouza 3-53, Sherwin 2-39, Beach 2-25, Murray 1-23, Brooks 2-23, Wonsley 2-18, Boyer 1-5.

Kickoff Returns—New England, Starring 6-125; Indianapolis, Wright 5-103.

Punt Returns—New England, Fryar 1-20, Starring 1-17; Indianapolis, Brooks 3-26.

Interceptions—Indianapolis, Prior 1-38.

Punting—New England, Camarillo 4-45.0; Indianapolis, Stark 5-44.6.

Field Goals—New England, Franklin 3-3; Indianapolis, Biasucci 3-3.

Sacks—New England, Lippett 2, Veris; Indianapolis, Bickett, Thompson.

Bills-Dolphins
SUNDAY, OCTOBER 25
SCORE BY PERIODS

Buffalo	0	3	14	14	3—34
Miami	14	7	0	10	0—31

SCORING

Miami—Duper 5 pass from Marino (Reveiz kick), 6:19 1st.

Miami—Pruitt 25 pass from Marino (Reveiz kick), 11:13 1st.

Miami—Hardy 2 pass from Marino (Reveiz kick), 8:33 2nd.

Buffalo—Field goal Norwood 41, 14:59 2nd.

Buffalo—Riddick 1 run (Norwood kick), 8:11 3rd.

Buffalo—Burkett 14 pass from Kelly (Norwood kick), 13:43 3rd.

Miami—Field goal Reveiz 46, 3:02 4th.

Buffalo—Riddick 1 run (Norwood kick), 7:47 4th.

Buffalo—Riddick 17 pass from Kelly (Norwood kick), 10:56 4th.

Miami—Clayton 12 pass from Marino (Reveiz kick), 13:57 4th.

Buffalo—Field goal Norwood 27, 4:12 OT.

TEAM STATISTICS

	Buffalo	Miami
First downs	29	21
Rushes-Yards	39-144	20-70
Passing yards	330	296
Sacked-Yards lost	3-29	1-7
3rd down eff.	7-13	5-10
Passes	29-39-0	24-36-0
Punts	3-38.3	3-34.3
Fumbles-Lost	1-0	3-2
Penalties-Yards	8-55	6-40
Time of possession	37:25	26:47
Attendance—61,295.		

INDIVIDUAL STATISTICS

Rushing—Buffalo, Harmon 2-45, Kelly 4-21, Byrum 3-5, Riddick 18-66, Mueller 2-7; Miami, W. Bennett 3-9, Hampton 13-52, Stradford 3-5, Clayton 1-4.

Passing—Buffalo, Kelly 29-39-0—359; Miami, Marino 24-36-0—303.

Receiving—Buffalo, Metzelaars 6-85, Harmon 5-43, Riddick 5-38, Burkett 9-130, Reed 4-63; Miami, Clayton 6-81, Duper 4-45, Pruitt 2-45, Hardy 2-6, Jensen 3-36, Hampton 1-18, Stradford 6-72.

Kickoff Returns—Buffalo, Tasker 2-43, Riddick 3-61, Mueller 1-20; Miami, Hardy 1-8, Stradford 2-36, Schwedes 2-58.

Punt Returns—Buffalo, Pitts 3-24; Miami, B. Brown 1-0, Schwedes 2-17.

Interceptions—None.

Punting—Buffalo, Kidd 3-38.3; Miami, Hayes 3-34.4.

Field Goals—Buffalo, Norwood 2-4 (missed: 22, 43); Miami, Reveiz 1-1.

Sacks—Buffalo, Smith; Miami, Graf, Brudzinski, Turner.

Bears-Buccaneers
SUNDAY, OCTOBER 25
SCORE BY PERIODS

Chicago	0	14	0	13—27	
Tampa Bay	20	3	3	0—26	

SCORING

Tampa Bay—Magee 7 pass from DeBerg (Igwebuike kick), 5:47 1st.

Tampa Bay—Smith 28 pass from DeBerg (Igwebuike kick), 10:13 1st.

Tampa Bay—Moss recovered fumble in end zone (kick blocked), 11:50 1st.

Chicago—Anderson 38 run (Butler kick), 2:23 2nd.

Chicago—McKinnon 65 punt return (Butler kick), 5:50 2nd.

Tampa Bay—Field goal Igwebuike 46, 13:04 2nd.

Tampa Bay—Field goal Igwebuike 37, 8:59 3rd.

Chicago—McMahon 1 run (kick failed), 9:29 4th.

Chicago—Anderson 6 pass from McMahon (Butler kick), 13:32 4th.

TEAM STATISTICS

	Chicago	Tampa Bay
First downs	19	20
Rushes-Yards	14-91	26-101
Passing yards	209	184
Sacked-Yards lost	4-31	7-65
3rd down eff.	2-6	5-16
Passes	23-34-1	23-38-0
Punts	2-40.5	5-32.8
Fumbles-Lost	4-3	4-0
Penalties-Yards	10-58	11-75
Time of possession	24:38	35:22
Attendance—70,747.		

INDIVIDUAL STATISTICS

Rushing—Chicago, Payton 6-30, Anderson 6-52, McMahon 2-9; Tampa Bay, Wilder 19-75, Smith 6-26, DeBerg 1-0.

Passing—Chicago, Tomczak 6-10-0—45, McMahon 17-24-1—195; Tampa Bay, DeBerg 23-38-0—249.

Receiving—Chicago, Anderson 7-45, Moorehead 2-13, McKinnon 3-25, Gault 4-67, Payton 2-0, Morris 3-55, Boso 2-35; Tampa Bay, Freeman 1-16, Hall 4-32, Smith 3-47, Carter 2-13, Magee 6-98, Miller 1-16, Wilder 4-7, Carrier 2-20.

Kickoff Returns—Chicago, Gentry 5-121, Sanders 1-31; Tampa Bay, Futrell 3-59.

Punt Returns—Chicago, McKinnon 3-89; Tampa Bay, Futrell 2-11.

Interceptions—Tampa Bay, Woods 1-21.

Punting—Chicago, Wagner 2-40.5; Tampa Bay, Garcia 5-32.8.

Field Goals—Chicago, Butler 0-1 (missed: 47); Tampa Bay, Igwebuike 2-2.

Sacks—Chicago, Dent 2, Wilson 1½, Hampton, McMichael ½, Duerson, Marshall; Tampa Bay, Holmes 2½, Keys ½, Cannon.

49ers-Saints
SUNDAY, OCTOBER 25
SCORE BY PERIODS

San Francisco	7	10	0	7—24	
New Orleans	3	3	6	10—22	

SCORING

New Orleans—Field goal Andersen 39, 5:55 1st.

San Francisco—Rice 8 pass from Montana (Wersching kick), 12:40 1st.

San Francisco—Heller 39 pass from Montana (Wersching kick), 5:18 2nd.

San Francisco—Field goal Wersching 31, 13:32 2nd.

New Orleans—Field goal Andersen 49, 14:58 2nd.

New Orleans—Field goal Andersen 19, 6:55 3rd.

New Orleans—Field goal Andersen 19, 14:22 3rd.

New Orleans—Toles 11 blocked punt return (Andersen kick), 1:36 4th.
San Francisco—Wilson 14 pass from Montana (Wersching kick), 3:34 4th.
New Orleans—Field goal Andersen 37, 9:10 4th.

TEAM STATISTICS

	San Francisco	New Orleans
First downs	23	20
Rushes-Yards	26-75	43-177
Passing yards	228	202
Sacked-Yards lost	4-28	0-0
3rd down eff.	6-13	4-13
Passes	18-32-0	14-27-1
Punts	6-34.3	3-45.0
Fumbles-Lost	2-2	4-1
Penalties-Yards	4-36	7-83
Time of possession	24:22	35:38

Attendance—60,497.

INDIVIDUAL STATISTICS

Rushing—San Francisco, Flagler 4-8, Craig 15-55, Montana 4-3, DuBose 3-9; New Orleans, Word 5-7, Mayes 29-144, Gray 2-minus 1, Hebert 1-9, Hilliard 6-18.

Passing—San Francisco, Montana 18-32-0—256; New Orleans, Hebert 14-27-1—202.

Receiving—San Francisco, Flagler 1-24, Francis 1-3, Rice 6-89, Wilson 3-38, Heller 1-39, Craig 5-50, Taylor 1-13; New Orleans, Jones 3-67, Mayes 2-8, Hill 4-93, Gray 2-8, Brenner 2-22, Tice 1-4.

Kickoff Returns—San Francisco, Sydney 1-22, Rodgers 2-35; New Orleans, Gray 4-88.

Punt Returns—San Francisco, McLemore 1-9; New Orleans, Gray 1-6.

Interceptions—San Francisco, McColl 1-0.

Punting—San Francisco, Runager 5-41.2; New Orleans, Hansen 3-45.0.

Field Goals—San Francisco, Wersching 1-1; New Orleans, Andersen 5-7 (missed: 51, 52).

Sacks—New Orleans, B. Clark, Wilks, Swilling 2.

Seahawks-Raiders
SUNDAY, OCTOBER 25
SCORE BY PERIODS

Seattle	7	21	0	7—35
Los Angeles Raiders	0	0	7	6—13

SCORING

Seattle—Warner 1 run (N. Johnson kick), 7:41 1st.
Seattle—R. Butler 15 pass from Krieg (N. Johnson kick), 5:00 2nd.
Seattle—Warner 6 run (N. Johnson kick), 12:00 2nd.
Seattle—Young 50 interception return (N. Johnson kick), 14:04 2nd.
Los Angeles—Christensen 7 pass from Wilson (Bahr kick), 3:59 3rd.
Los Angeles—Do. Williams 14 pass from Wilson (kick failed), 2:12 4th.
Seattle—R. Butler 31 pass from Krieg (N. Johnson kick), 10:42 4th.

TEAM STATISTICS

	Seattle	Los Angeles
First downs	21	18
Rushes-Yards	44-144	13-44
Passing yards	149	206
Sacked-Yards lost	5-43	5-45
3rd down eff.	14-19	2-11
Passes	14-20-1	20-40-3
Punts	5-44.0	5-41.4
Fumbles-Lost	2-1	0-0
Penalties-Yards	5-55	7-47
Time of possession	37:47	22:13

Attendance—52,735.

INDIVIDUAL STATISTICS

Rushing—Seattle, Warner 29-112, J. Williams 7-12, Morris 5-12, Krieg 3-8; Los Angeles, Allen 11-29, Mueller

1-10, Hilger 1-5.

Passing—Seattle, Krieg 14-20-1—192; Los Angeles, Hilger 7-13-1—78, Wilson 13-27-2—173.

Receiving—Seattle, Largent 5-56, R. Butler 4-73, Warner 2-33, B. Williams 1-15, Tice 1-6; Los Angeles, Christensen 8-124, Fernandez 3-33, Allen 3-14, Lofton 2-34, Mueller 2-24, Do. Williams 2-22.

Kickoff Returns—Seattle, Edmonds 1-15; Los Angeles, Adams 1-19, Do. Williams 1-14, Mueller 3-59.

Punt Returns—Seattle, Edmonds 2-17; Los Angeles, Fellows 2-19.

Interceptions—Seattle, Easley 2-25, Young 1-50; Los Angeles, McElroy 1-0.

Punting—Seattle, Rodriguez 5-44.0; Los Angeles, Talley 5-41.4.

Field Goals—Seattle, none attempted; Los Angeles, Bahr 0-1 (missed: 48).

Sacks—Seattle, Young, Bryant 3, Green; Los Angeles, Robinson, Long, Taylor, Townsend, Jones.

Chiefs-Chargers
SUNDAY, OCTOBER 25
SCORE BY PERIODS

Kansas City	0	14	7	0—21
San Diego	14	21	0	7—42

SCORING

San Diego—Chandler 10 pass from Fouts (Abbott kick), 5:14 1st.
San Diego—Anderson 1 run (Abbott kick), 14:50 1st.
San Diego—Miller recovered fumble in end zone (Abbott kick), 3:34 2nd.
San Diego—Fouts 1 run (Abbott kick), 8:37 2nd.
Kansas City—Carson 14 pass from Kenney (Lowery kick), 10:26 2nd.
San Diego—Winslow 19 pass from Fouts (Abbott kick), 13:43 2nd.
Kansas City—Carson 63 pass from Kenney (Lowery kick), 13:57 2nd.
Kansas City—Okoye 1 run (Lowery kick), 7:23 3rd.
San Diego—Anderson 1 run (Abbott kick), 3:16 4th.

TEAM STATISTICS

	Kansas City	San Diego
First downs	21	30
Rushes-Yards	15-66	39-114
Passing yards	305	277
Sacked-Yards lost	7-39	3-16
3rd down eff.	4-11	4-11
Passes	23-39-1	24-34-0
Punts	5-42.6	5-43.2
Fumbles-Lost	4-4	3-2
Penalties-Yards	12-141	11-118
Time of possession	23:00	37:00

Attendance—47,972.

INDIVIDUAL STATISTICS

Rushing—Kansas City, Okoye 8-44, Heard 7-22; San Diego, Spencer 8-15, Adams 6-20, Anderson 13-20, James 6-40, Fouts 1-1, Redden 5-18.

Passing—Kansas City, Kenney 22-38-1—328, Blackledge 1-1-0—16; San Diego, Fouts 24-34-0—293.

Receiving—Kansas City, Okoye 4-45, Carson 9-197, Paige 3-48, Marshall 3-30, Heard 2-10, Moriarty 2-14; San Diego, Ware 1-23, Winslow 4-58, Holohan 5-53, Chandler 2-25, Bernstine 1-15, James 5-72, Adams 1-21, Anderson 5-26.

Kickoff Returns—Kansas City, Robinson 1-12, Palmer 6-119; San Diego, Holland 3-73.

Punt Returns—Kansas City, Clemons 2-16, D. Colbert 1-11; San Diego, James 3-50.

Interceptions—San Diego, Smith 1-0.

Punting—Kansas City, Goodburn 5-42.6; San Diego, Mojsiejenko 5-43.2.

Field Goals—None attempted.

Sacks—Kansas City, Maas 1½, Koch ½, Bell; San Diego, Ehin 2, L. Williams, Phillips, Unrein, Benson, Bayless.

Cowboys-Eagles
SUNDAY, OCTOBER 25
SCORE BY PERIODS

Dallas	3	7	3	7—20
Philadelphia	3	10	7	17—37

SCORING
Dallas—Field goal Ruzek 23, 7:42 1st.
Philadelphia—Field goal McFadden 46, 14:15 1st.
Philadelphia—Field goal McFadden 45, 1:57 2nd.
Philadelphia—Spagnola 10 pass from Cunningham (McFadden kick), 8:46 2nd.
Dallas—Walker 1 run (Ruzek kick), 13:38 2nd.
Dallas—Field goal Ruzek 25, 4:32 3rd.
Philadelphia—Toney 1 run (McFadden kick), 9:39 3rd.
Philadelphia—Field goal McFadden 21, 2:50 4th.
Philadelphia—Spagnola 5 pass from Cunningham (McFadden kick), 6:53 4th.
Dallas—Dorsett 19 pass from D. White (Ruzek kick), 12:02 4th.
Philadelphia—Byars 1 run (McFadden kick), 14:59 4th.

TEAM STATISTICS

	Dallas	Philadelphia
First downs	18	18
Rushes-Yards	26-97	34-141
Passing yards	197	96
Sacked-Yards lost	5-60	4-31
3rd down eff.	4-14	5-14
Passes	22-36-0	10-24-0
Punts	4-39.5	4-36.8
Fumbles-Lost	5-3	2-1
Penalties-Yards	10-113	6-27
Time of possession	31:13	28:47
Attendance—61,630.		

INDIVIDUAL STATISTICS
Rushing—Dallas, Walker 12-54, Dorsett 11-32, Newsome 2-10, Pelluer 1-1; Philadelphia, Byars 20-94, Cunningham 8-39, Toney 6-8.

Passing—Dallas, D. White 22-36-0—257; Philadelphia, Cunningham 10-24-0—127.

Receiving—Dallas, Cosbie 6-31, Banks 4-59, Dorsett 3-40, Edwards 3-38, Renfro 2-41, Walker 2-14, Newsome 1-30, Barksdale 1-4; Philadelphia, Quick 3-61, Toney 3-43, Spagnola 2-15, Tautalatasi 2-8.

Kickoff Returns—Dallas, Newsome 1-12, Edwards 1-20, Chandler 1-7, Clack 3-80; Philadelphia, Morse 3-46, Cooper 1-11.

Punt Returns—Dallas, Edwards 1-9; Philadelphia, Garrity 2-2.

Interceptions—None.

Punting—Dallas, Saxon 4-39.5; Philadelphia, Teltschik 4-36.8.

Field Goals—Dallas, Ruzek 2-3 (missed: 49); Philadelphia, McFadden 3-4 (missed: 28).

Sacks—Dallas, R. White, Rohrer, Lockhart, Brooks; Philadelphia, Simmons 2, White 1½, Clarke ½, Joyner.

Jets-Redskins
SUNDAY, OCTOBER 25
SCORE BY PERIODS

New York Jets	0	3	10	3—16
Washington	0	7	0	10—17

SCORING
Washington—Clark 20 pass from Schroeder (Haji-Sheikh kick), 3:39 2nd.
New York—Field goal Leahy 33, 12:35 2nd.
New York—Field goal Leahy 23, 7:21 3rd.
New York—Shuler 15 pass from O'Brien (Leahy kick), 14:54 3rd.
New York—Field goal Leahy 39, 4:22 4th.
Washington—Bryant 2 pass from Schroeder (Haji-Sheikh kick), 9:45 4th.
Washington—Field goal Haji-Sheikh 28, 14:06 4th.

TEAM STATISTICS

	New York	Washington
First downs	14	16
Rushes-Yards	25-74	26-103
Passing yards	126	275
Sacked-Yards lost	7-48	0-0
3rd down eff.	1-14	4-15
Passes	18-27-1	15-38-1
Punts	8-37.7	7-32.4
Fumbles-Lost	1-0	2-1
Penalties-Yards	1-10	7-55
Time of possession	31:00	29:00
Attendance—53,497.		

INDIVIDUAL STATISTICS
Rushing—New York, McNeil 12-16, Vick 4-29, Hector 8-22, O'Brien 1-7; Washington, Griffin 20-79, Schroeder 2-2, Rogers 1-5, Bryant 3-17.

Passing—New York, O'Brien 18-27-1—174; Washington, Schroeder 15-38-1—275.

Receiving—New York, Toon 9-97, Shuler 3.31, McNeil 2-8, Sohn 1-15, Hector 2-11, Klever 1-12; Washington, Monk 3-70, Clark 3-52, Sanders 3-53, Warren 1-8, Bryant 4-67, Didier 1-25.

Kickoff Returns—New York, Townsell 1-57, Humphery 3-44; Washington, Griffin 2-23, Orr 1-16.

Punt Returns—New York, Townsell 4-60; Washington, Yarber 7-16.

Interceptions—New York, Miano 1-0; Washington, Wilburn 1-0.

Punting—New York, Jennings 8-37.7; Washington, Cox 7-32.4.

Field Goals—New York, Leahy 3-4 (missed: 62); Washington, Haji-Sheikh 1-2 (missed: 41).

Sacks—Washington, Mann 3, Coleman 2, Grant, Butz.

Bengals-Steelers
SUNDAY, OCTOBER 25
SCORE BY PERIODS

Cincinnati	7	7	6	0—20
Pittsburgh	3	0	7	13—23

SCORING
Cincinnati—Kinnebrew 2 run (Breech kick), 4:51 1st.
Pittsburgh—Field goal G. Anderson 45, 9:29 1st.
Cincinnati—Martin 41 pass from Esiason (Breech kick), 9:50 2nd.
Pittsburgh—Hall 25 run with lateral of interception (G. Anderson kick), 11:56 3rd.
Cincinnati—Jennings 9 pass from Esiason (kick blocked), 12:30 3rd.
Pittsburgh—Field goal G. Anderson 21, 2:33 4th.
Pittsburgh—Stallworth 12 pass from Malone (G. Anderson kick), 9:33 4th.
Pittsburgh—Field goal G. Anderson 20, 13:13 4th.

TEAM STATISTICS

	Cincinnati	Pittsburgh
First downs	17	17
Rushes-Yards	27-141	33-78
Passing yards	292	204
Sacked-Yards lost	1-11	2-14
3rd down eff.	5-14	4-14
Passes	20-32-2	18-30-0
Punts	6-41.0	7-45.3
Fumbles-Lost	0-0	2-0
Penalties-Yards	8-56	3-18
Time of possession	28:46	31:14
Attendance—53,692.		

INDIVIDUAL STATISTICS
Rushing—Cincinnati, Brooks 15-53, Kinnebrew 11-85, Esiason 1-3; Pittsburgh, Jackson 17-38, Abercrombie 15-39, Stone 1-1.

Passing—Cincinnati, Esiason 20-32-2—303; Pittsburgh, Malone 18-30-0—218.

Receiving—Cincinnati, Collinsworth 6-93, Brooks 6-67, Holman 1-19, Brown 2-19, Martin 2-56, Jennings 1-9,

McGee 2-40; Pittsburgh, Lee 1-7, Thompson 1-17, Abercrombie 2-30, Stallworth 7-100, Lockett 2-24, Sweeney 3-21, Jackson 2-19.

Kickoff Returns—Cincinnati, McGee 5-77; Pittsburgh, Stone 4-86.

Punt Returns—Cincinnati, Martin 5-54; Pittsburgh, Everett 4-22.

Interceptions—Pittsburgh, Hinkle 2-11, Hall 0-25.

Punting—Cincinnati, Horne 6-41.0; Pittsburgh, Newsome 7-45.3.

Field Goals—Cincinnati, none attempted; Pittsburgh, G. Anderson 3-3.

Sacks—Cincinnati, Skow, Williams; Pittsburgh, Willis.

Falcons-Oilers
SUNDAY, OCTOBER 25
SCORE BY PERIODS

Atlanta	3	10	14	6—33
Houston	3	10	7	17—37

SCORING

Atlanta—Field goal Luckhurst 39, 4:45 1st.
Houston—Field goal Zendejas 31, 11:03 1st.
Atlanta—Field goal Luckhurst 37, 0:26 2nd.
Houston—Field goal Zendejas 43, 4:17 2nd.
Atlanta—Dixon 10 pass from Campbell (Luckhurst kick), 7:43 2nd.
Houston—Duncan 41 pass from Moon (Zendejas kick), 13:40 2nd.
Houston—Givins 8 pass from Moon (Zendejas kick), 4:59 3rd.
Atlanta—Bailey 29 pass from Campbell (Luckhurst kick), 11:03 3rd.
Atlanta—Whisenhunt 3 pass from Campbell (Luckhurst kick), 14:01 3rd.
Houston—Rozier 14 run (Zendejas kick), 2:09 4th.
Houston—Field goal Zendejas 24, 5:38 4th.
Atlanta—Field goal Luckhurst 45, 8:15 4th.
Atlanta—Field goal Luckhurst 18, 12:36 4th.
Houston—Duncan 14 pass from Moon (Zendejas kick), 14:33 4th.

TEAM STATISTICS

	Atlanta	Houston
First downs	14	24
Rushes-Yards	26-121	43-205
Passing yards	183	234
Sacked-Yards lost	1-4	1-8
3rd down eff.	1-9	8-18
Passes	14-26-1	15-35-2
Punts	3-46.0	5-42.4
Fumbles-Lost	6-4	0-0
Penalties-Yards	4-27	6-46
Time of possession	24:19	35:41
Attendance—29,062.		

INDIVIDUAL STATISTICS

Rushing—Atlanta, Riggs 21-113, Campbell 3-1, Flowers 1-1, Stamps 1-6; Houston, Rozier 29-144, Wallace 4-13, Moon 6-26, Tillman 4-22.

Passing—Atlanta, Campbell 14-26-1—187; Houston, Moon 15-34-2—242, Hill 0-1-0—0.

Receiving—Atlanta, Whisenhunt 3-14, Riggs 1-31, Bailey 4-56, Dixon 3-50, Cox 1-19, Matthews 2-17; Houston, Rozier 3-14, Givins 5-99, Drewrey 1-16, Wallace 2-7, Duncan 2-55, D. Hill 2-51.

Kickoff Returns—Atlanta, Stamps 5-193, Griffin 1-21; Houston, Duncan 4-76, Pinkett 4-84.

Punt Returns—Atlanta, Johnson 2-43; Houston, Duncan 2-8.

Interceptions—Atlanta, B. Butler 1-31, Moore 1-18; Houston, R. Johnson 1-0.

Punting—Atlanta, Donnelly 3-46.0; Houston, L. Johnson 5-42.4.

Field Goals—Atlanta, Luckhurst 4-4; Houston, Zendejas 3-3.

Sacks—Atlanta, Gann; Houston, Bostic.

Packers-Lions
SUNDAY, OCTOBER 25
SCORE BY PERIODS

Green Bay	21	10	0	3—34
Detroit	0	16	3	14—33

SCORING

Green Bay—Fullwood 1 run (Del Greco kick), 4:03 1st.
Green Bay—Stanley 70 pass from Majkowski (Del Greco kick), 6:23 1st.
Green Bay—Davis 39 run (Del Greco kick), 9:40 1st.
Green Bay—Field goal Del Greco 22, 2:19 2nd.
Detroit—Bland 11 pass from Long (Murray kick), 8:55 2nd.
Green Bay—Davis 28 run (Del Greco kick), 13:07 2nd.
Detroit—Mandley 12 pass from Long (Murray kick), 14:43 2nd.
Detroit—Safety, Stanley tackled in end zone by Jamison, 14:45 2nd.
Detroit—Field goal Murray 23, 11:02 3rd.
Detroit—Mandley 22 pass from Long (Murray kick), 5:53 4th.
Detroit—James 2 run (Murray kick), 11:58 4th.
Green Bay—Field goal Del Greco 45, 14:00 4th.

TEAM STATISTICS

	Green Bay	Detroit
First downs	23	23
Rushes-Yards	38-172	12-17
Passing yards	293	336
Sacked-Yards lost	3-30	3-26
3rd down eff.	6-14	4-11
Passes	19-29-1	33-47-0
Punts	2-46.5	6-46.2
Fumbles-Lost	3-2	1-1
Penalties-Yards	4-20	6-30
Time of possession	34:57	25:03
Attendance—27,278.		

INDIVIDUAL STATISTICS

Rushing—Green Bay, Davis 23-129, Fullwood 7-27, Clark 4-9, Carruth 3-5, Majkowski 1-2; Detroit, James 8-8, Jones 3-8, Long 1-1.

Passing—Green Bay, Majkowski 19-29-1—323; Detroit, Long 33-47-0—362.

Receiving—Green Bay, Stanley 6-150, Epps 3-63, Neal 3-24, West 2-26, Clark 2-4, Davis 1-35, Carruth 1-15, Paskett 1-6; Detroit, Jones 9-81, James 7-91, Chadwick 7-81, Mandley 6-77, Nichols 2-17, Bland 1-11, Giles 1-4.

Kickoff Returns—Green Bay, Cook 3-44, Fullwood 1-32, Stanley 1-minus 2; Detroit, Lee 7-141, Bland 1-22.

Punt Returns—Green Bay, Stanley 3-9.

Interceptions—Detroit, Griffin 1-29.

Punting—Green Bay, Bracken 2-46.5; Detroit, Arnold 6-46.2.

Field Goals—Green Bay, Del Greco 2-3 (missed: 32); Detroit, Murray 1-2 (missed: 45).

Sacks—Green Bay, Boyarsky, Harris 2; Detroit, Griffin, Ball, Cofer.

Cardinals-Giants
SUNDAY, OCTOBER 25
SCORE BY PERIODS

St. Louis	0	0	0	7— 7
New York Giants	14	3	3	10—30

SCORING

New York—Bavaro 3 pass from Simms (Allegre kick), 4:14 1st.
New York—Manuel 16 pass from Simms (Allegre kick), 11:34 1st.
New York—Field goal Allegre 28, 12:24 2nd.
New York—Field goal Allegre 35, 11:54 3rd.
New York—Manuel 38 pass from Simms (Allegre kick), 5:27 4th.
New York—Field goal Allegre 32, 5:16 4th.

St. Louis—Novacek 18 pass from Lomax (Gallery kick), 13:05 4th.

TEAM STATISTICS

	St. Louis	New York
First downs	19	21
Rushes-Yards	19-51	43-162
Passing yards	257	232
Sacked-Yards lost	5-23	3-21
3rd down eff.	2-10	5-13
Passes	23-32-2	17-21-0
Punts	5-38.0	4-45.8
Fumbles-Lost	3-2	2-1
Penalties-Yards	7-63	6-40
Time of possession	24:22	35:38

Attendance—74,391.

INDIVIDUAL STATISTICS

Rushing—St. Louis, Mitchell 12-39, McAdoo 1-5, Ferrell 3-minus 10, Lomax 3-17; New York, Morris 22-88, Adams 5-24, Rouson 7-18, Galbreath 1-0, Baker 1-18, Carthon 5-17, Simms 2-minus 3.

Passing—St. Louis, Lomax 23-32-2—280; New York, Simms 17-21-0—253.

Receiving—St. Louis, Ferrell 3-31, Mitchell 5-49, Green 5-72, Novacek 4-53, McAdoo 1-6, J.T. Smith 3-49, T. Johnson 1-5, Wolfley 1-15; New York, Bavaro 3-38, Adams 6-78, Robinson 1-9, Manuel 2-54, Morris 1-9, Mowatt 2-38, McConkey 1-31, Galbreath 1-minus 4.

Kickoff Returns—St. Louis, Sikahema 5-97, McAdoo 2-45.

Punt Returns—St. Louis, Sikahema 2-19; New York, McConkey 3-29.

Interceptions—New York, Collins 1-0, Hill 1-1.

Punting—St. Louis, Cater 5-38.0; New York, Landeta 4-45.8.

Field Goals—St. Louis, none attempted; New York, Allegre 3-3.

Sacks—St. Louis, Nunn 2, Greer; New York, Banks 1½, Headen ½, Marshall, Howard 2.

Rams-Browns
MONDAY, OCTOBER 26
SCORE BY PERIODS

Los Angeles Rams	0	7	10	0—17
Cleveland	3	20	7	0—30

SCORING

Cleveland—Field goal Jaeger 23, 10:13 1st.
Cleveland—Mack 16 run (Jaeger kick), 1:34 2nd.
Cleveland—Wright 40 interception return (Jaeger kick), 3:07 2nd.
Cleveland—Field goal Jaeger 48, 7:15 2nd.
Los Angeles—Dickerson 27 run (Lansford kick), 13:29 2nd.
Cleveland—Field goal Jaeger 40, 15:00 2nd.
Cleveland—Brennan 53 pass from Kosar (Jaeger kick), 1:02 3rd.
Los Angeles—White 1 run (Lansford kick), 6:46 3rd.
Los Angeles—Field goal Lansford 27, 13:18 3rd.

TEAM STATISTICS

	Los Angeles	Cleveland
First downs	22	15
Rushes-Yards	24-101	23-65
Passing yards	227	202
Sacked-Yards lost	0-0	3-21
3rd down eff.	5-16	6-14
Passes	21-50-3	19-30-1
Punts	4-36.8	5-35.6
Fumbles-Lost	1-1	1-0
Penalties-Yards	9-67	11-113
Time of possession	30:13	29:47

Attendance—76,933.

INDIVIDUAL STATISTICS

Rushing—Los Angeles, White 13-54, McGee 2-4, Dickerson 7-38, Tyrrell 2-5; Cleveland, Mack 14-47, Byner 7-

15, Kosar 2-3.

Passing—Los Angeles, Everett 21-50-3—227; Cleveland, Kosar 19-30-1—223.

Receiving—Los Angeles, Brown 2-12, D. Johnson 6-69, House 1-13, Ellard 4-65, Hill 2-14, McGee 4-18, Tyrrell 1-10, Young 1-26; Cleveland, Slaughter 3-19, Brennan 4-75, Byner 5-70, Newsome 2-7, McNeil 1-15, Mack 3-17, Langhorne 1-20.

Kickoff Returns—Los Angeles, Hicks 1-20, Brown 4-71, Cox 1-12; Cleveland, Young 3-79, Fontenot 1-17.

Punt Returns—Los Angeles, Hicks 2-8, J. Johnson 1-5; Cleveland, McNeil 3-23.

Interceptions—Los Angeles, Wilcher 1-11; Cleveland, Wright 2-108, Harper 1-0.

Punting—Los Angeles, Hatcher 4-36.8; Cleveland, Gossett 5-35.6.

Field Goals—Los Angeles, Lansford 1-1; Cleveland, Jaeger 3-4 (missed: 47).

Sacks—Los Angeles, Collins, Wilcher, Miller.

Broncos-Vikings
MONDAY, OCTOBER 26
SCORE BY PERIODS

Denver	7	10	0	10—27
Minnesota	7	7	13	7—34

SCORING

Denver—V. Johnson 25 pass from Elway (Karlis kick), 7:53 1st.
Minnesota—Wilson 1 run (C. Nelson kick), 11:13 1st.
Denver—Elway 1 run (Karlis kick), 1:18 2nd.
Minnesota—Dozier 1 run (C. Nelson kick), 5:42 2nd.
Denver—Field goal Karlis 43, 14:23 2nd.
Minnesota—Dozier 3 run (kick failed), 1:16 3rd.
Minnesota—Dozier 5 run (C. Nelson kick), 14:02 3rd.
Minnesota—Lewis 5 pass from Wilson (C. Nelson kick), 12:15 4th.
Denver—Lang 4 pass from Elway (Karlis kick), 13:31 4th.
Denver—Field goal Karlis 51, 13:31 4th.

TEAM STATISTICS

	Denver	Minnesota
First downs	21	27
Rushes-Yards	27-123	36-197
Passing yards	206	196
Sacked-Yards lost	5-39	1-1
3rd down eff.	4-14	2-7
Passes	22-39-1	13-23-5
Punts	6-38.7	3-39.3
Fumbles-Lost	2-0	0-0
Penalties-Yards	10-128	4-29
Time of possession	23:34	36:26

Attendance—51,011.

INDIVIDUAL STATISTICS

Rushing—Denver, Willhite 8-57, Winder 9-26, Elway 7-37, Lang 2-minus 6, Sewell 1-9; Minnesota, D. Nelson 11-98, Anderson 8-38, Rice 6-24, Dozier 7-15, Wilson 4-22.

Passing—Denver, Elway 22-39-1—245; Minnesota, Wilson 13-23-5—197.

Receiving—Denver, Mobley 1-8, M. Jackson 5-52, V. Johnson 5-48, Nattiel 3-32, Lang 2-15, Kay 4-63, Bell 1-8, Massie 1-19; Minnesota, Jordan 3-57, Carter 3-53, Dozier 1-13, Anderson 1-12, Lewis 3-31, Rice 2-31.

Kickoff Returns—Denver, Bell 3-54, Lang 2-48, V. Johnson 1-34; Minnesota, Guggemos 3-80, Hilton 1-13, D. Nelson 2-38.

Punt Returns—Denver, Nattiel 2-17; Minnesota, Lewis 1-16.

Interceptions—Denver, Haynes 2-25, Harden 1-7, Lilly 1-5, Robbins 1-9; Minnesota, Harris 1-5.

Punting—Denver, Horan 6-38.7; Minnesota, Coleman 3-39.3.

Field Goals—Denver, Karlis 2-2; Minnesota, none attempted.

Sacks—Denver, Hunley ½, Bowyer ½; Minnesota, Solomon, Millard 2, Doleman ½, D. Martin, Thomas ½.

EIGHTH WEEK

Sunday, November 1

Chicago 31, Kansas City 28 at Chi.
Denver 34, Detroit 0 at Den.
Houston 31, Cincinnati 29 at Cin.
Indianapolis 19, N.Y. Jets 14 at N.Y.
Miami 35, Pittsburgh 24 at Mia.
New England 26, L.A. Raiders 23 at N.E.
New Orleans 38, Atlanta 0 at Atl.
Philadelphia 28, St. Louis 23 at St.L.
San Diego 27, Cleveland 24 (OT) at S.D.
San Francisco 31, L.A. Rams 10 at L.A.
Seattle 28, Minnesota 17 at Sea.
Tampa Bay 23, Green Bay 17 at Milw.
Washington 27, Buffalo 7 at Buff.

Monday, November 2

Dallas 33, N.Y. Giants 24 at Dall.

Eric Dickerson was the showcase, but Albert Bentley was the star.

When Dickerson, the most prolific running back in the National Football League, was traded by the Los Angeles Rams to the Indianapolis Colts on October 31, football fans wondered just how long it would take Dickerson—who had averaged 111 rushing yards per game in his Rams career—to turn around a moribund Colts franchise that had not made a playoff appearance in 10 seasons.

It didn't happen in one week. Dickerson rushed for only 38 yards on 10 carries in his first game as a Colt, a 19-14 Indianapolis victory over the New York Jets. He did catch one pass for 28 yards to set up the Colts' first touchdown, but the player most responsible for the team's success was Bentley, an unheralded 27-year-old running back from the University of Miami. Bentley, who played two seasons in the United States Football League and was in his third NFL campaign, rushed 29 times for 145 yards and caught three passes for 32 yards against the Jets.

Bentley had started the Colts' four non-strike games, but figured to lose his starting job with the arrival of Dickerson.

"I don't feel any pressure on me to do well and compete with him," Bentley said. "(The trade) bothered me a little. It was a distraction that they made the trade, but that was just until I got into the flow of the game. I understand when you can get a player of that caliber, you go out and get him.

"I accept it, but I don't like it. But if that's the way it has to be. . . ."

"Albert Bentley is a fine back," said Dickerson. "He ain't just going to roll over and say, 'Take my job.'

"But if my brother was on this team and was the starting halfback, I'd still go for his job. He's still my friend, my brother. But I'm a competitor and I want to play."

Albert Bentley stole the show in Week 8 by leading the Colts to a 19-14 win over the Jets in Eric Dickerson's Indianapolis debut.

Linebacker Duane Bickett led the defensive effort with 3½ sacks on Jets quarterback Ken O'Brien as the Colts swept the season series with New York for the first time since 1980.

Dickerson's former team, the Rams, could muster just 62 rushing yards on 24 attempts and were crushed at home by archrival San Francisco, 31-10. Dickerson's replacement, Charles White, carried 21 times for 52 yards.

The 49ers won for the sixth straight week, blowing open a close game with a 17-point second quarter. Two of quarterback Joe Montana's three touchdown passes came in the period, with his two-yard scoring pass to tight end John Frank in the final minute ending a 12-play, 95-yard drive.

Steve Grogan led the New England Patriots on a seven-play, 68-yard drive late in the fourth quarter as the Pats edged the Los Angeles Raiders, 26-23. Placekicker Tony Franklin kicked a 29-yard field goal with one second left for the game-winning points. Franklin, who had kicked three earlier field goals, got a second chance at his game-winner after missing a 34-yard attempt with nine seconds remaining when the Raiders' Lionel Washington was offside on the play.

Grogan, who had not played in five weeks because of neck problems, took over for starting quarterback Tony Eason in the first quarter after Eason suffered a shoulder separation. Grogan passed for 282 yards in his relief role, including 56 yards on three completions in the game-winning drive.

Grogan's biggest completion of the game was an 11-yard pass to tight end Greg Baty on a fourth-and-five play from the Raiders' 35-yard line with 21 seconds left.

The Philadelphia Eagles drove 70 yards in 70 seconds for the game-winning touchdown in a 28-23 NFC East Division victory at St. Louis. The touchdown came on a nine-yard pass from Randall Cunningham to wide receiver Gregg Garrity with 40 seconds left.

Cunningham threw three scoring passes in a game the Eagles led, 21-6, midway through the third period. But the Cardinals scored 17 unanswered points to take a 23-21 lead, with quarterback Neil Lomax's eight-yard touchdown pass to rookie Robert Awalt putting St. Louis in front with 1:50 left to play.

Lomax, who completed 29 of 50 passes for 288 yards, was sacked seven times and threw three interceptions, two of which came inside the Philadelphia 20-yard line.

The New Orleans defense intercepted five passes to lead the Saints to their largest victory margin ever, a 38-0 blowout of NFC West Division rival Atlanta. It was the Falcons' worst home loss in 20 years and their worst defeat anywhere since a 59-0 loss to the Rams in 1976.

The Saints rushed 42 times for 244 yards, with Rueben Mayes leading the attack with 112 yards on 19 carries. Another second-year running back, Dalton Hilliard, scored two touchdowns.

The Falcons, tied with Kansas City for fewest points scored through seven games, never moved the ball inside the New Orleans 30-yard line.

Another shutout was registered at Denver's Mile High Stadium, where the host Broncos pounded interconference rival Detroit, 34-0. It was the Broncos' first shutout victory in more than three years and may have been worse had it not been for six dropped passes by Denver wide receivers.

The Broncos got all the points they needed on their first possession, with a 10-play, 80-yard drive that ended with a three-yard touchdown run by quarterback John Elway. Denver also scored on its next two possessions and led, 17-0, after the first period.

The Lions offense held the ball for just 2:50 of the opening period and ran only six plays for a net gain of 10 yards.

The Tampa Bay Buccaneers jumped off to a 20-0 lead and then held off the Green Bay Packers for a 23-17 victory at Milwaukee. It was almost a case of deja vu for the Bucs, who led 20-0 against Chicago in Week 7 before losing, 27-26.

Packers Coach Forrest Gregg replaced starting quarterback Don Majkowski with Randy Wright after Tampa Bay grabbed its big lead. The move nearly resulted in a Green Bay victory. Wright completed 13 of his 19 pass attempts and led the Packers on scoring drives of 55, 65 and 69 yards.

Ironically, both teams finished the game with 89 yards rushing and 190 yards passing.

Chicago quarterback Jim McMahon, who was instrumental in leading his team to the comeback victory at Tampa Bay a week earlier, performed his magic again in Week 8, helping the Bears pull out a 31-28 victory over Kansas City. McMahon threw two fourth-quarter touchdown passes to Willie Gault, including the game-winner from 38 yards out with 4:44 remaining.

McMahon, who won for the 24th straight time as the Bears' starting quarterback, completed 23 of 34 attempts for 287 yards and three touchdowns in his first start of the season.

The Chiefs, who lost for the sixth straight week, led 28-24 with 9:16 left before a fumble by rookie Christian Okoye was recovered by the Bears' Dave Duerson at the Chicago 21-yard line. McMahon then led the Bears 79 yards in nine plays for the winning touchdown.

Kansas City's Bill Kenney threw four touchdown passes in the losing effort.

Miami quarterback Dan Marino also threw for four touchdowns in Week 8, but with better results. The Dolphins defeated Pittsburgh, 35-24, at Joe Robbie Stadium to give Coach Don Shula his 250th regular-season victory in his 25th year as an NFL head coach. Only former Chicago Bears Coach George Halas, with 320 wins in 40 seasons, recorded more regular-season victories.

The Steelers took a 14-0 lead in the first nine minutes by converting two Miami turnovers into touchdowns. The first score was set up by a fumble by running back Lorenzo Hampton on the Dolphins' first offensive play and the second touchdown came on strong safety Donnie Shell's 50-yard interception return of a Marino pass.

That was one of the few things Marino did wrong all day. He threw 41- and 33-yard touchdown passes to Mark Clayton and a 50-yarder to Mark Duper in the second half to help wipe out a 21-7 Pittsburgh halftime lead. He finished with 25 completions in 31 attempts for 332 yards.

Marino wasn't the only offensive star for the Dolphins, however. Running back Troy Stradford rushed for 110 yards on 19 attempts and scored Miami's final touchdown on a five-yard run with 9:02 left. Stradford's 100-yard game was the first by a Dolphin rookie since 1968 and only the third by a Miami player since 1984.

Washington running back George Rogers, a former Heisman Trophy winner in his seventh NFL season, put aside shoulder and toe ailments that had plagued him for most of the season to lead the Redskins to a 27-7 victory at Buffalo. Rogers exploded for 125 yards on 30 attempts after having gained only 20 yards on eight carries all season.

Quarterback Jay Schroeder threw two touchdown passes to Kelvin Bryant and ran for a third score to pace a Redskin offense that rolled up 406 total yards and had a better than 2-to-1 edge in time of possession.

The Cincinnati Bengals had a 504-227 edge in total yards in their AFC Central Division clash with Houston and still lost, 31-29, by blowing a 29-14 lead with less than six minutes left.

The comeback began when Oilers rookie Curtis Duncan returned a kickoff 62 yards to the Bengals' 34-yard line, setting up a 47-yard Tony Zendejas field goal with 5:38 left. Barney Bussey fumbled the ensuing kickoff and Kenny Johnson recovered for Houston at the Cincinnati 21-yard line. Oilers quarterback Warren Moon scrambled 20 yards to the 1, setting up a touchdown run by rookie Spencer Tillman on the next play and cutting the deficit to 29-24.

The Bengals were forced to punt on their next possession and punter Greg Horne shanked a 19-yard kick to the Cincinnati 45-yard line. Moon then hit Drew Hill for a 33-yard gain and, two plays later, ran seven yards himself to the 1. Tillman was stopped for no gain on two carries before Moon leaped over from a yard out for the game-winning score with 55 seconds left.

Oilers safety Keith Bostic intercepted a pass by quarterback Boomer Esiason on the Bengals' next offensive play to seal the win.

The San Diego Chargers beat the Cleveland Browns, 27-24, on placekicker Vince Abbott's 33-yard field goal 2:16 into overtime. Abbott's kick and the Chargers' sixth straight win came after Vencie Glenn intercepted a pass by Browns quarterback Bernie Kosar on the third play of overtime. A 30-yard return by Glenn and a facemasking penalty against Cleveland put the ball on the Browns' 20-yard line.

Ironically, the Chargers' first score of the game also was set up by an interception. Former Browns linebacker Chip Banks, who was traded to San Diego in the off-season, picked off a Kosar pass on the second play of the game and returned it 20 yards to the Cleveland 15. Lionel James scored for San Diego on the next play.

Dave Krieg threw three scoring passes to lead the Seattle Seahawks to a 28-17 interconference triumph over Minnesota. The loss was the first suffered by the Vikings' regular team after three victories.

The Dallas Cowboys scored 19 points in the final period to wipe out a 10-point deficit en route to a 33-24 victory over the New York Giants in the Monday night game. Twelve of Dallas' final 19 points came from the right leg of placekicker Roger Ruzek, who tied an NFL record with four fourth-quarter field goals.

Warren Moon was the guiding force behind Houston's come-from-behind victory at Cincinnati.

Four turnovers in their own territory in the final 15 minutes doomed the Giants to their 11th loss in 12 games at Texas Stadium. The biggest came when quarterback Phil Simms, throwing from deep in his own territory, had his pass tipped at the line of scrimmage by Dallas' Ed Jones. The ball deflected to the Cowboys' other defensive end, Jim Jeffcoat, who rambled 26 yards for a game-tying touchdown with 9:43 remaining. It was only the second interception return by Jeffcoat in his five-year NFL career, with both coming against Simms on passes tipped by Jones.

It was a rough night all around for Simms, who was sacked five times in addition to throwing two interceptions.

Steelers-Dolphins
SUNDAY, NOVEMBER 1
SCORE BY PERIODS

Pittsburgh	14	7	3	0—24
Miami	0	7	14	14—35

SCORING
Pittsburgh—Lockett 10 pass from Malone (Anderson kick), 7:31 1st.
Pittsburgh—Shell 50 interception return (Anderson kick), 9:09 1st.
Miami—Hardy 2 pass from Marino (Reveiz kick), 3:23 2nd.
Pittsburgh—Pollard 1 run (Anderson kick), 14:33 2nd.
Miami—Clayton 41 pass from Marino (Reveiz kick), 3:04 3rd.
Pittsburgh—Field goal Anderson 43, 10:41 3rd.

Miami—Duper 50 pass from Marino (Reveiz kick), 13:04 3rd.

Miami—Clayton 33 pass from Marino (Reveiz kick), 0:34 4th.

Miami—Stradford 5 run (Reveiz kick), 5:58 4th.

TEAM STATISTICS

	Pittsburgh	Miami
First downs	22	26
Rushes-Yards	30-116	31-146
Passing yards	199	332
Sacked-Yards lost	1-6	0-0
3rd down eff.	9-16	6-9
Passes	18-36-1	25-31-2
Punts	5-42.8	1-34.0
Fumbles-Lost	2-0	2-1
Penalties-Yards	5-35	2-15
Time of possession	26:50	33:10

Attendance—52,578.

INDIVIDUAL STATISTICS

Rushing—Pittsburgh, Jackson 12-32, Abercrombie 12-52, Malone 3-19, Pollard 3-13; Miami, Hampton 4-17, Stradford 19-110, T. Brown 3-3, Jensen 2-8, W. Bennett 3-8.

Passing—Pittsburgh, Malone 18-36-1—205; Miami, Marino 25-31-2—332.

Receiving—Pittsburgh, Abercrombie 6-55, Lockett 2-31, Pollard 1-4, Sweeney 3-49, Hoge 2-18, Stallworth 2-28, Jackson 2-20; Miami, Stradford 8-46, Hardy 2-22, Duper 5-100, Hampton 1-5, W. Bennett 2-12, T. Brown 1-6, Clayton 3-94, Jensen 1-2, Pruitt 2-45.

Kickoff Returns—Pittsburgh, Stone 5-92; Miami, Stradford 4-90, Hardy 1-15.

Punt Returns—Miami, Schwedes 3-22.

Interceptions—Pittsburgh, Cole 1-0, Shell 1-50; Miami, Blackwood 1-0.

Punting—Pittsburgh, Newsome 5-42.8; Miami, Roby 1-34.0.

Field Goals—Pittsburgh, Anderson 1-1; Miami, none attempted.

Sacks—Miami, Turner.

Redskins-Bills
SUNDAY, NOVEMBER 1
SCORE BY PERIODS

Washington	3	14	10	0—27
Buffalo	0	0	0	7— 7

SCORING

Washington—Field goal Haji-Sheikh 30, 4:15 1st.

Washington—Bryant 12 pass from Schroeder (Haji-Sheikh kick), 0:07 2nd.

Washington—Schroeder 13 run (Haji-Sheikh kick), 7:54 2nd.

Washington—Bryant 7 pass from Schroeder (Haji-Sheikh kick), 4:58 3rd.

Washington—Field goal Haji-Sheikh 33, 12:31 3rd.

Buffalo—Reed 17 pass from Kelly (Norwood kick), 0:03 4th.

TEAM STATISTICS

	Washington	Buffalo
First downs	24	14
Rushes-Yards	53-299	10-21
Passing yards	107	259
Sacked-Yards lost	2-25	3-33
3rd down eff.	5-13	2-11
Passes	11-18-0	25-43-3
Punts	5-44.4	5-41.6
Fumbles-Lost	2-1	2-1
Penalties-Yards	6-45	7-55
Time of possession	40:58	19:02

Attendance—71,640.

INDIVIDUAL STATISTICS

Rushing—Washington, Monk 3-54, Rogers 30-125, Bryant 9-46, Schroeder 3-15, Griffin 1-5, Smith 7-54; Buffalo, Byrum 2-minus 1, Riddick 6-19, Kelly 2-3.

Passing—Washington, Schroeder 11-18-0—132; Buffalo, Kelly 25-43-3—292.

Receiving—Washington, Monk 5-38, Clark 2-72, Bryant 3-19, Rogers 1-3; Buffalo, Metzelaars 2-18, Burkett 5-55, Reed 8-108, Harmon 6-70, T. Johnson 4-41.

Kickoff Returns—Washington, Griffin 1-15; Buffalo, Mueller 1-7, Tasker 1-21, Riddick 2-38.

Punt Returns—Washington, Yarber 2-25; Buffalo, Pitts 1-8.

Interceptions—Washington, Coleman 1-28, Wilburn 1-0, Bowles 1-24.

Punting—Washington, Cox 5-44.4; Buffalo, Kidd 5-41.6.

Field Goals—Washington, Haji-Sheikh 2-2; Buffalo, none attempted.

Sacks—Washington, Manley 2, Milot; Buffalo, Seals, Drane.

Raiders-Patriots
SUNDAY, NOVEMBER 1
SCORE BY PERIODS

Los Angeles Raiders	3	3	0	17—23
New England	3	7	6	10—26

SCORING

Los Angeles—Field goal Bahr 31, 5:02 1st.

New England—Field goal Franklin 50, 11:53 1st.

New England—Collins 15 pass from Tatupu (Franklin kick), 1:53 2nd.

Los Angeles—Field goal Bahr 31, 12:26 2nd.

New England—Field goal Franklin 27, 4:38 3rd.

New England—Field goal Franklin 25, 12:07 3rd.

New England—Fryar 25 pass from Grogan (Franklin kick), 0:50 4th.

Los Angeles—Christensen 8 pass from Hilger (Bahr kick), 3:24 4th.

Los Angeles—Allen 2 run (Bahr kick), 10:22 4th.

Los Angeles—Field goal Bahr 39, 14:14 4th.

New England—Field goal Franklin 4, 14:59 4th.

TEAM STATISTICS

	Los Angeles	New England
First downs	19	20
Rushes-Yards	28-81	37-110
Passing yards	249	296
Sacked-Yards lost	4-8	3-22
3rd down eff.	4-13	8-17
Passes	18-28-1	17-31-1
Punts	3-42.7	4-48.0
Fumbles-Lost	2-1	1-0
Penalties-Yards	5-30	3-20
Time of possession	28:45	31:15

Attendance—60,664.

INDIVIDUAL STATISTICS

Rushing—Los Angeles, Allen 16-41, Jackson 8-37, Mueller 2-8, Hilger 2-minus 5; New England, Collins 22-75, Tatupu 11-25, Grogan 2-14, Eason 1-4, Fryar 1-minus 8.

Passing—Los Angeles, Hilger 18-28-1—277; New England, Grogan 14-27-1—282, Eason 2-3-0—21, Tatupu 1-1-0—15.

Receiving—Los Angeles, Christensen 5-70, Allen 5-60, Lofton 4-76, Smith 2-42, Fernandez 1-23, Jackson 1-6; New England, Morgan 6-146, Fryar 6-107, Collins 2-34, Baty 2-16, Jones 1-15.

Kickoff Returns—Los Angeles, Mueller 6-141, Williams 1-minus 5; New England, Fryar 4-72, Perryman 1-16.

Punt Returns—Los Angeles, Woods 4-91.

Interceptions—Los Angeles, King 1-8; New England, Clayborn 1-24.

Punting—Los Angeles, Talley 3-42.7; New England, Camarillo 4-48.0.

Field Goals—Los Angeles, Bahr 3-4 (missed: 41); New England, Franklin 4-4.

Sacks—Los Angeles, Jones, Millen, Robinson ½, Long ½; New England, T. Williams ½, Sims ½, McGrew, Veris, B. Williams.

Lions-Broncos
SUNDAY, NOVEMBER 1
SCORE BY PERIODS

Detroit	0	0	0	0—	0
Denver	17	7	0	10—	34

SCORING
Denver—Elway 3 run (Karlis kick), 4:58 1st.
Denver—Field goal Karlis 28, 11:34 1st.
Denver—Winder 2 run (Karlis kick), 13:35 1st.
Denver—V. Johnson 35 pass from Elway (Karlis kick), 13:30 2nd.
Denver—Elway 7 run (Karlis kick), 1:30 4th.
Denver—Field goal Karlis 29, 12:28 4th.

TEAM STATISTICS

	Detroit	Denver
First downs	14	28
Rushes-Yards	17-63	39-212
Passing yards	128	248
Sacked-Yards lost	3-23	3-23
3rd down eff.	3-11	10-16
Passes	16-34-1	19-33-0
Punts	5-46.6	1-48.0
Fumbles-Lost	2-1	1-1
Penalties-Yards	4-37	7-59
Time of possession	23:44	36:16

Attendance—75,172.

INDIVIDUAL STATISTICS
Rushing—Detroit, James 9-34, Jones 5-23, Bernard 1-1, S. Williams 1-5, Long 1-0; Denver, Winder 21-94, Elway 4-42, Lang 4-15, Sewell 5-37, Kubiak 1-3, Bell 4-21.

Passing—Detroit, Long 16-34-1—151; Denver, Elway 16-30-0—246, Kubiak 3-3-0—25.

Receiving—Detroit, Jones 3-20, Mandley 2-7, Bland 1-3, Bernard 1-10, Giles 2-14, James 1-21, Woolfolk 3-29, Chadwick 3-37; Denver, Jackson 2-35, Kay 2-29, V. Johnson 4-87, Sewell 3-26, Nattiel 2-39, Winder 1-7, Lang 4-41, Mobley 1-7.

Kickoff Returns—Detroit, Lee 4-87, Woolfolk 2-29.

Punt Returns—Detroit, Mandley 1-11; Denver, Nattiel 3-25.

Interceptions—Denver, D. Smith 1-6.

Punting—Detroit, Arnold 5-46.6; Denver, Horan 1-48.0.

Field Goals—Detroit, Murray 0-3 (missed: 42, 47, 49); Denver, Karlis 2-3 (missed: 49).

Sacks—Detroit, J. Williams, Gay, Jamison; Denver, Kragen, R. Jones, Mecklenburg.

Saints-Falcons
SUNDAY, NOVEMBER 1
SCORE BY PERIODS

New Orleans	14	7	3	14—	38
Atlanta	0	0	0	0—	0

SCORING
New Orleans—Jones 7 pass from Hebert (Andersen kick), 9:44 1st.
New Orleans—Word 1 run (Andersen kick), 14:05 1st.
New Orleans—Hilliard 5 run (Andersen kick), 11:49 2nd.
New Orleans—Field goal Andersen 49, 3:38 3rd.
New Orleans—Hilliard 30 run (Andersen kick), 9:39 4th.
New Orleans—Gray 3 run (Andersen kick), 14:31 4th.

TEAM STATISTICS

	New Orleans	Atlanta
First downs	29	12
Rushes-Yards	42-244	16-55
Passing yards	166	128
Sacked-Yards lost	1-5	4-28
3rd down eff.	7-12	4-11
Passes	16-26-0	14-29-5
Punts	3-42.0	5-43.0
Fumbles-Lost	0-0	0-0
Penalties-Yards	8-73	6-51
Time of possession	37:37	22:23

Attendance—42,196.

INDIVIDUAL STATISTICS
Rushing—New Orleans, Mayes 19-112, Hilliard 10-63, Gray 5-27, Hebert 3-24, Word 5-18; Atlanta, Riggs 14-46, Dixon 1-7, Flowers 1-2.

Passing—New Orleans, Hebert 16-26-0—171; Atlanta, Campbell 14-29-5—156.

Receiving—New Orleans, Jones 4-54, Mayes 4-20, Brenner 2-40, Hilliard 2-25, Martin 2-24, Word 2-8; Atlanta, Bailey 6-89, Matthews 3-32, Dixon 2-24, Riggs 2-8, Cox 1-3.

Kickoff Returns—New Orleans, Hilliard 1-13; Atlanta, Flowers 3-52, Stamps 3-81.

Punt Returns—New Orleans, Gray 3-35; Atlanta, Johnson 2-22.

Interceptions—New Orleans, Gibson 1-17, Maxie 1-10, Jakes 1-3, Sutton 1-0, Mack 1-0.

Punting—New Orleans, Hansen 3-42.0; Atlanta, Donnelly 5-43.2.

Field Goals—New Orleans, Andersen 1-2 (missed: 43); Atlanta, Luckhurst 0-1 (missed: 51).

Sacks—New Orleans, Warren 2, Jackson 1½, B. Clark ½; Atlanta, Tuggle.

49ers-Rams
SUNDAY, NOVEMBER 1
SCORE BY PERIODS

San Francisco	7	17	0	7—	31
Los Angeles Rams	3	0	0	7—	10

SCORING
San Francisco—Rathman 9 run (Wersching kick), 8:40 1st.
Los Angeles—Field goal Lansford 22, 14:04 1st.
San Francisco—Field goal Wersching 22, 3:13 2nd.
San Francisco—Wilson 17 pass from Montana (Wersching kick), 8:45 2nd.
San Francisco—Frank 2 pass from Montana (Wersching kick), 14:38 2nd.
San Francisco—Rice 51 pass from Montana (Wersching kick), 9:19 4th.
Los Angeles—Young 7 pass from Everett (Lansford kick), 13:02 4th.

TEAM STATISTICS

	San Francisco	Los Angeles
First downs	23	19
Rushes-Yards	36-149	24-62
Passing yards	286	218
Sacked-Yards lost	1-8	3-13
3rd down eff.	7-14	5-14
Passes	21-30-1	20-35-0
Punts	3-31.7	6-43.8
Fumbles-Lost	0-0	1-1
Penalties-Yards	7-78	4-24
Time of possession	31:02	28:58

Attendance—55,328.

INDIVIDUAL STATISTICS
Rushing—San Francisco, Craig 23-104, Rathman 7-31, Montana 2-11, Cribbs 1-0, Rice 1-2, Sydney 1-2, Young 1-minus 1; Los Angeles, White 21-52, Everett 2-9, J. Francis 1-1.

Passing—San Francisco, Montana 21-30-1—294; Los Angeles, Everett 20-35-0—231.

Receiving—San Francisco, R. Francis 6-65, Wilson 5-91, Rathman 3-38, Rice 3-70, Craig 2-19, Frank 2-1; Los Angeles, White 5-44, D. Johnson 5-33, Ellard 4-91, Brown 2-37, Francis 2-11, House 1-8, Young 1-7.

Kickoff Returns—San Francisco, Rodgers 2-97; Los Angeles, Brown 3-53, Hicks 1-16.

Punt Returns—San Francisco, McLemore 4-35.

Interceptions—Los Angeles, Cromwell 1-28.

Punting—San Francisco, Runager 3-31.7; Los Angeles, Hatcher 6-43.8.

Field Goals—San Francisco, Wersching 1-1; Los Angeles, Lansford 1-1.

Sacks—San Francisco, Turner, Kugler, Roberts; Los Angeles, Meisner.

Buccaneers-Packers

SCORE BY PERIODS

Tampa Bay	0	3	17	3—23
Green Bay	0	0	3	14—17

SCORING

Tampa Bay—Field goal Igwebuike 48, 0:49 2nd.
Tampa Bay—Smith 1 run (Igwebuike kick), 5:31 3rd.
Tampa Bay—Carter 5 pass from DeBerg (Igwebuike kick), 6:39 3rd.
Tampa Bay—Field goal Igwebuike 36, 11:31 3rd.
Green Bay—Field goal Del Greco 36, 14:59 3rd.
Tampa Bay—Field goal Igwebuike 46, 4:56 4th.
Green Bay—Neal 4 pass from Wright (Del Greco kick), 8:35 4th.
Green Bay—Fullwood 1 run (Del Greco kick), 11:09 4th.

TEAM STATISTICS

	Tampa Bay	Green Bay
First downs	20	22
Rushes-Yards	41-89	24-89
Passing yards	190	190
Sacked-Yards lost	1-7	3-14
3rd down eff	8-16	4-11
Passes	17-30-1	17-33-0
Punts	4-38.8	5-40.0
Fumbles-Lost	0-0	5-2
Penalties-Yards	8-67	13-85
Time of possession	36:12	23:48
Attendance—50,308.		

INDIVIDUAL STATISTICS

Rushing—Tampa Bay, Smith 18-43, Howard 12-27, Wilder 5-22, Austin 3-3, DeBerg 3-minus 6; Green Bay, Majkowski 6-51, Davis 7-23, Wright 2-7, Carruth 2-4, Clark 5-3, Fullwood 2-1.

Passing—Tampa Bay, DeBerg 17-30-1—197; Green Bay, Majkowski 4-14-0—43, Wright 13-19-0—161.

Receiving—Tampa Bay, Magee 7-66, Carrier 3-66, Howard 2-30, Smith 2-13, Wilder 1-9, Miller 1-8, Carter 1-5; Green Bay, Epps 5-51, Neal 4-42, Stanley 3-45, Davis 2-12, Paskett 1-33, West 1-13, Clark 1-8.

Kickoff Returns—Tampa Bay, Futrell 3-60, Carrier 1-0; Green Bay, Fullwood 3-73, Carruth 1-8, Cook 1-0.

Punt Returns—Tampa Bay, Futrell 1-10; Green Bay, Stanley 3-12.

Interceptions—Green Bay, J. Morris 1-50.

Punting—Tampa Bay, Garcia 4-38.8; Green Bay, Bracken 5-40.0.

Field Goals—Tampa Bay, Igwebuike 3-3; Green Bay, Del Greco 1-2 (missed: 47).

Sacks—Tampa Bay, Washington 2, Cannon; Green Bay, Harris.

Browns-Chargers

SUNDAY, NOVEMBER 1

SCORE BY PERIODS

Cleveland	7	7	10	0	0—24
San Diego	14	0	0	10	3—27

SCORING

San Diego—James 15 run (Abbott kick), 1:05 1st.
Cleveland—Slaughter 20 pass from Kosar (Jaeger kick), 6:12 1st.
San Diego—Bernstine 10 pass from Fouts (Abbott kick), 10:30 1st.
Cleveland—Brennan 41 pass from Kosar (Jaeger kick), 9:20 2nd.
Cleveland—Field goal Jaeger 41, 9:48 3rd.
Cleveland—Byner 2 run (Jaeger kick), 11:48 3rd.
San Diego—James 22 pass from Fouts (Abbott kick), 9:52 4th.
San Diego—Field goal Abbott 20, 13:14 4th.
San Diego—Field goal Abbott 33, 2:16 OT.

TEAM STATISTICS

	Cleveland	San Diego
First downs	19	22
Rushes-Yards	21-72	27-128
Passing yards	267	286
Sacked-Yards lost	5-31	3-29
3rd down eff	3-12	4-13
Passes	24-42-2	25-42-1
Punts	7-43.1	5-46.4
Fumbles-Lost	1-1	1-1
Penalties-Yards	10-71	7-55
Time of possession	29:37	32:39
Attendance—55,381.		

INDIVIDUAL STATISTICS

Rushing—Cleveland, Mack 14-61, Byner 5-9, Kosar 1-minus 1, Manoa 1-3; San Diego, James 3-21, Adams 15-66, Spencer 3-19, Anderson 5-23, Fouts 1-minus 1.

Passing—Cleveland, Kosar 24-42-2—298; San Diego, Fouts 25-42-1—315.

Receiving—Cleveland, Newsome 2-10, Byner 6-62, Langhorne 2-20, Slaughter 5-74, McNeil 1-9, Brennan 4-94, Mack 3-14, Weathers 1-15; San Diego, Spencer 2-13, Holohan 2-31, Bernstine 4-31, Winslow 7-76, Chandler 3-49, Anderson 2-19, James 4-90, Adams 1-6.

Kickoff Returns—Cleveland, Young 4-84; San Diego, Adams 1-10, Holland 2-39.

Punt Returns—Cleveland, McNeil 2-30; San Diego, James 3-31.

Interceptions—Cleveland, Dixon 1-6; San Diego, Banks 1-20, Glenn 1-30.

Punting—Cleveland, Gossett 7-43.1; San Diego, Mojsiejenko 5-46.4.

Field Goals—Cleveland, Jaeger 1-1; San Diego, Abbott 2-4 (missed: 52, 32).

Sacks—Cleveland, Puzzuoli, M. Johnson, Hairston; San Diego, Bayless ½, Unrein ½, Glenn ½, Phillips 1½, L. Miller, L. Williams.

Colts-Jets

SUNDAY, NOVEMBER 1

SCORE BY PERIODS

Indianapolis	3	7	3	6—19
New York Jets	0	7	0	7—14

SCORING

Indianapolis—Field goal Biasucci 36, 7:04 1st.
Indianapolis—Bouza 44 pass from Trudeau (Biasucci kick), 4:37 2nd.
New York—Hector 12 run (Leahy kick), 12:46 2nd.
Indianapolis—Field goal Biasucci 45, 7:02 3rd.
Indianapolis—Field goal Biasucci 38, 0:04 4th.
Indianapolis—Field goal Biasucci 33, 5:39 4th.
New York—Hector 20 run (Leahy kick), 8:30 4th.

TEAM STATISTICS

	Indianapolis	New York
First downs	21	15
Rushes-Yards	45-186	20-101
Passing yards	191	129
Sacked-Yards lost	1-1	7-61
3rd down eff	7-16	6-13
Passes	14-23-0	16-30-1
Punts	3-40.0	5-35.8
Fumbles-Lost	1-0	2-2
Penalties-Yards	4-35	6-34
Time of possession	34:47	25:13
Attendance—60,863.		

INDIVIDUAL STATISTICS

Rushing—Indianapolis, Bentley 29-145, Dickerson 10-38, Trudeau 6-3; New York, McNeil 7-37, Hector 5-37, O'Brien 2-14, Faaola 2-8, Vick 4-5.

Passing—Indianapolis, Trudeau 14-23-0—192; New York, O'Brien 15-29-1—174, Jennings 1-1-0—16.

Receiving—Indianapolis, Beach 4-31, Bentley 3-32, Bouza 2-51, Brooks 2-37, Murray 2-13, Dickerson 1-28; New York, Toon 7-79, Shuler 2-26, Hector 2-18, McNeil 2-18, Klever 1-22, Faaola 1-16, Walker 1-11.

Kickoff Returns—Indianapolis, Wright 3-49; New York, Humphery 5-132.

Punt Returns—Indianapolis, Brooks 1-6; New York, Townsell 1-10.

Interceptions—Indianapolis, Robinson 1-18.

Punting—Indianapolis, Stark 3-40.0; New York, Jennings 5-35.8.

Field Goals—Indianapolis, Biasucci 4-5 (missed: 28); New York, none attempted.

Sacks—Indianapolis, Bickett 3½, Cooks 2½, Thompson; New York, Holmes.

Eagles-Cardinals
SUNDAY, NOVEMBER 1
SCORE BY PERIODS

Philadelphia	0	7	14	7—28
St. Louis	6	0	7	10—23

SCORING

St. Louis—Ferrell 8 run (kick blocked), 10:20 1st.

Philadelphia—Carter 22 pass from Cunningham (McFadden kick), 8:58 2nd.

Philadelphia—Byars 2 run (McFadden kick), 4:45 3rd.

Philadelphia—Jackson 70 pass from Cunningham (McFadden kick), 10:02 3rd.

St. Louis—J.T. Smith 14 pass from Lomax (Gallery kick), 14:35 3rd.

St. Louis—Field goal Gallery 43, 1:32 4th.

St. Louis—Awalt 8 pass from Lomax (Gallery kick), 13:10 4th.

Philadelphia—Garrity 9 pass from Cunningham (McFadden kick), 14:20 4th.

TEAM STATISTICS

	Philadelphia	St. Louis
First downs	14	27
Rushes-Yards	21-62	31-177
Passing yards	266	232
Sacked-Yards lost	4-25	7-56
3rd down eff.	4-13	6-18
Passes	17-33-1	29-50-3
Punts	5-50.8	4-37.8
Fumbles-Lost	3-1	1-0
Penalties-Yards	5-50	3-27
Time of possession	21:36	38:24
Attendance—24,586.		

INDIVIDUAL STATISTICS

Rushing—Philadelphia, Toney 7-27, Byars 8-17, Jackson 1-minus 2, Cunningham 5-20; St. Louis, Mitchell 18-57, Ferrell 8-79, Lomax 3-25, Wolfley 1-5, Cater 1-11.

Passing—Philadelphia, Cunningham 17-32-1—291, Carter 0-1-0—0; St. Louis, Lomax 29-50-3—288.

Receiving—Philadelphia, Byars 3-14, Quick 2-35, Toney 4-67, Carter 1-22, Spagnola 3-47, Jackson 1-70, Tautalatasi 2-27, Garrity 1-9; St. Louis, Green 1-13, Mitchell 5-18, Awalt 9-97, J.T. Smith 10-112, Johnson 1-7, Ferrell 2-25, Holmes 1-16.

Kickoff Returns—Philadelphia, Morse 4-83; St. Louis, McAdoo 3-45, Sikahema 1-50.

Punt Returns—Philadelphia, Morse 2-32; St. Louis, Sikahema 5-65.

Interceptions—Philadelphia, Brown 1-9, Cooper 1-0, Waters 1-63; St. Louis, Young 1-0.

Punting—Philadelphia, Teltschik 5-50.8; St. Louis, Cater 4-37.8.

Field Goals—Philadelphia, McFadden 0-2 (missed: 47, 41); St. Louis, Gallery 1-2 (missed: 31).

Sacks—Philadelphia, Jiles, Reichenbach, Joyner, White, Simmons, J. Brown; St. Louis, Mack, Noga, Greer, Nunn.

Oilers-Bengals
SUNDAY, NOVEMBER 1
SCORE BY PERIODS

Houston	7	0	7	17—31
Cincinnati	3	6	7	13—29

SCORING

Cincinnati—Field goal Breech 32, 1:59 1st.

Houston—J. Williams 7 pass from Moon (Zendejas kick), 6:56 1st.

Cincinnati—Field goal Breech 33, 3:56 2nd.

Cincinnati—Field goal Breech 26, 14:53 2nd.

Cincinnati—Brown 47 pass from Esiason (Breech kick), 2:32 3rd.

Houston—Duncan 16 pass from Moon (Zendejas kick), 6:07 3rd.

Cincinnati—Field goal Breech 39, 1:47 4th.

Cincinnati—Field goal Breech 32, 6:00 4th.

Cincinnati—Munoz 3 pass from Esiason (Breech kick), 8:19 4th.

Houston—Field goal Zendejas 47, 9:22 4th.

Houston—Tillman 1 run (Zendejas kick), 10:50 4th.

Houston—Moon 1 run (Zendejas kick), 14:05 4th.

TEAM STATISTICS

	Houston	Cincinnati
First downs	19	25
Rushes-Yards	20-82	33-121
Passing yards	145	383
Sacked-Yards lost	6-46	1-4
3rd down eff.	2-10	5-15
Passes	18-29-1	26-41-2
Punts	6-42.8	4-28.7
Fumbles-Lost	4-2	3-1
Penalties-Yards	3-42	15-132
Time of possession	24:51	35:09
Attendance—52,700.		

INDIVIDUAL STATISTICS

Rushing—Houston, Rozier 8-30, Moon 5-43, Jackson 3-8, Tillman 4-1; Cincinnati, Brooks 12-28, Esiason 4-25, Kinnebrew 13-49, Johnson 3-10, Jennings 1-9.

Passing—Houston, Moon 18-29-1—191; Cincinnati, Esiason 26-41-2—387.

Receiving—Houston, Wallace 1-7, Givins 6-55, D. Hill 4-79, Rozier 3-8, J. Williams 1-7, Duncan 2-30, Drewrey 1-5; Cincinnati, Collinsworth 8-121, Brown 6-90, Holman 3-50, Brooks 6-103, Kinnebrew 1-9, Munoz 1-5, Martin 1-11.

Kickoff Returns—Houston, Tillman 1-0, Duncan 4-120, Drewrey 1-27, K. Johnson 1-6, Davis 1-0; Cincinnati, Jennings 2-32, Bussey 4-72, Martin 3-36.

Punt Returns—Houston, K. Johnson 2-24; Cincinnati, Martin 3-36.

Interceptions—Houston, Donaldson 1-7, Bostic 1-minus 28; Cincinnati, Thomas 1-3.

Punting—Houston, L. Johnson 6-42.8; Cincinnati, Horne 4-28.7.

Field Goals—Houston, Zendejas 1-1; Cincinnati, Breech 5-6 (missed: 43).

Sacks—Houston, Cooks; Cincinnati, Skow, Williams, Fulcher, Buck, King, Hammerstein.

Chiefs-Bears
SUNDAY, NOVEMBER 1
SCORE BY PERIODS

Kansas City	14	7	7	0—28
Chicago	7	7	3	14—31

SCORING

Kansas City—Carson 29 pass from Kenney (Lowery kick), 5:42 1st.

Kansas City—Hayes 15 pass from Kenney (Lowery kick), 9:41 1st.

Chicago—Gentry 88 kickoff return (Butler kick), 10:00 1st.

Chicago—Boso 28 pass from McMahon (Butler kick), 9:55 2nd.

Kansas City—Moriarty 4 pass from Kenney (Lowery kick), 15:00 2nd.

Kansas City—Paige 43 pass from Kenney (Lowery kick), 3:17 3rd.

Chicago—Field goal Butler 27, 12:30 3rd.

Chicago—Gault 25 pass from McMahon (Butler kick), 1:37 4th.

Chicago—Gault 38 pass from McMahon (Butler kick), 10:16 4th.

TEAM STATISTICS

	Kansas City	Chicago
First downs	20	20
Rushes-Yards	34-111	30-80
Passing yards	256	263
Sacked-Yards lost	2-14	5-24
3rd down eff.	8-15	8-15
Passes	15-28-1	23-34-1
Punts	5-35.6	2-23.0
Fumbles-Lost	3-1	1-1
Penalties-Yards	7-45	3-25
Time of possession	30:36	29:24

Attendance—63,498.

INDIVIDUAL STATISTICS

Rushing—Kansas City, Okoye 22-93, Moriarty 7-12, Kenney 2-1, Heard 3-5; Chicago, Payton 8-15, Anderson 17-59, McMahon 5-6.

Passing—Kansas City, Kenney 15-28-1—270; Chicago, McMahon 23-34-1—287.

Receiving—Kansas City, Heard 1-13, Paige 5-121, Carson 7-117, Hayes 1-15, Moriarty 1-4; Chicago, Moorehead 1-5, Anderson 6-66, Boso 4-51, Gentry 2-24, Payton 5-31, Gault 4-98, McKinnon 1-12.

Kickoff Returns—Kansas City, Palmer 2-48; Chicago, Gentry 3-140.

Punt Returns—Chicago, McKinnon 3-29.

Interceptions—Kansas City, Cooper 1-0; Chicago, Phillips 1-0.

Punting—Kansas City, Goodburn 5-35.6; Chicago, Wagner 2-23.0.

Field Goals—Kansas City, Lowery 0-1 (missed: 35); Chicago, Butler 1-2 (missed: 52).

Sacks—Kansas City, Still 3, Bell 1½, Maas ½; Chicago, Marshall, Wilson.

Vikings-Seahawks
SUNDAY, NOVEMBER 1
SCORE BY PERIODS

Minnesota	7	3	0	7—17
Seattle	7	7	7	7—28

SCORING

Seattle—Turner 4 pass from Krieg (N. Johnson kick), 4:21 1st.

Minnesota—Wilson 1 run (Nelson kick), 10:39 1st.

Seattle—Warner 30 pass from Krieg (N. Johnson kick), 12:46 2nd.

Minnesota—Field goal Nelson 29, 14:49 2nd.

Seattle—Largent 27 pass from Krieg (N. Johnson kick), 3:46 3rd.

Minnesota—Dozier 5 run (Nelson kick), 8:12 4th.

Seattle—R. Butler 28 pass from Kemp (N. Johnson kick), 13:28 4th.

TEAM STATISTICS

	Minnesota	Seattle
First downs	23	19
Rushes-Yards	26-143	34-123
Passing yards	271	200
Sacked-Yards lost	4-19	1-5
3rd down eff.	4-12	6-12
Passes	23-39-1	14-21-1
Punts	4-34.5	5-42.2
Fumbles-Lost	2-1	0-0
Penalties-Yards	7-43	5-40
Time of possession	27:54	32:06

Attendance—61,134.

INDIVIDUAL STATISTICS

Rushing—Minnesota, Dozier 11-45, Fenney 7-42, Rice 4-32, Wilson 4-24; Seattle, Warner 23-94, J.L. Williams 10-30, Krieg 1-minus 1.

Passing—Minnesota, Wilson 23-39-1—27; Seattle, Krieg 11-17-1—148, Kemp 3-4-0—52.

Receiving—Minnesota, Rice 8-77, Carter 4-86, Dozier 4-29, Jordan 3-42, Lewis 3-40, Fenney 1-3; Seattle, R. Butler 3-62, J.L. Williams 3-34, Warner 2-38, Largent 2-29, Skansi 2-25, Turner 2-12.

Kickoff Returns—Minnesota, Guggemos 3-64, Dozier 2-23; Seattle, Morris 2-31, Hollis 1-26, Powell 1-9.

Punt Returns—Seattle, Edmonds 2-55.

Interceptions—Minnesota, Studwell 1-14; Seattle, Jenkins 1-0.

Punting—Minnesota, Coleman 4-34.5; Seattle, Rodriguez 5-42.2.

Field Goals—Minnesota, C. Nelson 1-2 (missed: 46); Seattle, N. Johnson 0-1 (missed: 39).

Sacks—Minnesota, Doleman; Seattle, J. Green, Moyer, F. Young, Scholtz ½, Bryant ½.

Giants-Cowboys
MONDAY, NOVEMBER 2
SCORE BY PERIODS

New York Giants	0	10	7	7—24
Dallas	7	7	0	19—33

SCORING

Dallas—Walker 1 run (Ruzek kick), 9:08 1st.

New York—Morris 5 run (Allegre kick), 0:50 2nd.

New York—Field goal Allegre 35, 4:47 2nd.

Dallas—Cosbie 2 pass from D. White (Ruzek kick), 14:34 2nd.

New York—Manuel 50 pass from Simms (Allegre kick), 6:29 3rd.

New York—Manuel 33 pass from Simms (Allegre kick), 0:06 4th.

Dallas—Field goal Ruzek 34, 3:02 4th.

Dallas—Jeffcoat 26 interception return (Ruzek kick), 5:17 4th.

Dallas—Field goal Ruzek 49, 10:49 4th.

Dallas—Field goal Ruzek 40, 12:06 4th.

Dallas—Field goal Ruzek 35, 14:14 4th.

TEAM STATISTICS

	New York	Dallas
First downs	16	15
Rushes-Yards	24-55	24-26
Passing yards	242	214
Sacked-Yards lost	6-48	4-31
3rd down eff.	6-12	3-13
Passes	20-27-2	24-33-1
Punts	5-49.4	6-38.2
Fumbles-Lost	3-3	2-1
Penalties-Yards	12-95	9-63
Time of possession	30:04	29:56

Attendance—55,730.

INDIVIDUAL STATISTICS

Rushing—New York, Morris 17-26, Simms 3-15, Adams 3-9, Galbreath 1-5; Dallas, Walker 9-28, Dorsett 14-3, Cosbie 1-minus 5.

Passing—New York, Simms 15-21-2—240, Rutledge 5-6-0—50; Dallas, D. White 24-33-1-245.

Receiving—New York, Manuel 7-151, Galbreath 4-32, Bavaro 3-43, Adams 3-40, Morris 1-9, Baker 1-8, Rouson 1-7; Dallas, Cosbie 6-72, Walker 6-62, Banks 4-56, Newsome 3-9, Renfro 2-32, Edwards 1-7, Chandler 1-5, Dorsett 1-2.

Kickoff Returns—New York, Rouson 5-119, Adams 1-16, Bavaro 1-16; Dallas, Edwards 5-103.

Punt Returns—New York, McConkey 2-17, Baker 2-11; Dallas, Edwards 3-35.

Interceptions—New York, Taylor 1-5; Dallas, R. White 1-0, Jeffcoat 1-26.

Punting—New York, Landeta 5-49.4; Dallas, Saxon 6-38.2.

Field Goals—New York, Allegre 1-1; Dallas, Ruzek 4-4.

Sacks—New York, Taylor, Marshall, Howard, Martin; Dallas, Rohrer, Hegman, Ed Jones 4.

NINTH WEEK

Sunday, November 8

Buffalo 21, Denver 14 at Buff.
Chicago 26, Green Bay 24 at G.B.
Cleveland 38, Atlanta 3 at Cleve.
Detroit 27, Dallas 17 at Det.
Miami 20, Cincinnati 14 at Cin.
Minnesota 31, L.A. Raiders 20 at Minn.
New Orleans 31, L.A. Rams 14 at L.A.
N.Y. Giants 17, New England 10 at N.Y.
Philadelphia 31, Washington 27 at Phila.
Pittsburgh 17, Kansas City 16 at K.C.
St. Louis 31, Tampa Bay 28 at St.L.
San Diego 16, Indianapolis 13 at Ind.
San Francisco 27, Houston 20 at S.F.

Monday, November 9

N.Y. Jets 30, Seattle 14 at N.Y.

"If you talk about all-time comebacks, this is it," said St. Louis Cardinals quarterback Neil Lomax. "We've come back from big deficits before, but never 28-3 in the fourth quarter."

No National Football League team ever had.

In what turned out to be the biggest fourth-quarter comeback in NFL history, the Cardinals erupted for four touchdowns in the final 12 minutes, 42 seconds to defeat the Tampa Bay Buccaneers, 31-28, in Week 9.

The Bucs, a team not accustomed to success in their 12 NFL seasons, were so confident of victory that they began the final period with rookie quarterback Vinny Testaverde warming up on the sideline, preparing to relieve veteran starter Steve DeBerg. They ended the period with placekicker Donald Igwebuike's 53-yard desperation field-goal attempt bouncing off the crossbar with five seconds left.

"There's no way I thought they were going to be able to come back," said DeBerg, who completed 23 of 37 passes for 303 yards and three touchdowns. "I have never felt this bad after a loss. There's no way I thought we were going to lose to these guys."

The Cardinals' comeback began when Lomax and running back Stump Mitchell hooked up for a 39-yard gain on a fourth-and-1 play at the Tampa Bay 43-yard line early in the period. On the next play, Lomax hit rookie tight end Robert Awalt with a four-yard scoring pass to cut the Bucs' lead to 28-10.

On Tampa Bay's second play from scrimmage after the ensuing kickoff, running back James Wilder fumbled and linebacker Niko Noga returned the ball 24 yards for another St. Louis touchdown.

The Tampa Bay lead was down to 11 points (28-17), and the Cardinals were confident.

"When Niko scored that touchdown," Lomax said, "I knew we could win this game. It changed everything. Our guys were going crazy, and the feeling in the huddle changed dramatically."

On the Cards' next possession, Lomax completed passes of 15 and 13 yards to Awalt before hooking up with wide receiver J.T. Smith for an 11-yard touchdown with 8:18 left. Bucs 28, Cards 24.

Tampa Bay was forced to punt on its next possession, and the Cardinals got the ball on their own 20-yard line with 5:41 left. From the 31, Lomax hit wide receiver Don Holmes for a 23-yard gain to the Tampa 46 and Awalt for 27 yards to the 19. On third-and-8, Lomax hit Smith from 17 yards out with 2:01 left, giving St. Louis its first lead of the game.

Lomax, who completed 25 of 36 passes for 314 yards, connected on 10 of 13 for 164 yards in the final period. Eighty of the Cardinals' 109 points in five non-strike games had been scored in the fourth period. Opponents, meanwhile, held a 72-12 advantage in the first halves of those games.

"If we could just get some points in the first three quarters, we'd be all right," said St. Louis Coach Gene Stallings, whose team won just its second non-strike game in five attempts.

Tampa Bay Coach Ray Perkins, on the other hand, had another problem. For the third straight game, his team had blown a huge lead. A 20-0 advantage against Chicago two weeks earlier ended in a 27-26 loss. The Bucs nearly squandered a 20-0 lead against Green Bay the previous week before holding on for a 23-17 victory. But blowing a 25-point fourth-quarter lead against St. Louis was by far the worst.

"(The Cardinals) deserved to win the game and we did not," said Perkins, whose team ran just eight offensive plays for 20 yards while the Cardinals were scoring their four touchdowns.

"In the fourth quarter, we're either not in as good of shape as I think we are, or we don't have enough guts to suck up what we need to suck up.

"We have not learned how to do it when we're really tired. And that's what winners do."

Chuck Long, the Detroit Lions' No. 1 draft choice in 1986, guided his team to a 27-17 victory over Dallas in the seventh and first winning start of his brief pro career. He completed 15 of 28 passes for 217 yards and threw a 20-yard scoring pass to tight end Rob Rubick for the Lions' first touchdown. Long also was not sacked by a defense that had sacked Giants quarterback Phil Simms five times the week before.

Detroit, which defeated Dallas for the third time in the teams' last four meetings, took the lead for good when safety James Griffin intercepted a Danny White pass and returned it 29 yards to the Cowboy 4-yard line early in the fourth quarter. Running back Garry James

Philadelphia quarterback Randall Cunningham was too much to handle for the Washington Redskins in Week 9, throwing for 268 yards and three touchdowns and rushing seven times for 80 yards in a 31-27 Eagles victory.

scored his second touchdown of the game on the next play to give the Lions a 24-17 lead.

Long, at age 24, figures to be the Detroit quarterback for many years. Jeff Rutledge, an eight-year NFL backup for both the Rams and Giants, also got his first victory as a starter at age 30. Rutledge, like Long, was making his seventh career start.

The veteran, 0-5-1 in his previous starting assignments, got the nod from Giants Coach Bill Parcells after regular quarterback Phil Simms was sidelined with ligament damage in his left knee. It marked the first time in 60 games that Simms was not in the starting lineup.

Rutledge started slowly by throwing interceptions on New York's first two possessions. But he made amends by throwing touchdown passes of 16 yards to Mark Bavaro and nine yards to George Adams in the second period, giving the Giants a 14-0 lead. Rutledge finished with 21 completions in 33 attempts for 233 yards as New York upended New England, 17-10.

Linebackers Carl Banks and Lawrence Taylor keyed a Giants defense that held the Pats to just 11 first downs and 232 total yards. Banks had 10 tackles, one interception and forced one fumble while Taylor, who had two sacks, sealed the victory with an interception of Pats quarterback Steve Grogan at the Giant 15-yard line with 1:09 remaining.

The most impressive performance by a linebacker in Week 9, however, came from a rookie playing in his first NFL game.

Cornelius Bennett, a former consensus All-America at Alabama and the second pick in the 1987 draft, made his professional debut with the Buffalo Bills and helped to fire up a defense that was instrumental in a 21-14 victory over the Denver Broncos. Bennett, who was acquired by the Bills from the Indianapolis Colts a week earlier, was used at left outside linebacker primarily on passing situations. He was credited with one of Buffalo's three sacks and forced the other two.

The Bills' offense was just as impressive. It rolled up 25 first downs and 428 total yards, including 258 yards rushing—the highest total for a Bills team in nine seasons. At halftime, Buffalo had an 18-0 lead and a 17-2 edge in first downs.

The New Orleans Saints swept their season series with the Los Angeles Rams for only the second time since 1970 with a 31-14 victory. The triumph was the Saints' first at Anaheim Stadium since 1981 and improved their record to 5-3, the best start in team history.

Second-year man Dalton Hilliard was the Saints' star, rushing 14 times for 92 yards, catching four passes for 84 yards, throwing a 23-yard touchdown pass and returning one kickoff for 14 yards. Hilliard's touchdown pass to tight end John Tice early in the second quarter gave New Orleans a 17-0 lead.

The loss was the eighth in a row for the Rams' regulars, whose last victory was a 29-10 decision over Dallas on December 7, 1986. L.A.'s average margin of defeat in those eight games was 11 points.

Another team in a tailspin was Kansas City, which lost for a team-record-tying seventh straight week, 17-16, to Pittsburgh. The Chiefs, whose 1-7 start was the worst in club history, scored 13 of their 16 points after Steeler turnovers.

A Kansas City turnover, however, led to the game-winning points. Rookie running back Christian Okoye, whose fumble a week earlier set up the decisive touchdown in a loss at Chicago, fumbled at his own 27-yard line with the Chiefs protecting a 16-14 fourth-quarter lead. Four plays later, Steelers placekicker Gary Anderson booted a 44-yard field goal for the game-winning points. Anderson had missed a 41-yard attempt on the play preceding Okoye's fumble.

Running backs Earnest Jackson (125 yards) and Walter Abercrombie (98) led a Pittsburgh ground attack that produced 250 yards rushing.

Eric Dickerson rushed for 138 yards on 35 attempts in his first start for the Indianapolis Colts, but it was his last carry of the game that proved most crucial in a 16-13 loss to San Diego.

With the score tied, 13-13, with 4:06 left to play, Dickerson fumbled at the Chargers' 1-yard line after a hit by linebacker Billy Ray Smith. Mike Humiston recovered in the end zone for San Diego and quarterback Dan Fouts then directed an 80-yard, game-winning drive. Fouts completed passes of 11 yards to Kellen Winslow, 18 to Wes Chandler and 11 to Rod Bernstine before placekicker Vince Abbott booted a 39-yard field goal with 12 seconds left, handing the Chargers their seventh straight win.

A crowd of 60,459—the largest since the Colts moved from Baltimore to Indianapolis in 1984—turned out at the Hoosierdome for Dickerson's home debut with the Colts. They saw the Colts score all 13 of their points in the first half and the Chargers all of their 16 in the second.

Kevin Butler's 52-yard field goal with four seconds left gave the Chicago Bears their third straight come-from-behind victory, a 26-24 NFC Central Division triumph over Green Bay. Butler had kicked just one other field goal of 50 yards or more in his career prior to the game-winner—a 52-yarder against the Packers a year earlier.

Butler's fourth field goal of the game came less than a minute after Al Del Greco's 47-yard field goal had given Green Bay a 24-23 advantage. Bears quarterback Jim McMahon completed passes of 21 yards to Ron Morris and 20 yards to Dennis McKinnon in the game-winning drive.

Even though it came in a losing effort, the Green Bay offensive line allowed no sacks in a game for the first time since October 21, 1974. The Bears' defense would finish the '87 season with a league-leading 70 sacks.

For the second straight week, quarterback Randall Cunningham and wide receiver Gregg Garrity combined for a touchdown in the final seconds to lead the Philadelphia Eagles to victory.

A week ago, the pair combined for a nine-yard touchdown with 40 seconds left for a 28-23 victory at St. Louis. This time, Cunningham threw a 40-yard pass to Garrity with 66 seconds left for a 31-27 upset victory over the Washington Redskins. The Eagles began their six-play, 77-yard game-winning drive with 2:29 remaining to snap a five-game Washington winning streak.

The play of the quarterbacks was critical to the outcome of this game. Cunningham was practically a one-man gang, completing 18 of 31 passes for 268 yards and three touchdowns and rushing seven times for 80 yards. The Redskins' Jay Schroeder, on the other hand, completed just two of his first 15 passes and 16 of 46 on the afternoon. He also threw two interceptions and fumbled one snap.

Freeman McNeil contributed two big plays off the bench in the Jets' 30-14 win over the Seahawks.

Veteran quarterback Tommy Kramer made his first start of the season for the Minnesota Vikings, but yielded to backup Wade Wilson after completing just five of 16 passes against the Los Angeles Raiders. Wilson attempted just two passes himself but completed both—for touchdowns. His 58-yard scoring pass to Hassan Jones and 11-yarder to Steve Jordan helped the Vikings to a 31-20 victory.

Wilson, who had led Minnesota to three wins in four earlier non-strike starts, also had a one-yard touchdown run.

The Viking defense also was responsible for handing the Raiders their fifth consecutive loss. The unit had five sacks, intercepted four passes and recovered one fumble. Both of Wilson's scoring passes came after Raider turnovers.

Running back Earnest Byner scored a career-high three touchdowns in the third quarter to lead the Cleveland Browns to a 38-3 interconference romp over Atlanta. The victory was the Browns' fifth straight over the Falcons and their seventh in eight meetings between the teams.

After having lost their previous four games,

the Cincinnati Bengals took the opening kick-off and drove 75 yards in eight plays for a touchdown in their Week 9 game against the Miami Dolphins. It was all downhill from there for the Bengals, however, as the Dolphins scored the next 17 points en route to a 20-14 victory.

The loss was Cincinnati's fifth in five 1987 home games.

Joe Montana completed 32 of 46 passes for 289 yards and three touchdowns to lead the San Francisco 49ers to their seventh straight victory, a 27-20 decision over the Houston Oilers. Montana's three scoring passes gave him 13 in his last four games.

San Francisco fullback Tom Rathman rushed 12 times for 57 yards and caught six passes for 60 yards and two touchdowns in only the third start of his two-year NFL career.

New York Jets running back Freeman McNeil was benched by Coach Joe Walton for the first time in his seven-year NFL career prior to the Jets' Monday night game against Seattle. McNeil, however, responded with two big plays once he entered the game to lead New York to a 30-14 victory.

The Jets, who at one time led 13-0, trailed 14-13 late in the third quarter with the ball on the Seattle 30-yard line. Quarterback Ken O'Brien handed off to rookie Roger Vick, who pitched the ball back to O'Brien. The Jet quarterback then shoveled the ball to McNeil, who sidestepped two tacklers for a 26-yard gain to the 4-yard line. On the next play, O'Brien hit tight end Billy Griggs for a touchdown and a 20-14 New York lead.

On the Jets' next possession, McNeil ripped off a 17-yard gain and, after a late-hit penalty against the Seahawks put the ball at the 17, Johnny Hector scored on a one-yard touchdown run.

The Jets' victory improved their record to 4-4, matching the record of each of the other four teams in the AFC East (the Bills, Colts, Dolphins and Patriots). It marked the first time since the NFL-AFL merger in 1970 that all teams in one division were tied so late in the regular season.

Broncos-Bills
SUNDAY, NOVEMBER 8
SCORE BY PERIODS

Denver	0	0	7	7—14
Buffalo	0	18	3	0—21

SCORING
Buffalo—Reed 9 pass from Kelly (Norwood kick), 3:23 2nd.
Buffalo—Safety, ball rolled out of end zone, 6:50 2nd.
Buffalo—Riddick 1 run (Norwood kick), 14:51 2nd.
Buffalo—Safety, ball rolled out of end zone, 15:00 2nd.
Buffalo—Field goal Norwood 30, 7:50 3rd.
Denver—Winder 6 run (Karlis kick), 9:27 3rd.
Denver—V. Johnson 15 pass from Elway (Karlis kick), 9:10 4th.

TEAM STATISTICS

	Denver	Buffalo
First downs	12	25
Rushes-Yards	22-76	58-258
Passing yards	139	170
Sacked-Yards lost	3-24	0-0
3rd down eff	2-12	9-19
Passes	13-30-0	15-24-1
Punts	9-30.8	7-39.1
Fumbles-Lost	2-2	4-2
Penalties-Yards	7-45	6-47
Time of possession	22:23	37:37

Attendance—63,698.

INDIVIDUAL STATISTICS

Rushing—Denver, Winder 12-40, Elway 3-9, Sewell 6-24, Lang 1-3; Buffalo, Harmon 18-60, Byrum 6-38, Kelly 6-17, Mueller 9-65, Riddick 19-78.

Passing—Denver, Elway 13-30-0—163; Buffalo, Kelly 14-23-1—135, Riddick 1-1-0—35.

Receiving—Denver, Nattiel 2-22, V. Johnson 5-95, Kay 4-38, Lang 2-8; Buffalo, Riddick 2-14, Metzelaars 2-13, Kelly 1-35, Reed 5-60, Burkett 2-21, Harmon 3-27.

Kickoff Returns—Denver, Lang 1-15; Buffalo, Tasker 3-32.

Punt Returns—Denver, Harden 2-11; Buffalo, Pitts 2-29.

Interceptions—Denver, Lilly 1-24.

Punting—Denver, Horan 7-39.6; Buffalo, Kidd 7-39.1.

Field Goals—Denver, none attempted; Buffalo, Norwood 1-1.

Sacks—Buffalo, Bennett, Smerlas, Smith.

Chargers-Colts
SUNDAY, NOVEMBER 8
SCORE BY PERIODS

San Diego	0	0	6	10—16
Indianapolis	3	10	0	0—13

SCORING

Indianapolis—Field goal Biasucci 37, 8:34 1st.
Indianapolis—Field goal Biasucci 27, 4:21 2nd.
Indianapolis—Bentley 8 run (Biasucci kick), 14:05 2nd.
San Diego—Field goal Abbott 42, 3:56 3rd.
San Diego—Field goal Abbott 37, 11:48 3rd.
San Diego—James 5 pass from Fouts (Abbott kick), 2:13 4th.
San Diego—Field goal Abbott 39, 14:48 4th.

TEAM STATISTICS

	San Diego	Indianapolis
First downs	15	18
Rushes-Yards	26-82	45-191
Passing yards	214	112
Sacked-Yards lost	0-0	3-15
3rd down eff	5-12	5-13
Passes	16-30-3	12-18-0
Punts	4-43.0	3-34.0
Fumbles-Lost	3-1	3-3
Penalties-Yards	10-80	9-65
Time of possession	22:11	37:49

Attendance—60,459.

INDIVIDUAL STATISTICS

Rushing—San Diego, Adams 13-52, Anderson 3-4, Redden 3-17, James 3-2, Spencer 2-5, Fouts 2-2; Indianapolis, Dickerson 35-138, Bentley 10-53.

Passing—San Diego, Fouts 16-30-3—214; Indianapolis, Trudeau 12-18-0—127.

Receiving—San Diego, Chandler 4-73, Holohan 1-16, Winslow 4-45, Anderson 3-36, Spencer 1-13, Bernstine 1-11, James 2-20; Indianapolis, Beach 3-37, Brooks 3-30, Bouza 3-53, Sherwin 2-11, Dickerson 1-minus 4.

Kickoff Returns—San Diego, Anderson 2-44, Adams 1-10; Indianapolis, Bentley 3-77, Prior 1-15.

Punt Returns—San Diego, Jones 2-28; Indianapolis, Brooks 2-24.

Interceptions—Indianapolis, Daniel 1-34, Glasgow 1-0, Prior 1-0.

Punting—San Diego, Mojsiejenko 4-43.0; Indianapolis, Stark 3-34.0.

Field Goals—San Diego, Abbott 3-3; Indianapolis, Biasucci 2-3 (missed: 53).

Sacks—San Diego, Miller 2, Banks.

Steelers-Chiefs
SUNDAY, NOVEMBER 8
SCORE BY PERIODS

Pittsburgh	0	7	7	3—17
Kansas City	7	3	0	6—16

SCORING

Kansas City—Maas 6 fumble return (Lowery kick), 1:15 1st.
Pittsburgh—Carter 4 pass from Malone (Anderson kick), 11:01 2nd.
Kansas City—Field goal Lowery 41, 14:28 2nd.
Pittsburgh—Carter 26 pass from Malone (Anderson kick), 5:05 3rd.
Kansas City—Field goal Lowery 27, 0:20 4th.
Kansas City—Field goal Lowery 38, 4:24 4th.
Pittsburgh—Field goal Anderson 44, 10:58 4th.

TEAM STATISTICS

	Pittsburgh	Kansas City
First downs	25	15
Rushes-Yards	48-250	28-101
Passing yards	141	123
Sacked-Yards lost	2-16	4-32
3rd down eff	10-19	4-12
Passes	14-31-2	14-29-4
Punts	3-42.8	3-47.0
Fumbles-Lost	2-2	3-1
Penalties-Yards	12-90	7-59
Time of possession	34:08	25:52

Attendance—45,249.

INDIVIDUAL STATISTICS

Rushing—Pittsburgh, Jackson 23-125, Abercrombie 16-98, Malone 4-14, Pollard 5-13; Kansas City, Okoye 19-72, Palmer 3-18, Heard 3-6, Moriarty 2-5, Kenney 1-0.

Passing—Pittsburgh, Malone 14-31-2—157; Kansas City, Kenney 14-29-4—155.

Receiving—Pittsburgh, Stallworth 6-66, Carter 3-39, Lee 2-14, Abercrombie 1-16, Sweeney 1-12, Thompson 1-10; Kansas City, Carson 5-70, Hayes 3-38, Paige 2-39, Moriarty 2-minus 3, Okoye 1-7, Coffman 1-4.

Kickoff Returns—Pittsburgh, Woodson 2-48, Stone 2-44; Kansas City, Palmer 3-61.

Punt Returns—Pittsburgh, Woodson 1-12; Kansas City, Clemons 2-39.

Interceptions—Pittsburgh, Merriweather 1-11, Woodruff 1-2, Everett 1-1, Hall 1-0; Kansas City, Cherry 1-30, Robinson 1-17.

Punting—Pittsburgh, Newsome 3-42.8; Kansas City, Goodburn 3-47.0.

Field Goals—Pittsburgh, Anderson 1-2 (missed: 41); Kansas City, Lowery 3-3.

Sacks—Pittsburgh, Merriweather 2½, G. Williams, Little ½; Kansas City, Del Rio, Bell.

Cowboys-Lions
SUNDAY, NOVEMBER 8
SCORE BY PERIODS

Dallas	0	10	7	0—17
Detroit	10	0	7	10—27

SCORING

Detroit—Field goal Murray 30, 9:39 1st.
Detroit—Rubick 20 pass from Long (Murray kick), 13:45 1st.

Dallas—Newsome 1 run (Ruzek kick), 12:14 2nd.
Dallas—Field goal Ruzek 38, 14:08 2nd.
Detroit—James 2 run (Murray kick), 3:02 3rd.
Dallas—Newsome 24 run (Ruzek kick), 5:42 3rd.
Detroit—James 4 run (Murray kick), 2:27 4th.
Detroit—Field goal Murray 19, 5:54 4th.

TEAM STATISTICS

	Dallas	Detroit
First downs	20	20
Rushes-Yards	29-123	30-76
Passing yards	167	217
Sacked-Yards lost	3-26	0-0
3rd down eff.	3-13	4-12
Passes	17-38-4	15-28-2
Punts	6-41.8	5-46.4
Fumbles-Lost	2-1	2-2
Penalties-Yards	11-94	6-38
Time of possession	32:11	27:49

Attendance—45,325.

INDIVIDUAL STATISTICS

Rushing—Dallas, Walker 13-65, Newsome 4-29, Dorsett 11-29, D. White 1-0; Detroit, Jones 9-46, James 18-32, Long 3-minus 2.

Passing—Dallas, D. White 17-38-4—193; Detroit, Long 15-28-2—217.

Receiving—Dallas, Walker 5-55, Renfro 4-67, Cosbie 3-26, Newsome 2-20, Edwards 2-20, Dorsett 1-5; Detroit, Mandley 8-97, Chadwick 3-72, Rubick 2-41, Jones 1-4, James 1-3.

Kickoff Returns—Dallas, Clack 4-87, Edwards 1-32; Detroit, Lee 2-46, Woolfolk 1-16.

Punt Returns—Dallas, Edwards 4-31; Detroit, Mandley 3-71.

Interceptions—Dallas, Downs 1-24, Bates 1-0; Detroit, Griffin 2-54, Gibson 1-5, Galloway 1-1.

Punting—Dallas, Saxon 6-41.8; Detroit, Arnold 5-46.4.

Field Goals—Dallas, Ruzek 1-2 (missed: 36); Detroit, Murray 2-2.

Sacks—Detroit, Cofer 2, Saleaumua.

Raiders-Vikings
SUNDAY, NOVEMBER 8
SCORE BY PERIODS

Los Angeles Raiders	3	0	10	7—20
Minnesota	0	7	14	10—31

SCORING
Los Angeles—Field goal Bahr 21, 11:21 1st.
Minnesota—Kramer 1 run (C. Nelson kick), 6:05 2nd.
Minnesota—Wilson 1 run (C. Nelson kick), 1:44 3rd.
Minnesota—Jones 58 pass from Wilson (C. Nelson kick), 4:45 3rd.
Los Angeles—Lofton 9 pass from Wilson (Bahr kick), 9:30 3rd.
Los Angeles—Field goal Bahr 35, 14:52 3rd.
Minnesota—Field goal C. Nelson 27, 3:15 4th.
Minnesota—Jordan 11 pass from Wilson (C. Nelson kick), 4:56 4th.
Los Angeles—Williams 27 pass from Wilson (Bahr kick), 7:46 4th.

TEAM STATISTICS

	Los Angeles	Minnesota
First downs	19	13
Rushes-Yards	30-157	38-116
Passing yards	219	84
Sacked-Yards lost	5-41	4-39
3rd down eff.	3-13	4-15
Passes	18-39-4	7-18-0
Punts	4-42.3	9-44.1
Fumbles-Lost	2-1	2-1
Penalties-Yards	8-66	4-26
Time of possession	30:18	29:42

Attendance—57,150.

INDIVIDUAL STATISTICS

Rushing—Los Angeles, Allen 11-50, Smith 4-18, Jackson 12-74, Hilger 1-4, Mueller 1-3, Wilson 1-8; Minnesota, D. Nelson 11-50, Rice 10-21, Dozier 11-24, Kramer 4-18, Wilson 1-1, Fenney 1-2.

Passing—Los Angeles, Hilger 8-19-3—105, Wilson 10-20-1—155; Minnesota, Kramer 5-16-0—54, Wilson 2-2-0—69.

Receiving—Los Angeles, Lofton 4-128, Smith 1-4, Christensen 4-44, Allen 4-12, Junkin 1-7, Fernandez 1-13, Jackson 1-7, Williams 2-45; Minnesota, Jordan 2-29, D. Nelson 1-minus 2, Dozier 1-0, Carter 1-26, Rice 1-12, H. Jones 1-58.

Kickoff Returns—Los Angeles, Mueller 1-24, D. Williams 3-53; Minnesota, Guggemos 5-112.

Punt Returns—Los Angeles, Woods 6-29; Minnesota, Lewis 2-5.

Interceptions—Minnesota, Browner 1-4, Thomas 1-0, Lee 1-36, Harris 1-1.

Punting—Los Angeles, Talley 4-42.3; Minnesota, Coleman 9-44.1.

Field Goals—Los Angeles, Bahr 2-2; Minnesota, C. Nelson 1-1.

Sacks—Los Angeles, Long ½, Jones, Townsend ½, King 2; Minnesota, Doleman 2, D. Martin 2, Mays.

Bears-Packers
SUNDAY, NOVEMBER 8
SCORE BY PERIODS

Chicago	7	6	0	13—26
Green Bay	14	7	0	3—24

SCORING
Chicago—Anderson 59 pass from McMahon (Butler kick), 2:24 1st.
Green Bay—West 27 pass from Wright (Del Greco kick), 6:45 1st.
Green Bay—Fullwood 2 run (Del Greco kick), 12:34 1st.
Chicago—Field goal Butler 27, 4:18 2nd.
Chicago—Field goal Butler 29, 11:20 2nd.
Green Bay—Epps 26 pass from Wright (Del Greco kick), 14:49 2nd.
Chicago—Payton 1 run (Butler kick), 3:24 4th.
Chicago—Field goal Butler 24, 11:01 4th.
Green Bay—Field goal Del Greco 47, 14:00 4th.
Chicago—Field goal Butler 52, 14:56 4th.

TEAM STATISTICS

	Chicago	Green Bay
First downs	22	17
Rushes-Yards	33-104	24-42
Passing yards	247	298
Sacked-Yards lost	2-12	0-00
3rd down eff.	5-18	6-15
Passes	21-42-2	20-42-0
Punts	3-52.0	6-38.0
Fumbles-Lost	1-0	2-1
Penalties-Yards	7-68	16-125
Time of possession	34:23	25:37

Attendance—53,320.

INDIVIDUAL STATISTICS

Rushing—Chicago, Anderson 13-22, Payton 12-49, Thomas 4-10, McMahon 1-13, Sanders 3-10; Green Bay, Carruth 5-13, Davis 11-5, Fullwood 8-24.

Passing—Chicago, McMahon 21-42-2—259; Green Bay, Wright 20-41-0—298, Neal 0-1-0—0.

Receiving—Chicago, Anderson 5-102, Morris 2-49, Boso 5-20, Gault 2-35, Payton 4-21, Moorehead 1-6, McKinnon 1-20, Suhey 1-6; Green Bay, Stanley 2-33, Neal 5-49, West 4-66, Davis 3-11, Epps 6-139.

Kickoff Returns—Chicago, Bell 1-18, Gentry 2-31; Green Bay, Cook 1-10, Fullwood 4-96.

Punt Returns—Chicago, McKinnon 4-16; Green Bay, Stanley 2-22.

Interceptions—Green Bay, Greene 1-11, Lee 1-0.

Punting—Chicago, Wagner 3-52.0; Green Bay, Bracken 6-38.0.

Field Goals—Chicago, Butler 4-6 (missed: 47, 48); Green Bay, Del Greco 1-3 (missed: 39, 26).

Sacks—Green Bay, Carreker, Johnson.

Patriots - Giants
SUNDAY, NOVEMBER 8
SCORE BY PERIODS

New England	0	0	7	3—10
New York Giants	0	14	3	0—17

SCORING

New York—Bavaro 16 pass from Rutledge (Allegre kick), 9:10 2nd.

New York—Adams 9 pass from Rutledge (Allegre kick), 12:11 2nd.

New England—Baty 15 pass from Grogan (Franklin kick), 6:42 3rd.

New York—Field goal Allegre 19, 14:43 3rd.

New England—Field goal Franklin 46, 12:38 4th.

TEAM STATISTICS

	New England	New York
First downs	11	24
Rushes-Yards	22-73	44-130
Passing yards	159	217
Sacked-Yards lost	2-16	3-16
3rd down eff	5-16	10-17
Passes	18-36-3	21-33-2
Punts	6-41.8	5-44.2
Fumbles-Lost	2-0	4-1
Penalties-Yards	2-8	7-76
Time of possession	24:10	35:50
Attendance—73,817.		

INDIVIDUAL STATISTICS

Rushing—New England, Collins 13-49, Tatupu 6-13, Grogan 1-6, Perryman 2-5; New York, Adams 12-32, Rutledge 4-3, Morris 26-88, Rouson 2-7.

Passing—New England, Grogan 18-36-3—175; New York, Rutledge 21-33-2—233.

Receiving—New England, Collins 4-25, Tatupu 3-21, Morgan 2-48, Jones 2-31, Baty 4-36, Perryman 1-1, Dawson 2-13, New York, Adams 6-36, Morris 2-16, Bavaro 5-63, Baker 4-69, McConkey 2-27, Manuel 2-22.

Kickoff Returns—New England, Starring 4-63; New York, McConkey 1-8, Rouson 1-20.

Punt Returns—New England, Fryar 3-84; New York, McConkey 4-47.

Interceptions—New England, Marion 1-19, Clayton 1-0; New York, Taylor 1-3, Banks 1-0, Welch 1-0.

Punting—New England, Camarillo 6-41.8; New York, Landeta 5-44.2.

Field Goals—New England, Franklin 1-2 (missed: 50); New York, Allegre 1-2 (missed: 41).

Sacks—New England, Reynolds, Tippett; New York, Taylor 2.

Dolphins - Bengals
SUNDAY, NOVEMBER 8
SCORE BY PERIODS

Miami	0	10	7	3—20
Cincinnati	7	0	0	7—14

SCORING

Cincinnati—Kattus 17 pass from Esiason (Breech kick), 4:32 1st.

Miami—Stradford 1 run (Reveiz kick), 5:48 2nd.

Miami—Field goal Reveiz 48, 15:00 2nd.

Miami—Clayton 30 pass from Marino (Reveiz kick), 10:50 3rd.

Cincinnati—Johnson 6 run (Breech kick), 5:03 4th.

Miami—Field goal Reveiz 34, 12:52 4th.

TEAM STATISTICS

	Miami	Cincinnati
First downs	22	24
Rushes-Yards	24-98	27-156
Passing yards	235	202
Sacked-Yards lost	3-27	1-26
3rd down eff	9-16	2-7
Passes	26-41-0	18-37-1
Punts	4-41.7	3-40.6
Fumbles-Lost	1-0	2-1
Penalties-Yards	6-61	3-35
Time of possession	34:13	25:47
Attendance—53,847.		

INDIVIDUAL STATISTICS

Rushing—Miami, Stradford 11-30, Hampton 9-50, Nathan 1-8, Bennett 3-10; Cincinnati, Brooks 1-8, Johnson 13-89, Kinnebrew 5-19, Jennings 6-25, Esiason 2-15.

Passing—Miami, Marino 26-41-0—262; Cincinnati, Esiason 18-37-1—228.

Receiving—Miami, Stradford 7-49, Clayton 3-53, Hampton 4-35, Pruitt 6-90, Nathan 2-9, Jensen 2-16, Bennett 1-3, Hardy 1-7; Cincinnati, Jennings 3-27, Brown 8-105, Kattus 5-70, Holman 1-15, Colllinsworth 1-11.

Kickoff Returns—Miami, Stradford 2-42, Lewis 1-0; Cincinnati, McGee 3-46, Bussey 1-12.

Punt Returns—Miami, Blackwood 1-1, Schwedes 1-8; Cincinnati, Martin 1-14.

Interceptions—Miami, Judson 1-10.

Punting—Miami, Roby 4-41.7; Cincinnati, Fulhage 3-40.6.

Field Goals—Miami, Reveiz 2-3 (missed: 45); Cincinnati, none attempted.

Sacks—Miami, Sochia ½, Offerdahl ½; Cincinnati, Williams, Krumrie, Edwards.

Redskins - Eagles
SUNDAY, NOVEMBER 8
SCORE BY PERIODS

Washington	7	14	0	6—27
Philadelphia	7	10	0	14—31

SCORING

Philadelphia—Toney 5 run (McFadden kick), 6:10 1st.

Washington—Rogers 3 run (Haji-Sheikh kick), 11:19 1st.

Washington—Monk 19 pass from Schroeder (Haji-Sheikh kick), 6:04 2nd.

Washington—Green 26 fumble return (Haji-Sheikh kick), 9:35 2nd.

Philadelphia—Field goal McFadden 37, 12:27 2nd.

Philadelphia—Quick 6 pass from Cunningham (McFadden kick), 14:46 2nd.

Philadelphia—Quick 32 pass from Cunningham (McFadden kick), 7:47 4th.

Washington—Clark 47 pass from Schroeder (kick blocked), 12:31 4th.

Philadelphia—Garrity 40 pass from Cunningham (McFadden kick), 13:54 4th.

TEAM STATISTICS

	Washington	Philadelphia
First downs	23	23
Rushes-Yards	28-129	41-195
Passing yards	231	238
Sacked-Yards lost	3-34	3-30
3rd down eff	4-14	3-13
Passes	16-46-2	18-31-3
Punts	8-35.1	6-41.7
Fumbles-Lost	2-2	2-1
Penalties-Yards	6-46	5-35
Time of possession	28:21	31:39
Attendance—63,609.		

INDIVIDUAL STATISTICS

Rushing—Washington, Rogers 19-80, Bryant 7-40, Schroeder 2-9; Philadelphia, Toney 20-87, Cunningham 7-

80, Byars 12-26, Tautalatasi 2-2.

Passing—Washington, Schroeder 16-46-2—265; Philadelphia, Cunningham 18-31-3—268.

Receiving—Washington, Clark 5-119, Monk 5-81, Bryant 5-57, Rogers 1-8; Philadelphia, Toney 6-38, Jackson 4-98, Garrity 3-63, Quick 2-38, Byars 1-12, Tautalatasi 1-11, Spagnola 1-8.

Kickoff Returns—Washington, Griffin 3-86, Orr 1-10; Philadelphia, Morse 3-32, C. Brown 1-13, Carter 1-28.

Punt Returns—Washington, Yarber 4-21; Philadelphia, Morse 3-19, A. Johnson 1-0.

Interceptions—Washington, Coleman 1-25, Wilburn 1-0, Bowles 1-0; Philadelphia, J. Brown 1-6, Young 1-30.

Punting—Washington, Cox 8-35.1; Philadelphia, Teltschik 6-41.7.

Field Goals—Washington, none attempted; Philadelphia, McFadden 1-1.

Sacks—Washington, Manley, Mann, Olkewicz; Philadelphia, Frizzell, Cobb, Reichenbach ½, Simmons ½.

Buccaneers-Cardinals
SUNDAY, NOVEMBER 8
SCORE BY PERIODS

Tampa Bay	7	7	14	0—28
St. Louis	0	3	0	28—31

SCORING

Tampa Bay—Carrier 5 pass from DeBerg (Igwebuike kick), 14:38 1st.

Tampa Bay—Carter 3 pass from DeBerg (Igwebuike kick), 9:50 2nd.

St. Louis—Field goal Gallery 31, 14:40 2nd.

Tampa Bay—Smith 34 pass from DeBerg (Igwebuike kick), 5:01 3rd.

Tampa Bay—Smith 3 run (Igwebuike kick), 13:09 3rd.

St. Louis—Awalt 4 pass from Lomax (Gallery kick), 2:18 4th.

St. Louis—Noga 24 fumble return (Gallery kick), 3:21 4th.

St. Louis—J.T. Smith 11 pass from Lomax (Gallery kick), 6:42 4th.

St. Louis—J.T. Smith 17 pass from Lomax (Gallery kick), 12:59 4th.

TEAM STATISTICS

	Tampa Bay	St. Louis
First downs	26	26
Rushes-Yards	33-83	31-137
Passing yards	294	278
Sacked-Yards lost	1-9	4-36
3rd down eff	12-16	7-14
Passes	23-37-0	25-36-1
Punts	3-39	3-39
Fumbles-Lost	1-1	2-1
Penalties-Yards	8-72	11-123
Time of possession	28:46	31:14
Attendance—22,449.		

INDIVIDUAL STATISTICS

Rushing—Tampa Bay, Wilder 11-49, Smith 19-48, DeBerg 1-minus 1, Howard 1-minus 3, Hill 1-minus 10; St. Louis, Mitchell 17-79, Lomax 4-23, Ferrell 9-33, Wolfley 1-2.

Passing—Tampa Bay, DeBerg 23-37-0—303; St. Louis, Lomax 25-36-1—314.

Receiving—Tampa Bay, Wilder 6-87, Carrier 1-5, Carter 6-82, Hill 4-56, Magee 1-11, Smith 3-43, Howard 2-19; St. Louis, Mitchell 4-58, Holmes 4-36, J.T. Smith 8-96, Awalt 9-124.

Kickoff Returns—Tampa Bay, Futrell 4-56, Miller 1-22; St. Louis, Sikahema 3-70, McAdoo 2-51.

Punt Returns—Tampa Bay, Futrell 1-5; St. Louis, Sikahema 2-12.

Interceptions—Tampa Bay, Jones 1-9.

Punting—Tampa Bay, Garcia 3-39.0; St. Louis, Cater 1-39.0.

Field Goals—Tampa Bay, Igwebuike 0-1 (missed: 53); St. Louis, Gallery 1-2 (missed: 38).

Sacks—Tampa Bay, Washington 2, Moss, Holmes; St. Louis, Greer.

Saints-Rams
SUNDAY, NOVEMBER 8
SCORE BY PERIODS

New Orleans	10	7	7	7—31
Los Angeles Rams	0	7	7	0—14

SCORING

New Orleans—Field goal Andersen 32, 4:23 1st.

New Orleans—Hilliard 38 pass from Hebert (Andersen kick), 13:18 1st.

New Orleans—Tice 23 pass from Hilliard (Andersen kick), 4:46 2nd.

Los Angeles—D. Johnson 8 pass from Everett (Lansford kick), 14:06 2nd.

Los Angeles—Bell 32 pass from Everett (Lansford kick), 3:16 3rd.

New Orleans—Mayes 2 run (Andersen kick), 10:04 3rd.

New Orleans—Hill 3 pass from Hebert (Andersen kick), 4:25 4th.

TEAM STATISTICS

	New Orleans	Los Angeles
First downs	20	18
Rushes-Yards	44-232	22-102
Passing yards	211	202
Sacked-Yards lost	0-0	0-0
3rd down eff	8-12	3-10
Passes	13-21-1	17-34-2
Punts	3-44.7	5-43.2
Fumbles-Lost	1-1	1-1
Penalties-Yards	8-62	5-41
Time of possession	36:54	23:06
Attendance—43,379.		

INDIVIDUAL STATISTICS

Rushing—New Orleans, Hilliard 14-92, Mayes 23-81, Word 4-31, Hebert 2-25, Jordan 1-3; Los Angeles, White 12-54, Bell 7-28, Everett 2-17, Guman 1-3.

Passing—New Orleans, Hebert 12-20-1—188, Hilliard 1-1-0—23; Los Angeles, Everett 17-34-2—202.

Receiving—New Orleans, Hilliard 4-84, Martin 2-33, Brenner 2-29, Jones 1-30, Tice 1-23, Gray 1-5, Mayes 1-4, Hill 1-3; Los Angeles, Ellard 5-73, Bell 5-59, D. Johnson 3-15, Hill 1-22, House 1-15, Young 1-14, Ron Brown 1-4.

Kickoff Returns—New Orleans, Gray 2-21, Hilliard 1-14; Los Angeles, Ron Brown 3-59.

Punt Returns—New Orleans, Gray 2-20; Los Angeles, Ellard 2-8.

Interceptions—New Orleans, Maxie 1-0, R. Sutton 1-26; Los Angeles, Gray 1-35.

Punting—New Orleans, Hansen 3-44.7; Los Angeles, Hatcher 5-43.2.

Field Goals—New Orleans, Andersen 1-1; Los Angeles, none attempted.

Sacks—None.

Falcons-Browns
SUNDAY, NOVEMBER 8
SCORE BY PERIODS

Atlanta	0	3	0	0— 3
Cleveland	0	14	21	3—38

SCORING

Cleveland—Slaughter 54 pass from Kosar (Jaeger kick), 6:50 2nd.

Cleveland—Mack 1 run (Jaeger kick), 11:04 2nd.

Atlanta—Field goal Luckhurst 42, 15:00 2nd.

Cleveland—Byner 2 run (Jaeger kick), 5:05 3rd.

Cleveland—Byner 5 run (Jaeger kick), 8:59 3rd.

Cleveland—Byner 4 pass from Kosar (Jaeger kick), 12:45 3rd.

Cleveland—Field goal Jaeger 38, 9:41 4th.

TEAM STATISTICS

	Atlanta	Cleveland
First downs	13	24
Rushes-Yards	23-117	40-173
Passing yards	126	192
Sacked-Yards lost	7-43	0-0
3rd down eff.	3-12	8-13
Passes	15-22-1	13-24-0
Punts	7-38.1	2-37.0
Fumbles-Lost	1-1	2-1
Penalties-Yards	16-90	6-47
Time of possession	31:36	28:24

Attendance—71,135.

INDIVIDUAL STATISTICS

Rushing—Atlanta, Riggs 16-93, Campbell 4-22, Flowers 1-1, Emery 1-5, Matthews 1-minus 4; Cleveland, Byner 10-29, Mack 18-52, Fontenot 4-24, Kosar 1-7, Manoa 7-61.

Passing—Atlanta, Campbell 15-22-1—169; Cleveland, Kosar 13-23-0—192, Danielson 0-1-0—0.

Receiving—Atlanta, Bailey 2-36, Emery 1-10, Dixon 2-14, Cox 2-18, Matthews 5-70, Whisenhunt 1-7, Riggs 2-14; Cleveland, Weathers 3-42, Slaughter 2-70, Newsome 3-33, Byner 4-40, Mack 1-7.

Kickoff Returns—Atlanta, Emery 6-120, Flowers 1-20; Cleveland, Young 1-44.

Punt Returns—Atlanta, B. Johnson 1-6; Cleveland, McNeil 5-92.

Interceptions—Cleveland, Dixon 1-0.

Punting—Atlanta, Donnelly 6-44.5; Cleveland, Winslow 2-37.0.

Field Goals—Atlanta, Luckhurst 1-1; Cleveland, Jaeger 1-2 (missed: 39).

Sacks—Cleveland, Harper, E. Johnson, Matthews, Baker ½, Puzzouli 2½, Hairston.

Oilers-49ers
SUNDAY, NOVEMBER 8
SCORE BY PERIODS

Houston	3	3	7	7—20
San Francisco	7	7	7	6—27

SCORING

Houston—Field goal Zendejas 20, 6:01 1st.
San Francisco—Rathman 8 pass from Montana (Wersching kick), 12:44 1st.
Houston—Field goal Zendejas 48, 11:42 2nd.
San Francisco—Rice 1 pass from Montana (Wersching kick), 14:57 2nd.
San Francisco—Rathman 5 pass from Montana (Wersching kick), 7:52 3rd.
Houston—Duncan 5 pass from Moon (Zendejas kick), 12:19 3rd.
San Francisco—Field goal Wersching 28, 2:05 4th.
San Francisco—Field goal Wersching 38, 6:35 4th.
Houston—Givins 8 pass from Moon (Zendejas kick), 10:03 4th.

TEAM STATISTICS

	Houston	San Francisco
First downs	15	33
Rushes-Yards	19-48	34-163
Passing yards	221	280
Sacked-Yards lost	1-12	1-9
3rd down eff.	7-14	6-11
Passes	18-38-3	32-46-2
Punts	1-54.0	3-42.0
Fumbles-Lost	2-1	1-0
Penalties-Yards	4-45	3-20
Time of possession	23:20	36:40

Attendance—59,740.

INDIVIDUAL STATISTICS

Rushing—Houston, Jackson 7-16, Moon 4-14, Pease 1-8, Tillman 4-6, Wallace 1-3, Highsmith 2-1; San Francisco, Craig 16-68, Rathman 12-57, Sydney 3-26, Young 1-15, Montana 2-minus 3.

Passing—Houston, Moon 17-36-3—198, Pease 1-2-0—35; San Francisco, Montana 32-46-2—289.

Receiving—Houston, Jackson 5-30, D. Hill 4-101, Givins 4-43, Duncan 2-14, Wallace 2-10, Drewrey 1-35; San Francisco, Craig 8-51, Rice 7-77, Rathman 6-60, Francis 6-44, Wilson 3-45, Clark 2-12.

Kickoff Returns—Houston, Duncan 5-111, K. Johnson 1-18; San Francisco, Rodgers 5-72.

Punt Returns—Houston, K. Johnson 1-11; San Francisco, Griffin 1-4.

Interceptions—Houston, Lyles 1-27, Bostic 1-7; San Francisco, Griffin 1-0, J. Fahnhorst 1-0, McKyer 1-0.

Punting—Houston, L. Johnson 1-54.0; San Francisco, Runager 2-46.0.

Field Goals—Houston, Zendejas 2-2; San Francisco, Wersching 2-3 (missed: 44).

Sacks—Houston, Baker; San Francisco, Kugler ½, Haley ½.

Seahawks-Jets
MONDAY, NOVEMBER 9
SCORE BY PERIODS

Seattle	0	0	14	0—14
New York Jets	0	10	10	10—30

SCORING

New York—Townsell 91 punt return (Leahy kick), 2:44 2nd.
New York—Field goal Leahy 35, 14:59 2nd.
New York—Field goal Leahy 36, 3:28 3rd.
Seattle—Warner 3 run (N. Johnson kick), 5:46 3rd.
Seattle—Largent 29 pass from Krieg (N. Johnson kick), 8:42 3rd.
New York—Griggs 4 pass from O'Brien (Leahy kick), 14:39 3rd.
New York—Hector 1 run (Leahy kick), 3:57 4th.
New York—Field goal Leahy 26, 13:34 4th.

TEAM STATISTICS

	Seattle	New York
First downs	17	23
Rushes-Yards	28-111	37-132
Passing yards	164	210
Sacked-Yards lost	2-24	2-16
3rd down eff.	2-10	9-16
Passes	12-29-2	23-30-0
Punts	5-38.8	5-36.2
Fumbles-Lost	2-2	2-1
Penalties-Yards	9-101	13-94
Time of possession	25:09	34:51

Attendance—60,452.

INDIVIDUAL STATISTICS

Rushing—Seattle, Warner 18-70, J.L. Williams 8-40, Krieg 1-1, Rodriguez 1-0; New York, Hector 20-63, McNeil 7-42, O'Brien 5-22, Vick 5-5.

Passing—Seattle, Krieg 12-29-2—188; New York, O'Brien 22-30-0—226.

Receiving—Seattle, Largent 4-88, J.L. Williams 3-45, Warner 2-8, Tice 1-27, R. Butler 1-9, Skansi 1-11; New York, Toon 4-66, Klever 4-26, Shuler 3-31, Sohn 3-31, McNeil 3-34, Vick 2-9, Griggs 1-4, Hector 3-25.

Kickoff Returns—Seattle, Hollis 2-35, Morris 2-36, Powell 1-14, Lane 1-22, Edmonds 1-19; New York, Townsell 1-13, Humphery 2-25.

Punt Returns—Seattle, Hollis 2-16; New York, Townsell 3-95.

Interceptions—New York, Hamilton 2-25.

Punting—Seattle, Rodriguez 5-38.8; New York, Jennings 5-36.2.

Field Goals—Seattle, none attempted; New York Leahy 3-3.

Sacks—Seattle, F. Young, Nash; New York, Howard, Nichols.

TENTH WEEK

RESULTS OF WEEK 10

Sunday, November 15

Cincinnati 16, Atlanta 10 at Atl.
Cleveland 27, Buffalo 21 at Cleve.
Dallas 23, New England 17 (OT) at N.E.
Houston 23, Pittsburgh 3 at Pitts.
Indianapolis 40, Miami 21 at Mia.
L.A. Rams 27, St. Louis 24 at St.L.
Minnesota 23, Tampa Bay 17 at Minn.
New Orleans 26, San Francisco 24 at S.F.
N.Y. Giants 20, Philadelphia 17 at Phila.
N.Y. Jets 16, Kansas City 9 at K.C.
San Diego 16, L.A. Raiders 14 at S.D.
Seattle 24, Green Bay 13 at Sea.
Washington 20, Detroit 13 at Wash.

Monday, November 16

Denver 31, Chicago 29 at Den.

The dawning of a new era and the end of another began Week 10 in Foxboro, Mass., when Herschel Walker replaced Tony Dorsett as the starting running back for the Dallas Cowboys in a game against the New England Patriots. Walker, who was named the starter just three days earlier by Cowboys Coach Tom Landry, responded by scoring the game-winning touchdown on a 60-yard dash on the fourth play in overtime. The Cowboys won, 23-17, and Walker's 173 yards rushing was the fourth highest total in club history. Walker carried the ball on 28 of Dallas' 30 rushing plays.

"I love to run the ball," said the 25-year-old Walker, who was picked by the Cowboys in the fifth round of the 1985 NFL draft while playing in the United States Football League. "Georgia gave me a chance in college. The New Jersey Generals (of the USFL) gave me a chance."

And so, too, would the Dallas Cowboys.

Walker had started nine games at three different positions during his 1986 NFL rookie season (running back, fullback and wide receiver), but the start against New England would be the first of seven straight at running back to close out the 1987 regular season.

Dorsett, the NFL's fourth all-time leading rusher, had held a hammerlock on the job since being Dallas' No. 1 draft choice in 1977. But he would never start another game as a Cowboy.

"I had a pretty good view of the game-winning touchdown, and all I could see was a blue flame," said Cowboys quarterback Danny White. "I couldn't see Herschel or who was after him or anything else. I just saw that blue flame and I knew he was smoking."

White played a key role in forcing the overtime by connecting with wide receiver Mike Renfro for a 43-yard gain on a fourth-and-13 play in the final minute of regulation. Roger Ruzek kicked a 20-yard field goal with 28 seconds remaining and Dallas won the coin flip to start the overtime.

On the touchdown run, Walker broke a tackle by linebacker Steve Nelson at the line of scrimmage and another by safety Fred Marion five yards later before outracing cornerback Raymond Clayborn to the end zone.

"It happened so fast," said Marion, "it's hard to remember the details."

"We have been quite well aware of his ability to do everything there is on a football field," said Patriots Coach Raymond Berry, whose team has never beaten the Cowboys in six tries and is now 0-9 in overtime games. "He showed that today."

Walker was impressive, but top rushing honors for the week went to Charles White of the Los Angeles Rams. White picked up a career-high 213 yards on 34 carries to lead the Rams to a 27-24 win over St. Louis. White's single-game total was the fifth best in Rams' history and the most ever against a Cardinal team.

Sixty-two of White's yards came on a mammoth 23-play, 94-yard drive that consumed the final 11:01 of the game. The Rams began the drive at their own 3-yard line with 11:04 left on the clock and didn't end it until Mike Lansford booted a game-winning, 20-yard field goal with three seconds left.

The Rams, who won their first non-strike game in more than 11 months, ran the ball on 19 of the 23 plays in the final drive.

Week 10's other outstanding rushing performance was turned in by the New York Jets' Freeman McNeil, who carried 26 times for 184 yards in a 16-9 victory over the Kansas City Chiefs. It was the second best regular-season rushing total in McNeil's seven-year NFL career. McNeil rushed for 135 yards in the 1986 AFC wild-card game against the Chiefs.

Kansas City, which set a team record with its eighth consecutive loss, opened the game with former University of Kansas star Frank Seurer at quarterback. Seurer, who became the fifth player to start a game at quarterback for the Chiefs in 1987 (following Todd Blackledge, Matt Stevens, Doug Hudson and Bill Kenney), completed 13 of 23 pass attempts for 233 yards while throwing three interceptions. He also was sacked five times and had one pass dropped in the end zone.

The Chiefs' only points came on three field goals by Nick Lowery, the last of which gave them a 9-6 lead after three quarters. But the Jets responded with a nine-play drive that ended with the game's only touchdown and the winning points—an 18-yard pass from Ken O'Brien to Al Toon with 11:04 left.

Another AFC West Division team in a tailspin was the Los Angeles Raiders, who dropped a 16-14 decision to division-rival San Diego. The loss was the Raiders' sixth straight after three season-opening wins and their 3-6 start was their worst since 1962.

Prior to the 1987 season, the Raiders had beaten the Chargers in nine of the previous 11 meetings between the teams. But the Chargers' victory, combined with a 23-17 win during the players' strike, gave them their first series sweep over the Raiders since 1981.

San Diego scored all of its points in the first half, with Dan Fouts throwing a nine-yard touchdown pass to Kellen Winslow and Vince Abbott kicking three field goals. The Raiders, who set one team record with 186 yards in penalties and tied another with 17 penalties, didn't score until quarterback Marc Wilson threw touchdown passes to Dokie Williams and James Lofton in the final eight minutes of the game.

The Chargers' victory gave them a team-record eight straight wins and improved their season record to 8-1, best in the NFL after nine games.

San Diego's closest competition in the AFC West, the Seattle Seahawks, remained two games back by posting a 24-13 interconference victory over Green Bay. Curt Warner led the Seahawks' attack by rushing 25 times for 123 yards, including a 57-yard touchdown run on the first play of the second quarter.

Seattle took control by scoring two touchdowns in the final 2:08 of the first half. With Green Bay leading, 13-7, reserve fullback Tony Burse blocked a punt by the Packers' Don Bracken and Eugene Robinson returned it eight yards for a touchdown. On the Packers' next possession, quarterback Randy Wright fumbled on a sack by defensive end Jacob Green and Paul Moyer returned the ball six yards to the Green Bay 8. Three plays later, Seahawks quarterback Dave Krieg ran eight yards for the score.

The game was one of the sloppiest of the season. Each team committed five turnovers, with the Seahawks and Packers combining for four in a forgettable one-minute span of the fourth period.

In a game someone had to win—barring a tie—the Cincinnati Bengals defeated the Atlanta Falcons, 16-10. Bengals fullback Larry Kinnebrew, who rushed for 100 yards on 27 attempts, scored the deciding touchdown on a two-yard run with 23 seconds left to snap a four-game Cincinnati losing streak and hand Atlanta its fourth straight loss.

The Falcons led, 10-6, midway through the final period and appeared ready to snap out of their midseason doldrums. Scott Campbell's 44-yard touchdown pass to Floyd Dixon late in the third period was Atlanta's first touchdown in 11 quarters—a span in which the Falcons had been outscored 96-9.

But Cincinnati cut the Falcons' lead to one point on Jim Breech's 30-yard field goal with 3:42 remaining. And on Atlanta's next posses-

Raul Allegre kicked field goals of 53 and 52 yards in the Giants' 20-17 victory over the Eagles in Week 10.

sion, Eddie Edwards and Reggie Williams sacked Campbell for 19 yards in losses on back-to-back plays, forcing the Falcons to punt from their own end zone. The Bengals took possession on their own 40-yard line with 2:14 left and, seven running plays later, Kinnebrew scored the game-winner.

The Houston Oilers won at Pittsburgh's Three Rivers Stadium for the first time since 1978 with a 23-3 AFC Central Division triumph over the Steelers. It was the fourth road win in six games for an Oilers team that entered the '87 season having lost 33 of 36 road games over five seasons.

The Oilers, who did not score until Tony Zendejas' 34-yard field goal on the final play of the first half, broke the game open on two Warren Moon touchdown passes in the third quarter. Moon, who completed 18 of 24 passes, threw a 14-yard touchdown pass to Curtis Duncan and a 42-yarder to Drew Hill for a 17-3 Houston lead.

The Steelers' only points came on a 22-yard field goal by Gary Anderson after linebacker Mike Merriweather recovered a Moon fumble at the Oilers' 33-yard line.

Morten Andersen of the New Orleans Saints, who supplanted Anderson as the NFL's all-time field-goal accuracy leader earlier in the season, booted four field goals to lead the Saints to a 26-24 victory over the San Francisco 49ers. Andersen's fourth field goal was the game-winner, a 40-yard kick with 1:06 remaining that snapped a seven-game 49ers winning streak and gave New Orleans its third win on the road in as many weeks.

The Saints began the winning drive at their own 22-yard line with 2:54 left when quarterback Bobby Hebert completed 23- and 31-yard passes, respectively, to Lonzell Hill and Eric Martin.

The game's biggest play came late in the third period, when the Saints' Reggie Sutton blocked a 47-yard field-goal attempt by San Francisco's Ray Wersching. Johnnie Poe scooped up the loose ball and returned it 61 yards for a touchdown.

If Wersching had a case of kicking blues, imagine how Paul McFadden of the Philadelphia Eagles felt after the Eagles' 20-17 NFC East Division loss to the New York Giants. McFadden was wide left on a 39-yard field goal attempt with 25 seconds left that would have forced the game into overtime.

McFadden's counterpart, Raul Allegre, kicked 53- and 52-yard field goals for New York to become the first player in Giants' history with two field goals of 50 or more yards in the same game.

Giant veteran Jeff Rutledge, who had never won a game as an NFL starting quarterback prior to a Week 9 triumph over New England, completed 16 of 30 passes for 298 yards to win his second straight game as a substitute for the injured Phil Simms.

Another pattern that continued for a second week was the Minnesota Vikings' ability to change quarterbacks at halftime and win with a second-half rally.

Vikings Coach Jerry Burns benched starter Wade Wilson in favor of Tommy Kramer after Minnesota trailed, 7-6, at intermission in a game against the Tampa Bay Buccaneers. Kramer went on to complete four of nine attempts in his relief role, including passes of 14 and 12 yards to Anthony Carter on Minnesota's first possession of the second half. Rookie Rick Fenney ended the drive with a one-yard scoring run to give the Vikings a 13-7 lead.

Kramer later threw a two-yard scoring pass to tight end Steve Jordan as the Vikings rallied for a 23-17 NFC Central Division victory. It was the first touchdown pass in 11 months for Kramer, who spent most of the 1987 preseason in an alcohol rehabilitation center and the first half of the regular season with a pinched nerve in his neck.

A week earlier, Burns had benched an ineffective Kramer in favor of Wilson and Minnesota responded with 24 second-half points in a 31-20 victory over the Raiders.

The Vikings, who got a 103-yard rushing performance from tailback Darrin Nelson, outgained the Bucs by a whopping 224-15 on the ground.

Bernie Kosar made it 2-for-2 in his head-to-head encounters with former University of Miami teammate Jim Kelly in the Cleveland Browns' 27-21 triumph over the Buffalo Bills at Cleveland Stadium. During the 1986 regular season, Kosar and the Browns won by a 21-17 score in a game played at Buffalo's Rich Stadium.

Kosar completed 24 of 34 passes for two touchdowns with one interception while Kelly hit on 22 of 35 attempts for two touchdowns and no interceptions.

Although Kosar (337 yards) and Kelly (206) combined for 543 net yards passing, each team's first touchdown, oddly, came on a fumble return. Buffalo's Mark Kelso returned a Kevin Mack fumble 56 yards late in the first period for a 7-3 Bills lead. Cleveland's Ray Ellis returned the favor 2:10 later, taking a Pete Metzelaars fumble 24 yards for a 10-7 Browns advantage.

The victory was the seventh for the Browns in the nine regular-season meetings between the teams.

After 14 consecutive losses, the Indianapolis Colts finally defeated the Miami Dolphins, 40-21, to end the longest-running domination by one team over another in the NFL. Prior to the Week 10 upset at Joe Robbie Stadium, the Colts' last victory over the Dolphins had occurred October 5, 1980, when the then-Baltimore Colts won 30-17 behind three Bert Jones touchdown passes.

Eric Dickerson rushed for 154 yards and Dean Biasucci kicked four field goals in the Colts' latest win, but the key to the game was five Miami turnovers that led to 24 Indianapolis points. The biggest Miami turnover came when running back Lorenzo Hampton fumbled at the Colts' goal line on the Dolphins' first possession of the second half, with Miami already holding a 21-20 lead. Instead of a 28-20 Dolphins' advantage, Nesby Glasgow recovered the loose ball for the Colts on the Indianapolis 3-yard line. Nineteen plays, 90 yards and nearly nine minutes later, Biasucci kicked a 25-yard field goal for a 23-21 Indianapolis lead.

One team that could not break a losing jinx in Week 10 was the Detroit Lions, who lost for the 12th straight time to the Washington Redskins, this time 20-13. The Lions have not beat-

Doug Williams came off the bench to lead the Washington Redskins to a 20-13 win over Detroit.

en the Redskins since a 14-10 triumph at Tiger Stadium on October 3, 1965.

Washington's latest win, however, did not come easily. The game was tied, 3-3, with seven minutes left in the first half when Redskins Coach Joe Gibbs replaced starting quarterback Jay Schroeder with veteran Doug Williams. Schroeder was coming off a poor performance against the Eagles a week earlier and had completed just five of 10 passes for 33 yards.

Williams was terrific in relief. He led the Redskins to touchdowns on his first two possessions after taking over, throwing a 16-yard touchdown pass to Kelvin Bryant on the first possession and a 42-yarder to Gary Clark on the second.

Turnovers, however, did in the Lions as much as Williams' play. Detroit quarterback Chuck Long threw four interceptions, three by Redskins cornerback Darrell Green. Trailing by seven points, the Lions drove into Washington territory four times in the final quarter and came up empty. Barry Wilburn picked off a Long pass at the Redskins' 1-yard line early in the period and Green intercepted Long at the Washington 15-yard line with a minute remaining.

Week 10's Monday night game between Denver and Chicago figured to be a quarterback duel between the Broncos' John Elway and the Bears' Jim McMahon.

It was. Elway threw for 341 yards and three touchdowns and McMahon a career-high 311 yards and three TDs as the Broncos prevailed, 31-29, in an interconference game. Ironically, the first 300-yard passing game of McMahon's six-year NFL career came in the same game

that snapped his string of 25 consecutive victories as the Bears' starting quarterback.

Chicago started fast, driving 90 and 86 yards for touchdowns on its first two possessions. McMahon capped the first drive with a 51-yard touchdown pass to Willie Gault and the second with a six-yard toss to tight end Cap Boso.

Elway responded by throwing all three of his TD passes—to Vance Johnson, Mark Jackson and Ricky Nattiel—in the second quarter to give the Broncos a 21-14 halftime lead.

Although the Bears botched the extra point attempts following their two third-quarter touchdowns, the momentum of the game probably shifted on a play in the second quarter. The Bears led, 14-7, and had the ball on the Denver 1-yard line. Bears Coach Mike Ditka sent in 325-pound defensive tackle William (The Refrigerator) Perry as a decoy for the next play.

McMahon, however, changed the play and handed the ball to Perry, who fumbled after a hit by cornerback Mike Harden. Mark Haynes recovered for Denver and returned the ball to the 24-yard line, setting up a 76-yard Broncos scoring drive to tie the game at 14-14.

Giants-Eagles
SUNDAY, NOVEMBER 15
SCORE BY PERIODS

New York Giants	7	3	7	3—20
Philadelphia	10	0	7	0—17

SCORING
Philadelphia—Cunningham 4 run (McFadden kick), 4:34 1st.

Philadelphia—Field goal McFadden 25, 8:21 1st.

New York—Manuel 36 pass from Rutledge (Allegre kick), 14:38 1st.

New York—Field goal Allegre 53, 12:38 2nd.
Philadelphia—Byars 8 pass from Cunningham (McFadden kick), 7:02 3rd.
New York—Adams 1 run (Allegre kick), 14:21 3rd.
New York—Field goal Allegre 52, 3:48 4th.

TEAM STATISTICS

	New York	Philadelphia
First downs	17	22
Rushes-Yards	28-116	39-191
Passing yards	268	146
Sacked-Yards lost	4-30	6-31
3rd down eff.	4-13	7-19
Passes	16-30-2	17-34-1
Punts	3-38.3	8-36.0
Fumbles-Lost	1-1	2-0
Penalties-Yards	6-48	5-45
Time of possession	27:53	32:07

Attendance—66,172.

INDIVIDUAL STATISTICS

Rushing—New York, Rouson 12-61, Adams 12-29, Rutledge 3-28, Morris 1-minus 2; Philadelphia, Cunningham 10-71, Toney 14-61, Byars 15-59.

Passing—New York, Rutledge 16-30-2—298; Philadelphia, Cunningham 17-34-1—177.

Receiving—New York, Bavaro 7-102, Manuel 4-105, Adams 3-31, Baker 2-60; Philadelphia, Quick 3-32, Toney 3-27, Tautalatasi 3-10, Garrity 2-50, Spagnola 2-26, Byars 2-17, Jackson 1-18, Cunningham 1-minus 3.

Kickoff Returns—New York, Adams 3-65, Rouson 1-17; Philadelphia, Morse 5-72.

Punt Returns—New York, McConkey 2-13; Philadelphia, Morse 3-11.

Interceptions—New York, P. Williams 1-minus 5; Philadelphia, Joyner 1-15, Foules 1-0.

Punting—New York, Landeta 4-37.8; Philadelphia, Teltschik 7-36.0.

Field Goals—New York, Allegre 2-4 (missed: 41, 44); Philadelphia, McFadden 1-3 (missed: 50, 37).

Sacks—New York, Howard, Taylor 2, Burt, Martin, Marshall; Philadelphia, White 3, Joyner ½, Clarke ½.

Jets-Chiefs
SUNDAY, NOVEMBER 15
SCORE BY PERIODS

New York Jets	3	0	3	10—16
Kansas City	0	3	6	0— 9

SCORING

New York—Field goal Leahy 39, 12:57 1st.
Kansas City—Field goal Lowery 42, 2:16 2nd.
Kansas City—Field goal Lowery 43, 4:02 3rd.
New York—Field goal Leahy 24, 9:17 3rd.
Kansas City—Field goal Lowery 18, 14:29 3rd.
New York—Toon 18 pass from O'Brien (Leahy kick), 3:56 4th.
New York—Field goal Leahy 18, 12:41 4th.

TEAM STATISTICS

	New York	Kansas City
First downs	19	18
Rushes-Yards	38-227	21-109
Passing yards	102	190
Sacked-Yards lost	4-30	5-43
3rd down eff.	7-15	3-10
Passes	14-23-0	13-24-3
Punts	4-38-7	3-37.7
Fumbles-Lost	0-0	1-0
Penalties-Yards	7-60	4-29
Time of possession	32:59	27:01

Attendance—40,718.

INDIVIDUAL STATISTICS

Rushing—New York, McNeil 26-184, Vick 7-40, Bligen 1-4, Faaola 1-1, O'Brien 3-minus 2; Kansas City, Okoye

13-58, Palmer 2-22, Seurer 2-16, Heard 3-7, Moriarty 1-6.

Passing—New York, O'Brien 14-22-0—132, Ryan 0-1-0—0; Kansas City, Seurer 13-23-3—233, Palmer 0-1-0—0.

Receiving—New York, Toon 3-36, Klever 3-17, Bligen 3-13, Sohn 2-34, Griggs 1-13, Vick 1-11, McNeil 1-8; Kansas City, Hayes 5-105, Paige 3-63, Carson 3-49, Colbert 1-8, Okoye 1-8.

Kickoff Returns—New York, Humphery 3-63, Barber 1-5; Kansas City, Palmer 4-81.

Punt Returns—New York, Townsell 2-8; Kansas City, Cocroft 1-0, Clemons 1-5.

Interceptions—New York, Holmes 1-20, Howard 2-29.

Punting—New York, Jennings 4-38.8; Kansas City, Goodburn 3-32.7.

Field Goals—New York, Leahy 3-4 (missed: 49); Kansas City, Lowery 3-3.

Sacks—New York, Gastineau 1½, Lyons 1½, Bennett, Klecko; Kansas City, Bell, Maas ½, Holle ½, Del Rio, Hackett.

Buccaneers-Vikings
SUNDAY, NOVEMBER 15
SCORE BY PERIODS

Tampa Bay	0	7	3	7—17
Minnesota	0	6	10	7—23

SCORING

Tampa Bay—Magee 20 pass from DeBerg (Igwebuike kick), 3:58 2nd.
Minnesota—Field goal C. Nelson 29, 8:02 2nd.
Minnesota—Field goal C. Nelson 27, 14:49 2nd.
Minnesota—Fenney 1 run (C. Nelson kick), 4:02 3rd.
Tampa Bay—Field goal Igwebuike 26, 8:06 3rd.
Minnesota—Field goal C. Nelson 27, 14:57 3rd.
Minnesota—Jordan 2 pass from Kramer (C. Nelson kick), 4:04 4th.
Tampa Bay—Freeman 64 pass from DeBerg (Igwebuike kick), 7:05 4th.

TEAM STATISTICS

	Tampa Bay	Minnesota
First downs	14	23
Rushes-Yards	9-15	47-224
Passing yards	244	106
Sacked-Yards lost	4-40	3-21
3rd down eff.	5-10	8-16
Passes	22-37-1	12-28-1
Punts	4-40.5	3-42.7
Fumbles-Lost	3-3	0-0
Penalties-Yards	9-66	9-70
Time of possession	22:01	37:59

Attendance—48,605.

INDIVIDUAL STATISTICS

Rushing—Tampa Bay, J. Smith 8-16, DeBerg 1-minus 1; Minnesota, Rice 10-22, Dozier 6-28, D. Nelson 17-103, Wilson 3-33, Fenney 9-40, Kramer 2-minus 2.

Passing—Tampa Bay, DeBerg 22-37-1—284; Minnesota, Wilson 8-19-0—97, Kramer 4-9-1—30.

Receiving—Tampa Bay, J. Smith 5-47, Wilder 5-38, Magee 6-25, Carter 3-56, Freeman 2-76, Carrier 1-2; Minnesota, Lewis 2-27, Jordan 3-28, Rice 2-21, Carter 3-37, H. Jones 1-12, Fenney 1-2.

Kickoff Returns—Tampa Bay, J. Smith 3-43, Futrell 1-40; Minnesota, Guggemos 3-94, Rice 1-18.

Punt Returns—Tampa Bay, Futrell 2-24; Minnesota, Lewis 4-56.

Interceptions—Tampa Bay, Isom 1-29; Minnesota, Henderson 1-17.

Punting—Tampa Bay, Garcia 4-40.5; Minnesota, Coleman 3-42.7.

Field Goals—Tampa Bay, Igwebuike 1-1; Minnesota, C. Nelson 3-5 (missed: 21, 41).

Sacks—Tampa Bay, Kellin, Washington, Moss; Minnesota, Browner, Doleman 2, D. Martin.

Cowboys-Patriots
SUNDAY, NOVEMBER 15
SCORE BY PERIODS

Dallas	7	7	0	3	6	23
New England	0	7	0	10	0	17

SCORING

Dallas—Francis 18 interception return (Ruzek kick), 13:06 1st.

New England—Grogan 2 run (Franklin kick), 2:36 2nd.

Dallas—Cosbie 3 pass from D. White (Ruzek kick), 14:50 2nd.

New England—Field goal Franklin 41, 5:12 4th.

New England—Morgan 5 pass from Ramsey (Franklin kick), 13:05 4th.

Dallas—Field goal Ruzek 20, 14:32 4th.

Dallas—Walker 60 run (no kick), 1:50 OT.

TEAM STATISTICS

	Dallas	New England
First downs	24	15
Rushes-Yards	30-181	33-88
Passing yards	257	177
Sacked-Yards lost	4-29	4-32
3rd down eff.	6-17	7-16
Passes	25-44-2	14-28-1
Punts	7-40.3	6-35.2
Fumbles-Lost	1-1	4-1
Penalties-Yards	15-112	5-35
Time of possession	33:43	28:07

Attendance—60,567.

INDIVIDUAL STATISTICS

Rushing—Dallas, Walker 28-173, Dorsett 1-5, Newsome 1-3; New England, Collins 14-40, Ramsey 3-17, Tatupu 6-14, Perryman 4-9, Dupard 3-7, Grogan 3-1.

Passing—Dallas, D. White 25-44-2—286; New England, Grogan 6-12-1—73, Ramsey 8-16-0—136.

Receiving—Dallas, Newsome 6-49, Walker 5-59, Renfro 4-79, Barksdale 3-40, Cosbie 3-26, Dorsett 2-19, Edwards 1-11, Chandler 1-3; New England, Morgan 5-56, Fryar 2-59, Starring 2-42, Dawson 2-18, Tatupu 1-23, Perryman 1-7, Collins 1-4.

Kickoff Returns—Dallas, Clack 5-91; New England, Starring 3-56, Dupard 1-21.

Punt Returns—Dallas, Martin 3-22; New England, Fryar 4-9.

Interceptions—Dallas, Francis 1-18; New England, E. Williams 1-51, R. James 1-27.

Punting—Dallas, Saxon 7-40.3; New England, Camarillo 6-35.2.

Field Goals—Dallas Ruzek 1-1; New England, Franklin 1-2 (missed: 35).

Sacks—Dallas, Ed Jones 2½, Jeffcoat ½, R. White ½, Hegman ½; New England, Tippett 3, Rembert.

Rams-Cardinals
SUNDAY, NOVEMBER 15
SCORE BY PERIODS

Los Angeles Rams	14	0	10	3	27
St. Louis	3	14	7	0	24

SCORING

Los Angeles—White 47 run (Lansford kick), 3:05 1st.

St. Louis—Field goal Gallery 44, 7:30 1st.

Los Angeles—D. Johnson 10 pass from Everett (Lansford kick), 9:59 1st.

St. Louis—Mitchell 5 run (Gallery kick), 7:00 2nd.

St. Louis—Awalt 19 pass from Lomax (Gallery kick), 14:27 2nd.

St. Louis—McAdoo recovered fumble in end zone (Gallery kick), 0:11 3rd.

Los Angeles—Gray recovered blocked punt in end zone (Lansford kick), 8:36 3rd.

Los Angeles—Field goal Lansford 28, 14:46 3rd.

Los Angeles—Field goal Lansford 20, 14:57 4th.

TEAM STATISTICS

	Los Angeles	St. Louis
First downs	21	19
Rushes-Yards	44-239	24-124
Passing yards	144	156
Sacked-Yards lost	1-10	3-29
3rd down eff.	10-15	4-11
Passes	14-26-1	19-29-0
Punts	3-37.0	4-34.8
Fumbles-Lost	3-1	1-1
Penalties-Yards	4-15	3-20
Time of possession	33:06	26:54

Attendance—27,730.

INDIVIDUAL STATISTICS

Rushing—Los Angeles, White 34-213, Everett 3-8, Bell 1-minus 2, Guman 6-20; St. Louis, Mitchell 14-78, Ferrell 9-44, McAdoo 1-2.

Passing—Los Angeles, Everett 14-26-1—154; St. Louis, Lomax 18-27-0—168, Mitchell 1-2-0—17.

Receiving—Los Angeles, R. Brown 3-78, D. Johnson 2-23, Hill 2-13, White 2-8, Ellard 3-20, House 1-7, Guman 1-5; St. Louis, Mitchell 5-34, J.T. Smith 2-29, Awalt 5-42, Ferrell 5-62, Wolfley 1-16, Green 1-2.

Kickoff Returns—Los Angeles, Brown 3-36, Guman 1-6; St. Louis, McAdoo 3-52.

Punt Returns—Los Angeles, Ellard 2-14; St. Louis, Sikahema 2-20.

Interceptions—St. Louis, Curtis 1-0.

Punting—Los Angeles, Hatcher 37.0; St. Louis, Cater 4-34.8.

Field Goals—Los Angeles, Lansford 2-2; St. Louis, Gallery 1-1.

Sacks—Los Angeles, Jeter 3; St. Louis, Nunn.

Lions-Redskins
SUNDAY, NOVEMBER 15
SCORE BY PERIODS

Detroit	3	0	10	0	13
Washington	0	17	3	0	20

SCORING

Detroit—Field goal Murray 40, 7:44 1st.

Washington—Field goal Haji-Sheikh 33, 0:09 2nd.

Washington—Bryant 16 pass from Williams (Haji-Sheikh kick), 12:33 2nd.

Washington—Clark 42 pass from Williams (Haji-Sheikh kick), 14:33 2nd.

Detroit—Field goal Murray 41, 3:42 3rd.

Washington—Field goal Haji-Sheikh 41, 9:23 3rd.

Detroit—Bernard 2 run (Murray kick), 13:09 3rd.

TEAM STATISTICS

	Detroit	Washington
First downs	23	18
Rushes-Yards	28-103	34-135
Passing yards	238	174
Sacked-Yards lost	1-11	2-20
3rd down eff.	6-13	4-12
Passes	23-37-4	16-28-0
Punts	3-37.3	4-32.7
Fumbles-Lost	1-0	3-2
Penalties-Yards	7-55	5-40
Time of possession	29:07	30:53

Attendance—53,593.

INDIVIDUAL STATISTICS

Rushing—Detroit, James 2-minus 1, Bernard 8-36, Jones 16—53, Long 2-15; Washington, Rogers 9-56, Bryant 4-11, Smith 8-22, Schroeder 1-2, Williams 4-4, Monk 1-8, Griffin 7-32.

Passing—Detroit, Long 23-37-4—249; Washington, Schroeder 5-10-0—33, Williams 11-18-0—161.

Receiving—Detroit, Mandley 7-70, Chadwick 7-94, Kab 2-10, James 4-44, Jones 2-13, Bernard 1-4, Woolfolk 1-11, Nichols 1-23, Lee 1-10; Washington, Monk 4-39, Clark 2-66, Didier 1-6, Sanders 2-28, Bryant 5-42, Rogers 1-4, Warren 1-9.

Kickoff Returns—Detroit, Lee 1-15, Saleaumua 1-21, Ball 1-20; Washington, Griffin 3-47, Branch 1-19.

Punt Returns—Detroit, Mandley 2-9; Washington, Yarber 1-3.

Interceptions—Washington, Green 3-65, Wilburn 1-13.

Punting—Detroit, Arnold 3-37.3; Washington, Cox 4-32.7.

Field Goals—Detroit, Murray 2-3 (missed: 34); Washington, Haji-Sheikh 2-2.

Sacks—Detroit, Cofer, Green; Washington, Coleman.

Bengals-Falcons
SUNDAY, NOVEMBER 15
SCORE BY PERIODS

Cincinnati	3	0	0	13	16
Atlanta	0	0	7	3	10

SCORING

Cincinnati—Field goal Breech 31, 9:05 1st.

Atlanta—Dixon 44 pass from Campbell (Luckhurst kick), 10:41 3rd.

Cincinnati—Field goal Breech 22, 0:03 4th.

Atlanta—Field goal Luckhurst 44, 6:04 4th.

Cincinnati—Field goal Breech 30, 11:18 4th.

Cincinnati—Kinnebrew 2 run (Breech kick), 14:37 4th.

TEAM STATISTICS

	Cincinnati	Atlanta
First downs	27	13
Rushes-Yards	50-270	25-119
Passing yards	146	147
Sacked-Yards lost	1-13	3-21
3rd down eff.	9-17	4-11
Passes	13-30-2	13-22-1
Punts	2-42	4-42
Fumbles-Lost	0-0	1-1
Penalties-Yards	4-27	6-50
Time of possession	35:08	24:52
Attendance—25,758.		

INDIVIDUAL STATISTICS

Rushing—Cincinnati, Kinnebrew 27-100, Jennings 12-91, Esiason 10-77, Johnson 1-2; Atlanta, Riggs 23-112, Campbell 2-7.

Passing—Cincinnati, Esiason 13-30-2—159; Atlanta, Campbell 12-21-1—167, Archer 1-1-0—1.

Receiving—Cincinnati, McGee 4-54, Jennings 4-22, Brown 3-52, Holman 1-22, Kattus 1-9; Atlanta, Dixon 3-64, Riggs 3-22, Johnson 2-18, Whisenhunt 2-15, Bailey 1-35, Cox 1-13, Middleton 1-1.

Kickoff Returns—Cincinnati, McGee 2-38, Bussey 1-22; Atlanta, Emery 5-80.

Punt Returns—Cincinnati, Martin 2-23; Atlanta, B. Johnson 1-6.

Interceptions—Cincinnati, Fulcher 1-0; Atlanta, Butler 1-10.

Punting—Cincinnati, Fulhage 2-42.5; Atlanta, Donnelly 4-42.5.

Field Goals—Cincinnati, Breech 3-4 (missed: 45); Atlanta, Luckhurst 1-1.

Sacks—Cincinnati, Kelly, Edwards, Williams; Atlanta, G. Brown.

Oilers-Steelers
SUNDAY, NOVEMBER 15
SCORE BY PERIODS

Houston	0	3	14	6	23
Pittsburgh	3	0	0	0	3

SCORING

Pittsburgh—Field goal Anderson 22, 14:05 1st.

Houston—Field goal Zendejas 34, 14:57 2nd.

Houston—Duncan 14 pass from Moon (Zendejas kick), 8:36 3rd.

Houston—D. Hill 42 pass from Moon (Zendejas kick), 13:30 3rd.

Houston—Field goal Zendejas 20, 3:36 4th.

Houston—Field goal Zendejas 40, 10:42 4th.

TEAM STATISTICS

	Houston	Pittsburgh
First downs	21	8
Rushes-Yards	41-139	20-86
Passing yards	234	84
Sacked-Yards lost	1-18	2-15
3rd down eff.	4-14	5-14
Passes	18-24-0	10-29-3
Punts	4-43.0	6-39.0
Fumbles-Lost	2-1	3-0
Penalties-Yards	12-100	8-50
Time of possession	36:34	23:26
Attendance—56,177.		

INDIVIDUAL STATISTICS

Rushing—Houston, Rozier 27-99, Wallace 5-26, Moon 4-6, Valentine 3-5, Highsmith 2-3; Pittsburgh, Jackson 4-1, Abercrombie 9-30, Newsome 1-0, Pollard 6-55.

Passing—Houston, Moon 18-24-0—252; Pittsburgh, Malone 7-22-1—89, Brister 3-7-2—10.

Receiving—Houston, Rozier 4-45, J. Williams 1-8, Valentine 2-10, Duncan 2-26, D. Hill 4-107, Givins 4-52, Wallace 1-4; Pittsburgh, Carter 1-22, Jackson 1-1, Abercrombie 4-28, Young 1-4, Stallworth 2-19, Lockett 1-25.

Kickoff Returns—Houston, Duncan 2-34; Pittsburgh, Stone 3-62, Woodson 2-24.

Punt Returns—Houston, K. Johnson 3-18; Pittsburgh, Woodson 3-22.

Interceptions—Houston, Bryant 1-29, Bostic 1-3, Lyles 1-15.

Punting—Houston, L. Johnson 4-43.0; Pittsburgh, Newsome 6-39.0.

Field Goals—Houston, Zendejas 3-3; Pittsburgh, Anderson 1-1.

Sacks—Houston, Childress, Bostic; Pittsburgh, Team.

Packers-Seahawks
SUNDAY, NOVEMBER 15
SCORE BY PERIODS

Green Bay	3	10	0	0	13
Seattle	0	21	0	3	24

SCORING

Green Bay—Field goal Zendejas 31, 4:53 1st.

Seattle—Warner 57 run (N. Johnson kick), 0:10 2nd.

Green Bay—Paskett 47 pass from Wright (Zendejas kick), 2:11 2nd.

Green Bay—Field goal Zendejas 48, 5:36 2nd.

Seattle—Robinson 8 blocked punt return (N. Johnson kick), 12:52 2nd.

Seattle—Krieg 8 run (N. Johnson kick), 14:17 2nd.

Seattle—Field goal N. Johnson 24, 0:48 4th.

TEAM STATISTICS

	Green Bay	Seattle
First downs	13	16
Rushes-Yards	25-100	42-193
Passing yards	198	88
Sacked-Yards lost	3-16	3-17
3rd down eff.	4-15	5-12
Passes	14-35-2	9-15-3
Punts	7-35.1	5-47.8
Fumbles-Lost	6-3	3-2
Penalties-Yards	9-70	7-61
Time of possession	28:19	31:41
Attendance—60,963.		

INDIVIDUAL STATISTICS

Rushing—Green Bay, Davis 14-75, Fullwood 4-11, Clark 1-5, Carruth 3-5, Majkowski 1-4, Wright 2-0; Seattle, Warner 25-123, J.L. Williams 13-57, Krieg 4-13.

Passing—Green Bay, Wright 10-19-1—134, Majkowski 4-16-1—80; Seattle, Krieg 9-15-3—105.

Receiving—Green Bay, Stanley 5-66, Neal 2-48, Epps 2-32, Clark 2-5, Paskett 1-47, West 1-9, Davis 1-7; Seattle, Largent 5-79, Skansi 2-19, Tice 1-5, Turner 1-2.

Kickoff Returns—Green Bay, Fullwood 4-88, Jefferson 1-18; Seattle, Hollis 4-99.

Punt Returns—Green Bay, Stanley 2-10; Seattle, Hollis 4-17.

Interceptions—Green Bay, Carreker 1-6, D. Brown 1-2, Holland 1-0; Seattle, Jenkins 1-12, Moyer 1-0.

Punting—Green Bay, Bracken 6-41.0; Seattle, Rodriguez 5-47.8.

Field Goals—Green Bay, Zendejas 2-2; Seattle N. Johnson 1-1.

Sacks—Green Bay, Harris 2, Browner; Seattle, Young, Green 1½, Nash ½.

Saints-49ers
SUNDAY, NOVEMBER 15
SCORE BY PERIODS

New Orleans	3	6	14	3—26
San Francisco	7	0	7	10—24

SCORING
New Orleans—Field goal Andersen 40, 8:55 1st.

San Francisco—Rice 46 pass from Young (Wersching kick), 13:53 1st.

New Orleans—Field goal Andersen 27, 13:08 2nd.

New Orleans—Field goal Andersen 51, 14:50 2nd.

New Orleans—Jones 43 pass from Hebert (Andersen kick), 3:34 3rd.

San Francisco—Rice 50 pass from Sydney (Wersching kick), 9:54 3rd.

New Orleans—Poe 61 blocked field goal return (Andersen kick), 14:57 3rd.

San Francisco—Field goal Wersching 35, 4:16 4th.

San Francisco—Heller 29 pass from Montana (Wersching kick), 12:06 4th.

New Orleans—Field goal Andersen 40, 13:54 4th.

TEAM STATISTICS

	New Orleans	San Francisco
First downs	16	20
Rushes-Yards	31-105	27-140
Passing yards	156	258
Sacked-Yards lost	3-25	3-16
3rd down eff	7-17	6-14
Passes	10-27-1	22-35-2
Punts	3-43.3	2-36.5
Fumbles-Lost	0-0	2-1
Penalties-Yards	5-35	7-67
Time of possession	31:07	28:53
Attendance—60,436.		

INDIVIDUAL STATISTICS
Rushing—New Orleans, Mayes 20-75, Hilliard 11-30; San Francisco, Craig 16-64, Young 4-25, Rice 2-22, Montana 2-16, Rathman 2-10, Sydney 1-4.

Passing—New Orleans, Hebert 10-27-1—181; San Francisco, Young 5-6-0—80, Montana 16-29-2—144, Sydney 1-1-0—50.

Receiving—New Orleans, Martin 3-59, Jones 1-43, Hill 1-23, Hilliard 1-15, Word 1-14, Brenner 1-11, Pattison 1-10, Tice 1-6; San Francisco, Craig 10-43, Rice 4-108, Frank 2-31, Rathman 2-23, Heller 1-29, Francis 1-16, Taylor 1-15, Wilson 1-9.

Kickoff Returns—New Orleans, Gray 4-98, Hilliard 1-25; San Francisco, Sydney 1-24, Rodgers 5-86.

Punt Returns—New Orleans, Gray 1-4; San Francisco, Griffin 1-8.

Interceptions—New Orleans, Waymer 1-17, Jackson 1-0; San Francisco, Lott 1-34.

Punting—New Orleans, Hansen 3-43.3; San Francisco, Runager 2-36.5.

Field Goals—New Orleans, Andersen 4-5 (missed: 41); San Francisco, Wersching 1-3 (missed: 46, 44).

Sacks—New Orleans, Warren, Wilks, Elliott; San Francisco, Stover 1½, Roberts ½.

Bills-Browns
SUNDAY, NOVEMBER 15
SCORE BY PERIODS

Buffalo	7	0	0	14—21
Cleveland	3	14	7	3—27

SCORING
Cleveland—Field goal Jaeger 22, 8:50 1st.

Buffalo—Kelso 56 fumble return (Norwood kick), 13:09 1st.

Cleveland—Ellis 24 fumble return (Jaeger kick), 0:19 2nd.

Cleveland—Langhorne 15 pass from Kosar (Jaeger kick), 6:51 2nd.

Cleveland—Slaughter 52 pass from Kosar (Jaeger kick), 2:46 3rd.

Cleveland—Field goal Jaeger 40, 2:07 4th.

Buffalo—Burkett 13 pass from Kelly (Norwood kick), 4:00 4th.

Buffalo—Reed 10 pass from Kelly (Norwood kick), 14:08 4th.

TEAM STATISTICS

	Buffalo	Cleveland
First downs	17	24
Rushes-Yards	20-61	31-84
Passing yards	206	337
Sacked-Yards lost	3-16	2-9
3rd down eff	3-11	7-12
Passes	22-35-0	24-34-1
Punts	3-39.3	1-45.0
Fumbles-Lost	2-2	2-2
Penalties-Yards	6-70	10-90
Time of possession	24:19	35:41
Attendance—78,409.		

INDIVIDUAL STATISTICS
Rushing—Buffalo, Harmon 6-2, Kelly 4-42, Byrum 3-13, Mueller 5-4, K. Porter 2-0; Cleveland, Mack 17-48, Byner 10-21, McNeil 1-17, Kosar 3-minus 2.

Passing—Buffalo, Kelly 22-35-0—222; Cleveland, Kosar 24-34-1—346.

Receiving—Buffalo, Burkett 6-91, Metzelaars 3-15, Harmon 6-52, Reed 4-36, R. Porter 1-4, T. Johnson 2-24; Cleveland, Langhorne 2-25, Newsome 3-70, Byner 6-64, Slaughter 4-78, Mack 4-46, NcNeil 1-10, Weathers 1-14, Brennan 2-15, Tennell 1-24.

Kickoff Returns—Buffalo, Tasker 1-39, Mueller 1-15, R. Porter 2-47, Rolle 1-6; Cleveland, Fontenot 2-25, McNeil 1-16.

Punt Returns—Cleveland, McNeil 3-19.

Interceptions—Buffalo, Burroughs 1-0.

Punting—Buffalo, Kidd 3-39.3; Cleveland, Winslow 1-45.0.

Field Goals—Buffalo, Norwood 0-2 (missed: 38, 36); Cleveland, Jaeger 2-3 (missed: 52).

Sacks—Buffalo, Smith 2; Cleveland, Baker, Hairston 2.

Raiders-Chargers
SUNDAY, NOVEMBER 15
SCORE BY PERIODS

Los Angeles Raiders	0	0	0	14—14
San Diego	7	9	0	0—16

SCORING
San Diego—Winslow 9 pass from Fouts (Abbott kick), 5:51 1st.

San Diego—Field goal Abbott 38, 0:50 2nd.

San Diego—Field goal Abbott 47, 2:42 2nd.

San Diego—Field goal Abbott 39, 11:21 2nd.

Los Angeles—Williams 5 pass from Wilson (Bahr kick), 6:59 4th.

Los Angeles—Lofton 47 pass from Wilson (Bahr kick), 14:44 4th.

TEAM STATISTICS

	Los Angeles	San Diego
First downs	12	16
Rushes-Yards	23-150	41-114
Passing yards	215	134
Sacked-Yards lost	2-13	2-15
3rd down eff.	1-12	2-14
Passes	15-32-1	15-32-1
Punts	9-43.7	8-40.3
Fumbles-Lost	2-1	1-0
Penalties-Yards	17-186	7-60
Time of possession	25:48	34:12

Attendance—60,639.

INDIVIDUAL STATISTICS

Rushing—Los Angeles, Jackson 8-45, Allen 13-82, Wilson 2-23; San Diego, Anderson 6-29, Spencer 8-18, James 4-minus 4, Adams 21-75, Redden 1-minus 2, Fouts 1-minus 2.

Passing—Los Angeles, Wilson 15-32-1—228; San Diego, Fouts 15-32-1—149.

Receiving—Los Angeles, Christensen 2-38, Jackson 3-26, Fernandez 1-16, Allen 3-21, Lofton 3-84, Williams 3-43; San Diego, Bernstine 1-7, Winslow 6-53, Holohan 3-24, Anderson 3-48, Chandler 1-15, James 1-2.

Kickoff Returns—Los Angeles, Mueller 4-58, Kimmel 1-0; San Diego, Anderson 2-40.

Punt Returns—Los Angeles, Woods 5-30; San Diego, James 5-39.

Interceptions—Los Angeles, Anderson 1-58; San Diego, Smith 1-0.

Punting—Los Angeles, Talley 9-43.7; San Diego, Mojsiejenko 8-40.3.

Field Goals—Los Angeles, Bahr 0-1 (missed: 41); San Diego, Abbott 3-4 (missed: 53).

Sacks—Los Angeles, Long, King; San Diego, Ehin, Smith.

Colts-Dolphins
SUNDAY, NOVEMBER 15
SCORE BY PERIODS

Indianapolis	7	13	3	17	40
Miami	14	7	0	0	21

SCORING

Miami—Hampton 6 run (Reveiz kick), 2:53 1st.

Miami—Johnson 4 pass from Marino (Reveiz kick), 9:52 1st.

Indianapolis—Dickerson 4 run (Biasucci kick), 14:04 1st.

Indianapolis—Brooks 4 pass from Hogeboom (Biasucci kick), 0:49 2nd.

Indianapolis—Field goal Biasucci 22, 10:41 2nd.

Miami—Banks 10 pass from Marino (Reveiz kick), 14:12 2nd.

Indianapolis—Field goal Biasucci 32, 15:00 2nd.

Indianapolis—Field goal Biasucci 25, 13:48 3rd.

Indianapolis—Field goal Biasucci 23, 5:38 4th.

Indianapolis—Bentley 17 run (Biasucci kick), 11:24 4th.

Indianapolis—Bentley 2 run (Biasucci kick), 13:57 4th.

TEAM STATISTICS

	Indianapolis	Miami
First downs	32	21
Rushes-Yards	44-239	23-77
Passing yards	218	209
Sacked-Yards lost	0-0	0-0
3rd down eff.	10-17	5-10
Passes	22-39-0	16-38-2
Punts	3-35.7	2-49.0
Fumbles-Lost	2-0	3-3
Penalties-Yards	12-116	8-63
Time of possession	35:23	24:37

Attendance—65,433.

INDIVIDUAL STATISTICS

Rushing—Indianapolis, Dickerson 30-154, Bentley 13-83, Hogeboom 1-2; Miami, Stradford 8-28, Hampton 7-19, Bennett 6-21, Nathan 2-9.

Passing—Indianapolis, Hogeboom 22-39-0—218;

Miami, Marino 14-34-1—194, Stradford 1-1-0—6, Strock 1-3-1—9.

Receiving—Indianapolis, Beach 5-33, Brooks 4-48, Brandes 2-16, Murray 1-15, Bentley 4-38, Dickerson 1-7, Bouza 5-61; Miami, Clayton 2-28, Hampton 2-43, Johnson 1-4, Stradford 2-19, Nathan 4-31, Hardy 2-26, Pruitt 2-48, Banks 1-10.

Kickoff Returns—Indianapolis, Bentley 4-105; Miami, Hardy 1-18, Hampton 1-21, Stradford 5-88, Johnson 1-10.

Punt Returns—Indianapolis, Brooks 2-14; Miami, Schwedes 3-58.

Interceptions—Indianapolis, Tullis 1-0, Robinson 1-68.

Punting—Indianapolis, Stark 3-35.7; Miami, Roby 2-49.0.

Field Goals—Indianapolis, Biasucci 4-4; Miami, none attempted.

Sacks—None.

Bears-Broncos
MONDAY, NOVEMBER 16
SCORE BY PERIODS

Chicago	14	0	15	0	29
Denver	0	21	0	10	31

SCORING

Chicago—Gault 51 pass from McMahon (Butler kick), 3:15 1st.

Chicago—Boso 6 pass from McMahon (Butler kick), 9:34 1st.

Denver—V. Johnson 22 pass from Elway (Karlis kick), 0:51 2nd.

Denver—Jackson 22 pass from Elway (Karlis kick), 13:06 2nd.

Denver—Nattiel 35 pass from Elway (Karlis kick), 14:49 2nd.

Chicago—Gault 26 pass from McMahon (kick failed), 6:50 3rd.

Chicago—McMahon 1 run (run failed), 9:08 3rd.

Chicago—Field goal Butler 42, 13:30 3rd.

Denver—Field goal Karlis 27, 2:20 4th.

Denver—Sewell 4 run (Karlis kick), 10:02 4th.

TEAM STATISTICS

	Chicago	Denver
First downs	24	25
Rushes-Yards	30-146	27-98
Passing yards	300	341
Sacked-Yards lost	3-20	0-0
3rd down eff.	4-11	6-11
Passes	23-36-1	21-41-2
Punts	3-52.9	4-46.5
Fumbles-Lost	3-1	0-0
Penalties-Yards	7-44	5-57
Time of possession	33:19	26:41

Attendance—75,783.

INDIVIDUAL STATISTICS

Rushing—Chicago, Payton 12-73, Gault 1-9, Anderson 11-44, McMahon 2-3, Perry 1-0, Gentry 2-16, Thomas 1-1; Denver, Nattiel 1-10, Winder 8-20, Lang 11-31, Elway 5-35, Sewell 2-2.

Passing—Chicago, McMahon 21-34-1—311, Tomczak 2-2-0—9; Denver, Elway 21-40-2—341, Johnson 0-1-0—0.

Receiving—Chicago, Moorehead 1-9, Gault 5-133, Anderson 7-38, Boso 2-20, Morris 1-27, McKinnon 4-67, Payton 3-26; Denver, V. Johnson 6-86, Lang 1-6, Sewell 5-78, Winder 1-3, Nattiel 4-93, Jackson 3-53, Kay 1-22.

Kickoff Returns—Chicago, Gentry 2-47, Sanders 2-16; Denver, V. Johnson 3-72, Bell 1-19.

Punt Returns—Chicago, McKinnon 3-8.

Interceptions—Chicago, Duerson 1-0, Rivera 1-15; Denver, Clark 1-20.

Punting—Chicago, Wagner 3-52.9; Denver, Horan 4-46.5.

Field Goals—Chicago, Butler 1-1; Denver, Karlis 1-1.

Sacks—Denver, Townsend, Jones, Mecklenburg.

ELEVENTH WEEK

RESULTS OF WEEK 11

Sunday, November 22

Buffalo 17, N.Y. Jets 14 at N.Y.
Chicago 30, Detroit 10 at Chi.
Cleveland 40, Houston 7 at Hous.
Denver 23, L.A. Raiders 17 at L.A.
Green Bay 23, Kansas City 3 at K.C.
Miami 20, Dallas 14 at Dall.
Minnesota 24, Atlanta 13 at Minn.
New England 24, Indianapolis 0 at N.E.
New Orleans 23, N.Y. Giants 14 at N.O.
Pittsburgh 30, Cincinnati 16 at Cin.
St. Louis 31, Philadelphia 19 at Phila.
San Francisco 24, Tampa Bay 10 at T.B.
Seattle 34, San Diego 3 at Sea.

Monday, November 23

L.A. Rams 30, Washington 26 at Wash.

As the 1987 season reached the home stretch, one of its big surprises was the New Orleans Saints, a team that entered the season with the ignominious distinction of being the only league member never to have made the playoffs. Things got so bad around the bayou in 1980 that Saints fans, in the midst of a 1-15 season, drew nationwide attention by wearing grocery bags over their heads and calling the team the "Aints."

But the fortunes of the franchise that had never had a winning season since its inception in 1967 took a turn for the better in '86 with the hiring of Jim Mora as head coach. Mora, a longtime assistant in both the college and pro ranks, led the Philadelphia/Baltimore Stars to three straight United States Football League title games (1983-85) and won two of them ('84 and '85). He led the Saints to a 7-9 record in 1986, his first year as an NFL head man.

"This may be the most important victory I've ever been around," Mora said after the Saints defeated the defending Super Bowl-champion New York Giants, 23-14, in Week 11. "It's a team win. I know that's a cliche, but it was a team win. And that is the key to a winning football team. We are playing as a team in what is a team game."

The Saints got off to a rousing start before the first sellout at the Superdome in three years (67,639) when Barry Word returned the opening kickoff 64 yards, setting up Morten Andersen's 19-yard field goal 3:57 into the game. After the Giants took a 7-3 lead with a touchdown early in the second quarter, Word's one-yard touchdown run capped a 15-play, 9½-minute drive with 4:14 remaining in the half. Andersen booted a 43-yard field goal on the final play before intermission to give New Orleans a 13-7 lead.

"They are an improved team, they're more confident than last year," said Giants Coach Bill Parcells, whose team registered a 20-17 tri-umph over New Orleans en route to their Super Bowl XXI championship. "I think they are going to make a good run in their division."

The Giants made a good run at the Saints in the second half, grabbing a 14-13 lead on Jeff Rutledge's 22-yard scoring pass to tight end Mark Bavaro 4:25 into the third quarter.

But Rutledge, who threw five interceptions in relief of the injured Phil Simms, fumbled after being sacked by linebacker Pat Swilling with eight minutes left in the game. Dave Waymer recovered for New Orleans at the New York 27-yard line and, three plays later, Saints quarterback Bobby Hebert threw a 22-yard touchdown pass to Eric Martin for the game-winning points.

On the Giants' next possession, Johnnie Poe blocked a punt by Sean Landeta and the Saints took over at the Giants' 8-yard line. Four plays later, Andersen's third field goal of the game, with 3:26 left, rounded out the scoring.

The victory was a club-record fourth straight for the Saints and gave them a 7-3 record, the team's best mark ever after 10 games. One victory in the remaining five games would ensure New Orleans its first winning season.

"We're looking to beat everybody now and it's going to be hard for somebody to beat us," said linebacker Rickey Jackson, a seven-year veteran with the Saints. "We're going to make the playoffs now, no doubt about that. We're looking to go far up in the playoffs, not just make them."

Another team looking to make the playoffs was Seattle, which missed out on the 1986 postseason party despite posting a 10-6 record in the tough AFC West Division. The Seahawks improved their '87 record to 7-3 and dropped division-leading San Diego to 8-2 with a 34-3 romp in Week 11, snapping the Chargers' team-record winning streak at eight games.

Quarterback Dave Krieg passed for two touchdowns and ran for another and running back Curt Warner rushed 23 times for 119 yards to lead the Seattle offense. The Seahawks, who won for the seventh straight time in the divisional series, dominated the Chargers in first downs (34-6), total yards (496-156) and time of possession (41:35 to 18:25).

San Diego's Gary Anderson set the tone for the game early by fumbling the opening kickoff. The Seahawks recovered at the Chargers' 22-yard line, leading to a 34-yard Norm Johnson field goal.

The Chicago Bears also won for the seventh straight time in a divisional series with a 30-10 victory over NFC Central Division rival Detroit. The Bears offense had a more than 2-to-1 edge in time of possession while the defense recorded three sacks and two interceptions while allowing just 30 yards rushing. Defensive back Shaun Gayle scored Chicago's first touch-

Frank Minnifield (31) intercepted three Warren Moon passes in Cleveland's 40-7 romp over Houston in Week 11.

down with a 20-yard interception return on the Lions' second possession of the game.

Although the Detroit defense sacked Bears' quarterback Jim McMahon seven times— the most against McMahon since his 1982 rookie season—the Lions offense was hapless. The Lions ran only 46 offensive plays (the Bears had 79), just four in the third quarter.

The Cleveland Browns manhandled the Houston Oilers in much the same manner the Bears pounded the Lions. The Browns won, 40-7, by holding the Oilers to just 43 yards rushing, forcing six turnovers and keeping possession for nearly 43 of the game's 60 minutes.

Houston quarterback Warren Moon, who lost for the seventh straight time as a starter against the Browns, had a horrendous performance: five completions in 23 attempts for 193 yards with three interceptions (all by cornerback Frank Minnifield), three sacks and one lost fumble. Moon completed just one of eight pass attempts in the second half.

Cleveland, which took over sole possession of first place in the AFC Central, got a 114-yard rushing performance from fullback Kevin Mack and two touchdowns each from running back Earnest Byner and quarterback Bernie Kosar. Twenty of the Browns' 40 points came after Oiler turnovers.

Philadelphia Coach Buddy Ryan predicted that his Eagles would rush for 400 yards against the St. Louis Cardinals in Week 11 after watching film of the Rams' Charles White scorching the Cardinal defense for 213 yards a week earlier.

The Eagles fell 340 yards short of fulfilling Ryan's prediction as St. Louis rolled to a 31-19 NFC East Division victory. Forty-three of the Eagles' 60 rushing yards came on scrambles by quarterback Randall Cunningham. Running backs Keith Byars and Anthony Toney combined for just 14 yards on 15 carries.

The Cards, inspired by Ryan's words, exploded for 318 total yards and 16 first downs in grabbing a commanding 31-3 halftime lead. Quarterback Neil Lomax threw for three touchdowns and 254 of his 263 passing yards in the first two periods.

The victory was the first for St. Louis in its last 10 road games.

The Cincinnati Bengals lost for the sixth straight time at home and for the fifth time in six games when the Pittsburgh Steelers beat them, 30-16, at Riverfront Stadium. The Bengals' last home win was a 52-21 decision over the Jets on December 21, 1986.

Defense played a large part in the Steelers' victory. The Pittsburgh defense had five sacks, three interceptions and two fumble recoveries. Rookie defensive back Rod Woodson, the club's No. 1 draft choice in 1987, scored the Steelers' first touchdown with a 45-yard interception return of a Boomer Esiason pass with 48 seconds left in the first half. Woodson, who missed half his rookie season in a contract dispute, was playing in just his third NFL game.

Steelers quarterback Mark Malone ran 42 yards for one touchdown and threw 14 yards to Weegie Thompson to help Pittsburgh sweep the season series with Cincinnati for the first time since 1978.

Like Woodson, New England's Ronnie Lippett returned an interception 45 yards for a touchdown to help the Patriots to a 24-0 AFC East Division victory over the Indianapolis Colts. Lippett grabbed a Gary Hogeboom pass intended for Matt Bouza and raced untouched down the left sideline for New England's final touchdown of the game.

Pats safety Jim Bowman intercepted two passes and recovered one fumble as the Colts committed five turnovers, four on consecutive possessions in the second half.

The New England offense didn't turn the ball over under the direction of third-string quarterback Tom Ramsey against a Colt defense that entered the game with a league-leading 31 takeaways. Ramsey, who got the starting nod from Coach Raymond Berry after injuries to both Tony Eason and Steve Grogan, completed 12 of 26 passes for 183 yards and no interceptions in the first starting assignment of his three-year NFL career.

The Buffalo Bills beat the New York Jets for

the first time in eight games with a 17-14 AFC East Division victory. The Bills, who could muster just 32 yards rushing in a first half that ended in a 7-7 tie, rushed for 49 yards on a 68-yard scoring drive to open the second half. Rookie Jamie Mueller scored the go-ahead touchdown from two yards out.

On the next Buffalo possession, quarterback Jim Kelly and wide receiver Walter Broughton hooked up for a 39-yard gain on a drive that ended in a 42-yard Scott Norwood field goal and 17-7 Bills lead. Broughton, who caught a 25-yard pass from Kelly for Buffalo's first touchdown, finished the game with three catches for 67 yards after catching just three passes for 71 yards in 11 previous NFL games.

Rookie Troy Stradford rushed for the third highest single-game total in Miami history to lead the Dolphins to a 20-14 interconference victory over the Dallas Cowboys. Stradford, a fourth-round draft choice from Boston College, rushed for 169 yards on 17 attempts to help the Dolphins keep pace with the rest of the AFC East. After 10 weeks of play, all five East teams sported 5-5 records.

What proved to be the game-winning touchdown was set up by a bizarre play. With the Dolphins leading, 13-7, early in the final quarter, quarterback Dan Marino threw a pass deep down the left sideline on a first-down play from the Dallas 45-yard line. Cowboys rookie Ron Francis appeared to have intercepted the ball, but the instant replay showed he never had control. When Francis fell on his back, however, the ball bounced off him straight into the air and right into the hands of Dolphins receiver Mark Clayton on the Dallas 4-yard line. Three plays later, Marino threw a two-yard scoring pass to James Pruitt for Miami's final victory.

San Francisco wide receiver Jerry Rice caught three touchdown passes from Joe Montana to lead the 49ers to a 24-10 win over the Tampa Bay Buccaneers. Rice, whose 11 touchdown receptions led the league after 10 weeks, beat second-year cornerback Rod Jones for all three scores.

The victory was San Francisco's seventh in eight games against Tampa Bay.

Two AFC West Division teams continued long losing streaks in Week 11.

The Denver Broncos handed the Los Angeles Raiders their seventh straight loss, 23-17. The last time the Raiders lost seven straight was in 1962, when the team finished with a 1-13 record.

The Broncos wasted little time in taking control. They drove 59 yards for a field goal on their first possession and added a touchdown later in the opening quarter after rookie Michael Brooks recovered a fumble by Raiders quarterback Marc Wilson on the L.A. 24-yard line.

About the only bright spot for the Raiders

were two touchdown runs by rookie running back Bo Jackson, the first of his NFL career.

The Kansas City Chiefs dropped their club-record ninth straight game, 23-3, at home to the Green Bay Packers. In the process, the Chiefs—whose 1-9 record was the NFL's worst—extended to 13 the number of quarters they had gone without an offensive touchdown.

The Packers, who snapped a three-game losing streak in winning for just the fourth time in 10 games, took command by scoring two touchdowns in a 55-second span of the third quarter. After Randy Wright and rookie Frankie Neal hooked up for a 13-yard score to increase the Packers' lead to 14-3, another Packer rookie, Norman Jefferson, recovered a fumble by the Chiefs' Aaron Pearson on the ensuing kickoff. Two plays later, Wright and Neal hooked up on a 26-yard touchdown pass and 20-3 Green Bay lead.

Leo Lewis became the first Minnesota player in 19 years to return a punt for a touchdown in the Vikings' 24-13 victory over Atlanta. Lewis' 78-yard punt return in the third quarter gave the Vikes a 17-7 lead and was the team's first since Charlie West returned one 98 yards against Washington in 1968.

Tight end Carl Hilton caught an eight-yard pass from Wade Wilson for Minnesota's first touchdown and blocked a punt by the Falcons' Rick Donnelly to set up the final Vikings score.

The Los Angeles Rams avenged a 19-7 loss to the Washington Redskins in the 1986 NFC wild-card game with a 30-26 upset victory in the Monday night game. Three of Los Angeles' four touchdowns were either scored by or set up by the Rams defense or special teams. Linebacker Mike Wilcher returned a fumble by Washington quarterback Doug Williams 35 yards for a touchdown on the third play of the game.

After the Redskins scored 10 points later in the opening period, speedster Ron Brown returned a kickoff 95 yards to give the Rams a 14-9 lead. In the second quarter, Nolan Cromwell's block of a Steve Cox punt was followed two plays later by a one-yard touchdown run by Charles White.

The Rams' victory over the Redskins was their first at RFK Stadium since 1969 and their first against Washington on any field since 1974.

Bills-Jets

SUNDAY, NOVEMBER 22

SCORE BY PERIODS

Buffalo	0	7	10	0—17
New York Jets	0	7	0	7—14

SCORING

New York—Shuler 32 pass from O'Brien (Leahy kick), 7:10 2nd.

Buffalo—Broughton 25 pass from Kelly (Norwood kick), 10:08 2nd.

Buffalo—Mueller 2 run (Norwood kick), 5:49 3rd.

Buffalo—Field goal Norwood 42, 11:43 3rd.
New York—Sohn 4 pass from O'Brien (Leahy kick), 14:03 4th.

TEAM STATISTICS

	Buffalo	New York
First downs	15	21
Rushes-Yards	31-127	30-126
Passing yards	204	192
Sacked-Yards lost	2-10	5-33
3rd down eff.	8-17	9-19
Passes	21-33-1	18-40-1
Punts	7-31.6	7-40.7
Fumbles-Lost	1-0	1-0
Penalties-Yards	2-15	6-38
Time of possession	29:32	30:28
Attendance—58,407.		

INDIVIDUAL STATISTICS

Rushing—Buffalo, Harmon 9-61, R. Porter 12-42, Mueller 7-20, Byrum 2-1, Kelly 1-3; New York, McNeil 20-103, Vick 3-12, O'Brien 4-8, Faaola 1-4, Hector 1-1, Townsell 1-minus 2.

Passing—Buffalo, Kelly 21-33-1—214; New York, O'Brien 18-40-1—225.

Receiving—Buffalo, Reed 4-21, R. Porter 4-30, Broughton 3-67, Burkett 3-35, Harmon 2-19, Metzelaars 2-16, T. Johnson 2-26; New York, Toon 4-54, Shuler 5-68, McNeil 2-26, Townsell 2-16, Sohn 2-35, Klever 1-11, Vick 1-7, Hector 1-8.

Kickoff Returns—Buffalo, R. Porter 1-18, Radecic 1-14; New York, Humphery 1-13, Sohn 1-18.

Punt Returns—Buffalo, Pitts 1-0.

Interceptions—Buffalo, Kelso 1-0; New York, Howard 1-0.

Punting—Buffalo, Kidd 7-31.6; New York, Jennings 7-40.7.

Field Goals—Buffalo, Norwood 1-1; New York, Leahy 0-1 (missed: 44).

Sacks—Buffalo, Bennett 1½, Smith 1½, Talley, Seals; New York, Zordich, Lyons.

Cardinals-Eagles
SUNDAY, NOVEMBER 22
SCORE BY PERIODS

St. Louis	7	24	0	0—31
Philadelphia	3	0	7	9—19

SCORING

Philadelphia—Field goal McFadden 44, 2:19 1st.
St. Louis—Green 20 pass from Lomax (Gallery kick), 5:27 1st.
St. Louis—J.T. Smith 6 pass from Lomax (Gallery kick), 0:52 2nd.
St. Louis—Field goal Gallery 20, 8:47 2nd.
St. Louis—J.T. Smith 32 pass from Lomax (Gallery kick), 13:15 2nd.
St. Louis—Ferrell 35 run (Gallery kick), 14:38 2nd.
Philadelphia—Quick 16 pass from Cunningham (McFadden kick), 3:08 3rd.
Philadelphia—Quick 27 pass from Cunningham (McFadden kick), 0:38 4th.
Philadelphia—Safety, Cater stepped out of end zone, 13:11 4th.

TEAM STATISTICS

	St. Louis	Philadelphia
First downs	18	17
Rushes-Yards	38-92	20-60
Passing yards	232	240
Sacked-Yards lost	5-31	6-32
3rd down eff.	6-16	5-18
Passes	18-30-2	26-51-2
Punts	7-26.3	8-37.9
Fumbles-Lost	2-1	4-1
Penalties-Yards	5-38	10-85
Time of possession	30:09	29:51
Attendance—55,592.		

INDIVIDUAL STATISTICS

Rushing—St. Louis, Ferrell 14-76, Mitchell 17-26, Lomax 5-minus 1, Awalt 1-minus 1, Cater 1-minus 8; Philadelphia, Cunningham 4-43, Toney 8-10, Byars 7-4, Jackson 1-3.

Passing—St. Louis, Lomax 18-30-2—263; Philadelphia, Cunningham 26-51-2—272.

Receiving—St. Louis, J.T. Smith 5-74, Mitchell 4-31, Awalt 3-57, Ferrell 2-47, T. Johnson 2-28, Green 2-26; Philadelphia, Quick 7-90, Toney 5-29, Spagnola 4-28, Tautalatasi 4-25, Jackson 3-51, Byars 1-21, Garrity 1-20, Giles 1-8.

Kickoff Returns—St. Louis, McAdoo 3-49, Sikahema 1-14; Philadelphia, Haddix 2-16, Lavette 2-37.

Punt Returns—St. Louis, Sikahema 3.34; Philadelphia, Garrity 1-4, C. Brown 1-minus 1.

Interceptions—St. Louis, Carter 1-0, Saddler 1-0; Philadelphia, J. Brown 1-1, Hoage 1-0.

Punting—St. Louis, Cater 7-26.3; Philadelphia, Teltschik 8-37.9.

Field Goals—St. Louis, Gallery 1-1; Philadelphia, McFadden 1-1.

Sacks—St. Louis, Alvord ½, Nunn 1½, Saddler 2, Clasby; Philadelphia, C. Brown, Hoage, White, Simmons, Allert.

Chargers-Seahawks
SUNDAY, NOVEMBER 22
SCORE BY PERIODS

San Diego	0	3	0	0— 3
Seattle	3	14	10	7—34

SCORING

Seattle—Field goal N. Johnson 34, 2:14 1st.
Seattle—J.L. Williams 12 pass from Krieg (N. Johnson kick), 0:07 2nd.
San Diego—Field goal Abbott 33, 4:33 2nd.
Seattle—Warner 5 run (N. Johnson kick), 8:47 2nd.
Seattle—Krieg 11 run (N. Johnson kick), 2:24 3rd.
Seattle—Field goal N. Johnson 22, 14:54 3rd.
Seattle—Largent 5 pass from Krieg (N. Johnson kick), 5:46 4th.

TEAM STATISTICS

	San Diego	Seattle
First downs	6	34
Rushes-Yards	12-17	54-277
Passing yards	139	219
Sacked-Yards lost	2-16	2-27
3rd down eff.	2-10	8-14
Passes	14-25-2	19-28-0
Punts	6-42.5	4-26.0
Fumbles-Lost	3-2	2-1
Penalties-Yards	5-35	3-20
Time of possession	18:25	41:35
Attendance—62,444.		

INDIVIDUAL STATISTICS

Rushing—San Diego, Adams 5-12, Spencer 3-4, Anderson 2-2, Herrmann 2-1; Seattle, Warner 23-119, J.L. Williams 14-61, Krieg 3-35, Burse 5-31, Morris 8-19, Largent 1-12.

Passing—San Diego, Herrmann 12-19-1—140, Fouts 2-6-1—15; Seattle, Krieg 19-26-0—246, Kemp 0-2-0—0.

Receiving—San Diego, Anderson 5-42, James 2-42, Redden 2-20, Holland 1-20, Chandler 1-9, Spencer 1-9, Holohan 1-7, Adams 1-6; Seattle, Largent 5-84, Skansi 4-48, Turner 3-42, J.L. Williams 3-31, Warner 3-25, R. Butler 1-16.

Kickoff Returns—San Diego, Anderson 6-107; Seattle, Edmonds 2-45.

Punt Returns—San Diego, James 1-14; Seattle, Edmonds 4-41.

Interceptions—Seattle, Taylor 1-9, Robinson 1-0.

Punting—San Diego, Mojsiejenko 6-42.5; Seattle, Rodriguez 4-26.0.

Field Goals—San Diego, Abbott 1-1; Seattle, N. Johnson 2-3 (missed: 48).

Sacks—San Diego, Charles, L. Williams; Seattle, Young 2.

Lions-Bears
SUNDAY, NOVEMBER 22
SCORE BY PERIODS

Detroit	0	10	0	0—10	
Chicago	14	13	0	3—30	

SCORING

Chicago—Gayle 20 interception return (Butler kick), 8:28 1st.

Chicago—McKinnon 31 pass from McMahon (Butler kick), 13:44 1st.

Detroit—Mandley 15 pass from Long (Murray kick), 3:32 2nd.

Detroit—Field goal Murray 36, 7:40 2nd.

Chicago—Anderson 16 run (Butler kick), 9:53 2nd.

Chicago—Field goal Butler 31, 13:10 2nd.

Chicago—Field goal Butler 37, 15:00 2nd.

Chicago—Field goal Butler 29, 11:12 4th.

TEAM STATISTICS

	Detroit	Chicago
First downs	10	29
Rushes-Yards	12-30	39-178
Passing yards	149	205
Sacked-Yards lost	3-21	8-63
3rd down eff.	1-10	7-16
Passes	14-31-2	20-32-1
Punts	6-48.3	3-31.7
Fumbles-Lost	3-0	0-0
Penalties-Yards	9-108	9-72
Time of possession	18:33	41:27

Attendance—63,357.

INDIVIDUAL STATISTICS

Rushing—Detroit, Jones 4-12, Bernard 4-3, Long 3-13, Woolfolk 1-2; Chicago, Payton 13-60, Anderson 13-67, Gentry 2-11, Sanders 6-32, McMahon 1-1, Thomas 3-6, Marshall 1-1.

Passing—Detroit, Long 14-31-2—170; Chicago, McMahon 16-27-1—206, Tomczak 4-5-0—62.

Receiving—Detroit, Mandley 3-42, Kab 1-28, Chadwick 2-29, Nichols 2-25, Woolfolk 5-39, Bernard 1-7; Chicago, Payton 4-42, Gentry 1-9, McKinnon 2-53, Anderson 2-23, Sanders 2-28, Moorehead 2-39, Gault 4-55, Boso 2-10, Morris 1-9.

Kickoff Returns—Detroit, Lee 2-33, Woolfolk 1-13, Green 1-0; Chicago, Sanders 2-37.

Punt Returns—Detroit, Mandley 1-12; Chicago, McKinnon 3-minus 4.

Interceptions—Detroit, McNorton 1-0; Chicago, Gayle 1-20, Rivera 1-4.

Punting—Detroit, Arnold 6-48.3; Chicago, Wagner 3-31.7.

Field Goals—Detroit, Murray 1-1; Chicago, Butler 3-3.

Sacks—Detroit, Cofer 3½, Ferguson 3, Williams, Green ½; Chicago, Dent 2, McMichael.

Dolphins-Cowboys
SUNDAY, NOVEMBER 22
SCORE BY PERIODS

Miami	7	3	3	7—20	
Dallas	7	0	0	7—14	

SCORING

Dallas—Newsome 8 pass from Pelluer (Ruzek kick), 3:47 1st.

Miami—Stradford 19 run (Reveiz kick), 7:08 1st.

Miami—Field goal Reveiz 26, 7:21 2nd.

Miami—Field goal Reveiz 33, 7:08 3rd.

Miami—Pruitt 2 pass from Marino (Reveiz kick), 6:18 4th.

Dallas—Newsome 18 pass from Pelluer (Ruzek kick), 9:42 4th.

TEAM STATISTICS

	Miami	Dallas
First downs	21	16
Rushes-Yards	25-184	33-190
Passing yards	256	129
Sacked-Yards lost	2-9	1-5
3rd down eff.	7-14	7-13
Passes	22-39-1	12-18-2
Punts	4-46.7	5-41.6
Fumbles-Lost	0-0	1-1
Penalties-Yards	7-55	6-80
Time of possession	31:56	28:04

Attendance—56,519.

INDIVIDUAL STATISTICS

Rushing—Miami, Stradford 17-169, Hampton 4-9, Davenport 2-5, Nathan 1-3, Marino 1-minus 2; Dallas, Pelluer 10-84, Walker 19-82, Newsome 4-24.

Passing—Miami, Marino 22-39-1—265; Dallas, Pelluer 12-18-2—134.

Receiving—Miami, Stradford 6-83, Clayton 4-95, Davenport 3-27, Nathan 2-23, Hampton 2-7, Jensen 1-11, Johnson 1-7, Hardy 1-6, Duper 1-4, Pruitt 1-2; Dallas, Newsome 7-53, Walker 4-74, Cosbie 1-7.

Kickoff Returns—Miami, Hampton 2-44, Schwedes 1-13; Dallas, Clack 3-62, Martin 2-59.

Punt Returns—Miami, Schwedes 1-3; Dallas, Martin 3-17.

Interceptions—Miami, B. Brown 1-0, Judson 1-1; Dallas, Francis 1-0.

Punting—Miami, Roby 4-46.7; Dallas, Saxon 5-41.6.

Field Goals—Miami, Reveiz 2-3 (missed: 48); Dallas, none attempted.

Sacks—Miami, Frye; Dallas, Rohrer, Jeffcoat.

Falcons-Vikings
SUNDAY, NOVEMBER 22
SCORE BY PERIODS

Atlanta	0	7	6	0—13	
Minnesota	0	10	7	7—24	

SCORING

Minnesota—Hilton 8 pass from Wilson (C. Nelson kick), 2:26 2nd.

Atlanta—Campbell 7 run (Luckhurst kick), 10:48 2nd.

Minnesota—Field goal C. Nelson 51, 14:57 2nd.

Minnesota—Lewis 78 punt return (C. Nelson kick), 10:12 3rd.

Atlanta—Matthews 23 pass from Campbell (kick failed), 12:49 3rd.

Minnesota—Rice 2 run (C. Nelson kick), 9:12 4th.

TEAM STATISTICS

	Atlanta	Minnesota
First downs	16	18
Rushes-Yards	25-96	36-134
Passing yards	194	172
Sacked-Yards lost	3-18	0-0
3rd down eff.	6-14	9-17
Passes	19-35-1	14-33-1
Punts	6-41.0	5-36.6
Fumbles-Lost	1-0	1-0
Penalties-Yards	3-20	7-45
Time of possession	29:42	30:18

Attendance—53,866.

INDIVIDUAL STATISTICS

Rushing—Atlanta, Riggs 15-41, Settle 5-8, Campbell 5-47; Minnesota, Fenney 9-44, D. Nelson 16-43, Anderson 5-28, Rice 3-3, Kramer 1-1, Wilson 2-15.

Passing—Atlanta, Campbell 19-35-1—212; Minnesota, Kramer 5-9-0—43, Wilson 7-18-0—111, Gannon 2-6-1—18.

Receiving—Atlanta, Dixon 3-69, C. Brown 1-19, Whisenhunt 4-27, Emery 1-minus 3, Riggs 5-24, Matthews 2-51, Cox 1-8, Sharp 1-5, Settle 1-12; Minnesota, Carter 3-80, Fenney 2-13, Jordan 3-40, D. Nelson 3-6, Hilton 1-8, Lewis 2-25.

Kickoff Returns—Atlanta, Emery 3-69, Settle 2-24; Minnesota, Guggemos 3-58.

Punt Returns—Atlanta, Johnson 4-36; Minnesota, Lewis 4-98.

Interceptions—Atlanta, Butler 1-0; Minnesota, Browner 1-5.

Punting—Atlanta, Donnelly 5-48.1; Minnesota, Coleman 6-36.6.

Field Goals—Atlanta, Luckhurst 0-1 (missed: 53); Minnesota, C. Nelson 1-2 (missed: 31).

Sacks—Minnesota, Doleman 1½, D. Martin 1½.

49ers-Buccaneers
SUNDAY, NOVEMBER 22
SCORE BY PERIODS

San Francisco	7	10	0	7—24
Tampa Bay	10	0	0	0—10

SCORING

Tampa Bay—Wilder 4 pass from DeBerg (Igwebuike kick), 5:46 1st.

San Francisco—Rice 21 pass from Montana (Wersching kick), 10:04 1st.

Tampa Bay—Field goal Igwebuike 29, 12:47 1st.

San Francisco—Rice 42 pass from Montana (Wersching kick), 8:10 2nd.

San Francisco—Field goal Wersching 43, 15:00 2nd.

San Francisco—Rice 3 pass from Montana (Wersching kick), 5:24 4th.

TEAM STATISTICS

	San Francisco	Tampa Bay
First downs	28	14
Rushes-Yards	34-137	20-60
Passing yards	295	196
Sacked-Yards lost	1-9	1-10
3rd down eff.	9-16	5-13
Passes	29-45-1	19-35-1
Punts	4-41.8	6-35.8
Fumbles-Lost	3-0	1-1
Penalties-Yards	5-37	6-35
Time of possession	32:48	27:12
Attendance—63,211.		

INDIVIDUAL STATISTICS

Rushing—San Francisco, Craig 15-60, Rathman 4-9, Montana 3-6, Cribbs 6-25, Rice 1-10, Sydney 5-27; Tampa Bay, Wilder 11-48, Smith 7-5, Bartalo 2-7.

Passing—San Francisco, Montana 29-45-1—304; Tampa Bay, DeBerg 19-35-1—206.

Receiving—San Francisco, Craig 5-28, Frank 2-21, Wilson 4-70, Rice 7-103, Francis 1-11, Cribbs 2-14, Clark 2-19; Tampa Bay, Carter 3-78, Wilder 8-39, Hill 2-18, Magee 1-18, Hall 1-3, Bartalo 1-5, Miller 2-42, Freeman 1-3.

Kickoff Returns—San Francisco, Rathman 1-16, Cribbs 1-12; Tampa Bay, Futrell 1-23, Miller 2-46.

Punt Returns—San Francisco, McLemore 4-27; Tampa Bay, Futrell 2-32.

Interceptions—San Francisco, Griffin 1-0; Tampa Bay, Isom 1-38.

Punting—San Francisco, Runager 4-41.8; Tampa Bay, Garcia 6-35.8.

Field Goals—San Francisco, Wersching 1-2 (missed: 40); Tampa Bay, Igwebuike 1-1.

Sacks—San Francisco, Shell; Tampa Bay, Washington.

Colts-Patriots
SUNDAY, NOVEMBER 22
SCORE BY PERIODS

Indianapolis	0	0	0	0— 0
New England	0	10	14	0—24

SCORING

New England—Fryar 8 pass from Ramsey (Franklin kick), 0:04 2nd.

New England—Field goal Franklin 34, 13:52 2nd.

New England—Scott 3 blocked punt return (Franklin kick), 5:27 3rd.

New England—Lippett 45 interception return (Franklin kick), 12:28 3rd.

TEAM STATISTICS

	Indianapolis	New England
First downs	18	15
Rushes-Yards	31-126	38-139
Passing yards	198	174
Sacked-Yards lost	3-20	3-9
3rd down eff.	3-14	4-16
Passes	17-38-4	12-26-0
Punts	5-34.8	8-33.6
Fumbles-Lost	1-1	0-0
Penalties-Yards	3-30	2-10
Time of possession	27:24	32:36
Attendance—56,906.		

INDIVIDUAL STATISTICS

Rushing—Indianapolis, Dickerson 27-117, Bentley 2-10, Wonsley 2-minus 1; New England, Perryman 10-73, Collins 8-31, Dupard 14-24, Tatupu 5-10, Ramsey 1-1.

Passing—Indianapolis, Hogeboom 10-20-3—122, Trudeau 7-18-1—96; New England, Ramsey 12-26-0—183.

Receiving—Indianapolis, Brooks 5-72, Beach 4-25, Bouza 2-40, Murray 2-32, Wonsley 1-16, Sherwin 1-14, Dickerson 1-12, Bentley 1-7; New England, Morgan 5-102, Jones 2-29, Tatupu 2-20, Collins 1-17, Fryar 1-8, Dawson 1-7.

Kickoff Returns—Indianapolis, Perryman 1-4, Wright 2-35, Prior 1-22; New England, Davis 1-23.

Punt Returns—Indianapolis, Brooks 3-5; New England, Marion 1-0, Fryar 2-22.

Interceptions—New England, Bowman 2-3, Lippett 1-45, Gibson 1-0.

Punting—Indianapolis, Stark 4-43.4; New England, Camarillo 8-33.6.

Field Goals—Indianapolis, Biasucci 0-1 (missed: 46); New England, Franklin 1-3 (missed: 37, 37).

Sacks—Indianapolis, Krauss, Thompson, Sally; New England, Tippett 3.

Broncos-Raiders
SUNDAY, NOVEMBER 22
SCORE BY PERIODS

Denver	10	10	0	3—23
Los Angeles Raiders	0	14	3	0—17

SCORING

Denver—Field goal Karlis 49, 8:45 1st.

Denver—Johnson 24 pass from Elway (Karlis kick), 9:59 1st.

Denver—Field goal Karlis 31, 0:21 2nd.

Los Angeles—Jackson 35 run (Bahr kick), 8:35 2nd.

Denver—Elway 1 run (Karlis kick), 13:29 2nd.

Los Angeles—Jackson 1 run (Bahr kick), 14:14 2nd.

Los Angeles—Field goal Bahr 34, 4:31 3rd.

Denver—Field goal Karlis 20, 7:55 4th.

TEAM STATISTICS

	Denver	Los Angeles
First downs	19	17
Rushes-Yards	38-127	26-149
Passing yards	276	122
Sacked-Yards lost	2-22	6-51
3rd down eff.	9-16	2-11
Passes	16-29-0	15-21-0
Punts	2-36.0	6-37.3
Fumbles-Lost	1-1	3-1
Penalties-Yards	7-48	5-30
Time of possession	34:12	25:48
Attendance—61,318.		

INDIVIDUAL STATISTICS

Rushing—Denver, Lang 14-67, Winder 13-27, Elway 7-25, Sewell 3-5, Nattiel 1-3; Los Angeles, Jackson 13-98, Allen 11-44, Wilson 2-7.

Passing—Denver, Elway 16-29-0—298; Los Angeles, Wilson 15-21-0—173.

Receiving—Denver, Johnson 5-115, Nattiel 3-87, Jackson 3-32, Kay 2-42, Sewell 1-15, Lang 1-6, Winder 1-1; Los Angeles, Jackson 5-20, Allen 4-60, Lofton 4-59, Williams 1-25, Christensen 1-9.

Kickoff Returns—Denver, Johnson 2-26, Nattiel 1-19, Bell 1-18; Los Angeles, Williams 1-13, Mueller 5-112.

Punt Returns—Denver, Nattiel 2-15, Johnson 1-9; Los Angeles, Woods 2-0.

Interceptions—None.

Punting—Denver, Horan 2-36.0; Los Angeles, Talley 6-37.3.

Field Goals—Denver, Karlis 3-4 (missed: 41); Los Angeles, Bahr 1-1.

Sacks—Denver, Jones, Mecklenburg 2, Kragen, Wilson, Fletcher; Los Angeles, Townsend, Jones.

Giants-Saints
SUNDAY, NOVEMBER 22
SCORE BY PERIODS

New York Giants	0	7	7	0—14
New Orleans	3	10	0	10—23

SCORING

New Orleans—Field goal Andersen 19, 3:57 1st.
New York—Baker 46 pass from Rutledge (Allegre kick), 1:16 2nd.
New Orleans—Word 1 run (Andersen kick), 10:46 2nd.
New Orleans—Field goal Andersen 43, 15:00 2nd.
New York—Bavaro 22 pass from Rutledge (Allegre kick), 4:25 3rd.
New Orleans—Martin 22 pass from Hebert (Andersen kick), 8:30 4th.
New Orleans—Field goal Andersen 28, 11:34 4th.

TEAM STATISTICS

	New York	New Orleans
First downs	16	16
Rushes-Yards	17-75	37-103
Passing yards	223	175
Sacked-Yards lost	5-41	3-19
3rd down eff.	3-11	7-18
Passes	20-36-5	17-27-1
Punts	4-37.0	7-37.7
Fumbles-Lost	3-2	1-1
Penalties-Yards	6-51	5-37
Time of possession	24:33	35:27
Attendance—67,639.		

INDIVIDUAL STATISTICS

Rushing—New York, Rouson 8-35, Adams 7-19, Rutledge 1-4, Galbreath 1-17; New Orleans, Mayes 24-84, Word 6-21, Hilliard 5-9, Hill 1-minus 9, Hebert 1-minus 2.

Passing—New York, Rutledge 20-36-5—264; New Orleans, Hebert 17-27-1—194.

Receiving—New York, Rouson 3-34, Adams 6-44, Baker 4-100, Manuel 3-36, Bavaro 3-43, Galbreath 1-7; New Orleans, Hilliard 8-81, Hill 3-53, Pattison 1-5, Brenner 2-14, Tice 1-8, Martin 2-33.

Kickoff Returns—New York, Ingram 1-17; New Orleans, Word 1-64, Gray 2-45.

Punt Returns—New York, McConkey 4-20; New Orleans, Gray 2-18, Atkins 1-0.

Interceptions—New York, Headen 1-20; New Orleans, Maxie 1-7, Atkins 2-4, Jakes 1-2, Waymer 1-9.

Punting—New York, Landeta 4-37.0; New Orleans, Hansen 7-37.7.

Field Goals—New York, Allegre 0-1 (missed: 40); New Orleans, Andersen 3-3.

Sacks—New York, Marshall, Banks, Reasons; New Orleans, Clark, Wilks 2½, Jackson ½, Swilling ½.

Browns-Oilers
SUNDAY, NOVEMBER 22
SCORE BY PERIODS

Cleveland	9	17	14	0—40
Houston	0	0	7	0— 7

SCORING

Cleveland—Byner 1 run (pass failed), 10:24 1st.
Cleveland—Field goal Jaeger 21, 12:15 1st.
Cleveland—Field goal Jaeger 32, 2:25 2nd.
Cleveland—Mack 5 run (Jaeger kick), 12:27 2nd.
Cleveland—Slaughter 27 pass from Kosar (Jaeger kick), 14:56 2nd.
Cleveland—Byner 17 run (Jaeger kick), 9:13 3rd.
Houston—Givins 83 pass from Moon (Zendejas kick), 9:41 3rd.
Cleveland—McNeil 39 pass from Kosar (Jaeger kick), 12:10 3rd.

TEAM STATISTICS

	Cleveland	Houston
First downs	27	11
Rushes-Yards	51-200	14-43
Passing yards	257	204
Sacked-Yards lost	0-0	3-22
3rd down eff.	7-18	3-13
Passes	15-28-0	11-34-4
Punts	3-25.7	5-34.2
Fumbles-Lost	3-0	2-2
Penalties-Yards	5-55	7-71
Time of possession	42:50	17:10
Attendance—51,161.		

INDIVIDUAL STATISTICS

Rushing—Cleveland, Mack 26-114, Byner 12-57, Manoa 6-24, Fontenot 7-5; Houston, Rozier 11-43, Moon 1-12, Givins 1-minus 1, Highsmith 1-1.

Passing—Cleveland, Kosar 15-26-0—257, Jaeger 0-1-0—0, Danielson 0-1-0—0; Houston, Moon 5-23-3—193, Pease 6-11-1—33.

Receiving—Cleveland, Byner 2-24, Newsome 2-47, Tennell 1-15, Slaughter 4-79, McNeil 3-66, Mack 2-17, Langhorne 1-9; Houston, Givins 3-126, Duncan 2-67, Jeffires 1-6, Drewrey 2-19, D. Hill 1-6, Rozier 1-minus 3, Highsmith 1-5.

Kickoff Returns—Cleveland, McNeil 4-77, Young 1-21; Houston, Duncan 7-104.

Punt Returns—Cleveland, Fontenot 1-24; Houston, K. Johnson 1-minus 1.

Interceptions—Cleveland, Minnifield 3-minus 3, Harper 1-16.

Punting—Cleveland, Winslow 3-25.7; Houston, L. Johnson 5-34.2.

Field Goals—Cleveland, Jaeger 2-3 (missed: 31); Houston, Zendejas 0-1 (missed: 48).

Sacks—Cleveland, Hairston, M. Johnson, Clancy.

Steelers-Bengals
SUNDAY, NOVEMBER 22
SCORE BY PERIODS

Pittsburgh	3	10	7	10—30
Cincinnati	3	3	3	7—16

SCORING

Pittsburgh—Field goal Anderson 43, 6:50 1st.
Cincinnati—Field goal Breech 35, 14:54 1st.
Pittsburgh—Field goal Anderson 52, 9:06 2nd.
Pittsburgh—Woodson 45 interception return (Anderson kick), 14:12 2nd.
Cincinnati—Field goal Breech 38, 15:00 2nd.
Cincinnati—Field goal Breech 41, 7:38 3rd.

Pittsburgh—Thompson 14 pass from Malone (Anderson kick), 10:36 3rd.
Pittsburgh—Field goal Anderson 46, 0:30 4th.
Cincinnati—Kinnebrew 2 run (Breech kick), 12:40 4th.
Pittsburgh—Malone 42 run (Anderson kick), 14:12 4th.

TEAM STATISTICS

	Pittsburgh	Cincinnati
First downs	14	28
Rushes-Yards	31-134	25-75
Passing yards	194	373
Sacked-Yards lost	0-0	5-36
3rd down eff.	3-13	4-15
Passes	15-28-2	30-53-3
Punts	6-41.0	4-42.0
Fumbles-Lost	0-0	4-2
Penalties-Yards	8-70	6-47
Time of possession	28:10	31:50

Attendance—52,795.

INDIVIDUAL STATISTICS

Rushing—Pittsburgh, Pollard 17-57, Abercrombie 10-20, Stone 2-16, Malone 2-41; Cincinnati, Jennings 10-14, Johnson 7-33, Esiason 7-26, Kinnebrew 1-2.

Passing—Pittsburgh, Malone 15-28-2—194; Cincinnati, Esiason 30-50-3—409.

Receiving—Pittsburgh, Pollard 4-22, Sweeney 2-42, Lee 2-12, Clinkscales 4-51, Thompson 3-67; Cincinnati, Brown 3-57, Jennings 7-57, McGee 8-139, Kattus 2-23, Martin 1-30, Hillary 4-50, Holman 4-49, Kinnebrew 1-4.

Kickoff Returns—Pittsburgh, Woodson 3-79, Stone 1-10; Cincinnati, McGee 5-81, Hillary 1-15, Kattus 1-9.

Punt Returns—Pittsburgh, Woodson 2-15; Cincinnati, Martin 3-20.

Interceptions—Pittsburgh, Everett 2-21, Woodson 1-45; Cincinnati, Fulcher 1-2, Jackson 1-0.

Punting—Pittsburgh, Newsome 6-41.0; Cincinnati, Fulhage 3-42.3, Esiason 1-41.0.

Field Goals—Pittsburgh, Anderson 3-3; Cincinnati, Breech 3-3.

Sacks—Pittsburgh, Merriweather 2, Hinkle, Willis, Gary.

Packers-Chiefs
SUNDAY, NOVEMBER 22
SCORE BY PERIODS

Green Bay	7	0	13	3—23
Kansas City	0	0	3	0— 3

SCORING

Green Bay—Carruth 6 run (Zendejas kick), 4:11 1st.
Kansas City—Field goal Lowery 34, 1:28 3rd.
Green Bay—Neal 13 pass from Wright (Zendejas kick), 11:14 3rd.
Green Bay—Neal 26 pass from Wright (kick failed), 12:09 3rd.
Green Bay—Field goal Zendejas 40, 13:08 4th.

TEAM STATISTICS

	Green Bay	Kansas City
First downs	14	10
Rushes-Yards	37-108	24-116
Passing yards	165	85
Sacked-Yards lost	0-0	5-40
3rd down eff.	4-16	5-17
Passes	9-26-0	14-34-1
Punts	9-42.7	7-42.4
Fumbles-Lost	1-1	4-2
Penalties-Yards	7-76	11-55
Time of possession	31:28	28:32

Attendance—34,611.

INDIVIDUAL STATISTICS

Rushing—Green Bay, Fullwood 23-68, Carruth 6-20, Davis 1-12, Wright 1-5, Epps 1-0; Kansas City, Okoye 15-67, Seurer 5-21, Palmer 1-12, Heard 1-12, Moriarty 2-4.

Passing—Green Bay, Majkowski 2-11-0—74, Wright 7-15-0—91; Kansas City, Seurer 13-32-1—107, Kenney 1-2-0—18.

Receiving—Green Bay, Neal 3-46, Epps 2-42, Paskett 1-41, Carruth 1-19, Stanley 1-11, West 1-6; Kansas City, Paige 3-36, Okoye 3-20, Carson 2-20, Coffman 2-17, Hayes 1-11, Marshall 1-7, Moriarty 1-3, Keel 1-2.

Kickoff Returns—Green Bay, Jefferson 1-12, Cherry 1-0; Kansas City, Robinson 1-25, Moriarty 1-16, Palmer 1-25, A. Pearson 2-4.

Punt Returns—Green Bay, Stanley 3-13; Kansas City, Clemons 6-79.

Interceptions—Green Bay, R. Brown 1-11.

Punting—Green Bay, Bracken 9-42.7; Kansas City, Goodburn 7-42.4.

Field Goals—Green Bay, Zendejas 1-1; Kansas City, Lowery 1-2 (missed: 49).

Sacks—Green Bay, Noble, Harris, Murphy, R. Brown, Anderson.

Rams-Redskins
MONDAY, NOVEMBER 23
SCORE BY PERIODS

Los Angeles Rams	14	9	7	0—30
Washington	9	7	3	7—26

SCORING

Los Angeles—Wilcher 35 fumble return (Lansford kick), 1:35 1st.
Washington—Monk 17 pass from Williams (kick failed), 9:14 1st.
Washington—Field goal Haji-Sheikh 22, 14:07 1st.
Los Angeles—Ron Brown 95 kickoff return (Lansford kick), 14:25 1st.
Los Angeles—Field goal Lansford 37, 6:28 2nd.
Los Angeles—White 1 run (kick failed), 10:54 2nd.
Washington—Williams 1 run (Haji-Sheikh kick), 13:45 2nd.
Washington—Field goal Haji-Sheikh 29, 7:57 3rd.
Los Angeles—Ron Brown 26 pass from Everett (Lansford kick), 11:22 3rd.
Washington—Monk 5 pass from Williams (Haji-Sheikh kick), 0:04 4th.

TEAM STATISTICS

	Los Angeles	Washington
First downs	14	20
Rushes-Yards	44-138	22-66
Passing yards	96	277
Sacked-Yards lost	1-10	4-31
3rd down eff.	3-13	5-17
Passes	7-13-1	24-47-1
Punts	8-36.1	7-36.8
Fumbles-Lost	0-0	1-1
Penalties-Yards	11-98	6-51
Time of possession	30:13	29:47

Attendance—53,614.

INDIVIDUAL STATISTICS

Rushing—Los Angeles, White 35-112, Guman 8-27, Everett 1-minus 1; Washington, Rogers 13-19, Bryant 7-46, Clark 1-0, Williams 1-1.

Passing—Los Angeles, Everett 7-13-1—106; Washington, Williams 24-46-1—308, Bryant 0-1-0—0.

Receiving—Los Angeles, Ron Brown 2-39, White 1-7, Guman 2-37, D. Johnson 1-6, Ellard 1-17; Washington, Monk 5-93, Clark 4-69, Didier 5-74, Sanders 2-13, Warren 2-11, Rogers 1-8, Bryant 5-40.

Kickoff Returns—Los Angeles, Ron Brown 5-172, McDonald 1-11; Washington, Branch 1-15, Orr 2-36, Griffin 3-57.

Punt Returns—Los Angeles, Hicks 3-9; Washington, Green 1-10, Yarber 4-26.

Interceptions—Los Angeles, Irvin 1-0; Washington, Walton 1-0.

Punting—Los Angeles, Hatcher 8-36.1; Washington, Cox 6-44.5.

Field Goals—Los Angeles, Lansford 1-1; Washington, Haji-Sheikh 2-2.

Sacks—Los Angeles, Jeter, Greene 2, Wilcher; Washington, Manley.

TWELFTH WEEK

RESULTS OF WEEK 12

Thursday, November 26

Kansas City 27, Detroit 20 at Det.
Minnesota 44, Dallas 38 (OT) at Dall.

Sunday, November 29

Buffalo 27, Miami 0 at Buff.
Chicago 23, Green Bay 10 at Chi.
Denver 31, San Diego 17 at S.D.
Indianapolis 51, Houston 27 at Ind.
L.A. Rams 35, Tampa Bay 3 at L.A.
New Orleans 20, Pittsburgh 16 at Pitts.
N.Y. Jets 27, Cincinnati 20 at N.Y.
Philadelphia 34, N. England 31 (OT) at N.E.
St. Louis 34, Atlanta 21 at Atl.
San Francisco 38, Cleveland 24 at S.F.
Washington 23, N.Y. Giants 19 at Wash.

Monday, November 30

L.A. Raiders 37, Seattle 14 at Sea.

Entering their Week 12 game against the New York Jets, the 1987 National Football League season had been like one long horror film for the Cincinnati Bengals. They had lost seven of their 10 games, including three in the final minutes when victory seemed inevitable. A 27-26 loss to San Francisco in Week 2 bordered on the unbelievable, with the Bengals blowing a six-point lead in the final minute despite having a first down at midfield.

The misery continued in New York. With the score tied, 20-20, with two minutes left in regulation, Bengals placekicker Jim Breech was wide left with a 46-yard potential game-winning field-goal attempt. The officials ruled, however, that the Cincinnati kicking team, which had lined up for the kick with 2:17 left, had failed to snap the ball before the two-minute warning. Breech was given a second chance and the beleaguered Bengals finally had received a break.

Or had they? The Jets' Barry Bennett answered that question by breaking through the line and blocking Breech's second kick. Teammate Rich Miano scooped up the loose ball and, using a block by Carl Howard, ran 67 yards for what proved to be the game-winning touchdown.

The Jets held on to win, 27-20, and the snake-bitten Bengals had been bitten again.

"If we don't find a way to lose it, the other team finds a way to win it," said Cincinnati quarterback Boomer Esiason, who sealed his team's fate by throwing an interception to Miano on the Bengals' next possession. "What's going on now with the Cincinnati Bengals is just terrible.

"The field goal called back looked like a break and it wasn't. It's a microcosm of our season."

On the block play, Bennett was lined up over left guard Tim Krumrie and next to Joe Klecko, who was over center Ed Brady.

"The guard became so engrossed with Joe that it left Barry with a gap to slip through," said Jets special teams coach Larry Pasquale. "Joe took a step and then withdrew, and (Krumrie's) momentum came forward. Barry's pretty clever. When you have an experienced line in the game, you can talk about adjustments."

"We were in deep trouble," Bennett said. "It's a feeling like first-and-goal at the 1. The odds are not in your favor."

But the Jets, who remained tied for first place in the AFC East at 6-5, made the big play when they had to. The Bengals, who dropped to 3-8 in the cellar of the AFC Central, once again did not.

"My insides are slowly eroding," said Bengals Coach Sam Wyche, whose team had won 10 of 16 games just one year earlier and whose own job security was very much in doubt.

The Kansas City Chiefs drove 67 yards for a touchdown on their first possession of the game to snap a string of 14 consecutive quarters without an offensive touchdown en route to a 27-20 interconference victory at Detroit in the Lions' annual Thanksgiving Day game. The Chiefs' victory was their first since opening day and snapped a club-record nine-game losing streak.

Bill Kenney made his first start at quarterback in four weeks and completed 14 of 17 passes for 198 yards and two touchdowns as the Chiefs grabbed a 24-10 halftime lead.

The Lions, whose record dropped to 2-9, pulled to within seven points on Chuck Long's 10-yard scoring pass to Gary Ellerson with 1:48 remaining. But rookie Gary Lee ended Detroit's hopes by dropping a fourth-down pass at the Kansas City 25-yard line with 30 seconds left.

The Minnesota Vikings also recorded a Thanksgiving Day road victory, defeating the Dallas Cowboys, 44-38 in overtime, at Texas Stadium. Vikings running back Darrin Nelson, who rushed for 118 yards, scored the game-winning touchdown on a 24-yard run 7:51 into the extra period. Vikings placekicker Chuck Nelson had missed a 46-yard field-goal attempt with nine seconds left in regulation.

Defense took a holiday as the Vikings (476) and Cowboys (403) combined for 879 total yards in offense. Dallas quarterback Danny White completed 25 of 41 pass attempts for 341 yards and four touchdowns, but also threw three interceptions and fumbled twice. White completed eight of 10 passes in two touchdown drives in the final six minutes of regulation, but was intercepted by Vikings linebacker Scott Studwell at the Minnesota 37-yard line in the overtime.

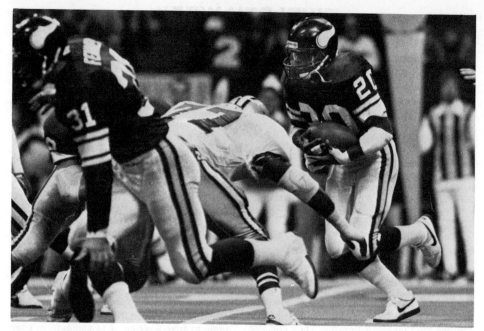

Darrin Nelson rushed for 118 yards and scored the game-winning touchdown in Minnesota's 44-38 overtime victory at Dallas on Thanksgiving Day.

The Chicago Bears maintained their two-game lead over the Vikings in the NFC Central Division with a 23-10 triumph over the Green Bay Packers. Kevin Butler kicked three field goals as the Bears won for the sixth straight time in the divisional series.

Butler's counterpart, Max Zendejas, had a day he'd just as soon forget. Zendejas, who entered the contest with a string of 10 successful field goals, had two kicks blocked and missed another in a 1-for-4 kicking performance. Bears safety Todd Bell, who had six tackles, two assists and one deflected pass, blocked one field-goal attempt while teammate Al Harris, who was credited with four tackles, one sack and one batted down pass, got the other. Bell's third-quarter block of a 50-yard Zendejas attempt led to a 27-yard Butler field goal for the game-winning points.

The kicking game also played a pivotal role in the Philadelphia Eagles' 34-31 overtime victory over the New England Patriots. The Patriots rallied from a 31-10 fourth-quarter deficit but still couldn't avoid their 12th loss in succession against an NFC East Division team and their 10th in as many overtime games in club history.

New England kicker Tony Franklin—a former Eagles player—missed a 31-yard field-goal attempt with five seconds left in regulation and a 46-yard try in the overtime. That opened the gates for Eagles kicker Paul McFadden, who promptly missed a 39-yard attempt of his own.

On the Patriots' next possession, however, running back Mosi Tatupu fumbled after a hit by Terry Hoage and Garry Cobb recovered for the Eagles on the New England 30-yard line. McFadden made the most of his second chance, booting a 38-yard game-winner with 2:44 left in overtime, just four plays after his earlier miss.

The NFL's top-rated passing offense met up with the league's No. 1-ranked defense against the pass in Week 12 and, in this game at least, the offense prevailed. The San Francisco 49ers, with quarterback Joe Montana completing 23 of 31 passes for 342 yards and four touchdowns, defeated the Cleveland Browns, 38-24, in an interconference game. Three of Montana's scoring passes were to wide receiver Jerry Rice, who had seven receptions for 126 yards in his third straight three-touchdown game.

The 49ers, who improved their NFC West Division-leading record to 9-2, entered the game with a league-high average of 250 yards passing. The Browns, who dropped to 7-4 but still had a one-game lead in the AFC Central, had allowed just 160 passing yards per game and nine touchdown passes in their 10 previous games.

One week after suffering a 24-0 shutout loss at New England, the Indianapolis Colts exploded for their highest point total in 11 years, defeating the Houston Oilers, 51-27. The Oilers, combined with a 40-7 loss to Cleveland one week earlier, had allowed 91 points in their last two games.

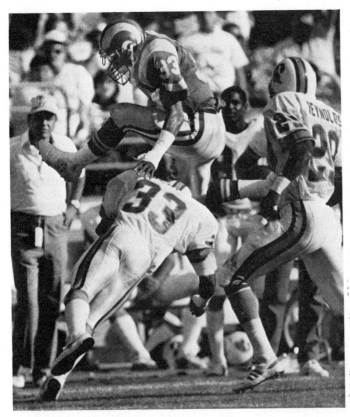

League-leading rusher Charles White ran for 137 yards and two touchdowns in the Rams' 35-3 win over Tampa Bay.

Running back Eric Dickerson led the Indianapolis attack with 136 yards rushing on 27 carries, including touchdown runs of 19 and 13 yards. Dickerson, who was making his fourth straight start after his celebrated trade from the Los Angeles Rams, set a Colts record with his fourth straight 100-yard rushing game. It also was Dickerson's second 100-yard rushing game of the season against the Oilers, who yielded 149 yards to the All-Pro in a 20-16 win over the Rams in Week 1.

Indianapolis took control of the game by scoring two touchdowns in a 1:02 span of the second period. After Gary Hogeboom and Albert Bentley hooked up for a 72-yard touchdown pass—the first touchdown reception by a Colts running back in 44 games—Allen Pinkett of the Oilers fumbled the ensuing kickoff at his own 27-yard line. Linebacker Dave Ahrens recovered for the Colts and, two plays later, Dickerson scored on a 13-yard run.

The Buffalo Bills swept a season series from the Miami Dolphins for the first time in 21 years with a 27-0 victory in Week 12. The Dolphins, who had won their last five games at Rich Stadium, were last swept by the Bills in 1966, Miami's first season as an NFL expansion franchise.

Dolphins quarterback Dan Marino also had a consecutive-games streak with at least one touchdown pass snapped at 30, the second-longest streak in league history to Johnny Unitas' NFL record of 47.

Bills quarterback Jim Kelly threw scoring passes to Butch Rolle and Chris Burkett while running back Ronnie Harmon rushed for 119 yards on 23 attempts for his first 100-yard rushing game.

The league's leading rusher, Charles White of the Los Angeles Rams, carried 29 times for 137 yards and scored two touchdowns in the Rams' 35-3 victory over Tampa Bay. White had 952 yards rushing on 219 attempts after 11 games.

The Rams drove 69 yards for a touchdown on their first possession en route to their third straight win and fourth in 11 games. The Buccaneers, who lost their fourth in a row, moved into Los Angeles territory only two times.

The Atlanta Falcons dropped their sixth straight game, this time a 34-21 decision to St. Louis. The Falcons, whose 2-9 record was tied with Detroit and Kansas City for the NFL's worst, had given up exactly twice as many points (328) as they had scored (164) in 11 games. Both figures were worst in the league.

The Cardinals, who won their second straight game for the first time in Coach Gene Stallings' two-year tenure, received a 369-yard passing performance from quarterback Neil

Lomax, including 279 in the first two periods as St. Louis grabbed a 24-14 halftime lead.

Jay Schroeder completed 28 of 46 attempts for 331 yards and three touchdowns to lead the Washington Redskins to a come-from-behind 23-19 victory over the New York Giants. Schroeder, who got the starting nod when Doug Williams injured his back in practice three days earlier, was 17 of 25 for 217 yards in the second half as the Redskins erased a 16-0 halftime deficit.

The Redskins, who got a measure of revenge for a 17-0 loss to the Giants in the 1986 NFC title game, scored the winning touchdown on Schroeder's 38-yard pass to Ricky Sanders with 4:56 left to play. Giants cornerback Perry Williams slipped and fell on a wet field, leaving Sanders wide open on the play.

The defending league-champion Giants, who dropped to 3-8, assured themselves of their first losing season since 1983 and were officially eliminated from playoff contention.

In contrast to the Giants' woes, the New Orleans Saints clinched their first winning season in franchise history with a 20-16 victory at Pittsburgh. The triumph gave New Orleans an 8-3 record with four games remaining.

The Saints defense sealed the win with two goal-line stands in the final 2:20, the first coming when linebacker Sam Mills stopped Steelers running back Frank Pollard at the New Orleans goal-line and the second when cornerback Dave Waymer intercepted a Mark Malone pass as time expired. The Saints successfully defended five Pittsburgh plays inside their own 4-yard line in the final four minutes.

The Saints trailed, 14-10, after three quarters before scoring the go-ahead touchdown on Bobby Hebert's 19-yard pass to Eric Martin with 8:16 left. Two plays before the touchdown, Waymer recovered a fumbled punt return by Steelers' rookie Rod Woodson on the Pittsburgh 21-yard line.

The Denver Broncos put together their best offensive performance of the season in a 31-17 AFC West Division win over San Diego. Quarterback John Elway completed 21 of 32 attempts for 347 yards and three touchdowns as the Broncos converted 12 of 15 third-down opportunities and punted only once—with 1:50 remaining in the game.

The Broncos led, 17-10, at halftime before driving 55 and 80 yards for touchdowns on their first two possessions of the second half to take a commanding 31-10 lead. Elway completed their first drive with a five-yard scoring pass to Gene Lang and the second with a nine-yarder to Vance Johnson.

The Chargers, who lost for the second week in succession after an eight-game winning streak, scored their first touchdown on safety Vencie Glenn's NFL-record 103-yard interception return in the first quarter. Glenn's return eclipsed the old record of 102 that had

been held by four other players.

Records fell in the Monday night game between the Los Angeles Raiders and Seattle Seahawks. Rookie Bo Jackson, who hit 22 home runs as an outfielder with the Kansas City Royals before joining the Raiders for his first NFL campaign, rushed 18 times for 221 yards and scored three touchdowns to lead L.A. to a 37-14 triumph over the Seahawks. The Raiders had lost in Seattle by scores of 33-3 and 37-0 the previous two seasons.

Jackson, who was celebrating his 25th birthday, set one Raider record with his 221 rushing yards and another with a spectacular 91-yard touchdown run in the second quarter. About the only mistake of the night for Jackson, who was playing in just his fifth NFL game, was a first-quarter fumble that led to Seattle's first touchdown.

The Raiders, who ended a club-record seven-game losing streak, won for the 25th time in 31 Monday night appearances since 1970.

Vikings-Cowboys
THURSDAY, NOVEMBER 26
SCORE BY PERIODS

Minnesota	14	7	7	10	6—44
Dallas	0	14	10	14	0—38

SCORING
Minnesota—Carter 11 pass from Kramer (C. Nelson kick), 3:35 1st.
Minnesota—Kramer 1 run (C. Nelson kick), 8:45 1st.
Dallas—D. White 1 run (Ruzek kick), 3:10 2nd.
Dallas—Walker 3 pass from D. White (Ruzek kick), 11:36 2nd.
Minnesota—Carter 37 pass from Kramer (C. Nelson kick), 13:48 2nd.
Minnesota—D. Nelson 52 run (C. Nelson kick), 4:26 3rd.
Dallas—Field goal Ruzek 38, 9:52 3rd.
Dallas—Renfro 8 pass from D. White (Ruzek kick), 11:50 3rd.
Minnesota—Field goal C. Nelson 33, 1:27 4th.
Minnesota—Fenney 1 run (C. Nelson kick), 6:36 4th.
Dallas—Renfro 14 pass from D. White (Ruzek kick), 8:56 4th.
Dallas—Renfro 18 pass from D. White (Ruzek kick), 12:52 4th.
Minnesota—D. Nelson 24 run (no kick), 7:51 OT.

TEAM STATISTICS

	Minnesota	Dallas
First downs	27	23
Rushes-Yards	40-188	34-112
Passing yards	288	291
Sacked-Yards lost	4-24	6-50
3rd down eff.	5-14	5-13
Passes	18-36-2	24-41-3
Punts	6-39.3	5-38.2
Fumbles-Lost	1-0	3-2
Penalties-Yards	5-53	8-64
Time of possession	33:50	34:01

Attendance—54,229.

INDIVIDUAL STATISTICS
Rushing—Minnesota, D. Nelson 16-118, Anderson 10-38, Fenney 10-31, Kramer 1-1, Rice 3-0; Dallas, Walker 21-76, Dorsett 7-19, Newsome 3-18, D. White 3-minus 1.

Passing—Minnesota, Wilson 9-18-1—189, Kramer 9-18-1—123; Dallas, D. White 25-41-3—341.

Receiving—Minnesota, Carter 8-184, D. Nelson 5-43, Jordan 3-41, Lewis 2-44; Dallas, Renfro 7-100, Walker

7-91, Newsome 5-34, Barksdale 3-60, Edwards 2-26, Cosbie 1-30.

Kickoff Returns—Minnesota, Guggemos 5-128, Mularkey 1-16; Dallas, Martin 3-44, Clack 3-54, Newsome 1-10.

Punt Returns—Minnesota, Lewis 3-43; Dallas, Martin 4-69.

Interceptions—Minnesota, Henderson 1-0, Holt 1-0, Studwell 1-12; Dallas, Lockhart 1-13, Walls 1-2.

Punting—Minnesota, Coleman 6-39.3; Dallas, Saxon 5-38.2.

Field Goals—Minnesota, C. Nelson 1-4 (missed: 44, 47, 46); Dallas, Ruzek 1-1.

Sacks—Minnesota, Doleman 3, Thomas, Mays, D. Martin; Dallas, Brooks, Hegman, Bates, Lockhart.

Chiefs-Lions
THURSDAY, NOVEMBER 26
SCORE BY PERIODS

Kansas City	7	17	3	0—	27
Detroit	0	10	3	7—	20

SCORING

Kansas City—Hayes 7 pass from Kenney (Lowery kick), 6:01 1st.

Kansas City—Coffman 13 pass from Kenney (Lowery kick), 1:31 2nd.

Detroit—Bernard 11 run (Murray kick), 7:33 2nd.

Kansas City—Field goal Lowery 52, 9:38 2nd.

Kansas City—Heard 1 run (Lowery kick), 13:27 2nd.

Detroit—Field goal Murray 48, 15:00 2nd.

Detroit—Field goal Murray 37, 8:43 3rd.

Kansas City—Field goal Lowery 54, 13:08 3rd.

Detroit—Ellerson 10 pass from Long (Murray kick), 13:12 4th.

TEAM STATISTICS

	Kansas City	Detroit
First downs	22	22
Rushes-Yards	34-162	26-151
Passing yards	246	206
Sacked-Yards lost	0-0	0-0
3rd down eff	4-9	4-12
Passes	18-26-1	21-41-0
Punts	3-49.0	4-44.3
Fumbles-Lost	2-1	0-0
Penalties-Yards	8-63	5-39
Time of possession	28:07	31:53
Attendance—43,820.		

INDIVIDUAL STATISTICS

Rushing—Kansas City, Heard 14-87, Okoye 14-58, Palmer 4-26, Carson 1-minus 2, Kenney 1-minus 7; Detroit, Bernard 20-99, Ellerson 5-43, Long 1-9.

Passing—Kansas City, Kenney 18-26-1—246; Detroit, Long 21-41-0—206.

Receiving—Kansas City, Carson 4-87, Paige 4-80, Okoye 4-25, Hayes 3-26, Palmer 2-15, Coffman 1-13; Detroit, Chadwick 5-50, Bernard 4-41, Woolfolk 3-18, Ellerson 3-16, Mandley 2-32, Rubick 2-15, Lee 1-22, Kab 1-12.

Kickoff Returns—Kansas City, Palmer 2-27, Moriarty 1-24, Clemons 1-3; Detroit, Lee 4-110, Bland 1-22.

Punt Returns—Kansas City, Clemons 2-11; Detroit, Mandley 3-47.

Interceptions—Detroit, McNorton 1-20.

Punting—Kansas City, Goodburn 3-49.0; Detroit, Arnold 4-44.3.

Field Goals—Kansas City, Lowery 2-2; Detroit, Murray 2-3 (missed: 33).

Sacks—None.

Saints-Steelers
SUNDAY, NOVEMBER 29
SCORE BY PERIODS

New Orleans	3	0	7	10—	20
Pittsburgh	0	14	0	2—	16

SCORING

New Orleans—Field goal Andersen 25, 12:18 1st.

Pittsburgh—Woodruff 33 interception return (Anderson kick), 2:30 2nd.

Pittsburgh—Abercrombie 5 run (Anderson kick), 14:14 2nd.

New Orleans—Mayes 5 run (Andersen kick), 6:53 3rd.

New Orleans—Martin 19 pass from Hebert (Andersen kick), 6:44 4th.

New Orleans—Field goal Andersen 32, 7:50 4th.

Pittsburgh—Safety, Hansen forced out of bounds in end zone by Carr, 13:55.

TEAM STATISTICS

	New Orleans	Pittsburgh
First downs	15	19
Rushes-Yards	38-114	32-112
Passing yards	144	172
Sacked-Yards lost	2-10	4-41
3rd down eff	3-14	5-13
Passes	14-24-1	16-31-3
Punts	6-42.0	6-38.0
Fumbles-Lost	4-1	5-3
Penalties-Yards	7-64	4-38
Time of possession	30:58	29:02
Attendance—47,896.		

INDIVIDUAL STATISTICS

Rushing—New Orleans, Mayes 22-73, Hilliard 11-39, Word 2-5, Hebert 2-0, Hansen 1-minus 3; Pittsburgh, Pollard 19-74, Abercrombie 9-36, Malone 2-minus 1, Carter 1-2, Hoge 1-1.

Passing—New Orleans, Hebert 14-23-1—154, Wilson 0-1-0—0; Pittsburgh, Malone 16-31-3—213.

Receiving—New Orleans, Hilliard 1-5, Mayes 2-1, Jones 5-65, Martin 3-43, Hill 1-13, Word 1-7, Brenner 1-20; Pittsburgh, Carter 3-30, Thompson 3-41, Pollard 1-minus 3, Stallworth 4-68, Sweeney 5-77.

Kickoff Returns—New Orleans, Gray 2-24, Brock 1-11; Pittsburgh, Stone 1-22, Woodson 3-73.

Punt Returns—New Orleans, Gray 4-47, Jordan 1-3; Pittsburgh, Woodson 2-10.

Interceptions—New Orleans, Poe 1-0, Mack 1-3, Waymer 1-35; Pittsburgh, Woodruff 1-33.

Punting—New Orleans, Hansen 6-42.0; Pittsburgh, Newsome 6-38.0.

Field Goals—New Orleans, Andersen 2-4 (missed: 53, 50); Pittsburgh, none attempted.

Sacks—New Orleans, Jackson 2, Swilling; Pittsburgh, Little, Merriweather.

Browns-49ers
SUNDAY, NOVEMBER 29
SCORE BY PERIODS

Cleveland	7	10	0	7—	24
San Francisco	7	14	3	14—	38

SCORING

Cleveland—Byner recovered fumble in end zone (Jaeger kick), 6:38 1st.

San Francisco—Rice 2 pass from Montana (Wersching kick), 9:05 1st.

Cleveland—Field goal Jaeger 28, 4:24 2nd.

San Francisco—Rice 30 pass from Montana (Wersching kick), 7:39 2nd.

San Francisco—Clark 40 pass from Montana (Wersching kick), 12:21 2nd.

Cleveland—Brennan 21 pass from Kosar (Jaeger kick), 14:09 2nd.

San Francisco—Field goal Wersching 38, 7:32 3rd.

San Francisco—Rice 29 pass from Montana (Wersching kick), 3:11 4th.

San Francisco—Cribbs 9 run (Wersching kick), 8:56 4th.

Cleveland—Grayson 17 fumble return (Jaeger kick), 10:26 4th.

TEAM STATISTICS

	Cleveland	San Francisco
First Downs	18	23
Rushes-Yards	20-88	34-119
Passing yards	268	336
Sacked-Yards lost	1-7	1-6
3rd down eff.	1-10	9-14
Passes	26-37-1	23-32-1
Punts	4-40.0	3-35.3
Fumbles-lost	1-0	2-1
Penalties-yards	6-63	9-78
Time of possession	26:09	33:51

Attendance—60,248.

INDIVIDUAL STATISTICS

Rushing—Cleveland, Byner 7-38, Mack 9-37, Kosar 3-10, Fontenot 1-3; San Francisco, Montana 4-43, Cribbs 6-33, Craig 13-26, Rathman 7-18, Sydney 2-2, Young 2-minus 3.

Passing—Cleveland, Kosar 26-37-1—275; San Francisco, Montana 23-31-1—342, Young 0-1-0—0.

Receiving—Cleveland, Byner 8-83, Brennan 6-65, Slaughter 4-66, Langhorne 2-19, Mack 2-17, Fontenot 2-10, McNeil 1-9, Newsome 1-6; San Francisco, Rice 7-126, Frank 6-76, Rathman 4-60, Clark 3-57, Craig 3-23.

Kickoff Returns—Cleveland, McNeil 5-101, Fontenot 2-34; San Francisco, Cribbs 2-47, Sydney 2-41.

Punt Returns—San Francisco, McLemore 2-4.

Interceptions—Cleveland, Wright 1-26; San Francisco, Holmoe 1-0.

Punting—Cleveland, Winslow 4-40.0; San Francisco, Runager 3-35.3.

Field Goals—Cleveland, Jaeger 1-3 (missed: 44, 48); San Francisco, Wersching 1-1.

Sacks—Cleveland, Grayson; San Francisco, Haley.

Cardinals-Falcons
SUNDAY, NOVEMBER 29
SCORE BY PERIODS

St. Louis	14	10	10	0—34
Atlanta	7	7	0	7—21

SCORING

St. Louis—T. Johnson 49 pass from Lomax (Gallery kick), 8:16 1st.
Atlanta—Riggs 1 run (Luckhurst kick), 13:26 1st.
St. Louis—Awalt 25 pass from Lomax (Gallery kick), 14:33 1st.
St. Louis—Ferrell 1 run (Gallery kick), 9:04 2nd.
Atlanta—Matthews 25 pass from Campbell (Luckhurst kick), 12:15 2nd.
St. Louis—Field goal Gallery 29, 13:47 2nd.
St. Louis—Field goal Gallery 29, 4:52 3rd.
St. Louis—Ferrell 1 run (Gallery kick), 13:18 3rd.
Atlanta—Matthews 4 pass from Campbell (Luckhurst kick), 4:18 4th.

TEAM STATISTICS

	St. Louis	Atlanta
First downs	24	18
Rushes-Yards	33-113	27-120
Passing yards	363	147
Sacked-Yards lost	1-6	3-34
3rd down eff.	7-16	6-15
Passes	25-42-1	15-39-1
Punts	3-34.3	5-47.2
Fumbles-Lost	2-1	3-3
Penalties-Yards	9-68	1-15
Time of possession	34:44	25:16

Attendance—15,909.

INDIVIDUAL STATISTICS

Rushing—St. Louis, Ferrell 13-58, Wolfley 7-16, Lomax 3-15, Mitchell 7-15, McAdoo 3-9; Atlanta, Riggs 15-60, Settle 9-44, Campbell 2-16, Donnelly 1-0.

Passing—St. Louis, Lomax 25-42-1—369; Atlanta, Campbell 15-39-1—181.

Receiving—St. Louis, J.T. Smith 10-109, Awalt 5-81, Ferrell 4-52, Green 3-62, T. Johnson 1-49, Wolfley 1-10, Mitchell 1-6; Atlanta, Matthews 7-115, Dixon 3-25, Johnson 2-27, Emery 1-6, Riggs 1-4, Settle 1-4.

Kickoff Returns—St. Louis, Sikahema 2-36, McAdoo 2-51; Atlanta, Everett 1-18, Emery 4-116, Settle 1-11.

Punt Returns—St. Louis, Sikahema 5-81; Atlanta, Johnson 1-13.

Interceptions—St. Louis, Bell 1-13; Atlanta, Croudip 1-40.

Punting—St. Louis, Horne 3-34.3; Atlanta, Donnelly 5-47.2.

Field Goals—Gallery 2-4 (missed: 44, 39); Atlanta, none attempted.

Sacks—St. Louis, Junior, Clasby, Alvord; Atlanta, Rade.

Giants-Redskins
SUNDAY, NOVEMBER 29
SCORE BY PERIODS

New York Giants	10	6	3	0—19
Washington	0	0	9	14—23

SCORING

New York—Field goal Allegre 24, 2:19 1st.
New York—Bavaro 30 pass from Simms (Allegre kick), 13:29 1st.
New York—Field goal Allegre 42, 9:02 2nd.
New York—Field goal Allegre 30, 13:07 2nd.
Washington—Field goal Haji-Sheikh 39, 7:57 3rd.
New York—Field goal Allegre 45, 11:23 3rd.
Washington—Clark 34 pass from Schroeder (kick failed), 11:43 3rd.
Washington—Griffin 6 pass from Schroeder (Haji-Sheikh kick), 4:33 4th.
Washington—Sanders 38 pass from Schroeder (Haji-Sheikh kick), 10:04 4th.

TEAM STATISTICS

	New York	Washington
First downs	16	20
Rushes-Yards	37-119	25-82
Passing yards	200	275
Sacked-Yards lost	5-36	6-56
3rd down eff.	4-17	6-16
Passes	12-29-1	28-46-2
Punts	8-44.0	5-40.8
Fumbles-Lost	0-0	3-2
Penalties-Yards	5-37	2-15
Time of possession	31:46	28:13

Attendance—45,815.

INDIVIDUAL STATISTICS

Rushing—New York, Morris 27-76, Carthon 8-16, Simms 2-27; Washington, Rogers 2-6, Bryant 11-45, Schroeder 4-19, Griffin 8-12.

Passing—New York, Simms 12-29-1—236; Washington, Schroeder 28-46-2—331.

Receiving—New York, Bavaro 2-37, Baker 1-6, Carthon 1-25, Morris 1-25, Ingram 1-18, Galbreath 4-54, Turner 1-36, Manuel 1-35; Washington, Monk 8-74, Clark 7-112, Sanders 6-96, Bryant 5-36, Warren 1-7, Griffin 1-6.

Kickoff Returns—New York, Rouson 4-89; Washington, Griffin 3-57, Sanders 3-82.

Punt Returns—New York, McConkey 1-10, Baker 1-5; Washington, Yarber 4-61, Green 1-10.

Interceptions—New York, Collins 1-28, Kinard 1-0; Washington, Bowles 1-0.

Punting—New York, Landeta 8-44.0; Washington, Cox 5-40.8.

Field Goals—New York, Allegre 4-4; Washington, Haji-Sheikh 1-2 (missed: 46).

Sacks—New York, Dorsey, Carson, Banks, Marshall, Martin, Headen; Washington, Manley 3, Grant, Walton.

Oilers-Colts

SUNDAY, NOVEMBER 29

SCORE BY PERIODS

Houston	0	10	7	10—27
Indianapolis	7	21	3	20—51

SCORING

Indianapolis—Dickerson 19 run (Biasucci kick), 3:53 1st.
Houston—Field goal Zendejas 28, 0:06 2nd.
Indianapolis—Bentley 72 pass from Hogeboom (Biasucci kick), 1:39 2nd.
Indianapolis—Dickerson 13 run (Biasucci kick), 2:41 2nd.
Houston—D. Hill 7 pass from Moon (Zendejas kick), 9:19 2nd.
Indianapolis—Bentley 22 pass from Hogeboom (Biasucci kick), 14:50 2nd.
Indianapolis—Field goal Biasucci 36, 5:21 3rd.
Houston—J. Williams 7 pass from Moon (Zendejas kick), 12:33 3rd.
Houston—Field goal Zendejas 44, 1:38 4th.
Indianapolis—Field goal Biasucci 44, 5:55 4th.
Indianapolis—Bouza 4 pass from Trudeau (Biasucci kick), 9:10 4th.
Houston—D. Hill 40 pass from Moon (Zendejas kick), 10:12 4th.
Indianapolis—Field goal Biasucci 49, 13:04 4th.
Indianapolis—Wonsley 1 run (Biasucci kick), 14:54 4th.

TEAM STATISTICS

	Houston	Indianapolis
First downs	25	18
Rushes-Yards	32-136	38-211
Passing yards	318	148
Sacked-Yards lost	1-9	1-11
3rd down eff.	8-16	2-9
Passes	24-44-2	10-19-0
Punts	1-36.0	5-33.8
Fumbles-Lost	3-3	1-1
Penalties-Yards	4-65	3-40
Time of possession	31:12	28:48
Attendance—54,999.		

INDIVIDUAL STATISTICS

Rushing—Houston, Rozier 26-122, Pinkett 3-12, Moon 2-4, Highsmith 1-minus 2; Indianapolis, Dickerson 27-136, Bentley 8-64, Wonsley 3-11.

Passing—Houston, Moon 24-44-2—327; Indianapolis, Hogeboom 8-15-0—149, Trudeau 2-4-0—10.

Receiving—Houston, D. Hill 7-134, Givins 3-53, Duncan 2-39, Drewrey 3-33, Rozier 5-28, Jeffires 1-23, J. Williams 2-11, Wallace 1-6; Indianapolis, Bentley 2-94, Bouza 3-29, Brandes 2-14, Brooks 1-9, Beach 1-7, Dickerson 1-6.

Kickoff Returns—Houston, Duncan 5-83, Pinkett 1-12, Drewrey 1-17, Fuller 1-0; Indianapolis, Goode 1-0, Wonsley 1-19, Bentley 4-79.

Punt Returns—Houston, K. Johnson 5-42; Indianapolis, Brooks 1-13.

Interceptions—Indianapolis, Cooks 1-2, Tullis 1-0.

Punting—Houston, L. Johnson 1-36.0; Indianapolis, Stark 5-33.8.

Field Goals—Houston, Zendejas 2-4 (missed: 48, 37); Indianapolis, Biasucci 3-3.

Sacks—Houston, Childress; Indianapolis, Darby.

Packers-Bears

SUNDAY, NOVEMBER 29

SCORE BY PERIODS

Green Bay	7	3	0	0—10
Chicago	0	10	3	10—23

SCORING

Green Bay—Fullwood 1 run (Zendejas kick), 5:35 1st.
Chicago—Anderson 20 pass from McMahon (Butler kick), 1:27 2nd.
Green Bay—Field goal Zendejas 32, 8:02 2nd.
Chicago—Field goal Butler 21, 15:00 2nd.
Chicago—Field goal Butler 27, 8:25 3rd.
Chicago—Sanders 7 run (Butler kick), 0:04 4th.
Chicago—Field goal Butler 52, 12:16 4th.

TEAM STATISTICS

	Green Bay	Chicago
First downs	20	20
Rushes-Yards	30-111	35-127
Passing yards	237	192
Sacked-Yards lost	3-18	1-3
3rd down eff.	6-16	2-10
Passes	18-36-2	16-27-1
Punts	3-33.3	4-36.5
Fumbles-Lost	1-0	4-2
Penalties-Yards	10-88	7-89
Time of possession	30:05	29:55
Attendance—61,638.		

INDIVIDUAL STATISTICS

Rushing—Green Bay, Fullwood 20-64, Carruth 4-8, Clark 2-13, Cook 2-3, Wright 2-23; Chicago, Payton 8-22, Anderson 13-32, McMahon 6-24, Sanders 5-37, Thomas 2-13, Tomczak 1-minus 1.

Passing—Green Bay, Wright 18-36-2—255; Chicago, McMahon 16-27-1—195.

Receiving—Green Bay, Stanley 2-72, Fullwood 1-12, Neal 5-55, West 2-23, Epps 6-81, Carruth 2-12; Chicago, Morris 3-51, Gault 2-39, McKinnon 3-42, Anderson 1-20, Moorehead 2-25, Payton 3-16, Gentry 2-2.

Kickoff Returns—Green Bay, Cook 2-15, Fullwood 2-21; Chicago, Sanders 2-40, Gentry 1-25.

Punt Returns—Green Bay, Stanley 1-2; Chicago, McKinnon 2-13.

Interceptions—Green Bay, Holland 1-4; Chicago, Duerson 1-0, Douglass 1-0.

Punting—Green Bay, Bracken 3-33.3; Chicago, Wagner 4-36.5.

Field Goals—Green Bay, Zendejas 1-4 (missed: 42, 50, 37); Chicago, Butler 3-3.

Sacks—Green Bay, E. Johnson; Chicago, Dent, Perry, A. Harris.

Buccaneers-Rams

SUNDAY, NOVEMBER 29

SCORE BY PERIODS

Tampa Bay	0	0	3	0— 3
Los Angeles Rams	7	14	7	7—35

SCORING

Los Angeles—Ellard 19 pass from Everett (Lansford kick), 5:04 1st.
Los Angeles—White 2 run (Lansford kick), 3:26 2nd.
Los Angeles—White 7 run (Lansford kick), 7:08 2nd.
Tampa Bay—Field goal Igwebuike 33, 2:02 3rd.
Los Angeles—Guman 1 run (Lansford kick), 7:47 3rd.
Los Angeles—Ron Brown 39 pass from Everett (Lansford kick), 0:43 4th.

TEAM STATISTICS

	Tampa Bay	Los Angeles
First downs	11	27
Rushes-Yards	14-79	50-213
Passing yards	122	212
Sacked-Yards lost	4-35	3-25
3rd down eff.	2-11	8-13
Passes	17-34-2	16-21-0
Punts	8-40.9	4-35.5
Fumbles-Lost	2-1	1-1
Penalties-Yards	5-34	6-35
Time of possession	24:31	35:29
Attendance—45,188.		

INDIVIDUAL STATISTICS

Rushing—Tampa Bay, Smith 3-47, Wilder 9-32, DeBerg 1-0, Testaverde 1-0; Los Angeles, White 29-137, Guman 10-23, Francis 7-22, Tyrrell 3-20, Ron Brown 1-11.

Passing—Tampa Bay, DeBerg 13-28-1—124, Testa-verde 4-6-1—33; Los Angeles, Everett 14-19-0—208, Dils 2-2-0—29.

Receiving—Tampa Bay, Magee 5-72, Wilder 3-17, Freeman 2-21, Carter 2-18, Smith 2-7, Hall 1-20, Carrier 1-6, Howard 1-minus 4; Los Angeles, Ellard 5-82, Ron Brown 4-91, Guman 2-15, White 2-6, Hill 1-24, Tyrrell 1-14, Francis 1-5.

Kickoff Returns—Tampa Bay, Futrell 3-66, Howard 1-5; Los Angeles, Guman 1-12, McDonald 1-15.

Punt Returns—Tampa Bay, Futrell 2-6; Los Angeles, Hicks 6-60.

Interceptions—Los Angeles, Owens 1-26, Sutton 1-4.

Punting—Tampa Bay, Garcia 8-40.9; Los Angeles, Hatcher 4-35.5.

Field Goals—Tampa Bay, Igwebuike 1-1; Los Angeles, Lansford 0-1 (missed: 33).

Sacks—Tampa Bay, Washington, Jarvis 2; Los Angeles, Wilcher, Greene 1½, Jeter, Stokes ½.

Broncos-Chargers
SUNDAY, NOVEMBER 29
SCORE BY PERIODS

Denver	7	10	14	0—31
San Diego	7	3	0	7—17

SCORING

San Diego—Glenn 103 interception return (Abbott kick), 12:51 1st.
Denver—Winder 1 run (Karlis kick), 14:38 1st.
Denver—Nattiel 46 pass from Elway (Karlis kick), 6:07 2nd.
San Diego—Field goal Abbott 32, 8:56 2nd.
Denver—Field goal Karlis 27, 13:51 2nd.
Denver—Lang 5 pass from Elway (Karlis kick), 5:33 3rd.
Denver—Johnson 9 pass from Elway (Karlis kick), 13:40 3rd.
San Diego—Adams 1 run (Abbott kick), 0:54 4th.

TEAM STATISTICS

	Denver	San Diego
First downs	31	18
Rushes-Yards	47-175	10-66
Passing yards	347	312
Sacked-Yards lost	0-0	2-10
3rd down eff.	12-15	2-9
Passes	21-32-1	23-40-2
Punts	1-49.0	3-45.7
Fumbles-Lost	0-0	0-0
Penalties-Yards	3-26	8-49
Time of possession	41:19	18:41
Attendance—61,880.		

INDIVIDUAL STATISTICS

Rushing—Denver, Lang 24-73, Winder 16-62, Elway 6-40, Bell 1-0; San Diego, Adams 5-38, Anderson 3-16, Spencer 1-9, James 1-3.

Passing—Denver, Elway 21-32-1—347; San Diego, Fouts 23-40-2—322.

Receiving—Denver, Johnson 7-88, Nattiel 4-118, Winder 3-27, Jackson 2-56, Mobley 2-30, Massie 1-13, Kay 1-10, Lang 1-5; San Diego, James 7-87, Winslow 5-49, Chandler 4-67, Anderson 3-85, Redden 2-10, Spencer 1-18, Bernstine 1-6.

Kickoff Returns—Denver, Nattiel 1-14, Johnson 1-8, Bell 2-59; San Diego, Holland 3-58, Anderson 1-20.

Punt Returns—Denver, Clark 1-7; San Diego, James 1-12.

Interceptions—Denver, Lilly 1-0, Dennison 1-10; San Diego, Glenn 1-103.

Punting—Denver, Horan 1-49.0; San Diego, Mojsiejenko 3-45.7.

Field Goals—Denver, Karlis 1-2 (missed: 39); San Diego, Abbott 1-1.

Sacks—Denver, R. Jones, Mecklenburg.

Bengals-Jets
SUNDAY, NOVEMBER 29
SCORE BY PERIODS

Cincinnati	0	10	7	3—20
New York Jets	7	10	0	10—27

SCORING

New York—McNeil 22 pass from O'Brien (Leahy kick), 2:24 1st.
New York—Field goal Leahy 24, 7:45 2nd.
Cincinnati—Brown 17 pass from Esiason (Breech kick), 10:23 2nd.
New York—Hector 1 run (Leahy kick), 13:51 2nd.
Cincinnati—Field goal Breech 31, 14:59 2nd.
Cincinnati—Kattus 3 pass from Esiason (Breech kick), 6:31 3rd.
Cincinnati—Field goal Breech 35, 1:02 4th.
New York—Field goal Leahy 23, 8:37 4th.
New York—Miano 67 blocked field goal return (Leahy kick), 13:12 4th.

TEAM STATISTICS

	Cincinnati	New York
First downs	21	20
Rushes-Yards	29-106	38-123
Passing yards	233	205
Sacked-Yards lost	3-17	2-19
3rd down eff.	4-13	8-18
Passes	16-34-2	19-33-2
Punts	6-42.3	6-40.7
Fumbles-Lost	1-0	1-0
Penalties-Yards	8-50	9-60
Time of possession	23:36	36:24
Attendance—41,135.		

INDIVIDUAL STATISTICS

Rushing—Cincinnati, Jennings 12-50, Johnson 5-39, Kinnebrew 8-28, Esiason 3-minus 1, McGee 1-minus 10; New York, McNeil 19-49, Vick 9-62, O'Brien 6-3, Hector 3-12, Faaola 1-minus 3.

Passing—Cincinnati, Esiason 16-34-2—250; New York, O'Brien 19-33-2—224.

Receiving—Cincinnati, Brown 4-42, McGee 3-44, Martin 2-45, Holman 2-21, Kinnebrew 1-25, Kattus 2-60, Jennings 2-13; New York, McNeil 7-79, Toon 6-83, Shuler 2-16, Klever 1-30, Hector 1-7, Sohn 1-6, Vick 1-3.

Kickoff Returns—Cincinnati, Bussey 2-48, Wright 3-71; New York, Townsell 2-16, Barber 1-0.

Punt Returns—Cincinnati, Martin 2-19; New York, Townsell 2-23.

Interceptions—Cincinnati, Breeden 1-4, Bussey 1-0; New York, Miano 1-21, Hamilton 1-0.

Punting—Cincinnati, Fulhage 6-42.3; New York, Jennings 6-40.7.

Field Goals—Cincinnati, Breech 2-3 (missed: 46); New York, Leahy 2-2.

Sacks—Cincinnati, Fulcher, Hammerstein; New York, Gastineau, Glenn ½, Crable ½, Howard.

Dolphins-Bills
SUNDAY, NOVEMBER 29
SCORE BY PERIODS

Miami	0	0	0	0— 0
Buffalo	0	21	3	3—27

SCORING

Buffalo—Mueller 5 run (Norwood kick), 0:09 2nd.
Buffalo—Rolle 3 pass from Kelly (Norwood kick), 9:02 2nd.
Buffalo—Burkett 22 pass from Kelly (Norwood kick), 13:58 2nd.
Buffalo—Field goal Norwood 39, 4:59 3rd.
Buffalo—Field goal Norwood 28, 7:08 4th.

TEAM STATISTICS

	Miami	Buffalo
First downs	13	21
Rushes-Yards	16-23	47-229
Passing yards	206	217
Sacked-Yards lost	1-8	0-0
3rd down eff.	3-13	7-14
Passes	20-42-3	15-21-0
Punts	5-48.2	4-42.0
Fumbles-Lost	4-0	1-0
Penalties-Yards	4-30	8-65
Time of possession	24:02	35:58

Attendance—68,055.

INDIVIDUAL STATISTICS

Rushing—Miami, Stradford 15-23, Marino 1-0; Buffalo, Harmon 23-119, Mueller 8-32, R. Porter 14-67, Kelly 2-11.

Passing—Miami, Marino 13-28-3—165, Strock 7-14-0—49; Buffalo, Kelly 15-21-0—217.

Receiving—Miami, Davenport 3-41, Stradford 3-38, Pruitt 3-36, Jensen 6-34, Duper 2-19, Clayton 2-33, Hampton 1-13; Buffalo, Harmon 3-20, Reed 4-96, Metzelaars 3-40, Rolle 1-3, Mueller 1-minus 4, Burkett 3-62.

Kickoff Returns—Miami, Hampton 3-41, Schwedes 2-30, Johnson 1-3; Buffalo, R. Porter 1-24.

Punt Returns—Miami, Schwedes 2-10; Buffalo, Pitts 2-8.

Interceptions—Buffalo, Radecic 1-0, Kelso 1-5, Burroughs 1-minus 3.

Punting—Miami, Roby 5-48.2; Buffalo, Kidd 4-42.0.

Field Goals—Miami, none attempted; Buffalo, Norwood 2-3 (missed: 47).

Sacks—Buffalo, Bennett.

Eagles-Patriots
SUNDAY, NOVEMBER 29
SCORE BY PERIODS

Philadelphia	3	14	7	7	3—34
New England	0	10	0	21	0—31

SCORING

Philadelphia—Field goal McFadden 19, 13:11 1st.

New England—Collins 24 pass from Ramsey (Franklin kick), 3:49 2nd.

Philadelphia—Quick 61 pass from Cunningham (McFadden kick), 4:47 2nd.

Philadelphia—Cunningham 1 run (McFadden kick), 7:18 2nd.

New England—Field goal Franklin 21, 14:10 2nd.

Philadelphia—Toney 1 run (McFadden kick), 6:04 3rd.

Philadelphia—Quick 29 pass from Cunningham (McFadden kick), 5:00 4th.

New England—Morgan 13 pass from Ramsey (Franklin kick), 6:57 4th.

New England—Scott 3 pass from Ramsey (Franklin kick), 9:42 4th.

New England—Ramsey 1 run (Franklin kick), 13:55 4th.

Philadelphia—Field goal McFadden 38, 12:16 OT.

TEAM STATISTICS

	Philadelphia	New England
First downs	23	31
Rushes-Yards	47-184	23-89
Passing yards	287	356
Sacked-Yards lost	3-27	6-46
3rd down eff.	7-18	8-15
Passes	18-31-1	34-53-2
Punts	5-29.4	3-41.7
Fumbles-Lost	1-0	2-2
Penalties-Yards	14-98	7-39
Time of possession	43:07	29:09

Attendance—54,198.

INDIVIDUAL STATISTICS

Rushing—Philadelphia, Toney 24-123, Haddix 15-35, Cunningham 7-31, Tautalatasi 1-minus 5; New England, Tatupu 14-58, Ramsey 4-17, Fryar 1-12, Dupard 2-1, Collins 2-1.

Passing—Philadelphia, Cunningham 18-31-1—314; New England, Ramsey 34-53-2—402.

Receiving—Philadelphia, Quick 5-121, Spagnola 5-58, Toney 3-46, Tautalatasi 2-28, Garrity 1-40, Carter 1-13, Morse 1-8; New England, Collins 11-100, Morgan 6-70, Fryar 4-80, Jones 4-62, Tatupu 4-41, Starring 3-37, Dawson 1-9, Scott 1-3.

Kickoff Returns—Philadelphia, Reid 4-58, Carter 2-39; New England, Dupard 1-16, Fryar 2-47, E. Davis 4-111.

Punt Returns—Philadelphia, Morse 2-9; New England, Fryar 3-24.

Interceptions—Philadelphia, Joyner 1-29, Foules 1-6; New England, Rembert 1-1.

Punting—Philadelphia, Teltschik 4-36.8; New England, Camarillo 3-41.7.

Field Goals—Philadelphia, McFadden 2-4 (missed: 44, 39); New England, Franklin 1-4 (missed: 43, 31, 46).

Sacks—Philadelphia, White 2, Pitts 2, Clarke, Joyner ½, Simmons ½; New England, Veris, T. Williams 1½, B. Williams ½.

Raiders-Seahawks
MONDAY, NOVEMBER 30
SCORE BY PERIODS

Los Angeles Raiders	7	20	10	0—37
Seattle	7	0	7	0—14

SCORING

Seattle—Turner 19 pass from Krieg (N. Johnson kick), 9:27 1st.

Los Angeles—Lofton 46 pass from Wilson (Bahr kick), 12:27 1st.

Los Angeles—Jackson 14 pass from Wilson (Bahr kick), 2:41 2nd.

Los Angeles—Jackson 91 run (Bahr kick), 5:18 2nd.

Los Angeles—Field goal Bahr 23, 11:18 2nd.

Los Angeles—Field goal Bahr 47, 14:16 2nd.

Los Angeles—Jackson 2 run (Bahr kick), 3:30 3rd.

Los Angeles—Field goal Bahr 23, 9:31 3rd.

Seattle—Tice 3 pass from Krieg (N. Johnson kick), 14:55 3rd.

TEAM STATISTICS

	Los Angeles	Seattle
First downs	24	14
Rushes-Yards	50-356	16-37
Passing yards	151	130
Sacked-Yards lost	1-8	4-40
3rd down eff.	6-12	6-12
Passes	11-18-0	17-31-2
Punts	2-35.0	5-42.0
Fumbles-Lost	1-1	2-1
Penalties-Yards	8-86	4-22
Time of possession	36:45	23:15

Attendance—62,802.

INDIVIDUAL STATISTICS

Rushing—Los Angeles, Jackson 18-221, Allen 18-76, Mueller 6-43, Strachan 6-12, Wilson 2-4; Seattle, Warner 11-26, J.L. Williams 3-6, Krieg 2-5.

Passing—Los Angeles, Wilson 11-18-0—159; Seattle, Krieg 17-31-2—170.

Receiving—Los Angeles, Williams 4-47, Allen 3-20, Christensen 2-32, Lofton 1-46, Jackson 1-14; Seattle, Skansi 4-54, J.L. Williams 3-30, Tice 3-18, Largent 2-25, R. Butler 2-10, Turner 1-19, Franklin 1-7, Warner 1-7.

Kickoff Returns—Los Angeles, Mueller 1-22, Williams 2-32; Seattle, Edmonds 8-147.

Punt Returns—Los Angeles, Woods 2-8; Seattle, Edmonds 1-4.

Interceptions—Los Angeles, Adams 1-8, McElroy 1-0.

Punting—Los Angeles, Talley 2-35.0; Seattle, Rodriguez 5-42.0.

Field Goals—Los Angeles, Bahr 3-3; Seattle, N. Johnson 0-1 (missed: 54).

Sacks—Los Angeles, Townsend 2, Robinson, King; Seattle, Bosworth.

THIRTEENTH WEEK

RESULTS OF WEEK 13
Sunday, December 6
Atlanta 21, Dallas 10 at Dall.
Chicago 30, Minnesota 24 at Minn.
Cincinnati 30, Kansas City 27 (OT) at Cin.
Denver 31, New England 20 at Den.
Houston 33, San Diego 18 at Hous.
Indianapolis 9, Cleveland 7 at Cleve.
L.A. Raiders 34, Buffalo 21 at L.A.
L.A. Rams 37, Detroit 16 at Det.
New Orleans 44, Tampa Bay 34 at N.O.
N.Y. Giants 23, Philadelphia 20 (OT) at N.Y.
Pittsburgh 13, Seattle 9 at Pitts.
San Francisco 23, Green Bay 12 at G.B.
Washington 34, St. Louis 17 at St.L.

Monday, December 7
Miami 37, N.Y. Jets 28 at Mia.

"Anytime you have first down on the 1-yard line and four shots, you better get it done," said Minnesota Vikings Coach Jerry Burns. "We didn't and the Bears deserved to win."

The Vikings blew a golden chance to pull within one game of the Chicago Bears in the NFC Central Division race with three games to play when they failed to score a touchdown on four straight plays from the Chicago 1-yard line in the last six minutes of the game. Instead of a morale-boosting victory, Minnesota suffered a heart-wrenching 30-24 loss that dropped them three games behind Chicago in the division race.

The Vikings led, 24-23, with 6:04 remaining when defensive end Chris Doleman sacked Bears quarterback Mike Tomczak and forced a fumble, Minnesota recovering on the 1-yard line. On first down, rookie running back Rick Fenney was stuffed for no gain by tackle Steve McMichael. Linebacker Mike Singletary did the same thing to Fenney on second down. Quarterback Wade Wilson was stopped by safety Todd Bell on third down before Bell dropped running back Darrin Nelson for a three-yard fourth-down loss to kill the threat.

The Bears later took over on their own 39-yard line with 1:25 left and put together a 61-yard drive. Tomczak capped the comeback by hitting wide receiver Dennis Gentry on a 38-yard touchdown pass with 40 seconds left. Tomczak replaced starting quarterback Jim McMahon with 11 minutes left after McMahon had suffered a hamstring injury.

"It's unbelievable," said Bears Coach Mike Ditka, whose team ran its record to 10-2 and clinched its fourth straight NFC Central title. "We played a heckuva team and came out ahead. I don't know how it happened, but the guys never gave up.

"I've been excited before, but I've never felt like this after a win."

The loss was particularly galling to the Vik-

ings, who had won 16 of their 32 regular-season games in 1985 and 1986 after having hit rock bottom with a 3-13 slate in '84. This was supposed to be the year that Minnesota knocked the big, bad Bears from their lofty perch.

"Something's wrong when you can't go in when the game's on the line," said Vikings offensive coordinator Bob Schnelker. "I guess it means they're a better team than we are."

Those sentiments were shared in Week 13 by the St. Louis Cardinals, who lost to Washington for the seventh straight time, 34-17. Quarterback Jay Schroeder threw two touchdown passes and ran for another as the Redskins improved their record to 9-3 and clinched the NFC East crown.

It appeared as though the Cardinals might be on their way to ending the Washington jinx when placekicker Jim Gallery hit a 48-yard field goal early in the third quarter for a 17-10 St. Louis lead. But the Redskins—with two big assists from the Cards—scored two touchdowns in a 1:43 span to take command.

After Schroeder threw an incomplete pass on a third-and-2 from the St. Louis 44-yard line, Cardinal defensive end Freddie Joe Nunn kept the drive alive by giving tackle Mark May a headslap after the play had ended. The personal foul gave Washington a first down and, five plays later, Schroeder ran seven yards for a touchdown to tie the score.

St. Louis rookie Derrick McAdoo fumbled the ensuing kickoff after being hit by Brian Davis and Reggie Branch. The Redskins recovered on the Cardinal 17-yard line and, three plays later, George Rogers scored on a six-yard run for a 24-17 Washington lead.

The Atlanta Falcons also took advantage of a fumbled kickoff to score two touchdowns in a 13-second span en route to a 21-10 victory over the Dallas Cowboys. The win was Atlanta's first in seven games.

After Falcons quarterback Scott Campbell and Floyd Dixon hooked up for a 28-yard touchdown pass on Atlanta's first possession, Elbert Shelley and Major Everett clobbered Dallas rookie Kelvin Martin on the ensuing kickoff. Martin fumbled and Falcons safety Robert Moore scooped up the loose ball and returned it 20 yards for a 14-0 Atlanta lead. It was Moore's first NFL touchdown.

The game was played before a crowd of 40,103 Dallas fans, the smallest crowd ever for a Cowboys game at Texas Stadium and the smallest crowd to see the Cowboys play in Dallas in 22 years. Cowboys President and General Manager Tex Schramm, who has been with the franchise since its inception in 1960, called the defeat—the Cowboys' 13th loss in 17 games —his "lowest point" in 38 years of professional football.

The New Orleans Saints, a team that began

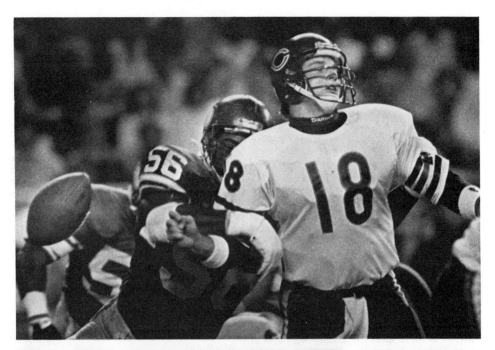

Chicago's Mike Tomczak (above) fumbles after a hit by Minnesota's Chris Doleman while San Francisco's Joe Montana (left) set a record for consecutive completions in Week 13.

Vinny Testaverde's first NFL start was not a memorable one.

playing in the NFL in 1967, clinched the first playoff berth in franchise history with a 44-34 triumph over Tampa Bay. The win improved the Saints' record to 9-3 and, coupled with Week 13 losses by the Cardinals and Philadelphia Eagles, assured New Orleans of a least a wild-card playoff spot.

Rueben Mayes and John Tice both scored two touchdowns as the Saints won for a club-record sixth successive week. Both of Tice's touchdowns came on passes from Bobby Hebert following turnovers by Bucs rookie quarterback Vinny Testaverde in the first six minutes of the game.

Testaverde, the No. 1 overall pick in the 1987 draft, was making the first start of his NFL career. On the Bucs' third play from scrimmage, he fumbled on a sack by defensive end Jim Wilks and Bruce Clark recovered for New Orleans on the Tampa Bay 19. Four plays later, Hebert hit Tice for an eight-yard touchdown and 7-0 Saints lead. On Tampa Bay's next play from scrimmage, Testaverde fumbled the center snap and Pat Swilling recovered for New Orleans on the Bucs' 38-yard line. Again four plays later, Hebert and Tice hooked up for another score, this time from six yards out.

The start of San Francisco quarterback Joe Montana's Week 13 performance was as spectacular as Testaverde's was inauspicious. Montana, who had completed his last five passes against Cleveland in Week 12, hit on his first 17 against Green Bay to establish a league record with 22 consecutive completions. The old mark of 20 had been set by Cincinnati's Ken Anderson in a 1983 game against Houston.

Montana's streak ended when he failed to connect with wide receiver Jerry Rice on a seven-yard pass into the end zone with 3:33 left

in the first half.

As it turned out, Montana's record performance came in a 23-12 victory that clinched a playoff spot for the 10-2 49ers. Montana finished with 26 completions in 35 attempts for 308 yards and two touchdowns, including a 57-yarder to Rice for the game's final points. Montana also ran 10 yards for another San Francisco touchdown.

Los Angeles Rams quarterback Jim Everett threw for a career-high 324 yards and Charles White became the first NFL running back to go over the 1,000-yard mark in the Rams' 37-16 victory over the Detroit Lions. The win was the Rams' fourth in succession while the loss was Detroit's fourth in a row.

Wide receiver Henry Ellard was Everett's main target with seven receptions for 171 yards, including an 81-yard touchdown pass on the first play of the fourth quarter. The Rams, who trailed 13-10 at halftime, scored on their first four possessions of the second half to take a commanding 34-16 lead.

White, who also scored two touchdowns, rushed 21 times for 102 yards for his fourth straight 100-yard game. He finished the day with a league-leading 1,054-yard total on 248 attempts.

The Indianapolis Colts ended a six-game losing streak against the Cleveland Browns and won at Cleveland Stadium for the first time in 25 years with a 9-7 victory. The Colts' last win in Cleveland had been a 36-14 triumph October 14, 1962.

Dean Biasucci kicked field goals of 33, 37 and 42 yards for the Colts' only points, but the game's pivotal play was a fumble by Browns running back Earnest Byner at the Indianapolis 4-yard line in the fourth quarter with Cleveland trailing by two points. Mike Prior recovered for the Colts and the Browns didn't threaten with either of their final two possessions.

A fumble by San Diego quarterback Dan Fouts on the third play of the game resulted in a Houston touchdown and set the stage for the Oilers' 33-18 victory over the Chargers. Fouts was sacked by safety Keith Bostic and his fumble was returned 55 yards by linebacker Robert Lyles for a 7-0 Houston lead just 2:35 into the game.

The Los Angeles Raiders won their second straight game after a club-record seven-game losing streak with a 34-21 decision over the Buffalo Bills. The Raiders, who trailed 14-13 at the half, drove 75 yards in three plays on their first possession of the second half for the go-ahead touchdown, a 41-yard Marc Wilson-to-James Lofton pass. Wilson completed 21 of 32 passes for 337 yards and three touchdowns.

Jim Breech kicked a 32-yard field goal with 5:16 left in overtime to give the Cincinnati Bengals their first home win of the season, a 30-27 triumph over the Kansas City Chiefs. Bengals quarterback Boomer Esiason, who completed 28 of 44 passes for 368 yards, hit on five of seven attempts for 50 yards in a 16-play, 79-yard drive to set up Breech's winning kick. The drive started on Cincinnati's 7-yard line.

The Chiefs, who lost for the 10th time in 11 games, tied the score at 27-27 on the final play of regulation when Nick Lowery kicked a 33-yard field goal.

For the second week in a row, the Bengals were the victim of a blocked field-goal attempt that was returned for a touchdown. Bill Maas blocked a 28-yarder that teammate Kevin Ross returned 65 yards with six minutes left to give Kansas City its first lead of the game. A week earlier, Barry Bennett and Rich Miano of the Jets did the same thing to a 46-yard Breech field-goal attempt.

The week's other overtime game was won by the New York Giants, who defeated NFC East Division rival Philadelphia, 23-20, on Raul Allegre's 28-yard field goal with 4:18 left in the extra period. Three plays prior to Allegre's field goal, Giants quarterback Phil Simms hit tight end Mark Bavaro for a 36-yard gain to the Eagles' 20-yard line.

Philadelphia, which lost for the sixth straight time in the series, had four possessions in the overtime but could muster just five net yards. Eagles punter John Teltschik set an NFL record with 15 punts.

The Giants led, 20-6, with less than four minutes left in regulation before Eagles quarterback Randall Cunningham threw two touchdown passes to force the overtime. It marked the fifth time in 1987 that the defending league champions had blown a fourth-quarter lead, but the first time they held on to win.

The Denver Broncos took over sole possession of first place in the AFC West with a come-from-behind 31-20 victory over New England. The Broncos, who improved to 8-3-1 with their fourth straight win, took a half-game lead over the 8-4 San Diego Chargers.

The Patriots led 17-3 at halftime before committing two costly turnovers early in the second half that helped Denver tie the score. Five of New England's six turnovers came in the second half.

An Irving Fryar fumble on the Patriots' first play from scrimmage in the third quarter was recovered by linebacker Jim Ryan on the New England 15-yard line. Two plays later, the Broncos' Tony Boddie scored from one yard out. On the Patriots' next possession, Karl Mecklenburg intercepted a pass by quarterback Tom Ramsey and returned it 16 yards to the Patriots' 19-yard line. Two plays later, John Elway and Rick Massie hooked up for a seven-yard touchdown to tie the game at 17-17.

Although the Pats regained the lead at 20-17 after three quarters on a Tony Franklin field goal, Elway threw a two-yard scoring pass to Mark Jackson with 12:41 left to give Denver its first lead at 24-20. Mark Haynes sealed the win

with a 14-yard interception return for a touchdown with 5:45 left.

Frank Pollard rushed for 106 yards on 22 carries and scored one touchdown to lead the Pittsburgh Steelers to a 13-9 victory over Seattle. Pollard's 11-yard touchdown run on the first play of the fourth quarter capped a 14-play, 81-yard drive.

The Seahawks missed a chance to take control when Paul Skansi fumbled at the Pittsburgh 19-yard line late in the third quarter with Seattle leading, 9-6. Linebacker Bryan Hinkle recovered for the Steelers.

Steelers rookie defensive back Delton Hall intercepted one Dave Krieg pass and broke up another in the end zone on the Seahawks' last two possessions.

Two rookies from Boston College played key roles in the Miami Dolphins' 37-28 victory over the New York Jets in the Monday night game. Defensive end John Bosa, Miami's No. 1 draft pick in '87, recorded his first two sacks of the season, recovered one fumble and stopped Jets rookie Roger Vick on a key fourth-down play with 2:32 remaining to lead the defense.

Troy Stradford, the Dolphins' fourth-round draft pick, led the Miami offense by rushing 30 times for 120 yards and scoring three, one-yard touchdown runs.

The Jets, who cut a 27-0 halftime deficit to 30-21 early in the fourth quarter, were held to just 40 yards rushing.

Chiefs-Bengals
SUNDAY, DECEMBER 6
SCORE BY PERIODS

Kansas City	0	3	14	10	0—27
Cincinnati	10	7	3	7	3—30

SCORING

Cincinnati—Kinnebrew 1 run (Breech kick), 11:36 1st.
Cincinnati—Field goal Breech 37, 14:53 1st.
Kansas City—Field goal Lowery 39, 8:46 2nd.
Cincinnati—McGee 8 pass from Esiason (Breech kick), 14:57 2nd.
Kansas City—Okoye 1 run (Lowery kick), 3:44 3rd.
Cincinnati—Field goal Breech 27, 8:07 3rd.
Kansas City—Paige 24 pass from Kenney (Lowery kick), 13:42 3rd.
Kansas City—Ross 65 blocked field goal return (Lowery kick), 8:00 4th.
Cincinnati—Brooks 23 pass from Esiason (Breech kick), 10:09 4th.
Kansas City—Field goal Lowery 33, 15:00 4th.
Cincinnati—Field goal Breech 32, 9:44 OT.

TEAM STATISTICS

	Kansas City	Cincinnati
First downs	21	31
Rushes-Yards	25-113	39-144
Paassing yards	209	359
Sacked-Yards lost	2-20	1-9
3rd down eff.	11-17	7-16
Passes	19-39-0	28-44-0
Punts	5-32.8	4-35.5
Fumbles-Lost	1-1	0-0
Penalties-Yards	5-34	9-75
Time of possession	27:11	42:33
Attendance—46,489.		

INDIVIDUAL STATISTICS

Rushing—Kansas City, Okoye 8-22, Palmer 5-41, Kenney 3-3, Moriarty 3-10, Heard 6-37; Cincinnati, Brooks 9-30, Kinnebrew 20-67, Jennings 7-27, Esiason 3-20.

Passing—Kansas City, Kenney 19-39-0—229; Cincinnati, Esiason 28-44-0—368.

Receiving—Kansas City, Okoye 2-12, Carson 6-80, Hayes 1-11, Palmer 1-9, Heard 1-4, Paige 6-88, Moriarty 1-8, Marshall 1-17; Cincinnati, Holman 5-90, Collinsworth 6-80, Brooks 2-32, Jennings 6-56, Martin 3-36, Brown 4-57, McGee 1-8, Kinnebrew 1-9.

Kickoff Returns—Kansas City, Palmer 2-35, Robinson 1-18, Moriarty 1-18, B. Colbert 1-13; Cincinnati, Bussey 1-8, Wright 5-95.

Punt Returns—Kansas City, Clemons 3-6; Cincinnati, Martin 3-36, Horton 1-0.

Interceptions—None.

Punting—Kansas City, Goodburn 5-32.8; Cincinnati, Fulhage 4-35.5.

Field Goals—Kansas City, Lowery 2-2; Cincinnati, Breech 3-4 (missed: 27).

Sacks—Kansas City, Bell; Cincinnati, King, Bussey.

Buccaneers-Saints
SUNDAY, DECEMBER 6
SCORE BY PERIODS

Tampa Bay	7	3	10	14—34
New Orleans	14	14	10	6—44

SCORING

New Orleans—Tice 8 pass from Hebert (Andersen kick), 3:41 1st.

New Orleans—Tice 6 pass from Hebert (Andersen kick), 6:09 1st.

Tampa Bay—Testaverde 1 run (Igwebuike kick), 12:29 1st.

New Orleans—Mayes 7 run (Andersen kick), 4:04 2nd.

New Orleans—Hilliard 3 run (Andersen kick), 7:20 2nd.

Tampa Bay—Field goal Igwebuike 37, 12:47 2nd.

New Orleans—Field goal Andersen 40, 4:04 3rd.

New Orleans—Mayes 2 run (Andersen kick), 6:49 3rd.

Tampa Bay—Carrier 37 pass from Testaverde (Igwebuike kick), 9:40 3rd.

Tampa Bay—Field goal Igwebuike 43, 14:35 3rd.

New Orleans—Field goal Andersen 24, 3:17 4th.

Tampa Bay—Hill 12 pass from Testaverde (Igwebuike kick), 5:11 4th.

New Orleans—Field goal Andersen 32, 11:26 4th.

Tampa Bay—Howard 2 run (Igwebuike kick), 13:04 4th.

TEAM STATISTICS

	Tampa Bay	New Orleans
First downs	27	19
Rushes-Yards	22-97	37-117
Passing yards	352	248
Sacked-Yards lost	3-17	1-7
3rd down eff.	6-14	6-13
Passes	22-47-2	16-24-0
Punts	3-41.0	4-44.8
Fumbles-Lost	2-2	1-1
Penalties-Yards	4-20	6-58
Time of possession	25:14	34:46
Attendance—66,471.		

INDIVIDUAL STATISTICS

Rushing—Tampa Bay, Smith 8.31, Wilder 6.30, Testaverde 5-19, Hill 1-9, Hunter 1-6, Howard 1-2; New Orleans, Mayes 21-55, Hilliard 16-62.

Passing—Tampa Bay, Testaverde 22-47-2—369; New Orleans, Hebert 16-24-0—255.

Receiving—Tampa Bay, Wilder 4-33, Carrier 8-212, Magee 1-6, Hill 5-73, Howard 1-8, Hall 1-12, Carter 2-25; New Orleans, Hill 3-27, Tice 2-14, Pattison 2-51, Mayes 1-0, Hilliard 1-12, Jones 2-20, Benson 1-5, Word 2-25, Martin 2-101.

Kickoff Returns—Tampa Bay, Futrell 3-81; New Orleans, Gray 3-73, Hilliard 2-47, Jordan 1-12.

Punt Returns—Tampa Bay, Futrell 3-24; New Orleans, Gray 2-130.

Interceptions—New Orleans, Jackson 1-4, Waymer 1-0.

Punting—Tampa Bay, Garcia 3-41.0; New Orleans, Hansen 4-41.8.

Field Goals—Tampa Bay, Igwebuike 2-2; New Orleans, Andersen 3-3.

Sacks—Tampa Bay, Jarvis; New Orleans, Wilks, Swilling, Warren.

Falcons-Cowboys
SUNDAY, DECEMBER 6
SCORE BY PERIODS

Atlanta	14	0	7	0—21
Dallas	3	7	0	0—10

SCORING

Atlanta—Dixon 28 pass from Campbell (Luckhurst kick), 8:51 1st.

Atlanta—Moore 20 fumble return (Luckhurst kick), 9:04 1st.

Dallas—Field goal Ruzek 44, 13:08 1st.

Dallas—Walker 1 run (Ruzek kick), 13:10 2nd.

Atlanta—Campbell 1 run (Luckhurst kick), 4:12 3rd.

TEAM STATISTICS

	Atlanta	Dallas
First downs	18	24
Rushes-Yards	32-111	27-91
Passing yards	253	263
Sacked-Yards lost	0-0	3-23
3rd down eff.	8-14	8-16
Passes	17-30-2	26-43-1
Punts	5-42.6	5-40.5
Fumbles-Lost	2-2	2-2
Penalties-Yards	5-68	3-42
Time of possession	29:30	30:30
Attendance—40,103.		

INDIVIDUAL STATISTICS

Rushing—Atlanta, Riggs 30-119, Campbell 1-1, Dixon 1-minus 9; Dallas, Walker 15-35, Dorsett 7-33, Newsome 3-13, Pelluer 1-11, Edwards 1-minus 1.

Passing—Atlanta, Campbell 17-30-2—253; Dallas, Pelluer 18-31-0—203, D. White 8-12-1—83.

Receiving—Atlanta, Dixon 7-80, Matthews 3-45, Settle 2-62, C. Brown 2-43, Emery 2-18, Riggs 1-5; Dallas, Edwards 7-88, Walker 7-62, Renfro 6-68, Newsome 4-35, Martin 1-17, Barksdale 1-16.

Kickoff Returns—Atlanta, Emery 3-55; Dallas, Martin 3-58, Clack 1-25.

Punt Returns—Atlanta, Johnson 3-6; Dallas, Martin 2-18.

Interceptions—Atlanta, Britt 1-4; Dallas, Downs 2-5.

Punting—Atlanta, Donnelly 5-42.6; Dallas, Saxon 5-40.5.

Field Goals—Atlanta, none attempted; Dallas, Ruzek 1-1.

Sacks—Atlanta, Casillas, G. Brown, Harrison.

Seahawks-Steelers
SUNDAY, DECEMBER 6
SCORE BY PERIODS

Seattle	3	6	0	0— 9
Pittsburgh	3	3	0	7—13

SCORING

Pittsburgh—Field goal Anderson 37, 5:53 1st.

Seattle—Field goal N. Johnson 33, 13:13 1st.

Seattle—Largent 12 pass from Krieg (pass failed), 7:13 2nd.

Pittsburgh—Field goal Anderson 24, 14:41 2nd.

Pittsburgh—Pollard 11 run (Anderson kick), 0:04 4th.

TEAM STATISTICS

	Seattle	Pittsburgh
First downs	16	18
Rushes-Yards	38-135	44-209
Passing yards	80	99
Sacked-Yards lost	1-11	0-0
3rd down eff	6-10	8-14
Passes	9-15-1	11-18-0
Punts	2-28.5	4-42.8
Fumbles-Lost	2-1	1-0
Penalties-Yards	0-0	7-63
Time of possession	29:02	30:58

Attendance—48,881.

INDIVIDUAL STATISTICS

Rushing—Seattle, Warner 22-69, J.L. Williams 13-61, Krieg 3-5; Pittsburgh, Pollard 22-106, Abercrombie 16-66, Stone 2-6, Malone 4-31.

Passing—Seattle, Krieg 9-15-1—91; Pittsburgh, Malone 11-18-0—99.

Receiving—Seattle, J.L. Williams 3-28, R. Butler 2-23, Largent 2-26, Skansi 1-7, Tice 1-7; Pittsburgh, Lee 1-4, Thompson 3-19, Lockett 1-19, Sweeney 2-16, Clinkscales 2-20, Carter 1-8, Pollard 1-13.

Kickoff Returns—Seattle, Morris 2-33, Edmonds 2-37; Pittsburgh, Stone 2-37, Woodson 1-24.

Punt Returns—Seattle, Edmonds 3-29.

Interceptions—Pittsburgh, Hall 1-0.

Punting—Seattle, Rodriguez 2-28.5; Pittsburgh, Newsome 4-42.8.

Field Goals—Seattle, N. Johnson 1-1; Pittsburgh, Anderson 2-2.

Sacks—Pittsburgh, Cole.

Bears-Vikings
SUNDAY, DECEMBER 6
SCORE BY PERIODS

Chicago	3	10	7	10—30
Minnesota	0	7	14	3—24

SCORING

Chicago—Field goal Butler 23, 14:32 1st.

Chicago—Gault 42 pass from McMahon (Butler kick), 7:20 2nd.

Chicago—Field goal Butler 26, 13:19 2nd.

Minnesota—Rice 1 pass from Wilson (C. Nelson kick), 14:54 2nd.

Chicago—Gault 16 pass from McMahon (Butler kick), 1:52 3rd.

Minnesota—Carter 60 pass from Wilson (C. Nelson kick), 4:12 3rd.

Minnesota—Carter 35 pass from Wilson (C. Nelson kick), 11:03 3rd.

Minnesota—Field goal C. Nelson 27, 1:13 4th.

Chicago—Field goal Butler 30, 6:09 4th.

Chicago—Gentry 38 pass from Tomczak (Butler kick), 14:20 4th.

TEAM STATISTICS

	Chicago	Minnesota
First downs	27	18
Rushes-Yards	32-159	27-75
Passing yards	264	281
Sacked-Yards lost	3-18	5-21
3rd down eff	6-12	9-17
Passes	17-34-1	22-39-1
Punts	4-40.0	6-40.0
Fumbles-Lost	1-0	1-0
Penalties-Yards	6-45	7-91
Time of possession	32:51	27:09

Attendance—62,331.

INDIVIDUAL STATISTICS

Rushing—Chicago, Anderson 13-75, McMahon 5-32, Payton 10-39, Sanders 4-13; Minnesota, D. Nelson 14-25, Anderson 5-15, Fenney 3-3, Kramer 1-15, Gustafson 1-minus 2, Rice 1-2, Wilson 2-17.

Passing—Chicago, McMahon 11-22-1—186, Tomczak 6-12-0—96; Minnesota, Kramer 10-20-1—91, Wilson 12-19-0—211.

Receiving—Chicago, Gentry 4-65, McKinnon 5-87, Payton 1-10, Morris 2-21, Gault 3-70, Moorehead 1-23, Anderson 1-6; Minnesota, Jordan 4-39, Lewis 2-39, Gustafson 3-48, D. Nelson 7-28, Fenney 1-8, Rice 1-1, Carter 3-106, Jones 1-33.

Kickoff Returns—Chicago, Sanders 3-44; Gentry 1-29, Suhey 1-5; Minnesota, Guggemos 6-106, D. Nelson 1-42.

Punt Returns—Chicago, McKinnon 4-21, Duerson 1-10; Minnesota, Carter 3-40.

Interceptions—Chicago, Duerson 1-0; Minnesota, Lee 1-12.

Punting—Chicago, Wagner 4-40.0; Minnesota, Coleman 6-40.0.

Field Goals—Chicago, Butler 3-3; Minnesota, C. Nelson 1-2 (missed: 26).

Sacks—Chicago, Rivera, Perry, McMichael 2½, Harris ½; Minnesota, Doleman, Mays 2.

Bills-Raiders
SUNDAY, DECEMBER 6
SCORE BY PERIODS

Buffalo	0	14	7	0—21
Los Angeles Raiders	10	3	14	7—34

SCORING

Los Angeles—Jackson 14 pass from Wilson (Bahr kick), 9:25 1st.

Los Angeles—Field goal Bahr 22, 13:45 1st.

Buffalo—Harmon 8 run (Norwood kick), 6:16 2nd.

Los Angeles—Field goal Bahr 33, 11:43 2nd.

Buffalo—Rolle 3 pass from Kelly (Norwood kick), 13:44 2nd.

Los Angeles—Lofton 41 pass from Wilson (Bahr kick), 1:34 3rd.

Los Angeles—Allen 2 run (Bahr kick), 8:08 3rd.

Buffalo—Harmon 8 run (Norwood kick), 10:23 3rd.

Los Angeles—Williams 23 pass from Wilson (Bahr kick), 12:32 4th.

TEAM STATISTICS

	Buffalo	Los Angeles
First downs	19	29
Rushes-Yards	21-84	40-144
Passing yards	303	350
Sacked-Yards lost	2-12	1-10
3rd down eff	3-9	9-15
Passes	22-36-0	22-33-0
Punts	4-46.0	3-42.3
Fumbles-Lost	1-1	0-0
Penalties-Yards	4-25	2-25
Time of possession	25:12	34:48

Attendance—43,143.

INDIVIDUAL STATISTICS

Rushing—Buffalo, Harmon 8-37, Mueller 6-28, R. Porter 3-14, Byrum 1-4, Kelly 3-1; Los Angeles, Jackson 19-78, Allen 15-47, Mueller 2-10, Wilson 2-6, Strachan 1-2, Lofton 1-1.

Passing—Buffalo, Kelly 22-36-0—315; Los Angeles, Wilson 21-32-0—337, Allen 1-1-0—23.

Receiving—Buffalo, Reed 7-153, Burkett 6-66, Harmon 3-26, Metzelaars 2-33, R. Porter 2-28, Johnson 1-6, Rolle 1-3; Los Angeles, Lofton 6-132, Allen 5-58, Jackson 4-59, Christensen 3-62, Williams 2-36, Junkin 1-8, Mueller 1-5.

Kickoff Returns—Buffalo, R. Porter 2-62, Tasker 1-16; Los Angeles, Williams 3-51.

Punt Returns—Buffalo, Pitts 1-2; Los Angeles, Woods 3-13.

Interceptions—None.

Punting—Buffalo, Kidd 4-46.0; Los Angeles, Talley 3-42.3.

Field Goals—Buffalo, none attempted; Los Angeles, Bahr 2-3 (missed: 44).

Sacks—Buffalo, Bentley; Los Angeles, Martin 2.

49ers-Packers
SUNDAY, DECEMBER 6
SCORE BY PERIODS

San Francisco	7	9	0	7—23
Green Bay	0	6	6	0—12

SCORING
San Francisco—Rathman 5 pass from Montana (Wersching kick), 7:56 1st.
San Francisco—Montana 10 run (kick failed), 3:31 2nd.
Green Bay—Field goal Zendejas 30, 7:50 2nd.
San Francisco—Field goal Wersching 25, 11:30 2nd.
Green Bay—Field goal Zendejas 45, 13:52 2nd.
Green Bay—Carruth 1 run (kick failed), 7:19 3rd.
San Francisco—Rice 57 pass from Montana (Wersching kick), 7:28 4th.

TEAM STATISTICS

	San Francisco	Green Bay
First downs	22	18
Rushes-Yards	38-143	30-188
Passing yards	296	127
Sacked-Yards lost	2-12	4-19
3rd down eff	9-16	2-13
Passes	26-35-1	19-32-3
Punts	5-37.6	4-35.3
Fumbles-Lost	3-3	2-2
Penalties-Yards	6-51	4-30
Time of possession	30:09	29:51

Attendance—51,118.

INDIVIDUAL STATISTICS
Rushing—San Francisco, Craig 14-48, Montana 7-33, Rathman 10-51, Sydney 2-minus 2, Cribbs 5-13; Green Bay, Clark 10-76, Carruth 17-68, Wright 2-28, Stanley 1-16.

Passing—San Francisco, Montana 26-35-1—308; Green Bay, Wright 19-32-3—146.

Receiving—San Francisco, Craig 6-46, Heller 2-19, Frank 2-18, Rice 4-90, Taylor 3-55, Clark 3-27, Jones 1-13, Rathman 5-40; Green Bay, Neal 2-17, Paskett 3-23, Stanley 5-57, Fullwood 1-minus 1, Epps 3-27, Clark 4-15, West 1-8.

Kickoff Returns—San Francisco, Cribbs 2-29, Sydney 1-2; Green Bay, Neal 1-10, Stanley 2-49, Fullwood 2-32.

Punt Returns—San Francisco, Taylor 1-9, McLemore 1-10; Green Bay, Stanley 3-4.

Interceptions—San Francisco, McKyer 1-0, Lott 2-2; Green Bay, D. Brown 1-3.

Punting—San Francisco, Runager 5-37.6; Green Bay, Bracken 4-35.3.

Field Goals—San Francisco, Wersching 1-1; Green Bay, Zendejas 2-2.

Sacks—San Francisco, Haley 2, Turner 2; Green Bay, E. Johnson, R. Brown.

Eagles-Giants
SUNDAY, DECEMBER 6
SCORE BY PERIODS

Philadelphia	0	6	0	14	0—20
New York Giants	7	0	6	7	3—23

SCORING
New York—Bavaro 19 pass from Simms (Allegre kick), 2:21 1st.
Philadelphia—Field goal McFadden 41, 10:32 2nd.
Philadelphia—Field goal McFadden 49, 15:00 2nd.
New York—Field goal Allegre 20, 10:13 3rd.
New York—Field goal Allegre 46, 11:52 3rd.
New York—Baker 16 pass from Simms (Allegre kick), 0:11 4th.
Philadelphia—Jackson 36 pass from Cunningham (McFadden kick), 11:38 4th.

Philadelphia—Giles 40 pass from Cunningham (McFadden kick), 14:12 4th.
New York—Field goal Allegre 28, 10:42 OT.

TEAM STATISTICS

	Philadelphia	New York
First downs	15	15
Rushes-Yards	29-95	39-78
Passing yards	164	221
Sacked-Yards lost	9-63	4-24
3rd down eff	1-18	2-18
Passes	20-43-0	16-34-1
Punts	15-36.0	10-38.0
Fumbles-Lost	3-1	0-0
Penalties-Yards	9-76	9-60
Time of possession	36:12	34:30

Attendance—65,874.

INDIVIDUAL STATISTICS
Rushing—Philadelphia, Toney 11-39, Cunningham 3-20, Haddix 15-36; New York, Simms 4-5, Morris 20-42, Adams 11-27, Galbreath 2-3, Rouson 1-1, Carthon 1-0.

Passing—Philadelphia, Cunningham 20-43-0—227; New York, Simms 16-34-1—245.

Receiving—Philadelphia, Carter 1-25, Toney 6-16, Quick 1-1, Haddix 2-31, Spagnola 1-8, Giles 5-78, Byars 1-7, Jackson 2-42, Garrity 1-19; New York, Bavaro 6-133, Morris 1-5, Adams 4-35, Galbreath 1-8, Carthon 1-9, Baker 2-25, Turner 1-30.

Kickoff Returns—Philadelphia, Carter 5-123, Reeves 0-1, Morse 1-7; New York, Rouson 2-47, Dorsey 1-13.

Punt Returns—Philadelphia, Morse 4-28; New York, McConkey 9-112.

Interceptions—Philadelphia, Hoage 1-3.

Punting—Philadelphia, Teltschik 15-36.1; New York, Landeta 10-38.2.

Field Goals—Philadelphia, McFadden 2-2; New York, Allegre 3-5 (missed: 31, 50).

Sacks—Philadelphia, White 2, J. Brown, Joyner; New York, Banks 2½, Martin, T. Johnson, Howard ½, Collins ½, Marshall, Taylor 2, Lasker ½.

Chargers-Oilers
SUNDAY, DECEMBER 6
SCORE BY PERIODS

San Diego	0	5	6	7—18
Houston	10	10	7	6—33

SCORING
Houston—Lyles 55 fumble return (Zendejas kick), 2:35 1st.
Houston—Field goal Zendejas 48, 11:09 1st.
Houston—Pinkett 4 run (Zendejas kick), 3:24 2nd.
Houston—Field goal Zendejas 47, 8:00 2nd.
San Diego—Safety, Williams tackled Moon in end zone, 10:07 2nd.
San Diego—Field goal Abbott 27, 14:56 2nd.
Houston—Rozier 1 run (Zendejas kick), 4:57 3rd.
San Diego—Winslow 6 pass from Fouts (kick failed), 9:40 3rd.
Houston—Moon 3 run (kick failed), 1:40 4th.
San Diego—Anderson 9 pass from Herrmann (Abbott kick), 14:34 4th.

TEAM STATISTICS

	San Diego	Houston
First downs	19	21
Rushes-Yards	12-43	45-140
Passing yards	289	184
Sacked-Yards lost	5-49	1-2
3rd down eff	2-13	3-14
Passes	28-48-0	13-25-1
Punts	8-44.0	7-42.4
Fumbles-Lost	4-4	4-4
Penalties-Yards	8-75	12-104
Time of possession	24:32	35:28

Attendance—31,714.

INDIVIDUAL STATISTICS

Rushing—San Diego, James 3-9, Adams 4-9, Bernstine 1-9, Spencer 4-16; Houston, Rozier 16-32, Pinkett 11-53, Highsmith 10-32, Valentine 2-5, Wallace 3-14, Moon 2-6, Pease 1-minus 2.

Passing—San Diego, Fouts 16-33-0—196, Herrmann 12-15-0—142; Houston, Moon 13-24-1—186, Pease 0-1-0—0.

Receiving—San Diego, James 6-91, Winslow 4-25, Chandler 10-140, Anderson 3-36, Holohan 1-15, Redden 1-3, Spencer 3-28; Houston, D. Hill 4-45, Highsmith 1-11, Givins 5-93, J. Williams 2-37, Rozier 1-0.

Kickoff Returns—San Diego, Kirk 1-0, Bernstine 1-13, Holland 5-103, James 1-20; Houston, Pinkett 3-56.

Punt Returns—San Diego, James 6-74; Houston, Drewrey 2-9.

Interceptions—San Diego, Glenn 1-15.

Punting—San Diego, Mojsiejenko 8-44.0; Houston, Gossett 7-42.4.

Field Goals—San Diego, Abbott 1-1; Houston, Zendejas 2-2.

Sacks—San Diego, Williams; Houston, Meads 2, Bostic, Newsom, Lyles.

Rams-Lions
SUNDAY, DECEMBER 6
SCORE BY PERIODS

Los Angeles Rams	3	7	10	17—37
Detroit	3	10	3	0—16

SCORING

Detroit—Field goal Murray 53, 3:14 1st.
Los Angeles—Field goal Lansford 48, 12:12 1st.
Detroit—Field goal Murray 39, 0:16 2nd.
Los Angeles—Francis 4 pass from Everett (Lansford kick), 2:53 2nd.
Detroit—Mandley 3 pass from Long (Murray kick), 12:34 2nd.
Los Angeles—White 1 run (Lansford kick), 5:20 3rd.
Detroit—Field goal Murray 36, 12:20 3rd.
Los Angeles—Field goal Lansford 47, 13:29 3rd.
Los Angeles—Ellard 81 pass from Everett (Lansford kick), 0:13 4th.
Los Angeles—White 1 run (Lansford kick), 5:47 4th.
Los Angeles—Field goal Lansford 48, 12:48 4th.

TEAM STATISTICS

	Los Angeles	Detroit
First downs	22	19
Rushes-Yards	36-110	17-57
Passing yards	313	271
Sacked-Yards lost	1-11	2-17
3rd down eff.	4-11	3-12
Passes	20-26-1	26-48-2
Punts	2-34	3-52.7
Fumbles-Lost	3-1	1-1
Penalties-Yards	8-56	6-55
Time of possession	29:21	30:39
Attendance—33,143.		

INDIVIDUAL STATISTICS

Rushing—Los Angeles, White 29-102, Francis 2-4, Guman 4-4, Everett 1-0; Detroit, Bernard 10-41, Jones 6-14, Paige 1-2.

Passing—Los Angeles, Everett 20-26-1—324; Detroit, Long 26-48-2—288.

Receiving—Los Angeles, Ellard 7-171, White 4-13, Ron Brown 3-93, Guman 2-21, Johnson 2-17, House 1-5, Francis 1-4; Detroit, Lee 7-69, Mandley 6-90, Jones 4-58, Rubick 4-34, Woolfolk 3-28, Bernard 2-9.

Kickoff Returns—Los Angeles, Hicks 1-53, Ron Brown 2-24; Detroit, Ball 1-3, Woolfolk 3-51, Lee 1-26, Glover 1-19.

Punt Returns—Los Angeles, Ellard 1-6, Hicks 1-7; Detroit, Mandley 1-0.

Interceptions—Los Angeles, Gray 1-0, Ekern 1-7; Detroit, McNorton 1-0.

Punting—Los Angeles, Hatcher 2-34.0; Detroit, Arnold 3-52.7.

Field Goals—Los Angeles, Lansford 3-3; Detroit, Murray 3-4 (missed: 44).

Sacks—Los Angeles, Jeter, Reed; Detroit, Green.

Colts-Browns
SUNDAY, DECEMBER 6
SCORE BY PERIODS

Indianapolis	0	9	0	0—9
Cleveland	0	0	7	0—7

SCORING

Indianapolis—Field goal Biasucci 33, 6:16 2nd.
Indianapolis—Field goal Biasucci 37, 11:00 2nd.
Indianapolis—Field goal Biasucci 42, 14:42 2nd.
Cleveland—Brennan 19 pass from Kosar (Jaeger kick), 11:22 3rd.

TEAM STATISTICS

	Indianapolis	Cleveland
First downs	18	15
Rushes-Yards	30-114	26-87
Passing yards	183	160
Sacked-Yards lost	1-9	3-18
3rd down eff.	2-12	4-14
Passes	20-34-0	16-35-0
Punts	7-38.7	8-32.5
Fumbles-Lost	1-1	2-1
Penalties-Yards	3-20	4-20
Time of possession	30:18	29:42
Attendance—70,661.		

INDIVIDUAL STATISTICS

Rushing—Indianapolis, Dickerson 27-98, Bentley 3-16; Cleveland, Mack 16-62, Byner 6-19, Manoa 3-6, Kosar 1-1.

Passing—Indianapolis, Trudeau 20-34-0—192; Cleveland, Kosar 16-35-0—178.

Receiving—Indianapolis, Boyer 5-38, Bentley 4-39, Brooks 7-85, Bouza 4-30; Cleveland, Brennan 4-51, Slaughter 4-56, Byner 4-45, Mack 2-7, Newsome 1-11, Weathers 1-8.

Kickoff Returns—Indianapolis, Bentley 2-46; Cleveland, Fontenot 2-27, Young 1-24, Manoa 1-13.

Punt Returns—Indianapolis, Brooks 2-2; Cleveland, McNeil 4-20.

Interceptions—None.

Punting—Indianapolis, Stark 7-38.1; Cleveland, Winslow 8-32.5.

Field Goals—Indianapolis, Biasucci 3-3; Cleveland, Jaeger 0-1 (missed: 38).

Sacks—Indianapolis, Cooks 2, Thompson; Cleveland, Puzzuoli.

Redskins-Cardinals
SUNDAY, DECEMBER 6
SCORE BY PERIODS

Washington	10	0	21	3—34
St. Louis	0	14	3	0—17

SCORING

Washington—Clark 84 pass from Schroeder (Haji-Sheikh kick), 11:22 1st.
Washington—Field goal Haji-Sheikh 22, 13:22 1st.
St. Louis—Mitchell 3 pass from Lomax (Gallery kick), 1:39 2nd.
St. Louis—J.T. Smith 4 pass from Lomax (Gallery kick), 14:12 2nd.
St. Louis—Field goal Gallery 48, 4:06 3rd.
Washington—Schroeder 7 run (Haji-Sheikh kick), 8:49 3rd.
Washington—Rogers 6 run (Haji-Sheikh kick), 10:32 3rd.
Washington—Didier 19 pass from Schroeder (Haji-Sheikh kick), 14:37 3rd.
Washington—Field goal Haji-Sheikh 40, 11:17 4th.

TEAM STATISTICS

	Washington	St. Louis
First downs	18	21
Rushes-Yards	41-180	26-128
Passing yards	231	195
Sacked-Yards lost	1-4	5-46
3rd down eff.	5-14	5-16
Passes	13-25-1	21-39-0
Punts	4-42.3	6-42
Fumbles-Lost	2-2	2-2
Penalties-Yards	4-51	10-85
Time of possession	31:05	28.55
Attendance—31,324.		

INDIVIDUAL STATISTICS

Rushing—Washington, Rogers 30-134, Schroeder 8-27, Griffin 3-19; St. Louis, Mitchell 20-101, Wolfley 5-16, Lomax 1-11.

Passing—Washington, Schroeder 13-25-1—235; St. Louis, Lomax 21-39-0—241.

Receiving—Washington, Clark 5-130, Monk 3-23, Sanders 2-56, Griffin 2-7, Didier 1-19; St. Louis, Mitchell 2-28, J.T. Smith 7-65, Awalt 3-32, Wolfley 2-13, Green 6-90, T. Johnson 1-13.

Kickoff Returns—Washington, Branch 1-15, Griffin 3-56; St. Louis, Sikahema 4-90, Sargent 1-27, Holmes 1-25, McAdoo 1-9.

Punt Returns—Washington, Yarber 4-36; St. Louis, Sikahema 2-4.

Interceptions—St. Louis, Curtis 1-15.

Punting—Washington, Cox 4-42.3; St. Louis, Horne 6-42.0.

Field Goals—Washington, Haji-Sheikh 2-2; St. Louis, Gallery 1-3 (missed: 40, 39).

Sacks—Washington, Kaufman, Butz, Coleman, Walton, Koch; St. Louis, Noga.

Patriots-Broncos
SUNDAY, DECEMBER 6
SCORE BY PERIODS

New England	7	10	3	0—20
Denver	0	3	14	14—31

SCORING

New England—Dupard 10 run (Franklin kick), 13:23 1st.
Denver—Field goal Karlis 24, 9:43 2nd.
New England—Collins 4 pass from Ramsey (Franklin kick), 13:47 2nd.
New England—Field goal Franklin 36, 14:56 2nd.
Denver—Boddie 1 run (Karlis kick), 1:49 3rd.
Denver—Massie 7 pass from Elway (Karlis kick), 7:55 3rd.
New England—Field goal Franklin 27, 13:58 3rd.
Denver—Jackson 2 pass from Elway (Karlis kick), 2:19 4th.
Denver—Haynes 14 interception return (Karlis kick), 9:15 4th.

TEAM STATISTICS

	New England	Denver
First downs	20	21
Rushes-Yards	35-211	32-112
Passing yards	158	259
Sacked-Yards lost	3-19	2-6
3rd down eff.	4-14	6-15
Passes	17-39-4	17-37-1
Punts	5-48.2	5-34.8
Fumbles-Lost	4-2	4-2
Penalties-Yards	5-37	6-51
Time of possession	30:46	29:14
Attendance—75,794.		

INDIVIDUAL STATISTICS

Rushing—New England, Collins 15-64, Dupard 11-91, Camarillo 1-0, Fryar 1-9, Tatupu 2-7, Ramsey 5-40; Denver, Elway 7-8, Winder 20-89, Lang 3-12, Boddie 2-3.

Passing—New England, Ramsey 17-39-4—177; Denver, Elway 17-37-1—265.

Receiving—New England, Fryar 3-22, Starring 2-26, Jones 3-61, D. Williams 2-21, Collins 5-37, Dawson 1-8, Dupard 1-2; Denver, Jackson 4-67, Nattiel 3-81, Kay 1-15, Massie 2-36, Lang 1-5, Boddie 4-26, Winder 1-7, Mobley 1-28.

Kickoff Returns—New England, Dupard 1-14; Denver, Bell 4-57.

Punt Returns—New England, Fryar 2-11; Denver, Clark 3-30.

Interceptions—New England, McSwain 1-17; Denver, Mecklenburg 2-25, Haynes 1-14, Robbins 1-0.

Punting—New England, Camarillo 5-48.2; Denver, Horan 4-35.8, Elway 1-31.0.

Field Goals—New England, Franklin 2-2; Denver, Karlis 1-2 (missed: 52).

Sacks—New England, Rembert, B. Williams; Denver, Jones, Ryan.

Jets-Dolphins
MONDAY, DECEMBER 7
SCORE BY PERIODS

New York Jets	0	0	14	14—28
Miami	14	13	3	7—37

SCORING

Miami—Johnson 2 pass from Marino (Reveiz kick), 6:37 1st.
Miami—Stradford 1 run (Reveiz kick), 11:37 1st.
Miami—Stradford 1 run (kick failed), 4:09 2nd.
Miami—Stradford 1 run (Reveiz kick), 14:46 2nd.
New York—Toon 44 pass from O'Brien (Leahy kick), 1:02 3rd.
Miami—Field goal Reveiz 18, 10:52 3rd.
New York—Ryan 8 run (Leahy kick), 12:28 3rd.
New York—Hector 14 run (Leahy kick), 0:07 4th.
Miami—Marino 5 run (Reveiz kick), 6:47 4th.
New York—Humphery 46 fumble return (Leahy kick), 7:59 4th.

TEAM STATISTICS

	New York	Miami
First downs	13	30
Rushes-Yards	12-40	41-139
Passing yards	216	293
Sacked-Yards lost	4-21	0-0
3rd down eff.	2-8	10-17
Passes	18-25-1	29-40-0
Punts	3-43.0	3-35.0
Fumbles-Lost	2-1	1-1
Penalties-Yards	9-32	4-35
Time of possession	16:21	43:39
Attendance—58,879.		

INDIVIDUAL STATISTICS

Rushing—New York, McNeil 1-1, Vick 3-3, Hector 7-28, Ryan 1-8; Miami, Stradford 30-120, Davenport 6-15, Hampton 2-1, Jensen 1-1, Marino 2-2.

Passing—New York, O'Brien 18-25-1—237; Miami, Marino 29-40-1—293.

Receiving—New York, Sohn 3-27, Vick 1-23, Hector 3-21, Shuler 3-23, Toon 5-100, McNeil 1-20, Klever 1-12, Townsell 1-11; Miami, Pruitt 2-27, Hardy 2-18, Johnson 2-24, Clayton 6-96, Stradford 3-20, Davenport 10-72, Bennett 1-3, Nathan 1-6, Duper 2-27.

Kickoff Returns—New York, Griggs 1-13, Klever 1-11, Humphery 1-47, Faaola 1-4; Miami, Hardy 1-1, Schwedes 1-17, Hampton 3-63.

Punt Returns—New York, Townsell 3-11; Miami, Schwedes 2-10.

Interceptions—Miami, Lankford 1-44.

Punting—New York, Jennings 4-43.0; Miami, Roby 3-35.0.

Field Goals—New York, none attempted; Miami, Reveiz 1-1.

Sacks—Miami, Bosa 2, M. Brown, Frye.

FOURTEENTH WEEK

RESULTS OF WEEK 14
Sunday, December 13

Buffalo 27, Indianapolis 3 at Ind.
Cleveland 38, Cincinnati 24 at Cleve.
Detroit 20, Tampa Bay 10 at T.B.
Green Bay 16, Minnesota 10 at G.B.
Kansas City 16, L.A. Raiders 10 at K.C.
L.A. Rams 33, Atlanta 0 at L.A.
Miami 28, Philadelphia 10 at Phil.
New England 42, N.Y. Jets 20 at N.E.
New Orleans 24, Houston 10 at N.O.
Pittsburgh 20, San Diego 16 at S.D.
St. Louis 27, N.Y. Giants 24 at St.L.
Seattle 28, Denver 21 at Sea.
Washington 24, Dallas 20 at Wash.

Monday, December 14

San Francisco 41, Chicago 0 at S.F.

A baseball player made a football homecoming in Week 14 and, even though his playing time was cut short by injury, he was the talk of the town before, during and after the game.

Bo Jackson, a rookie left fielder for the Kansas City Royals in 1987, returned to Kansas City as the celebrated rookie running back of the Los Angeles Raiders on December 13 for a National Football League game against the Chiefs. Although he played just eight minutes in Kansas City's 16-10 victory, Jackson's presence on the Raiders sideline was enough to fill Arrowhead Stadium and inspire a downtrodden Chiefs team.

"We respect Bo as a great athlete but we were getting pretty tired of all the talk about Bo this and Bo that," said Kansas City defensive end Mike Bell. "And I think all that talk helped get us fired up. We figured the only way to shut down the hype was to shut him down."

Kansas City's defense never really got a chance to show what it could do against Jackson. A first-quarter ankle injury limited the youngster to three rushing attempts for one yard and one pass reception for four yards. The Raiders, who committed four turnovers and came up with just one field goal on four possessions inside the Kansas City 25-yard line in the first half, rushed for only 88 yards in the game.

"I'm not going to kid myself," said Chiefs cornerback Albert Lewis. "I'm glad Bo didn't get to play. I hope he's not seriously hurt, but I'm not going to say I'm sorry he didn't play."

"No one really hit me," Jackson said of the play on which he was injured. "My shoe got caught and some people fell on it. I heard something pop and I thought it was something serious. I just said . . . well, I can't tell you what I said."

Jackson spent most of the afternoon on the Raider sideline in the company of Royals teammates George Brett, Steve Balboni, Jamie Quirk and former Royal Fred Patek. Royals co-Owner Avron Fogelman, who had as much interest in Jackson's injury as did the Raiders, watched from the stands.

Jackson's appearance drew a crowd of 63,834 to Arrowhead Stadium, the largest crowd for a Chiefs home game in December since 1973.

"The defense hasn't been playing that great the past few weeks," said Chiefs nose tackle Bill Maas. "But this was just the motivation to get us going. We had a lot of emotion today.

"It was pretty sad. Our own crowd, 65,000 of them, and all for him."

Kansas City's victory was its second in three weeks, but only its third in 13 games.

The Detroit Lions also finished the week with a 3-10 record after a 20-10 NFC Central Division victory over Tampa Bay. The Lions' victory—the team's first in a December game since 1983—snapped a four-game losing streak and handed the Buccaneers their sixth straight loss.

Detroit employed a ground attack that ranked at the bottom of the league. The Lions gained 190 yards rushing on 50 attempts despite entering the game with an NFL-low 78.3 rushing yards per game. Detroit rushed 32 times on 35 offensive plays in the second half while scoring 10 points.

The game marked the first home start for Bucs rookie quarterback Vinny Testaverde. Testaverde completed 20 of 39 attempts for 262 yards and one touchdown, but threw one interception and was sacked four times. The Buccaneers failed to convert any of their 10 third-down opportunities.

The Indianapolis Colts also were shut out in the third-down department (0 for 10) in a 27-3 loss to AFC East Division rival Buffalo. The division-leading Colts were held to nine first downs and 130 total yards—53 in the first half —while committing six turnovers. The longest Indianapolis drive consisted of six plays.

Colts running back Eric Dickerson was held to a career-low 19 yards rushing on 11 carries.

The Bills, who drove 75 yards in 13 plays on their opening possession for the only touchdown they needed, moved into a tie with the Colts and Miami Dolphins in the AFC East. Defensive end Bruce Smith led the Buffalo defense with five tackles, 2.5 sacks and a fumble recovery in the end zone with 1:11 left for the Bills' final touchdown.

The Dolphins kept pace with a 28-10 interconference win at Philadelphia. Quarterback Dan Marino completed 25 of 39 attempts for 376 yards and three touchdowns as Miami (7-6) went over the .500 mark for the first time in 1987.

The Dolphins, who drove 80 yards in 10 plays for a touchdown late in the first half to take a

14-10 lead, scored touchdowns on each of their first two possessions in the second half to take command. Marino threw touchdown passes of 11 and 20 yards to Mark Clayton to end both drives.

After having scored just one offensive touchdown in their previous seven quarters, the Cleveland Browns exploded for a team-record 28 points in the second quarter en route to a 38-24 victory over Cincinnati. Bernie Kosar threw four touchdown passes and Kevin Mack rushed 27 times for 133 yards to lead the Browns' offense, but the game's turning point came late in the first half.

Trailing 21-3, the Bengals had a third-and-three situation at the Cleveland 7-yard line with 1:55 left before intermission. Quarterback Boomer Esiason's pass, however, was intercepted by Browns linebacker Clay Matthews at the 4. Matthews returned the ball 36 yards before lateraling to teammate Carl Hairston, the league's oldest defensive end at 34, who lumbered 40 more yards to the Cincinnati 20. Two plays later, Kosar threw a two-yard scoring pass to rookie Derek Tennell for a 28-3 Cleveland lead.

New England quarterback Steve Grogan threw four touchdown passes and ran two yards for another score—all in the first half—to lead the Patriots to a 42-20 triumph over the New York Jets. Grogan, who was playing his first game in a month because of neck and shoulder ailments, took advantage of a beat-up Jets secondary that was missing three starters.

But Grogan's performance was no fluke. Grogan's four scoring passes gave him 25 touchdown passes and just six interceptions in his last 14 games against New York.

The San Diego Chargers continued their late-season swoon with a 20-16 loss to the visiting Pittsburgh Steelers. The Chargers, who at one time sported an NFL-best record of 8-1, fell to 8-5 with their fourth straight defeat, but still trailed Denver by just one-half game in the AFC West.

The Chargers lost four fumbles and committed five turnovers. Pittsburgh's first touchdown, an eight-yard run by Frank Pollard, came four plays after Lionel James' fumbled punt return was recovered by Steelers rookie Dwight Stone at the Chargers' 38-yard line.

Placekicker Vince Abbott missed field-goal attempts of 42, 48 and 46 yards as San Diego, despite an edge of 435-254 in total yards, failed to score an offensive touchdown until the final three minutes.

The Broncos maintained their half-game lead despite a 28-21 loss at Seattle that snapped a four-game winning streak. Denver quarterback John Elway, who had not been sacked in 14 quarters, was brought down five times by a swarming Seahawks defense. The Broncos rushed for just 72 yards against a Seattle defense that had given up 565 yards rushing in successive losses to the Raiders and Steelers.

After Denver (which had just four first downs in a scoreless first half) scored two touchdowns in the first 4:24 of the second half to forge a 14-14 tie, the Seahawks used a little razzle-dazzle to regain the lead. With a first down at the Broncos' 40-yard line, quarterback Dave Krieg handed the ball to running back Curt Warner on an apparent end run play. Warner, however, handed the ball to receiver Steve Largent on a reverse. Largent then threw a lateral back to Krieg, who fired 40 yards downfield to receiver Ray Butler in the Denver end zone.

The Los Angeles Rams didn't need trickery in their NFC West Division matchup with the Atlanta Falcons. The Rams pounded the Falcons, 33-0, for their fifth straight win and most lopsided victory in seven years. The Rams offense committed no turnovers, allowed no sacks and rolled up a season-high 494 total yards while hitting the 30-point barrier for the fourth consecutive week.

Los Angeles running back Charles White rushed for 159 yards on 29 carries and scored two touchdowns against the NFL's poorest defense against the run. It was White's fifth straight 100-yard rushing game.

The Falcons, who lost for the seventh time in eight games, trailed 26-0 at halftime with just 47 yards in total offense. That prompted the appearance of rookie quarterback Chris Miller, Atlanta's No. 1 draft choice in 1987, who made his NFL debut in the second half and completed 10 of 20 passes for 170 yards with one interception.

In what turned out to be their final home game in St. Louis, the Cardinals kept alive their slim hopes for a wild-card playoff berth by posting a 27-24 victory over the New York Giants. The Cardinals, who beat the Giants for the first time in six meetings, had scored just 23 points in their previous four games against New York.

The Cardinals took a 7-0 lead when Vai Sikahema returned a Sean Landeta punt 76 yards for a touchdown just over one minute into the game. After the Giants tied the score on Phil Simms' 11-yard touchdown pass to Mark Bavaro minutes later, Sikahema returned the ensuing kickoff 48 yards to set up the second St. Louis touchdown, a six-yard run by Ron Wolfley.

Stump Mitchell rushed 26 times for 111 yards for the first 100-yard rushing performance against the Giants in 36 non-strike games.

In another NFC East Division game, wide receiver Gary Clark caught nine passes for 187 yards to lead the Washington Redskins to a 24-20 victory over the Dallas Cowboys. Clark, who also caught a 56-yard scoring pass from Jay Schroeder with a minute left in the first half, caught six passes for 167 yards in the first two periods as the Redskins grabbed a 17-3 halftime lead.

The Cowboys, whose record dropped to 5-8

Bernie Kosar threw four touchdown passes to lead the Browns to a 38-24 victory over the Bengals in Week 14.

with their fourth straight loss, assured themselves (with only two games left) of their second consecutive losing season. Dallas had not suffered back-to-back losing years since finishing 4-10 and 5-8-1, respectively, in 1963 and 1964.

Bobby Hebert threw three touchdown passes in one game for the first time in his NFL career to lead the New Orleans Saints to their club-record seventh straight win, 24-10, over Houston. Hebert threw all three scoring passes in the first half as the Saints grabbed a 21-3 advantage. His counterpart, the Oilers' Warren Moon, completed just four of 16 attempts in the first half. The Oilers converted just one of 13 third-down opportunities.

Houston, which fell one game behind Cleveland and Pittsburgh in the AFC Central Division race, failed to score with a first down at the New Orleans 4-yard line with 5:09 left to play and at the Saints' 7 with 16 seconds left.

Kenneth Davis' seven-yard touchdown run from shotgun formation with 1:09 remaining propelled the Green Bay Packers to a 16-10 NFC Central Division triumph over Minnesota. Davis' touchdown capped a 10-play, 72-yard drive that began with Randy Wright's 33-yard completion to tight end Ed West.

The Vikings, who dropped to 7-6, failed to score with a first down at the Packers' 11-yard line at the end of the first half.

Joe Montana was forced to leave the game with a first-half injury, but backup Steve Young came off the bench to guide the San Francisco 49ers to a 41-0 pounding of the Chicago Bears in the Monday night game. The Bears, who committed six turnovers, suffered the worst defeat in Mike Ditka's six seasons as coach and the worst for any Chicago team since a 47-0 beating by the Houston Oilers on November 6, 1977.

Montana completed just four passes before knee and hamstring injuries forced him to give way to Young, who completed only nine himself the rest of the game. But four of Young's completions went for touchdowns, including three to wide receiver Jerry Rice.

Rice, who tied Mark Clayton's NFL record with his 18th touchdown catch of the season and another record with at least one touchdown reception in 11 straight games, caught eight passes for 75 yards.

The 49ers also rushed for 198 yards—116 in the first quarter—against a Bears defense that had yielded a league-low 82.3 per game.

Dolphins-Eagles
SUNDAY, DECEMBER 13
SCORE BY PERIODS

Miami	0	14	14	0—28
Philadelphia	0	10	0	0—10

SCORING

Philadelphia—Quick 44 pass from Cunningham (McFadden kick), 2:36 2nd.
Miami—Duper 20 pass from Marino (Tiffin kick), 3:40 2nd.
Philadelphia—Field goal McFadden 27, 7:54 2nd.
Miami—Davenport 1 run (Tiffin kick), 13:03 2nd.
Miami—Clayton 11 pass from Marino (Tiffin kick), 1:12 3rd.
Miami—Clayton 20 pass from Marino (Tiffin kick), 5:03 3rd.

TEAM STATISTICS

	Miami	Philadelphia
First downs	23	15
Rushes-Yards	30-119	25-155
Passing yards	357	155
Sacked-Yards lost	2-19	4-34
3rd down eff	5-13	3-16
Passes	25-39-1	22-38-0
Punts	5-40.0	8-37.8
Fumbles-Lost	5-3	2-1
Penalties-Yards	5.30	5-35
Time of possession	27:55	32:05
Attendance—63,841.		

INDIVIDUAL STATISTICS

Rushing—Miami, Davenport 10-49, Hampton 3-42, Stradford 13-24, Bennett 1-6, Marino 3-minus 2; Philadelphia, Byars 14-67, Toney 7-42, Cunningham 2-37, Jackson 1-10, Teltschik 1-minus 1.

Passing—Miami, Marino 25-39-1—376; Philadelphia, Cunningham 22-38-0—189.

Receiving—Miami, Clayton 7-104, Stradford 5-49, Davenport 4-35, Hardy 2-38, Jensen 2-34, Hampton 2-30, Duper 1-49, Pruitt 1-29, Nathan 1-8; Philadelphia, Byars 7-41, Quick 4-94, Spagnola 4-31, Jackson 2-20, Toney 2-3, Giles 1-9, Tautalatasi 1-2, Singletary 1-minus 11.

Kickoff Returns—Miami, Hampton 1-32; Philadelphia, Morse 3-46, Carter 2-16.

Punt Returns—Miami, Schwedes 5-1; Philadelphia, Morse 2-18.

Interceptions—Philadelphia, Cooper 1-0.

Punting—Miami, Roby 5-40.0; Philadelphia, Teltschik 8-37.8.

Field Goals—Miami, Tiffin 0-1 (missed: 45); Philadelphia, McFadden 1-2 (missed: 34).

Sacks—Miami, Offerdahl, Bosa, Turner 2; Philadelphia, White, Simmons.

Giants-Cardinals
SUNDAY, DECEMBER 13
SCORE BY PERIODS

New York Giants	7	3	7	7—24
St. Louis	14	13	0	0—27

SCORING

St. Louis—Sikahema 76 punt return (Del Greco kick), 1:08 1st.
New York—Bavaro 11 pass from Simms (Allegre kick), 5:30 1st.
St. Louis—Wolfley 6 run (Del Greco kick), 7:55 1st.
New York—Field goal Allegre 29, 4:03 2nd.
St. Louis—Awalt 20 pass from Lomax (Del Greco kick), 9:25 2nd.
St. Louis—Mitchell 6 run (kick failed), 13:50 2nd.
New York—Manuel 14 pass from Simms (Allegre kick), 6:48 3rd.
New York—Morris 1 run (Allegre kick), 2:08 4th.

TEAM STATISTICS

	New York	St. Louis
First downs	23	23
Rushes-Yards	16-62	38-158
Passing yards	335	164
Sacked-Yards lost	4-24	4-26
3rd down eff	7-14	4-13
Passes	30-48-1	17-30-0
Punts	4-47.3	6-42.2
Fumbles-Lost	2-1	1-0
Penalties-Yards	7-50	5-40
Time of possession	24:44	35:16
Attendance—29,623.		

INDIVIDUAL STATISTICS

Rushing—New York, Adams 5-11, Morris 10-36, Galbreath 1-15; St. Louis, Mitchell 26-111, Wolfley 4-21, Lomax 2-minus 4, Green 1-26, Sargent 4-12, Awalt 1-minus 8.

Passing—New York, Simms 30-48-1—359; St. Louis, Lomax 17-30-0—190.

Receiving—New York, Galbreath 5-47, Turner 4-56, McConkey 4-72, Bavaro 11-137, Adams 3-10, Manuel 2-27, Rouson 1-10; St. Louis, Mitchell 4-13, J.T. Smith 4-40, Awalt 5-78, Green 1-23, Holmes 1-17, Sargent 2-19.

Kickoff Returns—New York, Ingram 3-60, Rouson 2-60; St. Louis, McAdoo 3-63, Sikahema 2-67.

Punt Returns—New York, McConkey 4-54; St. Louis, Sikahema 2-96.

Interceptions—St. Louis, Curtis 1-0.

Punting—New York, Landeta 4-47.3; St. Louis, Horne 6-42.2.

Field Goals—New York, Allegre 1-2 (missed: 53); St. Louis, Del Greco 0-1 (missed: 27).

Sacks—New York, Collins, Taylor, Banks, Marshall; St. Louis, Noga, Galloway, Nunn, Clasby.

Falcons-Rams
SUNDAY, DECEMBER 13
SCORE BY PERIODS

Atlanta	0	0	0	0— 0
Los Angeles Rams	9	17	7	0—33

SCORING

Los Angeles—White 21 run (Lansford kick), 5:22 1st.
Los Angeles—Safety, Donnelly tackled in end zone by Stewart, 13:06 1st.
Los Angeles—Field goal Lansford 18, 3:50 2nd.
Los Angeles—Irvin 47 interception return (Lansford kick), 10:14 2nd.
Los Angeles—Ellard 50 pass from Everett (Lansford kick), 12:49 2nd.
Los Angeles—White 4 run (Lansford kick), 8:41 3rd.

TEAM STATISTICS

	Atlanta	Los Angeles
First downs	13	28
Rushes-Yards	15-59	46-238
Passing yards	210	256
Sacked-Yards lost	2-15	0-0
3rd down eff	1-9	7-14
Passes	17-33-2	18-29-0
Punts	6-40.0	3-49.0
Fumbles-Lost	2-0	0-0
Penalties-Yards	3-25	6-40
Time of possession	19:39	40:21
Attendance—43,310.		

INDIVIDUAL STATISTICS

Rushing—Atlanta, Riggs 9-31, Flowers 3-15, C. Miller 2-13, Donnelly 1-0; Los Angeles, White 29-159, Francis 8-32, Everett 2-26, Tyrrell 6-19, Guman 1-2.

Passing—Atlanta, Campbell 7-13-1—55, C. Miller 10-20-1—170; Los Angeles, Everett 13-24-0—193, Dils 5-5-0—63.

Receiving—Atlanta, Matthews 3-86, Settle 3-36, Flowers 3-29, C. Brown 2-41, Stamps 2-11, Riggs 2-minus 4, Dixon 1-25, Sharp 1-1; Los Angeles, Ellard 6-97, Guman

4-41, Baty 3-37, Ron Brown 2-45, Tyrrell 2-26, Hill 1-10.

Kickoff Returns—Atlanta, Stamps 4-68, Everett 1-15, Sharp 1-11; Los Angeles, Ellard 1-8, Ron Brown 1-14.

Punt Returns—Los Angeles, Irvin 1-0.

Interceptions—Los Angeles, Irvin 1-47, Hicks 1-9.

Punting—Atlanta, Donnelly 6-40.0; Los Angeles, Hatcher 3-49.0.

Field Goals—Atlanta, none attempted; Los Angeles, Lansford 1-2 (missed: 41).

Sacks—Los Angeles, Greene, Wilcher.

Oilers-Saints
SUNDAY, DECEMBER 13
SCORE BY PERIODS

Houston	0	3	7	0—10
New Orleans	7	14	3	0—24

SCORING

New Orleans—Martin 54 pass from Hebert (Andersen kick), 4:19 1st.

New Orleans—Martin 7 pass from Hebert (Andersen kick), 5:45 2nd.

Houston—Field goal Zendejas 21, 11:04 2nd.

New Orleans—Hill 26 pass from Hebert (Andersen kick), 14:04 2nd.

Houston—Givins 34 pass from Moon (Zendejas kick), 2:44 3rd.

New Orleans—Field goal Andersen 28, 10:39 3rd.

TEAM STATISTICS

	Houston	New Orleans
First downs	20	21
Rushes-Yards	26-110	39-151
Passing yards	244	240
Sacked-Yards lost	2-14	3-14
3rd down eff.	1-13	10-18
Passes	16-36-0	15-27-0
Punts	8-32.6	4-44.8
Fumbles-Lost	3-0	5-2
Penalties-Yards	6-43	10-89
Time of possession	26:23	33:37

Attendance—68,257.

INDIVIDUAL STATISTICS

Rushing—Houston, Rozier 22-91, Highsmith 3-7, Wallace 1-12; New Orleans, Mayes 17-54, Hilliard 19-93, Word 1-minus 1, Jordan 2-5.

Passing—Houston, Moon 16-36-0—258; New Orleans, Hebert 15-27-0—254.

Receiving—Houston, D. Hill 4-102, Drewrey 3-40, Pinkett 1-7, Givins 5-74, Rozier 2-32, Jeffires 1-3; New Orleans, Martin 6-130, Pattison 3-47, Hill 2-39, Hilliard 2-19, Jones 2-19.

Kickoff Returns—New Orleans, Gray 3-68.

Punt Returns—Houston, K. Johnson 1-5; New Orleans, Cook 1-3, Gray 3-45.

Interceptions—None.

Punting—Houston, Gossett 7-37.3; New Orleans, Hansen 4-44.8.

Field Goals—Houston, Zendejas 1-1; New Orleans, Andersen 1-3 (missed: 48, 46).

Sacks—Houston, Meads, Childress, D. Smith; New Orleans, Elliott, Jackson.

Vikings-Packers
SUNDAY, DECEMBER 13
SCORE BY PERIODS

Minnesota	7	0	0	3—10
Green Bay	0	7	3	6—16

SCORING

Minnesota—Carter 40 pass from Kramer (C. Nelson kick), 14:28 1st.

Green Bay—Carruth 1 run (Zendejas kick), 6:16 2nd.

Green Bay—Field goal Zendejas 43, 14:53 3rd.

Minnesota—Field goal C. Nelson 34, 5:45 4th.

Green Bay—Davis 7 run (kick failed), 13:51 4th.

TEAM STATISTICS

	Minnesota	Green Bay
First downs	15	19
Rushes-Yards	31-127	33-121
Passing yards	162	179
Sacked-Yards lost	1-6	2-13
3rd down eff.	1-9	6-14
Passes	14-21-0	18-31-1
Punts	4-34-5	5-38.6
Fumbles-Lost	4-2	0-0
Penalties-Yards	4-20	5-43
Time of possession	26:31	33:29

Attendance—47,059.

INDIVIDUAL STATISTICS

Rushing—Minnesota, Anderson 7-36, D. Nelson 13-33, Wilson 1-19, Kramer 2-12, Fenney 2-11, Rice 3-8, Dozier 2-8; Green Bay, Carruth 11-33, Stanley 2-32, Clark 11-30, Davis 7-28, Neal 1-0, Wright 1-minus 2.

Passing—Minnesota, Kramer 7-9-0—111, Wilson 7-12-0—57; Green Bay, Wright 18-31-1—192.

Receiving—Minnesota, D. Nelson 4-28; Carter 3-61, Jordan 3-45, Anderson 2-16, Jones 1-10, Lewis 1-8; Green Bay, Neal 5-57, Clark 4-14, West 3-80, Stanley 3-31, Davis 2-16, Carruth 1-minus 6.

Kickoff Returns—Minnesota, Guggemos 3-62, Rice 1-11; Green Bay, Neal 3-34.

Punt Returns—Minnesota, Lewis 5-45; Green Bay, Stanley 1-4.

Interceptions—Minnesota, Browner 1-0.

Punting—Minnesota, Scribner 4-34.5; Green Bay, Bracken 5-38.6.

Field Goals—Minnesota, C. Nelson 1-2 (missed: 35); Green Bay, Zendejas 1-1.

Sacks—Minnesota, Thomas, Solomon; Green Bay, Murphy.

Raiders-Chiefs
SUNDAY, DECEMBER 13
SCORE BY PERIODS

Los Angeles Raiders	0	3	7	0—10
Kansas City	0	7	3	6—16

SCORING

Kansas City—Carson 67 pass from Kenney (Lowery kick), 7:04 2nd.

Los Angeles—Field goal Bahr 23, 14:09 2nd.

Los Angeles—Allen 3 run (Bahr kick), 9:07 3rd.

Kansas City—Field goal Lowery 39, 14:01 3rd.

Kansas City—Field goal Lowery 22, 3:16 4th.

Kansas City—Field goal Lowery 35, 11:24 4th.

TEAM STATISTICS

	Los Angeles	Kansas City
First downs	26	17
Rushes-Yards	32-88	28-112
Passing yards	312	164
Sacked-Yards lost	4-27	4-30
3rd down eff.	6-12	6-14
Passes	22-38-3	10-27-1
Punts	4-40.0	4-33.3
Fumbles-Lost	2-1	5-1
Penalties-Yards	14-140	10-47
Time of possession	35:54	24:06

Attendance—63,834.

INDIVIDUAL STATISTICS

Rushing—Los Angeles, Allen 18-60, Mueller 11-27, Jackson 3-1; Kansas City, Okoye 13-48, Heard 10-41, Goodburn 1-16, Moriarty 2-9, Kenney 2-minus 2.

Passing—Los Angeles, Wilson 22-38-3—339; Kansas City, Kenney 10-27-1—194.

Receiving—Los Angeles, Lofton 5-112, Christensen 5-64, Mueller 5-36, Williams 3-70, Allen 3-53, Jackson 1-4; Kansas City, Carson 4-142, Heard 2-13, Marshall 1-16, Hayes 1-13, Paige 1-6, Okoye 1-4.

Kickoff Returns—Los Angeles, Woods 3-55, Williams 1-

— 231 —

16, Mueller 1-21; Kansas City, Palmer 2-43, Moriarty 1-19.

Punt Returns—Los Angeles, Woods 2-minus 3; Kansas City, Fields 3-6.

Interceptions—Kansas City, Robinson 1-25, Ross 2-40.

Punting—Los Angeles, Talley 4-40.0; Kansas City, Goodburn 4-35.8.

Field Goals—Los Angeles, Bahr 1-2 (missed: 32); Kansas City, Lowery 3-3.

Sacks—Los Angeles, Townsend, Long, Jones, Team; Kansas City, Still, Del Rio, Maas, Snipes.

Bills-Colts
SUNDAY, DECEMBER 13
SCORE BY PERIODS

Buffalo	7	6	0	14—27
Indianapolis	0	3	0	0— 3

SCORING

Buffalo—Harmon 12 pass from Kelly (Norwood kick), 7:11 1st.
Buffalo—Field goal Norwood 39, 1:17 2nd.
Indianapolis—Field goal Biasucci 30, 6:53 2nd.
Buffalo—Field goal Norwood 25, 13:03 2nd.
Buffalo—T. Johnson 8 pass from Kelly (Norwood kick), 5:22 4th.
Buffalo—Smith recovered fumble in end zone (Norwood kick), 13:49 4th.

TEAM STATISTICS

	Buffalo	Indianapolis
First downs	25	9
Rushes-Yards	49-218	17-33
Passing yards	167	97
Sacked-Yards lost	0-0	5-49
3rd down eff.	7-17	0-10
Passes	18-35-0	14-27-4
Punts	6-37.5	8-40.9
Fumbles-Lost	4-4	5-2
Penalties-Yards	5-45	4-25
Time of possession	39:08	20:52
Attendance—60,253.		

INDIVIDUAL STATISTICS

Rushing—Buffalo, Mueller 15-81, Harmon 18-85, Kelly 2-6, R. Porter 14-46; Indianapolis, Dickerson 11-19, Trudeau 2-1, Bentley 2-minus 1, Wonsley 2-14.

Passing—Buffalo, Kelly 18-34-0—167, Kidd 0-1-0—0; Indianapolis, Trudeau 6-15-2—78, Salisbury 8-12-2—68.

Receiving—Buffalo, T. Johnson 3-26, Metzelaars 2-9, Burkett 4-62, Harmon 3-10, Mueller 2-17, R. Porter 1-2, Reed 3-41; Indianapolis, Brooks 5-55, Bouza 2-18, Beach 1-11, Dickerson 2-31, Bentley 2-17, Wonsley 2-14.

Kickoff Returns—Buffalo, Tasker 2-38; Indianapolis, Prior 1-10, Bentley 4-82.

Punt Returns—Buffalo, Pitts 5-44; Indianapolis, Brooks 3-21.

Interceptions—Buffalo, Pitts 1-0, Davis 1-0, Burroughs 0-14, Kelso 2-18.

Punting—Buffalo, Kidd 6-37.5; Indianapolis, Stark 8-40.9.

Field Goals—Buffalo, Norwood 2-2; Indianapolis, Biasucci 1-1.

Sacks—Buffalo, Smith 2½, McNanie 1½, Talley.

Cowboys-Redskins
SUNDAY, DECEMBER 13
SCORE BY PERIODS

Dallas	3	0	10	7—20
Washington	7	10	7	0—24

SCORING

Washington—Rogers 1 run (Haji-Sheikh kick), 4:31 1st.
Dallas—Field goal Ruzek 22, 12:08 1st.
Washington—Field goal Haji-Sheikh 31, 7:18 2nd.

Washington—Clark 56 pass from Schroeder (Haji-Sheikh kick), 14:00 2nd.
Washington—Rogers 1 run (Haji-Sheikh kick), 4:15 3rd.
Dallas—Field goal Ruzek 37, 10:13 3rd.
Dallas—Renfro 25 pass from D. White (Ruzek kick), 11:54 3rd.
Dallas—Barksdale 5 pass from D. White (Ruzek kick), 3:06 4th.

TEAM STATISTICS

	Dallas	Washington
First downs	25	15
Rushes-Yards	25-87	31-68
Passing yards	341	249
Sacked-Yards lost	3-18	2-1
3rd down eff.	6-16	5-13
Passes	27-49-1	13-26-1
Punts	5-35.8	6-43.1
Fumbles-Lost	1-1	1-1
Penalties-Yards	7-75	6-35
Time of possession	32:05	27:55
Attendance—54,882.		

INDIVIDUAL STATISTICS

Rushing—Dallas, Walker 14-44, Dorsett 8-40, Newsome 2-1, D. White 1-2; Washington, Rogers 27-64, Schroeder 3-minus 4, Bryant 1-8.

Passing—Dallas, D. White 27-49-1—359; Washington, Schroeder 13-26-1—250.

Receiving—Dallas, Walker 5-54, Renfro 6-97, Newsome 2-20, Cosbie 5-79, Dorsett 2-9, Martin 2-55, Barksdale 2-20, Edwards 2-18, Chandler 1-7; Washington, Clark 9-187, Didier 1-2, Sanders 2-55, Warren 1-6.

Kickoff Returns—Dallas, Clack 3-93, Martin 1-9; Washington, Verdin 4-76.

Punt Returns—Dallas, Martin 3-22; Washington, Yarber 2-16.

Interceptions—Dallas, Walls 1-0; Washington, Wilburn 1-0.

Punting—Dallas, Saxon 5-35.8; Washington, Cox 6-43.1.

Field Goals—Dallas, Ruzek 2-3 (missed: 43); Washington, Haji-Sheikh 1-1.

Sacks—Dallas, Team, Bates; Washington, Mann, Kaufman.

Steelers-Chargers
SUNDAY, DECEMBER 13
SCORE BY PERIODS

Pittsburgh	0	7	10	3—20
San Diego	9	0	0	7—16

SCORING

San Diego—Brandon recovered blocked punt in end zone (Abbott kick), 5:47 1st.
San Diego—Safety, Ehin tackled Malone in end zone, 14:24 1st.
Pittsburgh—Pollard 8 run (Anderson kick), 9:37 2nd.
Pittsburgh—Malone 7 run (Anderson kick), 6:46 3rd.
Pittsburgh—Field goal Anderson 43, 14:23 3rd.
Pittsburgh—Field goal Anderson 33, 5:56 4th.
San Diego—James 15 pass from Fouts (Abbott kick), 12:04 4th.

TEAM STATISTICS

	Pittsburgh	San Diego
First downs	14	27
Rushes-Yards	31-104	29-114
Passing yards	150	321
Sacked-Yards lost	2-14	2-13
3rd down eff.	2-12	4-15
Passes	13-26-0	29-52-1
Punts	7-37.1	3-40.7
Fumbles-Lost	4-1	6-4
Penalties-Yards	7-39	6-40
Time of possession	27:07	32:53
Attendance—51,605.		

INDIVIDUAL STATISTICS

Rushing—Pittsburgh, Malone 5-34, Pollard 14-44, Abercrombie 8-13, Jackson 4-13; San Diego, Anderson 7-27, Fouts 3-0, Spencer 11-47, Adams 7-23, Holland 1-17.

Passing—Pittsburgh, Malone 13-26-0—164; San Diego, Fouts 29-52-1—334.

Receiving—Pittsburgh, Abercrombie 4-40, Thompson 4-73, Stallworth 1-13, Pollard 4-38; San Diego, Anderson 5-40, Holohan 3-52, Chandler 7-116, Winslow 6-74, Bernstine 1-5, Spencer 4-16, Ware 1-15, James 2-30.

Kickoff Returns—Pittsburgh, Stone 1-22; San Diego, Holland 3-52, Anderson 2-49, Hunter 1-0.

Punt Returns—Pittsburgh, Woodson 1-13; San Diego, James 3-17.

Interceptions—Pittsburgh, Woodruff 1-6.

Punting—Pittsburgh, Newsome 6-43.3; San Diego, Mojsiejenko 3-40.1.

Field Goals—Pittsburgh, Anderson 2-3 (missed: 49); San Diego, Abbott 0-3 (missed: 42, 48, 46).

Sacks—Pittsburgh, Carr 2; San Diego, Ehin, Williams.

Broncos-Seahawks

SUNDAY, DECEMBER 13

SCORE BY PERIODS

Denver	0	0	14	7—21
Seattle	0	14	7	7—28

SCORING

Seattle—Warner 3 run (N. Johnson kick), 9:10 2nd.

Seattle—R. Butler 3 pass from Krieg (N. Johnson kick), 14:38 2nd.

Denver—Winder 11 run (Karlis kick), 2:32 3rd.

Denver—Massie 39 pass from Elway (Karlis kick), 4:24 3rd.

Seattle—R. Butler 40 pass from Krieg (N. Johnson kick), 5:30 3rd.

Seattle—J.L. Williams 7 pass from Krieg (N. Johnson kick), 2:21 4th.

Denver—Winder 1 run (Karlis kick), 14:35 4th.

TEAM STATISTICS

	Denver	Seattle
First downs	20	24
Rushes-Yards	18-72	37-141
Passing yards	308	226
Sacked-Yards lost	5-27	1-12
3rd down eff.	8-16	8-15
Passes	21-43-2	23-34-2
Punts	6-40.7	4-43.0
Fumbles-Lost	1-0	2-2
Penalties-Yards	6-61	4-40
Time of possession	24:58	35:02

Attendance—61,759.

INDIVIDUAL STATISTICS

Rushing—Denver, Winder 13-50, Elway 3-12, Lang 1-6, Boddie 1-4; Seattle, Warner 22-76, J.L. Williams 10-37, Krieg 5-28.

Passing—Denver, Elway 21-42-2—335, Lang 0-1-0—0; Seattle, Krieg 23-33-2—238, Largent 0-1-0—0.

Receiving—Denver, Boddie 5-59, Winder 4-9, Jackson 3-85, Massie 3-82, Nattiel 3-68, Kay 2-26, Micho 1-6; Seattle, J.L. Williams 7-47, R. Butler 6-107, Warner 4-23, Largent 3-43, Turner 1-10, Skansi 1-8, Tice 1-0.

Kickoff Returns—Denver, Bell 3-92, Clark 1-8; Seattle, Morris 2-34, Edmonds 1-30.

Punt Returns—Denver, Clark 3-7; Seattle, Edmonds 4-39.

Interceptions—Denver, Ryan 1-5, Robbins 1-0; Seattle, Jenkins 1-34, Easley 1-22.

Punting—Denver, Horan 6-40.7; Seattle, Rodriguez 4-43.0.

Field Goals—Denver, Karlis 0-1 (missed: 55); Seattle, none attempted.

Sacks—Denver, Mecklenburg; Seattle, Bryant, Nash, Green 1½, Young 1½.

Bengals-Browns

SUNDAY, DECEMBER 13

SCORE BY PERIODS

Cincinnati	3	0	7	14—24
Cleveland	0	28	7	3—38

SCORING

Cincinnati—Field goal Breech 20, 7:55 1st.

Cleveland—Slaughter 22 pass from Kosar (Bahr kick), 2:17 2nd.

Cleveland—Mack 22 run (Bahr kick), 5:12 2nd.

Cleveland—Mack 2 pass from Kosar (Bahr kick), 10:11 2nd.

Cleveland—Tennell 2 pass from Kosar (Bahr kick), 14:14 2nd.

Cincinnati—Martin 54 pass from Esiason (Breech kick), 2:48 3rd.

Cleveland—Slaughter 18 pass from Kosar (Bahr kick), 11:06 3rd.

Cincinnati—Kinnebrew 2 run (Breech kick), 0:03 4th.

Cincinnati—Kinnebrew 1 run (Breech kick), 8:15 4th.

Cleveland—Field goal Bahr 27, 14:08 4th.

TEAM STATISTICS

	Cincinnati	Cleveland
First downs	24	19
Rushes-Yards	28-65	29-153
Passing yards	352	237
Sacked-Yards lost	1-9	1-4
3rd down eff.	7-16	7-11
Passes	22-39-2	17-26-0
Punts	5-35.6	3-44.3
Fumbles-Lost	0-0	2-1
Penalties-Yards	7-62	6-45
Time of possession	31:47	28:13

Attendance—77,331.

INDIVIDUAL STATISTICS

Rushing—Cincinnati, Brooks 9-11, Kinnebrew 16-44, Jennings 3-10; Cleveland, Mack 27-133, Byner 2-20.

Passing—Cincinnati, Esiason 22-39-2—361; Cleveland, Kosar 17-26-0—241.

Receiving—Cincinnati, Brown 2-34, Holman 2-17, Brooks 1-4, Martin 3-83, Jennings 5-53, McGee 4-117, Kattus 4-34, Kinnebrew 1-19; Cleveland, Newsome 3-18, Mack 3-19, Langhorne 2-43, Slaughter 5-119, Tennell 1-2, Brennan 1-12, Byner 2-28.

Kickoff Returns—Cincinnati, Bussey 5-88, Kattus 1-13; Cleveland, Byner 1-2, Young 2-40, Manoa 1-1.

Punt Returns—Cleveland, McNeil 4-7.

Interceptions—Cleveland, Wright 1-18, Matthews 1-36, Hairston 0-40.

Punting—Cincinnati, Fulhage 5-35.6; Cleveland, L. Johnson 3-44.3.

Field Goals—Cincinnati, Breech 1-1; Cleveland, Bahr 1-1.

Sacks—Cincinnati, Bussey; Cleveland, Puzzuoli ½, Matthews ½.

Jets-Patriots

SUNDAY, DECEMBER 13

SCORE BY PERIODS

New York Jets	3	3	0	14—20
New England	14	21	7	0—42

SCORING

New England—Jones 16 pass from Grogan (Franklin kick), 3:14 1st.

New York—Field goal Leahy 42, 7:53 1st.

New England—Grogan 2 run (Franklin kick), 12:26 1st.

New England—Fryar 26 pass from Grogan (Franklin kick), 1:33 2nd.

New York—Field goal Leahy 24, 6:25 2nd.

New England—Starring 28 pass from Grogan (Franklin kick), 13:52 2nd.

New England—Jones 17 pass from Grogan (Franklin kick), 14:54 2nd.

New England—Dupard 7 run (Franklin kick), 5:34 3rd.

New York—Hector 6 run (Leahy kick), 4:25 4th.

New York—Toon 28 pass from O'Brien (Leahy kick), 9:12 4th.

TEAM STATISTICS

	New York	New England
First downs	24	19
Rushes-Yards	29-111	36-129
Passing yards	197	171
Sacked-Yards lost	4-32	1-9
3rd down eff.	8-17	3-10
Passes	22-43-1	11-18-0
Punts	4-35.0	6-41.5
Fumbles-Lost	2-2	0-0
Penalties-Yards	14-121	9-80
Time of possession	31:12	28:48

Attendance—60,617.

INDIVIDUAL STATISTICS

Rushing—New York, Hector 22-104, Vick 5-8, Faaola 1-0, Bligen 1-minus 1; New England, Dupard 18-73, Collins 11-23, Fryar 3-19, Grogan 2-7, Tatupu 1-5, Hansen 1-2.

Passing—New York, O'Brien 22-43-1-229; New England, Grogan 11-18-0-180.

Receiving—New York, Toon 8-110, Sohn 4-42, Shuler 4-38, Vick 2-7, Hector 2-5, Klever 1-17, Townsell 1-10; New England, Fryar 4-71, Jones 3-58, Starring 2-51, Dupard 1-1, Collins 1-minus 1.

Kickoff Returns—New York, Martin 3-56, Townsell 1-49, Klever 1-4; New England, Starring 1-27, Dupard 1-10.

Punt Returns—New York, Townsell 2-12.

Interceptions—New England, Lippett 1-38.

Punting—New York, Jennings 4-35.0; New England, Camarillo 6-41.5.

Field Goals—New York, Leahy 2-2; New England, none attempted.

Sacks—New York, Gastineau; New England, Veris 2, B. Williams, Hodge.

Lions-Buccaneers
SUNDAY, DECEMBER 13
SCORE BY PERIODS

Detroit	7	3	3	7	—20
Tampa Bay	0	3	0	7	—10

SCORING

Detroit—Mandley 8 pass from Long (Murray kick), 8:31 1st.

Tampa Bay—Field goal Igwebuike 44, 7:30 2nd.

Detroit—Field goal Murray 24, 14:14 2nd.

Detroit—Field goal Murray 37, 12:18 3rd.

Detroit—Ellerson 5 run (Murray kick), 7:13 4th.

Tampa Bay—Hill 28 pass from Testaverde (Igwebuike kick), 8:32 4th.

TEAM STATISTICS

	Detroit	Tampa Bay
First downs	22	20
Rushes-Yards	50-190	14-47
Passing yards	108	216
Sacked-Yards lost	0-0	4-46
3rd down eff.	7-16	0-10
Passes	12-23-0	20-39-1
Punts	5-36.6	7-34.6
Fumbles-Lost	3-1	2-0
Penalties-Yards	7-50	8-66
Time of possession	36:07	23:53

Attendance—41,699.

INDIVIDUAL STATISTICS

Rushing—Detroit, James 18-67, Jones 14-40, Long 4-5, Woolfolk 5-59, Ellerson 9-19; Tampa Bay, Smith 3-3, Wilder 4-14, Testaverde 1-0, Hunter 6-30.

Passing—Detroit, Long 12-23-0—108; Tampa Bay, Testaverde 20-39-1—262.

Receiving—Detroit, Lee 3-36, Mandley 2-18, Rubick 2-22, Jones 3-24, James 2-8; Tampa Bay, Carter 4-78, Hill 5-86, Smith 1-7, Hall 4-34, Howard 2-18, Hunter 2-4, Carrier 2-35.

Kickoff Returns—Detroit, Lee 2-47, Saleaumua 1-18; Tampa Bay, Futrell 4-86, Hill 1-8.

Punt Returns—Detroit, Mandley 3-23; Tampa Bay, Futrell 1-0.

Interceptions—Detroit, J. Williams 1-48.

Punting—Detroit, Arnold 5-36.6; Tampa Bay, Garcia 7-34.6.

Field Goals—Detroit, Murray 2-2; Tampa Bay, Igwebuike 1-1.

Sacks—Detroit, Cofer 2, J. Williams, E. Williams.

Bears-49ers
MONDAY, DECEMBER 14
SCORE BY PERIODS

Chicago	0	0	0	0	— 0
San Francisco	10	10	14	7	—41

SCORING

San Francisco—Rice 1 pass from Young (Wersching kick), 8:49 1st.

San Francisco—Field goal Wersching 20, 14:57 1st.

San Francisco—Field goal Wersching 45, 5:35 2nd.

San Francisco—Clark 13 pass from Young (Wersching kick), 11:20 2nd.

San Francisco—McLemore 83 punt return (Wersching kick), 5:37 3rd.

San Francisco—Rice 16 pass from Young (Wersching kick), 10:02 3rd.

San Francisco—Rice 2 pass from Young (Wersching kick), 0:45 4th.

TEAM STATISTICS

	Chicago	San Francisco
First downs	16	20
Rushes-Yards	25-109	41-198
Passing yards	154	133
Sacked-Yards lost	3-30	2-14
3rd down eff.	4-13	6-14
Passes	19-36-4	13-27-0
Punts	6-39.2	5-40.4
Fumbles-Lost	3-2	1-1
Penalties-Yards	11-93	6-60
Time of possession	30:14	29:46

Attendance—63,509.

INDIVIDUAL STATISTICS

Rushing—Chicago, Anderson 10-47, Sanders 3-19, Payton 7-18, Harbaugh 3-15, Tomczak 2-10; San Francisco, Craig 12-51, Young 8-43, Cribbs 9-41, Rathman 5-22, Montana 2-15, Sydney 4-14, Rice 1-12.

Passing—Chicago, Tomczak 11-25-4—122, Harbaugh 8-11-0—62; San Francisco, Montana 4-8-0—47, Young 9-19-0—100.

Receiving—Chicago, Anderson 6-42, Gentry 3-18, Gault 2-30, McKinnon 2-30, Moorehead 2-17, Payton 2-16, Boso 1-21, Suhey 1-10; San Francisco, Rice 8-75, Clark 2-42, Rathman 1-18, Frank 1-9, Craig 1-3.

Kickoff Returns—Chicago, Sanders 3-60, Gentry 4-69; San Francisco, Cribbs 1-11.

Punt Returns—Chicago, McKinnon 3-7; San Francisco, McLemore 1-83.

Interceptions—San Francisco, Lott 1-26, Walter 1-16, Shell 1-1, Griffin 1-0.

Punting—Chicago, Wagner 6-39.2; San Francisco, Runager 5-40.4.

Field Goals—Chicago, Butler 0-1 (missed: 40); San Francisco, Wersching 2-2.

Sacks—Chicago, Duerson, Dent; San Francisco, Roberts, Haley, Fagan.

FIFTEENTH WEEK

RESULTS OF WEEK 15

Saturday, December 19

Denver 20, Kansas City 17 at Den.
N.Y. Giants 20, Green Bay 10 at N.Y.

Sunday, December 20

Cleveland 24, L.A. Raiders 17 at L.A.
Houston 24, Pittsburgh 16 at Hous.
Indianapolis 20, San Diego 7 at S.D.
Miami 23, Washington 21 at Mia.
Minnesota 17, Detroit 14 at Det.
New England 13, Buffalo 7 at Buff.
New Orleans 41, Cincinnati 24 at Cin.
Philadelphia 38, N.Y. Jets 27 at N.Y.
St. Louis 31, Tampa Bay 14 at T.B.
San Francisco 35, Atlanta 7 at S.F.
Seattle 34, Chicago 21 at Chi.

Monday, December 21

Dallas 29, L.A. Rams 21 at L.A.

Records are made to be broken, and nobody seems to understand that adage better than San Francisco 49ers wide receiver Jerry Rice.

Rice continued his assault on the National Football League record book in Week 15 while his team continued its assault on the rest of the league. Rice caught two touchdown passes and ran five yards for another score in a 35-7 victory over the Atlanta Falcons. The third-year pro, who scored three touchdowns in one game for the fourth time in five weeks, ran his league-leading touchdown reception total to 20 and recorded the 12th straight game in which he had caught at least one TD pass.

Rice, who was playing in just his 11th game of the season because of the strike, smashed the single-season touchdown reception record that Mark Clayton set in 15 games with the Miami Dolphins in 1984. The 12 consecutive games eclipsed the old mark of 11 set by the Rams' Elroy Hirsch in 1950-51 and equaled by Pittsburgh's Buddy Dial in 1959-60.

Both records fell on the same play, a 20-yard pass from Steve Young 3:49 into the second half that gave San Francisco a 14-0 lead.

"The most important thing to me is we won," Rice said. "Atlanta was a good team and we needed to win."

Rice was being much too kind to the Falcons, who dropped to 3-11. But he was right about the importance of the victory to the 49ers. The win improved San Francisco's record to 12-2, best in the league, and enabled them to maintain a one-game lead over the surging New Orleans Saints in the NFC West. With the playoffs just two weeks away, the 49ers were the NFL's best team and Rice was clearly the game's best player.

"I think it (the record-setting performance) is fantastic," said San Francisco center Randy Cross. "But we'd get more excited if he was

Jerry Rice broke two NFL records on the same play in the 49ers' 35-7 win over Atlanta.

more excited. He has so much talent and just seems to take things in stride.

"We want to jump up and down with him, but he just says, 'Thank you.'"

"He's just a good football player, quicker and better than most," said Falcons cornerback Bobby Butler, who was beaten by Rice on the record-setting play. "I saw Rice take off and thought, 'That's it.'"

Ironically, Rice's record play preceded another noteworthy performance. On San Francisco's ensuing kickoff, Atlanta's Sylvester Stamps returned the ball 97 yards for a touchdown. On the Falcons' kickoff, the 49ers' Joe Cribbs returned the favor, traveling 92 yards for a score. It marked only the third time in NFL history that teams had broken back-to-back kickoff returns for touchdowns.

The Saints kept pace with the 49ers by recording a 41-24 come-from-behind victory at Cincinnati. The win was the eighth in a row for New Orleans while the defeat was the Bengals' eighth in 10 games and seventh in eight 1987 home games.

The Saints trailed, 24-3, late in the first half when starting quarterback Bobby Hebert suf-

Walter Payton was showered with gifts in his final home appearance with the Chicago Bears but the Seattle Seahawks won the game, 34-21.

fered a sprained right knee and was forced to leave the game. In came backup Dave Wilson, who had thrown just eight passes all season.

But Wilson's inactivity didn't prove to be a factor. He led the Saints to a touchdown late in the half to cut the deficit to 14 points (24-10), and directed two New Orleans touchdown drives in the first six minutes of the third quarter to tie the score. Wilson threw a 29-yard pass to Mike Jones for the first touchdown and, after linebacker Pat Swilling recovered a fumble by Bengal quarterback Boomer Esiason at the Cincinnati 29, Dalton Hilliard ran three yards for his second touchdown of the game.

The Saints defense shut out Cincinnati in the second half, with five of the unit's six quarterback sacks coming after the intermission.

Cleveland quarterback Bernie Kosar was sacked six times in a 27-14 loss to the Los Angeles Raiders in a 1986 regular-season game. When the Browns and Raiders met in a Week 15 rematch, Kosar threw for 294 yards and two touchdowns and wasn't sacked once in a 24-17 Cleveland victory. It was only Cleveland's second victory ever over the Raiders in 10 regular-season games.

The Browns improved to 9-5 and regained first place in the AFC Central Division with one week left.

Houston and Pittsburgh finished the week tied at 8-6, one game behind the Browns, as a result of the Oilers' 24-16 victory at the Astrodome. The win gave Houston its first series sweep ever over the Steelers and guaranteed them their first winning season since 1980.

Warren Moon threw two touchdown passes to Drew Hill in a rough game in which tempers flared. Three players—Doug Smith and Richard Byrd of the Oilers and Frank Pollard of the Steelers—were ejected for fighting.

The Indianapolis Colts clinched the franchise's first winning season since 1977 with a 20-7 victory over the San Diego Chargers. The Colts ran their record to 8-6, tops in the AFC East, while handing the fast-fading Chargers their fifth straight loss. San Diego drove 74 yards for a touchdown on its first possession, but was held scoreless the remainder of the game.

Eric Dickerson led the Colts with 115 rushing yards to go over the 1,000-yard plateau for the fifth straight year. Dickerson also surpassed the 8,000-yard mark for his career in just his 74th regular-season game, the earliest any player has reached that milestone in NFL history.

The league's all-time leading rusher, Chicago's Walter Payton, played the final home game of his illustrious career, but the visiting Seattle Seahawks put a damper on the festivities with a 34-21 interconference win. Payton scored two touchdowns, but couldn't provide enough offense to overcome five Chicago turnovers.

The Seahawks exploded for 20 points in the third quarter to take command of a game that was tied, 7-7, at halftime. Seattle rookie Brian Bosworth stripped the ball from running back Neal Anderson on the Bears' first play of the second half and ran 38 yards to the Chicago

1-yard line. On the next play, Curt Warner scored for a 14-7 Seahawks lead.

After Payton's first touchdown tied the game, John L. Williams took a screen pass 75 yards for a touchdown on Seattle's next play from scrimmage.

The Bears, who were beaten 41-0 by San Francisco the previous week, had surrendered more points (75) in consecutive games than any time since 1968.

Seattle's victory kept the Seahawks a half game behind Denver in the AFC West Division race. The Broncos (9-4-1) maintained the lead with a 20-17 victory over Kansas City in a Saturday afternoon game and put themselves into position to nail down the division crown with a victory in their last game against San Diego.

The Broncos put together scoring drives of 76, 72 and 80 yards on their first three possessions to take a 17-3 halftime lead. The Chiefs battled back to cut the Denver lead to three points on Bill Kenney's eight-yard scoring pass to Stephone Paige with 6:36 remaining. But placekicker Nick Lowery missed a chance to send the game into overtime when he failed on a 37-yard field-goal attempt with 34 seconds left.

The week's other Saturday game was won by the New York Giants, who defeated Green Bay, 20-10. Phil Simms put on a passing display, connecting on 21 of 26 attempts to become the Giants' career passing leader. Simms, the Giants' No. 1 draft pick in 1979, finished the game with 19,551 passing yards to break Charlie Conerly's club record of 19,488 set from 1948 to '61.

New York's other team, the Jets, didn't fare nearly as well, losing their third straight game —a 38-27 decision to Philadelphia. Eagles receiver Mike Quick was the difference, taking advantage of a beat-up Jets secondary to catch two touchdown passes and set up two other scores with receptions. Quick finished the game with six catches for 148 yards against a Jets team that was missing three starting defensive backs because of injury.

The St. Louis Cardinals scored 31 straight points after spotting Tampa Bay an early 7-0 lead en route to a 31-14 victory over the Bucs, their fourth win in five weeks. Quarterback Neil Lomax threw three touchdown passes as the Cards improved their record to 7-7.

The Buccaneers, who scored on their first and last possessions, lost for the seventh week in a row. They had the ball on the St. Louis 6-yard line with a seven-point lead early in the game, but quarterback Vinny Testaverde was sacked by defensive end Freddie Joe Nunn on one play and running back Bobby Howard fumbled at the 15-yard line on the next. The Cardinals recovered and proceeded to drive 85 yards for the game-tying touchdown.

Turnovers also proved decisive in Minnesota's 17-14 NFC Central Division victory over

Detroit. The Lions turned the ball over on each of their first four possessions against a Vikings defense that intercepted four passes. Minnesota's Carl Lee killed the Lions' last chance with an interception of quarterback Chuck Long at the Vikings' 15 with six minutes left.

Detroit cornerback Bruce McNorton had a day to forget. He was penalized 43 yards for pass interference to set up the game-winning touchdown after earlier making an illegal block to wipe out teammate Pete Mandley's 73-yard punt return for a touchdown.

Miami quarterback Dan Marino completed 22 of 50 passes for 393 yards and three touchdowns to lead the Dolphins to a 23-21 interconference victory over Washington. Marino's final scoring pass, a six-yard throw to Mark Duper with 1:07 left, ended a 13-play, 80-yard drive that consumed more than five minutes. The Redskins had taken a 21-16 lead with 6:17 left on George Rogers' two-yard touchdown run.

Despite Marino attempting passes on 50 of Miami's 67 offensive plays, the Redskins failed to record a sack for the first time in 64 games. The Dolphins' offensive line had led the league in fewest sacks allowed each season from 1982-86 and had allowed just 13 in its first 14 games of 1987.

Buffalo's Jim Kelly failed to complete at least 50 percent of his pass attempts for the first time in 59 professional football games in the Bills' 13-7 AFC East Division loss to New England. Kelly, a former United States Football League standout who joined the Bills in 1986, completed only 13 of 31 attempts for 125 yards in a game played in winds that sometimes gusted up to 40 mph.

Buffalo's only touchdown came when linebacker Scott Radecic stripped the ball from Patriots running back Reggie Dupard and teammate Sean McNanie returned it 14 yards for a score.

Roger Ruzek kicked a club-record five field goals as the Dallas Cowboys defeated the Los Angeles Rams, 29-21, in the Monday night game. The Cowboys, who drove 80 yards for a touchdown on their first possession, snapped the Rams' five-game winning streak.

The game also marked the final appearance in the Dallas backfield for Tony Dorsett, who rushed 12 times for 52 yards to become just the fourth player in league history to surpass the 12,000-yard career mark. Dorsett, who joined Walter Payton, Jim Brown and Franco Harris at the 12,000 mark, finished his 11-year Dallas career with 12,036 yards rushing on 2,755 attempts. He later would be traded to the Denver Broncos.

Colts-Chargers

SUNDAY, DECEMBER 20

SCORE BY PERIODS

Indianapolis	7	6	0	7—20
San Diego	7	0	0	0— 7

SCORING

San Diego—Fouts 1 run (Abbott kick), 7:01 1st.
Indianapolis—Brooks 42 pass from Trudeau (Biasucci kick), 12:07 1st.
Indianapolis—Field goal Biasucci 35, 9:42 2nd.
Indianapolis—Field goal Biasucci 41, 14:59 2nd.
Indianapolis—Bentley 3 run (Biasucci kick), 13:07 4th.

TEAM STATISTICS

	Indianapolis	San Diego
First downs	19	17
Rushes-Yards	32-146	22-59
Passing yards	194	214
Sacked-Yards lost	1-7	5-43
3rd down eff.	7-18	3-14
Passes	20-39-0	22-37-3
Punts	9-41.9	7-39.1
Fumbles-Lost	2-0	1-0
Penalties-Yards	6-50	6-40
Time of possession	30:24	29:36
Attendance—46,211.		

INDIVIDUAL STATISTICS

Rushing—Indianapolis, Dickerson 23-115, Bentley 8-25, Trudeau 1-6; San Diego, Adams 7-26, Anderson 10-17, Spencer 3-12, Fouts 1-1, James 1-3.

Passing—Indianapolis, Trudeau 20-39-0—201; San Diego, Fouts 22-37-3—257.

Receiving—Indianapolis, Boyer 2-18, Bentley 3-29, Brooks 4-86, Dickerson 4-20, Bouza 5-35, Beach 2-13; San Diego, Anderson 7-68, James 3-32, Spencer 1-7, Winslow 6-45, Adams 1-5, Chandler 2-46, Holland 2-54.

Kickoff Returns—Indianapolis, Bentley 2-41; San Diego, Adams 1-1, Anderson 4-68.

Punt Returns—Indianapolis, Brooks 5-25; San Diego, James 2-10.

Interceptions—Indianapolis, Prior 1-4, E. Daniel 1-0, Tullis 1-0.

Punting—Indianapolis, Stark 9-41.9; San Diego, Mojsiejenko 7-39.1.

Field Goals—Indianapolis, Biasucci 2-2; San Diego, Abbott 1-1 (missed: 52).

Sacks—Indianapolis, Cooks, Krauss, Bickett, Perryman, Glasgow ½, Thompson ½; San Diego, L. Williams.

Patriots-Bills

SUNDAY, DECEMBER 20
SCORE BY PERIODS

New England	7	6	0	0—13
Buffalo	0	0	7	0— 7

SCORING

New England—Jones 7 pass from Grogan (Franklin kick), 9:44 1st.
New England—Dupard 36 run (kick failed), 13:09 2nd.
Buffalo—McNanie 14 fumble return (Norwood kick), 7:53 3rd.

TEAM STATISTICS

	New England	Buffalo
First downs	15	12
Rushes-Yards	47-150	24-84
Passing yards	85	64
Sacked-Yards lost	0-0	5-61
3rd down eff.	6-14	4-14
Passes	9-15-2	13-31-1
Punts	6-32.5	6-45.7
Fumbles-Lost	4-1	2-1
Penalties-Yards	2-10	5-25
Time of possession	35:47	24:13
Attendance—74,945.		

INDIVIDUAL STATISTICS

Rushing—New England, Dupard 31-78, Tatupu 1-9, Fryar 1-16, Perryman 8-42, Collins 1-1, Grogan 5-4; Buffalo, Harmon 6-15, Mueller 14-37, Kelly 2-19, Byrum 2-13.

Passing—New England, Grogan 9-15-2—85; Buffalo, Kelly 13-31-1—125.

Receiving—New England, Jones 4-57, Collins 3-21, Dawson 2-7; Buffalo, Harmon 3-42, Reed 4-19, R. Porter 1-6, Burkett 3-31, Byrum 1-7, Metzelaars 1-20.

Kickoff Returns—Buffalo, R. Porter 1-30, Tasker 1-8, Mueller 1-13.

Punt Returns—Buffalo, Pitts 1-2.

Interceptions—New England, Marion 1-25; Buffalo, Pitts 1-7, Kelso 1-2.

Punting—New England, Camarillo 6-32.5; Buffalo, Kidd 6-45.7.

Field Goals—None attempted.

Sacks—New England, Tippett 1½, B. Williams ½, T. Williams, Veris 2.

Eagles-Jets

SUNDAY, DECEMBER 20
SCORE BY PERIODS

Philadelphia	10	14	14	0—38
New York Jets	3	17	0	7—27

SCORING

Philadelphia—Toney 3 run (McFadden kick), 5:47 1st.
Philadelphia—Field goal McFadden 38, 8:42 1st.
New York—Field goal Leahy 42, 13:09 1st.
New York—Sohn 9 pass from O'Brien (Leahy kick), 3:11 2nd.
New York—Vick 5 run (Leahy kick), 6:52 2nd.
Philadelphia—Quick 45 pass from Cunningham (McFadden kick), 11:25 2nd.
Philadelphia—Quick 13 pass from Cunningham (McFadden kick), 14:23 2nd.
New York—Field goal Leahy 29, 14:58 2nd.
Philadelphia—Byars 2 run (McFadden kick), 3:15 3rd.
Philadelphia—Carter 14 pass from Cunningham (McFadden kick), 4:28 3rd.
New York—Toon 51 pass from O'Brien (Leahy kick), 12:37 4th.

TEAM STATISTICS

	Philadelphia	New York
First downs	22	21
Rushes-Yards	39-143	21-78
Passing yards	265	276
Sacked-Yards lost	3-15	3-25
3rd down eff.	7-16	3-13
Passes	19-32-0	25-49-0
Punts	7-39.6	7-36.0
Fumbles-Lost	4-1	5-3
Penalties-Yards	8-75	10-90
Time of possession	36:02	23:58
Attendance—30,752.		

INDIVIDUAL STATISTICS

Rushing—Philadelphia, Byars 16-51, Toney 12-30, Cunningham 5-47, Tautalatasi 4-15, Haddix 1-2, Cavanaugh 1-minus 2; New York, Hector 8-38, Vick 10-22, Faaola 1-18, O'Brien 2-0.

Passing—Philadelphia, Cunningham 19-31-0—280, Toney 0-1-0—0; New York, O'Brien 25-49-0—301.

Receiving—Philadelphia, Quick 6-148, Jackson 3-55, Byars 3-18, Toney 2-26, Tautalatasi 2-2, Carter 1-14, Garrity 1-10, Spagnola 1-7; New York, Toon 10-168, Shuler 6-66, Hector 5-40, Sohn 2-14, Bligen 1-10, Vick 1-3.

Kickoff Returns—Philadelphia, Morse 4-86, Carter 1-16; New York, Humphery 2-22, Klever 2-53, Martin 2-44, Townsell 1-19.

Punt Returns—Philadelphia, Morse 3-4; New York, Townsell 4-78.

Interceptions—None.

Punting—Philadelphia, Teltschik 7-39.6; New York, Jennings 7-36.0.

Field Goals—Philadelphia, McFadden 1-2 (missed: 39);

New York, Leahy 2-2.

Sacks—Philadelphia, White 2, J. Brown; New York, Gastineau, Gordon 2.

Steelers-Oilers
SUNDAY, DECEMBER 20
SCORE BY PERIODS

Pittsburgh	3	3	7	3—16
Houston	0	10	7	7—24

SCORING

Pittsburgh—Field goal Anderson 25, 7:05 1st.
Pittsburgh—Field goal Anderson 35, 5:21 2nd.
Houston—D. Hill 52 pass from Moon (Zendejas kick), 9:20 2nd.
Houston—Field goal Zendejas 34, 15:00 2nd.
Pittsburgh—Malone 1 run (Anderson kick), 5:51 3rd.
Houston—Pinkett 5 run (Zendejas kick), 11:48 3rd.
Pittsburgh—Field goal Anderson 20, 5:29 4th.
Houston—D. Hill 30 pass from Moon (Zendejas kick), 9:40 4th.

TEAM STATISTICS

	Pittsburgh	Houston
First downs	22	17
Rushes-Yards	42-176	30-62
Passing yards	172	221
Sacked-Yards lost	1-9	3-19
3rd down eff	4-12	4-13
Passes	12-27-3	12-25-1
Punts	4-42.4	7-42.0
Fumbles-Lost	0-0	4-0
Penalties-Yards	8-59	7-56
Time of possession	33:54	26:06

Attendance—38,683.

INDIVIDUAL STATISTICS

Rushing—Pittsburgh, Pollard 10-38, Abercrombie 10-35, Stone 2-24, Malone 2-4, Jackson 18-75; Houston, Rozier 19-37, Highsmith 1-3, Moon 4-2, Pinkett 6-20.

Passing—Pittsburgh, Malone 12-27-3—181; Houston, Moon 12-25-1—240.

Receiving—Pittsburgh, Stallworth 5-72, Carter 2-24, Abercrombie 2-1, Pollard 1-3, Lipps 1-18, Thompson 1-63; Houston, Highsmith 1-6, Givins 3-62, Rozier 2-34, D. Hill 4-109, J. Williams 2-29.

Kickoff Returns—Pittsburgh, Woodson 1-23, Stone 1-21; Houston, Drewrey 4-73.

Punt Returns—Pittsburgh, Woodson 5-37; Houston, K. Johnson 1-5.

Interceptions—Pittsburgh, Woodruff 1-25; Houston, Brown 1-35, Donaldson 2-0.

Punting—Pittsburgh, Newsome 4-42.4; Houston, Gossett 7-42.0.

Field Goals—Pittsburgh, Anderson 3-3; Houston, Zendejas 1-1.

Sacks—Pittsburgh, Gary 2, Willis; Houston, Martin.

Browns-Raiders
SUNDAY, DECEMBER 20
SCORE BY PERIODS

Cleveland	7	10	7	0—24
Los Angeles Raiders	3	0	0	14—17

SCORING

Los Angeles—Field goal Bahr 39, 8:36 1st.
Cleveland—Byner 2 pass from Kosar (Bahr kick), 11:09 1st.
Cleveland—Field goal Bahr 20, 4:02 2nd.
Cleveland—Byner 15 run (Bahr kick), 8:42 2nd.
Cleveland—Slaughter 18 pass from Kosar (Bahr kick), 13:25 3rd.
Los Angeles—Toran 48 interception return (Bahr kick), 1:00 4th.
Los Angeles—Lofton 28 pass from Wilson (Bahr kick), 13:09 4th.

TEAM STATISTICS

	Cleveland	Los Angeles
First downs	24	20
Rushes-Yards	31-127	20-71
Passing yards	294	228
Sacked-Yards lost	0-0	4-42
3rd down eff	8-15	8-15
Passes	21-32-1	23-36-0
Punts	2-39.5	5-41.4
Fumbles-Lost	2-1	1-1
Penalties-Yards	7-50	8-89
Time of possession	32:10	27:50

Attendance—40,275.

INDIVIDUAL STATISTICS

Rushing—Cleveland, Byner 12-74, Mack 17-55, Kosar 2-minus 2; Los Angeles, Allen 14-35, Wilson 4-33, Strachan 1-2, Mueller 1-1.

Passing—Cleveland, Kosar 21-32-1—294; Los Angeles, Wilson 23-36-0—270.

Receiving—Cleveland, Slaughter 7-115, Brennan 6-79, Weathers 2-28, Langhorne 2-25, Byner 2-21, Fontenot 1-25, Newsome 1-1; Los Angeles, Allen 10-84, Lofton 4-70, Christensen 4-49, Mueller 2-27, Strachan 2-26, Woods 1-14.

Kickoff Returns—Cleveland, Langhorne 1-8, McNeil 1-14, Young 2-48; Los Angeles, Williams 1-22, Adams 1-25, Mueller 2-49.

Punt Returns—Cleveland, McNeil 3-55.

Interceptions—Los Angeles, Toran 1-48.

Punting—Cleveland, L. Johnson 2-39.5; Los Angeles, Talley 5-41.4.

Field Goals—Cleveland, Bahr 1-2 (missed: 37); Los Angeles, Bahr 1-1.

Sacks—Cleveland, Clancy, Hairston, Baker, Golic.

Falcons-49ers
SUNDAY, DECEMBER 20
SCORE BY PERIODS

Atlanta	0	0	7	0— 7
San Francisco	0	7	14	14—35

SCORING

San Francisco—Rice 5 run (Wersching kick), 9:20 2nd.
San Francisco—Rice 20 pass from Young (Wersching kick), 3:49 3rd.
Atlanta—Stamps 97 kickoff return (Luckhurst kick), 4:05 3rd.
San Francisco—Cribbs 92 kickoff return (Wersching kick), 4:23 3rd.
San Francisco—Young 29 run (Wersching kick), 2:44 4th.
San Francisco—Rice 1 pass from Young (Wersching kick), 11:15 4th.

TEAM STATISTICS

	Atlanta	San Francisco
First downs	13	26
Rushes-Yards	17-51	48-255
Passing yards	165	206
Sacked-Yards lost	3-21	1-10
3rd down eff	1-11	5-13
Passes	13-36-4	13-30-0
Punts	7-38.1	6-40.2
Fumbles-Lost	0-0	1-1
Penalties-Yards	7-63	7-55
Time of possession	24:26	35:35

Attendance—54,698.

INDIVIDUAL STATISTICS

Rushing—Atlanta, Riggs 10-24, Settle 5-20, Flowers 1-4, C. Miller 1-3; San Francisco, Young 6-83, Craig 19-69, Cribbs 14-61, Rathman 7-26, Sydney 1-11, Rice 1-5.

Passing—Atlanta, C. Miller 13-36-4—186; San Francisco, Young 13-30-0—216.

Receiving—Atlanta, Matthews 4-59, Settle 3-34, Riggs 2-56, Dixon 2-24, Cox 2-13; San Francisco, Rice 4-58, Taylor 3-51, Frank 2-41, Craig 2-29, Jones 1-22, Rathman 1-15.

Kickoff Returns—Atlanta, Settle 1-22, Stamps 5-177; San Francisco, Cribbs 1-92.

Punt Returns—Atlanta, Johnson 1-3; San Francisco, McLemore 4-30.

Interceptions—San Francisco, Williamson 1-17, Lott 1-0, Griffin 1-0, Nixon 1-5.

Punting—Atlanta, Donnelly 7-38.1; San Francisco, Runager 6-40.2.

Field Goals—Atlanta, Luckhurst 0-1 (missed: 40); San Francisco, none attempted.

Sacks—Atlanta, Harrison ½, Bryan ½; San Francisco, Board, Stover, McColl.

Chiefs-Broncos
SATURDAY, DECEMBER 19
SCORE BY PERIODS

Kansas City	0	3	7	7—17
Denver	7	10	3	0—20

SCORING

Denver—Lang 3 run (Karlis kick), 8:27 1st.
Denver—Field goal Karlis 20, 2:46 2nd.
Kansas City—Field goal Lowery 33, 6:39 2nd.
Denver—Winder 8 pass from Elway (Karlis kick), 13:29 2nd.
Kansas City—Heard 64 run (Lowery kick), 1:16 3rd.
Denver—Field goal Karlis 43, 12:02 3rd.
Kansas City—Paige 8 pass from Kenney (Lowery kick), 8:24 4th.

TEAM STATISTICS

	Kansas City	Denver
First downs	20	22
Rushes-Yards	21-123	40-143
Passing yards	254	226
Sacked-Yards lost	2-18	1-11
3rd down eff.	6-14	8-15
Passes	26-39-0	18-31-0
Punts	5-46.8	4-51.5
Fumbles-Lost	2-1	2-2
Penalties-Yards	9-70	7-58
Time of possession	24:48	35:12
Attendance—75,053.		

INDIVIDUAL STATISTICS

Rushing—Kansas City, Heard 10-93, Palmer 2-8, Moriarty 6-22, Okoye 1-0, Kenney 2-0; Denver, Winder 23-98, Lang 5-24, Elway 11-20, Bell 1-1.

Passing—Kansas City, Kenney 26-39-0—272; Denver, Elway 18-31-0—237.

Receiving—Kansas City, Okoye 3-24, Heard 3-37, Moriarty 3-11, Coffman 1-8, Carson 5-59, D. Colbert 2-13, Paige 5-78, Keel 1-7, Hayes 3-35; Denver, Johnson 3-35, Winder 2-18, Nattiel 2-45, Kay 6-91, Lang 2-12, Watson 1-12, Mobley 1-7, Jackson 1-17.

Kickoff Returns—Kansas City, Robinson 1-17, Palmer 1-15; Denver, Bell 1-24.

Punt Returns—Kansas City, Fields 2-26; Denver, Clark 5-45.

Interceptions—None.

Punting—Kansas City, Goodburn 5-46.8; Denver, Horan 4-51.5.

Field Goals—Kansas City, Lowery 1-3 (missed: 49, 37); Denver, Karlis 2-2.

Sacks—Kansas City, Maas; Denver, Fletcher 2.

Seahawks-Bears
SUNDAY, DECEMBER 20
SCORE BY PERIODS

Seattle	0	7	20	7—34
Chicago	0	7	7	7—21

SCORING

Seattle—Turner 12 pass from Krieg (N. Johnson kick), 6:51 2nd.

Chicago—Moorehead 3 pass from Tomczak (Butler kick), 14:08 2nd.
Seattle—Warner 1 run (N. Johnson kick), 4:50 3rd.
Chicago—Payton 3 run (Butler kick), 9:18 3rd.
Seattle—J.L. Williams 75 pass from Krieg (N. Johnson kick), 9:46 3rd.
Seattle—Field goal N. Johnson 45, 11:59 3rd.
Seattle—Field goal N. Johnson 29, 13:52 3rd.
Chicago—Payton 5 run (Butler kick), 2:53 4th.
Seattle—Warner 4 run (N. Johnson kick), 12:50 4th.

TEAM STATISTICS

	Seattle	Chicago
First downs	16	31
Rushes-Yards	29-116	37-159
Passing yards	184	278
Sacked-Yards lost	3-30	3-20
3rd down eff.	4-12	6-12
Passes	17-26-0	21-36-2
Punts	6-37.7	2-34.5
Fumbles-Lost	4-0	3-3
Penalties-Yards	7-81	7-56
Time of possession	26:29	33:31
Attendance—62,518.		

INDIVIDUAL STATISTICS

Rushing—Seattle, Krieg 7-15, Warner 17-75, J.L. Williams 5-26; Chicago, Payton 17-79, Tomczak 8-24, Anderson 4-9, Suhey 1-2, Thomas 5-23, Gault 1-7, Gentry 1-9.

Passing—Seattle, Krieg 17-26-0—214; Chicago, Tomczak 21-36-2—298.

Receiving—Seattle, J.L. Williams 8-117, Largent 3-36, R. Butler 5-49, Turner 1-12; Chicago, Morris 3-55, Anderson 2-16, Payton 2-20, McKinnon 4-55, Boso 1-31, Moorehead 2-23, Gault 2-20, Gentry 3-58, Suhey 2-20.

Kickoff Returns—Seattle, Edmonds 3-59, Scholtz 1-1; Chicago, Sanders 5-73, Gentry 1-14.

Punt Returns—Seattle, Edmonds 1-15; Chicago, McKinnon 4-11.

Interceptions—Seattle, Robinson 2-75, Taylor 0-2.

Punting—Seattle, Rodriguez 6-37.7; Chicago, Barnhardt 2-34.5.

Field Goals—Seattle, N. Johnson 2-2; Chicago, Butler 0-2 (missed: 53, 48).

Sacks—Seattle, Bosworth, Green, Bryant; Chicago, McMichael, Wilson, Dent.

Packers-Giants
SATURDAY, DECEMBER 19
SCORE BY PERIODS

Green Bay	0	0	3	7—10
New York Giants	0	13	7	0—20

SCORING

New York—Morris 3 run (run failed), 0:37 2nd.
New York—Rouson 26 pass from Simms (Allegre kick), 13:00 2nd.
New York—Mowatt 1 pass from Simms (Allegre kick), 7:29 3rd.
Green Bay—Field goal Zendejas 26, 12:39 3rd.
Green Bay—Clark 3 pass from Carruth (Zendejas kick), 12:28 4th.

TEAM STATISTICS

	Green Bay	New York
First downs	10	21
Rushes-Yards	22-74	36-111
Passing yards	105	215
Sacked-Yards lost	4-29	4-18
3rd down eff.	3-16	11-16
Passes	20-34-1	21-26-0
Punts	8-40.5	5-36.8
Fumbles-Lost	0-0	6-4
Penalties-Yards	9-58	4-35
Time of possession	25:23	34:37
Attendance—51,013.		

INDIVIDUAL STATISTICS

Rushing—Green Bay, Carruth 2-11, Wright 3-9, Clark 8-20, Davis 9-34; New York, Morris 22-92, Adams 1-3, Carthon 6-10, Manuel 1-minus 10, Galbreath 2-20, Rutledge 4-minus 4.

Passing—Green Bay, Wright 19-33-1—131, Carruth 1-1-0—3; New York, Simms 21-26-0—233.

Receiving—Green Bay, Clark 6-31, Davis 1-9, Neal 2-11, Paskett 5-38, Stanley 2-9, Scott 1-10, West 3-26; New York, Rouson 4-61, Morris 3-37, Adams 2-12, McConkey 2-22, Carthon 2-8, Manuel 4-50, Bavaro 1-12, Galbreath 1-8, Turner 1-22, Mowatt 1-1.

Kickoff Returns—Green Bay, Fullwood 3-69, Scott 1-23; New York, Rouson 2-42.

Punt Returns—Green Bay, Stanley 2-58; New York, McConkey 6-40.

Interceptions—New York, Headen 1-5.

Punting—Green Bay, Bracken 8-40.5; New York, Landeta 5-36.8.

Field Goals—Green Bay, Zendejas 1-1; New York, none attempted.

Sacks—Green Bay, Carreker, Anderson 2, Harris; New York, Lasker, Taylor, Washington, Banks.

Cardinals-Buccaneers
SUNDAY, DECEMBER 20
SCORE BY PERIODS

St. Louis	0	14	10	7—31
Tampa Bay	7	0	0	7—14

SCORING

Tampa Bay—Hall 1 pass from Testaverde (Igwebuike kick), 4:49 1st.

St. Louis—Novacek 15 pass from Lomax (Del Greco kick), 1:03 2nd.

St. Louis—J.T. Smith 8 pass from Lomax (Del Greco kick), 13:57 2nd.

St. Louis—Field goal Del Greco 28, 4:08 3rd.

St. Louis—Awalt 5 pass from Lomax (Del Greco kick), 11:34 3rd.

St. Louis—Mitchell 3 run (Del Greco kick), 2:28 4th.

Tampa Bay—Carter 26 pass from Testaverde (Igwebuike kick), 14:15 4th.

TEAM STATISTICS

	St. Louis	Tampa Bay
First downs	24	19
Rushes-Yards	34-134	31-163
Passing yards	217	207
Sacked-Yards lost	3-16	6-33
3rd down eff	6-12	6-17
Passes	22-30-1	16-38-2
Punts	5-41.0	7-37.1
Fumbles-Lost	1-1	5-2
Penalties-Yards	10-65	7-55
Time of possession	30:43	29:17
Attendance—32,046.		

INDIVIDUAL STATISTICS

Rushing—St. Louis, Mitchell 23-101, Wolfley 5-17, Green 1-8, McAdoo 3-1, Lomax 1-9, Stoudt 1-minus 2; Tampa Bay, Wilder 10-80, Smith 14-40, Testaverde 2-19, Howard 3-15, Hill 1-4, Hunter 1-5.

Passing—St. Louis, Lomax 22-29-1—233, Stoudt 0-1-0—0; Tampa Bay, Testaverde 16-38-2—240.

Receiving—St. Louis, Mitchell 6-41, Awalt 3-15, Green 5-86, T. Johnson 2-22, J.T. Smith 5-54, Novacek 1-15; Tampa Bay, Carter 5-116, Hall 2-10, Magee 1-8, Hill 4-74, Smith 3-25, Howard 1-7.

Kickoff Returns—St. Louis, Sikahema 1-23, McAdoo 1-17; Tampa Bay, Smith 1-20, Futrell 2-27.

Punt Returns—St. Louis, Sikahema 4-53; Tampa Bay, Futrell 3-29.

Interceptions—St. Louis, Junior 1-25, Mack 1-0; Tampa Bay, Futrell 1-23.

Punting—St. Louis, Horne 5-41.0; Tampa Bay, Garcia 7-37.1.

Field Goals—St. Louis, Del Greco 1-1; Tampa Bay, Igwebuike 0-1 (missed: 49).

Sacks—St. Louis, Nunn 3, Clasby, Junior, Bell; Tampa Bay, Holmes 3.

Saints-Bengals
SUNDAY, DECEMBER 20
SCORE BY PERIODS

New Orleans	3	7	14	17—41
Cincinnati	14	10	0	0—24

SCORING

Cincinnati—Brown 10 pass from Esiason (Breech kick), 5:42 1st.

New Orleans—Field goal Andersen 21, 10:34 1st.

Cincinnati—Jennings 1 pass from Esiason (Breech kick), 11:46 1st.

Cincinnati—Field goal Breech 43, 0:05 2nd.

Cincinnati—Kinnebrew 1 run (Breech kick), 9:15 2nd.

New Orleans—Hilliard 2 run (Andersen kick), 13:06 2nd.

New Orleans—Jones 29 pass from Wilson (Andersen kick), 3:05 3rd.

New Orleans—Hilliard 3 run (Andersen kick), 5:26 3rd.

New Orleans—Field goal Andersen 30, 8:03 4th.

New Orleans—Jordan 1 run (Andersen kick), 9:05 4th.

New Orleans—Jordan 8 run (Andersen kick), 13:05 4th.

TEAM STATISTICS

	New Orleans	Cincinnati
First downs	24	24
Rushes-Yards	36-101	26-125
Passing yards	220	112
Sacked-Yards lost	3-24	6-58
3rd down eff	5-13	5-14
Passes	16-31-0	17-37-2
Punts	5-36.0	4-39.0
Fumbles-Lost	0-0	3-2
Penalties-Yards	7-67	7-43
Time of possession	32:28	27:32
Attendance—43,424.		

INDIVIDUAL STATISTICS

Rushing—New Orleans, Mayes 13-19, Hilliard 16-52, Hansen 1-minus 3, Word 4-24, Jordan 2-9; Cincinnati, Jennings 11-56, Esiason 5-34, Kinnebrew 10-35.

Passing—New Orleans, Hebert 7-16-0—84, Wilson 9-15-0—160; Cincinnati, Esiason 17-37-2—170.

Receiving—New Orleans, Martin 4-54, Hill 2-43, Hilliard 2-16, Tice 2-29, Mayes 1-16, Jones 4-67, Brenner 1-19; Cincinnati, Jennings 5-28, Brown 5-76, Martin 1-24, Holman 2-5, McGee 1-6, Kattus 2-19, Kinnebrew 1-12.

Kickoff Returns—New Orleans, Gray 2-48, Hilliard 2-42, Word 1-19; Cincinnati, Bussey 5-90.

Punt Returns—New Orleans, Maxie 1-12, Gray 1-minus 2; Cincinnati, Martin 3-19.

Interceptions—New Orleans, Jakes 1-27, Mack 1-26.

Punting—New Orleans, Hansen 5-36.0; Cincinnati, Fulhage 3-43.0, Esiason 1-27.0.

Field Goals—New Orleans, Andersen 2-2; Cincinnati, Breech 1-2 (missed: 46).

Sacks—New Orleans, Jackson 3, Swilling 2, Johnson; Cincinnati, Thomas, Buck, Krumrie.

Vikings-Lions
SUNDAY, DECEMBER 20
SCORE BY PERIODS

Minnesota	0	10	0	7—17
Detroit	0	7	0	7—14

SCORING

Minnesota—Dozier 20 pass from Wilson (C. Nelson kick), 11:04 2nd.

Detroit—Mandley 4 pass from Long (Murray kick), 13:51 2nd.

Minnesota—Field goal C. Nelson 22, 14:57 2nd.

Minnesota—Wilson 2 run (C. Nelson kick), 0:45 4th.
Detroit—James 16 run (Murray kick), 3:28 4th.

TEAM STATISTICS

	Minnesota	Detroit
First downs	20	17
Rushes-Yards	37-205	26-129
Passing yards	135	235
Sacked-Yards lost	2-30	1-5
3rd down eff.	4-12	5-12
Passes	16-27-0	16-31-4
Punts	7-42.7	4-42.0
Fumbles-Lost	1-0	3-1
Penalties-Yards	8-59	2-53
Time of possession	31:08	28:52

Attendance—27,693.

INDIVIDUAL STATISTICS

Rushing—Minnesota, Wilson 8-55, Anderson 7-51, Dozier 8-48, D. Nelson 11-41, Rice 2-6, Lewis 1-4; Detroit, James 17-94, Jones 4-16, Long 2-12, Paige 2-5, Woolfolk 1-2.

Passing—Minnesota, Wilson 16-27-0—165; Detroit, Long 16-30-3—240, Jones 0-1-1—0.

Receiving—Minnesota, Lewis 3-34, Carter 2-31, Dozier 2-24, Jordan 2-23, Fenney 2-7, D. Nelson 2-4, Anderson 1-22, Rice 1-13, Gustafson 1-7; Detroit, Mandley 7-78, Lee 3-85, James 3-58, Nichols 1-17, Kab 1-4, Paige 1-minus 2.

Kickoff Returns—Minnesota, D. Nelson 1-23; Detroit, Saleaumua 1-18, Woolfolk 2-30, Lee 1-21.

Punt Returns—Minnesota, Lewis 2-10; Detroit, Mandley 4-25.

Interceptions—Minnesota, Browner 2-43, Lee 1-5, J. Harris 1-14.

Punting—Minnesota, Scribner 7-42.7; Detroit, Arnold 4-42.0.

Field Goals—Minnesota, C. Nelson 1-2 (missed: 47); Detroit, none attempted.

Sacks—Minnesota, D. Martin; Detroit, K. Ferguson, Saleaumua.

Redskins-Dolphins
SUNDAY, DECEMBER 20
SCORE BY PERIODS

Washington	0	7	7	7—21
Miami	0	9	0	14—23

SCORING

Miami—Field goal Reveiz 48, 8:44 2nd.
Washington—Bryant 6 run (Haji-Sheikh kick), 10:53 2nd.
Miami—Duper 26 pass from Marino (kick failed), 13:06 2nd.
Washington—Schroeder 3 run (Haji-Sheikh kick), 9:14 3rd.
Miami—Duper 59 pass from Marino (Reveiz kick), 1:31 4th.
Washington—Rogers 2 run (Haji-Sheikh kick), 8:43 4th.
Miami—Duper 6 pass from Marino (Reveiz kick), 13:53 4th.

TEAM STATISTICS

	Washington	Miami
First downs	28	22
Rushes-Yards	39-204	17-66
Passing yards	268	393
Sacked-Yards lost	1-4	0-0
3rd down eff.	6-14	5-14
Passes	19-38-1	22-50-1
Punts	6-40.3	7-36.6
Fumbles-Lost	1-1	1-0
Penalties-Yards	4-30	6-60
Time of possession	34:52	25:08

Attendance—65,715.

INDIVIDUAL STATISTICS

Rushing—Washington, Rogers 16-59, Sanders 1-minus 4, Bryant 9-84, Smith 11-46, Schroeder 2-19; Miami,

Stradford 12-49, Davenport 2-5, Clayton 1-4, Marino 1-minus 1, Jensen 1-9.

Passing—Washington, Schroeder 19-38-1—272; Miami, Marino 22-50-1—393.

Receiving—Washington, Bryant 5-69, Didier 4-52, Smith 1-minus 2, Sanders 4-39, Clark 3-52, Verdin 2-62; Miami, Stradford 4-50, Duper 6-170, Clayton 4-65, Hardy 2-29, Jensen 2-20, Davenport 2-34, Pruitt 2-25.

Kickoff Returns—Washington, Verdin 4-100; Miami, Hampton 2-32.

Punt Returns—Washington, Yarber 2-5; Miami, B. Brown 1-8.

Interceptions—Washington, Wilburn 1-0; Miami, Lankford 1-0.

Punting—Washington, Cox 6-40.3; Miami, Roby 5-42.8, Strock 2-21.0.

Field Goals—Washington, Haji-Sheikh 0-1 (missed: 38), Cox 0-1 (missed: 67); Miami, Reveiz 1-1.

Sacks—Miami, Sochia.

Cowboys-Rams
MONDAY, DECEMBER 21
SCORE BY PERIODS

Dallas	10	6	10	3—29
Los Angeles Rams	7	0	7	7—21

SCORING

Dallas—Walker 1 run (Ruzek kick), 6:43 1st.
Los Angeles—White 8 run (Lansford kick), 9:37 1st.
Dallas—Field goal Ruzek 24, 14:36 1st.
Dallas—Field goal Ruzek 42, 5:44 2nd.
Dallas—Field goal Ruzek 44, 14:54 2nd.
Dallas—Field goal Ruzek 47, 2:44 3rd.
Dallas—Cosbie 27 pass from Pelluer (Ruzek kick), 8:25 3rd.
Los Angeles—Everett 1 run (Lansford kick), 12:18 3rd.
Dallas—Field goal Ruzek 37, 10:27 4th.
Los Angeles—House 15 pass from Dils (Lansford kick), 12:22 4th.

TEAM STATISTICS

	Dallas	Los Angeles
First downs	20	19
Rushes-Yards	42-194	30-74
Passing yards	171	237
Sacked-Yards lost	2-12	3-25
3rd down eff.	7-18	9-18
Passes	15-30-0	19-39-3
Punts	6-34.0	5-44.4
Fumbles-Lost	1-0	2-1
Penalties-Yards	8-56	3-18
Time of possession	31:07	28:53

Attendance—60,700.

INDIVIDUAL STATISTICS

Rushing—Dallas, Walker 23-108, Dorsett 12-52, Pelluer 5-29, Newsome 2-5; Los Angeles, White 26-66, Everett 3-8, Dils 1-0.

Passing—Dallas, Pelluer 15-30-0—183; Los Angeles, Everett 12-24-2—189, Dils 7-15-1—73.

Receiving—Dallas, Walker 6-54, Renfro 3-33, Cosbie 2-35, Martin 2-31, Dorsett 2-30; Los Angeles, Ellard 5-75, Guman 5-73, Ron Brown 3-52, Johnson 2-35, White 2-3, House 1-15, Tyrrell 1-9.

Kickoff Returns—Dallas, Martin 1-22, Clack 2-54; Los Angeles, Ron Brown 4-106, Tyrrell 1-39, Richard Brown 1-15.

Punt Returns—Dallas, Martin 4-34; Los Angeles, Ellard 2-0.

Interceptions—Dallas, Penn 1-21, Walls 1-0, Downs 1-27.

Punting—Dallas, Saxon 6-34.0; Los Angeles, Hatcher 5-44.4

Field Goals—Dallas, Ruzek 5-5; Los Angeles, Lansford 0-1 (missed: 47).

Sacks—Dallas, Jones, Jeffcoat, R. White; Los Angeles, Reed, Greene.

SIXTEENTH WEEK

RESULTS OF WEEK 16

Saturday, December 26

Cleveland 19, Pittsburgh 13 at Pitts.
Washington 27, Minnesota 24 (OT) at Minn.

Sunday, December 27

Chicago 6, L.A. Raiders 3 at L.A.
Dallas 21, St. Louis 16 at Dall.
Denver 24, San Diego 0 at Den.
Detroit 30, Atlanta 13 at Atl.
Houston 21, Cincinnati 17 at Hous.
Indianapolis 24, Tampa Bay 6 at Ind.
Kansas City 41, Seattle 20 at K.C.
N.Y. Giants 20, N.Y. Jets 7 at N.Y.
New Orleans 33, Green Bay 24 at N.O.
Philadelphia 17, Buffalo 7 at Phila.
San Francisco 48, L.A. Rams 0 at S.F.

Monday, December 28

New England 24, Miami 10 at Mia.

Given a choice, National Football League teams would prefer to have control of their own destiny as they jockey for late-season playoff positions. Winning your own games is much safer—and a lot less nerve-racking—than sitting in front of a television set and hoping another team can knock off your competition for you.

In other words, if you want something done right, do it yourself.

Entering the final weekend of the 1987 regular-season, the Houston Oilers, Indianapolis Colts, Minnesota Vikings and St. Louis Cardinals all faced the same situation: a victory would reserve them a spot in the NFL's postseason party and a defeat would keep them out. Or, in the case of the Vikings, force them to sit in front of a TV set.

The Oilers and Colts, two of the league's have-nots in recent years, came through in grand style with victories in Week 16 to nail down playoff spots. Although both were playing at home against teams they were favored to beat, they nonetheless came through big when the pressure was on.

The Oilers clinched an AFC wild-card berth and their first winning season (9-6) since 1980 with a 21-17 win over Cincinnati. Warren Moon threw for 280 yards and ran for a touchdown and rookie Alonzo Highsmith scored the first two touchdowns of his NFL career to lead the Oilers' attack. Mike Rozier rushed for 103 yards on 20 attempts.

"This is the most important game I ever played in the NFL," said Moon, who led Edmonton to five straight Canadian Football League championships before joining Houston in 1984. "I wanted this game more than any game I ever played.

"It's great for the fans. They've waited so long."

The Colts ended an even longer playoff drought when they beat Tampa Bay, 24-6, to win the AFC East Division title. The victory gave the Colts (9-6) their first winning season and playoff berth since 1977, when the franchise was located in Baltimore.

"I won't say this makes the whole experience even," said safety Nesby Glasgow, who suffered through eight straight losing seasons with the Colts after joining the team as a rookie in 1979. "There's no truth to the lie that losing builds character. I'm glad we've gained the heights after so long on the down side."

The Colts, who were led by Eric Dickerson's 196 yards rushing and two touchdowns, had finished 3-13 and last in the AFC East just one year earlier. But after Ron Meyer succeeded Rod Dowhower as coach with three games left in the '86 season, Indianapolis won 12 of 18 games.

The Vikings entered their Saturday afternoon game against Washington at the Metrodome with a chance to nail down an NFC wild-card berth. They led, 24-14, with less than six minutes left before the Redskins scored 10 points to send the game into overtime. The Redskins prevailed, 27-24, when Ali Haji-Sheikh kicked a 26-yard field goal 2:09 into the extra period.

"We've got to get the killer instinct," said Minnesota center Kirk Lowdermilk. "We had them by the throat and we should have killed them."

Washington forced the overtime on Doug Williams' 51-yard touchdown pass to Ricky Sanders with 1:46 left in regulation. Sanders then returned the overtime kickoff 36 yards to the Washington 47-yard line and caught passes of 22 and 10 yards to set up Haji-Sheikh's game-winning field goal.

Viking defensive end Keith Millard was not happy about the late-game collapse that dropped Minnesota's record to 8-7. The Vikes lost three of their final four games.

"We don't deserve to be in the playoffs," he said. "And if the Cardinals lose to Dallas, all I can say is 'Merry Christmas.'"

Christmas came two days late for the Vikings when the Cardinals lost, 21-16, at Texas Stadium the following day. Dallas' Herschel Walker rushed 25 times for 137 yards and scored two touchdowns to hand Minnesota the wild-card spot that neither the Vikings nor Cardinals could clinch on the field.

"We had it," said St. Louis quarterback Neil Lomax. "God, we had it. This team should not have lost to the Dallas Cowboys. They're down, they're out, their linebackers are all beat up."

The Cards simply did not come through in the clutch. Trailing by five points with two minutes left, they had a first down at the Dallas 23-yard line. Running back Stump Mitchell

Herschel Walker rushed for 137 yards and scored two touchdowns to help knock St. Louis out of the playoffs, 21-16.

was held to a one-yard gain on first down and on second, center Mike Ruether snapped the ball over his quarterback's head. Lomax recovered, but his pass intended for J.T. Smith fell incomplete. Lomax was sacked by Jim Jeffcoat for an eight-yard loss on third down and had a pass into the Dallas end zone knocked away on fourth down.

St. Louis drove into Dallas territory nine times but scored only one touchdown.

New Orleans, which already had assured itself of its first playoff appearance in franchise history, was the league's hottest team as the postseason approached. The Saints won for the ninth straight week, 33-24, over the Green Bay Packers, to close out the regular season with a 12-3 mark. The 12 victories and nine in a row were both New Orleans records.

The Saints trailed, 17-12, at halftime before taking control in the third quarter. They marched 72 yards with their first possession of the second half to take a 19-17 lead on a touchdown run by Rueben Mayes. But after Green Bay quarterback Don Majkowski drove his team 90 yards on 10 plays to regain the lead, the Saints' Dalton Hilliard returned the ensuing kickoff 74 yards to the Packers' 20-yard line. Three plays later, Bobby Hebert hit tight end John Tice with a five-yard touchdown pass to give the Saints the lead for good.

The Saints' victory forced the San Francisco

49ers to win their game that evening against the Los Angeles Rams to capture the NFC West Division title. The 49ers did just that, clobbering the Rams, 48-0, to win their fifth division crown in seven years.

The win improved the 49ers' record to a league-best 13-2 and guaranteed them home-field advantage throughout the NFC playoffs.

San Francisco dominated from start to finish, with starting quarterback Steve Young throwing three touchdown passes and Joe Montana, who had missed two games because of injury, coming off the bench to throw two more. Wide receiver Jerry Rice caught three passes, two for touchdowns, and finished as the league's regular-season scoring leader with 138 points. Rice's 23 touchdowns, however, fell one shy of equaling John Riggins' 1983 NFL record of 24.

The Cleveland Browns clinched their third straight AFC Central Division championship with a 19-13 victory over Pittsburgh in a Saturday afternoon game. The Browns' win was their fourth in succession against the Steelers and second in a row at Pittsburgh's Three Rivers Stadium, where the Browns had lost 16 straight games before winning there in 1986.

The Steelers' only touchdown came on rookie Cornell Gowdy's 45-yard interception return of a Bernie Kosar pass with 7:33 remaining. The Browns, however, controlled the ball for

Cornelius Bennett was a one-man wrecking crew in Buffalo's 17-7 victory at Philadelphia.

the rest of the game, keeping possession for all but 21 seconds of the fourth quarter.

Coming off impressive victories over Denver and Chicago, the Seattle Seahawks blew a chance to clinch home-field advantage for the AFC wild-card game with a 41-20 upset loss to Kansas City. Chiefs quarterback Bill Kenney engineered the upset by throwing for 320 yards and three touchdowns. Kansas City rolled up 512 yards in total offense and scored 24 points in the first 16 minutes. Running back Herman Heard ran 37 yards for a touchdown on the third play of the game.

The only bright spot for the Seahawks was wide receiver Steve Largent, who caught six passes to become the NFL's all-time leading pass receiver. Largent, in his 12th pro season out of Tulsa, finished the regular season with 752 receptions, two more than former Chargers great Charlie Joiner.

In the battle for the No. 1 overall choice in the 1988 draft, the Atlanta Falcons won top drafting honors with a 30-13 loss to the Detroit Lions. Both teams entered the game with records of 3-11, and the Falcons' 3-12 finish was their worst since 1968. A crowd of only 13,906 watched the game at Atlanta-Fulton County Stadium.

Gary Ellerson ran for two touchdowns and

Eddie Murray kicked three field goals to lead the Lions while rookie Chris Miller threw the first scoring pass of his NFL career for the Falcons' only touchdown. Miller, who was intercepted three times in the final period and four times in the game, finished his first season with one touchdown pass and nine interceptions in three games.

In the Battle of New York, the Giants beat the Jets, 20-7, to give both teams final 6-9 records. The Giants, who won three of their final four games, became the first Super Bowl champion in history to finish last in their division the following season. The Jets, who lost their final five games in 1986 but still made the playoffs, finished the '87 season with four straight defeats.

Another battle of non-playoff combatants saw the Philadelphia Eagles defeat the Buffalo Bills, 17-7, in an interconference game. Keith Byars rushed for 102 yards and running mate Anthony Toney scored two touchdowns to pace the Eagles' offense. Reggie White led the defense with two sacks of Bills quarterback Jim Kelly, giving him 21 in the strike-shortened season.

Bills rookie Cornelius Bennett had four sacks, 15 solo tackles and forced three fumbles in just his eighth NFL game.

The Chicago Bears registered nine sacks en route to a 6-3 interconference victory over the Los Angeles Raiders. End Richard Dent had 4½ sacks as the Bears finished the regular season with a league-high 70.

Chicago, which had lost its previous two games by a combined score of 75-21, beat the Raiders on Kevin Butler's 30-yard field goal with 4:56 left. Bears running back Walter Payton, who was playing in the final regular-season game of his 13-year career, kept the drive alive with a two-yard run on a fourth-and-one play at the Raiders' 40-yard line.

Payton, the NFL's all-time leading rusher, picked up 82 yards on 20 carries and finished his career with 16,726 yards on 3,838 attempts.

The AFC West-champion Denver Broncos clinched home-field advantage for the conference playoffs with a 24-0 victory over San Diego in a game played in blizzard conditions. The Broncos, who elected to kick off at the start of the game because of 25 mph winds and a minus-10 wind chill, got the only points they needed when the Chargers were forced to punt after just three plays from scrimmage. Denver rookie K.C. Clark returned Ralf Mojsiejenko's kick 71 yards for a touchdown.

The Chargers, who at one point of the season looked like a shoo-in for a playoff spot with an 8-1 record, lost their sixth game in a row to finish 8-7 and out of the playoffs.

Two other teams out of the playoff picture, the Miami Dolphins and New England Patriots, closed out the 1987 regular season with a Monday night game at Joe Robbie Stadium.

The Patriots' 24-10 triumph was their fifth win in a row over the Dolphins and left both AFC East teams with 8-7 records.

The tone for the game was set early when Miami rookie Troy Stradford fumbled on the first play from scrimmage. New England recovered and took a 7-0 lead minutes later on Steve Grogan's three-yard scoring pass to Irving Fryar. Grogan then threw a 34-yard touchdown pass to Stephen Starring on New England's next possession.

The Patriots scored on four of their five first-half possessions to take a 24-3 halftime lead.

Browns-Steelers
SATURDAY, DECEMBER 26
SCORE BY PERIODS

Cleveland	3	6	3	7—19
Pittsburgh	0	3	0	10—13

SCORING
Cleveland—Field goal Bahr 31, 11:33 1st.
Cleveland—Tennell 2 pass from Kosar (kick failed), 2:15 2nd.
Pittsburgh—Field goal Anderson 39, 6:12 2nd.
Cleveland—Field goal Bahr 30, 5:40 3rd.
Pittsburgh—Field goal Anderson 27, 0:03 4th.
Cleveland—Byner 2 run (Bahr kick), 5:24 4th.
Pittsburgh—Gowdy 45 interception return (Anderson kick), 7:27 4th.

TEAM STATISTICS

	Cleveland	Pittsburgh
First downs	22	10
Rushes-Yards	30-85	26-95
Passing yards	230	126
Sacked-Yards lost	2-11	0-0
3rd down eff	4-14	4-12
Passes	21-36-1	11-18-2
Punts	4-26.3	4-39.5
Fumbles-Lost	2-0	3-0
Penalties-Yards	3-25	11-90
Time of possession	32:58	27:02
Attendance—56,394.		

INDIVIDUAL STATISTICS
Rushing—Cleveland, Mack 18-37, Byner 12-48; Pittsburgh, Pollard 11-42, Malone 4-24, Abercrombie 5-1, Jackson 6-28.

Passing—Cleveland, Kosar 21-36-1—241; Pittsburgh, Malone 11-18-2—126.

Receiving—Cleveland, Mack 2-17, Newsome 6-94, Byner 3-19, Slaughter 4-65, Langhorne 2-30, Tennell 1-2, Weathers 1-2, Brennan 2-12; Pittsburgh, Stallworth 6-53, Lipps 2-34, Thompson 1-23, Abercrombie 1-10, Young 1-6.

Kickoff Returns—Cleveland, McNeil 4-74; Pittsburgh, Woodson 1-19, Stone 3-53.

Punt Returns—Cleveland, McNeil 2-16; Pittsburgh, Woodson 1-6.

Interceptions—Cleveland, E. Johnson 1-11, Dixon 1-minus 1; Pittsburgh, Gowdy 1-45.

Punting—Cleveland, L. Johnson 4-26.3; Pittsburgh, Newsome 4-39.5.

Field Goals—Cleveland, Bahr 2-2; Pittsburgh, Anderson 2-3 (missed: 42).

Sacks—Pittsburgh, Carr.

Redskins-Vikings
SATURDAY, DECEMBER 26
SCORE BY PERIODS

Washington	0	7	7	10	3—27
Minnesota	7	0	0	17	0—24

SCORING
Minnesota—Anderson 9 run (C. Nelson kick), 4:50 1st.
Washington—Wilburn 100 interception return (Haji-Sheikh kick), 9:47 2nd.
Washington—Sanders 46 pass from Williams (Haji-Sheikh kick), 9:04 3rd.
Minnesota—Anderson 1 run (C. Nelson kick), 0:02 4th.
Minnesota—Wilson 1 run (C. Nelson kick), 2:46 4th.
Minnesota—Field goal C. Nelson 20, 9:38 4th.
Washington—Field goal Haji-Sheikh 37, 9:55 4th.
Washington—Sanders 51 pass from Williams (Haji-Sheikh kick), 13:14 4th.
Washington—Field goal Haji-Sheikh 26, 2:09 OT.

TEAM STATISTICS

	Washington	Minnesota
First downs	18	24
Rushes-Yards	19-77	44-204
Passing yards	291	177
Sacked-Yards lost	1-11	4-29
3rd down eff	7-13	7-13
Passes	20-39-4	14-27-3
Punts	2-37.0	4-40.0
Fumbles-Lost	0-0	0-0
Penalties-Yards	6-40	3-35
Time of possession	24:28	37:41
Attendance—59,166.		

INDIVIDUAL STATISTICS
Rushing—Washington, Rogers 10-51, Smith 3-4, Bryant 4-7, Verdin 1-14, Williams 1-1; Minnesota, Anderson 8-29, D. Nelson 14-73, Rice 4-10, Wilson 10-75, Dozier 8-19, Lewis 2-minus 2.

Passing—Washington, Schroeder 9-17-2—85, Williams 11-22-2—217; Minnesota, Wilson 14-27-3—206.

Receiving—Washington, Bryant 4-50, Clark 5-53, Sanders 8-164, Orr 3-35; Minnesota, Lewis 3-63, Mularkey 1-6, Carter 2-47, Jordan 5-65, Rice 2-16, D. Nelson 1-9.

Kickoff Returns—Washington, Sanders 1-36, Verdin 4-68, Branch 1-12; Minnesota, D. Nelson 2-31, Guggemos 2-32.

Punt Returns—Washington, Green 2-18; Minnesota, Lewis 1-2.

Interceptions—Washington, Walton 1-28, Wilburn 1-100; Minnesota, Holt 1-7, Henderson 1-16, Howard 1-1, Browner 1-15.

Punting—Washington, Cox 2-37.0; Minnesota, Scribner 4-40.0.

Field Goals—Washington, Haji-Sheikh 2-4 (missed: 35, 33); Minnesota, C. Nelson 1-2 (missed: 51).

Sacks—Washington, Olkewicz, Mann 1½, Manley 1½; Minnesota, Millard.

Packers-Saints
SUNDAY, DECEMBER 27
SCORE BY PERIODS

Green Bay	14	3	7	0—24
New Orleans	9	3	14	7—33

SCORING
New Orleans—Field goal Andersen 31, 1:02 1st.
Green Bay—Stanley 29 pass from Majkowski (Zendejas kick), 3:20 1st.
Green Bay—Stanley 39 pass from Majkowski (Zendejas kick), 4:18 1st.
New Orleans—Field goal Andersen 52, 6:50 1st.
New Orleans—Field goal Andersen 48, 11:27 1st.
Green Bay—Field goal Zendejas 24, 0:49 2nd.
New Orleans—Field goal Andersen 32, 7:29 2nd.
New Orleans—Mayes 3 run (Andersen kick), 6:45 3rd.
Green Bay—Epps 20 pass from Majkowski (Zendejas kick), 12:25 3rd.
New Orleans—Tice 5 pass from Hebert (Andersen kick), 13:33 3rd.
New Orleans—Hilliard 1 run (Andersen kick), 8:24 4th.

TEAM STATISTICS

	Green Bay	New Orleans
First downs	17	22
Rushes-Yards	28-123	39-144
Passing yards	207	148
Sacked-Yards lost	1-12	2-12
3rd down eff.	3-10	5-12
Passes	14-29-1	16-24-1
Punts	5-45.6	3-39.7
Fumbles-Lost	2-2	3-3
Penalties-Yards	10-86	6-75
Time of possession	24:55	35:05
Attendance—68,364.		

INDIVIDUAL STATISTICS

Rushing—Green Bay, Majkowski 4-54, Davis 11-32, Clark 5-23, Fullwood 4-14, Carruth 3-10, Stanley 1-minus-10; New Orleans, Mayes 18-53, Word 7-27, Hilliard 11-42, Jordan 1-5, Hebert 2-17.

Passing—Green Bay, Majkowski 14-29-1—219; New Orleans, Hebert 16-23-1—160, Wilson 0-1-0—0.

Receiving—Green Bay, Stanley 4-109, Clark 1-11, Epps 5-44, Neal 2-31, Carruth 1-12, Davis 1-12; New Orleans, Jones 1-6, Hill 2-28, Benson 1-6, Hilliard 2-7, Brenner 2-30, Pattison 2-19, Mayes 2-16, Martin 2-25, Tice 2-23.

Kickoff Returns—Green Bay, Fullwood 2-33; New Orleans, Gray 2-51, Jordan 1-16, Hilliard 2-91.

Punt Returns—Green Bay, Stanley 2-6; New Orleans, Gray 4-49.

Interceptions—Green Bay, Anderson 1-13; New Orleans, Swilling 1-10.

Punting—Green Bay, Bracken 5-45.6; New Orleans, Hansen 3-39.7.

Field Goals—Green Bay, Zendejas 1-1; New Orleans, Andersen 4-4.

Sacks—Green Bay, Carreker, Boyarsky; New Orleans, Maxie.

Buccaneers-Colts
SUNDAY, DECEMBER 27
SCORE BY PERIODS

Tampa Bay	3	0	0	3— 6
Indianapolis	7	3	7	7—24

SCORING

Indianapolis—Dickerson 6 run (Biasucci kick), 3:17 1st.
Tampa Bay—Field goal Igwebuike 38, 10:58 1st.
Indianapolis—Field goal Biasucci 30, 14:52 2nd.
Indianapolis—Dickerson 34 run (Biasucci kick), 9:21 3rd.
Tampa Bay—Field goal Igwebuike 37, 3:11 4th.
Indianapolis—Bentley 2 run (Biasucci kick), 7:06 4th.

TEAM STATISTICS

	Tampa Bay	Indianapolis
First downs	10	23
Rushes-Yards	21-96	45-226
Passing yards	136	246
Sacked-Yards lost	3-27	0-0
3rd down eff.	6-16	9-16
Passes	8-32-1	17-27-0
Punts	7-38.4	5-42.2
Fumbles-Lost	1-0	4-1
Penalties-Yards	5-45	10-61
Time of possession	20:16	39:44
Attendance—60,468.		

INDIVIDUAL STATISTICS

Rushing—Tampa Bay, Wilder 7-45, Smith 9-27, Testaverde 4-12, Howard 1-12; Indianapolis, Dickerson 33-196, Brooks 1-1, Trudeau 4-minus 1, Bentley 4-10, Wonsley 3-20.

Passing—Tampa Bay, Testaverde 8-31-0—163, Bartalo 0-1-1—0; Indianapolis, Trudeau 17-27-0—246.

Receiving—Tampa Bay, Hill 3-96, Taylor 2-21, Wilder 1-7, Smith 1-8, Miller 1-31; Indianapolis, Bentley 2-69, Dickerson 2-33, Boyer 2-12, Bouza 4-82, Brooks 5-51, Beach 1-3, Utt 1-minus 4.

Kickoff Returns—Tampa Bay, Futrell 3-42, Bartalo 1-

15, Smith 1-21; Indianapolis, Bentley 3-70.

Punt Returns—Tampa Bay, Futrell 3-33; Indianapolis, Ahrens 1-0, Tullis 1-10.

Interceptions—Indianapolis, Prior 1-0.

Punting—Tampa Bay, Garcia 7-38.4; Indianapolis, Stark 5-42.2.

Field Goals—Tampa Bay, Igwebuike 2-3 (missed: 47); Indianapolis, Biasucci 1-1.

Sacks—Indianapolis, Bickett, Thompson, Darby.

Jets-Giants
SUNDAY, DECEMBER 27
SCORE BY PERIODS

New York Jets	7	0	0	0— 7
New York Giants	0	17	3	0—20

SCORING

Jets—Hector 14 run (Leahy kick), 12:09 1st.
Giants—Field goal Allegre 29, 0:44 2nd.
Giants—Bavaro 12 pass from Simms (Allegre kick), 9:51 2nd.
Giants—Turner 16 pass from Simms (Allegre kick), 14:52 2nd.
Giants—Field goal Allegre 23, 12:22 3rd.

TEAM STATISTICS

	Jets	Giants
First downs	13	23
Rushes-Yards	24-68	39-156
Passing yards	166	264
Sacked-Yards lost	3-26	0-0
3rd down eff.	5-15	5-16
Passes	20-36-0	20-40-0
Punts	6-39.0	4-44.3
Fumbles-Lost	1-0	0-0
Penalties-Yards	6-35	3-35
Time of possession	25:06	34:54
Attendance—68,318.		

INDIVIDUAL STATISTICS

Rushing—Jets, Hector 16-46, O'Brien 2-2, Jennings 1-1, Vick 5-19; Giants, Simms 2-minus 2, Morris 26-132, Galbreath 1-3, Carthon 2-10, Rouson 6-11, Rutledge 1-2, Adams 1-0.

Passing—Jets, O'Brien 19-34-0—185, Ryan 1-2-0—7; Giants, Simms 20-39-0—264, Rutledge 0-1-0—0.

Receiving—Jets, Hector 6-34, Vick 4-45, Toon 3-35, Shuler 2-15, Sohn 4-58, Klever 1-5; Giants, McConkey 1-22, Morris 1-9, Galbreath 3-30, Bavaro 6-109, Carthon 3-22, Rouson 1-9, Turner 3-51, Adams 2-12.

Kickoff Returns—Jets, Martin 3-80, Klever 1-17, Sohn 1-13; Giants, Ingram 1-25, Rouson 1-25.

Punt Returns—Jets, Townsell 2-15, Sohn 1-6; Giants, McConkey 3-20.

Interceptions—None.

Punting—Jets, Jennings 6-39.0; Giants, Landeta 4-44.3.

Field Goals—Jets, Leahy 0-1 (missed: 38); Giants, Allegre 2-4 (missed: 22, 48).

Sacks—Giants, Howard, Banks, Headen.

Bengals-Oilers
SUNDAY, DECEMBER 27
SCORE BY PERIODS

Cincinnati	7	0	7	3—17
Houston	7	14	0	0—21

SCORING

Cincinnati—Jennings 1 run (Breech kick), 3:14 1st.
Houston—Highsmith 33 pass from Moon (Zendejas kick), 7:13 1st.
Houston—Moon 1 run (Zendejas kick), 1:22 2nd.
Houston—Highsmith 1 run (Zendejas kick), 12:47 2nd.
Cincinnati—Martin 25 pass from Esiason (Breech kick), 12:36 3rd.
Cincinnati—Field goal Breech 43, 1:59 4th.

TEAM STATISTICS

	Cincinnati	Houston
First downs	16	25
Rushes-Yards	26-92	36-194
Passing yards	267	267
Sacked-Yards lost	2-3	3-13
3rd down eff	3-15	2-9
Passes	19-38-2	14-25-2
Punts	5-39.8	4-39.5
Fumbles-Lost	0-0	1-1
Penalties-Yards	4-35	8-50
Time of possession	28:04	31:56

Attendance—49,275.

INDIVIDUAL STATISTICS

Rushing—Cincinnati, Brooks 13-43, Johnson 7-25, Jennings 4-7, Esiason 2-17; Houston, Rozier 20-103, Pinkett 4-31, Moon 3-minus 1, Highsmith 9-61.

Passing—Cincinnati, Esiason 19-38-2—270; Houston, Moon 14-25-2—280.

Receiving—Cincinnati, Johnson 3-19, Brown 2-22, Collinsworth 4-119, Brooks 2-9, Jennings 1-5, Holman 2-16, Martin 5-80; Houston, Givins 4-93, Highsmith 1-33, D. Hill 6-109, Rozier 1-15, J. Williams 2-30.

Kickoff Returns—Cincinnati, Bussey 1-22, Brooks 2-42; Houston, Valentine 1-13, Pinkett 1-20.

Punt Returns—Cincinnati, Martin 1-7; Houston, K. Johnson 4-36.

Interceptions—Cincinnati, Breeden 1-5, Wilcox 1-37; Houston, Allen 1-37, Brown 1-10.

Punting—Cincinnati, Fulhage 5-39.8; Houston, Gossett 4-39.5.

Field Goals—Cincinnati, Breech 1-1; Houston, Zendejas 0-1 (missed: 42).

Sacks—Cincinnati, King 2, Skow ½, Krumrie ½; Houston, Meads, Childress.

Cardinals-Cowboys
SUNDAY, DECEMBER 27
SCORE BY PERIODS

St. Louis	3	7	0	6—16
Dallas	0	14	0	7—21

SCORING

St. Louis—Field goal Del Greco 32, 5:04 1st.
Dallas—Walker 11 run (Ruzek kick), 0:03 2nd.
Dallas—Walker 11 run (Ruzek kick), 13:06 2nd.
St. Louis—J.T. Smith 2 pass from Lomax (Del Greco kick), 14:40 2nd.
St. Louis—Field goal Del Greco 28, 2:46 4th.
Dallas—Pelluer 5 run (Ruzek kick), 4:47 4th.
St. Louis—Field goal Del Greco 37, 9:27 4th.

TEAM STATISTICS

	St. Louis	Dallas
First downs	26	17
Rushes-Yards	30-126	34-163
Passing yards	296	122
Sacked-Yards lost	3-18	0-0
3rd down eff	8-18	3-12
Passes	28-55-1	10-22-0
Punts	4-39.5	7-35.4
Fumbles-Lost	1-1	0-0
Penalties-Yards	7-65	9-55
Time of possession	33:45	26:15

Attendance—36,788.

INDIVIDUAL STATISTICS

Rushing—St. Louis, Mitchell 22-91, Lomax 2-14, McAdoo 3-11, Wolfley 3-10; Dallas, Walker 25-137, Pelluer 7-2, Newsome 2-4.

Passing—St. Louis, Lomax 28-54-1—314, Mitchell 0-1-0—0; Dallas, Pelluer 10-22-0—122.

Receiving—St. Louis, J.T. Smith 11-102, Green 7-112, Novacek 4-42, Wolfley 3-14, Mitchell 2-30, T. Johnson 1-14; Dallas, Walker 3-50, Edwards 2-41, Renfro 2-13, Chandler 1-9, Newsome 1-5, Cosbie 1-4.

Kickoff Returns—St. Louis, Sikahema 3-56, McAdoo 1-

22; Dallas, Clack 3-39, Martin 3-34.

Punt Returns—St. Louis, Sikahema 3-31; Dallas, Martin 3-34.

Interceptions—Dallas, Walls 1-30.

Punting—St. Louis, Horne 4-39.5; Dallas, Saxon 7-35.4.

Field Goals—St. Louis, Del Greco 3-3; Dallas, none attempted.

Sacks—Dallas, Noonan, Jeffcoat 2.

Chargers-Broncos
SUNDAY, DECEMBER 27
SCORE BY PERIODS

San Diego	0	0	0	0— 0
Denver	14	0	0	10—24

SCORING

Denver—Clark 71 punt return (Karlis kick), 1:50 1st.
Denver—Winder 1 run (Karlis kick), 13:55 1st.
Denver—Field goal Karlis 26, 3:50 4th.
Denver—Hunley 52 interception return (Karlis kick), 5:00 4th.

TEAM STATISTICS

	San Diego	Denver
First downs	7	15
Rushes-Yards	21-43	40-129
Passing yards	108	86
Sacked-Yards lost	2-23	2-12
3rd down eff	1-12	6-17
Passes	16-29-5	7-24-3
Punts	8-44.8	4-44.0
Fumbles-Lost	3-0	1-1
Penalties-Yards	4-38	2-10
Time of possession	25:26	34:34

Attendance—21,189.

INDIVIDUAL STATISTICS

Rushing—San Diego, Spencer 11-25, Redden 1-3, Adams 6-18, James 1-minus 3, Herrmann 2-0; Denver, Winder 23-67, Elway 5-24, Lang 7-23, Bell 5-15.

Passing—San Diego, Herrmann 13-23-4—123, Vlasic 3-6-1—8; Denver, Elway 7-20-1—98, Kubiak 0-4-2—0.

Receiving—San Diego, Winslow 6-44, Spencer 1-2, Holland 3-64, Anderson 3-7, Redden 2-13, Bernstine 1-1; Denver, Winder 1-2, Nattiel 2-24, Watson 1-15, Mobley 2-35, Kay 1-22.

Kickoff Returns—San Diego, Holland 3-85, Kirk 2-15.

Punt Returns—San Diego, James 3-33; Denver, Lilly 2-6, Clark 6-144.

Interceptions—San Diego, Smith 2-23, Glenn 1-18; Denver, Ryan 1-1, Harden 2-46, Hunley 2-64.

Punting—San Diego, Mojsiejenko 8-44.8; Denver, Horan 4-44.0.

Field Goals—San Diego, Abbott 0-1 (missed: 26); Denver, Karlis 1-2 (missed: 35).

Sacks—San Diego, Hunter, Williams; Denver, Jones, Mecklenburg.

Rams-49ers
SUNDAY, DECEMBER 27
SCORE BY PERIODS

Los Angeles Rams	0	0	0	0— 0
San Francisco	13	14	7	14—48

SCORING

San Francisco—Craig 1 run (kick failed), 5:49 1st.
San Francisco—Rice 22 pass from Young (Wersching kick), 12:03 1st.
San Francisco—Rice 50 pass from Young (Wersching kick), 2:55 2nd.
San Francisco—Wilson 7 pass from Young (Wersching kick), 9:02 2nd.
San Francisco—Frank 11 pass from Montana (Wersching kick), 9:13 3rd.
San Francisco—Wilson 46 pass from Montana (Wersching kick), 0:18 4th.

San Francisco—Taylor 26 fumble return (Wersching kick), 11:49 4th.

TEAM STATISTICS

	Los Angeles	San Francisco
First downs	9	23
Rushes-Yards	31-121	40-149
Passing yards	24	278
Sacked-Yards lost	3-26	1-3
3rd down eff.	1-12	6-11
Passes	6-18-1	16-22-0
Punts	7-43.7	5-38.6
Fumbles-Lost	2-1	2-0
Penalties-Yards	2-20	1-10
Time of possession	26:22	33:38
Attendance—57,950.		

INDIVIDUAL STATISTICS

Rushing—Los Angeles, White 21-95, Ron Brown 1-11, Evans 3-10, Francis 5-10, Dils 1-minus 5; San Francisco, Craig 15-56, Rathman 7-30, Young 4-29, Sydney 3-23, Cribbs 6-13, Frank 1-2, Montana 3-0, Rice 1-minus 4.

Passing—Los Angeles, Dils 5-17-1—50, Millen 1-1-0—0; San Francisco, Young 10-13-0—174, Montana 6-9-0—107.

Receiving—Los Angeles, Ellard 2-24, Ron Brown 2-22, Hill 1-4, Tyrrell 1-0; San Francisco, Frank 5-74, Rice 3-90, Wilson 2-53, Rathman 2-37, Craig 2-5, Cribbs 1-15, Margerum 1-7.

Kickoff Returns—Los Angeles, McDonald 1-5, Ron Brown 1-26, Tyrrell 3-77, Hicks 2-50; San Francisco, Rathman 1-21, Sydney 1-23.

Punt Returns—Los Angeles, Ellard 1-6, Hicks 1-26; San Francisco, McLemore 1-48.

Interceptions—San Francisco, Griffin 1-1.

Punting—Los Angeles, Hatcher 7-43.7; San Francisco, Runager 5-38.6.

Field Goals—None attempted.

Sacks—Los Angeles, Wilcher; San Francisco, Carter, Stover.

Bears-Raiders
SUNDAY, DECEMBER 27
SCORE BY PERIODS

Chicago	0	3	0	3—6
Los Angeles Raiders	3	0	0	0—3

SCORING

Los Angeles—Field goal Bahr 48, 14:58 1st.
Chicago—Field goal Butler 38, 6:36 2nd.
Chicago—Field goal Butler 30, 10:04 4th.

TEAM STATISTICS

	Chicago	Los Angeles
First downs	18	14
Rushes-Yards	35-121	26-101
Passing yards	146	92
Sacked-Yards lost	1-0	9-47
3rd down eff.	5-13	4-14
Passes	12-28-1	13-26-1
Punts	4-41.8	5-37.2
Fumbles-Lost	3-2	0-0
Penalties-Yards	5-30	4-41
Time of possession	31:12	28:48
Attendance—78,019.		

INDIVIDUAL STATISTICS

Rushing—Chicago, Payton 20-82, Suhey 6-22, Thomas 4-13, Tomczak 4-4, Harbaugh 1-0; Los Angeles, Allen 18-75, Mueller 3-11, Strachan 3-9, Wilson 2-6.

Passing—Chicago, Tomczak 12-27-0—146, Payton 0-1-1—0; Los Angeles, Wilson 13-26-1—139.

Receiving—Chicago, Gault 3-37, Morris 2-36, Payton 2-21, Gentry 2-7, Sanders 1-25, Moorehead 1-13, Suhey 1-7; Los Angeles, Allen 6-22, Christensen 4-54, Lofton 3-63.

Kickoff Returns—Chicago, Gentry 1-23, Sanders 1-6; Los Angeles, Adams 1-17, Mueller 2-45.

Punt Returns—Chicago, McKinnon 1-0; Los Angeles,

Woods 2-21.

Interceptions—Chicago, Douglass 1-0; Los Angeles, McElroy 1-0.

Punting—Chicago, Barnhardt 4-41.8; Los Angeles, Talley 5-37.2.

Field Goals—Chicago, Butler 2-2; Los Angeles, Bahr 1-3 (missed: 44, 46).

Sacks—Chicago, Dent 4½, Hampton 1½, McMichael 2, Duerson; Los Angeles, Townsend.

Bills-Eagles
SUNDAY, DECEMBER 27
SCORE BY PERIODS

Buffalo	0	0	0	7— 7
Philadelphia	0	10	7	0—17

SCORING

Philadelphia—Field goal McFadden 39, 6:09 2nd.
Philadelphia—Toney 18 pass from Cunningham (McFadden kick), 11:46 2nd.
Philadelphia—Toney 2 run (McFadden kick), 8:51 3rd.
Buffalo—Reed 4 pass from Kelly (Norwood kick), 8:07 4th.

TEAM STATISTICS

	Buffalo	Philadelphia
First downs	14	22
Rushes-Yards	14-57	52-210
Passing yards	154	134
Sacked-Yards lost	2-20	5-43
3rd down eff.	2-13	5-15
Passes	20-39-2	16-21-1
Punts	9-34.6	7-35.9
Fumbles-Lost	3-2	3-2
Penalties-Yards	5-40	7-64
Time of possession	19:28	40:32
Attendance—57,547.		

INDIVIDUAL STATISTICS

Rushing—Buffalo, Harmon 4-15, Mueller 7-33, R. Porter 3-9; Philadelphia, Byars 23-102, Toney 15-48, Cunningham 10-46, Jackson 2-10, Haddix 2-4.

Passing—Buffalo, Kelly 20-39-2—154; Philadelphia, Cunningham 16-21-1—177.

Receiving—Buffalo, Harmon 9-35, Burkett 4-50, Reed 5-46, Broughton 2-23; Philadelphia, Carter 1-10, Toney 5-46, Spagnola 3-24, Byars 2-37, Jackson 1-26, Quick 2-18, Garrity 1-13, Tautalatasi 1-3.

Kickoff Returns—Buffalo, Mueller 1-19, R. Porter 1-38; Philadelphia, Morse 1-14, Carter 1-19.

Punt Returns—Buffalo, Pitts 4-11; Philadelphia, Morse 1-0.

Interceptions—Buffalo, Radecic 1-4; Philadelphia, Evans 1-12, Waters 1-0.

Punting—Buffalo, Kidd 9-34.6; Philadelphia, Teltschik 7-35.9.

Field Goals—Buffalo, none attempted: Philadelphia, McFadden 1-1.

Sacks—Buffalo, Bennett 4, Smith; Philadelphia, White 2.

Seahawks-Chiefs
SUNDAY, DECEMBER 27
SCORE BY PERIODS

Seattle	7	13	0	0—20
Kansas City	17	10	7	7—41

SCORING

Kansas City—Heard 37 run (Lowery kick), 0:33 1st.
Seattle—Largent 15 pass from Krieg (N. Johnson kick), 4:29 1st.
Kansas City—Field goal Lowery 35, 10:00 1st.
Kansas City—Carson 81 pass from Kenney (Lowery kick), 12:06 1st.
Seattle—Skansi 8 pass from Krieg (N. Johnson kick), 0:49 2nd.
Kansas City—Palmer 92 kickoff return (Lowery kick), 1:07 2nd.

Seattle—Field goal N. Johnson 39, 4:58 2nd.
Seattle—Field goal N. Johnson 24, 13:10 2nd.
Kansas City—Field goal Lowery 44, 14:55 2nd.
Kansas City—Adickes 3 pass from Kenney (Lowery kick), 8:54 3rd.
Kansas City—Paige 46 pass from Kenney (Lowery kick), 1:14 4th.

TEAM STATISTICS

	Seattle	Kansas City
First downs	24	28
Rushes-Yards	29-169	32-199
Passing yards	195	313
Sacked-Yards lost	2-7	1-7
3rd down eff.	4-11	7-12
Passes	17-32-0	23-35-0
Punts	2-41.5	1-48.0
Fumbles-Lost	2-1	1-1
Penalties-Yards	4-20	6-51
Time of possession	28:52	31:08

Attendance—20,370.

INDIVIDUAL STATISTICS

Rushing—Seattle, Warner 15-85, J.L. Williams 10-40, Krieg 3-23, Largent 1-21; Kansas City, Heard 12-107, Okoye 12-63, Palmer 5-22, Moriarty 1-8, Seurer 1-1, Kenney 1-minus 2.

Passing—Seattle, Krieg 17-32-0—202; Kansas City, Kenney 23-35-0—320.

Receiving—Seattle, Largent 6-95, R. Butler 3-39, J.L. Williams 3-39, Tice 2-14, Skansi 2-12, Lane 1-12; Kansas City, Paige 7-100, Carson 4-120, Heard 4-34, Marshall 2-33, Hayes 2-18, Okoye 2-9, Palmer 1-3, Adickes 1-3.

Kickoff Returns—Seattle, Edmonds 4-85, Powell 1-0, Hollis 3-103; Kansas City, Moriarty 1-20, Palmer 3-133, Robinson 1-25.

Punt Returns—Seattle, Edmonds 1-23; Kansas City, Fields 1-6.

Interceptions—None.

Punting—Seattle, Rodriguez 2-41.5; Kansas City, Goodburn 1-48.0.

Field Goals—Seattle, N. Johnson 2-3 (missed: 32); Kansas City, Lowery 2-2.

Sacks—Seattle, Green; Kansas City, Maas 1½, Still ½.

Lions-Falcons
SUNDAY, DECEMBER 27
SCORE BY PERIODS

Detroit	7	3	10	10—30
Atlanta	0	13	0	0—13

SCORING

Detroit—Ellerson 8 run (Murray kick), 10:08 1st.
Atlanta—Field goal Luckhurst 50, 1:02 2nd.
Detroit—Field goal Murray 45, 2:46 2nd.
Atlanta—Dixon 51 pass from C. Miller (Luckhurst kick), 9:04 2nd.
Atlanta—Field goal Luckhurst 28, 14:18 2nd.
Detroit—Ellerson 2 run (Murray kick), 9:25 3rd.
Detroit—Field goal Murray 23, 12:18 3rd.
Detroit—Field goal Murray 36, 1:34 4th.
Detroit—Smith 34 interception return (Murray kick), 8:35 4th.

TEAM STATISTICS

	Detroit	Atlanta
First downs	18	14
Rushes-Yards	43-173	22-98
Passing yards	150	180
Sacked-Yards lost	1-7	2-16
3rd down eff.	5-16	3-13
Passes	11-25-2	16-36-4
Punts	3-36.3	4-44.5
Fumbles-Lost	0-0	2-1
Penalties-Yards	4-30	6-70
Time of possession	36:08	23:52

Attendance—13,906.

INDIVIDUAL STATISTICS

Rushing—Detroit, Ellerson 17-73, Jones 11-49, Woolfolk 5-19, James 6-15, Long 2-8, Paige 1-6, Mandley 1-3; Atlanta, Riggs 15-64, Flowers 5-35, C. Miller 1-5, Donnelly 1-minus 6.

Passing—Detroit, Long 11-24-2—157; Atlanta, C. Miller 16-36-4—196.

Receiving—Detroit, Lee 3-72, Jones 3-16, Ellerson 1-23, James 1-20, Woolfolk 1-13, Mandley 1-10, Paige 1-3; Atlanta, Dixon 4-87, Cox 3-27, Flowers 3-17, Matthews 1-21, Stamps 1-19, Bailey 1-8, Riggs 1-6, Johnson 1-6, Settle 1-5.

Kickoff Returns—Detroit, Woolfolk 2-50, Lee 2-55; Atlanta, Settle 6-101, Cox 1-11.

Punt Returns—Detroit, Mandley 2-16; Atlanta, Johnson 1-6.

Interceptions—Detroit, Griffin 1-7, Cherry 1-0, Smith 1-34, J. Williams 1-3; Atlanta, Gordon 1-27, Croudip 1-0, Britt 0-minus 5.

Punting—Detroit, Arnold 2-35.0, Murray 1-39.0; Atlanta, Donnelly 4-44.5.

Field Goals—Detroit, Murray 3-4 (missed: 37); Atlanta, Luckhurst 2-3 (missed: 41).

Sacks—Detroit, J. Williams, Green; Atlanta, Bryan.

Patriots-Dolphins
MONDAY, DECEMBER 28
SCORE BY PERIODS

New England	14	10	0	0—24
Miami	3	0	0	7—10

SCORING

New England—Fryar 3 pass from Grogan (Franklin kick), 4:10 1st.
Miami—Field goal Reveiz 47, 6:24 1st.
New England—Starring 34 pass from Grogan (Franklin kick), 11:52 1st.
New England—Collins 5 run (Franklin kick), 5:50 2nd.
New England—Field goal Franklin 31, 14:38 2nd.
Miami—Pruitt 9 pass from Marino (Reveiz kick), 2:45 4th.

TEAM STATISTICS

	New England	Miami
First downs	25	17
Rushes-Yards	44-138	16-54
Passing yards	238	243
Sacked-Yards lost	0-0	0-0
3rd down eff.	10-15	4-11
Passes	21-32-0	21-37-2
Punts	4-36.5	3-41.7
Fumbles-Lost	1-1	5-2
Penalties-Yards	4-42	4-25
Time of possession	37:48	22:12

Attendance—61,192.

INDIVIDUAL STATISTICS

Rushing—New England, Dupard 15-44, Perryman 15-52, Collins 3-16, Tatupu 4-12, Fryar 2-4, Starring 2-13, Grogan 3-minus 3; Miami, Stradford 9-27, Davenport 4-24, Hampton 1-3, Marino 2-0.

Passing—New England, Grogan 21-32-0—238; Miami, Marino 21-37-2—243.

Receiving—New England, Perryman 1-5, C. Jones 5-68, Fryar 6-70, Collins 4-30, Starring 2-53, D. Williams 1-9, Tatupu 1-5, Dupard 1-minus 2; Miami, Stradford 2-9, Hampton 1-13, Hardy 6-69, Clayton 3-22, Duper 1-24, Davenport 2-35, Pruitt 4-48, Jensen 2-23.

Kickoff Returns—New England, Starring 2-37; Miami, Hardy 1-15, Hampton 4-71.

Punt Returns—New England, Fryar 1-0; Miami, Schwedes 2-8.

Interceptions—New England, Gibson 1-17, Marion 1-0.

Punting—New England, Camarillo 4-36.5; Miami, Roby 3-41.7.

Field Goals—New England, Franklin 1-1; Miami, Reveiz 1-1.

Sacks—None.

DIVISIONAL PLAYOFFS AND CONFERENCE CHAMPIONSHIP GAMES

WILD-CARD GAMES

VIKINGS 44, SAINTS 10

NEW ORLEANS—The atmosphere in the Louisiana Superdome prior to the National Football Conference wild-card game between the New Orleans Saints and Minnesota Vikings more closely resembled a Super Bowl victory celebration than the 1987 season's first post-season game.

A crowd of 68,127, packing the Superdome for the 21-year-old Saints' first-ever playoff game, was screaming a good half hour before the opening kickoff. The consensus feeling was that the Saints, riding the crest of a nine-game winning streak, would easily dispose of a Vikings team that had lost three of its final four regular-season games.

What transpired in the next couple of hours, however, brought the Saints and their giddy fans back to earth—quickly. The Vikings won, 44-10, in the biggest blowout in the 10-year history of wild-card games. The Saints, who could do little wrong during a 12-3 regular season, did little right in their biggest game of the year.

"We learned we're not good enough," said nose tackle Tony Elliott. "We learned a lesson that the level of a playoff game cannot be misinterpreted as the same as a regular-season game. You've got to turn up your game another notch, and we didn't. It's a shame we had to pick this week to be terrible."

The Saints actually scored first, taking a 7-0 lead just 1:23 into the contest when quarterback Bobby Hebert and wide receiver Eric Martin combined on a 10-yard touchdown pass. The score came just two plays after New Orleans linebacker Rickey Jackson recovered a fumble by Vikings quarterback Tommy Kramer on the Minnesota 11-yard line.

An already-loud Superdome crowd got even louder.

But the noise subsided somewhat when Chuck Nelson kicked a 42-yard field goal for Minnesota's first points seven minutes into the game. And the Superdome got eerily quiet five minutes after that when the Vikings' Anthony Carter—who returned only three punts all season—returned a Brian Hansen punt 84 yards for a touchdown and a 10-7 Minnesota lead. Carter's return was the longest in NFL playoff history.

"This was a one-game shootout, and A.C. is a big-play guy," said Vikings Coach Jerry Burns. "He's got nerves of steel." Carter returned six punts for 143 yards and caught six passes for 79 yards.

The play that really broke the Saints' back, however, came on the final play before half-

The Vikings never trailed after Anthony Carter's NFL-record 84-yard punt return touchdown gave Minnesota a 10-7 first-quarter lead.

time. New Orleans was penalized for having 12 defenders on the field and the Vikings were given another play from the Saints' 44-yard line. Quarterback Wade Wilson threw a Hail Mary pass into the end zone that wide receiver Hassan Jones somehow caught with six New Orleans defenders in the area. The touchdown gave the Vikings a commanding 31-10 lead at the intermission.

"We really hadn't thought about it (a Hail Mary pass)," Burns said. "Then, when we got another chance on that last-second penalty, we decided, 'Why not?'"

The Saints' inability to stop the Vikings (28 first downs, 417 total yards) was matched by the inability of the New Orleans offense to move the ball. The Saints committed six turnovers and ran the ball on only 14 offensive plays, just eight times after star running back Rueben Mayes left in the second quarter with sprained ligaments in his right knee. They rushed for a total of 53 yards.

New Orleans led all teams with a 34:01 time-of-possession average during the regular season, but held the ball for just 18:42 against the Vikings.

"Things that went our way all season bounced the other way," said New Orleans offensive tackle Stan Brock. "A lot of dreams were riding on this game, and they were all shattered and shattered big today. It's hard to be upbeat now. Maybe a few weeks from now, I'll get over this."

Vikings-Saints
SUNDAY, JANUARY 3
SCORE BY PERIODS

Minnesota	10	21	3	10—44
New Orleans	7	3	0	0—10

SCORING

New Orleans—Martin 10 pass from Hebert (Andersen kick), 1:23 1st. Drive: 11 yards, 2 plays.

Minnesota—Field goal C. Nelson 42, 6:59 1st. Drive: 2 yards, 4 plays.

Minnesota—Carter 84 punt return (C. Nelson kick), 11:57 1st.

Minnesota—Jordan 5 pass from Wilson (C. Nelson kick), 3:19 2nd. Drive: 65 yards, 10 plays.

Minnesota—Carter 10 pass from Rice (C. Nelson kick), 8:50 2nd. Drive: 54 yards, 7 plays.

New Orleans—Field goal Andersen 40, 11:54 2nd. Drive: 40 yards, 8 plays.

Minnesota—Jones 44 pass from Wilson (C. Nelson kick), 15:00 2nd. Drive: 35 yards, 3 plays.

Minnesota—Field goal C. Nelson 32, 13:45 3rd. Drive: 68 yards, 11 plays.

Minnesota—Field goal C. Nelson 19, 7:46 4th. Drive: 54 yards, 13 plays.

Minnesota—Dozier 8 run (C. Nelson kick), 13:14 4th. Drive: 60 yards, 10 plays.

TEAM STATISTICS

	Minnesota	New Orleans
FIRST DOWNS	28	9
By rushing	14	0
By passing	14	7
By penalty	0	2
THIRD DOWN EFFICIENCY	12-19	2-10
TOTAL NET YARDS	417	149
Offensive plays	86	47
Average gain per play	4.8	3.2
NET YARDS RUSHING	210	53
Total rushes	50	14
Average gain per rush	4.2	3.8
NET YARDS PASSING	207	96
Sacked-Yards lost	6-42	2-8
Gross yards passing	249	104
PASSES	17-30-0	11-31-4
Average gain per pass	6.9	3.2
PUNTS	3-32.0	6-44.2
Had blocked	0	0
TOTAL RETURN YARDAGE	188	101
Punt returns	6-143	1-0
Kickoff returns	0-0	7-101
Interception returns	4-45	0-0
PENALTIES-YARDS	5-42	4-26
FUMBLES-LOST	4-2	3-2
TIME OF POSSESSION	41:18	18:42
Attendance—68,127.		

INDIVIDUAL STATISTICS

Rushing—Minnesota, D. Nelson 17-73, Kramer 2-5, Wil-son 2-5, Fenney 7-20, Dozier 8-45, Anderson 7-49, Rice 4-10, Gannon 3-3; New Orleans, Hebert 2-2, Jordan 1-1, Mayes 3-11, Hilliard 8-39.

Passing—Minnesota, Kramer 5-9-0—50, Wilson 11-20-0—189, Rice 1-1-0—10; New Orleans, Hebert 9-19-2—84, Wilson 2-12-2—20.

Receiving—Minnesota, Lewis 2-27, Rice 2-17, Gustafson 1-12, Carter 6-79, D. Nelson 2-56, Jordan 2-17, Anderson 1-minus 3, Jones 1-44; New Orleans, Martin 1-10; Pattison 2-18, Brenner 2-33, Hill 2-15, Hilliard 2-15, Tice 2-13.

Kickoff Returns—New Orleans, Word 4-53, Gray 1-16, Adams 1-19, Brock 1-13.

Punt Returns—Minnesota, Carter 6-143; New Orleans, Gray 1-0.

Interceptions—Minnesota, Holt 1-0, Harris 1-15, Rutland 1-0, Freeman 1-30.

Punting—Minnesota, Scribner 3-32.0; New Orleans, Hansen 6-44.2.

Field Goals—Minnesota, C. Nelson 3-3; New Orleans, Andersen 1-1.

Sacks—Minnesota, Millard, Doleman; New Orleans, Clark ½, Wilks ½, Elliott, Jackson, Swilling, Warren.

OILERS 23, SEAHAWKS 20 (OT)

HOUSTON—An old adage says that liars figure and figures lie. When it comes to the figures, or statistics, compiled by the Houston Oilers and Seattle Seahawks in the 1987 American Football Conference wild-card game, the figures lied.

The Oilers, who were playing in postseason competition for the first time since 1980, led the Seahawks in first downs (27-11), total yards (437-250) and time of possession (47:44 to 20:21). But it took a 42-yard field goal by Tony Zendejas more than eight minutes into overtime to give the Oilers their first playoff victory in eight years.

"We just didn't move the ball effectively, but we still had a chance to win the game," said Seattle wide receiver Steve Largent. "That would have been a grave injustice to the way the Oilers played. Their defense did a good job of stopping us, and their offense moved up and down the field."

At times, though, it looked as if the Oilers were trying to give the game away. They led, 20-13, with 1:47 left in regulation when Zendejas hit the left upright with a 29-yard field-goal attempt that would have given them a 10-point lead. Instead, the Seahawks, who were forced to play without injured star running back Curt Warner, drove 80 yards in 10 plays to force the overtime on Dave Krieg's 12-yard touchdown pass to Largent with 26 seconds left.

In the overtime, the Seahawks had to punt after three downs and the Oilers had a first down at their own 37-yard line. Quarterback Warren Moon's first-down pass, however, was batted into the air by defensive end Jeff Bryant and appeared to have been intercepted by a diving Fredd Young. Head linesman Dale Hamer ruled it incomplete and instant-replay official Tony Veteri concurred.

"I was fortunate that one wasn't picked off," said Moon, who was intercepted by Melvin

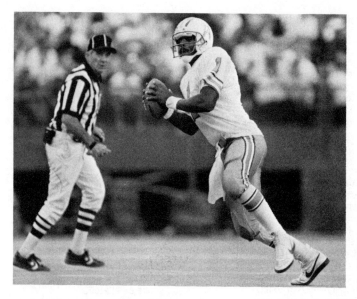

Warren Moon guided the Oilers to their first playoff victory in eight years.

Jenkins on Houston's first offensive play of the game to set up Seattle's first touchdown.

"I had it," said Young, Seattle's Pro Bowl linebacker. "There wasn't anything I could do but catch the ball. There was no possible way that ball hit the ground."

The officials disagreed, and the Oilers drove to the Seattle 24-yard line to give Zendejas a chance to redeem himself.

"I was grateful I got a second chance," said Zendejas, who kicked field goals of 47 and 49 yards in the first half. "After that horrible (29-yard) kick, I felt like I had let the whole team down. I didn't want Seattle to kick the winning field goal (in overtime) because it was all going to be on my shoulders. I would have blamed myself, and everyone would have blamed me."

Seahawks-Oilers
SUNDAY, JANUARY 3
SCORE BY PERIODS

Seattle	7	3	3	7	0—20
Houston	3	10	7	0	3—23

SCORING

Seattle—Largent 20 pass from Krieg (N. Johnson kick), 3:16 1st. Drive: 54 yards, 3 plays.

Houston—Field goal Zendejas 47, 10:16 1st. Drive: 51 yards, 11 plays.

Houston—Rozier 1 run (Zendejas kick), 1:43 2nd. Drive: 52 yards, 9 plays.

Houston—Field goal Zendejas 49, 8:11 2nd. Drive: 27 yards, 7 plays.

Seattle—Field goal N. Johnson 33, 11:50 2nd. Drive: 4 yards, 4 plays.

Seattle—Field goal N. Johnson 41, 6:37 3rd. Drive: 16 yards, 6 plays.

Houston—Drewrey 29 pass from Moon (Zendejas kick), 12:26 3rd. Drive: 84 yards, 9 plays.

Seattle—Largent 12 pass from Krieg (N. Johnson kick), 14:34 4th. Drive: 80 yards, 10 plays.

Houston—Field goal Zendejas 42, 8:05 OT. Drive: 61 yards, 12 plays.

TEAM STATISTICS

	Seattle	Houston
FIRST DOWNS	11	27
By rushing	1	9
By passing	10	18
By penalty	0	0
THIRD DOWN EFFICIENCY	2-12	10-18
TOTAL NET YARDS	250	437
Offensive plays	52	84
Average gain per play	4.8	5.2
NET YARDS RUSHING	29	178
Total rushes	11	50
Average gain per rush	2.6	3.6
NET YARDS PASSING	221	259
Sacked-Yards lost	2-16	2-14
Gross yards passing	237	273
PASSES	16-39-0	21-32-1
Average gain per pass	5.3	7.6
PUNTS	7-44.3	3-35.0
Had blocked	0	0
TOTAL RETURN YARDAGE	226	92
Punt returns	2-66	4-27
Kickoff returns	6-132	4-65
Interception returns	1-28	0-0
PENALTIES-YARDS	3-20	4-25
FUMBLES-LOST	1-1	2-1
TIME OF POSSESSION	20:21	47:44
Attendance—49,622.		

INDIVIDUAL STATISTICS

Rushing—Seattle, J.L. Williams 7-27, Morris 4-2; Houston, Rozier 21-66, Highsmith 12-74, Pinkett 11-29, Moon 4-minus 2, Wallace 2-11.

Passing—Seattle, Krieg 16-38-0—237, J.L. Williams 0-1-0—0; Houston, Moon 21-32-1—273.

Receiving—Seattle, Largent 7-132, Butler 3-73, J.L. Williams 2-5, Skansi 2-13, Morris 1-6, Tice 1-8; Houston, Rozier 1-7, D. Hill 6-84, Givins 7-89, Pinkett 1-3, Highsmith 2-17, Drewrey 3-62, Wallace 1-11.

Kickoff Returns—Seattle, Edmonds 5-109, Hollis 1-23; Houston, Pinkett 4-65.

Punt Returns—Seattle, Edmonds 2-66; Houston, K. Johnson 4-27.

Interceptions—Seattle, Jenkins 1-28.

Punting—Seattle, Rodriguez 7-44.3; Houston, Gossett 3-35.0.

Field Goals—Seattle, N. Johnson 2-2; Houston, Zendejas 3-5 (missed: 52, 29).

Sacks—Seattle, Gaines, Bryant; Houston, Childress, Meads ½, Lyles ½.

DIVISIONAL PLAYOFF GAMES

BROWNS 38, COLTS 21

CLEVELAND—Revenge can be a great motivator, whether it's in everyday life or the National Football League.

When the Indianapolis Colts upset the Cleveland Browns, 9-7, in Week 13 of the regular season, it marked the first time in 25 years that a Colts team had won a game at Cleveland Stadium. The Colts' victory was aided by running back Earnest Byner's fumble at the Indianapolis 4-yard line in the final period just as Cleveland appeared certain to take the lead. Instead, Mike Prior recovered for the Colts in the end zone and the Browns never threatened again.

As fate would have it, the two teams met again five weeks later in the same stadium in an American Football Conference playoff game. The Browns won this time, 38-21, as Byner rushed 23 times for 122 yards, caught four passes for 36 more and scored two touchdowns. The 100-yard rushing performance was the first in two years for Byner, who stepped into a huge void created when running mate Kevin Mack was forced out of the game with a stomach virus after Cleveland's first possession of the day.

"I sensed all week that Earnest Byner was going to have a big game," said Browns Coach Marty Schottenheimer. "You'd have to ask him why."

"I probably worked harder this past week than I have in a long time," said Byner. "I just decided to be the best that I could be. I'm not exactly sure why."

Byner's second touchdown, a two-yard run late in the third quarter, gave the Browns a 21-14 lead—one they never relinquished. It capped a 13-play, 86-yard drive after a crucial Indianapolis turnover.

The score was tied, 14-14, at the half when the Colts took the second-half kickoff and began a methodical march downfield. On the 12th play of the drive, with the ball on the Cleveland 20-yard line, Colts quarterback Jack Trudeau dropped back to pass. As he did, Browns linebackers Mike Johnson and Eddie Johnson blitzed. Mike Johnson was blocked by running back Eric Dickerson, but Eddie Johnson blasted Trudeau as he released the ball. The ball floated to Browns free safety Felix Wright, who grabbed it at the 14. Eighty-six yards later, the Browns had the lead.

"It was one of those things that's a nightmare for quarterbacks," said Trudeau, who had thrown two touchdown passes in the first half. "I was trying to throw the ball out of bounds, but right as I released the ball, he (Eddie Johnson) hit my arm.

"The momentum swing was really bad."

Indianapolis was unable to make a first down on either of its next two possessions.

Cleveland, meanwhile, scored 10 more points in the same span to take a commanding 31-14 lead. The Browns, who won the AFC Central Division title for the third straight year, were successful on 11 of 14 third-down conversion attempts and punted only once.

"We wanted the Colts because of what they did to us before," said Browns defensive end Sam Clancy. "That motivated us. We thought then we were the better team, and today we were."

The Browns' victory earned them a rematch with the Denver Broncos in the AFC championship game. The Broncos beat the Browns, 23-20 in overtime, in the 1986 title game.

"We're only four quarters away from the Super Bowl," said veteran Cleveland tight end Ozzie Newsome. "Maybe five."

Colts-Browns
SATURDAY, JANUARY 9
SCORE BY PERIODS

Indianapolis	7	7	0	7—	21
Cleveland	7	7	7	17—	38

SCORING

Cleveland—Byner 10 pass from Kosar (Bahr kick), 6:46 1st. Drive: 86 yards, 15 plays.

Indianapolis—Beach 2 pass from Trudeau (Biasucci kick), 12:44 1st. Drive: 74 yards, 10 plays.

Cleveland—Langhorne 39 pass from Kosar (Bahr kick), 13:09 2nd. Drive: 66 yards, 6 plays.

Indianapolis—Dickerson 19 pass from Trudeau (Biasucci kick), 14:18 2nd. Drive: 59 yards, 7 plays.

Cleveland—Byner 2 run (Bahr kick), 13:04 3rd. Drive: 86 yards, 13 plays.

Cleveland—Field goal Bahr 22, 3:51 4th. Drive: 43 yards, 8 plays.

Cleveland—Brennan 2 pass from Kosar (Bahr kick), 11:16 4th. Drive: 68 yards, 8 plays.

Indianapolis—Bentley 1 run (Biasucci kick), 13:53 4th. Drive: 82 yards, 10 plays.

Cleveland—Minnifield 48 interception return (Bahr kick), 14:21 4th.

TEAM STATISTICS

	Indianapolis	Cleveland
FIRST DOWNS	23	25
By rushing	4	10
By passing	16	13
By penalty	3	2
THIRD DOWN EFFICIENCY	7-12	11-14
TOTAL NET YARDS	315	404
Offensive plays	62	65
Average gain per play	5.1	6.2
NET YARDS RUSHING	63	175
Total rushes	21	34
Average gain per rush	3.0	5.1
NET YARDS PASSING	252	229
Sacked-Yards lost	2-14	0-0
Gross yards passing	266	229
PASSES	22-39-2	20-31-1
Average gain per pass	6.1	7.4
PUNTS	4-43.8	1-37.0
Had blocked	0	0
TOTAL RETURN YARDAGE	124	101
Punt returns	0-0	3-32
Kickoff returns	7-124	2-21
Interception returns	1-0	2-48
PENALTIES-YARDS	7-75	4-20
FUMBLES-LOST	1-0	2-0
TIME OF POSSESSION	27:34	32:26
Attendance—78,586.		

Earnest Byner exploded for 122 yards rushing and scored twice to lead the Cleveland Browns to a 38-21 victory over Indianapolis.

INDIVIDUAL STATISTICS

Rushing—Indianapolis, Dickerson 15-50, Bentley 4-9, Trudeau 2-4; Cleveland, Byner 23-122, Mack 6-38, Manoa 4-10, Kosar 1-5.

Passing—Indianapolis, Trudeau 21-33-1—251, Salisbury 1-6-1—15; Cleveland, Kosar 20-31-1—229.

Receiving—Indianapolis, Dickerson 7-65, Brooks 5-78, Bentley 4-47, Bouza 2-24, Beach 2-6, Murray 1-25, Bellini 1-21; Cleveland, Newsome 4-65, Byner 4-36, Brennan 3-25, Mack 3-17, Fontenot 2-20, Langhorne 1-39, Slaughter 1-14, McNeil 1-8, Weathers 1-5.

Kickoff Returns—Indianapolis, Bentley 6-114, Ahrens 1-10; Cleveland, Fontenot 1-3, McNeil 1-18.

Punt Returns—Cleveland, McNeil 3-32.

Interceptions—Indianapolis, Robinson 1-0; Cleveland, Minnifield 1-48, Wright 1-0.

Punting—Indianapolis, Stark 4-43.8; Cleveland, L. Johnson 1-37.0.

Field Goals—Indianapolis, none attempted; Cleveland, Bahr 1-1.

Sacks—Cleveland, Baker, Puzzuoli.

VIKINGS 36, 49ers 24

SAN FRANCISCO—All the talk preceding this National Football Conference playoff game between the San Francisco 49ers and Minnesota Vikings revolved around a fleet, young receiver who had made a mockery of the NFL record book during the regular season. When the game was over, all the talk revolved around a fleet, young receiver who had just made a mockery of the NFL playoff record book.

Trouble was, it wasn't the same person.

Anthony Carter, who is probably better remembered by football fans for his collegiate playing days at Michigan than for his professional football exploits, caught 10 passes for 227 yards to lead the Vikings to a 36-24 upset victory over the 49ers at Candlestick Park. Carter, who didn't score himself but set up numerous Minnesota points, broke the single-game playoff record of 198 yards set by Tom Fears of the Los Angeles Rams in 1950 against the Chicago Bears.

Surprisingly, the 49ers never seemed to adjust their defense once Carter started ripping it apart.

"They didn't do anything special at all," said Minnesota quarterback Wade Wilson. "I was surprised that they never really double-covered him. We just took advantage of it."

The player who garnered much of the pre-game attention, the 49ers' Jerry Rice, was coming off a regular season in which he caught 65 passes for 1,078 yards and an NFL-record 22 touchdowns. But he had the worst performance of his three-year career as a starter against the Vikings. He caught only three passes for 28 yards, his first reception coming with 1:08 left in the first half.

"Anthony didn't say anything all week, but I think he took this game as a personal challenge to go one-on-one with Rice and show the rest of the country he could play as well as anybody," said Wilson. "He had that look in his eyes today."

Carter's contributions were not limited to catching passes. He also returned two punts for 21 yards and rushed once for 30 to finish the game with 278 total yards. His 30-yard run on a reverse, in fact, may have been as important as any catch he made. His run set up Wilson's five-yard touchdown pass to Mike Jones after San Francisco had cut the Vikings' lead to 20-10 on Jeff Fuller's 48-yard interception return early in the second half.

The 49ers did not play like the team that had compiled the league's best record (13-2) during the regular season. Veteran Joe Montana opened at quarterback despite having played in only one half of one game since pulling a hamstring a month earlier. He was sacked four times and completed just 12 of 26 passes for 109 yards. His biggest mistake was hanging a sideline pass for wide receiver Dwight Clark midway through the second quarter. Rookie defensive back Reggie Rutland picked off Montana's pass and returned it 45 yards to give Minnesota a 20-3 halftime lead.

It marked the first time all season that the 49ers failed to score a touchdown in the opening half.

Montana was benched by Coach Bill Walsh for the first time in his eight-year career as a starter after San Francisco's second possession of the third period. His replacement, Steve Young, completed a 31-yard pass to Roger Craig on his first play and ended the drive by running five yards for a touchdown. But Young's efforts were too little, too late, and not enough to keep the 49ers from losing their opening playoff game for the third straight year and their first at Candlestick in six playoff games.

The Vikings' victory, combined with a 44-10 thrashing of New Orleans the previous week, meant that they had beaten teams with a combined regular-season record of 25-5 in successive weeks on the road. The Saints hadn't lost in nine games before the Vikings paid them a visit, and the 49ers hadn't lost in six.

Next up would be the Washington Redskins in the nation's capital for the NFC championship, and everyone knew who was responsible for getting them there.

"Anthony Carter tore us up," said 49ers linebacker Mike Walter. "He made some unreal catches. It was the first time we found out what it's like to play against Jerry Rice."

Vikings-49ers

SATURDAY, JANUARY 9
SCORE BY PERIODS

Minnesota	3	17	10	6	36
San Francisco	3	0	14	7	24

SCORING

Minnesota—Field goal C. Nelson 21, 5:43 1st. Drive: 77 yards, 15 plays.

San Francisco—Field goal Wersching 43, 13:23 1st. Drive: 74 yards, 10 plays.

Minnesota—Hilton 7 pass from Wilson (C. Nelson kick), 2:34 2nd. Drive: 70 yards, 9 plays.

Minnesota—Field goal C. Nelson 23, 6:33 2nd. Drive: 69 yards, 7 plays.

Minnesota—Rutland 45 interception return (C. Nelson kick), 7:24 2nd.

San Francisco—Fuller 48 interception return (Wersching kick), 1:42 3rd.

Minnesota—Jones 5 pass from Wilson (C. Nelson kick), 4:45 3rd. Drive: 68 yards, 11 plays.

San Francisco—Young 5 run (Wersching kick), 10:59 3rd. Drive: 35 yards, 5 plays.

Minnesota—Field goal C. Nelson 40, 13:38 3rd. Drive: 43 yards, 5 plays.

Minnesota—Field goal C. Nelson 46, 3:21 4th. Drive: 40 yards, 8 plays.

San Francisco—Frank 16 pass from Young (Wersching kick), 11:18 4th. Drive: 58 yards, 8 plays.

Minnesota—Field goal C. Nelson 23, 14:33 4th. Drive: 48 yards, 7 plays.

TEAM STATISTICS

	Minnesota	San Francisco
FIRST DOWNS	22	17
By rushing	5	6
By passing	15	10
By penalty	2	1
THIRD DOWN EFFICIENCY	7-17	4-15
TOTAL NET YARDS	397	358
Offensive plays	70	66
Average gain per play	5.7	5.4
NET YARDS RUSHING	117	115
Total rushes	34	18
Average gain per rush	3.4	6.4
NET YARDS PASSING	280	243
Sacked-Yards lost	2-18	4-24
Gross yards passing	298	267
PASSES	20-34-1	24-44-2
Average gain per pass	7.8	5.1
PUNTS	5-36.4	6-40.8
Had blocked	0	0
TOTAL RETURN YARDAGE	145	195
Punt returns	3-29	3-17
Kickoff returns	3-76	8-130
Interception returns	2-40	1-48
PENALTIES-YARDS	2-20	8-75
FUMBLES-LOST	0-0	1-0
TIME OF POSSESSION	33:43	26:17

Attendance—62,547.

INDIVIDUAL STATISTICS

Rushing—Minnesota, D. Nelson 11-42, Wilson 6-30, Carter 1-30, Anderson 7-9, Rice 6-8, Dozier 3-minus 2; San Francisco, Young 6-72, Montana 3-20, Craig 7-17, Rathman 1-12, Cribbs 1-minus 6.

Passing—Minnesota, Wilson 20-34-1—298; San Francisco, Montana 12-26-1—109, Young 12-17-1—158, Sydney 0-1-0—0.

Receiving—Minnesota, Carter 10-227, Rice 4-39, D. Nelson 2-17, Hilton 1-7, Jones 1-5, Lewis 1-5, Anderson 1-minus 2; San Francisco, Craig 9-78, Wilson 4-50, Rice 3-28, Taylor 2-48, Rathman 2-18, Frank 1-16, Clark 1-13, Cribbs 1-7, Jones 1-7, Young 0-2.

Kickoff Returns—Minnesota, D. Nelson 2-56, Rice 1-20; San Francisco, Rathman 3-45, Cribbs 3-28, Sydney 2-28, Taylor 0-29.

Punt Returns—Minnesota, Carter 2-21, Lewis 1-8; San Francisco, McLemore 3-17.

Interceptions—Minnesota, Rutland 1-45, Lee 1-minus 5; San Francisco, Fuller 1-48.

Punting—Minnesota, Scribner 5-36.4; San Francisco, Runager 6-40.8.

Field Goals—Minnesota, C. Nelson 5-5; San Francisco, Wersching 1-3 (missed: 26, 48).

Sacks—Minnesota, Studwell, Doleman 2, Thomas; San Francisco, Haley, Walter.

REDSKINS 21, BEARS 17

CHICAGO—When the Chicago Bears lost to the Washington Redskins, 27-13, in the first round of the 1986 National Football League playoffs, a scapegoat was needed. The Bears, heavily favored to roll past the Redskins in pursuit of a second straight Super Bowl championship, had lost in the first round at home to a team with a lesser record.

Quarterback Doug Flutie made a perfect scapegoat. He was small (5-foot-9), too cute to be a Bear, not particularly popular with his teammates and playing only because regular quarterback Jim McMahon had been felled by one of his numerous injuries. Flutie completed only 13 passes in the game—two to the Redskins—in just his second NFL start.

When Washington beat Chicago again, 21-17, in the teams' 1987 NFC playoff rematch at Soldier Field, the Bears this time had no excuses. Flutie was now a New England Patriot and McMahon played the entire game. The Bears were now 0 for 2 in the playoffs since their Super Bowl XX triumph, with the same team delivering the knockout punch both times.

"If Doug Flutie was too short, Jim McMahon was too tall," gloated Redskins defensive end Dexter Manley, who had engaged in a war of words with Chicago Coach Mike Ditka the week before the game.

"All week they were talking about Doug Flutie, blaming last year's loss on him. What's their excuse now?"

Just like the previous year, when they let a 13-7 halftime lead slip away, the Bears squandered a 14-0 advantage midway through the second quarter. George Rogers capped a 72-yard drive with a three-yard touchdown run and Doug Williams threw an 18-yard pass to Clint Didier with 51 seconds left in the first half to knot the score at 14-14.

Washington took the lead for good less than four minutes into the second half when starting cornerback Darrell Green—who returned only five punts all season—hauled in a Tommy Barnhardt punt on his own 48-yard line and ran it back 52 yards for a touchdown. Green pulled the muscles in his rib cage when he hurdled would-be tackler Cap Boso at the Chicago 30, but was able to score the Redskins' first kick-return touchdown of the year.

"Our special teams got us a touchdown, finally," said Washington Coach Joe Gibbs. "That ignited us as much as anything."

"I could easily have let (Boso) push me out of bounds," said Green, who played only one more down the rest of the game because of the injury. "Normally, that's what you do, but I just wanted to keep going.

"We haven't had a big play like that all year."

"Maybe I should have stayed up, I don't know," said Boso. "When he jumped over me, I didn't think he was going to land on his feet,

but he did."

The Bears' best late scoring opportunity came when they drove to the Redskins' 14-yard line midway through the final quarter. But on a second-down play, cornerback Barry Wilburn picked off a McMahon pass in the end zone, the last of three interceptions thrown by the Chicago quarterback in the game.

"I didn't throw the ball well in the second half," said McMahon, who had won 28 of his previous 29 starting assignments. "I know you guys (the media) are going to put heat on me, and I can take it."

Redskins-Bears
SUNDAY, JANUARY 10
SCORE BY PERIODS

Washington	0	14	7	0—21
Chicago	7	7	3	0—17

SCORING
Chicago—Thomas 2 run (Butler kick), 8:37 1st. Drive: 30 yards, 5 plays.
Chicago—Morris 14 pass from McMahon (Butler kick), 6:54 2nd. Drive: 68 yards, 14 plays.
Washington—Rogers 3 run (Haji-Sheikh kick), 11:09 2nd. Drive: 72 yards, 7 plays.
Washington—Didier 18 pass from Williams (Haji-Sheikh kick), 14:09 2nd. Drive: 69 yards, 7 plays.
Washington—Green 52 punt return (Haji-Sheikh kick), 3:20 3rd.
Chicago—Field goal Butler 25, 10:13 3rd. Drive: 62 yards, 7 plays.

TEAM STATISTICS

	Washington	Chicago
FIRST DOWNS	17	15
By rushing	4	8
By passing	11	7
By penalty	2	0
THIRD DOWN EFFICIENCY	7-14	4-13
TOTAL NET YARDS	272	280
Offensive plays	59	64
Average gain per play	4.6	4.4
NET YARDS RUSHING	72	110
Total rushes	29	30
Average gain per rush	2.5	3.7
NET YARDS PASSING	200	170
Sacked-Yards lost	1-7	5-27
Gross yards passing	207	197
PASSES	14-29-1	15-29-3
Average gain per pass	6.7	5.0
PUNTS	4-42.3	4-36.3
Had blocked	0	0
TOTAL RETURN YARDAGE	144	115
Punt returns	3-65	2-12
Kickoff returns	4-56	3-103
Interception returns	3-23	1-0
PENALTIES-YARDS	3-20	5-50
FUMBLES-LOST	1-1	1-0
TIME OF POSSESSION	27:03	32:57
Attendance—66,030.		

INDIVIDUAL STATISTICS

Rushing—Washington, Rogers 6-13, Bryant 3-8, Clark 1-minus 6, Smith 16-66, Schroeder 1-minus 8, Williams 2-minus 1; Chicago, Payton 18-85, Suhey 4-8, Thomas 2-3, Gentry 2-5, McMahon 2-5, Sanders 2-4.

Passing—Washington, Williams 14-29-1—207; Chicago, McMahon 15-29-3—197.

Receiving—Washington, Sanders 6-92, Rogers 1-11, Clark 4-56, Didier 2-32, Warren 1-16; Chicago, Gentry 3-43, Boso 3-19, Morris 2-47, Suhey 1-6, Payton 3-20, Gault 1-44, Sanders 1-2, McKinnon 1-16.

Kickoff Returns—Washington, Sanders 2-25, Smith 1-19, Branch 1-12; Chicago, Gentry 2-74, Gault 1-29.

Darrell Green's 52-yard punt return for a touchdown proved to be the winning points in the Redskins' 21-17 victory at Chicago.

Punt Returns—Washington, Yarber 2-13, Green 1-52; Chicago, McKinnon 2-12.

Interceptions—Washington, Davis 1-23, Wilburn 1-0, Woodberry 1-0; Chicago, Richardson 1-0.

Punting—Washington, Cox 4-42.3; Chicago, Barnhardt 4-36.3.

Field Goals—Washington, none attempted; Chicago, Butler 1-2 (missed: 48).

Sacks—Washington, Mann 3, Hamilton, Grant ½, Koch ½; Chicago, Dent.

BRONCOS 34, OILERS 10

DENVER—On their way to their first playoff appearance in seven years, the Houston Oilers didn't make many friends around the National Football League. The Oiler players often were accused of playing dirty and Coach Jerry Glanville had run-ins with numerous other coaches around the league, most notably Pittsburgh's Chuck Noll.

What does any of this have to do with the Oilers' 34-10 American Football Conference playoff loss to the Denver Broncos? Well, if a game can possibly turn around on a team's second play from scrimmage, this one did.

With second down and 11 at his own 4-yard line, Houston quarterback Warren Moon took the snap, dropped back quickly, and fired a lateral to running back Mike Rozier. Rozier dropped the ball and was swarmed under by the Broncos' Rulon Jones and Karl Mecklen-

burg. Cornerback Steve Wilson recovered for Denver on the 1-yard line. Two plays later, Gene Lang scored for a 7-0 Broncos lead.

"We had exactly what we wanted, but Mike didn't catch the ball," Glanville said. "He runs after he catches it on that play. There's no pass (by Rozier). With three blockers in front of him, Mike normally makes that play and makes it big. He just didn't catch the ball."

The play is called Stagger Lee in the Houston playbook, and it staggered the Oilers enough that they never recovered.

"I think that was the turning point right there," said Denver safety Tony Lilly. "I think that hurt them real bad, hurt them emotionally. They're not a playoff-experienced team, and they kind of panicked."

"We hadn't seen it on film," said Broncos defensive coordinator Joe Collier, but we knew they had it in their offense from having talked to some other coaches."

Who?

"I'd rather not say."

The Oilers weren't much better on their second possession. They drove 60 yards to the Denver 20, only to have the drive end when Mecklenburg intercepted a Moon pass. The Bronco offense then drove 72 yards on six plays, taking a 14-0 lead on John Elway's 27-yard touchdown pass to tight end Clarence

John Elway threw for two touchdowns and ran for another in Denver's 34-10 win over Houston.

Kay. Kay, who caught 31 passes in the regular season but none for touchdowns, made a lunging, fingertip grab for that score and later caught a one-yard touchdown pass just before halftime for a 24-3 Denver lead.

"After those first couple of touchdowns, you could see them kind of let down," said Denver running back Steve Sewell. "I'm not saying they quit, but you could tell they knew they were in for a long afternoon."

Three times the Oilers drove inside the Broncos' 20-yard line and came away scoreless, with two possessions ending with interceptions and one on downs.

"To go that far and not come away with anything doesn't do much for morale," said Houston guard Bruce Matthews.

The Broncos, on the other hand, had little trouble putting points on the board. Elway completed 14 of his 25 pass attempts for 259 yards and also ran three yards for the game's final touchdown.

"It brings us one step closer to our objective," said Denver Coach Dan Reeves. "This was just a great team effort. Everyone contributed. Nobody did more than anyone else and everyone did a good job."

Oilers-Broncos

SUNDAY, JANUARY 10

SCORE BY PERIODS

Houston	0	3	0	7	—10
Denver	14	10	3	7	—34

SCORING

Denver—Lang 1 run (Karlis kick), 7:29 1st. Drive: 1 yard, 2 plays.

Denver—Kay 27 pass from Elway (Karlis kick), 13:34 1st. Drive: 72 yards, 6 plays.

Denver—Field goal Karlis 43, 3:20 2nd. Drive: 14 yards, 7 plays.

Houston—Field goal Zendejas 46, 9:03 2nd. Drive: 54 yards, 12 plays.

Denver—Kay 1 pass from Elway (Karlis kick), 13:08 2nd. Drive: 80 yards, 9 plays.

Denver—Field goal Karlis 23, 2:29 3rd. Drive: 51 yards, 5 plays.

Houston—Givins 19 pass from Moon (Zendejas kick), 6:38 4th. Drive: 48 yards, 3 plays.

Denver—Elway 3 run (Karlis kick), 10:33 4th. Drive: 52 yards, 7 plays.

TEAM STATISTICS

	Houston	Denver
FIRST DOWNS	20	19
By rushing	5	9
By passing	14	9
By penalty	1	1
THIRD DOWN EFFICIENCY	8-16	4-9
TOTAL NET YARDS	337	316
Offensive plays	69	55
Average gain per play	4.9	5.7
NET YARDS RUSHING	73	61
Total rushes	26	29
Average gain per rush	2.8	2.1
NET YARDS PASSING	264	255
Sacked-Yards lost	0-0	1-4
Gross yards passing	264	259
PASSES	24-43-2	14-25-1
Average gain per pass	6.1	9.8
PUNTS	3-44.7	2-46.0
Had blocked	0	0
TOTAL RETURN YARDAGE	64	118
Punt returns	0-0	2-15
Kickoff returns	3-62	2-28
Interception returns	1-2	2-75
PENALTIES-YARDS	10-73	4-35
FUMBLES-LOST	2-1	0-0
TIME OF POSSESSION	32:33	27:27
Attendance—75,968.		

INDIVIDUAL STATISTICS

Rushing—Houston, Highsmith 5-13, Rozier 9-25, Moon 5-15, Givins 1-0, Pinkett 6-20; Denver, Sewell 5-9, Winder 13-46, Elway 4-8, Lang 3-minus 6, Bell 2-7, Kubiak 2-minus 3.

Passing—Houston, Moon 24-43-2—264; Denver, Elway 14-25-1—259.

Receiving—Houston, Duncan 4-32, Givins 6-84, D. Hill 5-93, J. Williams 1-7, Drewrey 2-17, Rozier 1-6, Highsmith 4-20, Pinkett 1-5; Denver, Johnson 4-105, Kay 3-57, Sewell 3-41, Boddie 1-15, Mobley 1-9, Nattiel 1-7, Lang 1-25.

Kickoff Returns—Houston, Pinkett 3-62, Denver, Bell 1-28, Clark 1-0.

Punt Returns—Denver, Clark 2-15.

Interceptions—Houston, Allen 1-2; Denver, Mecklenburg 1-18, Haynes 1-57.

Punting—Houston, Gossett 3-44.7; Denver, Horan 2-46.0.

Field Goals—Houston, Zendejas 1-1; Denver, Karlis 2-2.

Sacks—Houston, Martin.

NFC CHAMPIONSHIP GAME

REDSKINS 17, VIKINGS 10

WASHINGTON—Heading into the 1987 National Football Conference championship game, about the only thing that had been predictable about the NFC playoffs was their unpredictability. The visiting team had won each of the three playoff games played to that point, including the Minnesota Vikings' stunning 44-10 wild-card game victory at New Orleans and 36-24 thumping of the 49ers at San Francisco the following week. The Washington Redskins, on the other hand, had surprised observers by beating the Bears in Chicago for the second straight postseason, this time 21-17.

But when the Vikings and Redskins met in Washington for the conference title, the road magic came to an end. The 'Skins won, 17-10, for their ninth win in 10 playoff games at RFK Stadium since 1982.

The Vikings' Traveling Road Show simply ran out of gas.

"Nobody expected us to be here," said Vikings wide receiver Anthony Carter, the team's playoff star. "Our heads will be up."

The Redskins won largely because of their defense, which played well enough to offset numerous offensive breakdowns. The 'Skins defense sacked Minnesota quarterback Wade Wilson eight times—one short of the playoff record—and forced him to hurry his passes on at least a half-dozen other occasions. Carter, who had compiled 500 total yards of offense in the victories over New Orleans and San Francisco, was held to 142 yards (85 receiving, 57 in punt returns) by the Redskins.

Excluding their four-play, 71-yard touchdown drive in the second quarter, the Vikings had just 47 yards on 25 first-down plays. They converted just three of 16 third- and fourth-down tries.

"We couldn't hear the audibles," said offensive tackle Gary Zimmerman, alluding to the crowd noise at jam-packed RFK Stadium.

Minnesota blew a golden opportunity to take a four-point lead when it had a first-and-goal at the Washington 3-yard line with just over 10 minutes left in the game. Two runs by rookie Rick Fenney moved the ball to the 1 before another Vikings rookie, D.J. Dozier, was undercut by linebacker Neal Olkewicz on third down. The Vikings had to settle for a field goal and 10-10 tie.

But the Vikings were not the only ones to have offensive problems. Washington never seemed to get untracked behind quarterback Doug Williams. Williams drove the Redskins 98 yards in eight plays for a touchdown on the team's first possession—throwing 42 yards to Kelvin Bryant for the score—but completed just nine of 26 attempts overall.

Redskins Coach Joe Gibbs, who had sum-

Anthony Carter was a prime target of the Redskins' defense in the NFC championship game.

moned Williams from the bench to relieve Jay Schroeder on numerous occasions during the regular season, briefly contemplated making the reverse move.

"Jay wanted in there, and I think he could have done well," said the coach. "But you have to stay with your gut feeling."

Gibbs' patience paid off. With the game tied 10-10, Washington took over on its own 30-yard line with 9:57 remaining. After four running plays, Williams hit wide receiver Gary Clark for a 43-yard gain to the Vikes' 11-yard line. On a third-and-seven from the 8, Williams fired a low pass between two defenders into the hands of Clark, who fell into the Minnesota end zone for what proved to be the game-winning points.

Clark messed up by running the wrong route, but Williams adjusted in time to complete the seven-yard scoring pass with 5:15 left.

But the Vikings, who had played near-perfect games in their victories over the Saints and 49ers, weren't finished yet. They took possession at their own 33-yard line with 5:04 left and moved to the Redskin 6 with a little over a minute to go. Wilson then threw three straight incompletions, the last one when running back Darrin Nelson dropped what appeared to be a certain touchdown at the 1-yard line with 52

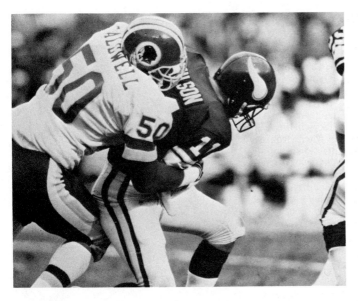

Wade Wilson was sacked eight times in the title game, one shy of the league record.

seconds left.

"The ball hit my hands, and then it was knocked away (by cornerback Darrell Green)," Nelson said. "Anytime the ball hits your hands, you should catch it."

"We were all in the huddle, telling each other to give it everything we had on the last play," said defensive end Dexter Manley. "There was a lot of talking. I guess I was doing most of it. I get excited in those moments."

"It felt like my heart stopped during that play," said 37-year-old tackle Dave Butz, who had two sacks and tipped a pass that was intercepted by teammate Mel Kaufman.

But the Redskins survived, thus earning a trip to San Diego for Super Bowl XXII, which would mark Washington's third appearance in the NFL title game in six years. They had come close in 1986, when they reached the conference championship game only to be whitewashed, 17-0, by the New York Giants.

"We didn't want to get this far again and blow the chance," Manley said. "You don't want to live a year with that hurt again."

Vikings-Redskins
SUNDAY, JANUARY 17
SCORE BY PERIODS

Minnesota	0	7	0	3	10
Washington	7	0	3	7	17

SCORING

Washington—Bryant 42 pass from Williams (Haji-Sheikh kick), 10:53 1st. Drive: 98 yards, 8 plays.

Minnesota—Lewis 23 pass from Wilson (C. Nelson kick), 13:00 2nd. Drive: 71 yards, 4 plays.

Washington—Field goal Haji-Sheikh 28, 10:30 3rd. Drive: 6 yards, 4 plays.

Minnesota—Field goal C. Nelson 18, 4:54 4th. Drive: 52 yards, 10 plays.

Washington—Clark 7 pass from Williams (Haji-Sheikh kick), 9:45 4th. Drive: 70 yards, 18 plays.

TEAM STATISTICS

	Minnesota	Washington
FIRST DOWNS	16	11
By rushing	5	7
By passing	10	4
By penalty	1	0
THIRD DOWN EFFICIENCY	3-15	5-16
TOTAL NET YARDS	259	280
Offensive plays	68	60
Average gain per play	3.8	4.7
NET YARDS RUSHING	76	161
Total rushes	21	34
Average gain per rush	3.6	4.7
NET YARDS PASSING	183	119
Sacked-Yards lost	8-60	0-0
Gross yards passing	243	119
PASSES	19-39-1	9-26-0
Average gain per pass	3.9	4.6
PUNTS	10-32.0	8-39.1
Had blocked	0	0
TOTAL RETURN YARDAGE	115	74
Punt returns	4-57	4-10
Kickoff returns	3-58	3-54
Interception returns	0-0	1-10
PENALTIES-YARDS	2-10	3-18
FUMBLES-LOST	0-0	0-0
TIME OF POSSESSION	33:02	26:58

Attendance—55,212.

INDIVIDUAL STATISTICS

Rushing—Minnesota, D. Nelson 8-15, Anderson 4-25, Dozier 2-minus 2, Rice 1-8, Wilson 4-28, Fenney 2-2; Washington, Rogers 12-46, Bryant 3-3, Sanders 1-28, Smith 13-72, Clark 1-5, Williams 4-7.

Passing—Minnesota, Wilson 19-39-1—243; Washington, Williams 9-26-0—119.

Receiving—Minnesota, Carter 7-85, Jordan 3-56, Lewis 4-54, D. Nelson 3-25, Anderson 1-8, Rice 1-15; Washington, Clark 3-57, Bryant 4-47, Allen 1-9, Warren 1-6.

Kickoff Returns—Minnesota, D. Nelson 2-43, Rice 1-15; Washington, Sanders 2-30, Smith 1-24.

Punt Returns—Minnesota, Carter 4-57; Washington, Dean 6-0, Green 1-1, Davis 1-0, Yarber 1-9.

Interceptions—Washington, Kaufman 1-10.

Punting—Minnesota, Scribner 10-32.0; Washington, Cox 8-39.1.

Field Goals—Minnesota, C. Nelson 1-1; Washington, Haji-Sheikh 1-3 (missed: 38, 47).

Sacks—Washington, Butz 2, Manley 1½, Walton, Vaughn, Gouveia, Caldwell, Mann ½.

AFC CHAMPIONSHIP GAME

BRONCOS 38, BROWNS 33

DENVER—As the Denver Broncos and Cleveland Browns were preparing for their showdown in the 1987 American Football Conference championship game, much time was spent looking back rather than ahead. At issue was Denver's 23-20 overtime victory in the 1986 AFC title game, made possible when Broncos quarterback John Elway engineered a dramatic 98-yard drive in the final minutes of regulation to tie the score.

The loss was particularly painful for Cleveland players and fans, who were hungry for the team's first-ever Super Bowl appearance.

"I'm sorry, but I just don't understand their so-called 'revenge' factor," said Elway. "They say they feel like we almost stole that game from them, as if we threw a 'Hail Mary' pass with two seconds left and it bounced off three Browns and we caught it and scored. I think the bottom line is that we played well on the drive and then we won in overtime."

The bottom line in '87 was the same even if the final score was different: Denver 38, Cleveland 33.

"This doesn't hurt any more than last year," said Cleveland Coach Marty Schottenheimer. "They all hurt. When you lose, they all hurt."

The Broncos jumped out to a big lead by scoring touchdowns on their first three possessions, the first two set up by turnovers. A pass by quarterback Bernie Kosar on Cleveland's first possession was deflected and intercepted by Denver's Freddie Gilbert at the Browns' 18-yard line. Four plays later, rookie wide receiver Ricky Nattiel split between safeties Ray Ellis and Felix Wright and hauled in an eight-yard scoring pass from Elway.

Less than four minutes later, Denver safety Tony Lilly stripped the ball from Browns fullback Kevin Mack and Steve Wilson recovered for the Broncos at his own 40-yard line. Eight running plays and 60 yards later, Steve Sewell's one-yard dash gave Denver a 14-0 lead.

Cleveland had entered the contest with the fewest turnovers (29) in the AFC during the regular season. And the Browns' defense finished tied with San Francisco for fewest touchdowns allowed (26).

The Broncos led by 18 points at the intermission, and with 75,993 fans at Mile High Stadium cheering their every move, the prospects were bleak at best for the visiting Browns.

But the three-time Central Division champion Browns rebounded in the final 30 minutes. Wright picked off an Elway pass on Denver's first second-half possession and returned it 13 yards to the Broncos 35. Three plays later, Kosar threw an 18-yard touchdown pass to Reggie Langhorne to cut the Denver lead to 21-10.

Bernie Kosar rallied the Browns to three third-period touchdowns but the Broncos held on to win their second straight AFC title game, 38-33.

"We decided we'd go out attacking in the second half, that we'd really throw it around," Kosar said. "We've lived and died with that all season. We didn't make it this far this season by quitting when we got behind."

Elway and wide receiver Mark Jackson hooked up for an 80-yard touchdown on Denver's next possession to restore the Broncos' 18-point advantage, but Kosar drove the Browns 80 yards in five plays, connecting with wide receiver Reggie Langhorne for a 30-yard gain before hitting running back Earnest Byner for a 32-yard touchdown to make the score 28-17.

Byner scored another touchdown on a four-yard run to cut the Browns' deficit to four. But a 38-yard field goal by Rich Karlis on the final play of the third period lifted Denver to a 31-24 lead.

Kosar responded by driving the Browns 86 yards on nine plays, including a 53-yard pass play to Byner. The touchdown came on a four-yard pass to Webster Slaughter, tying the game at 31-31 with 10:48 remaining.

The Browns, who appeared in need of life-support systems at the half, had scored touchdowns on four straight possessions in less than 16 minutes. Three of the touchdowns were on passes from Kosar, who completed 16 of 22 attempts for 246 yards on the four scoring drives.

"Everything we did defensively went right in the first half," said Denver linebacker Ricky Hunley. "But all of a sudden everything they did in the second half started clicking. They were running like a machine. Every play was executed perfectly." The Browns had 148 total yards in the first half, 316 in the second.

But the Broncos fought back. Taking over on his own 25 with 5:14 left, Elway guided his club 75 yards on five plays for what proved to be the game-winning score. He completed two 26-yard passes to Nattiel and then hooked up with Sammy Winder for a 20-yard touchdown with 4:01 left.

Like two punch-drunk fighters in a bar room brawl, Elway had responded in kind to Kosar's heavy blows. Now it was Kosar's chance once again.

Taking over at his own 25, Kosar handed to Byner on first down for a 17-yard gain. He then completed consecutive passes of 14 and 19 yards to wide receiver Brian Brennan before Byner ripped off another six-yard gain.

Cleveland worked the ball to the Denver 8 with 1:12 left, but disaster struck on second-and-five.

Byner, who would amass 120 receiving yards and 67 rushing, fumbled inside the Denver 5-yard line as he appeared headed for the go-ahead touchdown. Reserve defensive back Jeremiah Castille knocked the ball from Byner's grasp at the 3 and recovered it there with just 1:05 remaining.

"The play was supposed to go inside, but I saw that (Karl) Mecklenburg was plugging up the hole, so I slid to the outside," Byner said. "And I had daylight, too. There was no doubt in my mind that we were going to score."

"Last year I was elated at the end of the game," said Denver Coach Dan Reeves, whose team earned the right to make amends for last season's 39-20 Super Bowl blowout at the hands of the New York Giants. "This year I'm just numb."

Browns-Broncos
SUNDAY, JANUARY 17
SCORE BY PERIODS

Cleveland	0	3	21	9—33
Denver	14	7	10	7—38

SCORING

Denver—Nattiel 8 pass from Elway (Karlis kick), 3:38 1st. Drive: 18 yards, 4 plays.

Denver—Sewell 1 run (Karlis kick), 11:06 1st. Drive: 60 yards, 8 plays.

Cleveland—Field goal Bahr 24, 1:41 2nd. Drive: 64 yards, 13 plays.

Denver—Lang 1 run (Karlis kick), 6:59 2nd. Drive: 80 yards, 11 plays.

Cleveland—Langhorne 18 pass from Kosar (Bahr kick), 3:44 3rd. Drive: 35 yards, 3 plays.

Denver—Jackson 80 pass from Elway (Karlis kick), 5:03 3rd. Drive: 80 yards, 3 plays.

Cleveland—Byner 32 pass from Kosar (Bahr kick), 8:10 3rd. Drive: 80 yards, 5 plays.

Cleveland—Byner 4 run (Bahr kick), 11:15 3rd. Drive: 42 yards, 4 plays.

Denver—Field goal Karlis 38, 14:50 3rd. Drive: 59 yards, 9 plays.

Cleveland—Slaughter 4 pass from Kosar (Bahr kick), 4:12 4th. Drive: 86 yards, 9 plays.

Denver—Winder 20 pass from Elway (Karlis kick), 10:59 4th. Drive: 75 yards, 5 plays.

Cleveland—Safety, Horan ran out of end zone, 14:50 4th.

TEAM STATISTICS

	Cleveland	Denver
FIRST DOWNS	25	24
By rushing	8	10
By passing	15	11
By penalty	2	3
THIRD DOWN EFFICIENCY	8-14	7-14
TOTAL NET YARDS	464	412
Offensive plays	70	67
Average gain per play	6.6	6.1
NET YARDS RUSHING	128	156
Total rushes	27	39
Average gain per rush	4.7	4.0
NET YARDS PASSING	336	256
Sacked-Yards lost	2-20	2-25
Gross yards passing	356	281
PASSES	26-41-1	14-26-1
Average gain per pass	7.8	9.1
PUNTS	2-48.0	3-33.7
Had blocked	0	0
TOTAL RETURN YARDAGE	131	56
Punt returns	2-24	2-13
Kickoff returns	5-94	3-43
Interception returns	1-13	1-0
PENALTIES-YARDS	7-59	7-44
FUMBLES-LOST	3-3	2-0
TIME OF POSSESSION	31:37	28:23

Attendance—75,993.

INDIVIDUAL STATISTICS

Rushing—Cleveland, Byner 15-67, Mack 12-61; Denver, Winder 20-72, Elway 11-36, Lang 5-51, Sewell 1-1, Bodie 1-8, Horan 1-minus 12.

Passing—Cleveland, Kosar 26-41-1—356; Denver, Elway 14-26-1—281.

Receiving—Cleveland, Byner 7-120, Newsome 3-35, Tennell 1-5, Weathers 1-19, Slaughter 4-53, Brennan 4-48, Langhorne 2-48, Mack 4-28; Denver, Nattiel 5-95, Sewell 1-10, Winder 3-34, Jackson 1-134, Mobley 1-8.

Kickoff Returns—Cleveland, McNeil 5-94; Denver, Bell 3-43.

Punt Returns—Cleveland, McNeil 2-24; Denver, Clark 2-13.

Interceptions—Cleveland, Wright 1-13; Denver, Gilbert 1-0.

Punting—Cleveland, L. Johnson 2-48.0; Denver, Moran 2-41.5, Elway 1-18.

Field Goals—Cleveland, Bahr 0-1 (missed: 45); Denver, Karlis 1-2 (missed: 50).

Sacks—Cleveland, Baker, Clancy; Denver, Fletcher, Jones.

Williams Busts Broncos

By PAUL ATTNER
National Correspondent

SAN DIEGO—Super Bowl XXII will be remembered for the Washington Redskins' magnificent 35-point second quarter. It will be remembered, too, for the miseries endured by John Elway and for the stunning running of a rookie halfback named Tim Smith.

But more than anything, Super Bowl XXII should be remembered for the inspiring work of Redskins quarterback Doug Williams. Considering the burdens he carried with him into the game and the exceptional way he played during Washington's 42-10 trouncing of Denver, his performance rightly ranks among the best in pro football history.

Numbers alone carve out a special niche for Williams: a Super Bowl record 340 passing yards and a record-tying four touchdown passes as the Redskins gained a record 602 total yards. But realistically, he entered this already pressure-saturated game with a heavy load. He wasn't just the Redskins' quarterback; he also was the first black starting quarterback in Super Bowl history.

In the days preceeding the game, the Redskins' staff fretted over the pressures being placed upon Williams. The coaches were convinced they had Denver physically overmatched, but they wondered whether they could control Elway, the Broncos' quarterback, and if Williams would press too much, trying to live up to the expectations of his fans.

"Doug is the reason we are here," said one Redskins coach. "Since he became a starter, we're a different team. But you hope he doesn't go into the game feeling he's carrying all his fans on his shoulders. If he tries too hard, we could have problems."

But the stereotypical days when black quarterbacks weren't supposed to be able to start and win in the NFL were buried for good when Williams easily outperformed the more heralded Elway and gave the Redskins their second Super Bowl triumph in six years.

The Redskins, who had been 3½-point underdogs and had complained about not getting any respect despite their 11-4 regular-season record, gloated afterwards. "We've got six months of bragging to do," said cornerback Darrell Green.

But no Washington player overcame more odds than Williams, who seemingly was washed up just two years ago, unwanted by any NFL team, save the Redskins, when the United States Football League folded.

But the Redskins needed a veteran backup for young Jay Schroeder and Coach Joe Gibbs, who had tutored Williams when he was the quarterbacks coach in Tampa, thought of Williams, who quickly signed with Washington in August 1986. Williams never expected to play much—he attempted only one pass in 1986—but when Schroeder struggled in 1987, Williams was given the starting job. He lost it when he hurt his back, then got it back again for the playoffs.

The Redskins' march to the Super Bowl was hardly expected. This was a team that struggled all year, often coming from behind and hardly ever putting away opponents. There were controversies at quarterback and running back, wide receiver injuries and a 3-0 replacement team that kept them in the championship hunt. Then they wound up beating Denver, thanks to an unheralded defense that controlled Elway and to three offensive stars—Williams, Smith and receiver Ricky Sanders—who weren't even starters when the season began.

There had been expectations that this would be a dream game for Elway, the California golden boy who had dominated Super Bowl hype so much so that Denver Coach Dan Reeves sarcastically had suggested his one-man team needed to have a curfew only for the quarterback. He easily was the best-known player in the game and was the main reason the Broncos had come this far.

One day, Redskins defensive end Dexter Manley said his dream was to "catch the quarterback and hit him from behind, in between his two numbers, and cut his lights out." Reminded that Elway wore No. 7, Manley replied, "Oh."

Richie Petitbon, the Redskins' assistant head coach/defense, respected Elway so much that he changed his usual approach regarding blitzing. Instead of frequently sending six or seven defenders toward the quarterback, Petitbon and his staff decided to limit the pass rush to the front four plus blitzes by a fifth player, either safety Alvin Walton or linebackers Monte Coleman, Mel Kaufman or Clarence Vaughn. The idea was to have the front four rush straight, forgoing any stunting that would open up scramble lanes for Elway, and then try to confuse the quarterback by constantly blitzing from different points on the field.

"We didn't want to leave the middle of the field open, because he could hurt us there," said Petitbon. So free safety Todd Bowles manned the middle and Petitbon began what assistant coach Joe Bugel called "a chess game" with Elway.

John Elway gained 21 yards on this second-quarter run, but the Denver quarterback was kept under pretty tight reins by the Redskins' defense in Super Bowl XXII.

The Broncos almost had a checkmate in the first quarter. On their first play from scrimmage, Elway kept looking away from Redskins cornerback Barry Wilburn, who thought he wouldn't be involved in the play. Suddenly, Elway switched to Wilburn's side and connected with rookie wide receiver Ricky Nattiel, who was five yards behind the defender. The result was a 56-yard touchdown after only one minute and 57 seconds—the quickest score in Super Bowl history.

"He caught me asleep," said Wilburn. "Give him credit."

On Denver's next possession, a trick pass from halfback Steve Sewell to Elway gained 23 yards to the Washington 13-yard line. But Elway was stopped by tackle Dave Butz on a third-down quarterback draw and Denver settled for a 24-yard Rich Karlis field goal and a 10-0 lead. Had Sanders not recovered his own fumble on the ensuing kickoff, it might have gone to 17-0.

"We were too excited, too emotional," said Redskins defensive end Charles Mann. On the sideline, in between some pointed yelling by the coaches, the Washington players told each other to relax. "It was like someone was kicking us in the mouth and we weren't doing anything about it," said Bugel.

Williams saw four of his passes dropped before he twisted a knee and had to leave the game for one play. But he returned, telling Gibbs that he had played before in pain, so why should this be any different? He already had been thrown off by emergency root canal work the day before the game.

Now the Redskins were looking at a 10-point deficit with a gimpy, sore-mouthed quarterback, a defense stunned by Elway's strikes and an offensive game plan of run and ball control that suddenly looked out of place.

That all changed in the second quarter, which wound up being the most prolific by an offensive team in NFL postseason history.

On Washington's first play of the period, Williams wanted to throw a conservative, seven-yard pass to Sanders. But cornerback Mark Haynes bumped Sanders at the line and he adjusted by going deep. He got behind Haynes, caught the pass at midfield and scampered in for an 80-yard touchdown, tying the Super Bowl record for longest pass reception.

"The turning point," said Gibbs. "You could feel the sidelines come alive. We caught fire."

The rest almost defies imagination. The Redskins also scored on their next four possessions of the quarter, performing as if they were going up against their scout team in practice.

Receiver Gary Clark, running the same pattern as Sanders, got behind Steve Wilson and pulled in a 27-yard touchdown pass. After Karlis missed a 43-yard field-goal attempt,

Gary Clark and Eric Yarber (left) celebrate Clark's 27-yard touchdown catch in the second quarter while rookie Timmy Smith takes a handoff from Doug Williams en route to a Super Bowl-record 204-yard rushing performance.

Smith broke away on a counter play for a 58-yard touchdown. Then Sanders beat safety Tony Lilly for a 50-yard score and, following the first of two interceptions by Wilburn, tight end Clint Didier beat safety Tyrone Braxton and pulled in an 8-yard pass for a 35-10 lead.

The Washington numbers in the second quarter were astounding: 35 points, the most ever in one quarter in an NFL postseason game; 356 total yards, including 228 passing by Williams on nine of 11 completions; five touchdowns in 18 plays covering just 5:47 of possession time; 122 yards on five carries by Smith, and 168 yards on five receptions by Sanders.

The Broncos, who had reworked six defensive positions since their 39-20 loss to the Giants in Super Bowl XXI, couldn't stop the Redskins because they simply were unable to handle either Williams or the Hogs, Washington's wonderful and huge offensive line. The Hogs gave Williams enough time to wait for receivers to come open against an average, injury-plagued secondary and also wore down the smaller Denver front seven with the relentless pounding on running plays.

"I'll take a good physical team over a good finesse team nine out of 10 times," said Redskins tackle Mark May.

Washington was particularly effective using its counter gap play, where the running back follows the lead blocks of the right guard and tackle pulling around left end or the left guard and tackle moving to the right.

"It's the best way to neutralize a quick team like Denver that likes to slant its defense," said tackle Joe Jacoby. "They were guessing where we would run, and they guessed right in the first quarter. But they guessed wrong in the second and we got 'em."

The Redskins were determined to use the counter gap, their bread-and-butter running play, at least 15 times in the game.

Smith's 58-yard touchdown came on a counter gap behind left tackle Jacoby, left guard Raleigh McKenzie and tight end Clint Didier, who had the key block. Smith later had a 43-yard gain in the quarter, going left behind right guard R.C. Thielemann and right tackle May. Suddenly, Smith, a fifth-round draft pick from Texas Tech who missed most of his last two college seasons with injuries, was a Super Bowl star.

He really had run better than hobbled starter George Rogers for most of the season, but Gibbs had been reluctant to make a change. An internal team debate had raged for weeks, with most backing an increased use of Smith. Finally, Gibbs decided he needed more outside speed against Denver, so he switched to Smith, cementing the decision the night before the game. To keep Smith from becoming nervous, the Redskins didn't inform him of the change until they came out on the field before the opening kickoff.

He obviously never got too nervous. He rushed for a Super Bowl record 204 yards—78 more than he had gained during the regular season. At least Sanders, another USFL refugee, had some NFL experience, having caught 14 passes in 1986. Still, his nine catches for a Super Bowl record 193 yards also was unexpected.

Meanwhile, nothing was clicking for Elway. The Redskins' five-man rush got better and better, especially Walton, whose blitzing gave Elway particular problems. After a fast start (three of four passes for 96 yards) Elway labored (11 for 34, 161 yards, three interceptions) and Denver collapsed.

Elway was sacked five times. Just as importantly, the Redskins' disciplined rush prevented him from scrambling for more than 32 yards. The Broncos had 142 total yards and 10 points in the first 15 minutes and 185 yards and no points the rest of the game.

"We thought our cornerbacks could cover their wide receivers," said Petitbon. "But we had to get pressure on Elway. We gave him new stuff, with someone blitzing a lot from different spots to confuse him. He's a great player, but he had a big load to carry coming in."

Denver survived on defense in the regular season by causing turnovers (an AFC-high 47). But Williams was intercepted just once and Washington didn't lose a fumble. Thus, the Broncos had nothing to fall back on against the Washington onslaught, which included a Super Bowl record 280 rushing yards.

The Hogs, who were outclassed by the New York Giants' defense three times in 1986, were justifiably proud of their performance in the playoffs in '87. They allowed only three sacks and paved the way for the Redskins to rush for 513 yards.

"We caught fire," Gibbs said of the second quarter. "It was easily the best quarter of football I've been around."

And the key was Williams, who earns less money over three years than $2 million man Elway does in one season. But what is his value to Washington these days?

"I wasn't the quarterback of the Washington Redskins because I was black. That's the important thing," said Williams. "It's been a long week, but a good week. There have been a lot of black questions, but once we got on the practice field, the most important thing was working hard and doing what we did today. That's why I didn't let anything affect me."

Nearby, Eddie Robinson, Williams' former coach at Grambling State University, put it all in context.

"I've seen him do what he did today all the time at Grambling," Robinson said. "The only difference is, today he had a much bigger audience, that's all."

JACK MURPHY STADIUM, SAN DIEGO, CALIF.
SUNDAY, JANUARY 31

SCORE BY PERIODS

Washington	0	35	0	7—42
Denver	10	0	0	0—10

SCORING

Denver—Nattiel 56 pass from Elway (Karlis kick), 1:57 of first quarter. Drive: 56 yards, 1 play.

Denver—Field goal Karlis 24, 5:51 of first quarter. Drive: 61 yards, 7 plays.

Washington—Sanders 80 pass from Williams (Haji-Sheikh kick), 0:53 of second quarter. Drive: 80 yards, 1 play.

Washington—Clark 27 pass from Williams (Haji-Sheikh kick), 4:45 of second quarter. Drive: 64 yards, 5 plays.

Washington—Smith 58 run (Haji-Sheikh kick), 8:33 of second quarter. Drive: 74 yards, 2 plays.

Washington—Sanders 50 pass from Williams (Haji-Sheikh kick), 11:18 of second quarter. Drive: 60 yards, 3 plays.

Washington—Didier 8 pass from Williams (Haji-Sheikh kick), 13:56 of second quarter. Drive: 79 yards, 7 plays.

Washington—Smith 4 run (Haji-Sheikh kick), 1:51 of fourth quarter. Drive: 68 yards, 4 plays.

TEAM STATISTICS

	Washington	Denver
FIRST DOWNS	25	18
By rushing	13	6
By passing	11	10
By penalty	1	2
THIRD DOWN EFFICIENCY	9-15	2-12
TOTAL NET YARDS	602	327
Offensive plays	72	61
Average gain per play	8.4	5.4
NET YARDS RUSHING	280	97
Total rushes	40	17
Average gain per rush	7.0	5.7
NET YARDS PASSING	322	230
Sacked-Yards lost	2-18	5-50
Gross yards passing	340	280
PASSES	18-30-1	15-39-3
Average gain per pass	10.1	5.2
PUNTS	4-37.5	7-36.1
Had blocked	0	0
TOTAL RETURN YARDAGE	57	106
Punt returns	1-0	2-18
Kickoff returns	3-46	5-88
Interception returns	3-11	1-0
PENALTIES-YARDS	6-65	5-26
FUMBLES-LOST	1-0	0-0
TIME OF POSSESSION	35:15	24:45

Attendance—73,302.

INDIVIDUAL STATISTICS

Rushing—Washington, Sanders 1-minus 4, Smith 22-204, Williams 2-minus 2, Bryant 8-38, Clark 1-25, Rogers 5-17, Griffin 1-2; Denver, Elway 3-32, Sewell 1-minus 3, Winder 8-30, Lang 5-38.

Passing—Washington, Williams 18-29-1—340, Schroeder 0-1-0—0; Denver, Elway 14-38-3—257, Sewell 1-1-0—23.

Receiving—Washington, Sanders 9-193, Smith 1-9, Bryant 1-20, Monk 1-40, Warren 2-15, Clark 3-55, Didier 1-8; Denver, Nattiel 2-69, Elway 1-23, Jackson 4-76, Sewell 4-41, Winder 1-26, Lang 1-7, Kay 2-38.

Kickoff Returns—Washington, Sanders 3-46; Denver, Bell 5-88.

Punt Returns—Washington, Green 1-0; Denver, Clark 2-18.

Interceptions—Washington, Wilburn 2-11, Davis 1-0; Denver, Castille 1-0.

Punting—Washington, Cox 4-37.5; Denver, Horan 7-36.1.

Field Goals—Washington, Haji-Sheikh 0-1 (missed: 46); Denver, Karlis 1-2 (missed: 43).

Sacks—Washington, Walton 2, Coleman ½, Mann, Manley 1½; Denver, R. Jones, Mecklenburg.

SUPER BOWL SUMMARIES

SUPER BOWL I

January 15, 1967 at Los Angeles

Attendance—61,946

Kansas City (AFL) ...	0	10	0	0 — 10
Green Bay (NFL)	7	7	14	7 — 35

Winning coach—Vince Lombardi.
Most Valuable Player—Bart Starr.

SUPER BOWL II

January 14, 1968 at Miami

Attendance—75,546

Green Bay (NFL)	3	13	10	7 — 33
Oakland (AFL)	0	7	0	7 — 14

Winning coach—Vince Lombardi.
Most Valuable Player—Bart Starr.

SUPER BOWL III

January 12, 1969 at Miami

Attendance—75,389

New York (AFL)	0	7	6	3 — 16
Baltimore (NFL)	0	0	0	7 — 7

Winning coach—Weeb Ewbank.
Most Valuable Player—Joe Namath.

SUPER BOWL IV

January 11, 1970 at New Orleans

Attendance—80,562

Minnesota (NFL)	0	0	7	0 — 7
Kansas City (AFL) ...	3	13	7	0 — 23

Winning coach—Hank Stram.
Most Valuable Player—Len Dawson.

SUPER BOWL V

January 17, 1971 at Miami

Attendance—79,204

Baltimore (AFC)	0	6	0	10 — 16
Dallas (NFC)	3	10	0	0 — 13

Winning coach—Don McCafferty.
Most Valuable Player—Chuck Howley.

SUPER BOWL VI

January 16, 1972 at New Orleans

Attendance—81,023

Dallas (NFC)	3	7	7	7 — 24
Miami (AFC)	0	3	0	0 — 3

Winning coach—Tom Landry.
Most Valuable Player—Roger Staubach.

SUPER BOWL VII

January 14, 1973 at Los Angeles

Attendance—90,182

Miami (AFC)	7	7	0	0 — 14
Washington (NFC)...	0	0	0	7 — 7

Winning coach—Don Shula.
Most Valuable Player—Jake Scott.

SUPER BOWL VIII

January 13, 1974 at Houston

Attendance—71,882

Minnesota (NFC).....	0	0	0	7 — 7
Miami (AFC)	14	3	7	0 — 24

Winning coach—Don Shula.
Most Valuable Player—Larry Csonka.

SUPER BOWL IX

January 12, 1975 at New Orleans

Attendance—80,997

Pittsburgh (AFC)	0	2	7	7 — 16
Minnesota (NFC).....	0	0	0	6 — 6

Winning coach—Chuck Noll.
Most Valuable Player—Franco Harris.

SUPER BOWL X

January 18, 1976 at Miami

Attendance—80,187

Dallas (NFC)	7	3	0	7 — 17
Pittsburgh (AFC)	7	0	0	14 — 21

Winning coach—Chuck Noll.
Most Valuable Player—Lynn Swann.

SUPER BOWL XI

January 9, 1977 at Pasadena

Attendance—103,428

Oakland (AFC)	0	16	3	13 — 32
Minnesota (NFC).....	0	0	7	7 — 14

Winning coach—John Madden.
Most Valuable Player—Fred Biletnikoff.

SUPER BOWL XII

January 15, 1978 at New Orleans

Attendance—75,804

Dallas (NFC)	10	3	7	7 — 27
Denver (AFC)...........	0	0	10	0 — 10

Winning coach—Tom Landry.
Most Valuable Players—Harvey Martin and Randy White.

SUPER BOWL XIII

January 21, 1979 at Miami

Attendance—78,656

Pittsburgh (AFC)	7	14	0	14 — 35
Dallas (NFC)	7	7	3	14 — 31

Winning coach—Chuck Noll.
Most Valuable Player—Terry Bradshaw.

Joe Robbie Stadium in Miami will host Super Bowl XXIII on January 22, 1989.

SUPER BOWL XIV

January 20, 1980 at Pasadena

Attendance—103,985

Los Angeles (NFC)..	7	6	6	0 — 19
Pittsburgh (AFC)	3	7	7	14 — 31

Winning coach—Chuck Noll.
Most Valuable Player—Terry Bradshaw.

SUPER BOWL XV

January 25, 1981 at New Orleans

Attendance—75,500

Oakland (AFC)	14	0	10	3 — 27
Philadelphia (NFC)..	0	3	0	7 — 10

Winning coach—Tom Flores.
Most Valuable Player—Jim Plunkett.

SUPER BOWL XVI

January 24, 1982 at Pontiac

Attendance—81,270

San Fran. (NFC)	7	13	0	6 — 26
Cincinnati (AFC)......	0	0	7	14 — 21

Winning coach—Bill Walsh.
Most Valuable Player—Joe Montana.

SUPER BOWL XVII

January 30, 1983 at Pasadena

Attendance—103,667

Miami (AFC)	7	10	0	0 — 17
Washington (NFC)...	0	10	3	14 — 27

Winning coach—Joe Gibbs.
Most Valuable Player—John Riggins.

SUPER BOWL XVIII

January 22, 1984 at Tampa

Attendance—72,920

Washington (NFC)...	0	3	6	0 — 9
Los Angeles (AFC)..	7	14	14	3 — 38

Winning coach—Tom Flores.
Most Valuable Player—Marcus Allen.

SUPER BOWL XIX

January 20, 1985 at Palo Alto

Attendance—84,059

Miami (AFC)	10	6	0	0 — 16
San Fran. (NFC)	7	21	10	0 — 38

Winning coach—Bill Walsh.
Most Valuable Player—Joe Montana.

SUPER BOWL XX

January 26, 1986 at New Orleans

Attendance—73,818

Chicago (NFC)	13	10	21	2 — 46
New England (AFC)	3	0	0	7 — 10

Winning coach—Mike Ditka.
Most Valuable Player—Richard Dent.

SUPER BOWL XXI

January 25, 1987 at Pasadena

Attendance—101,063

Denver (AFC)	10	0	0	10 — 20
N.Y. Giants (NFC)	7	2	17	13 — 39

Winning coach—Bill Parcells.
Most Valuable Player—Phil Simms.

SUPER BOWL XXII

January 31, 1988 at San Diego

Attendance—73,302

Washington (NFC)...	0	35	0	7 — 42
Denver (AFC)	10	0	0	0 — 10

Winning coach—Joe Gibbs.
Most Valuable Player—Doug Williams.

1987 NFL Statistics

1987 RUSHING

MOST YARDS, SEASON
NFC: 1374—Charles White, L.A. Rams.
AFC: 1011—Eric Dickerson, Indianapolis.

MOST YARDS, GAME
AFC: 221—Bo Jackson, L.A. Raiders at Seattle, November 30 (18 attempts).
NFC: 213—Charles White, L.A. Rams at St. Louis, November 15 (34 attempts).

LONGEST GAIN
AFC: 91—Bo Jackson, L.A. Raiders at Seattle, November 30 (TD).
NFC: 72—Darrin Nelson, Minnesota vs. Denver, October 26.

MOST ATTEMPTS, SEASON
NFC: 324—Charles White, L.A. Rams.
AFC: 234—Curt Warner, Seattle.

MOST ATTEMPTS, GAME
AFC: 35—Mike LeBlanc, New England vs. Buffalo, October 11 (146 yards).
       Eric Dickerson, Indianapolis vs. San Diego, November 8 (138 yards).
NFC: 35—Dwight Beverly, New Orleans at St. Louis, October 11 (139 yards).
       Charles White, L.A. Rams at Washington, November 23 (112 yards).

AVERAGE YARDS PER ATTEMPT
NFC: 4.9—Darrin Nelson, Minnesota.
AFC: 4.5—Eric Dickerson, Indianapolis.

MOST TOUCHDOWNS
AFC: 11—Johnny Hector, N.Y. Jets.
NFC: 11—Charles White, L.A. Rams.

TEAM LEADERS
AFC: BUFFALO: 485, Ronnie Harmon; CINCINNATI: 570, Larry Kinnebrew; CLEVELAND: 735, Kevin Mack; DENVER: 741, Sammy Winder; HOUSTON: 957, Mike Rozier; INDIANAPOLIS: 1011, Eric Dickerson; KANSAS CITY: 660, Christian Okoye; L.A. RAIDERS: 754, Marcus Allen; MIAMI: 619, Troy Stradford; NEW ENGLAND: 474, Tony Collins; N.Y. JETS: 530, Freeman McNeil; PITTSBURGH: 696, Earnest Jackson; SAN DIEGO: 343, Curtis Adams; SEATTLE: 985, Curt Warner.
NFC: ATLANTA: 875, Gerald Riggs; CHICAGO: 586, Neal Anderson; DALLAS: 891, Herschel Walker; DETROIT: 342, James Jones; GREEN BAY: 413, Kenneth Davis; L.A. RAMS: 1374, Charles White; MINNESOTA: 642, Darrin Nelson; NEW ORLEANS: 917, Rueben Mayes; N.Y. GIANTS: 658, Joe Morris; PHILADELPHIA: 505, Randall Cunningham; ST. LOUIS: 781, Stump Mitchell; SAN FRANCISCO: 815, Roger Craig; TAMPA BAY: 488, James Wilder; WASHINGTON: 613, George Rogers.

TEAM CHAMPION
NFC: 2237—San Francisco.
AFC: 2197—L.A. Raiders.

RUSHING—TEAM

AMERICAN FOOTBALL CONFERENCE

	Att.	Yards	Avg.	Long	TDs.
L.A. Raiders	475	2197	4.6	t91	13
Cincinnati	538	2164	4.0	52	13
Pittsburgh	517	2144	4.1	51	11
Indianapolis	497	2143	4.3	53	14
Seattle	496	2023	4.1	t57	13
Denver	510	1970	3.9	29	18
Houston	486	1923	4.0	41	12
Buffalo	465	1840	4.0	30	9
Kansas City	419	1799	4.3	t64	7
New England	513	1771	3.5	49	12
Cleveland	474	1745	3.7	35	16
N.Y. Jets	458	1671	3.6	32	17
Miami	408	1662	4.1	51	16
San Diego	396	1308	3.3	25	11
Conference Total	6652	26360	.....	t91	182
Conference Average	475.1	1882.9	4.0	.....	13.0

NATIONAL FOOTBALL CONFERENCE

	Att.	Yards	Avg.	Long	TDs.
San Francisco	524	2237	4.3	35	11
New Orleans	569	2190	3.8	38	20
Washington	500	2102	4.2	31	18
L.A. Rams	512	2097	4.1	58	15
Philadelphia	509	2027	4.0	45	12
Minnesota	482	1983	4.1	72	20
Chicago	485	1954	4.0	t38	13
St. Louis	462	1873	4.1	42	15
Dallas	465	1865	4.0	t62	17
Green Bay	464	1801	3.9	61	13
N.Y. Giants	440	1457	3.3	34	4
Detroit	398	1435	3.6	33	9
Tampa Bay	394	1365	3.5	46	7
Atlanta	333	1298	3.9	44	5
Conference Total	6537	25684	.....	72	179
Conference Average	466.9	1834.6	3.9	.....	12.8
League Total	13189	52044	.....	t91	361
League Average	471.0	1858.7	3.9	.....	12.9

TOP TEN RUSHERS

	Att.	Yards	Avg.	Long	TDs.
WHITE, CHARLES, L.A. Rams	324	1374	4.2	58	11
Dickerson, Eric, L.A. Rams-Indianapolis	283	1288	4.6	57	6
Warner, Curt, Seattle	234	985	4.2	t57	8
Rozier, Mike, Houston	229	957	4.2	41	3
Mayes, Rueben, New Orleans	243	917	3.8	38	5
Walker, Herschel, Dallas	209	891	4.3	t60	7
Riggs, Gerald, Atlanta	203	875	4.3	44	2
Craig, Roger, San Francisco	215	815	3.8	25	3
Mitchell, Stump, St. Louis	203	781	3.8	42	3
Allen, Marcus, L.A. Raiders	200	754	3.8	44	5

AFC—INDIVIDUALS

Player—Team	Att.	Yds.	Avg.	Lng.	TD	Player—Team	Att.	Yds.	Avg.	Lng.	TD
DICKERSON, LA-Ind.	283	1288	4.6	57	6	Mueller, Buff.	82	354	4.3	20	2
Warner, Sea.	234	985	4.2	t57	8	Adams, S.D.	90	343	3.8	24	1
Rozier, Hou.	229	957	4.2	41	3	Dupard, N.E.	94	318	3.4	49	3
Allen, Raiders	200	754	3.8	44	5	Jennings, Cin.	70	314	4.5	18	1
Winder, Den.	196	741	3.8	19	6	Elway, Den.	66	304	4.6	29	4
Mack, Clev.	201	735	3.7	t22	5	Lang, Den.	89	303	3.4	28	2
Jackson, Pitt.	180	696	3.9	39	1	Brooks, Cin.	94	290	3.1	18	1
Okoye, K.C.	157	660	4.2	t43	3	Hampton, Mia.	75	289	3.9	34	1
Bentley, Ind.	142	631	4.4	t17	7	Byrum, Buff.	66	280	4.2	30	0
Stradford, Mia.	145	619	4.3	51	6	G. Anderson, S.D.	80	260	3.3	25	3
Kinnebrew, Cin.	145	570	3.9	52	8	Vick, Jets.	77	257	3.3	14	1
B. Jackson, Raiders	81	554	6.8	t91	4	Tatupu, N.E.	79	248	3.1	19	0
Pollard, Pitt.	128	536	4.2	33	3	C. Banks, Ind.	50	245	4.9	35	0
McNeil, Jets	121	530	4.4	30	0	Esiason, Cin.	52	241	4.6	19	0
Jo. Williams, Sea.	113	500	4.4	48	1	Jackson, Hou.	60	232	3.9	t16	1
Harmon, Buff.	116	485	4.2	21	2	Ti. Spencer, S.D.	73	228	3.1	16	0
Collins, N.E.	147	474	3.2	19	3	Riddick, Buff.	59	221	3.7	25	5
Heard, K.C.	82	466	5.7	t64	3	Mason, Clev.	56	207	3.7	22	2
Abercrombie, Pitt.	123	459	3.7	t28	2	B. Johnson, Cin.	39	205	5.3	20	1
Hector, Jets	111	435	3.9	t20	11	Logan, Cin.	37	203	5.5	51	1
Byner, Clev.	105	432	4.1	21	8	R. Scott, Mia.	47	199	4.2	24	3

Player—Team	Att.	Yds.	Avg.	Lng.	TD
Perryman, N.E.	41	187	4.6	48	0
R. Porter, Buff.	47	177	3.8	13	0
Mueller, Raiders	37	175	4.7	35	1
LeBlanc, N.E.	49	170	3.5	42	1
Malone, Pitt.	34	162	4.8	t42	3
Krieg, Sea.	36	155	4.3	17	2
Palmer, K.C.	24	155	6.5	35	0
Dudek, Den.	35	154	4.4	16	2
Parker, K.C.	47	150	3.2	10	1
Pinkett, Hou.	31	149	4.8	22	2
Evans, Raiders	11	144	13.1	24	1
Hunter, Hou.	34	144	4.2	21	0
Willhite, Den.	26	141	5.4	29	0
C. Ellis, Raiders	33	138	4.2	14	2
Stone, Pitt.	17	135	7.9	51	0
Kelly, Buff.	29	133	4.6	24	0
Bligen, Jets	31	128	4.1	15	1
Poole, Den.	28	126	4.5	15	1
Manoa, Clev.	23	116	5.0	35	0
Davenport, Mia.	32	114	3.6	27	1
C. Smith, K.C.	26	114	4.4	11	0
Moon, Hou.	34	112	3.3	20	3
Strachan, Raiders	28	108	3.9	20	0
Moriarty, K.C.	30	107	3.6	11	0
Highsmith, Hou.	29	106	3.7	25	1
W. Bennett, Mia.	25	102	4.1	18	0
James, S.D.	27	102	3.8	t15	2
Wallace, Hou.	19	102	5.4	19	0
Mackey, Mia.	17	98	5.8	17	2
Everett, Clev.	34	95	2.8	16	0
Horton, Raiders	31	95	3.1	14	0
McCluskey, Cin.	29	94	3.2	12	1
Wilson, Raiders	17	91	5.4	16	0
Jenkins, S.D.	22	88	4.0	9	0
G. Brown, Ind.	19	85	4.5	t18	1
Sewell, Den.	19	83	4.4	17	2
B. Green, Raiders	21	77	3.7	17	0
Ramsey, N.E.	13	75	5.8	19	1
Middleton, S.D.	28	74	2.6	21	1
Wright, Cin.	24	74	3.1	10	0
Morris, Sea.	21	71	3.4	13	0
Wonsley, Ind.	18	71	3.9	12	1
D. Walter, Cin.	16	70	4.4	16	0
Sanders, Pitt.	11	65	5.9	14	1
O'Brien, Jets	30	61	2.0	11	0
Rice, Cin.	18	59	3.3	8	0
McLemore, Ind.	17	58	3.4	9	0
Bailey, Mia.	10	55	5.5	13	0
Caldwell, Den.	16	53	3.3	7	0
Fryar, N.E.	9	52	5.8	16	0
Morton, Sea.	19	52	2.7	10	1
Sartin, S.D.	19	52	2.7	10	1
Harrison, Raiders	9	49	5.4	13	0
Lacy, K.C.	14	49	3.5	17	0
Konecny, Mia.	6	46	7.7	19	0
Tagliaferri, Mia.	13	45	3.5	7	1
Hansen, N.E.	16	44	2.8	7	0
Bell, Den.	13	43	3.3	11	0
Davis, N.E.	9	43	4.8	27	0
Faaola, Jets	14	43	3.1	18	2
Flutie, N.E.	6	43	7.2	13	0
Shepherd, Buff.	12	42	3.5	19	0
Christensen, Clev.	11	41	3.7	15	0
Isom, Mia.	9	41	4.6	8	1
Neuheisel, S.D.	6	41	6.8	18	1
Lane, Sea.	13	40	3.1	7	0
Grogan, N.E.	20	37	1.9	8	2
Burse, Sea.	7	36	5.1	16	0
Calhoun, Raiders	7	36	5.1	18	0
Redden, S.D.	11	36	3.3	7	0
Fontenot, Clev.	15	33	2.2	14	0
Largent, Sea.	2	33	16.5	21	0
Pease, Hou.	15	33	2.2	8	1
Seurer, K.C.	9	33	3.7	11	0
Parros, Sea.	13	32	2.5	7	1
Driver, Clev.	9	31	3.4	16	0
Kiel, Ind.	4	30	7.5	16	0
Tillman, Hou.	12	29	2.4	13	1
King, Buff.	9	28	3.1	8	0
Bono, Pitt.	8	27	3.4	23	1
Eason, N.E.	3	25	8.3	13	0
L. Williams, Buff.	9	25	2.8	9	0
Hawkins, Raiders	4	24	6.0	7	0
To. Spencer, S.D.	14	24	1.7	5	0
Cobble, Hou.	9	23	2.6	12	0
C. McSwain, N.E.	9	23	2.6	9	0
Chirico, Jets	12	22	1.8	4	1
Kosar, Clev.	15	22	1.5	7	1
R. Moore, Hou.	7	22	3.1	11	0
Blackledge, K.C.	5	21	4.2	11	0
Collier, Pitt.	4	20	5.0	12	0
Nathan, Mia.	4	20	5.0	8	0
Woods, N.E.	4	20	5.0	13	1
Meehan, Cin.	4	19	4.8	17	0
Breen, Cin.	6	18	3.0	9	0
Jensen, Mia.	4	18	4.5	9	0
Smith, Raiders	5	18	3.6	15	0
Bennett, Cin.	2	17	8.5	9	0
Harris, Hou.	1	17	17.0	17	0
Holland, S.D.	1	17	17.0	17	0
Kelley, S.D.	4	17	4.3	10	0
McNeil, Clev.	1	17	17.0	17	0
Goodburn, K.C.	1	16	16.0	16	0
Newsome, Pitt.	2	16	8.0	16	0
Pippens, K.C.	3	16	5.3	11	0
Mathison, Sea.	5	15	3.0	10	0
Moore, Det.	3	15	5.0	13	0
Nattiel, Den.	2	13	6.5	10	0
Partridge, Buff.	1	13	13.0	13	0
Starring, N.E.	2	13	6.5	10	0
Carter, Pitt.	5	12	2.4	4	0
Totten, Buff.	12	11	0.9	7	0
A. Williams, S.D.	1	11	11.0	11	0
C. James, N.E.	4	10	2.5	5	0
Roth, Mia.	3	10	3.3	9	0
Valentine, Hou.	5	10	2.0	4	0
Bernstine, S.D.	1	9	9.0	9	0
D. Foster, Jets	1	9	9.0	9	0
Kemp, Sea.	5	9	1.8	12	0
Verser, Clev.	1	9	9.0	9	0
Clayton, Mia.	2	8	4.0	4	0
Hilger, Raiders	8	8	1.0	6	0
Hoge, Pitt.	3	8	2.7	5	0
Micho, Den.	4	8	2.0	5	0
Reeder, Pitt.	2	8	4.0	4	0
Boddie, Den.	3	7	2.3	4	1
Clemons, K.C.	2	7	3.5	7	0
Davis, Clev.	1	7	7.0	7	0
Stevens, K.C.	3	7	2.3	6	0
Trudeau, Ind.	15	7	0.5	9	0
Manucci, Buff.	4	6	1.5	9	0
Espinoza, K.C.	1	5	5.0	5	0
Jennings, Jets	2	5	2.5	4	0
Norrie, Jets	5	5	1.0	2	0
Ryan, Jets	4	5	1.3	t8	1
Briggs, Jets	1	4	4.0	4	0
McClure, Buff.	2	4	2.0	3	0
T. Brown, Mia.	3	3	1.0	3	0
Carver, Ind.	2	3	1.5	3	0
Hagen, Sea.	2	3	1.5	4	0
Hogeboom, Ind.	3	3	1.0	2	0
Karcher, Den.	9	3	0.3	8	0
Kubiak, Den.	1	3	3.0	3	0
Steels, S.D.	1	3	3.0	3	0
Zachary, S.D.	1	3	3.0	3	0
Stockemer, K.C.	1	2	2.0	2	0
Aikens, Raiders	1	1	1.0	1	0
Browne, Raiders	2	1	0.5	2	0
Lofton, Raiders	1	1	1.0	1	0
Moffett, S.D.	1	1	1.0	1	0
Nugent, Ind.	2	1	0.5	3	0
Reed, Buff.	1	1	1.0	1	0
E. Brown, Cin.	1	0	0.0	0	0
Camarillo, N.E.	1	0	0.0	0	0
Danielson, Clev.	1	0	0.0	0	0
Fouts, S.D.	12	0	0.0	2	2
Griffith, Sea.	1	0	0.0	0	0
Hudson, K.C.	1	0	0.0	0	0
Katolin, Clev.	1	0	0.0	0	0
K. Porter, Buff.	2	0	0.0	1	0
Roby, Mia.	1	0	0.0	0	0
Rodriguez, Sea.	1	0	0.0	0	0

Player—Team	Att.	Yds.	Avg.	Lng.	TD
Herrmann, S.D.	4	−1	−0.3	0	0
Brooks, Ind.	2	−2	−1.0	1	0
Kenney, K.C.	12	−2	−0.2	6	0
Townsell, Jets	1	−2	−2.0	−2	0
May, Den.	2	−4	−2.0	−2	0
Bleier, N.E.	5	−5	−1.0	t1	1
Marino, Mia.	12	−5	−0.4	t5	1
Whitten, N.E.	2	−6	−3.0	−2	0
Carson, K.C.	1	−7	−7.0	−7	0
V. Johnson, Den.	1	−8	−8.0	−8	0
McGee, Cin.	1	−10	−10.0	−10	0
Givins, Hou.	1	−13	−13.0	−13	0

NFC—INDIVIDUALS

Player—Team	Att.	Yds.	Avg.	Lng.	TD
WHITE, Rams	324	1374	4.2	58	11
Mayes, N.O.	243	917	3.8	38	5
H. Walker, Dall.	209	891	4.3	t60	7
Riggs, Atl.	203	875	4.3	44	2
Craig, S.F.	215	815	3.8	25	3
Mitchell, St.L.	203	781	3.8	42	3
Morris, Giants	193	658	3.4	34	3
D. Nelson, Minn.	131	642	4.9	72	2
Rogers, Wash.	163	613	3.8	29	6
Anderson, Chi.	129	586	4.5	t38	3
W. Payton, Chi.	146	533	3.7	17	4
Ferrell, St.L.	113	512	4.5	t35	7
Hilliard, N.O.	123	508	4.1	t30	7
Cunningham, Phil.	76	505	6.6	45	3
Wilder, T.B.	106	488	4.6	21	0
Toney, Phil.	127	473	3.7	36	5
Dorsett, Dall.	130	456	3.5	24	1
Byars, Phil.	116	426	3.7	30	3
Davis, G.B.	109	413	3.8	t39	3
Bryant, Wash.	77	406	5.3	28	1
Vital, Wash.	80	346	4.3	t22	2
Jones, Det.	96	342	3.6	19	0
Anderson, Minn.	68	319	4.7	27	2
J. Smith, T.B.	100	309	3.1	46	2
Cribbs, S.F.	70	300	4.3	20	1
Fullwood, G.B.	84	274	3.3	18	5
James, Det.	82	270	3.3	17	4
W. Wilson, Minn.	41	263	6.4	38	5
Dozier, Minn.	69	257	3.7	19	5
Rathman, S.F.	62	257	4.1	35	1
Willhite, G.B.	53	251	4.7	61	0
Griffin, Wash.	62	242	3.9	13	0
McAdoo, St.L.	53	230	4.3	17	3
Beverly, N.O.	62	217	3.5	25	2
Clark, G.B.	56	211	3.8	57	0
E. Hunter, Jets-T.B.	56	210	3.8	23	0
Ellerson, Det.	47	196	4.2	33	3
Carruth, G.B.	64	192	3.0	23	3
Young, S.F.	26	190	7.3	t29	1
Bernard, Det.	45	187	4.2	14	2
Fenney, Minn.	42	174	4.1	12	2
Adams, Giants	61	169	2.8	14	1
Haddix, Phil.	59	165	2.8	11	0
Rouson, Giants	41	155	3.8	14	0
Pelluer, Dall.	25	142	5.7	21	1
Montana, S.F.	35	141	4.0	20	1
Francis, Rams	35	138	3.9	23	0
R. Brown, Phil.	39	136	3.5	23	0
J. Fourcade, N.O.	19	134	7.1	18	0
Word, N.O.	36	133	3.7	20	2
Rice, Minn.	51	131	2.6	13	1
Heimuli, Chi.	34	128	3.8	12	0
Majkowski, G.B.	15	127	8.5	33	0
Smith, Wash.	29	126	4.3	15	0
Blount, Dall.	46	125	2.7	15	3
Sydney, S.F.	29	125	4.3	15	0
Sanders, Chi.	23	122	5.3	17	1
Newsome, Dall.	25	121	4.8	t24	2
Schroeder, Wash.	26	120	4.6	31	3
Robinson, Phil.	24	114	4.8	18	0
Wester, Det.	33	113	3.4	14	0
Wright, T.B.	37	112	3.0	11	0
V. Williams, Giants	29	108	3.7	17	0
Lomax, St.L.	29	107	3.7	19	0
Campbell, Atl.	21	102	4.9	24	2
Howard, T.B.	30	100	3.3	31	1
Guman, Rams	36	98	2.7	7	1
Hebert, N.O.	13	95	7.3	19	0
DiRico, Giants	25	90	3.6	14	0
Sargent, St.L.	18	90	5.0	16	0
McMahon, Chi.	22	88	4.0	13	2
Thomas, Chi.	25	88	3.5	18	0
Badanjek, Atl.	29	87	3.0	31	1
Wolfley, St.L.	26	87	3.3	8	1
Bell, Buff.-Rams	22	86	3.9	13	0
Everett, Rams	18	83	4.6	16	1
Varajon, S.F.	18	82	4.6	11	0
Woolfolk, Det.	12	82	6.8	31	0
Mosley, Chi.	18	80	4.4	16	0
Ricks, T.B.	24	76	3.2	14	1
Galbreath, Giants	10	74	7.4	17	0
Settle, Atl.	19	72	3.8	12	0
Alexander, N.O.	21	71	3.4	16	1
Wright, G.B.	13	70	5.4	27	0
Edwards, Det.	32	69	2.2	13	0
Hold, T.B.	7	69	9.9	35	0
Tautalatasi, Phil.	26	69	2.7	17	0
Cherry, S.F.	13	65	5.0	16	1
Long, Det.	22	64	2.9	15	0
Risher, G.B.	11	64	5.8	15	1
Monk, Wash.	6	63	10.5	26	0
Edwards, Dall.	2	61	30.5	t62	1
Flowers, Atl.	14	61	4.4	14	0
Carthon, Giants	26	60	2.3	10	0
Hohensee, Chi.	9	56	6.2	26	0
Brewer, Chi.	24	55	2.3	16	2
W. Wilson, Wash.	18	55	3.1	11	2
Ross, Phil.	14	54	3.9	12	1
Tomczak, Chi.	18	54	3.0	10	1
Rice, S.F.	8	51	6.4	17	1
Testaverde, T.B.	13	50	3.8	17	1
Adams, Dall.	7	49	7.0	t27	1
Hons, Det.	5	49	9.8	23	0
M. Williams, Atl.	14	49	3.5	9	0
Hardy, S.F.	7	48	6.9	14	0
Rodgers, S.F.	11	46	4.2	15	1
Stevens, S.F.	10	45	4.5	16	1
Kramer, Minn.	10	44	4.4	15	2
Simms, Giants	14	44	3.1	20	0
Tyrrell, Rams	11	44	4.0	13	0
Gentry, Chi.	6	41	6.8	12	0
Hargrove, G.B.	11	38	3.5	7	1
Stanley, G.B.	4	38	9.5	24	0
Gray, N.O.	8	37	4.6	12	1
Jessie, Wash.	10	37	3.7	t14	1
Brim, Minn.	2	36	18.0	t38	1
Jordan, N.O.	12	36	3.0	t8	2
Rodenberger, N.O.	17	35	2.1	5	0
Green, St.L.	2	34	17.0	26	0
DuBose, S.F.	10	33	3.3	11	0
Parker, S.F.	8	33	4.1	17	0
Austin, T.B.	19	32	1.7	8	1
Teltschik, Phil.	3	32	10.7	23	0
Adams, Minn.	11	31	2.8	12	0
Garza, St.L.	8	31	3.9	10	1
Rubbert, Wash.	9	31	3.4	14	0
Rutledge, Giants	15	31	2.1	20	0
Bartalo, T.B.	9	30	3.3	6	1
Gladman, T.B.	12	29	2.4	6	0
S. Williams, Det.	8	29	3.6	8	0
S. Payton, Chi.	1	28	28.0	28	0
T. Wilson, Wash.	2	28	14.0	t16	1
Jackson, Phil.	6	27	4.5	10	0
Monroe, S.F.	2	26	13.0	17	0
Weigel, G.B.	10	26	2.6	7	0
Suhey, Chi.	7	24	3.4	6	0
A. Walker, Minn.	5	24	4.8	11	0
F. Harris, Chi.	6	23	3.8	18	0
Beecham, Giants	5	22	4.4	10	0
Ro. Brown, Rams	2	22	11.0	11	0
Dollinger, Det.	8	22	2.8	8	0
C. Miller, Atl.	4	21	5.3	11	0

Player—Team	Att.	Yds.	Avg.	Lng.	TD
Grant, Phil.	1	20	20.0	20	0
Land, T.B.	9	20	2.2	6	0
Sterling, G.B.	5	20	4.0	9	0
Womack, Minn.	9	20	2.2	13	0
L. Thomas, G.B.	5	19	3.8	5	0
Baker, Giants	1	18	18.0	18	0
Jean-Batiste, N.O.	8	18	2.3	7	0
La. Morris, G.B.	8	18	2.3	10	0
Gault, Chi.	2	16	8.0	9	0
B. Wilson, Minn.	5	16	3.2	6	0
Harbaugh, Chi.	4	15	3.8	9	0
Ingram, N.O.	2	14	7.0	9	0
Morse, Phil.	6	14	2.3	7	0
Verdin, Wash.	1	14	14.0	14	0
D. White, Dall.	10	14	1.4	8	1
Paige, Det.	4	13	3.3	6	0
J. Smith, Minn.	7	13	1.9	5	0
Granger, Atl.	6	12	2.0	6	0
Clark, Chi.	5	11	2.2	5	0
Flagler, S.F.	6	11	1.8	5	0
Lovelady, Giants	2	11	5.5	8	0
McIntosh, Atl.	5	11	2.2	5	0
Moore, Minn.	4	11	2.8	4	0
Park, Giants	6	11	1.8	4	0
Evans, Rams	3	10	3.3	5	0
Kramer, Atl.	2	10	5.0	11	0
Branch, Wash.	4	9	2.3	3	1
Ro. Brown, St.L.	1	9	9.0	9	0
T. Johnson, St.L.	1	9	9.0	9	0
Williams, Rams	2	9	4.5	7	0
D. Williams, Wash.	7	9	1.3	7	1
Archer, Atl.	2	8	4.0	7	0
Harrell, Minn.	5	8	1.6	4	0
Quarles, Rams	1	8	8.0	8	0
Sweeney, Dall.	5	8	1.6	5	0
Wolden, Chi.	2	8	4.0	7	0
Holman, Wash.	2	7	3.5	5	0
E.J. Jones, Dall.	2	7	3.5	5	0
Anderson, Giants	2	6	3.0	4	0
McGee, Rams	3	6	2.0	t2	1
Stamps, Atl.	1	6	6.0	6	0
Van Raaphorst, Atl.	1	6	6.0	6	0
Crocicchia, Giants	4	5	1.3	7	0
DiRenzo, Giants	1	5	5.0	5	0
Emery, Atl.	1	5	5.0	5	0
Streater, T.B.	1	5	5.0	5	0
Ellard, Rams	1	4	4.0	4	0
Frye, Minn.	4	4	1.0	2	0
A. Thomas, Minn.	6	4	0.7	5	0
Zorn, T.B.	4	4	1.0	5	0
Cater, St.L.	2	3	1.5	11	0
Cook, G.B.	2	3	1.5	2	0
S. Harris, Minn.	4	3	0.8	2	0
Hill, T.B.	3	3	1.0	9	0
Mandley, Det.	1	3	3.0	3	0
Riordan, N.O.	1	3	3.0	3	0
Boone, T.B.	1	2	2.0	2	0
Bryant, Rams	1	2	2.0	2	0
Frank, S.F.	1	2	2.0	2	0
Kowgios, Det.	1	2	2.0	2	0
Le. Morris, G.B.	2	2	1.0	4	0
Scott, G.B.	1	2	2.0	2	0
D. Thomas, T.B.	1	2	2.0	2	0
Tinsley, Phil.	4	2	0.5	2	0
J. Butler, Atl.	1	1	1.0	1	0
Freeman, T.B.	1	1	1.0	1	0
Marshall, Chi.	1	1	1.0	1	0
Black, Det.	1	0	0.0	0	0
Blount, S.F.	1	0	0.0	0	0
Brown, Chi.	1	0	0.0	0	0
Clark, Wash.	1	0	0.0	0	0
Clemons, Phil.	3	0	0.0	3	0
Covington, Giants	4	0	0.0	2	0
Criswell, T.B.	1	0	0.0	0	0
Epps, G.B.	1	0	0.0	0	0
Horn, Phil.	1	0	0.0	0	0
Hunter, G.B.	1	0	0.0	0	0
Neal, G.B.	1	0	0.0	0	0
Oliver, Atl.	1	0	0.0	0	0
Perry, Chi.	1	0	0.0	0	0
T. Robinson, Wash.	2	0	0.0	2	0
Snyder, Dall.	2	0	0.0	0	0
Miller, Minn.	1	−1	−1.0	−1	0
Cavanaugh, Phil.	1	−2	−2.0	−2	0
Griffin, Steve B., Atl.	1	−2	−2.0	−2	0
Gustafson, Minn.	1	−2	−2.0	−2	0
Stoudt, St.L.	1	−2	−2.0	−2	0
Bradley, Chi.	1	−3	−3.0	−3	0
Dixon, Atl.	3	−3	−1.0	7	0
Dils, Rams	7	−4	−0.6	5	0
Matthews, Atl.	1	−4	−4.0	−4	0
Sanders, Wash.	1	−4	−4.0	−4	0
G. White, Dall.	1	−4	−4.0	−4	0
Cosbie, Dall.	1	−5	−5.0	−5	0
Chadwick, Det.	1	−6	−6.0	−6	0
Donnelly, Atl.	3	−6	−2.0	0	0
Hansen, N.O.	2	−6	−3.0	−3	0
Lewis, Minn.	5	−7	−1.4	4	0
Scribner, Minn.	1	−7	−7.0	−7	0
DeBerg, T.B.	8	−8	−1.0	0	0
Merkens, Phil.	3	−8	−2.7	1	0
Awalt, St.L.	2	−9	−4.5	−1	0
Halloran, St.L.	3	−9	−3.0	2	0
Hill, N.O.	1	−9	−9.0	−9	0
Manuel, Giants	1	−10	−10.0	−10	0
Barnhardt, N.O.	1	−13	−13.0	−13	0
Taylor, Atl.	1	−13	−13.0	−13	0

t—Touchdown
Leader based on most yards gained

1987 PASSING

HIGHEST RATING
NFC: 102.1—Joe Montana, San Francisco.
AFC: 95.4—Bernie Kosar, Cleveland.

HIGHEST COMPLETION PERCENTAGE
NFC: 66.8—Joe Montana, San Francisco.
AFC: 62.0—Bernie Kosar, Cleveland.

MOST ATTEMPTS, SEASON
NFC: 463—Neil Lomax, St. Louis.
AFC: 444—Dan Marino, Miami.

MOST COMPLETIONS, SEASON
NFC: 275—Neil Lomax, St. Louis.
AFC: 263—Dan Marino, Miami.

MOST YARDS, SEASON
NFC: 3387—Neil Lomax, St. Louis.
AFC: 3321—Boomer Esiason, Cincinnati.

MOST YARDS, GAME
NFC: 457—Neil Lomax, St. Louis at San Diego, September 20 (32 completions, 61 attempts).
AFC: 409—Boomer Esiason, Cincinnati vs. Pittsburgh, November 22 (30 completions, 53 attempts).

LONGEST GAIN
NFC: 88—Ed Rubbert (to Anthony Allen) Washington vs. St. Louis, October 4 (TD).
AFC: 83—Warren Moon (to Ernest Givins) Houston vs. Cleveland, November 22 (TD).

AVERAGE YARDS PER ATTEMPT
NFC: 7.98—Wade Wilson, Minnesota.
AFC: 7.80—John Elway, Denver.

MOST TOUCHDOWN PASSES, SEASON
NFC: 31—Joe Montana, San Francisco.
AFC: 26—Dan Marino, Miami.

MOST TOUCHDOWN PASSES, GAME
AFC: 5—Gary Hogeboom, Indianapolis at Buffalo, October 4.
NFC: 5—Steve DeBerg, Tampa Bay vs. Atlanta, September 13.

LOWEST INTERCEPTION PERCENTAGE
AFC: 2.0—Ken O'Brien, N.Y. Jets.
NFC: 2.5—Steve DeBerg, Tampa Bay.

TEAM CHAMPION (Net Yards)
AFC: 3876—Miami.
NFC: 3750—San Francisco.

PASSING—TEAM

AMERICAN FOOTBALL CONFERENCE

	Atts.	Com.	Pct. Com.	Gross Yards	Tkd.-Yds. Lost	Net Yards	Avg. Yds. Att.	Avg. Yds. Com.	TD	Lng.	Had Int.
Miami	584	338	57.9	3977	13-101	3876	6.81	11.77	29	t59	20
Denver	530	285	53.8	3874	30-220	3654	7.31	13.59	24	t72	19
Cleveland	482	291	60.4	3625	29-170	3455	7.52	12.46	27	t54	12
Houston	482	240	49.8	3534	30-234	3300	7.33	14.73	24	t83	23
San Diego	516	303	58.7	3602	39-322	3280	6.98	11.89	13	67	23
Cincinnati	475	255	53.7	3468	32-255	3213	7.30	13.60	17	t61	20
L.A. Raiders	457	247	54.0	3429	53-359	3070	7.50	13.88	19	49	18
N.Y. Jets	517	302	58.4	3402	66-443	2959	6.58	11.26	18	59	15
Buffalo	516	292	56.6	3246	37-345	2901	6.29	11.12	21	47	19
Indianapolis	447	255	57.0	3042	24-190	2852	6.81	11.93	16	t72	16
Seattle	405	237	58.5	3028	36-316	2712	7.48	12.78	31	t75	21
New England	440	236	53.6	2929	33-246	2683	6.66	12.41	22	45	18
Kansas City	432	236	54.6	2985	48-366	2619	6.91	12.65	17	t81	17
Pittsburgh	429	198	46.2	2464	27-198	2266	5.74	12.44	13	63	25
Conf. Total	6712	3715	....	46605	497-3765	42840	....	....	291	t83	266
Conf. Average	479.4	265.4	55.3	3328.9	35.5-268.9	3060.0	6.94	12.55	20.8	.....	19.0

NATIONAL FOOTBALL CONFERENCE

	Atts.	Com.	Pct. Com.	Gross Yards	Tkd.-Yds. Lost	Net Yards	Avg. Yds. Att.	Avg. Yds. Com.	TD	Lng.	Had Int.
San Francisco	501	322	64.3	3955	29-205	3750	7.89	12.28	44	t57	14
Washington	478	247	51.7	3718	27-223	3495	7.78	15.05	27	t88	18
St. Louis	529	305	57.7	3850	54-397	3453	7.28	12.62	25	57	15
N.Y. Giants	499	265	53.1	3645	61-443	3202	7.30	13.75	26	t63	22
Dallas	500	288	57.6	3594	52-403	3191	7.19	12.48	19	t77	20
Chicago	493	272	55.2	3420	48-330	3090	6.94	12.57	23	t59	24
Philadelphia	520	283	54.4	3561	72-511	3050	6.85	12.58	26	t70	16
Tampa Bay	517	264	51.1	3377	43-361	3016	6.53	12.79	22	t64	17
Detroit	509	275	54.0	3150	26-194	2956	6.19	11.45	16	t53	26
Minnesota	446	232	52.0	3185	52-359	2826	7.14	13.73	21	t73	23
New Orleans	411	227	55.2	2987	29-213	2774	7.27	13.16	23	t82	12
Atlanta	501	247	49.3	3108	46-340	2768	6.20	12.58	17	57	32
Green Bay	455	234	51.4	2977	45-296	2681	6.54	12.72	15	t70	17
L.A. Rams	420	220	52.4	2750	25-196	2554	6.55	12.50	16	t81	18
Conf. Total	6779	3681	....	47277	609-4471	42806	....	....	320	t88	274
Conf. Average	484.2	262.9	54.3	3376.9	43.5-319.4	3057.6	6.97	12.84	22.9	.....	19.6
League Total	13491	7396	....	93882	1106-8236	85646	....	....	611	t88	540
League Avg.	481.8	264.1	54.8	3352.9	39.5-294.1	3058.8	6.96	12.69	21.8	.....	19.3

Leader based on net yards

TOP TEN PASSING QUALIFIERS

Player—Team	Att.	Cmp.	Pct. Cmp.	Yds.	Avg. Gain	TD	Pct. TD	Lg.	Int.	Pct. Int.	Rating Pts.
MONTANA, JOE, S.F.	398	266	66.8	3054	7.67	31	7.8	t57	13	3.3	102.1
Kosar, Bernie, Clev.	389	241	62.0	3033	7.80	22	5.7	t54	9	2.3	95.4
Simms, Phil, Giants	282	163	57.8	2230	7.91	17	6.0	t50	9	3.2	90.0
Marino, Dan, Mia.	444	263	59.2	3245	7.31	26	5.9	t59	13	2.9	89.2
Lomax, Neil, St.L.	463	275	59.4	3387	7.32	24	5.2	57	12	2.6	88.5
Krieg, Dave, Sea.	294	178	60.5	2131	7.25	23	7.8	t75	15	5.1	87.6
McMahon, Jim, Chi.	210	125	59.5	1639	7.80	12	5.7	t59	8	3.8	87.4
Kenney, Bill, K.C.	273	154	56.4	2107	7.72	15	5.5	t81	9	3.3	85.8
DeBerg, Steve, T.B.	275	159	57.8	1891	6.88	14	5.1	t64	7	2.5	85.3
Wilson, Marc, Raiders	266	152	57.1	2070	7.78	12	4.5	t47	8	3.0	84.6

AFC INDIVIDUAL QUALIFIERS

Player—Team	Att.	Cmp.	Pct. Cmp.	Yds.	Avg. Gain	TD	Pct. TD	Lg.	Int.	Pct. Int.	Rating Pts.
KOSAR, Clev.	389	241	62.0	3033	7.80	22	5.7	t54	9	2.3	95.4
Marino, Mia.	444	263	59.2	3245	7.31	26	5.9	t59	13	2.9	89.2
Krieg, Sea.	294	178	60.5	2131	7.25	23	7.8	t75	15	5.1	87.6
Kenney, K.C.	273	154	56.4	2107	7.72	15	5.5	t81	9	3.3	85.8
Wilson, Raiders	266	152	57.1	2070	7.78	12	4.5	t47	8	3.0	84.6
Kelly, Buff.	419	250	59.7	2798	6.68	19	4.5	47	11	2.6	83.8
Elway, Den.	410	224	54.6	3198	7.80	19	4.6	t72	12	2.9	83.4
O'Brien, Jets	393	234	59.5	2696	6.86	13	3.3	59	8	2.0	82.8
Trudeau, Ind.	229	128	55.9	1587	6.93	6	2.6	55	6	2.6	75.4
Moon, Hou.	368	184	50.0	2806	7.63	21	5.7	t83	18	4.9	74.2
Esiason, Cin.	440	240	54.5	3321	7.55	16	3.6	t61	19	4.3	73.1
Fouts, S.D.	364	206	56.6	2517	6.91	10	2.7	46	15	4.1	70.0
Malone, Pitt.	336	156	46.4	1896	5.64	6	1.8	63	19	5.7	46.7

AFC NON-QUALIFIERS

Player—Team	Att.	Cmp.	Pct. Cmp.	Yds.	Avg. Gain	TD	Pct. TD	Lg.	Int.	Pct. Int.	Rating Pts.
Danielson, Clev.	33	25	75.8	281	8.52	4	12.1	23	0	0.0	140.3
Kemp, Sea.	33	23	69.7	396	12.00	5	15.2	55	1	3.0	137.1
Kelley, S.D.	29	17	58.6	305	10.52	1	3.4	67	0	0.0	106.3
Flutie, N.E.	25	15	60.0	199	7.96	1	4.0	30	0	0.0	98.6
Ryan, Jets	53	32	60.4	314	5.92	4	7.5	t35	2	3.8	86.5
Neuheisel, S.D.	59	40	67.8	367	6.22	1	1.7	32	1	1.7	83.1
Hogeboom, Ind.	168	99	58.9	1145	6.82	9	5.4	t72	5	3.0	85.0
Grogan, N.E.	161	93	57.8	1183	7.35	10	6.2	40	9	5.6	78.2
Bono, Pitt.	74	34	45.9	438	5.92	5	6.8	57	2	2.7	76.3
Karcher, Den.	102	56	54.9	628	6.16	5	4.9	49	4	3.9	73.5
Evans, Raiders	83	39	47.0	630	7.59	5	6.0	47	4	4.8	72.9
Eason, N.E.	79	42	53.2	453	5.73	3	3.8	45	2	2.5	72.4
Stevens, K.C.	57	32	56.1	315	5.53	1	1.8	23	1	1.8	70.4
Ramsey, N.E.	134	71	53.0	898	6.70	6	4.5	40	6	4.5	70.4
D. Walter, Cin.	21	10	47.6	113	5.38	0	0.0	35	0	0.0	64.2
Pease, Hou.	113	56	49.6	728	6.44	3	2.7	51	5	4.4	60.6
Blackledge, K.C.	31	15	48.4	154	4.97	1	3.2	19	1	3.2	60.4
Mackey, Mia.	109	57	52.3	604	5.54	3	2.8	30	5	4.6	58.8
Hilger, Raiders	106	55	51.9	706	6.66	2	1.9	49	6	5.7	55.8
Herrmann, S.D.	57	37	64.9	405	7.11	1	1.8	34	5	8.8	55.1
Mathison, Sea.	76	36	47.4	501	6.59	3	3.9	47	5	6.6	54.8
Strock, Mia.	23	13	56.5	114	4.96	0	0.0	26	1	4.3	51.7
Totten, Buff.	33	13	39.4	155	4.70	2	6.1	37	2	6.1	49.4
Bleier, N.E.	39	14	35.9	181	4.64	1	2.6	35	1	2.6	49.2
Norrie, Jets	68	35	51.5	376	5.53	1	1.5	t41	4	5.9	48.4
Christensen, Clev.	58	24	41.4	297	5.12	1	1.7	34	3	5.2	42.1
Kiel, Ind.	33	17	51.5	195	5.91	1	3.0	21	3	9.1	41.9
Salisbury, Ind.	12	8	66.7	68	5.67	0	0.0	11	2	16.7	41.7
Seurer, K.C.	55	26	47.3	340	6.18	0	0.0	33	4	7.3	36.9
Espinoza, K.C.	14	9	64.3	69	4.93	0	0.0	16	2	14.3	36.6
McClure, Buff.	38	20	52.6	181	4.76	0	0.0	30	3	7.9	32.9
Manucci, Buff.	21	7	33.3	68	3.24	0	0.0	15	2	9.5	3.8
Brister, Pitt.	12	4	33.3	20	1.67	0	0.0	10	3	25.0	2.8

(Fewer than 10 attempts)

Player—Team	Att.	Cmp.	Pct. Cmp.	Yds.	Avg. Gain	TD	Pct. TD	Lg.	Int.	Pct. Int.	Rating Pts.
Allen, Raiders	2	1	50.0	23	11.50	0	0.0	23	0	0.0	91.7
Bennett, Cin.	6	2	33.3	25	4.17	0	0.0	18	1	16.7	7.6
Breen, Cin.	8	3	37.5	9	1.13	1	12.5	6	0	0.0	85.4
Briggs, Jets	2	0	0.0	0	0.00	0	0.0	0	1	50.0	0.0
Collier, Pitt.	7	4	57.1	110	15.71	2	28.6	49	1	14.3	101.8
Fontenot, Clev.	1	1	100.0	14	14.00	0	0.0	14	0	0.0	118.8
D. Hill, Hou.	1	0	0.0	0	0.00	0	0.0	0	0	0.0	39.6
Hillary, Cin.	0	0	......	0	......	0	......	0	0	......	0.0
Hudson, K.C.	1	0	0.0	0	0.00	0	0.0	0	0	0.0	39.6
Jaeger, Clev.	1	0	0.0	0	0.00	0	0.0	0	0	0.0	39.6
Jennings, Jets	1	1	100.0	16	16.00	0	0.0	16	0	0.0	118.8
V. Johnson, Den.	1	0	0.0	0	0.00	0	0.0	0	0	0.0	39.6
Ce. Jones, N.E.	1	0	0.0	0	0.00	0	0.0	0	0	0.0	39.6
Kidd, Buff.	1	0	0.0	0	0.00	0	0.0	0	0	0.0	39.6
Kubiak, Den.	7	3	42.9	25	3.57	0	0.0	17	2	28.6	13.1
Lang, Den.	1	0	0.0	0	0.00	0	0.0	0	0	0.0	39.6
Largent, Sea.	2	0	0.0	0	0.00	0	0.0	0	1	20.0	0.0
May, Den.	5	0	0.0	0	0.00	0	0.0	0	1	20.0	0.0
McGuire, Den.	3	2	66.7	23	7.67	0	0.0	13	0	0.0	89.6
Miller, Buff.	3	1	33.3	9	3.00	0	0.0	9	1	33.3	2.8
Nugent, Ind.	5	3	60.0	47	9.40	0	0.0	21	0	0.0	91.3
Palmer, K.C.	1	0	0.0	0	0.00	0	0.0	0	0	0.0	39.6
Riddick, Buff.	1	1	100.0	35	35.00	0	0.0	35	0	0.0	118.8
Sewell, Den.	0	0	......	0	......	0	......	0	0	......	0.0
Smith, S.D.	1	0	0.0	0	0.00	0	0.0	0	1	100.0	0.0
Stankavage, Mia.	7	4	57.1	8	1.14	0	0.0	8	1	14.3	22.6
Stradford, Mia.	1	1	100.0	6	6.00	0	0.0	6	0	0.0	91.7
Tatupu, N.E.	1	1	100.0	15	15.00	1	100.0	t15	0	0.0	158.3
Vlasic, S.D.	6	3	50.0	8	1.33	0	0.0	7	1	16.7	16.7
Willhite, Den.	1	0	0.0	0	0.00	0	0.0	0	0	0.0	39.6

NFC INDIVIDUAL QUALIFIERS

Player—Team	Att.	Cmp.	Pct. Cmp.	Yds.	Avg. Gain	TD	Pct. TD	Lg.	Int.	Pct. Int.	Rating Pts.
MONTANA, S.F.	398	266	66.8	3054	7.67	31	7.8	t57	13	3.3	102.1
Simms, Giants	282	163	57.8	2230	7.91	17	6.0	t50	9	3.2	90.0
Lomax, St.L.	463	275	59.4	3387	7.32	24	5.2	57	12	2.6	88.5
McMahon, Chi.	210	125	59.5	1639	7.80	12	5.7	t59	8	3.8	87.4
DeBerg, T.B.	275	159	57.8	1891	6.88	14	5.1	t64	7	2.5	85.3
Cunningham, Phil.	406	223	54.9	2786	6.86	23	5.7	t70	12	3.0	83.0
Hebert, N.O.	294	164	55.8	2119	7.21	15	5.1	67	9	3.1	82.9
W. Wilson, Minn.	264	140	53.0	2106	7.98	14	5.3	t73	13	4.9	76.7
D. White, Dall.	362	215	59.4	2617	7.23	12	3.3	43	17	4.7	73.2

Player—Team	Att.	Cmp.	Pct. Cmp.	Yds.	Avg. Gain	TD	Pct. TD	Lg.	Int.	Pct. Int.	Rating Pts.
Schroeder, Wash..................	267	129	48.3	1878	7.03	12	4.5	t84	10	3.7	71.0
Everett, Rams.....................	302	162	53.6	2064	6.83	10	3.3	t81	13	4.3	68.4
Campbell, Atl.....................	260	136	52.3	1728	6.65	11	4.2	t44	14	5.4	65.0
Long, Det..........................	416	232	55.8	2598	6.25	11	2.6	53	20	4.8	63.4
Wright, G.B.......................	247	132	53.4	1507	6.10	6	2.4	66	11	4.5	61.6

NFC NON-QUALIFIERS

Player—Team	Att.	Cmp.	Pct. Cmp.	Yds.	Avg. Gain	TD	Pct. TD	Lg.	Int.	Pct. Int.	Rating Pts.
Young, S.F.	69	37	53.6	570	8.26	10	14.5	t50	0	0.0	120.8
Wilson, N.O.	24	13	54.2	243	10.13	2	8.3	38	0	0.0	117.2
Sweeney, Dall.	28	14	50.0	291	10.39	4	14.3	t77	1	3.6	111.8
Rubbert, Wash.	49	26	53.1	532	10.86	4	8.2	t88	1	2.0	110.2
D. Williams, Wash.	143	81	56.6	1156	8.08	11	7.7	62	5	3.5	94.0
Hohensee, Chi.	52	28	53.8	343	6.60	4	7.7	28	1	1.9	92.1
Harbaugh, Chi....................	11	8	72.7	62	5.64	0	0.0	21	0	0.0	86.2
Crocicchia, Giants	15	6	40.0	89	5.93	1	6.7	t46	0	0.0	82.4
Risher, G.B.......................	74	44	59.5	564	7.62	3	4.1	t46	3	4.1	80.0
Gagliano, S.F.....................	29	16	55.2	229	7.90	1	3.4	50	1	3.4	78.1
J. Fourcade, N.O.	89	48	53.9	597	6.71	4	4.5	t82	3	3.4	75.9
Reaves, T.B.	16	6	37.5	83	5.19	1	6.3	t26	0	0.0	75.8
Pelluer, Dall......................	101	55	54.5	642	6.36	3	3.0	44	2	2.0	75.6
Tinsley, Phil......................	86	48	55.8	637	7.41	3	3.5	t62	4	4.7	71.7
Majkowski, G.B..................	127	55	43.3	875	6.89	5	3.9	t70	3	2.4	70.2
Kramer, Minn.	81	40	49.4	452	5.58	4	4.9	t40	3	3.7	67.5
Dils, Rams........................	114	56	49.1	646	5.67	5	4.4	51	4	3.5	66.6
Horn, Phil.	11	5	45.5	68	6.18	0	0.0	23	0	0.0	65.7
Merkens, Phil.	14	7	50.0	70	5.00	0	0.0	17	0	0.0	64.6
Adams, Minn.	89	49	55.1	607	6.82	3	3.4	t63	5	5.6	64.2
Garza, St.L.	20	11	55.0	183	9.15	1	5.0	t38	2	10.0	63.1
Tomczak, Chi.....................	178	97	54.5	1220	6.85	5	2.8	t56	10	5.6	62.0
Hold, T.B.	24	8	33.3	123	5.13	2	8.3	t61	1	4.2	61.6
Hons, Det.	92	43	46.7	552	6.00	5	5.4	t53	5	5.4	61.5
Busch, Giants.....................	47	17	36.2	278	5.91	3	6.4	t63	2	4.3	60.4
Testaverde, T.B.	165	71	43.0	1081	6.55	5	3.0	40	6	3.6	60.2
Kramer, Atl.	92	45	48.9	559	6.08	4	4.3	33	5	5.4	60.0
Halloran, St.L.	42	18	42.9	263	6.26	0	0.0	49	1	2.4	54.0
Rutledge, Giants	155	79	51.0	1048	6.76	5	3.2	50	11	7.1	53.9
Van Raaphorst, Atl.	34	18	52.9	174	5.12	1	2.9	24	2	5.9	52.8
T. Robinson, Wash.	18	11	61.1	152	8.44	0	0.0	42	2	11.1	48.6
Zorn, T.B.	36	20	55.6	199	5.53	0	0.0	26	2	5.6	48.3
Bradley, Chi.......................	18	6	33.3	77	4.28	2	11.1	t18	3	16.7	45.1
S. Payton, Chi....................	23	8	34.8	79	3.43	0	0.0	20	1	4.3	27.3
C. Miller, Atl.	92	39	42.4	552	6.00	1	1.1	57	9	9.8	26.4
Archer, Atl.	23	9	39.1	95	4.13	0	0.0	33	2	8.7	15.7

(Fewer than 10 attempts)

Player—Team	Att.	Cmp.	Pct. Cmp.	Yds.	Avg. Gain	TD	Pct. TD	Lg.	Int.	Pct. Int.	Rating Pts.
Bartalo, T.B.	1	0	0.0	0	0.00	0	0.0	0	1	100.0	0.0
Bryant, Wash.....................	1	0	0.0	0	0.00	0	0.0	0	0	0.0	39.6
Carruth, G.B......................	1	1	100.0	3	3.00	1	100.0	t3	0	0.0	118.8
Carter, Phil.	1	0	0.0	0	0.00	0	0.0	0	0	0.0	39.6
Gannon, Minn.	6	2	33.3	18	3.00	0	0.0	12	1	16.7	2.8
Gillus, G.B.	5	2	40.0	28	5.60	0	0.0	15	0	0.0	58.8
Grant, Phil.	1	0	0.0	0	0.00	0	0.0	0	0	0.0	39.6
Hilliard, N.O.	1	1	100.0	23	23.00	1	100.0	t23	0	0.0	158.3
Ingram, N.O.......................	2	1	50.0	5	2.50	1	50.0	t5	0	0.0	95.8
Jones, Det.	1	0	0.0	0	0.00	0	0.0	0	1	100.0	0.0
Millen, Rams	1	1	100.0	0	0.00	0	0.0	0	0	0.0	79.2
Miller, Minn.......................	6	1	16.7	2	0.33	0	0.0	2	1	16.7	0.0
Mitchell, St.L.	3	1	33.3	17	5.67	0	0.0	17	0	0.0	53.5
Neal, G.B.	1	0	0.0	0	0.00	0	0.0	0	0	0.0	39.6
W. Payton, Chi.	1	0	0.0	0	0.00	0	0.0	0	1	100.0	0.0
Quarles, Rams....................	3	1	33.3	40	13.33	1	33.3	t40	1	33.3	81.9
Riordan, N.O......................	1	0	0.0	0	0.00	0	0.0	0	0	0.0	39.6
Snyder, Dall.......................	9	4	44.4	44	4.89	0	0.0	22	0	0.0	59.5
Stevens, S.F.	4	2	50.0	52	13.00	1	25.0	t39	0	0.0	135.4
Stoudt, St.L.	1	0	0.0	0	0.00	0	0.0	0	0	0.0	39.6
Sydney, S.F.	1	1	100.0	50	50.00	1	100.0	t50	0	0.0	158.3
Teltschik, Phil.	0	0	......	0	......	0	......	0	0	......	0.0
Toney, Phil.	1	0	0.0	0	0.00	0	0.0	0	0	0.0	39.6

t—Touchdown   Leader based on rating points, minimum 210 attempts.

1987 PASS RECEIVING

MOST RECEPTIONS, SEASON
  NFC: 91—J.T. Smith, St. Louis.
  AFC: 68—Al Toon, N.Y. Jets.

MOST RECEPTIONS, GAME
  AFC: 15—Steve Largent, Seattle at Detroit, October 18 (261 yards).
  NFC: 11—Mark Bavaro, N.Y. Giants at St. Louis, December 13 (137 yards).
    J.T. Smith, St. Louis at Dallas, December 27 (102 yards).

MOST YARDS, SEASON
  NFC: 1117—J.T. Smith, St. Louis.
  AFC: 1044—Carlos Carson, Kansas City.

MOST YARDS, GAME
  AFC: 261—Steve Largent, Seattle at Detroit, October 18 (15 receptions).
  NFC: 255—Anthony Allen, Washington vs. St. Louis, October 4 (7 receptions).

LONGEST GAIN
  NFC: 88—Anthony Allen (from Ed Rubbert) Washington vs. St. Louis, September 20 (TD).
  AFC: 83—Ernest Givins (from Warren Moon) Houston vs. Cleveland, November 22 (TD).

AVERAGE YARDS PER RECEPTION
  NFC: 24.3—Anthony Carter, Minnesota.
  AFC: 21.5—James Lofton, L.A. Raiders.

MOST TOUCHDOWNS
  NFC: 22—Jerry Rice, San Francisco.
  AFC: 8—Mark Duper, Miami.
    Steve Largent, Seattle.

TEAM LEADERS
  AFC: BUFFALO: 57, Andre Reed; CINCINNATI: 44, Eddie Brown; CLEVELAND: 52, Earnest Byner; DENVER: 42, Vance Johnson; HOUSTON: 53, Ernest Givins; INDIANAPOLIS: 51, Bill Brooks; KANSAS CITY: 55, Carlos Carson; L.A. RAIDERS: 51, Marcus Allen; MIAMI: 48, Troy Stradford; NEW ENGLAND: 44, Tony Collins; N.Y. JETS: 68, Al Toon; PITTSBURGH: 41, John Stallworth; SAN DIEGO: 53, Kellen Winslow; SEATTLE: 58, Steve Largent.
  NFC: ATLANTA: 36, Floyd Dixon; CHICAGO: 47, Neal Anderson; DALLAS: 60, Herschel Walker; DETROIT: 58, Pete Mandley; GREEN BAY: 38, Walter Stanley; L.A. RAMS: 51, Henry Ellard; MINNESOTA: 38, Anthony Carter; NEW ORLEANS: 44, Eric Martin; N.Y. GIANTS: 55, Mark Bavaro; PHILADELPHIA: 46, Mike Quick; ST. LOUIS: 91, J.T. Smith; SAN FRANCISCO: 66, Roger Craig; TAMPA BAY: 40, James Wilder; WASHINGTON: 56, Gary Clark.

TOP TEN PASS RECEIVERS

Player—Team	No.	Yards	Avg.	Long	TDs.
SMITH, J.T., St.L.	91	1117	12.3	38	8
Toon, Al, Jets	68	976	14.4	t58	5
Craig, Roger, S.F.	66	492	7.5	t35	1
Rice, Jerry, S.F.	65	1078	16.6	t57	22
Walker, Herschel, Dall.	60	715	11.9	44	1
Largent, Steve, Sea.	58	912	15.7	55	8
Mandley, Pete, Det.	58	720	12.4	41	7
Reed, Andre, Buff.	57	752	13.2	40	5
Clark, Gary, Wash.	56	1066	19.0	t84	7
Burkett, Chris, Buff.	56	765	13.7	47	4
Harmon, Ronnie, Buff.	56	477	8.5	42	2

TOP TEN PASS RECEIVERS BY YARDS

Player—Team	Yards	No.	Avg.	Long	TDs.
SMITH, J.T., St.L.	1117	91	12.3	38	8
Rice, Jerry, S.F.	1078	65	16.6	t57	22
Clark, Gary, Wash.	1066	56	19.0	t84	7
Carson, Carlos, K.C.	1044	55	19.0	t81	7
Hill, Drew, Hou.	989	49	20.2	t52	6
Toon, Al, Jets	976	68	14.4	t58	5
Givins, Ernest, Hou.	933	53	17.6	t83	6
Carter, Anthony, Minn.	922	38	24.3	t73	7
Largent, Steve, Sea.	912	58	15.7	55	8
Lofton, James, Raiders	880	41	21.5	49	5

AFC—INDIVIDUALS

Player—Team	No.	Yds.	Avg.	Lng.	TD	Player—Team	No.	Yds.	Avg.	Lng.	TD
TOON, Jets	68	976	14.4	t58	5	Harper, Jets	18	225	12.5	t35	1
Largent, Sea.	58	912	15.7	55	8	Kattus, Cin.	18	217	12.1	57	2
Reed, Buff.	57	752	13.2	40	5	Dickerson, Rams-Ind.	18	171	9.5	28	0
Burkett, Buff.	56	765	13.7	47	4	Thompson, Pitt.	17	313	18.4	63	1
Harmon, Buff.	56	477	8.5	42	2	Starring, N.E.	17	289	17.0	t34	3
Carson, K.C.	55	1044	19.0	t81	7	Warner, Sea.	17	167	9.8	t30	2
Givins, Hou.	53	933	17.6	t83	6	Lang, Den.	17	130	7.6	29	2
Winslow, S.D.	53	519	9.8	30	3	Ti. Spencer, S.D.	17	123	7.2	18	0
Byner, Clev.	52	552	10.6	37	2	Mobley, Den.	16	228	14.3	28	1
Brooks, Ind.	51	722	14.2	t52	3	Sweeney, Pitt.	16	217	13.6	34	0
Allen, Raiders	51	410	8.0	39	0	Carter, Pitt.	16	180	11.3	t26	3
D. Hill, Hou.	49	989	20.2	t52	6	B. Jackson, Raiders	16	136	8.5	23	2
Stradford, Mia.	48	457	9.5	34	1	T. Johnson, Buff.	15	186	12.4	t26	2
Slaughter, Clev.	47	806	17.1	t54	7	Holman, Jets	15	155	10.3	30	0
Christensen, Raiders	47	663	14.1	33	2	Tatupu, N.E.	15	136	9.1	23	0
G. Anderson, S.D.	47	503	10.7	38	2	Riddick, Buff.	15	96	6.4	t17	3
Clayton, Mia.	46	776	16.9	43	7	Fernandez, Raiders	14	236	16.9	47	0
E. Brown, Cin.	44	608	13.8	t47	3	Teal, Sea.	14	198	14.1	47	2
Collins, N.E.	44	347	7.9	29	3	Turner, Sea.	14	153	10.9	t20	6
Paige, K.C.	43	707	16.4	51	4	Klever, Jets	14	152	10.9	30	0
Brennan, Clev.	43	607	14.1	t53	6	Heard, K.C.	14	118	8.4	15	0
Shuler, Jets	43	434	10.1	t32	3	Tice, Sea.	14	106	7.6	27	2
V. Johnson, Den.	42	684	16.3	t59	7	Pollard, Pitt.	14	77	5.5	17	0
Bouza, Ind.	42	569	13.5	t44	4	Winder, Den.	14	74	5.3	13	1
Lofton, Raiders	41	880	21.5	49	5	Massie, Den.	13	244	18.8	t39	4
James, S.D.	41	593	14.5	46	3	Clinkscales, Pitt.	13	240	18.5	57	1
Stallworth, Pitt.	41	521	12.7	45	2	Duncan, Hou.	13	237	18.2	48	5
Morgan, N.E.	40	672	16.8	45	3	Sewell, Den.	13	209	16.1	t72	1
Chandler, S.D.	39	617	15.8	27	2	J. Williams, Hou.	13	158	12.2	25	3
Jo. Williams, Sea.	38	420	11.1	t75	3	Vick, Jets	13	108	8.3	23	0
Jennings, Cin.	35	277	7.9	24	2	A. Williams, S.D.	12	247	20.6	57	1
Bentley, Ind.	34	447	13.1	t72	2	Kemp, Clev.	12	224	18.7	34	2
Newsome, Clev.	34	375	11.0	25	0	Lee, Pitt.	12	124	10.3	24	0
Duper, Mia.	33	597	18.1	t59	8	Tagliaferri, Mia.	12	117	9.8	27	0
R. Butler, Sea.	33	465	14.1	t40	5	Dawson, N.E.	12	81	6.8	14	0
Hector, Jets	32	249	7.8	27	0	Watson, Den.	11	167	15.2	49	1
Mack, Clev.	32	223	7.0	17	1	O. Williams, Hou.	11	165	15.0	t36	1
Nattiel, Den.	31	630	20.3	54	2	Lipps, Pitt.	11	164	14.9	27	0
Collinsworth, Cin.	31	494	15.9	53	0	Linne, N.E.	11	158	14.4	30	2
Fryar, N.E.	31	467	15.1	40	5	Weathers, Clev.	11	153	13.9	t37	2
Kay, Den.	31	440	14.2	30	0	Drewrey, Hou.	11	148	13.5	35	0
Holman, Cin.	28	438	15.6	t61	2	Mueller, Raiders	11	95	8.6	14	0
Hardy, Mia.	28	292	10.4	31	2	Bligen, Jets	11	81	7.4	19	0
Metzelaars, Buff.	28	290	10.4	34	0	Harris, Hou.	10	164	16.4	39	0
Beach, Ind.	28	239	8.5	16	0	Marshall, K.C.	10	126	12.6	19	0
Davenport, Mia.	27	249	9.2	29	1	Noble, Ind.	10	78	7.8	t18	2
Rozier, Hou.	27	192	7.1	27	0	Nathan, Mia.	10	77	7.7	14	0
M. Jackson, Den.	26	436	16.8	52	2	Bernstine, S.D.	10	76	7.6	15	1
Pruitt, Mia.	26	404	15.5	37	3	Boyer, Ind.	10	73	7.3	15	0
Jensen, Mia.	26	221	8.5	20	1	Jackson, Hou.	10	44	4.4	16	0
Ce. Jones, N.E.	25	388	15.5	29	3	Moriarty, K.C.	10	37	3.7	8	1
Micho, Den.	25	242	9.7	t26	2	Walker, Jets	9	190	21.1	59	1
McNeil, Jets	24	262	10.9	57	1	M. Brown, Buff.	9	120	13.3	30	1
Abercrombie, Pitt.	24	209	8.7	24	0	Gaines, Buff.	9	115	12.8	37	0
Okoye, K.C.	24	169	7.0	22	0	Kinnebrew, Cin.	9	114	12.7	25	0
McGee, Cin.	23	408	17.7	49	1	Tennell, Clev.	9	102	11.3	24	3
Sohn, Jets	23	261	11.3	31	2	Douglas, Mia.	9	92	10.2	17	1
Hampton, Mia.	23	223	9.7	24	0	Sherwin, Ind.	9	86	9.6	32	1
Brooks, Cin.	22	272	12.4	46	2	Boddie, Den.	9	85	9.4	26	0
Do. Williams, Raiders	21	330	15.7	33	5	McKeller, Buff.	9	80	8.9	22	0
Hayes, K.C.	21	272	13.0	33	2	R. Porter, Buff.	9	70	7.8	26	0
Martin, Cin.	20	394	19.7	t54	3	C. Banks, Ind.	9	50	5.6	18	0
Murray, Ind.	20	339	17.0	43	3	Willhite, Den.	9	25	2.8	6	0
Langhorne, Clev.	20	288	14.4	25	1	Pardridge, Sea.	8	145	18.1	47	1
Holohan, S.D.	20	239	12.0	18	0	Aikens, Raiders	8	134	16.8	t32	3
Skansi, Sea.	19	207	10.9	25	1	McNeil, Clev.	8	120	15.0	t39	2

Player—Team	No.	Yds.	Avg.	Lng.	TD	Player—Team	No.	Yds.	Avg.	Lng.	TD
Keel, Sea.-K.C.	8	97	12.1	t24	1	Logan, Cin.	3	14	4.7	18	0
R. Jones, K.C.	8	76	9.5	16	1	Mueller, Buff.	3	13	4.3	11	0
Sampleton, Mia.	8	64	8.0	19	0	Perryman, N.E.	3	13	4.3	7	0
Middleton, S.D.	8	43	5.4	17	0	Dupard, N.E.	3	1	0.3	2	0
Everett, Clev.	8	41	5.1	10	0	Muhammad, S.D.	2	87	43.5	67	0
Jenkins, S.D.	8	40	5.0	7	0	To. Spencer, S.D.	2	47	23.5	45	0
Lockett, Pitt.	7	116	16.6	25	1	Caterbone, Mia.	2	46	23.0	30	0
Chavis, Mia.	7	108	15.4	27	0	Pleasant, Cin.	2	45	22.5	35	0
Hoge, Pitt.	7	97	13.9	27	1	Ware, S.D.	2	38	19.0	23	0
Juma, Sea.	7	95	13.6	26	0	Bengen, Sea.	2	33	16.5	24	0
Jeffires, Hou.	7	89	12.7	23	0	Russell, Cin.	2	27	13.5	23	1
Holt, S.D.	7	56	8.0	17	0	Koss, K.C.	2	25	12.5	14	0
Jackson, Pitt.	7	52	7.4	23	0	Bynum, Buff.	2	24	12.0	17	0
Redden, S.D.	7	46	6.6	13	0	Frain, N.E.	2	22	11.0	11	0
Parker, K.C.	7	44	6.3	14	0	Nash, K.C.	2	22	11.0	14	0
Dudek, Den.	7	41	5.9	19	0	Pierce, Clev.	2	21	10.5	13	0
Wallace, Hou.	7	34	4.9	7	0	C. Smith, K.C.	2	21	10.5	16	0
Holland, S.D.	6	138	23.0	45	0	Harrison, Raiders	2	18	9.0	15	0
Swanson, Den.	6	87	14.5	t35	1	Griggs, Jets	2	17	8.5	13	1
Lewis, Mia.	6	53	8.8	22	1	Hairston, Pitt.	2	16	8.0	11	1
S. Hunter, Jets	6	50	8.3	12	1	Junkin, Raiders	2	15	7.5	8	0
Rome, S.D.	6	49	8.2	13	0	Munoz, Cin.	2	15	7.5	12	1
Konecny, Mia.	6	26	4.3	10	0	W. Smith, Mia.	2	13	6.5	8	1
Sartin, S.D.	6	19	3.2	8	0	Pippens, K.C.	2	12	6.0	7	0
Walters, Hou.	5	99	19.8	51	0	Valentine, Hou.	2	10	5.0	7	0
Lathan, Raiders	5	98	19.6	33	0	Young, Pitt.	2	10	5.0	6	0
Broughton, Buff.	5	90	18.0	39	1	Gothard, Pitt.	2	9	4.5	7	1
Moffett, S.D.	5	80	16.0	25	1	McLemore, Ind.	2	9	4.5	5	0
Reilly, Mia.	5	70	14.0	20	0	Browne, Raiders	2	8	4.0	5	0
Bellini, Ind.	5	69	13.8	19	0	R. Scott, Mia.	2	7	3.5	5	0
Brown, K.C.	5	69	13.8	23	0	Rolle, Buff.	2	6	3.0	t3	2
Hillary, Cin.	5	65	13.0	23	0	LeBlanc, N.E.	2	3	1.5	3	0
Gehring, Hou.	5	64	12.8	t31	1	Kurisko, Jets	1	41	41.0	t41	1
Wonsley, Ind.	5	48	9.6	16	0	Darrington, Hou.	1	38	38.0	38	0
Montagne, K.C.	5	47	9.4	16	0	Kelly, Buff.	1	35	35.0	35	0
Coffman, K.C.	5	42	8.4	t13	1	Hester, Raiders	1	30	30.0	30	0
C. Ellis, Raiders	5	39	7.8	15	0	Hansen, N.E.	1	22	22.0	22	0
Brandes, Ind.	5	35	7.0	13	0	Stone, Pitt.	1	22	22.0	22	0
Scott, N.E.	5	35	7.0	15	1	Calhoun, Raiders	1	17	17.0	17	0
Mason, Clev.	5	26	5.2	15	1	Tinsley, Clev.	1	17	17.0	17	0
Da. Williams, Raiders	4	104	26.0	44	0	Faaola, Jets	1	16	16.0	16	0
McDonald, Hou.	4	56	14.0	24	1	Johnson, Ind.	1	15	15.0	15	0
Highsmith, Hou.	4	55	13.8	t33	1	James, Hou.	1	14	14.0	14	0
Andrews, Den.	4	53	13.3	20	0	Woods, Raiders	1	14	14.0	14	0
E. Riley, Jets	4	42	10.5	16	0	R. Watson, Clev.	1	13	13.0	13	0
Strachan, Raiders	4	42	10.5	14	0	Bryant, Ind.	1	12	12.0	12	0
McFadden, Buff.	4	41	10.3	t13	1	Isom, Mia.	1	11	11.0	11	0
Brown, Den.	4	40	10.0	18	0	Sanders, Pitt.	1	11	11.0	11	0
Fontenot, Clev.	4	40	10.0	25	0	Banks, Mia.	1	10	10.0	t10	1
Trahan, K.C.	4	40	10.0	14	0	Gaffney, Jets	1	10	10.0	10	0
Adams, S.D.	4	38	9.5	21	0	Pickering, N.E.	1	10	10.0	10	0
Townsell, Jets	4	37	9.3	11	0	Chetti, Buff.	1	9	9.0	9	0
Da. Johnson, Mia.	4	35	8.8	22	2	D. Foster, Jets	1	9	9.0	9	0
Caldwell, Den.	4	34	8.5	14	0	Poole, Den.	1	9	9.0	9	0
Lane, Sea.	4	30	7.5	12	0	L. Watson, Clev.	1	9	9.0	9	0
Wright, Cin.	4	28	7.0	11	0	Bell, Den.	1	8	8.0	8	0
Palmer, K.C.	4	27	6.8	10	0	Manoa, Clev.	1	8	8.0	8	0
W. Bennett, Mia.	4	18	4.5	6	0	McCluskey, Cin.	1	8	8.0	8	0
Chirico, Jets	4	18	4.5	8	0	Payne, Den.	1	8	8.0	8	0
Alston, Pitt.	3	84	28.0	t42	2	Belk, Buff.	1	7	7.0	7	0
Coffey, N.E.	3	66	22.0	35	0	Franklin, Sea.	1	7	7.0	7	0
R. Wheeler, Raiders	3	61	20.3	29	0	Parros, Sea.	1	7	7.0	7	0
Kearse, Ind.	3	56	18.7	21	0	Pinkett, Hou.	1	7	7.0	7	0
Gadbois, N.E.	3	51	17.0	20	0	T. Brown, Mia.	1	6	6.0	6	0
Smith, Raiders	3	46	15.3	32	0	Hawkins, Raiders	1	6	6.0	6	0
Sweet, Jets	3	45	15.0	22	0	Farmer, Mia.	1	5	5.0	5	0
Horton, Raiders	3	44	14.7	t32	1	L. Williams, Buff.	1	5	5.0	5	0
Hawthorne, Ind.	3	41	13.7	21	0	Steels, S.D.	1	4	4.0	4	0
D. Williams, N.E.	3	30	10.0	12	0	Stockemer, K.C.	1	4	4.0	4	0
Arnold, K.C.	3	26	8.7	10	0	Adickes, K.C.	1	3	3.0	t3	1
J. Jones, Ind.	3	25	8.3	13	1	King, Buff.	1	3	3.0	3	0
Meehan, Cin.	3	25	8.3	12	0	Perry, Raiders	1	3	3.0	t3	1
Estell, K.C.	3	24	8.0	11	0	Bono, Pitt.	1	2	2.0	2	0
Byrum, Buff.	3	23	7.7	20	0	Shepherd, Buff.	1	2	2.0	2	0
Colbert, K.C.	3	21	7.0	9	0	Boyle, Pitt.	1	0	0.0	0	0
R. Moore, Hou.	3	21	7.0	10	0	Utt, Ind.	1	−4	−4.0	−4	0
B. Johnson, Cin.	3	19	6.3	9	0	Millard, Sea.	1	−5	−5.0	−5	0
Hunter, Hou.	3	17	5.7	11	0						

Player—Team	No.	Yds.	Avg.	Lng.	TD
J.T. SMITH, St.L.	91	1117	12.3	38	8
Craig, S.F.	66	492	7.5	t35	1
Rice, S.F.	65	1078	16.6	t57	22
H. Walker, Dall.	60	715	11.9	44	1
Mandley, Det.	58	720	12.4	41	7
Clark, Wash.	56	1066	19.0	t84	7
Bavaro, Giants	55	867	15.8	38	8
Ellard, Rams	51	799	15.7	t81	3
Anderson, Chi.	47	467	9.9	t59	3
Quick, Phil.	46	790	17.2	t61	11
Renfro, Dall.	46	662	14.4	43	4
Mitchell, St.L.	45	397	8.8	39	2
Martin, N.O.	44	778	17.7	67	7
Green, St.L.	43	731	17.0	57	4
Bryant, Wash.	43	490	11.4	39	5
Awalt, St.L.	42	526	12.5	35	6
Wilder, T.B.	40	328	8.2	32	1
Toney, Phil.	39	341	8.7	33	1
Carter, Minn.	38	922	24.3	t73	7
Stanley, G.B.	38	672	17.7	t70	3
G. Carter, T.B.	38	586	15.4	57	5
Monk, Wash.	38	483	12.7	62	6
Sanders, Wash.	37	630	17.0	57	3
Dixon, Atl.	36	600	16.7	t51	3
Cosbie, Dall.	36	421	11.7	30	3
Neal, G.B.	36	420	11.7	38	3
Spagnola, Phil.	36	350	9.7	22	2
Gault, Chi.	35	705	20.1	t56	7
Jordan, Minn.	35	490	14.0	38	2
Adams, Giants	35	298	8.5	25	1
Edwards, Dall.	34	521	15.3	t38	3
Epps, G.B.	34	516	15.2	40	2
Magee, T.B.	34	424	12.5	37	3
Newsome, Dall.	34	274	8.1	30	2
Jones, Det.	34	262	7.7	35	0
W. Payton, Chi.	33	217	6.6	16	1
Matthews, Atl.	32	537	16.8	57	3
Manuel, Giants	30	545	18.2	t50	6
Chadwick, Det.	30	416	13.9	36	0
Rathman, S.F.	30	329	11.0	29	3
Wilson, S.F.	29	450	15.5	t46	5
M. Jones, N.O.	27	420	15.6	t43	3
McKinnon, Chi.	27	406	15.0	33	1
Ro. Brown, Rams	26	521	20.0	52	2
Carrier, T.B.	26	423	16.3	38	3
Frank, S.F.	26	296	11.4	27	3
Galbreath, Giants	26	248	9.5	21	0
D. Nelson, Minn.	26	129	5.0	13	0
Riggs, Atl.	25	199	8.0	48	0
Tautalatasi, Phil.	25	176	7.0	22	0
Lewis, Minn.	24	383	16.0	36	2
Clark, S.F.	24	290	12.1	t40	5
Moorehead, Chi.	24	269	11.2	27	1
Hill, T.B.	23	403	17.5	40	2
Hilliard, N.O.	23	264	11.5	t38	1
Ferrell, St.L.	23	262	11.4	36	0
White, Rams	23	121	5.3	20	0
Guman, Rams	22	263	12.0	33	0
Francis, S.F.	22	202	9.2	19	0
Clark, G.B.	22	119	5.4	19	1
Jackson, Phil.	21	471	22.4	t70	3
D. Johnson, Rams	21	198	9.4	20	2
Byars, Phil.	21	177	8.4	30	1
Ro. Morris, Chi.	20	379	19.0	t42	1
Bailey, Atl.	20	325	16.3	35	3
Brenner, N.O.	20	280	14.0	29	2
Novacek, St.L.	20	254	12.7	25	3
J. Smith, T.B.	20	197	9.9	t34	2
Hill, N.O.	19	322	16.9	36	2
Lee, Det.	19	308	16.2	53	0
West, G.B.	19	261	13.7	40	1
Rice, Minn.	19	201	10.6	24	1
Dorsett, Dall.	19	177	9.3	33	1
Woolfolk, Det.	19	166	8.7	13	0
Brim, Minn.	18	282	15.7	t63	2
Baty, N.E.-Rams	18	175	9.7	22	2
Boso, Chi.	17	188	11.1	31	2
Gentry, Chi.	17	183	10.8	t38	1
Whisenhunt, Atl.	17	145	8.5	26	1
Grant, Phil.	16	280	17.5	41	0
Le. Morris, G.B.	16	259	16.2	t46	1
James, Det.	16	215	13.4	46	0
Tice, N.O.	16	181	11.3	t27	6
Hall, T.B.	16	169	10.6	29	1
T. Johnson, St.L.	15	308	20.5	t49	2
Baker, Giants	15	277	18.5	50	2
Banks, Dall.	15	231	15.4	34	1
Kozlowski, Chi.	15	199	13.3	28	3
Mayes, N.O.	15	68	4.5	16	0
Davis, G.B.	14	110	7.9	35	0
A. Allen, Wash.	13	337	25.9	t88	3
Didier, Wash.	13	178	13.7	25	1
Giles, Det.-Phil.	13	157	12.1	t40	1
Rubick, Det.	13	147	11.3	22	1
Dawsey, N.O.	13	142	10.9	29	0
Wright, T.B.	13	98	7.5	t15	1
Bernard, Det.	13	91	7.0	12	0
Garrity, Phil.	12	242	20.2	41	2
Truvillion, Det.	12	207	17.3	t53	1
Paskett, G.B.	12	188	15.7	t47	1
Taylor, Atl.	12	171	14.3	28	1
Barksdale, Dall.	12	165	13.8	22	1
Heller, S.F.	12	165	13.8	t39	3
McEwen, Wash.	12	164	13.7	42	0
Dozier, Minn.	12	89	7.4	t20	2
McConkey, Giants	11	186	16.9	31	0
Settle, Atl.	11	153	13.9	36	0
Holmes, St.L.	11	132	12.0	23	0
Rouson, Giants	11	129	11.7	t26	1
Morris, Giants	11	114	10.4	25	0
Hill, Rams	11	105	9.5	24	0
A. Cox, Atl.	11	101	9.2	19	0
Turner, Giants	10	195	19.5	36	1
Bennett, Giants	10	184	18.4	t46	1
Barney, Atl.	10	175	17.5	32	2
S. Holloway, T.B.	10	127	12.7	26	0
Lovelady, Giants	10	125	12.5	t23	2
Howard, T.B.	10	123	12.3	45	0
Carruth, G.B.	10	78	7.8	19	1
Taylor, S.F.	9	151	16.8	34	0
Grymes, Det.	9	140	15.6	t36	2
Siano, Phil.	9	137	15.2	34	1
Pattison, N.O.	9	132	14.7	36	0
Bell, Buff.-Rams	9	96	10.7	t32	1
Cribbs, S.F.	9	70	7.8	16	0
M. Williams, Atl.	9	70	7.8	15	0
Freeman, T.B.	8	141	17.6	t64	2
Mobley, Rams	8	107	13.4	t40	1
Johnson, Atl.	8	84	10.5	19	0
Scott, G.B.	8	79	9.9	16	0
Carthon, Giants	8	71	8.9	25	0
Bailey, Phil.	8	69	8.6	19	0
Wolfley, St.L.	8	68	8.5	16	0
R. Brown, Phil.	8	53	6.6	14	0
Francis, Rams	8	38	4.8	7	2
H. Jones, Minn.	7	189	27.0	t58	2
Burbage, Dall.	7	168	24.0	t77	2
Byrd, Atl.	7	125	17.9	33	0
Nichols, Det.	7	87	12.4	23	0
Summers, G.B.	7	83	11.9	17	1
Edwards, Det.	7	82	11.7	21	0
Anderson, Minn.	7	69	9.9	22	0
Haddix, Phil.	7	58	8.3	23	0
Suhey, Chi.	7	54	7.7	12	0
Kamana, Atl.	7	51	7.3	15	1
Bradley, Det.	7	50	7.1	14	2
Flowers, Atl.	7	50	7.1	24	0
Warren, Wash.	7	43	6.1	9	0
McGee, Rams	7	40	5.7	12	0
E. Hunter, Jets-T.B.	7	28	4.0	t8	2
Fenney, Minn.	7	27	3.9	18	0
Bowman, Phil.	6	127	21.2	t62	1
Greer, S.F.	6	111	18.5	50	1
Moore, Rams	6	107	17.8	26	1
J. Smith, Giants	6	72	12.0	19	0
House, Rams	6	63	10.5	t15	1
Tyrrell, Rams	6	59	9.8	16	0
Robinson, Giants	6	58	9.7	14	2
Word, N.O.	6	54	9.0	17	0
Willhite, G.B.	6	37	6.2	12	0

Player—Team	No.	Yds.	Avg.	Lng.	TD	Player—Team	No.	Yds.	Avg.	Lng.	TD
Badanjek, Atl.	6	35	5.8	16	0	Wheeler, Det.	2	17	8.5	9	0
Scott, N.O.	6	35	5.8	11	0	Anderson, Giants	2	16	8.0	9	0
Gray, N.O.	6	30	5.0	12	0	Ro. Brown, St.L.	2	16	8.0	9	0
Waters, N.O.	5	140	28.0	t82	1	Glasgow, Chi.	2	16	8.0	11	0
Streater, T.B.	5	117	23.4	t61	2	Hilton, Minn.	2	16	8.0	t8	2
T. Wilson, Wash.	5	112	22.4	t64	1	Mosley, Chi.	2	16	8.0	16	0
C. Brown, Atl.	5	103	20.6	23	0	W. Wilson, Wash.	2	16	8.0	9	0
K. Martin, Dall.	5	103	20.6	33	0	Alexander, N.O.	2	15	7.5	10	0
Miller, T.B.	5	97	19.4	33	0	Walker, N.O.	2	15	7.5	8	0
Carter, Phil.	5	84	16.8	25	2	Bland, Det.	2	14	7.0	t11	1
Brewer, Chi.	5	56	11.2	19	1	B. Wilson, Minn.	2	14	7.0	9	0
Kab, Det.	5	54	10.8	28	0	Jordan, N.O.	2	13	6.5	11	0
Austin, T.B.	5	51	10.2	20	0	A. Thomas, Minn.	2	13	6.5	10	0
Heimuli, Chi.	5	51	10.2	17	1	McAdoo, St.L.	2	12	6.0	6	0
Ellerson, Det.	5	48	9.6	23	1	Benson, N.O.	2	11	5.5	6	0
Repko, Phil.	5	46	9.2	12	0	Fullwood, G.B.	2	11	5.5	12	0
G. White, Dall.	5	46	9.2	14	0	Robinson, Phil.	2	9	4.5	5	0
Womack, Minn.	5	46	9.2	t23	1	Dennison, Wash.	2	8	4.0	5	0
Ross, Phil.	5	41	8.2	17	0	Gladman, T.B.	2	8	4.0	5	0
V. Williams, Giants	5	36	7.2	12	0	J. Butler, Atl.	2	7	3.5	4	0
Kindt, Chi.	5	34	6.8	11	1	Sharp, Atl.	2	6	3.0	5	0
Emery, Atl.	5	31	6.2	13	0	A. Walker, Minn.	2	3	1.5	2	0
Chandler, Dall.	5	25	5.0	9	1	Paige, Det.	2	1	0.5	3	0
McGowan, Giants	4	111	27.8	t63	1	Wolden, Chi.	1	26	26.0	26	0
Knapczyk, Chi.	4	62	15.5	22	0	May, Minn.	1	22	22.0	22	0
Gladney, S.F.	4	60	15.0	19	0	Witte, Det.	1	19	19.0	19	0
Young, Rams	4	56	14.0	26	1	Dixon, T.B.	1	18	18.0	18	0
Gustafson, Minn.	4	55	13.8	23	0	Redick, G.B.	1	18	18.0	18	0
Stamps, Atl.	4	40	10.0	19	0	Weigel, G.B.	1	17	17.0	17	0
DuBose, S.F.	4	37	9.3	14	0	C. Thomas, N.O.	1	14	14.0	14	0
J. McDonald, Rams	4	31	7.8	13	2	Clemons, Phil.	1	13	13.0	t13	1
Rogers, Wash.	4	23	5.8	8	0	Henry, Rams	1	13	13.0	13	0
S. Williams, Det.	4	16	4.0	7	1	Vital, Wash.	1	13	13.0	13	0
P. Smith, Rams	3	95	31.7	51	0	Walls, T.B.	1	13	13.0	13	0
Monroe, S.F.	3	66	22.0	t39	1	S. Carter, T.B.	1	12	12.0	12	0
Finch, Minn.	3	54	18.0	20	0	Ricks, T.B.	1	12	12.0	12	0
Sanders, Chi.	3	53	17.7	25	0	C. Scott, Dall.	1	11	11.0	11	0
Parks, Minn.	3	46	15.3	19	0	Schenk, Minn.	1	10	10.0	10	0
Gonzalez, Atl.	3	40	13.3	22	0	Covington, Giants	1	9	9.0	9	0
Mowatt, Giants	3	39	13.0	29	1	Adams, Dall.	1	8	8.0	8	0
R. Clark, N.O.	3	38	12.7	14	0	Beverly, N.O.	1	8	8.0	8	0
Orr, Wash.	3	35	11.7	23	0	Dressel, S.F.	1	8	8.0	8	0
Dollinger, Det.	3	25	8.3	15	0	Evans, Atl.	1	8	8.0	8	0
Frye, Minn.	3	25	8.3	12	0	Harris, St.L.	1	8	8.0	8	0
Varajon, S.F.	3	25	8.3	12	0	Jessie, Wash.	1	8	8.0	8	0
Parker, G.B.	3	22	7.3	13	0	Little, Phil.	1	8	8.0	8	0
Harrell, Minn.	3	20	6.7	8	0	Moore, Minn.	1	8	8.0	8	0
E.J. Jones, Dall.	3	16	5.3	10	0	Morse, Phil.	1	8	8.0	8	0
McIntosh, Atl.	3	15	5.0	9	1	Hardy, S.F.	1	7	7.0	7	0
Griffin, Wash.	3	13	4.3	t6	1	Margerum, S.F.	1	7	7.0	7	0
O'Neal, N.O.	3	10	3.3	5	1	Bowers, Chi.	1	6	6.0	6	0
Verdin, Wash.	2	62	31.0	55	0	Fowler, Dall.	1	6	6.0	6	0
L. Thomas, G.B.	2	52	26.0	t30	1	Hargrove, G.B.	1	6	6.0	6	0
Rodgers, S.F.	2	45	22.5	24	0	Lavette, Dall.	1	6	6.0	6	0
Jones, S.F.	2	35	17.5	22	0	Mularkey, Minn.	1	6	6.0	6	0
Granger, Atl.	2	34	17.0	26	0	Park, Giants	1	6	6.0	6	0
Spivey, Dall.	2	34	17.0	25	0	Bartalo, T.B.	1	5	5.0	5	0
Mullen, Chi.	2	33	16.5	20	0	Blount, Dall.	1	5	5.0	5	0
Ingram, Giants	2	32	16.0	18	0	Coleman, Giants	1	5	5.0	5	0
Caravello, Wash.	2	29	14.5	22	0	Johnson, Wash.	1	5	5.0	5	0
Harden, G.B.	2	29	14.5	15	0	Yarber, Wash.	1	5	5.0	5	0
Flagler, S.F.	2	28	14.0	24	0	Kowgios, Det.	1	3	3.0	3	0
Gillespie, Minn.	2	28	14.0	14	0	Sydney, S.F.	1	3	3.0	3	0
DiRico, Giants	2	22	11.0	15	0	Oliver, Atl.	1	2	2.0	2	0
Daugherty, Minn.	2	21	10.5	13	0	Middleton, Atl.	1	1	1.0	1	0
G. Taylor, T.B.	2	21	10.5	11	0	Smith, Wash.	1	−2	−2.0	−2	0
Sargent, St.L.	2	19	9.5	10	0	Cunningham, Phil.	1	−3	−3.0	−3	0
S. Harris, Minn.	2	17	8.5	16	0	Singletary, Phil.	1	−11	−11.0	−11	0
Rodenberger, N.O.	2	17	8.5	11	0						

t—Touchdown
Leader based on most passes caught.

1987 INTERCEPTIONS

MOST INTERCEPTIONS, SEASON
> NFC: 9—Barry Wilburn, Washington.
> AFC: 6—Keith Bostic, Houston.
> Mark Kelso, Buffalo.
> Mike Prior, Indianapolis.

MOST INTERCEPTIONS, GAME
> AFC: 3—Frank Minnifield, Cleveland at Houston, November 22.
> NFC: 3—Terry Kinard, N.Y. Giants vs. Dallas, September 20.
> Reggie Sutton, New Orleans at Chicago, October 18.
> Darrell Green, Washington vs. Detroit, November 15.

MOST YARDS RETURNING INTERCEPTIONS
> AFC: 166—Vencie Glenn, San Diego.
> NFC: 163—Terry Kinard, N.Y. Giants.

LONGEST INTERCEPTION RETURN
> AFC: 103—Vencie Glenn, San Diego vs. Denver, November 29 (TD).
> NFC: 100—Barry Wilburn, Washington at Minnesota, December 26 (TD).

MOST TOUCHDOWNS, SEASON
> AFC: 2—Ronnie Lippett, New England.
> NFC: 1—By 12 players.

TEAM LEADERS
> AFC: BUFFALO: 6, Mark Kelso; CINCINNATI: 3, Robert Jackson, David Fulcher; CLEVELAND: 4, Frank Minnifield, Felix Wright; DENVER: 4, Mike Harden; HOUSTON: 6, Keith Bostic; INDIANAPOLIS: 6, Mike Prior; KANSAS CITY: 3, Deron Cherry, Kevin Ross; L.A. RAIDERS: 4, Vann McElroy; MIAMI: 3, Glenn Blackwood, Paul Lankford; NEW ENGLAND: 4, Fred Marion; N.Y. JETS: 3, Harry Hamilton, Carl Howard, Rich Miano; PITTSBURGH: 5, Dwayne Woodruff; SAN DIEGO: 5, Billy Ray Smith; SEATTLE: 4, Kenny Easley.
> NFC: ATLANTA: 4, Bobby Butler; CHICAGO: 3, Dave Duerson; DALLAS: 5, Everson Walls; DETROIT: 6, James Griffin; GREEN BAY: 3, Dave Brown, Jim Bob Morris; L.A. RAMS: 2, Nolan Cromwell, Jerry Gray, LeRoy Irvin; MINNESOTA: 6, Joey Browner; NEW ORLEANS: 5, Reggie Sutton, Dave Waymer; N.Y. GIANTS: 5, Terry Kinard; PHILADELPHIA: 4, Elbert Foules; ST. LOUIS: 5, Travis Curtis; SAN FRANCISCO: 5, Don Griffin, Ronnie Lott; TAMPA BAY: 3, Paul Tripoli; WASHINGTON: 9, Barry Wilburn.

TEAM CHAMPION
> NFC: 30—New Orleans.
> AFC: 28—Denver.

INTERCEPTIONS—TEAM
AMERICAN FOOTBALL CONFERENCE

Team	No.	Yards	Avg.	Long	TDs.
Denver	28	403	14.4	t52	2
Pittsburgh	27	336	12.4	t50	5
Cleveland	23	366	15.9	76	2
Houston	23	274	11.9	t73	1
New England	21	307	14.6	51	2
Indianapolis	20	212	10.6	68	0
N.Y. Jets	18	239	13.3	45	0
Seattle	17	289	17.0	53	1
Buffalo	17	93	5.5	23	0
Miami	16	135	8.4	44	0
Cincinnati	14	187	13.4	44	0
San Diego	13	291	22.4	t103	2
L.A. Raiders	13	178	13.7	58	2
Kansas City	11	140	12.7	40	0
Conference Total	261	3450	....	t103	17
Conference Average	18.6	246.4	13.2	....	1.2

NATIONAL FOOTBALL CONFERENCE

Team	No.	Yards	Avg.	Long	TDs.
New Orleans	30	280	9.3	35	0
Minnesota	26	303	11.7	36	0
San Francisco	25	205	8.2	34	0
Washington	23	329	14.3	t100	1
Dallas	23	208	9.0	30	2
Philadelphia	21	197	9.4	63	0
N.Y. Giants	20	263	13.2	t70	1
Detroit	19	290	15.3	48	1
Green Bay	18	220	12.2	73	0
L.A. Rams	16	305	19.1	49	2
Tampa Bay	16	248	15.5	42	2
Atlanta	15	182	12.1	40	0
St. Louis	14	167	11.9	t60	1
Chicago	13	69	5.3	t23	2
Conference Total	279	3266	....	t100	12
Conference Average	19.9	233.3	11.7	....	0.9
League Total	540	6716	....	t103	29
League Average	19.3	239.9	12.4	....	1.0

TOP TEN INTERCEPTORS

Player—Team	No.	Yards	Avg.	Long	TDs.
WILBURN, BARRY, Wash.	9	135	15.0	t100	1
Griffin, James, Det.	6	130	21.7	29	0
Browner, Joey, Minn.	6	67	11.2	23	0
Prior, Mike, Ind.	6	57	9.5	38	0
Kelso, Mark, Buff.	6	25	4.2	12	0
Bostic, Keith, Hou.	6	−14	−2.3	7	0
Kinard, Terry, Giants	5	163	32.6	t70	1
Woodruff, Dwayne, Pitt.	5	91	18.2	t33	1
Waymer, Dave, N.O.	5	78	15.6	35	0
Sutton, Reggie, N.O.	5	68	13.6	26	0
Curtis, Travis, St.L.	5	65	13.0	31	0
Lott, Ronnie, S.F.	5	62	12.4	34	0
Walls, Everson, Dall.	5	38	7.6	30	0
Smith, Billy Ray, S.D.	5	28	5.6	12	0
Griffin, Don, S.F.	5	1	0.2	1	0

AFC—INDIVIDUALS

Player—Team	No.	Yds.	Avg.	Lng.	TD	Player—Team	No.	Yds.	Avg.	Lng.	TD
PRIOR, Ind.	6	57	9.5	38	0	Robinson, Sea.	3	75	25.0	44	0
KELSO, Buff.	6	25	4.2	12	0	Matthews, Clev.	3	62	20.7	36	1
BOSTIC, Hou.	6	−14	−2.3	7	0	Cherry, K.C.	3	58	19.3	30	0
Woodruff, Pitt.	5	91	18.2	t33	1	Jackson, Cin.	3	49	16.3	29	0
Smith, S.D.	5	28	5.6	12	0	Toran, Raiders	3	48	16.0	t48	1
Glenn, S.D.	4	166	41.5	t103	1	Jenkins, Sea.	3	46	15.3	34	0
Wright, Clev.	4	152	38.0	68	1	Lankford, Mia.	3	44	14.7	44	0
Harden, Den.	4	85	21.3	32	0	Ross, K.C.	3	40	13.3	40	0
Bryant, Hou.	4	75	18.8	29	0	Haynes, Den.	3	39	13.0	25	1
Marion, N.E.	4	53	13.3	25	0	Fulcher, Cin.	3	30	10.0	28	0
Easley, Sea.	4	47	11.8	22	0	Hall, Pitt.	3	29	9.7	t25	1
McElroy, Raiders	4	41	10.3	t35	1	Howard, Jets	3	29	9.7	29	0
Minnifield, Clev.	4	24	6.0	27	0	Lilly, Den.	3	29	9.7	24	0
Donaldson, Hou.	4	16	4.0	9	0	Hamilton, Jets	3	25	8.3	25	0
Clark, Den.	3	105	35.0	50	0	Miano, Jets	3	24	8.0	21	0
Lippett, N.E.	3	103	34.3	t45	2	Mecklenburg, Den.	3	23	7.7	16	0

Player—Team	No.	Yds.	Avg.	Lng.	TD
Everett, Pitt.	3	22	7.3	21	0
Pitts, Buff.	3	19	6.3	12	0
Blackwood, Mia.	3	17	5.7	17	0
Hinkle, Pitt.	3	15	5.0	8	0
Robbins, Den.	3	9	3.0	9	0
Ryan, Den.	3	7	2.3	5	0
Dixon, Clev.	3	5	1.7	6	0
Tullis, Ind.	3	0	0.0	0	0
Robinson, Ind.	2	86	43.0	68	0
Hunley, Den.	2	64	32.0	t52	1
Glaze, Sea.	2	53	26.5	53	0
Gowdy, Pitt.	2	50	25.0	t45	1
Breeden, Cin.	2	49	24.5	44	0
St. Brown, Hou.	2	45	22.5	35	0
Radachowsky, Jets	2	45	22.5	45	0
Lyles, Hou.	2	42	21.0	27	0
Robinson, K.C.	2	42	21.0	25	0
E. Daniel, Ind.	2	34	17.0	34	0
B. Jones, Ind.	2	26	13.0	23	0
Merriweather, Pitt.	2	26	13.0	15	0
Rockins, Clev.	2	25	12.5	15	0
Clayborn, N.E.	2	24	12.0	24	0
D. Smith, Den.	2	21	10.5	15	0
E. Gibson, N.E.	2	17	8.5	17	0
Harper, Clev.	2	16	8.0	16	0
Randle, Mia.	2	16	8.0	11	0
Burroughs, Buff.	2	11	5.5	14	0
Hooper, Mia.	2	11	5.5	11	0
Judson, Mia.	2	11	5.5	10	0
Haynes, Raiders	2	9	4.5	7	0
Hobley, Mia.	2	7	3.5	7	0
Radecic, Buff.	2	4	2.0	4	0
Bowman, N.E.	2	3	1.5	3	0
Griffin, Pitt.	2	2	1.0	2	0
D. Smith, Cin.	2	0	0.0	0	0
Patterson, S.D.	1	75	75.0	t75	1
Seale, Hou.	1	73	73.0	t73	1
Anderson, Raiders	1	58	58.0	58	0
E. Williams, N.E.	1	51	51.0	51	0
Shell, Pitt.	1	50	50.0	t50	1
F. Young, Sea.	1	50	50.0	t50	1
Woodson, Pitt.	1	45	45.0	t45	1
Robinson, Jets	1	38	38.0	38	0
P. Allen, Hou.	1	37	37.0	37	0
Wilcots, Cin.	1	37	37.0	37	0
Heath, Jets	1	35	35.0	35	0
Sowell, Mia.	1	29	29.0	29	0
Horn, Clev.	1	28	28.0	28	0
R. James, N.E.	1	27	27.0	27	0
Clark, Buff.	1	23	23.0	23	0
Banks, S.D.	1	20	20.0	20	0
Holmes, Jets	1	20	20.0	20	0
Niehoff, Cin.	1	19	19.0	19	0
R. McSwain, N.E.	1	17	17.0	17	0
E. Johnson, Clev.	1	11	11.0	11	0
Lucas, Den.	1	11	11.0	11	0
T. Taylor, Sea.	1	11	11.0	11	0
Dennison, Den.	1	10	10.0	10	0
Haslett, Jets	1	9	9.0	9	0
Adams, Raiders	1	8	8.0	8	0
Crable, Jets	1	8	8.0	8	0
King, Raiders	1	8	8.0	8	0
Davis, Ind.	1	7	7.0	7	0
Schankweiler, Buff.	1	7	7.0	7	0
Shegog, N.E.	1	7	7.0	7	0
Millen, Raiders	1	6	6.0	6	0
Hogan, Jets	1	5	5.0	5	0
Caldwell, Sea.	1	4	4.0	4	0
Cokeley, Buff.	1	4	4.0	4	0
Holmes, N.E.	1	4	4.0	4	0
A. Riley, Pitt.	1	4	4.0	4	0
Hunter, Sea.	1	3	3.0	3	0
M. Johnson, Clev.	1	3	3.0	3	0
Small, Hou.	1	3	3.0	3	0
Thomas, Cin.	1	3	3.0	3	0
Cooks, Ind.	1	2	2.0	2	0
Plummer, S.D.	1	2	2.0	2	0
Sheffield, Pitt.	1	2	2.0	2	0
Rembert, N.E.	1	1	1.0	1	0
Rose, Jets	1	1	1.0	1	0
Brazley, S.D.	1	0	0.0	0	0
B. Brown, Mia.	1	0	0.0	0	0
Bryant, K.C.	1	0	0.0	0	0
Bussey, Cin.	1	0	0.0	0	0
Cole, Pitt.	1	0	0.0	0	0
Cooper, K.C.	1	0	0.0	0	0
Curry, Ind.	1	0	0.0	0	0
Davis, Buff.	1	0	0.0	0	0
Edwards, Pitt.	1	0	0.0	0	0
Glasgow, Ind.	1	0	0.0	0	0
R. Johnson, Hou.	1	0	0.0	0	0
Lewis, K.C.	1	0	0.0	0	0
Moyer, Sea.	1	0	0.0	0	0
Perryman, Ind.	1	0	0.0	0	0
Peterson, N.E.	1	0	0.0	0	0
D. Robinson, Clev.	1	0	0.0	0	0
P. Williams, N.E.	1	0	0.0	0	0
R. Williams, Pitt.	1	0	0.0	0	0
Wilson, Clev.	1	0	0.0	0	0
Newsom, Hou.	1	−3	−3.0	−3	0
Hairston, Clev.	0	40	.....	40	0

NFC—INDIVIDUALS

Player—Team	No.	Yds.	Avg.	Lng.	TD
WILBURN, Wash.	9	135	15.0	t100	1
Griffin, Det.	6	130	21.7	29	0
Browner, Minn.	6	67	11.2	23	0
Kinard, Giants	5	163	32.6	t70	1
Waymer, N.O.	5	78	15.6	35	0
R. Sutton, N.O.	5	68	13.6	26	0
Curtis, St.L.	5	65	13.0	31	0
Lott, S.F.	5	62	12.4	34	0
Walls, Dall.	5	38	7.6	30	0
Griffin, S.F.	5	1	0.2	1	0
Downs, Dall.	4	56	14.0	27	0
B. Butler, Atl.	4	48	12.0	31	0
Henderson, Minn.	4	33	8.3	17	0
Mack, N.O.	4	32	8.0	26	0
Bowles, Wash.	4	24	6.0	24	0
Foules, Phil.	4	6	1.5	6	0
J.B. Morris, G.B.	3	135	45.0	73	0
Green, Wash.	3	65	21.7	56	0
Waters, Phil.	3	63	21.0	63	0
Lee, Minn.	3	53	17.7	36	0
Galloway, Det.	3	46	15.3	30	0
Jakes, N.O.	3	32	10.7	27	0
Bates, Dall.	3	28	9.3	28	0
Walton, Wash.	3	28	9.3	24	0
J. Harris, Minn.	3	20	6.7	14	0
McNorton, Det.	3	20	6.7	20	0
Maxie, N.O.	3	17	5.7	10	0
Tripoli, T.B.	3	17	5.7	t15	1
D. Brown, G.B.	3	16	5.3	11	0
L. Taylor, Giants	3	16	5.3	15	0
Atkins, N.O.	3	12	4.0	8	0
Haynes, Dall.	3	7	2.3	7	0
Duerson, Chi.	3	0	0.0	0	0
Isom, T.B.	2	67	33.5	38	0
Woods, T.B.	2	63	31.5	42	0
Coleman, Wash.	2	53	26.5	28	0
J. Williams, Det.	2	51	25.5	48	0
Irvin, Rams	2	47	23.5	t47	1
Futrell, T.B.	2	46	23.0	23	0
Joyner, Phil.	2	42	21.0	29	0
Croudip, Atl.	2	40	20.0	40	0
Gray, Rams	2	35	17.5	35	0
McLemore, S.F.	2	35	17.5	25	0
K. Walker, T.B.	2	30	15.0	t30	1
Collins, Giants	2	28	14.0	28	0
Cromwell, Rams	2	28	14.0	28	0
Gordon, Atl.	2	28	14.0	27	0
Studwell, Minn.	2	26	13.0	14	0
Headen, Giants	2	25	12.5	20	0
Kullman, Phil.	2	25	12.5	13	0
Moore, Atl.	2	23	11.5	18	0
J. Anderson, G.B.	2	22	11.0	13	0

San Diego safety Vencie Glenn returned one of his four interceptions of 1987 an NFL-record 103 yards for a touchdown against Denver.

Player—Team	No.	Yds.	Avg.	Lng.	TD	Player—Team	No.	Yds.	Avg.	Lng.	TD
Rivera, Chi.	2	19	9.5	15	0	Kemp, T.B.	1	11	11.0	11	0
Francis, Dall.	2	18	9.0	t18	1	Wilcher, Rams	1	11	11.0	11	0
Huff, Atl.	2	14	7.0	14	0	DeRose, Giants	1	10	10.0	10	0
Jones, T.B.	2	9	4.5	9	0	S. Leach, N.O.	1	10	10.0	10	0
J. Brown, Phil.	2	7	3.5	6	0	Noble, G.B.	1	10	10.0	10	0
Holt, Minn.	2	7	3.5	7	0	Swilling, N.O.	1	10	10.0	10	0
Welch, Giants	2	7	3.5	7	0	C. Brown, Phil.	1	9	9.0	9	0
Holland, G.B.	2	4	2.0	4	0	Hicks, Rams	1	9	9.0	9	0
Jackson, N.O.	2	4	2.0	4	0	Ekern, Rams	1	7	7.0	7	0
Hoage, Phil.	2	3	1.5	3	0	Gage, Wash.	1	7	7.0	7	0
R. Phillips, Chi.	2	1	0.5	1	0	Carreker, G.B.	1	6	6.0	6	0
Cooper, Phil.	2	0	0.0	0	0	Norris, Chi.	1	6	6.0	6	0
Douglass, Chi.	2	0	0.0	0	0	Gant, T.B.	1	5	5.0	5	0
C. Mack, St.L.	2	0	0.0	0	0	Gibson, Det.	1	5	5.0	5	0
McKyer, S.F.	2	0	0.0	0	0	Nixon, S.F.	1	5	5.0	5	0
P. Noga, St.L.	1	60	60.0	t60	1	Brown, Giants	1	4	4.0	4	0
H. Johnson, Rams	1	49	49.0	49	0	Mathis, St.L.	1	4	4.0	4	0
Jackson, Rams	1	36	36.0	36	0	Sutton, Rams	1	4	4.0	4	0
Smith, Det.	1	34	34.0	t34	1	Benson, Det.	1	2	2.0	2	0
Courtney, S.F.	1	30	30.0	30	0	Cherry, Det.	1	2	2.0	2	0
Solomon, Minn.	1	30	30.0	30	0	K. Johnson, G.B.	1	2	2.0	2	0
Young, Phil.	1	30	30.0	30	0	Hill, Giants	1	1	1.0	1	0
Williamson, Rams	1	28	28.0	28	0	Howard, Minn.	1	1	1.0	1	0
Guggemos, Minn.	1	26	26.0	26	0	V. Scott, Dall.	1	1	1.0	1	0
Jeffcoat, Dall.	1	26	26.0	t26	1	Shell, S.F.	1	1	1.0	1	0
Owens, Rams	1	26	26.0	26	0	Banks, Giants	1	0	0.0	0	0
Greene, Rams	1	25	25.0	t25	1	C. Carter, St.L.	1	0	0.0	0	0
Junior, St.L.	1	25	25.0	25	0	J. Fahnhorst, S.F.	1	0	0.0	0	0
W. Smith, Minn.	1	24	24.0	24	0	Green, Dall.	1	0	0.0	0	0
McCray, Chi.	1	23	23.0	t23	1	Hall, Det.	1	0	0.0	0	0
Penn, Dall.	1	21	21.0	21	0	Harrison, G.B.	1	0	0.0	0	0
Gayle, Chi.	1	20	20.0	t20	1	Holmoe, S.F.	1	0	0.0	0	0
Moss, Atl.	1	18	18.0	18	0	V. Jackson, Chi.	1	0	0.0	0	0
Gibson, N.O.	1	17	17.0	17	0	J. Johnson, Rams	1	0	0.0	0	0
Mitchell, Wash.	1	17	17.0	17	0	V. Johnson, N.O.	1	0	0.0	0	0
Williamson, S.F.	1	17	17.0	17	0	Lee, G.B.	1	0	0.0	0	0
Louallen, Minn.	1	16	16.0	16	0	McColl, S.F.	1	0	0.0	0	0
Walter, S.F.	1	16	16.0	16	0	Melka, G.B.	1	0	0.0	0	0
Turner, S.F.	1	15	15.0	15	0	Montoute, T.B.	1	0	0.0	0	0
Mansfield, G.B.	1	14	14.0	14	0	Poe, N.O.	1	0	0.0	0	0
Rehage, Giants	1	14	14.0	14	0	Saddler, St.L.	1	0	0.0	0	0
Bell, St.L.	1	13	13.0	13	0	H. Thomas, Minn.	1	0	0.0	0	0
Lockhart, Dall.	1	13	13.0	13	0	West, Phil.	1	0	0.0	0	0
Case, Atl.	1	12	12.0	12	0	R. White, Dall.	1	0	0.0	0	0
Evans, Phil.	1	12	12.0	12	0	Young, St.L.	1	0	0.0	0	0
Martin, S.F.	1	12	12.0	12	0	Britt, Atl.	1	−1	−1.0	−1	0
Cousineau, S.F.	1	11	11.0	11	0	P. Williams, Giants	1	−5	−5.0	−5	0
Greene, G.B.	1	11	11.0	11	0						

t—Touchdown
Leader based on most interceptions.

1987 SCORING

MOST POINTS, SEASON
NFC: 138—Jerry Rice, San Francisco.
AFC: 97—Jim Breech, Cincinnati.

MOST TOUCHDOWNS
NFC: 23—Jerry Rice, San Francisco.
AFC: 11—Johnny Hector, N.Y. Jets.

MOST EXTRA POINTS
NFC: 44—Ray Wersching, San Francisco.
AFC: 40—Norm Johnson, Seattle.

MOST FIELD GOALS
NFC: 28—Morten Andersen, New Orleans.
AFC: 24—Dean Biasucci, Indianapolis.
       Jim Breech, Cincinnati.

MOST FIELD GOALS ATTEMPTED
NFC: 36—Morten Andersen, New Orleans.
AFC: 30—Jim Breech, Cincinnati.

LONGEST FIELD GOAL
AFC: 54—Nick Lowery, Kansas City at Detroit, November 26.
NFC: 53—Raul Allegre, N.Y. Giants at Philadelphia, November 15.
       Ed Murray, Detroit vs. L.A. Rams, December 6.

MOST POINTS, GAME
AFC: 19—Norm Johnson, Seattle vs. Kansas City, September 20 (4 XP, 5 FG)
NFC: 18—Achieved by five players.

TEAM LEADERS
AFC: BUFFALO: 61, Scott Norwood; CINCINNATI: 97, Jim Breech; CLEVE-
     LAND: 75, Jeff Jaeger; DENVER: 91, Rich Karlis; HOUSTON: 92,
     Tony Zendejas; INDIANAPOLIS: 96, Dean Biasucci; KANSAS
     CITY: 83, Nick Lowery; L.A. RAIDERS: 84, Chris Bahr; MIAMI:
     55, Fuad Reveiz; NEW ENGLAND: 82, Tony Franklin; N.Y.
     JETS: 85, Pat Leahy; PITTSBURGH: 87, Gary Anderson; SAN
     DIEGO: 61, Vince Abbott; SEATTLE: 85, Norm Johnson.
NFC: ATLANTA: 44, Mick Luckhurst; CHICAGO: 85, Kevin Butler; DALLAS:
     92, Roger Ruzek; DETROIT: 81, Ed Murray; GREEN BAY: 61,
     Max Zendejas; L.A. RAMS: 87, Mike Lansford; MINNESOTA: 75,
     Chuck Nelson; NEW ORLEANS: 121, Morten Andersen; N.Y.
     GIANTS: 76, Raul Allegre; PHILADELPHIA: 84, Paul McFad-
     den; ST. LOUIS: 57, Jim Gallery; SAN FRANCISCO: 138, Jerry
     Rice; TAMPA BAY: 66, Donald Igwebuike; WASHINGTON: 68,
     Ali Haji-Sheikh.

TEAM CHAMPION
NFC: 459—San Francisco.
AFC: 390—Cleveland.

SCORING—TEAM

AMERICAN FOOTBALL CONFERENCE

	Tot. Tds.	Tds. R.	Tds. P.	Tds. Misc.	XP	XPA	FG	FGA	Saf.	Tot. Pts.
Cleveland	47	16	27	4	45	47	21	31	0	390
Denver	45	18	24	3	44	45	21	29	1	379
Seattle	46	13	31	2	44	46	17	22	0	371
Miami	47	16	29	2	44	47	12	16	0	362
Houston	38	12	24	2	37	38	26	32	1	345
N.Y. Jets	39	17	18	4	38	38	20	26	1	334
New England	39	12	22	5	38	39	16	28	0	320
L.A. Raiders	35	13	19	3	34	35	19	30	0	301
Indianapolis	31	14	16	1	31	31	27	32	1	300
Cincinnati	30	13	17	0	28	30	25	32	1	285
Pittsburgh	31	11	13	7	31	31	22	29	1	285
Kansas City	30	7	17	6	30	30	21	25	0	273
Buffalo	33	9	21	3	32	33	12	20	2	270
San Diego	29	11	13	5	27	29	16	28	2	253
Conference Total	520	182	291	47	503	519	275	380	10	4468
Conference Avg.	37.1	13.0	20.8	3.4	35.9	37.1	19.6	27.1	0.7	319.1

NATIONAL FOOTBALL CONFERENCE

	Tot. Tds.	Tds. R.	Tds. P.	Tds. Misc.	XP	XPA	FG	FGA	Saf.	Tot. Pts.
San Francisco	59	11	44	4	55	59	16	23	1	459
New Orleans	46	20	23	3	43	46	33	42	2	422
Washington	47	18	27	2	43	47	18	29	0	379
St. Louis	46	15	25	6	44	46	14	27	0	362
Chicago	42	13	23	6	38	42	22	32	0	356
Dallas	38	17	19	2	37	37	25	29	0	340
Philadelphia	40	12	26	2	38	40	19	31	1	337
Minnesota	42	20	21	1	40	41	14	29	1	336
L.A. Rams	38	15	16	7	36	38	17	21	1	317
Tampa Bay	33	7	22	4	31	33	19	24	0	286
N.Y. Giants	32	4	26	2	28	32	20	32	0	280
Detroit	27	9	16	2	27	27	26	39	1	269
Green Bay	28	13	15	0	24	27	21	29	0	255
Atlanta	24	5	17	2	23	24	12	17	1	205
Conference Total	542	179	320	43	507	539	276	404	8	4603
Conference Avg.	38.7	12.8	22.9	3.1	36.2	38.5	19.7	28.9	0.6	328.8
League Total	1062	361	611	90	1010	1058	551	784	18	9071
League Average	37.9	12.9	21.8	3.2	36.1	37.8	19.7	28.0	0.6	324.0

TOP TEN SCORERS

NON-KICKERS

Player—Team	Total TDs.	Rush TDs.	Pass TDs.	Misc. TDs.	Tot. Pts.
RICE, S.F.	23	1	22	0	138
Hector, Jets	11	11	0	0	66
Quick, Phil.	11	0	11	0	66
White, Rams	11	11	0	0	66
Byner, Clev.	10	8	2	0	60
Warner, Sea.	10	8	2	0	60
Bentley, Ind.	9	7	2	0	54
Riddick, Buff.	8	5	3	0	50
Bavaro, Giants	8	0	8	0	48
Duper, Mia.	8	0	8	0	48
Hilliard, N.O.	8	7	1	0	48
Kinnebrew, Cin.	8	8	0	0	48
Largent, Sea.	8	0	8	0	48
J.T. Smith, St.L.	8	0	8	0	48
H. Walker, Dall.	8	7	1	0	48

KICKERS

Player—Team	XP Made	XP Att.	FG. Made	FG. Att.	Tot. Pts.
ANDERSEN, N.O.	37	37	28	36	121
Breech, Cin.	25	27	24	30	97
Biasucci, Ind.	24	24	24	27	96
Ruzek, Dall.	26	26	22	25	92
Zendejas, Hou.	32	33	20	26	92
Karlis, Den.	37	37	18	25	91
G. Anderson, Pitt.	21	21	22	27	87
Lansford, Rams	36	38	17	21	87
Butler, Chi.	28	30	19	28	85
N. Johnson, Sea.	40	40	15	20	85
Leahy, Jets	31	31	18	22	85

AFC—INDIVIDUALS

KICKERS

Player—Team	XP Made	XP Att.	FG. Made	FG. Att.	Tot. Pts.
BREECH, Cin.	25	27	24	30	97
Biasucci, Ind.	24	24	24	27	96
Zendejas, Hou.	32	33	20	26	92
Karlis, Den.	37	37	18	25	91
G. Anderson, Pitt.	21	21	22	27	87
N. Johnson, Sea.	40	40	15	20	85
Leahy, Jets	31	31	18	22	85
Bahr, Raiders	27	28	19	29	84
Lowery, K.C.	26	26	19	23	83
T. Franklin, N.E.	37	38	15	26	82
Jaeger, Clev.	33	33	14	22	75
Abbott, S.D.	22	23	13	22	61
Norwood, Buff.	31	31	10	15	61
Reveiz, Mia.	28	30	9	11	55
Tiffin, T.B.-Mia.	11	11	5	7	26
Diettrich, Hou.	5	5	6	6	23
Bahr, Clev.	9	10	4	5	21
Beecher, Mia.	12	12	3	4	21
Clendenen, Den.	7	7	3	4	16
Jordan, Ind.	7	7	3	5	16
Gaffney, S.D.	4	5	3	6	13
Ragusa, Jets	7	7	2	4	13
Franco, Clev.	2	2	3	4	11
Hagler, Sea.	4	4	2	2	10
Hamrick, K.C.	4	4	2	2	10
Trout, Pitt.	10	10	0	2	10
Hardy, Raiders	7	7	0	1	7
Schlopy, Buff.	1	2	2	5	7
Manca, Cin.	3	3	1	2	6
Schubert, N.E.	1	1	1	2	4
Kelley, Clev.	1	1	0	0	1

NON-KICKERS

Player—Team	Total TDs.	Rush TDs.	Pass TDs.	Misc. TDs.	Tot. Pts.
HECTOR, Jets	11	11	0	0	66
Byner, Clev.	10	8	2	0	60
Warner, Sea.	10	8	2	0	60
Bentley, Ind.	9	7	2	0	54
Riddick, Buff.	8	5	3	0	*50
Duper, Mia.	8	0	8	0	48
Kinnebrew, Cin.	8	8	0	0	48
Largent, Sea.	8	0	8	0	48
Carson, K.C.	7	0	7	0	42
Clayton, Mia.	7	0	7	0	42
V. Johnson, Den.	7	0	7	0	42
Slaughter, Clev.	7	0	7	0	42
Stradford, Mia.	7	6	1	0	42
Winder, Den.	7	6	1	0	42
Brennan, Clev.	6	0	6	0	36
Collins, N.E.	6	3	3	0	36
Dickerson, Rams-Ind.	6	6	0	0	36
Givins, Hou.	6	0	6	0	36
D. Hill, Hou.	6	0	6	0	36
B. Jackson, Raiders	6	4	2	0	36
James, S.D.	6	2	3	1	36
Mack, Clev.	6	5	1	0	36
Turner, Sea.	6	0	6	0	36
Allen, Raiders	5	5	0	0	30
G. Anderson, S.D.	5	3	2	0	30
R. Butler, Sea.	5	0	5	0	30
Duncan, Hou.	5	0	5	0	30
Fryar, N.E.	5	0	5	0	30
Lofton, Raiders	5	0	5	0	30
Reed, Buff.	5	0	5	0	30
Toon, Jets	5	0	5	0	30

Player—Team	Total TDs.	Rush TDs.	Pass TDs.	Misc. TDs.	Tot. Pts.
Do. Williams, Raiders	5	0	5	0	30
Bouza, Ind.	4	0	4	0	24
Burkett, Buff.	4	0	4	0	24
Elway, Den.	4	4	0	0	24
Harmon, Buff.	4	2	2	0	24
Lang, Den.	4	2	2	0	24
Massie, Den.	4	0	4	0	24
Paige, K.C.	4	0	4	0	24
Jo. Williams, Sea.	4	1	3	0	24
Aikens, Raiders	3	0	3	0	18
Brooks, Ind.	3	0	3	0	18
Brooks, Cin.	3	1	2	0	18
E. Brown, Cin.	3	0	3	0	18
Carter, Pitt.	3	0	3	0	18
Dupard, N.E.	3	3	0	0	18
Heard, K.C.	3	3	0	0	18
Jennings, Cin.	3	1	2	0	18
Ce. Jones, N.E.	3	0	3	0	18
Malone, Pitt.	3	3	0	0	18
Martin, Cin.	3	0	3	0	18
Mason, Clev.	3	2	1	0	18
Moon, Hou.	3	3	0	0	18
Morgan, N.E.	3	0	3	0	18
Murray, Ind.	3	0	3	0	18
Okoye, K.C.	3	3	0	0	18
Pollard, Pitt.	3	3	0	0	18
Pruitt, Mia.	3	0	3	0	18
Rozier, Hou.	3	3	0	0	18
R. Scott, Mia.	3	3	0	0	18
Sewell, Den.	3	2	1	0	18
Shuler, Jets	3	0	3	0	18
Starring, N.E.	3	0	3	0	18
Tennell, Clev.	3	0	3	0	18
J. Williams, Hou.	3	0	3	0	18
Winslow, S.D.	3	0	3	0	18
Abercrombie, Pitt.	2	2	0	0	12
Alston, Pitt.	2	0	2	0	12
Baty, N.E.	2	0	2	0	12
Chandler, S.D.	2	0	2	0	12
Christensen, Raiders	2	0	2	0	12
Davenport, Mia.	2	1	1	0	12
Dudek, Den.	2	2	0	0	12
C. Ellis, Raiders	2	2	0	0	12
Faaola, Jets	2	2	0	0	12
Fouts, S.D.	2	2	0	0	12
Grogan, N.E.	2	2	0	0	12
Hall, Pitt.	2	0	0	2	12
Hardy, Mia.	2	0	2	0	12
Harper, Jets	2	0	1	1	12
Hayes, K.C.	2	0	2	0	12
Highsmith, Hou.	2	1	1	0	12
Holman, Cin.	2	0	2	0	12
E. Hunter, Jets	2	0	2	0	12
M. Jackson, Den.	2	0	2	0	12
Da. Johnson, Mia.	2	0	2	0	12
T. Johnson, Buff.	2	0	2	0	12
Kattus, Cin.	2	0	2	0	12
Kemp, Clev.	2	0	2	0	12
Krieg, Sea.	2	2	0	0	12
Linne, N.E.	2	0	2	0	12
Lippett, N.E.	2	0	0	2	12
Mackey, Mia.	2	2	0	0	12
McNeil, Clev.	2	0	2	0	12
Micho, Den.	2	0	2	0	12
Mueller, Buff.	2	2	0	0	12
Nattiel, Den.	2	0	2	0	12
Noble, Ind.	2	0	2	0	12
Palmer, K.C.	2	0	0	2	12
Pinkett, Hou.	2	2	0	0	12
Rolle, Buff.	2	0	2	0	12
Scott, N.E.	2	0	1	1	12
Shell, Pitt.	2	0	0	2	12
Sohn, Jets	2	0	2	0	12
Stallworth, Pitt.	2	0	2	0	12
Teal, Sea.	2	0	2	0	12
Tice, Sea.	2	0	2	0	12
Weathers, Clev.	2	0	2	0	12
Neuheisel, S.D.	1	1	0	0	†7
Adams, S.D.	1	1	0	0	6
Adickes, K.C.	1	0	1	0	6
Banks, Mia.	1	0	1	0	6
Bernstine, S.D.	1	0	1	0	6
Bleier, N.E.	1	1	0	0	6
Bligen, Jets	1	1	0	0	6
Boddie, Den.	1	1	0	0	6
Bono, Pitt.	1	1	0	0	6
Brandon, S.D.	1	0	0	1	6
Broughton, Buff.	1	0	1	0	6
G. Brown, Ind.	1	1	0	0	6
M. Brown, Buff.	1	0	1	0	6
Calhoun, Raiders	1	0	0	1	6
Chirico, Jets	1	1	0	0	6
Clark, Den.	1	0	0	1	6
Clayborn, N.E.	1	0	0	1	6
Clinkscales, Pitt.	1	0	1	0	6
Coffman, K.C.	1	0	1	0	6
Douglas, Mia.	1	0	1	0	6
Ellis, Clev.	1	0	0	1	6
Evans, Raiders	1	1	0	0	6
Fields, K.C.	1	0	0	1	6
Gehring, Hou.	1	0	1	0	6
Glenn, S.D.	1	0	0	1	6
Gothard, Pitt.	1	0	1	0	6
Gowdy, Pitt.	1	0	0	1	6
Grayson, Clev.	1	0	0	1	6
Griggs, Jets	1	0	1	0	6
Hairston, Pitt.	1	0	1	0	6
Hampton, Mia.	1	1	0	0	6
Harris, K.C.	1	0	0	1	6
Haynes, Den.	1	0	0	1	6
Hobley, Mia.	1	0	1	0	6
Hoge, Pitt.	1	0	1	0	6
Hooper, Mia.	1	0	0	1	6
Horton, Raiders	1	0	1	0	6
Humphery, Jets	1	0	0	1	6
Hunley, Den.	1	0	1	0	6
S. Hunter, Jets	1	0	1	0	6
Isom, Mia.	1	1	0	0	6
Jackson, Hou.	1	1	0	0	6
Jackson, Pitt.	1	1	0	0	6
Jensen, Mia.	1	0	1	0	6
B. Johnson, Cin.	1	1	0	0	6
J. Jones, Ind.	1	0	1	0	6
R. Jones, K.C.	1	0	1	0	6
Keel, Sea.	1	0	1	0	6
Kelso, Buff.	1	0	0	1	6
Kosar, Clev.	1	1	0	0	6
Kurisko, Jets	1	0	1	0	6
Langhorne, Clev.	1	0	1	0	6
LeBlanc, N.E.	1	1	0	0	6
Lewis, Mia.	1	0	1	0	6
Lockett, Pitt.	1	0	1	0	6
Logan, Cin.	1	1	0	0	6
Lyles, Hou.	1	0	0	1	6
Maas, K.C.	1	0	0	1	6
Marino, Mia.	1	1	0	0	6
Matthews, Clev.	1	0	0	1	6
McCluskey, Cin.	1	1	0	0	6
McDonald, Hou.	1	0	1	0	6
McElroy, Raiders	1	0	0	1	6
McFadden, Buff.	1	0	1	0	6
McGee, Cin.	1	0	1	0	6
McNanie, Buff.	1	0	0	1	6
McNeil, Jets	1	0	1	0	6
Miano, Jets	1	0	0	1	6
Middleton, S.D.	1	1	0	0	6
L. Miller, S.D.	1	0	0	1	6
Mobley, Den.	1	0	1	0	6
Moffett, S.D.	1	0	1	0	6
Moriarty, K.C.	1	0	1	0	6
Morton, Sea.	1	1	0	0	6
Mueller, Raiders	1	1	0	0	6
Munoz, Cin.	1	0	1	0	6
Pardridge, Sea.	1	0	1	0	6
Parker, K.C.	1	1	0	0	6
Parros, Sea.	1	1	0	0	6
Patterson, S.D.	1	0	0	1	6
Pease, Hou.	1	1	0	0	6
Perry, Raiders	1	0	1	0	6
Poole, Den.	1	1	0	0	6
Ramsey, N.E.	1	1	0	0	6
Robinson, Sea.	1	0	0	1	6

Player—Team	Total TDs.	Rush TDs.	Pass TDs.	Misc. TDs.	Tot. Pts.
Ross, K.C.	1	0	0	1	6
Russell, Cin.	1	0	1	0	6
Ryan, Jets	1	1	0	0	6
Sanders, Pitt.	1	1	0	0	6
Sartin, S.D.	1	1	0	0	6
Seale, Hou.	1	0	0	1	6
Sherwin, Ind.	1	0	1	0	6
Skansi, Sea.	1	0	1	0	6
Smith, Buff.	1	0	0	1	6
W. Smith, Mia.	1	0	1	0	6
Swanson, Den.	1	0	1	0	6
Tagliaferri, Mia.	1	1	0	0	6
Thompson, Ind.	1	0	0	1	6
Thompson, Pitt.	1	0	1	0	6
Tillman, Hou.	1	1	0	0	6
Tippett, N.E.	1	0	0	1	6
Toran, Raiders	1	0	0	1	6
Townsell, Jets	1	0	0	1	6
Vick, Jets	1	1	0	0	6
Walker, Jets	1	0	1	0	6
Watson, Den.	1	0	1	0	6
A. Williams, S.D.	1	0	1	0	6
O. Williams, Hou.	1	0	1	0	6
Wonsley, Ind.	1	1	0	0	6
Woodruff, Pitt.	1	0	0	1	6
Woods, N.E.	1	1	0	0	6
Woodson, Pitt.	1	0	0	1	6
Wright, Clev.	1	0	0	1	6
F. Young, Sea.	1	0	0	1	6
Baker, Hou.	0	0	0	0	*2
Carr, Pitt.	0	0	0	0	*2
Leiding, Ind.	0	0	0	0	*2
Lyons, Jets	0	0	0	0	*2
Ryan, Den.	0	0	0	0	*2
Schutt, Cin.	0	0	0	0	*2
Tasker, Buff.	0	0	0	0	*2
L. Williams, S.D.	0	0	0	0	*2

NFC—INDIVIDUALS

KICKERS

Player—Team	XP Made	XP Att.	FG Made	FG Att.	Tot. Pts.
Andersen, N.O.	37	37	28	36	121
Ruzek, Dall.	26	26	22	25	92
Lansford, Rams	36	38	17	21	87
Butler, Chi.	28	30	19	28	85
McFadden, Phil.	36	36	16	26	84
Wersching, S.F.	44	46	13	17	83
Murray, Det.	21	21	20	32	81
Allegre, Giants	25	26	17	27	76
C. Nelson, Minn.	36	37	13	24	75
Haji-Sheikh, Wash.	29	32	13	19	68
Igwebuike, T.B.	24	26	14	18	66
Zendejas, G.B.	13	15	16	19	61
Gallery, St.L.	30	31	9	19	57
Del Greco, G.B.-St.L.	19	20	9	15	46
Luckhurst, Atl.	17	17	9	13	44
Prindle, Det.	6	6	6	7	24
Brockhaus, S.F.	11	13	3	6	20
Lashar, Chi.	10	10	3	4	19
Zendejas, Dall.	10	10	3	4	19
Ariri, Wash.	6	6	3	5	15
Davis, Atl.	6	6	3	4	15
Kempf, N.O.	1	1	4	5	13
Benyola, Giants	3	3	3	5	12
Jacobs, Phil.	2	4	3	5	11
Staurovsky, St.L.	6	6	1	3	9
Cofer, N.O.	5	7	1	1	8
Dawson, Minn.	4	4	1	5	7
Cox, Wash.	3	3	1	2	6
Atkinson, Wash.	1	1	1	1	4
Toibin, Wash.	4	4	0	2	4
Brady, Dall.	1	1	0	0	1

NON-KICKERS

Player—Team	Total TDs.	Rush TDs.	Pass TDs.	Misc. TDs.	Tot. Pts.
Rice, S.F.	23	1	22	0	138
Quick, Phil.	11	0	11	0	66
White, Rams	11	11	0	0	66
Bavaro, Giants	8	0	8	0	48
Hilliard, N.O.	8	7	1	0	48
J.T. Smith, St.L.	8	0	8	0	48
H. Walker, Dall.	8	7	1	0	48
Carter, Minn.	7	0	7	0	42
Clark, Wash.	7	0	7	0	42
Dozier, Minn.	7	5	2	0	42
Ferrell, St.L.	7	7	0	0	42
Gault, Chi.	7	0	7	0	42
Mandley, Det.	7	0	7	0	42
Martin, N.O.	7	0	7	0	42
Anderson, Chi.	6	3	3	0	36
Awalt, St.L.	6	0	6	0	36
Bryant, Wash.	6	1	5	0	36
Manuel, Giants	6	0	6	0	36
Monk, Wash.	6	0	6	0	36
Rogers, Wash.	6	6	0	0	36

Player—Team	Total TDs.	Rush TDs.	Pass TDs.	Misc. TDs.	Tot. Pts.
Tice, N.O.	6	0	6	0	36
Toney, Phil.	6	5	1	0	36
G. Carter, T.B.	5	0	5	0	30
Clark, S.F.	5	0	5	0	30
Dixon, Atl.	5	0	5	0	30
Fullwood, G.B.	5	5	0	0	30
Mayes, N.O.	5	5	0	0	30
Mitchell, St.L.	5	3	2	0	30
W. Payton, Chi.	5	4	1	0	30
Wilson, S.F.	5	0	5	0	30
W. Wilson, Minn.	5	5	0	0	30
Byars, Phil.	4	3	1	0	24
Carruth, G.B.	4	3	1	0	24
Craig, S.F.	4	3	1	0	24
Edwards, Dall.	4	1	3	0	24
Ellerson, Det.	4	3	1	0	24
Green, St.L.	4	0	4	0	24
James, Det.	4	4	0	0	24
McAdoo, St.L.	4	3	0	1	24
Newsome, Dall.	4	2	2	0	24
Rathman, S.F.	4	1	3	0	24
Renfro, Dall.	4	0	4	0	24
J. Smith, T.B.	4	2	2	0	24
A. Allen, Wash.	3	0	3	0	18
Bailey, Atl.	3	0	3	0	18
Blount, Dall.	3	3	0	0	18
Brewer, Chi.	3	2	1	0	18
Brim, Minn.	3	1	2	0	18
Ro. Brown, Rams	3	0	2	1	18
Carrier, T.B.	3	0	3	0	18
Cosbie, Dall.	3	0	3	0	18
Cunningham, Phil.	3	3	0	0	18
Davis, G.B.	3	3	0	0	18
Ellard, Rams	3	0	3	0	18
Frank, S.F.	3	0	3	0	18
Heller, S.F.	3	0	3	0	18
Jackson, Phil.	3	0	3	0	18
M. Jones, N.O.	3	0	3	0	18
Kozlowski, Chi.	3	0	3	0	18
Lewis, Minn.	3	0	2	1	18
Magee, T.B.	3	0	3	0	18
Matthews, Atl.	3	0	3	0	18
McKinnon, Chi.	3	0	1	2	18
Morris, Giants	3	3	0	0	18
Neal, G.B.	3	0	3	0	18
Novacek, St.L.	3	0	3	0	18
Sanders, Wash.	3	0	3	0	18
Schroeder, Wash.	3	3	0	0	18
Stanley, G.B.	3	0	3	0	18
Adams, Giants	2	1	1	0	12
Anderson, Minn.	2	2	0	0	12
Baker, Giants	2	0	2	0	12
Barney, Atl.	2	0	2	0	12
Bernard, Det.	2	2	0	0	12
Beverly, N.O.	2	2	0	0	12
Boso, Chi.	2	0	2	0	12
Bradley, Det.	2	0	2	0	12

Player—Team	Total TDs.	Rush TDs.	Pass TDs.	Misc. TDs.	Tot. Pts.
Brenner, N.O.	2	0	2	0	12
Burbage, Dall.	2	0	2	0	12
Campbell, Atl.	2	2	0	0	12
Carter, Phil.	2	0	2	0	12
Cribbs, S.F.	2	1	0	1	12
Dorsett, Dall.	2	1	1	0	12
Epps, G.B.	2	0	2	0	12
Fenney, Minn.	2	2	0	0	12
Francis, Rams	2	0	2	0	12
Freeman, T.B.	2	0	2	0	12
Garrity, Phil.	2	0	2	0	12
Gentry, Chi.	2	0	1	1	12
Grymes, Det.	2	0	2	0	12
Hill, T.B.	2	0	2	0	12
Hill, N.O.	2	0	2	0	12
Hilton, Minn.	2	0	2	0	12
D. Johnson, Rams	2	0	2	0	12
T. Johnson, St.L.	2	0	2	0	12
H. Jones, Minn.	2	0	2	0	12
Jordan, N.O.	2	2	0	0	12
Jordan, Minn.	2	0	2	0	12
Kramer, Minn.	2	2	0	0	12
Lovelady, Giants	2	0	2	0	12
J. McDonald, Rams	2	0	2	0	12
McMahon, Chi.	2	2	0	0	12
D. Nelson, Minn.	2	2	0	0	12
Rice, Minn.	2	1	1	0	12
Riggs, Atl.	2	2	0	0	12
Robinson, Giants	2	0	2	0	12
Spagnola, Phil.	2	0	2	0	12
Streater, T.B.	2	0	2	0	12
Vital, Wash.	2	2	0	0	12
T. Wilson, Wash.	2	1	1	0	12
W. Wilson, Wash.	2	2	0	0	12
Word, N.O.	2	2	0	0	12
Adams, Dall.	1	1	0	0	6
Alexander, N.O.	1	1	0	0	6
Austin, T.B.	1	1	0	0	6
Badanjek, Atl.	1	1	0	0	6
Banks, Dall.	1	0	1	0	6
Barksdale, Dall.	1	0	1	0	6
Bartalo, T.B.	1	1	0	0	6
Bell, Rams	1	0	1	0	6
Bennett, Giants	1	0	1	0	6
Bland, Det.	1	0	1	0	6
Bowman, Phil.	1	0	1	0	6
Branch, Wash.	1	1	0	0	6
Chandler, Dall.	1	0	1	0	6
Cherry, S.F.	1	1	0	0	6
Clark, G.B.	1	0	1	0	6
Clemons, Phil.	1	0	1	0	6
Didier, Wash.	1	0	1	0	6
Everett, Rams	1	1	0	0	6
Flynn, Giants	1	0	0	1	6
Francis, Dall.	1	0	0	1	6
Garza, St.L.	1	1	0	0	6
Gayle, Chi.	1	0	0	1	6
Giles, Phil.	1	0	1	0	6
Gray, Rams	1	0	0	1	6
Gray, N.O.	1	1	0	0	6
Green, Wash.	1	0	0	1	6
Greene, Rams	1	0	0	1	6
Greer, S.F.	1	0	1	0	6
Griffin, Wash.	1	0	1	0	6
Guman, Rams	1	1	0	0	6
Hall, T.B.	1	0	1	0	6
Hargrove, G.B.	1	1	0	0	6
Heimuli, Chi.	1	0	1	0	6
House, Rams	1	0	1	0	6
Howard, T.B.	1	1	0	0	6
Irvin, Rams	1	0	0	1	6
Jackson, Rams	1	0	0	1	6
Jackson, St.L.	1	0	0	1	6
Jeffcoat, Dall.	1	0	0	1	6
Jessie, Wash.	1	1	0	0	6
J. Johnson, Rams	1	0	0	1	6
Joyner, Phil.	1	0	0	1	6
Kamana, Atl.	1	0	1	0	6
Kinard, Giants	1	0	0	1	6
Kindt, Chi.	1	0	1	0	6
King, Det.	1	0	0	1	6
McCray, Chi.	1	0	0	1	6
McGee, Rams	1	1	0	0	6
McGowan, Giants	1	0	1	0	6
McIntosh, Atl.	1	0	1	0	6
McLemore, S.F.	1	0	0	1	6
Mobley, Rams	1	0	1	0	6
Monroe, S.F.	1	0	1	0	6
Montana, S.F.	1	1	0	0	6
Moore, Rams	1	0	1	0	6
Moore, Atl.	1	0	0	1	6
Moorehead, Chi.	1	0	1	0	6
Le. Morris, G.B.	1	0	1	0	6
Ro. Morris, Chi.	1	0	1	0	6
Mosley, Chi.	1	0	0	1	6
Moss, T.B.	1	0	0	1	6
Mowatt, Giants	1	0	1	0	6
N. Noga, St.L.	1	0	0	1	6
P. Noga, St.L.	1	0	0	1	6
O'Neal, N.O.	1	0	1	0	6
Paskett, G.B.	1	0	1	0	6
Pelluer, Dall.	1	1	0	0	6
Poe, N.O.	1	0	0	1	6
Ricks, T.B.	1	1	0	0	6
Risher, G.B.	1	1	0	0	6
Rodgers, S.F.	1	1	0	0	6
Ross, Phil.	1	1	0	0	6
Rouson, Giants	1	0	1	0	6
Rubick, Det.	1	0	1	0	6
Sanders, Chi.	1	1	0	0	6
Siano, Phil.	1	0	1	0	6
Sikahema, St.L.	1	0	0	1	6
Le. Smith, St.L.	1	0	0	1	6
Smith, Det.	1	0	0	1	6
Stamps, Atl.	1	0	0	1	6
Stevens, S.F.	1	0	1	0	6
Summers, G.B.	1	0	1	0	6
R. Sutton, N.O.	1	0	0	1	6
Taylor, S.F.	1	0	0	1	6
Taylor, Atl.	1	0	1	0	6
Testaverde, T.B.	1	1	0	0	6
L. Thomas, G.B.	1	0	1	0	6
Toles, N.O.	1	0	0	1	6
Tomczak, Chi.	1	1	0	0	6
Tripoli, T.B.	1	0	0	1	6
Truvillion, Det.	1	0	1	0	6
Turner, Giants	1	0	1	0	6
K. Walker, T.B.	1	0	0	1	6
Waters, N.O.	1	0	1	0	6
Wells, T.B.	1	0	1	0	6
Wells, S.F.	1	0	0	1	6
West, G.B.	1	0	1	0	6
Whisenhunt, Atl.	1	0	1	0	6
D. White, Dall.	1	1	0	0	6
White, Phil.	1	0	0	1	6
Wilburn, Wash.	1	0	0	1	6
Wilcher, Rams	1	0	0	1	6
Wilder, T.B.	1	0	1	0	6
D. Williams, Wash.	1	1	0	0	6
S. Williams, Det.	1	0	1	0	6
Wolfley, St.L.	1	1	0	0	6
Womack, Minn.	1	0	1	0	6
Wright, T.B.	1	0	1	0	6
Young, Rams	1	0	1	0	6
Young, S.F.	1	1	0	0	6
B. Clark, N.O.	0	0	0	0	*2
Fuller, S.F.	0	0	0	0	*2
Jamison, Det.	0	0	0	0	*2
Maxie, N.O.	0	0	0	0	*2
Stepanek, Minn.	0	0	0	0	*2
Stewart, Rams	0	0	0	0	*2

*Safety.
†Extra Point.

1987 PUNTING

AVERAGE YARDS PER PUNT
  NFC: 44.0—Rick Donnelly, Atlanta.
  AFC: 42.9—Ralf Mojsiejenko, San Diego.

NET AVERAGE YARDS PER PUNT
  NFC: 39.6—Jim Arnold, Detroit.
  AFC: 35.6—Scott Fulhage, Cincinnati.

LONGEST PUNT
  AFC: 77—Reggie Roby, Miami at Buffalo, November 29.
  NFC: 77—Steve Cox, Washington at Buffalo, November 1.

MOST PUNTS, SEASON
  NFC: 82—John Teltschik, Philadelphia.
  AFC: 67—Ralf Mojsiejenko, San Diego.

MOST PUNTS, GAME
  NFC: 15—John Teltschik, Philadelphia at N.Y. Giants, December 6 (OT).
  AFC: 10—Scott Fulhage, Cincinnati vs. San Diego, October 4.

TEAM CHAMPION
  AFC: 42.0—San Diego.
  NFC: 41.8—Detroit.

PUNTING—TEAM

AMERICAN FOOTBALL CONFERENCE

	Total Punts	Yards	Long	Avg.	TB.	Blk.	Opp. Ret.	Ret. Yds.	In 20	Net Avg.
San Diego	84	3529	57	42.0	13	0	43	429	16	33.8
Cincinnati	73	2995	58	41.0	9	0	42	299	13	34.5
Kansas City	69	2789	55	40.4	6	0	43	442	13	32.3
Pittsburgh	82	3297	57	40.2	17	2	46	395	13	31.2
Denver	65	2595	61	39.9	6	2	34	424	16	31.6
L.A. Raiders	71	2796	63	39.4	5	2	34	256	15	34.4
Houston	75	2929	59	39.1	6	1	43	454	7	31.4
Seattle	61	2370	63	38.9	5	0	32	251	18	33.1
Miami	63	2424	77	38.5	3	1	26	141	20	35.3
Buffalo	83	3173	67	38.2	9	1	35	179	23	33.9
Indianapolis	78	2941	63	37.7	8	3	39	376	15	30.8
New England	89	3350	73	37.6	12	2	41	397	15	30.5
N.Y. Jets	82	3046	58	37.1	7	0	33	162	14	33.5
Cleveland	57	2102	66	36.9	8	0	17	93	14	32.4
Conference Total	1032	40336	77	....	114	14	508	4298	212	....
Conference Average	73.7	2881.1	....	39.1	8.1	1.0	36.3	307.0	15.1	32.7

NATIONAL FOOTBALL CONFERENCE

	Total Punts	Yards	Long	Avg.	TB.	Blk.	Opp. Ret.	Ret. Yds.	In 20	Net Avg.
Detroit	70	2927	60	41.8	6	0	34	177	22	37.6
New Orleans	63	2587	60	41.1	7	0	29	199	23	35.7
L.A. Rams	77	3140	62	40.8	4	1	43	317	19	35.6
Atlanta	83	3375	62	40.7	11	2	48	541	11	31.5
N.Y. Giants	91	3604	64	39.6	7	2	51	811	14	29.2
Dallas	84	3324	63	39.6	6	0	45	376	21	33.7
Green Bay	93	3659	65	39.3	6	1	54	422	17	33.5
Chicago	62	2439	71	39.3	8	2	26	339	15	31.3
Tampa Bay	88	3455	61	39.3	10	0	50	621	15	29.9
Washington	78	3053	77	39.1	8	1	37	231	19	34.1
Minnesota	79	3077	54	38.9	5	1	44	424	11	32.3
St. Louis	70	2663	68	38.0	5	1	36	489	16	29.6
San Francisco	68	2541	56	37.4	8	1	29	195	16	32.1
Philadelphia	102	3770	60	37.0	5	3	54	469	18	31.4
Conference Total	1108	43614	77	....	96	15	580	5611	237	....
Conference Average	79.1	3115.3	....	39.4	6.9	1.1	41.4	400.8	16.9	32.6
League Total	2140	83950	77	....	210	29	1088	9909	449	....
League Average	76.4	2998.2	....	39.2	7.5	1.0	38.9	353.9	16.0	32.6

TOP TEN PUNTERS

Player—Team	Net Punts	Yards	Long	Avg.	Total Punts	TB.	Blk.	Opp. Ret.	Ret. Yds.	In 20	Net Avg.
DONNELLY, RICK, Atl.	61	2686	62	44.0	63	8	2	38	501	9	32.1
Arnold, Jim, Det.	46	2007	60	43.6	46	4	0	22	104	17	39.6
Mojsiejenko, Ralf, S.D.	67	2875	57	42.9	67	12	0	37	392	15	33.5
Landeta, Sean, Giants	65	2773	64	42.7	66	6	1	38	606	13	31.0
Newsome, Harry, Pitt.	64	2678	57	41.8	65	13	1	36	373	8	31.5
Fulhage, Scott, Cin.	52	2168	58	41.7	52	5	0	31	216	10	35.6
Hatcher, Dale, Rams.	76	3140	62	41.3	77	4	1	43	317	19	35.6
Horan, Mike, Den.	44	1807	61	41.1	46	5	2	22	186	11	33.1
Bracken, Don, G.B.	72	2947	65	40.9	73	5	1	45	354	13	34.2
Goodburn, Kelly, K.C.	59	2412	55	40.9	59	5	0	39	403	13	32.4

AFC—INDIVIDUALS

Player—Team	Net Punts	Yards	Long	Avg.	Total Punts	TB.	Blk.	Opp. Ret.	Ret. Yds.	In 20	Net Avg.
MOJSIEJENKO, S.D.	67	2875	57	42.9	67	12	0	37	392	15	33.5
Newsome, Pitt.	64	2678	57	41.8	65	13	1	36	373	8	31.5
Fulhage, Cin.	52	2168	58	41.7	52	5	0	31	216	10	35.6
Horan, Den.	44	1807	61	41.1	46	5	2	22	186	11	33.1
Goodburn, K.C.	59	2412	55	40.9	59	5	0	39	403	13	32.4
Talley, Raiders	56	2277	63	40.7	57	5	1	28	207	13	34.6
Gossett, Clev.-Hou.	44	1777	55	40.4	45	6	1	23	234	4	31.6
Camarillo, N.E.	62	2489	73	40.1	63	8	1	34	333	14	31.7
Rodriguez, Sea.	47	1880	63	40.0	47	5	0	22	182	17	34.0
Stark, Ind.	61	2440	63	40.0	63	7	2	33	353	12	30.9
L. Johnson, Hou.-Clev.	50	1969	66	39.4	50	4	0	25	249	8	32.8
Kidd, Buff.	64	2495	67	39.0	64	7	0	26	148	20	34.5
Jennings, Jets	64	2444	58	38.2	64	6	0	24	100	12	34.8

(Non-Qualifiers)

Player—Team	Net Punts	Yards	Long	Avg.	Total Punts	TB.	Blk.	Opp. Ret.	Ret. Yds.	In 20	Net Avg.
Roby, Mia.	32	1371	77	42.8	32	3	0	16	87	8	38.3
Herline, N.E.	25	861	50	34.4	26	4	1	7	64	1	27.6
Giacomarro, Den.	18	757	50	42.1	18	1	0	12	238	4	27.7
O'Connor, Jets	18	602	47	33.4	18	1	0	9	62	2	28.9
Winslow, Clev.	18	616	45	34.2	18	2	0	6	11	5	31.4
Partridge, Buff.	18	678	52	37.7	19	2	1	9	31	3	31.9
Prokop, S.D.	17	654	50	38.5	17	1	0	6	37	1	35.1
Bruno, Pitt.	16	619	56	38.7	17	4	1	10	22	5	30.4
Gore, Mia.	14	502	60	35.9	14	0	0	4	21	6	34.4
Gamache, Raiders	13	519	53	39.9	14	0	1	6	49	2	33.6
Kiel, Ind.	12	440	50	36.7	12	1	0	5	16	3	33.7
Griffith, Sea.	11	386	51	35.1	11	0	0	7	57	1	29.9
Walters, Clev.	11	400	56	36.4	11	1	0	2	28	2	32.0
Colbert, K.C.	10	377	47	37.7	10	1	0	4	39	0	31.8
Strock, Mia.	9	277	44	30.8	9	0	0	1	0	5	30.8
Superick, Hou.	8	269	45	33.6	8	1	0	4	25	2	28.0
Hayes, Mia.	7	274	51	39.1	8	0	1	5	33	1	30.1
Bowman, Sea.	3	104	36	34.7	3	0	0	3	12	0	30.7
Esiason, Cin.	2	68	41	34.0	2	0	0	1	12	1	28.0
Colquitt, Ind.	2	61	33	30.5	3	0	1	1	7	0	18.0
Elway, Den.	1	31	31	31.0	1	0	0	0	0	1	31.0

NFC—INDIVIDUALS

Player—Team	Net Punts	Yards	Long	Avg.	Total Punts	TB.	Blk.	Opp. Ret.	Ret. Yds.	In 20	Net Avg.
DONNELLY, Atl.	61	2686	62	44.0	63	8	2	38	501	9	32.1
Arnold, Det.	46	2007	60	43.6	46	4	0	22	104	17	39.6
Landeta, Giants	65	2773	64	42.7	66	6	1	38	606	13	31.0
Hatcher, Rams	76	3140	62	41.3	77	4	1	43	317	19	35.6
Bracken, G.B.	72	2947	65	40.9	73	5	1	45	354	13	34.2
Cox, Wash.	63	2571	77	40.8	64	7	1	29	193	14	35.0
Hansen, N.O.	52	2104	60	40.5	52	6	0	23	135	19	35.6
Horne, Cin.-St.L.	43	1730	57	40.2	43	7	0	25	237	6	31.5
G. Coleman, Minn.	45	1786	54	39.7	46	3	1	30	323	5	30.5
Saxon, Dall.	68	2685	63	39.5	68	5	0	36	260	20	34.2
Runager, S.F.	55	2157	56	39.2	56	7	1	23	167	13	33.0
Garcia, T.B.	62	2409	58	38.9	62	5	0	38	553	12	28.3
Teltschik, Phil.	82	3131	60	38.2	83	4	1	47	399	13	32.0
Cater, St.L.	39	1470	68	37.7	40	2	1	17	204	10	30.7

(Non-Qualifiers)

Player—Team	Net Punts	Yards	Long	Avg.	Total Punts	TB.	Blk.	Opp. Ret.	Ret. Yds.	In 20	Net Avg.
Wagner, Chi.	36	1461	71	40.6	37	4	1	12	195	9	32.1
Criswell, T.B.	26	1046	61	40.2	26	5	0	12	68	3	33.8
Renner, G.B.	20	712	49	35.6	20	1	0	9	68	4	31.2
Scribner, Minn.	20	827	54	41.3	20	1	0	10	79	4	36.4
Brown, Chi.	18	742	58	41.2	19	4	1	11	108	4	29.2
Barnhardt, N.O.-Chi.	17	719	52	42.3	17	1	0	9	100	6	35.2
Sawyer, Dall.	16	639	54	39.9	16	1	0	9	116	1	31.4

Detroit's Jim Arnold led the NFL with a 39.6-yard net punting average in 1987 and was voted to the NFC Pro Bowl team.

(More Non-Qualifiers)

Player—Team	Net Punts	Yards	Long	Avg.	Total Punts	TB.	Blk.	Opp. Ret.	Ret. Yds.	In 20	Net Avg.
Weil, Wash.	14	482	51	34.4	14	1	0	8	38	5	30.3
Moore, Giants	14	486	46	34.7	15	0	1	9	154	0	22.1
Bruno, Minn.	13	464	53	35.7	13	1	0	4	22	2	32.5
Asmus, S.F.	12	384	51	32.0	12	1	0	6	28	3	28.0
Royals, St.L.-Phil.	11	431	48	39.2	11	1	0	6	155	3	23.3
Miller, Giants	10	345	53	34.5	10	1	0	4	51	1	27.4
Jacobs, Phil.	10	369	44	36.9	11	0	1	5	34	4	30.5
Berry, Atl.	7	258	51	36.9	7	1	0	5	15	0	31.9
Kinzer, Det.	7	238	42	34.0	7	0	0	3	35	2	29.0
Black, Det.	6	233	47	38.8	6	0	0	4	12	1	36.8
Davis, Atl.	6	191	55	31.8	6	1	0	2	6	0	27.5
Misko, Det.	6	242	51	40.3	6	0	0	4	23	1	36.5
Starnes, Atl.	6	203	49	33.8	6	0	0	3	19	2	30.7
Murray, Det.	4	155	46	38.8	4	2	0	1	3	1	28.0
Merkens, Phil.	2	61	38	30.5	3	0	1	0	0	0	20.3
Erxleben, Det.	1	52	52	52.0	1	0	0	0	0	0	52.0
Luckhurst, Atl.	1	37	37	37.0	1	1	0	0	0	0	17.0

Leader based on average, minimum 38 punts.

1987 PUNT RETURNS

AVERAGE YARDS PER RETURN
NFC: 14.7—Mel Gray, New Orleans.
AFC: 12.6—Bobby Joe Edmonds, Seattle.

MOST YARDS, SEASON
NFC: 550—Vai Sikahema, St. Louis.
AFC: 400—Lionel James, San Diego.

MOST YARDS, GAME
AFC: 144—Kevin Clark, Denver vs. San Diego, December 27 (6 returns).
NFC: 142—Ted Wilson, Washington at N.Y. Giants, October 11 (7 returns).

LONGEST PUNT RETURN
NFC: 94—Dennis McKinnon, Chicago vs. N.Y. Giants, September 14 (TD).
AFC: 91—JoJo Townsell, N.Y. Jets vs. Seattle, November 9 (TD).

MOST RETURNS, SEASON
NFC: 44—Vai Sikahema, St. Louis.
AFC: 34—Gerald McNeil, Cleveland.

MOST RETURNS, GAME
NFC: 9—Phil McConkey, N.Y. Giants vs. Philadelphia, December 6 (OT).
AFC: 6—Achieved by seven players.

MOST FAIR CATCHES
NFC: 14—Phil McConkey, N.Y. Giants.
AFC: 12—Ron Pitts, Buffalo.

TOUCHDOWNS
NFC: 2—Dennis McKinnon, Chicago.
AFC: 1—Rick Calhoun, L.A. Raiders.
    Kevin Clark, Denver.
    Jitter Fields, Kansas City.
    Michael Harper, N.Y. Jets.
    Lionel James, San Diego.
    JoJo Townsell, N.Y. Jets.

TEAM CHAMPION
NFC: 12.5—St. Louis.
AFC: 11.8—N.Y. Jets.

PUNT RETURNS—TEAM
AMERICAN FOOTBALL CONFERENCE

	No.	FC	Yards	Avg.	Long	TDs
N.Y. Jets	42	12	497	11.8	t91	2
San Diego	45	9	508	11.3	t81	1
Cleveland	44	12	487	11.1	40	0
Kansas City	32	8	346	10.8	t85	1
Denver	48	4	486	10.1	t71	1
Seattle	32	8	322	10.1	40	0
Cincinnati	34	9	293	8.6	21	0
New England	25	17	213	8.5	36	0
L.A. Raiders	44	7	356	8.1	t55	1
Miami	37	13	290	7.8	31	0
Buffalo	31	15	232	7.5	23	0
Pittsburgh	36	5	244	6.8	20	0
Houston	37	14	249	6.7	26	0
Indianapolis	38	12	210	5.5	17	0
Conference Total	525	145	4733	.....	t91	6
Conference Average	37.5	10.4	338.1	9.0	.....	0.4

NATIONAL FOOTBALL CONFERENCE

	No.	FC	Yards	Avg.	Long	TDs
St. Louis	44	7	550	12.5	t76	1
Minnesota	36	12	420	11.7	t78	1
New Orleans	41	7	468	11.4	80	0
Washington	56	10	615	11.0	73	0
San Francisco	34	9	365	10.7	t83	1
Chicago	50	6	484	9.7	t94	2
Detroit	35	12	303	8.7	54	0
Dallas	41	6	353	8.6	38	0
Tampa Bay	31	8	257	8.3	22	0
N.Y. Giants	55	14	448	8.1	37	0
Atlanta	31	7	221	7.1	45	0
Green Bay	35	6	245	7.0	48	0
L.A. Rams	40	10	245	6.1	29	0
Philadelphia	34	24	202	5.9	37	0
Conference Total	563	138	5176	.....	t94	5
Conference Average	40.2	9.9	369.7	9.2	.....	0.4
League Total	1088	283	9909	.....	t94	11
League Average	38.9	10.1	353.9	9.1	.....	0.4

TOP TEN PUNT RETURNERS

	No.	FC	Yards	Avg.	Long	TDs
GRAY, MEL, N.O.	24	5	352	14.7	80	0
McLemore, Dana, S.F.	21	7	265	12.6	t83	1
Edmonds, Bobby Joe, Sea.	20	4	251	12.6	40	0
James, Lionel, S.D.	32	7	400	12.5	t81	1
Lewis, Leo, Minn.	22	7	275	12.5	t78	1
Sikahema, Vai, St.L.	44	7	550	12.5	t76	1
Townsell, JoJo, Jets	32	11	381	11.9	t91	1
McNeil, Gerald, Clev.	34	9	386	11.4	40	0
Mandley, Pete, Det.	23	6	250	10.9	54	0
McKinnon, Dennis, Chi.	40	4	405	10.1	t94	2

AFC—INDIVIDUALS

Player—Team	No.	FC.	Yds.	Avg.	Lng.	TD	Player—Team	No.	FC.	Yds.	Avg.	Lng.	TD
EDMONDS, Sea.	20	4	251	12.6	40	0	Johnson, Ind.	9	2	42	4.7	12	0
James, S.D.	32	7	400	12.5	t81	1	Fields, K.C.	8	3	161	20.1	t85	1
Townsell, Jets	32	11	381	11.9	t91	1	Calhoun, Raiders	8	1	92	11.5	t55	1
McNeil, Clev.	34	9	386	11.4	40	0	McFadden, Buff.	8	3	83	10.4	23	0
Martin, Cin.	28	5	277	9.9	21	0	Duncan, Hou.	8	2	23	2.9	9	0
Clemons, K.C.	19	4	162	8.5	44	0	Lipps, Pitt.	7	1	46	6.6	12	0
Schwedes, Mia.	24	6	203	8.5	31	0	M. Anderson, Pitt.	7	1	38	5.4	10	0
K. Johnson, Hou.	24	5	196	8.2	26	0	Teal, Sea.	6	4	38	6.3	13	0
Woods, Raiders	26	4	189	7.3	34	0	Hollis, Sea.	6	0	33	5.5	15	0
Pitts, Buff.	23	12	149	6.5	19	0	Adams, Raiders	5	2	39	7.8	12	0
Brooks, Ind.	22	9	136	6.2	17	0	Linne, N.E.	5	2	22	4.4	16	0
							K. Brown, Cin.	5	3	16	3.2	10	0
(Non-Qualifiers)							Harper, Jets	4	1	93	23.3	t78	1
Clark, Den.	18	1	233	12.9	t71	1	Tullis, Ind.	4	1	27	6.8	10	0
Fryar, N.E.	18	12	174	9.7	36	0	Everett, Pitt.	4	2	22	5.5	11	0
Woodson, Pitt.	16	1	135	8.4	20	0	Willhite, Den.	4	1	22	5.5	9	0
Nattiel, Den.	12	1	73	6.1	14	0	Rome, S.D.	3	1	12	4.0	6	0
Wilson, Clev.	10	3	101	10.1	17	0	Drewrey, Hou.	3	1	11	3.7	5	0
A. Williams, S.D.	10	1	96	9.6	25	0	Fellows, Raiders	2	0	19	9.5	18	0
Swanson, Den.	9	1	132	14.7	33	0	Walters, Hou.	2	6	19	9.5	12	0
Caterbone, Mia.	9	4	78	8.7	21	0	Harkey, Raiders	2	0	17	8.5	9	0

Player—Team	No.	FC.	Yds.	Avg.	Lng.	TD	Player—Team	No.	FC.	Yds.	Avg.	Lng.	TD
Harden, Den.	2	0	11	5.5	7	0	Sohn, Jets	1	0	6	6.0	6	0
R. Smith, Jets	2	0	9	4.5	7	0	Blackwood, Mia.	1	1	1	1.0	1	0
B. Brown, Mia.	2	1	8	4.0	8	0	Ahrens, Ind.	1	0	0	0.0	0	0
D. Foster, Jets	2	0	8	4.0	4	0	Cocroft, K.C.	1	0	0	0.0	0	0
Lilly, Den.	2	0	6	3.0	4	0	Collins, Jets	1	0	0	0.0	0	0
Simmons, Ind.	2	0	5	2.5	5	0	J. Davis, Raiders	1	0	0	0.0	0	0
Wyatt, K.C.	2	0	4	2.0	4	0	Hooper, Mia.	1	0	0	0.0	0	0
Lockett, Pitt.	2	0	3	1.5	5	0	Horton, Cin.	1	0	0	0.0	0	0
Starring, N.E.	1	1	17	17.0	17	0	Marion, N.E.	1	2	0	0.0	0	0
D. Colbert, K.C.	1	0	11	11.0	11	0	Jackson, Cin.	0	1	0	.....	.....	0
V. Johnson, Den.	1	0	9	9.0	9	0	Stradford, Mia.	0	1	0	.....	.....	0
Montague, K.C.	1	1	8	8.0	8	0							

NFC—INDIVIDUALS

Player—Team	No.	FC.	Yds.	Avg.	Lng.	TD	Player—Team	No.	FC.	Yds.	Avg.	Lng.	TD
GRAY, N.O.	24	5	352	14.7	80	0	Richardson, Minn.	4	2	19	4.8	7	0
McLemore, S.F.	21	7	265	12.6	t83	1	Garrity, Phil.	4	10	16	4.0	10	0
Lewis, Minn.	22	7	275	12.5	t78	1	Walls, T.B.	4	2	12	3.0	11	0
Sikahema, St.L.	44	7	550	12.5	t76	1	S. Johnson, Rams	4	1	—4	—1.0	5	0
Mandley, Det.	23	6	250	10.9	54	0	Carter, Minn.	3	0	40	13.3	22	0
McKinnon, Chi.	40	4	405	10.1	t94	2	Curry, T.B.	3	0	32	10.7	14	0
K. Martin, Dall.	22	2	216	9.8	38	0	Baker, Giants	3	0	16	5.3	6	0
McConkey, Giants	42	14	394	9.4	37	0	Moss, Atl.	3	1	15	5.0	11	0
Futrell, T.B.	24	6	213	8.9	22	0	Rutledge, Rams.	3	0	10	3.3	7	0
Johnson, Atl.	21	6	168	8.0	45	0	Caterbone, Phil.	2	0	13	6.5	13	0
Yarber, Wash.	37	9	273	7.4	33	0	Martin, S.F.	2	0	12	6.0	9	0
Stanley, G.B.	28	4	173	6.2	48	0	J. Butler, Atl.	2	0	10	5.0	9	0
Morse, Phil.	20	13	121	6.1	23	0	Ulmer, Phil.	2	0	10	5.0	5	0

(Non-Qualifiers)

Player—Team	No.	FC.	Yds.	Avg.	Lng.	TD	Player—Team	No.	FC.	Yds.	Avg.	Lng.	TD
							P. Smith, Rams	2	0	5	2.5	5	0
Ellard, Rams	15	6	107	7.1	29	0	Jordan, N.O.	1	0	13	13.0	13	0
Martin, N.O.	14	2	88	6.3	15	0	Maxie, N.O.	1	0	12	12.0	12	0
Hicks, Rams	13	1	110	8.5	26	0	Mobley, Rams	1	0	12	12.0	12	0
Bradley, Det.	12	5	53	4.4	13	0	Duerson, Chi.	1	1	10	10.0	10	0
Lovelady, Giants	10	0	38	3.8	14	0	Taylor, S.F.	1	0	9	9.0	9	0
Griffin, S.F.	9	2	79	8.8	29	0	Jeffries, Chi.	1	0	5	5.0	5	0
T. Wilson, Wash.	8	0	143	17.9	40	0	J. Johnson, Rams	1	0	5	5.0	5	0
Edwards, Dall.	8	1	75	9.4	13	0	Cook, N.O.	1	0	3	3.0	3	0
Duarte, Chi.	8	1	64	8.0	16	0	Le. Morris, G.B.	1	0	1	1.0	1	0
Bess, Minn.	7	3	86	12.3	28	0	Irvin, Rams	1	0	0	0.0	0	0
Shepard, Wash.	6	0	146	24.3	73	0	A. Johnson, Phil.	1	0	0	0.0	0	0
Scott, G.B.	6	2	71	11.8	36	0	Livingston, Dall.	1	0	0	0.0	0	0
Green, Wash.	5	1	53	10.6	15	0	Pollard, S.F.	1	0	0	0.0	0	0
Banks, Dall.	5	1	33	6.6	12	0	C. Brown, Phil.	1	0	—1	—1.0	—1	0
Burbage, Dall.	5	1	29	5.8	13	0	Bland, Det.	0	1	0	.....	.....	0
Barney, Atl.	5	0	28	5.6	11	0	Lavette, Dall.	0	1	0	.....	.....	0
Bowman, Phil.	4	1	43	10.8	37	0	Sutton, Rams	0	2	0	.....	.....	0

t—Touchdown
Leader based on average return, minimum 19 returns

1987 KICKOFF RETURNS

YARDS PER RETURN
  NFC: 27.5—Sylvester Stamps, Atlanta.
  AFC: 24.3—Paul Palmer, Kansas City.

MOST YARDS, SEASON
  AFC: 923—Paul Palmer, Kansas City.
  NFC: 808—Neal Guggemos, Minnesota.

MOST YARDS, GAME
  AFC: 221—Paul Palmer, Kansas City at Seattle, September 20 (9 returns).
  NFC: 193—Sylvester Stamps, Atlanta at Houston, October 25 (5 returns).

LONGEST KICKOFF RETURN
  NFC: 97—Sylvester Stamps, Atlanta at San Francisco, December 20 (TD).
  AFC: 95—Paul Palmer, Kansas City vs. San Diego, September 13 (TD).

MOST RETURNS, SEASON
  AFC: 38—Paul Palmer, Kansas City.
  NFC: 36—Neal Guggemos, Minnesota.

MOST RETURNS, GAME
  AFC: 9—Paul Palmer, Kansas City at Seattle, September 20 (221 yards).
  NFC: 7—Gary Lee, Detroit vs. Green Bay, October 25 (141 yards).

TOUCHDOWNS
  AFC: 2—Paul Palmer, Kansas City.
  NFC: 1—Ron Brown, L.A. Rams.
         Joe Cribbs, San Francisco.
         Dennis Gentry, Chicago.
         Sylvester Stamps, Atlanta.

TEAM CHAMPION
  NFC: 21.5—Atlanta.
  AFC: 20.7—Denver.

KICKOFF RETURNS—TEAM
AMERICAN FOOTBALL CONFERENCE

Team	No.	Yards	Avg.	Long	TDs.
Denver	46	952	20.7	50	0
Kansas City	70	1437	20.5	t95	2
Indianapolis	55	1115	20.3	45	0
L.A. Raiders	60	1174	19.6	50	0
Buffalo	45	872	19.4	40	0
Seattle	64	1236	19.3	43	0
Pittsburgh	56	1060	18.9	36	0
N.Y. Jets	65	1221	18.8	60	0
New England	48	901	18.8	43	0
San Diego	62	1137	18.3	46	0
Houston	67	1225	18.3	62	0
Miami	54	952	17.6	34	0
Cleveland	48	846	17.6	44	0
Cincinnati	67	1161	17.3	34	0
Conference Total	807	15289	....	t95	2
Conference Average	57.6	1092.1	18.9	.....	0.1

NATIONAL FOOTBALL CONFERENCE

Team	No.	Yards	Avg.	Long	TDs.
Atlanta	79	1700	21.5	t97	1
Chicago	57	1193	20.9	t88	1
St. Louis	63	1317	20.9	50	0
New Orleans	55	1147	20.9	74	0
San Francisco	55	1144	20.8	t92	1
L.A. Rams	63	1282	20.3	t95	1
Dallas	64	1295	20.2	48	0
N.Y. Giants	56	1128	20.1	49	0
Detroit	71	1428	20.1	50	0
Minnesota	71	1421	20.0	42	0
Washington	59	1139	19.3	54	0
Tampa Bay	56	1037	18.5	40	0
Green Bay	59	1032	17.5	46	0
Philadelphia	66	1112	16.8	33	0
Conference Total	874	17375	......	t97	4
Conference Average	62.4	1241.1	19.9	.....	0.3
League Total	1681	32664	......	t97	6
League Average	60.0	1166.6	19.4	.....	0.2

TOP TEN KICKOFF RETURNERS

Player—Team	No.	Yards	Avg.	Long	TDs.
STAMPS, SYLVESTER, Atl.	24	660	27.5	t97	1
Gentry, Dennis, Chi.	25	621	24.8	t88	1
Palmer, Paul, K.C.	38	923	24.3	t95	2
Bentley, Albert, Ind.	22	500	22.7	45	0
Rouson, Lee, Giants	22	497	22.6	49	0
Lee, Gary, Det.	32	719	22.5	50	0
Guggemos, Neal, Minn.	36	808	22.4	42	0
Sikahema, Vai, St.L.	34	761	22.4	50	0
Clack, Darryl, Dall.	29	635	21.9	48	0
Mueller, Vance, Raiders	27	588	21.8	46	0

AFC—INDIVIDUALS

Player—Team	No.	Yds.	Avg.	Lng.	TD
PALMER, K.C.	38	923	24.3	t95	2
Bentley, Ind.	22	500	22.7	45	0
Mueller, Raiders	27	588	21.8	46	0
Holland, S.D.	19	410	21.6	46	0
Edmonds, Sea.	27	564	20.9	43	0
Stone, Pitt.	28	568	20.3	34	0
G. Anderson, S.D.	22	433	19.7	31	0
Duncan, Hou.	28	546	19.5	62	0
Starring, N.E.	23	445	19.3	43	0
Bussey, Cin.	21	406	19.3	34	0

(Non-Qualifiers)

Player—Team	No.	Yds.	Avg.	Lng.	TD
Young, Clev.	18	412	22.9	44	0
Humphery, Jets	18	357	19.8	47	0
Pinkett, Hou.	17	322	18.9	30	0
Hampton, Mia.	16	304	19.0	32	0
Bell, Den.	15	323	21.5	42	0
McGee, Cin.	15	242	16.1	24	0
Stradford, Mia.	14	258	18.4	32	0
Do. Williams, Raiders	14	221	15.8	27	0
Woodson, Pitt.	13	290	22.3	36	0
Wright, Cin.	13	266	20.5	30	0
Townsell, Jets	11	272	24.7	60	0
McNeil, Clev.	11	205	18.6	33	0
Tasker, Buff.	11	197	17.9	39	0
Hollis, Sea.	10	263	26.3	41	0
K. Daniel, Ind.	10	225	22.5	29	0
Wright, Ind.	10	187	18.7	27	0
Swanson, Den.	9	234	26.0	50	0
Calhoun, Raiders	9	217	24.1	50	0
Schwedes, Mia.	9	177	19.7	34	0
Morris, Sea.	9	149	16.6	20	0
Fontenot, Clev.	9	130	14.4	24	0
R. Porter, Buff.	8	219	27.4	40	0
Martin, Jets	8	180	22.5	47	0
Drewrey, Hou.	8	136	17.0	27	0
E. Hunter, Jets	8	123	15.4	27	0
Riddick, Buff.	7	151	21.6	31	0
V. Johnson, Den.	7	140	20.0	34	0
McFadden, Buff.	7	121	17.3	26	0
Fryar, N.E.	6	119	19.8	31	0
Sanchez, Pitt.	6	116	19.3	27	0
Moriarty, K.C.	6	102	17.0	24	0

Player—Team	No.	Yds.	Avg.	Lng.	TD
Johnson, Ind.	6	98	16.3	28	0
Teal, Sea.	6	95	15.8	23	0
Davis, N.E.	5	134	26.8	43	0
Wyatt, K.C.	5	121	24.2	29	0
Sartin, S.D.	5	117	23.4	28	0
Robinson, K.C.	5	97	19.4	25	0
Klever, Jets	5	85	17.0	29	0
Mueller, Buff.	5	74	14.8	20	0
Hardy, Mia.	5	62	12.4	18	0
Hunter, Hou.	4	79	19.8	28	0
Lang, Den.	4	78	19.5	25	0
Nattiel, Den.	4	78	19.5	25	0
Harper, Jets	4	75	18.8	22	0
Dupard, N.E.	4	61	15.3	21	0
R. Smith, Jets	4	60	15.0	20	0
Lacy, K.C.	4	44	11.0	20	0
Adams, S.D.	4	32	8.0	11	0
Harris, Hou.	3	87	29.0	43	0
Adams, Raiders	3	61	20.3	25	0
Brown, Den.	3	57	19.0	28	0
Farmer, Mia.	3	56	18.7	23	0
Woods, Raiders	3	55	18.3	22	0
Martin, Cin.	3	51	17.0	20	0
Parker, K.C.	3	49	16.3	25	0
Prior, Ind.	3	47	15.7	22	0
Sohn, Jets	3	47	15.7	18	0
K. Brown, Cin.	3	45	15.0	20	0
Perryman, N.E.	3	43	14.3	16	0
Logan, Cin.	3	31	10.3	16	0
Powell, Sea.	3	23	7.7	14	0
Kirk, S.D.	3	15	5.0	10	0
Roth, Mia.	2	49	24.5	26	0
Bengen, Sea.	2	47	23.5	36	0
Jenkins, S.D.	2	46	23.0	25	0
Brooks, Cin.	2	42	21.0	23	0
James, S.D.	2	41	20.5	21	0
Jones, Pitt.	2	38	19.0	22	0
Lane, K.C.	2	37	18.5	21	0
M. Brown, Buff.	2	35	17.5	18	0
Noble, Ind.	2	35	17.5	18	0
Lane, Sea.	2	34	17.0	22	0
Clark, Den.	2	33	16.5	25	0
Jennings, Cin.	2	32	16.0	18	0

Player—Team	No.	Yds.	Avg.	Lng.	TD	Player—Team	No.	Yds.	Avg.	Lng.	TD
C. McSwain, N.E.	2	32	16.0	24	0	Griggs, Jets	1	13	13.0	13	0
LeBlanc, N.E.	2	31	15.5	24	0	Hoge, Pitt.	1	13	13.0	13	0
Tinsley, Clev.	2	31	15.5	18	0	Valentine, Hou.	1	13	13.0	13	0
Pardridge, Sea.	2	29	14.5	16	0	Foster, Raiders	1	12	12.0	12	0
Rome, S.D.	2	28	14.0	17	0	Isom, Mia.	1	11	11.0	11	0
Armstrong, Buff.	2	25	12.5	18	0	Scholtz, Sea.	1	11	11.0	11	0
K. Johnson, Hou.	2	24	12.0	18	0	B. Smith, K.C.	1	10	10.0	10	0
Kattus, Cin.	2	22	11.0	13	0	Meehan, Cin.	1	9	9.0	9	0
Manoa, Clev.	2	14	7.0	13	0	M. Anderson, Pitt.	1	8	8.0	8	0
Da. Johnson, Mia.	2	13	6.5	10	0	Langhorne, Clev.	1	8	8.0	8	0
Britt, Pitt.	2	9	4.5	5	0	Grayson, Clev.	1	6	6.0	6	0
Ryan, Den.	2	9	4.5	9	0	Rolle, Buff.	1	6	6.0	6	0
Barber, Jets.	2	5	2.5	5	0	Alexander, N.E.	1	4	4.0	4	0
A. Pearson, K.C.	2	4	2.0	4	0	Faaola, Jets	1	4	4.0	4	0
Harmon, Buff.	1	30	30.0	30	0	Perryman, Ind.	1	4	4.0	4	0
Beauford, Clev.	1	22	22.0	22	0	Clemons, K.C.	1	3	3.0	3	0
R. Scott, Mia.	1	22	22.0	22	0	Byner, Clev.	1	2	2.0	2	0
B. Green, Sea.	1	20	20.0	20	0	Zachary, S.D.	1	2	2.0	2	0
Harkey, Raiders	1	20	20.0	20	0	Burse, Sea.	1	1	1.0	1	0
Wonsley, Ind.	1	19	19.0	19	0	J. Davis, Hou.	1	0	0.0	0	0
Clark, Pitt.	1	18	18.0	18	0	Fulcher, Cin.	1	0	0.0	0	0
D. Colbert, K.C.	1	18	18.0	18	0	Fuller, Hou.	1	0	0.0	0	0
Collins, N.E.	1	18	18.0	18	0	Gowdy, Pitt.	1	0	0.0	0	0
Walters, Hou.	1	18	18.0	18	0	Hunter, S.D.	1	0	0.0	0	0
Driver, Clev.	1	16	16.0	16	0	Lewis, Mia.	1	0	0.0	0	0
S. Griffin, K.C.	1	16	16.0	16	0	Mason, Clev.	1	0	0.0	0	0
Hillary, Cin.	1	15	15.0	15	0	Millen, Raiders	1	0	0.0	0	0
Hansen, N.E.	1	14	14.0	14	0	A. Riley, Pitt.	1	0	0.0	0	0
Radecic, Buff.	1	14	14.0	14	0	Tillman, Hou.	1	0	0.0	0	0
Bernstine, S.D.	1	13	13.0	13	0	R. Washington, Raiders	1	0	0.0	0	0
Fields, K.C.	1	13	13.0	13	0	Wallace, Hou.	†0	0	.....	....	0

NFC—INDIVIDUALS

Player—Team	No.	Yds.	Avg.	Lng.	TD	Player—Team	No.	Yds.	Avg.	Lng.	TD
STAMPS, Atl.	24	660	27.5	t97	1	J. Smith, T.B.	5	84	16.8	21	0
Gentry, Chi.	25	621	24.8	t88	1	Womack, Minn.	5	77	15.4	20	0
Rouson, Giants	22	497	22.6	49	0	Hicks, Rams.	4	119	29.8	53	0
Lee, Det.	32	719	22.5	50	0	Sanders, Wash.	4	118	29.5	39	0
Guggemos, Minn.	36	808	22.4	42	0	Byrd, Giants	4	99	24.8	34	0
Sikahema, St.L.	34	761	22.4	50	0	Richardson, Minn.	4	76	19.0	24	0
Clack, Dall.	29	635	21.9	48	0	Jessie, Wash.	4	73	18.3	24	0
Ro. Brown, Rams.	27	581	21.5	t95	1	Flowers, Atl.	4	72	18.0	20	0
Fullwood, G.B.	24	510	21.3	46	0	Harden, G.B.	4	72	18.0	20	0
Gray, N.O.	30	636	21.2	43	0	Norris, Giants	4	70	17.5	29	0
Emery, Atl.	21	440	21.0	66	0	Orr, Wash.	4	62	15.5	19	0
Futrell, T.B.	31	609	19.6	40	0	Branch, Wash.	4	61	15.3	19	0
McAdoo, St.L.	23	444	19.3	30	0	Reid, Phil.	4	58	14.5	19	0
Griffin, Wash.	25	478	19.1	54	0	Bernard, Det.	4	54	13.5	32	0
Sanders, Chi.	20	349	17.5	42	0	Adams, N.O.	4	52	13.0	20	0
Morse, Phil.	24	386	16.1	28	0	Neal, G.B.	4	44	11.0	18	0
						McIntosh, Atl.	3	108	36.0	71	0
(Non-Qualifiers)						Word, N.O.	3	100	33.3	64	0
Rodgers, S.F.	17	358	21.1	50	0	White, Rams	3	73	24.3	26	0
Cribbs, S.F.	13	327	25.2	t92	1	Kozlowski, Chi.	3	72	24.0	31	0
Verdin, Wash.	12	244	20.3	38	0	Beecham, Giants	3	70	23.3	30	0
Sydney, S.F.	12	243	20.3	30	0	Miller, T.B.	3	68	22.7	25	0
Carter, Phil.	12	241	20.1	33	0	Lynch, Chi.	3	66	22.0	37	0
K.Martin, Dall.	12	237	19.8	38	0	Saleaumua, Det.	3	57	19.0	21	0
Woolfolk, Det.	11	219	19.9	44	0	Curry, N.O.	3	53	17.7	20	0
Hilliard, N.O.	10	248	24.8	74	0	Tautalatasi, Phil.	3	53	17.7	32	0
Bess, Minn.	10	169	16.9	33	0	Stanley, G.B.	3	47	15.7	29	0
Settle, Atl.	10	158	15.8	22	0	Beverly, N.O.	3	46	15.3	21	0
Cook, G.B.	10	147	14.7	38	0	Sargent, St.L.	3	37	12.3	27	0
Bradley, Det.	9	188	20.9	27	0	Flagler, S.F.	3	31	10.3	16	0
Adams, Giants	9	166	18.4	27	0	M. McDonald, Rams	3	31	10.3	15	0
Tiumalu, Rams	8	158	19.8	25	0	Spivey, Dall.	2	49	24.5	29	0
D. Nelson, Minn.	7	164	23.4	42	0	Bland, Det.	2	44	22.0	22	0
Edwards, Dall.	7	155	22.1	32	0	J. Smith, Minn.	2	42	21.0	22	0
Bowman, Phil.	7	153	21.9	32	0	Rathman, S.F.	2	37	18.5	21	0
Walls, T.B.	6	136	22.7	39	0	Sutton, Rams	2	37	18.5	19	0
Tyrrell, Rams	6	116	19.3	30	0	Everett, Atl.	2	33	16.5	18	0
Ingram, Giants	6	114	19.0	25	0	Scott, G.B.	2	32	16.0	23	0
Adams, Dall.	6	113	18.8	27	0	W. Wilson, Wash.	2	32	16.0	18	0
Lavette, Dall.-Phil.	6	109	18.2	22	0	DiRico, Giants	2	31	15.5	25	0
Hall, Det.	6	105	17.5	25	0	Vital, Wash.	2	31	15.5	18	0
Le. Morris, G.B.	6	104	17.3	28	0	Jefferson, G.B.	2	30	15.0	18	0
Williams, Rams	5	114	22.8	47	0	Rice, Minn.	†2	29	14.5	18	0
Monroe, S.F.	5	91	18.2	24	0	Jordan, N.O.	2	28	14.0	16	0
Oliver, Atl.	5	90	18.0	28	0	Badanjek, Atl.	2	27	13.5	16	0
Cooper, Phil.	5	86	17.2	24	0	Ball, Det.	2	23	11.5	20	0

Atlanta's Sylvester Stamps led the NFL in kickoff returns with a 27.5-yard average and had a 97-yard touchdown return against San Francisco.

Player—Team	No.	Yds.	Avg.	Lng.	TD	Player—Team	No.	Yds.	Avg.	Lng.	TD
Dozier, Minn.	2	23	11.5	13	0	Hilton, Minn.	1	13	13.0	13	0
Newsome, Dall.	2	22	11.0	12	0	Siano, Phil.	1	13	13.0	13	0
Guman, Rams	2	18	9.0	12	0	Urch, Giants	1	13	13.0	13	0
Haddix, Phil.	2	16	8.0	9	0	Varajon, S.F.	1	13	13.0	13	0
M. Williams, Atl.	2	15	7.5	15	0	R. Cox, Rams	1	12	12.0	12	0
Ro. Brown, St.L.	1	40	40.0	40	0	Brock, N.O.	1	11	11.0	11	0
Ricks, T.B.	1	26	26.0	26	0	A. Cox, Atl.	1	11	11.0	11	0
Holmes, St.L.	1	25	25.0	25	0	Cummings, Giants	1	11	11.0	11	0
McLemore, S.F.	1	23	23.0	23	0	Sharp, Atl.	1	11	11.0	11	0
Moss, Atl.	1	23	23.0	23	0	C. Thomas, N.O.	1	11	11.0	11	0
Steve B. Griffin, Atl.	1	21	21.0	21	0	Ferrell, St.L.	1	10	10.0	10	0
Henley, S.F.	1	21	21.0	21	0	Milton, Chi.	1	10	10.0	10	0
Turrall, Phil.	1	21	21.0	21	0	Suhey, Chi.	1	9	9.0	9	0
R. Brown, Phil.	1	20	20.0	20	0	Carruth, G.B.	1	8	8.0	8	0
Coleman, Giants	1	20	20.0	20	0	Ellard, Rams	1	8	8.0	8	0
Shepard, Wash.	1	20	20.0	20	0	Hill, T.B.	1	8	8.0	8	0
T. Wilson, Wash.	1	20	20.0	20	0	McConkey, Giants	1	8	8.0	8	0
Glover, Det.	1	19	19.0	19	0	Ulmer, Phil.	1	8	8.0	8	0
T. Bell, Chi.	1	18	18.0	18	0	Chandler, Dall.	1	7	7.0	7	0
Croudip, Atl.	1	18	18.0	18	0	Alexander, Phil.	1	6	6.0	6	0
Mosley, Chi.	1	17	17.0	17	0	Borresen, Dall.	1	5	5.0	5	0
White, Chi.	1	17	17.0	17	0	Howard, T.B.	1	5	5.0	5	0
Wright, T.B.	1	17	17.0	17	0	Harrell, Minn.	1	4	4.0	4	0
Bavaro, Giants	1	16	16.0	16	0	Weishuhn, G.B.	1	1	1.0	1	0
Gladman, T.B.	1	16	16.0	16	0	Carrier, T.B.	1	0	0.0	0	0
Mularkey, Minn.	1	16	16.0	16	0	Cherry, G.B.	1	0	0.0	0	0
Bartalo, T.B.	1	15	15.0	15	0	Clemons, Phil.	1	0	0.0	0	0
Ri. Brown, Rams	1	15	15.0	15	0	Green, Det.	1	0	0.0	0	0
Martin, N.O.	1	15	15.0	15	0	Sterling, G.B.	1	0	0.0	0	0
Knapczyk, Chi.	1	14	14.0	14	0	K. Walker, T.B.	1	0	0.0	0	0
C. Brown, Phil.	1	13	13.0	13	0	Willhite, G.B.	0	37	.....	37	0
J. Butler, Atl.	1	13	13.0	13	0	Reeves, Phil.	0	1	.....	1	0
Dorsey, Giants	1	13	13.0	13	0						

t—Touchdown   †—Fair Catch
Leader based on average return, minimum 19 returns

1987 SACKS

MOST SACKS, SEASON
NFC: 21.0—Reggie White, Philadelphia.
AFC: 12.5—Andre Tippett, New England.

MOST SACKS, GAME
NFC: 4.5—Richard Dent, Chicago at L.A. Raiders, December 27.
AFC: 4.0—Duane Bickett, Indianapolis at N.Y. Jets, November 1.
 Cornelius Bennett, Buffalo at Philadelphia, December 27.

TEAM CHAMPION
NFC: 70—Chicago.
AFC: 45—San Diego.

TOP TEN IN SACKS

Player—Team	Sacks	Player—Team	Sacks
WHITE, REGGIE, Phil.	21.0	Nunn, Freddie Joe, St.L.	11.0
Dent, Richard, Chi.	12.5	Swilling, Pat, N.O.	10.5
Tippett, Andre, N.E.	12.5	Jones, Ed L., Dall.	10.0
Smith, Bruce, Buff.	12.0	Green, Jacob, Sea.	9.5
Taylor, Lawrence, Giants	12.0	Jackson, Rickey, N.O.	9.5
Doleman, Chris, Minn.	11.0	Mann, Charles, Wash.	9.5

AFC—TEAM

	Sacks	Yds.
San Diego	45	298
L.A. Raiders	44	361
New England	43	339
Cincinnati	40	303
Indianapolis	39	313
Seattle	37	238
Houston	35	271
Buffalo	34	267
Cleveland	34	257
Denver	31	244
N.Y. Jets	29	206
Kansas City	26	167
Pittsburgh	26	196
Miami	21	183
Conference Total	484	3643
Conference Average	34.6	260.2

NFC—TEAM

	Sacks	Yds.
Chicago	70	484
Philadelphia	57	452
N.Y. Giants	55	382
Washington	53	424
Dallas	51	337
New Orleans	47	355
Detroit	42	355
Minnesota	41	307
St. Louis	41	285
Tampa Bay	39	306
L.A. Rams	38	304
San Francisco	37	287
Green Bay	34	197
Atlanta	17	118
Conference Total	622	4593
Conference Average	44.4	328.1
League Total	1106	8236
League Average	39.5	294.1

AFC—INDIVIDUALS

Player—Team	Sacks	Player—Team	Sacks
TIPPETT, N.E.	12.5	Bosworth, Sea.	4.0
Smith, Buff.	12.0	Bryant, Sea.	4.0
J. Green, Sea.	9.5	Edwards, Cin.	4.0
F. Young, Sea.	9.0	Fletcher, Den.	4.0
Bennett, Buff.	8.5	Gary, Pitt.	4.0
Townsend, Raiders	8.5	King, Cin.	4.0
Bickett, Ind.	8.0	Long, Raiders	4.0
Hairston, Clev.	8.0	Martin, G.B.-Hou.	4.0
L. Williams, S.D.	8.0	Meads, Hou.	4.0
R. Jones, Den.	7.0	Turner, Mia.	4.0
Mecklenburg, Den.	7.0	Winter, S.D.	4.0
Veris, N.E.	7.0	A. Baker, Clev.	3.5
Bell, K.C.	6.5	Ehin, S.D.	3.5
Childress, Hou.	6.0	Krumrie, Cin.	3.5
Jones, Raiders	6.0	Lyons, Jets	3.5
Maas, K.C.	6.0	Martin, Raiders	3.5
Williams, Cin.	6.0	Nash, Sea.	3.5
Merriweather, Pitt.	5.5	Seals, Buff.	3.5
Puzzuoli, Clev.	5.5	D. Smith, Hou.	3.5
Still, K.C.	5.5	Sochia, Mia.	3.5
Thompson, Ind.	5.5	Banks, S.D.	3.0
Cooks, Ind.	5.0	Bosa, Mia.	3.0
Gordon, Jets	5.0	Bostic, Hou.	3.0
Phillips, S.D.	5.0	Carr, Pitt.	3.0
B. Williams, N.E.	5.0	Crawford, Clev.	3.0
Gastineau, Jets	4.5	Darby, Ind.	3.0
King, Raiders	4.5	Del Rio, K.C.	3.0
Robinson, Raiders	4.5	Fulcher, Cin.	3.0
Skow, Cin.	4.5	L. Miller, S.D.	3.0
T. Williams, N.E.	4.5	Smith, S.D.	3.0

Player—Team	Sacks	Player—Team	Sacks
Taylor, Raiders	3.0	Frye, Mia.	1.0
Thorp, Ind.	3.0	Graf, Mia.	1.0
Willis, Pitt.	3.0	Grayson, Clev.	1.0
Baker, Hou.	2.5	Grimsley, Ind.	1.0
Bayless, S.D.	2.5	Hammerstein, Cin.	1.0
Berthusen, Cin.	2.5	Hand, Ind.	1.0
Catchings, Cin.	2.5	Harper, Clev.	1.0
Crable, Jets	2.5	Hodge, N.E.	1.0
Matthews, Clev.	2.5	Holmes, Jets	1.0
McNanie, Buff.	2.5	Hunley, Den.	1.0
Nichols, Jets	2.5	Hunter, S.D.	1.0
Unrein, S.D.	2.5	Jackson, S.D.	1.0
Armstrong, Buff.	2.0	E. Johnson, Clev.	1.0
Brown, Raiders	2.0	Kelly, Cin.	1.0
Buck, Cin.	2.0	Kirk, S.D.	1.0
Bussey, Cin.	2.0	Klecko, Jets	1.0
Clancy, Clev.	2.0	Leiding, Ind.	1.0
Cooks, Hou.	2.0	Lippett, N.E.	1.0
Fuller, Hou.	2.0	Mangiero, N.E.	1.0
Glaze, Sea.	2.0	Martin, Buff.	1.0
Hackett, K.C.	2.0	Mattiace, Ind.	1.0
Hinkle, Pitt.	2.0	McCabe, N.E.	1.0
Howard, Jets	2.0	McGrew, N.E.	1.0
B. Johnson, Hou.	2.0	McMillen, Raiders	1.0
M. Johnson, Clev.	2.0	Millen, Raiders	1.0
Kragen, Den.	2.0	Moyer, Sea.	1.0
Krauss, Ind.	2.0	Newsom, Hou.	1.0
Lucas, Den.	2.0	Perryman, Ind.	1.0
Lyles, Hou.	2.0	Pickel, Raiders	1.0
Readon, Mia.	2.0	Prior, Ind.	1.0
Rembert, N.E.	2.0	Robbins, Den.	1.0
Reynolds, N.E.	2.0	Ross, K.C.	1.0
Snipes, S.D.-K.C.	2.0	Rusinek, Clev.	1.0
Bennett, Jets	1.5	Sally, Ind.	1.0
Dorning, Sea.	1.5	Schutt, Cin.	1.0
Golic, Clev.	1.5	S. Scott, Mia.	1.0
Lambrecht, Mia.	1.5	Seale, Hou.	1.0
Little, Pitt.	1.5	T. Simmons, S.D.	1.0
Mersereau, Jets	1.5	Smerlas, Buff.	1.0
Offerdahl, Mia.	1.5	Talley, Buff.	1.0
Rose, Jets	1.5	Thomas, Cin.	1.0
Ryan, Den.	1.5	Townsend, Den.	1.0
K. Simmons, S.D.	1.5	Ward, Cin.	1.0
Sims, N.E.	1.5	Warren, Pitt.	1.0
Tupper, Den.	1.5	R. Washington, Raiders	1.0
Ackerman, Raiders	1.0	Wichard, N.E.	1.0
Benjamin, Ind.	1.0	Wilburn, N.E.	1.0
Benson, S.D.	1.0	Wiley, Sea.	1.0
Bentley, Buff.	1.0	G. Williams, Pitt.	1.0
Blackmon, N.E.	1.0	J. Williams, Pitt.	1.0
Brooks, Den.	1.0	L. Williams, Sea.	1.0
Brophy, Jets	1.0	K. Wilson, S.D.	1.0
M. Brown, Mia.	1.0	Wilson, Den.	1.0
Brudzinski, Mia.	1.0	Wright, Ind.	1.0
Buczkowski, Raiders	1.0	Zander, Cin.	1.0
Bulluck, Ind.	1.0	Zordich, Jets	1.0
Byrd, Hou.	1.0	A. Anderson, S.D.	0.5
Camp, Clev.	1.0	Bowman, N.E.	0.5
Carter, Clev.	1.0	Bowyer, Den.	0.5
Charles, S.D.	1.0	Conlan, Buff.	0.5
Chatman, Ind.	1.0	Glasgow, Ind.	0.5
Cole, Pitt.	1.0	Glenn, Jets	0.5
Cormier, Raiders	1.0	Glenn, S.D.	0.5
Dawkins, Pitt.	1.0	Holle, K.C.	0.5
Donaldson, Hou.	1.0	Koch, K.C.	0.5
Drane, Buff.	1.0	Scholtz, Sea.	0.5
Elko, Ind.	1.0	Wimberly, Mia.	0.5
Fox, Hou.	1.0	Woodard, Den.	0.5

NFC—INDIVIDUALS

Player—Team	Sacks	Player—Team	Sacks
WHITE, Phil.	21.0	Banks, Giants	9.0
Dent, Chi.	12.5	D. Martin, Minn.	9.0
L. Taylor, Giants	12.0	Cofer, Det.	8.5
Doleman, Minn.	11.0	Manley, Wash.	8.5
Nunn, St.L.	11.0	Holmes, T.B.	8.0
Swilling, N.O.	10.5	Marshall, Giants	8.0
E.L. Jones, Dall.	10.0	T. Harris, G.B.	7.0
Jackson, N.O.	9.5	Jeter, Rams	7.0
Mann, Wash.	9.5	Mays, Minn.	7.0

Player—Team	Sacks	Player—Team	Sacks
McMichael, Chi.	7.0	E. Johnson, G.B.	2.0
Greene, Rams	6.5	Junior, St.L.	2.0
Haley, S.F.	6.5	Kaufman, Wash.	2.0
McInerney, Chi.	6.5	Koch, Wash.	2.0
Washington, T.B.	6.5	Lockhart, Dall.	2.0
Wilson, Chi.	6.5	Maxie, N.O.	2.0
K. Ferguson, Det.	6.0	McCoy, N.O.	2.0
Greer, St.L.	6.0	McDuffie, Det.	2.0
Miller, Rams	6.0	Murphy, G.B.	2.0
Simmons, Phil.	6.0	Norris, Chi.	2.0
Warren, N.O.	6.0	Olkewicz, Wash.	2.0
R. White, Dall.	6.0	Perkins, Dall.	2.0
E. Howard, Giants	5.5	Phillips, Phil.	2.0
Wilks, N.O.	5.5	Pitts, Phil.	2.0
Jeffcoat, Dall.	5.0	Reed, Rams	2.0
Marshall, Chi.	5.0	Riggins, T.B.	2.0
Martin, Giants	5.0	Saleaumua, Det.	2.0
Martin, Wash.	5.0	Scotts, St.L.	2.0
Wilcher, Rams	5.0	Singletary, Chi.	2.0
B. Clark, N.O.	4.5	Le. Smith, St.L.	2.0
Clasby, St.L.	4.5	Solomon, Minn.	2.0
Kugler, S.F.	4.5	Thompson, Det.	2.0
J. Anderson, G.B.	4.0	Thompson, Giants	2.0
J. Brown, Phil.	4.0	Turpin, T.B.	2.0
Carreker, G.B.	4.0	Eric M. Williams, Det.	2.0
Coleman, Wash.	4.0	Wright, Rams	2.0
Joyner, Phil.	4.0	Alvord, St.L.	1.5
Moor, Atl.	4.0	Clarke, Phil.	1.5
Norvell, Chi.	4.0	Collins, Giants	1.5
Rohrer, Dall.	4.0	A. Harris, Chi.	1.5
J. Williams, Det.	4.0	Harrison, Atl.	1.5
Althoff, Chi.	3.5	Jiles, Phil.	1.5
B. Bell, Chi.	3.5	Korff, S.F.	1.5
Hampton, Chi.	3.5	Lasker, Giants	1.5
Kellin, T.B.	3.5	S. Leach, N.O.	1.5
Millard, Minn.	3.5	Montoute, T.B.	1.5
Stover, S.F.	3.5	Moss, T.B.	1.5
Turner, T.B.	3.5	Teafatiller, Chi.	1.5
Bates, Dall.	3.0	Ball, Det.	1.0
Brooks, Dall.	3.0	Battaglia, Phil.	1.0
R. Brown, G.B.	3.0	Bell, St.L.	1.0
Butz, Wash.	3.0	T. Bell, Chi.	1.0
Duerson, Chi.	3.0	Benson, Det.	1.0
Haynes, Dall.	3.0	Boyd, Det.	1.0
Hegman, Dall.	3.0	C. Brown, Phil.	1.0
Jarvis, T.B.	3.0	Browner, Minn.	1.0
Meisner, Rams	3.0	Browner, G.B.	1.0
N. Noga, St.L.	3.0	Carson, Giants	1.0
Perry, Chi.	3.0	Carter, S.F.	1.0
Saddler, St.L.	3.0	M. Clark, T.B.	1.0
Turner, S.F.	3.0	Cobb, Phil.	1.0
Walton, Wash.	3.0	Collins, Rams	1.0
Watts, Dall.	3.0	Courtney, S.F.	1.0
Bryan, Atl.	2.5	Cromwell, Rams	1.0
Garalczyk, St.L.	2.5	Curtis, Wash.	1.0
Green, Det.	2.5	Deforest, N.O.	1.0
Headen, Giants	2.5	Dorsey, Giants	1.0
Roberts, S.F.	2.5	Dwyer, Dall.	1.0
Smalls, Phil.	2.5	Edwards, Rams	1.0
H. Thomas, Minn.	2.5	Federico, Det.	1.0
Benish, Wash.	2.0	Frizzell, Phil.	1.0
Board, S.F.	2.0	Galloway, St.L.	1.0
Borland, Rams	2.0	Gann, Atl.	1.0
Boyarsky, G.B.	2.0	Gibson, Det.	1.0
G. Brown, Atl.	2.0	Green, Atl.	1.0
Burt, Giants	2.0	Griffin, Det.	1.0
Cannon, T.B.	2.0	Griffin, Phil.	1.0
Carr, Det.	2.0	Hamilton, Wash.	1.0
Casillas, Atl.	2.0	Harris, T.B.	1.0
Cofer, Wash.	2.0	Hill, Giants	1.0
D. Coleman, Minn.	2.0	Hoage, Phil.	1.0
Collins, S.F.	2.0	Holland, G.B.	1.0
Drost, G.B.	2.0	Jamison, Det.	1.0
Duliban, Dall.	2.0	January, Chi.	1.0
Elliott, N.O.	2.0	K. Johnson, G.B.	1.0
Fagan, S.F.	2.0	T. Johnson, Giants	1.0
Fuller, S.F.	2.0	V. Johnson, N.O.	1.0
Gay, Det.	2.0	Johnson, Dall.	1.0
Glover, S.F.	2.0	Jordan, G.B.	1.0
Grant, Wash.	2.0	Karras, Wash.	1.0
Grooms, Phil.	2.0	Lee, Phil.	1.0

Reggie White of the Philadelphia Eagles dominated the NFL with 21 sacks in 1987, just one shy of Mark Gastineau's 1984 league record despite playing in only 12 games.

Player—Team	Sacks	Player—Team	Sacks
Lockett, Det.	1.0	Shell, S.F.	1.0
C. Mack, St.L.	1.0	Studwell, Minn.	1.0
McCallister, T.B.	1.0	Swoopes, N.O.	1.0
McColl, S.F.	1.0	Thompson, Wash.	1.0
Milot, Wash.	1.0	Tuggle, Atl.	1.0
R. Mitchell, Phil.	1.0	Waechter, Wash.	1.0
Molden, Minn.	1.0	Walen, Dall.	1.0
J.B. Morris, G.B.	1.0	J. Walker, Minn.	1.0
Ra. Morris, Chi.	1.0	Washington, Giants	1.0
Noble, G.B.	1.0	West, Phil.	1.0
Noonan, Dall.	1.0	Auer, Phil.	0.5
Nordgren, T.B.	1.0	Browner, S.F.	0.5
Owens, Rams	1.0	Caldwell, G.B.	0.5
Rade, Atl.	1.0	Dulin, St.L.	0.5
Reasons, Giants	1.0	Keys, T.B.	0.5
Reichenbach, Phil.	1.0	Morris, Atl.	0.5
Rivera, Chi.	1.0	Stokes, Rams	0.5
Rose, Wash.	1.0	Studaway, Atl.	0.5
Ross, Det.	1.0	Sullivan, G.B.	0.5
Sagnella, Wash.	1.0	Taylor, N.O.	0.5

1987 FUMBLES

MOST FUMBLES, SEASON
    NFC: 12—Randall Cunningham, Philadelphia.
    AFC: 11—Dave Krieg, Seattle.

MOST FUMBLES, GAME
    AFC: 5—Willie Totten, Buffalo vs. Indianapolis, October 4.
             Dave Walter, Cincinnati at Seattle, October 11.
    NFC: 3—By 9 players.

OWN FUMBLES RECOVERED, SEASON
    AFC: 6—Steve Grogan, New England.
             Warren Moon, Houston.
    NFC: 6—Randall Cunningham, Philadelphia.

OWN FUMBLES RECOVERED, GAME
    AFC: 3—Dave Krieg, Seattle at Chicago, December 20.
    NFC: 2—By 10 players.

OPPONENTS' FUMBLES RECOVERED, SEASON
    NFC: 5—Brian Noble, Green Bay.
    AFC: 4—Fredd Young, Seattle.

OPPONENTS' FUMBLES RECOVERED, GAME
    AFC: 2—By 9 players.
    NFC: 2—By 9 players.

MOST YARDS RETURNING FUMBLES
    NFC: 77—Mark Jackson, St. Louis.
    AFC: 59—Trell Hooper, Miami.

LONGEST FUMBLE RETURN
    NFC: 77—Mark Jackson, St. Louis vs. New Orleans, October 11 (TD).
    AFC: 59—Trell Hooper, Miami vs. Kansas City, October 11 (TD).

FUMBLES—TEAM

AMERICAN FOOTBALL CONFERENCE

	Fum.	Own Rec.	Fum. *O.B.	TDs.	Opp. Rec.	Yds.	TDs.	Tot. Rec.
L.A. Raiders	24	10	1	0	15	—7	0	25
Cincinnati	29	17	0	0	12	—34	0	29
Denver	29	12	0	0	19	34	0	31
Seattle	31	16	0	0	21	19	0	37
Houston	32	15	3	0	14	39	1	29
Cleveland	33	15	1	0	13	46	2	28
N.Y. Jets	33	13	1	0	11	25	1	24
Indianapolis	36	13	5	0	25	44	1	38
New England	36	21	2	0	21	35	1	42
Miami	37	18	2	0	16	87	2	34
Pittsburgh	37	28	1	0	17	80	2	45
San Diego	38	17	1	0	15	4	1	32
Buffalo	41	17	0	0	14	57	3	31
Kansas City	41	14	3	0	17	—20	1	31
Conference Total	477	226	20	0	230	409	15	456
Conference Average	34.1	16.1	1.4	0.0	16.4	29.2	1.1	32.6

NATIONAL FOOTBALL CONFERENCE

	Fum.	Own Rec.	Fum. *O.B.	TDs.	Opp. Rec.	Yds.	TDs.	Tot. Rec.
St. Louis	23	8	3	0	19	127	4	27
San Francisco	25	13	0	1	13	63	0	26
L.A. Rams	26	9	2	0	11	47	1	20
Washington	26	5	2	0	11	35	1	16
Atlanta	27	9	1	0	12	57	1	21
Minnesota	28	13	5	0	11	42	0	24
Detroit	29	15	3	0	13	−30	1	28
Dallas	30	10	0	0	20	32	0	30
Chicago	33	13	0	0	11	22	0	24
New Orleans	33	14	3	0	18	52	0	32
Green Bay	35	16	1	0	24	−2	0	40
Tampa Bay	35	21	0	0	19	61	2	40
N.Y. Giants	38	14	4	0	14	−14	0	28
Philadelphia	44	23	2	0	27	189	2	50
Conference Total	432	183	26	1	223	681	12	406
Conference Average	30.9	13.1	1.9	0.7	15.9	48.6	0.9	29.0
League Total	909	409	46	1	453	1090	27	862
League Average	32.5	14.6	1.6	0.4	16.2	38.9	1.0	30.8

*Fumbled out of bounds.
Total yards include all fumble yardage (aborted plays, own and opponents recoveries).

AFC—INDIVIDUALS

Player-Team	Fum.	Own Rec.	Opp. Rec.	Yds.	Tot. Rec.
Abercrombie, Pitt.	4	3	0	2	3
Ackerman, Raiders	0	0	1	0	1
Adams, S.D.	1	0	0	0	0
Adickes, K.C.	0	1	0	0	1
Ahrens, Ind.	0	0	2	0	2
Alexander, Jets	0	2	0	0	2
Allen, Raiders	3	0	0	0	0
P. Allen, Hou.	0	1	0	0	1
Anderson, Raiders	0	1	0	0	1
G. Anderson, S.D.	4	1	0	0	1
Armstrong, Ind.	0	1	1	0	2
Armstrong, Buff.	1	0	0	0	0
Aydelette, Pitt.	0	1	0	5	1
Ayers, Den.	0	1	0	0	1
A. Baker, Clev.	0	0	1	0	1
R. Baldinger, K.C.	0	1	0	0	1
Banker, Jets	0	1	0	0	1
Banks, S.D.	0	0	2	0	2
C. Banks, Ind.	1	0	0	0	0
Baugh, K.C.	1	2	0	0	2
Bell, Den.	2	1	0	0	1
Bell, K.C.	0	0	2	0	2
Benjamin, Ind.	0	0	1	0	1
Benson, S.D.	0	0	1	0	1
Bentley, Ind.	3	3	0	0	3
Bernstine, S.D.	0	1	0	0	1
Berthusen, Cin.	0	0	1	1	1
Bickett, Ind.	1	0	2	32	2
Billups, Cin.	0	0	1	0	1
Blackledge, K.C.	2	0	0	−6	0
Bleier, N.E.	2	2	0	0	2
Bligen, Jets	1	1	0	0	1
Boddie, Den.	0	0	1	0	1
Bono, Pitt.	5	3	0	0	3
Bosa, Mia.	0	0	2	0	2
Bostic, Hou.	1	0	1	2	1
Bosworth, Sea.	0	0	2	38	2
Bouza, Ind.	2	0	0	0	0
Bowman, N.E.	0	0	1	6	1
Brady, Cin.	0	0	1	0	1
Breen, Cin.	1	1	0	0	1
Brennan, Clev.	1	1	0	0	1
Britt, Pitt.	1	1	0	0	1
Brooks, Ind.	3	0	0	0	0
Brooks, Den.	0	0	1	0	1
Brown, Sea.	0	1	0	0	1
B. Brown, Mia.	1	1	0	0	1
E. Brown, Cin.	3	1	0	0	1
G. Brown, Ind.	1	0	0	0	0
M. Brown, Mia.	0	0	1	1	1
Brown, Raiders	0	0	1	0	1
St. Brown, Hou.	1	0	1	0	1
B. Bryan, Den.	0	0	1	0	1
Bryant, Hou.	0	0	1	0	1
Bryant, Sea.	0	0	1	0	1
Burkett, Buff.	1	0	0	0	0
Burnham, Sea.	1	0	0	0	0
Burroughs, Buff.	0	1	0	0	1
Burse, Sea.	1	0	0	0	0
Bussey, Cin.	1	0	0	0	0
K. Butler, Sea.	0	0	1	0	1
R. Butler, Sea.	1	0	0	0	0
Byner, Clev.	5	1	0	0	1
Byrd, S.D.	0	0	1	0	1
Byrum, Buff.	4	1	0	0	1
Carson, K.C.	1	0	0	0	0
Carter, Jets	0	0	1	0	1
Catchings, Cin.	0	0	1	0	1
Caterbone, Mia.	1	1	0	0	1
Chandler, S.D.	1	1	0	0	1
Chapman, Raiders	0	0	1	0	1
Cherry, K.C.	0	0	1	0	1
Childress, Hou.	0	0	1	1	1
Chirico, Jets	1	0	2	0	2
Christensen, Clev.	3	0	0	−3	0
Clancy, Clev.	0	0	2	0	2
Clark, Den.	1	1	0	0	1
Clay, Raiders	0	1	0	0	1
Clayborn, N.E.	0	0	1	0	1
Clemons, K.C.	3	1	0	0	1
Coffman, K.C.	0	0	2	0	2
Cofield, K.C.	0	0	1	0	1
Cole, Pitt.	0	0	1	0	1
Collins, N.E.	6	2	0	0	2
Collins, Jets	1	0	1	0	1
Colton, N.E.	0	1	0	0	1
Cooks, Ind.	1	0	1	0	1
K. Daniel, Ind.	2	0	0	0	0
Danielson, Clev.	2	2	0	−2	2
J. Davis, Raiders	1	0	1	0	1
J. Davis, Hou.	1	0	0	0	0
Davis, Clev.	1	1	0	0	1
Davis, Ind.	0	1	0	0	1
DeAyala, Cin.	0	1	1	0	1
Dellenbach, Mia.	1	0	0	−13	0
Dickerson, Rams-Ind.	7	3	0	0	3
Donaldson, Hou.	0	0	2	0	2
Drane, Buff.	0	0	1	0	1
Driver, Clev.	1	0	0	0	0
Dudek, Den.	4	1	0	0	1
Dunn, Pitt.	0	0	1	0	1
Dupard, N.E.	2	1	0	0	1
Easley, Sea.	0	0	1	0	1
Eason, N.E.	1	0	0	0	0
Echols, Clev.	0	1	0	0	1
Edmonds, Sea.	1	1	0	0	1

Player—Team	Fum.	Own Rec.	Opp. Rec.	Yds.	Tot. Rec.	Player—Team	Fum.	Own Rec.	Opp. Rec.	Yds.	Tot. Rec.
Edwards, Cin.	0	0	1	0	1	Jackson, S.D.	0	0	1	0	1
Ehin, S.D.	1	0	1	27	1	Jackson, Cin.	0	0	1	0	1
Elko, Ind.	0	0	1	0	1	Jaeger, Clev.	0	1	0	0	1
C. Ellis, Raiders	1	0	0	0	0	James, S.D.	6	0	0	−8	0
Ellis, Clev.	0	1	1	27	2	Jenkins, Sea.	1	0	0	0	0
Elway, Den.	2	0	0	−1	0	Jennings, Cin.	0	0	1	0	1
Esiason, Cin.	10	4	0	−8	4	Jensen, Mia.	1	0	3	2	3
Everett, Pitt.	1	2	0	7	2	Da. Johnson, Mia.	1	0	0	0	0
Faaola, Jets	0	0	1	3	1	E. Johnson, Clev.	0	0	1	0	1
Farren, Clev.	0	1	0	0	1	Johnson, Ind.	1	0	0	0	0
Feasel, Sea.	1	1	0	−19	1	K. Johnson, Hou.	3	0	1	0	1
Fernandez, Raiders	1	0	0	0	0	M. Johnson, Clev.	0	0	1	0	1
Fields, Jets	0	1	0	0	1	V. Johnson, Den.	1	0	0	0	0
Flaherty, Cin.	0	0	1	0	1	L. Jones, Den.	0	0	2	24	2
Fletcher, Den.	0	0	1	0	1	R. Jones, K.C.	1	0	0	0	0
Flutie, N.E.	1	1	0	0	1	Jones, Raiders	0	0	2	0	2
Foster, Hou.	0	1	0	0	1	Jordan, N.E.	0	1	0	0	1
Fouts, S.D.	10	4	0	−10	4	Justin, Sea.	0	0	1	0	1
Fryar, N.E.	2	0	0	0	0	Kaiser, Buff.	0	0	1	0	1
Fulcher, Cin.	0	0	1	0	1	Karcher, Den.	2	3	0	−11	3
Fuller, Hou.	0	0	1	0	1	Katolin, Clev.	1	0	0	0	0
Gaines, Sea.	0	0	1	0	1	Kay, Den.	3	0	0	0	0
Gaines, Buff.	1	0	0	0	0	Keel, Sea.	0	2	0	0	2
Gilbert, Den.	0	0	1	0	1	Kelly, Buff.	6	2	0	0	2
Givins, Hou.	2	0	0	0	0	Kelso, Buff.	0	0	2	56	2
Glasgow, Ind.	0	0	1	0	1	Kemp, Sea.	2	1	0	−8	1
Glenn, S.D.	0	0	1	0	1	Kenney, K.C.	8	2	0	−8	2
Gowdy, Pitt.	0	0	2	1	2	Kidd, Hou.	0	1	0	0	1
Graf, Mia.	0	0	1	0	1	Kimmel, Raiders	0	1	0	0	1
Graham, Sea.	0	0	2	0	2	King, Raiders	0	0	1	0	1
Grayson, Clev.	0	0	1	17	1	Kinnebrew, Cin.	1	0	0	0	0
J. Green, Sea.	0	0	1	0	1	Kirk, S.D.	1	1	0	0	1
Griffith, Sea.	0	1	0	0	1	Klecko, Jets	0	0	1	0	1
Grimsley, Ind.	0	0	1	0	1	Konecny, Mia.	0	1	0	0	1
Grimsley, Hou.	0	0	1	0	1	Kosar, Clev.	2	1	0	−3	1
Grogan, N.E.	8	6	0	−6	6	Kowalski, S.D.	0	1	0	0	1
Hairston, Clev.	0	0	1	0	1	Kozerski, Cin.	0	1	0	0	1
Hairston, Pitt.	1	0	0	0	0	Kragen, Den.	0	0	1	0	1
Hall, Pitt.	1	0	2	50	2	Krauss, Ind.	0	0	2	0	2
Hamilton, Jets	0	0	1	0	1	Krieg, Sea.	11	5	0	−2	5
Hampton, Mia.	4	1	0	0	1	Lacy, K.C.	2	0	0	0	0
Hannah, Raiders	0	1	0	2	1	Lankford, Mia.	0	0	1	4	1
Hansen, N.E.	0	1	0	0	1	Largent, Sea.	2	0	0	0	0
Harden, Den.	0	0	1	14	1	LeBlanc, N.E.	2	0	0	0	0
Hardy, Mia.	1	0	0	−7	0	Lee, Pitt.	0	0	1	0	1
Harmon, Buff.	2	0	0	0	0	L. Lee, Den.	0	1	0	0	1
Harrell, K.C.	0	0	2	0	2	Lewis, K.C.	0	0	1	0	1
Harris, K.C.	0	0	1	0	1	Lilly, Den.	0	0	1	0	1
Harris, S.D.	0	0	1	0	1	Lingner, Buff.	0	0	1	0	1
Harrison, Raiders	2	0	0	0	0	Linne, N.E.	1	1	0	0	1
Haslett, Jets	0	0	1	0	1	Little, Pitt.	0	0	1	0	1
Hayes, K.C.	0	1	0	0	1	Lockett, Pitt.	1	1	0	0	1
Haynes, Den.	0	0	1	24	1	Long, Raiders	0	0	2	0	2
Heard, K.C.	5	2	0	0	2	Lowry, Ind.	0	0	1	0	1
Hector, Jets	2	1	0	0	1	Lucas, Den.	0	0	1	0	1
Herrmann, S.D.	1	1	0	−5	1	Lyles, Hou.	0	0	3	55	3
Highsmith, Hou.	2	0	0	0	0	Maas, K.C.	0	0	1	6	1
Hilger, Raiders	3	1	0	0	1	Macek, S.D.	1	1	0	0	1
D. Hill, Hou.	1	0	0	0	0	Mack, Clev.	6	1	0	0	1
Hinkle, Pitt.	1	0	1	0	1	Mackey, Mia.	3	0	0	−6	0
Hinton, Ind.	0	0	1	0	1	Malone, Pitt.	10	5	0	−3	5
Hobley, Mia.	0	1	3	55	4	Manoa, Clev.	1	1	0	0	1
Hogeboom, Ind.	1	1	0	−1	1	Manos, Cin.	0	1	0	0	1
Holman, Cin.	1	0	0	0	1	Manucci, Buff.	1	0	0	−7	0
Holman, Jets	1	0	0	0	0	Marino, Mia.	5	4	0	−25	4
Holmes, N.E.	0	0	1	0	1	Marion, N.E.	0	0	1	0	1
Holohan, S.D.	0	1	0	0	1	Martin, Hou.	0	0	1	0	1
Holt, S.D.	1	0	0	0	0	Martin, Cin.	1	0	0	0	0
Hooper, Mia.	1	0	1	59	1	Mason, Clev.	4	1	0	0	1
Horton, Raiders	2	0	0	0	0	Matthews, Clev.	0	0	2	0	2
Howard, K.C.	0	0	1	0	1	McCluskey, Cin.	2	0	0	0	0
Hudson, K.C.	1	1	0	−3	1	McGrew, N.E.	0	0	1	0	1
Humiston, S.D.	0	0	1	0	1	McLemore, Ind.	1	0	0	0	0
Humphery, Jets	1	1	1	46	2	McNanie, Buff.	0	0	1	14	1
Hunter, S.D.	1	0	0	0	0	McNeil, Jets	1	0	0	0	0
E. Hunter, Jets	3	0	0	−12	0	McNeil, Clev.	2	0	0	0	0
Hunter, Hou.	1	0	0	0	0	C. McSwain, N.E.	0	0	1	11	1
Hyde, K.C.	1	0	1	0	1	Mecklenburg, Den.	0	0	1	0	1
B. Jackson, Raiders	2	1	0	0	1	Meehan, Cin.	1	0	0	0	0
Jackson, Pitt.	2	3	0	0	3	Merritts, Ind.	0	0	1	0	1

Player—Team	Fum.	Own Rec.	Opp. Rec.	Yds.	Tot. Rec.
Merriweather, Pitt.	0	1	3	4	4
Mersereau, Jets	0	0	1	0	1
Metzelaars, Buff.	3	1	0	0	1
Micho, Den.	1	0	0	0	0
Millard, Sea.	0	2	0	0	2
Millen, Raiders	1	0	0	0	0
L. Miller, S.D.	0	0	2	0	2
Mobley, Den.	1	0	0	0	0
Moon, Hou.	8	6	0	−7	6
G. Moore, N.E.	0	0	1	0	1
Morriss, N.E.	1	0	0	0	0
Morton, Sea.	1	0	0	0	0
Moyer, Sea.	0	0	3	10	3
Mueller, Buff.	5	1	0	−22	1
Mueller, Raiders	3	1	0	0	1
Munchak, Hou.	0	0	1	0	1
Munford, Den.	0	0	2	0	2
Nathan, Mia.	1	0	0	0	0
Nattiel, Den.	2	1	0	0	1
Nelson, Pitt.	0	0	1	0	1
Nelson, N.E.	0	0	1	0	1
T. Nelson, K.C.	0	0	1	0	1
Neuheisel, S.D.	1	1	0	0	1
Newsome, Pitt.	1	1	0	−17	1
Nickerson, Pitt.	0	1	0	0	1
Noble, Ind.	2	0	0	0	0
Noble, Raiders	0	0	1	0	1
Norrie, Jets	4	2	0	−2	2
O'Brien, Jets	8	1	0	−10	1
O'Connor, Jets	1	1	0	0	1
Odom, Ind.	0	0	3	8	3
Odomes, Buff.	0	1	0	0	2
Okoye, K.C.	5	0	0	0	0
Oubre, Mia.	0	1	0	0	1
Palmer, K.C.	2	0	0	0	0
Parker, Raiders	0	1	0	0	1
Parker, K.C.	1	0	0	0	0
Partridge, Buff.	0	1	0	0	1
Patterson, S.D.	0	0	1	0	1
A. Pearson, K.C.	2	0	0	0	0
Pease, Hou.	2	2	0	0	2
Peavey, Den.	1	0	0	−16	0
Pennison, Hou.	1	1	0	−12	1
Perryman, N.E.	1	2	0	0	2
Perryman, Ind.	0	0	1	5	1
Peterson, N.E.	0	0	1	0	1
Pickel, Raiders	0	0	2	0	2
Pidgeon, Mia.	0	0	1	17	1
Pinkett, Hou.	1	0	0	0	0
Pitts, Buff.	3	1	0	0	1
Pollard, Pitt.	3	1	0	1	1
Polley, Clev.	0	0	1	0	1
Powell, Sea.	1	0	0	0	0
Prior, Ind.	0	0	3	0	3
Pruitt, Mia.	1	0	0	0	0
Radecic, Buff.	0	0	2	0	2
Ramsey, N.E.	4	1	0	0	1
Reimers, Cin.	0	1	0	0	1
Riddick, Buff.	2	1	0	0	1
A. Riley, Pitt.	1	0	0	0	0
E. Riley, Jets	0	0	1	0	1
Rimington, Cin.	2	0	0	−18	0
D. Robinson, Clev.	0	1	0	10	1
Robinson, Sea.	0	0	1	0	1
Robinson, Ind.	0	0	1	0	1
Robinson, N.E.	0	1	0	0	1
Robinson, K.C.	0	0	2	0	2
Roby, Mia.	0	1	0	0	1
Rockins, Clev.	0	0	1	0	1
Romasko, Cin.	0	1	0	0	1
Rose, Mia.	0	0	1	0	1
Roth, Mia.	0	0	1	0	1
Rozier, Hou.	5	2	0	0	2
Rusinek, Clev.	0	0	1	0	1
Ryan, Den.	1	1	1	0	2
Salisbury, Ind.	1	0	0	0	0
Sampleton, Mia.	1	0	0	0	0
Sanchez, Pitt.	1	0	0	0	0
Sartin, S.D.	2	1	0	0	1
Schulte, Buff.	0	1	0	0	1
Schwedes, Mia.	7	3	0	0	3
R. Scott, Mia.	1	1	0	0	1
Sealby, N.E.	0	0	1	0	1
Seale, Raiders	0	0	1	−9	1
Seurer, K.C.	2	1	0	0	1
Sewell, Den.	1	0	0	0	0
Shell, Pitt.	0	0	1	19	1
Shuler, Jets	2	0	0	0	0
Sims, N.E.	0	0	1	0	1
Skansi, Sea.	1	0	0	0	0
Slaughter, Clev.	1	0	0	0	0
Smith, S.D.	0	0	3	0	3
B. Smith, K.C.	1	1	0	0	1
Smith, Buff.	0	0	2	15	2
C. Smith, K.C.	2	0	0	0	0
Smith, Sea.	0	0	2	0	2
D. Smith, Den.	0	0	2	0	2
R. Smith, Jets	1	0	0	0	0
Smith, Raiders	0	1	0	0	1
Ti. Spencer, S.D.	1	0	0	0	0
To. Spencer, S.D.	2	2	0	0	2
Stallworth, Pitt.	1	0	0	0	0
Starring, N.E.	2	1	0	0	1
Stephenson, Mia.	1	0	0	0	0
Stevens, K.C.	0	1	0	−9	1
Stone, Pitt.	0	0	1	0	1
Strachan, Raiders	1	0	0	0	0
Stradford, Mia.	6	2	0	0	2
Swanson, Den.	1	0	0	0	0
Talley, Buff.	0	0	1	1	1
Tasker, Buff.	2	0	0	0	0
Tatupu, N.E.	1	0	0	0	0
Teal, Sea.	1	0	0	0	0
Thomas, K.C.	0	0	1	0	1
Thompson, Ind.	0	0	1	28	1
Thompson, Pitt.	0	1	0	0	1
Tillman, Hou.	1	0	0	0	0
Tippett, N.E.	0	0	3	29	3
Toran, Raiders	0	0	1	0	1
Totten, Buff.	9	3	0	0	3
Townsell, Jets	3	2	0	0	2
Trudeau, Ind.	10	2	0	−28	2
Turner, Mia.	0	0	1	0	1
Utt, Ind.	0	2	0	0	2
Veris, N.E.	0	0	2	0	2
Vick, Jets	3	0	0	0	0
Villa, N.E.	1	0	0	−13	0
Vlasic, S.D.	1	1	0	0	1
Vogler, Buff.	0	2	0	0	2
Walczak, Buff.	1	0	0	0	0
Wallace, Hou.	1	1	0	0	1
D. Walter, Cin.	6	3	0	−9	3
J. Walter, Cin.	0	2	0	0	2
Warner, Sea.	4	1	0	0	1
Warren, Pitt.	0	1	0	11	1
Watters, Buff.	0	0	2	0	2
R. Wheeler, Raiders	1	0	0	0	0
Wichard, N.E.	0	0	2	0	2
Willhite, Den.	1	0	0	0	0
A. Williams, S.D.	1	0	0	0	0
B. Williams, Pitt.	0	0	1	0	1
D. Williams, N.E.	0	0	1	0	1
Do. Williams, Raiders	0	0	1	0	1
E. Williams, N.E.	0	0	2	8	2
G. Williams, Pitt.	0	0	1	0	1
J. Williams, Hou.	0	1	0	0	1
Jo. Williams, Sea.	2	1	0	0	1
L. Williams, Buff.	0	1	0	0	1
O. Williams, Hou.	1	0	0	0	0
Williams, Cin.	0	0	2	0	2
Wilson, Raiders	1	0	0	0	0
Wilson, Clev.	2	0	0	0	0
Winder, Den.	5	2	0	0	2
Winn, Den.	0	0	1	0	1
Winslow, S.D.	1	0	0	0	0
Winters, Clev.	1	0	0	0	0
Wolfley, Pitt.	0	1	0	0	1
Wonsley, Ind.	1	0	0	0	0
Woods, Raiders	2	1	0	0	1
Woods, Sea.	0	0	1	0	1

Player—Team	Fum.	Own Rec.	Opp. Rec.	Yds.	Tot. Rec.	Player—Team	Fum.	Own Rec.	Opp. Rec.	Yds.	Tot. Rec.
Woodson, Pitt.	3	2	0	0	2	Wyatt, K.C.	1	0	0	0	0
Wright, Cin.	1	0	0	0	0	F. Young, Sea.	0	0	4	0	4
Wright, Clev.	0	1	0	0	1	Zachary, S.D.	1	0	0	0	0
Wright, Ind.	0	0	1	0	1						

Touchdowns: Ellis, Cleve.; Grayson, Cleve.; Hall, Pitt.; Hobley, Mia.; Hooper, Mia.; Humphery, Jets; Kelso, Buff.; Lyles, Hou.; Maas, K.C.; McNanie, Buff.; Miller, S.D.; Shell, Pitt.; Smith, Buff.; Thompson, Ind.; Tippett, N.E., 1 each.

NFC—INDIVIDUALS

Player—Team	Fum.	Own Rec.	Opp. Rec.	Yds.	Tot. Rec.	Player—Team	Fum.	Own Rec.	Opp. Rec.	Yds.	Tot. Rec.
Adams, Dall.	2	1	0	0	1	Choate, G.B.	0	0	1	4	1
Adams, Giants	3	1	0	0	1	Clack, Dall.	1	0	0	0	0
Adams, N.O.	1	1	1	0	2	B. Clark, N.O.	0	0	2	0	2
Adams, Minn.	3	0	0	0	0	Clark, S.F.	1	0	0	0	0
Alexander, N.O.	2	0	0	0	0	Clark, Wash.	3	0	0	0	0
Allen, Chi.	0	0	2	0	2	Clasby, St.L.	0	0	1	0	1
Althoff, Chi.	0	0	1	0	1	Cobb, Phil.	0	0	3	0	3
Anderson, Minn.	1	0	0	0	0	Cofer, Det.	0	0	1	0	1
Anderson, T.B.	0	0	1	38	1	Collins, Rams	0	0	2	0	2
J. Anderson, G.B.	0	0	3	0	3	Cooper, Phil.	1	0	0	0	0
Anderson, Chi.	2	0	0	0	0	Courtney, S.F.	0	0	2	0	2
Atkins, N.O.	0	0	1	0	1	Covert, Chi.	0	1	0	0	1
Awalt, St.L.	0	1	0	0	1	A. Cox, Atl.	2	0	0	0	0
Badanjek, Atl.	1	0	0	0	0	Craig, S.F.	5	2	0	0	2
Bailey, Atl.	1	0	0	0	0	Crawford, Phil.	0	0	1	0	1
Baker, Phil.	0	1	0	0	1	Cribbs, S.F.	1	0	0	0	0
Baker, Giants	1	0	0	0	0	Criswell, T.B.	1	0	0	0	0
Banks, Dall.	1	1	0	0	1	Crocicchia, Giants	2	1	0	0	1
Barney, Atl.	1	0	0	0	0	Cunningham, Phil.	12	6	0	−7	6
Barrows, Det.	0	1	0	0	1	Curtis, Wash.	0	0	2	0	2
Barton, S.F.	0	1	0	0	1	Darwin, Phil.	0	1	0	0	1
Bavaro, Giants	2	0	0	0	0	Davis, Wash.	0	0	1	11	1
Bell, St.L.	1	0	0	0	0	C. Davis, Giants	0	0	2	0	2
B. Bell, Chi.	0	0	1	0	1	Davis, T.B.	0	0	2	3	2
Bell, Rams	1	0	0	0	0	Davis, G.B.	2	0	0	0	0
T. Bell, Chi.	1	0	1	0	1	Dawsey, N.O.	2	1	0	9	1
Benish, Wash.	0	0	1	0	1	Dean, Wash.	0	1	0	0	1
Bennett, Giants	0	0	1	0	1	DeBerg, T.B.	7	2	0	−2	2
Benson, Det.	0	0	1	0	1	Dent, Chi.	0	0	2	11	2
Bernard, Det.	3	1	0	0	1	DiBernardo, Rams	0	0	2	5	2
Berry, Minn.	0	1	0	0	1	Dils, Rams	2	1	0	−1	1
Bess, Minn.	4	0	0	0	0	DiRico, Giants	2	1	0	0	1
Beverly, N.O.	1	0	0	0	0	Donnelly, Atl.	2	1	0	−4	1
Black, Det.	1	1	0	0	1	Dorsett, Dall.	3	0	0	0	0
Blount, Dall.	1	0	0	0	0	Douglass, Chi.	0	1	0	0	1
Blount, S.F.	1	1	0	−4	1	Downs, Dall.	0	0	1	0	1
Board, S.F.	0	0	1	0	1	Dozier, Minn.	2	0	0	0	0
Borcky, Giants	0	0	1	0	1	Duarte, Chi.	1	1	0	0	1
Bowles, Wash.	0	0	1	0	1	Duerson, Chi.	0	0	1	10	1
Bowman, Phil.	1	1	0	0	1	Dwyer, Dall.	0	0	2	0	2
Bradley, Phil.	0	0	2	0	2	Edwards, Dall.	1	0	0	0	0
Bradley, Det.	2	2	0	0	2	Edwards, Det.	3	0	0	−23	0
Bramlett, Minn.	0	1	0	0	1	Ellard, Rams	3	1	0	0	1
Brantley, T.B.	0	0	1	0	1	Epps, G.B.	1	0	0	0	0
Brooks, Dall.	0	0	1	0	1	Evans, Phil.	0	0	1	0	1
A. Brown, Atl.	0	0	1	0	1	Evans, Minn.	0	0	1	0	1
Brown, Giants	0	0	1	0	1	Everett, Rams	2	1	0	0	1
J. Brown, Phil.	0	0	1	37	1	Fagan, S.F.	0	0	1	6	1
Brown, Chi.	1	0	0	−6	0	K. Ferguson, Det.	0	0	1	0	1
R. Brown, Phil.	2	1	1	0	2	Ferrell, St.L.	1	0	0	0	1
R. Brown, G.B.	0	0	4	0	4	Flagler, S.F.	2	1	0	0	1
Ro. Brown, Rams	2	1	0	0	1	Flowers, Atl.	1	1	0	0	1
Browner, Minn.	0	0	1	0	1	J. Fourcade, N.O.	1	0	0	0	0
Bryan, Atl.	0	0	1	0	1	Francis, Dall.	0	0	1	2	1
Bryant, Wash.	4	1	0	0	1	Frank, S.F.	2	0	0	0	0
Burton, Dall.	0	0	1	0	1	Freeman, T.B.	1	0	0	0	0
Butcher, Det.	0	1	0	0	1	Frizzell, Phil.	0	1	0	0	1
Byars, Phil.	3	2	0	0	2	Fuller, S.F.	0	0	3	0	3
Campbell, Atl.	4	2	0	0	2	Fullwood, G.B.	2	1	0	0	1
Campen, N.O.	0	1	0	0	1	Futrell, T.B.	2	2	0	0	2
Cannon, T.B.	0	0	1	0	1	Galbreath, Giants	1	0	0	0	0
Cannon, G.B.	1	0	0	−8	0	Garalczyk, St.L.	0	0	1	0	1
Caravello, Wash.	0	0	1	0	1	Garrity, Phil.	2	0	0	0	0
Carr, Det.	0	0	1	0	1	Gary, Phil.	0	0	1	19	1
Carson, Giants	0	0	1	0	1	Garza, St.L.	1	0	0	0	0
C. Carter, St.L.	0	0	1	0	1	Gault, Chi.	0	1	0	0	1
Carter, T.B.	0	1	0	0	1	Gentry, Chi.	2	0	0	0	0
Casillas, Atl.	0	0	1	0	1	Gogan, Dall.	0	1	0	0	1

Player—Team	Fum.	Own Rec.	Opp. Rec.	Yds.	Tot. Rec.	Player—Team	Fum.	Own Rec.	Opp. Rec.	Yds.	Tot. Rec.
Goode, T.B.	0	1	0	0	1	Kennard, St.L.	2	0	0	−4	0
Gordon, Atl.	0	0	1	0	1	King, Det.	0	0	1	9	1
Granger, Atl.	1	0	0	0	0	Kirchbaum, Phil.	0	0	1	0	1
Grant, Wash.	0	0	1	0	1	Klingel, Phil.	0	0	1	0	1
Gray, Rams.	0	0	1	0	1	Kramer, Minn.	2	0	0	0	0
Gray, N.O.	3	1	0	0	1	Lee, Det.	1	0	0	0	0
Green, Det.	1	0	0	0	0	Lewis, Minn.	1	2	0	0	2
Green, Wash.	0	0	1	26	1	Lilja, Dall.	1	0	0	0	0
Green, St.L.	1	0	0	0	0	Livingston, Dall.	1	0	0	0	0
Green, Atl.	0	0	2	35	2	Lockett, Det.	0	0	1	0	1
Greene, G.B.	0	0	2	0	2	Lockhart, Dall.	0	0	1	0	1
Griffin, S.F.	0	0	1	7	1	Lomax, St.L.	7	3	0	−3	3
Griffin, Phil.	0	0	1	0	1	Long, Det.	8	3	0	−8	3
Griffin, Wash.	3	0	0	0	0	Lott, S.F.	0	1	1	33	2
Guggemos, Minn.	4	3	0	0	3	Lovelady, Giants	5	2	0	0	2
Haddix, Phil.	1	0	0	0	0	C. Mack, St.L.	0	0	2	0	2
Hadley, S.F.	0	0	1	0	1	Majkowski, G.B.	5	0	0	0	0
Hall, Det.	1	1	0	0	1	Mandley, Det.	0	1	0	0	1
Halloran, St.L.	1	0	0	0	0	Mann, Wash.	0	0	1	0	1
Hallstrom, G.B.	0	0	1	0	1	Mansfield, G.B.	1	0	0	0	0
Hamilton, Wash.	0	1	0	0	1	Manuel, Giants	1	0	0	0	0
Harden, G.B.	1	0	0	0	0	Marshall, Chi.	0	0	1	0	1
Harrell, Minn.	1	0	0	0	0	C. Martin, Minn.	0	0	1	0	1
J. Harris, Minn.	0	0	1	0	1	Martin, S.F.	1	0	0	0	0
S. Harris, Minn.	0	1	0	0	1	Martin, N.O.	3	1	0	0	1
Harrison, G.B.	0	0	1	0	1	K. Martin, Dall.	1	0	0	0	0
Headen, Giants	0	0	1	0	1	Matthews, Atl.	2	0	1	0	1
Hebert, N.O.	4	2	0	0	2	May, Minn.	1	0	0	0	0
Hegman, Dall.	0	0	1	0	1	May, Wash.	0	0	1	0	1
Heimuli, Chi.	1	0	0	0	0	Mayes, N.O.	8	1	0	0	1
Heller, S.F.	1	0	0	0	0	Mayes, St.L.	0	0	1	0	1
M. Hendrix, Dall.	0	0	1	0	1	Mays, Minn.	0	0	2	0	2
Hicks, Rams.	1	0	0	0	0	McAdoo, St.L.	2	1	2	0	3
Hilgenberg, N.O.	0	1	0	0	1	McCallister, T.B.	0	0	1	0	1
Hill, T.B.	1	1	0	0	1	McConkey, Giants	2	1	0	0	1
Hill, Rams	0	1	0	0	1	McHale, T.B.	0	0	1	0	1
Hill, Giants	0	0	1	6	1	McKinnon, Chi.	6	3	0	0	3
Hill, N.O.	0	1	0	0	1	McLemore, S.F.	1	1	0	0	1
Hilliard, N.O.	4	0	0	0	0	McMahon, Chi.	2	0	0	0	0
Hoage, Phil.	0	0	2	0	2	Merkens, Phil.	3	1	0	0	1
Hobbins, G.B.	0	1	0	0	1	Mikolas, S.F.	0	0	1	0	1
Hohensee, Chi.	2	2	0	0	2	Millard, Minn.	0	0	2	8	2
Holland, G.B.	0	0	1	0	1	Millen, Rams	1	0	0	0	0
Holloway, St.L.	0	0	1	0	1	Mills, N.O.	0	0	3	0	3
S. Holloway, T.B.	0	1	0	0	1	Milot, Wash.	0	0	1	0	1
Holmes, T.B.	0	0	1	0	1	Mitchell, St.L.	3	1	0	0	1
Hons, Det.	2	2	0	−8	2	Monroe, S.F.	1	1	0	0	1
Horn, Phil.	1	0	0	0	0	Montana, S.F.	3	2	0	−5	2
Howard, Giants	0	0	2	0	2	Moore, Atl.	0	0	2	20	2
Howard, T.B.	0	0	0	0	0	Moorehead, Chi.	1	0	0	0	0
E. Howard, Giants	0	0	1	0	1	Moran, G.B.	1	1	0	3	1
Ingram, N.O.	2	0	0	0	0	Morris, Giants	2	0	0	0	0
Jackson, Phil.	1	1	0	0	1	Le. Morris, G.B.	1	2	0	0	2
Jackson, St.L.	0	0	1	77	1	Morse, Phil.	1	0	1	0	1
Jakes, N.O.	0	0	1	30	1	Moss, T.B.	0	0	1	0	1
James, Det.	3	1	0	0	1	Murphy, G.B.	0	0	2	0	2
James, N.O.	0	1	0	0	1	Neal, G.B.	1	0	0	0	0
January, Chi.	0	0	1	7	1	D. Nelson, Minn.	2	0	0	0	0
Jeffcoat, Dall.	0	0	2	8	2	Neville, G.B.	0	1	0	0	1
Jefferson, G.B.	2	0	1	0	1	Newsome, Dall.	1	0	0	0	0
A. Johnson, Phil.	1	0	0	0	0	Newsome, Rams	0	0	1	7	1
Johnson, Atl.	2	0	0	0	0	Noble, G.B.	0	0	5	0	5
G. Johnson, St.L.	0	0	2	0	2	N. Noga, St.L.	0	0	1	23	1
H. Johnson, Rams	0	1	0	0	1	Novacek, St.L.	1	0	0	0	0
S. Johnson, Rams	2	0	0	0	0	Oates, Giants	0	1	0	0	1
T. Johnson, Giants	0	0	1	0	1	Ori, Minn.	0	2	0	0	2
V. Johnson, N.O.	0	0	1	0	1	Owens, Rams	0	0	1	0	1
C. Jones, Giants	1	0	0	−18	0	Paige, Det.	0	0	1	0	1
D. Jones, Dall.	0	0	2	26	2	S. Payton, Chi.	1	0	0	0	0
E.L. Jones, Dall.	0	0	1	0	1	W. Payton, Chi.	5	0	0	0	0
Jones, Det.	2	0	0	0	0	Penn, Dall.	0	0	1	0	1
M. Jones, N.O.	1	0	0	0	0	Perry, Chi.	1	0	0	0	0
Jones, T.B.	0	0	1	8	1	Pitts, Phil.	0	0	4	21	4
Jordan, T.B.	0	1	0	0	1	Pointer, G.B.	0	0	1	0	1
Jordan, Minn.	1	0	0	0	0	Quick, Phil.	3	1	0	0	1
Joyner, Phil.	0	0	2	18	2	Quinn, T.B.	0	0	1	0	1
Junior, St.L.	1	0	2	5	2	Rafferty, Dall.	0	1	0	0	1
Kab, Det.	0	1	0	0	1	Randle, T.B.	0	0	1	0	1
Kamana, Atl.	1	0	0	0	0	Rathman, S.F.	1	0	0	0	0
Keever, S.F.	0	0	1	0	1	Reaves, T.B.	1	0	0	0	0

Player—Team	Fum.	Own Rec.	Opp. Rec.	Yds.	Tot. Rec.
Renfro, Dall.	1	0	0	0	0
Rice, Minn.	1	1	0	0	1
Rice, S.F.	2	1	0	0	1
Richardson, Minn.	1	0	0	0	0
R. Richardson, Rams	0	0	1	0	1
Ricks, T.B.	3	2	0	0	2
Riggs, Atl.	4	1	0	0	1
Risher, G.B.	4	1	0	0	1
Robinson, Phil.	1	1	0	0	1
Robinson, Det.	0	0	2	0	2
Rodenberger, N.O.	0	1	0	0	1
Rodgers, S.F.	1	0	0	0	0
Rogers, Wash.	2	0	0	0	0
Rohrer, Dall.	0	0	2	0	2
Rouson, Giants	3	1	0	0	1
Rubbert, Wash.	1	0	0	−2	0
Rutledge, Rams	1	0	0	0	0
Rutledge, Giants	7	3	0	−3	3
Saindon, Atl.	0	1	0	6	1
Sanders, Chi.	1	0	0	0	0
Sargent, St.L.	1	0	0	0	0
Schroeder, Wash.	5	0	0	0	0
Scott, G.B.	2	2	0	0	2
V. Scott, Dall.	0	0	1	3	1
Scribner, Minn.	1	0	0	0	0
Settle, Atl.	2	1	0	0	1
Sharpe, St.L.	0	1	0	0	1
Simmons, Phil.	0	0	1	0	1
Simms, Giants	4	1	0	0	1
Singletary, Chi.	0	0	1	0	1
J.T. Smith, St.L.	2	0	0	0	0
J. Smith, T.B.	2	0	0	0	0
Le. Smith, St.L.	0	0	1	29	1
P. Smith, Rams	1	0	0	0	0
Smith, Chi.	0	1	0	0	1
Snyder, Dall.	1	0	0	0	0
Solomon, Minn.	0	0	1	33	1
Spagnola, Phil.	2	0	0	0	0
Stamps, Atl.	1	1	0	0	1
Stanley, G.B.	5	3	0	0	3
Stensrud, T.B.	0	0	1	3	1
Sterling, G.B.	1	0	0	0	0
Stills, G.B.	0	1	0	0	1
Studwell, Minn.	0	0	1	0	1
Sully, Det.	0	0	1	0	1
Sutton, Rams	0	0	2	0	2
R. Sutton, N.O.	0	0	1	0	1
Sweeney, Dall.	0	1	0	0	1
Swilling, N.O.	0	0	3	1	3
Sydney, S.F.	2	0	0	0	0
Tamburello, Phil.	0	1	0	0	1
Tautalatasi, Phil.	1	0	0	0	0
Taylor, S.F.	0	1	0	26	1
Testaverde, T.B.	7	4	0	−3	4
Thomas, Chi.	0	1	0	0	1
H. Thomas, Minn.	0	0	1	0	1
Thomas, Rams	0	1	0	1	1
L. Thomas, G.B.	0	1	1	3	2
Thomasson, Atl.	0	0	1	0	1
Thompson, Det.	0	0	1	0	1
Tinsley, Phil.	3	0	0	0	0
Tomczak, Chi.	6	1	0	0	1
Toney, Phil.	5	3	0	0	3
Tripoli, T.B.	0	0	3	0	3
Truvillion, Det.	1	0	0	0	0
Tuinei, Dall.	0	1	0	0	1
Vann, Rams	0	1	0	0	1
Van Raaphorst, Atl.	1	0	0	0	0
Vital, Wash.	3	0	0	0	0
Walker, N.O.	0	1	0	0	1
H. Walker, Dall.	4	1	0	0	1
Wallace, S.F.	0	1	0	0	1
Walls, T.B.	1	1	0	0	1
Walter, S.F.	0	0	1	0	1
Washington, G.B.	0	1	0	0	1
Waters, Phil.	0	0	2	11	2
Wattelet, N.O.	0	0	1	0	1
Watts, Dall.	0	0	1	0	1
Waymer, N.O.	0	0	3	2	3
Weaver, Atl.	0	0	1	0	1
Weddington, G.B.	0	0	1	0	1
Wells, T.B.	0	0	1	0	1
Wenzel, Phil.	0	1	0	0	1
Whisenhunt, Atl.	1	1	0	0	1
B. White, Dall.	2	0	0	0	0
White, Rams	8	1	0	0	1
D. White, Dall.	9	3	0	−7	3
White, Phil.	0	0	1	70	1
Wilcher, Rams	0	0	1	35	1
Wilder, T.B.	3	2	0	0	2
Wilks, N.O.	0	0	1	10	1
Willhite, G.B.	2	0	0	0	0
D. Williams, Wash.	3	0	0	0	0
J. Williams, Det.	0	0	2	0	2
P. Williams, Giants	0	0	2	1	2
Williams, Dall.	0	0	1	0	1
V. Williams, Giants	2	2	0	0	2
Wilson, Atl.	0	0	1	0	1
W. Wilson, Minn.	3	0	0	−3	0
W. Wilson, Wash.	1	1	0	0	1
Wojciechowski, Chi.	0	1	0	0	1
Womack, Minn.	0	1	0	0	1
Woodberry, Wash.	0	0	1	0	1
Woods, T.B.	1	0	2	14	2
Woolfolk, Det.	1	0	0	0	0
Word, N.O.	1	1	0	0	1
Wright, T.B.	1	1	0	0	1
Wright, G.B.	3	1	0	−4	1
Yarber, Wash.	1	0	0	0	0
Young, St.L.	0	0	3	0	3
Young, Phil.	0	1	1	20	2
Zimmerman, Minn.	0	1	0	4	1
Zorn, T.B.	3	2	0	0	2

Touchdowns: Green, Wash.; Jackson, St.L.; Joyner, Phil.; King, Det.; McAdoo, St.L.; Moore, Atl.; Moss, T.B.; P. Noga, St.L.; Le. Smith, St.L.; Taylor, S.F.; Wells, T.B.; White, Phil.; Wilcher, Rams, 1 each.

1987 AFC FIELD GOALS—TEAM

	Made	Att.	Pct.	Long
Indianapolis	27	32	.844	50
Kansas City	21	25	.840	54
Houston	26	32	.813	52
Cincinnati	25	32	.781	46
Seattle	17	22	.773	49
N.Y. Jets	20	26	.769	42
Pittsburgh	22	29	.759	52
Miami	12	16	.750	48
Denver	21	29	.724	51
Cleveland	21	31	.677	48
L.A. Raiders	19	30	.633	48
Buffalo	12	20	.600	45
New England	16	28	.571	50
San Diego	16	28	.571	47
Conference Totals	275	380	....	54
Conference Average	19.6	27.1	.724	....

1987 NFC FIELD GOALS—TEAM

	Made	Att.	Pct.	Long
Dallas	25	29	.862	50
L.A. Rams	17	21	.810	48
Tampa Bay	19	24	.792	50
New Orleans	33	42	.786	52
Green Bay	21	29	.724	48
Atlanta	12	17	.706	50
San Francisco	16	23	.696	45
Chicago	22	32	.688	52
Detroit	26	39	.667	53
N.Y. Giants	20	32	.625	53
Washington	18	29	.621	41
Philadelphia	19	31	.613	49
St. Louis	14	27	.519	48
Minnesota	14	29	.483	51
Conference Totals	276	404	....	53
Conference Average	19.7	28.9	.683	....
League Totals	551	784	....	54
League Average	19.7	28.0	.703	....

1987 AFC FIELD GOALS—INDIVIDUAL

Kicker and Club	1-19	20-29	30-39	40-49	50 & over	Totals	Avg. Yds. Att.	Avg. Yds. Made	Avg. Yds. Miss	Lg.
Biasucci, Dean	0-0	5-6	12-12	6-7	1-2	24-27	36.4	35.7	42.3	50
Indianapolis	......	.833	1.000	.857	.500	.889				
Lowery, Nick	1-1	4-4	8-10	4-6	2-2	19-23	37.1	35.9	42.5	54
Kansas City	1.000	1.000	.800	.667	1.000	.826				
Leahy, Pat	0-0	11-11	5-6	2-4	0-1	18-22	32.7	29.3	48.3	42
N.Y. Jets	......	1.000	.833	.500	.000	.818				
Anderson, Gary	0-0	8-9	5-5	7-11	2-2	22-27	36.1	35.0	40.6	52
Pittsburgh	......	.889	1.000	.636	1.000	.815				
Breech, Jim	0-0	6-7	12-12	6-11	0-0	24-30	34.9	33.3	41.5	46
Cincinnati	......	.857	1.000	.545	......	.800				
Zendejas, Tony	2-2	5-5	4-6	8-12	1-1	20-26	36.5	34.6	42.8	52
Houston	1.000	1.000	.667	.667	1.000	.769				
Johnson, Norm	0-0	7-7	4-7	4-5	0-1	15-20	35.6	33.3	42.4	49
Seattle	......	1.000	.571	.800	.000	.750				
Karlis, Rich	0-0	9-9	4-6	4-7	1-3	18-25	36.4	33.3	44.4	51
Denver	......	1.000	.667	.571	.333	.720				
Norwood, Scott	0-0	3-4	4-6	3-5	0-0	10-15	36.0	35.4	37.2	45
Buffalo	......	.750	.667	.600	......	.667				
Bahr, Chris	0-0	6-6	10-13	3-10	0-0	19-29	35.7	32.7	41.3	48
L.A. Raiders	......	1.000	.769	.300	......	.655				
Jaeger, Jeff	0-0	6-6	3-6	5-9	0-1	14-22	36.9	33.1	43.5	48
Cleveland	......	1.000	.500	.556	.000	.636				
Abbott, Vince	0-0	2-3	9-10	2-6	0-3	13-22	38.5	34.8	43.9	47
San Diego	......	.667	.900	.333	.000	.591				
Franklin, Tony	0-0	5-5	6-11	3-7	1-3	15-26	37.8	34.5	42.3	50
New England	......	1.000	.545	.429	.333	.577				

Kicker and Club	1-19	20-29	30-39	40-49	50 & over	Totals	Avg. Yds. Att.	Avg. Yds. Made	Avg. Yds. Miss	Lg.
Diettrich, John	0-0	2-2	1-1	3-3	0-0	6-6	36.8	36.8	0.0	45
Houston	......	1.000	1.000	1.000	......	1.000				
Hagler, Scott	0-0	2-2	0-0	0-0	0-0	2-2	22.0	22.0	0.0	24
Seattle	......	1.000	......	......	......	1.000				
Hamrick, James	0-0	1-1	0-0	1-1	0-0	2-2	32.5	32.5	0.0	40
Kansas City	......	1.000	......	1.000	......	1.000				
Reveiz, Fuad	1-1	2-2	2-2	4-6	0-0	9-11	38.2	36.3	46.5	48
Miami	1.000	1.000	1.000	.667	......	.818				
Bahr, Matt	0-0	2-2	2-3	0-0	0-0	4-5	29.0	27.0	37.0	31
Cleveland	......	1.000	.667	......	......	.800				
Beecher, Willie	1-1	0-0	1-1	1-2	0-0	3-4	35.5	31.0	40.0	40
Miami	1.000	......	1.000	.500	......	.750				
Clendenen, Mike	0-0	1-1	2-2	0-1	0-0	3-4	33.5	31.3	40.0	35
Denver	......	1.000	1.000	.000	......	.750				
Franco, Brian	0-0	3-3	0-1	0-0	0-0	3-4	28.0	25.0	37.0	28
Cleveland	......	1.000	.000	......	......	.750				
Tiffin, Van*	0-0	1-1	1-2	2-3	1-1	5-7	38.7	38.8	38.5	50
Tampa Bay-Miami	......	1.000	.500	.667	1.000	.714				
Jordan, Steve	0-0	1-1	2-2	0-2	0-0	3-5	36.0	32.0	42.0	36
Indianapolis	......	1.000	1.000	.000	......	.600				
Gaffney, Jeff	0-0	3-3	0-3	0-0	0-0	3-6	29.3	24.0	34.7	27
San Diego	......	1.000	.000	......	......	.500				
Manca, Massimo	0-0	1-1	0-0	0-1	0-0	1-2	36.5	28.0	45.0	28
Cincinnati	......	1.000	......	.000	......	.500				
Ragusa, Pat	0-0	1-1	1-2	0-1	0-0	2-4	33.3	27.0	39.5	34
N.Y. Jets	......	1.000	.500	.000	......	.500				
Schubert, Eric	0-0	1-1	0-0	0-1	0-0	1-2	31.5	23.0	40.0	23
New England	......	1.000	......	.000	......	.500				
Schlopy, Todd	0-0	1-1	1-3	0-1	0-0	2-5	33.4	29.0	36.3	31
Buffalo	......	1.000	.333	.000	......	.400				
Hardy, David	0-0	0-0	0-1	0-0	0-0	0-1	34.0	0.0	34.0	—
L.A. Raiders	......	......	.000	......	......	.000				
Trout, David	0-0	0-1	0-1	0-0	0-0	0-2	61.0	0.0	61.0	—
Pittsburgh	......	.000	.000	......	......	.000				
Conference Totals	5-5	98-104	98-132	66-120	8-19	275-380	35.7	33.4	41.8	54
	1.000	.942	.742	.550	.421	.724				

*Includes record with Tampa Bay.

1987 NFC FIELD GOALS—INDIVIDUAL

Kicker and Club	1-19	20-29	30-39	40-49	50 & over	Totals	Avg. Yds. Att.	Avg. Yds. Made	Avg. Yds. Miss	Lg.
Ruzek, Roger	0-0	8-8	6-7	8-10	0-0	22-25	35.8	34.9	42.7	49
Dallas	......	1.000	.857	.800	......	.880				
Zendejas, Max	0-0	3-3	6-7	7-8	0-1	16-19	37.8	36.8	43.0	48
Green Bay	......	1.000	.857	.875	.000	.842				
Lansford, Mike	1-1	6-6	3-4	7-9	0-1	17-21	36.6	35.2	42.8	48
L.A. Rams	1.000	1.000	.750	.778	.000	.810				
Andersen, Morten	3-3	6-6	9-9	8-12	2-6	28-36	37.6	34.7	48.0	52
New Orleans	1.000	1.000	1.000	.667	.333	.778				
Igwebuike, Donald	0-0	2-2	6-6	6-9	0-1	14-18	41.0	38.8	48.8	48
Tampa Bay	......	1.000	1.000	.667	.000	.778				
Wersching, Ray	0-0	5-5	5-5	3-7	0-0	13-17	35.3	32.5	44.3	45
San Francisco	......	1.000	1.000	.429	......	.765				
Haji-Sheikh, Ali	0-0	5-5	6-10	2-4	0-0	13-19	33.5	31.6	37.5	41
Washington	......	1.000	.600	.500	......	.684				
Butler, Kevin	0-0	11-11	5-5	1-6	2-6	19-28	36.9	31.3	48.8	52
Chicago	......	1.000	1.000	.167	.333	.679				
Allegre, Raul	1-1	7-8	4-5	3-9	2-4	17-27	36.6	33.5	41.9	53
N.Y. Giants	1.000	.875	.800	.333	.500	.630				
Murray, Ed	1-1	6-6	7-12	5-11	1-2	20-32	37.0	34.4	41.4	53
Detroit	1.000	1.000	.583	.455	.500	.625				
McFadden, Paul	1-1	3-4	6-10	6-9	0-2	16-26	38.0	35.8	41.7	49
Philadelphia	1.000	.750	.600	.667	.000	.615				
Del Greco, Al	0-0	3-5	4-6	2-4	0-0	9-15	35.3	34.1	37.2	47
G.B.-St. Louis	......	.600	.667	.500	......	.600				
Nelson, Chuck	0-0	10-12	2-4	0-6	1-2	13-24	33.7	28.8	39.5	51
Minnesota	......	.833	.500	.000	.500	.542				
Gallery, Jim	0-0	4-5	2-7	3-7	0-0	9-19	36.1	33.9	38.1	48
St. Louis	......	.800	.286	.429	......	.474				

Non-Qualifiers (Fewer than 15 attempts)

Atkinson, Jess	0-0	1-1	0-0	0-0	0-0	1-1	27.0	27.0	0.0	27
Washington		1.000				1.000				
Cofer, Mike	0-0	1-1	0-0	0-0	0-0	1-1	27.0	27.0	0.0	27
New Orleans		1.000				1.000				
Prindle, Mike	0-0	3-3	3-3	0-1	0-0	6-7	30.4	28.5	42.0	35
Detroit		1.000	1.000	.000		.857				
Kempf, Florian	0-0	1-1	1-2	2-2	0-0	4-5	35.0	35.5	33.0	48
New Orleans		1.000	.500	1.000		.800				
Davis, Greg	0-0	1-1	1-1	1-2	0-0	3-4	37.3	34.7	45.0	42
Atlanta		1.000	1.000	.500		.750				
Lashar, Tim	0-0	3-3	0-0	0-1	0-0	3-4	29.3	25.0	42.0	27
Chicago		1.000		.000		.750				
Zendejas, Luis	0-0	0-0	1-1	1-2	1-1	3-4	44.0	42.3	49.0	50
Dallas			1.000	.500	1.000	.750				
Luckhurst, Mick	1-1	1-1	2-2	3-5	2-4	9-13	41.4	39.2	46.3	50
Atlanta	1.000	1.000	1.000	.600	.500	.692				
Ariri, Obed	1-1	1-1	1-1	0-2	0-0	3-5	33.0	26.7	42.5	39
Washington	1.000	1.000	1.000	.000		.600				
Benyola, George	0-0	2-2	0-1	1-2	0-0	3-5	32.8	29.0	38.5	45
N.Y. Giants		1.000	.000	.500		.600				
Jacobs, Dave	0-0	1-1	0-1	2-3	0-0	3-5	38.2	37.0	40.0	44
Philadelphia		1.000	.000	.667		.600				
Brockhaus, Jeff	0-0	2-3	1-2	0-1	0-0	3-6	31.3	27.0	35.7	39
San Francisco		.667	.500	.000		.500				
Cox, Steve	0-0	0-0	0-0	1-1	0-1	1-2	53.5	40.0	67.0	40
Washington				1.000	.000	.500				
Staurovsky, Jason	0-0	1-2	0-0	0-1	0-0	1-3	30.0	24.0	33.0	24
St. Louis		.500		.000		.333				
Dawson, Dale	0-0	0-0	1-2	0-3	0-0	1-5	39.4	34.0	40.8	34
Minnesota			.500	.000		.200				
Toibin, Brendan	0-0	0-0	0-1	0-1	0-0	0-2	39.5	0.0	39.5	....
Washington			.000	.000		.000				
Conference Totals	9-9	98-107	83-116	74-140	12-32	276-404	36.5	34.0	42.0	53
	1.000	.916	.716	.529	.375	.683				
League Totals	14-14	196-211	181-248	140-260	20-51	551-784	36.1	33.7	41.9	54
	1.000	.929	.730	.538	.392	.703				

CLUB RANKINGS BY YARDS

	OFFENSE			DEFENSE		
	Total	Rush	Pass	Total	Rush	Pass
Atlanta	28	28	22	28	28	18
Buffalo	16	17	18	12	22	9
Chicago	12	13	12	2	*1	7
Cincinnati	5	4	9	8	8	14
Cleveland	9	21	5	3	2	8
Dallas	11	16	11	20	6	27
Denver	2	12	3	9	20	5
Detroit	26	25	17	24	23	19
Green Bay	22	18	25	14	18	13
Houston	8	14	7	17	17	17
Indianapolis	13	6	19	6	15	3
Kansas City	24	19	26	27	27	22
L.A. Raiders	7	2	13	5	7	2
L.A. Rams	19	8	27	21	12	26
Miami	4	23	*1	26	25	21
Minnesota	15	11	20	10	11	16
New England	23	20	24	11	14	15
New Orleans	14	3	21	4	3	6
N.Y. Giants	18	24	10	7	13	10
N.Y. Jets	20	22	16	19	16	20
Philadelphia	10	9	14	23	9	28
Pittsburgh	25	5	28	13	4	23
St. Louis	6	15	6	25	19	25
San Diego	21	27	8	15	24	4
San Francisco	*1	*1	2	*1	5	*1
Seattle	17	10	23	22	26	12
Tampa Bay	27	26	15	16	21	11
Washington	3	7	4	18	10	24

*League leader.

TAKEAWAYS/GIVEAWAYS

AMERICAN FOOTBALL CONFERENCE

	Takeaways			Giveaways			Net
	Int.	Fum.	Total	Int.	Fum.	Total	Diff.
Denver	28	19	47	19	17	36	+11
Indianapolis	20	25	45	16	18	34	+11
New England	21	21	42	18	13	31	+11
Pittsburgh	27	17	44	25	8	33	+11
Cleveland	23	13	36	12	17	29	+ 7
Seattle	17	21	38	21	15	36	+ 2
Houston	23	14	37	23	14	37	0
Los Angeles Raiders	13	15	28	18	13	31	− 3
New York Jets	18	11	29	15	19	34	− 5
Miami	16	16	32	20	17	37	− 5
Cincinnati	14	12	26	20	12	32	− 6
Buffalo	17	14	31	19	24	43	−12
Kansas City	11	17	28	17	24	41	−13
San Diego	13	15	28	23	20	43	−15

NATIONAL FOOTBALL CONFERENCE

	Takeaways			Giveaways			Net
	Int.	Fum.	Total	Int.	Fum.	Total	Diff.
New Orleans	30	18	48	12	16	28	+20
Philadelphia	21	27	48	16	19	35	+13
San Francisco	25	13	38	14	12	26	+12
Green Bay	18	24	42	17	18	35	+ 7
St. Louis	14	19	33	15	12	27	+ 6
Tampa Bay	16	20	36	17	14	31	+ 5
Minnesota	26	11	37	23	10	33	+ 4
Dallas	23	20	43	20	20	40	+ 3
Washington	23	11	34	18	19	37	− 3
Detroit	19	13	32	26	11	37	− 5
Los Angeles Rams	16	11	27	18	15	33	− 6
New York Giants	20	14	34	22	20	42	− 8
Chicago	13	11	24	24	20	44	−20
Atlanta	15	12	27	32	17	49	−22

CLUB LEADERS

	Offense	Defense
First Downs	San Francisco 357	San Francisco 250
Rushing	San Francisco 134	Chicago 77
Passing	San Francisco 202	San Francisco 132
Penalty	Chicago 42	Washington 15
Rushes	New Orleans 569	New Orleans 388
Net Yards Gained	San Francisco 2297	Chicago 1413
Average Gain	Raiders 4.6	Chicago 3.4
Passes Attempted	Miami 584	Raiders 425
Completed	Miami 338	Raiders & San Francisco 224
Percent Completed	San Francisco 64.3	San Francisco 48.0
Total Yards Gained	Miami 3977	San Francisco 2771
Times Sacked	Miami 13	Chicago 70
Yards Lost	Miami 101	Chicago 484
Net Yards Gained	Miami 3876	San Francisco 2484
Net Yards per Pass Play	San Francisco 7.08	Chicago 4.86
Yards Gained per Completion	Washington 15.05	New York Giants 11.21
Combined Net Yards Gained	San Francisco 5987	San Francisco 4095
Percent Total Yards Rushing	Pittsburgh 48.6	Philadelphia 31.3
Percent Total Yards Passing	San Diego 71.5	Atlanta 53.7
Ball Control Plays	Philadelphia 1101	Cleveland 902
Average Yards per Play	San Francisco 5.7	Chicago 4.3
Average Time of Possession	New Orleans 34:01	—
Third Down Efficiency	Seattle 48.7	San Francisco 28.9
Interceptions		New Orleans 30
Yards Returned		Denver 403
Returned for TD		Pittsburgh 5
Punts	Philadelphia 102	
Yards Punted	Philadelphia 3770	
Average Yards per Punt	San Diego 42.0	
Punt Returns	Washington 56	Cleveland 17
Yards Returned	Washington 615	Cleveland 93
Average Yards per Return	St. Louis 12.5	New York Jets 4.9
Returned for TD	Chicago & N.Y. Jets 2	
Kickoff Returns	Atlanta 79	Buffalo 43
Yards Returned	Atlanta 1700	Buffalo 679
Average Yards per Return	Atlanta 21.5	Buffalo 15.8
Returned for TD	Kansas City 2	
Total Points Scored	San Francisco 459	Indianapolis 238
Total TDs	San Francisco 59	Cleveland & San Fran. 26
TDs Rushing	Minn. & N.O. 20	Chicago 5
TDs Passing	San Francisco 44	San Francisco 13
TDs on Returns and Recoveries	Pittsburgh & Rams 7	Buffalo & New York Jets 1
Extra Points	San Francisco 55	Indianapolis & San Fran. 25
Safeties	Three with 2	
Field Goals Made	New Orleans 33	St. Louis 11
Field Goals Attempted	New Orleans 42	New Orleans & St. Louis 18
Percent Successful	Dallas 86.2	Indianapolis 57.7

1987 NFL TEAM-BY-TEAM STATISTICAL SUMMARY

AMERICAN FOOTBALL CONFERENCE

OFFENSE

	Buff.	Cin.	Clev.	Den.	Hou.	Ind.	K.C.	Raid.	Mia.	N.E.	N.Y.J.	Pitt.	S.D.	Sea.
First Downs	294	319	310	331	294	285	265	300	331	266	292	263	264	301
Rushing	111	130	110	132	118	122	97	107	109	84	97	114	68	120
Passing	151	159	171	173	150	138	141	158	197	158	169	126	175	154
Penalty	32	30	29	26	26	25	27	35	25	24	26	23	21	27
Rushes	465	538	474	510	486	497	419	475	408	513	458	517	396	496
Net Yards Gained	1840	2164	1745	1970	1923	2143	1799	2197	1662	1771	1671	2144	1308	2023
Average Gain	4.0	4.0	3.7	3.9	4.0	4.3	4.3	4.6	4.1	3.5	3.6	4.1	3.3	4.1
Average Yards per Game	122.7	144.3	116.3	131.3	128.2	142.9	119.9	146.5	110.8	118.1	111.4	142.9	87.2	134.9
Passes Attempted	516	475	482	530	482	447	432	457	584	440	517	429	516	405
Completed	292	255	291	285	240	255	236	247	338	236	302	198	303	237
Percent Completed	56.6	53.7	60.4	53.8	49.8	57.0	54.6	54.0	57.9	53.6	58.4	46.2	58.7	58.5
Total Yards Gained	3246	3468	3625	3874	3534	3042	2985	3429	3977	2929	3402	2464	3602	3028
Times Sacked	37	32	29	30	30	24	48	53	13	33	66	27	39	36
Yards Lost	345	255	170	220	234	190	366	359	101	246	443	198	322	316
Net Yards Gained	2901	3213	3455	3654	3300	2852	2619	3070	3876	2683	2959	2266	3280	2712
Average Yards per Game	193.4	214.2	230.3	243.6	220.0	190.1	174.6	204.7	258.4	178.9	197.3	151.1	218.7	180.8
Net Yards per Pass Play	5.25	6.34	6.76	6.53	6.45	6.06	5.46	6.02	6.49	5.67	5.08	4.97	5.91	6.15
Yards Gained per Completion	11.12	13.60	12.46	13.59	14.73	11.93	12.65	13.88	11.77	12.41	11.26	12.44	11.89	12.78
Combined Net Yards Gained	4741	5377	5200	5624	5223	4995	4418	5267	5538	4454	4630	4410	4588	4735
Percent Total Yards Rushing	38.8	40.2	33.6	35.0	36.8	42.9	40.7	41.7	30.0	39.8	36.1	48.6	28.5	42.7
Percent Total Yards Passing	61.2	59.8	66.4	65.0	63.2	57.1	59.3	58.3	70.0	60.2	63.9	51.4	71.5	57.3
Average Yards per Game	316.1	358.5	346.7	374.9	348.2	333.0	294.5	351.1	369.2	296.9	308.7	294.0	305.9	315.7
Ball Control Plays	1018	1045	985	1070	998	968	899	985	1005	986	1041	973	951	937
Average Yards per Play	4.7	5.1	5.3	5.3	5.2	5.2	4.9	5.3	5.5	4.5	4.4	4.5	4.8	5.1
Average Time of Possession	28:41	30:24	31:44	31:52	30:17	30:10	27:11	30:45	29:43	29:37	30:28	29:45	28:08	30:35
Third Down Efficiency	37.0	37.5	41.6	47.1	35.1	34.8	40.1	37.5	47.5	37.3	40.6	39.7	30.1	48.7

AFC OFFENSE—Continued

	Buff.	Cin.	Clev.	Den.	Hou.	Ind.	K.C.	Raid.	Mia.	N.E.	N.Y.J.	Pitt.	S.D.	Sea.
Had Intercepted	19	20	12	19	23	16	17	18	20	18	15	25	23	21
Yards Opponents Returned	177	336	173	362	225	181	141	371	298	160	210	330	266	146
Returned by Opponents for TD	0	2	2	2	1	1	0	2	2	2	0	1	1	0
Punts	83	73	57	65	75	78	69	71	63	89	82	82	84	61
Yards Punted	3173	2995	2102	2595	2929	2941	2789	2796	2424	3350	3046	3297	3529	2370
Average Yards per Punt	38.2	41.0	36.9	39.9	39.1	37.7	40.4	39.4	38.5	37.6	37.1	40.2	42.0	38.9
Punt Returns	31	34	44	48	37	38	32	44	37	25	42	36	45	32
Yards Returned	232	293	487	486	249	210	346	356	290	213	497	244	508	322
Average Yards per Return	7.5	8.6	11.1	10.1	6.7	5.5	10.8	8.1	7.8	8.5	11.8	6.8	11.3	10.1
Returned for TD	0	0	0	1	0	0	1	1	0	0	2	0	1	0
Kickoff Returns	45	67	48	46	67	55	70	60	54	48	65	56	62	64
Yards Returned	872	1161	846	952	1225	1115	1437	1174	952	901	1221	1060	1137	1236
Average Yards per Return	19.4	17.3	17.6	20.7	18.3	20.3	20.5	19.6	17.6	18.8	18.8	18.9	18.3	19.3
Returned for TD	0	0	0	0	0	0	2	0	0	0	0	0	0	0
Fumbles	41	29	33	29	32	36	41	24	37	36	33	37	38	31
Lost	24	12	17	17	14	18	24	13	17	13	19	8	20	15
Out of Bounds	0	0	1	0	3	5	3	1	2	0	1	1	1	0
Own Recovered for TD	0	0	0	0	0	0	0	0	0	0	0	0	0	0
Opponent Recovered by	14	12	13	19	14	25	17	15	16	21	11	17	15	21
Opponent Recovered for TD	3	0	2	0	1	1	1	0	2	1	1	2	1	0
Penalties	94	99	100	95	114	90	108	114	76	64	135	105	98	79
Yards Penalized	762	791	857	812	1029	742	861	1048	634	506	1055	801	743	668
Total Points Scored	270	285	390	379	345	300	273	301	362	320	334	285	253	371
Total TDs	33	30	47	45	38	31	30	35	47	39	39	31	29	46
TDs Rushing	9	13	16	18	12	14	7	13	16	12	17	11	11	13
TDs Passing	21	17	27	24	24	16	17	19	29	22	18	13	13	31
TDs on Returns and Recoveries	3	0	4	3	2	1	6	3	2	5	4	7	5	2
Extra Points	32	28	45	44	37	31	30	34	44	38	38	31	27	44
Safeties	2	1	0	1	1	1	0	0	0	0	1	1	2	0
Field Goals Made	12	25	21	21	26	27	21	19	12	16	20	22	16	17
Field Goals Attempted	20	32	31	29	32	32	25	30	16	28	26	29	28	22
Percent Successful	60.0	78.1	67.7	72.4	81.3	84.4	84.0	63.3	75.0	57.1	76.9	75.9	57.1	77.3

AMERICAN FOOTBALL CONFERENCE

DEFENSE

	Buff.	Cin.	Clev.	Den.	Hou.	Ind.	K.C.	Raid.	Mia.	N.E.	N.Y.J.	Pitt.	S.D.	Sea.
First Downs	297	286	251	277	287	276	344	267	314	293	300	289	280	297
Rushing	114	99	86	103	98	97	139	98	115	112	117	94	120	133
Passing	162	169	134	148	153	161	172	135	176	159	153	170	136	148
Penalty	21	18	31	26	36	18	33	34	23	22	30	25	24	16
Rushes	541	441	401	454	446	463	535	469	498	490	476	455	522	472
Net Yards Gained	2052	1641	1433	2017	1848	1790	2333	1637	2198	1778	1835	1610	2171	2201
Average Gain	3.8	3.7	3.6	4.4	4.1	3.9	4.4	3.5	4.4	3.6	3.9	3.5	4.2	4.7
Average Yards per Game	136.8	109.4	95.5	134.5	123.2	119.3	155.5	109.1	146.5	118.5	122.3	107.3	144.7	146.7
Passes Attempted	447	456	467	456	495	501	484	425	494	520	488	481	441	445
Completed	249	267	246	261	266	250	279	224	295	273	260	290	227	255
Percent Completed	55.7	58.6	52.7	57.2	53.7	49.9	57.6	52.7	59.7	52.5	53.3	60.3	51.5	57.3
Total Yards Gained	3121	3359	3088	3040	3416	3073	3473	3088	3430	3438	3412	3506	3080	3196
Times Sacked	34	40	34	31	35	39	26	44	21	43	29	26	45	37
Yards Lost	267	303	257	244	271	313	167	361	183	339	206	196	298	238
Net Yards Gained	2854	3056	2831	2796	3145	2760	3306	2727	3247	3099	3206	3310	2782	2958
Average Yards per Game	190.3	203.7	188.7	186.4	209.7	184.0	220.4	181.8	216.5	206.6	213.7	220.7	185.5	197.2
Net Yards per Pass Play	5.93	6.16	5.65	5.74	5.93	5.11	6.48	5.81	6.30	5.50	6.20	6.53	5.72	6.14
Yards Gained per Completion	12.53	12.58	12.55	11.65	12.84	12.29	12.45	13.79	11.63	12.59	13.12	12.09	13.57	12.53
Combined Net Yards Gained	4906	4697	4264	4813	4993	4550	5639	4364	5445	4877	5041	4920	4953	5159
Percent Total Yards Rushing	41.8	34.9	33.6	41.9	37.0	39.3	41.4	37.5	40.4	36.5	36.4	32.7	43.8	42.7
Percent Total Yards Passing	58.2	65.1	66.4	58.1	63.0	60.7	58.6	62.5	59.6	63.5	63.6	67.3	56.2	57.3
Average Yards per Game	327.1	313.1	284.3	320.9	332.9	303.3	375.9	290.9	363.0	325.1	336.1	328.0	330.2	343.9
Ball Control Plays	1022	937	902	941	976	1003	1045	938	1013	1053	993	962	1008	954
Average Yards per Play	4.8	5.0	4.7	5.1	5.1	4.5	5.4	4.7	5.4	4.6	5.1	5.1	4.9	5.4
Average Time of Possession	31:19	29:36	28:16	28:09	29:43	29:50	32:49	29:15	30:17	30:23	29:32	30:15	31:52	29:25
Third Down Efficiency	37.3	40.7	35.5	35.0	32.3	39.0	44.7	39.1	45.5	36.8	38.6	34.4	34.9	43.4
Intercepted by	17	14	23	28	23	20	11	13	16	21	18	27	13	17
Yards Returned by	93	187	366	403	274	212	140	178	135	307	239	336	291	289
Returned for TD	0	0	2	2	1	0	0	2	0	2	0	5	2	1

AFC DEFENSE—Continued

	Buff.	Cin.	Clev.	Den.	Hou.	Ind.	K.C.	Raid.	Mia.	N.E.	N.Y.J.	Pitt.	S.D.	Sea.
Punts	88	75	81	75	77	82	56	78	71	77	80	70	89	63
Yards Punted	3229	3017	3035	3158	3033	3048	2260	3321	2753	2937	3073	2741	3694	2465
Average Yards per Punt	36.7	40.2	37.5	42.1	39.4	37.2	40.4	42.6	38.8	38.1	38.4	39.2	41.5	39.1
Punt Returns	35	42	17	34	43	39	43	34	26	41	33	46	43	32
Yards Returned	179	299	93	424	454	376	442	256	141	397	162	395	429	251
Average Yards per Return	5.1	7.1	5.5	12.5	10.6	9.6	10.3	7.5	5.4	9.7	4.9	8.6	10.0	7.8
Returned for TD	0	0	0	2	0	0	0	0	0	0	0	0	1	1
Kickoff Returns	43	62	72	61	57	60	55	59	67	63	54	65	50	67
Yards Returned	679	1145	1343	1168	1177	1068	1263	1136	1222	1130	1013	1083	985	1379
Average Yards per Return	15.8	18.5	18.7	19.1	20.6	17.8	23.0	19.3	18.2	17.9	18.8	16.7	19.7	20.6
Returned for TD	0	0	0	0	0	0	1	0	0	0	0	0	1	1
Fumbles	37	26	26	35	37	43	24	28	32	42	23	41	26	38
Lost	14	12	13	19	14	25	17	15	16	21	11	17	15	21
Out of Bounds	3	1	1	1	2	0	2	3	2	2	0	4	1	0
Own Recovered for TD	0	0	0	0	0	0	0	0	0	0	0	0	0	0
Opponent Recovered by	24	12	17	17	14	18	24	13	17	13	19	8	20	15
Opponent Recovered for TD	1	0	2	0	0	1	3	0	1	2	1	1	1	0
Penalties	103	79	120	96	101	85	112	95	103	110	96	95	107	104
Yards Penalized	840	669	1008	785	874	689	936	652	850	846	881	771	869	890
Total Points Scored	305	370	239	288	349	238	388	289	335	293	360	299	317	314
Total TDs	37	43	26	35	37	28	45	33	42	34	43	34	37	36
TDs Rushing	11	15	7	16	10	6	16	12	18	13	15	8	14	14
TDs Passing	25	24	15	15	25	19	25	18	21	17	27	22	19	20
TDs on Returns and Recoveries	1	4	4	4	2	3	4	3	3	4	1	4	4	2
Extra Points	36	43	26	32	35	25	44	31	41	33	42	31	36	35
Safeties	0	0	3	2	1	1	1	0	0	0	0	2	0	0
Field Goals Made	15	23	17	14	30	15	24	20	14	18	20	20	19	21
Field Goals Attempted	20	26	25	21	36	26	35	29	22	27	29	26	29	26
Percent Successful	75.0	88.5	68.0	66.7	83.3	57.7	68.6	69.0	63.6	66.7	69.0	76.9	65.5	80.8

NATIONAL FOOTBALL CONFERENCE

OFFENSE

	Atl.	Chi.	Dall.	Det.	G.B.	Rams	Minn.	N.O.	N.Y.G.	Phil.	St.L.	S.F.	T.B.	Wash.
First Downs	230	319	293	270	248	276	293	304	266	289	325	357	263	301
Rushing	73	121	93	81	97	118	129	128	80	112	115	134	62	119
Passing	139	156	176	156	133	136	136	151	168	154	189	202	168	153
Penalty	18	42	24	33	18	22	28	25	18	23	21	21	33	29
Rushes	333	485	465	398	464	512	482	569	440	509	462	524	394	500
Net Yards Gained	1298	1954	1865	1435	1801	2097	1983	2190	1457	2027	1873	2237	1365	2102
Average Gain	3.9	4.0	4.0	3.6	3.9	4.1	4.1	3.8	3.3	4.0	4.1	4.3	3.5	4.2
Average Yards per Game	86.5	130.3	124.3	95.7	120.1	139.8	132.2	146.0	97.1	135.1	124.9	149.1	91.0	140.1
Passes Attempted	501	493	500	509	455	420	446	411	499	520	529	501	517	478
Completed	247	272	288	275	234	220	232	227	265	283	305	322	264	247
Percent Completed	49.3	55.2	57.6	54.0	51.4	52.4	52.0	55.2	53.1	54.4	57.7	64.3	51.1	51.7
Total Yards Gained	3108	3420	3594	3150	2977	2750	3185	2987	3645	3561	3850	3955	3377	3718
Times Sacked	46	48	52	26	45	25	52	29	61	72	54	29	43	27
Yards Lost	340	330	403	194	296	196	359	213	443	511	397	205	361	223
Net Yards Gained	2768	3090	3191	2956	2681	2554	2826	2774	3202	3050	3453	3750	3016	3495
Average Yards per Game	184.5	206.0	212.7	197.1	178.7	170.3	188.4	184.9	213.5	203.3	230.2	250.0	201.1	233.0
Net Yards per Pass Play	5.06	5.71	5.78	5.53	5.36	5.74	5.67	6.30	5.72	5.15	5.92	7.08	5.39	6.92
Yards Gained per Completion	12.58	12.57	12.48	11.45	12.72	12.50	13.73	13.16	13.75	12.58	12.62	12.28	12.79	15.05
Combined Net Yards Gained	4066	5044	5056	4391	4482	4651	4809	4964	4659	5077	5326	5987	4381	5597
Percent Total Yards Rushing	31.9	38.7	36.9	32.7	40.2	45.1	41.2	44.1	31.3	39.9	35.2	37.4	31.2	37.6
Percent Total Yards Passing	68.1	61.3	63.1	67.3	59.8	54.9	58.8	55.9	68.7	60.1	64.8	62.6	68.8	62.4
Average Yards per Game	271.1	336.3	337.1	292.7	298.8	310.1	320.6	330.9	310.6	338.5	355.1	399.1	292.1	373.1
Ball Control Plays	680	1026	1017	933	964	957	980	1009	1000	1101	1045	1054	954	1005
Average Yards per Play	4.6	4.9	5.0	4.7	4.6	4.9	4.9	4.9	4.7	4.6	5.1	5.7	4.6	5.6
Average Time of Possession	26:01	31:58	30:41	28:19	29:02	29:59	29:20	34:01	28:20	31:41	30:33	31:43	28:37	30:30
Third Down Efficiency	30.5	35.6	38.7	30.9	31.3	36.8	37.1	44.8	35.0	31.1	37.4	47.8	39.5	40.0

NFC OFFENSE—Continued

	Atl.	Chi.	Dall.	Det.	G.B.	Rams	Minn.	N.O.	N.Y.G.	Phil.	St.L.	S.F.	T.B.	Wash.
Had Intercepted	32	24	20	26	17	18	23	12	22	16	15	14	17	18
Yards Opponent Returned	342	334	279	335	115	226	399	173	164	68	227	258	227	193
Returned by Opponent for TD	2	1	0	2	1	1	3	1	1	0	0	0	0	1
Punts	83	62	84	70	93	77	79	63	91	102	70	68	88	78
Yards Punted	3375	2439	3324	2927	3659	3140	3077	2587	3604	3770	2663	2541	3455	3053
Average Yards per Punt	40.7	39.3	39.6	41.8	39.3	40.8	38.9	41.1	39.6	37.0	38.0	37.4	39.3	39.1
Punt Returns	31	50	41	35	35	40	36	41	55	34	44	34	31	56
Yards Returned	221	484	353	303	245	245	420	468	448	202	550	365	257	615
Average Yards per Return	7.1	9.7	8.6	8.7	7.0	6.1	11.7	11.4	8.1	5.9	12.5	10.7	8.3	11.0
Returned for TD	0	2	0	0	0	0	1	0	0	0	1	1	0	0
Kickoff Returns	79	57	64	71	59	63	71	55	56	66	63	55	56	59
Yards Returned	1700	1193	1295	1428	1032	1282	1421	1147	1128	1112	1317	1144	1037	1139
Average Yards per Return	21.5	20.9	20.2	20.1	17.5	20.3	20.0	20.9	20.1	16.8	20.9	20.8	18.5	19.3
Returned for TD	1	1	0	0	0	1	0	0	0	0	0	1	0	0
Fumbles	27	33	30	29	35	26	28	33	38	44	23	25	35	26
Lost	17	20	20	11	18	15	10	16	20	19	12	12	14	19
Out of Bounds	0	0	0	3	1	2	5	3	4	2	3	0	0	2
Own Recovered for TD	0	0	0	0	0	0	0	0	0	0	0	1	0	0
Opponent Recovered by	12	11	20	13	24	11	11	18	14	27	19	13	19	11
Opponent Recovered for TD	1	0	0	1	0	1	0	0	0	2	4	0	2	1
Penalties	98	103	131	86	135	91	96	107	100	116	101	88	115	82
Yards Penalized	807	821	1091	737	1103	677	814	994	835	919	797	792	894	691
Total Points Scored	205	356	340	269	255	317	336	422	280	337	362	459	286	379
Total TDs	24	42	38	27	28	38	42	46	32	40	46	59	33	47
TDs Rushing	5	13	17	9	13	15	20	20	4	12	15	11	7	18
TDs Passing	17	23	19	16	15	16	21	23	26	26	25	44	22	27
TDs on Returns and Recoveries	2	6	2	2	0	7	1	3	2	2	6	4	4	2
Extra Points	23	38	37	27	24	36	40	43	28	38	44	55	31	43
Safeties	1	0	0	1	0	1	1	2	0	1	0	1	0	0
Field Goals Made	12	22	25	26	21	17	14	33	20	19	14	16	19	18
Field Goals Attempted	17	32	29	39	29	21	29	42	32	31	27	23	24	29
Percent Successful	70.6	68.8	86.2	66.7	72.4	81.0	48.3	78.6	62.5	61.3	51.9	69.6	79.2	62.1

DEFENSE

	Atl.	Chi.	Dall.	Det.	G.B.	Rams	Minn.	N.O.	N.Y.G.	Phil.	St.L.	S.F.	T.B.	Wash.
First Downs	354	261	294	314	296	279	281	270	275	301	306	250	314	296
Rushing	162	77	85	122	118	95	95	81	97	85	116	95	124	104
Passing	164	158	175	162	152	162	159	155	148	186	168	132	163	177
Penalty	28	26	34	30	26	22	27	34	30	30	22	23	27	15
Rushes	600	412	459	504	521	419	440	388	493	428	492	429	500	441
Net Yards Gained	2734	1413	1617	2070	1920	1732	1724	1550	1768	1643	2001	1611	2038	1679
Average Gain	4.6	3.4	3.5	4.1	3.7	4.1	3.9	4.0	3.6	3.8	4.1	3.8	4.1	3.8
Average Yards per Game	182.3	94.2	107.8	138.0	128.0	115.5	114.9	103.3	117.9	109.5	133.4	107.4	135.9	111.9
Passes Attempted	453	507	502	459	469	504	498	489	508	561	490	467	457	527
Completed	243	255	269	259	279	281	278	246	292	305	276	224	271	276
Percent Completed	53.6	50.3	53.6	56.4	59.5	55.8	55.8	50.3	57.5	54.4	56.3	48.0	59.3	52.4
Total Yards Gained	3291	3286	3781	3558	3200	3693	3407	3155	3272	4058	3668	2771	3256	3767
Times Sacked	17	70	51	42	34	38	41	47	55	57	41	37	39	53
Yards Lost	118	484	337	355	197	304	307	355	382	452	285	287	306	424
Net Yards Gained	3173	2802	3444	3203	3003	3389	3100	2800	2890	3606	3383	2484	2949	3343
Average Yards per Game	211.5	186.8	229.6	213.5	200.2	225.9	206.7	186.7	192.7	240.4	225.5	165.6	196.6	222.9
Net Yards per Pass Play	6.75	4.86	6.23	6.39	5.97	6.25	5.75	5.22	5.13	5.83	6.37	4.93	5.95	5.76
Yards Gained per Completion	13.54	12.89	14.06	13.74	11.47	13.14	12.26	12.83	11.21	13.30	13.29	12.37	12.01	13.65
Combined Net Yards Gained	5907	4215	5061	5273	4923	5121	4824	4350	4658	5249	5384	4095	4987	5022
Percent Total Yards Rushing	46.3	33.5	32.0	39.3	39.0	33.8	35.7	35.6	38.0	31.3	37.2	39.3	40.9	33.4
Percent Total Yards Passing	53.7	66.5	68.0	60.7	61.0	66.2	64.3	64.4	62.0	68.7	62.8	60.7	59.1	66.6
Average Yards per Game	393.8	281.0	337.4	351.5	328.2	341.4	321.6	290.0	310.5	349.9	358.9	273.0	332.5	334.8
Ball Control Plays	1070	989	1012	1005	1024	961	979	924	1056	1046	1023	933	996	1021
Average Yards per Play	5.5	4.3	5.0	5.2	4.8	5.3	4.9	4.7	4.4	5.0	5.3	4.4	5.0	4.9
Average Time of Possession	33:59	28:02	29:19	31:41	30:58	30:01	30:40	25:59	31:40	28:19	29:27	28:17	31:23	29:30
Third Down Efficiency	50.9	35.4	43.0	40.3	39.1	37.9	36.9	31.3	32.5	31.9	46.1	28.9	45.0	33.6
Intercepted by	15	13	23	19	18	16	26	30	20	21	14	25	16	23
Yards Returned by	182	69	208	290	220	305	303	280	263	197	167	205	248	329
Returned for TD	0	2	2	1	0	2	0	0	1	0	1	0	2	1

NFC DEFENSE—Continued

	Atl.	Chi.	Dall.	Det.	G.B.	Rams	Minn.	N.O.	N.Y.G.	Phil.	St.L.	S.F.	T.B.	Wash.
Punts	60	86	75	65	77	83	74	73	96	88	74	72	64	91
Yards Punted	2383	3408	3042	2461	3084	3097	2954	2740	3653	3262	3049	2850	2634	3569
Average Yards per Punt	39.7	39.6	40.6	37.9	40.1	37.3	39.9	37.5	38.1	37.1	41.2	39.6	41.2	39.2
Punt Returns	48	26	45	34	54	43	44	29	51	54	36	29	50	37
Yards Returned	541	339	376	177	422	317	424	199	811	469	489	195	621	231
Average Yards per Return	11.3	13.0	8.4	5.2	7.8	7.4	9.6	6.9	15.9	8.7	13.6	6.7	12.4	6.2
Returned for TD	1	1	1	0	0	0	0	0	2	0	1	0	1	0
Kickoff Returns	44	58	65	56	61	57	64	55	68	59	59	76	61	63
Yards Returned	915	1054	1281	1089	1140	1112	1173	1115	1463	1276	1063	1598	1242	1352
Average Yards per Return	20.8	18.2	19.7	19.4	18.7	19.5	18.3	20.3	21.5	21.6	18.0	21.0	20.4	21.5
Returned for TD	1	0	0	0	0	0	0	0	0	0	0	1	0	1
Fumbles	18	37	29	36	42	28	30	31	31	41	34	30	42	22
Lost	12	11	20	13	24	11	11	18	14	27	19	13	20	11
Out of Bounds	2	2	1	1	2	4	0	2	3	0	0	0	0	0
Own Recovered for TD	0	0	0	0	0	1	0	0	0	0	0	0	0	0
Opponent Recovered by	17	20	20	11	18	15	10	16	20	19	11	12	14	19
Opponent Recovered for TD	0	1	1	0	0	1	1	3	0	1	0	2	2	2
Penalties	92	120	100	115	104	100	107	84	97	105	88	80	125	97
Yards Penalized	729	1108	851	907	852	888	964	685	802	830	718	660	926	801
Total Points Scored	436	282	348	384	300	361	335	283	312	380	368	253	360	285
Total TDs	54	33	42	43	31	43	38	35	35	47	48	26	44	33
TDs Rushing	24	5	19	18	15	8	9	6	14	16	16	8	18	10
TDs Passing	26	24	21	23	14	31	24	25	17	29	30	13	23	19
TDs on Returns and Recoveries	4	4	2	2	2	4	5	4	4	2	2	5	3	4
Extra Points	51	30	39	42	29	40	35	35	33	44	45	25	42	30
Safeties	2	0	0	0	2	0	1	1	0	0	1	0	0	0
Field Goals Made	19	18	19	28	27	21	24	12	23	18	11	24	18	19
Field Goals Attempted	30	31	29	34	36	24	31	18	34	29	18	35	30	28
Percent Successful	63.3	58.1	65.5	82.4	75.0	87.5	77.4	66.7	67.6	62.1	61.1	68.6	60.0	67.9

1987 AFC, NFC, AND NFL SUMMARY

	AFC Offense Total	AFC Offense Average	AFC Defense Total	AFC Defense Average	NFC Offense Total	NFC Offense Average	NFC Defense Total	NFC Defense Average	NFL Total	NFL Average
First Downs	4115	293.9	4058	289.9	4034	288.1	4091	292.2	8149	291.0
Rushing	1519	108.5	1525	108.9	1462	104.4	1456	104.0	2981	106.5
Passing	2220	158.6	2176	155.4	2217	158.4	2261	161.5	4437	158.5
Penalty	376	26.9	357	25.5	355	25.4	374	26.7	731	26.1
Rushes	6652	475.1	6663	475.9	6537	466.9	6526	466.1	13,189	471.0
Net Yards Gained	26,360	1882.9	26,544	1896.0	25,684	1834.6	25,500	1821.4	52,044	1858.7
Average Gain	......	4.0	......	4.0	......	3.9	......	3.9	......	3.9
Average Yards per Game	......	125.5	......	126.4	......	122.3	......	121.4	......	123.9
Passes Attempted	6712	479.4	6600	471.4	6779	484.2	6891	492.2	13,491	481.8
Completed	3715	265.4	3642	260.1	3681	262.9	3754	268.1	7396	264.1
Percent Completed	......	55.3	......	55.2	......	54.3	......	54.5	......	54.8
Total Yards Gained	46,605	3328.9	45,720	3265.7	47,277	3376.9	48,162	3440.1	93,882	3352.9
Times Sacked	497	35.5	484	34.6	609	43.5	622	44.4	1106	39.5
Yards Lost	3765	268.9	3643	260.2	4471	319.4	4593	328.1	8236	294.1
Net Yards Gained	42,840	3060.0	42,077	3005.5	42,806	3057.6	43,569	3112.1	85,646	3058.8
Average Yards per Game	......	204.0	......	200.4	......	203.8	......	207.5	......	203.9
Net Yards per Pass Play	......	5.94	......	5.94	......	5.79	......	5.80	......	5.87
Yards Gained per Completion	......	12.55	......	12.55	......	12.84	......	12.83	......	12.69
Combined Net Yards Gained	69,200	4942.9	68,621	4901.5	68,490	4892.1	69,069	4933.5	137,690	4917.5
Percent Total Yards Rushing	......	38.1	......	38.7	......	37.5	......	36.9	......	37.8
Percent Total Yards Passing	......	61.9	......	61.3	......	62.5	......	63.1	......	62.2
Average Yards per Game	......	329.5	......	326.8	......	326.1	......	328.9	......	327.8
Ball Control Plays	13,861	990.1	13,747	981.9	13,925	994.6	14,039	1002.8	27,786	992.4
Average Yards per Play	......	5.0	......	5.0	......	4.9	......	4.9	......	5.0
Third Down Efficiency	......	39.6	......	38.4	......	36.9	......	38.1	......	38.3
Interceptions	261	18.6	266	19.0	279	19.9	274	19.6	540	19.3
Yards Returned	3450	246.4	3376	241.1	3266	233.3	3340	238.6	6716	239.9
Returned for TD	17	1.2	16	1.1	12	0.9	13	0.9	29	1.0

1987 AFC, NFC, AND NFL SUMMARY—Continued

	AFC Offense Total	AFC Offense Average	AFC Defense Total	AFC Defense Average	NFC Offense Total	NFC Offense Average	NFC Defense Total	NFC Defense Average	NFL Total	NFL Average
Punts	1032	73.7	1062	75.9	1108	79.1	1078	77.0	2140	76.4
Yards Punted	40,336	2881.1	41,764	2983.1	43,614	3115.3	42,186	3013.3	83,950	2998.2
Average Yards per Punt	……	39.1	……	39.3	……	39.4	……	39.1	……	39.2
Punt Returns	525	37.5	508	36.3	563	40.2	580	41.4	1088	38.9
Yards Returned	4733	338.1	4298	307.0	5176	369.7	5611	400.8	9909	353.9
Average Yards per Return	……	9.0	……	8.5	……	9.2	……	9.7	……	9.1
Returned for TD	6	0.4	4	0.3	5	0.4	7	0.5	11	0.4
Kickoff Returns	807	57.6	835	59.6	874	62.4	846	60.4	1681	60.0
Yards Returned	15,289	1092.1	15,791	1127.9	17,375	1241.1	16,873	1205.2	32,664	1166.6
Average Yards per Return	……	18.9	……	18.9	……	19.9	……	19.9	……	19.4
Returned for TD	2	0.1	3	0.2	4	0.3	3	0.2	6	0.2
Fumbles	477	34.1	458	32.7	432	30.9	451	32.2	909	32.5
Lost	231	16.5	230	16.4	223	15.9	224	16.0	454	16.2
Out of Bounds	20	1.4	22	1.6	26	1.9	24	1.7	46	1.6
Own Recovered for TD	0	0.0	0	0.0	1	0.1	1	0.1	1	0.0
Opponent Recovered	230	16.4	231	16.5	223	15.9	222	15.9	453	16.2
Opponent Recovered for TD	15	1.1	13	0.9	12	0.9	14	1.0	27	1.0
Penalties	1371	97.9	1406	100.4	1449	103.5	1414	101.0	2820	100.7
Yards Penalized	11,309	807.8	11,560	825.7	11,972	855.1	11,721	837.2	23,281	831.5
Total Points Scored	4468	319.1	4384	313.1	4603	328.8	4687	334.8	9071	324.0
Total TDs	520	37.1	510	36.4	542	38.7	552	39.4	1062	37.9
TDs Rushing	182	13.0	175	12.5	179	12.8	186	13.3	361	12.9
TDs Passing	291	20.8	292	20.9	320	22.9	319	22.8	611	21.8
TDs on Returns and Recoveries	47	3.4	43	3.1	43	3.1	47	3.4	90	3.2
Extra Points	503	35.9	490	35.0	507	36.2	520	37.1	1010	36.1
Safeties	10	0.7	12	0.9	8	0.6	6	0.4	18	0.6
Field Goals Made	275	19.6	270	19.3	276	19.7	281	20.1	551	19.7
Field Goals Attempted	380	27.1	377	26.9	404	28.9	407	29.1	784	28.0
Percent Successful	……	72.4	……	71.6	……	68.3	……	69.0	……	70.3

COACHES WITH 100 CAREER VICTORIES
(Ranked according to career wins)

	Yrs.	REGULAR SEASON				POST-SEASON			CAREER			
		Won	Lost	Tied	Pct.	Won	Lost	Pct.	Won	Lost	Tied	Pct.
George Halas	40	320	148	30	.673	6	3	.667	326	151	30	.673
*Don Shula	25	255	101	6	.713	18	13	.581	273	114	6	.702
*Tom Landry	28	247	149	6	.622	21	18	.538	268	167	6	.615
Curly Lambeau	33	231	133	23	.627	3	2	.600	234	135	43	.626
*Chuck Noll	19	163	114	1	.588	15	7	.682	178	121	1	.595
Paul Brown	21	166	100	6	.621	4	9	.308	170	109	6	.607
Bud Grant	18	158	96	5	.620	10	13	.435	168	109	5	.605
Steve Owen	23	151	100	17	.595	3	8	.273	154	108	17	.582
*Chuck Knox	15	139	82	1	.628	7	10	.412	146	92	1	.613
Hank Stram	17	131	97	10	.571	5	3	.625	136	100	10	.573
Weeb Ewbank	20	130	129	7	.502	4	1	.800	134	130	7	.507
Sid Gillman	18	122	99	7	.550	1	5	.167	123	104	7	.541
George Allen	12	116	47	5	.705	4	7	.364	120	54	5	.684
Don Coryell	14	111	83	1	.572	3	6	.333	114	89	1	.561
John Madden	10	103	32	7	.750	9	7	.563	112	39	7	.731
Buddy Parker	15	104	75	9	.577	3	2	.600	107	77	9	.578
Vince Lombardi	10	96	34	6	.728	8	2	.800	104	36	6	.733

*Active NFL coaches in 1988.

ACTIVE COACHES CAREER RECORDS
(Ranked according to career percentages)

	Yrs.	REGULAR SEASON				POST-SEASON			CAREER			
		Won	Lost	Tied	Pct.	Won	Lost	Pct.	Won	Lost	Tied	Pct.
Joe Gibbs	7	74	30	0	.712	11	3	.786	85	33	0	.720
Don Shula	25	255	101	6	.713	18	13	.581	273	114	6	.702
Mike Ditka	6	61	27	0	.693	4	3	.571	65	30	0	.684
Dan Reeves	7	66	37	1	.639	4	4	.500	70	41	1	.629
Raymond Berry	4	34	21	0	.618	3	2	.600	37	23	0	.617
Tom Landry	28	247	149	6	.622	21	18	.538	268	167	6	.615
Chuck Knox	15	139	82	1	.628	7	10	.412	146	92	1	.613
Bill Walsh	9	82	53	1	.607	7	4	.636	89	57	1	.609
Marty Schottenheimer	4	34	21	0	.618	2	3	.400	36	24	0	.600
Chuck Noll	19	163	114	1	.588	15	7	.682	178	121	1	.595
Jim Mora	2	19	12	0	.613	0	1	.000	19	13	0	.594
USFL Totals	3	41	12	1	.769	7	1	.875	48	13	1	.782
Ron Meyer	5	30	21	0	.588	0	2	.000	30	23	0	.566
John Robinson	5	46	33	0	.582	2	4	.333	48	37	0	.565
Jerry Burns	2	17	14	0	.548	2	1	.667	19	15	0	.559
Bill Parcells	5	42	36	1	.538	5	2	.714	47	38	1	.552
Joe Walton	5	41	38	0	.519	1	2	.333	42	40	0	.512
Al Saunders	2	11	12	0	.478	0	0	.000	11	12	0	.478
Sam Wyche	4	29	34	0	.460	0	0	.000	29	34	0	.460
Jerry Glanville	3	14	19	0	.424	1	1	.500	15	20	0	.429
Marv Levy	7	40	55	0	.421	0	0	.000	40	55	0	.421
CFL Totals	5	43	31	4	.577	7	3	.700	50	34	4	.591
USFL Totals	1	5	13	0	.278	0	0	.000	5	13	0	.278
Buddy Ryan	2	12	18	1	.403	0	0	.000	12	18	1	.403
Ray Perkins	5	27	45	0	.375	1	1	.500	28	46	0	.378
Gene Stallings	2	11	19	1	.371	0	0	.000	11	19	1	.371
Darryl Rogers	3	16	31	0	.340	0	0	.000	16	31	0	.340
Marion Campbell	7	26	60	1	.305	0	0	.000	26	60	1	.305
Frank Gansz	1	4	11	0	.267	0	0	.000	4	11	0	.267
Lindy Infante	0	0	0	0	.000	0	0	.000	0	0	0	.000
USFL Totals	2	15	21	0	.417	0	0	.000	15	21	0	.417
Mike Shanahan	0	0	0	0	.000	0	0	.000	0	0	0	.000

LEADING NFC ACTIVE PASSERS
(1000 or More Attempts)

	Yrs.	Att.	Comp.	Pct.	Yds.	Avg. Gain	TD	Pct. TD	Int.	Pct. Int.	Pts.
Joe Montana, S.F.	9	3276	2084	63.6	24552	7.49	172	5.3	89	2.7	92.7
Danny White, Dall.	12	2908	1732	59.6	21685	7.46	154	5.3	129	4.4	82.2
Neil Lomax, Phoe.	7	2710	1562	57.6	19376	7.15	116	4.3	79	2.9	82.1
Jim McMahon, Chi.	6	1321	760	57.5	9857	7.46	61	4.6	49	3.7	81.0
Phil Simms, N.Y.	8	2774	1489	53.7	19815	7.14	121	4.4	112	4.0	74.6
Tommy Kramer, Minn.	11	3339	1851	55.4	22605	6.77	147	4.4	141	4.2	73.6
Jay Schroeder, Wash.	4	1017	517	50.8	7445	7.32	39	3.8	37	3.6	72.6
Eric Hipple, Det.	7	1501	811	54.0	10463	6.97	55	3.7	67	4.5	69.7
Joe Ferguson, T.B.	15	4375	2292	52.4	28895	6.60	190	4.3	200	4.6	68.4
Doug Williams, Wash.	7	2034	976	48.0	13804	6.79	84	4.1	78	3.8	68.2
Dave Wilson, N.O.	6	1023	546	53.4	6914	6.76	36	3.5	54	5.3	64.3

LEADING AFC ACTIVE PASSERS

(1000 or More Attempts)

	Yrs.	Att.	Comp.	Pct.	Yds.	Avg. Gain	TD	Pct. TD	Int.	Pct. Int.	Pts.
Dan Marino, Mia.	5	2494	1512	60.6	19422	7.79	168	6.7	80	3.2	94.1
Ken O'Brien, N.Y.	5	1566	947	60.5	11676	7.46	69	4.4	43	2.7	87.0
Bernie Kosar, Clev.	3	1168	675	57.8	8465	7.25	47	4.0	26	2.2	84.6
Dave Krieg, Sea.	8	2116	1224	57.8	15808	7.47	130	6.1	88	4.2	84.2
Boomer Esiason, Cin.	4	1442	815	56.5	11253	7.80	70	4.9	51	3.5	83.4
Tony Eason, N.E.	5	1352	791	58.5	9722	7.19	57	4.2	42	3.1	81.9
Bill Kenney, K.C.	9	2316	1272	54.9	16728	7.22	105	4.5	81	3.5	78.3
Gary Danielson, Clev.	10	1880	1074	57.1	13440	7.15	81	4.3	77	4.1	76.7
John Elway, Den.	5	2158	1168	54.1	14835	6.87	85	3.9	77	3.6	73.8
Ron Jaworski, Mia.	14	4042	2142	53.0	27682	6.85	176	4.4	159	3.9	73.2
Steve Grogan, N.E.	13	3100	1629	52.5	23466	7.66	165	5.3	178	5.7	71.7
Steve DeBerg, K.C.	11	2997	1698	56.7	19582	6.53	116	3.9	139	4.6	70.4
Steve Fuller, S.D.	8	1066	605	56.8	7156	6.71	28	2.6	41	3.8	70.2
Warren Moon, Hou.	4	1683	899	53.4	12342	7.33	61	3.6	77	4.6	70.0
Jim Plunkett, L.A.	16	3701	1943	52.5	25882	6.99	164	4.4	198	5.3	67.6
Mike Pagel, Clev.	6	1157	589	50.9	7527	6.51	39	3.4	47	4.1	65.9
Mark Malone, S.D.	8	1374	690	50.2	8582	6.25	54	3.9	68	4.9	62.6

NOTE: Marc Wilson was not active at press time. After seven years, his statistics include 871 completions in 1,666 attempts for 11,760 yards, 77 touchdown passes, 86 interceptions and a 68.8 rating.

LEADING NFC ACTIVE SCORERS

(300 or More Points)

	Yrs.	TDs.	FGs.	XPs.	Pts.
Ray Wersching, San Francisco	15	0	222	456	1122
Ed Murray, Detroit	8	0	172	249	765
Morten Andersen, New Orleans	6	0	125	171	546
Mike Lansford, Los Angeles	6	0	96	177	465
Raul Allegre, New York	5	0	98	130	424
Paul McFadden, Philadelphia	4	0	91	117	390
Kevin Butler, Chicago	3	0	78	115	349
Wes Chandler, San Francisco	10	56	0	0	336
Mike Quick, Philadelphia	6	54	0	0	324
Ali Haji-Sheikh, Washington	5	0	76	95	323
Ottis Anderson, New York	9	52	0	0	312
Roy Green, Phoenix	9	51	0	0	306

NOTE: George Rogers was not active at press time. After seven years, his statistics include 54 touchdowns for 324 points.

LEADING AFC ACTIVE SCORERS

(300 or More Points)

	Yrs.	TDs.	FGs.	XPs.	Pts.
Pat Leahy, New York	14	0	218	424	1078
Chris Bahr, Los Angeles	12	0	206	424	1042
Tony Franklin, New England	9	0	173	335	854
Jim Breech, Cincinnati	10	0	161	325	808
Nick Lowery, Kansas City	9	0	174	281	803
Matt Bahr, Cleveland	9	0	142	277	703
Gary Anderson, Pittsburgh	6	0	137	198	609
Steve Largent, Seattle	12	96	0	1	577
Rich Karlis, Denver	6	0	157	208	550
Norm Johnson, Seattle	6	0	99	234	531
Tony Dorsett, Denver	11	86	0	0	516
Marcus Allen, Los Angeles	6	70	0	0	420
Wesley Walker, New York	11	64	0	0	†386
Eric Dickerson, Indianapolis	5	63	0	0	378
Stanley Morgan, New England	11	61	0	0	366
James Lofton, Los Angeles	10	55	0	0	330

†Credited with one safety.

LEADING NFC ACTIVE RUSHERS

(2000 or More Yards)

	Yrs.	Att.	Yds.	TDs.		Yrs.	Att.	Yds.	TDs.
Ottis Anderson, N.Y.	9	1884	8086	47	Darrin Nelson, Minn.	6	800	3512	15
Gerald Riggs, Atl.	6	1474	6143	47	James Jones, Det.	5	864	3138	23
James Wilder, T.B.	7	1419	5370	36	Charles White, L.A.	7	692	2752	23
Joe Cribbs, S.F.	7	1294	5335	27	Matt Suhey, Chi.	8	721	2642	17
Joe Morris, N.Y.	6	1011	4213	43	Greg Bell, L.A.	4	597	2446	19
Roger Craig, S.F.	5	964	4069	34	Rueben Mayes, N.O.	2	529	2270	13
Stump Mitchell, Phoe.	7	779	3758	28					

NOTE: George Rogers was not active at press time. After seven years, his statistics include 1,692 attempts, 7,176 yards and 54 touchdowns.

LEADING AFC ACTIVE RUSHERS
(2000 or More Yards)

	Yrs.	Att.	Yds.	TDs.		Yrs.	Att.	Yds.	TDs.
Tony Dorsett, Den.	11	2755	12036	72	Walter Abercrombie, Pitt.	6	842	3343	22
Eric Dickerson, Ind.	5	1748	8256	61	Larry Kinnebrew, Cin.	5	639	2582	37
Marcus Allen, L.A.	6	1489	6151	54	Kevin Mack, Cle.	3	597	2504	22
Freeman McNeil, N.Y.	7	1306	5850	22	Craig James, N.E.	4	581	2454	10
Curt Warner, Sea.	5	1189	5049	42	Mosi Tatupu, N.E.	10	563	2246	16
Sammy Winder, Den.	6	1194	4413	31	Johnny Hector, N.Y.	5	560	2228	26
James Brooks, Cin.	7	917	4173	27	Steve Grogan, N.E.	13	426	2150	34
Frank Pollard, Pitt.	8	922	3896	20	Earnest Byner, Cle.	4	515	2137	20
Randy McMillan, Ind.	6	990	3876	24	Mike Rozier, Hou.	3	561	2081	15
Earnest Jackson, Pitt.	5	985	3852	19	Herman Heard, K.C.	4	482	2040	13

LEADING NFC ACTIVE RECEIVERS
(200 or More Receptions)

	Yrs.	No.	Yds.	TDs.		Yrs.	No.	Yds.	TDs.
Wes Chandler, S.F.	10	555	8933	56	Kevin House, L.A.	8	299	5169	34
Art Monk, Wash.	8	504	7033	34	Doug Cosbie, Dall.	9	288	3616	30
J. T. Smith, St. L.	10	381	4985	23	James Jones, Det.	5	256	2059	10
James Wilder, T.B.	7	379	3033	6	John Spagnola, Phi.	8	256	2833	14
Roger Craig, S.F.	5	358	3234	14	Gerald Carter, T.B.	8	239	3443	17
David Hill, Det.	12	358	4212	28	Matt Suhey, Chi.	8	231	1886	4
Roy Green, Phoe.	9	357	5899	48	Joe Cribbs, S.F.	7	224	2199	15
Paul Coffman, N.O.	10	339	4340	42	Steve Jordan, Minn.	6	217	2812	12
Jimmie Giles, Phila.	11	328	4802	38	Emery Moorehead, Chi.	11	210	2847	13
Mike Renfro, Dall.	10	323	4708	28	Darrin Nelson, Minn.	6	209	1903	5
Mike Quick, Phila.	6	319	5593	54	Gary Clark, Wash.	3	202	3257	19
Ottis Anderson, N.Y.	9	310	2557	5	Jerry Rice, S.F.	3	200	3575	40

LEADING AFC ACTIVE RECEIVERS
(200 or More Receptions)

	Yrs.	No.	Yds.	TDs.		Yrs.	No.	Yds.	TDs.
Steve Largent, Sea.	12	752	12041	95	Billy Johnson, Ind.	13	337	4211	25
Ozzie Newsome, Cle.	10	575	7073	42	Marcus Allen, L.A.	6	334	3167	15
James Lofton, L.A.	10	571	10536	54	Carlos Carson, K.C.	8	299	5554	29
Kellen Winslow, S.D.	9	541	6741	45	Jerry Butler, Buf.	7	278	4301	29
Stanley Morgan, N.E.	11	475	9364	60	Mark Duper, Mia.	6	257	4869	40
Todd Christensen, L.A.	9	446	5682	41	Mark Clayton, Mia.	5	255	4425	40
Henry Marshall, K.C.	12	416	6545	33	Bruce Hardy, Mia.	10	251	2407	25
Cris Collinsworth, Cin.	7	404	6471	35	James Brooks, Cin.	7	249	2412	16
Wesley Walker, N.Y.	11	404	7666	64	Drew Hill, Hou.	8	238	4617	30
Tony Dorsett, Den.	11	382	3432	13	Ray Butler, Sea.	8	221	3706	33
Russ Francis, N.E.	12	382	5042	40	Charlie Brown, Ind.	6	220	3548	25
Steve Watson, Den.	9	353	6112	36	Matt Bouza, Ind.	7	209	2722	13
Mickey Shuler, N.Y.	10	339	3692	32					

LEADING NFC ACTIVE INTERCEPTORS
(20 or More Interceptions)

	Yrs.	No.	Yds.	TDs.		Yrs.	No.	Yds.	TDs.
Dave Brown, G.B.	13	53	659	5	Andre Waters, Phi.	4	26	495	1
John Harris, Minn.	10	47	514	2	Mark Lee, G.B.	8	25	202	0
Everson Walls, Dall.	7	42	391	0	John Anderson, G.B.	10	24	166	1
Ronnie Lott, S.F.	7	38	524	5	Bobby Butler, Atl.	7	23	200	1
Nolan Cromwell, L.A.	11	37	671	4	Steve Freeman, Minn.	13	23	329	3
Michael Downs, Dall.	7	32	430	1	Roynell Young, Phi.	8	21	101	0
LeRoy Irvin, L.A.	8	28	586	5	Bobby Watkins, Det.	6	20	85	0
Dave Waymer, N.O.	8	28	238	0					

LEADING AFC ACTIVE INTERCEPTORS
(20 or More Interceptions)

	Yrs.	No.	Yds.	TDs.		Yrs.	No.	Yds.	TDs.
Mike Haynes, L.A.	12	43	658	2	Charles Romes, Sea.	11	28	493	1
Deron Cherry, K.C.	7	34	539	1	Dwayne Woodruff, Pitt.	8	26	413	2
Louis Breeden, Ind.	10	33	558	2	Vann McElroy, L.A.	6	25	279	1
Kenny Easley, Sea.	7	32	538	3	Hanford Dixon, Cleve.	7	23	199	0
Ray Clayborn, N.E.	11	31	490	1	Roland James, N.E.	8	23	303	0
Glenn Blackwood, Mia.	9	29	398	1	Albert Lewis, K.C.	5	21	176	0
Mike Harden, Den.	8	29	607	4	Steve Wilson, Den.	9	21	257	0

NOTE: Lester Hayes was not active at press time. After 10 years, his statistics include 39 interceptions for 572 yards and four touchdowns.

TOP 1987 REGULAR-SEASON PERFORMANCES

(NOTE: In this section, statistics compiled during the strike replacement games of October 4 through 19 are not recognized.)

*Denotes overtime game.

TOP 40 RUSHING PERFORMANCES BY YARDS

Player—Team Opp. Date	Att.	Yds.	TDs.
Bo Jackson, L.A. Raiders at Seattle, November 30	18	221	2
Charles White, L.A. Rams at St. Louis, November 15	34	213	1
Eric Dickerson, Indianapolis vs. Tampa Bay, December 27	33	196	2
Freeman McNeil, N.Y. Jets at Kansas City, November 15	26	184	0
Herschel Walker, Dallas at New England, November 15	*28	173	1
Troy Stradford, Miami at Dallas, November 22	17	169	1
Charles White, L.A. Rams vs. Atlanta, December 13	29	159	2
Eric Dickerson, Indianapolis at Miami, November 15	30	154	1
Mike Rozier, Houston at Buffalo, September 20	29	150	1
Eric Dickerson, L.A. Rams at Houston, September 13	27	149	0
Rueben Mayes, New Orleans vs. Cleveland, September 13	24	147	0
Albert Bentley, Indianapolis at N.Y. Jets, November 1	29	145	0
Rueben Mayes, New Orleans vs. San Francisco, October 25	29	144	0
Mike Rozier, Houston vs. Atlanta, October 25	29	144	1
Eric Dickerson, Indianapolis vs. San Diego, November 8	35	138	0
Charles White, L.A. Rams vs. Tampa Bay, November 29	29	137	2
Herschel Walker, Dallas vs. St. Louis, December 27	25	137	2
Marcus Allen, L.A. Raiders at Green Bay, September 13	33	136	1
Eric Dickerson, Indianapolis vs. Houston, November 29	27	136	2
George Rogers, Washington at St. Louis, December 6	30	134	1
Kevin Mack, Cleveland vs. Cincinnati, December 13	27	133	1
Joe Morris, N.Y. Giants vs. N.Y. Jets, December 27	26	132	0
Kenneth Davis, Green Bay at Detroit, October 25	23	129	2
George Rogers, Washington at Buffalo, November 1	30	125	0
Earnest Jackson, Pittsburgh at Kansas City, November 8	23	125	0
Curt Warner, Seattle vs. Green Bay, November 15	25	123	1
Anthony Toney, Philadelphia at New England, November 29	*24	123	1
Mike Rozier, Houston at Indianapolis, November 29	26	122	0
Gerald Riggs, Atlanta vs. Washington, September 20	23	120	1
Troy Stradford, Miami vs. N.Y. Jets, December 7	30	120	3
Curt Warner, Seattle vs. San Diego, November 22	23	119	1
Ronnie Harmon, Buffalo vs. Miami, November 29	23	119	0
Gerald Riggs, Atlanta at Dallas, December 6	30	119	0
Darrin Nelson, Minnesota at Dallas, November 26	*16	118	2
Eric Dickerson, Indianapolis at New England, November 22	27	117	0
Neal Anderson, Chicago vs. Tampa Bay, September 20	16	115	1
Eric Dickerson, Indianapolis at San Diego, December 20	23	115	0
Kevin Mack, Cleveland at Houston, November 22	26	114	1
Gerald Riggs, Atlanta at Houston, October 25	21	113	0

TOP 40 PASSING PERFORMANCES BY YARDS

Player—Team Opp. Date	Att.	Cmp.	Yds.	TDs.	Int.
Neil Lomax, St. Louis at San Diego, September 20	61	32	457	3	1
Boomer Esiason, Cincinnati vs. Pittsburgh, November 22	50	30	409	0	3
Tom Ramsey, New England vs. Philadelphia, November 29	*53	34	402	3	2
Dan Marino, Miami vs. Washington, December 20	50	22	393	3	1
Boomer Esiason, Cincinnati vs. Houston, November 1	41	26	387	2	2
Dan Marino, Miami at Philadelphia, December 13	39	25	376	3	1
Neil Lomax, St. Louis at Atlanta, November 29	42	25	369	2	1
Vinny Testaverde, Tampa Bay at New Orleans, December 6	47	22	369	2	2
Boomer Esiason, Cincinnati at Kansas City, December 6	*44	28	368	2	0
Chuck Long, Detroit vs. Green Bay, October 25	47	33	362	3	0
Boomer Esiason, Cincinnati at Cleveland, December 13	39	22	361	1	2
Jim Kelly, Buffalo at Miami, October 25	*39	29	359	2	0
Phil Simms, N.Y. Giants at St. Louis, December 13	48	30	359	2	1
Danny White, Dallas at Washington, December 13	49	27	359	2	1
John Elway, Denver at San Diego, November 29	32	21	347	3	1
Bernie Kosar, Cleveland vs Buffalo, November 15	34	24	346	2	1
Joe Montana, San Francisco vs. Cleveland, November 29	31	23	342	4	1
John Elway, Denver vs. Chicago, November 16	40	21	341	3	2
Danny White, Dallas vs. Minnesota, November 26	*41	25	341	4	3
Marc Wilson, L.A. Raiders at Kansas City, December 13	38	22	339	0	3
John Elway, Denver vs. Seattle, September 13	32	22	338	4	1
Marc Wilson, L.A. Raiders vs. Buffalo, December 6	32	21	337	3	0
John Elway, Denver at Seattle, December 13	42	21	335	1	2
Dan Fouts, San Diego vs. Pittsburgh, December 13	52	29	334	1	1
Steve DeBerg, Tampa Bay vs. Atlanta, September 13	34	24	333	5	1
Dan Marino, Miami vs. Pittsburgh, November 1	31	25	332	4	2
Jay Schroeder, Washington vs. N.Y. Giants, November 29	46	28	331	3	2
Bill Kenney, Kansas City at San Diego, October 25	38	22	328	2	1
Warren Moon, Houston at Indianapolis, November 29	44	24	327	3	2
Jim Everett, L.A. Rams at Detroit, December 6	26	20	324	2	1

TOP 40 PASSING PERFORMANCES BY YARDS

Player—Team Opp. Date	Att.	Cmp.	Yds.	TDs.	Int.
Don Majkowski, Green Bay at Detroit, October 25	29	19	323	1	1
Dan Fouts, San Diego vs. Denver, November 29	40	23	322	0	2
Bill Kenney, Kansas City vs. Seattle, December 27	35	23	320	3	0
Joe Montana, San Francisco at Pittsburgh, September 13	49	34	316	2	3
Dan Fouts, San Diego vs. Cleveland, November 1	*42	25	315	2	1
Jim Kelly, Buffalo at L.A. Raiders, December 6	36	22	315	1	0
Bernie Kosar, Cleveland at New Orleans, September 13	39	28	314	2	1
Neil Lomax, St. Louis vs. Tampa Bay, November 8	36	25	314	3	1
Randall Cunningham, Philadelphia at New England, November 29	*31	18	314	2	1
Neil Lomax, St. Louis at Dallas, December 27	54	28	314	1	1

TOP 40 RECEIVING PERFORMANCES BY YARDS

Player—Team Opp. Date	Rec.	Yds.	TDs.
Mark Carrier, Tampa Bay at New Orleans, December 6	8	212	1
Carlos Carson, Kansas City at San Diego, October 25	9	197	2
Gary Clark, Washington vs. Dallas, December 13	9	187	1
Anthony Carter, Minnesota at Dallas, November 26	*8	184	2
Henry Ellard, L.A. Rams at Detroit, December 6	7	171	1
Mark Duper, Miami vs. Washington, December 20	6	170	3
Al Toon, N.Y. Jets vs. Philadelphia, December 20	10	168	1
Ricky Sanders, Washington at Minnesota, December 26	*8	164	2
Andre Reed, Buffalo at L.A. Raiders, December 6	7	153	0
Lionel Manuel, N.Y. Giants at Dallas, November 2	7	151	2
Walter Stanley, Green Bay at Detroit, October 25	6	150	1
Mike Quick, Philadelphia at N.Y. Jets, December 20	6	148	2
Bill Brooks, Indianapolis vs. Cincinnati, September 13	6	146	1
Stanley Morgan, New England vs. L.A. Raiders, November 1	6	146	0
Carlos Carson, Kansas City vs. L.A. Raiders, December 13	4	142	1
Wes Chandler, San Diego at Houston, December 6	10	140	0
Roy Green, St. Louis at San Diego, September 20	7	139	1
Tim McGee, Cincinnati vs. Pittsburgh, November 22	8	139	0
Mark Bavaro, N.Y. Giants at St. Louis, December 13	11	137	1
Drew Hill, Houston at Indianapolis, November 29	7	134	2
Willie Gault, Chicago at Denver, November 16	5	133	2
Mark Bavaro, N.Y. Giants vs. Philadelphia, December 6	*6	133	1
James Lofton, L.A. Raiders vs. Buffalo, December 6	6	132	1
Chris Burkett, Buffalo at Miami, October 25	*9	130	1
Gary Clark, Washington at St. Louis, December 6	5	130	1
Eric Martin, New Orleans vs. Houston, December 13	6	130	2
James Lofton, L.A. Raiders at Minnesota, November 8	4	128	1
Ernest Givins, Houston vs. Cleveland, November 22	3	126	1
Jerry Rice, San Francisco vs. Cleveland, November 29	7	126	3
Todd Christensen, L.A. Raiders vs. Seattle, October 25	8	124	1
Robert Awalt, St. Louis vs. Tampa Bay, November 8	9	124	1
Mark Duper, Miami at New England, September 13	9	123	2
Cris Collinsworth, Cincinnati vs. Houston, November 1	8	121	0
Stephone Paige, Kansas City at Chicago, November 1	5	121	1
Mike Quick, Philadelphia at New England, November 29	*5	121	2
Carlos Carson, Kansas City vs. Seattle, December 27	4	120	1
Gary Clark, Washington at Philadelphia, November 8	5	119	1
Webster Slaughter, Cleveland vs. Cincinnati, December 13	5	119	2
Cris Collinsworth, Cincinnati at Houston, December 27	4	119	0

NATIONAL FOOTBALL CONFERENCE
INDIVIDUAL LEADERS, 1960-87
(National Football League, 1960-69)

RUSHING

Year	Player	Net Yds.	Att.	TD
1987	Charles White, LA	1,374	324	11
1986	Eric Dickerson, LA	1,821	404	11
1985	Gerald Riggs, Atlanta	1,719	397	10
1984	Eric Dickerson, LA	2,105	379	14
1983	Eric Dickerson, LA	1,808	390	18
1982	Tony Dorsett, Dallas	745	177	5
1981	George Rogers, NO	1,674	378	13
1980	Walter Payton, Chicago	1,460	317	6
1979	Walter Payton, Chicago	1,610	369	14
1978	Walter Payton, Chicago	1,395	333	11
1977	Walter Payton, Chicago	1,852	339	14
1976	Walter Payton, Chicago	1,390	311	13
1975	Jim Otis, St. Louis	1,076	269	5
1974	Lawrence McCutcheon, LA	1,109	236	3
1973	John Brockington, GB	1,144	265	3
1972	Larry Brown, Washington	1,216	285	8
1971	John Brockington, GB	1,105	216	4
1970	Larry Brown, Washington	1,125	237	5
1969	Gale Sayers, Chicago	1,032	236	8
1968	Leroy Kelly, Cleveland	1,239	248	16
1967	Leroy Kelly, Cleveland	1,205	235	11
1966	Gale Sayers, Chicago	1,231	229	8
1965	Jim Brown, Cleveland	1,544	289	17
1964	Jim Brown, Cleveland	1,446	280	7
1963	Jim Brown, Cleveland	1,863	291	12
1962	Jim Taylor, Green Bay	1,474	272	19
1961	Jim Brown, Cleveland	1,408	305	8
1960	Jim Brown, Cleveland	1,257	215	9

PASSING

Year	Player	Passes	Com.	Yds.	TD	Int.
1987	Joe Montana, San Francisco	398	266	3,054	31	13
1986	Tommy Kramer, Minnesota	372	208	3,000	24	10
1985	Joe Montana, San Francisco	494	303	3,653	27	13
1984	Joe Montana, San Francisco	432	279	3,630	28	10
1983	Steve Bartkowski, Atlanta	432	274	3,167	22	5
1982	Joe Theismann, Washington	252	161	2,033	13	9
1981	Joe Montana, San Francisco	488	311	3,565	19	12
1980	Ron Jaworski, Philadelphia	451	257	3,529	27	12
1979	Roger Staubach, Dallas	461	267	3,586	27	11
1978	Roger Staubach, Dallas	413	231	3,190	25	16
1977	Roger Staubach, Dallas	361	210	2,620	18	9
1976	James Harris, Los Angeles	158	91	1,460	8	6
1975	Fran Tarkenton, Minnesota	425	273	2,994	25	13
1974	Sonny Jurgensen, Washington	167	107	1,185	11	5
1973	Roger Staubach, Dallas	286	179	2,428	23	15
1972	Norm Snead, New York	325	196	2,307	17	12
1971	Roger Staubach, Dallas	211	126	1,882	15	4
1970	John Brodie, San Francisco	378	223	2,941	24	10
1969	Sonny Jurgensen, Washington	442	274	3,102	22	15
1968	Earl Morrall, Baltimore	317	182	2,909	26	17
1967	Sonny Jurgensen, Washington	508	288	3,747	31	16
1966	Bart Starr, Green Bay	251	156	2,257	14	3
1965	Rudy Bukich, Chicago	312	176	2,641	20	9
1964	Bart Starr, Green Bay	272	163	2,144	15	4
1963	Y. A. Tittle, New York	367	221	3,145	36	14
1962	Bart Starr, Green Bay	285	178	2,438	12	9
1961	Milt Plum, Cleveland	302	177	2,416	18	10
1960	Milt Plum, Cleveland	250	151	2,297	21	5

PASS RECEIVING

Year	Player	No.	Yds.	TD
1987	J. T. Smith, St. Louis	91	1,117	8
1986	Jerry Rice, SF	86	1,570	15
1985	Roger Craig, SF	92	1,016	6
1984	Art Monk, Washington	106	1,372	7
1983	Roy Green, St. Louis	78	1,227	14
1982	Dwight Clark, SF	60	913	5
1981	Dwight Clark, SF	85	1,105	4
1980	Earl Cooper, San Francisco	83	567	4
1979	Ahmad Rashad, Minnesota	80	1,156	9
1978	Rickey Young, Minnesota	88	704	5
1977	Ahmad Rashad, Minnesota	51	681	2
1976	Drew Pearson, Dallas	58	806	6
1975	Chuck Foreman, Minnesota	73	691	9
1974	Charles Young, Phila.	63	696	3
1973	Harold Carmichael, Phila.	67	1,116	9
1972	Harold Jackson, Phila.	62	1,048	4
1971	Bob Tucker, New York	59	791	4
1970	Dick Gordon, Chicago	71	1,026	13
1969	Dan Abramowicz, NO	73	1,015	7
1968	Clifton McNeil, San Fran.	71	994	7
1967	Charley Taylor, Wash.	70	990	9
1966	Charley Taylor, Wash.	72	1,119	12
1965	Dave Parks, San Francisco	80	1,344	12
1964	Johnny Morris, Chicago	93	1,200	10
1963	Bobby Joe Conrad, St. Louis	73	967	10
1962	Bobby Mitchell, Wash.	72	1,384	11
1961	Jim Phillips, Los Angeles	78	1,092	5
1960	Raymond Berry, Baltimore	74	1,298	10

SCORING

Year	Player	TD	PAT	FG	Tot.
1987	Jerry Rice, SF	23	0	0	138
1986	Kevin Butler, Chicago	0	36	28	120
1985	Kevin Butler, Chicago	0	51	31	144
1984	Ray Wersching, SF	0	56	25	131
1983	Mark Moseley, Wash.	0	62	33	161
1982	Wendell Tyler, LA	13	0	0	78
1981	Ed Murray, Detroit	0	46	25	121
	Rafael Septien, Dallas	0	40	27	121
1980	Ed Murray, Detroit	0	35	27	116
1979	Mark Moseley, Wash.	0	39	25	114
1978	Frank Corral, Los Angeles	0	31	29	118
1977	Walter Payton, Chicago	16	0	0	96
1976	Mark Moseley, Wash.	0	31	22	97
1975	Chuck Foreman, Minn.	22	0	0	132
1974	Chester Marcol, GB	0	19	25	94
1973	David Ray, Los Angeles	0	40	30	130
1972	Chester Marcol, GB	0	29	33	128
1971	Curt Knight, Washington	0	27	29	114
1970	Fred Cox, Minnesota	0	35	30	125
1969	Fred Cox, Minnesota	0	43	26	121
1968	Leroy Kelly, Cleveland	20	0	0	120
1967	Jim Bakken, St. Louis	0	36	27	117

SCORING

	TD	PAT	FG	Tot.		TD	PAT	FG	Tot.
1966—Bruce Gossett, LA	0	29	28	113	1962—Jim Taylor, Green Bay	19	0	0	114
1965—Gale Sayers, Chicago	22	0	0	132	1961—Paul Hornung, GB	10	41	15	146
1964—Lenny Moore, Baltimore	20	0	0	120	1960—Paul Hornung, GB	15	41	15	176
1963—Don Chandler, New York	0	52	18	106					

FIELD GOALS

1987—Morten Andersen, New Orleans	28	1973—David Ray, Los Angeles	30
1986—Kevin Butler, Chicago	28	1972—Chester Marcol, Green Bay	33
1985—Morten Andersen, New Orleans	31	1971—Curt Knight, Washington	29
Kevin Butler, Chicago	31	1970—Fred Cox, Minnesota	30
1984—Paul McFadden, Philadelphia	30	1969—Fred Cox, Minnesota	26
1983—Ali Haji-Sheikh, New York	35	1968—Mac Percival, Chicago	25
1982—Mark Moseley, Washington	20	1967—Jim Bakken, St. Louis	27
1981—Rafael Septien, Dallas	27	1966—Bruce Gossett, Los Angeles	28
1980—Ed Murray, Detroit	27	1965—Fred Cox, Minnesota	23
1979—Mark Moseley, Washington	25	1964—Jim Bakken, St. Louis	25
1978—Frank Corral, Los Angeles	29	1963—Jim Martin, Baltimore	24
1977—Mark Moseley, Washington	21	1962—Lou Michaels, Pittsburgh	26
1976—Mark Moseley, Washington	22	1961—Steve Myhra, Baltimore	21
1975—Toni Fritsch, Dallas	22	1960—Tommy Davis, San Francisco	19
1974—Chester Marcol, Green Bay	25		

PASS INTERCEPTIONS

	No.	Yds.		No.	Yds.
1987—Barry Wilburn, Washington	9	135	1972—Bill Bradley, Philadelphia	9	73
1986—Ronnie Lott, San Francisco	10	134	1971—Bill Bradley, Philadelphia	11	248
1985—Everson Walls, Dallas	9	31	1970—Dick Le Beau, Detroit	9	96
1984—Tom Flynn, Green Bay	9	106	1969—Mel Renfro, Dallas	10	118
1983—Mark Murphy, Washington	9	127	1968—Willie Williams, New York	10	103
1982—Everson Walls, Dallas	7	61	1967—Lem Barney, Detroit	10	232
1981—Everson Walls, Dallas	11	133	Dave Whitsell, New Orleans	10	178
1980—Nolan Cromwell, Los Angeles	8	140	1966—Larry Wilson, St. Louis	10	180
1979—Lemar Parrish, Washington	9	65	1965—Bobby Boyd, Baltimore	9	78
1978—Ken Stone, St. Louis	9	139	1964—Paul Krause, Washington	12	140
Willie Buchanon, Green Bay	9	93	1963—Dick Lynch, New York Giants	9	251
1977—Rolland Lawrence, Atlanta	7	138	Rosie Taylor, Chicago	9	172
1976—Monte Jackson, Los Angeles	10	173	1962—Willie Wood, Green Bay	9	132
1975—Paul Krause, Minnesota	10	201	1961—Dick Lynch, New York Giants	9	60
1974—Ray Brown, Atlanta	8	164	1960—Dave Baker, San Francisco	10	96
1973—Bob Bryant, Minnesota	7	105	Jerry Norton, St. Louis	10	96

PUNTING

	No.	Avg.		No.	Avg.
1987—Rick Donnelly, Atlanta	61	44.0	1973—Tom Wittum, San Francisco	79	43.7
1986—Sean Landeta, New York	79	44.8	1972—Dave Chapple, Los Angeles	53	44.2
1985—Rick Donnelly, Atlanta	59	43.6	1971—Tom McNeill, Philadelphia	73	42.0
1984—Brian Hansen, New Orleans	69	43.8	1970—Julian Fagan, New Orleans	77	42.5
1983—Frank Garcia, Tampa Bay	95	42.2	1969—David Lee, Baltimore	50	45.3
1982—Carl Birdsong, St. Louis	54	43.8	1968—Billy Lothridge, Atlanta	75	44.3
1981—Tom Skladany, Detroit	64	43.5	1967—Billy Lothridge, Atlanta	87	43.7
1980—Dave Jennings, New York	94	44.8	1966—David Lee, Baltimore	49	45.6
1979—Dave Jennings, New York	104	42.7	1965—Gary Collins, Cleveland	65	46.7
1978—Tom Skladany, Detroit	86	42.5	1964—Bobby Walden, Minnesota	72	46.4
1977—Tom Blanchard, New Orleans	82	42.4	1963—Yale Lary, Detroit	35	48.9
1976—John James, Atlanta	101	42.1	1962—Tommy Davis, San Francisco	48	45.8
1975—Herman Weaver, Detroit	80	42.0	1961—Yale Lary, Detroit	52	48.4
1974—Tom Blanchard, New Orleans	88	42.1	1960—Jerry Norton, St. Louis	39	45.6

PUNT RETURNS

	No.	Yds.	Avg.		No.	Yds.	Avg.
1987—Mel Gray, New Orleans	24	352	14.7	1973—Bruce Taylor, San Francisco	15	207	13.8
1986—Vai Sikahema, St. Louis	43	522	12.1	1972—Ken Ellis, Green Bay	14	215	15.4
1985—Henry Ellard, Los Angeles	37	501	13.5	1971—Les Duncan, Washington	22	233	10.6
1984—Henry Ellard, Los Angeles	30	403	13.4	1970—Bruce Taylor, San Francisco	43	516	12.0
1983—Henry Ellard, Los Angeles	16	217	13.6	1969—Alvin Haymond, Los Angeles	33	435	13.2
1982—Billy Johnson, Atlanta	24	273	11.4	1968—Bob Hayes, Dallas	15	312	20.8
1981—LeRoy Irvin, Los Angeles	46	615	13.4	1967—Ben Davis, Cleveland	18	229	12.7
1980—Kenny Johnson, Atlanta	23	281	12.2	1966—Johnny Roland, St. Louis	20	221	11.1
1979—John Sciarra, Philadelphia	16	182	11.4	1965—Leroy Kelly, Cleveland	17	265	15.6
1978—Jackie Wallace, Los Angeles	52	618	11.9	1964—Tommy Watkins, Detroit	16	238	14.9
1977—Larry Marshall, Philadelphia	46	489	10.6	1963—Dick James, Washington	16	214	13.4
1976—Eddie Brown, Washington	48	646	13.5	1962—Pat Studstill, Detroit	29	457	15.8
1975—Terry Metcalf, St. Louis	23	285	12.4	1961—Willie Wood, Green Bay	14	225	16.1
1974—Dick Jauron, Detroit	17	286	16.8	1960—Abe Woodson, San Francisco	13	174	13.4

KICKOFF RETURNS

	No.	Yds.	Avg.		No.	Yds.	Avg.
1987—Sylvester Stamps, Atlanta.....	24	660	27.5	1973—Carl Garrett, Chicago..............	16	486	30.4
1986—Dennis Gentry, Chicago	20	576	28.8	1972—Ron Smith, Chicago.................	30	924	30.8
1985—Ron Brown, Los Angeles	28	918	32.8	1971—Travis Williams, Los Angeles	25	743	29.7
1984—Barry Redden, Los Angeles ...	23	530	23.0	1970—Cecil Turner, Chicago	23	752	32.7
1983—Darrin Nelson, Minnesota......	18	445	24.7	1969—Bobby Williams, Detroit	17	563	33.1
1982—Alvin Hall, Detroit..................	16	426	26.6	1968—Preston Pearson, Baltimore...	15	527	35.1
1981—Mike Nelms, Washington.......	37	1099	29.7	1967—Travis Williams, Green Bay...	18	739	41.1
1980—Rich Mauti, New Orleans......	31	798	27.6	1966—Gale Sayers, Chicago..............	23	718	31.2
1979—Jimmy Edwards, Minnesota.	44	1103	25.1	1965—Tommy Watkins, Detroit	17	584	34.4
1978—Steve Odom, Green Bay	25	677	27.1	1964—Clarence Childs, NYG	34	987	29.0
1977—Wilbert Montgomery, Phila...	23	619	26.9	1963—Abe Woodson, San Francisco.	29	935	32.3
1976—Cullen Bryant, Los Angeles...	16	459	28.7	1962—Abe Woodson, San Francisco.	37	1157	31.3
1975—Walter Payton, Chicago.........	14	444	31.7	1961—Dick Bass, Los Angeles...........	23	698	30.3
1974—Terry Metcalf, St. Louis..........	20	623	31.2	1960—Tom Moore, Green Bay..........	12	397	33.1

SACKS

1987—Reggie White, Philadelphia.....................21.0	1984—Richard Dent, Chicago 17.5
1986—Lawrence Taylor, New York 20.5	1983—Fred Dean, San Francisco 17.5
1985—Richard Dent, Chicago 17.0	1982—Doug Martin, Minnesota.........................11.5

AMERICAN FOOTBALL CONFERENCE
INDIVIDUAL LEADERS, 1960-87
(American Football League, 1960-69)

RUSHING

	Net Yds.	Att.	TD		Net Yds.	Att.	TD
1987—Eric Dickerson, Ind...............	1,288	283	6	1973—O. J. Simpson, Buffalo...........	2,003	332	12
1986—Curt Warner, Seattle	1,481	319	13	1972—O. J. Simpson, Buffalo...........	1,251	292	6
1985—Marcus Allen, Los Angeles...	1,759	380	11	1971—Floyd Little, Denver..............	1,133	284	6
1984—Earnest Jackson, S.D............	1,179	296	8	1970—Floyd Little, Denver..............	901	209	3
1983—Curt Warner, Seattle	1,449	335	13	1969—Dick Post, San Diego	873	182	6
1982—Freeman McNeil, N.Y.........	786	151	6	1968—Paul Robinson, Cincinnati ...	1,023	238	8
1981—Earl Campbell, Houston.......	1,376	361	10	1967—Jim Nance, Boston.................	1,216	269	7
1980—Earl Campbell, Houston.......	1,934	373	13	1966—Jim Nance, Boston.................	1,458	299	11
1979—Earl Campbell, Houston.......	1,697	368	19	1965—Paul Lowe, San Diego	1,121	222	7
1978—Earl Campbell, Houston.......	1,450	302	13	1964—Cookie Gilchrist, Buffalo	981	230	6
1977—Mark van Eeghen, Oakland.	1,273	324	7	1963—Clem Daniels, Oakland	1,099	215	3
1976—O. J. Simpson, Buffalo...........	1,503	290	8	1962—Cookie Gilchrist, Buffalo	1,096	214	13
1975—O. J. Simpson, Buffalo...........	1,817	329	16	1961—Billy Cannon, Houston	948	200	6
1974—Otis Armstrong, Denver........	1,407	263	9	1960—Abner Haynes, Dallas............	875	156	9

PASSING

	Passes	Com.	Yds.	TD	Int.
1987—Bernie Kosar, Cleveland	389	241	3,033	22	9
1986—Dan Marino, Miami...	623	378	4,746	44	23
1985—Ken O'Brien, New York	488	297	3,888	25	8
1984—Dan Marino, Miami...	564	362	5,084	48	17
1983—Dan Marino, Miami...	296	173	2,210	20	6
1982—Ken Anderson, Cincinnati...	309	218	2,495	12	9
1981—Ken Anderson, Cincinnati...	479	300	3,754	29	10
1980—Brian Sipe, Cleveland..	554	337	4,132	30	14
1979—Dan Fouts, San Diego...	530	332	4,082	24	24
1978—Terry Bradshaw, Pittsburgh....................................	368	207	2,915	28	20
1977—Bob Griese, Miami...	307	180	2,252	22	13
1976—Ken Stabler, Oakland..	291	194	2,737	27	17
1975—Ken Anderson, Cincinnati...	377	228	3,169	21	11
1974—Ken Anderson, Cincinnati...	328	213	2,667	18	10
1973—Ken Stabler, Oakland..	260	163	1,997	14	10
1972—Earl Morrall, Miami...	150	83	1,360	11	7
1971—Bob Griese, Miami...	263	145	2,089	19	9
1970—Daryle Lamonica, Oakland.......................................	356	179	2,516	22	15
1969—Greg Cook, Cincinnati...	197	106	1,854	15	11
1968—Len Dawson, Kansas City	224	131	2,109	17	9
1967—Daryle Lamonica, Oakland.......................................	425	220	3,228	30	20
1966—Len Dawson, Kansas City	284	159	2,527	26	10
1965—John Hadl, San Diego	348	174	2,798	20	21
1964—Len Dawson, Kansas City	354	199	2,879	30	18
1963—Tobin Rote, San Diego	286	170	2,510	20	17
1962—Len Dawson, Dallas...	310	189	2,759	29	17
1961—George Blanda, Houston	362	187	3,330	36	22
1960—Jack Kemp, Los Angeles...	406	211	3,018	20	25

PASS RECEIVING

Year	Player	No.	Yds.	TD
1987	Al Toon, New York	68	976	5
1986	Todd Christensen, LA	95	1,153	8
1985	Lionel James, San Diego	86	1,027	6
1984	Ozzie Newsome, Cleveland	89	1,001	5
1983	Todd Christensen, LA	92	1,247	12
1982	Kellen Winslow, San Diego	54	721	6
1981	Kellen Winslow, San Diego	88	1,075	10
1980	Kellen Winslow, San Diego	89	1,290	9
1979	Joe Washington, Baltimore	82	750	3
1978	Steve Largent, Seattle	71	1,168	8
1977	Lydell Mitchell, Baltimore	71	620	4
1976	MacArthur Lane, KC	66	686	1
1975	Reggie Rucker, Cleveland	60	770	3
1974	Lydell Mitchell, Baltimore	72	544	2
1973	Fred Willis, Houston	57	371	1
1972	Fred Biletnikoff, Oakland	58	802	7
1971	Fred Biletnikoff, Oakland	61	929	9
1970	Marlin Briscoe, Buffalo	57	1,036	8
1969	Lance Alworth, San Diego	64	1,003	4
1968	Lance Alworth, San Diego	68	1,312	10
1967	George Sauer, New York	75	1,189	6
1966	Lance Alworth, San Diego	73	1,383	13
1965	Lionel Taylor, Denver	85	1,131	6
1964	Charley Hennigan, Houston	101	1,546	8
1963	Lionel Taylor, Denver	78	1,101	10
1962	Lionel Taylor, Denver	77	908	4
1961	Lionel Taylor, Denver	100	1,176	4
1960	Lionel Taylor, Denver	92	1,235	12

SCORING

Year	Player	TD	PAT	FG	Tot.
1987	Jim Breech, Cincinnati	0	25	24	97
1986	Tony Franklin, N.E.	0	44	32	140
1985	Gary Anderson, Pitts.	0	40	33	139
1984	Gary Anderson, Pitts.	0	45	24	117
1983	Gary Anderson, Pitts.	0	38	27	119
1982	Marcus Allen, Los Angeles	14	0	0	84
1981	Jim Breech, Cincinnati	0	49	22	115
	Nick Lowery, Kansas City	0	37	26	115
1980	John Smith, New England	0	51	26	129
1979	John Smith, New England	0	46	23	115
1978	Pat Leahy, New York	0	41	22	107
1977	Errol Mann, Oakland	0	39	20	99
1975	O. J. Simpson, Buffalo	23	0	0	138
1974	Roy Gerela, Pittsburgh	0	33	20	93
1973	Roy Gerela, Pittsburgh	0	36	29	123
1972	Bobby Howfield, N.Y.	0	40	27	121
1971	Garo Yepremian, Miami	0	33	28	117
1970	Jan Stenerud, Kansas City	0	26	30	116
1969	Jim Turner, New York	0	33	32	129
1968	Jim Turner, New York	0	43	34	145
1967	George Blanda, Oakland	0	56	20	116
1966	Gino Cappelletti, Boston	6	35	16	119
1965	Gino Cappelletti, Boston	9	27	17	132
1964	Gino Cappelletti, Boston	7	36	25	155
1963	Gino Cappelletti, Boston	2	35	22	113
1962	Gene Mingo, Denver	4	32	27	137
1961	Gino Cappelletti, Boston	8	48	17	147
1960	Gene Mingo, Denver	6	33	18	123

FIELD GOALS

Year	Player	FG
1987	Dean Biasucci, Indianapolis	24
	Jim Breech, Cincinnati	24
1986	Tony Franklin, New England	32
1985	Gary Anderson, Pittsburgh	33
1984	Gary Anderson, Pittsburgh	24
	Matt Bahr, Cleveland	24
1983	Raul Allegre, Baltimore	30
1982	Nick Lowery, Kansas City	19
1981	Nick Lowery, Kansas City	26
1980	John Smith, New England	26
	Fred Steinfort, Denver	26
1979	John Smith, New England	23
1978	Pat Leahy, New York	22
1977	Errol Mann, Oakland	20
1975	Jan Stenerud, Kansas City	22
1974	Roy Gerela, Pittsburgh	20
1973	Roy Gerela, Pittsburgh	29
1972	Roy Gerela, Pittsburgh	28
1971	Garo Yepremian, Miami	28
1970	Jan Stenerud, Kansas City	30
1969	Jim Turner, New York	32
1968	Jim Turner, New York	34
1967	Jan Stenerud, Kansas City	21
1966	Mike Mercer, Oakland-Kansas City	21
1965	Pete Gogolak, Buffalo	28
1964	Gino Cappelletti, Boston	25
1963	Gino Cappelletti, Boston	22
1962	Gene Mingo, Denver	27
1961	Gino Cappelletti, Boston	17
1960	Gene Mingo, Denver	18

PASS INTERCEPTIONS

Year	Player	No.	Yds.
1987	Mike Prior, Indianapolis	6	57
	Mark Kelso, Buffalo	6	25
	Keith Bostic, Houston	6	−14
1986	Deron Cherry, Kansas City	9	150
1985	Eugene Daniel, Indianapolis	8	53
	Albert Lewis, Kansas City	8	59
1984	Kenny Easley, Seattle	10	126
1983	Ken Riley, Cincinnati	8	89
	Vann McElroy, Los Angeles	8	68
1982	Ken Riley, Cincinnati	5	88
	Bobby Jackson, New York	5	84
	Dwayne Woodruff, Pittsburgh	5	53
	Donnie Shell, Pittsburgh	5	27
1981	John Harris, Seattle	10	155
1980	Lester Hayes, Oakland	13	273
1979	Mike Reinfeldt, Houston	12	205
1978	Thom Darden, Cleveland	10	200
1977	Lyle Blackwood, Baltimore	10	163
1976	Ken Riley, Cincinnati	9	141
1975	Mel Blount, Pittsburgh	11	121
1974	Emmitt Thomas, Kansas City	12	214
1973	Dick Anderson, Miami	8	136
	Mike Wagner, Pittsburgh	8	134
1972	Mike Sensibaugh, Kansas City	8	65
1971	Ken Houston, Houston	9	220
1970	Johnny Robinson, Kansas City	10	155
1969	Emmitt Thomas, Kansas City	9	146
1968	Dave Grayson, Oakland	10	195
1967	Miller Farr, Houston	10	264
	Tom Janik, Buffalo	10	222
	Dick Westmoreland, Miami	10	127
1966	Johnny Robinson, Kansas City	10	136
	Bobby Hunt, Kansas City	10	113
1965	W. K. Hicks, Houston	9	156
1964	Dainard Paulson, New York	12	157
1963	Fred Glick, Houston	12	180
1962	Lee Riley, New York	11	122
1961	Bill Atkins, Buffalo	10	158
1960	Austin Gonsoulin, Denver	11	98

PUNTING

	No.	Avg.		No.	Avg.
1987—Ralf Mojsiejenko, San Diego	67	42.9	1973—Jerrel Wilson, Kansas City	80	45.5
1986—Rohn Stark, Indianapolis	76	45.2	1972—Jerrel Wilson, Kansas City	66	44.8
1985—Rohn Stark, Indianapolis	78	45.9	1971—Dave Lewis, Cincinnati	72	44.8
1984—Jim Arnold, Kansas City	98	44.9	1970—Dave Lewis, Cincinnati	79	46.2
1983—Rohn Stark, Baltimore	91	45.3	1969—Dennis Partee, San Diego	71	44.6
1982—Luke Prestridge, Denver	45	45.0	1968—Jerrel Wilson, Kansas City	63	45.1
1981—Pat McInally, Cincinnati	72	45.4	1967—Bob Scarpitto, Denver	105	44.9
1980—Luke Prestridge, Denver	70	43.9	1966—Bob Scarpitto, Denver	76	45.8
1979—Bob Grupp, Kansas City	89	43.6	1965—Jerrel Wilson, Kansas City	69	45.4
1978—Pat McInally, Cincinnati	91	43.1	1964—Jim Fraser, Denver	73	44.2
1977—Ray Guy, Oakland	59	43.4	1963—Jim Fraser, Denver	81	44.4
1976—Marv Bateman, Buffalo	86	42.8	1962—Jim Fraser, Denver	55	43.6
1975—Ray Guy, Oakland	68	43.8	1961—Bill Atkins, Buffalo	85	44.5
1974—Ray Guy, Oakland	74	42.2	1960—Paul Maguire, Los Angeles	43	40.5

PUNT RETURNS

	No.	Yds.	Avg.		No.	Yds.	Avg.
1987—Bobby Joe Edmonds, Seattle	20	251	12.6	1973—Ron Smith, San Diego	27	352	15.0
1986—Bobby Joe Edmonds, Seattle	34	419	12.3	1972—Chris Farasopolous, NYJ	17	179	10.5
1985—Irving Fryar, New England	37	520	14.1	1971—Leroy Kelly, Cleveland	30	292	9.7
1984—Mike Martin, Cincinnati	24	376	15.7	1970—Ed Podolak, Kansas City	23	311	13.5
1983—Kirk Springs, New York	23	287	12.5	1969—Bill Thompson, Denver	25	288	11.5
1982—Rick Upchurch, Denver	15	242	16.1	1968—Noland Smith, Kansas City	18	270	15.0
1981—James Brooks, San Diego	22	290	13.2	1967—Floyd Little, Denver	16	270	16.9
1980—J. T. Smith, Kansas City	40	581	14.5	1966—Leslie Duncan, San Diego	18	238	13.2
1979—Tony Nathan, Miami	28	306	10.9	1965—Leslie Duncan, San Diego	30	464	15.5
1978—Rick Upchurch, Denver	36	493	13.7	1964—Bobby Jancik, Houston	12	220	18.3
1977—Billy Johnson, Houston	30	539	15.4	1963—Claude Gibson, Oakland	26	307	11.8
1976—Rick Upchurch, Denver	39	536	13.7	1962—Dick Christy, New York	15	250	16.7
1975—Billy Johnson, Houston	40	612	18.8	1961—Dick Christy, New York	18	383	21.3
1974—Lemar Parrish, Cincinnati	18	338	18.8	1960—Abner Haynes, Dallas	14	215	15.4

KICKOFF RETURNS

	No.	Yds.	Avg.		No.	Yds.	Avg.
1987—Paul Palmer, Kansas City	38	923	24.3	1973—Wallace Francis, Buffalo	23	687	29.9
1986—Lupe Sanchez, Pittsburgh	25	591	23.6	1972—Bruce Laird, Baltimore	29	843	29.1
1985—Glen Young, Cleveland	35	898	25.7	1971—Mercury Morris, Miami	15	423	28.2
1984—Bobby Humphery, New York	22	675	30.7	1970—Jim Duncan, Baltimore	20	707	35.4
1983—Fulton Walker, Miami	36	962	26.7	1969—Bill Thompson, Denver	19	594	31.3
1982—Mike Mosley, Buffalo	18	487	27.1	1968—George Atkinson, Oakland	32	802	25.1
1981—Carl Roaches, Houston	28	769	27.5	1967—Zeke Moore, Houston	14	405	28.9
1980—Horace Ivory, New England	36	992	27.6	1966—Goldie Sellers, Denver	19	541	28.5
1979—Larry Brunson, Oakland	17	441	25.9	1965—Abner Haynes, Denver	34	901	26.5
1978—Keith Wright, Cleveland	30	789	26.3	1964—Bo Roberson, Oakland	36	975	27.1
1977—Raymond Clayborn, NE	20	869	31.0	1963—Bobby Jancik, Houston	45	1,317	29.3
1976—Duriel Harris, Miami	17	559	32.9	1962—Bobby Jancik, Houston	24	726	30.3
1975—Harold Hart, Oakland	17	518	30.5	1961—Dave Grayson, Dallas	16	453	28.3
1974—Greg Pruitt, Cleveland	22	606	27.5	1960—Ken Hall, Houston	19	594	31.3

SACKS

1987—Andre Tippett, New England	12.5	1984—Mark Gastineau, New York	22.0
1986—Sean Jones, Los Angeles	15.5	1983—Mark Gastineau, New York	19.0
1985—Andre Tippett, New England	16.5	1982—Jesse Baker, Houston	7.5

ALL-TIME PRO FOOTBALL RECORDS

(Through 1987 season)

RUSHING

LEADING LIFETIME RUSHERS

(Courtesy of Pro Football's Hall of Fame, Canton, Ohio)

Player	League	Yrs.	Att.	Yards	Avg.	TD
WALTER PAYTON	NFL	13	3838	16726	4.4	110
JIM BROWN	NFL	9	2359	12312	5.2	106
FRANCO HARRIS	NFL	13	2949	12120	4.1	91
TONY DORSETT	NFL	11	2755	12036	4.4	72
JOHN RIGGINS	NFL	14	2916	11352	3.9	104
O.J. SIMPSON	AFL-NFL	11	2404	11236	4.7	61
JOE PERRY	AAFC-NFL	16	1929	9723	5.0	71
EARL CAMPBELL	NFL	8	2187	9407	4.3	74
JIM TAYLOR	NFL	10	1941	8597	4.4	83
ERIC DICKERSON	NFL	5	1778	8256	4.6	61
O. J. ANDERSON	NFL	9	1884	8086	4.3	47
LARRY CSONKA	AFL-NFL	11	1891	8081	4.3	64
MIKE PRUITT	NFL	11	1844	7378	4.0	51
LEROY KELLY	NFL	10	1727	7274	4.2	74
GEORGE ROGERS	NFL	7	1692	7176	4.2	54
JOHN HENRY JOHNSON	NFL-AFL	13	1571	6803	4.3	48
WILBERT MONTGOMERY	NFL	9	1540	6789	4.4	45
CHUCK MUNCIE	NFL	9	1561	6702	4.3	71
MARK VAN EEGHEN	NFL	10	1652	6651	4.0	37
LAWRENCE McCUTCHEON	NFL	10	1521	6578	4.3	26

NOTE—No new players entered the Top Twenty in 1987. Of those players active in 1987, Marcus Allen (6151 yards), Gerald Riggs (6143) and Freeman McNeil (5850) stand next in line to enter the Top Twenty.

AAFC—All-America Football Conference

AFL—American Football League

NFL—National Football League

Most Yards Gained, Season

2,105—Eric Dickerson, Los Angeles Rams, 1984

1,000-Yard Rushing Seasons by First-Year Players
Beattie Feathers, Chicago Bears, 1934, 1,004 yards
Cookie Gilchrist, Buffalo Bills, 1962, 1,096 yards
Paul Robinson, Cincinnati Bengals, 1968, 1,023 yards
John Brockington, Green Bay Packers, 1971, 1,105 yards
Franco Harris, Pittsburgh Steelers, 1972, 1,055 yards
Larry McCutcheon, Los Angeles Rams, 1973, 1,097 yards. (McCutcheon considered a 1973 rookie as he played only 3 games in 1972 and did not carry the ball, playing only on special teams.)
Don Woods, San Diego Chargers, 1974, 1,162 yards
Tony Dorsett, Dallas Cowboys, 1977, 1,007 yards
Earl Campbell, Houston Oilers, 1978, 1,450 yards
Terry Miller, Buffalo Bills, 1978, 1,060 yards
Ottis Anderson, St. Louis Cardinals, 1979, 1,605 yards
William Andrews, Atlanta Falcons, 1979, 1,023 yards
Billy Sims, Detroit Lions, 1980, 1,303 yards
Joe Cribbs, Buffalo Bills, 1980, 1,185 yards
George Rogers, New Orleans Saints, 1981, 1,674 yards
Joe Delaney, Kansas City Chiefs, 1981, 1,121 yards
Eric Dickerson, Los Angeles Rams, 1983, 1,808 yards
Curt Warner, Seattle Seahawks, 1983, 1,449 yards
Greg Bell, Buffalo Bills, 1984, 1,100 yards
Kevin Mack, Cleveland Browns, 1985, 1,104 yards. (Mack played in the United States Football League in 1984.)
Rueben Mayes, New Orleans Saints, 1986, 1,353 yards

Most Seasons, 1,000 or More Yards Rushing

10—Walter Payton, Chicago Bears, 1976-1981, 1983-1986

Most Yards Gained, Game

275—Walter Payton, Chicago Bears vs. Minnesota Vikings, November 20, 1977

Longest Run From Scrimmage

99—Tony Dorsett, Dallas Cowboys vs. Minnesota Vikings, January 3, 1983

Most Games, 100 Yards or More, Season

12—Eric Dickerson, Los Angeles Rams, 1984

Most Games, 100 Yards or More, Career

77—Walter Payton, Chicago Bears, 1975-1987

Most Consecutive Games, 100 Yards or More

11—Marcus Allen, Los Angeles Raiders, October 28, 1985, through September 14, 1986

Most Games, 200 Yards or More, Career
    6—O. J. Simpson, Buffalo Bills, 1969-1976

Most Games, 200 Yards or More, Season
    4—Earl Campbell, Houston Oilers, 1980

Most Touchdowns Rushing, Career
    110—Walter Payton, Chicago Bears, 1975-1987

Most Touchdowns Rushing, Season
    24—John Riggins, Washington Redskins, 1983

Most Touchdowns Rushing, Game
    6—Ernie Nevers, Chicago Cardinals vs. Chicago Bears, November 28, 1929

Most Rushing Attempts, Season
    407—James Wilder, Tampa Bay Buccaneers, 1984

Most Rushing Attempts, Game
    43—Butch Woolfolk, New York Giants vs. Philadelphia Eagles, November 20, 1983
        James Wilder, Tampa Bay Buccaneers vs. Green Bay Packers, September 30, 1984 (OT)

PASSING

LEADING LIFETIME PASSERS
Minimum 1500 attempts
(Courtesy of Pro Football's Hall of Fame, Canton, Ohio)

Player	League	Yrs.	Att.	Comp.	Yds.	TD	Int.	Rating Pts.
DAN MARINO	NFL	5	2494	1512	19422	168	80	94.1
JOE MONTANA	NFL	9	3276	2084	24552	172	89	92.5
KEN O'BRIEN	NFL	5	1566	947	11676	69	43	86.8
OTTO GRAHAM	AAFC-NFL	10	2626	1464	23584	174	135	86.6
DAVE KRIEG	NFL	8	2116	1224	15808	130	88	84.5
ROGER STAUBACH	NFL	11	2958	1685	22700	153	109	83.4
SONNY JURGENSEN	NFL	18	4262	2433	32224	255	189	82.62
LEN DAWSON	NFL-AFL	19	3741	2136	28711	252	187	82.55
DANNY WHITE	NFL	12	2908	1732	21685	154	129	82.0
NEIL LOMAX	NFL	7	2710	1562	19376	116	79	82.0
KEN ANDERSON	NFL	16	4475	2654	32838	197	160	81.8
BART STARR	NFL	16	3149	1808	24718	152	138	80.5
FRAN TARKENTON	NFL	18	6467	3686	47003	342	266	80.4
DAN FOUTS	NFL	15	5604	3297	43040	254	242	80.2
BILL KENNEY	NFL	9	2316	1272	16728	105	81	78.4
BERT JONES	NFL	10	2551	1430	18190	124	101	78.2
JOHNNY UNITAS	NFL	18	5186	2830	40239	290	253	78.2
FRANK RYAN	NFL	13	2133	1090	16042	149	111	77.6
JOE THEISMANN	NFL	12	3602	2044	25206	160	138	77.4
BOB GRIESE	AFL-NFL	14	3429	1926	25092	192	172	77.1

NOTE—Ken O'Brien entered the Top Twenty during the 1987 season. He displaced Gary Danielson (76.8). Of those players active in 1987 who have the 1500 attempts needed to qualify for the career leadership, Danielson, Phil Simms (74.3), John Elway (74.1) and Tommy Kramer (73.6) rank the highest. Other active passers who would be ranked in the Top Twenty if they had the required 1500 attempts include Boomer Esiason (1442 att., 82.3), Tony Eason (1353 att., 81.9) and Jim McMahon (1321 att., 81.0).

    Rating points based on a combination of performances in the following four categories: percentage of completions, percentage of touchdown passes, percentage of interceptions and average gain per pass attempt.

    AAFC—All-America Football Conference
    AFL—American Football League
    NFL—National Football League

Most Yards Gained, Season
    5,084—Dan Marino, Miami Dolphins, 1984

Most Yards Gained, Game
    554—Norm Van Brocklin, Los Angeles Rams vs. New York Yankees, September 28, 1951 (27 completions in 41 attempts)

Most Games, 300 or More Yards Passing, Season
    9—Dan Marino, Miami Dolphins, 1984

Longest Pass Completion (99 Yards; All Touchdowns)
    Frank Filchock to Andy Farkas, Washington Redskins vs. Pittsburgh Steelers, October 15, 1939
    Otto Graham to Mac Speedie, Cleveland Browns vs. Buffalo Bills, November 2, 1947
    George Izo to Bobby Mitchell, Washington Redskins vs. Cleveland Browns, September 15, 1963
    Karl Sweetan to Pat Studstill, Detroit Lions vs. Baltimore Colts, October 16, 1966
    Sonny Jurgensen to Gerry Allen, Washington Redskins vs. Chicago Bears, September 15, 1968
    Jim Plunkett to Cliff Branch, Los Angeles Raiders vs. Washington Redskins, October 2, 1983
    Ron Jaworski to Mike Quick, Philadelphia Eagles vs. Atlanta Falcons, November 10, 1985

Most Touchdowns Passing, Career
　342—Fran Tarkenton, Minnesota Vikings, 1961-65; New York Giants 1967-71; Minnesota Vikings, 1972-78

Most Touchdowns Passing, Season
　48—Dan Marino, Miami Dolphins, 1984

Most Touchdowns Passing, Game
　7—Sid Luckman, Chicago Bears vs. New York Giants, November 14, 1943
　　Adrian Burk, Philadelphia Eagles vs. Washington Redskins, October 17, 1954
　　George Blanda, Houston Oilers vs. New York Titans, November 19, 1961
　　Y. A. Tittle, New York Giants vs. Washington Redskins, October 28, 1962
　　Joe Kapp, Minnesota Vikings vs. Baltimore Colts, September 28, 1969

Most Consecutive Games, Touchdown Passes
　47—Johnny Unitas, Baltimore Colts, 1956-60

Most Passing Attempts, Season
　623—Dan Marino, Miami Dolphins, 1986

Most Passing Attempts, Game
　68—George Blanda, Houston Oilers vs. Buffalo Bills, November 1, 1964 (37 completions)

Most Passes Completed, Season
　378—Dan Marino, Miami Dolphins, 1986

Most Passes Completed, Game
　42—Richard Todd, New York Jets vs. San Francisco 49ers, September 21, 1980

Most Consecutive Passes Completed
　22—Joe Montana, San Francisco 49ers vs. Cleveland Browns (5), November 29, 1987, and Green Bay Packers (17), December 6, 1987

Highest Completion Percentage, Season (Qualifiers)
　70.55—Ken Anderson, Cincinnati Bengals, 1982 (309-218)

Highest Completion Percentage, Game (20 attempts)
　90.91—Ken Anderson, Cincinnati Bengals vs. Pittsburgh Steelers, November 10, 1974 (22-20)

Most Passes Had Intercepted, Game
　8—Jim Hardy, Chicago Cardinals vs. Philadelphia Eagles, September 24, 1950 (39 attempts)

Most Passes Had Intercepted, Season
　42—George Blanda, Houston Oilers, 1962 (418 attempts)

Most Passes Had Intercepted, Career
　277—George Blanda, Chicago Bears, 1949, 1950-1958; Baltimore Colts 1950; Houston Oilers, 1960-1966; Oakland Raiders, 1967-1975 (4,007 attempts)

Most Consecutive Passes Attempted Without Interception
　294—Bart Starr, Green Bay Packers, 1964-1965

PASS RECEIVING

LEADING LIFETIME RECEIVERS
(Courtesy of Pro Football's Hall of Fame, Canton, Ohio)

Player	League	Yrs.	No.	Yards	Avg.	TD
STEVE LARGENT	NFL	12	752	12041	16.0	95
CHARLIE JOINER	AFL-NFL	18	750	12146	16.2	65
CHARLEY TAYLOR	NFL	13	649	9110	14.0	79
DON MAYNARD	NFL-AFL	15	633	11834	18.7	88
RAYMOND BERRY	NFL	13	631	9275	14.7	68
HAROLD CARMICHAEL	NFL	14	590	8985	15.2	79
FRED BILETNIKOFF	AFL-NFL	14	589	8974	15.2	76
HAROLD JACKSON	NFL	16	579	10372	17.9	76
OZZIE NEWSOME	NFL	10	575	7073	12.3	42
JAMES LOFTON	NFL	10	571	10536	18.4	54
LIONEL TAYLOR	NFL-AFL	10	567	7195	12.7	45
WES CHANDLER	NFL	10	555	8933	16.1	56
LANCE ALWORTH	AFL-NFL	11	542	10266	18.9	85
KELLEN WINSLOW	NFL	10	541	6741	12.5	45
JOHN STALLWORTH	NFL	14	537	8723	16.2	63
BOBBY MITCHELL	NFL	11	521	7954	15.3	65
NAT MOORE	NFL	13	510	7546	14.8	74
DWIGHT CLARK	NFL	9	506	6750	13.3	48
ART MONK	NFL	8	504	7033	14.0	34
BILLY HOWTON	NFL	12	503	8459	16.8	61

NOTE—Kellen Winslow, Dwight Clark and Art Monk all attained Top Twenty ranking during the 1987 season. They replaced Cliff Branch (501 catches), Tommy McDonald (495) and Ahmad Rashad (495). Of those players active in 1987, Tony Galbreath (490 catches) and Stanley Morgan (475) are the closest to a Top Twenty ranking.

　AFL—American Football League
　NFL—National Football League

Most Yards Gained, Season
   1,746—Charley Hennigan, Houston Oilers, 1961

Most Yards Gained, Game
   309—Stephone Paige, Kansas City Chiefs vs. San Diego Chargers, December 22, 1985 (8 receptions)

Longest Pass Reception
   (See receivers mentioned under Longest Pass Completion)

Most Pass Receptions, Season
   106—Art Monk, Washington Redskins, 1984

Most Pass Receptions, Game
   18—Tom Fears, Los Angeles Rams vs. Green Bay Packers, December 3, 1950 (189 yards)

Most Consecutive Games, Pass Receptions
   152—Steve Largent, Seattle Seahawks, 1976-1987 (current)

Most Touchdown Receptions, Career
   99—Don Hutson, Green Bay Packers, 1935-1945

Most Touchdown Receptions, Season
   22—Jerry Rice, San Francisco 49ers, 1987

Most Touchdowns Receptions, Game
   5—Bob Shaw, Chicago Cardinals vs. Baltimore Colts, October 2, 1950
      Kellen Winslow, San Diego Chargers vs. Oakland Raiders, November 22, 1981

Most Consecutive Games, Touchdown Receptions
   13—Jerry Rice, San Francisco 49ers, 1986-1987

PASS INTERCEPTIONS

Most Interceptions, Game
   4—Sammy Baugh, Washington Redskins vs. Detroit Lions, November 14, 1943
      Dan Sandifer, Washington Redskins vs. Boston Yanks, October 31, 1948
      Don Doll, Detroit Lions vs. Chicago Cardinals, October 23, 1949
      Bob Nussbaumer, Chicago Cardinals vs. New York Bulldogs, November 13, 1949
      Russ Craft, Philadelphia Eagles vs. Chicago Cardinals, September 24, 1950
      Bob Dillon, Green Bay Packers vs. Detroit Lions, November 26, 1953
      Jack Butler, Pittsburgh Steelers vs. Washington Redskins, December 13, 1953
      Jerry Norton, St. Louis Cardinals vs. Washington Redskins, November 20, 1960; vs. Pittsburgh
         Steelers, November 26, 1961
      Goose Gonsoulin, Denver Broncos vs. Buffalo Bills, September 18, 1960
      Dave Baker, San Francisco 49ers vs. Los Angeles Rams, December 4, 1960
      Bobby Ply, Dallas Texans vs. San Diego Chargers, December 16, 1962
      Bobby Hunt, Kansas City Chiefs vs. Houston Oilers, October 4, 1964
      Willie Brown, Denver Broncos vs. New York Jets, November 15, 1964
      Dick Anderson, Miami Dolphins vs. Pittsburgh Steelers, December 3, 1973
      Willie Buchanon, Green Bay Packers vs. San Diego Chargers, September 24, 1978
      Deron Cherry, Kansas City Chiefs vs. Seattle Seahawks, September 29, 1985

Most Interceptions, Season
   14—Dick Lane, Los Angeles Rams, 1952

Most Interceptions, Career
   81—Paul Krause, Washington Redskins, 1964-1967; Minnesota Vikings, 1968- 1979

Most Consecutive Games, Passes Intercepted By
   8—Tom Morrow, Oakland Raiders, 1962 (4), 1963 (4)

Most Yardage Gained via Pass Interceptions, Career
   1,282—Emlen Tunnell, New York Giants, 1948-1958; Green Bay Packers, 1959- 1961

Most Yardage Gained via Pass Interceptions, Season
   349—Charley McNeil, San Diego Chargers, 1961

Most Yardage Gained via Pass Interceptions, Game
   177—Charley McNeil, San Diego Chargers vs. Houston Oilers, September 24, 1961

Longest Run With Intercepted Pass (Touchdown)
   103—Vencie Glenn, San Diego Chargers vs. Denver Broncos, November 29, 1987.

Most Touchdowns Scored via Pass Interceptions, Lifetime
   9—Ken Houston, Houston Oilers, 1967 (2), 1968 (2), 1969, 1971 (4)

Most Touchdowns Scored via Pass Interceptions, Season
   4—Ken Houston, Houston Oilers, 1971
      Jim Kearney, Kansas City Chiefs, 1972

Most Touchdowns Scored via Pass Interceptions, Game
   2—Bill Blackburn, Chicago Cardinals vs. Boston Yanks, October 24, 1948
      Dan Sandifer, Washington Redskins vs. Boston Yanks, October 31, 1948
      Bob Franklin, Cleveland Browns vs. Chicago Bears, December 11, 1960

Bill Stacy, St. Louis Cardinals vs. Dallas Cowboys, November 5, 1961
Jerry Norton, St. Louis Cardinals vs. Pittsburgh Steelers, November 26, 1961
Miller Farr, Houston Oilers vs. Buffalo Bills, December 7, 1968
Ken Houston, Houston Oilers vs. San Diego Chargers, December 19, 1971
Jim Kearney, Kansas City Chiefs vs. Denver Broncos, October 1, 1972
Lemar Parrish, Cincinnati Bengals vs. Houston Oilers, December 17, 1972
Dick Anderson, Miami Dolphins vs. Pittsburgh Steelers, December 3, 1973
Prentice McCray, New England Patriots vs. New York Jets, November 21, 1976
Kenny Johnson, Atlanta Falcons vs. Green Bay Packers, November 27, 1983
Mike Kozlowski, Miami Dolphins vs. New York Jets, December 16, 1983
Dave Brown, Seattle Seahawks vs. Kansas City Chiefs, November 4, 1984
Lloyd Burruss, Kansas City Chiefs vs. San Diego Chargers, October 19, 1986

SCORING

LEADING LIFETIME SCORERS
(Courtesy of Pro Football's Hall of Fame, Canton, Ohio)

Player	League	Yrs.	TD	PAT	FG	Tot.
GEORGE BLANDA	NFL-AFL	26	9	943	335	2002
JAN STENERUD	AFL-NFL	19	0	580	373	1699
LOU GROZA	AAFC-NFL	21	1	810	264	1608
JIM TURNER	AFL-NFL	16	1	521	304	1439
MARK MOSELEY	NFL	16	0	482	300	1382
JIM BAKKEN	NFL	17	0	534	282	1380
FRED COX	NFL	15	0	519	282	1365
GINO CAPPELLETTI	AFL	11	42	350	176	1130
RAY WERSCHING	NFL	15	0	456	222	1122
DON COCKROFT	NFL	13	0	432	216	1080
PAT LEAHY	NFL	14	0	424	218	1078
GARO YEPREMIAN	NFL-AFL	14	0	444	210	1074
CHRIS BAHR	NFL	12	0	424	218	1042
BRUCE GOSSETT	NFL	11	0	374	219	1031
SAM BAKER	NFL	15	2	428	179	977
RAFAEL SEPTIEN	NFL	10	0	420	180	960
LOU MICHAELS	NFL	13	1	386	187	*955
ROY GERELA	AFL-NFL	11	0	351	184	903
BOBBY WALSTON	NFL	12	46	365	80	881
PETE GOGOLAK	AFL-NFL	10	0	344	173	863

NOTE—There were no new players added to the Top Twenty in 1987. Of those players who were active in 1987, Tony Franklin (844 points), Jim Breech (808), Nick Lowery (803) and Ed Murray (765) stand next in line to enter the Top Twenty.

*Includes safety.

AAFC—All-America Football Conference
AFL—American Football League
NFL—National Football League

Most Consecutive Games Scoring
151—Fred Cox, Minnesota Vikings, 1963-1973

Most Points, Season
176—Paul Hornung, Green Bay Packers, 1960 (15 TDs, 41 PATs, 15 FGs)

Most Points, Game
40—Ernie Nevers, Chicago Cardinals vs. Chicago Bears, November 28, 1929 (6 TDs, 4 PATs)

Most Touchdowns, Career
126—Jim Brown, Cleveland Browns, 1957-1965

Most Consecutive Games, Scoring Touchdowns
18—Lenny Moore, Baltimore Colts, 1963-1965

Most Touchdowns, Season
24—John Riggins, Washington Redskins, 1983 (all rushing)

Most Touchdowns, Game
6—Ernie Nevers, Chicago Cardinals vs. Chicago Bears, November 28, 1929 (6 rushing)
    Dub Jones, Cleveland Browns vs. Chicago Bears, November 25, 1951 (4 rushing, 2 pass receptions)
    Gale Sayers, Chicago Bears vs. San Francisco 49ers, December 12, 1965 (4 rushing, 1 pass reception, 1 punt return)

Most Points After Touchdown, Game
9—Pat Harder, Chicago Cardinals vs. New York Giants, October 17, 1948
    Joe Vetrano, San Francisco 49ers vs. Brooklyn Dodgers, November 21, 1948
    Bob Waterfield, Los Angeles Rams vs. Baltimore Colts, October 22, 1950
    Charlie Gogolak, Washington Redskins vs. New York Giants, November 27, 1966

Most Points After Touchdown, Season
66—Uwe von Schamann, Miami Dolphins, 1984 (70 attempts)

Most Consecutive Points After Touchdown
234—Tommy Davis, San Francisco 49ers, 1959-1965

Most Points After Touchdown (no misses), Season
56—Danny Villanueva, Dallas Cowboys, 1966
Ray Wersching, San Francisco 49ers, 1984

Most Points After Touchdown (no misses), Game
9—Pat Harder, Chicago Cardinals vs. New York Giants, October 17, 1948
Joe Vetrano, San Francisco 49ers vs. Brooklyn Dodgers, November 21, 1948
Bob Waterfield, Los Angeles Rams vs. Baltimore Colts, October 22, 1950

Most Points After Touchdown Attempted, Season
70—Uwe von Schamann, Miami Dolphins, 1984 (66 successful)

Most Points After Touchdown Attempted, Game
10—Charlie Gogolak, Washington Redskins vs. New York Giants, November 27, 1966 (9 successful)

Most Field Goals, Game
7—Jim Bakken, St. Louis Cardinals vs. Pittsburgh Steelers, September 24, 1967

Most Field Goals, Season
35—Ali Haji-Sheikh, New York Giants, 1983

Most Field Goals Attempted, Season
49—Bruce Gossett, Los Angeles Rams, 1966
Curt Knight, Washington Redskins, 1971

Most Field Goals Attempted, Game
9—Jim Bakken, St. Louis Cardinals vs. Pittsburgh Steelers, September 24, 1967 (7 successful)

Most Consecutive Field Goals
23—Mark Moseley, Washington Redskins, 1981-82

Most Consecutive Games, Field Goal
31—Fred Cox, Minnesota Vikings, 1968-1970

Longest Field Goal
63—Tom Dempsey, New Orleans Saints vs. Detroit Lions, November 8, 1970

Highest Field Goal Completion Percentage, Season (20 attempts)
95.2—Mark Moseley, Washington Redskins, 1982 (20 FGs in 21 attempts)

Highest Field Goal Percentage, Game (6 attempts)
100—Gino Cappelletti, Boston Patriots vs. Denver Broncos, October 4, 1964 (6 FGs in 6 attempts)
Joe Danelo, New York Giants vs. Seattle Seahawks, October 18, 1981 (6 FGs in 6 attempts)
Ray Wersching, San Francisco 49ers vs. New Orleans Saints, October 16, 1983 (6 FGs in 6 attempts)

Most Safeties, Career
4—Ted Hendricks, Baltimore Colts, 1969-73; Green Bay Packers, 1974; Oakland Raiders, 1975-81; Los Angeles Raiders, 1982-83
Doug English, Detroit Lions, 1975-79; 1981-85

Most Safeties, Season
2—Tom Nash, Green Bay Packers, 1932
Roger Brown, Detroit Lions, 1962
Ron McDole, Buffalo Bills, 1964
Alan Page, Minnesota Vikings, 1971
Benny Barnes, Dallas Cowboys, 1973
Fred Dryer, Los Angeles Rams, 1973
James Young, Houston Oilers, 1977
Tom Hannon, Minnesota Vikings, 1981
Doug English, Detroit Lions, 1983
Don Blackmon, New England Patriots, 1985

Most Safeties, Game
2—Fred Dryer, Los Angeles Rams vs. Green Bay Packers, October 21, 1973

PUNT RETURNS

Most Yardage Returning Punts, Career
3,291—Billy (White Shoes) Johnson, Houston Oilers, 1974-1980; Atlanta Falcons, 1982-1987

Most Yardage Returning Punts, Season
692—Fulton Walker, Los Angeles Raiders, 1985

Most Yardage Returning Punts, Game
207—LeRoy Irvin, Los Angeles Rams vs. Atlanta Falcons, October 11, 1981

Most Touchdowns Scored via Punt Returns, Career
8—Jack Christiansen, Detroit Lions, 1951 (4), 1952 (2), 1954, 1956
Rick Upchurch, Denver Broncos, 1976 (4), 1977 (1), 1978 (1), 1982 (2)

Most Touchdowns Scored via Punt Returns, Season
4—Jack Christiansen, Detroit Lions, 1951
Rick Upchurch, Denver Broncos, 1976

Most Touchdowns Scored via Punt Returns, Game

2—Jack Christiansen, Detroit Lions vs. Los Angeles Rams, October 14, 1951; vs. Green Bay Packers, November 22, 1951
Dick Christy, New York Titans vs. Denver Broncos, September 24, 1961
Rick Upchurch, Denver Broncos vs. Cleveland Browns, September 26, 1976
LeRoy Irvin, Los Angeles Rams vs. Atlanta Falcons, October 11, 1981
Vai Sikahema, St. Louis Cardinals vs. Tampa Bay Buccaneers, December 21, 1986

Most Punt Returns, Career

279—Billy (White Shoes) Johnson, Houston Oilers, 1974-1980; Atlanta Falcons, 1982-1987

Most Punt Returns, Season

70—Danny Reece, Tampa Bay Buccaneers, 1979

Most Punt Returns, Game

11—Eddie Brown, Washington Redskins vs. Tampa Bay Buccaneers, October 9, 1977

Longest Punt Return (All Touchdowns)

98—Gil LeFebvre, Cincinnati Reds vs. Brooklyn Dodgers, December 3, 1933
Charlie West, Minnesota Vikings vs. Washington Redskins, November 3, 1968
Dennis Morgan, Dallas Cowboys vs. St. Louis Cardinals, October 13, 1974

KICKOFF RETURNS

Most Yardage Returning Kickoffs, Career

6,922—Ron Smith, Chicago Bears, 1965; Atlanta Falcons, 1966-67; Los Angeles Rams, 1968-1969; Chicago Bears, 1970-1972; San Diego Chargers, 1973; Oakland Raiders, 1974

Most Yardage Returning Kickoffs, Season

1,345—Buster Rhymes, Minnesota Vikings, 1985

Most Yardage Returning Kickoffs, Game

294—Wally Triplett, Detroit Lions vs. Los Angeles Rams, October 29, 1950 (4 returns)

Most Touchdowns Scored via Kickoff Returns, Career

6—Ollie Matson, Chicago Cardinals, 1952 (2), 1954, 1956, 1958 (2)
Gale Sayers, Chicago Bears, 1965, 1966 (2), 1967 (3)
Travis Williams, Green Bay Packers, 1967 (4), 1969; Los Angeles Rams, 1971

Most Touchdowns Scored via Kickoff Returns, Season

4—Travis Williams, Green Bay Packers, 1967
Cecil Turner, Chicago Bears, 1970

Most Touchdowns Scored via Kickoff Returns, Game

2—Tim Brown, Philadelphia Eagles vs. Dallas Cowboys, November 6, 1966
Travis Williams, Green Bay Packers vs. Cleveland Browns, November 12, 1967
Ron Brown, Los Angeles Rams vs. Green Bay Packers, November 24, 1985

Most Kickoff Returns, Career

275—Ron Smith, Chicago Bears, 1965; Atlanta Falcons, 1966-67; Los Angeles Rams, 1968-1969; Chicago Bears, 1970-1972; San Diego Chargers, 1973; Oakland Raiders, 1974

Most Kickoff Returns, Season

60—Drew Hill, Los Angeles Rams, 1981

Most Kickoff Returns, Game

9—Noland Smith, Kansas City Chiefs vs. Oakland Raiders, November 23, 1967
Dino Hall, Cleveland Browns vs. Pittsburgh Steelers, October 7, 1979
Paul Palmer, Kansas City Chiefs vs. Seattle Seahawks, September 20, 1987

Longest Kickoff Return (All Touchdowns)

106—Al Carmichael, Green Bay Packers vs. Chicago Bears, October 7, 1956
Noland Smith, Kansas City Chiefs vs. Denver Broncos, December 17, 1967
Roy Green, St. Louis Cardinals vs. Dallas Cowboys, October 21, 1979

PUNTING

Highest Punting Average, Career (300 Punts)

44.5—Rohn Stark, Indianapolis Colts, 1982-1987 (450 punts)

Highest Punting Average, Season (Qualifiers)

51.4—Sammy Baugh, Washington Redskins, 1940 (35 punts)

Highest Punting Average, Game (4 Punts)

61.8—Bob Cifers, Detroit Lions vs. Chicago Bears, November 24, 1946

Longest Punt

98—Steve O'Neal, New York Jets vs. Denver Broncos, September 21, 1969

Most Punts, Career

1,154—Dave Jennings, New York Giants, 1974-1984; New York Jets, 1985-1987

Most Punts, Season

114—Bob Parsons, Chicago Bears, 1981

Most Punts, Game
   15—John Teltschik, Philadelphia Eagles vs. New York Giants (OT), December 6, 1987

MISCELLANEOUS RECORDS

Most Seasons, Active Player
   26—George Blanda, Chicago Bears, 1949, 1950-1958; Baltimore Colts, 1950; Houston Oilers, 1960-1966; Oakland Raiders, 1967-1975

Most Games Played, Career
   340—George Blanda, Chicago Bears, 1949, 1950-1958; Baltimore Colts, 1950; Houston Oilers, 1960-1966; Oakland Raiders, 1967-1975

Most Consecutive Games Played, Career
   282—Jim Marshall, Cleveland Browns, 1960; Minnesota Vikings, 1961-1979

Most Seasons, Coach
   40—George Halas, Chicago Bears, 1920-1929; 1933-1942; 1946-1955; 1958-1967

Most Fumbles, Career
   105—Roman Gabriel, Los Angeles Rams, 1962-72; Philadelphia Eagles, 1973-77

Most Fumbles, Season
   17—Dan Pastorini, Houston Oilers, 1973
       Warren Moon, Houston Oilers, 1984

Most Fumbles, Game
   7—Len Dawson, Kansas City Chiefs vs. San Diego Chargers, November 15, 1964

Longest Run With Recovered Fumble
   104—Jack Tatum, Oakland Raiders vs. Green Bay Packers, September 24, 1972

Philadelphia's John Teltschik set an NFL record by punting 15 times in the Eagles' 23-20 overtime loss to the Giants on December 6.

TEAM YEAR-BY-YEAR STANDINGS

ATLANTA FALCONS (1966-87)

Year	W.	L.	T.	Pct.	Pts.	Opp.	Head Coach
1987	3	12	0	.200	205	436	Marion Campbell
1986	7	8	1	.469	280	280	Dan Henning
1985	4	12	0	.250	282	452	Dan Henning
1984	4	12	0	.250	281	382	Dan Henning
1983	7	9	0	.438	370	389	Dan Henning
1982‡	5	4	0	.556	183	199	Leeman Bennett
1981	7	9	0	.438	426	355	Leeman Bennett
1980†	12	4	0	.750	405	272	Leeman Bennett
1979	6	10	0	.375	300	388	Leeman Bennett
1978*	9	7	0	.563	240	290	Leeman Bennett
1977	7	7	0	.500	179	129	Leeman Bennett
1976	4	10	0	.286	172	312	Marion Campbell, Pat Peppler
1975	4	10	0	.286	240	289	Marion Campbell
1974	3	11	0	.214	111	271	Norm Van Brocklin, Marion Campbell
1973	9	5	0	.643	318	224	Norm Van Brocklin
1972	7	7	0	.500	269	274	Norm Van Brocklin
1971	7	6	1	.538	274	277	Norm Van Brocklin
1970	4	8	2	.333	206	261	Norm Van Brocklin
1969	6	8	0	.429	276	268	Norm Van Brocklin
1968	2	12	0	.143	170	389	Norb Hecker, Norm Van Brocklin
1967	1	12	1	.077	175	422	Norb Hecker
1966	3	11	0	.214	204	437	Norb Hecker

*NFC wild-card team.
†NFC Western Division champion.
‡NFC playoff qualifier.

BUFFALO BILLS (1960-87)

Year	W.	L.	T.	Pct.	Pts.	Opp.	Head Coach
1987	7	8	0	.467	270	305	Marv Levy
1986	4	12	0	.250	287	348	Hank Bullough, Marv Levy
1985	2	14	0	.125	200	381	Kay Stephenson, Hank Bullough
1984	2	14	0	.125	250	454	Kay Stephenson
1983	8	8	0	.500	283	351	Kay Stephenson
1982	4	5	0	.444	150	154	Chuck Knox
1981‡	10	6	0	.625	311	276	Chuck Knox
1980§	11	5	0	.688	320	260	Chuck Knox
1979	7	9	0	.438	268	279	Chuck Knox
1978	5	11	0	.313	302	354	Chuck Knox
1977	3	11	0	.214	160	313	Jim Ringo
1976	2	12	0	.143	245	363	Lou Saban, Jim Ringo
1975	8	6	0	.571	420	355	Lou Saban
1974‡	9	5	0	.643	264	244	Lou Saban
1973	9	5	0	.643	259	230	Lou Saban
1972	4	9	1	.321	257	377	Lou Saban
1971	1	13	0	.071	184	394	Harvey Johnson
1970	3	10	1	.231	204	337	John Rauch
1969	4	10	0	.286	230	359	John Rauch
1968	1	12	1	.077	199	367	Joel Collier, Harvey Johnson
1967	4	10	0	.286	237	285	Joel Collier
1966†	9	4	1	.692	358	255	Joel Collier
1965*	10	3	1	.769	313	226	Lou Saban
1964*	12	2	0	.857	400	242	Lou Saban
1963	7	6	1	.538	304	291	Lou Saban
1962	7	6	1	.538	309	272	Lou Saban
1961	6	8	0	.429	294	342	Garrard Ramsey
1960	5	8	1	.385	296	303	Garrard Ramsey

*AFL champion.
†AFL Eastern Division champion.
‡AFC wild-card team.
§AFC Eastern Division champion.

CHICAGO BEARS (1920-87)

Year	W.	L.	T.	Pct.	Pts.	Opp.	Head Coach
1987x	11	4	0	.733	356	282	Mike Ditka
1986x	14	2	0	.875	352	187	Mike Ditka
1985y	15	1	0	.938	456	198	Mike Ditka
1984x	10	6	0	.625	325	248	Mike Ditka
1983	8	8	0	.500	311	301	Mike Ditka
1982	3	6	0	.333	141	174	Mike Ditka

Year	W.	L.	T.	Pct.	Pts.	Opp.	Head Coach
1981	6	10	0	.375	253	324	Neill Armstrong
1980	7	9	0	.438	304	264	Neill Armstrong
1979§	10	6	0	.625	306	249	Neill Armstrong
1978	7	9	0	.438	253	274	Neill Armstrong
1977§	9	5	0	.643	255	253	Jack Pardee
1976	7	7	0	.500	253	216	Jack Pardee
1975	4	10	0	.286	191	379	Jack Pardee
1974	4	10	0	.286	152	279	Abe Gibron
1973	3	11	0	.214	195	334	Abe Gibron
1972	4	9	1	.321	225	275	Abe Gibron
1971	6	8	0	.429	185	276	Jim Dooley
1970	6	8	0	.429	256	261	Jim Dooley
1969	1	13	0	.071	210	339	Jim Dooley
1968	7	7	0	.500	250	333	Jim Dooley
1967	7	6	1	.538	239	218	George Halas
1966	5	7	2	.417	234	272	George Halas
1965	9	5	0	.643	409	275	George Halas
1964	5	9	0	.357	260	379	George Halas
1963*	11	1	2	.917	301	144	George Halas
1962	9	5	0	.643	321	287	George Halas
1961	8	6	0	.571	326	302	George Halas
1960	5	6	1	.455	194	299	George Halas
1959	8	4	0	.667	252	196	George Halas
1958	8	4	0	.667	298	230	George Halas
1957	5	7	0	.417	203	211	John (Paddy) Driscoll
1956‡	9	2	1	.818	363	246	John (Paddy) Driscoll
1955	8	4	0	.667	294	251	George Halas
1954	8	4	0	.667	301	279	George Halas
1953	3	8	1	.273	218	262	George Halas
1952	5	7	0	.417	245	326	George Halas
1951	7	5	0	.583	286	282	George Halas
1950	9	3	0	.750	279	207	George Halas
1949	9	3	0	.750	332	218	George Halas
1948	10	2	0	.833	375	151	George Halas
1947	8	4	0	.667	363	241	George Halas
1946*	8	2	1	.800	289	193	George Halas
1945	3	7	0	.300	192	235	Hunk Anderson, Luke Johnsos (co-coaches)
1944	6	3	1	.667	258	172	Hunk Anderson, Luke Johnsos (co-coaches)
1943*	8	1	1	.889	303	157	Hunk Anderson, Luke Johnsos (co-coaches)
1942†	11	0	0	1.000	376	84	George Halas, Hunk Anderson, Luke Johnsos
1941*	10	1	0	.909	396	147	George Halas
1940*	8	3	0	.727	238	152	George Halas
1939	8	3	0	.727	298	157	George Halas
1938	6	5	0	.545	194	148	George Halas
1937†	9	1	1	.900	201	100	George Halas
1936	9	3	0	.750	222	94	George Halas
1935	6	4	2	.600	192	106	George Halas
1934†	13	0	0	1.000	286	86	George Halas
1933*	10	2	1	.833	133	82	George Halas
1932*	7	1	6	.875			Ralph Jones
1931	8	4	0	.667			Ralph Jones
1930	9	4	1	.692			Ralph Jones
1929	4	8	2	.333			George Halas
1928	7	5	1	.583			George Halas
1927	9	3	2	.750			George Halas
1926	12	1	3	.923			George Halas
1925	9	5	3	.643			George Halas
1924	6	1	4	.857			George Halas
1923	9	2	1	.818			George Halas
1922	9	3	0	.750			George Halas

Chicago Staleys

Year	W.	L.	T.	Pct.	Pts.	Opp.	Head Coach
1921*	10	1	1	.909			George Halas

Decatur Staleys

Year	W.	L.	T.	Pct.	Pts.	Opp.	Head Coach
1920	10	1	1	.909			George Halas

*NFL champion.
†NFL Western Division champion.
‡NFL Western Conference champion.
§NFC wild-card team.
xNFC Central Division champion.
ySuper Bowl champion.

CINCINNATI BENGALS (1968-87)

Year	W.	L.	T.	Pct.	Pts.	Opp.	Head Coach
1987	4	11	0	.267	285	370	Sam Wyche
1986	10	6	0	.625	409	394	Sam Wyche
1985	7	9	0	.438	441	437	Sam Wyche
1984	8	8	0	.500	339	339	Sam Wyche
1983	7	9	0	.438	346	302	Forrest Gregg
1982§	7	2	0	.778	232	177	Forrest Gregg
1981‡	12	4	0	.750	421	304	Forrest Gregg
1980	6	10	0	.375	244	312	Forrest Gregg
1979	4	12	0	.250	337	421	Homer Rice
1978	4	12	0	.250	252	284	Bill Johnson, Homer Rice
1977	8	6	0	.571	238	235	Bill Johnson
1976	10	4	0	.714	335	210	Bill Johnson
1975†	11	3	0	.786	340	246	Paul Brown
1974	7	7	0	.500	283	259	Paul Brown
1973*	10	4	0	.714	286	231	Paul Brown
1972	8	6	0	.571	299	229	Paul Brown
1971	4	10	0	.286	284	265	Paul Brown
1970*	8	6	0	.571	312	255	Paul Brown
1969	4	9	1	.308	280	367	Paul Brown
1968	3	11	0	.214	215	329	Paul Brown

*AFC Central Division champion.
†AFC wild-card team.
‡AFC champion.
§AFC playoff qualifier.

CLEVELAND BROWNS (1946-87)

Year	W.	L.	T.	Pct.	Pts.	Opp.	Head Coach
1987y	10	5	0	.667	390	239	Marty Schottenheimer
1986y	12	4	0	.750	391	310	Marty Schottenheimer
1985y	8	8	0	.500	287	294	Marty Schottenheimer
1984	5	11	0	.313	250	297	Sam Rutigliano, Marty Schottenheimer
1983	9	7	0	.562	356	342	Sam Rutigliano
1982a	4	5	0	.444	140	182	Sam Rutigliano
1981	5	11	0	.313	276	375	Sam Rutigliano
1980y	11	5	0	.688	357	310	Sam Rutigliano
1979	9	7	0	.563	359	352	Sam Rutigliano
1978	8	8	0	.500	334	356	Sam Rutigliano
1977	6	8	0	.429	269	267	Forrest Gregg, Dick Modzelewski
1976	9	5	0	.643	267	287	Forrest Gregg
1975	3	11	0	.214	218	372	Forrest Gregg
1974	4	10	0	.286	251	344	Nick Skorich
1973	7	5	2	.571	234	255	Nick Skorich
1972z	10	4	0	.714	268	249	Nick Skorich
1971y	9	5	0	.643	285	273	Nick Skorich
1970	7	7	0	.500	286	265	Blanton Collier
1969‡	10	3	1	.769	351	300	Blanton Collier
1968‡	10	4	0	.714	394	273	Blanton Collier
1967x	9	5	0	.643	334	297	Blanton Collier
1966	9	5	0	.643	403	259	Blanton Collier
1965‡	11	3	0	.786	363	325	Blanton Collier
1964†	10	3	1	.769	415	293	Blanton Collier
1963	10	4	0	.714	343	262	Blanton Collier
1962	7	6	1	.538	291	257	Paul Brown
1961	8	5	1	.615	319	270	Paul Brown
1960	8	3	1	.727	362	217	Paul Brown
1959	7	5	0	.583	270	214	Paul Brown
1958	9	3	0	.750	302	217	Paul Brown
1957‡	9	2	1	.818	269	172	Paul Brown
1956	5	7	0	.417	167	177	Paul Brown
1955†	9	2	1	.818	349	218	Paul Brown
1954†	9	3	0	.750	336	162	Paul Brown
1953‡	11	1	0	.917	348	162	Paul Brown
1952§	8	4	0	.667	310	213	Paul Brown
1951‡	11	1	0	.917	331	152	Paul Brown
1950†	10	2	0	.833	310	144	Paul Brown
1949*	9	1	2	.900	339	171	Paul Brown
1948*	14	0	0	1.000	389	190	Paul Brown
1947*	12	1	1	.923	410	185	Paul Brown
1946*	12	2	0	.857	423	137	Paul Brown

*AAFC champion.
†NFL champion.
‡NFL Eastern Conference champion.
§NFL American Conference champion.
xNFL Century Division champion.
yAFC Central Division champion.
zAFC wild-card team.
aAFC playoff qualifier.

DALLAS COWBOYS (1960-87)

Year	W.	L.	T.	Pct.	Pts.	Opp.	Head Coach
1987	7	8	0	.467	340	348	Tom Landry
1986	7	9	0	.438	346	337	Tom Landry
1985y	10	6	0	.625	357	333	Tom Landry
1984	9	7	0	.563	308	308	Tom Landry
1983x	12	4	0	.750	479	360	Tom Landry
1982z	6	3	0	.667	226	145	Tom Landry
1981y	12	4	0	.750	367	277	Tom Landry
1980x	12	4	0	.750	454	311	Tom Landry
1979y	11	5	0	.688	371	313	Tom Landry
1978‡	12	4	0	.750	384	208	Tom Landry
1977§	12	2	0	.857	345	212	Tom Landry
1976y	11	3	0	.786	296	194	Tom Landry
1975‡	10	4	0	.714	350	266	Tom Landry
1974	8	6	0	.571	297	235	Tom Landry
1973*	10	4	0	.714	382	203	Tom Landry
1972x	10	4	0	.714	319	240	Tom Landry
1971§	11	3	0	.786	406	222	Tom Landry
1970‡	10	4	0	.714	299	221	Tom Landry
1969†	11	2	1	.846	369	223	Tom Landry
1968†	12	2	0	.857	431	186	Tom Landry
1967*	9	5	0	.643	342	268	Tom Landry
1966*	10	3	1	.769	445	239	Tom Landry
1965	7	7	0	.500	325	280	Tom Landry
1964	5	8	1	.385	250	289	Tom Landry
1963	4	10	0	.286	305	378	Tom Landry
1962	5	8	1	.385	398	402	Tom Landry
1961	4	9	1	.308	236	380	Tom Landry
1960	0	11	1	.000	177	369	Tom Landry

*NFL Eastern Conference champion.
†NFL Capitol Division champion.
‡NFC champion.
§Super Bowl champion.
xNFC wild-card team.
yNFC Eastern Division champion.
zNFC playoff qualifier.

DENVER BRONCOS (1960-87)

Year	W.	L.	T.	Pct.	Pts.	Opp.	Head Coach
1987*	10	4	1	.700	379	288	Dan Reeves
1986*	11	5	0	.688	378	327	Dan Reeves
1985	11	5	0	.688	380	329	Dan Reeves
1984†	13	3	0	.813	353	241	Dan Reeves
1983‡	9	7	0	.562	302	327	Dan Reeves
1982	2	7	0	.222	148	226	Dan Reeves
1981	10	6	0	.625	321	289	Dan Reeves
1980	8	8	0	.500	310	323	Red Miller
1979‡	10	6	0	.625	289	262	Red Miller
1978†	10	6	0	.625	282	198	Red Miller
1977*	12	2	0	.857	274	148	Red Miller
1976	9	5	0	.643	315	206	John Ralston
1975	6	8	0	.429	254	307	John Ralston
1974	7	6	1	.586	302	294	John Ralston
1973	7	5	2	.571	354	296	John Ralston
1972	5	9	0	.357	325	350	John Ralston
1971	4	9	1	.308	203	275	Lou Saban, Jerry Smith
1970	5	8	1	.385	253	264	Lou Saban
1969	5	8	1	.385	297	344	Lou Saban
1968	5	9	0	.357	255	404	Lou Saban
1967	3	11	0	.214	256	409	Lou Saban
1966	4	10	0	.286	196	381	Mac Speedie, Ray Malavasi
1965	4	10	0	.286	303	392	Mac Speedie
1964	2	11	1	.154	240	438	Jack Faulkner, Mac Speedie
1963	2	11	1	.154	301	473	Jack Faulkner
1962	7	7	0	.500	353	334	Jack Faulkner
1961	3	11	0	.214	251	432	Frank Filchock
1960	4	9	1	.308	309	393	Frank Filchock

*AFC champion.
†AFC Western Division champion.
‡AFC wild-card team.

DETROIT LIONS (1930-87)

Year	W.	L.	T.	Pct.	Pts.	Opp.	Head Coach
1987	4	11	0	.267	269	384	Darryl Rogers
1986	5	11	0	.313	277	326	Darryl Rogers
1985	7	9	0	.438	307	366	Darryl Rogers
1984	4	11	1	.281	283	408	Monte Clark

Year	W.	L.	T.	Pct.	Pts.	Opp.	Head Coach
1983x	9	7	0	.562	347	286	Monte Clark
1982§	4	5	0	.444	181	176	Monte Clark
1981	8	8	0	.500	397	322	Monte Clark
1980	9	7	0	.563	334	272	Monte Clark
1979	2	14	0	.125	219	365	Monte Clark
1978	7	9	0	.438	290	300	Monte Clark
1977	6	8	0	.429	183	252	Tommy Hudspeth
1976	6	8	0	.429	262	220	Rick Forzano, Tommy Hudspeth
1975	7	7	0	.500	245	262	Rick Forzano
1974	7	7	0	.500	256	270	Rick Forzano
1973	6	7	1	.464	271	247	Don McCafferty
1972	8	5	1	.607	339	290	Joe Schmidt
1971	7	6	1	.538	341	286	Joe Schmidt
1970‡	10	4	0	.714	347	202	Joe Schmidt
1969	9	4	1	.692	259	188	Joe Schmidt
1968	4	8	2	.333	207	241	Joe Schmidt
1967	5	7	2	.417	260	259	Joe Schmidt
1966	4	9	1	.308	206	317	Harry Gilmer
1965	6	7	1	.462	257	295	Harry Gilmer
1964	7	5	2	.583	280	260	George Wilson
1963	5	8	1	.385	326	265	George Wilson
1962	11	3	0	.786	315	177	George Wilson
1961	8	5	1	.615	270	258	George Wilson
1960	7	5	0	.583	239	212	George Wilson
1959	3	8	1	.273	203	275	George Wilson
1958	4	7	1	.364	261	276	George Wilson
1957*	8	4	0	.667	251	231	George Wilson
1956	9	3	0	.750	300	188	Buddy Parker
1955	3	9	0	.250	230	275	Buddy Parker
1954†	9	2	1	.818	337	189	Buddy Parker
1953*	10	2	0	.833	271	205	Buddy Parker
1952*	9	3	0	.750	344	192	Buddy Parker
1951	7	4	1	.636	336	259	Buddy Parker
1950	6	6	0	.500	321	285	Alvin (Bo) McMillin
1949	4	8	0	.333	237	259	Alvin (Bo) McMillin
1948	2	10	0	.167	200	407	Alvin (Bo) McMillin
1947	3	9	0	.250	231	305	Gus Dorais
1946	1	10	0	.091	142	310	Gus Dorais
1945	7	3	0	.700	195	194	Gus Dorais
1944	6	3	1	.667	216	151	Gus Dorais
1943	3	6	1	.333	178	218	Gus Dorais
1942	0	11	0	.000	38	263	Bill Edwards, John Karcis
1941	4	6	1	.400	121	195	Bill Edwards
1940	5	5	1	.500	138	153	George (Potsy) Clark
1939	6	5	0	.545	145	150	Elmer (Gus) Henderson
1938	7	4	0	.636	119	108	Earl (Dutch) Clark
1937	7	4	0	.636	180	105	Earl (Dutch) Clark
1936	8	4	0	.667	235	102	George (Potsy) Clark
1935*	7	3	2	.700	191	111	George (Potsy) Clark
1934	10	3	0	.769	238	59	George (Potsy) Clark

Portsmouth Spartans

Year	W.	L.	T.	Pct.	Pts.	Opp.	Head Coach
1933	6	5	0	.545	128	87	George (Potsy) Clark
1932	6	2	4	.750			George (Potsy) Clark
1931	11	3	0	.786			George (Potsy) Clark
1930	5	6	3	.455			George (Potsy) Clark

*NFL champion.
†NFL Western Conference champion.
‡NFC wild-card team.
§NFC playoff qualifier.
xNFC Central Division champion.

GREEN BAY PACKERS (1921-87)

Year	W.	L.	T.	Pct.	Pts.	Opp.	Head Coach
1987	5	9	1	.367	255	300	Forrest Gregg
1986	4	12	0	.250	254	418	Forrest Gregg
1985	8	8	0	.500	337	355	Forrest Gregg
1984	8	8	0	.500	390	309	Forrest Gregg
1983	8	8	0	.500	429	439	Bart Starr
1982x	5	3	1	.611	226	169	Bart Starr
1981	8	8	0	.500	324	361	Bart Starr
1980	5	10	1	.44	231	371	Bart Starr
1979	5	11	0	.313	246	316	Bart Starr
1978	8	7	1	.531	249	269	Bart Starr
1977	4	10	0	.286	134	219	Bart Starr
1976	5	9	0	.357	218	299	Bart Starr
1975	4	10	0	.286	226	285	Bart Starr
1974	6	8	0	.429	210	206	Dan Devine
1973	5	7	2	.429	202	259	Dan Devine
1972§	10	4	0	.714	304	226	Dan Devine
1971	4	8	2	.333	274	298	Dan Devine
1970	6	8	0	.429	196	293	Phil Bengtson
1969	8	6	0	.571	269	221	Phil Bengtson
1968	6	7	1	.462	281	227	Phil Bengtson
1967‡	9	4	1	.692	332	209	Vince Lombardi
1966‡	12	2	0	.857	335	163	Vince Lombardi
1965*	10	3	1	.769	316	224	Vince Lombardi
1964	8	5	1	.615	342	245	Vince Lombardi
1963	11	2	1	.846	369	206	Vince Lombardi
1962*	13	1	0	.929	415	148	Vince Lombardi
1961*	11	3	0	.786	391	223	Vince Lombardi
1960†	8	4	0	.667	332	209	Vince Lombardi
1959	7	5	0	.583	248	246	Vince Lombardi
1958	1	10	1	.091	193	382	Ray (Scooter) McLean
1957	3	9	0	.250	218	311	Lisle Blackbourn
1956	4	8	0	.333	264	342	Lisle Blackbourn
1955	6	6	0	.500	258	276	Lisle Blackbourn
1954	4	8	0	.333	234	251	Lisle Blackbourn
1953	2	9	1	.182	200	338	Gene Ronzani
1952	6	6	0	.500	295	312	Gene Ronzani
1951	3	9	0	.250	254	375	Gene Ronzani
1950	3	9	0	.250	244	406	Gene Ronzani
1949	2	10	0	.167	114	329	Earl (Curly) Lambeau
1948	3	9	0	.250	154	290	Earl (Curly) Lambeau
1947	6	5	1	.545	274	210	Earl (Curly) Lambeau
1946	6	5	0	.545	148	158	Earl (Curly) Lambeau
1945	6	4	0	.600	258	173	Earl (Curly) Lambeau
1944*	8	2	0	.800	238	141	Earl (Curly) Lambeau
1943	7	2	1	.778	264	172	Earl (Curly) Lambeau
1942	8	2	1	.800	300	215	Earl (Curly) Lambeau
1941	10	1	0	.909	258	120	Earl (Curly) Lambeau
1940	6	4	1	.600	238	155	Earl (Curly) Lambeau
1939*	9	2	0	.818	233	153	Earl (Curly) Lambeau
1938†	7	4	0	.636	220	122	Earl (Curly) Lambeau
1937	7	4	0	.636	220	122	Earl (Curly) Lambeau
1936*	10	1	1	.909	248	118	Earl (Curly) Lambeau
1935	8	4	0	.667	181	96	Earl (Curly) Lambeau
1934	7	6	0	.538	156	112	Earl (Curly) Lambeau
1933	5	7	1	.417	170	107	Earl (Curly) Lambeau
1932	10	3	1	.769			Earl (Curly) Lambeau
1931*	12	2	0	.857			Earl (Curly) Lambeau
1930*	10	3	1	.769			Earl (Curly) Lambeau
1929*	12	0	1	1.000			Earl (Curly) Lambeau
1928	6	4	3	.600			Earl (Curly) Lambeau
1927	7	2	1	.778			Earl (Curly) Lambeau
1926	7	3	3	.700			Earl (Curly) Lambeau
1925	8	5	0	.615			Earl (Curly) Lambeau
1924	8	4	0	.667			Earl (Curly) Lambeau
1923	7	2	1	.778			Earl (Curly) Lambeau
1922	4	3	3	.571			Earl (Curly) Lambeau
1921	6	2	2	.750			Earl (Curly) Lambeau

*NFL champion.
†NFL Western Conference champion.
‡Super Bowl champion.
§NFC Central Division champion.
xNFC playoff qualifier.

HOUSTON OILERS (1960-87)

Year	W.	L.	T.	Pct.	Pts.	Opp.	Head Coach
1987‡	9	6	0	.600	345	349	Jerry Glanville
1986	5	11	0	.313	274	329	Jerry Glanville
1985	5	11	0	.313	284	412	Hugh Campbell, Jerry Glanville
1984	3	13	0	.188	240	437	Hugh Campbell
1983	2	14	0	.125	288	460	Ed Biles, Chuck Studley
1982	1	8	0	.111	136	245	Ed Biles
1981	7	9	0	.438	281	355	Ed Biles
1980‡	11	5	0	.688	295	251	O.A. (Bum) Phillips
1979‡	11	5	0	.688	362	331	O.A. (Bum) Phillips
1978‡	10	6	0	.625	283	298	O.A. (Bum) Phillips
1977	8	6	0	.571	299	230	O.A. (Bum) Phillips
1976	5	9	0	.357	222	273	O.A. (Bum) Phillips
1975	10	4	0	.714	293	226	O.A. (Bum) Phillips
1974	7	7	0	.500	236	282	Sid Gillman
1973	1	13	0	.071	199	447	Bill Peterson, Sid Gillman
1972	1	13	0	.071	164	380	Bill Peterson
1971	4	9	1	.308	251	330	Ed Hughes

Year	W.	L.	T.	Pct.	Pts.	Opp.	Head Coach
1970	3	10	1	.231	217	352	Wally Lemm
1969	6	6	2	.500	278	279	Wally Lemm
1968	7	7	0	.500	303	248	Wally Lemm
1967†	9	4	1	.692	258	199	Wally Lemm
1966	3	11	0	.214	335	396	Wally Lemm
1965	4	10	0	.286	298	429	Hugh (Bones) Taylor
1964	4	10	0	.286	310	355	Sammy Baugh
1963	6	8	0	.429	302	372	Frank (Pop) Ivy
1962†	11	3	0	.786	387	270	Frank (Pop) Ivy
1961*	10	3	1	.769	513	242	Lou Rymkus, Wally Lemm
1960*	10	4	0	.714	379	285	Lou Rymkus

*AFL champion.
†AFL Eastern Division champion.
‡AFC wild-card team.

INDIANAPOLIS COLTS (1953-87)

Year	W.	L.	T.	Pct.	Pts.	Opp.	Head Coach
1987x	9	6	0	.600	300	238	Ron Meyer
1986	3	13	0	.188	229	400	Rod Dowhower, Ron Meyer
1985	5	11	0	.313	320	386	Rod Dowhower
1984	4	12	0	.250	239	414	Frank Kush, Hal Hunter

Baltimore Colts

Year	W.	L.	T.	Pct.	Pts.	Opp.	Head Coach
1983	7	9	0	.438	264	354	Frank Kush
1982	0	8	1	.056	113	236	Frank Kush
1981	2	14	0	.125	259	533	Mike McCormack
1980	7	9	0	.438	355	387	Mike McCormack
1979	5	11	0	.313	271	351	Ted Marchibroda
1978	5	11	0	.313	239	421	Ted Marchibroda
1977x	10	4	0	.714	295	221	Ted Marchibroda
1976x	11	3	0	.786	417	246	Ted Marchibroda
1975x	10	4	0	.714	395	269	Ted Marchibroda
1974	2	12	0	.143	190	321	Howard Schn'lenberger, Joe Thomas
1973	4	10	0	.286	226	341	Howard Schnellenberger
1972	5	9	0	.357	235	252	Don McCafferty, John Sandusky
1971§	10	4	0	.714	313	140	Don McCafferty
1970‡	11	2	1	.846	321	234	Don McCafferty
1969	8	5	1	.615	279	268	Don Shula
1968*	13	1	0	.929	402	144	Don Shula
1967	11	1	2	.917	398	198	Don Shula
1966	9	5	0	.643	314	226	Don Shula
1965	10	3	1	.769	389	284	Don Shula
1964†	12	2	0	.857	428	225	Don Shula
1963	8	6	0	.571	316	285	Don Shula
1962	7	7	0	.500	293	288	Weeb Ewbank
1961	8	6	0	.571	302	307	Weeb Ewbank
1960	6	6	0	.500	288	234	Weeb Ewbank
1959*	9	3	0	.750	374	251	Weeb Ewbank
1958*	9	3	0	.750	381	203	Weeb Ewbank
1957	7	5	0	.583	303	235	Weeb Ewbank
1956	5	7	0	.417	270	322	Weeb Ewbank
1955	5	6	1	.455	214	239	Weeb Ewbank
1954	3	9	0	.250	131	279	Weeb Ewbank
1953	3	9	0	.250	182	350	Keith Molesworth

*NFL champion.
†Western Conference champion.
‡Super Bowl champion.
§AFC wild-card team.
xAFC Eastern Division champion.

KANSAS CITY CHIEFS (1960-87)

Year	W.	L.	T.	Pct.	Pts.	Opp.	Head Coach
1987	4	11	0	.267	273	388	Frank Gansz
1986x	10	6	0	.625	358	326	John Mackovic
1985	6	10	0	.375	317	360	John Mackovic
1984	8	8	0	.500	314	324	John Mackovic
1983	6	10	0	.375	386	367	John Mackovic
1982	3	6	0	.333	176	184	Marv Levy
1981	9	7	0	.563	343	290	Marv Levy
1980	8	8	0	.500	319	336	Marv Levy
1979	7	9	0	.438	238	262	Marv Levy
1978	4	12	0	.250	243	327	Marv Levy
1977	2	12	0	.143	225	349	Paul Wiggin, Tom Bettis

Year	W.	L.	T.	Pct.	Pts.	Opp.	Head Coach
1976	5	9	0	.357	290	376	Paul Wiggin
1975	5	9	0	.357	282	341	Paul Wiggin
1974	5	9	0	.357	233	293	Hank Stram
1973	7	5	2	.583	231	192	Hank Stram
1972	8	6	0	.571	287	254	Hank Stram
1971§	10	3	1	.769	302	208	Hank Stram
1970	7	5	2	.583	272	244	Hank Stram
1969‡	11	3	0	.786	359	177	Hank Stram
1968†	12	2	0	.857	371	170	Hank Stram
1967	9	5	0	.643	408	254	Hank Stram
1966*	11	2	1	.846	448	276	Hank Stram
1965	7	5	2	.583	322	285	Hank Stram
1964	7	7	0	.500	366	306	Hank Stram
1963	5	7	2	.417	347	263	Hank Stram

Dallas Texans

Year	W.	L.	T.	Pct.	Pts.	Opp.	Head Coach
1962*	11	3	0	.786	389	233	Hank Stram
1961	6	8	0	.429	334	343	Hank Stram
1960	8	6	0	.571	362	253	Hank Stram

*AFL champion.
†AFL Western Division co-champion.
‡Super Bowl champion.
§AFC Western Division champion.
xAFC wild-card team.

LOS ANGELES RAIDERS (1960-87)

Year	W.	L.	T.	Pct.	Pts.	Opp.	Head Coach
1987	5	10	0	.333	301	289	Tom Flores
1986	8	8	0	.500	323	346	Tom Flores
1985‡	12	4	0	.750	354	308	Tom Flores
1984x	11	5	0	.688	368	278	Tom Flores
1983§	12	4	0	.750	442	338	Tom Flores
1982y	8	1	0	.889	260	200	Tom Flores

Oakland Raiders

Year	W.	L.	T.	Pct.	Pts.	Opp.	Head Coach
1981	7	9	0	.438	273	343	Tom Flores
1980§	11	5	0	.688	364	306	Tom Flores
1979	9	7	0	.563	365	337	Tom Flores
1978	9	7	0	.563	311	283	John Madden
1977x	11	3	0	.786	351	230	John Madden
1976§	13	1	0	.929	350	237	John Madden
1975‡	11	3	0	.786	375	255	John Madden
1974‡	12	2	0	.857	355	228	John Madden
1973‡	9	4	1	.679	292	175	John Madden
1972‡	10	3	1	.750	365	248	John Madden
1971	8	4	2	.667	344	278	John Madden
1970‡	8	4	2	.667	300	293	John Madden
1969†	12	1	1	.923	377	242	John Madden
1968†	12	2	0	.857	453	233	John Rauch
1967*	13	1	0	.929	468	233	John Rauch
1966	8	5	1	.615	315	288	John Rauch
1965	8	5	1	.615	298	239	Al Davis
1964	5	7	2	.417	303	350	Al Davis
1963	10	4	0	.714	363	288	Al Davis
1962	1	13	0	.071	213	370	Marty Feldman, William Conkright
1961	2	12	0	.143	237	458	Eddie Erdelatz, Marty Feldman
1960	6	8	0	.429	319	399	Eddie Erdelatz

*AFL champion.
†AFL Western Division champion.
‡AFC Western Division champion.
§Super Bowl champion.
xAFC wild-card team.
yAFC playoff qualifier.

LOS ANGELES RAMS (1937-87)

Year	W.	L.	T.	Pct.	Pts.	Opp.	Head Coach
1987	6	9	0	.400	317	361	John Robinson
1986y	10	6	0	.625	309	267	John Robinson
1985§	11	5	0	.688	340	277	John Robinson
1984y	10	6	0	.625	346	316	John Robinson
1983y	9	7	0	.562	361	344	John Robinson
1982	2	7	0	.222	200	250	Ray Malavasi
1981	6	10	0	.375	303	351	Ray Malavasi
1980y	11	5	0	.688	424	289	Ray Malavasi
1979x	9	7	0	.563	323	309	Ray Malavasi

Year	W.	L.	T.	Pct.	Pts.	Opp.	Head Coach
1978§	12	4	0	.750	316	245	Ray Malavasi
1977§	10	4	0	.714	302	146	Chuck Knox
1976§	10	3	1	.750	351	190	Chuck Knox
1975§	12	2	0	.857	312	135	Chuck Knox
1974§	10	4	0	.714	263	181	Chuck Knox
1973§	12	2	0	.857	388	178	Chuck Knox
1972	6	7	1	.464	291	286	Tommy Prothro
1971	8	5	1	.615	313	260	Tommy Prothro
1970	9	4	1	.692	325	202	George Allen
1969‡	11	3	0	.786	320	243	George Allen
1968	10	3	1	.769	312	200	George Allen
1967‡	11	1	2	.917	398	196	George Allen
1966	8	6	0	.571	289	212	George Allen
1965	4	10	0	.286	269	328	Harland Svare
1964	5	7	2	.417	283	339	Harland Svare
1963	5	9	0	.357	210	350	Harland Svare
1962	1	12	1	.077	220	334	Bob Waterfield, Harland Svare
1961	4	10	0	.286	263	333	Bob Waterfield
1960	4	7	1	.364	265	297	Bob Waterfield
1959	2	10	0	.167	242	315	Sid Gillman
1958	8	4	0	.667	344	278	Sid Gillman
1957	6	6	0	.500	307	278	Sid Gillman
1956	4	8	0	.333	291	307	Sid Gillman
1955†	8	3	1	.727	260	231	Sid Gillman
1954	6	5	1	.545	314	285	Hampton Pool
1953	8	3	1	.727	366	236	Hampton Pool
1952	9	3	0	.750	349	234	Hampton Pool
1951*	8	4	0	.667	392	261	Joe Stydahar
1950†	9	3	0	.750	466	309	Joe Stydahar
1949†	8	2	2	.800	360	239	Clark Shaughnessy
1948	6	5	1	.545	327	269	Clark Shaughnessy
1947	6	6	0	.500	259	214	Bob Snyder
1946	6	4	1	.600	277	257	Adam Walsh

Cleveland Rams

Year	W.	L.	T.	Pct.	Pts.	Opp.	Head Coach
1945*	9	1	0	.900	244	136	Adam Walsh
1944	4	6	0	.400	188	224	Aldo (Buff)Donelli
1943	(Rams did not play in 1943)						

Year	W.	L.	T.	Pct.	Pts.	Opp.	Head Coach
1942	5	6	0	.455	150	207	Earl (Dutch) Clark
1941	2	9	0	.182	116	244	Earl (Dutch) Clark
1940	4	6	1	.400	171	191	Earl (Dutch) Clark
1939	5	5	1	.500	195	164	Earl (Dutch) Clark
1938	4	7	0	.363	131	215	Hugo Bezdek, Art Lewis
1937	1	10	0	.091	75	207	Hugo Bezdek

*NFL champion.
†NFL Western Conference champion.
‡NFL Coastal Division champion.
§NFC Western Division champion.
xNFC champion.
yNFC wild-card team.

MIAMI DOLPHINS (1966-87)

Year	W.	L.	T.	Pct.	Pts.	Opp.	Head Coach
1987	8	7	0	.533	362	335	Don Shula
1986	8	8	0	.500	430	405	Don Shula
1985§	12	4	0	.750	428	320	Don Shula
1984†	14	2	0	.875	513	298	Don Shula
1983§	12	4	0	.750	389	250	Don Shula
1982†	7	2	0	.778	198	131	Don Shula
1981§	11	4	1	.719	345	275	Don Shula
1980	8	8	0	.500	266	305	Don Shula
1979§	10	6	0	.625	341	257	Don Shula
1978*	11	5	0	.688	372	254	Don Shula
1977	10	4	0	.714	313	197	Don Shula
1976	6	8	0	.429	263	264	Don Shula
1975	10	4	0	.714	357	222	Don Shula
1974§	11	3	0	.786	327	216	Don Shula
1973‡	12	2	0	.857	343	150	Don Shula
1972‡	14	0	0	1.000	385	171	Don Shula
1971†	10	3	1	.769	315	174	Don Shula
1970*	10	4	0	.714	297	228	Don Shula
1969	3	10	1	.231	233	332	George Wilson
1968	5	8	1	.385	276	355	George Wilson
1967	4	10	0	.286	219	407	George Wilson

Year	W.	L.	T.	Pct.	Pts.	Opp.	Head Coach
1966	3	11	0	.214	213	362	George Wilson

*AFC wild-card team.
†AFC champion.
‡Super Bowl champion.
§AFC Eastern Division champion.

MINNESOTA VIKINGS (1961-87)

Year	W.	L.	T.	Pct.	Pts.	Opp.	Head Coach
1987y	8	7	0	.533	336	335	Jerry Burns
1986	9	7	0	.563	398	273	Jerry Burns
1985	7	9	0	.438	346	359	Harry (Bud) Grant
1984	3	13	0	.188	276	484	Les Steckel
1983	8	8	0	.500	316	348	Harry (Bud) Grant
1982x	5	4	0	.556	187	198	Harry (Bud) Grant
1981	7	9	0	.438	325	369	Harry (Bud) Grant
1980‡	9	7	0	.563	317	308	Harry (Bud) Grant
1979	7	9	0	.438	259	337	Harry (Bud) Grant
1978‡	8	7	1	.531	294	306	Harry (Bud) Grant
1977‡	9	5	0	.643	231	227	Harry (Bud) Grant
1976§	11	2	1	.821	305	176	Harry (Bud) Grant
1975‡	12	2	0	.857	377	180	Harry (Bud) Grant
1974§	10	4	0	.714	310	195	Harry (Bud) Grant
1973§	12	2	0	.857	296	168	Harry (Bud) Grant
1972	7	7	0	.500	301	252	Harry (Bud) Grant
1971‡	11	3	0	.786	245	139	Harry (Bud) Grant
1970‡	12	2	0	.857	335	143	Harry (Bud) Grant
1969†	12	2	0	.857	379	133	Harry (Bud) Grant
1968*	8	6	0	.571	282	242	Harry (Bud) Grant
1967	3	8	3	.273	233	294	Harry (Bud) Grant
1966	4	9	1	.308	292	304	Norm Van Brocklin
1965	7	7	0	.500	383	403	Norm Van Brocklin
1964	8	5	1	.615	355	296	Norm Van Brocklin
1963	5	8	1	.385	309	390	Norm Van Brocklin
1962	2	11	1	.154	254	410	Norm Van Brocklin
1961	3	11	0	.214	285	407	Norm Van Brocklin

*NFL Central Division champion.
†NFL champion.
‡NFC Central Division champion.
§NFC champion.
xNFC playoff qualifier.
yNFC wild-card team.

NEW ENGLAND PATRIOTS (1960-87)

Year	W.	L.	T.	Pct.	Pts.	Opp.	Head Coach
1987	8	7	0	.533	320	293	Raymond Berry
1986‡	11	5	0	.688	412	307	Raymond Berry
1985x	11	5	0	.688	362	290	Raymond Berry
1984	9	7	0	.563	362	352	Ron Meyer, Raymond Berry
1983	8	8	0	.500	274	289	Ron Meyer
1982§	5	4	0	.556	143	157	Ron Meyer
1981	2	14	0	.125	322	370	Ron Erhardt
1980	10	6	0	.625	441	325	Ron Erhardt
1979	9	7	0	.563	411	326	Ron Erhardt
1978‡	11	5	0	.688	358	286	C. Fairbanks, R. Erhardt, Hank Bullough
1977	9	5	0	.643	278	217	Chuck Fairbanks
1976†	11	3	0	.786	376	236	Chuck Fairbanks
1975	3	11	0	.214	258	358	Chuck Fairbanks
1974	7	7	0	.500	348	289	Chuck Fairbanks
1973	5	9	0	.357	258	300	Chuck Fairbanks
1972	3	11	0	.214	192	446	John Mazur, Phil Bengtson
1971	6	8	0	.429	238	325	John Mazur

Boston Patriots

Year	W.	L.	T.	Pct.	Pts.	Opp.	Head Coach
1970	2	12	0	.143	149	361	Clive Rush, John Mazur
1969	4	10	0	.286	266	316	Clive Rush
1968	4	10	0	.286	229	406	Mike Holovak
1967	3	10	1	.231	280	389	Mike Holovak
1966	8	4	2	.667	315	283	Mike Holovak
1965	4	8	2	.333	244	302	Mike Holovak
1964	10	3	1	.769	365	297	Mike Holovak
1963*	7	6	1	.538	327	257	Mike Holovak
1962	9	4	1	.692	346	295	Mike Holovak

Year	W.	L.	T.	Pct.	Pts.	Opp.	Head Coach
1961	9	4	1	.692	413	313	Lou Saban,
							Mike Holovak
1960	5	9	0	.357	286	349	Lou Saban

*AFL Eastern Division champion.
†AFC wild-card team.
‡AFC Eastern Division champion.
§AFC playoff qualifier.
xAFC champion.

NEW ORLEANS SAINTS (1967-87)

Year	W.	L.	T.	Pct.	Pts.	Opp.	Head Coach
1987*	12	3	0	.800	422	283	Jim Mora
1986	7	9	0	.438	288	287	Jim Mora
1985	5	11	0	.313	294	401	O.A. (Bum) Phillips,
							Wade Phillips
1984	7	9	0	.438	298	361	O.A. (Bum) Phillips
1983	8	8	0	.500	319	337	O.A. (Bum) Phillips
1982	4	5	0	.444	129	160	O.A. (Bum) Phillips
1981	4	12	0	.250	207	378	O.A. (Bum) Phillips
1980	1	15	0	.063	291	487	Dick Nolan, Dick Stanfel
1979	8	8	0	.500	370	360	Dick Nolan
1978	7	9	0	.438	281	298	Dick Nolan
1977	3	11	0	.214	232	336	Hank Stram
1976	4	10	0	.286	253	346	Hank Stram
1975	2	12	0	.143	165	360	John North,
							Ernie Hefferle
1974	5	9	0	.357	166	263	John North
1973	5	9	0	.357	163	312	John North
1972	2	11	1	.154	215	361	J.D. Roberts
1971	4	8	2	.333	266	347	J.D. Roberts
1970	2	11	1	.154	172	347	Tom Fears, J.D. Roberts
1969	5	9	0	.357	311	393	Tom Fears
1968	4	9	1	.308	246	327	Tom Fears
1967	3	11	0	.214	233	379	Tom Fears

*NFC wild-card team.

NEW YORK GIANTS (1925-87)

Year	W.	L.	T.	Pct.	Pts.	Opp.	Head Coach
1987	6	9	0	.400	280	312	Bill Parcells
1986x	14	2	0	.875	371	236	Bill Parcells
1985§	10	6	0	.625	399	283	Bill Parcells
1984§	9	7	0	.563	299	301	Bill Parcells
1983	3	12	1	.219	267	347	Bill Parcells
1982	4	5	0	.444	164	160	Ray Perkins
1981§	9	7	0	.563	295	257	Ray Perkins
1980	4	12	0	.250	249	425	Ray Perkins
1979	6	10	0	.375	237	323	Ray Perkins
1978	6	10	0	.375	264	298	John McVay
1977	5	9	0	.357	181	265	John McVay
1976	3	11	0	.214	170	250	Bill Arnsparger,
							John McVay
1975	5	9	0	.357	216	306	Bill Arnsparger
1974	2	12	0	.143	195	299	Bill Arnsparger
1973	2	11	1	.179	226	362	Alex Webster
1972	8	6	0	.571	331	247	Alex Webster
1971	4	10	0	.286	228	362	Alex Webster
1970	9	5	0	.643	301	270	Alex Webster
1969	6	8	0	.429	264	298	Alex Webster
1968	7	7	0	.500	294	325	Allie Sherman
1967	7	7	0	.500	369	379	Allie Sherman
1966	1	12	1	.077	263	501	Allie Sherman
1965	7	7	0	.500	270	338	Allie Sherman
1964	2	10	2	.167	241	399	Allie Sherman
1963‡	11	3	0	.786	448	280	Allie Sherman
1962‡	12	2	0	.857	398	283	Allie Sherman
1961‡	10	3	1	.769	368	220	Allie Sherman
1960	6	4	2	.600	271	261	Jim Lee Howell
1959‡	10	2	0	.833	284	170	Jim Lee Howell
1958‡	9	3	0	.750	246	183	Jim Lee Howell
1957	7	5	0	.583	254	211	Jim Lee Howell
1956*	8	3	1	.727	264	197	Jim Lee Howell
1955	6	5	1	.545	267	223	Jim Lee Howell
1954	7	5	0	.583	293	184	Jim Lee Howell
1953	3	9	0	.250	179	277	Steve Owen
1952	7	5	0	.583	234	231	Steve Owen
1951	9	2	1	.818	254	161	Steve Owen
1950	10	2	0	.833	268	150	Steve Owen
1949	6	6	0	.500	287	298	Steve Owen
1948	4	8	0	.333	297	388	Steve Owen
1947	2	8	2	.200	190	309	Steve Owen

Year	W.	L.	T.	Pct.	Pts.	Opp.	Head Coach
1946†	7	3	1	.700	236	162	Steve Owen
1945	3	6	1	.333	179	198	Steve Owen
1944†	8	1	1	.889	206	75	Steve Owen
1943	6	3	1	.667	197	170	Steve Owen
1942	5	5	1	.500	155	139	Steve Owen
1941†	8	3	0	.727	238	114	Steve Owen
1940	6	4	1	.600	131	133	Steve Owen
1939†	9	1	1	.900	168	85	Steve Owen
1938*	8	2	1	.800	194	79	Steve Owen
1937	6	3	2	.667	128	109	Steve Owen
1936	5	6	1	.455	115	163	Steve Owen
1935†	9	3	0	.750	180	96	Steve Owen
1934*	8	5	0	.615	147	107	Steve Owen
1933†	11	3	0	.786	244	101	Steve Owen
1932	4	6	2	.400	93	113	Steve Owen
1931	7	6	1	.538	154	100	Steve Owen
1930	13	4	0	.765	308	98	LeRoy Andrews
1929	13	1	1	.929	312	86	LeRoy Andrews
1928	4	7	2	.364	79	136	Earl Potteiger
1927*	11	1	1	.917	197	20	Earl Potteiger
1926	8	4	1	.667	147	51	Joe Alexander
1925	8	4	0	.667	122	67	Robert Folwell

*NFL champion.
†NFL Eastern Division champion.
‡NFL Eastern Conference champion.
§NFC wild-card team.
xSuper Bowl champion.

NEW YORK JETS (1960-87)

Year	W.	L.	T.	Pct.	Pts.	Opp.	Head Coach
1987	6	9	0	.400	334	360	Joe Walton
1986‡	10	6	0	.625	364	386	Joe Walton
1985‡	11	5	0	.688	393	264	Joe Walton
1984	7	9	0	.438	332	364	Joe Walton
1983	7	9	0	.438	313	331	Joe Walton
1982§	6	3	0	.667	245	166	Walt Michaels
1981‡	10	5	1	.656	355	287	Walt Michaels
1980	4	12	0	.250	302	395	Walt Michaels
1979	8	8	0	.500	337	383	Walt Michaels
1978	8	8	0	.500	359	364	Walt Michaels
1977	3	11	0	.214	191	300	Walt Michaels
1976	3	11	0	.214	169	383	Lou Holtz, Mike Holovak
1975	3	11	0	.214	256	433	Charley Winner,
							Ken Shipp
1974	7	7	0	.500	279	300	Charley Winner
1973	4	10	0	.286	240	306	Weeb Ewbank
1972	7	7	0	.500	367	324	Weeb Ewbank
1971	6	8	0	.429	212	299	Weeb Ewbank
1970	4	10	0	.286	255	286	Weeb Ewbank
1969†	10	4	0	.714	353	269	Weeb Ewbank
1968*	11	3	0	.786	419	280	Weeb Ewbank
1967	8	5	1	.615	371	329	Weeb Ewbank
1966	6	6	2	.500	322	312	Weeb Ewbank
1965	5	8	1	.385	285	303	Weeb Ewbank
1964	5	8	1	.385	278	315	Weeb Ewbank
1963	5	8	1	.385	249	399	Weeb Ewbank

New York Titans

Year	W.	L.	T.	Pct.	Pts.	Opp.	Head Coach
1962	5	9	0	.357	278	423	Clyde (Bulldog) Turner
1961	7	7	0	.500	301	390	Sammy Baugh
1960	7	7	0	.500	382	399	Sammy Baugh

*Super Bowl champion.
†AFL Eastern Division champion.
‡AFC wild-card team.
§AFC playoff qualifier.

PHILADELPHIA EAGLES (1933-87)

Year	W.	L.	T.	Pct.	Pts.	Opp.	Head Coach
1987	7	8	0	.467	337	380	Buddy Ryan
1986	5	10	1	.344	256	312	Buddy Ryan
1985	7	9	0	.438	286	310	Marion Campbell,
							Fred Bruney
1984	6	9	1	.406	278	320	Marion Campbell
1983	5	11	0	.313	233	322	Marion Campbell
1982	3	6	0	.333	191	195	Dick Vermeil
1981‡	10	6	0	.625	368	221	Dick Vermeil
1980§	12	4	0	.750	384	222	Dick Vermeil
1979‡	11	5	0	.688	339	282	Dick Vermeil

Year	W.	L.	T.	Pct.	Pts.	Opp.	Head Coach
1978‡	9	7	0	.563	270	250	Dick Vermeil
1977	5	9	0	.357	220	207	Dick Vermeil
1976	4	10	0	.286	165	286	Dick Vermeil
1975	4	10	0	.286	225	302	Mike McCormack
1974	7	7	0	.500	242	217	Mike McCormack
1973	5	8	1	.393	310	393	Mike McCormack
1972	2	11	1	.179	145	352	Ed Khayat
1971	6	7	1	.462	221	302	Jerry Williams, Ed Khayat
1970	3	10	1	.231	241	332	Jerry Williams
1969	4	9	1	.308	279	377	Jerry Williams
1968	2	12	0	.143	202	351	Joe Kuharich
1967	6	7	1	.462	351	409	Joe Kuharich
1966	9	5	0	.643	326	340	Joe Kuharich
1965	5	9	0	.357	363	359	Joe Kuharich
1964	6	8	0	.429	312	313	Joe Kuharich
1963	2	10	2	.167	242	381	Nick Skorich
1962	3	10	1	.231	282	356	Nick Skorich
1961	10	4	0	.714	361	297	Nick Skorich
1960†	10	2	0	.833	321	246	Lawrence (Buck) Shaw
1959	7	5	0	.583	268	278	Lawrence (Buck) Shaw
1958	2	9	1	.182	235	306	Lawrence (Buck) Shaw
1957	4	8	0	.333	173	230	Hugh Devore
1956	3	8	1	.273	143	215	Hugh Devore
1955	4	7	1	.364	248	231	Jim Trimble
1954	7	4	1	.636	284	230	Jim Trimble
1953	7	4	1	.636	352	215	Jim Trimble
1952	7	5	0	.583	252	271	Jim Trimble
1951	4	8	0	.333	234	264	Alvin (Bo) McMillin, Wayne Millner
1950	6	6	0	.500	254	141	Earle (Greasy) Neale
1949†	11	1	0	.917	364	134	Earle (Greasy) Neale
1948†	9	2	1	.818	376	156	Earle (Greasy) Neale
1947*	8	4	0	.667	308	242	Earle (Greasy) Neale
1946	6	5	0	.545	231	220	Earle (Greasy) Neale
1945	7	3	0	.700	272	133	Earle (Greasy) Neale
1944	7	1	2	.875	267	131	Earle (Greasy) Neale

Phil-Pitt Steagles
(Combined Philadelphia and Pittsburgh squads.)

Year	W.	L.	T.	Pct.	Pts.	Opp.	Head Coach
1943	5	4	1	.556	225	230	Greasy Neale, Walt Kiesling (co-coaches)

Philadelphia Eagles

Year	W.	L.	T.	Pct.	Pts.	Opp.	Head Coach
1942	2	9	0	.182	134	239	Earle (Greasy) Neale
1941	2	8	1	.200	119	218	Earle (Greasy) Neale
1940	1	10	0	.091	111	211	Bert Bell
1939	1	9	1	.100	105	200	Bert Bell
1938	5	6	0	.455	154	164	Bert Bell
1937	2	8	1	.200	86	177	Bert Bell
1936	1	11	0	.083	51	206	Bert Bell
1935	2	9	0	.182	60	179	Lud Wray
1934	4	7	0	.364	127	85	Lud Wray
1933	3	5	1	.375	77	158	Lud Wray

*NFL Eastern Division champion.
†NFL champion.
‡NFC wild-card team.
§NFC champion.

PITTSBURGH STEELERS (1933-87)

Year	W.	L.	T.	Pct.	Pts.	Opp.	Head Coach
1987	8	7	0	.533	285	299	Chuck Noll
1986	6	10	0	.375	307	336	Chuck Noll
1985	7	9	0	.438	379	355	Chuck Noll
1984*	9	7	0	.563	387	310	Chuck Noll
1983*	10	6	0	.625	355	303	Chuck Noll
1982§	6	3	0	.667	204	146	Chuck Noll
1981	8	8	0	.500	356	297	Chuck Noll
1980	9	7	0	.563	352	313	Chuck Noll
1979‡	12	4	0	.750	416	262	Chuck Noll
1978‡	14	2	0	.875	356	195	Chuck Noll
1977*	9	5	0	.643	283	243	Chuck Noll
1976*	10	4	0	.714	342	138	Chuck Noll
1975‡	12	2	0	.857	373	162	Chuck Noll
1974‡	10	3	1	.750	305	189	Chuck Noll
1973†	10	4	0	.714	347	210	Chuck Noll
1972*	11	3	0	.786	343	175	Chuck Noll
1971	6	8	0	.429	246	292	Chuck Noll
1970	5	9	0	.357	210	272	Chuck Noll

Year	W.	L.	T.	Pct.	Pts.	Opp.	Head Coach
1969	1	13	0	.071	218	404	Chuck Noll
1968	2	11	1	.154	244	397	Bill Austin
1967	4	9	1	.308	281	320	Bill Austin
1966	5	8	1	.385	316	347	Bill Austin
1965	2	12	0	.143	202	397	Mike Nixon
1964	5	9	0	.357	253	315	Buddy Parker
1963	7	4	3	.636	321	295	Buddy Parker
1962	9	5	0	.643	312	363	Buddy Parker
1961	6	8	0	.429	295	287	Buddy Parker
1960	5	6	1	.455	240	275	Buddy Parker
1959	6	5	1	.545	257	216	Buddy Parker
1958	7	4	1	.636	261	230	Buddy Parker
1957	6	6	0	.500	161	178	Buddy Parker
1956	5	7	0	.417	217	250	Walt Kiesling
1955	4	8	0	.333	195	285	Walt Kiesling
1954	5	7	0	.417	219	263	Walt Kiesling
1953	6	6	0	.500	211	263	Joe Bach
1952	5	7	0	.417	300	273	Joe Bach
1951	4	7	1	.364	183	235	John Michelosen
1950	6	6	0	.500	180	195	John Michelosen
1949	6	5	1	.545	224	214	John Michelosen
1948	4	8	0	.333	200	243	John Michelosen
1947	8	4	0	.667	240	259	Jock Sutherland
1946	5	5	1	.500	136	117	Jock Sutherland
1945	2	8	0	.200	79	220	Jim Leonard

Card-Pitt
(Combined Pittsburgh and Chicago Cardinals squads.)

Year	W.	L.	T.	Pct.	Pts.	Opp.	Head Coach
1944	0	10	0	.000	108	328	Walt Kiesling, Phil Handler (co-coaches)

Phil-Pitt Steagles
(Combined Pittsburgh and Philadelphia squads.)

Year	W.	L.	T.	Pct.	Pts.	Opp.	Head Coach
1943	5	4	1	.556	225	230	Walt Kiesling, Greasy Neale (co-coaches)

Pittsburgh Steelers

Year	W.	L.	T.	Pct.	Pts.	Opp.	Head Coach
1942	7	4	0	.636	167	119	Walt Kiesling
1941	1	9	1	.100	103	276	Bert Bell, Aldo (Buff) Donelli, Walt Kiesling

Pittsburgh Pirates

Year	W.	L.	T.	Pct.	Pts.	Opp.	Head Coach
1940	2	7	2	.222	60	178	Walt Kiesling
1939	1	9	1	.100	114	216	Johnny Blood (McNally), Walt Kiesling
1938	2	9	0	.182	79	169	Johnny Blood (McNally)
1937	4	7	0	.364	122	145	Johnny Blood (McNally)
1936	6	6	0	.500	98	187	Joe Bach
1935	4	8	0	.333	100	209	Joe Bach
1934	2	10	0	.167	51	206	Luby DiMelio
1933	3	6	2	.333	67	208	Forrest Douds

*AFC Central Division champion.
†AFC wild-card team.
‡Super Bowl champion.
§AFC playoff qualifier.

ST. LOUIS CARDINALS (1920-87)

Year	W.	L.	T.	Pct.	Pts.	Opp.	Head Coach
1987	7	8	0	.467	362	368	Gene Stallings
1986	4	11	1	.281	218	351	Gene Stallings
1985	5	11	0	.313	278	414	Jim Hanifan
1984	9	7	0	.563	423	345	Jim Hanifan
1983	8	7	1	.531	374	428	Jim Hanifan
1982§	5	4	0	.556	135	170	Jim Hanifan
1981	7	9	0	.438	315	408	Jim Hanifan
1980	5	11	0	.313	299	350	Jim Hanifan
1979	5	11	0	.313	307	358	Bud Wilkinson, Larry Wilson
1978	6	10	0	.375	248	296	Bud Wilkinson
1977	7	7	0	.500	272	287	Don Coryell
1976	10	4	0	.714	309	267	Don Coryell
1975‡	11	3	0	.786	356	276	Don Coryell
1974‡	10	4	0	.714	285	218	Don Coryell
1973	4	9	1	.308	286	365	Don Coryell
1972	4	9	1	.308	193	303	Bob Hollway
1971	4	9	1	.308	231	279	Bob Hollway
1970	8	5	1	.615	325	228	Charley Winner
1969	4	9	1	.308	314	389	Charley Winner

Year	W.	L.	T.	Pct.	Pts.	Opp.	Head Coach
1968	9	4	1	.692	325	289	Charley Winner
1967	6	7	1	.462	333	356	Charley Winner
1966	8	5	1	.615	264	265	Charley Winner
1965	5	9	0	.357	296	309	Wally Lemm
1964	9	3	2	.750	357	331	Wally Lemm
1963	9	5	0	.643	341	283	Wally Lemm
1962	4	9	1	.308	287	361	Wally Lemm
1961	7	7	0	.500	279	267	Frank (Pop) Ivy
1960	6	5	1	.545	288	230	Frank (Pop) Ivy

Chicago Cardinals

Year	W.	L.	T.	Pct.	Pts.	Opp.	Head Coach
1959	2	10	0	.167	234	324	Frank (Pop) Ivy
1958	2	9	1	.182	261	356	Frank (Pop) Ivy
1957	3	9	0	.250	200	299	Ray Richards
1956	7	5	0	.583	240	182	Ray Richards
1955	4	7	1	.364	224	252	Ray Richards
1954	2	10	0	.167	183	347	Joe Stydahar
1953	1	10	1	.091	190	337	Joe Stydahar
1952	4	8	0	.333	172	221	Joe Kuharich
1951	3	9	0	.250	210	287	Earl (Curly) Lambeau
1950	5	7	0	.417	233	287	Earl (Curly) Lambeau
1949	6	5	1	.545	360	301	Phil Handler, Buddy Parker (co-coaches)
1948†	11	1	0	.917	395	226	Jimmy Conzelman
1947*	9	3	0	.750	306	231	Jimmy Conzelman
1946	6	5	0	.545	260	198	Jimmy Conzelman
1945	1	9	0	.100	98	228	Phil Handler

Card-Pitt
(Combined Chicago Cardinals and Pittsburgh squads.)

Year	W.	L.	T.	Pct.	Pts.	Opp.	Head Coach
1944	0	10	0	.000	108	328	Phil Handler, Walt Kiesling (co-coaches)

Chicago Cardinals

Year	W.	L.	T.	Pct.	Pts.	Opp.	Head Coach
1943	0	10	0	.000	95	238	Phil Handler
1942	3	8	0	.273	98	209	Jimmy Conzelman
1941	3	7	1	.300	127	197	Jimmy Conzelman
1940	2	7	2	.222	139	222	Jimmy Conzelman
1939	1	10	0	.091	84	254	Ernie Nevers
1938	2	9	0	.182	111	168	Milan Creighton
1937	5	5	1	.500	135	165	Milan Creighton
1936	3	8	1	.273	74	143	Milan Creighton
1935	6	4	2	.600	99	97	Milan Creighton
1934	5	6	0	.455	80	84	Paul Schissler
1933	1	9	1	.100	52	101	Paul Schissler
1932	2	6	2	.250			Jack Chevigny
1931	5	4	0	.556			LeRoy Andrews, Ernie Nevers
1930	5	6	2	.455			Ernie Nevers
1929	6	6	1	.500			Ernie Nevers
1928	1	5	0	.167			Guy Chamberlin
1927	3	7	1	.300			Fred Gillies
1926	5	6	1	.455			Norman Barry
1925*	11	2	1	.846			Norman Barry
1924	5	4	1	.556			Arnold Horween
1923	8	4	0	.667			Arnold Horween
1922	8	3	0	.727			John (Paddy) Driscoll
1921	2	3	2	.400			John (Paddy) Driscoll
1920	5	2	1	.714			Marshall Smith

*NFL champion.
†NFL Western Division champion.
‡NFC Eastern Division champion.
§NFC playoff qualifier.

SAN DIEGO CHARGERS (1960-87)

Year	W.	L.	T.	Pct.	Pts.	Opp.	Head Coach
1987	8	7	0	.533	253	317	Al Saunders
1986	4	12	0	.250	335	396	Don Coryell, Al Saunders
1985	8	8	0	.500	467	435	Don Coryell
1984	7	9	0	.438	394	413	Don Coryell
1983	6	10	0	.375	358	462	Don Coryell
1982§	6	3	0	.667	288	221	Don Coryell
1981‡	10	6	0	.625	478	390	Don Coryell
1980‡	11	5	0	.688	418	327	Don Coryell
1979‡	12	4	0	.750	411	246	Don Coryell
1978	9	7	0	.563	355	309	Tommy Prothro, Don Coryell
1977	7	7	0	.500	222	205	Tommy Prothro
1976	6	8	0	.429	248	285	Tommy Prothro

Year	W.	L.	T.	Pct.	Pts.	Opp.	Head Coach
1975	2	12	0	.143	189	345	Tommy Prothro
1974	5	9	0	.357	212	285	Tommy Prothro
1973	2	11	1	.179	188	386	Harland Svare, Ron Waller
1972	4	9	1	.308	264	344	Harland Svare
1971	6	8	0	.429	311	341	Sid Gillman, Harland Svare
1970	5	6	3	.455	282	278	Charlie Waller
1969	8	6	0	.571	288	276	Sid Gillman, Charlie Waller
1968	9	5	0	.643	382	310	Sid Gillman
1967	8	5	1	.615	360	352	Sid Gillman
1966	7	6	1	.538	335	284	Sid Gillman
1965*	9	2	3	.818	340	227	Sid Gillman
1964*	8	5	1	.615	341	300	Sid Gillman
1963†	11	3	0	.786	399	256	Sid Gillman
1962	4	10	0	.286	314	392	Sid Gillman
1961*	12	2	0	.857	396	219	Sid Gillman

Los Angeles Chargers

Year	W.	L.	T.	Pct.	Pts.	Opp.	Head Coach
1960*	10	4	0	.714	373	336	Sid Gillman

*AFL Western Division champion.
†AFL champion.
‡AFC Western Division champion.
§AFC playoff qualifier.

SAN FRANCISCO 49ers (1946-87)

Year	W.	L.	T.	Pct.	Pts.	Opp.	Head Coach
1987*	13	2	0	.867	459	253	Bill Walsh
1986*	10	5	1	.656	374	247	Bill Walsh
1985‡	10	6	0	.625	411	263	Bill Walsh
1984†	15	1	0	.938	475	227	Bill Walsh
1983*	10	6	0	.625	432	293	Bill Walsh
1982	3	6	0	.333	209	206	Bill Walsh
1981†	13	3	0	.813	357	250	Bill Walsh
1980	6	10	0	.375	320	415	Bill Walsh
1979	2	14	0	.125	308	416	Bill Walsh
1978	2	14	0	.125	219	350	Pete McCulley, Fred O'Connor
1977	5	9	0	.357	220	260	Ken Meyer
1976	8	6	0	.571	270	190	Monte Clark
1975	5	9	0	.357	255	286	Dick Nolan
1974	6	8	0	.429	226	236	Dick Nolan
1973	5	9	0	.357	262	319	Dick Nolan
1972*	8	5	1	.607	353	249	Dick Nolan
1971*	9	5	0	.643	300	216	Dick Nolan
1970*	10	3	1	.769	352	267	Dick Nolan
1969	4	8	2	.333	277	319	Dick Nolan
1968	7	6	1	.538	303	310	Dick Nolan
1967	7	7	0	.500	273	337	Jack Christiansen
1966	6	6	2	.500	320	325	Jack Christiansen
1965	7	6	1	.538	421	402	Jack Christiansen
1964	4	10	0	.286	236	330	Jack Christiansen
1963	2	12	0	.143	198	391	Howard (Red) Hickey, Jack Christiansen
1962	6	8	0	.429	282	331	Howard (Red) Hickey
1961	7	6	1	.538	346	272	Howard (Red) Hickey
1960	7	5	0	.583	208	205	Howard (Red) Hickey
1959	7	5	0	.583	255	237	Howard (Red) Hickey
1958	6	6	0	.500	257	324	Frankie Albert
1957	8	4	0	.667	260	264	Frankie Albert
1956	5	6	1	.455	233	284	Frankie Albert
1955	4	8	0	.333	216	298	Norman (Red) Strader
1954	7	4	1	.636	313	251	Lawrence (Buck) Shaw
1953	9	3	0	.750	372	237	Lawrence (Buck) Shaw
1952	7	5	0	.583	285	221	Lawrence (Buck) Shaw
1951	7	4	1	.636	255	205	Lawrence (Buck) Shaw
1950	3	9	0	.250	213	300	Lawrence (Buck) Shaw
1949	9	3	0	.750	416	227	Lawrence (Buck) Shaw
1948	12	2	0	.857	495	248	Lawrence (Buck) Shaw
1947	8	4	2	.667	327	264	Lawrence (Buck) Shaw
1946	9	5	0	.643	307	189	Lawrence (Buck) Shaw

*NFC Western Division champion.
†Super Bowl champion.
‡NFC wild-card team.

SEATTLE SEAHAWKS (1976-87)

Year	W.	L.	T.	Pct.	Pts.	Opp.	Head Coach
1987*	9	6	0	.600	371	314	Chuck Knox

Year	W.	L.	T.	Pct.	Pts.	Opp.	Head Coach
1986	10	6	0	.625	366	293	Chuck Knox
1985	8	8	0	.500	349	313	Chuck Knox
1984*	12	4	0	.750	418	282	Chuck Knox
1983*	9	7	0	.562	403	397	Chuck Knox
1982	4	5	0	.444	127	147	Jack Patera, Mike McCormack
1981	6	10	0	.375	322	388	Jack Patera
1980	4	12	0	.250	291	408	Jack Patera
1979	9	7	0	.563	378	372	Jack Patera
1978	9	7	0	.563	345	358	Jack Patera
1977	5	9	0	.357	282	373	Jack Patera
1976	2	12	0	.143	229	429	Jack Patera

*AFC wild-card team.

TAMPA BAY BUCCANEERS (1976-87)

Year	W.	L.	T.	Pct.	Pts.	Opp.	Head Coach
1987	4	11	0	.267	286	360	Ray Perkins
1986	2	14	0	.125	239	473	Leeman Bennett
1985	2	14	0	.125	294	448	Leeman Bennett
1984	6	10	0	.375	335	380	John McKay
1983	2	14	0	.125	241	380	John McKay
1982†	5	4	0	.556	158	178	John McKay
1981*	9	7	0	.563	315	268	John McKay
1980	5	10	1	.344	271	341	John McKay
1979*	10	6	0	.625	273	237	John McKay
1978	5	11	0	.313	241	259	John McKay
1977	2	12	0	.143	103	223	John McKay
1976	0	14	0	.000	125	412	John McKay

*NFC Central Division champion.
†NFC playoff qualifier.

WASHINGTON REDSKINS (1932-87)

Year	W.	L.	T.	Pct.	Pts.	Opp.	Head Coach
1987x	11	4	0	.733	379	285	Joe Gibbs
1986‡	12	4	0	.750	368	296	Joe Gibbs
1985	10	6	0	.625	297	312	Joe Gibbs
1984y	11	5	0	.688	426	310	Joe Gibbs
1983§	14	2	0	.875	541	332	Joe Gibbs
1982x	8	1	0	.889	190	128	Joe Gibbs
1981	8	8	0	.500	347	349	Joe Gibbs
1980	6	10	0	.375	261	293	Jack Pardee
1979	10	6	0	.625	348	295	Jack Pardee
1978	8	8	0	.500	273	283	Jack Pardee
1977	9	5	0	.643	196	189	George Allen
1976‡	10	4	0	.714	291	217	George Allen
1975	8	6	0	.571	325	276	George Allen
1974‡	10	4	0	.714	320	196	George Allen
1973‡	10	4	0	.714	325	198	George Allen
1972§	11	3	0	.786	336	218	George Allen
1971‡	9	4	1	.692	276	190	George Allen
1970	6	8	0	.429	297	314	Bill Austin
1969	7	5	2	.583	307	319	Vince Lombardi
1968	5	9	0	.357	249	358	Otto Graham
1967	5	6	3	.455	347	353	Otto Graham
1966	7	7	0	.500	351	355	Otto Graham
1965	6	8	0	.429	257	301	Bill McPeak
1964	6	8	0	.429	307	305	Bill McPeak
1963	3	11	0	.214	279	398	Bill McPeak
1962	5	7	2	.417	305	376	Bill McPeak
1961	1	12	1	.077	174	392	Bill McPeak
1960	1	9	2	.100	178	309	Mike Nixon
1959	3	9	0	.250	185	350	Mike Nixon
1958	4	7	1	.364	214	268	Joe Kuharich
1957	5	6	1	.455	251	230	Joe Kuharich
1956	6	6	0	.500	183	225	Joe Kuharich
1955	8	4	0	.667	246	222	Joe Kuharich
1954	3	9	0	.250	207	432	Joe Kuharich
1953	6	5	1	.545	208	215	Earl (Curly) Lambeau
1952	4	8	0	.333	240	287	Earl (Curly) Lambeau
1951	5	7	0	.417	183	296	Herman Ball, Dick Todd
1950	3	9	0	.250	232	326	Herman Ball
1949	4	7	1	.364	268	339	John Whelchel, Herman Ball
1948	7	5	0	.583	291	287	Glen (Turk) Edwards
1947	4	8	0	.333	295	367	Glen (Turk) Edwards
1946	5	5	1	.500	171	191	Glen (Turk) Edwards

Joe Gibbs guided Washington to its second Super Bowl title in 1987.

Year	W.	L.	T.	Pct.	Pts.	Opp.	Head Coach
1945*	8	2	0	.800	209	121	Dudley DeGroot
1944	6	3	1	.667	169	180	Dudley DeGroot
1943*	6	3	1	.667	229	137	Arthur Bergman
1942†	10	1	0	.909	227	102	Ray Flaherty
1941	6	5	0	.545	176	174	Ray Flaherty
1940*	9	2	0	.818	245	142	Ray Flaherty
1939	8	2	1	.800	242	94	Ray Flaherty
1938	6	3	2	.667	148	154	Ray Flaherty
1937†	8	3	0	.727	195	120	Ray Flaherty

Boston Redskins

Year	W.	L.	T.	Pct.	Pts.	Opp.	Head Coach
1936*	7	5	0	.583	149	110	Ray Flaherty
1935	2	8	1	.200	65	123	Eddie Casey
1934	6	6	0	.500	107	94	William Dietz
1933	5	5	2	.500	103	97	William Dietz

Boston Braves

Year	W.	L.	T.	Pct.	Pts.	Opp.	Head Coach
1932	4	4	2	.500	55	79	Lud Wray

*NFL Eastern Division champion.
†NFL champion.
‡NFC wild-card team.
§NFC champion.
xSuper Bowl champion.
yNFC Eastern Division champion.

ALL-TIME SERIES RECORDS

Listed below are the all-time regular-season series records for all 28 NFL teams. The date to the right indicates the last time the two teams met in regular-season play. Although many current teams have played in different cities (in parentheses) and with different nicknames, for the purpose of this section franchises are recognized to have started in the following years: Atlanta, 1966; Buffalo, 1960; Chicago, 1920 (Decatur); Cincinnati, 1968; Cleveland, 1950; Dallas, 1960; Denver, 1960; Detroit, 1934; Green Bay, 1921; Houston, 1960; Indianapolis, 1953 (Baltimore); Kansas City, 1960 (Dallas); Los Angeles Raiders, 1960 (Oakland); Los Angeles Rams, 1946; Miami, 1966; Minnesota, 1961; New England, 1960 (Boston); New Orleans, 1967; New York Giants, 1925; New York Jets, 1960; Philadelphia, 1933; Pittsburgh, 1933; St. Louis, 1920 (Chicago); San Diego, 1960 (Los Angeles); San Francisco, 1950; Seattle, 1976; Tampa Bay, 1976; Washington, 1937. American Football League results (1960-69) are recognized; All-America Football Conference results (1946-49) are not.

Atlanta vs. Buffalo (1983)
(Series tied, 2-2)

Atlanta vs. Chicago (1986)
(Atlanta leads series, 9-6)

Atlanta vs. Cincinnati (1987)
(Cincinnati leads series, 5-1)

Atlanta vs. Cleveland (1987)
(Cleveland leads series, 7-1)

Atlanta vs. Dallas (1987)
(Dallas leads series, 6-3)

Atlanta vs. Denver (1985)
(Series tied, 3-3)

Atlanta vs. Detroit (1987)
(Detroit leads series, 13-5)

Atlanta vs. Green Bay (1983)
(Green Bay leads series, 8-6)

Atlanta vs. Houston (1987)
(Atlanta leads series, 4-2)

Atlanta vs. Indianapolis (1986)
(Indianapolis leads series, 9-0)

Atlanta vs. Kansas City (1985)
(Kansas City leads series, 2-0)

Atlanta vs. Los Angeles Raiders (1985)
(Raiders leads series, 4-1)

Atlanta vs. Los Angeles Rams (1987)
(Rams lead series, 30-10-2)

Atlanta vs. Miami (1986)
(Miami leads series, 4-1)

Atlanta vs. Minnesota (1987)
(Minnesota leads series, 10-6)

Atlanta vs. New England (1986)
(New England leads series, 3-2)

Atlanta vs. New Orleans (1987)
(Atlanta leads series, 24-13)

Atlanta vs. New York Giants (1984)
(Atlanta leads series, 6-5)

Atlanta vs. New York Jets (1986)
(Series tied, 2-2)

Atlanta vs. Philadelphia (1986)
(Philadelphia leads series, 7-5-1)

Atlanta vs. Pittsburgh (1987)
(Pittsburgh leads series, 7-1)

Atlanta vs. St. Louis (1987)
(St. Louis leads series, 7-4)

Atlanta vs. San Diego (1979)
(Atlanta leads series, 2-0)

Atlanta vs. San Francisco (1987)
(San Francisco leads series, 24-17-1)

Atlanta vs. Seattle (1985)
(Seattle leads series, 3-0)

Atlanta vs. Tampa Bay (1987)
(Tampa Bay leads series, 4-3)

Atlanta vs. Washington (1987)
(Washington leads series, 9-3-1)

Buffalo vs. Chicago (1979)
(Chicago leads series, 2-1)

Buffalo vs. Cincinnati (1986)
(Cincinnati leads series, 9-5)

Buffalo vs. Cleveland (1987)
(Cleveland leads series, 7-2)

Buffalo vs. Dallas (1984)
(Dallas leads series, 3-1)

Buffalo vs. Denver (1987)
(Buffalo leads series, 14-9-1)

Buffalo vs. Detroit (1979)
(Series tied, 1-1-1)

Buffalo vs. Green Bay (1982)
(Buffalo leads series, 2-1)

Buffalo vs. Houston (1987)
(Houston leads series, 18-10)

Buffalo vs. Indianapolis (1987)
(Series tied, 17-17-1)

Buffalo vs. Kansas City (1986)
(Buffalo leads series, 15-11-1)

Buffalo vs. Los Angeles Raiders (1987)
(Raiders lead series, 13-11)

Buffalo vs. Los Angeles Rams (1983)
(Rams lead series, 3-1)

Buffalo vs. Miami (1987)
(Miami leads series, 34-9-1)

Buffalo vs. Minnesota (1985)
(Minnesota leads series, 4-1)

Buffalo vs. New England (1987)
(New England leads series, 32-23-1)

Buffalo vs. New Orleans (1983)
(Buffalo leads series, 2-1)

Buffalo vs. New York Giants (1987)
(Series tied, 2-2)

Buffalo vs. New York Jets (1987)
(Jets lead series, 28-27)

Buffalo vs. Philadelphia (1987)
(Philadelphia leads series, 4-1)

Buffalo vs. Pittsburgh (1986)
(Pittsburgh leads series, 5-4)

Buffalo vs. St. Louis (1986)
(St. Louis leads series, 3-2)

Buffalo vs. San Diego (1985)
(San Diego leads series, 16-7-2)

Buffalo vs. San Francisco (1983)
(Buffalo leads series, 2-1)

Buffalo vs. Seattle (1984)
(Seattle leads series, 2-0)

Buffalo vs. Tampa Bay (1986)
(Tampa Bay leads series, 3-1)

Buffalo vs. Washington (1987)
(Washington leads series, 3-2)

Chicago vs. Cincinnati (1986)
(Cincinnati leads series, 2-1)
Chicago vs. Cleveland (1986)
(Cleveland leads series, 6-3)
Chicago vs. Dallas (1986)
(Dallas leads series, 7-5)
Chicago vs. Denver (1987)
(Series tied, 4-4)
Chicago vs. Detroit (1987)
(Chicago leads series, 62-42-3)
Chicago vs. Green Bay (1987)
(Chicago leads series, 74-55-6)
Chicago vs. Houston (1986)
(Series tied, 2-2)
Chicago vs. Indianapolis (1985)
(Indianapolis leads series, 21-14)
Chicago vs. Kansas City (1987)
(Chicago leads series, 3-1)
Chicago vs. Los Angeles Raiders (1987)
(Series tied, 3-3)
Chicago vs. Los Angeles Rams (1986)
(Chicago leads series, 31-22-3)
Chicago vs. Miami (1985)
(Miami leads series, 4-0)
Chicago vs. Minnesota (1987)
(Minnesota leads series, 26-25-2)
Chicago vs. New England (1985)
(Series tied, 2-2)
Chicago vs. New Orleans (1987)
(Chicago leads series, 8-4)
Chicago vs. New York Giants (1987)
(Chicago leads series, 23-14-2)
Chicago vs. New York Jets (1985)
(Chicago leads series, 2-1)
Chicago vs. Philadelphia (1987)
(Chicago leads series, 22-3-1)
Chicago vs. Pittsburgh (1986)
(Chicago leads series, 17-4-1)
Chicago vs. St. Louis (1984)
(Chicago leads series, 52-25-6)
Chicago vs. San Diego (1984)
(San Diego leads series, 4-1)
Chicago vs. San Francisco (1987)
(Chicago leads series, 24-23-1)
Chicago vs. Seattle (1987)
(Seattle leads series, 4-1)
Chicago vs. Tampa Bay (1987)
(Chicago leads series, 16-4)
Chicago vs. Washington (1985)
(Chicago leads series, 13-8)

Cincinnati vs. Cleveland (1987)
(Cleveland leads series, 18-17)
Cincinnati vs. Dallas (1985)
(Dallas leads series, 2-1)
Cincinnati vs. Denver (1986)
(Denver leads series, 9-6)
Cincinnati vs. Detroit (1986)
(Series tied, 2-2)
Cincinnati vs. Green Bay (1986)
(Cincinnati leads series, 4-2)
Cincinnati vs. Houston (1987)
(Cincinnati leads series, 21-16-1)
Cincinnati vs. Indianapolis (1987)
(Series tied, 5-5)
Cincinnati vs. Kansas City (1987)
(Kansas City leads series, 9-8)
Cincinnati vs. Los Angeles Raiders (1985)
(Raiders lead series, 11-4)
Cincinnati vs. Los Angeles Rams (1984)
(Cincinnati leads series, 3-2)
Cincinnati vs. Miami (1987)
(Miami leads series, 8-3)

Cincinnati vs. Minnesota (1986)
(Cincinnati leads series, 3-2)
Cincinnati vs. New England (1986)
(New England leads series, 6-4)
Cincinnati vs. New Orleans (1987)
(Series tied, 3-3)
Cincinnati vs. New York Giants (1985)
(Cincinnati leads series, 3-0)
Cincinnati vs. New York Jets (1987)
(Jets lead series, 7-4)
Cincinnati vs. Philadelphia (1982)
(Cincinnati leads series, 4-0)
Cincinnati vs. Pittsburgh (1987)
(Pittsburgh leads series, 20-15)
Cincinnati vs. St. Louis (1985)
(Cincinnati leads series, 2-1)
Cincinnati vs. San Diego (1987)
(San Diego leads series, 11-6)
Cincinnati vs. San Francisco (1987)
(San Francisco leads series, 4-1)
Cincinnati vs. Seattle (1987)
(Cincinnati leads series, 5-2)
Cincinnati vs. Tampa Bay (1983)
(Cincinnati leads series, 2-1)
Cincinnati vs. Washington (1985)
(Washington leads series, 3-1)

Cleveland vs. Dallas (1985)
(Cleveland leads series, 13-8)
Cleveland vs. Denver (1984)
(Denver leads series, 8-3)
Cleveland vs. Detroit (1986)
(Detroit leads series, 9-3)
Cleveland vs. Green Bay (1986)
(Green Bay leads series, 7-5)
Cleveland vs. Houston (1987)
(Cleveland leads series, 23-12)
Cleveland vs. Indianapolis (1987)
(Cleveland leads series, 10-4)
Cleveland vs. Kansas City (1986)
(Series tied, 5-5-1)
Cleveland vs. Los Angeles Raiders (1987)
(Raiders lead series, 8-2)
Cleveland vs. Los Angeles Rams (1987)
(Cleveland leads series, 7-6)
Cleveland vs. Miami (1986)
(Cleveland leads series, 4-1)
Cleveland vs. Minnesota (1986)
(Minnesota leads series, 6-2)
Cleveland vs. New England (1987)
(Cleveland leads series, 7-2)
Cleveland vs. New Orleans (1987)
(Cleveland leads series, 8-2)
Cleveland vs. New York Giants (1985)
(Cleveland leads series, 25-15-2)
Cleveland vs. New York Jets (1985)
(Cleveland leads series, 7-3)
Cleveland vs. Philadelphia (1982)
(Cleveland leads series, 29-11-1)
Cleveland vs. Pittsburgh (1987)
(Cleveland leads series, 45-31)
Cleveland vs. St. Louis (1985)
(Cleveland leads series, 30-10-3)
Cleveland vs. San Diego (1987)
(San Diego leads series, 6-5-1)
Cleveland vs. San Francisco (1987)
(Cleveland leads series, 8-5)
Cleveland vs. Seattle (1985)
(Seattle leads series, 7-2)
Cleveland vs. Tampa Bay (1983)
(Cleveland leads series, 3-0)
Cleveland vs. Washington (1985)
(Cleveland leads series, 31-8-1)

Dallas vs. Denver (1986)
(Series tied, 2-2)

Dallas vs. Detroit (1987)
(Dallas leads series, 6-4)

Dallas vs. Green Bay (1984)
(Green Bay leads series, 7-3)

Dallas vs. Houston (1985)
(Dallas leads series, 4-1)

Dallas vs. Indianapolis (1984)
(Dallas leads series, 6-2)

Dallas vs. Kansas City (1983)
(Dallas leads series, 2-1)

Dallas vs. Los Angeles Raiders (1987)
(Raiders lead series, 3-1)

Dallas vs. Los Angeles Rams (1987)
(Series tied, 7-7)

Dallas vs. Miami (1987)
(Miami leads series, 4-1)

Dallas vs. Minnesota (1987)
(Dallas leads series, 7-5)

Dallas vs. New England (1987)
(Dallas leads series, 6-0)

Dallas vs. New Orleans (1984)
(Dallas leads series, 11-1)

Dallas vs. New York Giants (1987)
(Dallas leads series, 35-14-2)

Dallas vs. New York Jets (1987)
(Dallas leads series, 4-0)

Dallas vs. Philadelphia (1987)
(Dallas leads series, 36-18)

Dallas vs. Pittsburgh (1985)
(Dallas leads series, 11-10)

Dallas vs. St. Louis (1987)
(Dallas leads series, 32-18-1)

Dallas vs. San Diego (1986)
(Dallas leads series, 3-1)

Dallas vs. San Francisco (1985)
(San Francisco leads series, 7-5-1)

Dallas vs. Seattle (1986)
(Dallas leads series, 3-1)

Dallas vs. Tampa Bay (1983)
(Dallas leads series, 4-0)

Dallas vs. Washington (1987)
(Dallas leads series, 31-21-2)

Denver vs. Detroit (1987)
(Denver leads series, 4-2)

Denver vs. Green Bay (1987)
(Denver leads series, 3-1-1)

Denver vs. Houston (1987)
(Houston leads series, 18-10-1)

Denver vs. Indianapolis (1985)
(Denver leads series, 6-1)

Denver vs. Kansas City (1987)
(Kansas City leads series, 34-21)

Denver vs. Los Angeles Raiders (1987)
(Raiders lead series, 36-17-2)

Denver vs. Los Angeles Rams (1985)
(Rams lead series, 3-2)

Denver vs. Miami (1985)
(Miami leads series, 5-2-1)

Denver vs. Minnesota (1987)
(Minnesota leads series, 3-2)

Denver vs. New England (1987)
(Denver leads series, 13-12)

Denver vs. New Orleans (1985)
(Denver leads series, 4-0)

Denver vs. New York Giants (1986)
(Series tied, 2-2)

Denver vs. New York Jets (1986)
(Jets lead series, 11-10-1)

Denver vs. Philadelphia (1986)
(Philadelphia leads series, 3-2)

Denver vs. Pittsburgh (1986)
(Denver leads series, 7-3-1)

Denver vs. St. Louis (1977)
(Denver leads series, 1-0-1)

Denver vs. San Diego (1987)
(San Diego leads series, 28-27-1)

Denver vs. San Francisco (1985)
(Denver lead series, 3-2)

Denver vs. Seattle (1987)
(Denver leads series, 13-8)

Denver vs. Tampa Bay (1981)
(Denver leads series, 2-0)

Denver vs. Washington (1986)
(Series tied, 2-2)

Detroit vs. Green Bay (1987)
(Green Bay leads series, 56-47-6)

Detroit vs. Houston (1986)
(Series tied, 2-2)

Detroit vs. Indianapolis (1985)
(Series tied, 17-17-2)

Detroit vs. Kansas City (1987)
(Kansas City leads series, 3-2)

Detroit vs. Los Angeles Raiders (1987)
(Raiders lead series, 4-2)

Detroit vs. Los Angeles Rams (1987)
(Rams lead series, 31-25-1)

Detroit vs. Miami (1985)
(Miami leads series, 2-1)

Detroit vs. Minnesota (1987)
(Minnesota leads series, 33-18-2)

Detroit vs. New England (1985)
(Series tied, 2-2)

Detroit vs. New Orleans (1980)
(Series tied, 4-4-1)

Detroit vs. New York Giants (1983)
(Detroit leads series, 13-8-1)

Detroit vs. New York Jets (1985)
(Series tied, 2-2)

Detroit vs. Philadelphia (1985)
(Detroit leads series, 11-9-2)

Detroit vs. Pittsburgh (1986)
(Detroit leads series, 13-9-1)

Detroit vs. St. Louis (1980)
(Detroit leads series, 26-13-3)

Detroit vs. San Diego (1984)
(Detroit leads series, 3-2)

Detroit vs. San Francisco (1985)
(Detroit leads series, 25-22-1)

Detroit vs. Seattle (1987)
(Seattle leads series, 3-1)

Detroit vs. Tampa Bay (1987)
(Detroit leads series, 11-9)

Detroit vs. Washington (1987)
(Washington leads series, 19-3)

Green Bay vs. Houston (1986)
(Houston leads series, 3-2)

Green Bay vs. Indianapolis (1985)
(Series tied, 17-17-1)

Green Bay vs. Kansas City (1987)
(Series tied, 1-1-1)

Green Bay vs. Los Angeles Raiders (1987)
(Raiders lead series, 5-0)

Green Bay vs. Los Angeles Rams (1985)
(Rams lead series, 36-21-1)

Green Bay vs. Miami (1985)
(Miami leads series, 4-0)

Green Bay vs. Minnesota (1987)
(Series tied, 26-26-1)

Green Bay vs. New England (1985)
(New England leads series, 2-1)

Green Bay vs. New Orleans (1987)
(Green Bay leads series, 10-4)

Green Bay vs. New York Giants (1987)
(Green Bay leads series, 21-19-2)

Green Bay vs. New York Jets (1985)
(Jets lead series, 4-1)

Green Bay vs. Philadelphia (1987)
(Green Bay leads series, 18-4)

Green Bay vs. Pittsburgh (1986)
(Green Bay leads series, 19-11)

Green Bay vs. St. Louis (1985)
(Green Bay leads series, 39-21-4)

Green Bay vs. San Diego (1984)
(Green Bay leads series, 3-1)

Green Bay vs. San Francisco (1987)
(San Francisco leads series, 24-20-1)

Green Bay vs. Seattle (1987)
(Green Bay leads series, 3-2)

Green Bay vs. Tampa Bay (1987)
(Green Bay leads series, 10-7-1)

Green Bay vs. Washington (1986)
(Washington leads series, 10-9)

Houston vs. Indianapolis (1987)
(Indianapolis leads series, 6-4)

Houston vs. Kansas City (1986)
(Kansas City leads series, 20-12)

Houston vs. Los Angeles Raiders (1986)
(Raiders lead series, 19-10)

Houston vs. Los Angeles Rams (1987)
(Rams lead series, 3-2)

Houston vs. Miami (1986)
(Miami leads series, 10-9)

Houston vs. Minnesota (1986)
(Series tied, 2-2)

Houston vs. New England (1987)
(New England leads series, 15-12-1)

Houston vs. New Orleans (1987)
(New Orleans leads series, 3-2-1)

Houston vs. New York Giants (1985)
(Giants lead series, 3-0)

Houston vs. New York Jets (1984)
(Houston leads series, 15-10-1)

Houston vs. Philadelphia (1982)
(Philadelphia leads series, 3-0)

Houston vs. Pittsburgh (1987)
(Pittsburgh leads series, 24-11)

Houston vs. St. Louis (1985)
(St. Louis leads series, 3-1)

Houston vs. San Diego (1987)
(San Diego leads series, 17-10-1)

Houston vs. San Francisco (1987)
(San Francisco leads series, 4-2)

Houston vs. Seattle (1982)
(Houston leads series, 3-2)

Houston vs. Tampa Bay (1983)
(Houston leads series, 2-1)

Houston vs. Washington (1985)
(Series tied, 2-2)

Indianapolis vs. Kansas City (1985)
(Kansas City leads series, 6-3)

Indianapolis vs. Los Angeles Raiders (1986)
(Raiders lead series, 3-2)

Indianapolis vs. Los Angeles Rams (1986)
(Indianapolis leads series, 20-16-2)

Indianapolis vs. Miami (1987)
(Miami leads series, 26-10)

Indianapolis vs. Minnesota (1982)
(Indianapolis leads series, 11-5-1)

Indianapolis vs. New England (1987)
(New England leads series, 19-16)

Indianapolis vs. New Orleans (1986)
(Indianapolis leads series, 3-1)

Indianapolis vs. New York Giants (1979)
(Indianapolis leads series, 5-3)

Indianapolis vs. New York Jets (1987)
(Indianapolis leads series, 18-17)

Indianapolis vs. Philadelphia (1984)
(Series tied, 5-5)

Indianapolis vs. Pittsburgh (1987)
(Pittsburgh leads series, 9-4)

Indianapolis vs. St. Louis (1984)
(St. Louis leads series, 5-4)

Indianapolis vs. San Diego (1987)
(San Diego leads series, 5-4)

Indianapolis vs. San Francisco (1986)
(Indianapolis leads series, 21-15)

Indianapolis vs. Seattle (1978)
(Indianapolis leads series, 2-0)

Indianapolis vs. Tampa Bay (1987)
(Indianapolis leads series, 3-1)

Indianapolis vs. Washington (1984)
(Indianapolis leads series, 15-6)

Kansas City vs. Los Angeles Raiders (1987)
(Raiders lead series, 31-22-2)

Kansas City vs. Los Angeles Rams (1985)
(Rams lead series, 3-0)

Kansas City vs. Miami (1987)
(Kansas City leads series, 7-6)

Kansas City vs. Minnesota (1981)
(Minnesota leads series, 2-1)

Kansas City vs. New England (1981)
(Kansas City leads series, 11-7-3)

Kansas City vs. New Orleans (1985)
(Series tied, 2-2)

Kansas City vs. New York Giants (1984)
(Giants lead series, 4-1)

Kansas City vs. New York Jets (1987)
(Series tied, 12-12)

Kansas City vs. Philadelphia (1972)
(Philadelphia leads series, 1-0)

Kansas City vs. Pittsburgh (1987)
(Pittsburgh leads series, 10-5)

Kansas City vs. St. Louis (1986)
(Kansas City leads series, 3-1-1)

Kansas City vs. San Diego (1987)
(Series tied, 27-27-1)

Kansas City vs. San Francisco (1985)
(San Francisco leads series, 3-1)

Kansas City vs. Seattle (1987)
(Kansas City leads series, 10-9)

Kansas City vs. Tampa Bay (1986)
(Kansas City leads series, 4-2)

Kansas City vs. Washington (1983)
(Kansas City leads series, 2-1)

L. A. Raiders vs. L. A. Rams (1985)
(Raiders lead series, 4-1)

Los Angeles Raiders vs. Miami (1986)
(Raiders lead series, 13-2-1)

Los Angeles Raiders vs. Minnesota (1987)
(Raiders lead series, 4-2)

Los Angeles Raiders vs. New England (1987)
(New England leads series, 12-11-1)

Los Angeles Raiders vs. New Orleans (1985)
(Raiders lead series, 3-0-1)

Los Angeles Raiders vs. N. Y. Giants (1986)
(Raiders lead series, 3-1)

Los Angeles Raiders vs. New York Jets (1985)
(Raiders lead series, 12-9-2)

Los Angeles Raiders vs. Philadelphia (1986)
(Series tied, 2-2)

Los Angeles Raiders vs. Pittsburgh (1984)
(Raiders lead series, 6-3)

Los Angeles Raiders vs. **St. Louis (1983)**
(Series tied, 1-1)

Los Angeles Raiders vs. **San Diego (1987)**
(Raiders lead series, 34-20-2)

Los Angeles Raiders vs. **San Francisco (1985)**
(Raiders lead series, 3-2)

Los Angeles Raiders vs. **Seattle (1987)**
(Series tied, 10-10)

Los Angeles Raiders vs. **Tampa Bay (1981)**
(Raiders lead series, 2-0)

Los Angeles Raiders vs. **Washington (1986)**
(Raiders lead series, 3-2)

Los Angeles Rams vs. **Miami (1986)**
(Miami leads series, 4-1)

Los Angeles Rams vs. **Minnesota (1987)**
(Minnesota leads series, 12-11-2)

Los Angeles Rams vs. **New England (1986)**
(New England leads series, 3-1)

Los Angeles Rams vs. **New Orleans (1987)**
(Rams lead series, 24-12)

Los Angeles Rams vs. **New York Giants (1985)**
(Rams lead series, 14-5)

Los Angeles Rams vs. **New York Jets (1986)**
(Rams lead series, 3-2)

Los Angeles Rams vs. **Philadelphia (1986)**
(Rams lead series, 14-9-1)

Los Angeles Rams vs. **Pittsburgh (1987)**
(Rams lead series, 15-3-2)

Los Angeles Rams vs. **St. Louis (1987)**
(Rams lead series, 14-8-2)

Los Angeles Rams vs. **San Diego (1979)**
(Rams lead series, 2-1)

Los Angeles Rams vs. **San Francisco (1987)**
(Rams lead series, 45-29-2)

Los Angeles Rams vs. **Seattle (1985)**
(Rams lead series, 3-0)

Los Angeles Rams vs. **Tampa Bay (1987)**
(Rams lead series, 6-2)

Los Angeles Rams vs. **Washington (1987)**
(Washington leads series, 12-5-1)

Miami vs. **Minnesota (1982)**
(Miami leads series, 3-1)

Miami vs. **New England (1987)**
(Miami leads series, 24-18)

Miami vs. **New Orleans (1986)**
(Miami leads series, 4-1)

Miami vs. **New York Giants (1972)**
(Miami leads series, 1-0)

Miami vs. **New York Jets (1987)**
(Miami leads series, 23-20-1)

Miami vs. **Philadelphia (1987)**
(Miami leads series, 4-2)

Miami vs. **Pittsburgh (1987)**
(Miami leads series, 6-2)

Miami vs. **St. Louis (1984)**
(Miami leads series, 5-0)

Miami vs. **San Diego (1986)**
(San Diego leads series, 8-4)

Miami vs. **San Francisco (1986)**
(Miami leads series, 4-1)

Miami vs. **Seattle (1987)**
(Miami leads series, 2-1)

Miami vs. **Tampa Bay (1985)**
(Miami leads series, 2-1)

Miami vs. **Washington (1987)**
(Miami leads series, 4-1)

Minnesota vs. **New England (1979)**
(New England leads series, 2-1)

Minnesota vs. **New Orleans (1986)**
(Minnesota leads series, 9-4)

Minnesota vs. **New York Giants (1986)**
(Minnesota leads series, 6-2)

Minnesota vs. **New York Jets (1982)**
(Jets lead series, 3-1)

Minnesota vs. **Philadelphia (1985)**
(Minnesota leads series, 9-3)

Minnesota vs. **Pittsburgh (1986)**
(Minnesota leads series, 6-3)

Minnesota vs. **St. Louis (1983)**
(St. Louis leads series, 7-2)

Minnesota vs. **San Diego (1985)**
(Series tied, 3-3)

Minnesota vs. **San Francisco (1986)**
(Minnesota leads series, 14-11-1)

Minnesota vs. **Seattle (1987)**
(Seattle leads series, 3-1)

Minnesota vs. **Tampa Bay (1987)**
(Minnesota leads series, 14-6)

Minnesota vs. **Washington (1987)**
(Washington leads series, 5-3)

New England vs. **New Orleans (1986)**
(New England leads series, 5-0)

New England vs. **New York Giants (1987)**
(Giants lead series, 2-1)

New England vs. **New York Jets (1987)**
(Jets lead series, 31-23-1)

New England vs. **Philadelphia (1987)**
(Philadelphia leads series, 4-2)

New England vs. **Pittsburgh (1986)**
(Pittsburgh leads series, 5-3)

New England vs. **St. Louis (1984)**
(St. Louis leads series, 4-1)

New England vs. **San Diego (1983)**
(New England leads series, 13-11-2)

New England vs. **San Francisco (1986)**
(San Francisco leads series, 4-1)

New England vs. **Seattle (1986)**
(New England leads series, 5-2)

New England vs. **Tampa Bay (1985)**
(New England leads series, 2-0)

New England vs. **Washington (1984)**
(Washington leads series, 3-1)

New Orleans vs. **New York Giants (1987)**
(Giants lead series, 7-6)

New Orleans vs. **New York Jets (1986)**
(Jets lead series, 4-1)

New Orleans vs. **Philadelphia (1987)**
(Philadelphia leads series, 9-6)

New Orleans vs. **Pittsburgh (1987)**
(New Orleans leads series, 5-4)

New Orleans vs. **St. Louis (1987)**
(St. Louis leads series, 10-5)

New Orleans vs. **San Diego (1979)**
(San Diego leads series, 3-0)

New Orleans vs. **San Francisco (1987)**
(San Francisco leads series, 24-11-2)

New Orleans vs. **Seattle (1985)**
(Seattle leads series, 2-1)

New Orleans vs. **Tampa Bay (1987)**
(New Orleans leads series, 7-3)

New Orleans vs. **Washington (1986)**
(Washington leads series, 8-4)

New York Giants vs. **New York Jets (1987)**
(Giants lead series, 3-2)

New York Giants vs. **Philadelphia (1987)**
(Giants lead series, 59-45-2)

New York Giants vs. **Pittsburgh (1985)**
(Giants lead series, 43-27-3)

New York Giants vs. **St. Louis (1987)**
(Giants lead series, 57-32-2)

New York Giants vs. San Diego (1986)
(Giants lead series, 3-2)
New York Giants vs. San Francisco (1987)
(Giants lead series, 10-6)
New York Giants vs. Seattle (1986)
(Giants lead series, 3-2)
New York Giants vs. Tampa Bay (1985)
(Giants lead series, 6-3)
New York Giants vs. Washington (1987)
(Giants lead series, 53-45-2)

New York Jets vs. Philadelphia (1987)
(Philadelphia leads series, 4-0)
New York Jets vs. Pittsburgh (1986)
(Pittsburgh leads series, 9-0)
New York Jets vs. St. Louis (1978)
(St. Louis leads series, 2-1)
New York Jets vs. San Diego (1983)
(San Diego leads series, 14-7-1)
New York Jets vs. San Francisco (1986)
(San Francisco leads series, 4-1)
New York Jets vs. Seattle (1987)
(Seattle leads series, 7-3)
New York Jets vs. Tampa Bay (1985)
(Jets lead series, 3-1)
New York Jets vs. Washington (1987)
(Washington leads series, 4-0)

Philadelphia vs. Pittsburgh (1979)
(Philadelphia leads series, 41-25-3)
Philadelphia vs. St. Louis (1987)
(St. Louis leads series, 41-35-5)
Philadelphia vs. San Diego (1986)
(Series tied, 2-2)
Philadelphia vs. San Francisco (1985)
(San Francisco leads series, 10-4-1)
Philadelphia vs. Seattle (1986)
(Philadelphia leads series, 2-1)
Philadelphia vs. Tampa Bay (1981)
(Philadelphia leads series, 2-0)
Philadelphia vs. Washington (1987)
(Washington leads series, 56-42-6)

Pittsburgh vs. St. Louis (1985)
(Pittsburgh leads series, 29-20-3)
Pittsburgh vs. San Diego (1987)
(Pittsburgh leads series, 9-3)
Pittsburgh vs. San Francisco (1987)
(Pittsburgh leads series, 7-6)
Pittsburgh vs. Seattle (1987)
(Pittsburgh leads series, 4-3)
Pittsburgh vs. Tampa Bay (1983)
(Pittsburgh leads series, 3-0)
Pittsburgh vs. Washington (1985)
(Washington leads series, 37-24-4)

St. Louis vs. San Diego (1987)
(San Diego leads series, 3-1)
St. Louis vs. San Francisco (1987)
(San Francisco leads series, 8-7)
St. Louis vs. Seattle (1983)
(St. Louis leads series, 2-0)
St. Louis vs. Tampa Bay (1987)
(St. Louis leads series, 5-3)
St. Louis vs. Washington (1987)
(Washington leads series, 50-30-1)

San Diego vs. San Francisco (1982)
(San Diego leads series, 3-1)
San Diego vs. Seattle (1987)
(Series tied, 9-9)
San Diego vs. Tampa Bay (1987)
(San Diego leads series, 3-0)
San Diego vs. Washington (1986)
(Washington leads series, 4-0)

San Francisco vs. Seattle (1985)
(San Francisco leads series, 2-1)
San Francisco vs. Tampa Bay (1987)
(San Francisco leads series, 7-1)
San Francisco vs. Washington (1986)
(San Francisco leads series, 7-6-1)

Seattle vs. Tampa Bay (1977)
(Seattle leads series, 2-0)
Seattle vs. Washington (1986)
(Washington leads series, 3-1)

Tampa Bay vs. Washington (1982)
(Washington leads series, 2-0)

NFL ANNUAL SELECTION MEETING

APRIL 24, 1988

Start of Round:
12:03 p.m.

FIRST ROUND

1. Atlanta	BRUCE, Aundray (1)	LB	Auburn
2. Kansas City from Detroit	SMITH, Neil (2)	DE	Nebraska
3. Detroit from Kansas City	BLADES, Bennie (3)	DB	Miami (Fla.)
4. Tampa Bay	GRUBER, Paul (4)	T	Wisconsin
5. Cincinnati	DIXON, Rickey (5)	DB	Oklahoma
6. Los Angeles Raiders	BROWN, Tim (6)	WR	Notre Dame
7. Green Bay	SHARPE, Sterling (7)	WR	South Carolina
8. New York Jets	CADIGAN, Dave (8)	T	Southern Cal
9. Los Angeles Raiders from L.A. Rams through Houston	McDANIEL, Terry (9)	DB	Tennessee
10. New York Giants	MOORE, Eric (10)	T	Indiana
11. Dallas	IRVIN, Michael (11)	WR	Miami (Fla.)
12. Phoenix	HARVEY, Ken (12)	LB	California
13. Philadelphia	JACKSON, Keith (13)	TE	Oklahoma
14. Los Angeles Rams from Buffalo	GREEN, Gaston (14)	RB	UCLA
15. San Diego	MILLER, Anthony (15)	WR	Tennessee
16. Miami	KUMEROW, Eric (16)	DE	Ohio State
17. New England	STEPHENS, John (17)	RB	N.W. Louisiana
18. Pittsburgh	JONES, Aaron (18)	DE	Eastern Kentucky
19. Minnesota Seattle	McDANIEL, Randall (19)	G	Arizona State

Choice exercised in 1987 Supplemental Draft
for Brian Bosworth, LB, Oklahoma

20. Los Angeles Rams from Indianapolis	COX, Aaron (20)	WR	Arizona State
21. Cleveland*	CHARLTON, Clifford (21)	LB	Florida
22. Houston	WHITE, Lorenzo (22)	RB	Michigan State
23. Chicago	MUSTER, Brad (23)	RB	Stanford
24. New Orleans	HEYWARD, Craig (24)	RB	Pittsburgh
25. Los Angeles Raiders from San Francisco	DAVIS, Scott (25)	DE	Illinois
26. Denver	GREGORY, Ted (26)	NT	Syracuse
27. Chicago from Washington	DAVIS, Wendell (27)	WR	Louisiana State

*Selected ahead of Houston, which passed.

End of Round:	**Time of Round:**	**Elapsed Time:**
3:32 p.m.	3 hours, 29 minutes	3 hours, 29 minutes

NFL ANNUAL SELECTION MEETING

APRIL 24, 1988

SECOND ROUND

1. Atlanta	COTTON, Marcus (28)	LB	Southern Cal
2. Detroit from Kansas City	SPIELMAN, Chris (29)	LB	Ohio State
3. Philadelphia from Tampa Bay	ALLEN, Eric (30)	DB	Arizona State
4. Cincinnati	WOODS, Ickey (31)	RB	Nevada-Las Vegas
5. Detroit	CARTER, Pat (32)	TE	Florida State
6. San Francisco from L.A. Raiders	STUBBS, Danny (33)	DE	Miami (Fla.)
7. Green Bay	PATTERSON, Shawn (34)	DT	Arizona State
8. Los Angeles Rams	NEWMAN, Anthony (35)	DB	Oregon
9. New York Giants	ELLIOTT, John (36)	T	Michigan
10. New York Jets	WILLIAMS, Terry (37)	DB	Bethune-Cookman
11. Phoenix	JEFFERY, Tony (38)	RB	Texas Christian
12. San Francisco from Philadelphia through Tampa Bay	HOLT, Pierce (39)	DT	Angelo State
13. Buffalo	THOMAS, Thurman (40)	RB	Oklahoma State
14. Dallas	NORTON, Ken (41)	LB	UCLA
15. Miami	WILLIAMS, Jarvis (42)	DB	Florida
16. New England	BROWN, Vincent (43)	LB	Miss. Valley St.
17. Pittsburgh	DAWSON, Dermontti (44)	G	Kentucky
18. Denver from Minnesota	PERRY, Gerald (45)	T	Southern U.
19. Los Angeles Rams from San Diego	ANDERSON, Willie (46)	WR	UCLA
20. Los Angeles Rams from Indianapolis	STRICKLAND, Fred (47)	LB	Purdue
21. Houston	JONES, Quintin (48)	DB	Pittsburgh
22. Seattle	BLADES, Brian (49)	WR	Miami (Fla.)
23. Cleveland	PERRY, Michael Dean (50)	DT	Clemson
24. Chicago	JONES, Dante (51)	LB	Oklahoma
25. New Orleans	PERRIMAN, Brett (52)	WR	Miami (Fla.)
26. Tampa Bay from San Francisco	TATE, Lars (53)	RB	Georgia
27. Minnesota from Denver	EDWARDS, Brad (54)	DB	South Carolina
28. Washington	LOHMILLER, Chip (55)	K	Minnesota

End of Round: 5:59 p.m.	Time of Round: 2 hours, 27 minutes	Elapsed Time: 5 hours, 56 minutes

NFL ANNUAL SELECTION MEETING

APRIL 24, 1988

Start of Round:
5:59 p.m.

THIRD ROUND

1. Atlanta   HIGDON, Alex (56)   TE   Ohio State
   Tampa Bay
   Choice exercised in 1987 Supplemental Draft
   for Dan Sileo, DT, Miami (Fla.)
2. Cincinnati   WALKER, Kevin (57)   LB   Maryland
3. Detroit   ROUNDTREE, Ray (58)   WR   Penn State
4. Kansas City   PORTER, Kevin (59)   DB   Auburn
5. San Diego   EARLY, Quinn (60)   WR   Iowa
   from L.A. Raiders through Houston
6. Green Bay   WOODSIDE, Keith (61)   RB   Texas A&M
7. New York Giants   WHITE, Sheldon (62)   DB   Miami (Ohio)
8. New York Jets   McMILLAN, Erik (63)   DB   Missouri
9. Philadelphia*   PATCHAN, Matt (64)   T   Miami (Fla.)
10. Buffalo*   FORD, Bernard (65)   WR   Central Florida
11. Washington   OLIPHANT, Mike (66)   KR   Puget Sound
    from L.A. Rams
12. Dallas   HUTSON, Mark (67)   G   Oklahoma
13. Phoenix   TUPA, Tom (68)   P   Ohio State
14. New England   REHDER, Tom (69)   T   Notre Dame
15. Pittsburgh   LANZA, Chuck (70)   C   Notre Dame
16. Minnesota   NOGA, Al (71)   DT   Hawaii
17. Houston   MONTGOMERY, Greg (72)   P   Michigan State
    from San Diego
18. Miami   EDMUNDS, Ferrell (73)   TE   Maryland
19. New York Jets   HASTY, James (74)   DB   Washington State
    from Houston through L.A. Raiders
20. Seattle   KANE, Tommy (75)   WR   Syracuse
21. Indianapolis   CHANDLER, Chris (76)   QB   Washington
22. Cleveland   WAITERS, Van (77)   LB   Indiana
23. Chicago   JARVIS, Ralph (78)   DE   Temple
24. Denver   GUIDRY, Kevin (79)   DB   Louisiana State
    from New Orleans
25. San Francisco   ROMANOWSKI, Bill (80)   LB   Boston College
26. New Orleans   STEPHENS, Tony (81)   NT   Clemson
    from Denver
27. Los Angeles Rams   PIEL, Mike (82)   DT   Illinois
    from Washington

*Selected ahead of Washington, which passed.

End of Round: Time of Round: Elapsed Time:
7:17 p.m.   1 hour, 18 minutes   7 hours, 14 minutes

NFL ANNUAL SELECTION MEETING

APRIL 24, 1988

FOURTH ROUND

1. Tampa Bay   GOFF, Robert (83)   DT   Auburn
   from Atlanta through Philadelphia
2. Cincinnati   GRANT, David (84)   NT   West Virginia
3. Detroit   WHITE, William (85)   DB   Ohio State
4. Tampa Bay   BRUHIN, John (86)   G   Tennessee
   from Kansas City
5. New England   GOAD, Tim (87)   NT   North Carolina
   from Tampa Bay
6. Green Bay   PUTZIER, Rollin (88)   DT   Oregon
   from L.A. Raiders
7. Green Bay   CECIL, Chuck (89)   DB   Arizona
8. Los Angeles Raiders   ROTHER, Tim (90)   DT   Nebraska
   from N.Y. Jets
9. San Diego   CAMPBELL, Joe (91)   DE   New Mexico State
   from L.A. Rams
10. New York Giants   SHAW, Ricky (92)   LB   Oklahoma State
11. San Diego   SEARELS, Stacy (93)   T   Auburn
    from Buffalo
12. Dallas   WIDELL, Dave (94)   T   Boston College
13. Phoenix   BRIM, Michael (95)   DB   Virginia Union

    Philadelphia
    Choice exercised in 1987 Supplemental Draft
    for Cris Carter, WR, Ohio State

14. Kansas City   AMBROSE, J.R. (96)   WR   Mississippi
    from Pittsburgh
15. New England   MARTIN, Sammy (97)   WR   Louisiana State
    from Minnesota
16. San Diego   RICHARDS, David (98)   T   UCLA
17. Miami   JOHNSON, Greg (99)   T   Oklahoma
18. New England   GARCIA, Teddy (100)   K   N.E. Louisiana
19. Seattle   HARMON, Kevin (101)   RB   Iowa
20. San Francisco*   HELTON, Barry (102)   P   Colorado
    from Houston through L.A. Raiders
21. Cleveland*   BLAYLOCK, Anthony (103)   DB   Winston-Salem
22. Indianapolis   BALL, Michael (104)   DB   Southern U.
23. Chicago   THORNTON, Jim (105)   TE   Fullerton State
24. New Orleans   CARR, Lydell (106)   RB   Oklahoma
25. Tampa Bay   ROBBINS, Monte (107)   P   Michigan
    from San Francisco
26. Minnesota   KALIS, Todd (108)   G   Arizona State
    from Denver
27. Washington   MORRIS, Jamie (109)   RB   Michigan

*Selected ahead of Indianapolis, which passed.

End of Round:	Time of Round:	Elapsed Time:
8:21 p.m.	1 hour, 4 minutes	8 hours, 18 minutes

NFL ANNUAL SELECTION MEETING

APRIL 24, 1988

Start of Round:
8:21 p.m.

FIFTH ROUND

1. Atlanta	DIMRY, Charles (110)	DB	Nevada-Las Vegas
2. Detroit	ANDOLSEK, Eric (111)	G	Louisiana State
3. New Orleans from Kansas City	SCALES, Greg (112)	TE	Wake Forest
4. Tampa Bay	HOWARD, William (113)	RB	Tennessee
5. Cincinnati	WESTER, Herb (114)	T	Iowa
6. New England from L.A. Raiders	WOLKOW, Troy (115)	G	Minnesota
7. Green Bay	REED, Darrell (116)	LB	Oklahoma
8. Los Angeles Rams	DELPINO, Robert (117)	RB	Missouri
9. New York Giants	CARTER, Jon (118)	DE	Pittsburgh
10. New York Jets	WITHYCOMBE, Mike (119)	T	Fresno State
11. Phoenix from Dallas through Seattle	GAINES, Chris (120)	LB	Vanderbilt
12. Pittsburgh from Phoenix	JORDAN, Darin (121)	LB	Northeastern
13. Philadelphia	EVERETT, Eric (122)	DB	Texas Tech
14. Buffalo	GADSON, Ezekial (123)	DB	Pittsburgh
15. Minnesota	FULLINGTON, Darrell (124)	DB	Miami (Fla.)
16. Houston from San Diego	DISHMAN, Cris (125)	DB	Purdue
17. Miami	THOMAS, Rodney (126)	DB	Brigham Young
18. Washington from New England	MIMS, Carl (127)	DB	Sam Houston State
19. Pittsburgh	REESE, Jerry (128)	NT	Kentucky
20. Indianapolis	BAYLOR, John (129)	DB	So. Mississippi
21. Houston	VERHULST, Chris (130)	TE	Chico State
22. Los Angeles Raiders from Sea. through S.F. & N.Y. Jets	PRICE, Dennis (131)	DB	UCLA
23. Phoenix from Cleveland	JORDAN, Tony (132)	RB	Kansas State
24. Chicago	JOHNSON, Troy (133)	LB	Oklahoma
25. New Orleans	TAYLOR, Keith (134)	DB	Illinois
26. Buffalo from San Francisco	ROACH, Kirk (135)	K	Western Carolina
27. Denver	ERVIN, Corris (136)	DB	Central Florida
28. Los Angeles Rams from Washington	WASHINGTON, James (137)	DB	UCLA

End of Round: | **Time of Round:** | **Elapsed Time:**
9:31 p.m. | **1 hour, 10 minutes** | **9 hours, 28 minutes**

NFL ANNUAL SELECTION MEETING

APRIL 25, 1988

SIXTH ROUND

1. Atlanta	THOMAS, George (138)	WR	Nevada-Las Vegas
2. Kansas City	SAXON, James (139)	RB	San Jose State
3. Atlanta from Tampa Bay	HOOVER, Houston (140)	G	Jackson State
4. Cincinnati	JETTON, Paul (141)	G	Texas
5. Detroit	PAINTER, Carl (142)	RB	Hampton (Va.)
6. Los Angeles Raiders	GRABISNA, Erwin (143)	LB	Case Western (O.)
7. Green Bay	HILL, Nate (144)	DE	Auburn
8. New York Giants	HOULE, David (145)	G	Michigan State
9. New York Jets	FRASE, Paul (146)	DE	Syracuse
10. Los Angeles Rams	JONES, Keith (147)	RB	Nebraska
11. Phoenix	PHILLIPS, Jon (148)	G	Oklahoma
12. Philadelphia	McPHERSON, Don (149)	QB	Syracuse
13. Buffalo	MURRAY, Dan (150)	LB	E. Str'dsbrg (Pa.)
14. Dallas	SECULES, Scott (151)	QB	Virginia
15. San Diego	FIGARO, Cedric (152)	LB	Notre Dame
16. Miami	BRATTON, Melvin (153)	RB	Miami (Fla.)
17. New England	JOHNSON, Steve (154)	TE	Virginia Tech
18. Pittsburgh	WILLIAMS, Warren (155)	RB	Miami (Fla.)
19. Miami from Minnesota	COOPER, George (156)	RB	Ohio State
20. Houston	CRAIN, Kurt (157)	LB	Auburn
21. Seattle	HART, Roy (158)	NT	South Carolina
22. Washington from Indianapolis	HUMPHRIES, Stan (159)	QB	N.E. Louisiana
23. Philadelphia from Cleveland	STERLING, Rob (160)	DB	Maine
24. Chicago	STINSON, Lemuel (161)	DB	Texas Tech
25. New Orleans	SIMS, Bob (162)	G	Florida
26. Tampa Bay from San Francisco	LEE, Shawn (163)	DT	North Alabama
27. Minnesota from Denver	WHITE, Derrick (164)	DB	Oklahoma
28. Los Angeles Rams from Washington	KNAPTON, Jeff (165)	DT	Wyoming

End of Round: **10:57 a.m.**	**Time of Round:** **57 minutes**	**Elapsed Time:** **10 hours, 25 minutes**

NFL ANNUAL SELECTION MEETING

APRIL 25, 1988

SEVENTH ROUND

1. Atlanta	HAYNES, Michael (166)	WR	Northern Arizona
2. Tampa Bay	GOODE, Kerry (167)	RB	Alabama
3. Cincinnati	ROMER, Rich (168)	LB	Union (N.Y.)
4. Detroit	JAMES, Jeff (169)	WR	Stanford
5. Kansas City	STEDMAN, Troy (170)	LB	Washburn (Kan.)
6. Los Angeles Raiders	CRUDUP, Derrick (171)	DB	Oklahoma
7. New York Jets*	PATTON, Gary (172)	RB	Eastern Michigan
8. Green Bay	RICHARD, Gary (173)	DB	Pittsburgh
9. Denver from L.A. Rams	KELLY, Pat (174)	TE	Syracuse
10. New York Giants	PEREZ, Mike (175)	QB	San Jose State
11. Philadelphia	WHITE, Todd (176)	WR	Fullerton State
12. Buffalo	BORCKY, Tim (177)	T	Memphis State
13. Dallas	HOOVEN, Owen (178)	T	Oregon State
14. Phoenix	JONES, Ernie (179)	WR	Indiana
15. Miami	BELL, Kerwin (180)	QB	Florida
16. New England	USHER, Darryl (181)	WR	Illinois
17. Pittsburgh	ZENO, Marc (182)	WR	Tulane
18. Minnesota	BECKMAN, Brad (183)	TE	Nebraska-Omaha
19. Buffalo from San Diego	WRIGHT, Bo (184)	RB	Alabama
20. Seattle	JACKSON, Ray (185)	DB	Ohio State
21. New York Giants from Indianapolis	WHITAKER, Danta (186)	TE	Miss. Valley St.
22. Houston	EATON, Tracey (187)	DB	Portland State
23. Cleveland	GASH, Thane (188)	DB	East Tennessee St.
24. Chicago	RENTIE, Caesar (189)	T	Oklahoma
25. New Orleans	FORDE, Brian (190)	LB	Washington State
26. San Francisco	BRYANT, Kevin (191)	LB	Delaware State
27. Denver	FRANK, Garry (192)	G	Mississippi State
28. Washington	HICKS, Harold (193)	DB	San Diego State

*Selected ahead of Green Bay, which passed.

End of Round:	Time of Round:	Elapsed Time:
12:03 p.m.	1 hour, 6 minutes	11 hours, 31 minutes

NFL ANNUAL SELECTION MEETING

APRIL 25, 1988

Start of Round:
12:03 p.m.

EIGHTH ROUND

1. Atlanta	BROWN, Phillip (194)	LB	Alabama
2. Cincinnati	MAXEY, Curtis (195)	NT	Grambling
3. Detroit	HADD, Gary (196)	DE	Minnesota
4. Kansas City	ROBERTS, Alfredo (197)	TE	Miami (Fla.)
5. Tampa Bay	SIMPSON, Anthony (198)	RB	East Carolina
6. Los Angeles Raiders	ALEXANDER, Mike (199)	WR	Penn State
7. Green Bay	COLLINS, Patrick (200)	RB	Oklahoma
8. Los Angeles Rams	FRANKLIN, Darryl (201)	WR	Washington
9. New York Giants	LILLY, Sammy (202)	DB	Georgia Tech
10. New York Jets	NEUBERT, Keith (203)	TE	Nebraska
11. Buffalo	HAGY, John (204)	DB	Texas
12. Dallas	HIGGS, Mark (205)	RB	Kentucky
13. Phoenix	MOORE, Tim (206)	LB	Michigan State
14. Philadelphia	SMITH, David (207)	RB	Western Kentucky
15. Chicago from New England	TATE, David (208)	DB	Colorado
16. Pittsburgh	NICHOLS, Mark (209)	NT	Michigan State
17. Minnesota	CAIN, Joe (210)	LB	Oregon Tech
18. Pittsburgh from San Diego	HINNANT, Mike (211)	TE	Temple
19. Miami	GALBREATH, Harry (212)	G	Tennessee
20. Buffalo from Indianapolis	WRIGHT, Jeff (213)	NT	Central Missouri
21. Houston	VIAENE, Dave (214)	C	Minnesota-Duluth
22. Seattle	TYLER, Robert (215)	TE	South Carolina St.
23. Cleveland	BIRDEN, J.J. (216)	WR	Oregon
24. Chicago	REED, Harvey (217)	RB	Howard
25. New Orleans	DERBY, Glenn (218)	T	Wisconsin
26. San Francisco	CLARKSON, Larry (219)	T	Montana
27. Miami from Denver	CHEEK, Louis (220)	T	Texas A&M
28. Washington	McGILL, Darryl (221)	RB	Wake Forest

End of Round:
1:08 p.m.

Time of Round:
1 hour, 5 minutes

Elapsed Time:
12 hours, 36 minutes

NFL ANNUAL SELECTION MEETING
APRIL 25, 1988

NINTH ROUND

1. Atlanta	PRIMUS, James (222)	RB	UCLA
2. Detroit	CORRINGTON, Kip (223)	DB	Texas A & M
3. Kansas City	ABDUR-RA'OOF, A. (224)	WR	Maryland
4. Tampa Bay	DAVIS, Reuben (225)	DT	North Carolina
5. Cincinnati	WELLS, Brandy (226)	DB	Notre Dame
6. Los Angeles Raiders	WARE, Reggie (227)	RB	Auburn
7. Green Bay	WILKINSON, Neal (228)	TE	James Madison
8. Los Angeles Raiders from N.Y. Giants	TABOR, Scott (229)	P	California
9. New York Jets	TAMM, Ralph (230)	G	West Chester (Pa.)
10. Los Angeles Rams	FOSTER, Pat (231)	DT	Montana
11. Dallas	BEDFORD, Brian (232)	WR	California
12. Phoenix	DILL, Scott (233)	G	Memphis State
13. Detroit from Philadelphia	IRVIN, Todd (234)	T	Mississippi
14. Buffalo	BAILEY, Carlton (235)	NT	North Carolina
15. Pittsburgh	LOCKBAUM, Gordie (236)	RB	Holy Cross
16. Minnesota	McGOWAN, Paul (237)	LB	Florida State
17. San Diego	HOWARD, Joey (238)	T	Tennessee
18. Miami	CROSS, Jeff (239)	DE	Missouri
19. New England	GALBRAITH, Neil (240)	DB	Central State (O.)
20. Houston	SPRADLIN, David (241)	LB	Texas Christian
21. Seattle	WISE, Deatrich (242)	NT	Jackson State
22. Indianapolis	HERROD, Jeff (243)	LB	Mississippi
23. Cleveland	COPELAND, Danny (244)	DB	Eastern Kentucky
24. Chicago	MAGEE, Rogie (245)	WR	Louisiana State
25. New Orleans	NUNN, Clarence (246)	DB	San Diego State
26. San Francisco	BONNER, Brian (247)	LB	Minnesota
27. Denver	FARR, Mel (248)	RB	UCLA
28. Washington	PETERSON, Blake (249)	LB	Mesa (Colo.)

End of Round:
2:11 p.m.

Time of Round:
1 hour, 3 minutes

Elapsed Time:
13 hours, 39 minutes

NFL ANNUAL SELECTION MEETING
APRIL 25, 1988

Start of Round:
2:11 p.m.

TENTH ROUND

1. Atlanta	CLAYTON, Stan (250)	T	Penn State
2. Kansas City	GAMBLE, Kenny (251)	RB	Colgate
3. Pittsburgh from Tampa Bay	JACKSON, John (252)	T	Eastern Kentucky
4. Cincinnati	DILLAHUNT, Ellis (253)	DB	East Carolina
5. Detroit	CRAIG, Paco (254)	WR	UCLA
6. Los Angeles Raiders	HARRELL, Newt (255)	T	West Texas State
7. Green Bay	KEYES, Bud (256)	QB	Wisconsin
8. New York Jets	BOOTY, John (257)	DB	Texas Christian
9. Los Angeles Rams	MULLIN, R.C. (258)	T	S.W. Louisiana
10. New York Giants	HICKERSON, Eric (259)	DB	Indiana
11. Phoenix	SCHILLINGER, Andy (260)	WR	Miami (O.)
12. Philadelphia	SCHUSTER, Joe (261)	DT	Iowa
13. Buffalo	MAYHEW, Martin (262)	DB	Florida State
14. Dallas	OWENS, Billy (263)	DB	Pittsburgh
15. Minnesota	HABIB, Brian (264)	DT	Washington
16. New York Giants from San Diego	WILKES, Steve (265)	TE	Appalachian State
17. Miami	JACKSON, Artis (266)	NT	Texas Tech
18. New England	LOSSOW, Rodney (267)	C	Wisconsin
19. Denver from Pittsburgh	WILLIAMS, Channing (268)	RB	Arizona State
20. Seattle	JONES, Derwin (269)	DE	Miami (Fla.)
21. Indianapolis	ALSTON, O'Brien (270)	LB	Maryland
22. Houston	JOHNSON, Marco (271)	WR	Hawaii
23. Cleveland	WASHINGTON, Brian (272)	DB	Nebraska
24. Chicago	PORTER, Joel (273)	G	Baylor
25. New Orleans	SANTOS, Todd (274)	QB	San Diego State
26. San Francisco	FOLEY, Tim (275)	K	Georgia Southern
27. New Orleans from Denver	FIZER, Vincent (276)	LB	Southern U.
28. Washington	BROWN, Henry (277)	T	Ohio State

End of Round: **Time of Round:**   **Elapsed Time:**
3:18 p.m.   **1 hour, 7 minutes**   **14 hours, 46 minutes**

NFL ANNUAL SELECTION MEETING

APRIL 25, 1988

ELEVENTH ROUND

1. Atlanta	MILLING, James (278)	WR	Maryland
2. Tampa Bay	PILLOW, Frank (279)	WR	Tennessee State
3. Cincinnati	HICKERT, Paul (280)	K	Murray State
4. Detroit	McCOIN, Danny (281)	QB	Cincinnati
5. Kansas City	McMANUS, Danny (282)	QB	Florida State
6. Los Angeles Raiders	WEBER, David (283)	QB	Carroll (Wis.)
7. Seattle from Green Bay	McLEOD, Rick (284)	T	Washington
8. San Diego from L.A. Rams	MILLER, Ed (285)	C	Pittsburgh
9. New York Giants	HARRIS, Greg (286)	WR	Troy State
10. New York Jets	GALVIN, John (287)	LB	Boston College
11. Philadelphia	JENKINS, Izel (288)	DB	North Carolina St.
12. Buffalo	CURKENDALL, Pete (289)	NT	Penn State
13. Dallas	HENNINGS, Chad (290)	DE	Air Force
14. Phoenix	McCOY, Keith (291)	DB	Fresno State
15. Miami*	KELLEHER, Tom (292)	RB	Holy Cross
16. San Diego	HINKLE, George (293)	NT	Arizona
17. New England	ALLEN, Marvin (294)	RB	Tulane
18. Pittsburgh	DAWSON, Bobby (295)	DB	Illinois
19. Minnesota	FLOYD, Norman (296)	DB	South Carolina
20. Indianapolis	DEE, Donnie (297)	TE	Tulsa
21. Houston	FRANKLIN, Jethro (298)	DE	Fresno State
22. Seattle	HARPER, Dwayne (299)	DB	South Carolina St.
23. Cleveland	HAWKINS, Hendley (300)	WR	Nebraska
24. Chicago	FORCH, Steve (301)	LB	Nebraska
25. New Orleans	COUCH, Gary (302)	WR	Minnesota
26. San Francisco	BROOKS, Chet (303)	DB	Texas A & M
27. Denver	CALVIN, Richard (304)	RB	Washington State
28. Washington	KOCH, Curt (305)	DE	Colorado

*Selected ahead of San Diego, which passed.

End of Round:	Time of Round:	Elapsed Time:
4:22 p.m.	1 hour, 4 minutes	15 hours, 50 minutes

NFL ANNUAL SELECTION MEETING

APRIL 25, 1988

TWELFTH ROUND

1. Atlanta	WILEY, Carter (306)	DB	Virginia Tech
2. Cincinnati	PARKER, Carl (307)	WR	Vanderbilt
3. Indianapolis from Detroit	KENNEY, Aatron (308)	WR	Stevens Pt., (Wis.)
4. Buffalo from Kansas City	DRISCOLL, John (309)	T	New Hampshire
5. Tampa Bay	JONES, Victor (310)	LB	Virginia Tech
6. Los Angeles Raiders	KUNKEL, Greg (311)	G	Kentucky
7. Green Bay	BOLTON, Scott (312)	WR	Auburn
8. New York Giants	FUTRELL, David (313)	NT	Brigham Young
9. New York Jets	GOSS, Albert (314)	NT	Jackson State
10. Washington from L.A. Rams	ROSS, Wayne (315)	P	San Diego State
11. Buffalo	ERLANDSON, Tom (316)	LB	Washington
12. Dallas	HUMMEL, Ben (317)	LB	UCLA
13. Phoenix	CARRIER, Chris (318)	DB	Louisiana State
14. Philadelphia	KAUFUSI, Steve (319)	DE	Brigham Young
15. Miami	KINCHEN, Brian (320)	TE	Louisiana State
16. New England	NUGENT, Dave (321)	NT	Boston College
17. Pittsburgh	EARLE, James (322)	LB	Clemson
18. New York Giants from Minnesota	McCORMACK, Brendan (323)	DT	South Carolina
19. San Diego	PHILLIPS, Wendell (324)	DB	North Alabama
20. Houston	BRANTLEY, John (325)	LB	Georgia
21. Seattle	DesROCHERS, Dave (326)	T	San Diego State
22. Indianapolis	VESLING, Tim (327)	K	Syracuse
23. Cleveland	SLAYDEN, Steve (328)	QB	Duke
24. Chicago	CLARK, Greg (329)	LB	Arizona State
25. New Orleans	JURGENSEN, Paul (330)	DE	Georgia Tech
26. San Francisco	MIRA, George (331)	LB	Miami (Fla.)
27. Denver	CARTER, Johnny (332)	NT	Grambling
28. Los Angeles Rams from Washington	BEATHARD, Jeff (333)	WR	Southern Oregon

End of Round:
5:16 p.m.

Time of Round:
54 minutes

Elapsed Time:
16 hours, 44 minutes

TEAM-BY-TEAM NO. 1 DRAFT CHOICES

*—Designates first player chosen in draft.

ATLANTA FALCONS

1988—Aundray Bruce, LB, Auburn*
1987—Chris Miller, QB, Oregon
1986—Tony Casillas, DT, Oklahoma
　　　Tim Green, LB, Syracuse
1985—Bill Fralic, T, Pittsburgh
1984—Rick Bryan, DT, Oklahoma
1983—Mike Pitts, DE, Alabama
1982—Gerald Riggs, RB, Arizona State
1981—Bobby Butler, DB, Florida State
1980—Junior Miller, TE, Nebraska
1979—Don Smith, DE, Miami (Fla.)
1978—Mike Kenn, T, Michigan
1977—Warren Bryant, T, Kentucky
　　　Wilson Faumuina, DT, San Jose State
1976—Bubba Bean, RB, Texas A & M
1975—Steve Bartkowski, QB, California*
1974—(No Number One Selection)
1973—(No Number One Selection)
1972—Clarence Ellis, DB, Notre Dame
1971—Joe Profit, RB, Northeast Louisiana
1970—John Small, LB, Citadel
1969—George Kunz, T, Notre Dame
1968—Claude Humphrey, DE, Tennessee State
1967—(No Number One Selection)
1966—Tommy Nobis, LB, Texas*
　　　Randy Johnson, QB, Texas A & I

BUFFALO BILLS

1988—(No Number One Selection)
1987—Shane Conlan, LB, Penn State
1986—Ronnie Harmon, RB, Iowa
　　　Will Wolford, T, Vanderbilt
1985—Bruce Smith, DT, Virginia Tech*
　　　Derrick Burroughs, DB, Memphis State
1984—Greg Bell, RB, Notre Dame
1983—Tony Hunter, TE, Notre Dame
　　　Jim Kelly, QB, Miami (Fla.)
1982—Perry Tuttle, WR, Clemson
1981—Booker Moore, RB, Penn State
1980—Jim Ritcher, C, North Carolina State
1979—Tom Cousineau, LB, Ohio State*
　　　Jerry Butler, WR, Clemson
1978—Terry Miller, RB, Oklahoma State
1977—Phil Dokes, DT, Oklahoma State
1976—Mario Clark, DB, Oregon
1975—Tom Ruud, LB, Nebraska
1974—Reuben Gant, TE, Oklahoma State
1973—Paul Seymour, T, Michigan
　　　Joe DeLamielleure, G, Michigan State
1972—Walt Patulski, DE, Notre Dame*
1971—J.D. Hill, WR, Arizona State
1970—Al Cowlings, DE, Southern California
1969—O.J. Simpson, RB, Southern California*
1968—Haven Moses, WR, San Diego State
1967—John Pitts, DB, Arizona State
1966—Mike Dennis, RB, Mississippi
1965—Jim Davidson, T, Ohio State
1964—Carl Eller, DE, Minnesota
1963—Dave Behrman, C, Michigan State
1962—Ernie Davis, RB, Syracuse
1961—Ken Rice, T, Auburn* (AFL)
1960—Richie Lucas, QB, Penn State

CHICAGO BEARS

1988—Brad Muster, RB, Stanford
　　　Wendell Davis, WR, Louisiana State
1987—Jim Harbaugh, QB, Michigan
1986—Neal Anderson, RB, Florida
1985—William Perry, DT, Clemson
1984—Wilber Marshall, LB, Florida
1983—Jimbo Covert, T, Pittsburgh
　　　Willie Gault, WR, Tennessee
1982—Jim McMahon, QB, Brigham Young
1981—Keith Van Horne, T, Southern California
1980—Otis Wilson, LB, Louisville
1979—Dan Hampton, DT, Arkansas
　　　Al Harris, DE, Arizona State
1978—(No Number One Selection)
1977—Ted Albrecht, T, California
1976—Dennis Lick, T, Wisconsin
1975—Walter Payton, RB, Jackson State
1974—Waymond Bryant, LB, Tennessee State
　　　Dave Gallagher, DE, Michigan
1973—Wally Chambers, DE, Eastern Kentucky
1972—Lionel Antoine, T, Southern Illinois
　　　Craig Clemons, DB, Iowa
1971—Joe Moore, RB, Missouri
1970—(No Number One Selection)
1969—Rufus Mayes, T, Ohio State
1968—Mike Hull, RB, Southern California
1967—Loyd Phillips, DE, Arkansas
1966—George Rice, DT, Louisiana State
1965—Dick Butkus, LB, Illinois
　　　Gale Sayers, RB, Kansas
　　　Steve DeLong, DE, Tennessee
1964—Dick Evey, DT, Tennessee
1963—Dave Behrman, C, Michigan State
1962—Ron Bull, RB, Baylor
1961—Mike Ditka, E, Pittsburgh
1960—Roger Davis, G, Syracuse
1959—Don Clark, B, Ohio State
1958—Chuck Howley, LB, West Virginia
1957—Earl Leggett, DT, Louisiana State
1956—Menan (Tex) Schriewer, E, Texas
1955—Ron Drzewiecki, B, Marquette
1954—Stan Wallace, B, Illinois
1953—Billy Anderson, B, Compton (Calif.) JC
1952—Jim Dooley, B, Miami
1951—Bob Williams, B, Notre Dame
　　　Billy Stone, B, Bradley
1950—Chuck Hunsinger, B, Florida
1949—Dick Harris, C, Texas
1948—Bobby Layne, QB, Texas
　　　Max Baumgardner, E, Texas
1947—Bob Fenimore, B, Oklahoma A & M*
1946—Johnny Lujack, QB, Notre Dame
1945—Don Lund, B, Michigan
1944—Ray Evans, B, Kansas
1943—Bob Steuber, B, Missouri
1942—Frankie Albert, B, Stanford
1941—Tom Harmon, B, Michigan*
　　　Norm Standlee, B, Stanford
　　　Don Scott, B, Ohio State
1940—Clyde Turner, C, Hardin-Simmons
1939—Sid Luckman, B, Columbia
　　　Bill Osmanski, B, Holy Cross
1938—Joe Gray, B, Oregon State
1937—Les McDonald, E, Nebraska
1936—Joe Stydahar, T, West Virginia

CINCINNATI BENGALS

1988—Rickey Dixon, S, Oklahoma
1987—Jason Buck, DT, Brigham Young
1986—Joe Kelly, LB, Washington
　　　Tim McGee, WR, Tennessee
1985—Eddie Brown, WR, Miami (Fla.)
　　　Emanuel King, LB, Alabama
1984—Ricky Hunley, LB, Arizona
　　　Pete Koch, DE, Maryland
　　　Brian Blados, T, North Carolina
1983—Dave Rimington, C, Nebraska
1982—Glen Collins, DE, Mississippi State
1981—David Verser, WR, Kansas
1980—Anthony Munoz, T, Southern California
1979—Jack Thompson, QB, Washington State
　　　Charles Alexander, RB, Louisiana State
1978—Ross Browner, DE, Notre Dame
　　　Blair Bush, C, Washington
1977—Eddie Edwards, DT, Miami
　　　Wilson Whitley, DT, Houston
　　　Mike Cobb, TE, Michigan State
1976—Billy Brooks, WR, Oklahoma
　　　Archie Griffin, RB, Ohio State
1975—Glenn Cameron, LB, Florida

1974—Bill Kollar, DT, Montana State
1973—Issac Curtis, WR, San Diego State
1972—Sherman White, DE, California
1971—Vernon Holland, T, Tennessee State
1970—Mike Reid, DT, Penn State
1969—Greg Cook, QB, Cincinnati
1968—Bob Johnson, C, Tennessee

CLEVELAND BROWNS

1988—Clifford Charlton, LB, Florida
1987—Mike Junkin, LB, Duke
1986— (No Number One Selection)
1985— (No Number One Selection)
1984—Don Rogers, DB, UCLA
1983— (No Number One Selection)
1982—Chip Banks, LB, Southern California
1981—Hanford Dixon, CB, Southern Mississippi
1980—Charles White, RB, Southern California
1979—Willis Adams, WR, Houston
1978—Clay Matthews, LB, Southern California
Ozzie Newsome, WR, Alabama
1977—Robert Jackson, LB, Texas A & M
1976—Mike Pruitt, RB, Purdue
1975—Mack Mitchell, DE, Houston
1974— (No Number One Selection)
1973—Steve Holden, WR, Arizona State
Pete Adams, G, Southern California
1972—Thom Darden, DB, Michigan
1971—Clarence Scott, DB, Kansas State
1970—Mike Phipps, QB, Purdue
Bob McKay, T, Texas
1969—Ron Johnson, RB, Michigan
1968—Marvin Upshaw, DE, Trinity (Tex.)
1967—Bob Matheson, LB, Duke
1966—Milt Morin, TE, Massachusetts
1965— (No Number One Selection)
1964—Paul Warfield, WR, Ohio State
1963—Tom Hutchinson, TE, Kentucky
1962—Gary Collins, WR, Maryland
Leroy Jackson, B, Western Illinois
1961— (No Number One Selection)
1960—Jim Houston, DE, Ohio State
1959—Rich Kreitling, DE, Illinois
1958—Jim Shofner, DB, Texas Christian
1957—Jim Brown, B, Syracuse
1956—Preston Carpenter, B, Arkansas
1955—Kent Burris, C, Oklahoma
1954—Bobby Garrett, QB, Stanford*
John Bauer, G, Illinois
1953—Doug Atkins, DT, Tennessee
1952—Bert Rechichar, DB, Tennessee
Harry Agganis, QB, Boston U.
1951—Ken Konz, B, Louisiana State
1950—Ken Carpenter, B, Oregon State

DALLAS COWBOYS

1988—Michael Irvin, WR, Miami (Fla.)
1987—Danny Noonan, DT, Nebraska
1986—Mike Sherrard, WR, UCLA
1985—Kevin Brooks, DE, Michigan
1984—Billy Cannon, Jr., LB, Texas A & M
1983—Jim Jeffcoat, DE, Arizona State
1982—Rod Hill, DB, Kentucky State
1981—Howard Richards, T, Missouri
1980—(No Number One Selection)
1979—Robert Shaw, C, Tennessee
1978—Larry Bethea, DE, Michigan State
1977—Tony Dorsett, RB, Pittsburgh
1976—Aaron Kyle, DB, Wyoming
1975—Randy White, LB, Maryland
Thomas Henderson, LB, Langston
1974—Ed Jones, DE, Tennessee State*
Charles Young, RB, North Carolina State
1973—Billy Joe DuPree, TE, Michigan State
1972—Bill Thomas, RB, Boston College
1971—Tody Smith, DE, Southern California
1970—Duane Thomas, RB, West Texas State
1969—Calvin Hill, RB, Yale
1968—Dennis Homan, WR, Alabama
1967—(No Number One Selection)
1966—John Niland, G, Iowa
1965—Craig Morton, QB, California

1964—Scott Appleton, DT, Texas
1963—Lee Roy Jordan, LB, Alabama
1962— (No Number One Selection)
1961—Bob Lilly, DT, Texas Christian

DENVER BRONCOS

1988—Ted Gregory, DT, Syracuse
1987—Ricky Nattiel, WR, Florida
1986— (No Number One Selection)
1985—Steve Sewell, RB, Oklahoma
1984— (No Number One Selection)
1983—Chris Hinton, G, Northwestern
1982—Gerald Willhite, RB, San Jose State
1981—Dennis Smith, DB, Southern California
1980— (No Number One Selection)
1979—Kelvin Clark, T, Nebraska
1978—Don Latimer, DT, Miami (Fla.)
1977—Steve Schindler, G, Boston College
1976—Tom Glassic, G, Virginia
1975—Louis Wright, DB, San Jose State
1974—Randy Gradishar, LB, Ohio State
1973—Otis Armstrong, RB, Purdue
1972—Riley Odoms, TE, Houston
1971—Marv Montgomery, T, Southern California
1970—Bob Anderson, RB, Colorado
1969—(No Number One Selection)
1968—(No Number One Selection)
1967—Floyd Little, RB, Syracuse
1966—Jerry Shay, DT, Purdue
1965—(No Number One Selection)
1964—Bob Brown, T, Nebraska
1963—Kermit Alexander, DB, UCLA
1962—Merlin Olsen, DT, Utah State
1961—Bob Gaiters, RB, New Mexico State
1960—Roger Leclerc, C, Trinity (Conn.)

DETROIT LIONS

1988—Bennie Blades, S, Miami (Fla.)
1987—Reggie Rogers, DE, Washington
1986—Chuck Long, QB, Iowa
1985—Lomas Brown, T, Florida
1984—David Lewis, TE, California
1983—James Jones, RB, Florida
1982—Jimmy Williams, LB, Nebraska
1981—Mark Nichols, WR, San Jose State
1980—Billy Sims, RB, Oklahoma*
1979—Keith Dorney, T, Penn State
1978—Luther Bradley, DB, Notre Dame
1977—(No Number One Selection)
1976—James Hunter, DB, Grambling
Lawrence Gaines, FB, Wyoming
1975—Lynn Boden, G, South Dakota State
1974—Ed O'Neil, LB, Penn State
1973—Ernie Price, DE, Texas A & I
1972—Herb Orvis, DE, Colorado
1971—Bob Bell, DT, Cincinnati
1970—Steve Owens, RB, Oklahoma
1969—(No Number One Selection)
1968—Greg Landry, QB, Massachusetts
Earl McCullouch, E. Southern California
1967—Mel Farr, RB, UCLA
1966—(No Number One Selection)
1965—Tom Nowatzke, RB, Indiana
1964—Pete Beathard, QB, Southern California
1963—Daryl Sanders, T, Ohio State
1962—John Hadl, QB, Kansas
1961—(No Number One Selection)
1960—John Robinson, DB, Louisiana State
1959—Nick Pietrosante, B, Notre Dame
1958—Alex Karras, DT, Iowa
1957—Bill Glass, G, Baylor
1956—Howard Cassidy, B, Ohio State
1955—Dave Middleton, B, Auburn
1954—Dick Chapman, T, Rice
1953—Harley Sewell, G, Texas
1952—(No Number One Selection)
1951—(No Number One Selection)
1950—Leon Hart, E, Notre Dame*
1949—John Rauch, B, Georgia
1948—Y.A. Tittle, B, Louisiana State
1947—Glenn Davis, B, Army
1946—Bill Dellastatious, B, Missouri

1945—Frank Szymanski, B, Notre Dame
1944—Otto Graham, B, Northwestern
1943—Frank Sinkwich, B, Georgia*
1942—Bob Westfall, B, Michigan
1941—Jim Thomason, B, Texas A&M
1940—Doyle Nave, B, Southern California
1939—John Pingel, B, Michigan State
1938—Alex Wojciechowicz, C, Fordham
1937—Lloyd Cardwell, B, Nebraska
1936—Sid Wagner, G, Michigan State

GREEN BAY PACKERS

1988—Sterling Sharpe, WR, South Carolina
1987—Brent Fullwood, RB, Auburn
1986—(No Number One Selection)
1985—Ken Ruettgers, T, Southern California
1984—Alphonso Carreker, DT, Florida State
1983—Tim Lewis, DB, Pittsburgh
1982—Ron Hallstrom, G, Iowa
1981—Rich Campbell, QB, California
1980—Bruce Clark, DT, Penn State
       George Cumby, LB, Oklahoma
1979—Eddie Lee Ivery, RB, Georgia Tech
1978—James Lofton, WR, Stanford
       John Anderson, LB, Michigan
1977—Mike Butler, DE, Kansas
       Ezra Johnson, DE, Morris Brown
1976—Mark Koncar, T, Colorado
1975—(No Number One Selection)
1974—Barty Smith, RB, Richmond
1973—Barry Smith, WR, Florida State
1972—Willie Buchanon, DB, San Diego State
       Jerry Tagge, QB, Nebraska
1971—John Brockington, RB, Ohio State
1970—Mike McCoy, DT, Notre Dame
       Rich McGeorge, TE, Elon
1969—Rich Moore, DT, Villanova
1968—Fred Carr, LB, Texas-El Paso
       Bill Lueck, G, Arizona
1967—Bob Hyland, C, Boston College
       Don Horn, QB, San Diego State
1966—Gale Gillingham, G, Minnesota
       Jim Grabowski, RB, Illinois
1965—Donny Anderson, RB, Texas Tech
       Larry Elkins, E, Baylor
1964—Lloyd Voss, DT, Nebraska
1963—Dave Robinson, LB, Penn State
1962—Earl Gros, RB, Louisiana State
1961—Herb Adderley, DB, Michigan State
1960—Tom Moore, RB, Vanderbilt
1959—Randy Duncan, B, Iowa*
1958—Dan Currie, C, Michigan State
1957—Paul Hornung, B, Notre Dame*
       Ron Kramer, E, Michigan
1956—Jack Losch, B, Miami
1955—Tom Bettis, G, Purdue
1954—Art Hunter, T, Notre Dame
1953—Al Carmichael, B, Southern California
1952—Babe Parilli, QB, Kentucky
1951—Bob Gain, T, Kentucky
1950—Clayton Tonnemaker, G, Minnesota
1949—Stan Heath, B, Nevada
1948—Earl Girard, B, Wisconsin
1947—Ernie Case, B, UCLA
1946—Johnny Strzykalski, B, Marquette
1945—Walt Schlinkman, G, Texas Tech
1944—Merv Pregulman, G, Michigan
1943—Dick Wildung, T, Minnesota
1942—Urban Odson, T, Minnesota
1941—George Paskvan, B, Wisconsin
1940—Hal Van Every, B, Marquette
1939—Larry Buhler, B, Minnesota
1938—Cecil Isbell, B, Purdue
1937—Ed Jankowski, B, Wisconsin
1936—Russ Letlow, G, San Francisco

HOUSTON OILERS

1988—Lorenzo White, RB, Michigan State
1987—Alonzo Highsmith, FB, Miami (Fla.)
       Haywood Jeffires, WR, N.C. State
1986—Jim Everett, QB, Purdue

1985—Ray Childress, DE, Texas A&M
       Richard Johnson, DB, Wisconsin
1984—Dean Steinkuhler, G, Nebraska
1983—Bruce Matthews, G, Southern California
1982—Mike Munchak, G, Penn State
1981—(No Number One Selection)
1980—(No Number One Selection)
1979—(No Number One Selection)
1978—Earl Campbell, RB, Texas*
1977—Morris Towns, T, Missouri
1976—(No Number One Selection)
1975—Robert Brazile, LB, Jackson State
       Don Hardeman, RB, Texas A&I
1974—(No Number One Selection)
1973—John Matuszak, DE, Tampa*
       George Amundson, RB, Iowa State
1972—Greg Sampson, DE, Stanford
1971—Dan Pastorini, QB, Santa Clara
1970—Doug Wilkerson, G, North Carolina Centra.
1969—Ron Pritchard, LB, Arizona State
1968—(No Number One Selection)
1967—George Webster, LB, Michigan State
       Tom Regner, G, Notre Dame
1966—Tommy Nobis, LB, Texas
1965—Lawrence Elkins, WR, Baylor* (AFL)
1964—Scott Appleton, DT, Texas
1963—Danny Brabham, LB, Arkansas
1962—Ray Jacobs, DT, Howard Payne
1961—Mike Ditka, E, Pittsburgh
1960—Billy Cannon, RB, Louisiana State

INDIANAPOLIS COLTS

1988—(No Number One Selection)
1987—Cornelius Bennett, LB, Alabama
1986—Jon Hand, DT, Alabama
1985—Duane Bickett, LB, Southern California
1984—Leonard Coleman, DB, Vanderbilt
       Ron Solt, G, Maryland
1983—John Elway, QB, Stanford*
1982—Johnie Cooks, LB, Mississippi State
       Art Schlichter, QB, Ohio State
1981—Randy McMillan, RB, Pittsburgh
       Donnell Thompson, DT, North Carolina
1980—Curtis Dickey, RB, Texas A&M
       Derrick Hatchett, DB, Texas
1979—Barry Krauss, LB, Alabama
1978—Reese McCall, TE, Auburn
1977—Randy Burke, WR, Kentucky
1976—Ken Novak, DT, Purdue
1975—Ken Huff, G, North Carolina
1974—John Dutton, DE, Nebraska
       Roger Carr, WR, Louisiana Tech
1973—Bert Jones, QB, Louisiana State
       Joe Ehrmann, DT, Syracuse
1972—Tom Drougas, T, Oregon
1971—Don McCauley, RB, North Carolina
       Leonard Dunlap, DB, North Texas State
1970—Norm Bulaich, RB, Texas Christian
1969—Eddie Hinton, WR, Oklahoma
1968—John Williams, G, Minnesota
1967—Bubba Smith, DT, Michigan State*
       Jim Detwiler, RB, Michigan
1966—Sam Ball, T, Kentucky
1965—Mike Curtis, LB, Duke
1964—Marv Woodson, DB, Indiana
1963—Bob Vogel, T, Ohio State
1962—Wendell Harris, DB, Louisiana State
1961—Tom Matte, RB, Ohio State
1960—Ron Mix, T, Southern California
1959—Jackie Burkett, C, Auburn
1958—Lenny Lyles, B, Louisville
1957—Jim Parker, T, Ohio State
1956—Lenny Moore, B, Penn State
1955—George Shaw, B, Oregon*
       Alan Ameche, B, Wisconsin
1954—Cotton Davidson, B, Baylor
1953—Billy Vessels, B, Oklahoma

KANSAS CITY CHIEFS

1988—Neil Smith, DE, Nebraska
1987—Paul Palmer, RB, Temple
1986—Brian Jozwiak, T, West Virginia

1985—Ethan Horton, RB, North Carolina
1984—Bill Maas, DT, Pittsburgh
    John Alt, T, Iowa
1983—Todd Blackledge, QB, Penn State
1982—Anthony Hancock, WR, Tennessee
1981—Willie Scott, TE, South Carolina
1980—Brad Budde, G, Southern California
1979—Mike Bell, DE, Colorado State
    Steve Fuller, QB, Clemson
1978—Art Still, DE, Kentucky
1977—Gary Green, DB, Baylor
1976—Rod Walters, G, Iowa
1975—(No Number One Selection)
1974—Woody Green, RB, Arizona State
1973—(No Number One Selection)
1972—Jeff Kinney, RB, Nebraska
1971—Elmo Wright, WR, Houston
1970—Sid Smith, T, Southern California
1969—Jim Marsalis, DB, Tennessee State
1968—Mo Moorman, G, Texas A & M
    George Daney, G, Texas-El Paso
1967—Gene Trosch, DE, Miami
1966—Aaron Brown, DE, Minnesota
1965—Gale Sayers, RB, Kansas
1964—Pete Beathard, QB, Southern California
1963—Buck Buchanan, DT, Grambling* (AFL)
    Ed Budde, G, Michigan State
1962—Ronnie Bull, RB, Baylor
1961—E.J. Holub, C, Texas Tech
1960—Don Meredith, QB, Southern Methodist

LOS ANGELES RAIDERS

1988—Tim Brown, WR, Notre Dame
    Terry McDaniel, CB, Tennessee
    Scott Davis, DE, Illinois
1987—John Clay, T, Missouri
1986—Bob Buczkowski, DT, Pittsburgh
1985—Jessie Hester, WR, Florida State
1984—(No Number One Selection)
1983—Don Mosebar, T, Southern California
1982—Marcus Allen, RB, Southern California
1981—Ted Watts, DB, Texas Tech
    Curt Marsh, G, Washington
1980—Marc Wilson, QB, Brigham Young
1979—(No Number One Selection)
1978—(No Number One Selection)
1977—(No Number One Selection)
1976—(No Number One Selection)
1975—Neal Colzie, DB, Ohio State
1974—Henry Lawrence, T, Florida A & M
1973—Ray Guy, P, Southern Mississippi
1972—Mike Siani, WR, Villanova
1971—Jack Tatum, DB, Ohio State
1970—Raymond Chester, TE, Morgan State
1969—Art Thoms, DT, Syracuse
1968—Eldridge Dickey, QB, Tennessee State
1967—Gene Upshaw, G, Texas A & I
1966—Rodger Bird, DB, Kentucky
1965—Harry Schuh, T, Memphis State
1964—Tony Lorick, RB, Arizona State
1963—(No Number One Selection)
1962—Roman Gabriel, QB, N.C. State* (AFL)
1961—Joe Rutgens, DT, Illinois
1960—Dale Hackbart, DB, Wisconsin

LOS ANGELES RAMS

1988—Gaston Green, RB, UCLA
    Aaron Cox, WR, Arizona State
1987—(No Number One Selection)
1986—Mike Schad, T, Queens College (Ont.)
1985—Jerry Gray, DB, Texas
1984—(No Number One Selection)
1983—Eric Dickerson, RB, Southern Methodist
1982—Barry Redden, RB, Richmond
1981—Mel Owens, LB, Michigan
1980—Johnnie Johnson, DB, Texas
1979—George Andrews, LB, Nebraska
    Kent Hill, G, Georgia Tech
1978—Elvis Peacock, RB, Oklahoma
1977—Bob Brudzinski, LB, Ohio State
1976—Kevin McLain, LB, Colorado State

1975—Mike Fanning, DT, Notre Dame
    Dennis Harrah, G, Miami
    Doug France, T, Ohio State
1974—John Cappelletti, RB, Penn State
1973—(No Number One Selection)
1972—(No Number One Selection)
1971—Isiah Robertson, LB, Southern
    Jack Youngblood, DE, Florida
1970—Jack Reynolds, LB, Tennessee
1969—Larry Smith, RB, Florida
    Jim Seymour, E, Notre Dame
    Bob Klein, TE, Southern California
1968—(No Number One Selection)
1967—(No Number One Selection)
1966—Tom Mack, G, Michigan
1965—Clancy Williams, DB, Washington State
1964—Bill Munson, QB, Utah State
1963—Terry Baker, QB, Oregon State*
    Rufus Guthrie, G, Georgia Tech
1962—Roman Gabriel, QB, North Carolina State
    Merlin Olsen, DT, Utah State
1961—Marlin McKeever, LB, Southern California
1960—Billy Cannon, RB, Louisiana State*
1959—Paul Dickson, G, Baylor
    Dick Bass, B, Pacific
1958—Lou Michaels, T, Kentucky
    Jim Phillips, E, Auburn
1957—Jon Arnett, B, Southern California
    Del Shofner, B, Baylor
1956—Joe Marconi, B, West Virginia
    Charlie Horton, B, Vanderbilt
1955—Larry Morris, C, Georgia Tech
1954—Ed Beatty, C, Cincinnati
1953—Donn Moomaw, C, UCLA
    Ed Barker, E, Washington State
1952—Bill Wade, B, Vanderbilt*
    Bob Carey, E, Michigan State
1951—Bud McFadin, G, Texas
1950—Ralph Pasquariello, B, Villanova
    Stan West, G, Oklahoma
1949—Bobby Thomason, B, Virginia Military
1948—(No Number One Selection)
1947—Herman Wedemeyer, B, St. Mary's (Calif.)
1946—Emil Sitko, B, Notre Dame
1945—Elroy Hirsch, B, Wisconsin
1944—Tony Butkovich, B, Illinois
1943—Mike Holovak, B, Boston College
1942—Jack Wilson, B, Baylor
1941—Rudy Mucha, C, Washington
1940—Ollie Cordill, B, Rice
1939—Parker Hall, B, Mississippi
1938—Corbett Davis, B, Indiana*
1937—Johnny Drake, B, Purdue

MIAMI DOLPHINS

1988—Eric Kumerow, DE, Ohio State
1987—John Bosa, DE, Boston College
1986—(No Number One Selection)
1985—Lorenzo Hampton, RB, Florida
1984—Jackie Shipp, LB, Oklahoma
1983—Dan Marino, QB, Pittsburgh
1982—Roy Foster, G, Southern California
1981—David Overstreet, RB, Oklahoma
1980—Don McNeal, DB, Alabama
1979—Jon Giesler, T, Michigan
1978—(No Number One Selection)
1977—A.J. Duhe, DE, Louisiana State
1976—Larry Gordon, LB, Arizona State
    Kim Bokamper, LB, San Jose State
1975—Darryl Carlton, T, Tampa
1974—Don Reese, DE, Jackson State
1973—(No Number One Selection)
1972—Mike Kadish, DT, Notre Dame
1971—(No Number One Selection)
1970—(No Number One Selection)
1969—Bill Stanfill, DE, Georgia
1968—Larry Csonka, RB, Syracuse
    Doug Crusan, T, Indiana
1967—Bob Griese, QB, Purdue
1966—Jim Grabowski, RB, Illinois*
    Rick Norton, QB, Kentucky

MINNESOTA VIKINGS

1988—Randall McDaniel, G, Arizona State
1987—D.J. Dozier, RB, Penn State
1986—Gerald Robinson, DE, Auburn
1985—Chris Doleman, LB, Pittsburgh
1984—Keith Millard, DE, Washington State
1983—Joey Browner, DB, Southern California
1982—Darrin Nelson, RB, Stanford
1981—(No Number One Selection)
1980—Doug Martin, DT, Washington
1979—Ted Brown, RB, North Carolina State
1978—Randy Holloway, DE, Pittsburgh
1977—Tommy Kramer, QB, Rice
1976—James White, DT, Oklahoma State
1975—Mark Mullaney, DE, Colorado State
1974—Fred McNeill, LB, UCLA
       Steve Riley, T, Southern California
1973—Chuck Foreman, RB, Miami (Fla.)
1972—Jeff Siemon, LB, Stanford
1971—Leo Hayden, RB, Ohio State
1970—John Ward, DT, Oklahoma State
1969—(No Number One Selection)
1968—Ron Yary, T, Southern California*
1967—Clint Jones, RB, Michigan State
       Gene Washington, WR, Michigan State
       Alan Page, DT, Notre Dame
1966—Jerry Shay, DT, Purdue
1965—Jack Snow, WR, Notre Dame
1964—Carl Eller, DE, Minnesota
1963—Jim Dunaway, T, Mississippi
1962—(No Number One Selection)
1961—Tommy Mason, RB, Tulane*

NEW ENGLAND PATRIOTS

1988—John Stephens, RB, Northwestern (La.) St.
1987—Bruce Armstrong, G, Louisville
1986—Reggie Dupard, RB, Southern Methodist
1985—Trevor Matich, C, Brigham Young
1984—Irving Fryar, WR, Nebraska*
1983—Tony Eason, QB, Illinois
1982—Kenneth Sims, DT, Texas*
       Lester Williams, DT, Nebraska
1981—Brian Holloway, T, Stanford
1980—Roland James, DB, Tennessee
       Vagas Ferguson, RB, Notre Dame
1979—Rick Sanford, DB, South Carolina
1978—Bob Cryder, G, Alabama
1977—Raymond Clayborn, DB, Texas
       Stanley Morgan, WR, Tennessee
1976—Mike Haynes, DB, Arizona State
       Pete Brock, C, Colorado
       Tim Fox, DB, Ohio State
1975—Russ Francis, TE, Oregon
1974—(No Number One Selection)
1973—John Hannah, G, Alabama
       Sam Cunningham, RB, Southern California
       Darryl Stingley, WR, Purdue
1972—(No Number One Selection)
1971—Jim Plunkett, QB, Stanford*
1970—Phil Olsen, DT, Utah State
1969—Ron Sellers, WR, Florida State
1968—Dennis Byrd, DE, North Carolina State
1967—John Charles, DB, Purdue
1966—Karl Singer, T, Purdue
       Willie Townes, T, Tulsa
1965—Jerry Rush, DE, Michigan State
       Dave McCormick, T, Louisiana State
1964—Jack Concannon, QB, Boston Col* (AFL)
1963—Art Graham, E, Boston College
1962—Gary Collins, WR, Maryland
1961—Tommy Mason, RB, Tulane
1960—Ron Burton, RB, Northwestern

NEW ORLEANS SAINTS

1988—Craig Heyward, RB, Pittsburgh
1987—Shawn Knight, DE, Brigham Young
1986—Jim Dombrowski, T, Virginia
1985—Alvin Toles, LB, Tennessee
1984—(No Number One Selection)
1983—(No Number One Selection)
1982—Lindsay Scott, WR, Georgia

1981—George Rogers, RB, South Carolina*
1980—Stan Brock, T, Colorado
1979—Russell Erxleben, P, Texas
1978—Wes Chandler, WR, Florida
1977—Joe Campbell, DE, Maryland
1976—Chuck Muncie, RB, California
1975—Larry Burton, WR, Purdue
       Kurt Schumacher, G, Ohio State
1974—Rick Middleton, LB, Ohio State
1973—(No Number One Selection)
1972—Royce Smith, G, Georgia
1971—Archie Manning, QB, Mississippi
1970—Ken Burrough, WR, Texas Southern
1969—John Shinners, G, Xavier (Ohio)
1968—Kevin Hardy, DE, Notre Dame
1967—Les Kelley, RB, Alabama

NEW YORK GIANTS

1988—Eric Moore, T, Indiana
1987—Mark Ingram, WR, Michigan State
1986—Eric Dorsey, DT, Notre Dame
1985—George Adams, RB, Kentucky
1984—Carl Banks, LB, Michigan State
       Bill Roberts, T, Ohio State
1983—Terry Kinard, DB, Clemson
1982—Butch Woolfolk, RB, Michigan
1981—Lawrence Taylor, LB, North Carolina
1980—Mark Haynes, DB, Colorado
1979—Phil Simms, QB, Morehead State
1978—Gordon King, T, Stanford
1977—Gary Jeter, DT, Southern California
1976—Troy Archer, DE, Colorado
1975—(No Number One Selection)
1974—John Hicks, G, Ohio State
1973—(No Number One Selection)
1972—Eldridge Small, DB, Texas A & I
       Larry Jacobson, DT, Nebraska
1971—Rocky Thompson, RB, West Texas State
1970—Jim Files, LB, Oklahoma
1969—Fred Dryer, DE, San Diego State
1968—(No Number One Selection)
1967—(No Number One Selection)
1966—Francis Peay, T, Missouri
1965—Tucker Frederickson, RB, Auburn*
1964—Joe Don Looney, RB, Oklahoma
1963—(No Number One Selection)
1962—Jerry Hillebrand, LB, Colorado
1961—(No Number One Selection)
1960—Lou Cordileone, G, Clemson
1959—Lee Grosscup, B, Utah
1958—Phil King, B, Vanderbilt
1957—(No Number One Selection)
1956—Henry Moore, B, Arkansas
1955—Joe Heap, B, Notre Dame
1954—(No Number One Selection)
1953—Bobby Marlow, B, Alabama
1952—Frank Gifford, B, Southern California
1951—Kyle Rote, B, Southern Methodist*
1950—Travis Tidwell, B, Auburn
1949—Paul Page, B, Southern Methodist
1948—Tony Minisi, B, Pennsylvania
1947—Vic Schwall, B, Northwestern
1946—George Connor, T, Notre Dame
1945—Elmer Barbour, B, Wake Forest
1944—Billy Hillenbrand, B, Indiana
1943—Steve Filipowicz, B, Fordham
1942—Merle Hapes, B, Mississippi
1941—George Franck, B, Minnesota
1940—Grenville Lansdell, B, Southern California
1939—Walt Nielson, B, Arizona
1938—George Karamatic, B, Gonzaga
1937—Ed Widseth, T, Minnesota
1936—Art Lewis, T, Ohio

NEW YORK JETS

1988—Dave Cadigan, T, Southern California
1987—Roger Vick, FB, Texas A & M
1986—Mike Haight, T, Iowa
1985—Al Toon, WR, Wisconsin
1984—Russell Carter, DB, Southern Methodist
       Ron Faurot, DE, Arkansas
1983—Ken O'Brien, QB, California-Davis

1982—Bob Crable, LB, Notre Dame
1981—Freeman McNeil, RB, UCLA
1980—Lam Jones, WR, Texas
1979—Marty Lyons, DT, Alabama
1978—Chris Ward, T, Ohio State
1977—Marvin Powell, T, Southern California
1976—Richard Todd, QB, Alabama
1975—(No Number One Selection)
1974—Carl Barzilauskas, DT, Indiana
1973—Burgess Owens, DB, Miami
1972—Jerome Barkum, WR, Jackson State
    Mike Taylor, LB, Michigan
1971—John Riggins, RB, Kansas
1970—Steve Tannen, DB, Florida
1969—Dave Foley, T, Ohio State
1968—Lee White, RB, Weber State
1967—Paul Seiler, G, Notre Dame
1966—Bill Yearby, DT, Michigan
1965—Joe Namath, QB, Alabama
    Tom Nowatzke, RB, Indiana
1964—Matt Snell, RB, Ohio State
1963—Jerry Stovall, RB, Louisiana State
1962—Sandy Stephens, QB, Minnesota
1961—Tom Brown, G, Minnesota
1960—George Izo, QB, Notre Dame

PHILADELPHIA EAGLES

1988—Keith Jackson, TE, Oklahoma
1987—Jerome Brown, DT, Miami (Fla.)
1986—Keith Byars, RB, Ohio State
1985—Kevin Allen, T, Indiana
1984—Kenny Jackson, WR, Penn State
1983—Michael Haddix, RB, Mississippi State
1982—Mike Quick, WR, North Carolina State
1981—Leonard Mitchell, DE, Houston
1980—Roynell Young, DB, Alcorn State
1979—Jerry Robinson, LB, UCLA
1978—(No Number One Selection)
1977—(No Number One Selection)
1976—(No Number One Selection)
1975—(No Number One Selection)
1974—(No Number One Selection)
1973—Jerry Sisemore, T, Texas
    Charle Young, TE, Southern California
1972—John Reaves, QB, Florida
1971—Richard Harris, DE, Grambling
1970—Steve Zabel, E, Oklahoma
1969—Leroy Keyes, RB, Purdue
1968—Tim Rossovich, DE, Southern California
1967—Harry Jones, RB, Arkansas
1966—Randy Beisler, T, Indiana
1965—(No Number One Selection)
1964—Bob Brown, T, Nebraska
1963—Ed Budde, T, Michigan State
1962—(No Number One Selection)
1961—Art Baker, B, Syracuse
1960—Ron Burton, B, Northwestern
1959—(No Number One Selection)
1958—Walter Kowalczyk, B, Michigan State
1957—Clarence Peaks, B, Michigan State
1956—Bob Pellegrini, C, Maryland
1955—Dick Bielski, B, Maryland
1954—Neil Worden, B, Notre Dame
1953—(No Number One Selection)
1952—John Bright, B, Drake
1951—Ebert Van Buren, B, Louisiana State
1950—Harry Grant, E, Minnesota ·
1949—Chuck Bednarik, C, Pennsylvania*
    Frank Tripucka, QB, Notre Dame
1948—Clyde Scott, B, Arkansas
1947—Neil Armstrong, E, Oklahoma A&M
1946—Leo Riggs, B, Southern California
1945—John Yonaker, E, Notre Dame
1944—Steve Van Buren, B, Louisiana State
1943—Joe Muha, B, Virginia Military
1942—Pete Kmetovic, B, Stanford
1941—(No Number One Selection)
1940—Wes McAfee, B, Duke
1939—Davey O'Brien, QB, Texas Christian
1938—John McDonald, B, Nebraska
1937—Sam Francis, B, Nebraska*
1936—Jay Berwanger, B, Chicago*

PHOENIX CARDINALS

1988—Ken Harvey, LB, California
1987—Kelly Stouffer, QB, Colorado State
1986—Anthony Bell, LB, Michigan State
1985—Freddie Joe Nunn, LB, Mississippi
1984—Clyde Duncan, WR, Tennessee
1983—Leonard Smith, DB, McNeese State
1982—Luis Sharpe, T, UCLA
1981—E.J. Junior, LB, Alabama
1980—Curtis Greer, DE, Michigan
1979—Ottis Anderson, RB, Miami (Fla.)
1978—Steve Little, K, Arkansas
    Ken Greene, DB, Washington State
1977—Steve Pisarkiewicz, QB, Missouri
1976—Mike Dawson, DT, Arizona
1975—Tim Gray, DB, Texas A&M
1974—J.V. Cain, TE, Colorado
1973—Dave Butz, DT, Purdue
1972—Bobby Moore, RB, Oregon
1971—Norm Thompson, DB, Utah
1970—Larry Stegent, RB, Texas A&M
1969—Roger Wehrli, DB, Missouri
1968—MacArthur Lane, RB, Utah State
1967—Dave Williams, WR, Washington
1966—Carl McAdams, LB, Oklahoma
1965—Joe Namath, QB, Alabama
1964—Ken Kortas, DT, Louisville
1963—Jerry Stovall, DB, Louisiana State
    Don Brumm, E, Purdue
1962—Fate Echols, DT, Northwestern
    Irv Goode, C, Kentucky
1961—Ken Rice, T, Auburn
1960—George Izo, QB, Notre Dame
1959—Billy Stacy, B, Mississippi State
1958—King Hill, B, Rice*
1957—Jerry Tubbs, C, Oklahoma
1956—Joe Childress, B, Auburn
1955—Max Boydston, E, Oklahoma
1954—Lamar McHan, B, Arkansas
1953—Johnny Olszewski, QB, California
1952—Ollie Matson, B, San Francisco
1951—Jerry Groom, C, Notre Dame
1950—(No Number One Selection)
1949—Bill Fischer, G, Notre Dame
1948—Jim Spavital, B, Oklahoma A&M
1947—DeWitt (Tex) Coulter, T, Army
1946—Dub Jones, B, Louisiana State
1945—Charley Trippi, B, Georgia*
1944—Pat Harder, B, Wisconsin
1943—Glenn Dobbs, B, Tulsa
1942—Steve Lach, B, Duke
1941—John Kimbrough, B, Texas A&M
1940—George Cafego, B, Tennessee*
1939—Charles Aldrich, C, Texas Christian*
1938—Jack Robbins, B, Arkansas
1937—Ray Buivid, B, Marquette
1936—Jim Lawrence, B, Texas Christian

PITTSBURGH STEELERS

1988—Aaron Jones, DE, Eastern Kentucky
1987—Rod Woodson, DB, Purdue
1986—John Rienstra, G, Temple
1985—Darryl Sims, DT, Wisconsin
1984—Louis Lipps, WR, Southern Mississippi
1983—Gabriel Rivera, DT, Texas Tech
1982—Walter Abercrombie, RB, Baylor
1981—Keith Gary, DE, Oklahoma
1980—Mark Malone, QB, Arizona State
1979—Greg Hawthorne, RB, Baylor
1978—Ron Johnson, DB, Eastern Michigan
1977—Robin Cole, LB, New Mexico
1976—Bennie Cunningham, TE, Clemson
1975—Dave Brown, DB, Michigan
1974—Lynn Swann, WR, Southern California
1973—James Thomas, DB, Florida State
1972—Franco Harris, RB, Penn State
1971—Frank Lewis, WR, Grambling
1970—Terry Bradshaw, QB, Louisiana Tech*
1969—Joe Greene, DT, North Texas State
1968—Mike Taylor, T, Southern California
1967—(No Number One Selection)
1966—Dick Leftridge, RB, West Virginia

1965— (No Number One Selection)
1964—Paul Martha, RB, Pittsburgh
1963— (No Number One Selection)
1962—Bob Ferguson, RB, Ohio State
1961— (No Number One Selection)
1960—Jack Spikes, B, Texas Christian
1959— (No Number One Selection)
1958— (No Number One Selection)
1957—Len Dawson, QB, Purdue
1956—Gary Glick, B, Colorado State*
    Art Davis, B, Mississippi State
1955—Frank Varrichione, T, Notre Dame
1954—John Lattner, B, Notre Dame
1953—Ted Marchibroda, QB, St. Bonaventure
1952—Ed Modzelewski, B, Maryland
1951—Clarence Avinger, B, Alabama
1950—Lynn Chandnois, B, Michigan State
1949—Bobby Gage, B, Clemson
1948—Dan Edwards, E, Georgia
1947—Hub Bechtol, E, Texas
1946—Doc Blanchard, B, Army
1945—Paul Duhart, B, Florida
1944—Johnny Podesto, B, St. Mary's (Calif.)
1943—Bill Daley, B, Minnesota
1942—Bill Dudley, B, Virginia*
1941—Chet Gladchuk, C, Boston College
1940—Kay Eakin, B, Arkansas
1939— (No Number One Selection)
1938—Byron White, B, Colorado
    Frank Filchock, B, Indiana
1937—Mike Basrak, C, Duquesne
1936—Bill Shakespeare, B, Notre Dame

SAN DIEGO CHARGERS

1988—Anthony Miller, WR, Tennessee
1987—Rod Bernstine, TE, Texas A & M
1986—Leslie O'Neal, DE, Oklahoma State
    Jim FitzPatrick, T, Southern California
1985—Jim Lachey, G, Ohio State
1984—Mossy Cade, DB, Texas
1983—Billy Ray Smith, LB, Arkansas
    Gary Anderson, WR, Arkansas
    Gill Byrd, DB, San Jose State
1982— (No Number One Selection)
1981—James Brooks, RB, Auburn
1980— (No Number One Selection)
1979—Kellen Winslow, TE, Missouri
1978—John Jefferson, WR, Arizona State
1977—Bob Rush, C, Memphis State
1976—Joe Washington, RB, Oklahoma
1975—Gary Johnson, DT, Grambling
    Mike Williams, DB, Louisiana State
1974—Bo Matthews, RB, Colorado
    Don Goode, LB, Kansas
1973—Johnny Rodgers, WR, Nebraska
1972— (No Number One Selection)
1971—Leon Burns, RB, Long Beach State
1970—Walker Gillette, WR, Richmond
1969—Marty Domres, QB, Columbia
    Bob Babich, LB, Miami (Ohio)
1968—Russ Washington, T, Missouri
    Jim Hill, DB, Texas A & I
1967—Ron Billingsley, DT, Wyoming
1966—Don Davis, T, Los Angeles State
1965—Steve DeLong, DE, Tennessee
1964—Ted Davis, E, Georgia Tech
1963—Walt Sweeney, E, Syracuse
1962—Bob Ferguson, RB, Ohio State
1961—Earl Faison, E, Indiana
1960—Monty Stickles, E, Notre Dame

SAN FRANCISCO 49ers

1988— (No Number One Selection)
1987—Harris Barton, T, North Carolina
    Terrence Flager, RB, Clemson
1986— (No Number One Selection)
1985—Jerry Rice, WR, Mississippi Valley
1984—Todd Shell, LB, Brigham Young
1983— (No Number One Selection)
1982— (No Number One Selection)
1981—Ronnie Lott, DB, Southern California

1980—Earl Cooper, RB, Rice
    Jim Stuckey, DE, Clemson
1979— (No Number One Selection)
1978—Ken McAfee, TE, Notre Dame
    Dan Bunz, LB, Long Beach State
1977— (No Number One Selection)
1976— (No Number One Selection)
1975—Jimmy Webb, DT, Mississippi State
1974—Wilbur Jackson, RB, Alabama
    Bill Sandifer, DT, UCLA
1973—Mike Holmes, DB, Texas Southern
1972—Terry Beasley, WR, Auburn
1971—Tim Anderson, DB, Ohio State
1970—Cedrick Hardman, DE, North Texas State
    Bruce Taylor, DB, Boston U.
1969—Ted Kwalick, TE, Penn State
    Gene Washington, WR, Stanford
1968—Forrest Blue, C, Auburn
1967—Steve Spurrier, QB, Florida
    Cas Banaszek, LB, Northwestern
1966—Stan Hindman, DE, Mississippi
1965—Ken Willard, RB, North Carolina
    George Donnelly, DB, Illinois
1964—Dave Parks, E, Texas Tech*
1963—Kermit Alexander, RB, UCLA
1962—Lance Alworth, RB, Arkansas
1961—Jim Johnson, RB, UCLA
    Bernie Casey, RB, Bowling Green
    Bill Kilmer, QB, UCLA
1960—Monty Stickles, E, Notre Dame
1959—Dave Baker, RB, Oklahoma
    Dan James, C, Ohio State
1958—Jim Pace, RB, Michigan
    Charles Krueger, T, Texas A & M
1957—John Brodie, QB, Stanford
1956—Earl Morrall, QB, Michigan State
1955—Dick Moegel, HB, Rice
1954—Bernie Faloney, QB, Maryland
1953—Harry Babcock, E, Georgia*
    Tom Stolhandske, E, Texas
1952—Hugh McElhenny, RB, Washington
1951—Y.A. Tittle, QB, Louisiana State
1950—Leo Nomellini, T, Minnesota

SEATTLE SEAHAWKS

1988— (No Number One Selection)
1987—Tony Woods, LB, Pittsburgh
1986—John L. Williams, RB, Florida
1985— (No Number One Selection)
1984—Terry Taylor, DB, Southern Illinois
1983—Curt Warner, RB, Penn State
1982—Jeff Bryant, DE, Clemson
1981—Kenny Easley, DB, UCLA
1980—Jacob Green, DE, Texas A & M
1979—Manu Tuiasosopo, DT, UCLA
1978—Keith Simpson, DB, Memphis State
1977—Steve August, G, Tulsa
1976—Steve Niehaus, DT, Notre Dame

TAMPA BAY BUCCANEERS

1988—Paul Gruber, T, Wisconsin
1987—Vinny Testaverde, QB, Miami (Fla.)*
1986—Bo Jackson, RB, Auburn*
    Rod Jones, DB, Southern Methodist
1985—Ron Holmes, DE, Washington
1984— (No Number One Selection)
1983— (No Number One Selection)
1982—Sean Farrell, G, Penn State
1981—Hugh Green, LB, Pittsburgh
1980—Ray Snell, T, Wisconsin
1979— (No Number One Selection)
1978—Doug Williams, QB, Grambling
1977—Ricky Bell, RB, Southern California*
1976—Lee Roy Selmon, DE, Oklahoma*

WASHINGTON REDSKINS

1988— (No Number One Selection)
1987— (No Number One Selection)
1986— (No Number One Selection)
1985— (No Number One Selection)
1984— (No Number One Selection)
1983—Darrell Green, DB, Texas A & I

1982— (No Number One Selection)
1981—Mark May, T, Pittsburgh
1980—Art Monk, WR, Syracuse
1979— (No Number One Selection)
1978— (No Number One Selection)
1977— (No Number One Selection)
1976— (No Number One Selection)
1975— (No Number One Selection)
1974— (No Number One Selection)
1973— (No Number One Selection)
1972— (No Number One Selection)
1971— (No Number One Selection)
1970— (No Number One Selection)
1969— (No Number One Selection)
1968—Jim Smith, DB, Oregon
1967—Ray McDonald, RB, Idaho
1966—Charlie Gogolak, K, Princeton
1965— (No Number One Selection)
1964—Charley Taylor, RB, Arizona State
1963—Pat Richter, TE, Wisconsin
1962—Ernie Davis, RB, Syracuse*
    Leroy Jackson, RB, Illinois Central
1961—Joe Rutgens, T, Illinois
    Norm Snead, QB, Wake Forest
1960—Richie Lucas, QB, Penn State

1959—Don Allard, QB, Boston College
1958— (No Number One Selection)
1957—Don Bosseler, RB, Miami (Fla.)
1956—Ed Vereb, RB, Maryland
1955—Ralph Guglielmi, QB, Notre Dame
1954—Steve Meilinger, TE, Kentucky
1953—Jack Scarbath, QB, Maryland
1952—Larry Isbell, QB, Baylor
1951—Leon Heath, RB, Oklahoma
1950—George Thomas, RB, Oklahoma
1949—Rob Goode, RB, Texas A & M
1948—Harry Gilmer, QB, Alabama*
1947—Cal Rossi, B, UCLA
1946—Cal Rossi, B, UCLA
1945—Jim Hardy, B, Southern California
1944—Mike Micka, B, Colgate
1943—Jack Jenkins, B, Missouri
1942—Orban Sanders, B, Texas
1941—Forrest Evashevski, B, Michigan
1940—Ed Boell, B, New York U.
1939—I.B. Hale, T, Texas Christian
1938—Andy Farkas, B, Detroit
1937—Sammy Baugh, QB, Texas Christian
1936—Riley Smith, QB, Alabama

Auburn linebacker Aundray Bruce was selected by the Atlanta Falcons as the No. 1 overall choice in the 1988 NFL draft.

1987-88 NFL TRADES
(Covering June 1987 through June 1988)

Tight end CHRIS DRESSEL from Houston to Washington for conditional draft choice (6/22).

Quarterback DAVID WOODLEY from Pittsburgh to Green Bay for conditional draft choice (6/22).

Cornerback CHARLES ROMES from Buffalo to Kansas City for 12th-round choice in 1988 draft (7/14). Buffalo subsequently selected tackle JOHN DRISCOLL (New Hampshire).

Wide receiver CLINT SAMPSON from Denver to Buffalo for conditional draft choice (7/14).

Linebacker TIM LUCAS from St. Louis to San Diego for conditional draft choice (7/18).

Wide receiver JOHNNY (LAM) JONES from New York Jets to San Francisco for 5th-round choice in 1988 draft (7/23). Jets subsequently traded choice and 4th-round choice in 1988 draft to Los Angeles Raiders for 3rd-round choice in 1988 draft (4/24).

Tackle DARRYL HALEY from New England to Tampa Bay for conditional draft choice (7/27).

Cornerback RON FELLOWS from Dallas to Los Angeles Raiders for wide receiver ROD BARKSDALE (8/2).

Tackle LEONARD MITCHELL from Philadelphia to Houston for conditional draft choice (8/3). Trade voided when Mitchell failed physical (8/6).

Tackle LEONARD MITCHELL from Philadelphia to Atlanta for 4th-round choice in 1988 draft (8/7). Philadelphia subsequently traded choice and 2nd-round choice in 1988 draft to Tampa Bay for 2nd-round choice in 1988 draft (4/24).

Running back KEITH WILLIAMS from Atlanta to Tampa Bay for conditional draft choice (8/13).

Center JIM ROMANO from Houston to New England for conditional draft choice (8/17).

Linebacker JACK DEL RIO from New Orleans to Kansas City for 5th-round choice in 1988 draft (8/17). New Orleans subsequently selected tight end GREG SCALES (Wake Forest).

Guard LARRY LEE from Miami to Denver for 8th-round choice in 1988 draft (8/19). Miami subsequently selected tackle LOUIS CHEEK (Texas A&M).

Tight end GLENN DENNISON from New England to Washington for conditional draft choice (8/20).

Wide receiver BOBBY JOHNSON from New York Giants to San Diego for 10th-round choice in 1988 draft (8/20). Giants subsequently selected tight end STEVE WILKES (Appalachian State).

Safety DEMETRIOUS JOHNSON from Detroit to Indianapolis for conditional 1989 draft choice (8/24).

Tackle RON ESSINK from Seattle to Dallas for 5th-round choice in 1988 draft (8/25). Seattle subsequently traded choice and 1st- and 5th-round choices in 1989 to Phoenix for rights to quarterback KELLY STOUFFER (4/22).

Safety DENNIS WOODBERRY from Atlanta to Green Bay for cash (8/25).

Guard STEFAN HUMPHRIES from Chicago to Denver for punter BRYAN WAGNER and draft choice (8/25).

Cornerback DAVE BROWN from Seattle to Green Bay for 11th-round choice in 1988 draft (8/26). Seattle subsequently selected tackle RICK McLEOD (Washington).

Cornerback WAYNE DAVIS from San Diego to Buffalo for safety MARTIN BAYLESS (8/26).

Linebacker KEN WOODARD from Denver to Pittsburgh for 10th-round choice in 1988 draft (8/27). Denver subsequently selected running back CHANNING WILLIAMS (Arizona State).

Wide receiver TRUMAINE JOHNSON and 7th-round choice in 1988 draft from San Diego to Buffalo for linebacker DAVID BRANDON and 4th-round choice in 1988 draft (8/31). San Diego subsequently selected tackle STACY SEARELS (Auburn). Buffalo subsequently selected running back BO WRIGHT (Alabama).

Tackle GREG FEASEL from Green Bay to Houston for conditional draft choice (8/31).

Defensive tackle WILLARD GOFF from Los Angeles Raiders to San Francisco for conditional draft choice (8/31).

Kicker ROLF BENIRSCHKE from San Diego to Dallas for conditional draft choice (8/31).

Tackle BRIAN HOLLOWAY from New England to Los Angeles Raiders for 5th-round choice in 1988 draft and conditional 1989 choice (9/1). New England subsequently selected guard TROY WOLKOW (Minnesota).

Tight end DERRICK RAMSEY from Indianapolis to Detroit for 12th-round choice in 1988 draft (9/1). Indianapolis subsequently selected wide receiver AATRON KENNEY (Wisconsin-Stevens Point).

Safety RICK WOODS from Pittsburgh to Tampa Bay for 10th-round choice in 1988 draft (9/1). Pittsburgh subsequently selected tackle JOHN JACKSON (Eastern Kentucky).

Nose tackle JEROME SALLY from New York Giants to Indianapolis for 7th-round choice in 1988 draft (9/2). Giants subsequently selected tight end DANTA WHITAKER (Mississippi Valley State).

Defensive end AL BAKER from St. Louis to Cleveland for 5th-round choice in 1988 draft (9/3). Phoenix subsequently selected running back TONY JORDAN (Kansas State).

Running back JEFF SMITH from Kansas City to Tampa Bay for 8th-round choice in 1988 draft (9/3). Kansas City subsequently traded choice, 4th-round choice in 1988 draft and safety MARK ROBINSON to Tampa Bay for quarterback STEVE DeBERG (3/31).

Defensive end GREG BROWN from Philadelphia to Atlanta for defensive end MIKE PITTS (9/7).

Cornerback HARVEY CLAYTON from Pittsburgh to Detroit for conditional draft choice (9/7).

Nose tackle DON SMITH from Buffalo to New York Jets for conditional draft choice (9/7).

Running back CLIFF AUSTIN from Atlanta to Tampa Bay for 6th-round choice in 1988 draft (9/7). Atlanta subsequently selected guard HOUSTON HOOVER (Jackson State).

Guard JEFF WALKER from San Diego to Los Angeles Rams for 11th-round choice in 1988 draft (9/8). San Diego subsequently selected center ED MILLER (Pittsburgh).

Note: The following trades, preceded by an asterisk (*), were consummated during the strike.

*Defensive tackle MARK SMYTHE from Indianapolis to Pittsburgh for cash (10/1).

*Kicker JOHN DIETTRICH from Green Bay to Houston for cash (10/2).

*Guard MITCH GEIER from Tampa Bay to New York Jets for cash (10/6).

*Cornerback ERIC JEFFRIES from Washington to Chicago for cash (10/6).

*Linebacker KEITH BROWNER from San Francisco to Los Angeles Raiders for cash (10/7).

*Running back ANDRE HARDY from San Francisco to Seattle for conditional draft choice (10/7).

*Quarterback DOUG FLUTIE from Chicago to New England for 8th-round choice in 1988 draft (10/13). Chicago subsequently selected defensive back DAVID TATE (Colorado).

*Linebacker JAMES JOHNSON from San Francisco to San Diego for past consideration (10/13).

*Defensive tackle VAN HUGHES from Seattle to Atlanta for cash (10/14).

*Defensive end ROBERT BRANNON and running back KIRK JONES from Cleveland to New Orleans for conditional draft choices (10/15).

*Safety JON SUTTON from New Orleans to Tampa Bay for past consideration (10/15).

*Center JOE BOCK from St. Louis to Buffalo for cash (10/16).

Tackle GREG KOCH from Miami to Minnesota for 6th-round choice in 1988 draft and conditional 1989 choice (10/20). Miami subsequently selected running back GEORGE COOPER (Ohio State).

Quarterback JOHN WITKOWSKI from Houston to Green Bay for past consideration (10/20).

Running back ERIC DICKERSON from Los Angeles Rams to Indianapolis and rights to linebacker CORNELIUS BENNETT from Indianapolis to Buffalo with Rams receiving 1st- and 2nd-round choices in 1988 draft, 2nd-round choice in 1989 draft and running back OWEN GILL from Indianapolis and 1st-round choice in 1988 draft, 1st- and 2nd-round choices in 1989 draft and running back GREG BELL from Buffalo (10/31). With picks from Indianapolis, Rams subsequently selected wide receiver AARON COX (Arizona State) and linebacker FRED STRICKLAND (Purdue). With pick from Buffalo, Rams subsequently selected running back GASTON GREEN (UCLA).

Tackle BRUCE DAVIS from Los Angeles Raiders to Houston for 2nd-round choice in 1988 draft (11/3). Raiders subsequently traded choice, 3rd-round choice in 1988 draft and defensive end SEAN JONES to Houston for 1st-, 3rd- and 4th-round choices in 1988 draft (4/21).

Tight end JIMMIE GILES from Detroit to Philadelphia for 9th-round choice in 1988 draft (11/3). Detroit subsequently selected tackle TODD IRVIN (Mississippi).

Linebacker DAVID WYMAN and 6th-round choice in 1988 draft from Seattle to San Francisco for 2nd-round choice in 1988 draft (11/3). Trade voided when Wyman failed physical (11/5).

Defensive tackle BARRY BENNETT from New York Jets to Los Angeles Raiders for 1989 draft choice (3/9).

Linebacker WILBER MARSHALL from Chicago to Washington as veteran free agent and Chicago received 1st-round choices in 1988 and 1989 drafts as compensation (3/18). Chicago subsequently selected wide receiver WENDELL DAVIS (Louisiana State).

Rights to defensive tackle CHRIS PIKE from Philadelphia to Cleveland for 6th-round choice in 1988 draft, conditional choice in 1989 draft and cornerback D.D. HOGGARD (3/25). Philadelphia subsequently selected defensive back ROB STERLING (Maine).

Tackle EMIL SLOVACEK from San Diego to Denver for past consideration (3/25).

Quarterback TODD BLACKLEDGE from Kansas City to Pittsburgh for 4th-round choice in 1988 draft (3/29). Kansas City subsequently selected wide receiver J.R. AMBROSE (Mississippi).

Wide receiver CLARENCE VERDIN from Washington to Indianapolis for 6th-round choice in 1988 draft (3/29). Washington subsequently selected quarterback STAN HUMPHRIES (Northeast Louisiana).

Quarterback STEVE DeBERG from Tampa Bay to Kansas City for 4th- and 8th-round choices in 1988 draft and safety MARK ROBINSON (3/31). Tampa Bay subsequently selected guard JOHN BRUHIN (Tennessee) and running back ANTHONY SIMPSON (East Carolina).

Quarterback MARK MALONE from Pittsburgh to San Diego for 8th-round choice in 1988 draft and conditional 1989 choice (4/12). Pittsburgh subsequently selected tight end MIKE HINNANT (Temple).

Kansas City traded 1st- and 2nd-round choices in 1988 draft to Detroit for 1st-round choice in 1988 draft (4/20). Kansas City subsequently selected defensive end NEIL SMITH (Nebraska). Detroit subsequently selected safety BENNIE BLADES (Miami, Fla.) and linebacker CHRIS SPIELMAN (Ohio State).

Defensive end SEAN JONES and 2nd- and 3rd-round choices in 1988 draft from Los Angeles Raiders to Houston for 1st-, 3rd- and 4th-round choices in 1988 draft (4/21). Raiders subsequently selected cornerback TERRY McDANIEL (Tennessee), traded 3rd-round choice to New York Jets for 4th- and 5th-round choices in 1988 draft (4/24) and traded 4th-round choice, 2nd-round choice in 1988 draft and wide receiver DOKIE WILLIAMS to San Francisco for 1st-round choice in 1988 draft (4/24). Houston subsequently selected defensive back QUINTIN JONES (Pittsburgh) and traded 3rd-round choice to San Diego for 3rd- and 5th-round choices in 1988 draft (4/24).

Rights to quarterback KELLY STOUFFER from Phoenix to Seattle for 5th-round choice in 1988 draft and 1st- and 5th-round choices in 1989 draft (4/22). Phoenix subsequently selected linebacker CHRIS GAINES (Vanderbilt).

Wide receiver DOKIE WILLIAMS and 2nd- and 4th-round choices in 1988 draft from Los Angeles Raiders to San Francisco for 1st-round choice in 1988 draft (4/24). Raiders subsequently selected defensive end SCOTT DAVIS (Illinois). San Francisco subsequently selected defensive end DAN STUBBS (Miami, Fla.) and punter BARRY HELTON (Colorado).

Tampa Bay traded 2nd-round choice in 1988 draft to Philadelphia for 2nd- and 4th-round choices in 1988 draft (4/24). Tampa Bay subsequently selected defensive tackle ROBERT GOFF (Auburn) and traded 2nd-round choice to San Francisco for 2nd- and 4th-round choices in 1988 draft (4/24). Philadelphia subsequently selected cornerback ERIC ALLEN (Arizona State).

Tampa Bay traded 2nd-round choice in 1988 draft to San Francisco for 2nd- and 4th-round choices in 1988 draft (4/24). Tampa Bay subsequently selected running back LARS TATE (Georgia) and punter MONTE ROBBINS (Michigan). San Francisco subsequently selected defensive tackle PIERCE HOLT (Angelo State).

Minnesota traded 2nd-round choice in 1988 draft to Denver for 2nd-, 4th- and 6th-round choices in 1988 draft (4/24). Minnesota subsequently selected safety BRAD EDWARDS (South Carolina), guard TODD KALIS (Arizona State) and defensive back DERRICK WHITE (Oklahoma). Denver subsequently selected tackle GERALD PERRY (Southern).

Houston traded 3rd-round choice in 1988 draft to San Diego for 3rd- and 5th-round choices in 1988 draft (4/24). Houston subsequently selected punter GREG MONTGOMERY (Michigan State) and defensive back CRIS DISHMAN (Purdue). San Diego subsequently selected wide receiver QUINN EARLY (Iowa).

Los Angeles Rams traded 3rd-round choice in 1988 draft to Washington for 3rd-, 5th- and 6th-round choices in 1988 draft (4/24). Rams subsequently selected defensive tackle MIKE PIEL (Illinois), defensive back JAMES WASHINGTON (UCLA) and defensive tackle JEFF KNAPTON (Wyoming). Washington subsequently selected running back MIKE OLIPHANT (Puget Sound).

Los Angeles Raiders traded 3rd-round choice in 1988 draft to New York Jets for 4th- and 5th-round choices in 1988 draft (4/24). Raiders subsequently selected defensive tackle TIM ROTHER (Nebraska) and defensive back DENNIS PRICE (UCLA). Jets subsequently selected cornerback JAMES HASTY (Washington State).

New Orleans traded 3rd-round choice in 1988 draft to Denver for 3rd- and 10th-round choices in 1988 draft (4/24). New Orleans subsequently selected nose tackle TONY STEPHENS (Clemson) and linebacker VINCENT FIZER (Southern). Denver subsequently selected cornerback KEVIN GUIDRY (Louisiana State).

Tight end PETE HOLOHAN from San Diego to Los Angeles Rams for 4th-round choice in 1988 draft (4/24). San Diego subsequently selected defensive end JOE CAMPBELL (New Mexico State).

New England traded 5th-round choice in 1988 draft to Washington for 4th-round choice in 1989 draft (4/24). Washington subsequently selected cornerback CARL MIMS (Sam Houston State).

New England traded 11th-round choice in 1988 draft to Minnesota for 9th-round choice in 1989 draft (4/25). Minnesota subsequently selected defensive back NORMAN FLOYD (South Carolina).

Los Angeles Rams traded 12th-round choice in 1988 draft to Washington for 12th-round choice in 1988 draft and 11th-round choice in 1989 draft (4/24). Rams subsequently selected wide receiver JEFF BEATHARD (Southern Oregon). Washington subsequently selected punter WAYNE ROSS (San Diego State).

Wide receiver CHARLIE BROWN from Atlanta to Indianapolis for conditional 1989 draft choice (4/27).

Quarterback MARK HERRMANN from San Diego to Indianapolis for conditional 1989 draft choice (4/27).

Defensive end BLAISE WINTER from San Diego to Green Bay for past consideration (4/28).

Quarterback JOE FERGUSON from Indianapolis to Tampa Bay for 12th-round choice in 1989 draft (4/29).

Tackle RON HELLER from Tampa Bay to Seattle for defensive end RANDY EDWARDS and 1989 draft choice (5/4).

Linebacker KEN WOODARD from Pittsburgh to Indianapolis for conditional 1989 draft choice (5/5). Deal voided when Woodard failed physical (5/23).

Defensive end ANDREW PROVENCE from Atlanta to Denver for conditional 10th-round choice in 1989 draft (5/10).

Rights to defensive back KIP CORRINGTON (Texas A&M) from Detroit to Denver for conditional 9th-round choice in 1989 draft (5/13).

Cornerback RUSSELL CARTER from New York Jets to Los Angeles Raiders for conditional 6th-round choice in 1989 draft (5/21).

Cornerback TIM MORRISON from Washington to Seattle for conditional choice in 1989 draft (5/23).

Running back TONY DORSETT from Dallas to Denver for conditional choice in 1989 draft (6/3).

Wide receiver WES CHANDLER and a conditional 1989 draft choice from San Diego to San Francisco for center FRED QUILLAN and a conditional 1989 draft choice (6/3).

Safety BO EASON from Houston to San Francisco for conditional 5th-round choice in 1989 draft and conditional 4th round choice in 1990 draft (6/6).

Rights to Kicker TIM FOLEY from San Francisco to Atlanta for conditional 10th-round choice in 1989 draft (6/8).

Also Played With in 1987

ATLANTA FALCONS

Also played with Falcons in '87—QB David Archer (9 games), C Doug Barnett (10), WR Milton Barney (3), P Louis Berry (2), DE Dwight Bingham (3), LB Ken Bowen (1), CB James Britt (12), LB Aaron Brown (6), WR Charlie Brown (6), RB Jerry Butler (1), S Wendell Cason (3), G Randy Clark (3), TE Arthur Cox (12), LB Buddy Curry (4), K Greg Davis (3), TE John Evans (1), WR Leon Gonzalez (2), RB Norm Granger (3), LB Paul Gray (2), WR Steve B. Griffin (4), WR Kwante Hampton (1), DE Dennis Harrison (11), C James Hendley (3), G Howard Hood (active for 1 game, but did not play), DE Van Hughes (active for 1 game, but did not play), WR Billy Johnson (12), CB Lyndell Jones (3), RB John Kamana (2), G Jeff Kiewel (12), LB Jim Laughlin (5), K Mick Luckhurst (12), S Mike Lush (3), T Doug Mackie (3), RB Joe McIntosh (2), DE Buddy Moor (3), DE Dwaine Morris (3), S Gary Moss (3), S Jerome Norris (3), RB Darryl Oliver (2), TE Charles Phillips (active for 1 game, but did not play), RB Shelley Poole (1), LB Art Price (3), DL Andrew Provence (5), G/T Greg Quick (1), T/G Don Robinson (2), G Pat Saindon (3), TE Dan Sharp (9), WR James Shibest (1), T Reggie Smith (2), LB Herb Spencer (3), P John Starnes (1), DE Mark Studaway (3), WR Lenny Taylor (3), CB Leon Thomasson (3), LB Jesse Tuggle (12), CB Jimmy Turner (2), QB Jeff Van Raaphorst (2), NT Emanuel Weaver (2), C Eric Wiegand (2), LB Reggie Wilkes (6), RB Mike Williams (3), S Brenard Wilson (8), DE Leonard Wingate (1), TE Geno Zimmerlink (3).

BUFFALO BILLS

Also played with Bills in '87—NT/FB Ira Albright (3 games), CB John Armstrong (3), TE Veno Belk (2), RB Greg Bell (2), CB Gerald Bess (2), C Joe Bock (1), DE Jack Brayvak (1), WR Marc Brown (3), S Bill Callahan (3), DE Arnold Campbell (3), FB Joe Chetti (2), S Steve Clark (3), LB Will Cokeley (3), T Sean Dowling (3), G Mike Estep (2), S Larry Friday (1), WR Sheldon Gaines (3), DE Scott Garnett (3), C Will Grant (1), WR Kris Haines (1), NT Scott Hernandez (2), S Lawrence Johnson (3), LB Mike Jones (1), FB Bruce King (3), G Kevin Lamar (1), LB Bob LeBlanc (3), CB John Lewis (3), LB Steve Maidlow (2), QB Dan Manucci (3), CB Dave Martin (3), WR Thad McFadden (3), NT Joe McGrail (2), TE Keith McKeller (1), QB Mark Miller (1), S Chip Nuzzo (3), RB Mike Panepinto (1), CB Kerry Parker (2), P Rick Partridge (3), S Durwood Roquemore (5), C Erik Rosenmeier (1), LB Scott Schankweiler (3), K Todd Schlopy (2), G Rick Schulte (3), RB Johnny Shepherd (2), C Mark Shupe (2), C Joe Silipo (1), T Don Sommer (3), DE Richard Tharpe (3), QB Willie Totten (3), TE Mark Walczak (2), LB Craig Walls (3), LB Scott Watters (3), LB Al Wenglikowski (1), TE Gary Wilkins (1), RB Leonard Williams (2), DE Billy Witt (2).

CHICAGO BEARS

Also played with Bears in '87—T John Arp (3 games), LB Bobby Bell (3), S Todd Bell (12), WR Todd Black (1), QB Steve Bradley (1), TE Sam Bowers (3), RB Chris Brewer (3), P Kevin Brown (3), RB Daryl Clark (3), CB/S George Duarte (3), DT Greg Fitzgerald (3), QB Doug Flutie (1), TE Brian Glasgow (3), T/G Charles Harris (3), RB Frank Harris (3), RB Lakei Heimuli (3), CB/S Mike Hintz (3), QB Mike Hohensee (3), DE Leonard Jackson (1), LB Mike January (3), C/G Brent Johnson (3), WR Herbert Johnson (3), TE Don Kindt (3), WR Ken Knapczyk (3), LB Wilber Marshall (12), CB/S Bruce McCray (3), DT Sean McInerney (3), LB Paul Migliazzo (3), LB Eldridge Milton (3), LB Raymond Morris (3), WR Gary Mullen (3), T Jack Oliver (3), QB Sean Payton (3), G/T Stuart Rindy (2), CB/S Garland Rivers (2), G Jon Roehlk (3), LB Doug Rothschild (3), DT Gene Rowell (1), S Mike Stoops (3), DT Guy Teafatiller (3), S/CB Steve Trimble (3), WR Lawrence White (2), RB Alan Wolden (3).

CINCINNATI BENGALS

Also played with Bengals in '87—QB Ben Bennett (1 game), NT Bill Berthusen (3), S Nate Borders (3), CB Louis Breeden (8), WR Kenneth Brown (3), WR Tom Brown (2), LB Toney Catchings (3), T Keith Cupp (3), NT James Eaddy (2), DE Willie Fears (3), LB Tom Flaherty (3), G John Fletcher (3), RB Pat Franklin (2), P Greg Horne (4), CB Gary Hunt (3), TE Curtis Jeffries (3), S Mark Johnson (3), RB Marc Logan (3), K Massimo Manca (3), CB Aaron Manning (3), RB David McCluskey (3), S Rob Niehoff (3), WR Marquis Pleasant (3), G Bill Poe (3), G Tom Richey (3), T Bob Riley (3), TE Dave Romasko (3), T Wade Russell (3), LB Scott Schutt (3), LB Lance Sellers (3), TE Reginald Sims (1), DE Jeff Smith (3), G Ken Smith (3), T Mark Tigges (3), WR Rodney Tweet (2), QB Dave Walter (3), LB David Ward (3).

CLEVELAND BROWNS

Also played with Browns in '87—S/CB Vincent Barnett (3 games), WR Clayton Beauford (1), DE Robert Brannon (1), LB Dave Butler (1), DE/LB James Capers (3), S/CB Vincent Carreker (2), DE Alex Carter (3), QB Jeff Christensen (3), DT Scott Cooper (active for 1 game, but did not play), LB Tim Crawford (3), RB Johnny Davis (1), RB Stacey Driver (3), TE Don Echols (3), S Ray Ellis (12), RB Major Everett (4), K Brian Franco (2), P Jeff Gossett (5), LB Rusty Guilbeau (1), LB Cliff Hannemann (3), CB D.D. Hoggard (1), CB/S Enis Jackson (1), RB Kirk Jones (1), QB Homer Jordan (active for 2 games, but did not play), C Mike Katolin (3), TE Chris Kelley (3), WR Perry Kemp (3), LB Mike Kovaleski (1), G Mark Krerowicz (3), K Goran Lingmerth (1), RB Larry Mason (3), DE Aaron Moog (3), LB Steve Nave (3), LB Jerry Parker (3), WR Steve Pierce (2), LB Tom Polley (3), S/CB Billy Robinson (3), CB DeJuan Robinson (3), LB Lucius Sanford (11), G Dave Sparenberg (1), WR Keith Tinsley (3), T Ralph Van Dyke (2), WR David Verser (2), P Dale Walters (2), CB Troy Wilson (3), G Blake Wingle (3), P George Winslow (5).

DALLAS COWBOYS

Also played with Cowboys in '87—RB David Adams (3 games), CB Jimmy Armstrong (2), T/G Brian Baldinger (3), RB Alvin Blount (2), TE Rich Borresen (3), K Kerry Brady (1), T Dave Burnette (1), G Sal Cesario (3), CB/S Anthony Coleman (3), WR Vince Courville (2), RB Tony Dorsett (12), LB Chris Duliban (3), DT John Dutton (4), DT Mike Dwyer (3), LB Harry Flaherty (2), S Alex Green (3), TE Tim Hendrix (3), CB Bill Hill (3), T Glen Howe (active for 1 game, but did not play), DT/DE Walter Johnson (1), LB Dale Jones (3), RB E.J. Jones (3), RB Robert Lavette (4), CB/S Bruce Livingston (3), DE Ray Perkins (2), P Buzz Sawyer (3), WR Chuck Scott (2), C Joe Shearin (1), T/G Jon Shields (1), LB Victor Simmons (3), QB Loren Snyder (2), WR Sebron Spivey (2), LB Russ Swan (5), LB Kirk Timmer (1), T/G Gary Walker (1), K Luis Zendejas (2), C Mike Zentic (3).

DENVER BRONCOS

Also played with Broncos in '87—G John Ayers (9 games), T Kevin Belcher (1), RB Scott Caldwell (3), K Mike Clendenen (3), G Mark Cooper (5), LB Stan David (active for 1 game, but did not play), LB Kirk Dodge (3), S Steve Fitzhugh (3), P Ralph Glacomarro (3), G/T Archie Harris (3), S Roger Jackson (3), S Earl Johnson (3), LB Tim Joiner (3), G David Jones (3), LB Mike Knox (3), RB Zeph Lee (1), LB Kerry Locklin (3), TE Kerry Locklin (3), LB Dan MacDonald (3), QB Dean May (3), QB Monte McGuire (2), RB Bruce McIntyre (active for 1 game, but did not play), DE/DT Ron McLean (3), TE Russell Payne (1), C Jack Peavey (3), CB Lyle Pickens (1), RB Nathan Poole (2), CB Martin Rudolph (3), CB/S Darryl Russell (3), C Carlos Scott (active for 1 game, but did not play), LB Matt Smith (3), WR Shane Swanson (3), WR Robert Thompson (2), NT Jeff Tupper (4), DE Ray Woodard (3).

DETROIT LIONS

Also played with Lions in '87—LB Earnest Adams (3 games), WR Stan Baker (active for 1 game, but did not play), P Mike Black (1), LB Steve Boadway (2), CB Jon Bostic (3), LB Thomas Boyd (4), WR Danny Bradley (3), C Pat Cain (3), CB/S Dexter Clark (2), TE Jerry Diorio (2), RB Tony Dollinger (2), RB Stan Edwards (3), P Russell Erxleben (1), RB Kelvin Farmer (active for 1 game, but did not play), S Creig Federico (3), G Joe Felton (2), QB Joe Ferguson (active for 12 games, but did not play), CB Anthony Fields (3), DE/DT Bill Lobenstein (3), DE William Gay (11), G Chris Geile (3), TE Jimmie Giles (4), S William Graham (3), S Alvin Hall (3), CB Maurice Harvey (2), CB/S Ivan Hicks (1), LB Mark Hicks (1), CB Steve Hirsch (3), QB Todd Hons (3), WR Mel Hoover (2), T Mark Jenkins (active for 1 game, but did not play), WR Gilvanni Johnson (3), NT Jeff Kacmarek (3), LB Angelo King (1), P Matt Kinzer (1), G Paul Kiser (1), RB Nick Kowgios (3), CB/S Bob McDonough (3), P John Misko (1), LB Anthony Office (3), G Greg Orton (3), K Mike Prindle (3), T Jerry Quaerna (3), TE Derrick Ramsey (1), LB Tim Ross (3), C Chuck Steele (3), T Rich Strenger (3), S Ivory Sully (11), LB Robert Thompson (3), NT Stuart Tolle (1), WR Eric Truvillion (3), T Jim Warne (3), CB Eric T. Williams (1), TE Mark Witte (3).

GREEN BAY PACKERS

Also played with Packers in '87—LB Eric Anderson (3 games), LB Todd Auer (3), LB Warren Bone (1), NT David Caldwell (3), LB Putt Choate (2), CB/S Chuck Compton (2), K Al Del Greco (5), G Mike Estep (1), TE Kevin Fitzgerald (1), QB Willie Gillus (1), T Bob Gruber (1), WR Derrick Harden (3), RB Jimmy Hargrove (2), S Anthony Harrison (3), G Perry Hartnett (1), CB/S Carlos Henderson (active for 1 game, but did not play), G Jim Hobbins (3), RB Tony Hunter (1), TE Craig Jay (3), G Greg Jensen (1), DE Ezra Johnson (6), LB Kenneth Jordan (3), CB/S David King (3), T Ed Konopasek (3), DE Tony Leiker (1), TE Mark Lewis (3), NT Dave Logan (2), LB Rydell Malancon (3), CB/S Von Mansfield (3), DE Charles Martin (2), QB John McCarthy (active for 1 game, but did not play), G John McGarry (2), DE Sylvester McGrew (3), LB James Melka (1), T Jim Meyer (2), LB John Miller (1), LB Ron Monaco (2), RB Larry Morris (2), RB Freddie Parker (1), LB John Pointer (3), C Vince Rafferty (3), CB/S Louis Rash (3), WR Cornelius Redick (1), P Bill Renner (3), QB Alan Risher (3), C Travis Simpson (3), WR Wes Smith (1), RB John Sterling (2), DE Carl Sullivan (3), NT Vince Villanucci (2), DE Calvin Wallace (1), CB/S Charles Washington (3), RB Lee Weigel (2).

HOUSTON OILERS

Also played with Oilers in '87—LB Robert Abraham (2 games), CB Earl Allen (1), DE Jesse Baker (9), T Scott Boucher (2), LB Tom Briehl (3), S Sonny Brown (3), CB Charles Clinton (2), RB Eric Cobble (3), WR Chris Darrington (3), TE Mitch Daum (3), K John Diettrich (2), NT Joe Dixon (2), S Bo Eason (3), TE Scott Eccles (1), LB Scott Fox (2), T Jerrell Franklin (3), TE Mark Gehring (6), NT Mike Golic (2), G Kent Hill (12), RB Herman Hunter (3), RB Andrew Jackson (7), LB Thad Jefferson (3), LB Byron Johnson (3), P Lee Johnson (9), S Larry Joyner (1), T Doug Kellermeyer (3), G Mike Kelley (1), C Billy Kidd (7), DE Eric Larkin (1), S Allan Lyday (7), FB Ricky Moore (3), DE Kenny Neil (1), CB Tony Newsom (5), DE Bob Otto (3), T Barry Pettyjohn (2), S Donovan Small (1), LB Larry Smith (3), T Scott Stroughton (active for 1 game, but did not play), G Vince Stroth (9), P Steve Superick (2), CB Emmuel Thompson (3), NT Dwain Turner (1), LB Paul Vogel (1), WR Joey Walters (5), CB Robert White (3), WR Oliver Williams (3), QB John Witkowski (active for 3 games, but did not play), G Almon Young (3).

INDIANAPOLIS COLTS

Also played with Colts in '87—T Sid Abramowitz (3 games), CB/S Pat Ballage (3), WR Roy Banks (1), T Mark Boggs (1), RB Gordon Brown (3), WR Steve Bryant (1), LB Brian Bulluck (2), T Milt Carthens (1), RB Mel Carver (1), LB Ricky Chatman (3), G Jeff Criswell (3), CB/S Craig Curry (3), CB Kenny Daniel (2), S/CB Lee Davis (3), NT Bill Elko (3), CB Jitter Fields (1), T Marsharne Graves (3), DE Bob Hamm (3), LB Kevin Hancock (1), WR Greg Hawthorne (3), DT Marcus Jackson (1), WR Kelley Johnson (3), CB Bryant Jones (3), TE Joe Jones (3), K Steve Jordan (3), WR Tim Kearse (3), QB Blair Kiel (3), G Steve Knight (3), TE Keith Lester (1), DT Frank Mattiace (3), RB Chris McLemore (2), DT Jim Merritts (1), WR James Noble (3), QB Terry Nugent (1), LB Bob Ontko (3), LB Gary Padjen (3), C/G Ron Plantz (3), LB Roger Remo (3), LB Brad Saar (1), S John Simmons (2), RB John Williams (2).

KANSAS CITY CHIEFS

Also played with Chiefs in '87—NT Bill Acker (2 games), C Kevin Adkins (2), G John Aimonetti (active for 1 game, but did not play), TE Walt Arnold (5), T James Black (1), WR Eric Brown (2), CB Trent Bryant (3), TE Paul Coffman (12), CB Jeff Colter (1), C Rick Donnalley (6), T Dan Doubiago (3), S Cornelius Dozier (2), S Jack Epps (3), WR Richard Estell (2), RB James Evans (2), DT Jeff Faulkner (3), LB Randy Frazier (3), G Lee Getz (3), RB Stephen Griffin (1), K James Hamrick (3), LB Bob Harris (3), WR Eric Hodges (1), DE Tony Holloway (1), LB Bruce Holmes (3), T Doug Hoppock (3), C Glenn Hyde (7), DE Ken Johnson (3), LB Fred Jones (2), TE Stein Koss (2), RB Ken Lacy (3), CB Garcia Lane (1), DE Chris Lindstrom (3), LB Ken McAlister (1), WR David Montagne (3), DE Mitchell Morris (active for 1 game, but did not play), LB Gary Moten (1), DT Lloyd Mumphrey (3), WR Kenny Nash (1), T Mark Nelson (1), C Jim Pietrzak (2), RB Woodie Pippins (2), T Steve Rogers (3), S Blane Smith (3), RB Chris Smith (3), QB Matt Stevens (3), RB Ralph Stockemer (2), T Terry Summers (active for 1 game, but did not play), G Arland Thompson (3), WR John Trahan (3), DL John Walker (3), TE Riley Walton (2), K Paul Woodside (active for 1 game, but did not play), CB Kevin Wyatt (2).

LOS ANGELES RAIDERS

Also played with Raiders in '87—DT Rick Ackerman (3 games), WR Carl Aikens (3), DE Brian Belway (1), G Barry Black (3), RB Jim Browne (2), LB Keith Browner (1), LB Darryl Byrd (3), RB Rick Calhoun (3), CB Chetti Carr (2), DE Ted Chapman (2), LB Joe Cormier (2), T Bruce Davis (4), G Andy Dickerson (1), C Paul Dufault (1), RB Craig Ellis (3), LB Jim Ellis (3), S Ron Foster (3), P Vince Gamache (3), DE Rick Goltz (1), LB Darryl Goodlow (2), K David Hardy (2), CB/S Lance Harkey (2), CB/S Rob Harrison (2), RB Frank Hawkins (2), CB Greg Hill (3), CB Rod Hill (4), LB Leonard Jackson (1), S Victor Jackson (2), DE Sean Jones (12), WR Greg Lathan (3), WR Wade Lockett (2), LB Dan McMillen (1), LB Mike Noble (1), TE Mario Perry (3), T Robert Pyles (2), C Shawn Regent (3), DT Mike Rodriguez (1), CB Willie Teal (1), CB Tony Tillmon (3), LB Ronnie Washington (2), TE Ron Wheeler (3), WR David Williams (3), S Demise Williams (1), WR Dokie Williams (11), CB Ricky Williams (1), QB Marc Wilson (15), QB Scott Woolf (1), G Jon Zogg (1).

LOS ANGELES RAMS

Also played with Rams in '87—LB Sam Anno (3 games), LB David Aupiu (1), LB Kyle Borland (2), RB Cullen Bryant (3), LB Dan Clark (1), T Tom Cox (3), LB Rick DiBernardo (3), RB Eric Dickerson (3), DE Reggie Doss (12), NT Dennis Edwards (3), TE Jon Embree (1), DE Donald Evans (1), RB Owen Gill (1), T Hank Goebel (3), CB/S Darryl Hall (1), WR Bernard Henry (3), DE Tom Hensley (active for 1 game, but did not play), TE David Hill (12), LB Neil Hope (3), CB Kirby Jackson (5), WR Samuel Johnson (3), LB Jim Kalafat (1), NT Marion Knight (2), WR Steve Marks (active for 1 game, but did not play), G Chris Matau (3), TE James McDonald (5), WR Stacey Mobley (3), G/T Joe Murray (3), TE Don Noble (2), NT Christopher Pacheco (3), NT Dave Purling (3), S Reggie Richardson (3), TE Joe Rose (1), S Craig Rutledge (3), T Greg Sinnott (1), LB Tommy Taylor (3), T Kelly Thomas (3), RB Casey Tiumalu (3), LB Cary Whittingham (3), LB Kyle Whittingham (3), RB Alonzo Williams (3), CB Greg Williamson (3), CB/S Ed Zeman (3).

MIAMI DOLPHINS

Also played with Dolphins in '87—RB Clarence Bailey (3 games), T Bill Bealles (3), K Willie Beecher (3), LB Laz Chavez (3), WR Eddie Chavis (3), T Greg Cleveland (2), WR Leland Douglas (3), WR George Farmer (1), WR Scott Feldman (1), LB Dennis Fowlkes (3), C Guy Goar (active for 1 game, but did not play), P Stacy Gore (3), P Jeff Hayes (2), CB Trell Hooper (3), G Jim Huddleston (active for 2 games, but did not play), S Mark Irvin (3), FB Rickey Isom (3), G Steve Jacobson (3), S Demetrious Johnson (3), T Greg Koch (1), RB Mark Konecny (3), TE David Lewis (5), LB Steve Lubischer (1), QB Kyle Mackey (3), LB David Marshall (2), LB Victor Morris (3), RB Tony Nathan (6), G Louis Oubre (1), C Greg Ours (3), LB Tim Pidgeon (3), CB Floyd Raglin (2), S Tate Randle (3), NT Ike Readon (3), WR Dameon Reilly (3), S Donovan Rose (12), RB Pete Roth (3), TE Lawrence Sampleton (3), LB Duke Schamel (3), RB Ronald Scott (3), DE Stanley Scott (3), TE Rich Siler (1), TE Willie Smith (3), CB Robert Sowell (3), QB Scott Stankavage (3), LB Greg Storr (3), CB John Swain (1), RB John Tagliaferri (3), K Van Tiffin (3), TE Joel Williams (3), G Jeff Wiska (3).

MINNESOTA VIKINGS

Also played with Vikings in '87—LB Steve Ache (3 games), QB Tony Adams (3), CB Rufus Bess (3), QB Keith Bishop (active for 3 games, but did not play), DT Don Bramlett (3), WR Larry Brown (1), P Dave Bruno (2), LB Tim Bryant (1), S Chuck Clanton (active for 1 game, but did not play), DE Daniel Coleman (3), LB Fabrey Collins (3), WR Ron Daugherty (3), K Dale Brown (3), LB Jim Dick (3), TE Clifton Eley (2), CB David Evans (3), WR Steve Finch (1), RB Phil Frye (1), WR Willie Gillespie (1), G Mark Hanson (1), RB Sam Harrell (1), RB Steve Harris (2), DE Mike Hartenstine (5), G Wayne Jones (6), WR Keith Kidd (3), QB Todd Krueger (active for 1 game, but did not play), WR Terry LeCount (3), DB Terry Love (1), TE Marc May (3), G Mike McCurry (3), DE Phil Micech (3), LB Larry Miller (2), G Ted Million (1), RB Leonard Moore (1), LB Pete Najarian (5), DE Tony Norman (2), G Frank Ori (3), WR Rickey Parks (2), DT Kurt Ploeger (1), LB Kelly Quinn (3), S Ted Rosnagle (3), T John Scardina (3), TE Ed Schenk (3), LB Randy Scott (2), G Ron Selesky (2), DE Mike Slaton (1), RB Jimmy Smith (1), DB Tim Starks (1), DT Joe Stepanek (1), RB Andre Thomas (1), DB John Turner (2), DB Mike Turner (2), RB Adam Walker (2), DT Jimmy Walker (2), C Kevin Webster (3), DT Brad White (1), RB Brett Wilson (3), RB Jeff Womack (2).

NEW ENGLAND PATRIOTS

Also played with Patriots in '87—DE Julius Adams (10 games), LB Rogers Alexander (3), CB Ricky Atkinson (1), TE Greg Baty (5), WR Mike Benson (active for 1 game, but did not play), RB Frank Bianchini (1), LB Mel Black (3), QB Bob Bleier (3), WR Brian Carey (2), S Duffy Cobbs (3), WR Wayne Coffey (3), RB Tony Collins (13), T George Colton (3), LB Rico Corsetti (2), LB Steve Doig (1), TE Todd Frain (3), TE Arnold Franklin (3), NT John Guzik (3), CB David Hendley (2), P Alan

Herline (3), WR Harold Jackson (active for 1 game, but did not play), WR Bill LaFreniere (active for 1 game, but did not play), RB Michael LeBlanc (4), WR Larry Linne (3), NT Dino Mangiero (2), LB Joe McHale (3), RB Chuck McSwain (3), LB Greg Moore (3), CB Joe Peterson (3), WR Clay Pickering (1), NT Tom Porell (1), DE Benton Reed (3), T Greg Robinson (3), LB Frank Sacco (2), G Todd Sandham (2), G Brian Saranovitz (active for 2 games, but did not play), CB Jon Sawyer (2), K Eric Schubert (1), TE Willie Scott (9), LB Randy Sealby (2), S Ron Shegog (3), G Eric Stokes (1), DE Bill Turner (2), C Darren Twombly (1), QB Todd Whitten (1), DE Murray Wichard (3), WR Derwin Williams (10), CB Perry Williams (3), RB Carl Woods (2).

NEW ORLEANS SAINTS

Also played with Saints in '87—RB Vincent Alexander (1 game), NT Sheldon Andrus (3), P Tommy Barnhardt (3), RB Dwight Beverly (3), DE Robert Brannon (1), K Mike Cofer (2), NT Ted Elliott (3), TE Darren Gottschalk (1), WR Vic Harrison (3), T/G Walter Housman (3), QB Kevin Ingram (2), C Phillip James (3), RB Garland Jean-Batiste (3), RB Nate Johnson (1), K Florian Kempf (1), LB Scott Leach (3), G/T William Leach (1), G Greg Loberg (3), LB Ken Marchiol (3), LB Larry McCoy (3), TE Ken O'Neal (3), CB Johnnie Poe (12), QB Tim Riordan (1), RB Jeff Rodenberger (3), LB Bill Roe (3), TE Malcolm Scott (3), CB/S John Sutton (2), CB Reggie Sutton (11), S Derrick Taylor (3), WR Curtland Thomas (3), G Henry Thomas (3), WR Joe Thomas (1), CB/S Junior Thurman (3), CB/S Darrell Toussaint (2), WR Dwight Walker (2), S Frank Wattelet (2), LB Ron Weissenhofer (1), S Scott Woerner (1), DE Kevin Young (1).

NEW YORK GIANTS

Also played with Giants in '87—WR Beau Almodobar (2 games), RB Earl Beecham (1), WR Lewis Bennett (3), K George Benyola (3), CB Don Brown (3), LB Charlie Burgess (2), QB Mike Busch (2), CB Boris Byrd (3), DE Reggie Carr (3), TE Charles Coleman (3), RB Jamie Covington (2), QB Jim Crocicchia (1), LB Chris Davis (3), G Kelvin Davis (3), LB Dan DeRose (3), RB Fred DiRenzo (1), RB Robert DiRico (3), G Bill Dugan (3), RB Tony Galbreath (12), DE Curtis Garrett (3), G Anthony Howard (3), C Brian Johnston (5), CB Chris Jones (3), DE James Jones (active for 1 game, but did not play), LB Robbie Jones (12), QB Paul Kelly (active for 2 games, but did not play), LB Jerry Kimmel (2), WR Edwin Lovelady (3), WR Reggie McGowan (3), T Kevin Meuth (3), P Jim Miller (1), C Russell Mitchell (3), P Dana Moore (2), S Pat Morrison (3), LB Frank Nicholson (3), CB Jimmy Norris (3), RB Kaulana Park (2), CB Elvis Patterson (1), T Marty Peterson (active for 1 game, but did not play), S Robert Porter (3), S Steve Rehage (3), WR Warren Seitz (2), CB Doug Smith (3), TE Jeff Smith (3), DE Torin Smith (1), T Frank Sutton (2), T Gregg Swarthwoudt (1), DE Joe Taibi (3), LB Warren Thompson (3), LB Jeff Tootle (3), G Scott Urch (3), RB Van Williams (3), S Jim Yarbrough (3).

NEW YORK JETS

Also played with Jets in '87—LB Lynwood Alford (1 game), DT Adam Bethea (active for 1 game, but did not play), QB Walter Briggs (1), LB Jay Brophy (3), T Chris Brown (1), RB Joe Burke (2), CB Russell Carter (8), DE Tony Chickillo (2), RB John Chirico (3), S Trent Collins (3), C Martin Cornelson (3), G/T Anthony Corvino (2), G/C Eric Coss (3), C/G Joe Fields (10), RB Derrick Foster (3), WR Derrick Gaffney (2), DE Tony Garbarczyk (2), G/T Mitch Geier (active for 1 game, but did not play), CB/S Jo Jo Heath (3), CB Marc Hogan (3), WR Scott Holman (3), G Tom Humphrey (3), RB Eddie Hunter (3), WR Stan Hunter (3), G Vince Jasper (3), P Dave Jennings (12), T Ken Jones (5), T Gordon King (2), NT Joe Klecko (7), TE Jamie Kurisko (3), G Pete McCartney (3), RB Tim Newman (1), QB David Norrie (2), P Tom O'Connor (3), K Pat Ragusa (3), TE Eric Riley (3), CB Larry Robinson (3), DE Don Smith (3), WR/KR Reggie Smith (1), CB Treg Songy (2), TE Tony Sweet (3), T John Thomas (3), RB Maurice Turner (1), C Vinny Tuzeo (active for 1 game, but did not play), LB Henry Walls (3), LB Ladell Wills (3), LB Mike Witteck (3).

PHILADELPHIA EAGLES

Also played with Eagles in '87—G Jim Angelo (1 game), DE Jim Auer (1), DE Marvin Ayers (2), LB Matt Battaglia (3), CB Vic Bellamy (3), WR Jesse Bendross (3), DT Gary Bolden (3), WR Kevin Bowman (3), LB Carlos Bradley (3), LB Dave Brown (1), RB Reggie Brown (3), CB Thomas Caterbone (2), NT Ken Clarke (11), DT Ray Conlin (1), LB George Cumby (1), TE Ron Fazio (1), S Chris Gerhard (3), LB Chuck Gorecki (3), WR Otis Grant (3), S Jeff Griffin (2), DE/DT Elois Grooms (3), DT Skip Hamilton (1), CB/S Greg Harding (1), QB Marty Horn (3), WR Kenny Jackson (12), K Dave Jacobs (3), CB Angelo James (3), CB/S Christopher Johnson (2), LB Kelly Kirchbaum (3), S Mike Kullman (3), RB Robert Lavette (3), LB Byron Lee (3), G Scott Leggett (3), DE Greg Liter (1), C Matt Long (3), TE Mike McCloskey (1), DE Dan McMillen (3), QB Guido Merkens (3), NT Mike Mitchell (active for 1 game, but did not play), NT Randall Mitchell (3), DE Tim Mooney (2), G Mike Nease (2), T Mike Perrino (3), DE/LB Ray Phillips (3), TE Jay Repko (3), FB Jacque Robinson (3), RB Alvin Ross (3), P Mark Royals (1), C Paul Ryczek (3), LB Jody Schulz (7), WR Mike Siano (3), LB Fred Smalls (3), RB Willie Turrall (1), CB/S Mike Ulmer (1), G Pete Walters (3), S Troy West (3), CB Brenard Wilson (1).

PHOENIX CARDINALS

Also played with Cardinals in '87—S Dwayne Anderson (1 game), LB Terrence Anthony (1), LB Joe Bock (1), DE Ron Bohm (3), LB Tony Buford (2), DT Anthony Burke (1), DT Victor Burnett (3), LB Jimmie Carter (1), P Greg Cater (9), WR Clarence Collins (1), RB Larry Cowan (active for 3 games, but did not play), DE Gary Dulin (3), LB Phil Forney (3), RB Don Goodman (3), QB Shawn Halloran (3), CB Johnny Holloway (3), TE Bob Keseday (3), LB Terrence Mack (5), CB Mark Mathis (2), S Tony Mayes (3), WR Adrian McBride (3), LB Peter Noga (3), LB Jeff Paine (1), G Ron Pasquale (1), DT Victor Perry (1), S John Preston (5), C Keith Radecic (3), S Ed Scott (3), CB Ken Sims (3), K Jason Staurovsky (2), QB Gregg Tipton (active for 3 games, but did not play), CB Charles Wright (3).

PITTSBURGH STEELERS

Also played with Steelers in '87—WR Mel Anderson (2 games), LB Steve Apke (3), LB Craig Bingham (3), TE Ralph Britt (3), RB Mike Clark (1), DE Jackie Cline (1), QB Reggie Collier (2), DE Tommy Dawkins (2), G Charlie Dickey (1), S Dave Edwards (3), WR Moses Ford (1), WR Russell Hairston (3), NT Alan Huff (2), CB/S Bruce Jones (2), LB Darryl Knox (3), G Ben Lawrence (1), C John Lott (1), S Kelvin Middleton (2), DL Edmund Nelson (10), NT David Opfar (3), C Paul Oswald (2), G Ted Petersen (2), T Ray Pinney (12), RB Dan Reeder (2), CB Rock Richmond (2), LB Avon Riley (3), RB Chuck Sanders (5), CB Chris Sheffield (5), DE Bret Shugarts (2), WR Calvin Sweeney (9), K David Trout (3), CB Anthony Tuggle (2), DE Xavier Warren (2), T Robert Washington (3), LB Albert Williams (3), LB Joe Williams (3), CB/S Ray Williams (1), LB Ken Woodard (7).

SAN DIEGO CHARGERS

Also played with Chargers in '87—LB Ty Allert (3), S Anthony Anderson (3), DE Monte Bennett (3), CB Ed Berry (2), CB Carl Brazley (2), WR Wes Chandler (12), WR Bruce Davis (active for 1 game, but did not play), C/G David Diaz-Infante (3), T Greg Feasel (3), TE Kevin Ferguson (3), K Jeff Gaffney (3), DE Willard Goff (1), S Walt Harris (3), LB Andy Hawkins (2), TE Pete Holohan (12), TE Harry Holt (3), CB/S Darrel Hopper (4), LB Mike Humiston (7), LB Brian Ingram (1), FB Keyvan Jenkins (3), LB James Johnson (1), RB Frank Middleton (3), WR Calvin Muhammad (2), QB Rick Neuheisel (3), RB Jeff Powell (1), P/K Joe Prokop (3), WR Tag Rome (3), CB Charles Romes (5), RB Martin Sartin (3), T Gary Schippang (active for 1 game, but did not play), S King Simmons (3), DE Tony Simmons (3), T Emil Slovacek (3), LB Angelo Snipes (2), RB Todd Spencer (3), RB Anthony Steels (2), CB Danny Walters (12), S Ted Watts (1), G/T Dwight Wheeler (3), DE Earl Wilson (1).

SAN FRANCISCO 49ers

Also played with 49ers in '87—K Jim Asmus (3 games), QB Ed Blount (1), K Jeff Brockhaus (3), RB Raynard Brown (1), LB Keith Browner (1), S John Butler (3), RB Tony Cherry (1), DE Glen Collins (3), CB Matt Courtney (3), LB Tom Cousineau (4), NT Joe Drake (3), TE Chris Dressel (1), G Michael Durrette (3), S John Faylor (3), TE Russ Francis (8), T Tracy Franz (3), WR Tony Gladney (2), WR Terry Greer (3), FB Andre Hardy (1), WR Thomas Henley (1), T Gary Hoffman (3), LB James Johnson (1), LB Jerry Keeble (3), LB Carl Keever (3), LB Mark Korff (2), DE Greg Liter (1), C Tim Long (2), CB Derrick Martin (3), CB Dana McLemore (12), WR Carl Monroe (3), T Limbo Parks (3), NT Reno Patterson (1), CB Darryl Pollard (3), C Fred Quillan (11), G Kevin Reach (3), DE Elston Ridgle (3), RB Del Rodgers (7), CB Jonathan Shelley (1), QB Mark Stevens (2), S John Sullivan (1), RB Mike Varajon (3), TE Mike Wells (1).

SEATTLE SEAHAWKS

Also played with Seahawks in '87—S Harvey Allen (2 games), C Tom Andrews (2), CB Curtis Baham (3), WR Brant Bengen (3), CB Anthony Blue (3), P Barry Bowman (1), CB Arnold Brown (2), LB Tony Caldwell (1), TE Chris Corley (1), LB Julio Cortes (3), CB Fred Davis (1), LB Rob DeVita (1), DE Dale Dorning (3), DE Randy Edwards (7), NT John Eisenhooth (1), WR Russell Evans (1), DE Don Fairbanks (3), CB Charles Glaze (3), NT David Graham (3), RB Boyce Green (2), P Russell Griffith (2), RB Mike Hagan (2), K Scott Hagler (2), G Matt Hanousek (3), C Doug Hire (3), DE Van Hughes (1), LB Joe Jackson (3), WR Kevin Juma (3), TE Mark Keel (3), LB Paul Lavine (3), S Kim Mack (1), LB John McVeigh (3), RB Alvin Moore (1), RB Michael Morton (2), TE John O'Callaghan (1), LB Fred Orns (3), WR Curtis Pardridge (3), RB Rick Parros (1), C Dean Perryman (1), DE Greg Ramsey (2), T Howard Richards (2), TE Ken Sager (3), T Ron Scoggins (3), G Jack Sims (3), S Dallis Smith (3), WR Donald Snell (1), RB Chad Stark (2), LB Joe Terry (3), G Garth Thomas (1), S Ricky Thomas (1), S Chris White (1), NT Charles Wiley (1), RB James Williams (1), CB Renard Young (3).

TAMPA BAY BUCCANEERS

Also played with Buccaneers in '87—CB Don Anderson (11 games), RB Steve Bartalo (9), RB Greg Boone (2), LB Scot Brantley (12), G Rufus Brown (2), WR Steve Carter (3), DE Walter Carter (2), DE Mike Clark (3), CB/S Torin Clark (2), CB Ivory Curry (3), WR Dwayne Dixon (2), P Frank Garcia (12), CB Jeff George (2), RB Charles Gladman (2), T Conrad Goode (11), DB Roy Harris (3), T Ron Heller (12), WR Derek Holloway (1), TE Steve Holloway (6), G Jim Huddleston (1), G John Hunt (1), WR David Jackson (1), LB Cam Jacobs (3), T Hoss Johnson (1), G David Jordan (3), S Bobby Kemp (12), DE Tyrone Keys (3), CB Tim King (3), RB Dan Land (3), LB Fred McCallister (3), CB Vito McKeever (1), TE Jeff Modesitt (1), LB Sankar Montoute (3), NT Fred Nordgren (3), G Paul O'Connor (2), CB Lee Paige (3), LB Leon Pennington (3), C Chuck Pitcock (2), T Marvin Powell (6), DE James Ramey (3), QB John Reaves (2), RB Harold Ricks (3), DE Charles Riggins (3), WR Stanley Shakespeare (1), T Reggie Smith (3), NT Mike Stensrud (12), WR Eric Streater (3), S Craig Swoope (1), RB Derrick Thomas (1), K Van Tiffin (3), LB Miles Turpin (3), CB Kevin Walker (3), WR Herkie Walls (2), TE Arthur Wells (2), S Rick Woods (5), C George Yarno (11), QB Jim Zorn (1).

WASHINGTON REDSKINS

Also played with Redskins in '87—K Obed Ariri (2 games), TE Cliff Benson (2), WR Keiron Bigby (1), LB Derek Bunch (3), S Danny Burmeister (3), S Joe Cofer (3), LB Anthony Copeland (3), C John Cowne (3), CB Vernon Dean (12), TE Glenn Dennison (3), TE K.D. Dunn (3), CB David Etherly (3), G Frank Frazier (3), DT Alec Gibson (3), RB Allen Harvin (1), RB Walter Holman (3), S Charles Jackson (1), WR Richard Johnson (1), DT Ted Karras (3), CB Garry Kimble (3), LB Jon Kimmel (1), DT Kit Lathrop (1), QB Babe Laufenberg (active for 1 game, but did not play), S Skip Lane (3), DE Steve Martin (3), DT Curtis McGriff (1), T Dan McQuaid (1), LB Rich Milot (9), CB Michael Mitchell (3), CB Tim Morrison (7), G Phil Pettey (3), WR Joe Phillips (3), QB Tony Robinson (1), RB George Rogers (11), QB Ed Rubbert (3), DT Anthony Sagnella (3), G Willard Scissum (3), LB Tony Settles (3), QB Jack Stanley (active for 3 games, but did not play), DT Steve Thompson (1), K Brendan Toibin (1), TE Dave Truitt (1), WR Clarence Verdin (3), RB Lionel Vital (3), DT Henry Waechter (1), P Jack Weil (1), G T Marvin Williams (2), LB Eric Wilson (3), WR Ted Wilson (3), RB Wayne Wilson (2), LB David Windham (3), C Mike Wooten (3).

The Sporting News AWARDS

NFL Coach of the Year (since 1970)

1970—Don Shula, Miami
1971—George Allen, Washington
1972—Don Shula, Miami
1973—Chuck Knox, Los Angeles
1974—Don Coryell, St. Louis
1975—Ted Marchibroda, Baltimore
1976—Chuck Fairbanks, New England
1977—Red Miller, Denver
1978—Jack Patera, Seattle
1979—Dick Vermeil, Philadelphia
1980—Chuck Knox, Buffalo
1981—Bill Walsh, San Francisco
1982—Joe Gibbs, Washington
1983—Joe Gibbs, Washington
1984—Chuck Knox, Seattle
1985—Mike Ditka, Chicago
1986—Bill Parcells, N.Y. Giants
1987—Jim Mora, New Orleans

Player of the Year (since 1957)

1957—Jim Brown, RB, Cleveland
1958—Jim Brown, RB, Cleveland
1959—Johnny Unitas, QB, Baltimore
1960—Norm Van Brocklin, QB, Philadelphia
1961—Paul Hornung, HB, Green Bay
1962—Y.A. Tittle, QB, New York
1963—Y.A. Tittle, QB, New York
1964—Johnny Unitas, QB, Baltimore
1965—Jim Brown, RB, Cleveland
1966—Bart Starr, QB, Green Bay
1967—Johnny Unitas, QB, Baltimore
1968—Earl Morrall, QB, Baltimore
1969—Roman Gabriel, QB, Los Angeles
1970—NFC: John Brodie, QB, San Francisco   AFC: George Blanda, QB-PK, Oakland
1971—NFC: Roger Staubach, QB, Dallas   AFC: Bob Griese, QB, Miami
1972—NFC: Larry Brown, RB, Washington   AFC: Earl Morrall, QB, Miami
1973—NFC: John Hadl, QB, Los Angeles   AFC: O.J. Simpson, RB, Buffalo
1974—NFC: Chuck Foreman, RB, Minnesota   AFC: Ken Stabler, QB, Oakland
1975—NFC: Fran Tarkenton, QB, Minnesota   AFC: O.J. Simpson, RB, Buffalo
1976—NFC: Walter Payton, RB, Chicago   AFC: Ken Stabler, QB, Oakland
1977—NFC: Walter Payton, RB, Chicago   AFC: Craig Morton, QB, Denver
1978—NFC: Archie Manning, QB, New Orleans   AFC: Earl Campbell, RB, Houston
1979—NFC: Ottis Anderson, RB, St. Louis   AFC: Dan Fouts, QB, San Diego
1980—Brian Sipe, QB, Cleveland
1981—Ken Anderson, QB, Cincinnati
1982—Mark Moseley, PK, Washington
1983—Eric Dickerson, RB, L.A. Rams
1984—Dan Marino, QB, Miami
1985—Marcus Allen, RB, L.A. Raiders
1986—Lawrence Taylor, LB, N.Y. Giants
1987—Jerry Rice, WR, San Francisco

NOTE: From 1970-79, a player was selected as Player of the Year for both the NFC and AFC. In 1980, The Sporting News reinstated the selection of one player as Player of the Year for the entire NFL.

Rookie of the Year (since 1970)

1970—NFC: Bruce Taylor, CB, San Francisco   AFC: Dennis Shaw, QB, Buffalo
1971—NFC: John Brockington, RB, Green Bay   AFC: Jim Plunkett, QB, New England
1972—NFC: Chester Marcol, PK, Green Bay   AFC: Franco Harris, RB, Pittsburgh
1973—NFC: Chuck Foreman, RB, Minnesota   AFC: Boobie Clark, RB, Cincinnati
1974—NFC: Wilbur Jackson, RB, San Francisco   AFC: Don Woods, RB, San Diego
1975—NFC: Steve Bartkowski, QB, Atlanta   AFC: Robert Brazile, LB, Houston
1976—NFC: Sammy White, WR, Minnesota   AFC: Mike Haynes, CB, New England
1977—NFC: Tony Dorsett, RB, Dallas   AFC: A.J. Duhe, DT, Miami
1978—NFC: Al Baker, DE, Detroit   AFC: Earl Campbell, RB, Houston
1979—NFC: Ottis Anderson, RB, St. Louis   AFC: Jerry Butler, WR, Buffalo
1980—Billy Sims, RB, Detroit
1981—George Rogers, RB, New Orleans
1982—Marcus Allen, RB, L.A. Raiders
1983—Dan Marino, QB, Miami
1984—Louis Lipps, WR, Pittsburgh
1985—Eddie Brown, WR, Cincinnati
1986—Rueben Mayes, RB, New Orleans
1987—Robert Awalt, TE, St. Louis

NOTE: In 1980, The Sporting News began selecting one rookie as Rookie of the Year for the entire NFL.

1987 Pro Bowl Squads

*Denotes starter.

AFC OFFENSE

WR—Al Toon, N.Y. Jets*
    Steve Largent, Seattle*
    Carlos Carson, Kansas City
    Stanley Morgan, New England
TE—Kellen Winslow, San Diego*
    Todd Christensen, L.A. Raiders
T—Anthony Munoz, Cincinnati*
    Chris Hinton, Indianapolis*
    Cody Risien, Cleveland
G—Keith Bishop, Denver*
    Mike Munchak, Houston*
    Ron Solt, Indianapolis
C—Ray Donaldson, Indianapolis*
    Dwight Stephenson, Miami
QB—John Elway, Denver*
    Dan Marino, Miami
RB—Eric Dickerson, Indianapolis*
    Curt Warner, Seattle*
    Kevin Mack, Cleveland
    Mike Rozier, Houston
NOTE: T Munoz replaced due to injury by Jim Lachey, San Diego; C Stephenson replaced due to injury by Mike Webster, Pittsburgh; QB Marino replaced due to injury by Jim Kelly, Buffalo.

AFC DEFENSE

DE—Bruce Smith, Buffalo*
    Jacob Green, Seattle*
    Howie Long, L.A. Raiders
DT—Bill Maas, Kansas City*
    Bob Golic, Cleveland
OLB—Andre Tippett, New England*
    Duane Bickett, Indianapolis*
    Clay Matthews, Cleveland
ILB—Fredd Young, Seattle*
    Karl Mecklenburg, Denver*
    John Offerdahl, Miami
CB—Frank Minnifield, Cleveland*
    Hanford Dixon, Cleveland*
    Albert Lewis, Kansas City
S—Kenny Easley, Seattle*
    Deron Cherry, Kansas City*
    Keith Bostic, Houston
NOTE: DT Golic replaced due to injury by Tim Krumrie, Cincinnati.

AFC SPECIALISTS

P—Ralf Mojsiejenko, San Diego
PK—Dean Biasucci, Indianapolis
KR—Gerald McNeil, Cleveland

ST—Steve Tasker, Buffalo

NFC OFFENSE

WR—Jerry Rice, San Francisco*
    Mike Quick, Philadelphia*
    Anthony Carter, Minnesota
    Gary Clark, Washington
TE—Mark Bavaro, N.Y. Giants*
    Steve Jordan, Minnesota
T—Jackie Slater, L.A. Rams*
    Gary Zimmerman, Minnesota*
    Luis Sharpe, St. Louis
G—Bill Fralic, Atlanta*
    Dennis Harrah, L.A. Rams*
    Brad Edelman, New Orleans
C—Jay Hilgenberg, Chicago*
    Doug Smith, L.A. Rams
QB—Joe Montana, San Francisco*
    Neil Lomax, St. Louis
RB—Rueben Mayes, New Orleans*
    Charles White, L.A. Rams*
    Herschel Walker, Dallas
    Roger Craig, San Francisco
NOTE: TE Bavaro replaced due to injury by Hoby Brenner, New Orleans; RB Mayes replaced due to injury by Gerald Riggs, Atlanta.

NFC DEFENSE

DE—Reggie White, Philadelphia*
    Chris Doleman, Minnesota*
    Charles Mann, Washington
DT—Michael Carter, San Francisco*
    Steve McMichael, Chicago
OLB—Carl Banks, N.Y. Giants*
    Wilber Marshall, Chicago*
    Lawrence Taylor, N.Y. Giants
ILB—Mike Singletary, Chicago*
    Harry Carson, N.Y. Giants*
    Sam Mills, New Orleans
CB—Darrell Green, Washington*
    Jerry Gray, L.A. Rams*
    Dave Waymer, New Orleans
S—Joey Browner, Minnesota*
    Ronnie Lott, San Francisco*
    Dave Duerson, Chicago

NFC SPECIALISTS

P—Jim Arnold, Detroit
PK—Morten Andersen, New Orleans
KR—Vai Sikahema, St. Louis
ST—Ron Wolfley, St. Louis

1988 NATIONAL FOOTBALL LEAGUE SCHEDULE
(All times local)

FIRST WEEK
SUNDAY, SEPTEMBER 4
1. Atlanta at Detroit 1:00
2. Cleveland at Kansas City 3:00
3. Dallas at Pittsburgh......................... 1:00
4. Houston at Indianapolis...................... 3:00
5. Los Angeles Rams at Green Bay............... 12:00
6. Miami at Chicago 12:00
7. Minnesota at Buffalo......................... 1:00
8. New York Jets at New England 4:00
9. Philadelphia at Tampa Bay.................... 1:00
10. Phoenix at Cincinnati....................... 1:00
11. San Diego at Los Angeles Raiders........... 1:00
12. San Francisco at New Orleans 12:00
13. Seattle at Denver........................... 2:00

MONDAY, SEPTEMBER 5
14. Washington at New York Giants 9:00

SECOND WEEK
SUNDAY, SEPTEMBER 11
15. Chicago at Indianapolis 12:00
16. Cincinnati at Philadelphia 4:00
17. Detroit at Los Angeles Rams................. 1:00
18. Kansas City at Seattle...................... 1:00
19. Los Angeles Raiders at Houston............. 3:00
20. Miami at Buffalo............................ 1:00
21. New England at Minnesota.................... 3:00
22. New Orleans at Atlanta...................... 1:00
23. New York Jets at Cleveland 4:00
24. Pittsburgh at Washington.................... 1:00
25. San Diego at Denver......................... 2:00
26. San Francisco at New York Giants........... 1:00
27. Tampa Bay at Green Bay...................... 12:00

MONDAY, SEPTEMBER 12
28. Dallas at Phoenix 6:00

THIRD WEEK
SUNDAY, SEPTEMBER 18
29. Atlanta at San Francisco.................... 1:00
30. Buffalo at New England...................... 1:00
31. Cincinnati at Pittsburgh.................... 1:00
32. Denver at Kansas City 12:00
33. Green Bay at Miami.......................... 1:00
34. Houston at New York Jets.................... 1:00
35. Los Angeles Rams at Los Angeles Raiders ... 1:00
36. Minnesota at Chicago 12:00
37. New Orleans at Detroit 1:00
38. New York Giants at Dallas................... 3:00
39. Philadelphia at Washington.................. 1:00
40. Phoenix at Tampa Bay 1:00
41. Seattle at San Diego........................ 1:00

MONDAY, SEPTEMBER 19
42. Indianapolis at Cleveland................... 8:00

FOURTH WEEK
SUNDAY, SEPTEMBER 25
43. Atlanta at Dallas........................... 12:00
44. Chicago at Green Bay........................ 12:00
45. Cleveland at Cincinnati 1:00
46. Los Angeles Rams at New York Giants........ 4:00
47. Miami at Indianapolis....................... 12:00
48. New England at Houston...................... 12:00
49. New York Jets at Detroit.................... 1:00
50. Philadelphia at Minnesota 12:00
51. Pittsburgh at Buffalo 1:00
52. San Diego at Kansas City 3:00
53. San Francisco at Seattle.................... 1:00
54. Tampa Bay at New Orleans 12:00
55. Washington at Phoenix 1:00

MONDAY, SEPTEMBER 26
56. Los Angeles Raiders at Denver............... 6:00

FIFTH WEEK
SUNDAY, OCTOBER 2
57. Buffalo at Chicago 12:00
58. Cincinnati at Los Angeles Raiders 1:00
59. Cleveland at Pittsburgh 1:00
60. Denver at San Diego 1:00
61. Detroit at San Francisco.................... 1:00
62. Green Bay at Tampa Bay 1:00
63. Houston at Philadelphia 1:00
64. Indianapolis at New England................. 1:00
65. Kansas City at New York Jets 4:00
66. Minnesota at Miami 4:00
67. New York Giants at Washington 1:00
68. Phoenix at Los Angeles Rams 1:00
69. Seattle at Atlanta......................... 1:00

MONDAY, OCTOBER 3
70. Dallas at New Orleans 8:00

SIXTH WEEK
SUNDAY, OCTOBER 9
71. Chicago at Detroit.......................... 1:00
72. Denver at San Francisco..................... 1:00
73. Indianapolis at Buffalo 1:00
74. Kansas City at Houston...................... 12:00
75. Los Angeles Rams at Atlanta 1:00
76. Miami at Los Angeles Raiders................ 1:00
77. New England vs. Green Bay at Milwaukee 12:00
78. New Orleans at San Diego 1:00
79. New York Jets at Cincinnati 1:00
80. Pittsburgh at Phoenix 1:00
81. Seattle at Cleveland 1:00
82. Tampa Bay at Minnesota 12:00
83. Washington at Dallas........................ 12:00

MONDAY, OCTOBER 10
84. New York Giants at Philadelphia 9:00

SEVENTH WEEK
SUNDAY, OCTOBER 16
85. Atlanta at Denver 2:00
86. Cincinnati at New England 1:00
87. Dallas at Chicago 12:00
88. Detroit at New York Giants 1:00
89. Green Bay at Minnesota 12:00
90. Houston at Pittsburgh 1:00
91. Los Angeles Raiders at Kansas City 12:00
92. New Orleans at Seattle 1:00
93. Philadelphia at Cleveland 1:00
94. Phoenix at Washington 1:00
95. San Diego at Miami 1:00
96. San Francisco at Los Angeles Rams.......... 1:00
97. Tampa Bay at Indianapolis 12:00

MONDAY, OCTOBER 17
98. Buffalo at New York Jets.................... 9:00

EIGHTH WEEK
SUNDAY, OCTOBER 23
99. Cleveland at Phoenix........................ 1:00
100. Dallas at Philadelphia..................... 1:00
101. Denver at Pittsburgh....................... 1:00
102. Detroit at Kansas City 12:00
103. Houston at Cincinnati...................... 1:00
104. Indianapolis at San Diego.................. 1:00
105. Los Angeles Raiders at New Orleans......... 12:00
106. Minnesota at Tampa Bay..................... 1:00
107. New England at Buffalo..................... 1:00
108. New York Giants at Atlanta 1:00
109. New York Jets at Miami 4:00
110. Seattle at Los Angeles Rams 1:00
111. Washington vs. Green Bay at Milwaukee 12:00

MONDAY, OCTOBER 24
112. San Francisco at Chicago 8:00

NINTH WEEK

SUNDAY, OCTOBER 30
113. Atlanta at Philadelphia 1:00
114. Chicago at New England 1:00
115. Cincinnati at Cleveland 1:00
116. Green Bay at Buffalo 1:00
117. Kansas City at Los Angeles Raiders 1:00
118. Los Angeles Rams at New Orleans 12:00
119. Miami at Tampa Bay 1:00
120. Minnesota at San Francisco 1:00
121. New York Giants at Detroit 1:00
122. Phoenix at Dallas 12:00
123. Pittsburgh at New York Jets 1:00
124. San Diego at Seattle 1:00
125. Washington at Houston 7:00

MONDAY, OCTOBER 31
126. Denver at Indianapolis 9:00

TENTH WEEK

SUNDAY, NOVEMBER 6
127. Buffalo at Seattle 1:00
128. Dallas at New York Giants 1:00
129. Detroit at Minnesota 12:00
130. Green Bay at Atlanta 1:00
131. Kansas City at Denver 2:00
132. Los Angeles Rams at Philadelphia 1:00
133. Miami at New England 1:00
134. New Orleans at Washington 4:00
135. New York Jets at Indianapolis 4:00
136. Pittsburgh at Cincinnati 1:00
137. San Francisco at Phoenix 2:00
138. Tampa Bay at Chicago 12:00
139. Los Angeles Raiders at San Diego 5:00

MONDAY, NOVEMBER 7
140. Cleveland at Houston 8:00

ELEVENTH WEEK

SUNDAY, NOVEMBER 13
141. Chicago at Washington 1:00
142. Cincinnati at Kansas City 12:00
143. Cleveland at Denver 2:00
144. Houston at Seattle 1:00
145. Indianapolis at Green Bay 12:00
146. Los Angeles Raiders at San Francisco 1:00
147. New England at New York Jets 1:00
148. New Orleans at Los Angeles Rams 1:00
149. New York Giants at Phoenix 2:00
150. Philadelphia at Pittsburgh 1:00
151. San Diego at Atlanta 1:00
152. Tampa Bay at Detroit 1:00
153. Minnesota at Dallas 7:00

MONDAY, NOVEMBER 14
154. Buffalo at Miami 9:00

TWELFTH WEEK

SUNDAY, NOVEMBER 20
155. Atlanta at Los Angeles Raiders 1:00
156. Chicago at Tampa Bay 1:00
157. Cincinnati at Dallas 12:00
158. Denver at New Orleans 12:00
159. Detroit vs. Green Bay at Milwaukee 12:00
160. Indianapolis at Minnesota 12:00
161. New York Jets at Buffalo 1:00
162. Philadelphia at New York Giants 4:00
163. Phoenix at Houston 12:00
164. Pittsburgh at Cleveland 1:00
165. San Diego at Los Angeles Rams 1:00
166. Seattle at Kansas City 12:00
167. New England at Miami 8:00

MONDAY, NOVEMBER 21
168. Washington at San Francisco 6:00

THIRTEENTH WEEK

THURSDAY, NOVEMBER 24
169. Minnesota at Detroit 12:30
170. Houston at Dallas 3:00

SUNDAY, NOVEMBER 27
171. Buffalo at Cincinnati 1:00
172. Cleveland at Washington 1:00
173. Green Bay at Chicago 12:00
174. Kansas City at Pittsburgh 1:00
175. Los Angeles Rams at Denver 2:00
176. Miami at New York Jets 1:00
177. New England at Indianapolis 4:00
178. Phoenix at Philadelphia 1:00
179. San Francisco at San Diego 1:00
180. Tampa Bay at Atlanta 1:00
181. New York Giants at New Orleans 7:00

MONDAY, NOVEMBER 28
182. Los Angeles Raiders at Seattle 6:00

FOURTEENTH WEEK

SUNDAY, DECEMBER 4
183. Buffalo at Tampa Bay 1:00
184. Dallas at Cleveland 1:00
185. Denver at Los Angeles Raiders 1:00
186. Green Bay at Detroit 1:00
187. Indianapolis at Miami 1:00
188. New Orleans at Minnesota 12:00
189. New York Jets at Kansas City 3:00
190. Phoenix at New York Giants 1:00
191. San Diego at Cincinnati 1:00
192. San Francisco at Atlanta 1:00
193. Seattle at New England 1:00
194. Washington at Philadelphia 1:00
195. Pittsburgh at Houston 7:00

MONDAY, DECEMBER 5
196. Chicago at Los Angeles Rams 6:00

FIFTEENTH WEEK

SATURDAY, DECEMBER 10
197. Indianapolis at New York Jets 12:30
198. Philadelphia at Phoenix 2:00

SUNDAY, DECEMBER 11
199. Atlanta at Los Angeles Rams 1:00
200. Cincinnati at Houston 12:00
201. Dallas at Washington 1:00
202. Detroit at Chicago 12:00
203. Kansas City at New York Giants 1:00
204. Los Angeles Raiders at Buffalo 1:00
205. Minnesota at Green Bay 12:00
206. New Orleans at San Francisco 1:00
207. Pittsburgh at San Diego 1:00
208. Tampa Bay at New England 1:00
209. Denver at Seattle 5:00

MONDAY, DECEMBER 12
210. Cleveland at Miami 9:00

SIXTEENTH WEEK

SATURDAY, DECEMBER 17
211. New England at Denver 2:00
212. Washington at Cincinnati 12:30

SUNDAY, DECEMBER 18
213. Atlanta at New Orleans 12:00
214. Buffalo at Indianapolis 1:00
215. Detroit at Tampa Bay 1:00
216. Green Bay at Phoenix 2:00
217. Houston at Cleveland 1:00
218. Kansas City at San Diego 1:00
219. Miami at Pittsburgh 1:00
220. New York Giants at New York Jets 1:00
221. Philadelphia at Dallas 12:00
222. Seattle at Los Angeles Raiders 1:00
223. Los Angeles Rams at San Francisco 5:00

MONDAY, DECEMBER 19
224. Chicago at Minnesota 8:00

NFL PRESEASON GAMES

(All times local)

HALL OF FAME GAME

SATURDAY, JULY 30
Cincinnati vs. Los Angeles Rams at Canton, O. 2:00

FIRST WEEK

WEDNESDAY, AUGUST 3
Denver at Los Angeles Rams.................................7:00

THURSDAY, AUGUST 4
Buffalo at Houston...7:00
Phoenix at Seattle 7:30

FRIDAY, AUGUST 5
Pittsburgh at Washington.....................................8:00

SATURDAY, AUGUST 6
Atlanta at New England 7:00
Cincinnati at Kansas City......................................7:35
Dallas at San Diego...6:00
Detroit at Cleveland...7:00
Indianapolis at Tampa Bay....................................6:00
Los Angeles Raiders at San Francisco.................7:00
Miami at Chicago...6:00
New York Giants at Green Bay..............................7:00
New York Jets at Philadelphia 7:30

SUNDAY, AUGUST 7
New Orleans at Minnesota....................................7:00

SECOND WEEK

THURSDAY, AUGUST 11
Seattle at Detroit 7:30

SATURDAY, AUGUST 13
Cincinnati at Buffalo 7:30
Cleveland at Tampa Bay 7:00
Dallas at Los Angeles Raiders.............................1:00
Green Bay at Indianapolis.....................................7:30
Houston vs. New England at Memphis, Tenn........7:00
Kansas City at Atlanta 7:30
New Orleans at Phoenix.......................................7:30
New York Jets vs. New York Giants....................8:00
San Diego at Los Angeles Rams 7:00
San Francisco at Denver 7:00
Washington at Miami..8:00

SUNDAY, AUGUST 14
Chicago vs. Minnesota at Gothenburg, Sweden ...1:00
Philadelphia at Pittsburgh.....................................8:00

THIRD WEEK

THURSDAY, AUGUST 18
Cleveland vs. New York Jets at Montreal 7:30

FRIDAY, AUGUST 19
Buffalo at Seattle..7:30
Denver at Miami..9:00
Kansas City vs. Green Bay at Milwaukee.............7:00

SATURDAY, AUGUST 20
Detroit at Cincinnati 7:30
Houston at Los Angeles Rams.............................7:00
New England at Philadelphia 7:30
New Orleans at Indianapolis 7:30
Pittsburgh at New York Giants.............................8:00
San Francisco at San Diego..................................6:00
Tampa Bay at Atlanta..7:30
Washington at Los Angeles Raiders.....................7:00

SUNDAY, AUGUST 21
Minnesota at Phoenix...5:00

MONDAY, AUGUST 22
Chicago at Dallas...7:00

FOURTH WEEK

THURSDAY, AUGUST 25
Buffalo vs. Tampa Bay at Nashville, Tenn............7:00
Indianapolis at Denver 6:00
Philadelphia at Detroit..7:30
Phoenix at Kansas City 5:30

FRIDAY, AUGUST 26
Cincinnati at New England....................................7:00
Los Angeles Raiders at Chicago 8:00
Los Angeles Rams at San Diego 8:00
Miami at Minnesota..8:00
New York Giants at Cleveland..............................9:00
Seattle at San Francisco 6:00

SATURDAY, AUGUST 27
Atlanta vs. Washington at Birmingham, Ala....... 12:00
Houston at Dallas...8:00
New York Jets vs. Green Bay at Madison, Wis....1:00
Pittsburgh at New Orleans 11:30

1988 NATIONALLY TELEVISED GAMES
(All games carried on CBS Radio Network)

REGULAR SEASON

Monday,   Sept. 5—Washington at New York Giants (night, ABC)
Monday,   Sept. 12—Dallas at Phoenix (night, ABC)
Monday,   Sept. 19—Indianapolis at Cleveland (night, ABC)
Monday,   Sept. 26—Los Angeles Raiders at Denver (night, ABC)
Monday,   Oct. 3—Dallas at New Orleans (night, ABC)
Monday,   Oct. 10—New York Giants at Philadelphia (night, ABC)
Monday,   Oct. 17—Buffalo at New York Jets (night, ABC)
Monday,   Oct. 24—San Francisco at Chicago (night, ABC)
Sunday,   Oct. 30—Washington at Houston (night, ESPN)
Monday,   Oct. 31—Denver at Indianapolis (night, ABC)
Sunday,   Nov. 6—Los Angeles Raiders at San Diego (night, ESPN)
Monday,   Nov. 7—Cleveland at Houston (night, ABC)
Sunday,   Nov. 13—Minnesota at Dallas (night, ESPN)
Monday,   Nov. 14—Buffalo at Miami (night, ABC)
Sunday,   Nov. 20—New England at Miami (night, ESPN)
Monday,   Nov. 21—Washington at San Francisco (night, ABC)
Thursday,   Nov. 24—(Thanksgiving) Minnesota at Detroit (day, CBS)
                       Houston at Dallas (day, NBC)
Sunday,   Nov. 27—New York Giants at New Orleans (night, ESPN)
Monday,   Nov. 28—Los Angeles Raiders at Seattle (night, ABC)
Sunday,   Dec. 4—Pittsburgh at Houston (night, ESPN)
Monday,   Dec. 5—Chicago at Los Angeles Rams (night, ABC)
Saturday,   Dec. 10—Indianapolis at New York Jets (day, NBC)
                       Philadephia at Phoenix (day, CBS)
Sunday,   Dec. 11—Denver at Seattle (night, ESPN)
Monday,   Dec. 12—Cleveland at Miami (night, ABC)
Saturday,   Dec. 17—Washington at Cincinnati (day, CBS)
                       New England at Denver (day, NBC)
Sunday,   Dec. 18—Los Angeles Rams at San Francisco (night, ESPN)
Monday,   Dec. 19—Chicago at Minnesota (night, ABC)

POSTSEASON

Saturday,   Dec. 24—AFC First Round Playoff (NBC)
Monday,   Dec. 26—NFC First Round Playoff (CBS)
Saturday,   Dec. 31—AFC and NFC Divisional Playoffs (NBC and CBS)
Sunday,   Jan. 1—AFC and NFC Divisional Playoffs (NBC and CBS)
Sunday,   Jan. 8—AFC and NFC Championship Games (NBC and CBS)
Sunday,   Jan. 22—Super Bowl XXIII at Joe Robbie Stadium,
                       Miami, Florida (NBC)
Sunday,   Jan. 29—AFC-NFC Pro Bowl at Honolulu, Hawaii (ESPN)

SUNDAY AND MONDAY NIGHT GAMES

(All times local; Sunday on ESPN, Monday on ABC-TV; all on CBS Radio Network)

Monday,   Sept. 5—Washington at New York Giants (ABC) 9:00
Monday,   Sept. 12—Dallas at Phoenix (ABC) 6:00
Monday,   Sept. 19—Indianapolis at Cleveland (ABC) 8:00
Monday,   Sept. 26—Los Angeles Raiders at Denver (ABC) 6:00
Monday,   Oct. 3—Dallas at New Orleans (ABC) 8:00
Monday,   Oct. 10—New York Giants at Philadelphia (ABC) 9:00
Monday,   Oct. 17—Buffalo at New York Jets (ABC) 9:00
Monday,   Oct. 24—San Francisco at Chicago (ABC) 8:00
Sunday,   Oct. 30—Washington at Houston (ESPN) 7:00
Monday,   Oct. 31—Denver at Indianapolis (ABC) 9:00
Sunday,   Nov. 6—Los Angeles Raiders at San Diego (ESPN) 5:00
Monday,   Nov. 7—Cleveland at Houston (ABC) 8:00
Sunday,   Nov. 13—Minnesota at Dallas (ESPN) 7:00
Monday,   Nov. 14—Buffalo at Miami (ABC) 9:00
Sunday,   Nov. 20—New England at Miami (ESPN) 8:00

Monday,	Nov. 21—Washington at San Francisco (ABC)	6:00
Sunday,	Nov. 27—New York Giants at New Orleans (ESPN)	7:00
Monday,	Nov. 28—Los Angeles Raiders at Seattle (ABC)	6:00
Sunday,	Dec. 4—Pittsburgh at Houston (ESPN)	7:00
Monday,	Dec. 5—Chicago at Los Angeles Rams (ABC)	6:00
Sunday,	Dec. 11—Denver at Seattle (ESPN)	5:00
Monday,	Dec. 12—Cleveland at Miami (ABC)	9:00
Sunday,	Dec. 18—Los Angeles Rams at San Francisco (ESPN)	5:00
Monday,	Dec. 19—Chicago at Minnesota (ABC)	8:00

NFL POST-SEASON PLAN,
1988 TIE-BREAKING PROCEDURES

DIVISION TIES

Two Clubs

1. Head-to-head (best won-lost-tied percentage in games between the clubs).
2. Best won-lost-tied percentage in games played within the division.
3. Best won-lost-tied percentage in games played within the conference.
4. Best won-lost-tied percentage in common games, if applicable.
5. Best net points in division games.
6. Best net points in all games.
7. Strength of schedule.
8. Best net touchdowns in all games.
9. Coin toss.

Three or More Clubs

(Note: If two clubs remain tied after other clubs are eliminated during any step, tie-breaker reverts to step 1 of two-club format.)

1. Head-to-head (best won-lost-tied percentage in games among the clubs).
2. Best won-lost-tied percentage in games played within the division.
3. Best won-lost-tied percentage in games played within the conference.
4. Best won-lost-tied percentage in common games.
5. Best net points in division games.
6. Best net points in all games.
7. Strength of schedule.
8. Best net touchdowns in all games.
9. Coin toss.

WILD CARD TIES

If necessary to break ties to determine the two wild card clubs from each conference, the following steps will be taken:

1. If all the tied clubs are from the same division, apply division tie-breaker.
2. If the tied clubs are from different divisions, apply the following steps:

Two Clubs

1. Head-to-head, if applicable.
2. Best won-lost-tied percentage in games played within the conference.
3. Best won-lost-tied percentage in common games, minimum of four.
4. Best net points in conference games.
5. Best net points in all games.
6. Strength of schedule.
7. Best net touchdowns in all games.
8. Coin toss.

Three or More Clubs

(Note: If two clubs remain tied after other clubs are eliminated, tie-breaker reverts to step 1 of applicable two-club format.)

1. Head-to-head sweep (applicable only if one club has defeated each of the others or one club has lost to each of the others).
2. Best won-lost-tied percentage in games within the conference.
3. Best won-lost-tied percentage in common games, minimum of four.
4. Best net points in conference games.
5. Best net points in all games.
6. Strength of schedule.
7. Best net touchdowns in all games.
8. Coin toss.

1988 AFC-NFC INTERCONFERENCE GAMES

(All times local. All games Sunday unless noted otherwise.)

Sept.	4—Dallas at Pittsburgh	1:00
	Miami at Chicago	12:00
	Minnesota at Buffalo	1:00
	Phoenix at Cincinnati	1:00
Sept.	11—Chicago at Indianapolis	12:00
	Cincinnati at Philadelphia	4:00
	New England at Minnesota	3:00
	Pittsburgh at Washington	1:00
Sept.	18—Green Bay at Miami	1:00
	Los Angeles Rams at Los Angeles Raiders	1:00
Sept.	25—New York Jets at Detroit	1:00
	San Francisco at Seattle	1:00
Oct.	2—Buffalo at Chicago	12:00
	Houston at Philadelphia	1:00
	Minnesota at Miami	4:00
	Seattle at Atlanta	1:00
Oct.	9—Denver at San Francisco	1:00
	New England at Green Bay	12:00
	New Orleans at San Diego	1:00
	Pittsburgh at Phoenix	1:00
Oct.	16—Atlanta at Denver	2:00
	New Orleans at Seattle	1:00
	Philadelphia at Cleveland	1:00
	Tampa Bay at Indianapolis	12:00
Oct.	23—Cleveland at Phoenix	1:00
	Detroit at Kansas City	12:00
	Los Angeles Raiders at New Orleans	12:00
	Seattle at Los Angeles Rams	1:00
Oct.	30—Chicago at New England	1:00
	Green Bay at Buffalo	1:00
	Miami at Tampa Bay	1:00
	Washington at Houston	7:00
Nov.	13—Indianapolis at Green Bay	12:00
	Los Angeles Raiders at San Francisco	1:00
	Philadelphia at Pittsburgh	1:00
	San Diego at Atlanta	1:00
Nov.	20—Atlanta at Los Angeles Raiders	1:00
	Cincinnati at Dallas	12:00
	Denver at New Orleans	12:00
	Indianapolis at Minnesota	12:00
	Phoenix at Houston	12:00
	San Diego at Los Angeles Rams	1:00
Nov.	24—Houston at Dallas (Thanksgiving)	3:00
Nov.	27—Cleveland at Washington	1:00
	Los Angeles Rams at Denver	2:00
	San Francisco at San Diego	1:00
Dec.	4—Buffalo at Tampa Bay	1:00
	Dallas at Cleveland	1:00
Dec.	11—Kansas City at New York Giants	1:00
	Tampa Bay at New England	1:00
Dec.	17—Washington at Cincinnati	12:30
Dec.	18—New York Giants vs. New York Jets	1:00

1987 NFL PAID ATTENDANCE OF 10,032,493
ACHIEVED IN 12 NON-STRIKE WEEKENDS

National Football League total paid attendance for all 278 games played during the 1987 season was 15,180,013. This total includes a paid total of 10,032,493 and an average of 59,717 for the 168 games played during the 12 non-strike weekends of the abbreviated '87 regular season.

The 59,717 average for the non-strike games compares favorably with the top regular-season averages which have surpassed 60,000 twice (1981 and 1986) in the NFL's 68-year history.

The regular season was reduced to 210 games from the scheduled 224 by a 24-day players strike that forced cancellation of the 14 games of September 27-28. Forty-two games were played with replacement players during the fourth, fifth and sixth weekends. Paid attendance for the 210 games was 11,406,166, for an average of 54,315, and included 1,373,673 (32,707 average) for the 42 replacement games.

The 1987 preseason total of 3,116,870 paid tickets and the average of 53,739 for the 58 games were the highest since the NFL adopted the four-game preseason format (from six games) in 1978.

ACTUAL 1987 REGULAR-SEASON ATTENDANCE

(Unused tickets not included. Listed after each city for both home and road attendance are two numbers. The first number designates how many home or road games that club played in 1987 and the second number designates how many of those games were strike games played by replacement players).

HOME GAMES		ROAD GAMES	
1. Denver (8, 2)	498,714	1. New England (7, 1)	431,739
2. Cleveland (7, 1)	492,939	2. Houston (8, 2)	425,828
3. Chicago (8, 2)	459,190	3. L.A. Raiders (7, 1)	421,302
4. Buffalo (8, 2)	437,187	4. Dallas (8, 1)	416,141
5. Indianapolis (8, 1)	436,867	5. Washington (8, 2)	411,874
6. N.Y. Giants (8, 2)	432,433	6. Chicago (7, 1)	407,782
7. Philadelphia (8, 1)	429,949	7. N.Y. Jets (7, 1)	393,674
8. Seattle (8, 2)	421,956	8. Miami (8, 2)	392,125
9. New Orleans (7, 1)	420,873	9. Detroit (8, 1)	390,867
10. Minnesota (8, 1)	403,101	10. Cleveland (8, 2)	378,359
11. San Francisco (7, 1)	394,675	11. Kansas City (8, 2)	375,074
12. Miami (7, 1)	390,959	12. Buffalo (7, 1)	370,932
13. Green Bay (8, 2)	379,033	13. Denver (7, 1)	370,586
14. New England (8, 2)	374,302	14. San Francisco (8, 2)	364,534
15. San Diego (7, 0)	371,676	15. Tampa Bay (8, 1)	361,959
16. Cincinnati (8, 2)	360,989	16. Pittsburgh (8, 2)	357,338
17. L.A. Raiders (8, 2)	360,039	17. New Orleans (8, 2)	353,424
18. Pittsburgh (7, 1)	353,402	18. N.Y. Giants (7, 1)	346,420
19. N.Y. Jets (8, 2)	353,075	19. Indianapolis (7, 2)	344,561
20. Dallas (7, 2)	344,406	20. Atlanta (7, 0)	343,424
21. Washington (7, 1)	341,257	21. Cincinnati (7, 1)	338,317
22. L.A. Rams (7, 1)	331,690	22. Seattle (7, 1)	329,265
23. Tampa Bay (7, 2)	303,676	23. St. Louis (8, 2)	328,536
24. Kansas City (7, 1)	282,018	24. L.A. Rams (8, 2)	328,114
25. Houston (7, 1)	259,375	25. Green Bay (7, 1)	317,778
26. St. Louis (7, 1)	194,748	26. Minnesota (7, 2)	306,643
27. Detroit (7, 2)	190,488	27. Philadelphia (7, 2)	304,002
28. Atlanta (8, 3)	189,815	28. San Diego (8, 3)	298,234
Total	10,208,832	Total	10,208,832

PAID ATTENDANCE
NATIONAL FOOTBALL LEAGUE

	Regular Season		Average	*Post-Season	
1987‡	10,032,493	(168 games)	59,717	606,864	(9)
1986	13,588,551	(224 games)	60,663	683,901	(9)
1985	13,345,047	(224 games)	59,567	660,667	(9)
1984	13,398,112	(224 games)	59,813	614,809	(9)
1983	13,277,222	(224 games)	59,273	625,068	(9)
1982†	7,367,438	(126 games)	58,472	985,952	(15)
1981	13,606,990	(224 games)	60,745	587,361	(9)
1980	13,392,230	(224 games)	59,787	577,186	(9)
1979	13,182,039	(224 games)	58,848	582,266	(9)
1978	12,771,800	(224 games)	57,017	578,107	(9)
1977	11,018,632	(196 games)	56,218	483,588	(7)
1976	11,070,543	(196 games)	56,482	428,733	(7)
1975	10,213,193	(182 games)	56,116	443,811	(7)
1974	10,236,322	(182 games)	56,224	412,180	(7)
1973	10,730,933	(182 games)	58,961	458,515	(7)
1972	10,445,827	(182 games)	57,395	435,446	(7)
1971	10,076,035	(182 games)	55,363	430,244	(7)
1970	9,533,333	(182 games)	52,381	410,371	(7)
1969	6,096,127	(112 games)	54,430	242,841	(4)
1968	5,882,313	(112 games)	52,521	291,279	(4)
1967	5,938,924	(112 games)	53,026	241,754	(4)
1966	5,337,044	(105 games)	50,829	135,098	(2)
1965	4,634,021	(98 games)	47,296	100,304	(2)
1964	4,563,049	(98 games)	46,562	79,544	(1)
1963	4,163,643	(98 games)	42,486	45,801	(1)
1962	4,003,421	(98 games)	40,851	64,892	(1)
1961	3,986,159	(98 games)	40,675	39,029	(1)
1960	3,128,296	(78 games)	40,106	67,325	(1)
1959	3,140,000	(72 games)	43,617	57,545	(1)
1958	3,006,124	(72 games)	41,752	123,659	(2)
1957	2,836,318	(72 games)	39,393	119,579	(2)
1956	2,551,263	(72 games)	35,434	56,836	(1)
1955	2,521,836	(72 games)	35,026	85,693	(1)
1954	2,190,571	(72 games)	30,425	43,827	(1)
1953	2,164,585	(72 games)	30,064	54,577	(1)
1952	2,052,126	(72 games)	28,502	97,507	(2)
1951	1,913,019	(72 games)	26,570	57,522	(1)
1950	1,977,753	(78 games)	25,356	136,647	(3)
1949	1,391,735	(60 games)	23,196	27,980	(1)
1948	1,525,243	(60 games)	25,421	36,309	(1)
1947	1,837,437	(60 games)	30,624	66,268	(2)
1946	1,732,135	(55 games)	31,493	58,346	(1)
1945	1,270,401	(50 games)	25,408	32,178	(1)
1944	1,019,649	(50 games)	20,393	46,016	(1)
1943	969,128	(50 games)	19,383	71,315	(2)
1942	887,920	(55 games)	16,144	36,006	(1)
1941	1,108,615	(55 games)	20,157	55,870	(2)
1940	1,063,025	(55 games)	19,328	36,034	(1)
1939	1,071,200	(55 games)	19,476	32,279	(1)
1938	937,197	(55 games)	17,040	48,120	(1)
1937	963,039	(55 games)	17,510	15,878	(1)
1936	816,007	(54 games)	15,111	29,545	(1)
1935	638,178	(53 games)	12,041	15,000	(1)
1934	492,684	(60 games)	8,211	35,059	(1)

*Includes conference and league championship and AFL-NFL championship (Super Bowl) games; number of post-season games in parentheses. Pro Bowl not included.

†A 57-day players' strike reduced 224-game schedule to 126 games.

‡A 24-day players' strike reduced 224-game schedule to 168 non-strike games.

AMERICAN FOOTBALL LEAGUE

Season	Attendance	Teams-Games	Avg. per Game	AFL-NFL Championship	AFL Championship
1969***	2,843,373	10 teams—70 games	40,620	80,562	53,564
1968**	2,635,004	10 teams—70 games	37,643	75,377	62,627
1967	2,295,697	9 teams—63 games	36,439	75,546	53,330
1966	2,160,369	9 teams—63 games	34,291	61,946	42,080
1965	1,782,384	8 teams—56 games	31,828		30,361
1964	1,447,875	8 teams—56 games	25,855		40,242
1963*	1,241,741	8 teams—56 games	22,174		30,127
1962	1,147,302	8 teams—56 games	20,487		37,981
1961	1,002,657	8 teams—56 games	17,904		29,556
1960	926,156	8 teams—56 games	16,538		32,183

***Inter-divisional playoffs: Kansas City-New York, 61,832; Houston-Oakland, 51,692.

**Kansas City-Oakland playoff, 51,811.

*Boston-Buffalo playoff, 33,044.

NATIONAL PROFESSIONAL FOOTBALL
HALL OF FAME

The Pro Football Hall of Fame in Canton, Ohio.

FOUR NEW INDUCTEES IN 1988

Fred Biletnikoff, Mike Ditka, Jack Ham and Alan Page were inducted into Pro Football's Hall of Fame in 1988, expanding the list of former stars honored at Canton, Ohio, to 144.

Pro Football Hall of Fame

The National Professional Football Hall of Fame is located in Canton, Ohio, site of the organizational meeting in 1920 from which the National Football League grew.

The League recognized Canton as the Hall of Fame site on April 27, 1961, and ground was broken for the Hall on August 11, 1962. Dedication ceremonies were held September 7, 1963.

The National Board of Selectors, consisting of representatives from professional football cities, elected 17 charter members to the Hall. The selections were announced on January 29, 1963.

Subsequent selections were announced on February 28, 1964, January 19, 1965, March 23, 1966, February 8, 1967, February 19, 1968, February 6, 1969, February 2, 1970, February 4, 1971, February 8, 1972, February 6, 1973, February 5, 1974, January 20, 1975, January 26, 1976, January 17, 1977, January 23, 1978, January 30, 1979, January 26, 1980, January 31, 1981, January 28, 1982, February 5, 1983, January 28, 1984, January 22, 1985, January 27, 1986, January 27, 1987 and February 2, 1988.

ROSTER OF MEMBERS (144)

HERB ADDERLEY (Michigan State), 1980, cornerback, Green Bay Packers (1961-69), Dallas Cowboys (1970-72).

LANCE ALWORTH (Arkansas), 1978, wide receiver, San Diego Chargers (1962-70), Dallas Cowboys (1971-72).

DOUG ATKINS (Tennessee), 1982, defensive end, Cleveland Browns (1953-54), Chicago Bears (1955-66), New Orleans Saints (1967-69).

MORRIS (RED) BADGRO (Southern California), 1981, end, New York Yankees (1926), New York Giants (1930-35).

CLIFF BATTLES (West Virginia Wesleyan), 1968, halfback-quarterback, Boston Braves, Boston Redskins, Washington Redskins (1932-37); coach, Brooklyn Dodgers (1946-47).

SAMMY BAUGH (Texas Christian), Charter 1963, quarterback, Washington Redskins (1937-52); coach, New York Titans (1960-61); Houston Oilers (1964).

CHUCK BEDNARIK (Pennsylvania), 1967, center and linebacker, Philadelphia Eagles (1949-62).

BERT BELL (Pennsylvania), Charter 1963, NFL Commissioner (1946-59).

BOBBY BELL (Minnesota), 1983, linebacker, Kansas City Chiefs (1963-74).

RAYMOND BERRY (Southern Methodist), 1973, offensive end, Baltimore Colts (1955-67), coach, New England Patriots, (1984-present).

CHARLES W. BIDWILL (Loyola), 1967, owner, Chicago Cardinals (1933-47).

FRED BILETNIKOFF (Florida State), 1988, wide receiver, Oakland Raiders (1965-78).

GEORGE BLANDA (Kentucky), 1981, quarterback-placekicker, Chicago Bears (1949-58), Baltimore Colts (1950), Houston Oilers (1960-66), Oakland Raiders (1967-73).

JIM BROWN (Syracuse), 1971, fullback, Cleveland Browns (1957-65).

PAUL BROWN (Miami, Ohio), 1967, coach, Cleveland Browns (1946-62), Cincinnati Bengals (1968-75).

ROOSEVELT BROWN (Morgan State), 1975, tackle, New York Giants (1953-66).

WILLIE BROWN (Grambling), 1984, defensive back, Denver Broncos (1963-66), Oakland Raiders (1967-78).

DICK BUTKUS (Illinois), 1979, linebacker, Chicago Bears (1965-73).

TONY CANADEO (Gonzaga), 1974, halfback, Green Bay Packers (1941-44, 1946-52).

JOE CARR, Charter 1963, NFL President (1921-39).

GUY CHAMBERLIN (Nebraska), 1965, player-coach, Canton Bulldogs, Cleveland, Frankford Yellowjackets, Chicago Bears, and Chicago Cardinals (1919-28).

JACK CHRISTIANSEN (Colorado A&M), 1970, defensive back, Detroit Lions (1951-58); coach, San Francisco 49ers (1963-67).

DUTCH CLARK (Colorado College), Charter 1963, quarterback, Portsmouth Spartans and Detroit Lions (1931-38).

Fred Biletnikoff (left) played 14 seasons as a wide receiver for the Oakland Raiders while current Chicago Coach Mike Ditka in 1988 became the first tight end ever elected to the Pro Football Hall of Fame.

GEORGE CONNOR (Notre Dame), 1975, tackle and linebacker, Chicago Bears (1948-55).

JIMMY CONZELMAN (Washington, Mo.), 1964, halfback, coach, executive, Decatur, Rock Island, Milwaukee, Detroit, Providence, Chicago Cardinals (1920-48).

LARRY CSONKA (Syracuse), 1987, running back, Miami Dolphins (1968-74, 79), New York Giants (1976-78).

WILLIE DAVIS (Grambling), 1981, defensive end, Cleveland Browns (1958-59), Green Bay Packers (1960-69).

LEN DAWSON (Purdue), 1987, quarterback, Pittsburgh Steelers (1957-58), Cleveland Browns (1960-61), Dallas Texans (1962), Kansas City Chiefs (1963-75).

MIKE DITKA (Pittsburgh), 1988, tight end, Chicago Bears (1961-66), Philadelphia Eagles (1967-68), Dallas Cowboys (1969-72), coach, Chicago Bears (1982-present).

ART DONOVAN (Boston College), 1968, defensive tackle, Baltimore Colts, New York Yanks, Dallas Texans, Baltimore Colts (1950-61).

PADDY DRISCOLL (Northwestern), 1965, player-coach, Chicago Cardinals and Chicago Bears (1919-31, 1941-68).

BILL DUDLEY (Virginia), 1966, halfback, Pittsburgh Steelers, Detroit Lions and Washington Redskins (1942-53).

TURK EDWARDS (Washington State), 1969, tackle, Boston Braves, Boston Redskins, Washington Redskins (1932-40).

WEEB EWBANK (Miami, O.), 1978, coach, Baltimore Colts (1954-1962) and New York Jets (1963-1973).

TOM FEARS (Santa Clara, UCLA), 1970, end, Los Angeles Rams (1948-56), coach, New Orleans Saints (1967-70).

RAY FLAHERTY (Gonzaga), 1976, player-coach, Los Angeles Wildcats, New York Yankees (AFL), New York Giants, Boston Redskins, Washington Redskins, New York Yankees (AAFC), Chicago Hornets (1926-1949).

LEN FORD (Michigan), 1976, end, Los Angeles Dons and Cleveland Browns (1948-1958).

DANNY FORTMANN (Colgate), 1965, guard, Chicago Bears (1936-43).

FRANK GATSKI (Marshall), 1985, center, Cleveland Browns (1946-56), Detroit Lions (1957).

BILL GEORGE (Wake Forest), 1974, linebacker, Chicago Bears, and Los Angeles Rams (1952-66).

FRANK GIFFORD (Southern California), 1977, halfback and end, New York Giants (1952-60 and 1962-64).

SID GILLMAN (Ohio State), 1983, end, Cleveland Rams (1936); coach, Los Angeles Rams (1955-59), Los Angeles Chargers (1960), San Diego Chargers (1961-69, 71), Houston Oilers (1973-74).

OTTO GRAHAM (Northwestern), 1965, quarterback, Cleveland Browns (1946-55), coach, Washington Redskins (1966-68).

RED GRANGE (Illinois), Charter 1963, halfback, Chicago Bears (1925, 1929-34), New York Yankees (1926-27).

JOE GREENE (North Texas State), 1987, defensive tackle, Pittsburgh Steelers (1969-81).

FORREST GREGG (Southern Methodist), 1977, tackle, Green Bay Packers and Dallas Cowboys (1956; 1958-71); coach, Cleveland Browns (1975-77), Cincinnati Bengals (1980-83) and Green Bay Packers (1984-87).

LOU GROZA (Ohio State), 1974, offensive tackle and placekicker, Cleveland Browns (1946-59, 1961-67).

JOE GUYON (Carlisle, Georgia Tech), 1966, halfback, Canton Bulldogs, Cleveland Indians, Oorang Indians, Rock Island Independents, Kansas City Cowboys and New York Giants (1918-27).

GEORGE HALAS (Illinois), Charter 1963, player, coach, founder, Chicago Bears (1920-83).

JACK HAM (Penn State), 1988, linebacker, Pittsburgh Steelers (1971-82).

ED HEALEY (Dartmouth), 1964, tackle, Rock Island and Chicago Bears (1920-27).

MEL HEIN (Washington State), Charter 1963, center, New York Giants (1931-45).

WILBUR HENRY (Washington & Jefferson), Charter 1963, tackle, Canton Bulldogs, Akron Indians, New York Giants, Pottsville Maroons, Pittsburgh Steelers (1920-30).

ARNIE HERBER (Regis), 1966, halfback, Green Bay Packers and New York Giants (1930-45).

BILL HEWITT (Michigan), 1971, end, Chicago Bears (1932-36), Philadelphia Eagles (1937-39), Philadelphia-Pittsburgh (1943).

CLARKE HINKLE (Bucknell), 1964, fullback, Green Bay Packers (1932-41).

ELROY (CRAZYLEGS) HIRSCH (Wisconsin), 1968, end-halfback, Chicago Rockets, Los Angeles Rams (1946-57).

PAUL HORNUNG (Notre Dame), 1986, running back, Green Bay Packers (1957-62, 64-66).

KEN HOUSTON (Prairie View), 1986, defensive back, Houston Oilers (1967-72), Washington Redskins (1973-80).

CAL HUBBARD (Centenary, Geneva), Charter 1963, tackle and end, New York Giants, Green Bay Packers and Pittsburgh Steelers (1927-36).

SAM HUFF (West Virginia), 1982, linebacker, New York Giants (1956-63), Washington Redskins (1964-67, 69).

LAMAR HUNT (Southern Methodist), 1972, founder, American Football League, 1959; president, Dallas Texans (1960-62), Kansas City Chiefs (1963-present).

DON HUTSON (Alabama), Charter 1963, end, Green Bay Packers (1935-45).

JOHN HENRY JOHNSON (Arizona State), 1987, fullback, San Francisco 49ers (1954-56), Detroit Lions (1957-59), Pittsburgh Steelers (1960-65), Houston Oilers (1966).

DEACON JONES (South Carolina State), 1980, defensive end, Los Angeles Rams (1961-71), San Diego Chargers (1972-73), Washington Redskins (1974).

SONNY JURGENSEN (Duke), 1983, quarterback, Philadelphia Eagles (1957-63), Washington Redskins (1964-74).

Former Vikings tackle Alan Page (left) and ex-Steelers linebacker Jack Ham were two of the NFL's outstanding defensive players of the 1970s.

WALTER KIESLING (St. Thomas), 1966, player-coach, Duluth Eskimos, Pottsville Maroons, Boston Braves, Chicago Cardinals, Chicago Bears, Green Bay Packers and Pittsburgh Steelers (1926-56).

FRANK (BRUISER) KINARD (Mississippi), 1971, tackle, Brooklyn Dodgers (1938-45) New York Yankees (1946-47).

CURLY LAMBEAU (Notre Dame), Charter 1963, founder, player, coach, Green Bay Packers (1919-49).

DICK (NIGHT TRAIN) LANE (Scottsbluff JC), 1974, defensive back, Los Angeles Rams, Chicago Cardinals, Detroit Lions (1952-65).

JIM LANGER (South Dakota State), 1987, center, Miami Dolphins (1970-79), Minnesota Vikings (1980-81).

WILLIE LANIER (Morgan State), 1986, linebacker, Kansas City Chiefs (1967-77).

YALE LARY (Texas A & M), 1979, defensive back, Detroit Lions (1952-53, 1956-64).

DANTE LAVELLI (Ohio State), 1975, end, Cleveland Browns (1946-56).

BOBBY LAYNE (Texas), 1967, quarterback, Chicago Bears, New York Bulldogs, Detroit Lions, Pittsburgh Steelers (1948-62).

TUFFY LEEMANS (George Washington), 1978, fullback, New York Giants (1936-1943).

BOB LILLY (Texas Christian), 1980, defensive tackle, Dallas Cowboys (1961-1974).

VINCE LOMBARDI (Fordham), 1971, coach, Green Bay Packers (1959-67), Washington Redskins (1969).

SID LUCKMAN (Columbia), 1965, quarterback, Chicago Bears (1939-50).

ROY (LINK) LYMAN, 1964, tackle, Canton Bulldogs, Cleveland, Chicago Bears (1922-34).

TIM MARA, Charter 1963, founder, New York Giants (1925-65).

GINO MARCHETTI (San Francisco), 1972, defensive end, Dallas Texans (1952), Baltimore Colts (1953-66).

GEORGE PRESTON MARSHALL, Charter 1963, founder, Washington Redskins (1932-1965).

OLLIE MATSON (San Francisco), 1972, halfback, Chicago Cardinals (1952, 1954-58), Los Angeles Rams (1959-62), Detroit Lions (1963), Philadelphia Eagles (1964-66).

DON MAYNARD (Texas Western College), 1987, wide receiver, New York Giants (1958), New York Jets (1960-72), St. Louis Cardinals (1973).

GEORGE McAFEE (Duke), 1966, halfback, Chicago Bears (1940-41, 1945-50).

MIKE McCORMACK (Kansas), 1984, tackle, New York Yanks (1951), Cleveland Browns (1954-62).

HUGH McELHENNY (Washington), 1970, halfback, San Francisco 49ers, Minnesota Vikings, New York Giants and Detroit Lions (1952-64).

JOHNNY BLOOD (McNALLY) (St. John's, Minn.), Charter 1963, halfback, Milwaukee Badgers, Duluth Eskimos, Pottsville Maroons, Green Bay Packers, Pittsburgh Steelers (1925-39).

AUGUST (MIKE) MICHALSKE (Penn State), 1964, guard, New York Yankees and Green Bay Packers (1927-37).

WAYNE MILLNER (Notre Dame), 1968, end, Boston Redskins, Washington Redskins (1936-41, 1945).

BOBBY MITCHELL (Illinois), 1983, running back and receiver, Cleveland Browns (1958-61), Washington Redskins (1962-68).

RON MIX (Southern California), 1979, offensive tackle, Los Angeles Chargers (1960), San Diego Chargers (1961-69), Oakland Raiders (1971).

LENNY MOORE (Penn State), 1975, halfback, Baltimore Colts (1956-67).

MARION MOTLEY (Nevada), 1968, fullback-linebacker, Cleveland Browns, Pittsburgh Steelers (1946-1955).

GEORGE MUSSO (Millikin), 1982, offensive guard and defensive tackle, Chicago Bears (1933-44).

BRONKO NAGURSKI (Minnesota), Charter 1963, fullback and tackle, Chicago Bears (1930-37, 1943).

JOE NAMATH (Alabama), 1985, quarterback, New York Jets (1965-76), Los Angeles Rams (1977).

EARLE (GREASY) NEALE (West Virginia Wesleyan), 1969, coach, Philadelphia Eagles (1941-50).

ERNIE NEVERS (Stanford), Charter 1963, fullback, Duluth Eskimos and Chicago Cardinals (1926-37).

RAY NITSCHKE (Illinois), 1978, linebacker, Green Bay Packers (1958-72).

LEO NOMELLINI (Minnesota), 1969, defensive tackle, San Francisco 49ers (1953-63).

MERLIN OLSEN (Utah State), 1982, defensive tackle, Los Angeles Rams (1962-76).

JIM OTTO (Miami, Fla.), 1980, center, Oakland Raiders (1960-1974).

STEVE OWEN (Phillips), 1966, player-coach, Kansas City Cowboys and New York Giants (1924-53).

ALAN PAGE (Notre Dame), 1988, defensive tackle, Minnesota Vikings (1967-78), Chicago Bears (1978-81).

CLARENCE (ACE) PARKER (Duke), 1972, halfback, Brooklyn Dodgers (1937-41), Boston Yanks (1945), New York Yankees (1946).

JIM PARKER (Ohio State), 1973, guard, Baltimore Colts (1957-67).

JOE PERRY (Compton JC), 1969, fullback, San Francisco 49ers, Baltimore Colts (1948-63).

PETE PIHOS (Indiana), 1970, end, Philadelphia Eagles (1947-55).

HUGH (SHORTY) RAY (Illinois), 1966, NFL technical adviser and supervisor of officials (1938-56).

DANIEL F. REEVES (Georgetown), 1967, founder, Los Angeles Rams (1941-71).

JIM RINGO (Syracuse), 1981, center, Green Bay Packers (1953-63), Philadelphia Eagles (1964-67).

ANDY ROBUSTELLI (Arnold), 1971, defensive end, Los Angeles Rams (1951-55), New York Giants (1956-64).

ARTHUR J. ROONEY (Georgetown), 1964, founder, Pittsburgh Steelers (1933-82).

PETE ROZELLE (San Francisco), 1985, NFL Commissioner (1960-present).

GALE SAYERS (Kansas), 1977, running back, Chicago Bears (1965-71).

JOE SCHMIDT (Pittsburgh), 1973, linebacker, Detroit Lions (1953-65); coach, Detroit Lions (1967-72).

O.J. SIMPSON (Southern California), 1985, running back, Buffalo Bills (1969-77), San Francisco 49ers (1978).

BART STARR (Alabama), 1977, quarterback, Green Bay Packers (1956-71); coach, Green Bay Packers (1975-83).

ROGER STAUBACH (Navy), 1985, quarterback, Dallas Cowboys (1969-79).

ERNIE STAUTNER (West Virginia), 1969, defensive tackle, Pittsburgh Steelers (1950-63).

KEN STRONG (New York U.), 1967, halfback-placekicker, Staten Island Stapletons, New York Yankees and New York Giants (1929-39, 1944-47).

JOE STYDAHAR (West Virginia), 1967, tackle, Chicago Bears (1936-42, 1945-46).

FRAN TARKENTON (Georgia), 1986, quarterback, Minnesota Vikings (1961-66, 72-78), New York Giants (1967-71).

CHARLEY TAYLOR (Arizona State), 1984, wide receiver, Washington Redskins (1964-75, 77).

JIM TAYLOR (Louisiana State), 1976, fullback, Green Bay Packers (1958-1966), New Orleans Saints (1967).

JIM THORPE (Carlisle), Charter 1963, halfback, Canton Bulldogs, Oorang Indians, Cleveland Indians, Toledo Maroons, Rock Island Independents, New York Giants (1915-26, 1929).

Y.A. TITTLE (Louisiana State), 1971, quarterback, Baltimore Colts (1948-50), San Francisco 49ers (1951-60), New York Giants (1961-64).

GEORGE TRAFTON (Notre Dame), 1964, center, Chicago Bears (1920-32).

CHARLIE TRIPPI (Georgia), 1968, halfback, Chicago Cardinals (1947-55).

EMLEN TUNNELL (Iowa), 1967, defensive back, New York Giants and Green Bay Packers (1948-61).

CLYDE (BULLDOG) TURNER (Hardin-Simmons), 1966, center-linebacker, Chicago Bears (1940-52); coach, New York Titans (1962).

JOHN UNITAS (Louisville), 1979, quarterback, Baltimore Colts (1956-72), San Diego Chargers (1973).

GENE UPSHAW (Texas A&I), 1987, guard, Oakland Raiders (1967-81).

NORM VAN BROCKLIN (Oregon), 1971, quarterback, Los Angeles Rams (1949-57), Philadelphia Eagles (1958-60), coach, Minnesota Vikings (1961-66), Atlanta Falcons (1968-74).

STEVE VAN BUREN (Louisiana State), 1965, halfback, Philadelphia Eagles (1944-51).

DOAK WALKER (Southern Methodist), 1986, running back, Detroit Lions (1950-55).

PAUL WARFIELD (Ohio State), 1983, receiver, Cleveland Browns (1964-69, 76-77), Miami Dolphins (1970-74).

BOB WATERFIELD (UCLA), 1965, quarterback, Cleveland Rams and Los Angeles Rams (1945-52); coach, Los Angeles Rams (1960-62).

ARNIE WEINMEISTER (Washington), 1984, tackle, New York Yankees (1948-49), New York Giants (1950-53).

BILL WILLIS (Ohio State), 1977, guard, Cleveland Browns (1946-53).

LARRY WILSON (Utah), 1978, defensive back, St. Louis Cardinals (1960-72).

ALEX WOJCIECHOWICZ (Fordham), 1968, center-linebacker Detroit Lions, Philadelphia Eagles (1938-50).

1988 ROSTER OF OFFICIALS

Art McNally, Supervisor of Officials
Jack Reader, Assistant Supervisor of Officials
Joe Gardi, Assistant Supervisor of Officials
Tony Veteri, Assistant Supervisor of Officials

REFEREES

No. Name	College	Yrs.
14—Gene Barth	St. Louis	18
43—Red Cashion	Texas A & M	17
6—Tom Dooley	Virginia Military	11
12—Ben Dreith	Colorado State	29
23—Johnny Grier	D.C. Teachers	8
40—Pat Haggerty	Colorado State	24
105—Dick Hantack	Southeast Missouri	11
60—Dick Jorgensen	Wisconsin	21
9—Jerry Markbreit	Illinois	13
48—Gordon McCarter	Western Reserve	22
95—Bob McElwee	Navy	13
70—Jerry Seeman	Winona State	14
7—Fred Silva	San Jose State	22
32—Jim Tunney	Occidental	29
11—Fred Wyant	West Virginia	23

UMPIRES

No. Name	College	Yrs.
115—Hendi Ancich	Harbor College	7
110—Ron Botchan	Occidental	9
101—Bob Boylston	Alabama	11
27—Al Conway	Army	20
78—Art Demmas	Vanderbilt	21
57—Ed Fiffick	Marquette	10
50—Neil Gereb	California	8
42—Dave Hamilton	Utah	14
67—John Keck	Cornell	17
117—Ben Montgomery	Morehouse	7
88—Dave Moss	Dartmouth	9
30—Dennis Riggs	Bellarmine	1
103—Rex Stuart	Appalachian St.	5
100—Bob Wagner	Penn State	4
89—Gordon Wells	Occidental	17

HEAD LINESMEN

No. Name	College	Yrs.
81—Dave Anderson	Salem College	5
55—Tom Barnes	Minnesota	3
17—Jerry Bergman	Duquesne	23
111—Earnie Frantz	None	8
72—Terry Gierke	Portland State	8
85—Frank Glover	Morris Brown	17
104—Dale Hamer	California St., Pa.	11
114—Tom Johnson	Miami-Ohio	7
26—Ed Marion	Pennsylvania	29
35—Leo Miles	Virginia State	20
10—Ron Phares	Virginia Polytechnic	4
79—Aaron Pointer	Pacific Lutheran	2
109—Sid Semon	Southern California	11
37—Burl Toler	San Francisco	24
87—Paul Weidner	Cincinnati	3
8—Dale Williams	California State	9

LINE JUDGES

No. Name	College	Yrs.
116—Bob Baker	East Texas St.	2
56—Ron Baynes	Auburn	2
59—Bob Beeks	Lincoln	21
83—Ron Blum	Marin	4
45—Ron DeSouza	Morgan State	9
74—Ray Dodez	Wooster	21
15—Bama Glass	Colorado	10
112—Joe Haynes	Alcorn State	5
54—Jack Johnson	Pacific Lutheran	13
94—Vern Marshall	Linfield College	13
41—Dick McKenzie	Ashland	11
51—Dale Orem	Louisville	9
5—Jim Quirk	Delaware	1
53—Bill Reynolds	West Chester State	14
33—Howard Roe	Wichita State	5
3—Boyce Smith	Vanderbilt	8

BACK JUDGES

No. Name	College	Yrs.
22—Paul Baetz	Heidelberg	11
24—Roy Clymer	New Mexico State	9
106—Al Jury	S. Bernardino Valley	11
107—Jim Kearney	Pennsylvania	11
21—Pete Liske	Penn State	6
49—Dean Look	Michigan State	16
38—Bruce Maurer	Ohio State	2
36—Bob Moore	Dayton	5
92—Jim Poole	San Diego State	14
68—Louis Richard	Southwestern La.	3
98—Jimmy Rosser	Auburn	12
118—Tom Sifferman	Seattle	3
52—Ben Tompkins	Texas	18
4—Doug Toole	Stanford	1
28—Don Wedge	Ohio Wesleyan	17
99—Banks Williams	Houston	11

SIDE JUDGES

No. Name	College	Yrs.
34—Gerald Austin	Western Carolina	7
61—Dick Creed	Louisville	11
102—Merrill Douglas	Utah	8
47—Tom Fincken	Kansas State	5
62—Duwayne Gandy	Tulsa	8
66—Dave Hawk	Southern Methodist	17
16—Doyle Jackson	Central Arkansas	1
97—Nate Jones	Lewis and Clark	12
108—Stan Kemp	Michigan	3
120—Gary Lane	Missouri	7
90—Gil Mace	Westminster	15
20—Larry Menners	Upper Iowa	4
64—Dave Parry	Wabash	14
58—William Quinby	Iowa State	11
29—Howard Slavin	Southern California	2

FIELD JUDGES

No. Name	College	Yrs.
31—Dick Dolack	Ferris State	23
113—Don Dorkowski	Cal St.-Los Angeles	3
96—Don Hakes	Bradley	12
44—Donnie Hampton	Georgia	1
86—Bernie Kukar	St. John's	5
18—Bob Lewis	None	13
82—Pat Mallette	Nebraska	20
76—Ed Merrifield	Missouri	14
77—Don Orr	Vanderbilt	18
46—John Robison	Utah	1
73—Bob Skelton	Alabama	4
119—Ron Spitler	Panhandle State	7
91—Bill Stanley	Redlands	15
93—Jack Vaughn	Mississippi State	13
84—Bob Wortman	Findlay	23